M000314201

Table of Contents

Table of Contents

Appendices

Preface

The *Far East Pinyin Chinese-English English-Chinese Dictionary* is an adaptation of two widely-acclaimed references for learning Chinese, the *Far East Pinyin Chinese-English Dictionary* and the *Far East English-Chinese Pinyin Dictionary*. The best of these two dictionaries is brought together to produce a reference that is both effective and convenient.

Over 14,000 entries were selected for the Chinese-English section, including the vocabulary for both the HSK and TOP Chinese proficiency tests as well as the words most commonly used on both sides of the Taiwan Straits. To better suit the needs of non-native learners, entries are ordered alphabetically by word according to their Hanyu Pinyin spellings, thus breaking with the Chinese tradition of ordering entries by head character. Detailed explanations are given for each entry, along with clarification for any differences in pronunciation or usage between Mainland China and Taiwan. Additionally, the latest scientific and technical terms have been added. The end result is a dictionary which meets the needs of learners from all around the world.

The English-Chinese section consists of more than 12,000 entries and includes the latest new words that have made their way into common use. Each entry is

annotated with Hanyu pinyin. For those with multiple meanings, a bilingual explanation in both Chinese and English is provided in order to help the reader distinguish the various meanings. Any differences in pronunciation or usage between Mainland China and Taiwan are also given.

This two-way dictionary is not only rich in content, but contains more than a few important appendices, including: Tips on Pronunciation, Introduction to Chinese Characters, Essential Measure Words, Numbers, Practical Daily Usage, Countries · Cities · Regions, Important Chinese Festivals, Introduction to Chinese Culture, Principles of Simplified Characters, Simplified vs. Traditional Character Comparison Chart, Comparison Chart for Hanyu Pinyin (HP) and Mandarin Phonetic Symbols (MPS), and the Hanyu Pinyin Table. These practical appendices can aid non-native learners of Chinese to better understand Chinese culture and thereby provide additional support for learning the Chinese language.

The Far East Book Co., Editorial Committee

序

《远东拼音汉英英汉双向辞典》改编自《远东拼音汉英辞典》及《远东英汉拼音辞典》这两本广受欢迎的华语学习工具书，将两本辞典的精华结合在一起，是一本方便而有效率的工具书。

汉英部分精选逾14,000个词条，包含HSK、TOP汉语考试之基本词汇及其它两岸常用词语。以词条作为排列方式，突破传统汉英辞典以字条排列的模式，更符合外籍学习者的使用习惯。所有词条根据汉语拼音的字母顺序排列，列有详细的英文解释，并呈现两岸音读差异及用语，另收录现今常用之科技新词，适合世界各国人士学习中文之用。

英汉部分收录逾12,000个词条，并加收现今常用之新词。每字加注汉语拼音，遇有一词多义时则附以英文说明，帮助读者清楚分辨中文词义。同时提供大陆及台湾两地说法有异的用语及发音。

本双向辞典内容丰富，另增加许多重要的附录，包括：发音说明、汉字简介、常用量词、数词的用法、日常实用语句、国家都市地区、中国重要节日、中国文化概说、简繁字比较说明、简繁字对照表、拼音注音对照表及汉语拼音表，这些实用的附录可帮助外国人士对中国文化的了解，更有助于汉语的学习。

远东图书公司编审委员会

辞典编审、编校人员

企划编辑　傅国忠

编辑校对人员

王文君	方君宁	史晓文	吴珮华
林芳如	周彦伶	郑雅方	林筱卿
郭韦吟	萧贸元	黄晓倩	黄晴玉
詹登渊	蔡孟儒	廖婉筑	蔡筑晶

（上述人员依姓名笔画为序）

Pinyin
Chinese-English
Dictionary

拼音汉英辞典

User's Guide

• Arrangement of Entries

All entries are listed in alphabetical order. Characters whose pronunciation differs by tone only are arranged in ascending order by tone number (i.e. 1st, 2nd, 3rd, and 4th, followed by the neutral tone.) Entries with identical pronunciation (including tone) are arranged in ascending order by stroke count.

• Pronunciation Standard

Putonghua pronunciation is used as the standard in this dictionary. If the pronunciation commonly used in Taiwan differs from this standard, then it is also provided as a reference.

When giving the pronunciation for phrases, a slash (/) is used to indicate a pronunciation difference between Putonghua and common Taiwanese pronunciation (e.g., qī / qí 期). For example, the character "期" is pronounced as qī in Putonghua but as qí in Taiwan.

> qī / qí 期 ① periods; times ② a
> designated time; a time limit
> ③ to expect; to hope; to wait
> qīdài / qídài 期待 to expect; to hope

"⇨" indicates that the given character has one or more standard pronunciations.

> jī 奇 odd (numbers)
> ⇨qí
> qí 奇 ① strange; uncanny; occult;
> rare ② wonderful ③ to feel strange
> about
> ⇨jī

The symbol "⇨" is also used to indicate when a multi-

character word has different pronunciations and meanings for the same written form. This type of word is split into two separate entries. The symbol "⇨" in each entry indicates that there is a separate entry for this word. Take "澄清" for example:

> chéngqīng 澄清 ① to clarify ② to set right ③ clear
> ⇨dèngqīng
> dèngqīng 澄清 (of liquid) to become clear; to settle
> ⇨chéngqīng

For each main entry, the common standard pronunciation is given. Variant pronunciations that appear only in formal, written contexts are given in parentheses after the main pronunciation. For example:

> jiáo 嚼 (jué) to chew; to
> masticate; to munch

• "Neutral Tone" and the "-r" Suffix

The "neutral tone" (as in fúqi 福气) and "-r" suffix (as in hǎohāor 好好儿) are marked in this dictionary; however, these words may be pronounced differently by some dialect speakers.

• Tone Changes

All syllables are marked with their primary tones. The tone of certain characters (i.e. yī 一, bù 不) may change when under the influence of the following syllable. However, in this dictionary, the primary tone is annotated to explain this phenomenon of the tone change.

• The Use of "C" "T"

Some words may have different meanings in China and Taiwan. An italic "C" or "T" is used to indicate these differing usage. For example:

> tǔdòu 土豆 ① C potatoes ② T peanuts

• Segmentation

Idioms or proverbs which are made up of a combination of two or more phrases are connected with a hyphen (-). For example:

fāyáng-guāngdà 发扬光大 to enhance and glorify

Multi-character words that are not idioms or proverbs are made up of loosely combined phrases or words and thus are transcribed separately without hyphens. For example:

bǎihuò gōngsī 百货公司 a department store

Phrases or words that either contain function words or that are inseparable phrases themselves are transcribed as one word. For example:

bùxiāngshàngxià 不相上下 equal; equally matched

dǎjiāodao 打交道 to associate with; to have dealings with

Two vowels appearing in succession, but belonging to different syllables, are separated by an apostrophe (') to avoid ambiguity.

bàntú'érfèi 半途而废 to stop (a task) halfway

chāo'é 超额 to exceed a quota or target amount

Entries containing characters whose pronunciation end in "-n" or "-ng" and are followed by a syllable starting with a vowel are separated by an apostrophe (') to avoid ambiguity.

biǎn'é 匾额 a (wooden) tablet; a horizontal inscribed board

cóng'ér 从而 and; thereupon; thus; as a result; then; so then

体 例 说 明

- **词条排列**

所有词目根据汉语拼音的字母顺序排列。相同字首之词目，依声调顺序排列（一声→二声→三声→四声→轻声）。同音之词目，则依笔画数顺序排列。

- **音读**

音读以大陆音为主。若遇有台湾音与大陆音相异时，会一并呈列台湾音，并以"/"分隔大陆音与台湾音（如：qī / qí 期）。例如"期"字大陆音念 qī 而台湾音念 qí，则其呈现方式如下：

> qī / qí 期 ① periods; times ② a
>
>   designated time; a time limit
>
>   ③ to expect; to hope; to wait
>
>   qīdài / qídài 期待 to expect; to hope

当一字有多音现象时，以"⇨"标示此字之其他音读，代表此字为多音字。例如：

> jī 奇 odd (numbers)
>
>   ⇨ qí
>
> qí 奇 ① strange; uncanny; occult;
>
>   rare ② wonderful ③ to feel strange
>
>   about
>
>   ⇨ jī

相同词目但有不同音读与意义时，也以"⇨"标示，并于书中分列两个词目，读者可以根据⇨符号查索词目的其他音读与意义，例如：

> chéngqīng 澄清 ① to clarify ② to set right ③ clear
>
>   ⇨ dèngqīng
>
> dèngqīng 澄清 (of liquid) to become clear; to settle
>
>   ⇨ chéngqīng

每一词目均以普通音读为主，若有语音与读音之差异时，则于词目后以括号标示，例如：

> jiáo 嚼 (jué) to chew; to
>
>   masticate; to munch

- **"轻声字"与"儿化音"**

部分词目会依据实际用法而标示轻声（如：fúqi 福气）与儿化音（如：hǎohāor 好好儿），但这些音读并非是各地通用的，在某些地区也许不会有这些音读的变化。

- **声调的改变**

所有词目均标示本调，但词目遇有"yī 一"字与"bù 不"字时，则标示变调。"一"字后接一声、二声、三声字时，则变读为四声。"一"字与"不"字后接四声字时，则变读为二声。这些声调的变化均于词目下附注说明。

- **"C"、"T"的用法**

部分词目因大陆与台湾的用法不同而有不同的意义，因此以"C"、"T"分别代表大陆与台湾相异的用法与词义，例如：

> tǔdòu 土豆 ① *C* potatoes ② *T* peanuts

- **词目之分连写**

成语或谚语是由两个以上的词语或惯用语组合而成，其结构紧密，因此以"-"来连结这些不同的词语，例如：

> fāyáng-guāngdà 发扬光大 to enhance and glorify

某些非成语或谚语的词语，结构较为松散，则不以"-"加以区隔，仅以分写的形式呈现。如：

> bǎihuò gōngsī 百货公司 a department store

部分词语其结构难以分割，或内含虚词，则会连写为一个词目。如：

> bùxiāngshàngxià 不相上下 equal; equally matched
> dǎjiāodao 打交道 to associate with; to have dealings with

词目音读中相连的两个元音，但不属于同一个音节的，在两个元音之间加隔音符号（'）。如：

> bàntú'érfèi 半途而废 to stop (a task) halfway
> chāo'é 超额 to exceed a quota or target amount

词目音读中，前一个音节以"-n"或"-ng"结尾，而下一个音节由元音开始的，则在其间加隔音符号（'）。如：

> biǎn'é 匾额 a (wooden) tablet; a horizontal inscribed board
> cóng'ér 从而 and; thereupon; thus; as a result; then; so then

Radical List

Radicals are arranged according to the stroke numbers used in writing them. The page number to the right of each radical indicates where the radical is located in the Radical Index.

Radical	Page Number	Radical	Page Number	Radical	Page Number	Radical	Page Number	Radical	Page Number
一画		刀(⺈)	7	广	11	支	15	五画	
一	4	力	7	门	11	日	15	示	17
丨	4	厶	7	氵	11	曰	15	石	17
丿	4	又	7	忄(⺗)	12	水(氺)	15	龙	18
丶	4	廴	7	宀	12	贝	15	业	18
乙(乛乚)	4			辶	12	见	16	目	18
		三画		彐(⺕)	13	牛(牜牛)	16	田	18
二画		工	7	尸	13	手	16	罒	18
二	4	土	8	己(巳)	13	毛	16	皿	18
十	4	士	8	弓	13	气	16	钅	18
厂	5	艹	8	屮	13	攵	16	矢	18
匚	5	廾	8	女	13	片	16	禾	18
卜(⺊)	5	大	8	子	13	斤	16	白	19
刂	5	尢	9	纟	14	爪(⺥)	16	瓜	19
冂	5	扌	9	马	14	父	16	鸟	19
亻	5	寸	9	幺	14	月(⺼)	16	疒	19
八(丷)	5	弋	9	巛	14	欠	17	立	19
人(入)	6	小(⺌)	9	四画		风	17	穴	19
勹	6	口	10	王	14	殳	17	⻊(⻌)	19
儿	6	囗	10	韦	14	文	17	皮	19
几(凢)	6	巾	10	木	14	方	17	矛	19
亠	6	山	10	犬	15	火	17		
冫	6	彳	11	歹	15	斗	17	六画	
冖	6	彡	11	车	15	灬	17	耒	19
冂(巳)	6	犭	11	戈	15	户	17	老	19
阝(在左)	7	夂	11	比	15	礻	17	耳	19
阝(在右)	7	饣	11	瓦	15	心	17	臣	19
凵	7	爿	11	止	15	毋(母)	17	西(覀)	19

Radical Index

In this index the characters are listed under their respective radicals. Characters with the same radical are arranged in the ascending order according to the number of strokes used in writing them. The figure to the right of each character is the page number under which the character can be found in the body of the dictionary.

The first step in looking for a character is to find out the radical under which it is listed. The next step is to look for the character in the index according to the number of strokes (i.e. the total number of strokes used in writing the whole character minus the number of strokes used in writing the radial). With the page number as a guide, one can locate in the dictionary the character and the entries beneath it.

一		世	211	整	301	友	63	**2**		乱	152
一	273	丝	219	**21**		氏	211	凡	63	**7**	
1		未	243	襄	166		303	丸	239	承	30
丁	54	右	286	**丨**		乌	245	义	277	乳	196
七	178	正	301	**3**		午	246	之	303	**10**	
2			302	丰	69	**4**		**3**		乾	183
才	21	**5**		内	166	乎	98	为	242	**二**	
干	74	百	4	书	215	乐	141		243	二	61
	76	而	60	中	307		290	**4**		**1**	
三	197	夹	110		309	丘	188	半	6	亏	138
上	201		111	**4**		生	206	头	234	于	286
万	240	死	220	北	9	失	217	永	282	**2**	
下	250	亚	268	出	33	甩	282	主	311	井	125
于	286	有	285	电	52	乍	295	**5**		无	245
与	286	再	292	甲	111	**5**		农	169	五	246
	287	在	292	旧	126	丢	55	州	310	元	288
丈	297	**6**		且	185	后	97	**8**		云	291
3		甫	72	凸	235	年	168	举	127	**6**	
不	17	更	79	由	283	兵	176	叛	172	些	258
丑	33	来	139	**5**		乔	277	**乙(乛乚)**		**十**	
互	98	丽	144	曲	189	向	255	乙	277	十	209
井	125	两	147	**6**		兆	298	**1**		**1**	
开	130	求	189	串	36	**6**		了	141	千	182
廿	168	束	217	**7**		系	109		147	**2**	
卅	197	严	268	畅	26		250	**2**		午	246
天	229	**7**		**8**		卵	152	飞	66	支	303
屯	237	表	14	临	148	每	157	乞	180	**3**	
无	245	事	212	**丿**		我	245	习	249	古	83
五	246	**8**		**1**		**7**		乡	253	**4**	
牙	268	甫	10	九	126	秉	15	也	273	毕	11
友	284	面	112	乃	165	垂	37	**3**		华	99
专	313	面	159	**2**		乖	85	巴	3		100
4		甚	205	川	35	**8**		尺	31	协	258
丙	15	歪	238	久	126	重	32	丑	33	**6**	
册	23	巷	256	么	156		310	书	215	卑	9
东	55	昼	310	千	182	**9**		以	277	卖	155
甘	75	奏	320	**3**		乘	30	予	287	丧	198
击	105	**10**		长	25		208	**4**		直	304
末	162	爽	218		297	**13**		民	160	卓	316
平	176	**11**		丹	45	舞	247	**5**		**7**	
且	185	棘	107	乏	62	**丶**		买	154	南	165
丘	188	**15**						**6**		**8**	

8
调 53, 230
读 56, 57
诽 67
课 135
谅 147
诺 170
请 188
谁 204
谈 225
诸 311
9
逸 25
谎 102
谜 159
谋 163
谓 243
谘 317
10
谦 182
谢 259
谣 272
11
谨 122
谬 162
12
谱 178
13
遭 183

卩(㔾)
1
卫 243
3
印 280
4
危 241
5
即 107
却 191
6
卷 128
7
卸 258

阝(在左)
2
队 58
4
防 65
阶 118
阳 270
阴 279
阵 300
5
阿 1, 60
陈 28
附 72
际 109
陆 151
陀 237
阻 320
6
降 115, 255
7
除 34
陡 56
险 252
院 290
陨 291
8
陪 173
陶 227
陷 253
9
隆 150
随 222
隐 280
10
隔 78
11
障 297
12
隧 223

阝(在右)
邓 50
4
那 165
邪 258
5
邻 148
邱 188
邮 284
6
郊 116
耶 272
郑 302
7
郝 94
8
部 20
都 56, 255
郭 89

凵
2
凶 263
3
凹 3
出 33
击 105
6
函 92
画 100
7
幽 283

刀(⺈)
刀 47
2
分 67, 69
切 185
3
召 298
4
色 198, 199
危 241
争 301
5
龟 88, 130
免 159
6
券 191
兔 235
9
剪 113
象 256
13
劈 174

力
力 144
2
办 6
劝 191
3
功 81
加 110
务 247
幼 286
4
动 55
劣 147
5
劫 119
劲 123, 125
劳 140
男 165
努 170
助 312
6
势 212
7
勉 159
勇 282
9
勘 132
10
募 164
11
勤 186

厶
2
云 291
允 291
3
去 190
台 224
4
牟 163
5
车 163
6
参 22, 204
8
能 167

又
又 286
1
叉 23
2
邓 50
反 63
劝 191
双 218
友 23
支 303
3
对 58
发 61, 63
圣 207
4
观 86
欢 100
戏 249
6
变 13
艰 112
舰 114
取 189
受 215
叔 216
7
叛 172
竖 217
叙 264
8
难 166
桑 198
曼 155
11
叠 54

廴
4
延 268
6
建 114

工
工 79
2
功 81
巧 185
左 322
3
巩 82
式 212
4
攻 82
汞 82
贡 83
巫 245
6

7	抖 56	169	换 101	搭 41	**14**
套 227	扶 71	拍 171	捡 112	提 50	擦 21
8	抚 71	拚 172	捐 128	228	**16**
奢 203	护 99	披 174	捆 138	揪 77	攒 39
爽 218	技 109	拓 224	捞 140	搅 117	293
9	拒 128	237	揭 168	掂 119	**【寸】**
奥 3	抉 129	抬 225	捎 202	揪 126	寸 40
奠 53	抗 132	拖 237	损 223	搂 150	**2**
【九】	抠 136	押 268	捅 233	151	对 58
1	抡 152	择 294	挽 239	揉 195	**3**
尤 283	拟 167	招 297	挹 278	搜 221	导 47
2	扭 169	拄 312	振 300	握 245	寺 220
龙 150	抛 172	**6**	捉 316	援 289	寻 267
9	批 174	按 2	**8**	揍 320	**4**
就 127	抢 184	持 31	掺 24	**10**	寿 215
10	扰 192	挡 47	捶 37	摆 5	**6**
尴 75	折 203	拱 82	措 40	搬 5	封 70
【扌】	299	挂 85	掎 52	搏 16	耐 165
1	抒 216	挥 102	掉 53	搞 77	**7**
扎 292	投 234	挤 108	接 118	摸 162	射 203
295	抑 278	拷 133	捷 120	摄 203	**9**
2	找 298	挪 170	据 128	摊 225	尊 321
扒 3	抓 313	拼 175	掘 129	携 258	**【弋】**
171	**5**	拾 211	控 136	摇 272	**3**
打 41	拔 4	试 213	掠 152	**11**	式 212
扑 178	拌 6	拴 218	描 160	摧 39	**6**
扔 194	抱 8	挑 230	捻 168	撇 175	贰 61
3	拨 16	挺 232	排 171	摔 217	**【小(⺌)】**
扛 132	拆 24	挖 238	捧 173	摘 295	小 256
扣 136	抽 32	挟 258	掐 181	**12**	**1**
扩 138	担 45	挣 301	授 215	播 16	少 202
扫 198	抵 50	303	探 226	撤 197	**2**
托 237	拐 85	指 305	掏 226	撑 29	尔 61
扬 270	拣 112	**7**	推 236	撮 40	劣 147
执 304	拘 127	挨 1	掀 251	撺 168	**3**
4	拉 139	捌 4	掩 269	撒 197	尘 28
把 4	拦 139	捕 17	掷 307	撕 220	当 46
扳 5	拢 150	挫 40	**9**	撰 314	光 87
扮 8	抹 162	捣 48	揣 24	撞 315	尖 111
报 8	163	捍 92	搀 24	**13**	**4**
抄 26	拧 168		揎 35	操 23	肖 257
扯 28			搓 40	擅 200	

5
岸 2
岭 149
岩 269
6
峡 250
7
峰 70
峭 185
8
崩 10
崇 32
崖 268
崭 296
9
嵌 183

彳
3
行 92, 261
4
彻 28
彷 66
役 278
5
彼 11
径 125
往 240
征 301
6
待 44, 45
很 96
律 152
衍 269
7
徒 235
徐 264
8
得 49
徘 171
衔 252
9
街 119
循 267
10
微 241
12
德 49
13
衡 96

彡
4
形 262
5
参 22, 204
6
须 264
8
彩 22
9
彭 173
11
彰 297
12
影 281

犭
2
犯 64
4
狂 138
犹 284
5
狗 83
狐 98
6
独 57
狠 96
狡 117
狮 209
狩 215
狭 250
狱 287
7
狼 140
8
猜 21
猖 25
猎 148
猫 156
猛 158
猪 311
9
猴 97
猩 261
10
猿 289

夕
夕 248
2
外 238
3
多 59
名 161
岁 223
5
罗 153
8
够 83
梦 158
11
夥 104

夂
2
处 35
冬 55
务 247
3
各 78
4
条 230
5
备 9
6
复 73
7
夏 251

饣
2
饥 105
4
饭 64
饮 280
5
饱 7
饰 212
饲 221
6
饼 15
饵 61
饺 117
饶 192
7
饿 60
8
馆 86
馅 253
9
馋 25
11
馒 155

丬
3
妆 314
壮 315
4
状 315
6
将 115, 116

广
广 87
3
庆 188
庄 314
4
床 36
库 137
庐 151
序 264
应 280, 282
5
底 50
店 53
废 67
府 72
庙 160
庞 172
6
度 57, 59
庭 231
7
席 249
座 322
8
康 132
庸 282
10
廉 146
11
腐 72
廖 147
15
鹰 281

门
门 158
2
闪 200
3
闭 11
闯 36
问 245
4
间 112, 114
闷 157, 158
闰 196
闲 252
5
闹 166
闸 295
6
阁 78
闺 88
闽 160
闻 244
7
阅 291
8
阐 25
阎 269
9
阔 138

氵
2
汉 92
汇 103
汁 304
3
池 31
汗 92
汲 107
江 114
汤 226
污 245
4
沉 28
泛 64
沟 83
沥 144
沦 152
没 156, 162
沐 164
沏 179
汽 181
沙 198
沈 205

贪 225	觅 159	毛 156	敦 59	爵 219	胜 207
贤 252	视 212	**3**	敬 126	**父**	胎 224
责 294	**5**	尾 242	散 197	父 72	胃 243
账 297	觉 117	**7**	**9**	**2**	**6**
质 306	129	毫 93	数 217	爷 273	脆 40
5	觎 140	**8**	**11**	**4**	胳 77
贷 45	**6**	毽 114	敷 71	爸 4	脊 108
贰 61	舰 114	毯 226	**片**	斧 72	胶 116
费 67	**牛(牜 牛)**	**气(气)**	片 174	**6**	朗 140
贵 88	牛 169	气 180	175	爹 53	脑 166
贺 96	**2**	**5**	**4**	**月(月)**	能 167
贱 114	牟 163	氚 71	版 5	月 290	胸 263
贸 156	**4**	氢 186	**8**	**2**	脏 293
贴 231	牧 164	**6**	牌 171	有 285	朕 300
6	物 247	氧 271	**斤**	肌 106	脂 304
贿 103	**5**	**8**	斤 121	**3**	**7**
赃 293	牵 182	氨 46	**1**	肠 26	脖 16
贼 294	牲 207	**攵**	斥 31	肚 57	脚 117
资 316	**6**	**2**	**4**	肝 75	脯 146
8	特 227	收 213	斧 72	肖 257	脱 237
赐 38	牺 248	**3**	所 223	**4**	望 241
赌 57	**7**	改 74	欣 259	肮 2	**8**
赋 73	犁 143	攻 82	斩 296	肥 67	朝 27
赔 173	**8**	**4**	**7**	肺 67	298
赏 201	犀 249	放 66	断 58	肤 71	腊 139
赎 216	**11**	条 230	**8**	服 71	腌 174
9	靠 133	**5**	斯 220	72	期 179
赖 139	**手**	故 84	**9**	股 84	腔 184
10	手 214	政 303	新 260	肩 112	**9**
赛 197	**5**	**6**	**爪(爫)**	**5**	腹 73
赚 314	拜 5	敖 3	爪 313	肯 135	腻 168
12	**6**	效 258	**3**	朋 173	腮 197
赞 293	拿 164	致 307	妥 237	肾 205	腾 236
赠 295	拳 190	**7**	**4**	育 287	腿 236
13	掰 4	敌 12	采 21	胀 297	腥 261
赢 281	掌 297	敢 75	觅 159	肢 304	腰 271
见	**11**	**11**	爬 171	肿 309	**10**
见 113	摩 162	敝 117	乳 196	**5**	膜 162
2	**15**	救 126	受 215	背 9	**11**
观 86	攀 172	敏 160	爱 1	胆 46	膝 249
4	**毛**	**8**	**13**	胡 98	**12**
规 88		敞 26		脉 155	膨 173
				胖 172	

矽	248
4	
砍	132
砌	181
砂	199
研	269
砖	314
5	
破	177
砸	292
6	
硕	219
7	
硫	150
确	191
硬	282
8	
碍	2
碑	9
碰	174
碎	223
碗	240
9	
碧	12
磁	38
磋	40
碟	54
碳	226
10	
磅	6
	172
磕	133
11	
磨	162
	163
12	
磷	148
龙	
龙	150
3	
垄	150
6	

聋	150
袭	249
业	
业	273
7	
龇	293
目	
目	164
2	
盯	54
3	
盲	155
4	
看	132
眉	156
盼	172
省	207
	262
眨	295
5	
眼	159
6	
睿	129
眯	158
	159
着	298
	299
	316
睁	301
8	
督	56
睛	124
睡	219
10	
瞄	155
瞎	250
11	
瞥	175
12	
瞪	50
瞧	185

瞬	219
瞩	312
13	
瞻	296
田	
电	52
甲	111
申	204
田	230
由	283
2	
宙	163
男	165
3	
备	9
4	
界	121
思	220
畏	243
胃	243
5	
畜	35
	265
留	149
畔	172
6	
累	142
略	152
7	
番	63
	172
8	
畸	106
⺲	
四	220
3	
罗	153
4	
罚	62
5	
罢	4

8	
署	216
罩	299
置	307
罪	321
11	
罹	143
12	
羁	107
皿	
3	
孟	158
盆	173
盈	281
5	
盘	2
监	112
盐	269
益	278
盏	296
6	
盗	48
盖	74
盒	96
盘	172
盛	208
8	
盟	158
钅	
钉	54
针	299
3	
钓	53
4	
钞	26
钙	74
钢	76
钩	83
钮	169

钦	185
钥	272
钟	309
5	
铃	148
铅	182
钱	183
钳	183
铁	231
铀	284
钻	321
6	
铲	25
铝	152
铜	233
银	279
7	
锄	35
锋	70
锅	89
链	146
铺	178
锐	196
锁	224
销	256
锌	260
锈	264
铸	313
8	
锤	37
错	40
键	114
锦	122
锯	128
锣	153
锡	249
9	
镀	57
锻	58
镁	157
锹	184
10	

镇	301
11	
镜	126
13	
镰	146
17	
镶	255
矢	
3	
知	304
4	
矩	127
6	
矫	117
7	
短	57
8	
矮	1
9	
疑	277
禾	
禾	94
2	
利	144
私	220
秃	235
秀	264
3	
秉	15
秆	75
和	95
	96
	104
季	109
委	243
4	
科	133
秒	160
秋	188
香	254
种	309
	310

5
称 28, 29, 30
乘 30, 208
秤 30
积 106
秘 159
秦 186
秩 307
租 320
6
移 276
7
程 30
稍 202
税 219
稀 249
8
稠 33
9
稳 244
10
稻 48
稿 77
稽 106
黎 143
11
穆 164
12
黏 168
穗 223

白
白 4
1
百 4
3
的 49, 50, 51
4
皇 101
皆 118
泉 190

瓜
瓜 85
14
瓣 6

鸟
鸟 168
2
鸡 106
3
鸣 162
4
鸦 268
5
鸭 268
6
鸽 77
7
鹅 60
13
鹰 281

疒
2
疗 147
3
疙 77
4
疤 4
疮 36
疯 70
疫 278
5
病 15
疾 107
痉 125
疲 174
疼 228
疹 300
症 301, 303
6
痕 96
痊 190
痒 271
7
痞 174
痛 233
痣 307
8
痰 225
9
瘦 215
瘟 244
10
瘫 225
11
瘸 191
12
癌 1

立
立 144
1
产 25
4
亲 185, 188
竖 217
5
竞 125
站 296
6
竟 125
翌 278
章 297
7
童 233
8
意 278
9
端 57
竭 120

穴
穴 266
2
究 126
穷 188
3
空 135, 136
帘 145
4
穿 35
窃 185
突 235
5
窄 295
6
窑 272
7
窗 36
窜 39
窝 245
8
窟 136

衤
2
补 16
初 34
3
衬 28
衫 199
4
袄 3
5
被 9
袜 238
袖 264
7
裤 137
裙 191
8
裸 153
9
褐 96

疋(⺪)
7
疏 216
9
疑 277

皮
皮 174
5
皱 310
6
颇 177

矛
矛 156
4
柔 195

耒
4
耕 79
耗 94

老
考 133
老 140

耳
耳 61
2
取 189
耶 272
3
闻 244
4
耽 46
耸 221
5
聊 147
聆 148
聋 150
职 305
6
联 145
7
聘 176
8
聚 128
9
聪 38

臣
2
卧 245

西(覀)
西 248
3
要 271, 272
4
栗 145
5
票 175
12
覆 73

而
而 60
3
耐 165
耍 217

页
页 273
2
顶 54
3
顺 219
项 255
须 264
4
颁 5
顿 59
顾 84
顽 239
预 287
5
颈 125
领 149
颇 177
硕 219
6

Stroke Numbers Index

In this index the characters are arranged according to the total number of strokes used in writing the character. Characters with the same number of strokes are arranged according to the order of their appearance in this dictionary. The figure to the right of each character is the page number under which the character can be found in the body of the dictionary. Using the page number as a guide, one can locate in the dictionary the character and the entries beneath it.

果	90	迥	126	弥	158	祈	179	拓	224	夜	273
函	92	拘	127	觅	159	浅	183		237	依	276
杭	93	居	127	苗	160	枪	184	抬	225	宜	276
呵	94	沮	127	庙	160	侨	184	态	225	易	278
和	95	具	128	明	161	茄	185	贪	225	英	280
	96	卷	128	鸣	162	青	189	坦	225	拥	282
	104	咖	130	命	162	屈	189	图	235	油	284
河	95	凯	132	抹	162	取	189	兔	235	鱼	286
戋	96	炕	133		163	诠	190	拖	237	雨	287
呼	98	苛	133	茉	163	券	191	玩	239	育	287
忽	98	刻	134	陌	163	若	192	宛	239	枣	294
狐	98	肯	135	牧	163		196	往	240	责	294
虎	98	空	135	闹	166	乳	196	委	241	择	294
画	100		136	呢	166	软	196	味	243	咋	295
话	100	苦	136		167	丧	198	卧	243	闸	295
环	101	矿	138	泥	167	衫	199	武	247	沾	295
昏	103	昆	138	念	168	尚	202	物	247	斩	296
或	104	垃	139	拧	168	舍	204	昔	248	账	297
贷	105	拉	139		169	呻	204	矽	248	胀	297
奇	106	拦	139	欧	170	绅	204	细	250	招	297
	179	泪	142	殴	170	审	205	贤	252	沼	298
季	109	例	145	爬	171	肾	205	弦	252	者	299
剂	109	隶	145	怕	171	诗	209	现	252	侦	299
佳	110	帘	145	拍	171	实	210	限	253	枕	300
驾	111	练	146	拚	172	使	211	线	253	征	301
肩	112	林	148	庞	172	驶	211	详	255	郑	302
艰	112	岭	149	泡	172	势	212	享	255	枝	304
拣	112	拢	150	佩	173	事	212	些	258	知	304
建	114	奎	150	抨	173	侍	212	泄	258	肢	304
降	115	炉	151	朋	173	饰	212	泻	258	织	304
	255	录	151	坯	174	试	212	欣	259	直	304
郊	116	轮	152	披	174	视	212	幸	262	侄	304
佼	117	罗	153	贫	176	受	215	性	262	制	306
杰	119	码	154	凭	177	叔	216	姓	263	质	306
姐	120	卖	155	坪	177	述	217	学	266	治	307
届	121	盲	155	苹	177	刷	217	询	267	忠	308
金	121	茅	156	坡	177	饲	221	押	268	终	309
茎	123	茂	156	泼	177	丛	221	炎	269	肿	309
京	123	玫	156	迫	179	炎	222	松	269	宙	310
经	123	枚	156	妻	179	沿	222	沿	269	侏	311
径	125	妹	157	其	179	書	222	耶	272	挂	312
净	125	孟	158	歧	179	所	223				

A

ā 阿 ① a prefix to a name or a term of address ② a word often used in transliterations
⇨ē

Āgēntíng 阿根廷 Argentina; the Argentine

Ālābó 阿拉伯 ① Arabia ② Arab

Ālābóyǔ 阿拉伯语 Arabic (the language)

Ālǐshān 阿里山 Mt. Ali, Taiwan

Āmàn 阿曼 Oman

Āměizú 阿美族 the Ami tribe among the aborigines in Taiwan

āyí 阿姨 ① an aunt ② a step-mother

ā 啊 an exclamatory particle
⇨á

a 啊 a sentence-final particle
⇨ā

āi 哎 an interjection of surprise mixed with regret

āiyā 哎呀 an interjection of surprise

āiyō/āiyāo 哎哟 an interjection of surprise or grief

āi 哀 ① to grieve; to mourn; to lament ② to pity; to sympathize; to commiserate; compassion ③ sad; sorrowful; lamentable ④ sadness; sorrow; grief

āidào 哀悼 to mourn over or lament (someone's death)

āiqiú 哀求 to beg or appeal pathetically

Āijí 埃及 Egypt

āi 挨 ① (to stay) near, next to, close to; to lean to ② according to order ③ (now rarely) to rub
⇨ái

āi 唉 (an interjection of regret or disgust) alas

āi/èi 欸 the sound of answering
⇨èi

ái/āi 挨 ① to suffer (from cold, hunger, etc.) ② to wait; to delay;

to put off
⇨āi

ái'è/āi'è 挨饿 to suffer from hunger or starvation

ái 癌 cancer

áixìbāo 癌细胞 cancer cells

áizhèng 癌症 cancer

ǎi 矮 ① a short person; a dwarf ② short; low; low-ranking

àizībìng 艾滋病 AIDS (Acquired Immune Deficiency Syndrome)

ài 爱 ① to love; to like; to be fond of; to be kind to ② love; affection; kindness; benevolence; likes ③ to be apt to

àidài 爱戴 to love and support

Àidíshēng 爱迪生 Thomas Alva Edison, 1847-1931, American inventor

Àidīngbǎo 爱丁堡 Edinburgh, Scotland

Ài'ěrlán 爱尔兰 Ireland

àifǔ 爱抚 to caress

àiguó 爱国 patriotic

àihào 爱好 to be interested in or to love (sport, art, etc.)

àihù 爱护 to give kind protection to; to take kind care of

àimiànzi 爱面子 to be concerned about face-saving; to be sensitive about one's reputation

àiqíng 爱情 love

àiren 爱人 ① a spouse ② a sweetheart; a lover ③ to love others

àixī/àixì 爱惜 to prize; to cherish; to value

àixīn 爱心 compassion; kindness

Àiyīnsītǎn 爱因斯坦 Albert Einstein, 1879-1955, Jewish physicist and mathematician known for his theory of relativity

àizībìng 爱滋病 AIDS (Acquired Immune Deficiency Syndrome)

àizībìngdú 爱滋病毒 AIDS virus

A

ài 碍 ① to obstruct; to hinder; to be in the way ② harmful; detrimental

àishì 碍事 to be in the way

ān 安 ① to quiet; to stabilize; to pacify; to console ② to be content with ③ peaceful; quiet; calm; tranquil ④ safe; secure; stable ⑤ to put; to place; to arrange ⑥ a surname

āndǎ 安打 (baseball) a safe hit, a safety hit, or a safety

āndìng 安定 stable; steadfast; to stabilize

āndùn 安顿 to put in order; to help settle down

ānfēitāmìng 安非他命 amphetamine

ānfǔ 安抚 to pacify

Ānhuī 安徽 Anhui Province

ānjìng 安静 quiet; tranquil; still; peaceful

Ānlǐhuì 安理会 the Security Council (of the United Nations)

Ānnán 安南 Annam

ānníng 安宁 peace; repose; tranquility

ānpái 安排 arrangements; to arrange

ānquán 安全 ① safe; secure ② safety; security

ānquángǎn 安全感 a sense of security

ānquánmào 安全帽 a safety helmet

ānrán 安然 ① safely ② peacefully; at rest

ānwèi 安慰 to console; to soothe

ānwěn 安稳 ① smoothly ② peacefully

ānxiáng 安详 (said of one's manner) undisturbed; composed

ānxīn 安心 to have peace of mind; to be relieved

ānzhì 安置 ① to put in a proper place ② to settle (people in need of employment, refugees, etc.)

ānzhuāng 安装 to install (a device)

àn 岸 a shore; a bank; a beach; a coast

àn 按 ① to place the hand on; to press, control, etc. with one's hand ② according to; in (good order); as ③ to follow (a map, river, etc.) ④ to stop; to halt; to repress ⑤ a note; a comment

ànmó 按摩 ① massage ② to massage

ànniǔ 按钮 ① a push button ② to push the button

ànqī/ànqí 按期 according to the dates, periods, etc. agreed upon or specified

ànshí 按时 ① according to the time specified or agreed upon ② on time ③ regularly

ànzhào 按照 in accordance with; according to

àn 案 ① a legal case; legal records; a legal offense ② according to; on the strength of; following this precedent ③ to note

ànjiàn 案件 a legal case; a crime

ànqíng 案情 the ins and outs of a crime

ànzi 案子 a legal case; a project

àn 暗 ① dim; dark; obscure ② stupid; ignorant ③ secret; clandestine; stealthy ④ hidden

àn'àn 暗暗 ① obscure ② secret

àndàn 暗淡 ① (said of colors, etc.) faded, dull, and not fresh ② (said of business, etc.) dim

ànhào 暗号 a secret mark, sign, signal, or password

ànshā 暗杀 assassination; to assassinate

ànshì 暗示 ① to hint; to suggest ② a hint; a suggestion

ànzhōng 暗中 ① in secret ② (to do something) in the dark or without light

ànzì 暗自 inwardly; to oneself; secretly

āngzāng 肮脏 dirty

ángguì 昂贵 expensive; costly

ángyáng 昂扬 high-spirited

àngrán 盎然 abundant; full; exuberant

āo 凹 ① indented; an indention ② hollow; concave

āo/áo 熬 ① to cook; to stew ② to be worn down by worries, cares; discouraged or despondent; dejected ⇨áo

áo 翱 leisurely; idle

áo 熬 ① to extract (oil, etc.) by applying heat ② to cook; to stew or simmer ③ to endure with perseverance; to suffer with patience (an ordeal, etc.); to sustain ⇨āo

áoyè 熬夜 to burn the midnight oil

ǎo 袄 a coat; a jacket or top garment padded with cotton or lined with fur

Àodìlì 奥地利 Austria

Àolínpǐkè/Àolínpǐkè 奥林匹克 Olympic

àomì 奥秘 deep, profound, and mysterious; subtle

àomiào 奥妙 ① mysterious; marvelous ② the secret of doing something

Ào-Yùn 奥运 abbr. for the Olympic Games

ào 澳 ① deep waters—where seagoing vessels can moor ② name of various places

Àomén 澳门 Macao

Àozhōu 澳洲 Australia

àonǎo 懊恼 to feel remorseful and angry

B

bā 八 eight (Note: When bā precedes a 4th-tone sound, it is pronounced as bá.)

bāchéng 八成 nearly; almost; very likely

bāguà 八卦 the Eight Diagrams, consisting of an arrangement of single and divided lines in eight groups of three lines each as specified in the *Book of Changes*

bāzì 八字 ① a general term for the Celestial Stems and the Terrestrial Branches (干支), denoting the time, date, month and year of a person's birth; now used by fortuneteller as a reference to see if the betrothed are well matched; the horoscope ② character 八

bā 巴 ① name of an ancient state which occupied today's eastern Sichuan ② a crust formed as a result of heat or dryness ③ to expect; to hope for anxiously ④ used with parts of human body (such as hands, cheeks, chin, etc.) ⑤ to be close to ⑥ (physics) a bar

Bāgédá 巴格达 Bagdad or Baghdad, capital of Iraq

Bāhā 巴哈 Johann Sebastian Bach (1685-1750), German musician and composer

bājie 巴结 ① to curry favor; to toady; to flatter ② to exert oneself for advancement

Bālí 巴黎 Paris

Bālín 巴林 Bahrain

bāshì 巴士 a bus

Bāxī 巴西 Brazil

bā 扒 ① to claw; to strip ② to rake ③ to climb; to scale ⇨pá

bājiāo 芭蕉 a plantain

bāléiwǔ 芭蕾舞 ballet

bā 疤 ① a scar ② something that resembles a scar

bā 捌 an elaborate form of 八 (eight) used in documents or checks to prevent forgery

bá 拔 ① to pull out; to uproot ② to attack and take (a city); to capture ③ to promote (another to a higher position, etc.) ④ to stand out; outstanding; remarkable

bǎ 把 ① a handle; a hold ② a bundle; a grasp; a handful ③ to take ④ to hold ⑤ to guard; to watch over; to keep under surveillance ⑥ around; about; approximately; more or less ⑦ sworn
⇨bà

bǎbǐng 把柄 a hold (on somebody); a handle

bǎchí 把持 to monopolize; to dominate or control

bǎguān 把关 ① to guard a pass ② to check on

bǎshou 把手 ① a handle ② to hold hands

bǎwò 把握 ① something one holds in hand ② confident ③ to have a firm grasp of the situation

bǎxì 把戏 ① acrobatic performances as juggling, etc. ② a trick or scheme

bà 坝 ① an embankment; a dike ② a dam

bà 把 a handle
⇨bǎ

bà 爸 father

bàba 爸爸 father; papa

bà 罢 to cease; to stop; to finish; to be done with

bàgōng 罢工 (said of workers) to strike

bàle 罢了 (as a sentence-final phrase) merely; only; that's all

bàdào 霸道 to throw one's weight or to bully around; overbearing; high-handed

bàdao 霸道 a strong or heavy dosage (of liquor, medicine, etc.)

bàquán 霸权 the authority of a powerful feudal prince; hegemony

bàzhàn 霸占 to occupy or take by force

ba 吧 a sentence-final particle used to solicit agreement

bāi 掰 to pull apart with hands

bái 白 ① white; clear; bright; clean; pure; plain ② empty; blank ③ in vain; for nothing ④ free of charge; gratis ⑤ the spoken part in an opera, etc. ⑥ to state; to explain ⑦ a surname

báibái 白白 ① for no reason ② in vain; without purpose ③ to watch helplessly

báibān 白斑 white specks; white spots

báicài 白菜 ① Chinese cabbage ② white rape

báichī 白痴 an idiot

Báigōng 白宫 the White House, Washington, D.C.

báijiǔ 白酒 spirits usually distilled from sorghum or maize; white spirits

báilù 白鹭 an egret

báimǐ 白米 white polished rice

báipíshū 白皮书 a white paper (in the sense of an official government report)

báirèhuà 白热化 (said of a contest, movement, etc.) to reach the climax

báirén 白人 a white man or woman

báisè 白色 white

báitian 白天 daytime

báitù 白兔 ① a white rabbit ② the rabbit in the moon—the moon

báiyún 白云 white clouds

bǎi 百 ① hundred ② many; numerous ③ all

bǎibān 百般 all sorts; every kind

bǎibèi 百倍 one hundred times

bǎifēnbǐ 百分比 a percentage

bǎifēnzhībǎi 百分之百 absolutely

bǎihuā-qífàng 百花齐放 All flowers are in bloom.

bǎihuò 百货 general merchan-

dise; products for daily use

bǎihuò gōngsī 百货公司 a department store

bǎijiā-zhēngmíng 百家争鸣 All schools of thoughts contend for attention.

bǎixìng 百姓 the common people; the people

bǎizhàn-bǎishèng 百战百胜 victorious in every battle

bǎishù/bóshù 柏树 a cypress

bǎi 摆 ① to arrange; to display; to place; to put ② to wave; to swing; to oscillate; to wag ③ to assume; to put on ④ a pendulum

bǎidòng 摆动 to sway; to swing

bǎishè 摆设 to furnish and decorate (a room)

bǎishe 摆设 articles for interior decoration

bǎituō 摆脱 to free oneself from; to cast off; to shake off (a tailer)

bài 败 ① to defeat or be defeated; to fail; to go down ② to decline; to decay; to wither ③ to spoil or be spoiled; to corrupt or be corrupted

bàihuài 败坏 to ruin or be ruined

bài 拜 ① to do obeisance; to salute; to pay respects to ② to appoint (as a government official); an appointment ③ to visit; to pay a visit to; to call on (or at)

bàibai 拜拜 ① to bring hands together and take a bow ② a worshipping festival in Taiwan

bàifǎng 拜访 to pay a visit to; to visit

bàihuì 拜会 to visit; to call on

bàinián 拜年 to call on another and offer New Year's greetings

bàituō 拜托 a polite expression in asking another to do something for oneself

bān 扳 ① to pull ② to count (on one's fingers)

bān 班 ① a grade; a seat or position ② a class or company; a set; a group ③ a shift; duty ④ a squad (of soldiers) ⑤ scheduled runs (of the bus, etc.) ⑥ to distribute

⑦ to return ⑧ of equal rank, same generation, etc. ⑨ a surname

bānchē 班车 a regular bus

bāncì 班次 ① the flight number of an airliner ② the designated number of a scheduled train ③ the grade or class (of a student) ④ sequence

bānjī 班机 an airliner on the scheduled flight

bānjí 班级 ① a grade ② a class

bānzhǎng 班长 ① (military) a squad leader ② (in school) the leader of a class

bānzi 班子 ① an operatic company ② a brothel

bān 般 kind; sort; class ⇨bō

bān 颁 ① to bestow on; to grant; to confer on ② to proclaim; to make public ③ to promulgate ③ to distribute; to send out

bānbù 颁布 to proclaim or promulgate

bānfā 颁发 to bestow; to award or distribute (prizes, etc.)

bānjiǎng 颁奖 to hand out an award or prize

bān 斑 ① speckles; spots; mottles ② mottled; variegated; motley

bānmǎxiàn 斑马线 a zebra crossing

bān 搬 ① to move; to transport ② to present

bānjiā 搬家 to move from one dwelling to another

bānyùn 搬运 to move; to transport; to carry

bǎn 板 ① a board; a plank ② a plate (of tin, aluminum, etc.); a slab ③ printing blocks ④ rigid; stern; stiff

bǎnqiáo 板桥 ① a bridge built of wooden planks ② a city in Taipei County, Taiwan

bǎn 版 ① edition ② printing plate ③ household registers ④ supporting boards used in building walls

bǎnběn 版本 an edition; a ver-

sion

bǎnhuà 版画 a print

bǎnmiàn 版面 ① space of a whole page ② layout of a printed sheet

bǎnquán 版权 copyright

bàn 办 ① to manage; to handle; to transact; to deal with; to attend to ② to purchase ③ to try and punish

bàn'àn 办案 to handle a (legal or business) case

bànfǎ 办法 means; schemes; ways; resources

bàngōng 办公 to attend to business; to do office work

bàngōngshì 办公室 an office

bànlǐ 办理 to handle; to manage

bànshì 办事 to handle business; to manage an affair

bànshìchù 办事处 a branch office (of an organization)

bànxué 办学 to run a school

bàn 半 ① half ② very little ③ in the middle ④ partly; about half

bànbiāntiān 半边天 half the sky

bànchéngpǐn 半成品 semi-finished products or articles; half-finished products or goods

bàndǎo 半岛 a peninsula

bàndǎotǐ 半导体 a semiconductor

bànjié 半截 a half part; half (a section)

bànjìng 半径 a radius

bànlā/bànlā 半拉 (colloquial) half; half a piece

bànlù 半路 halfway; midway

bànshù 半数 half the number; half

bàntiān 半天 ① half-day; half a day ② quite a while ③ midair; in the air

bàntú'érfèi 半途而废 to stop (a task) halfway

bànyè 半夜 ① half a night ② midnight

bànzhēn-bànjiǎ 半真半假 partly true, partly false

bàn 扮 to dress up; to disguise;

to play

bànyǎn 扮演 to play or act (a part or role)

bàn 伴 ① to accompany ② a companion

bànlǚ 伴侣 a companion; a pal

bànsuí 伴随 to accompany; to follow

bànzòu 伴奏 to accompany (a soloist)

bàn 拌 to mix

bàn 瓣 ① petals ② sections (as of oranges) ③ a valve; a lamella ④ fragments

bāng 帮 ① to help; to assist ② the sides of a shoe or gutter ③ a gang; a group; a class; a fleet

bāngmáng 帮忙 help; assistance; to help or assist

bāngpài 帮派 a faction

bāngshou 帮手 a helper; an assistant

bāngzhù 帮助 help; assistance; to help or assist

bǎng 绑 to tie; to bind; to fasten

bǎngjià 绑架 to kidnap for ransoms

bǎng 榜 a publicly posted roll of successful examinees

bǎngyàng 榜样 an example; a model

bàng 棒 ① a club; a stick; a truncheon ② good; strong; wonderful ③ to hit with a club

bàngqiú 棒球 baseball

bàngzi 棒子 ① a short and thick club ② Indian corn

bàngwǎn/bāngwǎn 傍晚 dusk; twilight; nightfall

bàng 磅 ① a pound ② scales ③ to weigh
⇨páng

bāo 包 ① a parcel; a package; a bundle ② to wrap ③ to surround ④ to guarantee ⑤ to include; to contain ⑥ a surname

bāobàn 包办 to undertake completely

bāofu 包袱 ① a bundle in a

cloth wrapper ② a cloth wrapper ③ a burden

bāogānr 包干儿 to be responsible for a task

bāoguǒ 包裹 ① a parcel ② to wrap up

bāohán 包含 to contain; to comprise

bāokuò/bāoguā 包括 to include; to comprise

bāoluó-wànxiàng 包罗万象 inclusive of everything

bāoróng 包容 to tolerate; to forgive

bāowéi 围围 to surround; to encircle

bāozhuāng 包装 to pack; packing

bāozi 包子 a steamed stuffed bun

bāo 炮 quick-fry ⇨**páo, pào**

bāo/bō 剥 to strip ⇨**bō**

bàozi 电子 hail; a hailstone

bǎo 饱 ① to eat to the full; surfeited ② full; plump ③ fully; to the full ④ satisfied

bǎohé 饱和 saturation; saturated

bǎomǎn 饱满 well-stacked (figures, etc.); full; plump

bǎoshòu 饱受 to suffer (insult, grievances, etc.) to the fullest extent

bǎo 宝 ① treasure ② precious; valuable ③ respectable; honorable

bǎobao 宝宝 baby

bǎobèi 宝贝 ① a cherished thing ② darling

bǎodǎo 宝岛 a treasure island

bǎoguì 宝贵 valuable; precious

bǎokù 宝库 a treasury; a treasure house

bǎoshí 宝石 a precious stone; a gem; a jewel

bǎowù 宝物 a treasure; a treasury

bǎozàng 宝藏 a treasure; a treasury

bǎozuò 宝座 the throne

bǎo 保 ① to guard; to shelter; to protect ② to be responsible; to guarantee; to insure ③ to keep; to maintain

bǎo'ān 保安 ① to ensure local security ② to ensure the workers' safety ③ public security

bǎochí 保持 to maintain; to keep

bǎocún 保存 ① to preserve ② to safeguard

bǎoguǎn 保管 to safeguard; safekeeping

bǎohù 保护 to protect; to guard; protection

bǎohùqū 保护区 a protected area

bǎojiàn 保健 health protection; health care

bǎolíngqiú 保龄球 bowling

bǎoliú 保留 to preserve; to reserve

bǎoliúdì 保留地 ① the land reserved for a certain purpose ② a reservation (as the territory set apart for a certain class of people, like aborigines)

bǎomì 保密 to keep the secret

bǎomǔ 保姆 a nurse who looks after small children

bǎoquán 保全 to assure the safety of

bǎoquán rényuán 保全人员 security personnel

bǎoshǒu 保守 conservative

bǎowèi 保卫 to defend; to guard against

bǎowēn 保温 ① to keep (water, etc.) hot; to preserve heat ② heat preservation

bǎoxiǎn 保险 ① insurance ② to guarantee

bǎoxiǎn gōngsī 保险公司 an insurance company

bǎoxiǎntào 保险套 a condom; a sheath

bǎoxiǎnxiāng 保险箱 a safe; a strongbox

bǎoyǎng 保养 ① to take care (of health) ② to maintain ③ maintenance

B

bǎoyǒu 保有 to keep

bǎoyòu 保佑 ① to protect or bless ② a blessing

bǎoyù 保育 to raise (a kid)

bǎozhàng 保障 to safeguard; to protect

bǎozhèng 保证 to guarantee; to assure

bǎozhèngjīn 保证金 guaranty money

bǎozhòng 保重 Please take good care (of yourself).

bǎolěi 堡垒 a fortress; a bastion

bào 报 ① a report; a newspaper ② to report; to announce ③ to repay; to recompense; to requite ④ a reward; a retribution

bào'àn 报案 to report a case (such as a theft, murder, etc.) to the police

bàobiǎo 报表 forms for reporting statistics, etc.; report forms

bàochóu 报仇 to avenge (a grievance, etc.)

bàochou 报酬 ① remuneration; reward ② pay; a salary

bàodá 报答 to repay another's kindness

bàodǎo 报导 ① to report (news) ② a news report

bàodào 报到 to check in; to register

bàodào 报道 ① to report (news) ② to transmit; to convey

bàofù 报复 ① to avenge; to revenge ② to report back (after investigation)

bàogào 报告 ① to report ② a report

bàoguān 报关 to declare something at the customs

bàojià 报价 (economics) ① a quoted price ② to quote

bàojǐng 报警 ① to report an alarm or emergency ② to report to the police

bàokān 报刊 newspapers and periodicals

bàokǎo 报考 to enter one's name in an examination

bàomíng 报名 to enroll; to enlist

bàoqǐng 报请 to request for permission to do something

bàoshè 报社 a newspaper office

bàoxiāo 报销 ① to give a statement on one's expenses ② to write off

bàoyìng 报应 retribution

bàozhāng 报章 ① newspapers ② reply letters

bàozhǐ 报纸 ① a newspaper ② newsprint

bào 抱 ① to embrace; to enfold; to hold in the arms ② to harbor; to cherish; to bosom ③ to adopt ④ ambition

bàofù 抱负 aspirations; ambition

bàoqiàn 抱歉 to feel sorry about; to regret

bàoyuàn 抱怨 to complain; to grumble

bào 豹 a leopard; a panther

bào 鲍 ① an abalone ② salted fish ③ a surname

bào 暴 ① cruel; savage; fierce; violent ② short-tempered ③ sudden

bàodòng 暴动 a riot; a rebellion

bàofēng-zhòuyǔ / bàofēng-zòuyǔ 暴风骤雨 a storm; a tempest

bàolì 暴力 violence; brute force

bàomín 暴民 mobs or mobsters

bàoyǔ 暴雨 torrential rain; a squall

bàozào 暴躁 irritable; fretful; irascible

bàozhǎng 暴涨 (said of a water level or a commodity price) to rise sharply or quickly

bào 爆 ① to explode; to burst; to crack ② to quick-boil; to quick-fry

bàofā 爆发 ① to break out; to erupt; to flare up ② to explode; to blow up

bàomǐhuā 爆米花 popcorn

bàopò 爆破 to demolish by explosives; demolition

bàozhà 爆炸 to explode; to blow

up

bàozhú 爆竹 firecrackers

bēi 杯 a cup; a tumbler; a glass; a goblet

bēizi 杯子 a cup; a tumbler; a glass

bēibǐ 卑鄙 ① mean ② low; inferior

bēi 背 to bear or shoulder (a load, burden, etc.); to carry on the back
⇨**bèi**

bēibāo 背包 a knapsack

bēifù 背负 to carry on the back

bēi 悲 ① sad; sorrowful; mournful; woeful; rueful; doleful ② to lament; to deplore; to mourn; to pity; to sympathize

bēiāi 悲哀 mournful; woeful

bēicǎn 悲惨 tragic(al); pathetic; miserable

bēifèn 悲愤 ① grief and indignation ② to lament and resent (an injustice)

bēiguān 悲观 pessimistic

bēijù 悲剧 a tragedy

bēishāng 悲伤 sad; sorrowful

bēitòng 悲痛 grieved; deep sorrow

bēi 碑 a stone tablet

bēiwén 碑文 an inscription on a tablet

běi 北 ① north; northern; northerly ② northward

běibian 北边 the north; the northern part

běibù 北部 northern part; north

běifāng 北方 ① the north ② the northern region

Běi Hán 北韩 North Korea

Běijīng 北京 Beijing; Peking

Běi Měizhōu 北美洲 North America

běimiàn 北面 ① the north; the northern part ② to have an audience (with the emperor); to pay homage to

Běi Ōu 北欧 northern Europe

Běipíng 北平 see **Běijīng** 北京

běishàng 北上 to go north

Bèiduōfēn 贝多芬 Ludwig van Beethoven (1770-1827), German composer

bèiké 贝壳 seashells; shells

bèi 备 ① a sense of completeness; perfection ② to be equipped with ③ to get ready ④ to prepare against

bèiwànglù 备忘录 a memorandum

bèiyòng 备用 reserve; spare; alternate

bèizhù 备注 ① remarks or footnotes ② space reserved for footnotes

bèi 背 ① the back ② the reverse side; the back side ③ to remember by rote; to commit to memory in detail ④ to cast away; to turn one's back on; to give up ⑤ to go against; to rebel
⇨**bèi**

bèibù 背部 the back (of a man or an animal, etc.)

bèihòu 背后 behind one's back

bèijǐ 背脊 the back of human body; the spine

bèijǐng 背景 background

bèimiàn 背面 the reverse side; the back side

bèipàn 背叛 to rebel; to betray

bèishū 背书 ① to recite a lesson ② to endorse a check ③ endorsement

bèisòng 背诵 to recite

bèixīn 背心 a vest; a waistcoat

bèiyǐng 背影 the sight of one's back

bèi 倍 ① (joined to a numeral) -times; -fold ② double; to double ③ to rebel; to be insubordinate

bèishù 倍数 a multiple

bèi 被 ① placed before verbs to show the passive voice ② bedding; a coverlet; a quilt ③ to cover; to shroud ④ to spread; to reach ⑤ because of; due to

bèidān 被单 a bedsheet; a bedspread

B

bèidòng 被动 passive; to act on orders

bèigào 被告 the accused; the defendant

bèihàizhě 被害者 the injured or wronged party; a victim; an injured person

bèipò 被迫 to be compelled or forced to

bèizi 被子 a quilt

bèi 辈 ① a generation ② rank; a grade

bèizi 辈子 ① all one's life; a lifetime ② a generation

bēn 奔 ① to move quickly; to run; to hurry ② to run for one's life; to flee ③ to elope
⇨bèn

bēnbō 奔波 to be on the run; to work very hard

bēnchí 奔驰 to travel quickly; to move fast

bēnpǎo 奔跑 to run in a great hurry

bēnténg 奔腾 ① to gallop ② to surge forward; to roll in surges

bēnzǒu 奔走 ① to solicit help (in trying to land a job, get an appointment, etc.) ② to do a job on orders; to run errands

běn 本 ① a book; a copy ② original ③ our; this; the present ④ capital (in business) ⑤ the root; the origin; the source; the basis; the foundation ⑥ the root of a plant ⑦ according to; based on ⑧ the beginning; the starting point

běndì 本地 the local area

běnjīn 本金 principal as distinct from interest

běnlái 本来 ① originally ② of course

běnlǐng 本领 ability; skill; talent

běnnéng 本能 instinct

běnqián 本钱 capital (in business)

běnrén 本人 ① I; me ② himself; herself; yourself ③ personally

běnshēn 本身 oneself; personal-

ly; itself

běnshì 本事 a story (or a plot) of a play, movie, etc.

běnshi 本事 ability; skill; talent

běntǔ 本土 the mainland; a country proper

běnwèi 本位 ① a basic unit ② a standard

běnxìng 本性 the real nature

běnyè 本业 ① (in ancient China) farming which was considered the most important sector of the economy ② one's own occupation

běnzhe 本着 in the light of; in accordance with

běnzhì/běnzhí 本质 essence; the intrinsic nature

běnzi 本子 a book; a notebook

bēn/bèn 奔 to go straightforward; to head for
⇨bēn

bèn 笨 ① stupid; dull ② clumsy; awkward

bèndàn 笨蛋 a fool

bènzhòng 笨重 ① cumbersome; too heavy for convenient handling ② clumsy

bènzhuō/bènzhuó 笨拙 unskilled; clumsy; awkward

bēngkuì 崩溃 to collapse; to break down; to fall to pieces

bēng 绷 to tight; to stretch tight
⇨bèng

bēngdài 绷带 a bandage

béng 甭 unnecessary; do not have to

běng 绷 ① taut; tense ② to endure or bear
⇨bēng

bèng 蹦 to skip; to caper; to trip; to jump; to leap

bī 逼 ① to press; to compel; to pressure; to force; to coerce ② to importune; to harass; to annoy ③ to close in; to draw near

bījìn 逼近 to draw near; to press

bīpò 逼迫 to compel; to force

bīzhēn 逼真 (said of acting, performances, etc.) lifelike; almost

B

real

bí 鼻 a nose

bíkǒng 鼻孔 nostrils

bítì 鼻涕 nasal mucus or drips; snivel

bíyān'ái 鼻咽癌 nasopharyngeal carcinoma

bíyán 鼻炎 nasal catarrh

bízi 鼻子 a nose

bǐ 比 ① to compare with ② to liken; to compare to ③ than ④ to compete ⑤ to (in a score) ⑥ ratio ⑦ gesture

bǐbúshàng 比不上 to be inferior to; to be no peer for

bǐduì 比对 to collate

bǐfang 比方 an example

bǐfāngshuō 比方说 for example; for instance

bǐfēn 比分 (sports) score

bǐjià 比价 to compare prices or bids

bǐjiào 比较 ① comparative; relatively ② to compare

bǐlì 比例 ratio; proportion

Bǐlìshí 比利时 Belgium

bǐlǜ 比率 ratio; rate

bǐnǐ 比拟 ① to liken; to compare to ② a parallel

bǐrú 比如 such as; like

bǐrúshuō 比如说 for example; for instance; such as

bǐsài 比赛 a contest; a match; a tournament

bǐyù 比喻 ① a metaphor; a simile ② to compare to; to liken

bǐzhào 比照 according to; in the light of

bǐzhòng 比重 specific gravity

bǐ 彼 ① that; those ② another; the other ③ there

bǐcǐ 彼此 you and me; both parties; that and this; each other

bǐ 笔 ① a writing brush; a pen; a pencil ② a stroke; a touch ③ a unit of amount ④ writer's skill or style ⑤ to write ⑥ (formerly) prose

bǐchù 笔触 the touch of writing or drawing

bǐhuà 笔画 the number of strokes (in a character)

bǐjì/bǐjì 笔迹 one's handwriting

bǐjì 笔记 notes taken (of lectures, speeches, etc.)

bǐjìxíng diànnǎo 笔记型电脑 a portable computer

bǐlù 笔录 ① to write down; to take down ② notes; a record

bǐmò 笔墨 ① pen and ink ② writing words

bǐshì 笔试 a written examination

bǐzhě 笔者 the (present) writer

bǐzhí 笔直 perfectly straight

bì 币 ① currency; money ② a present; an offering

bìzhí 币值 the purchasing power of a currency

bì 必 ① must; necessarily ② an emphatic particle

bìbèi 必备 essential; necessary; indispensible

bìdìng 必定 most certainly; to be sure to

bìjiāng 必将 to have to; to be sure to

bìrán 必然 to have to be (like this)

bìxiūkē 必修科 a required course; an obligatory course

bìxū 必须 must; to have to

bìxū 必需 what is essential or indispensable

bìyào 必要 necessary; need

bì 毕 ① to complete; to finish; to end ② a surname

bìjìng 毕竟 after all; in the long run; ultimately

Bìkǎsuǒ 毕卡索 Pablo Picasso, 1881-1973, Spanish painter

bìshēng 毕生 in one's whole life; throughout one's lifetime; lifelong

bìyè 毕业 to be graduated; to graduate; graduation

bìyèshēng 毕业生 a graduate

bì 闭 ① to close; to shut ② (said of a conference, etc.) to conclude; to end ③ to block up; to

B

stop; to obstruct ④ to restrain

bìmù 闭幕 (said of shows, meetings, etc.) to close or conclude

bìmùshì 闭幕式 a closing ceremony

bìsè 闭塞 ① to block up; to obstruct ② backward ③ hard to get to

bì 敝 (a self-depreciatory term) my or our

bìlǜ 碧绿 verdant; emerald green

bìbìng 弊病 corrupt practices

bìduān 弊端 corrupt practices

bì 壁 ① a partition wall; the walls of a room ② a military breastwork ③ a cliff

bìhuà 壁画 a mural painting; a fresco

bì 避 ① to avoid; to shun; to evade; to hide ② to prevent; to keep away; to repel

bìkāi 避开 to get out of the way

bìmiǎn 避免 to avoid; to forestall

bìnàn 避难 to escape a calamity; to avoid disaster; to take refuge

bìyùn 避孕 to avoid pregnancy; contraception

bì 臂 the arms (of a human being or a tool, machine, etc.)

biān 边 ① an edge; the end of something; a verge; a margin ② a side ③ a hem; a decorative border ④ nearby; near to ⑤ the border of a nation's territory; a boundary ⑥ limits; bounds

biān...biān...... 边……边…… a speech pattern indicating two actions taking place simultaneously

biānfáng 边防 border defense; frontier defense

biānjì 边际 ① a boundary ② (Buddhism) the extremity of things ③ the substance of one's speech or writing

biānjiāng 边疆 a borderland; a frontier

biānjiè 边界 the national boundary

biānjìng 边境 the national boundary or border; the frontier

biānyuán 边缘 the edge; the verge

biān 编 ① to compile; to edit ② to put together; to organize; to form; to arrange ③ to fabricate; to make up; to invent ④ to knit; to weave ⑤ a volume

biānhào 编号 ① a serial number ② to arrange under numbers; to number

biānjí 编辑 ① to edit; to compile ② an editor

biānjíbù 编辑部 an editorial department; the editorial office

biānjù 编剧 ① to write a play ② a playwright

biānliè 编列 to list (the expenses for a project in the budget); to compile

biānmǎ 编码 coding

biānmù 编目 to prepare or compile a catalogue; to arrange a table of contents; to catalogue

biānpái 编排 ① to arrange in order ② to write and present (a play, etc.)

biānxiě 编写 ① to compile ② to compose

biānzhě'àn 编者按 editorial footnote; editorial annotation

biānzhī 编织 to knit

biānzhì 编制 ① to work out; to draw up ② organization ③ to knit; to weave

biāncè 鞭策 ① a horsewhip ② to urge or goad on; to encourage

biānpào 鞭炮 (a long string of) firecrackers

biānzi 鞭子 a whip; a lash

biǎn 贬 ① to reduce or lower (prices, etc.); to devalue ② to degrade; to reduce; to demote ③ to disparage; to condemn; to censure ④ to dismiss; to send away

biǎndī 贬低 to belittle; to depreciate; to play down

biǎnyì 贬义 derogatory sense;

pejorative connotation

biǎnzhí 贬值 to devalue or debase (especially referring to a currency); devaluation; depreciation

biǎn 扁 ① flat ② a tablet
⇨piǎn

biǎn'é 匾额 a (wooden) tablet; a horizontal inscribed board

biàn 变 ① to change; to alter; to become different ② to turn into; to become ③ extraordinary; uncommon ④ changeable ⑤ an accident; misfortune; tragedy; upheaval; disturbance

biànchéng 变成 to become; to change into

biànde 变得 to become

biàndòng 变动 ① (said of organizations, arrangements, etc.) to change; to reorganize ② alteration ③ variation

biàngé 变革 (said of an institution, etc.) to change or reform

biàngēng 变更 to change (plans, methods, etc.); to alter; to modify

biànhuà 变化 ① to transform; to transmute ② to change ③ changeable

biànhuàn 变换 ① to convert (foreign money, etc.) ② to change; to vary; to switch

biànqiān 变迁 evolution; change; vicissitudes

biànshù 变数 (mathematics) a variable

biànsùxiāng 变速箱 a gearbox; a transmission

biàntài 变态 ① (zoology) metamorphosis ② abnormality

biàntōng 变通 to adapt oneself to circumstances

biànwéi 变为 to become; to be converted or transformed into

biànxíng 变形 to transfigure; to transform

biànyì 变异 (biology) variation; mutation

biànzhì/biànzhì 变质 ① to change in quality or objectives

② to deteriorate; to go bad ③ to degenerate

biàn 便 ① in that case; even if ② then ③ expedient; convenient; handy ④ fitting; appropriate ⑤ advantageous ⑥ excrement and urine; to relieve oneself ⑦ informal; at ease; ordinary
⇨pián

biàndāng 便当 a box lunch

biàndang 便当 easy; convenient

biàndào 便道 ① sidewalks; paths flanking the main road ② a shortcut; a snap course ③ to do something on the way

biànjié 便捷 easy and convenient

biànlì 便利 convenience; facility

biànlì shāngdiàn 便利商店 a convenience store

biànmín 便民 to offer greater convenience to the people

biànshì 便是 even if

biàntiáo 便条 a note; a memo

biànyú 便于 easy to; convenient to

biàn 遍 ① (for action) a time; once through ② all over; everywhere ③ the whole (world, etc.)

biàndì 遍地 everywhere; all places

biànjí 遍及 all over

biàntǐ-línshāng 遍体鳞伤 to suffer injuries all over one's body

biànbié 辨别 to distinguish between; to see the difference between

biànrèn 辨认 to recognize; to identify

biànshí/biànshì 辨识 to recognize; to identify

biàn 辩 ① to debate; to argue; to dispute ② to use specious arguments

biànhù 辩护 ① to speak in defense of; to defend verbally; to defend ② (law) to plead; to defend; defense

biànjiě 辩解 to provide an expla-

nation; to try to defend oneself

biànlùn 辩论 ① to debate; a debate

biànzhèng 辩证 ① to analyze and verify a point ② dialectical

biànzhèngfǎ 辩证法 dialectic

biànzi 辫子 ① a queue; a pigtail; a braid; a plait ② a mistake or defect that may be exploited by an opponent

biāo 标 ① to show; to indicate; to mark; to symbolize ② a mark; a sign; a symbol; an indication; a label ③ a model; a paragon ④ to bid; to tender

biāobǎng 标榜 ① to glorify ② to profess ③ to boost

biāoběn 标本 ① a specimen ② appearance and substance

biāodì 标的 a target; an objective; a purpose; an aim

biāodiǎn 标点 punctuation

biāogān 标竿 a guidepost

biāojì 记 a mark; an indication

biāoqiān 标签 a label; a tag

biāoshì 标示 to indicate; to mark

biāotí 标题 a heading; a title; a headline

biāoyǔ 标语 a slogan; a motto

biāozhì 标志 a mark; a sign; a symbol

biāozhǔn 标准 ① a standard; a criterion ② typical

Biāozhǔn Jú 标准局 the Nation-al Bureau of Standards

biāochē 飙车 to speed a car or a motorcycle

biǎo 表 ① a table; a schedule; a chart ② a form ② outside; external; apparent; appearance; exteriors; superficial ③ to announce; to manifest; to show ④ relatives on the side of one's mother's sisters or brothers; relatives on the side of one's father's sisters ⑤ a watch; a timepiece

biǎobái 表白 to express or state clearly

biǎodá 表达 to convey or transmit (one's feelings, meaning, etc.); to present; to express; to

make known

biǎodì 表弟 a cousin (a son of one's father's sister or of one's mother's brother or sister, who is younger than oneself)

biǎogē 表哥 a cousin (a son of one's father's sister or of one's mother's brother or sister, who is older than oneself)

biǎogé 表格 a form or blank (for filling); a table or chart

biǎojué 表决 to vote; to put to the vote

biǎomèi 表妹 a cousin (a daughter of one's father's sister or of one's mother's brother or sister, who is younger than oneself)

biǎomiàn 表面 on the surface; externally; outwardly; superficial

biǎomíng 表明 to indicate or state clearly or plainly

biǎopí 表皮 ① the epidermis ② the cuticle (of plants)

biǎoqíng 表情 facial expression

biǎoshì 表示 to express; to show; to indicate; expression; reaction

biǎotài 表态 to make known one's position towards an issue

biǎoxiàn 表现 ① to appear ② to behave ③ to distinguish oneself

biǎoyǎn 表演 to perform; to demonstrate; a performance; demonstration; a show

biǎoyáng 表扬 to praise in public; to cite for all to know

biǎozhāng 表彰 to honor; to cite; citation

biē 憋 ① to suppress inner feelings with efforts ② to feel oppressed

bié 别 ① (in imperative expressions) do not ② other; another; different ③ to part ④ to distinguish; to differentiate

biéchù 别处 other places; elsewhere

biéde 别的 other; different

biérén 别人 someone else

biéren 别人 other people; others

biéshù 别墅 a villa; a country house

biézì 别字 ① a word which is not correctly written or pronounced ② an alias

bièniu 别扭 ① awkward; refractory ② an awkward situation

bīn 宾 ① a guest; a visitor ② to treat as a guest ③ to obey; to follow instructions; to submit ④ a surname

bīnguǎn 宾馆 a guesthouse

bīnyǔ 宾语 (grammar) the object of a transitive verb

bīnfēn 缤纷 ① flourishing; thriving ② chaotic

bīnlín 濒临 near; on the brink of

bīng 冰 ① ice; icicles ② cold; frost

bīnggùnr 冰棍儿 ice-lolly; popsicle; ice-sucker

bīnghé 冰河 a glacier

bīngkuài 冰块 ice cubes; ice blocks

bīnglěng 冰冷 ① icy cold; cold as ice ② cold or frosty (expressions, etc.)

bīngqílín 冰淇淋 ice cream

bīngshān 冰山 an iceberg

bīngxiāng 冰箱 an icebox; a refrigerator

bīng 兵 ① a soldier; a serviceman ② arms; weapons ③ a piece in Chinese chess—a pawn

bīnglì 兵力 military strength

bīngyì 兵役 (compulsory) military service

bīngláng/bīnláng 槟榔 the areca (nut); the betel (nut)

bǐng 丙 the third of the ten Celestial Stems (tiāngān 天干)

bǐngchí 秉持 ① to adhere to (one's principles, etc.) ② to hold in hand (a spear, etc.)

bǐngxìng 秉性 nature; a natural disposition or temperament

bǐng 柄 ① the handle of something ② a handle

bǐng 饼 ① cakes; biscuits; pastry ② anything round and flat, as a disc

bǐnggān 饼干 biscuits or crackers

bìng 并 ① on the same level with; even; equal ② and; also; at the same time ③ entirely; completely ④ to combine; to annex ⑤ together ⑥ all; entire

bìngcún 并存 to coexist; coexistent; coexistence

bìngfā 并发 to begin, explode, erupt, attack, occur, etc. at the same time

bìngfāzhèng 并发症 (medicine) a complication

bìngfēi 并非 by no means

bìngliè 并列 to stand side by side; to juxtapose

bìngpái 并排 side by side; in the same row

bìngqiě 并且 moreover; furthermore; and

bìngzhòng 并重 to lay equal stress on

bìng 病 ① illness; disease; ailment ② to be ill ③ blemish; fault

bìngbiàn 病变 pathological changes

bìngchónghài 病虫害 blight

bìngchuáng 病床 a sickbed

bìngdú 病毒 a virus

bìngfáng 病房 a sickroom; a ward

bìnghào 病号 a hospitalized patient who is numbered for easy identification

bìnghuàn 病患 a patient

bìngjūn/bìngjùn 病菌 germs; bacteria; viruses

bìnglì 病历 medical history (of a patient)

bìnglì 病例 number of cases of a particular disease

bìngqíng 病情 the condition of a patient

bìngrén 病人 a sick man; a patient

bìngtòng 病痛 slight illness; indisposition

B

bìngyǒu 病友 a friend made in hospital or people who become friends in hospital

bō 拨 ① to dispel; to remove ② to poke ③ to move; to transfer ④ to distribute; to issue ⑤ to set aside; to set apart; to appropriate

bōkuǎn 拨款 to issue or appropriate funds; an appropriation

bō 波 ① waves; breakers ② to undulate; undulation; to fluctuate; fluctuations ③ to affect; to involve; to implicate; to entangle

bōcháng 波长 (physics) wavelength

bōdòng 波动 ① undulation ② (said of prices) fluctuations

bōduàn 波段 a wave band

bōjí 波及 ① to affect; to involve ② (said of a fire) to engulf; to spread to

Bōlán 波兰 Poland

bōlán 波澜 ① waves or billows ② the turns and twists of a piece of writing

bōlàng 波浪 billows; breakers; waves

Bōshìdùn 波士顿 Boston

Bōsīwān 波斯湾 the Persian Gulf

bōtāo/bòtáo 波涛 billows; breakers; large waves

bōli 玻璃 glass

bō 般 (Buddhism) intelligence ⇨bān

bō 剥 to strip; to skin; to make bare; to peel; to peel off; to shell ⇨bāo

bōduó 剥夺 to deprive or strip one of (rights, property, etc.)

bōxuē/bòxuè 剥削 to exploit (people)

bōcài 菠菜 spinach

bō/bò 播 ① to sow; to seed ② to spread; to propagate

bōchū/bòchū 播出 to broadcast; to transmit

bōfàng/bòfàng 播放 to broadcast (news, etc.) on the air

bōsòng/bòsòng 播送 to broadcast (messages, programs, etc.)

bōyīn/bòyīn 播音 to make broadcasts; to transmit

bōzhǒng/bòzhǒng 播种 to sow seed; to sow; to seed

bōzhòng/bòzhòng 播种 to sow by seeding

bóbo 伯伯 an uncle (one's father's elder brother)

bófù 伯父 ① an elder brother of one's father ② a respectful term for the senior

bómǔ 伯母 ① the wife of father's elder brother ② a respectful term for the senior

bóchì 驳斥 ① to refute; to rebut; to disprove ② to reject (an appeal)

Bólín 柏林 Berlin, Germany

bózi 脖子 the neck

bó 博 ① wide; extensive ② abundant; ample; rich ③ broadly knowledgeable; well-read; learned; erudite ④ to exchange; to barter for ⑤ to win; to gain

bólǎnhuì 博览会 a trade fair; an exhibition

bóshì 博士 a doctorate

bówùguǎn 博物馆 a museum

bó 搏 ① to pounce on (or at); to spring upon ② to grasp; to catch; to arrest; to seize ③ to strike; to box; to engage in a hand-to-hand combat

bódòu 搏斗 to battle; to wrestle; to fight

bó 薄 ① thin; light; slight ② to despise; to slight; to disdain ③ barren; not fertile ④ a screen ⑤ a patch of grass ⑥ frivolous ⇨báo

bómó 薄膜 ① a membrane ② film

bóruò 薄弱 weak; fragile

bò 薄 peppermint ⇨bó

bǔ 卜 ① to divine; to consult the oracle ② a surname

bǔ 补 ① to repair; to patch; to mend ② to fill; to add to; to sup-

B

plement; to supply ③ addenda; supplements; complements ④ to appoint to or fill a post ⑤ to nourish ⑥ nutritious; nutrient ⑦ rich foods; tonics ⑧ to make up; to help (finance, etc.); to subsidize

bǔcháng 补偿 to compensate; to make up

bǔchōng 补充 to add; to supplement

bǔjǐ 补给 (military) provisions; supplies; to supply

bǔjiù 补救 to save the situation

bǔkè 补课 a compensatory class

bǔtiē 补贴 to subsidize; a subsidy; an allowance

bǔxí 补习 private tutoring to supplement regular schooling; to tutor

bǔxíbān 补习班 a class for supplementary schooling

bǔzhèng 补正 (said of printed materials) additions and corrections

bǔzhù 补助 to subsidize; to help (finance, etc.)

bǔzú 补足 to make up a deficit; to make complete or whole

bǔ 捕 ① to arrest; to catch; to seize ② (formerly) a policeman

bǔlāo 捕捞 to fish for (aquatic animals and plants); to catch

bǔyú 捕鱼 to catch fish; to fish

bǔzhuō 捕捉 to chase or hunt down

bǔrǔlèi 哺乳类 mammals

bù 不 no; not; negative (Note: When bù precedes a 4th-tone sound, it is pronounced as bú.)

bù'ān 不安 ① uneasy; disturbed ② intranquil

bùbēi-bùkàng 不卑不亢 to conduct oneself properly

bùbǐ 不比 unlike

búbì 不必 not necessary

búbiàn 不便 inconvenience; inconvenient

bùcéng 不曾 to have never done something

bùchéng 不成 ① will not do ② an expression used at the end of a question

bùcí'érbié 不辞而别 to leave without bidding goodbye

búcuò 不错 ① not bad ② to be right ③ granted that; to be sure that

búdà 不大 ① not very; not too ② not often; rarely

bùdān 不单 ① not the only ② not merely; not simply

búdàn 不但 not only...

búdàng 不当 unsuitable; improper; inappropriate

búdào 不到 insufficient; less than

bùdé 不得 must not

bùdébù 不得不 to have to; must

bùdéliǎo 不得了 ① Good heavens! ② It's serious!

bùdéyǐ 不得已 cannot help but...

bùděng 不等 differently

búdìng 不定 ① not certain ② indefinite

búdòngchǎn 不动产 real estate; immovable assets

búduàn 不断 continuous; constant

búduì 不对 not right; wrong

búduìjìn/búduìjìng 不对劲 not in harmony; listless

bùfá 不乏 there is no lack of; not rare

bùfǎ 不法 unlawful; illegal

bùfán 不凡 extraordinary; unusual; outstanding

bùfáng 不妨 no harm in (trying doing, etc.)

bùfú 不服 to recalcitrate; to disobey

bùfú 不符 do not tally

bùfúqì 不服气 recalcitrant; unwilling to submit; rebellious; disobedient

bùgān 不甘 unreconciled to

bùgǎn 不敢 dare not

bùgǎndāng 不敢当 I don't deserve it.

bùgōng 不公 unjust; unfair

B

bùgòu 不够 not enough; insufficient; inadequate

bùgù 不顾 in disregard of; regardless of; despite; in spite of

bùguǎn 不管 in disregard of; regardless of

bùguāng 不光 ① not the only one ② not only

bùguīzé 不规则 irregular

bùguò 不过 ① but; nevertheless ② only; merely

bùhǎo 不好 ① not good ② to be spoiled; to become worse

bùhǎoyìsi 不好意思 to feel embarrassed, shy, bashful, or ashamed

bùhé 不合 unsuitable; in disagreement with (rules, etc.)

bùhé 不和 at loggerheads; not on good terms

bùhuì 不会 unable; can not; will not; do not know how

bùjí 不及 not so (good, tall, early, etc.) as...; to be inferior to

bùjiàn 不见 do not see; do not meet

bùjiànde 不见得 not likely; not necessarily so

bùjiànle 不见了 missing; disappeared

bùjiě 不解 ① do not understand ② indissoluble

bùjìn 不禁 cannot help...

bùjǐn 不仅 not only

bùjīngyì 不经意 inattentive(ly); careless(ly)

bùjǐngqì 不景气 (economics) depression

bùjiǔ 不久 within a short time; soon

bùjū 不拘 ① no limit; not to be bound ② whatever

bùjù 不具 ① not encompassing or complete enough (usually used at the end of a letter) ② crippled

bùjué 不觉 ① unconsciously; do not feel at all ② unexpectedly; never thought

bùkān 不堪 cannot suffer; unendurable

bùkě 不可 ① cannot ② no; negative ③ not allowed

bùkě-sīyì 不可思议 mysterious; unimaginable

bùkèqi 不客气 ① impolite; rude; blunt ② You are welcome.

bùkuì 不愧 to be worthy of; to deserve to be

bùlǐ 不理 in disregard of; to ignore

bùlì 不力 (said of the performance of duties) half-heartedly; perfunctorily

bùlì 不利 ① bad; adverse; harmful ② not going smoothly

bùliáng 不良 bad; harmful; unhealthy

bùliǎo 不了 without end

bùliào 不料 unexpectedly; never thought

bùlìn 不吝 not stingy; without sparing; do not stint

bùlùn 不论 no matter; regardless

bùmǎn 不满 discontent; dissatisfaction

bùmiǎn 不免 have to; must; unavoidable

bùmíng 不明 not clear; nebulous; unknown

búnàifán 不耐烦 impatient

bùnéng 不能 cannot; unable

bùnéngbù 不能不 to have to; must; cannot but

bùnénggòu 不能够 cannot; unable

búpà 不怕 not afraid

bùpíng 不平 ① unjust ② complaint; a grudge

bùrán 不然 ① otherwise; or ② not so

bùrěn 不忍 disturbed (characterized by pity); cannot bear to...

bùróng 不容 ① do not tolerate; do not allow ② do not welcome

bùrú 不如 ① not equal to; can do no better than; inferior to ② might as well; it would be better to

bùshàn 不善 ① bad; ill ② improper(ly); not proper(ly) ③ not

good at

bùshǎo 不少 some; quite a few

bùshèng/bùshēng 不胜 ① cannot bear; to be unequal to ② very; extremely

bùshí 不时 ① frequently ② at any time

búshì 不适 ill; indisposed; unwell

búshì 不是 in the wrong

búshì…érshì… 不是……而是…… not...but...

búshì…jiùshì… 不是……就是…… either...or...

búshìma 不是吗 ① Isn't that so? ②..., right?;..., isn't it?;..., aren't you?

bùshūfu 不舒服 unwell; not feeling well; uncomfortable; indisposed

bùtíng 不停 without stop

bùtōng 不通 ① (said of writings) poor; illogical; inarticulate ② blocked; not passable

bùtóng 不同 different; distinct; difference

bùtuǒ 不妥 not the right way; improper

búwài 不外 invariably; most likely; no other than; nothing more than; only

bùwěn 不稳 unsteady; unstable (market, position)

bùxī/búxì 不惜 to be ready to go to extreme lengths

bùxià 不下 ① no less than ② unable to capture (a city or position)

bùxiānggān 不相干 irrelevant; to have nothing to do with

bùxiāngshàngxià 不相上下 equal; equally matched

bùxiǎng 不想 do not want

búxiànghuà 不像话 absurd or ludicrous (talks, acts, etc.)

bùxiǎode 不晓得 do not know; ignorant of; to know nothing about

búxiào 不肖 ① a son who is not so good as his father ② good-for-nothing

búxiè 不懈 untiring; indefatigable

bùxíng 不行 ① not allowed; nothing doing ② unsuccessful; to no avail ③ not qualified ④ do not work

búxìng 不幸 misfortune; unfortunate

bùxiū 不休 endlessly; ceaselessly

bùxiǔ 不朽 immortal; immortality

bùxū 不须 need not

bùxū 不需 do not need

bùxǔ 不许 not allowed; must not; prohibited

bùyán'éryù 不言而喻 self-evident; to understand without explanation

búyànqífán 不厌其烦 to be very patient

búyào 不要 ① don't ② don't want

búyàojǐn 不要紧 ① unimportant; not serious ② never mind

búyàoliǎn 不要脸 shameless; brazen

bùyī 不一 to vary; to differ

bùyí 不宜 not suitable; inadvisable

bùyídìng 不一定 uncertain; not sure

bùyí-yúlì 不遗余力 to spare no effort; to do one's best (or utmost)

búyì 不已 continuously; endlessly; incessantly

bùyǐwéirán 不以为然 to object; to take exception to

búyòng 不用 ① need not ② not necessary

búyòngshuō 不用说 it goes without saying; needless to say

bùyóude 不由得 cannot help; cannot but

bùyuē'értóng 不约而同 to accord without consulting each other

búzài 不再 not anymore; no longer

búzài 不在 ① dead ② not in;

absent

búzàihu 不在乎 do not care; do not mind

bùzěnmeyàng 不怎么样 not up to much; very indifferent

búzhèngzhīfēng 不正之风 an unhealthy trend; an immoral trend

bùzhī-bùjué 不知不觉 imperceptibly; unnoticed

bùzhīdao 不知道 do not know; to be unconscious

bùzhīqíng 不知情 to know nothing about...; to be ignorant of...

bùzhǐ 不止 ① do not stop ② and more than...; over

bùzhǐ 不只 not only; not merely

búzhì 不治 to die of illness or injury despite medical help

búzhì 不致 not likely to; cannot be

búzhìyú 不至于 will not go so far as...; will not be so serious as...

búzhìyú 不致于 not to the extent of; not go so far as to

búzhù 不住 continuously; incessantly

bùzhǔn 不准 not allowed; forbidden

bùzú 不足 ① insufficient; not enough ② not deserving

bù 布 ① cloth; textiles ② to display; to distribute or disseminate; to spread out ③ to declare, announce, or proclaim

bùdàixì 布袋戏 a kind of puppet show typical in southeast China featuring figures of tiny sacks topped with painted heads manipulated with hands and fingers

bùgào 布告 ① a public notice; a bulletin ② to make a public announcement

bùgàolán 布告栏 a notice board; a bulletin board

bùjǐng 布景 sets; a setting

bùjú 布局 ① overall arrangement ② the composition (of a picture, a piece of writing, etc.) ③ the position (of pieces on a chessboard)

bùzhì 布置 to fix up; to decorate

bù 步 ① a pace; a step ② to walk; on foot ③ situation; state; degree ④ fortune; doom

bùbīng 步兵 foot soldiers; infantry

bùdào 步道 a sidewalk; a footpath

bùdiào 步调 marching order; gaits

bùfá/bùfā 步伐 steps or paces

bùxíng 步行 to walk; to march on foot

bùzhòu/bùzòu 步骤 procedure or sequence of doing something

bùzi 步子 a step; a pace

bù 部 ① a department; a section; a division; a class; a sort ② a cabinet ministry ③ a volume; a complete work, novel, writing, etc.

bùduì 部队 troops; a military unit

bùfen 部分 a portion; a part; partial; partly

bùhuì 部会 the ministries and commissions under the Executive Yuan of the Chinese government

bùjiàn 部件 parts; components

bùluò 部落 a tribe

bùmén 部门 a class; a section; a department

bùshǔ 部属 subordinates

bùshǔ/bùshù 部署 to make preparations or arrangements

bùwèi 部位 location (of an injury, etc.)

bùzhǎng 部长 ① a cabinet minister ② (in U.S.) the Secretary (of the army, the navy, the air force, the Defense Department, the Agriculture Department, etc.)

bù 埠 ① a harbor; a port; a pier ② a mart on the bank of a river or seacoast

C

cā 擦 ① to wipe; to mop; to scrub; to polish ② to spread on; to put on ③ to rub; to graze; to scratch ④ to brush; to shave

cāi 猜 ① to guess; to suspect; to doubt ② cruel and suspicious

cāicè 猜测 to guess; to speculate; to conjecture

cāijì 猜忌 to be jealous and suspicious

cāixiǎng 猜想 to guess; to speculate; to conjecture

cái 才 ① just; just now ② natural abilities; a gift; talent; a mental faculty ③ a gifted person; a talented person; a brilliant man; a talent ④ people of a certain type ⑤ certainly; indeed

cáigàn 才干 talent or ability to get things done; competence

cáihuá 才华 brilliance (of mind); a gift; talent

cáinéng 才能 talent; abilities; a gift

cáinǚ 才女 a talented woman

cáizhì 才智 intelligence; brilliance

cáiliào 材料 ① raw materials ② materials (such as data, statistics, figure, information for writing an article, story, novel, etc.) ③ ingredients of a preparation (of food, medicine, etc.) ④ makings; stuff

cái 财 wealth; riches; money

cáichǎn 财产 property; belongings

cáichǎnquán 财产权 ownership of property; property right

cáifù 财富 wealth or fortune; riches

cáijīng 财经 finance and economy

cáikuài 财会 finance and accounting

cáilì 财力 financial resources

cáituán 财团 a consortium

cáituán fǎrén 财团法人 a juridical person

cáiwù 财务 finance; financial affairs

cáiwù 财物 property; belongings

cáiyuán 财源 financial resources

cáizhèng 财政 finance; financial administration

Cáizhèng Bù 财政部 Ministry of Finance

cáizhèngbùzhǎng 财政部长 the minister of finance

cái 裁 ① to diminish; to reduce ② to cut paper, cloth, etc. with a knife or scissors ③ to delete ④ to consider; to decide; to judge ⑤ a form; a style ⑥ sanctions ⑦ to weight; to measure ⑧ to kill

cáidìng 裁定 (law) a court decision on the legality of a case, or the property or appropriateness of a verdict

cáiféng 裁缝 to tailor; to make dress

cáifeng 裁缝 a tailor; a dressmaker

cáijiǎn 裁减 ① to reduce (personnel, the staff, etc.) ② reduction

cáijué 裁决 ① to judge and decide ② a ruling; a judgment; a decision

cáijūn 裁军 disarmament

cáipàn 裁判 ① a judge; a referee; an umpire ② a verdict or judgment by law

cáiyuán 裁员 to eliminate unnecessary personnel; to lay off workers

cǎi 采 ① to pick; to select; to adopt ② to pluck (flowers, etc.); to gather; to collect ③ bright colors

cǎifǎng 采访 to cover (a news item or story); to interview

C

căigòu 采购 to purchase

căiguāng 采光 lighting

căijí 采集 to gather (samples, etc.); to collect (materials, etc.)

căinà 采纳 to accept or adopt (an idea, opinion, proposal, etc.)

căiqŭ 采取 to take or adopt (an attitude, a measure, etc.)

căiyòng 采用 to adopt (a suggestion, new technique, etc.)

căi 彩 ① colors; variegated colors ② makeup in various Chinese operas ③ special feats or stunts in Chinese operas ④ ornamental; brilliant; gay ⑤ prize money; stakes in a gambling game

căihóng 彩虹 a rainbow

căihuì 彩绘 a colored drawing or pattern

căisè 彩色 color

căiquàn 彩券 a lottery ticket

căi 踩 to tread upon; to trample; to step upon

cài 菜 ① vegetables; greens ② food eaten with rice or alcoholic drinks ③ a dish; a course

càidān 菜单 a bill of fare; a menu

càiniăo 菜鸟 a rookie; a beginner

càisè 菜色 pallor due to hunger; a famished or emaciated look

càiyáo 菜肴 food eaten with rice or alcoholic drinks

Cài 蔡 ① name of an ancient state in the Epoch of Spring and Autumn ② a surname

cān 参 ① to take part in; to get involved in ② to visit; to interview; to call on ③ to impeach; to censure ④ to recommend ⑤ to counsel; to consult together ⑥ to consider; to collate; to compare
⇨shēn

cānguān 参观 to visit, inspect, or tour (a place, etc.)

cānjiā 参加 to attend; to join

cānjūn 参军 ① a military staff officer ② to join the army

cānkăo 参考 ① to consult; to collate ② reference

cānmóu 参谋 the staff; a counselor

cānshù 参数 (mathematics) a parameter

Cānyì Yuàn 参议院 the upper house of a parliament

cānyù 参与 to take part in; to participate in

cānyuè 参阅 to see; to consult

cānzhào 参照 in accordance with; with reference to

cān 餐 ① a meal ② to eat ③ food

cānchē 餐车 a diner; a dining car

cānjù 餐具 a dinner set; tableware; a dinner service

cāntīng 餐厅 a restaurant; a dining hall; a mess hall

cānzhuō 餐桌 a dining table

cán 残 ① cruel and fierce; heartless and relentless ② to wither; to destroy; to injure; to damage; to spoil ③ crippled; disfigured ④ remnants or residues; the little amount of something left ⑤ incomplete ⑥ to kill

cánbào 残暴 cruel and heartless

cánjí 残疾 physical deformity

cánkù 残酷 cruelty; heartlessness; cold-bloodedness; savagery

cánrĕn 残忍 cruel; heartless; brutal; savage

cánshā 残杀 to massacre; to slaughter

cányú 残余 remnants; survivals; remains

cánzhàng 残障 handicapped

cán 蚕 a silkworm

cánkuì 惭愧 ashamed

căn 惨 ① sorrowful; tragic; miserable; sad ② cruel; merciless; brutal ③ dark; gloomy; dull ④ disastrously

cănzhòng 惨重 heavy; grievous; disastrous

cànlàn 灿烂 resplendent; brilliant; glorious

cāngchŭ/cāngchú 仓储 to keep grain, goods, etc. in a store-

house

cāngcù 仓促 in haste; hurriedly

cāngkù 仓库 a warehouse; a storehouse

cāngbái 苍白 pale; pallid

cāngying 苍蝇 the fly

cāng 舱 the hold or cabin (of a ship)

cáng 藏 ① to hide; to conceal ② to store; to save; to hoard ⇨zàng

cāo 操 ① to handle; to manage ② to hold; to grasp ③ to exercise; to drill ④ to speak

cāochǎng 操场 an athletic ground; a playground

cáoláo 操劳 ① to work hard ② to look after

cāoliàn 操练 to drill; to practice

cāoxīn 操心 ① to worry about ② to rack one's brains

cāozòng 操纵 to manage, control, manipulate, or operate

cāozuò 操作 to manipulate or operate (a machine)

Cáo 曹 a surname

Cáo Cāo 曹操 Cao Cao (155-220), father of Cao Pi and Cao Zhi, skilled in strategy and versed in literature

cáo 槽 ① a manger ② a trough; a flume; a chute

cǎo 草 ① grass; straw; a herb; a weed ② coarse; crude ③ the script type of Chinese calligraphy

cǎo'àn 草案 a draft plan; a proposed plan

cǎocóng 草丛 a thick growth of grass

cǎodì 草地 a lawn; meadow; pasture

cǎoméi 草莓 a strawberry

cǎopíng 草坪 a lawn; meadow; pasture

cǎoshuài 草率 careless; perfunctory

cǎoxí 草席 a straw mat

cǎoyào 草药 herb medicine

cǎoyuán 草原 a prairie; grassland; a steppe

cè 册 ① (in ancient China) a register; a book or books in general; volumes ② a list; statistical tables; to record; records

cèsuǒ 厕所 a toilet; a lavatory; a latrine; a restroom

cè 侧 ① the side; sideways ② to slant; to incline towards ③ low and narrow-minded; prejudiced

cèmén 侧门 a side door

cèmiàn 侧面 the side; the flank

cè 测 to measure; to survey

cèdìng 测定 to determine

cèliáng 测量 ① survey ② to survey

cèshì 测试 to test; to measure

cèsuàn 测算 to measure and calculate; to survey

cèyàn 测验 ① to test; to examine ② a quiz or test

cè 策 ① expository writings on government affairs ② orders of appointment ③ to whip; to spur; to urge; to impel

cèhuà 策划 to plan; to make plans

cèlüè 策略 a stratagem; a scheme; tactics

céng 层 a layer; a stratum; a story (of a building)

céngchū-bùqióng 层出不穷 to happen again and again

céngcì 层次 ① order (of importance or priority) ② the arrangement of ideas (in writing or speech)

céng 曾 ever; once ⇨zēng

céngjīng 曾经 to have had the experience of

cèng 蹭 ① deprived of power ② to stroll ③ to protract

chā 叉 a prong; a fork (used in catching fish, etc.)

chāzi 叉子 a fork

chā 差 ① errors; mistakes ② difference; discrepancy ③ (mathematics) difference ⇨chà, chāi, cī

chābié 差别 discrepancy; distinction

chācuò 差错 ① errors; mistakes ② accidents

chā'é 差额 the difference between two amounts or figures

chājià 差价 price differences

chājù 差距 gap; disparity; difference

chāyì 差异 ① discrepancy; difference ② to differ

chā 插 ① to insert; to put in; to stick into ② to plant ③ to take part in ④ to interpose; to get a word in edgeways

chāhuā 插花 to arrange flowers

chāqǔ 插曲 ① a musical interlude ② songs and tunes used in motion picture dubbing ③ an episode

chārù 插入 to stick into; to insert

chāshǒu 插手 to take part in; to meddle

chātú 插图 illustrations or plates

chāyāng 插秧 to transplant rice seedlings

chāzuǐ 插嘴 to interrupt a narration, conversation, etc.; to chip in

chá 茶 tea

cháguǎn 茶馆 a tearoom; a teahouse

cháhuì 茶会 a tea party; a tea reception

chájù 茶具 tea utensils; teathings

cháyè 茶叶 tea leaves

chá 查 ① to investigate; to check; to seek out; to look into ② (used at the beginning of the official correspondence) It appears....; It seems....; It is known....; It is found that.... ③ a wooden raft ⇨Zhā

cháchǔ 查处 to investigate (a crime) and enforce (the law)

cháchu 查出 to find out; to discover

cháfēng 查封 the execution of a court order by which all property of a debtor would be placed under legal custody until further action

cháhuò 查获 to hunt down and seize

chákàn 查看 to investigate; to look into (a matter)

chámíng 查明 to investigate and clarify

cháxún 查询 to inquire about; to inquire

cháyuè 查阅 to consult (a book, etc.); to study (the Bible, etc.)

cházhèng 查证 to investigate and verify

chájué 察觉 to be conscious of; to perceive

chà 岔 ① to branch; to fork ② a fork; a branching point

chànà 刹那 a moment; an instant

chàyì 诧异 to be surprised

chà/chā 差 ① to differ ② to want; to fall short of ③ not up to standard ④ wrong
⇨chā, chāi, cī

chàbuduō/chābuduō 差不多 ① almost the same ② almost; nearly ③ just about enough

chàdiǎn/chādiǎnr 差点儿 ① almost; nearly ② nearly the same ③ not good enough

chāi 拆 ① to split; to break; to rip open ② to take down; to tear down (a house, etc.); to destroy; to dismantle ③ to analyze; to scrutinize

chāichú 拆除 to dismantle and get rid of

chāi 差 ① a messenger; an errand man ② to dispatch; to send (a person) ③ one's duty or job
⇨chā, chà, cī

chái 柴 ① firewood; brushwood; fagots ② thin; emaciated ③ a surname

cháiyóu 柴油 diesel oil

chān 掺 to mix; to blend

chān 搀 ① to lead (a person) by the hand ② to mix; to blend

chán 单 the chief of the Huns (a common term during the Han Dynasty)
⇨dān, Shàn

C

chányán 谗言 malicious or slanderous talk

chán 馋 piggish; gluttonous; greedy

chán 禅 ① Zen Buddhism ② meditation; intense contemplation ⇨shàn

chánshī 禅师 a master, or teacher, of meditation, or of the Zen school

chán 缠 ① to wind round; to twine round; to bind; to wrap; to tangle ② to bother persistently ③ to pester; to worry

chán 蝉 ① a cicada ② continuous; uninterrupted

chánchán 潺潺 the murmuring of flowing water

chǎn 产 ① to bear (offsprings); to lay (eggs) ② to produce; to bring about

chǎndì 产地 a producing center

chǎnfù 产妇 a lying-in woman

chǎnliàng 产量 production; output; yield

chǎnpǐn 产品 products

chǎnqū 产区 origin

chǎnshēng 产生 to produce

chǎnwù 产物 products; outcomes

chǎnyè 产业 ① property; estate ② industry

chǎnzhí 产值 the value of output; output value

chǎn 铲 ① to shovel; to level off; to raze to the ground ② a shovel; a scoop ③ to shovel; to scoop

chǎnmíng 阐明 to elucidate; to clarify

chǎnshì 阐释 to explain; to expound

chǎnshù 阐述 to expound; to elaborate

chàn/zhàn 颤 to tremble; to shake; to shiver; to quiver; to vibrate ⇨zhàn

chàndòng/zhàndòng 颤动 to shake; to tremble

chāngshèng 昌盛 ① prosperous ② glory

chāngjué 猖獗 rampant; on the rampage

chāngkuáng 猖狂 wild; unrestrained; unbridled

cháng 长 ① long; length ② a forte; strong points ③ to be good at; to excel ⇨zhǎng

Cháng'ān 长安 Changan, an ancient name of Xian, capital of the Chinese empire during several dynasties

Chángchéng 长城 ① the Great Wall ② someone who can be trusted

chángchéng 长程 long-term

chángchu 长处 merits; good points; advantages

chángdù 长度 length

chángduǎn 长短 ① length ② mishaps or accidents which may endanger one's life ③ good or bad; malicious criticism ④ long or short

chángfāngxíng 长方形 a rectangle; an oblong

Chánggēng 长庚 (astronomy) Hesperus; an ancient Chinese name for Venus

Chángjiāng 长江 the Yangzi River

chángjiǔ 长久 permanent; a very long time

chángnián 长年 yearlong; all the year round

chángqī/chángqí 长期 ① long-term; long-range; long-standing ② a long time

chángshòu 长寿 longevity; a long life

chángtú 长途 a long distance; a long journey

chángyuǎn 长远 for a long time; long-range; long-term

chángzhēng 长征 an expedition (usually military); to take a long journey to a distant place

cháng/chǎng 场 ① a thresh-

ing ground ② a measure word used to indicate a process ⇨chǎng

cháng 肠 the intestines; the bowels

chángwèi 肠胃 intestines and the stomach

cháng 尝 ① to taste; to savor ② to try

chángshì 尝试 ① to try; a try; to experience ② to taste; to savor

cháng 常 ① regular; frequent; often ② long; lasting; eternal ③ common; normal ④ ordinarily; usually ⑤ a rule; a principle ⑥ a surname

chángcháng 常常 often; frequently

chángguī 常规 ordinary rules or practices

chángjiàn 常见 to see or to be seen frequently

chángnián 常年 all the year round

chángshí/chángshì 常识 ① common sense ② general knowledge (as distinct from expertise)

chángtài 常态 a normal carriage or manner

chángwù 常务 ① routine business ② to be in charge of day-to-day work

chángyòng 常用 to use often; used often

cháng 偿 ① to make restitution; to compensate ② to fulfill (a wish) ③ to repay ④ to offset

chánghuán 偿还 to repay (what one owes)

chǎng 厂 a factory; a plant; a workshop

chǎngfáng 厂房 a factory building

chǎngjiā 厂家 a factory; a plant

chǎngshāng 厂商 manufacturers

chǎngzhǎng 厂长 a factory manager

chǎng 场 ① an act of a play; an act of an opera ② an area of level ground; an open space ③ the stage ④ an arena for drill; a playground ⑤ a farm ⑥ a place for a special purpose ⑦ (physics) a field ⇨cháng

chǎngcì 场次 the number of showings of a film, play, etc.

chǎngdì 场地 a playground; a site

chǎnghé 场合 an occasion; a condition

chǎngmiàn 场面 ① a scene; a spectacle ② pageantry ③ an appearance

chǎngsuǒ 场所 a location; a place; an arena

chǎngkāi 敞开 to open; to unfold

chàngtán 畅谈 to talk to one's heart's content

chàngtōng 畅通 unimpeded; unblocked

chàngxiāo 畅销 a booming sale; to sell well

chàngxiāoshū 畅销书 a best seller

chàngdǎo 倡导 to lead; to advocate; to promote

chàngyì 倡议 to make a motion; to advocate

chàng 唱 ① to sing; to chant ② to crow; cry ③ a song or a singing part of a Chinese opera

chànggē 唱歌 to sing songs; to sing

chàngpiàn 唱片 a (phonograph) record or a disc

chàngqiāng 唱腔 the music for voices in a Chinese opera

chāo 抄 ① to copy; to transcribe; transcription; to plagiarize ② to confiscate; to seize; to take

chāoxí 抄袭 ① to plagiarize; to copy off ② to attack the flank of

chāoxiě 抄写 to make a copy of; to transcribe

chāo 钞 ① to copy; to transcribe ② bank notes

chāopiào 钞票 bank notes; paper money

chāo 超 ① to be more than; to exceed ② to be better than; to excel; to surpass ③ to rise above; to transcend ④ to overtake

chāochǎn 超产 to overproduce; overproduction

chāochū 超出 to exceed; to surpass; to overtake

chāo'é 超额 to exceed a quota or target amount

chāoguò 超过 ① to exceed; to be more than ② to excel; to surpass; to outweigh

chāojí 超级 super

chāojí shìchǎng 超级市场 a supermarket

chāorén 超人 a superman

chāoshāng 超商 a convenience store

chāoshì 超市 abbr. for a supermarket

chāosù 超速 speeding

chāotuō 超脱 to transcend worldliness; to detach oneself from

chāoyīnbō 超音波 supersonic waves

chāoyuè 超越 ① to excel; to surpass ② to fly across; to jump over

chāozhòng 超重 ① an overload ② excess; overweight

cháo 巢 ① living quarters in the trees ② a bird's nest ③ a haunt; a den

cháo 朝 ① to face ② an imperial court ③ a dynasty ④ to go to imperial court
⇨zhāo

cháodài 朝代 a dynasty

cháotíng 朝廷 the court (of a sovereign); an imperial court

cháoyě 朝野 the government and the people

cháoxiào 嘲笑 to laugh at; to jeer at; to sneer at; to deride

cháo 潮 ① the tide ② damp; moist; wet ③ (now rarely, said of gold, silver, etc.) inferior in skill or fineness

cháoliú 潮流 ① tides ② a current; a trend

cháoshī 潮湿 humid; damp

chǎo 吵 ① to disturb; to annoy ② to quarrel; to wrangle; to dispute

chǎojià 吵架 to quarrel; to brawl; to argue

chǎonào 吵闹 to quarrel noisily; to brawl

chǎozuǐ 吵嘴 to dispute

chǎo 炒 to fry; to stir-fry

chǎozuò 炒作 to sensationalize; to play up

chē 车 ① a vehicle ② a wheeled machine ③ to carry in a cart ④ to shape (things) on a lathe; to lathe ⑤ to lift water by a waterwheel
⇨jū

chēchǎng 车厂 a shop in which motorcars are repaired or serviced

chēchuāng 车窗 car windows; train windows

chēchuáng 车床 a lathe

chēdào 车道 roads or lanes for vehicular traffic

chēdēng 车灯 the headlight of an automobile or a motorcycle or bicycle

chēduì 车队 a motorcade

chēháng 车行 ① a vehicle dealer's shop ② a taxi company

chēhuò 车祸 a traffic accident

chējiān 车间 a workshop; a shop

chēkù 车库 a garage; a vehicle barn

chēliàng 车辆 vehicles; rolling stock

chēpái 车牌 the license plate (on a vehicle)

chēpiào 车票 a train or bus ticket

chēshēn 车身 the car body; the vehicle body; the automobile body

chētóu 车头 the engine or locomotive of a train

chēxiāng 车厢 cars (of a train); railway carriages; compartments

chēzhàn 车站 ① a railway station ② a bus station; a bus stop; a bus terminal

chēzi 车子 a vehicle

chě 扯 ① to pull; to drag; to haul; to strain ② to tear ③ to talk nonsense; to lie; to prevaricate; to digress ④ to lump

chèdǐ 彻底 ① to get to the bottom of; thorough ② (said of a stream, etc.) to be able to see the bottom

chèyè 彻夜 all through the night

chè 撤 to remove; to withdraw; to take back

chèchu 撤出 (said of troops) to withdraw or pull out

chèhuí 撤回 to take back or withdraw

chèlí 撤离 (said of troops) to move away or withdraw

chètuì 撤退 (said of troops) to move back or withdraw

chèxiāo 撤销 to abolish; to do away with

chén 尘 ① dust; dirt ② trace; trail ③ this world; ways of the world ④ vice; sensual pleasures

chéntǔ 尘土 dust; dirt

chén 沉 ① to sink; to submerge ② heavy (in weight) ③ to straighten (one's face); to put on a grave expression ④ to retain (one's composure); to restrain; to contain ⑤ (said of sleep) deep; sound; fast ⑥ to indulge in; to be addicted to ⑦ for a long time ⑧ delaying; postponement ⑨ latent; hidden

chénchuán 沉船 ① a shipwreck ② to scuttle a ship

chéndiàn 沉淀 to precipitate; to settle

chénjìn 沉浸 ① to permeate; to submerge; to be steeped in ② very erudite

chénjìng 沉静 calm; quiet; placid

chénmèn 沉闷 ① dull and heavy (atmosphere); hot and humid ② depressed

chénmò 沉默 silence; silent; reticent

chénsī 沉思 to ponder; to contemplate; to meditate

chéntòng 沉痛 to be deeply grieved

chénzhòng 沉重 ① heavy (in weight) ② heavy (at heart); serious (looks) ③ calm, steady, and graceful

chénzhuó 沉着 calm and steady; composed

chén 陈 ① to arrange; to display; to spread out ② to tell, state, or narrate; to explain ③ old; stale; preserved for a long time ④ a surname ⑤ name of a dynasty (557-589 A.D.) ⑥ to make public

chénjiù 陈旧 old; worn-out; outmoded; obsolete; shabby

chénliè 陈列 to arrange and display; to set out; to exhibit

chénpí 陈皮 (Chinese medicine) dried tangerine or orange peel

chénqíng 陈情 to give a full statement or account of a situation, etc.

chénshè 陈设 to display; to decorate; to exhibit; to set out; to furnish

chénshù 陈述 to tell; to narrate; to state

chènshān 衬衫 a shirt

chèntuō 衬托 to bring into relief; to set off; to supplement; to embellish; to provide a contrast; a foil

chènyī 衬衣 undergarments

chèn/chèng 称 fit; suitable; in accordance with
⇨ chēng, chèng

chènxīn/chèngxīn 称心 to have something as one's wish

chèn 趁 ① while ② to take advantage of; to avail oneself of

chènjī 趁机 to take advantage

of an opportunity

chēng 称 ① to call; to name; a name; an appellation ② to weigh; to measure weight ③ to claim; to report; to declare ④ to say; to tell; to state ⑤ to speak laudatory words; to praise
➪**chèn, chèng**

chēngdeqǐ 称得起 to deserve to be called; to be worthy of the name of

chēnghào 称号 a title; a designation

chēnghu 称呼 a name by which one addresses another; to address; to name

chēngwéi 称为 to call; to designate

chēngzàn 称赞 to praise; to acclaim

chēng 撑 ① to prop; to support ② to pole or punt (a raft or a boat) ③ to maintain; to keep up; to go on with ④ to open ⑤ to stretch tight; to burst

chēngyāo 撑腰 to support; to give backing to someone

chéng 成 ① completed; accomplished; finished; fixed; settled; to accomplish; to succeed; to complete ② to achieve ③ to become ④ one tenth ⑤ acceptable; all right ⑥ able; capable ⑦ a surname

chéngbài 成败 success or failure

chéngběn 成本 (commerce) cost

chéngfèn 成分 ① an ingredient; a component ② personal background ③ a factor

chénggōng 成功 success; to succeed

chéngguǒ 成果 achievements; the fruits (of efforts)

chéngjī/chéngjì 成绩 records established or set

chéngjìdān/chéngjīdān 成绩单/成绩单 a report card

chéngjiàn 成见 a prejudice; a bias

chéngjiāo 成交 to get accepted by both parties or to go through a

business deal; to strike

chéngjiù 成就 an achievement; an accomplishment; to accomplish

chéngjiùgǎn 成就感 a sense of fulfillment

chénglì 成立 ① to establish; to found; to set up ② (said of a relation, theory, etc.) to hold good or to be recognized as irrefutable

chéngmíng 成名 to become famous

chéngnián 成年 to reach adulthood; to come of age

chéngpǐn 成品 finished products

chéngqiān-chéngwàn 成千成万 countless; numerous

chéngquán 成全 to help (others) accomplish something

chéngqún 成群 in groups; in large numbers

chéngrén 成人 an adult; a grown-up

chéngshú/chéngshóu 成熟 to mature; to ripen

chéngtào 成套 to form a complete set

chéngtiān 成天 all day long; the whole day

chéngwéi 成为 to become; to turn into

chéngxiào 成效 result; effect

chéngxīn 成心 ① intentionally; on purpose; with deliberate intent ② a preconceived notion

chéngxíng 成形 to take shape

chéngyī 成衣 ready-made clothes; garments

chéngyǔ 成语 an idiom; a phrase

chéngyuán 成员 a member

chéngzhǎng 成长 to grow up; growth

chéng 呈 ① to show, manifest, expose, display, disclose, exhibit, etc. ② to submit, present, or hand in (to a superior) ③ a petition or appeal

chéngbào 呈报 to present or submit a report

chéngxiàn 呈现 to appear; to

C

emerge

chéngxiàn 呈献 to present (to a superior)

chéng 诚 sincere; honest; cordial; sincerity

chéngkěn 诚恳 sincere; true-hearted; cordial

chéngshí 诚实 honest; upright; trustworthy; honesty

chéngxīn 诚心 sincerity; whole-heartedness

chéngxīn-chéngyì 诚心诚意 earnestly and sincerely

chéngyì 诚意 sincerity; good faith

chéngzhì 诚挚 sincere; true-hearted; cordial

chéng 承 ① to receive; to inherit; to succeed ② to undertake; to make it one's responsibility ③ by (order of) ④ to continue; to carry on ⑤ to hold; to contain; to support; to bear ⑥ to confess ⑦ with thanks; obliged ⑧ to please

chéngbàn 承办 to handle (a case); to be responsible for (a task); to undertake

chéngbāo 承包 to contract

chéngdān 承担 to take or to shoulder (the responsibility, task, etc.)

chéngjiē 承接 to receive and carry on; to continue; to succeed to

chéngnuò 承诺 a promise; to promise

chéngrèn 承认 ① to confess; to admit ② to recognize (a nation, etc.)

chéngshòu 承受 to take; to receive; to accept; to bear

chéngzū 承租 to rent

chéng 城 ① the walls of a city ② a city; a town ③ to surround a city with walls

chéngbǎo 城堡 a fort; a castle

chéngqiáng 城墙 the city wall

chéngshì 城市 a city or town

chéngzhèn 城镇 cities and towns

chéng 乘 ① to ride; to mount ② to multiply ③ to avail oneself of; to take advantage of

chéng/shèng 乘 Buddhist teaching—a conveyance to bring the truth to men and help them ⇨shèng

chéngjī 乘机 ① to avail oneself of an opportunity; to seize the right time ② to ride an airplane

chéngkè 乘客 a passenger

chéngwùyuán 乘务员 conductors on a train, bus, etc.; a general term for flight attendants, or attendants on passenger ships or passenger trains

chéng 程 ① degree; extent ② a schedule; an agenda; order ③ distance ④ a journey; a road ⑤ a form; a pattern ⑥ a surname

chéngdù 程度 ① degree; extent ② standard ③ general achievement in academic studies

chéngshì 程式 ① standard procedures ② (computer) a program

chéngxù 程序 ① procedures; processes ② (computer) program

chéng 惩 ① to punish; to chastise; to reprimand; to reprove; to warn ② to stop

chéngbàn 惩办 to take disciplinary action against

chéngfá 惩罚 to punish; to penalize; a penalty

chéngjiè 惩戒 to reprimand; to punish

chéngqīng 澄清 ① to clarify ② to set right ③ clear ⇨dèngqīng

chèng 秤 to weigh with a scale, etc.

chèng/píng 秤 a weighing scale; a balance; a steelyard

chèng 称 a steelyard; a weighing machine ⇨chèn, chéng

chī 吃 ① to eat ② to sustain

chī/jí 吃 to stammer; to stutter

chībǎo 吃饱 to have had enough food; to be stuffed with food

chīfàn 吃饭 to eat, take, or have

a meal

chīhē-wánlè 吃喝玩乐 to idle away one's time in seeking pleasure

chījīng 吃惊 surprised; frightened; startled

chīkǔ 吃苦 to suffer hardship

chīkuī 吃亏 to be at a disadvantage; to suffer a loss

chīlì 吃力 tired; exhausted

chīyào 吃药 to take medicine

chí 池 ① a pond; a pool ② an enclosed space with raised sides

chítáng 池塘 a pond

chízi 池子 ① a pond ② orchestra stalls in a theater

chí 驰 to go swiftly; to fleet; to rush; to speed ② to exert; to exercise ③ to spread; to propagate

chí 迟 ① late ② slow; dilatory; tardy ③ to delay ④ (said of a person) dull; stupid ⑤ a surname

chíchí 迟迟 ① slow; tardy ② slow and easy; leisurely

chídào 迟到 to come or arrive late

chídùn 迟钝 stupid; awkward; clumsy

chíhuǎn 迟缓 slow; tardy; tardiness

chíyí 迟疑 to hesitate; hesitancy

chízǎo 迟早 sooner or later

chí 持 ① to hold; to grasp ② to maintain; to support; to keep ③ to manage ④ to resist; to oppose

chíjiǔ 持久 to hold out; to last for a long time; lasting; durable

chípíng 持平 fair and unbiased

chíxù 持续 continuous; incessant; uninterrupted

chíyǒu 持有 to hold

chí 匙 a spoon
⇨shi

chǐ 尺 ① a unit in Chinese linear measurement (equal to 1/3 meter) ② a ruler; a rule

chǐcùn 尺寸 a small quantity

chǐdù 尺度 measure; a scale

chǐguī 尺规 a sector

chǐzi 尺子 a rule; a ruler

chǐ 呎 a foot (equal to 0.3048 meter)

chǐ 齿 ① teeth ② a toothlike part of anything

chǐlún 齿轮 a cogwheel; a gear wheel; a gear

chīzī 斥资 a contribute money

chìdào 赤道 ① the equator ② (astronomy) the celestial equator

chìzì 赤字 a deficit

chì 翅 ① wings ② fins

chìbǎng 翅膀 wings

chōng 冲 ① to soar; to rise rapidly or shoot up ② to pour water (to powder, etc.); to infuse ③ to wash away; to rinse; to flush ④ empty; void ⑤ to dash against; to clash with ⑥ childhood ⑦ to neutralize; to make void ⑧ to rush; to thrust; to forge ahead ⑨ to charge forward; to hit with force ⑩ a thoroughfare; a hub; a strategic place ⑪ to offend
⇨chòng

chōngcì 冲刺 a spurt; a sprint

chōngdàn 冲淡 ① to dilute ② to play down ③ to make few demands on life

chōngdòng 冲动 ① an impulse; a sudden urge ② to be excited

chōngfēng 冲锋 (military) to charge; a charge; an assault

chōngjī/chōngjí 冲击 to strike against; to pound against; to charge

chōngpò 冲破 to break through; to breach; to smash

chōngtiān 冲天 to shoot up to the sky

chōngtū/chōngtú 冲突 a conflict; a fight; a clash

chōngxǐ 冲洗 ① to flush ② (photography) to develop or process negatives

chōngzhuàng 冲撞 ① to collide; to ram ② to offend; to treat impolitely

chōng 充 ① full; sufficient ② to

fill ③ to fake; to cheat; to pretend

chōngchì 充斥 filled with; rife

chōngdāng 充当 to serve as; to act as

chōngdiàn 充电 to recharge (a battery)

chōngfèn 充分 fully; sufficient; enough

chōngmǎn 充满 to fill up; full of; filled with

chōngpèi 充沛 brimming (with energy)

chōngshí 充实 ① rich; abundant ② to fill out ③ to strengthen or improve

chōngyù 充裕 abundance; sufficiency; rich

chōngzú 充足 plenty; abundant; sufficient

chōngjǐng 憧憬 to imagine something or a place with yearning or longing

chóng 虫 insects; worms

chóngzi 虫子 worms; insects

chóng 重 ① to repeat; to duplicate ② layers ③ to pile one upon another ④ double; manifold ⑤ numerous
⇨zhòng

chóngchóng 重重 ring upon ring; one after another

chóngdié 重叠 to pile one upon another; to superimpose

chóngfǎn 重返 to go back; to return

chóngfù 重复 ① to repeat; repetition ② to duplicate

chóngjiàn 重建 to rebuild; to reconstruct

Chóngqìng 重庆 Chongqing, Sichuan

chóngshēn 重申 to reaffirm; to reiterate; to restate

chóngxiàn 重现 to appear again; to reappear

chóngxīn 重新 anew; afresh

chóngyǎn 重演 to repeat the performance of; to repeat

chóngzhěng 重整 to readjust (debts or credit)

chóngbài 崇拜 to worship; to idolize; to adore

chónggāo 崇高 lofty; sublime; high

chóngjìng 崇敬 to honor; to revere

chóngshàng 崇尚 to uphold; to advocate

chǒng 宠 ① a concubine ② to favor; to dote on; to patronize ③ favor or love

chǒng'ài 宠爱 to favor or patronize

chǒngwù 宠物 a pet

chòng 冲 ① to head or go (south, north, etc.) ② for (your, his, etc.) sake ③ brave and fierce ④ strong (smell) ⑤ to direct (one's attack, etc.) toward

chòng/chōng 冲 aggressiveness
⇨chōng

chōu 抽 ① to draw out; to pull out; to take out ② to rid; to take away ③ to smoke (cigarettes, etc.) ④ to whip; to lash ⑤ to sprout; to put forth shoots; to bud ⑥ to shrink

chōuchá 抽查 to investigate, survey, or test a part of a group

chōuchu 抽出 to draw out; to pull out

chōujiǎng 抽奖 to draw a lottery or raffle

chōukòng 抽空 to find time (to do something)

chōuqiān 抽签 to draw (or cast) lots

chōuti 抽屉 a drawer

chōuxiàng 抽象 abstract

chōuxiànghuà 抽象画 abstract painting

chōuyān 抽烟 to smoke (a pipe, cigars, cigarettes, etc.)

chōuyàng 抽样 ① a sample ② sampling

chóu 仇 ① a foe; an enemy; a rival; an adversary ② hatred; enmity; antagonism; hostility ③ to hate

chóuhèn 仇恨 ① hatred; enmity ② to hate

chóuzi 绸子 a general name of

silk fabrics

chóumì 稠密 crowded; dense

chóu 愁 ① to worry about; to be anxious about ② distressed; worried; unhappy; sad; melancholy ③ depressing; saddening; gloomy ④ sorrow; woe

chóu 筹 ① chips, tallies, etc. for calculating purposes ② to plan; to prepare ③ to raise (money) ④ to assess or estimate

chóubèi 筹备 to prepare and plan; to arrange

chóubèichù 筹备处 a preparatory office

chóubèihuì 筹备会 a preparatory meeting, committee, etc.; an organizing committee

chóucuò 筹措 to raise (funds)

chóuhuà 筹划 to deliberate and plan

chóujiàn 筹建 to prepare the construction of

chóukuǎn 筹款 to raise funds

chóumǎ 筹码 chips (in gambling, etc.); a counter

chóuchú 踌躇 ① to hesitate; to waver; to falter; to vacillate ② confident; complacent

chóu 雠 ① an enemy; a rival; a foe ② to collate; to compare ③ to toast ④ an answer

chǒu 丑 ① ugly; homely ② abominable; vile; bad ③ shameful; infamous

chǒu'è 丑恶 ugly; repulsive; hideous

chòu 臭 ① stinking; smelly ② notorious; flagrant; disreputable ③ very; much; soundly; sternly ④ foul and petty; worthless ⑤ an odor; a stench
⇨xiù

chòuyǎngcéng 臭氧层 the ozone layer

chū 出 ① to go out; to come out ② to put forth; to bud ③ to appear ④ to vent (one's anger, etc.) ⑤ to produce; to reproduce ⑥ to expend; to pay out ⑦ to happen or occur; to incur ⑧ to beget ⑨ to divorce (a wife, etc.) ⑩ to chase away; to banish ⑪ to take office ⑫ to escape; to leave (one's home, etc.) ⑬ a chapter (of old-style novels) ⑭ a measure word for plays

chūbǎn 出版 to publish

chūchāi 出差 to go out of town on business

chūchǎn 出产 to produce or grow

chūchǎng 出厂 (said of a product) to leave the factory

chūchǎng 出场 ① (said of a player) to go on the stage ② (said of an athlete) to enter the stadium or go on to the playground

chūchāo 出超 a favorable balance of trade

chūcuò 出错 to make mistakes

chūdòng 出动 to dispatch or send out

chūfā 出发 to set out; to leave for

chūfādiǎn 出发点 ① the starting point ② a basis; premises ③ a motive

chūfǎng 出访 to visit other cities, countries, etc.

chūguó 出国 to go abroad

chūhǎi 出海 to leave (a) port; to go to sea

chūhuò 出货 ① to produce goods ② to get delivered goods ③ to contribute money

chūjī/chūjí 出击 to leave (a base, camp, position, etc.) to attack or raid (the enemy)

chūjiā 出家 (Buddhism) to leave home and become a monk or nun

chūjià 出价 to bid; to offer a price

chūjìng 出境 to leave a place or country

chūjú 出局 (baseball) out

chūkǒu 出口 ① to export ② to utter; to speak ③ an exit (in a theater, etc.)

chūlái 出来 ① to come out; to appear ② to make out ③ to bring to pass

chūlì 出力 to devote one's efforts to

chūlù 出路 ① an outlet ② the prospects (of a career, etc.)

chūmǎ 出马 to go out and face something

chūmài 出卖 ① to sell ② to betray

chūmén 出门 to leave one's home; to take a trip

chūmiàn 出面 to assume the responsibility (in mediation, negotiations, etc.)

chūmíng 出名 to become famous; famous

chū nántí 出难题 to make things difficult for someone

chūpǐn 出品 products

chūqián 出钱 to provide the funds

chūqù 出去 ① to go out ② Get out!

chūrèn 出任 to take up the post of

chūrù 出入 ① to come and go ② receipts and expenditures

chūsè 出色 outstanding; remarkable

chūshēn 出身 backgrounds; qualifications

chūshén 出神 ① absorbed in ② absent-minded

chūshēng 出生 to be born

chūshì 出示 to show (to someone)

chūshì 出世 (Buddhism) ① to come into the world; to be born ② to leave the mundane world (as a monk or nun) ③ beyond or outside this world; not of this world; of nirvana character ④ appearance in the world, e.g. the Buddha's appearance

chūshì 出事 to be in trouble; to have an accident

chūshǒu 出手 ① to sell ② to take on a job ③ an offer ④ to reach out with one's hand

chūshòu 出售 to sell

chūshū 出书 to publish books

chūtóu 出头 to make good or to succeed

chūtǔ 出土 to come out of earth

chūwài 出外 to leave for a distant place

chūxí 出席 to attend or to be present at

chūxi 出息 ① promising ② profit

chūxiàn 出现 to appear; to emerge

chūxuè/chūxiě 出血 bleeding; hemorrhage

chūyángxiàng 出洋相 to make a fool of oneself (especially in public)

chūyóu 出游 to go on an excursion

chūyú 出于 to start from; to proceed from; to stem from

chūyuàn 出院 to leave the hospital

chūzī 出资 to put up capital

chūzǒu 出走 to run away from one's home

chūzū 出租 to let (a house, equipment, etc.)

chūzū qìchē 出租汽车 a taxicab; a taxi

chū 初 ① first ② original ③ junior ④ early; initial

chūbù 初步 ① the first or initial step ② a primer or the rudimentary knowledge of something

chūcì 初次 the first time

chūgǎo 初稿 the first draft

chūjí 初级 elementary; primary

chūqī/chūqí 初期 the first or initial stage

chūshì 初试 ① to try for the first time ② a preliminary examination or test

chūxuǎn 初选 a primary election

chūzhōng 初中 junior high school

chú 除 ① to remove; to rid of; to wipe out ② (mathematics) to divide; division ③ to subtract; to deduct ④ except; besides; unless ⑤ to change or turn, as a new

year

chúcízhīwài 除此之外 besides this (or these); in addition; except

chúfēi 除非 unless

chúle 除了 ① except that; except ② aside from; besides

chúle...yǐwài 除了……以外 except (for); aside from; other than

chúqù 除去 to remove; to except

chúwài 除外 except; to except; in addition

Chúxī/Chúxì 除夕 Lunar New Year's Eve

chúfáng 厨房 a kitchen

chúshī 厨师 a chef; a cook

chú 锄 ① a hoe ② to hoe

chútou 锄头 a hoe

chúxíng 雏形 an embryonic form

chúchuāng 橱窗 a show window; a showcase

chúguì 橱柜 a closet; a sideboard; a cupboard; a cabinet; etc.

chǔ 处 ① to get along ② to place oneself in; to live in ③ to be faced with; to live in ③ to sentence; to punish ④ to dispose of; to handle ⑤ to dwell; to live
⇨chù

chǔfá 处罚 to punish

chǔfāng 处方 to prescribe

chǔfèn 处分 ① to take action against; to punish ② to deal with (a matter)

chǔjìng 处境 the position or situation one is in

chǔjué 处决 ① to decide; to resolve ② to execute (an offender)

chǔlǐ 处理 ① to handle; to deal with ② to treat by a special process

chǔnǚ 处女 a virgin

chǔshì 处事 to deal with affairs; to manage business

chǔyú 处于 to be in a certain condition

chǔzhì 处置 to dispose of

chǔ/chú 储 ① to save; to store; saving ② a deputy; an alternate

chǔbèi/chúbèi 储备 savings

and/or reserves

chǔcáng/chúcáng 储藏 ① to store up; to hoard; to save and preserve ② a deposit

chǔcún/chúcún 储存 ① to store or stockpile ② storage; saving

chǔxù/chúxù 储蓄 ① to save (money) ② savings

chǔ 楚 ① name of a powerful feudal state which existed 740-223 B.C. ② a surname ③ clear; neat ④ distress; suffering

chù 处 ① a place; a spot; a location; a locality ② a department in a government agency ③ a special quality
⇨chǔ

chùchù 处处 ① everywhere ② in all respects

chùzhǎng 处长 the head of a department in a government agency

chù 畜 ① a dumb creature; an animal ② livestock
⇨xù

chù 触 ① to touch; to contact ② to move or touch emotionally ③ (said of an animal) to ram with the horn; to ram; to butt ④ to offend; to infuriate

chùfàn 触犯 ① to offend; to incur the displeasure of ② to violate or infringe (regulations, rules, etc.)

chùjiǎo 触角 feelers; tentacles; antennae

chuǎicè 揣测 to conjecture; to fathom; to speculate

chuǎimó 揣摩 ① to learn; to examine ② to assume; to speculate

chuānliú-bùxī / chuānliú--bùxí 川流不息 continuous; a constant flow

chuān 穿 ① to wear (clothes, shoes, etc.) ② to cross (a street, etc.) ③ to pierce through; to penetrate or bore through; to thread

chuānsuō 穿梭 ① busy comings and goings of people ② to shuttle back and forth

chuāntòu 穿透 to penetrate; to pierce through

chuānyuè 穿越 to pass through; to cross (a bridge, street, tunnel, etc.)

chuānzhuó 穿着 ① attire; dress ② dressed in

chuán 传 ① to pass (a ball, an order, learning, etc.) on to ② to propagate; to disseminate ③ to preach ④ to summon
⇨zhuàn

chuánbō/chuánbò 传播 to disseminate; to spread

chuándá 传达 ① to forward (a message) ② to inform or notify ③ a messenger

chuándān 传单 handbills; leaflets

chuándì 传递 to forward; to deliver

chuándòng 传动 transmission; drive

chuánqí 传奇 a legend, saga, romance, etc.

chuánrǎn 传染 to infect; to be contagious

chuánrǎnbìng 传染病 infectious diseases

chuánshén 传神 a vivid portrayal

chuánshòu 传授 to teach; to teach by demonstration

chuánshū 传输 (electricity) transmission

chuánshuō 传说 hearsay; legends

chuánsòng 传送 to convey; to deliver

chuántǒng 传统 tradition; convention

chuánwén 传闻 hearsay; unconfirmed reports

chuányán 传言 ① hearsay; rumor ② to pass on a message

chuánzhēn 传真 ① to transmit photos, printed matter, etc.; to fax ② a fax; a facsimile ③ a lifelike portrait by a painter

chuánzhēnjī 传真机 a fax machine

chuán 船 a ship; a boat; a vessel; a craft

chuánbó 船舶 ships; vessels; boats; crafts

chuányuán 船员 the crew (of a ship)

chuánzhǎng 船长 the captain or skipper (of a boat)

chuánzhī 船只 ships; boats; crafts; vessels

chuǎn 喘 ① to pant; to gasp; to breathe hard ② (pathology) asthma

chuàn 串 ① to string together ② a string (of coins, etc.)

chuāng 创 ① a wound ② a sore; a boil; an ulcer
⇨chuàng

chuāngshāng 创伤 a wound; a cut

chuāng 疮 ① an ulcer; a sore; a boil ② a wound

chuāng 窗 a window; a skylight

chuānghu 窗户 a window

chuāngkǒu 窗口 ① a window ② a wicket ③ (computer) window

chuānglián 窗帘 a screen, blind, or window curtain

chuāngtái 窗台 a window sill

chuáng 床 ① a bed; a couch ② the ground under a body of water

chuángdān 床单 bed linen; a bedsheet; sheets

chuángpù 床铺 a bed and bedding

chuángwèi 床位 berths or bunks (in a ship or on a train)

chuáng 幢 ① a curtain for carriage ② a numerary adjunct for buildings of more than one story ③ flickering; waving

chuǎng 闯 ① to rush in all of a sudden; to intrude into ② to be trained by experience; to hew out one's way ③ to cause (a disaster, etc.)

chuàng 创 ① to start; to begin; to initiate; to create; to establish;

to found ② original; unprecedented

⇨**chuāng**

chuàngbàn 创办 to start; to found

chuàngbànrén 创办人 a founder

chuàngjiàn 创建 to found; to establish

chuàngjǔ 创举 an unprecedented undertaking

chuànglì 创立 to start, found, or establish

chuàngxīn 创新 to bring forth new ideas

chuàngyè 创业 to start a business

chuàngyì 创意 creativity

chuàngzào 创造 to create; to produce

chuàngzàolì 创造力 originality; creative ability

chuàngzuò 创作 ① to write (original works of literature) ② an original work of literature or art

chuī 吹 ① to blow; to puff ② to brag or boast; to praise in exaggerated words ③ to break up

chuīniú 吹牛 to brag; to boast

chuīpěng 吹捧 to boast (before equals or inferiors) and to flatter (superiors)

chuīshìyuán 炊事员 a cook or the kitchen staff

chuí 垂 ① to hang down; to let fall ② nearly; almost; approaching ③ to condescend

chuídiào 垂钓 to go fishing

chuízhí 垂直 perpendicular; vertical

chuí 捶 ① to beat; to thrash; to pound ② a stick for beating

chuí 锤 ① to hammer; to pound ② a hammer ③ a weight on a steelyard ④ an ancient unit of weight

chūn 春 ① spring, the first of the four seasons ② alive; vitality; living ③ sensuality; lustful; lewd; pornographic ④ joyful ⑤ youth

chūngēng 春耕 spring cultivation

chūnjì 春季 spring

chūnjià 春假 spring holidays; the spring vacation

Chūnjié 春节 the Lunar New Year

chūnqiū 春秋 ① a year ② spring and autumn ③ age ④ annals of any state during the period of Warring States ⑤ Spring and Autumn Annals ⑥ annals; history

chūntiān 春天 spring; springtime

chún 纯 ① pure; net (profits, etc.); unalloyed ② sincere; honest; simple; faithful ③ completely; purely; entirely ④ (now rare) great; large

chúncuì 纯粹 ① pure; genuine ② completely

chúnjié 纯洁 innocent; pure and clean

chúnjìng 纯净 pure and clean

chúnpǔ/**chúnpú** 纯朴 simple and sincere

chúnyì 纯益 net income

chúnzhēn 纯真 pure, sincere, and faithful

chún 唇 the lips; the labia

chúngāo 唇膏 lipstick

chǔn 蠢 stupid; foolish; dull; silly

chuòhào 绰号 a nickname; a sobriquet

cī 差 uneven; irregular

⇨**chā, chà, chāi**

cí 词 ① words; phrases; statements; speech; expressions ② a part of speech in grammar ③ (Chinese literature) a form of poetry

cídiǎn 词典 a dictionary; a lexicon; a thesaurus

cíhuì 词汇 vocabulary

cíjù 词句 expressions; words and phrases

cílèi 词类 the parts of speech

cí 瓷 porcelain; chinaware

cíqì 瓷器 porcelain; porcelain

ware; chinaware; china

cí 辞 ① language; words; a phrase; an expression ② to decline; to refuse ③ to leave; to part from; to depart ④ to resign

cíxíng 辞行 to take leave of; to say goodbye to

cízhí 辞职 to resign from one's post; resignation

cí'ài 慈爱 (said of elderly persons) benevolence; affection; love; kindness

cíbēi 慈悲 benevolence; pity; mercy

císhàn 慈善 benevolence; charity; philanthropy

Cíxǐ / Cíxī 慈禧 Empress Dowager Ci Xi, 1835-1908, who dominated the Manzhou court for 47 years toward the end of the Qing Dynasty

cíxiáng 慈祥 (said of elderly persons) benevolent; kind; benign

cídài 磁带 a magnetic tape

cídié 磁碟 a magnetic disk

cídiéjī 磁碟机 (computer) a disk drive

cídiépiàn 磁碟片 (computer) a diskette; a floppy disk

cípiàn 磁片 (computer) a diskette; a floppy disk

cítiě 磁铁 a magnet; magnetic iron

cí / cī 雌 ① female; feminine; womanlike; soft (voice, etc.) ② weak; retiring ③ to scold ④ to expose or show (the teeth)

cǐ 此 ① this; these ② such; thus ③ if so; in this case ④ here

cǐdì 此地 this place; here

cǐhòu 此后 from now on; hereafter

cǐkè 此刻 at this moment; at present

cǐshí 此时 now; at this time; at present

cǐwài 此外 besides; in addition

cì 次 ① time (each occasion of a recurring action or event) ② the next in order; secondary ③

inferior; lower ④ vice or deputy (ministers, etc.) ⑤ a grade; grading; order; sequence

cìpǐn 次品 goods of inferior quality

cìrì 次日 the next day; the following day

cìshù 次数 the number of times

cìxù 次序 order, sequence, succession, etc.

cìyào 次要 secondary; not very important

cìyú 次于 next to...; inferior to...

cìzhǎng 次长 a vice minister; a deputy minister

cìzǐ 次子 the second son

cìhòu 伺候 to wait or attend upon; to serve

cì 刺 ① to pierce; to stab; to prick ② to irritate; to stimulate ③ to assassinate ④ a thorn; a splinter; small fishbones; a sting

cìjī 刺激 to stimulate; to irritate; exciting

cìshā 刺杀 ① to assassinate ② (baseball) to put out (a base runner)

cì / sì 赐 ① to bestow or confer on an inferior; to grant ② to order; to appoint

cōngcōng 匆匆 hurriedly

cōngmáng 匆忙 haste; in haste; hastily; hurriedly

cōng 葱 scallions; onions ② bright green

cōngmíng 聪明 ① clever; bright; intelligent ② sharp hearing and seeing faculties

cóng 从 ① from; by; whence; through ② to undertake; to manage; to engage in ③ to follow; to yield to; to listen to; to obey

cóng / cōng 从 lax; easy

cóng / zòng 从 a follower; an attendant

cóngbù 从不 never

cóng...chūfā 从……出发 to set off from...; to depart from...

cóngcǐyǐhòu 从此以后 from now on; henceforth

cóng...dào... 从……到…… from...to...

cóng'ér 从而 and; thereupon; thus; as a result; then; so then

cónglái 从来 from the beginning

cóng...láikàn 从……来看 from the viewpoint of...; from the perspective of...

cóngméi 从没 to have never...

cóngqián 从前 once upon a time; a long time ago

cóngróng/cōngróng 从容 ① unhurried; calm; composed ② plentiful; plenty of

cóngróng-búpò/cōngróng-búpò 从容不迫 in an unhurried or leisurely manner

cóngshì 从事 to be engaged in (a task); to devote oneself to

cóngtóu 从头 from the beginning

cóngwèi 从未 to have never (happened, etc.)

cóngxiǎo 从小 from one's childhood

cóngzhōng 从中 ① in the process (of doing something) ② from the inside (of something) ③ in the middle

cóng 丛 ① to crowd together; to meet in large numbers ② a shrub (plant); a thicket

cónglín 丛林 ① a jungle ② a Buddhist monastery

cóngshēng 丛生 ① lush growth; dense growth ② full of (shortcomings)

còu 凑 ① to put together ② to raise (fund) ③ to move close to; to press near ④ to happen by chance

còuhe 凑合 ① to manage to collect or gather together ② to make do with what is available ③ to improvise ④ not too bad; passable

còuqiǎo 凑巧 by chance; by coincidence

cū 粗 ① thick; bulky; big ② coarse; rough; crude ③ gruff; husky ④ rude; vulgar ⑤ brief; sketchy

cūbào 粗暴 rude; violent; rough

cūcāo 粗糙 (said of a surface, etc.) coarse; rough; unpolished

cūdà 粗大 thick and big

cūliáng 粗粮 coarse grain (e.g. corn, sorghum, millet, etc. as distinct from wheat and rice)

cūlǔ 粗鲁 rude; impolite; rough

cūxì 粗细 ① thickness (of the thread, stick, rope, or anything which is long and round) ② roughness ③ thick and thin ④ crudeness or fitness; quality of work

cūxīn 粗心 careless (in work)

cūxīn-dàyi 粗心大意 rash and careless; inadvertency

cù 促 ① to urge; to hurry; to promote ② close; crowded; near ③ hurried; urgent

cùchéng 促成 to help to materialize

cùjìn 促进 to urge to proceed; to promote

cùshǐ 促使 to impel; to urge; to spur

cùxiāo 促销 sales promotion

cù 醋 vinegar

cùyōng/cùyǒng 簇拥 attended by a crowd

cuán 攒 to bring together; to gather; to assemble; to collect ⇨zǎn

cuàn 窜 ① to escape; to run away; to flee ② to change or alter (the wording)

cuī 催 to hasten; to urge; to press; to hurry

cuīcù 催促 to hasten; to urge; to press

cuīmián 催眠 to hypnotize; to mesmerize

cuīshēng 催生 ① a present from the parental home of the expectant mother usually one month before the childbirth ② a drug to hasten the birth of a child

cuīcán 摧残 ① to destroy; to ruin ② to humiliate

cuīhuǐ 摧毁 to destroy (enemy positions, heavy weapons, etc.)

cuì 脆 ① brittle; fragile; hard but easily broken (as glass, porcelain, etc.) ② crisp ③ light; shallow; thin

cuìruò 脆弱 weak; fragile; delicate

cuìlǜ 翠绿 emerald; bluish green

cūn 村 ① a village; the countryside; a hamlet ② vulgar; coarse ③ simple-minded; naive

cūnluò 村落 a village; a hamlet

cūnzhǎng 村长 the village chief

cūnzhuāng 村庄 a village; a farmstead

cūnzi 村子 a village; a hamlet

cún 存 ① to live; to exist; to survive; to remain ② to keep; to deposit

cúndàng/cúndǎng 存档 to place on file; to file

cúnfàng 存放 to deposit (money); to leave (something somewhere) for safekeeping

cúnhuó 存活 to survive; to keep alive

cúnhuò 存货 remaining (still unsold) goods

cúnkuǎn 存款 ① to make a deposit ② a deposit

cúnkuǎnbù 存款簿 a deposit book

cúnqǔ 存取 (computer) access

cúnyǒu 存有 being

cúnzài 存在 to exist; to be present

cúnzhé 存折 a bankbook; a passbook

cùn 寸 ① a measure of length (equal to about 1/10 foot) ② as small as an inch; small; tiny; little

cùn 吋 inch—a unit of length

cuō 搓 ① to rub hands; to rub between the hands ② to scrub ③ to twist (a thread, etc.) between the hands

cuōshāng 磋商 to exchange views; to hold a discussion or consultation

cuōhé/cuòhé 撮合 to bring (two persons or parties) together; to make a match

cuò 挫 ① to defeat; to frustrate ② to damp ③ to humiliate; to treat harshly

cuòzhé 挫折 a setback; defeat; failure

cuò 厝 house

cuòshī 措施 a (political, financial, etc.) measure; a step

cuò 错 ① wrong; mistaken; erroneous ② a mistake; an error ③ untidy; uneven; irregular; intricate

cuòguò 错过 to let (a chance) slip by; to miss

cuòshī 错失 ① to miss ② an error; a mistake; a fault

cuòwù 错误 ① an error; a mistake; a fault ② erroneous; wrong

cuòzì 错字 misspelling; a misprint

D

dā 搭 ① to raise; to build (a shed, etc.); to put up; to pitch (a tent, etc.) ② to attach to; to join together; to add to ③ to hang over ④ to travel by; to take (a passage on a bus, train, boat, etc.) ⑤ to help; to rescue ⑥ a short garment ⑦ a cover; to cover

dāchéng 搭乘 to travel by (air, ship, bus, etc.)

dādàng/dādǎng 搭档 ① a partner ② to cooperate

dāpèi 搭配 ① to match (colors, etc.) ② to select (items as a present to a person or dishes for a feast)

dāshang 搭上 ① to take (a bus, ship, plane, etc.) ② to add to ③ to make contact or liaison with

dāzài 搭载 to carry (passengers)

dā 答 ① to respond ② to promise ⇨ dá

dāying 答应 ① to answer ② to assent or agree to (a request); to promise (to do something)

dá/dǎ 打 a dozen ⇨ dǎ

dá 达 ① to reach; to arrive at ② to inform; to tell ③ intelligent; smart; understanding; reasonable ④ prominent; successful ⑤ open-minded

dáchéng 达成 to succeed in (a mission, etc.); to accomplish; to reach (an agreement)

dádào 达到 to reach (a decision or conclusion); to achieve or attain (a goal, etc.)

dá 答 ① to answer; to reply ② to reciprocate; to return ⇨ dā

dá'àn 答案 solution; answers (to examination questions, puzzles, etc.)

dábiàn 答辩 to reply (to a verbal attack); to speak in self-defense

dáfù 答复 to reply to or answer (an inquiry, etc.); an answer; a reply

dájuàn 答卷 a test paper; an answer sheet

dálùjī 答录机 an answering machine

dǎ 打 ① to strike; to beat ② to smash ③ to do, make, get, fetch, play, buy, etc. (depending on the object) ④ to attack; to fight ⑤ to; from; toward ⇨ dá

dǎbài 打败 ① to defeat ② to suffer a defeat

dǎban 打扮 to make up

dǎbāo 打包 to pack

dǎcóng 打从 from; since

dǎdǎo 打倒 to knock down; to overthrow

dǎ diànhuà 打电话 to make a telephone call; to telephone

dǎdòng 打动 to move (a person mentally)

dǎdòu 打斗 a fight; a skirmish; to fight

dǎdǔ 打赌 to make a bet

dǎduàn 打断 ① to break ② to interrupt

dǎfa 打发 ① to dispatch; to send away ② to fire; to dismiss ③ to spend (time)

dǎgōng 打工 to do odd jobs as distinct from a regular employment

dǎhūlu 打呼噜 to snore

dǎjī/dǎjí 打击 to give a blow to

dǎjià 打架 to have a brawl, a blow, a row, or a fight

dǎjiāodao 打交道 to associate with; to have dealings with

dǎkāi 打开 ① to open ② to turn on

dǎkēshuì 打瞌睡 to doze; to take a nap

dǎliang 打量 to size up; to look someone up and down

dǎliè 打猎 to go hunting

dǎpái 打牌 to play a card game, mahjong, etc.

dǎpì 打屁 to chat; to gossip

dǎpò 打破 to smash to pieces; to break

dǎqì 打气 ① to inflate ② (figuratively) to pep up

dǎqiú 打球 to play a ball game

dǎrǎo 打扰 to disturb; to bother; to trouble

dǎrù 打入 ① to work one's way into (a secret organization, a tight-knit group, etc.) ② to enter by attacking ③ to throw into; to banish...to

dǎsǎo 打扫 to clean (a room, house, etc.)

dǎshou 打手 thugs hired by men of wealth or power

dǎsǐ 打死 to beat to death; to shoot to death

dǎsuàn 打算 ① to plan; to intend; to prepare ② a plan; intention

dǎtīng 打听 to inquire; to find out through inquiries

dǎyàng/dǎyáng 打烊 to close the store for the night

dǎzhàng 打仗 to engage in a battle; to fight

dǎzhāohu 打招呼 ① to say hello ② to use one's influence in other's behalf

dǎzhé 打折 at a discount

dǎzhēn 打针 to give or receive an injection

dǎzhuàn 打转 ① to revolve ② to go round

dǎzì 打字 to do typing work; to typewrite; to type

dǎzuò 打坐 (said of a Buddhist) to sit in meditation

dà 大 ① big; large ② great ③ much ④ very; highly; extremely; greatly ⑤ the eldest; senior ⑥ (polite expression) your ⑦

full-grown; an adult ⑧ (referring to date only) before; after ⑨ to make large or great

dàbàn 大半 ① for the most part; mostly ② probably; likely

dàbāo-dàlǎn 大包大揽 to take full responsibility for everything; to take on everything

dàbiàn 大便 ① stool; shit ② to empty the bowels

dàbùfen 大部分 for the most part; mainly

dàcān 大餐 ① a sumptuous feast or meal ② Western-style foods

dàchén 大臣 a ranking official

dàdà 大大 greatly; enormously

dàdà-xiǎoxiǎo 大大小小 the big and the small—the whole

dàdǎn 大胆 bold; boldness

dàdào 大道 ① a wide road ② the way of virtue and justice

dàdǐ 大抵 generally speaking; for the most part

dàdì 大地 ① the earth ② the whole territory of a nation

dàdū/dàdōu 大都 most probably; almost; for the most part; generally

dàduì 大队 ① (said of military cadets, militia, or paramilitary units) a battalion ② a group (in air force organization)

dàduō 大多 for the most part; mostly

dàduōshù 大多数 the majority

dàfǎguān 大法官 a grand justice

dàfāng 大方 experts; connoisseurs

dàfang 大方 ① generous ② elegant and composed

dàgài 大概 most probably; generally

dàgē 大哥 ① the eldest brother ② elder brother (a polite form of address for a man about one's own age)

dàgēdà 大哥大 a walkie-talkie (a mobile phone); a cellular phone

dàgōng-wúsī 大公无私 all for

the public without selfish considerations

dàguān 大观 a grand sight; a magnificent spectacle

dàguān 大官 ranking officials

dàguīmó 大规模 large-scale

dàguōfàn 大锅饭 food prepared in a large canteen cauldron; a mess

dàhǎi 大海 ① the ocean ② a wide-mouthed bowl or wine cup

dàhǎn-dàjiào 大喊大叫 ① to shout at the top of one's voice ② to conduct vigorous propaganda

dàhuì 大会 a rally; a conference

dàhuǒr 大伙儿 ① us; we ② a group of people

dàjiā 大家 ① all of us; we ② a rich and influential family of long standing ③ a famous expert; a master

dàjiē 大街 a main street; a street

dàjiě 大姐 the eldest sister

dàjú 大局 ① the situation in general ② the fate of a nation

dàjǔ 大举 ① large-scale (invasions, etc.) ② a great undertaking

dàjūn 大军 a great concentration of troops

dàkāi-yǎnjiè 大开眼界 to see something completely new or very strange

dàlǐshí 大理石 marble

dàlì 大力 energetically; vigorously; with a great effort

dàliàng 大量 ① a large quantity; mass ② magnanimous

dàlóu 大楼 a multistory building

dàlù 大陆 a continent; the mainland

dàmá 大麻 ① hemp ② marijuana

dàmén 大门 the main door or gate

dàmǐ 大米 a variety of Chinese rice known to Westerners as "pearl rice"; white rice; rice (as opposed to wheat)

dàmíng 大名 ① your name (used in formal speech) ② a reputation

dàmǔzhǐ 大拇指 thumb

dànǎo 大脑 ① the cerebrum ② a sarcastic reference to intellectual capacity

dàpào 大炮 ① a gun; a battery; a cannon ② (slang) one who talks big

dàpī 大批 a large batch of; a good deal of

dàqì 大气 ① the atmosphere; atmospheric ② heavy breathing

dàqi 大气 ① a grand air or deportment ② magnanimity; open-mindedness

dàqì yālì 大气压力 atmospheric pressure

dàqīngzǎo 大清早 very early in the morning

dàrén 大人 (in ancient China) a respectful salutation for one's parents, seniors, etc.

dàren 大人 an adult

dàsǎo 大嫂 ① one's eldest sister-in-law ② a polite name for women of similar age as oneself

dàsǎochú 大扫除 to make a thorough cleanup

dàshà/dàxià 大厦 a big building; a mansion

dàshēng 大声 ① loud (voice) ② aloud; in a loud voice

dàshī 大师 ① a master ② a reverent title for a Buddhist monk ③ maestro

dàshǐ 大使 an ambassador

dàshǐguǎn 大使馆 an embassy

dàshì 大势 the general trend of events; the prevailing situation

dàshì 大事 important events; serious matters

dàshǒubǐ 大手笔 the work or handwriting of a great author or calligrapher

dàsì 大肆 unbridled; without restraint; wantonly

dàsuàn 大蒜 garlic

dàtíqín 大提琴 a cello

dàtǐ 大体 ① generally; on the whole ② the main principle

dàtīng 大厅 the main hall; the

parlor

dàtóng-xiǎoyì 大同小异 almost the same

dàtuǐ 大腿 the thigh

dàwáng 大王 ① Your Majesty ② magnate or tycoon of a monopoly ③ master
⇨**dàiwang**

dàwéi 大为 greatly; significantly; markedly

dàwúwèi 大无畏 dauntless; fearless

Dàxīyáng 大西洋 the Atlantic Ocean

dàxiàng 大象 an elephant

dàxiǎo 大小 ① adults and children ② sizes (of shoes, etc.) ③ degree of seniority

dàxiào 大笑 to laugh heartily

dàxíng 大型 (said of machines, etc.) large-sized; large-scale

dàxuǎn 大选 ① a presidential election ② general elections for congressmen

dàxué 大学 ① a university or college ② *The Great Learning* (one of the *Four Classics*)

dàxuéshēng 大学生 a college or university student; a collegian

dàyàn 大雁 a wild goose

dàyī 大衣 an overcoat

dàyì 大意 ① the general idea; the gist ② high ambitions

dàyi 大意 negligent

dàyìqíqù 大异其趣 very different; totally different

dàyǒu 大有 ① to be rich in...; to be extremely... ② a harvest year

dàyǒukěwéi 大有可为 very promising (projects, etc.); very hopeful

dàyú 大于 greater than; bigger than; more than

dàyǔ 大雨 heavy rain

dàyuē 大约 about; around; probably; likely

dàyuèjìn 大跃进 (Communist terminology) "the great leap forward"

dàzhì 大致 ① for the most part ② about

dàzhòng 大众 the masses; the public

dàzhòng chuánbō/dàzhòng chuánbò 大众传播 mass communications

dàzhuān yuànxiào 大专院校 colleges and universities

dàzìrán 大自然 nature

dàzōng 大宗 a large batch; lots of

dāi 呆 ① dull; dull-witted; stupid; unintelligent ② blank; wooden

dāizhàng 呆账 a bad debt

dāi 待 ① to stay ② later
⇨**dài**

dāihuìr/dāihuǐr 待会儿 just a little while

dǎitú 歹徒 a hoodlum; a ruffian; a scoundrel

dǎi 逮 to capture; to catch
⇨**dài**

dàifu 大夫 a doctor

dàiwang/dàwáng 大王 the chief of brigands
⇨**dàwáng**

dài 代 ① a dynasty ② an era ③ a generation ④ to be a substitute or an equivalent; to take the place of

dàibàn 代办 to manage on behalf of another

dàibiǎo 代表 ① a representative; a delegate; a proxy ② to represent; to stand for

dàibiǎotuán 代表团 a delegation

dàigōu 代沟 the generation gap

dàihào 代号 a code name

dàijià 代价 price; cost; reward

dàikè 代课 to teach on behalf of another teacher

dàilǐ 代理 ① to serve as agent of; to act for ② an agent

dàilǐshāng 代理商 a business agent; an agent

dàimíngcí 代名词 a pronoun

dàishù 代数 algebra

dàitì 代替 to take the place of; to

substitute

dàixiè 代谢 ① to express thanks to someone on behalf of others ② to metabolize

dàiyánrén 代言人 a spokesperson; a mouthpiece

dài 带 ① to bear; to bring along ② to wear (a smile, sword, etc.) ③ to lead (the way, troops, etc.); to head (an army, etc.) ④ a girdle; a sash; a belt; a band ⑤ a climatic zone

dàidòng 带动 to drive; to spur on

dàihui 带回 to bring back

dàijìn/dàijìng 带劲 ① energetic ② interesting; exciting

dàilai 带来 to bring here

dàilǐng 带领 to lead (an army, a party, etc.)

dàilù 带路 to lead the way

dàir 带儿 a girdle; a sash; a belt; a band

dàitóu 带头 to pioneer; to initiate; to lead

dàizi 带子 ① a ribbon; laces (of shoes, boots, etc.) ② a tape ③ a belt

dài 贷 ① to loan; to lend or borrow; a loan ② the credit side in bookkeeping ③ to pardon; to be lenient ④ to shift (responsibility); to shirk

dàikuǎn 贷款 a loan (of money)

dài 待 ① to treat; to entertain ② to await; to wait for ③ need ④ until
⇨dāi

dàimìng 待命 to await orders

dàiyè 待业 to wait for employment

dàiyù 待遇 ① the manner of treating people ② pay, salary, or remuneration

dàigōng 怠工 ① a slowdown ② to goof off

dàimàn 怠慢 ① lax and crude; idle and remiss ② to neglect a visitor or guest (often used as a polite expression)

dài 袋 a bag; a sack; a pocket; a pouch

dàizi 袋子 a bag; a sack; a pocket

dài/dǎi 逮 to hunt; to chase and make arrest
⇨dǎi

dàibǔ/dǎibǔ 逮捕 to make arrest

dài 戴 ① to wear on the head, the nose, the ear, or the hand; to put on ② to support; to sustain; to bear ③ a surname ④ to respect; to honor

dān 丹 ① red; scarlet ② a medical pill, ointment, and powder ③ cinnabar ④ a sophisticated decoction

Dānmài 丹麦 Denmark

dān 担 to shoulder; to take upon oneself
⇨dàn

dānbǎo 担保 to guarantee; to pledge

dāndāng 担当 to take (responsibility) upon oneself or undertake (a task)

dānfù 担负 ① to assume a responsibility; to undertake ② a burden; responsibility

dānrèn 担任 to take charge of (a task); to hold the post of

dānxīn 担心 to worry; to feel anxious

dānyōu 担忧 to be anxious; to worry; to be apprehensive

dān 单 ① single; individual ② of an odd number ③ alone; only ④ simple ⑤ a slip of paper ⑥ a list
⇨chán, Shàn

dānchē 单车 a bicycle

dānchún 单纯 ① simple; plain ② unpretending

dāncí 单词 ① an individual word; a word; a singular term ② a single-morpheme word

dāndǎ 单打 (sports) singles

dāndiào 单调 dull; monotonous; dry; boring

dāndú 单独 independent; alone

dānjià 单价 a unit price

dānjù 单据 a receipt

D

dānqīn 单亲 ① a single parent ② of a single-parent family

dānshēn 单身 ① alone; unaccompanied ② unmarried; single

dānwèi 单位 ① a unit (in measurement) ② a military unit or organization

dānxiàng 单项 (sports) an individual event

dānxíngdào 单行道 a one-way path or a one-way street

dānyī 单一 single; unitary

dānyuán 单元 a unit; a complete entity; a whole

dānzì 单字 a single character or word

dānzi 单子 a list; a bill; a form

dānwu 耽误 to delay; to hold up

dǎn 胆 ① the gall ② courage; bravery; audacity ③ the internal parts, etc. of a vessel ④ the tube of a tire, basketball, etc.

dǎngùchún 胆固醇 cholesterol; cholesterin

dǎnliàng 胆量 courage; bravery; guts

dǎnqiè/dǎnquè 胆怯 frightened; afraid; fainthearted

dǎnzi 胆子 courage; bravery; audacity; nerve

dàn 石 ① a dry measure for grains roughly equivalent to 120-160 pounds; picul ② a weight measure equivalent to about 110 pounds ⇨**shí**

dàn 但 but; however; yet

dànshì 但是 but; however; yet

dànyuàn 但愿 to wish; to hope

dàn 担 ① a unit of weight or capacity ② a load; a burden ⇨**dān**

dànzi 担子 a load or burden upon the shoulder or the back

dànchén 诞辰 birthday

dànshēng 诞生 birth

dàn 淡 ① weak or thin (tea, etc.) ② tasteless; insipid ③ light (in color); slight ④ without worldly desires ⑤ off-season; slack

dànhuà 淡化 ① desalination ② to play down

dànjì 淡季 slack seasons (for business)

Dànjiāng Dàxué 淡江大学 the Tamkang University

dànshuǐ 淡水 ① fresh water ② Tamsui, Taiwan

dàn 弹 a pellet; a bullet; a bomb ⇨**tán**

dànyào 弹药 ammunition

dàn 蛋 ① an egg ② a fellow

dànbái 蛋白 egg white; albumen

dànbáizhí/dànbáizhì 蛋白质 protein; albumen

dàngāo 蛋糕 cake

dàn 氮 nitrogen

dāng 当 ① just at (a time or a place) ② to work as; to serve as ③ to face ④ to undertake or assume (responsibilities, etc.); to accept ⑤ ought to; should; must ⑥ equal; well-matched ⇨**dàng**

dāngbīng 当兵 to serve in the army; to be a soldier

dāngchǎng 当场 on the spot; then and there

dāngchū 当初 at first; in the beginning

dāngdài 当代 in the present age

dāngdào 当道 ① to be in power ② to block one's way

dāng...de shíhou 当……的时候 when...; while...

dāngdì 当地 this place; local

dāngguī 当归 ligusticum, or levisticum, whose root is used as medicine

dāngjiā 当家 to housekeep; to be the master of a family, an organization, etc.

dāngjīn 当今 ① the present time; today ② the reigning emperor

dāngjú 当局 the authorities

dāngmiàn 当面 right in one's face; face to face

dāngnián 当年 that year

dāngqián 当前 present; current

dāngrán 当然 ① as it should

dāngshí 当时 at that time; then ⇨dàngshí

dāngshírén 当事人 those directly involved

dāngxià 当下 presently; immediately

dāngxīn 当心 to be careful; to be cautious

dāngxuǎn 当选 to get elected; to be elected; to win an election

dāngxuǎnrén 当选人 as in 总统当选人 (the president-elect), 市长当选人 (the mayor-elect), etc.

dāngzhōng 当中 right in the middle

dǎng 挡 ① to obstruct; to impede; to stop; to resist; to ward off ② a fender ⇨dàng

dǎng 党 ① a party; a faction; a clique; a gang; an association ② the village

dǎngbù 党部 the headquarters of a political party

dǎnggāng 党纲 the platform of a political party

dǎngpài 党派 factions; parties; cliques

dǎngqí 党旗 the flag of a political party

dǎngwěi 党委 committees of a political party

dǎngyuán 党员 a party member; a partisan

dǎngzhāng 党章 the constitution of a political party

dàng 当 ① proper; appropriate ② to take as; to regard as; to consider as ③ to mistake something for another ④ to pawn; to mortgage; to pledge ⑤ to flunk ⑥ to break down ⑦ that very same (place, year, day, etc.) ⇨dāng

dàngjī 当机 ① to break down ② (computer) unexpected failure or shut down

dàngrì 当日 on the same day; on that very day

dàngdàng 当当 at that very moment; immediately ⇨dàngshí

dàngtiān 当天 on the same day; on that very day

dàngwǎn 当晚 on the same night; on that very night

dàngzuò 当做 to regard as; to treat as

dàng 挡 used in the combination of bìngdàng 摒挡—to arrange in order; to pack up for traveling ⇨dǎng

dàng 荡 ① to shake; to oscillate; to move to and fro; to loaf about; unsettled; vagrant ② to cleanse; to wash away ③ a pond; a pool ④ dissipated; wanton; debauched; licentious; of loose morals ⑤ agitated; disturbed ⑥ vast; large; magnificent

dàng/dǎng 档 ① files ② shelves; pigeonholes ③ a wooden crosspiece, as the rung of a ladder, etc.

dàngàn/dǎngàn 档案 archives; official files (of government offices)

dàngcì/dǎngcì 档次 ① grade; bracket ② a listing of movie times at a movie theater

dàngmíng/dǎngmíng 档名 file names

dàngqī/dǎngqī 档期 a schedule for showing motion picture in a theater

dāo 刀 ① a knife; a blade; a sword ② knife-shaped coins of ancient China

dāorèn 刀刃 ① the blade or edge of a knife ② an occasion on which money can be spent to advantage

dāozi 刀子 a small knife; a dagger

dǎo 导 to guide; to lead; to instruct; to conduct; to direct

dǎodàn 导弹 a guided missile

dǎoháng 导航 to navigate; navigation

dǎomángquǎn 导盲犬 a Seeing

Eye dog

dǎoshī 导师 ① a tutor ② a spiritual guide

dǎotǐ 导体 an electric conductor

dǎoyǎn 导演 the director

dǎoyǐn 导引 Taoist breathing exercises

dǎoyóu 导游 a tourist guide

dǎozhì 导致 to lead to; to cause something to happen

dǎo 岛 an island; an isle

dǎoyǔ 岛屿 islands; islets and islands

dǎo 捣 ① to beat; to pound ② to thresh (grains); to hull or unhusk ③ to sabotage ④ to drive; to attack

dǎodàn 捣蛋 to make trouble; to be mischievous; to sabotage

dǎoluàn 捣乱 to cause disturbance; to sabotage

dǎo 倒 to fall down; to lie down ⇨dào

dǎobì 倒闭 to close down a shop; to go bankrupt

dǎoméi 倒楣 to be out of luck

dǎoteng 倒腾 to turn upside down

dǎoyé 倒爷 (used chiefly in mainland China) a profiteer

dào 到 to reach; to arrive

dào'àn 到案 to answer a court summons

dàochǎng 到场 to show up; to be present

dàochù 到处 everywhere; far and wide

dàodá 到达 to reach; to arrive

dàodǐ 到底 ① after all; at length; finally ② to reach the extremity

dàolái 到来 arrival; coming; the advent

dàoqī/dàoqí 到期 to reach the deadline or date of termination; to expire

dàoshí 到时 by that time; when that time comes; by then

dàotóulái 到头来 after all; in the end

dào...wéizhǐ 到……为止 up

to...; until...

dào 倒 ① to inverse; to place upside down; in reverse order or the wrong direction ② to pour out; to empty ③ on the contrary ④ after all ⑤ but; and yet ⇨dǎo

dàoshì 倒是 actually; really

dàoshǔ 倒数 to count from bottom to top

dàotuì 倒退 ① to retreat; to fall back ② to retrospect

dào 盗 to steal; to rob; to misappropriate

dàobǎn 盗版 a pirated edition

dàoqiè 盗窃 theft; larceny

dàoniàn 悼念 to mourn; to grieve over

dào 道 ① to say; to speak ② a road; a path; a street ③ the "way" (in the metaphysical sense) ④ a way; a method ⑤ a theory; a doctrine ⑥ Taoism; a Taoist ⑦ to think; to suppose ⑧ an administrative district in old China ⑨ to govern; to lead ⑩ a skill; an art; craft

dàobié 道别 to say goodbye; to bid farewell

dàochǎng 道场 ① sites of Taoist or Buddhist rituals ② a Buddhist temple

dàodé 道德 morality; morals

dàodì 道地 ① (of a product) produced in its place of origin ② genuine; real; pure

Dàojiā 道家 the Taoist school

Dàojiào 道教 (religion) Taoism

dàojù 道具 stage properties

dàolǐ 道理 ① the right way; the proper way ② reason; rationality

dàolù 道路 a road

dàoqiàn 道歉 to make an apology; to apologize

dàoshi 道士 a Taoist priest

dàoyì 道义 morals; morality; a sense of righteousness; honor

dàocǎorén 稻草人 a scarecrow

dàogǔ 稻谷 paddy

dàomǐ 稻米 rice or paddy

dàotián 稻田 a paddy field; a rice field

dàozi 稻子 unhulled rice

dé 得 ① to get; to obtain; to acquire ② can; may ③ complacent ④ agreement ⑤ All right! That's enough!
⇨**de, děi**

débiāo 得标 to win the contract

débìng 得病 to get sick or ill; to fall sick

débùchángshī 得不偿失 not worth the effort

dédào 得到 to succeed in getting or obtaining

défēn 得分 to score; a score

déjiǎng 得奖 to win a prize

déle 得了 ① Stop it!; Hold it!; Well! ② finished; completed

délì 得力 ① capable (assistants, etc.) ② thanks to ③ to get help from

déshī 得失 gain and loss; success and failure; merits and faults

déyǐ 得以 to be able to

déyì 得意 to be complacent; to be very satisfied

dézhī 得知 to have learned; to have become acquainted with

dézuì 得罪 ① to offend ② to violate the law

dé 德 ① morality; decency; virtues ② favor; kindness ③ behavior; conduct ④ to feel grateful ⑤ Germany; German

Déguó 德国 Germany; Deutschland

Déyǔ 德语 the German (language)

Dézhōu 德州 the state of Texas, U.S.A.

de 地 a suffix used to form a manner adverb
⇨**dì**

de 的 ① a bound subordinate particle translatable by "'s" or with terms interchanged by "of" ② by an adjectival ending, a prepositional phrase, or a relative ③ by "-ly"

⇨**dí, dì**

de 得 a structural particle
⇨**dé, děi**

děi 得 ① to need; to take ② must; should; ought to
⇨**dé, de**

dēng 灯 ① a lamp; a lantern; a burner ② Buddha dharma; the Buddhist doctrine ③ a valve; a tube

dēngguāng 灯光 lamplight; lights; illumination

dēnghuǒ 灯火 lamplight; lights; illumination

dēngjù 灯具 lamps and lanterns

dēnglong 灯笼 a lantern

dēngpào 灯泡 an electric bulb; a light bulb

dēngtǎ 灯塔 a lighthouse

dēngzhào 灯罩 a lampshade

dēng 登 ① to ascend; to climb; to rise ② to record; to register; to enter ③ to board ④ to step on; to tread ⑤ to take; to employ

dēngchǎng/dēngchǎng 登场 to be gathered and taken to the threshing ground
⇨**dēngchǎng**

dēngchǎng 登场 ① (said of actors, entertainers, etc.) to appear on the stage ② (said of products) to appear in the market
⇨**dēngchǎng**

dēnggérè 登革热 dengue fever

dēngjī 登机 to board a plane

dēngjì 登记 to check in; to register

dēnglù 登陆 to go ashore; to land

dēnglù 登录 to check in; to register

dēngshān 登山 to climb a mountain; to mountaineer

děng 等 ① to wait ② and so on; etc.; and the like ③ rank; grade ④ same; equal ⑤ when; till ⑥ common

děngbùjí 等不及 ① too impatient to wait ② unable to wait any longer

děngdài 等待 to wait for; to

awAit

děngdào 等到 by the time; when

děngděng 等等 and so forth; et cetera; etc.

děnghòu 等候 to wait; to await; to expect

děngjí 等级 grade; rank

děngjià 等价 equal in value or prices

děngyíxià 等一下 to wait a little while

děngyú 等于 ① to be equal to ② tantamount to; the same as

Dèng 邓 a surname

dèngzi 凳子 a stool

dèngqīng 澄清 (of liquid) to become clear; to settle ⇨chéngqīng

dèng 瞪 to stare at; to open (one's eyes) wide; to glare at

dèng 蹬 ① to tread on; to step on ② deprived of power or influence

dī 低 ① low ② to lower

dījí 低级 ① elementary; rudimentary ② vulgar; low

dīlián 低廉 cheap; low

dīliè 低劣 poor in quality

dīluò 低落 low; downcast

dīmí 低迷 ① (said of the sky, clouds, etc.) turbid ② (said of business) sluggish; depressed; slack

dītóu 低头 to bow one's head

dīwēn 低温 low temperature

dīxià 低下 low; lowly

dī/tí 堤 a dike, levee, or embankment

dī/tí 提 to hold or take in hand ⇨tí

dī 滴 ① water drops ② to drip

dí 的 ① accurate; exact; proper ⇨de, dì

díquè 的确 certainly; surely

díquèliáng 的确良 dacron, a light strong cloth made from artificial fibers

dí 敌 ① an enemy; a foe; a rival ② to oppose; to resist ③ to match; to rival; to equal

díduì 敌对 to be hostile to; to oppose

dírén 敌人 an enemy; a foe

díshì 敌视 to regard with hostility

dízi 笛子 a flute

dígu 嘀咕 ① to murmur; to whisper ② apprehensive; uneasy

dǐ 抵 ① to resist; to oppose ② to prop; to sustain ③ to substitute; to give as an equivalent ④ to offer as collateral ⑤ to offset; to balance ⑥ to arrive at; to reach (a place) ⑦ to go against; to offend against (the law and regulations)

dǐdá 抵达 to arrive at or reach (a place)

dǐkàng 抵抗 to resist; to oppose; to withstand

dǐyā 抵押 to mortgage; to collateralize

dǐzhì 抵制 ① to resist ② to boycott

dǐ 底 ① underside; base; foundation ② the end

dǐcéng 底层 ① the bottom layer ② the ground floor

dǐpán 底盘 a chassis (of an automobile, a car, a radio, etc.)

dǐpiàn 底片 (photography) a negative

Dǐtèlǜ 底特律 Detroit, in Michigan

dǐxia 底下 the underside; the downward position

dì 地 ① land; soil; ground ② the earth ③ a region; a territory; a belt; a place; a locality ④ a position; a place; a situation ⇨de

dìbǎn 地板 floor

dìbiǎo 地表 the surface of the earth

dìbù 地步 ① a situation; a condition ② extent ③ room for action

dìcéng 地层 (geology) a stratum of earth; a single layer of

sedimentary rock, representing the deposition of a single geological period

dìchǎn 地产 landed property; real estate

dìdài 地带 a place and its vicinity

dìdào 地道 a tunnel

dìdao 地道 ① (of a product) produced in its place origin ② genuine; real; pure ③ (quality of work) good; up to standard

dìdiǎn 地点 a site; a location; a place

dìduàn 地段 the locality of a piece of land (especially referring to the numbered land plots on government file)

dìfāng 地方 ① a locality (in contrast with the central government) ② local

dìfang 地方 ① a place ② space; room ③ part; respect

dìfāng fǎyuàn 地方法院 a district court

dìfāng zhèngfǔ 地方政府 the local government

dìguā 地瓜 ① sweet potatoes ② yam beans

dìjià 地价 a land price

dìlǐ 地理 ① geographical characteristics of a place ② geography

dìmiàn 地面 ① the surface of the earth ② a region; a territory

dìpán 地盘 ① a region under one's sphere of influence; a domain ② the foundation of a building or house

dìqiú 地球 the earth

dìqiúcūn 地球村 the global village

dìqū 地区 an area; a region; a zone

dìshì 地势 topography; terrain

dìtān 地摊 a stall with goods displaying on the ground for sale

dìtǎn 地毯 a carpet or rug

dìtiě 地铁 the subway

dìtú 地图 a map

dìwèi 地位 the ranking or position (of a person)

dìxià 地下 ① underground ② in the grave

dìxia 地下 on the ground

dìxiàdào 地下道 an underpass

dìxiàshì 地下室 a basement

dìxíng 地形 topography; terrain

dìyù 地狱 hell; Hades; the inferno

dìyù 地域 ① boundaries of a piece of land ② a district; a region

dìzhèn 地震 earthquakes; seism

dìzhǐ 地址 the address of a place; a location

dìzhì/dìzhí 地质 geology

Dìzhōnghǎi 地中海 the Mediterranean Sea

dìzhǔ 地主 ① a land-owner ② a host

dì 弟 ① a younger brother ② a junior

dìdi 弟弟 a younger brother

dìxiōng 弟兄 ① brothers ② soldiers

dìzǐ 弟子 ① a disciple; a pupil ② a youth

dì 的 ① clear; manifest ② a target; a goal
⇨de, dí

dìguó 帝国 an empire; a monarchy

dìguó zhǔyì 帝国主义 imperialism

dìwáng 帝王 the emperor; the throne; the king

dì 递 ① to forward; to transmit; to hand or pass over to ② to substitute; to alternate

dìjiāo 递交 to hand over; to deliver

dìzēng 递增 to increase progressively

dì 第 ① sequence; order ② a mansion; a residence

dìsānzhě 第三者 a third person; a disinterested person; a third party

dìsìtái 第四台 cable television

dì-yī 第一 first; primary

dìjié 缔结 to conclude (treaties,

agreements, etc.)

dìzào 缔造 to construct; to compose; to build; to found; to create

diān 掂 to estimate the weight of something by weighing it with hands

diānbǒ 颠簸 to shake; to joggle or jolt; to bump; to toss

diāndǎo 颠倒 ① upside down; to reverse ② mentally deranged; infatuated

diānfù 颠覆 to topple; to subvert

diānxián 癫痫 epilepsy

diǎn 典 ① a rule; a statute; a law; a canon ② a tale or story from the classics; an allusion ③ to pawn; to mortgage

diǎnfàn 典范 an example; a paragon

diǎnlǐ 典礼 a ceremony; a rite

diǎnxíng 典型 a model; a pattern

diǎnyǎ 典雅 refined (writing); elegant (style)

diǎn 点 ① a dot; a spot; a speck ② to dot; to mark ③ to nod (the head) ④ a drop; a small amount; a little ⑤ hours ⑥ a point ⑦ to light; to ignite ⑧ to check; to examine; to investigate; to review ⑨ to instruct; to teach ⑩ to touch; to point at ⑪ to select; to pick out ⑫ snacks; refreshments

diǎnbō/diǎnbò 点播 ① (agriculture) dibble seeding; dibbling ② to request a radio or TV station to broadcast a program

diǎncài 点菜 to order dishes at a restaurant

diǎndiǎn 点点 ① small and numerous ② to have a snack ③ to supply punctuation marks

diǎnhuǒ 点火 to light a fire

diǎnmíng 点名 ① to call the roll; to make a roll call ② to mention somebody by name

diǎnrán 点燃 to light; to kindle; to ignite

diǎntóu 点头 to nod

diǎnxin 点心 snacks; refreshments

diǎnzhōng 点钟 hours; o'clock

diǎnzhuì 点缀 to provide decorative accessories; to embellish

diǎnzi 点子 ① a dot; a spot; a speck ② a little; a bit ③ a key point ④ ideas

diàn 电 ① electricity; power ② short for cable or telegram

diànbào 电报 a cable; a telegram; a wire

diànbīngxiāng 电冰箱 a refrigerator; an ice box

diànbō 电波 electric waves

diànchǎng 电厂 a power plant

diànchē 电车 a tramcar; a streetcar; a trolley car

diànchí 电池 an electric battery; a dry cell

diàndēng 电灯 electric lights or lamps

diàndòng 电动 powered by electricity

diàndòngjī 电动机 an electric moto; an induction motor

diànfēngshàn 电风扇 an electric fan

diàngōng 电工 an electrician

diànhuà 电话 telephone; phone

diànjī 电机 electrical machinery

diànjí 电极 an electrode

diànjīngtǐ 电晶体 a transistor

diànlì 电力 electric power

diànlíng 电铃 an electric bell; a buzzer

diànliú 电流 an electric current

diànlú 电炉 an electric stove; a hot plate

diànlù 电路 an electric circuit

diànnǎo 电脑 a computer; an electronic computer

diànniǔ 电钮 a button that controls electric currents

diànqì 电气 electric

diànqì 电器 electric appliances

diànróng 电容 electric capacity

diànshàn 电扇 an electric fan

diànshì 电视 television; TV

diànshìjī 电视机 a TV set

diànshìjù 电视剧 a teleplay

diànshìtái 电视台 a television station

diàntái 电台 a radio station

diàntī 电梯 an electric lift; an elevator

diànwán 电玩 video games; computer games; electronic games

diànxiàn 电线 electric wires

diànxìn 电信 telecommunications

Diànxìn Jú 电信局 a telephone and telegraph office

diànxùn 电讯 telecommunications; wire communications

diànyā 电压 voltage

diànyǐng 电影 movies; motion pictures

diànyǐngyuàn 电影院 a movie theater; a cinema

diànyuán 电源 the source of electricity

diànzǐ 电子 an electron

diànzǐ bùgàolán 电子布告栏 electronic bulletin boards

diànzǐ shāngwù 电子商务 e-commerce

diànzǐ yóujiàn 电子邮件 e-mail

diàn diàn 店 ① a shop; a store ② an inn; a hotel

diànjiā 店家 a manager (of an inn, shop, etc.)

diànmiàn 店面 a shop front

diànpù 店铺 a store; a shop

diànyuán 店员 a shop clerk; a shopman

diànfěn 淀粉 starch

diànjì 惦记 to feel concern about someone far away

diàndìng 奠定 to lay foundation and consolidate it; to settle

diàn 殿 ① a palace; a palace hall; a temple; a sanctuary ② the rear; the rear guard

diàntáng 殿堂 a palace; a sanctuary

diāo 刁 low and cunning; crafty; wicked; artful; knavish

diāo 叼 to hold in the mouth

diāolíng 凋零 ① withered ② to

pass away

diāo 貂 the sable; the marten; the mink

diāo 雕 ① to engrave; to carve or cut, as in sculpture ② an eagle; a hawk

diāokè 雕刻 ① sculpture ② to engrave

diāosù 雕塑 ① sculpture ② to cut wood or clay for a statue or idol

diāoxiàng 雕像 ① a sculptured statue ② portrayal of a person

diào 吊 to hang; to suspend; suspended

diàoqiáo 吊桥 ① a suspension bridge ② a drawbridge over the moat

diào 钓 ① to fish (with a hook and line); to angle ② to lure; to tempt

diàogān 钓竿 a fishing rod; a fishing pole

diàoyú 钓鱼 to fish; to angle

diào 调 ① to transfer; to move ② to collect; to mobilize ③ a tune; a melody; an accent ⇨tiáo

diàochá 调查 to investigate; to study; to probe; to survey; investigation

diàocháyuán 调查员 an investigator

diàodòng 调动 to transfer; to shift; to move (troops)

diàodù 调度 ① to move (available equipment or manpower) about according to needs ② a dispatcher

diàohuàn 调换 to exchange; to replace; to swap

diàopài 调派 to assign

diào 掉 ① to fall; to drop; to shed ② to fall behind; to lag behind ③ to lose ④ to turn ⑤ to change; to substitute ⑥ to move; to shake; to wag ⑦ used as an adverbial particle after verbs expressing conditions of fulfillment

diàoxiàlai 掉下来 to fall down

diē 爹 father

D

diē/dié 跌 ① to fall; to drop ② to stamp ③ a fall

diēdǎo/diédǎo 跌倒 to stumble and fall; to fall down

diētíngbǎn/diétíngbǎn 跌停板 (stock trading) to fall to the lowest point allowed for a single trading day; to hit the rock bottom

dié 叠 ① to fold up ② to pile up ③ to repeat; to duplicate ④ a stack of (bank notes)

diézi 碟子 a small dish or plate

dié 蝶 a butterfly

dīng 丁 ① the fourth of the Ten Celestial Stems (tiāngān 天干) ② population ③ small cubes of meat or vegetable ④ fourth ⑤ attendants ⑥ a surname

dīng 叮 ① the chimes of a bell ② to exhort or enjoin repeatedly ③ to sting, as a mosquito, etc.

dīngníng 叮咛 to exhort repeatedly

dīngzhǔ 叮嘱 to enjoin and urge repeatedly

dīng 盯 to stare at; to gaze at; to fix one's eyes on; to keep a close watch

dīng 钉 ① to look steadily ② nails (for fastening things) ⇨dìng

dīngzi 钉子 nails (for fastening)

dīng 顶 ① the top of anything ② the crown of the head ③ to carry (a weight) on one's head; to push the head against; to wear on the head ④ topmost; extremely; very ⑤ to gore; to butt ⑥ to offend intentionally; to retort; to turn down ⑦ a measure word for hats, etc. ⑧ to substitute ⑨ to equal; to be equivalent to ⑩ to push up; to prop up ⑪ to cope with; to stand up to

dīngdiǎn 顶点 the pinnacle; the topmost

dīngduān 顶端 the top; the peak; the apex

dīngduō 顶多 at (the) most; at best

dīngjiān 顶尖 the peak; the highest point; the top; the best

dìng 订 ① to draw up or conclude (a contract, etc.) ② to subscribe to (a magazine, etc.) ③ to make reservations ④ to edit; to collate; to revise ⑤ to arrange; to settle; to fix

dìngdān 订单 an order (for goods)

dìngdìng 订定 ① to fix or arrange beforehand ② specified in a contract between the two parties concerned

dìnggòu 订购 to order (goods, etc.)

dìnghūn 订婚 to be betrothed

dìnghuò 订货 to order goods; to place an order for goods

dìngwèi 订位 to make a reservation for seats

dìngyuè 订阅 to subscribe to (a publication)

dìngzuò 订做 to be made to order; to custom-tailor

dìng 钉 to fasten (with nails, etc.) ⇨dīng

dìng 定 ① to decide; to fix; to settle ② definite; sure ③ stable ④ to remain

dìng'àn 定案 ① to decide on a verdict ② a verdict

dìngdiǎn 定点 a fixed location

dìng'é 定额 a fixed amount or number

dìngjià 定价 ① to fix a price ② a list price

dìngjū 定居 to settle down

dìnglǐ 定理 (mathematics) a theorem

dìngliàng 定量 fixed amount

dìnglǜ 定律 (science) a law

dìngqī/dìngqí 定期 periodic; regular

dìngshí 定时 ① to set time ② at fixed time

dìngwèi 定位 ① a location; orientation ② to position

dìngxiàng 定向 to fix the direction; to orientate

dìngxìng 定性 ① steadiness; stability ② to determine the chemical composition and properties of a substance

dìngyì 定义 a definition

diū 丢 ① to throw ② to lose ③ to put (or lay) aside

diūdiào 丢掉 ① to lose ② to cast away; to throw away

diūliǎn 丢脸 to lose face; to disgrace

diūqì 丢弃 to cast away; to get rid of

diūrén 丢人 to lose face; to disgrace

diūshī 丢失 to lose

dōng 东 ① the east; eastern ② the host; the master ③ to travel eastward

dōngběi 东北 ① northeast ② Manchuria

dōngbēn-xīzǒu 东奔西走 to run about busily

dōngbian 东边 the east side; on the east

dōngbù 东部 the eastern part (of a territory); the East

dōngdàozhǔ 东道主 the host at a dinner party

dōngfāng 东方 ① the east ② Oriental ③ a surname

Dōnghǎi 东海 the East China Sea

Dōngjīng 东京 ① Tokyo ② (in the Han Dynasty) Luoyang ③ (in the Song Dynasty) Kaifeng

dōngmiàn 东面 east; towards the east

dōngnán 东南 southeast

Dōngnán Yà 东南亚 Southeast Asia

Dōng Ōu 东欧 Eastern Europe

dōngxī 东西 ① east and west ② from east to west

dōngxi 东西 ① things; objects; matters ② a contemptible fellow

Dōngxié 东协 short for the Association of Southeast Asian

Nations (ASEAN)

Dōng Yà 东亚 East Asia

dōng 冬 ① winter ② (the lunar calendar) the period from the 10th to the 12th month

dōngchóng-xiàcǎo 冬虫夏草 Cordyceps sinensis, a parasitic fungus in a wintry insect's body growing in summer as part of a plant

dōngguā 冬瓜 a white gourd; a wax gourd

dōngjì 冬季 the winter season

dōngtiān 冬天 winter

dǒngshì 董事 a director (on the board of a school, company, etc.); a trustee

dǒngshìhuì 董事会 a board of directors

dǒngshìzhǎng 董事长 a board director; the chairman of the board of directors

dǒng 懂 to understand; to comprehend; to know

dǒngde 懂得 to understand; to comprehend

dǒngshì 懂事 (said of the young) familiar with human affairs

dòng 动 ① to move; to stir ② to change; to alter ③ to act ④ movement; action ⑤ to take up ⑥ to use ⑦ to touch (one's heart); to arouse; to excite ⑧ to eat or drink

dòngbudòng 动不动 to be apt to

dòngcí 动词 a verb

dòngdàng 动荡 uneasy; unstable

dònggōng 动工 to start (construction) work

dònghuà 动画 an animation picture

dòngjī 动机 motives; intentions

dòngjìng 动静 signs of action

dònglì 动力 ① power; dynamic force ② impetus

dòngluàn 动乱 disturbance; commotion

dòngmài 动脉 an artery

dòngrén 动人 ① moving ② (said

of the beauty of a woman) to arouse interest

dòngróng 动容 to change one's facial expression when one is moved

dòngshēn 动身 to set out (on a trip); to depart

dòngshǒu 动手 ① to start work ② to use hands; to touch ③ to raise a hand to strike

dòng shǒushù 动手术 ① to operate on a patient ② to have an operation

dòngtài 动态 ① development ② the movement

dòngwǔ 动武 to resort to violence

dòngwù 动物 an animal; a creature

dòngwùyuán 动物园 a zoo

dòngxiàng 动向 trends

dòngyáo 动摇 to waver; to shake

dòngyì 动议 a motion; a proposal

dòngyòng 动用 to use or employ

dòngyuán 动员 to mobilize; mobilization

dòngzhé 动辄 easily; frequently

dòngzuò 动作 motions; movements; actions

dòng 冻 ① to freeze ② cold; icy

dòngjié 冻结 to freeze (an account, etc.)

dòng 栋 ① the main beam of a house ② a measure word for a building

dòng 洞 a cave; a hole

dòngkū 洞窟 a cave; a cavern

dòngxué/dòngxuè 洞穴 a cave; a cavern

dōu 都 ① all; altogether ② even ③ already
⇨dū

dōushì 都是 all; no exception

dōu 兜 ① to surround; to wrap up ② a small pocket in clothes ③ a head-covering; a helmet ④ to go for a drive around; to move around ⑤ overalls ⑥ to solicit

dōur 兜儿 a small pocket

dǒu 抖 ① to shiver; to tremble ② to shake; to jerk ③ to rouse ④ (colloquial) to make good; to become well-to-do

dǒu 陡 ① steep; precipitous ② suddenly; abruptly

dǒuqiào 陡峭 steep; precipitous

dòu 斗 to struggle

dòuzhēng 斗争 struggle; conflict; strife

dòuzhì 斗志 the determination to compete or fight; pugnacious spirit

dòu 豆 beans and peas collectively

dòufu 豆腐 bean curd; tofu

dòufunǎor 豆腐脑儿 jellied bean curd; tofu pudding

dòuhuār 豆花儿 jellied bean curd; tofu pudding

dòujiāng 豆浆 soybean milk

dòuzi 豆子 beans or peas

dòu 逗 ① to stir; to rouse; to tickle ② to stay; to linger; to remain; to pause ③ funny ④ a slight pause in reading

dòuliú 逗留 to stay; to stop over; to linger

dòuqùr 逗趣儿 to amuse; to entertain (with jokes, etc.)

dòu 读 pauses in a sentence
⇨dú

dū 都 ① a large town; a city; a metropolis ② the capital of a nation; to make a city the national capital
⇨dōu

dūhuì 都会 a big city; a metropolis

dūshì 都市 a big city; a metropolis

dūcù 督促 to urge; to press

dūdǎo 督导 to direct and supervise

dú 毒 ① poison; toxins ② poisonous; noxious ③ to poison

dúhài 毒害 to injure atrociously; to murder

dúpǐn 毒品 narcotic drugs; nar-

cotics

dúsǐ 毒死 to poison to death

dúsù 毒素 poisonous matter; toxins

dúxìng 毒性 toxicity; poisonousness

dú 独 ① alone; solitary; single ② only ③ to monopolize ④ to be old and without a son

dúcái 独裁 dictatorship; dictatorial

dúchuàng 独创 (literally) to create all by oneself—unique; original

dúdào 独到 original

dújiā 独家 the only one; exclusive (interviews, reports, etc.)

dúlì 独立 independence; independent

dúlì-zìzhǔ 独立自主 ① the independence of sovereignty ② to act independently and with the initiative in one's own hands

dútè 独特 unique

dúyī-wú'èr 独一无二 unique

dúzhàn 独占 to monopolize

dúzì 独自 alone; personally

dú 读 ① to read ② to attend school; to go to school, college, etc. ③ to study
⇨dòu

dúshū 读书 ① to read books ② to study

dúshūrén 读书人 a scholar; an intellectual

dúwù 读物 reading matter; reading

dúzhě 读者 the reader

dǔ 肚 tripe (as food)
⇨dù

dǔ 堵 to stop; to block up; to shut off

dǔsè 堵塞 to stop up; to block up; a jam

dǔ 赌 ① to gamble; to bet; to wager ② to compete ③ to swear

dǔbó 赌博 to gamble; gambling

dǔchǎng 赌场 a gambling joint; a gambling den or house; a casino

dùjuān 杜鹃 a cuckoo

dùjué 杜绝 ① to stop (a bad practice, etc.) for good; to eradicate ② to cut off (relations with) ③ irrevocable (contracts, title deeds, etc.)

dù 肚 the belly; the abdomen; the bowels
⇨dǔ

dùzi 肚子 the abdomen; the belly

dù 度 ① a kilowatt-hour ② a unit of measurement for angles, etc.; a degree ③ (number of) times ④ to pass ⑤ an instrument for measuring length ⑥ a manner; bearing ⑦ a system ⑧ consideration; careful thought
⇨duó

dùguò 度过 to pass through; to go through

dùjià 度假 to spend one's holidays (or vacation)

dùliànghéng 度量衡 weights and measures

dù 渡 ① to cross (a river or ocean) ② a ferry

dùchuán 渡船 a ferryboat

dùkǒu 渡口 a ferry

dù 镀 to plate; to gilt

duān 端 ① to carry carefully ② an extreme; an end ③ correct; proper; upright ④ leads; a clue ⑤ a beginning ⑥ cause

duānní 端倪 an outline; a clue; signs

Duānwǔjié 端午节 the Dragon Boat Festival

duānzhèng 端正 ① correct; proper ② to correct; to rectify ③ regular; well-formed; symmetric

duǎn 短 ① short; brief ② shortcomings; faults; mistakes ③ to be deficient; to want; to lack; to owe

duǎnchu 短处 shortcomings; faults; defects

duǎncù 短促 (said of time) brief; short; transient

duǎndǎ 短打 (baseball) to bunt; a bunt

duǎnkù 短裤 knee pants; shorts; short pants

D

duǎnqī/duǎnqí 短期 short-term; a short period

duǎnqī lìlǜ/duǎnqí lìlǜ 短期利率 short-term interest

duǎnquē 短缺 to fall short; deficient

duǎnzàn/duǎnzhàn 短暂 (said of time) brief; short; transient

duàn 段 ① a section; a division; a part; a paragraph ② a stage ③ a surname

duàn 断 ① to cut apart; to sever ② to give up; to abstain from ③ to judge; to decide; to conclude ④ to break; broken

duàncéng 断层 (geology) a fault

duàndiàn 断电 power failure; a blackout

duàndìng 断定 to determine; to conclude

duànduàn-xùxù 断断续续 intermittent; off and on

duànjiāo 断交 ① to break off relations with someone ② to sever diplomatic relations

duànjué 断绝 to break off (relations); to sever

duànzi 缎子 satin

duànliàn 锻炼 ① to forge (metal); to temper ② to train (oneself)

duī 堆 ① to heap up; to pile; to stack ② a heap; a pile; a mass; a crowd

duījī 堆积 to store up; to heap up

duì 队 ① a group; a team; a batch ② the troops

duìwǔ 队伍 ① troops in ranks and files ② a line of (people)

duìyuán 队员 members of a team or group

duìzhǎng 队长 the team leader; the captain of a sports team; the commanding officer of a small military unit

duì 对 ① right; correct; proper ② to be directed at ③ to; as to; with regard to ④ parallel; opposing ⑤ a pair; a couple ⑥ to check; ascertain

duìàn 对岸 the opposite shore

duìbái 对白 dialogue

duìbǐ 对比 contrast; correlation

duìbuqǐ 对不起 ① to let a person down ② I am sorry.

duìcè 对策 a measure (to deal with a problem, etc.); a counter-measure

duìchèn/duìchèng 对称 symmetry; symmetrical

duìdài 对待 to treat (a person kindly, cruelly, etc.)

duìdeqǐ 对得起 not let somebody down; to treat somebody fairly

duìfāng 对方 the other side (or party)

duìfu 对付 to deal with; to cope with

duìhuà 对话 a dialogue; a conversation

duìkàng 对抗 to be opposed to each other

duì...láishuō 对……来说 as far as...is concerned; where...is concerned

duìle 对了 by the way...

duìlì 对立 to be opposed to each other

duìlián 对联 a Chinese couplet

duìmén 对门 ① the family, or household, right across the front street ② (two buildings) opposite to (each other)

duìmiàn 对面 on the opposite side

duìshǒu 对手 an opponent; a match

duìtóu 对头 ① correct ② normal; right ③ to get on well

duìtou 对头 an opponent; an adversary

duìwài 对外 for foreign or overseas (consumption, use, etc.)

duìxiàng 对象 the object (of an action); the subject (of consideration)

duìyìng 对应 corresponding; homologous

duìyú 对于 to; as to; with regard

to

duìzhào 对照 to compare; to contrast

duìzhì 对峙 to face (or confront) each other

duìzhǔn 对准 ① to adjust (a machine part needing adjustment) to the right or proper position ② to aim at

duì 兑 ① to exchange; to barter ② (said of wine, etc.) to water; to weaken by adding water

duìhuàn 兑换 exchange; to exchange

duìxiàn 兑现 ① to cash ② to fulfill; to carry out

dūn/dùn 吨 ton (a unit of weight)

Dūnhuáng 敦煌 Dunhuang, Gansu Province

dūn 蹲 ① to squat; to crouch ② to stay

dùn 炖 ① to stew; to simmer ② to warm

dùn 顿 ① a time; a turn ② immediately; promptly ③ to stop or halt; to pause ④ to arrange; to put in order ⑤ to stamp (the foot) ⑥ to kowtow ⑦ to be tired; to fall apart ⑧ to be broken

dùnshí 顿时 immediately; promptly

duō 多 ① many; much; too much ② to praise ③ how, what, etc.—in exclamations ④ more than; much more; over ⑤ only ⑥ greatly; highly

duōbàn 多半 ① most ② probably; most likely

duōbiàn 多变 changeable; changeful; varied

duōcǎi-duōzī 多彩多姿 colorful; many-faceted

duōduō-shǎoshǎo 多多少少 more or less

duōfāng 多方 by all means; in every way

duōguǎ 多寡 number; amount

duōkuī 多亏 It is fortunate that....; We are lucky to....; Thanks to

Duōlúnduō 多伦多 Toronto,

a Canadian city

duōme 多么 how (good, beautiful, etc.); what

duōméitǐ 多媒体 multimedia

duōshǎo 多少 more or less; somewhat

duōshao 多少 How much? How many?

duōshù 多数 the majority; many

duōtóu 多头 (said of stock exchange) to buy long; taking a long position

duōxiè 多谢 Thanks a lot.

duōyànghuà 多样化 to diversify; to make varied

duōyú 多余 unnecessary; superfluous

duōyuán 多元 multiple; plural; poly-

duōsuo 哆嗦 to shiver with cold or tremble with fear

duó 夺 ① to take by force; to rob ② to snatch; to grasp; to carry away (the first prize, etc.) ③ to settle; to decide

duódé 夺得 ① to take by force ② to win

duókuí 夺魁 to win a race or tournament

duóqǔ 夺取 to take by force; to wrest from

duó/duò 度 to consider; to measure; to infer
⇨dù

duǒ 朵 ① a flower; a cluster of flowers; a bud ② a lobe of the ear

duǒ 躲 ① to escape; to shun; to avoid ② to hide

duǒbì 躲避 to dodge; to ward off; to shun

duǒbìqiú 躲避球 dodge ball; a kind of ball game played by children)

duǒcáng 躲藏 to hide oneself; to hide

duò 舵 a rudder; a helm

duòshǒu 舵手 a helmsman; a steersman

duòluò 堕落 ① to indulge in evil

D

ways; to degenerate ② the fall (of a nation, family, etc.)

duòtāi 堕胎 abortion; to abort
duò 跥 to stamp the feet

E

ē 阿 ① to favor; to toady; to assent; to pander to; to play up to ② to rely on ③ a pillar ④ slender and beautiful ⑤ to discharge (night soil, urine, etc.)
⇨ā

é 讹 ① rumors ② errors; erroneous; wrong ③ to extort; to swindle; to deceive; to bluff ④ to move about ⑤ to change

É 俄 Russia
Éguó 俄国 Russia
Éhài'ézhōu 俄亥俄州 Ohio, U.S.A.
Éluósī 俄罗斯 Russia
Éyǔ 俄语 Russian (language)
é 鹅 a goose; a gander
ézi 蛾子 a moth
é 额 ① the forehead ② a fixed number, amount, value, etc.; a quota ③ a horizontal tablet
étóu 额头 the forehead
éwài 额外 extra
ěxin 恶心 ① nauseated ② disgust
è 呃 to hiccup or hiccough
è 恶 ① bad; evil; wickedness; vice; wicked ② fierce; ferocious
⇨wù
èdú 恶毒 venomous; vicious; malicious
èguǐ 恶鬼 a bad spirit; a fiend; a demon
èhuà 恶化 to get worse; to degenerate
èliè 恶劣 ① of very poor quality; very inferior ② rude; distasteful ③ vile; satanic
èmèng 恶梦 a nightmare
èxìng 恶性 malignant; virulent;

vicious
èyì 恶意 ① malicious; spiteful ② malice; evil intentions
è 饿 ① hungry; hunger ② to starve ③ greedy; covetous
èsǐ 饿死 to be starved to death
èzhǐ 遏止 to check; to hold back; to stop
èi 欸 an exclamation
⇨āi
ēn 恩 favor; grace; gratitude; kindness; benevolence; mercy; charity
ēn'ài 恩爱 (said of a married couple) mutual affection
ēnqíng 恩情 loving-kindness; devotion (between friends, teacher and student, husband and wife, etc.)
ēnrén 恩人 a benefactor
ēnyuàn 恩怨 ① gratitude and grudges ② resentment; grievance
ér 儿 ① a child; a baby ② a son ③ referring to oneself when addressing parents ④ as a particle after noun, pronoun, adjective, adverb, and verb
érnǚ 儿女 ① sons and daughters; children ② young men and women
értóng 儿童 children
érzi 儿子 a son
ér 而 ① and; also ② and yet; but; nevertheless ③ on the condition that; supposing that; if ④ accordingly; otherwise
érhòu 而后 then; afterward; later; thenceforward; thereafter
érjīn 而今 now
érqiě 而且 ① and ② moreover;

furthermore; besides

éryĭ 而已 merely; only; and that is all

ěrhòu 尔后 thereafter; afterward

ěr 耳 ears

ěrbíhóukē 耳鼻喉科 otorhinolaryngology; otolaryngology

ěrduo 耳朵 ears

ěrguāng 耳光 a box on the ear

ěrhuán 耳环 earrings

ěrmù-yìxīn 耳目一新 to have a completely new impression

ěrshú-néngxiáng/ěrshóu--néngxiáng 耳熟能详 so frequently heard about that it can be told (in detail or word by word)

ěr 饵 ① bait ② cakes ③ food ④ to eat

èr 二 two; second; twice

èrhú 二胡 a two-stringed Chinese musical instrument

èrshǒu 二手 secondhand

èryǎnghuàtàn 二氧化碳 carbon dioxide

èr 贰 ① an elaborate form of 二 (two), used in writing checks, etc. to prevent forgery ② to repeat ③ doubleness ④ a surname

F

⇨fā

fā 发 ① to shoot; to launch ② to issue; to publish ③ to utter; to express; to speak ④ to reveal; to disclose; to uncover ⑤ to begin; to start ⑥ to become; to come to be ⑦ to set off; to set out ⑧ to illuminate; to help out

⇨fā

fābāo 发包 to contract with a contractor for a construction program

fābiǎo 发表 to make public; to publish; to announce

fābìng 发病 to get sick; to fall ill

fābù 发布 to announce; to promulgate

fācái 发财 to acquire wealth; to become rich

fāchóu 发愁 to worry

fāchū 发出 to send forth; to generate

fādá 发达 to evolve; developed; prosperous; thriving

fādāi 发呆 to look absent-minded

fādiàn 发电 ① to generate electric power ② to send a telegram

fādòng 发动 to start; to launch; to initiate

fādòngjī 发动机 a motor; an engine

fādǒu 发抖 to tremble; to shiver

fāfàng 发放 ① to issue; to distribute; to provide; to extend ② to dispose of

fāfèn-túqiáng 发愤图强 (said of a nation) to strive for progress with determination

fāfēng 发疯 to go mad; to become insane

fāgěi 发给 to issue (supplies, allowances, etc.)

fāguāng 发光 to emit light

fāhuī 发挥 to bring (skill, talent, etc.) into full play

fāhuǒ 发火 ① to become angry ② to burst into flames ③ to go off

fājué 发觉 ① to discover; to find ② (said of crimes, plots, etc.) to be uncovered

fājué 发掘 to unearth; to dig out; to excavate

fāmíng 发明 ① to invent; to devise ② an invention

F

fāpíqi 发脾气 to lose one's temper; to get angry; to get mad

fāpiào 发票 an invoice; a bill of sale

fāqǐ 发起 to initiate; to start; to originate

fāqǐrén 发起人 an originator; an initiator

fāqiú 发球 to serve a ball (in tennis, handball, etc.)

fārè 发热 to have a temperature; to have a fever

fāshāo 发烧 to have a temperature; to have a fever

fāshè 发射 to launch; to shoot; to catapult

fāshēng 发生 to happen; to occur; to arise

fāshì 发誓 to swear; to take an oath

fāshòu 发售 to go on sale

fāsòng 发送 ① to transmit radio-signals by a transmitter ② to send out

fāwèn 发问 to ask questions; to raise questions

fāxiàn 发现 to discover; to find; discovery

fāxiè 发泄 to give vent to; to vent; to let out

fāxíng 发行 (said of currency, bonds, books, etc.) to issue; to publish

fāxíngrén 发行人 a publisher

fāyán 发言 to speak; to voice one's views

fāyán 发炎 to become inflamed; to become infected

fāyánrén 发言人 a spokesman

fāyáng 发扬 to exalt; to enhance

fāyáng-guāngdà 发扬光大 to enhance and glorify

fāyīn 发音 to pronounce; pronunciation

fāyù 发育 ① to grow up; to develop ② to send forth and nourish

fāzhǎn 发展 to develop; to grow; to expand

fāzuò 发作 ① to show effect ② to have a fit (of anger) ③ (said of ill-ness) to have a relapse

fá 乏 ① in want of; deficient; lack ② exhausted; tired ③ poverty-stricken; poor

fá/fā 伐 ① to cut (wood) ② to attack; to smite

fá 罚 to punish; to penalize; to fine

fáhuán 罚锾 a fine

fákuǎn 罚款 ① a fine ② to fine

fǎ 法 ① an institution ② law; regulations; rules; the statutes; legal ③ methods; ways of doing things ④ to pattern or model after; to emulate ⑤ (Buddhism) the "way"—doctrines, etc. ⑥ tricks; magic arts ⑦ expert or standard (calligraphy, painting, etc.) ⑧ penalty; punishment ⑨ France; French

fǎ'àn 法案 a law; a statute

fǎbǎo 法宝 ① dharmaratna, one of the three Buddhist trea-sures ② something of uncanny or occult power—for killing or subduing the enemy

fǎdìng 法定 legal

fǎguān 法官 a judge (at court); a justice

fǎguī 法规 laws and regulations

Fǎguó 法国 France

Fǎguórén 法国人 the French; a Frenchman

fǎjǐng 法警 ① the judicial police ② a bailiff

fǎláng 法郎 franc (an old mone-tary unit of France)

fǎlìng 法令 a general term for laws and regulations

fǎlǜ 法律 laws

fǎlǜxì 法律系 the Department of Law (at a university)

fǎrén 法人 a juridical person; a corporate person; a legal person; legalis homo

fǎshī 法师 ① a salutation for a Buddhist monk ② a Taoist high priest

fǎtíng 法庭 a law court; a tribu-nal

Făwén 法文 French (language)

Făwù Bù 法务部 the Ministry of Justice

făxīsī 法西斯 ① fascism ② a fascist

făyī 法医 an expert in forensic medicine employed by a court of law, such as a coroner

Făyǔ 法语 the spoken French; French

făyuàn 法院 a court of justice; a court of law

făzé 法则 ① a way or method; a pattern or model considered as a standard ② a formula in mathematics ③ an agreement which has the same binding force as law

făzhì 法制 the legal system; laws and institutions

făzhì 法治 rule of law

făzi / fázi 法子 a method; a way

fà / fǎ 发 ① hair (covering human heads) ② a hairbreadth; a hair's breadth
⇨**fā**

fàjiā / fǎjiá 发夹 a hairpin; a bobby pin

fàxíng / fǎxíng 发型 a hairstyle; a hairdo; a coiffure

fān / fán 帆 canvas; sailcloth

fānchuán / fánchuán 帆船 a sailboat

fān 番 ① a time ② a kind of; a sort of ③ to take turns ④ order in series ⑤ barbarians
⇨**Pān**

fānqié 番茄 a tomato

fānlí / fánlí 藩篱 ① a fence; a hedge ② anything acting as a hedge ③ a barrier

fān 翻 ① to turn; to upset; to capsize ② to rummage ③ to translate ④ to fall out ⑤ to fly; to flutter

fānkai 翻开 to turn open

fānliǎn 翻脸 to show displeasure; to get angry; to turn hostile

fānshēn 翻身 ① to turn the body over ② to rise from poverty to affluence; to have a break of fortune

fānxīn 翻新 to overhaul; to rebuild; to recondition; to revamp

fānyì 翻译 to translate; to interpret

fán 凡 ① every; whenever; wherever ② worldly; mortal; earthly ③ common; ordinary; dull

fánshì 凡事 everything

fánshì 凡是 all (who are present, etc. or which are black, heavy, etc.)

fán 烦 ① to vex; to annoy; to worry ② annoying ③ to trouble ④ superfluous and confusing

fánmèn 烦闷 annoyed; downcast; bored; depressed; vexed; worried

fánnǎo 烦恼 worries; cares; worried

fánzào 烦躁 vexed; short-tempered

fán 繁 ① many; numerous; abundant; prolific ② complex; complicated; intricate

fánduō 繁多 many; numerous

fánfù 繁复 complex; complicated; intricate

fánhuá 繁华 ① prosperous; flourishing; booming ② pompous; extravagant

fánmáng 繁忙 very busy; hectic

fánróng 繁荣 prosperous; flourishing; thriving

fántǐzì 繁体字 the original complex form of a simplified Chinese character

fánzhí 繁殖 to propagate; to breed

fánzhòng 繁重 (said of work loads) heavy; arduous

fǎn 反 ① reverse; opposite; contrary ② to return (something); to turn back; to retreat ③ to introspect; to retrospect ④ to rebel; rebellion; to revolt ⑤ to infer

fǎnbó 反驳 to refute; to retort

fǎncháng 反常 out-of-the-ordinary; abnormal

fǎndào 反倒 instead; on the contrary

fǎndòng 反动 reaction; reac-

tionary

fǎnduì 反对 to oppose; to object

fǎnduìdǎng 反对党 the opposition party

fǎn'ér 反而 unexpectedly; contrarily

fǎnfù 反复 ① repeatedly; again and again ② to relapse ③ not dependable

fǎngǎn 反感 antipathy

fǎngémìng 反革命 counter-revolution

fǎngōng 反攻 to counterattack; a counterattack; a counteroffensive

fǎngòng 反共 anticommunism

fǎnjí/fǎnjí 反击 to fight back; to strike back

fǎnkàng 反抗 to counter; to resist; to rebel; to rise up against

fǎnkuì 反馈 (electricity) feedback

fǎnmiàn 反面 ① the reverse side of the back side; the other side ② to turn away from; to be cold towards

fǎnshè 反射 to reflect; reflection

fǎnsī 反思 introspection; self-examination

fǎntán 反弹 ① to rebound; to bounce back ② to revolt; to rebel; to resent

fǎnwèn 反问 to rebut

fǎnxǐng 反省 reflection; self-examination

fǎnyìng 反应 ① response ② chemical reaction

fǎnyìng 反映 to reflect

fǎnzhèng 反正 in any case; anyway

fǎnzhī 反之 on the other hand

fǎn 返 to go back; to come back; to return ② to send back; to give back

fǎnguó 返国 to return from abroad

fǎnhuí 返回 to return; to come or go back

fàn 犯 ① to violate; to offend; to break (regulations or laws) ②

to commit (crimes, etc.) ③ to have a recurrence of ④ a criminal ⑤ to invade; to attack

fàn'àn 犯案 to commit a crime; to commit an offense

fàncuò 犯错 to make a mistake

fànfǎ 犯法 to violate the law

fànguī 犯规 (sports) to commit a foul

fànhún 犯浑 to act or speak improperly

fànrén 犯人 a criminal; a prisoner

fànzuì 犯罪 to commit (a crime, an offense or a sin)

fànzuìlǜ 犯罪率 the crime rate

fàn 饭 ① cooked rice; cooked grain for food ② a meal ③ to feed ④ a profession; a means of living

fàncài 饭菜 ① dishes to go with rice ② a meal; a repast; food

fàndiàn 饭店 ① a restaurant ② a hotel

fànguǎn 饭馆 a restaurant

fànwǎn 饭碗 ① a rice bowl ② (slang) one's job

fàn 泛 ① to be suffused with ② generally (speaking); as a whole; pan- ③ not exact or precise; not practical ④ not sincere; not intimate

fànlàn 泛滥 ① to overflow; in flood ② to spread far and wide

fànchóu 范畴 a domain

fànlì 范例 an example; a model

fànwéi 范围 range; scope; a sphere

fàn 贩 ① to buy and sell; to deal in; to trade in ② to carry about for sale; to peddle ③ a seller of goods; a peddler; a monger

fàndú 贩毒 to deal in narcotics

fànmài 贩卖 to deal in; to sell; to peddle

fāng 方 ① a method; a way ② an aspect ③ square; rectangular ④ a direction ⑤ a prescription; a recipe ⑥ honest; morally upright ⑦ a region; an area; a place ⑧

F

(classifier) short for square meter or cubic meter ⑨ side; party ⑩ occultism ⑪ (mathematics) power ⑫ one side ⑬ a surname

fāng'àn 方案 a plan; a project; a design; a scheme; a program

fāngbiàn 方便 ① convenient; handy to do somebody a favor ② (colloquial) to go to the lavatory

fāngbiànmiàn 方便面 instant noodles

fāngcái 方才 just a moment ago

fāngchéngshì 方程式 an equation

fāngfǎ 方法 a method; a way

fāngmiàn 方面 ① (in this or that) respect; (on the one or other) hand; (on this or that) topic, subject, etc. ② a direction; a quarter; a district; a sphere; a field

fāngshì 方式 a mode; a manner; a way

fāngwèi 方位 the points of the compass; a direction

fāngxiàng 方向 orientation; a direction; a course

fāngxiàngpán 方向盘 a steering wheel

fāngxīng-wèi'ài 方兴未艾 to be still growing

fāngxíng 方形 a rectangle

fāngzhēn 方针 a principle; a policy

fāngzhèng 方正 irreproachable (conduct)

fāng 坊 ① a community; a subdivision of a city; a neighborhood; a city quarter; a street; a lane ② an archlike memorial building
⇨**fáng**

fāngjiān 坊间 city quarters; in the streets

fāngxiāng 芳香 fragrance; aroma

fáng 防 ① to prepare for; to take precautions; to prevent ② to defend; defense

fángbèi 防备 to get ready or prepared (for an incident, etc.); to guard against

fángdào 防盗 prevention of burglary; to guard against burglary

fángdú 防毒 anti-poison; gas defense

fángfàn 防范 to be alert against; to take precautions; to guard against

fánghù 防护 ① to protect or safeguard ② first aid

fánghuǒ 防火 to guard against fire hazards; fireproof

fángshǒu 防守 to defend; to guard

fángshuǐ 防水 ① waterproof; watertight ② to guard against flood; anti-flood

fángwèi 防卫 to defend; to guard

fángxiàn 防线 a line of defense

fángyì 防疫 to guard against or prevent an epidemic

fángyù 防御 to defend; to guard

fángzhǐ 防止 to prevent; to guard against; to prohibit

fángzhì 防治 prevention and treatment (of diseases)

fáng/fāng 坊 a workshop of a trade; a mill
⇨**fāng**

fáng'ài 妨碍 to hinder; to hamper

fánghài 妨害 to impair; to be harmful to

fáng 房 ① a room; a chamber ② a house; a building ③ a compartmentalized structure ④ a wife; a concubine ⑤ a surname

fángdìchǎn 房地产 real estates

fángdōng 房东 the landlord (of a house)

fángjiān 房间 a room; a chamber

fángkè 房客 the tenant (of a house); a guest (at a hotel, etc.)

fángmén 房门 a door to a room

fángshè 房舍 a house

fángwū 房屋 a house; a building

fángzi 房子 a house; a building

fángzū 房租 a house rental

fǎng 仿 to imitate; to copy

fǎngfú 仿佛 as if; as though

fǎngmào 仿冒 to forge; to

F

counterfeit

fǎngzào 仿造 to manufacture an imitation of something already in market

fǎng 访 ① to visit; to call on ② to look for; to find out

fǎngchá 访查 to inquire about and investigate

fǎngkè 访客 a visitor; a caller

fǎngwèn 访问 to visit; to call upon

fǎngwèntuán 访问团 a visiting mission

fǎngfú 彷彿 ① to seem; as if ② to be more or less the same; to be alike

fǎng 纺 ① to reel; to spin ② reeled pongee (a kind of thin silk)

fǎngzhī 纺织 to spin and weave; spinning and weaving

fàng 放 ① to put; to place ② to put in; to add ③ to let go; to release; to free; to liberate; to loosen; to relax ④ to dissipate; to debauch; to indulge

fàngchu 放出 to give forth; to send out; to emit

fàngdà 放大 to magnify; to enlarge

fàngdàng 放荡 dissolute; debauched; dissipated

fàngguo 放过 to let go

fànghuǒ 放火 to set fire; to commit arson

fàngjià 放假 to have or give a holiday or vacation

fàngkai 放开 to relax or loosen (a grasp, etc.); to let go

fàngkuān 放宽 to ease or relax (restrictions, etc.); to liberalize

fàngkuǎn 放款 a loan; loaning; to loan

fàngmù 放牧 to put out to pasture; to graze; to herd

fàngqì 放弃 ① to give up; to abandon ② (law) to waive

fàngrèn 放任 to let (a person) do as he pleases; to let (a matter) take its own course

fàngshè 放射 to emit; to radiate; to send out; to emanate

fàngshèxiàn 放射线 radioactive rays

fàngshǒu 放手 ① to let go ② to have a free hand ③ to give up

fàngsōng 放松 to relax; to ease; to loosen; to slacken

fàngxia 放下 to put (or lay) down

fàngxīn 放心 to be free from anxiety

fàngxué 放学 to return home from school at the end of the day's classes

fàngyǎn 放眼 to take a broad view; to scan widely

fàngyìng 放映 to project (on the screen); to show

fàngzhì 放置 to place; to put down

fàngzhú 放逐 to exile; to banish

fēi 飞 ① to fly; to flit ② quickly; rapidly ③ high, as a bridge ④ to hang in the air; in the air

fēichuán 飞船 an airship

fēidàn 飞弹 ① a stray bullet or shell ② a missile

fēidié 飞碟 a flying saucer; an unidentified flying object (UFO)

fēijī 飞机 an airplane; a plane

fēikuài 飞快 ① with lightning speed; at full speed; fast ② extremely sharp

fēimáotuǐ 飞毛腿 a fast runner; fleet-footed

fēiniǎo 飞鸟 flying birds

fēiwǔ 飞舞 ① to dance in the wind ② to flutter

fēixiáng 飞翔 to fly; to glide in the air; to hover in the air

fēixíng 飞行 ① to fly, as a plane ② flight; flying

fēixíngyuán 飞行员 the pilot of a plane

fēiyuè 飞跃 by leaps and bounds; advancing rapidly

fēi 非 ① negative; not; not to be; non- ② faults; mistakes; evils; wrong ③ to object; to refute; to consider as wrong; to censure; to blame ④ short for Africa

fēi...bùkě 非……不可 a phrase used to express that someone or something is indispensible

fēi...cái... 非……才…… a phrase used to express that something must be done in order to...; have got to

fēicháng 非常 ① extraordinary; unusual; emergency ② very; terribly

fēidàn 非但 not only

fēifǎ 非法 illegal; unlawful; illicit

fēifán 非凡 extraordinary; remarkable

fēizhèngshì 非正式 informal; unofficial

Fēizhōu 非洲 Africa

fēi 菲 ① fragrant ② the Philippines ③ luxuriant
⇨fěi

Fēilǜbīn 菲律宾 the Philippines

fēiwén 绯闻 sexy news

féi 肥 ① fat; plump; portly; obese; corpulent ② fertile ③ fertilizers ④ baggy ⑤ to fertilize (land) ⑥ sufficiency; affluence; plenty ⑦ fat (of meat)

féiliào 肥料 fertilizers; manure

féipàng 肥胖 fat; obese

féiwò 肥沃 fertile (land)

féizào 肥皂 soap

fěitú 匪徒 bandits; brigands; robbers

fěibàng 诽谤 to libel; to slander

fěi 菲 a kind of radish
⇨fēi

fěicuì 翡翠 ① a kingfisher or halcyon ② emerald

fèi 肺 the lungs

fèi'ái 肺癌 lung cancer

fèiyán 肺炎 pneumonia

fèi 废 ① to give up; to abandon ② to reject ③ useless; disused ④ disabled

fèichú 废除 to abolish; to annul; to repeal

fèihuà 废话 rubbish; nonsense; a meaningless remark

fèipǐn 废品 ① a waste product ② scrap; waste

fèiqì 废气 waste gas; exhaust

fèiqì 废弃 to abandon as useless; to discard

fèishuǐ 废水 wastewater; liquid waste

fèiwù 废物 waste material; rubbish

fèiwu 废物 a good-for-nothing

fèixū 废墟 ruins (of a city, castle, etc.)

fèizhǐ 废止 to abolish; to annul; to repeal

fèizhǐ 废纸 wastepaper

fèiténg 沸腾 ① boiling—when liquid turns to steam ② bubbling and boiling—unrest; seething

fèi 费 ① expenditure; expenses; fees; dues; charges ② to waste; to use more than is needed; wasteful; consuming too much ③ to consume; to use; to spend; to cost; to expend ④ a surname

fèilì 费力 ① to need or use great effort ② difficult (tasks)

fèishí 费时 to take, need, or waste a lot of time; time-consuming

fèiyong 费用 expenditure; expenses; costs

fēn 分 ① to divide ② one minute ③ one cent ④ one hundredth of a tael ⑤ to part ⑥ to distinguish ⑦ to distribute ⑧ to share ⑨ a centimeter ⑩ located separately; a branch
⇨fèn

fēnbèi 分贝 a decibel

fēnbiàn 分辨 to distinguish; to tell apart

fēnbiàn 分辩 to make excuses; to explain

fēnbié 分别 ① to part (from a person) ② to distinguish or tell apart ③ separately

fēnbù 分布 to be scattered; to spread

fēncùn 分寸 judgment for propriety (in speech, behavior, etc.)

fēndān 分担 to undertake different portions of or share the responsibility for

fēnduì 分队 a unit of soldiers or policemen corresponding to the platoon or squad

fēnfā 分发 ① to issue ② to assign

fēngē 分割 ① to divide up; to cut apart ② segmentation

fēngōng 分工 to divide the work; division of labor

fēnháng 分行 a branch office; a branch store

fēnhóng 分红 to distribute a dividend

fēnhuà 分化 ① differentiation ② to disunite

fēnhuì 分会 a branch association

fēnjī 分机 (telephone) an extension

fēnjí 分级 to grade; to classify

fēnjiā 分家 to divide family property

fēnjiě 分解 ① to resolve; to dissolve

fēnjū 分居 to separate without a legal divorce; to live apart

fēnjú 分局 a police precinct office

fēnjù 分句 (grammar) a clause

fēnkāi 分开 to separate; to set apart

fēnlèi 分类 ① to classify ② taxonomy

fēnlí 分离 to separate; to part; to divide

fēnliè 分裂 to break up; to split; to disunite

fēnmì 分泌 to secrete; secretion

fēnmíng 分明 clear; distinct; unambiguous

fēnmǔ 分母 the denominator of a fraction

fēnpèi 分配 ① to distribute; to share out; to allocate ② distribution

fēnpī 分批 in batches; in turn

fēnqī/fēnqī 分期 (to pay, publish, etc.) in installments

fēnqí 分歧 ① difference ② to diverge

fēnqīng 分清 to distinguish; to draw a clear distinction between

fēnqū 分区 to divide into districts; to zone

fēnsàn 分散 to scatter; to disperse

fēnshǒu 分手 to part; to separate

fēnshù 分数 ① a fraction ② grades

fēnsuì 分碎 to break into pieces; to smash

fēnxī 分析 to analyze; to investigate

fēnxīshī 分析师 an analyst

fēnxiǎng 分享 to share; to take part in

...fēnzhī... ……分之…… used to express fractions; part of a whole number

fēnzhōng 分钟 a minute

fēnzǐ 分子 ① a numerator ② a molecule ⇨**fènzǐ**

fēnzǔ 分组 to divide into groups

fēnfāng 芬芳 fragrant; aromatic

fēnfu 吩咐 to instruct or direct (someone to do something)

fēn 纷 ① confused; disorderly ② numerous; many; varied

fēnfēn 纷纷 ① numerous and disorderly ② (said of people moving) in droves; numerous and in great confusion

fēnluàn 纷乱 confusion; chaotic

fēnzhēng 纷争 a dispute; to dispute; to wrangle; to quarrel

fén 坟 ① a grave; a mound ② great; large; big ③ the banks of a river

fénmù 坟墓 a grave; a tomb

fěn 粉 ① powder ② to make up; to doll up; to powder ③ flour ④ white (color) ⑤ to whitewash; to plaster

fěnbǐ 粉笔 chalk

fěnhóngsè 粉红色 pink

fěnmò 粉末 fine dust of anything; powder

fěnshuā 粉刷 to plaster or whitewash (a wall, etc.)

fěnsuì 粉碎 ① to shatter; to crush up; to smash ② broken into pieces

fèn 分 ① a role or part (played by a person in life) ② a part or portion (of a whole); a component
⇨**fēn**

fènliàng 分量 ① an amount ② (said of statements) weight or impact

fènwài 分外 ① particularly ② undeserved

fènzǐ 分子 a member (of some organization)
⇨**fēnzǐ**

fèndòu 奋斗 to struggle; to strive

fènlì 奋力 to do one's best

fènyǒng 奋勇 courageously; bravely

fènzhàn 奋战 to fight bravely

fèn 粪 night soil; manure; dung

fènhèn 愤恨 resentment

fènnù 愤怒 anger; wrath; indignation; rage

fēng 丰 ① abundant; luxuriant; copious; fruitful; plentiful; plenty; thick; big ② a crop; a harvest

fēngchǎn 丰产 a rich harvest; a bumper crop

fēngfù 丰富 ① abundant ② to enrich

fēnghòu 丰厚 handsome (pay, gifts, etc.); plentiful or rich

fēngmǎn 丰满 ① rich; affluence; plentiful ② (said of a woman's figure) plump; buxom ③ full-fledged

fēngshèng 丰盛 luxuriant; sumptuous

fēngshōu 丰收 a rich harvest; a bumper crop

fēngshuò 丰硕 rich; plenty

fēng 风 ① wind; a breeze; gust; a gale ② a fad; customs; practices; fashion; fashionable ③ a scene ④ a style; a manner; deportment; taste ⑤ rumor ⑥ education; influence ⑦ fame; reputation ⑧ ailments supposedly caused by wind and dampness

fēngbào 风暴 a storm; a windstorm

fēngbō 风波 disputes; quarrels; disturbances

fēngcǎi 风采 an elegant manner and appearance; fine deportment; graceful bearing

fēngcháo 风潮 ① directions of wind and tide ② disturbance; upheaval ③ a storm

fēngdù 风度 a manner; poise; bearing

fēngfàn 风范 ① appearance; an air; a manner ② a model; a paragon

fēnggé 风格 a style

fēngguāng 风光 scenery

fēngguang 风光 glory; good reputation

fēnghuà 风化 ① customs and cultural influence; decency ② (chemistry) efflorescence ③ erosion by the elements

fēngjǐng 风景 scenery; a landscape

fēngjǐngqū 风景区 scenic spots

fēnglàng 风浪 ① wind and waves at sea ② difficult experience

fēnglì 风力 wind power; the force of the wind

fēngliú 风流 ① an elegant style; a refined taste ② to have a weakness for women

fēngmào 风貌 ① style and features ② a view; a scene

fēngqì 风气 ① customs; a general mood; common practices; traditions ② air; manner; bearing

fēngqíng 风情 ① romantic feelings ② flirtatious expressions ③ fine taste; refined feelings

fēngqù 风趣 interesting; funny; humorous; witty; wit

fēngshā 风沙 a sandy wind; a sandstorm

fēngshàng 风尚 fashion; a custom; a vogue; a fad; taste of the time

fēngshui 风水 the direction and surroundings of a house or tomb, supposed to have an influence on the fortune of a family and their offsprings; a geomantic omen

fēngsú 风俗 customs; accepted practices

fēngwèi 风味 ① the bearing and taste of a person ② elegance ③ the taste and style of food

fēngxiǎn 风险 risk; danger

fēngxiàng 风向 the direction of wind

fēngxíng 风行 to become fashionable

fēngyǔ 风雨 wind and rain; the elements—trials and hardships

fēngzheng 风筝 a kite

fēng 封 ① a measure word for letters ② a wrapper; an envelope ③ to install as a feudal lord or a nobleman ④ to seal; to block

fēngbì 封闭 to seal; to close completely

fēngjiàn 封建 feudal; feudalism

fēngmiàn 封面 the cover (of a book)

fēngsuǒ 封锁 to blockade (a place)

fēngtiáo 封条 a sealing tape

fēng 疯 insane; crazy; mad; mentally deranged; lunatic; wild

fēngkuáng 疯狂 crazy; mad; insane; wild; irrational

fēngzi 疯子 a lunatic; a madman; a maniac

fēng 峰 ① a peak; a summit ② a hump

fēnglì 锋利 ① sharp-pointed; sharp ② vigorous; energetic; keen; incisive

fēngmiàn 锋面 (meteorology) frontal surface; a front

fēng 蜂 a bee; a wasp

fēngmì 蜂蜜 honey

Féng 冯 a surname

féng 逢 ① to meet; to come across ② to happen; to fall in with ③ to talk or act in order to please (a superior, etc.)

féng 缝 ① to sew; to stitch ② to suture ⇨fèng

fěngcì/fèngcì 讽刺 ① to satirize; to mock ② irony

fènghuáng 凤凰 phoenixes (fèng 凤 being male and huáng 凰 being female)

Fèngshān 凤山 Fengshan, a city in Taiwan

fèng 奉 ① to receive with respect ② an expression of respect ③ to offer; to present ④ to admire; to love and respect ⑤ pay; salary ⑥ to serve; to wait on

fèngmìng 奉命 to receive orders from above; (to do something) as ordered

fèngxiàn 奉献 to offer (something to a deity, superior, etc.)

fèngxíng 奉行 to act or perform something as ordered

fèngyǎng/fèngyàng 奉养 to support (one's parents)

fèng 缝 ① a suture ② a crack; an opening ⇨féng

fó 佛 ① Buddha (Shìjiāmóuní 释迦牟尼) ② of Buddhism

fófǎ 佛法 the Buddhist doctrines

fójiā 佛家 a Buddhist

Fójiào 佛教 Buddhism

Fójīng 佛经 the Buddhist scriptures; the Sutras

Fótuó 佛陀 Buddha

fóxiàng 佛像 a statue of Buddha

fóxué 佛学 Buddhistic study

fǒu 否 ① no; not ② negative ⇨pǐ

fǒudìng 否定 ① to deny; to negate; to refute ② denial; negation

fǒujué 否决 to veto; to vote down

fǒurèn 否认 ① to deny; to reject ② denial; rejection; repudiation

fǒuzé 否则 otherwise; if not, then...

fū 夫 ① a man; a male adult ② those eligible for military service ③ a master ④ a husband

fūfù 夫妇 husband and wife; a couple

fūqī 夫妻 husband and wife; a couple

fūrén 夫人 ① the wives of high officials ② Lady; Madame; Mrs.

fūxù 夫婿 a reference to one's own husband

fū 肤 ① the skin; the surface ② skin-deep; shallow; superficial

fūqiǎn 肤浅 shallow or superficial (views, etc.)

fūyǎn 敷衍 ① to act in a perfunctory manner ② to deal with a person insincerely

fú 伏 ① to prostrate; to yield ② to hide; to lie in ambush

fú 扶 ① to support; to prop up; to aid; to help; to shield; to shelter; to harbor; to protect ② to lean upon

fúchí 扶持 to back up; to support

fú 服 ① clothes; dress; garments; costume ② to wear (clothes) ③ to obey; to be convinced; to yield; to concede
⇨fù

fúcóng 服从 to obey; to follow; to submit to

fúqì 服气 to yield or submit willingly

fúshí 服食 ① to take Taoist pills ② to take food

fúshì 服饰 costume and accessories

fúwù 服务 ① service ② to work as an employee

fúwùqì 服务器 (computer) a server

fúwùshēng 服务生 an attendant; a server

fúwùtái 服务台 a service desk

fúwùyè 服务业 service industry

fúwùyuán 服务员 an attendant; a steward

fúwù zhōngxīn 服务中心 a service center

fúxíng 服刑 to serve a prison term

fúyào 服药 to take medicine

fúyì 服役 ① to undergo hard labor ② to undergo military service

fúyòng 服用 to take (medicine, etc.)

fúzhuāng 服装 costumes; dress; clothes

fú 氟 fluorine

fúlǔ 俘虏 ① to take prisoner ② a prisoner of war

fú 浮 ① to float; to waft ② to overflow; to exceed ③ empty; superficial; unsubstantial; unfounded; groundless

fúbiāo 浮标 a buoy

fúdiāo 浮雕 (sculpture) relief

fúdòng 浮动 ① to waft; to float; to drift ② to be unsteady; to fluctuate

fúqián 浮潜 snorkeling

fúxiàn 浮现 (said of memories, etc.) to rise before one's mind

fúyóu 浮游 an ephemera

fú 符 ① a tally carried for identification, as a warrant, etc.; an identification tag or label ② an auspicious omen ③ a charm; a talisman; a spell ④ to tally; to correspond; to match; to accord ⑤ a symbol; a sign

fúhào 符号 a symbol; a sign

fúhé 符合 to correspond; to match; to tally

fú 幅 ① a measure word for pictures, scrolls, etc. ② the breadth of cloth; a width (of cloth) ③ a border

fúdù 幅度 ① (said of stocks, commodity prices, etc.) the rate of rise or fall ② a range; an extent

fúshè 辐射 to radiate; radiation

fú 福 happiness; good fortune; good luck; a blessing; bliss

Fújiàn 福建 Fujian Province

fúlì 福利 welfare

fúqì 福气 good luck

Fútè 福特 ① Henry Ford, 1863-1947, American inventor of the automobile and philanthropist ② Gerald Rudolph Ford, born 1913, 38th U.S. President (1974-1977)

fúyīn 福音 ① good news ② the gospel

fǔmō 抚摸 to pass one's hand over; to stroke

fǔyǎng 抚养 to bring up; to rear

fǔyù 抚育 to bring up; to rear

F

fǔ 甫 ① (euphemism) a man ② (euphemism) father

fǔtou 斧头 an ax; a hatchet

fǔzi 斧子 an ax; a hatchet

fǔ 府 ① a mansion ② a government office (or agency) ③ an administrative district in former times; a prefecture ④ to call one's home respectfully

fǔ 俯 ① to face down; to come down; to bow down; to stoop ② to condescend; to deign

fǔkàn 俯瞰 to look down at; to overlook

fǔ 辅 ① human cheeks ② protective bars on both sides of a cart or carriage ③ to assist; to help; to complement

fǔdǎo 辅导 ① to assist and guide ② guidance

fǔzhù 辅助 to assist

fǔbài 腐败 ① corrupt and rotten (practice, administration, etc.) ② putrid; decayed; to decay; to decompose

fǔhuà 腐化 corrupt or rotten elements; a depraved person

fǔlàn 腐烂 to rot or decay

fǔshí 腐蚀 ① to erode; erosion; to corrode; corrosion ② (chemistry) to etch; etching

fǔxiǔ 腐朽 decayed; rotten

fù 父 ① father ② a male relative of an elder generation ③ to do father's duties

fùmǔ 父母 parents; father and mother

fùqīn 父亲 father

fùquán 父权 paternal power; patriarchate

fùzǐ 父子 father and son

fù 讣 an obituary

fù 付 ① to pay (money) ② to consign; to deliver (goods)

fùchū 付出 ① to pay ② to give

fùkuǎn 付款 to pay (money)

fùqián 付钱 to pay (money)

fù 负 ① to bear; to sustain; to shoulder ② to owe ③ defeat(ed); beaten; to lose; to fail ④ to let (someone) down; to disappoint ⑤ to take refuge in ⑥ negative; minus ⑦ to turn one's back on; ungrateful ⑧ to be proud and complacent

fùdān 负担 ① a burden; a load ② to support (a family, etc.) or pay the expenses ③ liability

fùhè 负荷 ① to bear or sustain ② the load (of electricity, etc.)

fùshāng 负伤 to be wounded; to sustain injuries

fùzài 负载 (electricity) load

fùzé 负责 to be responsible

fùzhài 负债 to be in debt; to owe; to incur debts

fù 妇 ① a woman; a female ② the wife of one's son ③ a wife ④ a married woman; a matron

fùchǎnkē 妇产科 the department of gynecology and obstetrics

fùnǚ 妇女 women; females; womenfolk

fùrén 妇人 ① a woman; a female ② a married woman

fù 附 ① to rely on; to be dependent on; to attach to; to adhere to ② to enclose; to send along with; to append ③ near or close to ④ to add to; to increase ⑤ (said of an evil spirit) to be possessed by

fùdài 附带 ① supplementary ② to attach in passing

fùhè 附和 to agree without conviction

fùjiā 附加 ① to add to ② supplementary

fùjiā jiàzhí 附加价值 value added

fùjìn 附近 around; nearby; the vicinity

fùshàng 附上 enclosed herewith

fùshè 附设 to have as an attached institution

fùshǔ 附属 accessory; subordinate; to affiliate with; to be attached to

fù/fú 服 (Chinese medicine) a dose
⇨fú

fù 赴 to go to; to proceed to

fù 复 ① to recover; a recovery ② to answer; to reply ③ to repeat; again; repeatedly ④ to return; to come back ⑤ to return to a normal state ⑥ double; overlapping ⑦ complex (concepts, etc.); compound (interest, etc.)

fùbì 复辟 ① (said of a monarch) to return to the throne after being deposed ② the restoration of monarchy (after revolution ushers in a republican government)

fùchū 复出 to come out again

fùfā 复发 (said of illness) a relapse; to relapse

fùgǔ 复古 to revive old customs, etc.

fùhé 复合 compound; complex; composite

fùhuó 复活 resurrection; to revive

Fùhuójié 复活节 the Easter holiday

fùjiàn 复健 rehabilitation

fùjù 复句 a complex sentence

fùsài 复赛 (sports) a semifinal; a play-off

fùshù 复述 ① to repeat ② to retell (a story)

fùsū 复苏 to come to life again; to revive; recovery

fùxí 复习 to review lessons learned

fùxīng 复兴 to revive; to restore

fùyìn 复印 duplication

fùyuán 复原 to restore

fùzá 复杂 complex; complicated

fùzhì 复制 to make a reproduction; to reproduce; to duplicate

fù 副 ① a set ② secondary; auxiliary; subsidiary ③ deputy; assistant; vice ④ to assist

fùcí 副词 an adverb that modifies an adjective, a verb, or another adverb

fùjiàoshòu 副教授 an associate professor

fùshí 副食 foods other than the staple food; nonstaple foods

fùyánjiūyuán / fùyánjiùyuán 副研究员 an associate research fellow

fùyè 副业 a side job; on the side

fùzhǔxí 副主席 a vice-chairman

fùzǒngcái 副总裁 ① a vice director general (of a political party) ② a vice-governor (of a bank)

fùzǒngtǒng 副总统 a vice-president

fùzuòyòng 副作用 (medicine) side effects; by-effects

fùyǔ 赋予 to give; to endow

fù 富 rich; wealthy; affluent; abundant; plentiful

fùguì 富贵 wealth and high position

fùháo 富豪 a man of wealth and influence

fùqiáng 富强 (said of a state) wealthy and powerful

Fùshìshān 富士山 Mt. Fuji, in Japan

fùwēng 富翁 a rich man

fùyǒu 富有 ① rich; wealthy ② to abound in; to teem with

fùyú 富余 to have more than needed; to have enough and to spare

fùyù 富裕 rich; wealthy; prosperous

fù 腹 ① the belly; under the chest; the abdomen ② the front part ③ the inside; inner

fùbù 腹部 the abdomen; the belly

fù 覆 ① to pour out ② to overturn; to topple ③ a reply; to reply; to respond ④ to defeat; to destroy ⑤ to cover; to screen ⑥ to repeat; a second time; again

fùgài 覆盖 to cover

F

G

gá 轧 (in the Wu dialect) ① to crowd ② to make friends ③ to check
⇨yà

gāi 该 ① should; ought to ② to be somebody's turn to do something ③ that; the said (person, etc.) ④ to owe ⑤ to deserve ⑥ fated to ⑦ inclusive

gāisǐ 该死 to deserve death; Go to hell!

gǎi 改 ① to change; to transform; to convert; to alter ② to correct ③ to revise ④ to switch over to

gǎibiān 改编 ① (said of a movie, stage play, etc.) adapted from or based on (a book, novel, etc.) ② to reorganize (a military unit, etc.) ③ to make a revision (of a book)

gǎibiàn 改变 to change; to alter

gǎigé 改革 to reform

gǎiguān 改观 to assume a new look

gǎijiàn 改建 to remodel; to rebuild

gǎijìn 改进 to improve; to better

gǎiliáng 改良 to ameliorate; to improve

gǎishàn 改善 to ameliorate; to improve

gǎitiān 改天 some other day

gǎixié-guīzhèng 改邪归正 to give up evil and return to virtue

gǎixuǎn 改选 to hold a new election

gǎizào 改造 to remodel; to rebuild

gǎizhèng 改正 to correct; to amend

gǎizhuāng 改装 ① to change dress ② to convert (a machine, vehicle, etc.) for a new use; to refit; to reequip

gǎizǔ 改组 to reshuffle (an organization); to reorganize

gài 钙 calcium

gàizhì/gàizhí 钙质 calcium content

gài 盖 ① to cover; to hide ② a lid; a covering ③ to build; to construct; to erect ④ to affix (a seal) ⑤ to surpass; to excel ⑥ to brag; to boast

gàizhāng 盖章 to affix the seal

gàizi 盖子 ① a lid; a cover ② a shell (of a tortoise, etc.)

gài 概 ① general; overall; roughly ② without exception; categorically ③ the manner of carrying oneself; deportment

gàikuàng 概况 a general situation

gàikuò/gàiguā 概括 to summarize; to sum up

gàilǎn 概览 a general view

gàiniàn 概念 a concept; a conception

gān 干 ① to interfere; to intervene ② to concern; to involve ③ (how) many or much; a group ④ a stem ⑤ dry; dried ⑥ exhausted ⑦ clean
⇨gàn

gānbēi 干杯 to toast; Bottoms up!

gānchéng 干城 defenders; protectors; champions

gāncuì 干脆 straightforward

gāngān-jìngjìng 干干净净 ① clean ② entirely; all gone

gānhàn 干旱 drought

gānjìng 干净 clean

gānrǎo 干扰 ① to disturb; to interfere ② (physics) interference; to jam

gānshè 干涉 to interfere; interference

gānyù 干预 to intervene; to interfere; intervention

gānzào 干燥 dry

gān 甘 ① luscious; sweet ② tasty; delicious ③ willing ④ to enjoy ⑤ pleasant; pleasing ⑥ a surname

Gānsù 甘肃 Gansu Province

gānxīn 甘心 ① willingly; willing ② joyous; happy

gānzhe 甘蔗 sugarcane

gān 杆 ① a wooden pole; the shaft of a spear ② rod, a unit of measurement which equals to 5.5 yards ③ a wooden fence; a balustrade; a railing
⇨gǎn

gān 肝 the liver

gān'ái 肝癌 liver cancer; hepatoma

gānbìng 肝病 a liver ailment

gānyán 肝炎 hepatitis

gānyìnghuà 肝硬化 cirrhosis of liver

gānzàng 肝脏 the liver

gān 竿 a bamboo pole; a bamboo rod

gāngà 尴尬 embarrassing; embarrassed

gǎn 杆 a wooden pole, cane, stick, or club
⇨gān

gǎn 秆 the stalk of grain; straw

gǎn 赶 ① to pursue; to catch up with; to overtake; to keep up with ② to drive; to expel ③ to hurry; to hasten ④ to try to catch; to make a dash for; to rush for

gǎndào 赶到 ① to arrive in haste; to come hurriedly ② by the time when...

gǎnjǐn 赶紧 to make haste; quickly; at once; to hurry

gǎnkuài 赶快 to make haste; quickly; at once; to hurry

gǎnmáng 赶忙 with haste; hurriedly

gǎnshang 赶上 ① to catch up with; to overtake; to keep pace with ② to be in time for ③ to chance upon

gǎn 敢 ① to dare ② to have the confidence to; to be sure; to be certain ③ bold; courageous; daring

gǎnyú 敢于 to dare to; to be bold in

gǎn 感 ① feeling; sensation; emotion ② to find; to feel; to sense; to perceive; to respond to ③ to affect, move, or touch ④ to be grateful

gǎnchù 感触 feeling; mental reaction

gǎndào 感到 to feel; to sense

gǎndòng 感动 (mentally) to move, affect, or touch

gǎn'ēn 感恩 to be grateful; to feel thankful

gǎnguān 感官 ① the senses ② a sensory organ

gǎnhuà 感化 to reform (a person); to influence (a person) by personal examples of moral uprightness

gǎnjī 感激 to feel grateful

gǎnjué 感觉 ① to feel; to sense ② sense; feeling

gǎnkǎi 感慨 emotional excitement; regrets

gǎnmào 感冒 ① a cold ② to catch a cold

gǎnniàn 感念 to remember with gratitude

gǎnqíng 感情 feelings; emotions; devotion (between friends, relatives, etc.)

gǎnrǎn 感染 to be infected with; to affect

gǎnshòu 感受 to perceive; to feel

gǎntàn 感叹 to exclaim

gǎnxiǎng 感想 mental reaction; an impression

gǎnxiè 感谢 to thank; gratitude

gǎnxìng 感性 perceptual; sensibility; sentimental

gǎnxìngqù 感兴趣 to be interested in...

gǎnyìng 感应 ① to feel and respond ② (physics) induction

G

gǎnlǎnyóu 橄榄油 olive oil

gàn 干 ① to do; to attend to business; to manage ② the main part of anything ③ talents; capable; skillful ④ the trunk (of a tree, etc.) ⑤ (slang) to kill
⇨gān

gànbù 干部 a cadre

gànhuó 干活 to work; to do a job

gànjìn/gànjìng 干劲 enthusiasm; drive; vigor

gànmá 干嘛 ① Why? Why (are you) doing this? ② What (do you do)?

gànshénme 干什么 ① What are you doing? ② What do you want? ③ Why (do you...)?

gànxiàn 干线 a trunk (or main) line

gànyuán 干员 a very capable officer or official

gāng 刚 ① just now ② just; exactly ③ barely; only ④ tough; unyielding; inflexible; hard; firm; strong; indomitable

gāngcái 刚才 just a moment ago; a very short while ago

gānggāng 刚刚 ① just now; just a moment ago ② just; only

gānghǎo 刚好 exactly; precisely

gāngqiáng 刚强 tough and strong; staunch

gāng 纲 ① the large rope of a net, round which it is netted, and by which it is drawn ② main points; an outline ③ a principle; discipline

gānglǐng 纲领 an outline

gāngyào 纲要 main points; an outline

gāng 钢 steel

gāngbǐ 钢笔 a fountain pen

gāngcái 钢材 steel product; steel; rolled steel

gāngjīn 钢筋 steel bars; steel rods; wire mesh

gāngqín 钢琴 a piano

gāngtiě 钢铁 steel; steel and iron

gāng 缸 a cistern; a crock

gǎngwèi 岗位 one's post; one's duty

gǎng 港 ① harbor; a seaport ② a bay; a gulf ③ short for Hongkong

Gǎngbì 港币 Hongkong currency

gǎngkǒu 港口 a harbor; a seaport; a port

Gǎngwù Jú 港务局 the harbor bureau

gànggǎn 杠杆 a lever; a pry

gāo 高 ① high; tall ② of a high level or degree; above the average ③ lofty ④ a surname

gāo'áng 高昂 (said of prices, morale, etc.) rising high

gāochǎn 高产 a high yield; high production

gāochāo 高超 surpassing; superior; outstanding

gāocháo 高潮 ① a high tide ② a climax

gāodà 高大 tall and big; colossal

gāodàng/gāodǎng 高档 ① a high grade; a high class; superior ② advanced (courses)

gāoděng 高等 high or advanced (in the grade)

gāodī 高低 ① height ② a sense of propriety; discretion ③ relative superiority or inferiority ④ (dialect) on any account; simply ⑤ (dialect) at last; after all

gāodù 高度 ① an altitude; a height; an elevation ② highly; great

gāo'ěrfūqiú 高尔夫球 golf

gāo'ěrfū qiúchǎng 高尔夫球场 a golf course; a golf links

gāofēng 高峰 the peak; the summit; the climax

gāogēnrxié 高跟儿鞋 high-heeled shoes

gāoguì 高贵 noble; exalted

gāojí 高级 ① a high grade; a high class; superior ② advanced (courses)

gāojiàn 高见 your esteemed opinion or advice

gāokǎo 高考 ① C college en-

G

trance examination ② *T* the Senior Examination (of civil service examinations)

gāokèjì 高科技 high technology; high-tech

gāokōng 高空 high altitude; upper air

gāoliang 高粱 sorghum; kafir

gāolíng 高龄 advanced age; great age; old age

gāolóu dàshà/gāolóu dàxià 高楼大厦 skyscrapers; tall buildings

gāomíng 高明 ① clever; wise; superior ② an expert; a master; a qualified person

gāoshàng 高尚 ① noble; exalted ② high-class; refined; respectable

gāoshāo 高烧 a high fever

gāoshǒu 高手 a master; an expert

gāosǒng 高耸 to tower; to rise high

gāosù 高速 high speed

gāosù gōnglù 高速公路 a freeway; a motorway; an expressway

gāotāng 高汤 ① consommé ② thin soup

gāowēn 高温 a high temperature

gāoxìng 高兴 glad; elated; delighted

Gāoxióng 高雄 Kaohsiung, a port city in southern Taiwan

gāoxuèyā/gāoxiěyā 高血压 high blood pressure; hypertension

gāoyā 高压 ① high pressure ② high-handed persecution

gāoyǎ 高雅 elegant; noble and graceful

gāoyīn 高音 treble

gāoyuán 高原 highlands; plateaus

gāozhǎng 高涨 to rise

gāozhōng 高中 a senior high school
⇨gāozhòng

gāozhòng 高中 to pass an examination
⇨gāozhōng

gǎo 搞 ① to do; to carry on; to be engaged in ② to set up; to start; to organize ③ to get; to secure ④ to stir up; to cause trouble

gǎoguǐ 搞鬼 (said of a person) to cause trouble or pull legs in secret

gǎohuó 搞活 to vitalize; to enliven

gǎo 稿 ① a manuscript; a sketch; a rough draft or copy ② a pattern or copy book for drawing

gǎojiàn 稿件 ① contribution to a publication; writings ② manuscripts; a sketch

gǎozhǐ 稿纸 manuscript or draft paper

gǎozi 稿子 ① manuscripts; drafts ② plans in one's mind; a plan formulated beforehand

gào 告 ① to tell; to inform; to report ② to accuse

gàobié 告别 to bid farewell; to say good-bye

gàocí 告辞 to take leave; to say good-bye

gàojiè 告诫 to admonish; to warn

gàosù 告诉 to file a lawsuit

gàosu 告诉 to tell (a person)

gàozhī 告知 to let know; to notify

gàozhuàng 告状 ① to file a lawsuit ② to say something bad against a colleague, fellow student, etc. before a superior

gēda 疙瘩 ① a wart; a pustule; a pimple ② a knot in one's heart; a hang-up

gē 哥 an elder brother

gēge 哥哥 an elder brother

Gēlúnbǐyà 哥伦比亚 ① Columbia, an American city ② the Republic of Colombia

Gēsīdàlíjiā 哥斯大黎加 Costa Rica

gēbo 胳膊 (a person's) arms

gēzi 鸽子 a pigeon

gē 搁 ① to lay; to leave; to put ② to add ③ to delay; to put aside

gē 割 to cut; to sever; to divide

G

gē'ài 割爱 to give up what one treasures

gēlǐ 割礼 (religion) circumcision

gē 歌 ① to sing; to chant ② to praise ③ a song ④ a ballad

gēchàng 歌唱 to sing; to chant

gēcí 歌词 lyrics or words of a song

gējù 歌剧 an opera

gēmí 歌迷 a fan of singing; a fan of a singer or music group

gēqǔ 歌曲 a song; a tune; a ballad

gēshēng 歌声 the singing voice

gēshǒu 歌手 a songster; a vocalist

gēsòng 歌颂 to sing praises

gēwǔ 歌舞 singing and dancing; song and dance

gēxīng 歌星 a singing star; an accomplished vocalist

gēyáo 歌谣 a ballad; a folk song

gēyǒng 歌咏 to sing praises; to sing; to eulogize

gémìng 革命 a revolution

géxīn 革新 to reform; to renovate; innovation

géyuán 阁员 cabinet ministers; members of the cabinet

gé 格 ① a frame; a trellis ② squares formed by crossed lines ③ a standard; a form; a rule; a pattern ④ to correct; to adjust or regulate ⑤ to reach; to come or go to ⑥ to influence ⑦ to resist; to attack; to fight

gédiào 格调 ① literary or artistic style; form; pattern ② personality

gége 格格 a princess in the Ching Dynasty

gégébúrù 格格不入 totally incompatible

géjú 格局 structure and form; style; setup

géshì 格式 a form; a pattern

géwài 格外 extraordinary; exceptional; especially

gézi 格子 a trellis; a lattice

gé 隔 ① at a distance from; at an interval of ② to separate; to divide; to partition ③ blocked; to obstruct; to be veiled

gébì 隔壁 next door

géhé 隔阂 no meeting of minds; a mental barrier

géjiān 隔间 a partition

géjué 隔绝 blocked or obstructed; to separate; to cut off

gélí 隔离 to separate; to isolate; to segregate; to quarantine

géyīn 隔音 soundproof

gè 个 ① a measure word ② piece ③ single ④ roughly ⑤ an adjunct to an indefinite pronoun, as this, that

gè'àn 个案 an individual case

gèbié 个别 individual; separately

gègè 个个 (each and) every one

gèr 个儿 size; height; stature

gèrén 个人 ① the individual as contrasted with the group ② oneself ③ personal

gèrén diànnǎo 个人电脑 a personal computer

gètǐ 个体 a matter, etc. having an independent and distinct quality

gètǐhù 个体户 an individual business or shop

gèxìng 个性 personality; individuality

gèzi 个子 physical size of a person; build

gè 各 ① each; every ② all

gèbèn-qiánchéng; gèbèn-qiánchéng 各奔前程 Each pursues his own goal (without caring about others' affairs).

gèbié 各别 individual; isolated (case); separate

gèdì 各地 various places or localities

gèháng-gèyè 各行各业 each and every trade

gèjiè 各界 all walks of life; all circles

gèrén 各人 everybody

gèshì-gèyàng 各式各样 all sorts, kinds, or varieties; various

gèwèi 各位 everybody (a term of address)

gèzhǒng 各种 various kinds, species, categories, etc.

gèzì 各自 each; respective; respectively

gěi 给 ① to give ② for; for the benefit of ③ to let; to allow
⇨jǐ

gěiyǐ 给以 to give; to grant

gēn 根 ① the root of a plant ② a piece (of string, rope, etc.); a (stick, spear, or thing of slender shape) ③ a base; a foundation ④ the beginning, cause, or source of something ⑤ (mathematics) the root of a number ⑥ (chemistry) radical

gēnběn 根本 ① a root; a base; a foundation ② basically

gēnjī 根基 foundation (in learning)

gēnjù 根据 ① a basis; grounds ② in accordance with (the regulation, etc.)

gēnjùdì 根据地 a base (of operations); a home base

gēnshēn-dìgù 根深蒂固 time-honored; deep-rooted

gēnyuán 根源 the source, origin, or cause of something

gēn 跟 ① and ② to follow ③ to attend upon ④ the heel

gēnjìn 跟进 to follow suit

gēnqián 跟前 the front, side, or presence (of a person)

gēnqian 跟前 used with reference to children in the presence of their parents

gēnsuí 跟随 ① to go closely behind; to follow ② a retainer; an attendant

gēntou 跟头 ① a somersault ② failure; a frustration

gēnzōng 跟踪 to keep track of; to tail

gēng 更 ① to alternate ② to change; to alter; to shift ③ (formerly) the watches of the night
⇨gèng

gēngdòng 更动 to shift; to switch; to change

gēnggǎi 更改 to change (over); to alter

gēnghuàn 更换 to change; to alter

gēngmíng 更名 to change one's name

gēngniánqī/gēngniánqí 更年期 (physiology) the menopause

gēngshēng 更生 to start life anew; to have a new life; to regenerate; to revive

gēngxīn 更新 to renew; to renovate

gēngzhèng 更正 to correct; to put right

gēng 耕 to till; to plow; to cultivate

gēngdì 耕地 ① cultivated land ② to till land

gēngyún 耕耘 to till and weed; to cultivate

gēngzhòng 耕种 ① to plow and sow; to cultivate ② cultivation

gěng 梗 ① the branch or stem of a plant ② to straighten ③ to block; to obstruct ④ fierce and fearless ⑤ an ailment; bane; distress ⑥ an outline; a synopsis; a summary ⑦ honest; straight

gèng 更 more; further; to a greater degree
⇨gēng

gèngduō 更多 more; still more

gèngjiā 更加 even more

gōng 工 ① a laborer; a worker ② work ③ an engineering or building project ④ a day's work ⑤ a defense work ⑥ a shift ⑦ fine; delicate ⑧ to be skilled in

gōngchǎng 工厂 a factory; a plant; a workshop

gōngchéng 工程 an engineering or building project—(figuratively) a job or task

gōngchéngshī 工程师 an engineer

Gōngdǎng 工党 ① the British Labor Party ② a labor party

gōngdì 工地 a building site

gōngdú 工读 to work on a job in

order to finance one's study or education

gōngdúshēng 工读生 a worker-student

gōngfu 工夫 ① time ② efforts put into a piece of work ③ skill; art

gōnghuì 工会 a labor union; a trade union

gōngjù 工具 tools; implements

gōngjùshū 工具书 reference books

gōnglíng 工龄 ① a year spent working for the same company or organization ② seniority

gōngqián 工钱 pay; wages

gōngrén 工人 a laborer; a workman

gōngrén jiējí 工人阶级 the working class; labor class

gōngshāngjiè 工商界 the industrial and business circles

gōngshāngyè 工商业 industry and commerce

gōngshì 工事 ① defense works; military fortifications ② matters pertaining to civil engineering work

Gōngwù Jú 工务局 the (municipal) bureau of public works

gōngxiào 工效 work efficiency

gōngxù 工序 working procedure; process; order

gōngxuéyuàn 工学院 a college of engineering

gōngyè 工业 industry; industrial

Gōngyè Gémìng 工业革命 Industrial Revolution

gōngyèhuà 工业化 industrialization

gōngyèqū 工业区 an industrial park

gōngyì 工艺 technology; a craft

gōngyìpǐn 工艺品 handicrafts; handmade products

gōngyǒu 工友 an office boy; an office errand man

gōngzī 工资 wages

gōngzuò 工作 ① to work ② one's job or duty

gōngzuò rényuán 工作人员 workers

gōngzuòzhě 工作者 workers

gōng 弓 ① a bow ② bent; arching; arched

gōng 公 ① to make public; open to all ② public ③ a respectful salutation ④ the male (of animals) ⑤ office; official duties ⑥ unselfish; unbiased; fair ⑦ the first of old China's five grades of the nobility ⑧ the father of one's husband (one's husband's father) ⑨ one's grandfather

gōng'ān 公安 public security

gōngbào 公报 an official bulletin; a gazette; a communique

gōngbù 公布 to promulgate; to announce

gōngchē 公车 a bus

gōngchēzhàn 公车站 a bus stop; a bus station

gōngchǐ 公尺 a meter

gōngdào 公道 justice

gōngdào 公道 reasonable (prices); just; fair

gōngdéxīn 公德心 public-mindedness

gōngdūn/gōngdùn 公吨 a metric ton

gōngfèi 公费 public funds; government funds

gōngfēn 公分 ① a centimeter (cm.) ② a gram (g.)

gōnggào 公告 ① a proclamation ② to make an announcement

gōnggong 公公 ① one's grandfather ② the father of one's husband ③ a respectful designation for an elder ④ a eunuch

gōnggòng 公共 public (relations, health, etc.)

gōnggòng gōngchéng 公共工程 public works

gōnggòng qìchē 公共汽车 a bus; an omnibus

gōngguān 公关 abbr. for public relations (PR)

gōngguǎn 公馆 ① an official residence ② a residence (a polite reference to other's residence)

gōnghài 公害 social effects of pollution

gōnghuì 公会 a union, league, society, federation, etc. of a certain trade

gōngjiā 公家 the nation, government, state, public, etc. as distinct from the private

gōngjīn 公斤 a kilogram (kg)

gōngkāi 公开 to make known to the public; to make public

gōngkè 公克 a gram

gōnglǐ 公里 a kilometer

gōnglì 公立 established and maintained by the government; public

gōnglù 公路 a highway

gōngmín 公民 citizens

gōngmù 公墓 a public cemetery

gōngpíng 公平 fair; unbiased; just

gōngqǐng 公顷 a hectare (ha.)

gōngquánlì 公权力 government power or authority

gōngrán 公然 openly; in public

gōngrèn 公认 generally recognized

gōngshè 公社 a commune

gōngshì 公式 a formula

gōngshì 公事 official business; public affairs

gōngsī 公司 a company; a corporation

gōngtīnghuì 公听会 a public hearing

gōngwén 公文 official documents

gōngwù 公务 official matters, business, duties, etc.

gōngwùyuán 公务员 government employees; civil servants

gōngxìnlì 公信力 government credibility

gōngyǎn 公演 to stage shows for public viewing

gōngyáng 公羊 ① a ram ② a surname

gōngyì 公益 public interests or welfare

gōngyíng 公营 publicly owned

gōngyòng 公用 public (telephones, etc.)

gōngyòng diànhuà 公用电话 a public telephone

gōngyǒu 公有 publicly-owned; public

gōngyǒuzhì 公有制 publicly owned; public ownership

gōngyù 公寓 an apartment house

gōngyuán 公元 in the year of our Lord...; the Christian era

gōngyuán 公园 a park; a public garden

gōngyuē 公约 ① a convention; a pact ② joint pledge

gōngzhài 公债 ① government bonds ② the public debt

gōngzhèng 公正 justice; fairness; just; impartial

gōngzhèng 公证 to notarize

gōngzhí 公职 government offices; official posts or ranks

gōngzhòng 公众 the public

gōngzhǔ 公主 a princess

gōngzhuàn 公转 (said of the earth or other major planets) to revolve around the sun

gōng 功 ① a function ② usefulness; effectiveness ③ a merit; an achievement; an accomplishment; an exploit ④ (physics) work

gōngfu 功夫 ① efforts (devoted to a task) ② accomplishments ③ skill

gōngjì/gōngjī 功绩 meritorious records; achievements; a contribution

gōngkè 功课 schoolwork; homework

gōngláo 功劳 merits; contribution

gōnglì 功力 efficacy; effectiveness; potency

gōnglì 功利 utility; material gain

gōngnéng 功能 use; a function; effect

gōngnéngbiǎo 功能表 ①

G

(computer) a menu ② (mathematics) a function table

gōngxiào 功效 effectiveness; efficacy

gōngyòng 功用 use; a function; effect

gōng 红 work; working
⇨**hóng**

gōng 攻 ① to attack; to raid; to assail; to accuse; to charge; to assail; to criticize; to rebuke ③ to work at; to apply oneself to; to study

gōngdǎ 攻打 to attack; to raid; to invade

gōngdú 攻读 to apply oneself diligently to study

gōngguān 攻关 surmount a fortification

gōngjī/gōngjí 攻击 ① to attack ② to accuse

gōngkè 攻克 to attack and conquer

gōngshì 攻势 the offensive

gōngxia 攻下 ① to succeed in capturing (a city, a fort, etc.) by attack ② to overcome

gōng 供 to supply; to contribute to
⇨**gòng**

gōngbúyìngqiú 供不应求 The supply is unable to meet the demand.

gōngjǐ 供给 to supply; to equip; to provide

gōngshuǐ 供水 to supply water; water supply

gōngxiāo 供销 supply and marketing

gōngyìng 供应 ① to furnish ② to supply

gōng 宫 ① a palace ② castration

gōngdiàn 宫殿 a palace

gōngtíng 宫廷 the living quarters of a monarch in his palace

gōngjìng 恭敬 respectful; reverent

gōngwéi 恭维 to praise; to flatter

gōngxǐ 恭喜 to congratulate

gǒnggù 巩固 ① strong; well-guarded; secure ② to consolidate

gǒng 汞 mercury (an element)

gǒng 拱 ① to fold hands before the breast when making a bow; to salute ② to raise up (in the middle); to hump up; to arch ③ to surround ④ (architecture) arched (doors, windows, etc.) ⑤ to encircle with the hands

gòng 共 ① common; same ② all; collectively ③ to share; to work together ④ together ⑤ an abbreviation of the word "Communism" or "Communist"

Gòngchǎndǎng 共产党 the Communist Party

Gòngchǎn zhǔyì 共产主义 communism

gòngcún 共存 to coexist; coexistent

gòngfàn 共犯 ① collusion ② an accomplice

gònghé 共和 a republic; the republican form of government

gònghéguó 共和国 a republic

gòngjì 共计 the sum total; to come to; to add up to

gòngmíng 共鸣 ① (physics) resonance or sympathetic vibration ② (to inspire) the same feeling in others

gòngshí/gòngshì 共识 common consensus

gòngshì 共事 to work together; to be colleagues

gòngtōng 共通 applicable to both or all

gòngtóng 共同 common; to cooperate in (an undertaking, etc.)

gòngtóng jījīn 共同基金 mutual fund

gòngxiāng-shèngjǔ 共襄盛举 Let's all work together for this worthy project.

gòngxiǎng 共享 to enjoy together; to share

gòngxìng 共性 general character; generality; common character-

acteristics

gòngyǒu 共有 owned by all; common (traits, customs, etc.)

gòngxiàn 贡献 to offer or contribute (oneself to the national cause, etc.); contribution

gòng 供 to offer in worship

gòng/gōng 供 to give a statement or an account of a criminal act; to give evidence ⇨gōng

gòngfèng 供奉 ① to provide for one's elders (especially parents) ② to offer sacrifices in worshipping

gòngyǎng/gòngyàng 供养 to offer provisions

gōu 勾 ① a hook ② to hook ③ to join; to connect ④ to mark; to put a check; to mark on ⑤ to evoke ⑥ to entice; to seduce ⑦ to cancel; to cross out (or off) ⇨gòu

gōujié 勾结 to collude or collaborate

gōu 沟 ① a ditch; a waterway; a moat ② a groove; a rut

gōutōng 沟通 to bring about an unobstructed interflow of (feelings, ideas, etc.); to communicate

gōu 钩 ① a hook ② to hook ③ to probe; to investigate ④ to entice; to lure

gōuzi 钩子 a hook

gǒu 狗 ① a dog ② (figuratively) a lackey; a footman; a servile person; a follower

gòu 勾 ① to manage ② business; affairs ⇨gōu

gòu 构 to frame; to form; to build; to establish; to constitute; to scheme

gòuchéng 构成 to constitute; to form

gòusī 构思 ① to weigh something mentally ② to plot; a plot

gòutú 构图 composition (in drawing)

gòuxiǎng 构想 an idea; a plan; a scheme

gòuzào 构造 structure; construction

gòu 购 to buy; to purchase

gòumǎi 购买 to buy

gòumǎilì 购买力 purchasing power

gòuwù 购物 to go shopping

gòuzhì 购置 to buy; to purchase

gòu 够 ① enough; too much; sufficient ② fully; quite

gū 估 to estimate; to calculate; to evaluate ⇨gù

gūjì 估计 to estimate; to calculate; to reckon; to conjecture

gūjià 估价 to evaluate; to appraise

gū 孤 ① solitary; lone; lonely; friendless; helpless; unaided ② fatherless; orphaned ③ (said of disposition) eccentric ④ negligent in an obligation

gūdān 孤单 solitary; alone

gūdú 孤独 solitary; alone

gū'ér 孤儿 an orphan

gūjì/gūjí 孤寂 lonely; friendless

gūlì 孤立 isolation; isolated; unaided

gūgu 姑姑 an aunt

gūniang 姑娘 an unmarried girl; a maiden

gūqiě 姑且 for the time being

gū 菇 mushrooms; a fungus

gūfù 辜负 to fail to live up to (another's expectation, etc.)

gǔ 古 ① ancient; antiquated; old; antiquity ② a surname ③ not following current customs or practices

Gǔbā 古巴 Cuba

gǔdài 古代 ancient times

gǔdiǎn 古典 classics; classical

gǔdiǎnyuè 古典乐 classical music

gǔdǒng 古董 antiques; curios

gǔguài 古怪 ① anachronistic ② queer; eccentric; strange; odd

gǔjí 古籍 ancient books

gǔjì/gǔjī 古迹 relics

G

gǔjīn 古今 in ancient and modern times

gǔlǎo 古老 old; antiquated; ancient

gǔrén 古人 ancient people

gǔwén 古文 ① ancient written language ② an old Chinese literary style

gǔwù 古物 antiques; curios; relics

gǔ 谷 ① a valley; a waterway between two mountains; a ravine ② a hollow; a pit ③ a dilemma; a difficult situation; a pre-dicament

gǔdǐ 谷底 the bottom of a valley

gǔzi 谷子 millet; grain

gǔ 股 ① the thigh; the haunches; the hips ② a puff; a blast (of hot air) ③ a bunch or band (of bandits) ④ shares; stock ⑤ a department; a section

gǔdōng 股东 a shareholder or stockholder

gǔfèn 股份 shares or stock

gǔlì 股利 interest on shares

gǔpiào 股票 stocks

gǔpiào shìchǎng 股票市场 the stock market

gǔquán 股权 the ownership of a share or stock

gǔzhǎng 股长 the head of a subdivision

gǔ 骨 a framework; a frame; a skeleton

gǔ/gú 骨 a bone

gǔgàn 骨干 ① the backbone; a mainstay ② (anatomy) a diaphysis

gǔròu 骨肉 one's own flesh and blood—blood relations

gǔsuǐ 骨髓 marrow

gǔtou/gútóu 骨头 ① bone ② strong character; fortitude; guts ③ a contemptible person

gǔzhé 骨折 a bone fracture

gǔ 鼓 ① drums ② to drum; to beat a drum ③ to vibrate; to quiver ④ to rouse; to stir up; to instigate

gǔchuī 鼓吹 ① to advocate; to uphold; to promote; to propagate ② a kind of ancient court music

gǔdòng 鼓动 to instigate; to rouse; to incite; to stir up; to excite

gǔlì 鼓励 to encourage; to hearten

gǔwǔ 鼓舞 ① to rouse; to inspire; to stir up; to excite; to spur on ② to dance for joy; to rejoice

gǔzhǎng 鼓掌 to clap the hands; to give applause

gù 估 to sell (used clothing)
⇨gū

gù 固 ① stable; firm; sturdy; secure; solid; hard; strong ② obstinate; stubborn; insistent; steadfast ③ chronic ④ to become solid; to solidify ⑤ to strengthen; to guard; to secure; to consolidate

gùdìng 固定 ① to fix ② fixed; regular

gùrán 固然 ① no doubt; true ② of course

gùtǐ 固体 solid

gùyǒu 固有 intrinsic; inherent; innate

gùzhi 固执 obstinate; stubborn

gù 故 ① intentional; willful; on purpose ② former; past; earlier; previous; old; ancient ③ cause; reason ④ to die ⑤ an incident; an event; a matter ⑥ consequently; hence; therefore ⑦ a friend; an acquaintance

gùshì 故事 old practice; routine

gùshì 故事 a story; a narrative; a tale

gùxiāng 故乡 one's homeland

gùyì 故意 intentional; on purpose

gùzhàng 故障 a bug or breakdown (of a machine)

gù 顾 ① to attend to; to mind; to care for; to concern oneself about; to regard; to look after ② to turn the head around and look at; to gaze ③ to visit; to call on ④ indeed; really ⑥ a surname

gùbude 顾不得 unable to take care of; to have to disregard

gùjí 顾及 to care about; to attend

to
gùkè 顾客 a customer; a patron; a client

gùlù 顾虑 to show concern about; misgivings; concern; scruple

gùquán 顾全 to have consideration for and take care to preserve

gùquán-dàjú 顾全大局 in the interest of the whole; for the sake of the country, organization, etc.

gùwèn 顾问 an advisor; a consultant; a counselor

gù 雇 to employ or hire

gùyòng 雇用 to hire; to employ; to recruit

gùyuán 雇员 an auxiliary employee of very low rank in a government office

gùzhǔ 雇主 the employer

guā 瓜 melons, gourds, cucumbers, etc.

guāfēn 瓜分 to apportion; to partition

guāzǐ 瓜子 melon seeds

guā 刮 to pare; to shave; to scrape

guǎfu 寡妇 a widow

guà 挂 ① to hang up; to suspend ② to worry; to think of; anxious ③ to ring off ④ with one's name registered or listed; recorded ⑤ to hitch; to get caught

guàgōu 挂钩 a hook for hanging clothes, etc. (usually nailed to the wall)

guàhào 挂号 ① to register (at the outpatient department of a hospital) ② registered (mail, etc.); to register a mail

guàhàoxìn 挂号信 a registered letter

guàniàn 挂念 to be anxious about; to worry about

guàshuài 挂帅 to be appointed commander-in-chief

guāi 乖 obedient; well-behaved

guāiguāi 乖乖 ① submissive; docile; obedient ② an endearing name for children

guāiguai 乖乖 (expressing surprise or admiration) wow

guǎi 拐 ① to turn or change direction ② to kidnap; to abduct ③ to swindle ④ a staff for an old person; a cane

guǎiwān 拐弯 to turn the corner

guài 怪 ① strange; queer; monstrous; odd; peculiar ② rather; very (interesting, tired, etc.) ③ to blame ④ uncanny; weird ⑤ to be surprised at ⑥ a ghost; a goblin; an apparition; a monster; an evil spirit

guàibude 怪不得 ① No wonder! ② cannot put the blame on

guàiyì 怪异 eerie; weird

guān 关 ① to shut; to close ② a frontier pass or checkpoint ③ a customs house; a customs barrier ④ a key point; a turning point ⑤ related; relationship; to involve; to concern ⑥ the bar across the door ⑦ to negotiate; to go between ⑧ to draw (money or pay) ⑨ a surname

guān'ài 关爱 to express solicitude for the well-being of someone

guānbì 关闭 ① to close ② to close down; to shut down (a store, etc.)

Guāndǎo 关岛 Guam

guānhuái 关怀 to be concerned about; to show concern

guānjiàn 关键 a key (to a problem); an important turning point

guānjié 关节 ① joints in the human body ② to bribe; a bribe ③ illegal transactions between the examiner and the examinee ④ key links; crucial links

guānjiéyán 关节炎 (pathology) arthrosis

guānlián 关联 related; involved; connection

guānmén 关门 ① to close the door ② to close a shop ③ to close its door—to go bankrupt

guānqiǎ/guānkǎ 关卡 a customs station or barrier

guānqiè 关切 to concern; a concern

guānshang 关上 to close; to shut; to slam

guānshuì 关税 customs duty

guāntóu 关头 a key point; a crucial period; a crux

Guānxī 关西 the land west of the Han Gu Pass, including Shanxi and Gansu Provinces

guānxi 关系 ① relation; connection; ties ② to matter

guānxìrén 关系人 (law) persons or parties concerned

guānxīn 关心 to be concerned about; to show concern; concern

guānyú 关于 concerning; with regard to

guānzhào 关照 ① to take care of; to look after ② to notify; to inform

guānzhù 关注 to be concerned about; to show concern

guān 观 ① to see; to observe; to behold; to view; to take a view of; to look; to inspect ② a point of view; a conception ③ to display ④ sights; views

guāncè 观测 to observe and survey

guānchá 观察 to observe; to watch; to inspect

guāndiǎn 观点 a point of view; one's view on a certain matter

guāngǎn 观感 one's feelings or emotional reactions after seeing or reading something

guānguāng 观光 sightseeing; to see the sights

guānguāngkè 观光客 a tourist

guānkàn 观看 to look at; to see

guānmó 观摩 to emulate the good points of others; to compare notes

guānniàn 观念 a conception; an idea; a view

guānshǎng 观赏 to see and enjoy

guānwàng 观望 a wait-and-see attitude; to wait and see; to hesitate

guānzhòng 观众 the audience

or spectators

guān 官 ① a government official ② of, or having to do with the government or the state ③ (biology) an organ ④ a surname

guānbīng 官兵 officers and men

guānchāi 官差 ① official business ② a government messenger

guānchǎng 官场 officialdom

guāndǐ 官邸 an official residence

guānfāng 官方 the government (as opposed to private citizens); official (information, sources, etc.)

guānliáo 官僚 bureaucrats

guānliáo zhǔyì 官僚主义 bureaucratism

guānsi 官司 a lawsuit

guānyuán 官员 an official

guān 冠 ① a cap ② the comb or crest of a bird
⇨ guàn

guāncai 棺材 a coffin

guǎn 馆 ① a house; a guesthouse; a hotel ② to stay or lodge ③ an official residence ④ an embassy; a legation; a consulate ⑤ a place for cultural activities ⑥ premises ⑦ a suffix for a library, teahouse, restaurant, etc.

guǎnzhǎng 馆长 a superintendent; a curator; the head of a library or an institute, etc.

guǎn 管 ① to control; to manage; to take care of; to keep ② to heed; to pay attention to ③ to provide ④ to guarantee ⑤ to meddle in; to interfere in; to bother about ⑥ a tube; a pipe; a duct ⑦ a wind instrument ⑧ a key ⑨ a surname

guǎndào 管道 ① a pipeline; a conduit ② a channel (for communication, etc.)

guǎnjiào 管教 to direct and teach (children, students, etc.)

guǎnlǐ 管理 to manage; to administer; to handle; to take care of

Guǎnlǐ Chù 管理处 a government agency in charge of the administration of national rail-

ways, highways, forestry, etc.; a special administration

Guǎnlǐ Jú 管理局 a government agency in charge of the administration of national railways, highways, forestry, etc.; a special administration

guǎnlǐyuán 管理员 a keeper; an administrator; a custodian; a janitor

guǎnxiá 管辖 to have jurisdiction over

guǎnxiàn 管线 a general term for pipes, wires, and cables

guǎnzhì 管制 to control; control

guànchè 贯彻 thoroughly; from beginning to end; to adhere to; to carry out

guànchuān 贯穿 ① to run through ② to penetrate or pierce through ③ to understand thoroughly

guàn 冠 first-rate
⇨ guān

guànjūn 冠军 a champion

guàn 惯 ① habitual; customary; usual; accustomed ② to be accustomed to; to be used to ③ to spoil (a child)

guànlì 惯例 custom; usual (or established) practice

guànyòngyǔ 惯用语 an idiom; an expression whose meaning cannot be inferred from the meaning of the individual words

guàn 灌 ① to water; to fill; to pour (on, into, at); to irrigate ② to offer a libation ③ shrubs; bushy clumps

guàngài 灌溉 to irrigate; irrigation

guànmù 灌木 shrubs

guànshū 灌输 to instill; to teach; to impart (knowledge to someone); to inculcate

guàn 罐 a vessel; a container; a jar; a jug; a can

guàntou 罐头 canned goods

guànzi 罐子 a can; a jar; a jug

guāng 光 ① light; brightness; light rays ② glossy; smooth ③

alone; only ④ to exhaust; to use up ⑤ bare; naked; to bare ⑥ glory; honor

guāngcǎi 光彩 ① luster; splendor; radiance ② honorable; glorious

guāngdiàn 光电 photoelectricity

guāngdié 光碟 a compact disc

guāngdiéjī 光碟机 an optical disc player

guāngfù 光复 to recover (a lost land)

guānggù 光顾 to patronize; to honor with one's presence

guānggùnr 光棍儿 a bachelor or unmarried man

guānghuá 光华 brilliance; splendor

guānghuá 光滑 smooth and glossy

guānghuī 光辉 radiance; brightness

guāngliàng 光亮 brightness; radiant; light; shiny

guānglín 光临 Please grace our place with your presence.

guāngmáng 光芒 rays of light; brilliant rays

guāngmíng 光明 ① light ② bright; promising ③ open-hearted; guileless

guāngquān 光圈 the diaphragm of a camera

guāngróng 光荣 glory; honor; glorious

guāngshì 光是 only; merely

guāngxiān 光纤 an optical fiber

guāngxiān 光鲜 fresh and bright

guāngxiàn 光线 a ray of light

guāngxué 光学 optics

guāngyuán 光源 (physics) a light source

guāngzé 光泽 luster

guǎng 广 ① wide; broad; spacious ② to extend Guangdong or Guangxi

guǎngbō/guǎngbò 广播 ① to broadcast; to telecast ② a broadcast

guǎngchǎng 广场 a square (in

G

a city); a plaza

guǎngdà 广大 vast

Guǎngdǎo 广岛 Hiroshima, Japan

Guǎngdōng 广东 Guangdong Province

guǎngfàn 广泛 extensive; widespread

guǎnggào 广告 advertisement

guǎnggào gōngsī 广告公司 an advertising agency

guǎngkuò 广阔 wide; extensive; vast; spacious

guǎngyì 广义 the broad definition

Guǎngzhōu 广州 a city in Guangdong

guàng 逛 to stroll; to roam; to ramble; to wander about

guàngjiē 逛街 to stroll down the street; to go window-shopping

guī 归 ① to come back; to return ② to return (something to its owner) ③ to belong; to attribute ④ to turn over to; to put in somebody's charge ⑤ (said of a woman) to marry ⑥ to pledge allegiance to ⑦ a surname

guīgēn-jiédǐ 归根结底 fundamentally; basically

guīhuán 归还 to return (something to its owner)

guījié 归结 to sum up

guīlèi 归类 to categorize; to classify

guīnà 归纳 to induct (a theory, natural law, etc.); to sum up

guīshǔ 归属 ① ownership ② to belong

guī 龟 a tortoise; a turtle
⇨jūn

guī 规 ① regulations; laws; rules; customs or usages ② to plan; to scheme ③ a pair of compasses ④ to advise so as to correct

guībì 规避 to evade; to shun or avoid

guīchéng 规程 regulations and rules

guīdìng 规定 ① to rule; to specify; to stipulate; to regulate ② rules or regulations

guīfàn 规范 a norm; a standard

guīgé 规格 specifications

guīhuà 规划 ① to map out or draw up (a plan) ② a plan or scheme

guīju 规矩 ① rules; practices ② well-behaved; well-disciplined ③ the compass and square

guīlǜ 规律 ① laws, rules, or regulations; discipline ② regular; regularity

guīmó 规模 ① scale; magnitude; scope; extent ② patterns; formulas

guīzé 规则 ① a rule or regulation ② regular; fixed; inflexible

guīzhāng 规章 rules; regulations

guīnǚ 闺女 a maiden; an unmarried girl

guīdào 轨道 ① a railway track ② an orbit ③ laws and conventions ④ a course; a track

guǐjì/guǐjī 轨迹 ① (mathematics) a locus ② (astronomy) an orbit ③ a track

guǐjué 诡谲 ① changing; cunning; crafty; treacherous ② strange; odd; weird

guǐyì 诡异 strange; odd; abnormal; weird

guǐ 鬼 ① spirits; ghosts; demons; devils ② sinister; evil; a dirty trick, work, etc. ③ cunning; wily; deceitful

guǐguài 鬼怪 monsters; goblins; bogies

guǐshén 鬼神 ghosts and deities; spirits and gods; spiritual beings

guǐzi 鬼子 a devil or monster (a term of abuse for foreigners)

guì 柜 ① a cabinet; a wardrobe; a cupboard ② a shop counter

guìtái 柜台 the counter in a store

guìzi 柜子 a cabinet; a sideboard

guì 贵 ① expensive; costly; high-priced ② a polite expression referring to another person—you or your ③ valuable; precious ④ to

treasure; to value highly; to prize ⑤ to esteem; to treat with respect ⑥ high-placed; high-ranking; honorable; distinguished ⑦ a surname ⑧ a short name of Guizhou Province

guìbīn 贵宾 distinguished guests

guìbīnshì 贵宾室 a VIP room; a VIP lounge

guìxìng 贵姓 May I know your distinguished name?

guìzhòng 贵重 precious; expensive; rare; valuable; highly treasured

guìzú 贵族 the nobility; an aristocrat

guìguān 桂冠 ① laurels (as an emblem of victory, success, and distinction) ② a garland made of laurel flowers

guìhuā 桂花 sweet osmanthus

guì 跪 to kneel

gǔn 滚 ① to turn round and round; to roll; to rotate ② boiling

gǔndòng 滚动 to roll; to trundle

gùnzi 棍子 a club; a stick

guō 郭 ① a town ② the outer part of anything ③ a surname

Guō 涡 name of a river ⇨wō

guō 锅 a cooking pot; a pan; a boiler; a caldron

guōlú 锅炉 a boiler (especially of a steam engine)

guōzi 锅子 a cooking pot; a pan

guó 国 ① a country; a nation; a kingdom; a state ② national; governmental ③ Chinese

guóbǎo 国宝 a national treasure

guóchǎn 国产 (said of products) native or locally manufactured

Guódà 国大 National Assembly

Guódà Dàibiǎo 国大代表 a member of the National Assembly; a National Assemblyman

guódù 国度 ① institutions of a country ② national expenditure

guófǎ 国法 the laws of the land, or the laws of the nation

guófáng 国防 national defense

Guófáng Bù 国防部 Ministry of National Defense; the Department of Defense (of the United States)

guófù 国父 ① the father of a nation ② Father of the Republic of China—Sun Zhongshan (Dr. Sun Yat-sen)

guógē 国歌 a national anthem

guóhuà 国画 a Chinese painting

guóhuì 国会 parliament, congress, the diet, etc.

guójí 国籍 nationality

guójì 国际 international

guójìfǎ 国际法 international law

guójìhuà 国际化 internationalization

guójì zhǔyì 国际主义 internationalism

guójiā 国家 a nation; a country

guójiā gōngyuán 国家公园 a national park

guójiè 国界 border; national boundary

guójìng 国境 ① national territory ② border; national boundary

guójù 国剧 Beijing (Peking) opera

guójūn 国军 the armed forces of the Republic of China

guójūn 国君 a sovereign; a monarch

guókùquàn 国库券 an exchequer bond

guólì 国力 national power (usually connoting resources and potentialities)

guólì 国立 (said of an institution) nationally supported or operated; national

guómín 国民 a citizen; the people

Guómíndǎng 国民党 Kuomintang (founded by Dr. Sun Yat-sen); the Nationalist Party

guómín suǒdé 国民所得 national income

guómín zhōngxué 国民中学 junior high school

guónèi 国内 domestic or internal

guóqí 国旗 the national flag

guóqíng 国情 the condition of a

G

country

Guóqìngrì 国庆日 the National Day (of a country)

guórén 国人 compatriots; people; fellow countrymen

guóshǒu 国手 (said of athletes, etc.) national representatives, who are the national champions in any lines of activities, especially of sports and games

guótǔ 国土 territory of a nation

guówài 国外 outside the country; abroad

guówáng 国王 a king; a monarch

guówén 国文 ① the written national language ② national language and literature ③ Chinese literature (a course in Chinese schools)

Guówùyuàn 国务院 ① the Department of State (of the U.S. Federal Government) ② the Cabinet (of the early Chinese Republican Government) ③ State Council (in mainland China)

guóxiǎo 国小 elementary school

guóyíng 国营 state-operated; state-run

guóyǒu 国有 state-owned

guóyǔ 国语 the national language

guóyuè 国乐 Chinese music

guǒ 果 ① surely; really; exactly ② the fruit of a plant ③ effect (in cause and effect); result; a consequence ④ to stuff; to fill ⑤ to succeed

guǒduàn 果断 (said of a person) resolute

guǒlíng 果岭 (golf) green

guǒrán 果然 exactly as one expected

guǒshí 果实 fruit

guǒshù 果树 fruit trees

guǒsuān 果酸 tartaric acid

guǒyuán 果园 an orchard

guǒzhēn 果真 really; if really

guǒzhī 果汁 fruit juice

guǒ 裹 ① to tie up; to wrap or bind ② things wrapped, as a par-

cel ③ to surround; to encompass ④ to close in and force obedience

guò 过 ① to pass; to pass through or by; to ford ② across; past; through; over ③ after; past ④ to spend or pass (time) ⑤ an experiential marker ⑥ too much; excessive ⑦ to go beyond the ordinary or proper limits; to surpass ⑧ a mistake; a demerit ⑨ contagious ⑩ to transfer ⑪ to die; death ⑫ to arrive; to get to

guòchéng 过程 (in) the process; (in) the course (of)

guòcuò 过错 mistakes; faults

guòdù 过度 ① to go beyond the normal limits; to overdo ② excessive

guòdù 过渡 ① (an) intermediate (state, stage, etc.); (a) transitional (period) ② to cross a river, stream, etc. by ferry

guòduō 过多 too many or much; excessive

guòfèn 过分 to go beyond the normal or proper limits; to overdo

guòguān 过关 ① to go through a checkpoint ② to pass a critical test ③ to come up to the standard

guòhòu 过后 later; afterward

guòjié 过节 ① to pass (or celebrate) a festival ② a grudge

guòjìng 过境 to pass through; in transit

guòlai 过来 Come here.

guòliàng 过量 an overdose; to go beyond the limits

guòlǜ 过滤 to filter; to filtrate

guòmǐn 过敏 allergy

guòmù 过目 to take a look; to go over

guònián 过年 to pass the New Year

guònian 过年 next year

guòqī/guòqí 过期 to have passed the deadline; (said of permits, etc.) to have passed the date of expiration; overdue

guòqù 过去 in the past; for-

guòqu 过去 ① to go over ② to pass; to pass by ③ to die; to pass away

guòrén 过人 to surpass others

guòrìzi 过日子 to live

guòshèng 过剩 a surplus

guòshī 过失 errors committed unintentionally; faults

guòshí 过时 old-fashioned; anachronistic; outdated; to out-date

guòshì 过世 to pass away; to die; dead

guòwǎng 过往 ① comings and goings ② social contacts

guòwèn 过问 ① to make inquiry about; to ask about ② to interfere with ③ to care

guòyè 过夜 ① to pass the night; to overnight ② to spend a whole night with a prostitute (as distinct from "short-time quickies")

guòyǐn 过瘾 ① to do something to one's heart's content ② to satisfy the urge of an addiction

guòyú 过于 too much; excessive; over

guòzhòng 过重 overweight

H

hā 哈 ① a form used in transliteration ② a sound of hearty laughter

Hāsàkè 哈萨克 Kazakh; Kazakhstan

hāi 咳 an interjection of regret or remorse
⇨ké

hāi 嗨 ① hi; hello ② alas; the sound of a sigh

hái 还 ① yet; still ② passably; fairly; quite ③ also ④ even ⑤ at the same time ⑥ or ⑦ had better
⇨huán

háibùrú 还不如 ① not as good as; can do no better than ② might as well; it would be better to

háihǎo 还好 ① passable; so-so; not bad ② fortunately

háishi 还是 ① still; nevertheless ② again ③ or (showing doubt) ④ had better

háiyào 还要 still want to...

háiyǒu 还有 ① There are still some left. ② furthermore; in addition

háitóng 孩童 a child

háizi 孩子 a child

hǎi 海 ① the sea; the ocean ② a great number of people, etc. coming together—(figuratively) a huge gathering ③ an area; a field ④ great; unlimited

hǎi'àn 海岸 the coast; the seaside; the seashore

hǎi'ànxiàn 海岸线 the coastal line

hǎibá 海拔 the elevation or height above sea level

hǎibào 海报 a poster

hǎibiān 海边 the seashore; the seaside; the beach

hǎibīn 海滨 the seashore; the beach

hǎidǐ 海底 the bed or bottom of the sea

hǎifēng 海风 a sea wind; a sea breeze

hǎigǎng 海港 a seaport; a harbor

hǎiguān 海关 the customs; a custom house

hǎijūn 海军 the navy; naval

hǎilàng 海浪 seas; sea waves

hǎimiàn 海面 the sea surface

hǎitān 海滩 the seashore; the beach

hǎitún 海豚 a dolphin

hǎiwài 海外 overseas; abroad

hǎiwān 海湾 a bay; a gulf

hǎixiá 海峡 straits; a channel

hǎixiān 海鲜 fresh seafood; marine delicacies

hǎiyáng 海洋 seas and oceans; the ocean

hǎiyù 海域 a sea area; a marine area

hǎiyùn 海运 marine transportation

hàikè 骇客 a hacker

hài 害 ① to injure; to hurt; to damage; to destroy ② damage; injury; harm; detriment ③ to kill ④ a vital point

hàichóng 害虫 injurious or noxious insects

hàichu 害处 shortcomings; harm; disadvantages

hàipà 害怕 to be afraid of; to fear

hàixiū 害羞 shy; bashful

hán 汗 as in kèhán 可汗—a khan ⇨hàn

hán 含 ① to hold in the mouth ② to contain; to include ③ to bear

hánhu 含糊 (said of a statement, manners, etc.) vague; ambiguous

hánliàng 含量 content

hányì 含义 a meaning; an implication

hányǒu 含有 ① to contain; to include ② to imply; to import

hán 函 ① a letter; correspondence ② armor ③ to contain; to envelop

hánshòu 函授 teaching by mail or correspondence

hánshù 函数 (mathematics) function

hán 韩 ① a fence ② name of two feudal states in the late Zhou Dynasty ③ short for the Republic of Korea ④ a surname

Hánguó 韩国 Korea

Hánzhàn 韩战 the Korean War (1950-1953)

hán 寒 ① cold; chilly; wintry ② poor

hánfēng 寒风 a cold wind

hánjià 寒假 the winter vacation

hánlěng 寒冷 cold; chilly; chilling

hánxuān 寒暄 to talk about the weather (in a conversation)

hǎnjiàn 罕见 rarely found; rare

hǎn 喊 ① to shout; to scream; to cry; a loud call or cry; a shout or scream ② to call

hǎnjiào 喊叫 to shout, scream, or cry loudly

Hàn 汉 ① of the Han Dynasty (206 B.C.-220 A.D.) ② of the Chinese people or language ③ a man; a fellow ④ name of a tributary of the Changjiang (Yangzi) River

Hànbǎo 汉堡 Hamburg, Germany

hànbǎo 汉堡 a hamburger

Hànjiān 汉奸 a traitor (to China)

Hànrén 汉人 the Han people—the predominant ethnic group in China

Hànxué 汉学 Sinology

Hànyǔ 汉语 the Chinese language

Hànzì 汉字 the Chinese characters

hànzi 汉子 ① a man ② a husband

hàn 汗 sweat; perspiration ⇨hán

hàn 旱 ① drought; dry ② (by) land route (as opposed to waterway)

hànzāi 旱灾 a drought

hànwèi 捍卫 to defend (a nation's territory, etc.); to protect

hàn 焊 to solder; to weld

háng 行 ① a row; a line; a series ② a business firm; a company ③ a trade; a line; a profession ④ order of brothers (and sisters) according to seniority ⑤ a generation ⇨xíng

hánghào 行号 shops; stores;

H

business establishments

hángliè 行列 the rank and file; rows and columns

hángqíng 行情 ① market prices of certain commodities; a quotation; market ② general standing of a person in terms of finance, influence, popularity, etc.

hángyè 行业 a trade; an occupation

Hángzhōu 杭州 Hangzhou, capital city of Zhejiang Province

háng 航 ① a ship; a boat; a vessel ② to navigate

hángbān 航班 a scheduled flight

hángchéng 航程 the distance of an air or a sea trip; sail

hángdào 航道 a navigation route

hánghǎi 航海 maritime navigation; a voyage; to sail on the seas

hángjī 航机 a scheduled airplane

hángkōng 航空 aviation; aeronautics

hángkōng gōngsī 航空公司 airlines

hángkōng mǔjiàn 航空母舰 an aircraft carrier; a flattop

hángkōngxìn 航空信 airmail

hángquán 航权 the right of navigation

hángtài gōngyè 航太工业 aerospace industry

hángtiān 航天 spaceflight

hángxiàn 航线 routes (of an airline or shipping company)

hángxíng 航行 ① to sail ② to fly

hángyùn 航运 shipping

háo 号 to cry; to shout; to howl; to wail
⇨**hào**

háo 毫 ① fine hair ② a measure of length ③ a writing brush ④ a dime ⑤ a measure of weight

háobù 毫不 not at all; not in the least

háomǐ 毫米 millimeter (mm.)

háowú 毫无 not at all; not in the least

háo 豪 ① a person outstanding

in intelligence or talent; a heroic person ② a leader; a ringleader ③ a proclivity to the use of force, bullying ways, etc.

háohuá 豪华 luxurious; swanky; plush

hǎo 好 ① good; nice; fine ② very; much ③ a friendly meeting ④ pleasing (looks, taste, etc.); easy (to deal with, etc.) ⑤ to finish (dressing, eating, etc.) ⑥ Wonderful! ⑦ an exclamatory expression ⑧ so that ⑨ fit; suitable; proper
⇨**hào**

hǎobǐ 好比 to be like

hǎobùhǎo 好不好 ① Is it all right? Okay? ② Won't you...?

hǎobùróngyì 好不容易 ① very difficult ② after all the trouble

hǎochī 好吃 good to eat; tasty; delicious

hǎochu 好处 ① good points; advantages ② profit

hǎoduō 好多 a good deal; so much; so many

hǎogǎn 好感 a favorable impression

hǎohàn 好汉 a brave man; a hero

hǎohāor 好好儿 ① delighted; joyful ② in perfectly good condition; when everything is all right

hǎohuài 好坏 ① good and bad; what's good and what's bad ② to be really bad

hǎojǐ 好几 many; much; quite a lot

hǎojiǔ 好久 a long time

hǎojiǔ bújiàn 好久不见 haven't seen you for a long time; long time no see

hǎokàn 好看 good-looking; beautiful; nice

Hǎoláiwù 好莱坞 Hollywood

hǎole 好了 ① well; all right; OK ② an expression used to express completion, similar to perfect tense ③ Just.... or Let's just....

hǎopíng 好评 favorable comment

hǎorén 好人 ① a beauty ② a person of virtue ③ a person who gets along very well with everyone

hǎoróngyì 好容易 with great difficulty; have a hard time (doing something)

hǎoshì 好事 ① good things ② charity ③ marriage

hǎoshǒu 好手 an expert

hǎoshòu 好受 pleasant; comfortable; much better

hǎoshuō 好说 Thanks for your kind word or compliments.

hǎosì 好似 (it) seems; (it) looks like

hǎotīng 好听 pleasant to hear

hǎowánr 好玩儿 interesting; full of fun

hǎoxiàng 好像 to seem; to look like

hǎoxiào 好笑 laughable; funny; ridiculous

hǎoxiē 好些 ① many (people, etc.) ② a little better

hǎoxīn 好心 kind-hearted

hǎoyàngrde 好样儿的 a person of integrity, courage, or action

hǎoyìsi 好意思 to have the nerve

hǎozài 好在 fortunately; luckily

hǎozhuǎn 好转 to take a turn for the better

Hǎo 郝 ① name of an ancient place in today's Shanxi Province ② a surname

hào 号 ① a number ② a mark; a sign ③ date ④ sizes ⑤ a bugle ⑥ a store; a shop ⑦ a designation; a title ⑧ a call
⇨hǎo

hàochēng 号称 ① to claim; to profess ② to be known as

hàomǎ 号码 a number (for identification)

hàozhào 号召 a call; to summon

hàozi 号子 (slang) a stock exchange

hào 好 ① to love to; to like to; to be fond of ② to be addicted to ③ what one likes or prefers
⇨hǎo

hàokè 好客 to be hospitable

hàoqí 好奇 to be curious; curiosity

hàoqíxīn 好奇心 curiosity

hàowán 好玩 pleasure-seeking

hàoxué 好学 to be fond of studying

hào 耗 ① to expend; to use up; to waste; to squander; to consume ② news; a report

hàofèi 耗费 to expend; to squander

hàohào-dàngdàng 浩浩荡荡 (said of an army in march) moving in an imposing manner

hē 呵 ① to scold in a loud voice ② to yawn

hēhù 呵护 divine protection

hē 喝 to drink
⇨hè

hējiǔ 喝酒 to drink (alcoholic beverages)

hémiáo 禾苗 rice seedlings

hé 合 ① to combine; to unite; to gather; to collect ② to close; to shut ③ to suit

hébàn 合办 to operate, or run jointly

hébìng 合并 to combine; to unite; to conjoin; to consolidate

hébùlái 合不来 cannot get along with (somebody)

héchàng 合唱 to sing in chorus

héchàngtuán 合唱团 a chorus; a choir

héchéng 合成 ① to combine into ② (chemistry) synthesis

hédelái 合得来 to get along well; to be congenial

héfǎ 合法 lawful; legal; legitimate

hégé 合格 qualified; up to the standard

héhū 合乎 to qualify; to tally with

héhuǒ 合伙 to enter into partnership

héjì 合计 a total; to add up to

héjì 合计 ① to think over ② to consult

héjīn 合金 an alloy

H

hélǐ 合理 reasonable; logical; rational

hélǐhuà 合理化 to rationalize

hélì 合力 ① to cooperate; to collaborate; to unite efforts; to join forces ② (physics) a resultant (of more than one force)

héqíng-hélǐ 合情合理 fair and reasonable

héshēn 合身 to fit

héshì 合适 suitable; fitting

hésuàn 合算 ① to reckon up ② worthwhile

hétong 合同 an agreement; a contract

héyì 合意 (said of a thing) to suit one's fancy

héyìzhì 合议制 a joint consultation (as distinct from dictatorship)

héyíng 合营 to run (a business) in partnership

héyuē 合约 an agreement; a contract

hézī 合资 to pool capital for a business

hézuò 合作 to cooperate; to collaborate

hézuòshè 合作社 a co-op

hé 何 ① what; how; where; why ② a surname

hébì 何必 why should; why is it necessary

hébù 何不 why not

hécháng 何尝 How (could it be an exception)?

héchù 何处 where; in what place

héděng 何等 ① how ② what sort of

hékuàng 何况 much less; not to mention; let alone

héshí 何时 when; at what time

héwèi 何谓 what is meant by

héyǐ 何以 why; wherefore; how

hézài 何在 ① Where is (that particular thing)? ② What is (that particular reason)?

hé 和 ① harmony; harmonious ② peace(ful) ③ to be affable ④ the sum or aggregate ⑤ of Japan

hé/hàn 和 and
⇨hè, huó, huò

hé'ǎi 和蔼 amiable; benign

héhǎo 和好 ① to be on friendly terms ② to make up

héjiě 和解 to be reconciled; reconciliation

hémù 和睦 to be on friendly terms

hépíng 和平 ① peaceful; mild (such as the weather, etc.) ② peace

héqì 和气 gentle; affable; friendly; cordial

héshang 和尚 a Buddhist monk

héxié 和谐 in harmony; harmony

héyuē 和约 a peace treaty

hé 河 ① a general name for rivers, streams, and waterways ② the Huanghe (Yellow) River in northern China, 4,450 km long

héchuáng 河床 the riverbed; the floor of a river

hédào 河道 the course of a river; a waterway

hékǒu 河口 a river mouth; a stream outlet

héliú 河流 streams, rivers, or channels of water

Hénán 河南 Henan Province

hébao 荷包 a purse; a pouch (carried with oneself)

héhuā 荷花 a lotus flower

Hélán 荷兰 Holland; the Netherlands

héyè 荷叶 lotus leaves

hé 核 ① a kernel; a fruit stone; a walnut; a pit ② a nucleus; nuclear ③ to investigate; to examine; to verify; to check

hédìng 核定 ① to decide after examination ② to check and ratify

héduì 核对 to verify; to check (the facts)

héfā 核发 to consider and issue

hénéng 核能 nuclear energy

hésuān 核酸 nucleic acid

hésuàn 核算 to examine and calculate

hétao 核桃 a walnut

héxīn 核心 ① the core (of a matter, etc.) ② the inner circle (of a political party, government, etc.)

hézhǔn 核准 to approve; approval

hézǐ 核子 a nucleus; a nucleon

hézǐ wǔqì 核子武器 nuclear weapons

hé 盒 a small box; a case

hézi 盒子 a small case; a small box

hè 吓 ① to intimidate; to threaten ② to show disapproval
⇨xià

hè 和 ① to match; to harmonize ② to write a poem in reply
⇨hé, huó, huò

hè 贺 ① to congratulate; to send a present in congratulation ② a surname

hècí 贺词 greetings; congratulations

hè 喝 to shout; to call out aloud
⇨hē

hèrán 赫然 ① looking angry; in flaming anger ② astonishing; shocking; consternation

hèsè/hésè 褐色 brown

hēi 黑 ① black; dark ② evil; sinister; gloomy

hēi'àn 黑暗 darkness; dark

hēibái 黑白 black and white—right and wrong, good and bad, etc.

hēibǎn 黑板 a blackboard

hēibāng 黑帮 a reactionary gang

hēidào 黑道 ① an unlighted road; a road in the dark ② the underworld; gangland

hēidòng 黑洞 (astronomy) a black hole

hēimíngdān 黑名单 a blacklist

hēirén 黑人 a Negro; a black

hēisè 黑色 black

hēishèhuì 黑社会 underworld society; the underworld

hēixióng 黑熊 a black bear

hēiyè 黑夜 a dark night; night

hēi 嘿 an interjection

hénjì/hénjī 痕迹 a trace

hěn 很 ① very; quite ② fierce; cruel ③ disobedient; quarrelsome ④ dispute; quarrel

hěn 狠 ① vicious; cruel; atrocious ② severe(ly); extreme(ly)

hěndú 狠毒 atrocious; malicious

hěnxīn 狠心 heartless; pitiless

hèn 恨 ① to resent; to hate; hatred; hate ② to regret

hènbude 恨不得 to wish that one could (do something which is not proper to do)

hēng 哼 ① to groan; to moan ② the grunt of disapproval or contempt ③ to croon; to hum

héng 恒 ① constant; regular; persevering ② lasting; continual; continually

Héngchūn 恒春 Hengchun, a town on the southernmost end of Taiwan

héngxīng 恒星 fixed stars

héng 横 ① horizontal; crosswise; lateral ② east to west or vice versa ③ by the side of; sideways ④ to move crosswise; to traverse ⑤ unrestrainedly; turbulently

héng/hèng 横 to overflow
⇨hèng

héngkuà 横跨 to stretch over or across

héngxíng 横行 ① to run wild ② to move sideways—as crabs

héngliáng 衡量 to weigh; to measure; to consider

hèng 横 ① presumptuous and unreasonable ② violent; cross ③ cross-grained; perverse ④ unexpected; uncalled for
⇨héng

hōng 轰 ① noise of a number of vehicles ② noise; an uproar ③ grand; magnificent ④ to bombard; to blast

hōngdòng 轰动 ① to cause an uproar; to create a sensation ② to excite (the public)

hōnghōng-lièliè 轰轰烈烈 in a grand fashion; on a grand and spectacular scale

hōngzhà 轰炸 to bomb (from an airplane)

hōng 哄 (said of a group of people) to make a roaring noise
⇨**hǒng**

hōng 烘 ① to bake; to roast ② to dry or warm near a fire

hóng 红 ① red; vermilion; rosy ② to blush; to redden ③ eminent; influential; (said of players) very popular ④ specially favored; a favorite
⇨**gōng**

hóngbāo 红包 ① a red paper bag containing money as a gift ② a bribe or kickback

hóngchá 红茶 black tea

hóngdēng 红灯 ① the red traffic light ② a red light

hóngdòu 红豆 ① Abrus precatorius, the red bean—a love pea ② Ormosia

hónglì 红利 a net profit; a bonus

hónglǜdēng 红绿灯 red and green lights; traffic lights

hóngluóbo 红萝卜 a carrot

hóngmǐ 红米 red rice

hóngqí 红旗 ① a red flag or banner (as a symbol of revolution) ② a red flag used as a symbol of danger

hóngsè 红色 red color

hóngshāo 红烧 to braise or stew in soy sauce

hóngshùlín 红树林 a mangrove forest

hóngwàixiàn 红外线 infrared rays

hóngxuèqiú/hóngxiěqiú 红血球 red blood cells; erythrocyte

hóngdà 宏大 great; grand; vast; immense

hóngwěi 宏伟 magnificent; grand

hóng 虹 a rainbow

hóng 洪 ① great; immense; magnificent ② floods; turbulent waters; torrents ③ a surname

hóngshuǐ 洪水 a flood; a deluge

hǒng 哄 to beguile; to cheat; to defraud
⇨**hōng**

hóulong 喉咙 the throat; the gullet

hóu 猴 ① the monkey ② naughty or impish (child)

hóuzi 猴子 ① a monkey ② a clever person with a glib and sharp tongue

hǒu 吼 (said of beasts) to roar or howl

hòu 后 ① behind; at the back of ② afterwards; to come after ③ an auxiliary to indicate "then" or "afterwards" ④ descendants; posterity

hòubian 后边 behind; at the back of

hòudài 后代 descendants or posterity

hòudùn 后盾 a support; a backing

hòufāng 后方 the rear (as contrasted to the war front)

hòuguǒ 后果 consequences

hòuhuǐ 后悔 to regret; remorse

hòulái 后来 then; afterwards

hòumiàn 后面 ① behind ② afterwards

hòunián 后年 the year after next

hòuqī/hòuqí 后期 ① to be behind schedule ② the latter part of an era

hòuqín 后勤 logistic service in the rear

hòurén 后人 ① one's descendants or posterity ② to be behind others (in doing good things, charity work, etc.)

hòushì 后世 descendants; future generations; posterity

hòushì 后市 the afternoon market

hòutái 后台 ① a backstage ② (usually in politics) one's backing or backers

hòutiān 后天 ① the day after tomorrow ② acquired; postnatal

hòutou 后头 ① behind ② in the future

hòutuì 后退 to retreat; to withdraw; retreat

hòuwèi 后卫 ① the rear guard (in military operations) ② the fullback (in football); the guard (in basketball)

hòuxiàndài 后现代 postmodern

hòuxù 后续 follow-up

hòuyízhèng 后遗症 (pathology) aftereffect; sequela

hòuyuàn 后院 a backyard

hòuzhě 后者 the latter

hòu 厚 ① thick; thickness ② deep friendship ③ substantial ④ to treat kindly; generous ⑤ kind; considerate; virtuous

hòudù 厚度 thickness

hòubǔ 候补 waiting to fill a vacancy, such as an alternate member of a committee, etc.

hòuniǎo 候鸟 migratory birds

hòuxuǎnrén 候选人 a candidate

hū 乎 at; in; from; than

hū 呼 ① to call; to cry ② to exhale

hūhū 呼呼 ① the howling of winds ② the regular breathing sound of a heavy sleeper

hūhuàn 呼唤 to call; to shout; to cry out

hūjiào 呼叫 to shout; to cry out; to yell

hūjiàoqì 呼叫器 a pager; a beeper

hūshēng 呼声 loud cries

hūxī 呼吸 to breathe

hūxiào 呼啸 to roar or howl

hūyìng 呼应 to act in coordination with each other; to echo

hūyù 呼吁 to appeal; to petition

hū 忽 ① suddenly; abruptly ② to disregard; to be indifferent to; to neglect ③ to forget

hūlüè 忽略 to overlook; to neglect

hūrán 忽然 suddenly; unexpectedly

hūshì 忽视 to disregard; to overlook; to neglect

húli 狐狸 a fox

húyí 狐疑 suspicious; doubt; suspicion

hú 胡 ① to blunder; reckless;

wildly; disorderly ② stupidly; blindly; confusedly ③ (in ancient China) a general name of the northern tribes ④ (now rarely) long and lasting ⑤ a surname

húguā 胡瓜 a cucumber; a zucchini

hújiāo 胡椒 pepper

húlái 胡来 to proceed (with a matter, etc.) recklessly and without thought

húluàn 胡乱 ① at random ② not choosy

húqín 胡琴 the two-stringed Chinese violin

húshuō 胡说 wild talk; to talk nonsense

hútòng 胡同 a lane

húzi 胡子 beard; mustache

hú 壶 ① a pot; a jug ② any potbellied container with a small opening

húlu 葫芦 a bottle gourd or a calabash

hú 湖 ① a lake ② a surname

Húnán 湖南 Hunan Province

húpō 湖泊 lakes

húdié 蝴蝶 a butterfly

hú 糊 ① to paste ② paste ③ scorched ④ not clear; blurred; confused; ambiguous; unintelligible

hútu 糊涂 ① mixed-up; confused ② stupid; foolish

hǔ 虎 ① a tiger ② fierce; savage; vigorous; brave

hù 互 each other; mutually; reciprocally

hùbǔ 互补 complementary

hùdòng 互动 to interact; interaction

hùhuì 互惠 mutually beneficial

hùlì 互利 mutually beneficial

hùxiāng 互相 mutually; each other; one another

hùzhù 互助 to help each other; mutual help

hù 户 ① a household; a family ② a door

hùjí 户籍 a domicile

hùkǒu 户口 households

hùmíng 户名 a depositor (in banking)

hùtóu 户头 an account; a depositor (in banking)

hùwài 户外 outdoor; outdoors

hùzhèng 户政 the administration with regard to residents and residence

hù 护 ① to protect; to guard; to defend; to shield ② to take sides; to be partial to

hùlǐ 护理 ① to act for a senior official ② nursing

hùshi 护士 a nurse

hùzhào 护照 a passport

huā 花 ① a flower ② a flowering plant ③ to spend ④ varicolored ⑤ fireworks ⑥ a prostitute ⑦ a surname

huābàn 花瓣 the petal (of a flower or blossom)

huābiān xīnwén 花边新闻 a sidebar

huācǎo 花草 flowers and grass

huāchē 花车 a float; a decorated vehicle in parade

huāduǒ 花朵 flowers

huāfèi 花费 to spend; to expend

huāhuì 花卉 flowering plants

huālán 花蓝 a flower basket

Huāliánxiàn 花莲县 Hualien County in Taiwan

huāpén 花盆 a flower pot

huāpíng 花瓶 a vase

huāqián 花钱 to spend money

huār 花儿 ① a flower; a blossom ② a flowering plant ③ smallpox

huāsè 花色 varieties; patterns

huāshēng 花生 a peanut plant

huāwén 花纹 a decorative design or pattern

huāyàng 花样 a pattern; a style; a model

huāyuán 花园 a flower garden; a garden

huāhuā 哗哗 an onomatopoeia, such as gurgle, clang, crack, etc.

huá 划 ① to oar; to row ② to cut

⇨**huà**

huábulái 划不来 not worthwhile; it doesn't pay to

huásuàn 划算 ① to calculate; to weigh ② profitable

huá 华 ① Cathay; China ② splendid; majestic; gorgeous; colorful; brilliant; bright; fine; beautiful; luxurious ③ prosperous; thriving

⇨**Huà**

Huáfǔ 华府 Washington D.C.

huálì 华丽 magnificent; resplendent; gorgeous

Huáqiáo 华侨 overseas Chinese

Huárén 华人 Chinese people (especially those living abroad)

Huáshèngdùn 华盛顿 ① George Washington, 1732-1799, founder of the U.S.A. ② Washington D.C., capital of the U.S.A. ③ the state of Washington , U.S.A.

Huáwén 华文 the Chinese language; Chinese

Huáxià 华夏 Cathay

Huáyì 华裔 foreign citizens of Chinese origin

huázú 华族 ① the peerage; the aristocracy; the nobility ② Chinese people

huá 滑 ① to slip; to slide; to glide ② smooth; slippery ③ insincere; dishonest; cunning ④ funny; comical; ridiculous

huábīng 滑冰 ice-skating

huáshǔ 滑鼠 (computer) a mouse

huáxuě 滑雪 to ski; to slide or travel on skis

huà 化 ① to melt ② to change; to convert; to transform; to influence ③ short for "chemistry"

huàféi 化肥 chemical fertilizer

huàgōng 化工 ① chemical engineering ② Nature's work; operations of Nature

huàhé 化合 to combine (chemically)

huàjiě 化解 to settle (disputes)

huàshēn 化身 an incarnation; an embodiment

H

huàshí 化石 a fossil

huàxiān 化纤 chemical fiber

huàxué 化学 chemistry

huàyàn 化验 to subject to chemical analysis

huàzhuāng 化妆 to make up; to apply cosmetics

huàzhuāng 化装 to masquerade

huàzhuāngpǐn 化妆品 cosmetics

huà 划 ① to set aside; to divide ② to lay boundaries ③ to draw a line; to mark; to delineate ④ to plan or design ⑤ to unify ⇨huá

huàbō 划拨 to deposit money under the account of a seller in payment of goods purchased; to transfer funds

huàfēn 划分 to differentiate

huàshídài 划时代 epoch-making; epochal

Huà 华 ① Mountain Hua in Shaanxi Province ② a surname ⇨huá

huà 画 ① to paint or draw (a picture); a painting; a drawing ② to plan; to design; a plan ③ to mark off; to delimit ④ a stroke in a Chinese character

huàbào 画报 a pictorial

huàbù 画布 a canvas (for painting)

huàfǎ 画法 a method of painting or drawing

huàfēng 画风 style of painting

huàhuàr 画画儿 to paint pictures; to draw pictures

huàjiā 画家 a painter; an artist

huàláng 画廊 a gallery (for paintings)

huàmiàn 画面 general appearance of a picture; tableau

huàr 画儿 a painting; a drawing

huàshé-tiānzú 画蛇添足 to make undesirable additions; superfluous

huàzhǎn 画展 an art exhibition

huà 话 ① words; sayings ② to speak; to talk; to converse; to say ③ language

huàjù 话剧 a play or drama (as distinct from opera)

huàshuōhuílái 话说回来 a colloquial expression which indicates a return to a subject discussed previously

huàtí 话题 the topic of conversation or discussion

huái 怀 ① bosom; breast ② to hold; to harbor ③ to think of; to recollect ④ to conceive (a child)

huáibào 怀抱 an embrace; a hug; to embrace; to hug

huáiniàn 怀念 to have a sweet memory of

huáiyí 怀疑 to doubt; to suspect

huáiyùn 怀孕 to become pregnant; to conceive

huáishù 槐树 a pagoda tree; a Chinese scholar tree

huài 坏 ① broken-down; decaying; rotten; out of order; useless ② bad; poor (scores, etc.) ③ vicious; mean; evil (persons, etc.)

huàichu 坏处 bad points; shortcomings

huàidàn 坏蛋 a bad fellow; a villain

huàirén 坏人 a bad guy; an evil person

huàishì 坏事 ① a bad thing; an evil deed ② to make things worse

huān 欢 ① pleased; glad; jubilant ② pleasures; joys ③ a lover ④ in full swing; active and energetic; quick

huānhū 欢呼 to cheer with jubilation; to hurrah

huānlè 欢乐 joy; happiness; gaiety

huānsòng 欢送 to send off; to give a farewell party

huānxǐ 欢喜 joyful; happy

huānxiào 欢笑 cheer and laughter—great joy; jubilation

huānyíng 欢迎 to welcome; a welcome

huán 还 ① to return; to come

back; return ② to repay; to pay back; to restore ⇨**hái**

huányuán 还原 ① to return to normal or original status ② (chemistry) reduction

huán 环 ① a jade ring or bracelet; a ring; a bracelet ② earrings for women; ear-ornaments ③ a link ④ around; round; to surround ⑤ (sports) a ring

huánbǎo 环保 environmental protection

Huánbǎo Jú 环保局 the Bureau of Environment Protection (BEP) in the local government

Huánbǎo Shǔ 环保署 the Environmental Protection Agency (EPA) in the Central Government

huánjié 环节 a segment; a link

huánjìng 环境 surroundings; environment

huánqiú 环球 around the globe

huánrào 环绕 to surround; to move round; to circle

huǎn 缓 ① slow; gradual; tardy; leisurely; unhurried ② to delay; to slacken; to put off; to postpone; to defer ③ to revive; to refresh

huǎnhé 缓和 ① to subside; to relax; to alleviate ② calm; mild

huǎnmàn 缓慢 slow

huàndēng 幻灯 a magic lantern

huànxiǎng 幻想 to daydream; reverie; a vision

huànxiàng 幻象 a vision; an illusion; a phantasm or fantasm

huàn 换 to exchange; to change; to alter; to substitute

huànqǔ 换取 to change; to exchange

huànshang 换上 to make changes; to change into; to substitute

huànyánzhī 换言之 in other words

huàn 唤 ① to call ② to summon ③ to arouse

huànqǐ 唤起 ① to arouse to action ② to call; to evoke

huànxǐng 唤醒 to arouse; to awaken

huàn 患 ① suffering; adversity; disaster; peril ② trouble; worry ③ to be troubled by; to be worried about

huànzhě 患者 a patient (at a hospital)

huāng 荒 ① uncultivated; desolate; wild; waste; deserted; barren ② absurd; ridiculous ③ famine; scarcity; deficiency ④ to neglect

huāngdì 荒地 uncultivated land; waste land; the wilderness

huāngliáng 荒凉 desolate; deserted; wild

huāngmiù 荒谬 grossly absurd; ridiculous; preposterous

huāngtáng 荒唐 absurd; nonsensical

huāngyě 荒野 the wilderness

huāng 慌 to lose self-possession; to lose one's head; panic; confused

huāngluàn 慌乱 in a hurry and confusion

huāngmáng 慌忙 hurried and flustered; hurry-scurry

huāngzhāng 慌张 flustered; nervous and confused

huángdì 皇帝 an emperor

huánggōng 皇宫 an imperial palace

huánghòu 皇后 an empress

huángjiā 皇家 the imperial family (or house)

huángshang 皇上 His Majesty

huángshì 皇室 the imperial household; the royal household

huáng 黄 ① yellow ② a surname

huángdòu 黄豆 soybean

huángguā 黄瓜 a cucumber

Huánghé 黄河 the Huanghe (Yellow) River

huánghūn 黄昏 dusk

huángjīn 黄金 gold

huángjiǔ 黄酒 ① same as 绍兴酒—wine from Shaoxing ② a kind of yellowish rice wine

brewed in Taiwan

huángsè 黄色 ① yellow ② decadent; obscene; pornographic

huángyóu 黄油 ① butter oil ② tallow

huánglùn 遑论 not to mention...

huángkǒng 惶恐 apprehensive; fearful; afraid

huángchóng 蝗虫 a locust

huǎnghū 恍惚 ① in a trance; absent-minded ② dimly; faintly

huǎng 晃 ① dazzling; glaring ② a flash; to flash past; to appear and disappear very quickly ③ brightness
⇨**huàng**

huǎngyán 谎言 a lie

huàng 晃 to rock; to sway; to shake
⇨**huǎng**

huàngdòng 晃动 to rock; to sway

huī 灰 ① gray (color) ② lime ③ ashes; dust ④ disheartened; disappointed or discouraged ⑤ (now rarely) to break into tiny pieces or particles

huīchén 灰尘 dust

huīsè 灰色 gray color

huīxīn 灰心 disappointed; discouraged; disheartened

huī 挥 ① to wield (a sword, pen, etc.); to move; to shake; to wave; to brandish; to make a light or rapid stroke ② to swing (fists) ③ to wipe away (sweat, tears, etc.) ④ to scatter; to sprinkle ⑤ to squander (money, etc.) ⑥ to conduct; to direct (troop movements, a concert, a course of action, etc.)

huīhuò 挥霍 to spend freely; to squander

huīsǎ 挥洒 to write or paint freely

huīfù 恢复 to restore; to regain; to recover

huīhuáng 辉煌 magnificent; splendid; glorious; brilliant

huí 回 ① to return; to go back; to bring back; to turn back ② to

reply; to answer ③ the number of times ④ to turn round ⑤ a kind; a sort ⑥ chapters in a novel ⑦ of Mohammedanism; Moslems ⑧ the Hui nationality

huíbào 回报 ① to bring back a report ② to repay (a favor or an injury)

huíbì 回避 ① to avoid meeting (another person) ② (law) to withdraw; withdrawal ③ to decline an offer or resign from a job, in order to avoid likely suspicion of favoritism

huíchéng 回程 the return trip

huídá 回答 to reply; to answer; a reply

huídiàn 回电 ① a cable or telegram sent in reply ② to wire back

huífù 回复 to reply; to answer; a reply

huígù 回顾 to look back

huíguī 回归 ① regression ② to regress

huíguó 回国 to return to one's own country

huíhé 回合 an encounter; a round; a bout

huíjī/huíjí 回击 to fight back; to counterattack

huíjiā 回家 to return home; to go home

Huíjiào 回教 Mohammedanism; Islam

huíjué 回绝 to decline; to refuse

huíkuì 回馈 to feedback

huílái 回来 to come back; to return

huíláng 回廊 a winding corridor

huíqu 回去 ① to return ② to go back

huíshēng 回升 to rise again (after a fall)

huíshōu 回收 ① to retrieve; to recover; to reclaim ② to recycle

huítóu 回头 ① after a while; later ② to turn back ③ to return ④ to repent

huíwèi 回味 to ponder over

huíxiǎng 回响 response; to

echo; to resound; to reverberate

huíxiǎng 回想 to recollect; to recall

huíxìn 回信 ① a letter in reply ② to write back ③ a reply

huíyì 回忆 to recollect; to recall

huíyóu 回邮 return mail

huǐ 悔 to regret; to repent; remorse

huǐgǎi 悔改 to repent of (a sin); to be repentant of

huǐhèn 悔恨 to feel remorse for; to regret; remorse

huǐ 毁 ① to destroy; to ruin; to damage; to injure ② to libel; to slander; to abuse; to revile; to defame

huǐhuài 毁坏 to destroy; to injure; to damage

huǐmiè 毁灭 to demolish; to ruin; to destroy

huǐsǔn 毁损 to damage; to injure; to disfigure

huì 汇 ① to remit money ② to converge ③ to flow into ④ a category; a class; a series ⑤ to categorize ⑥ to collect

huìbào 汇报 to collect (all information) and report

huìjí 汇集 to gather in one place; to collect (materials, etc.)

huìkuǎn 汇款 ① a remittance ② to remit money

huìlǜ 汇率 the exchange rate

huìpiào 汇票 a money order; a draft; a bill of exchange

huì 会 ① to meet ② to assemble; to gather; to converge ③ a meeting; a convention; a conference ④ to be able to ⑤ to understand; to comprehend; to realize ⑥ shall; will ⑦ an association; a society ⑧ a private banking cooperative ⑨ a chief city; a capital

huì/huí 会 a brief period of time; a moment
⇨**kuài**

huìbúhuì 会不会 ① Is it likely that...? ② Can (you, he, etc.) do...or not?

huìchǎng 会场 the place of a

meeting; the site of a conference

huìhuà 会话 a conversation; a dialogue

huìjiàn 会见 to meet (a person)

huìkè 会客 to receive callers (or visitors)

huìmiàn 会面 to meet face to face

huìqī/huìqí 会期 ① the time of a meeting ② the duration of a meeting

huìsuǒ 会所 the office of an association or organization

huìtán 会谈 talks

huìtóng 会同 together with

huìwù 会晤 to meet

huìyì 会议 a conference; a meeting

huìyì 会意 ① to understand the meaning ② associative compounds, one of six categories under which Chinese characters are grouped

huìyuán 会员 a member of an association, society, etc.

huìyuánguó 会员国 a member nation (or state)

huìzhǎng 会长 the president of an association or organization

huì 绘 to draw (pictures)

huìhuà 绘画 painting; drawing

huìtú 绘图 ① to draw pictures ② to prepare (engineering) drawings

huìlù 贿赂 to bribe; bribery

huìxuǎn 贿选 to try to win in an election by means of bribery

huìxīng 彗星 a comet

huì 惠 ① to benefit; benefit; to profit; profit; to favor; a favor ② kind; benevolent; gracious ③ gentle and yielding

hūn 昏 ① dusk; dark ② confused; muddled; mixed-up; demented ③ unclear of sight; dizzy

hūndǎo 昏倒 to faint; to swoon

hūnmí 昏迷 in a coma; delirious; stupor

hūn 婚 ① to wed; to marry ② marriage

hūnhòu 婚后 after marriage; after wedding

hūnlǐ 婚礼 a wedding (ceremony)

hūnyīn 婚姻 marriage

húnshēn 浑身 one's entire body; from head to toe

hún/hùn 混 turbid; muddy; not clear
⇨hùn

hùn 混 ① to mix; mixed; to mingle or blend ② to fool around; just to get along ③ to do things at random or without purpose ④ disorderly; confused
⇨hún

hùnfǎng 混纺 (said of textiles) mixture of natural and synthetic fibers

hùnhé 混合 to mix, mingle, or blend together

hùnhéwù 混合物 a mixture; a blend

hùnluàn 混乱 confusion; chaos

hùnníngtǔ 混凝土 concrete

hùnxiáo/hùnyáo 混淆 mixed, confused, and indistinguishable

hùnzhuó 混浊 turbid; not clean or pure

huó/huò 豁 ① a crack; a break; a breach ② to crack; to break open; to split ③ to give up; to sacrifice; to risk one's life for
⇨huò

huó/huò 和 to mix with water, etc.
⇨hé, hè, huò

huó 活 ① to live; to survive; to be alive ② work ③ active; lively; vivacious ④ moveable; mobile; flexible ⑤ to save the life of

huódòng 活动 ① to exercise ② activities ③ to lobby; to canvass ④ active; lively ⑤ movable; mobile ⑥ loose

huógāi 活该 It serves you (him, them) right.

huólì 活力 vitality; vigor

huóluò 活络 ① loose ② indefinite

huópō 活泼 active; lively; sprightly

huóqī/huóqí 活期 due on demand

huór 活儿 ① jobs; work; labor ② products

huóshēngshēng 活生生 alive and kicking

huóyuè 活跃 active; actively

huǒ 火 ① fire; flames; to burn with fire ② fury; anger; temper ③ urgency; urgent; imminent; pressing ④ (Chinese herbal medicine) the latent "heat" in human body

huǒchái 火柴 a match

huǒchē 火车 a train

huǒchēzhàn 火车站 a railway station

huǒguō 火锅 a chafing pot; a chafing dish

huǒhuā 火花 sparks

huǒjī 火鸡 a turkey

huǒjiàn 火箭 a rocket

huǒjǐng 火警 a fire alarm

huǒlì 火力 ① firepower ② thermal power

huǒshān 火山 a volcano

huǒshì 火势 the intensity and scope of a fire

huǒtuǐ 火腿 Chinese ham; ham

huǒxīng 火星 ① the planet Mars ② sparks

huǒyàn 火焰 flames

huǒyào 火药 gunpowder

huǒzāi 火灾 a fire disaster

huǒ 伙 ① a partner; a company ② a clerk ③ a crowd

huǒbàn 伙伴 a companion; a colleague

huǒji 伙计 ① a clerk ② buddy

huǒshí 伙食 meals

huǒ 夥 many; much; lots of

huò 或 ① or ② perhaps; probably

huòduō-huòshǎo 或多或少 more or less

huòshì 或是 ① perhaps ② or

huòxǔ 或许 perhaps; probably; maybe

huòzhě 或者 ① or ② perhaps

huò 和 to blend; to mix
⇨hé, hè, huó

huò 货 ① commodities; goods;

products; freight; cargo ② money; currency; property ③ to bribe; bribery ④ used as a term of reviling with an abusive suffix

huòbì 货币 currency; money

huòchē 货车 a freight car; a lorry; a cargo truck

huòpǐn 货品 commodities; goods

huòwù 货物 commodities; goods

huòyùn 货运 transportation service

huò 获 ① to get; to obtain; to incur; to capture; to catch; to reap ② can; able

huòdé 获得 to get or obtain; to acquire

huòjiǎng 获奖 to win a prize

huòlì 获利 to get or obtain

profit; to earn profit

huòqǔ 获取 to get; to acquire; to obtain

huòshèng 获胜 to triumph; to obtain victory; to win

huòxī 获悉 to be informed; to learn (of an event)

huòyì 获益 to get profit

huò 祸 ① calamity; disaster; misfortune; evil ② to bring disaster upon; to harm; to injure; to do evil to

huòhai 祸害 harm; injury; evil

huò 豁 ① to open up; clear ② to exempt from (duties, etc.)
⇨huō

huòdá 豁达 ① open and clear ② open-minded

J

jī 几 ① small; tiny; slight ② nearly ③ an omen; a portent
⇨jǐ

jīhū 几乎 almost; nearly

jīxiào 讥笑 to laugh at; taunts; sneers

jī/jí 击 to beat; to strike; to attack

jībài/jíbài 击败 to defeat; to beat; to conquer

jīluò/jíluò 击落 to shoot down (aircraft)

jīqiú/jíqiú 击球 (baseball) batting

jīzhòng/jízhòng 击中 to hit (the target)

jī'è 饥饿 hunger; hungry; starvation

jī 机 ① mechanics; machinery ② opportune; an opportunity ③ a crucial point; a pivot ④ an aircraft; a plane; an airplane ⑤ tricky; cunning

jīcāng 机舱 the cockpit of a small airplane; the cabin of an airliner

jīchǎng 机场 an airport; an airfield

jīchē 机车 ① a locomotive ② a motorcycle

jīchuáng 机床 a machine tool

jīdòng 机动 mobile

jīgòu 机构 an organization

jīguān 机关 ① an organization; an institution ② a stratagem; an intrigue ③ a machine

jīhuì 机会 an opportunity

jījǐng 机警 alert

jīlíng 机灵 clever; smart; sharp; intelligent

jīlǜ 机率 the probability

jīmì 机密 secret; confidential; classified

jīnéng 机能 functions; functional

jīpiào 机票 an airline ticket

jīqì 机器 machinery; a machine

jīqìrén 机器人 a robot

jīqiāng 机枪 a machine gun

jīshēn 机身 the fuselage

jīshī 机师 a pilot (of an airplane)

jītǐ 机体 an organism

jīxiè 机械 ① a machine ② mechanical ③ (said of persons) cunning or shrewd

jīxièhuà 机械化 mechanization

jīxíng 机型 ① the type (of an aircraft) ② the model (of a machine)

jīyì 机翼 wings of an airplane

jīyóu 机油 lubricating oil; lubricant

jīyù 机遇 a chance; an opportunity; luck

jīyuán 机缘 a chance and an opportunity

jīzhǎng 机长 an aircraft (or crew) commander

jīzhì 机制 mechanism

jīzhì 机智 alertness; quick wit; tact

jīzǔ 机组 ① (machinery) a unit; a set ② the aircrew; the flight crew

jīfū 肌肤 the skin and flesh

jīròu 肌肉 muscles

jī 鸡 a chicken; a hen; a cock; a fowl

jīdàn 鸡蛋 a hen's egg

jīròu 鸡肉 chicken (as food)

jī 奇 odd (numbers)
⇨qí

jī 积 ① to accumulate; to store up; to amass ② long (time); old; deep-rooted; longstanding ③ (mathematics) product

jīfēn 积分 ① accumulated points ② integral calculus

jījí 积极 active(ly); positive(ly); persistent(ly)

jījíxìng 积极性 initiative; positivism; enthusiasm

jīlěi 积累 to accumulate

jīqiàn 积欠 accumulated debts; outstanding debts; arrears

jīshuǐ 积水 to accumulate water; accumulated water (in low-lying areas after a shower)

jīyā 积压 to neglect handling official papers, legal cases, etc.

jī 基 ① a foundation; a base an origin; a basis; a root ③ on the basis of; according to; on the strength of ④ the base of a chemical compound

jīběn 基本 ① a root, foundation, or base ② fundamental; basic; elementary ③ basically; on the whole; by and large

jīběnshang 基本上 basically; fundamentally

jīcéng 基层 basic level; a grass-roots unit

jīchǔ 基础 ① the foundation of a building ② the basis of an argument, etc.

jīdì 基地 a base (of operations)

Jīdū 基督 Jesus Christ

Jīdūjiào 基督教 Christianity

Jīdūtú 基督徒 a Christian

jījīn 基金 a reserve fund

jījīnhuì 基金会 a foundation

Jīlóng 基隆 Keelung—the northern port city of Taiwan

jīyīn 基因 a gene

jīyú 基于 because of; in view of

jīzhǔn 基准 a pattern; a standard; a model

jīxíng 畸形 malformation; abnormality; deformity

jīchá 稽查 to examine and investigate

jīhé 稽核 to examine and audit

jī 激 ① to stir up; to rouse; to arouse; to urge; to excite ② to turn back the current—as a dike ③ heated (debate, battle, etc.); fierce; angry; vexed ④ abnormal; unusual; drastic ⑤ sudden; great; very

jīdàng 激荡 to surge; turmoil; stirring

jīdòng 激动 aroused; excited; agitated

jīfā 激发 to stir up; to arouse

jīguāng 激光 laser

jījìn 激进 radical

jīlì 激励 to arouse and encourage;

to impel

jīliè 激烈 heated (debates, battles, etc.)

jīqǐ 激起 to arouse; to excite; to stir up

jīqíng 激情 fervor; ardor; passion

jīshǎng 激赏 to heap high praise on (a work, person, etc.)

jīsù 激素 (physiology) hormone

jīzēng 激增 to shoot up; to increase sharply

jīyā 羁押 to take into custody

jí 及 ① and; as well as; with ② just at the moment; timely; when ③ to reach; to attain; to come up to ④ as long as; up to; until ⑤ to continue ⑥ to extend

jígé 及格 to pass an examination; to be qualified

jíshí 及时 in time

jízǎo 及早 as soon as possible; before it is too late

jílì 吉利 good luck; propitiousness

jípǔchē 吉普车 a jeep

jítā 吉他 a guitar

jíxiáng 吉祥 propitious; auspicious

jíqǔ 汲取 to draw; to derive

jí 级 ① a grade; a class (at school) ② a level; a degree; a mark of merit; a rank ③ a step (of a flight of steps) ④ a decapitated head

jíbié 级别 ranks; levels; grades; scales

jí 极 ① extreme(ly); utmost; highest; topmost; farthest ② to exhaust ③ poles ④ to reach; to arrive at

jídù 极度 extremely; exceedingly

jíduān 极端 an extreme; extremely

jílì 极力 to make the utmost effort

jípǐn 极品 a thing of the highest grade

jíqí 极其 very; exceedingly; highly

jíwéi 极为 extremely; exceedingly; highly

jíxiàn 极限 (mathematics) limit

jízhì 极致 the ultimate attain-

ment; the acme

jí 即 ① promptly; immediately; now ② then; accordingly ③ even if—indicating supposition or sequence

jíbiàn 即便 ① although; even if; even though ② at this moment; forthwith

jíjiāng 即将 to be about to

jíkè 即刻 immediately; promptly; now

jírì 即日 on the very day; immediately; as soon as possible; at once

jíshí 即时 immediately; at once

jíshǐ 即使 even if

jí 急 ① anxious; very eager; worried ② urgent; hurried; hasty ③ quick; quickly; with expedition

jíjiù 急救 first-aid; first aid

jíjù 急剧 rapid; sudden; hasty

jímáng 急忙 urgently; hastily; hurriedly; quickly; in a hurry

jíqiè 急切 ① urgent; anxiously (awaiting, etc.) ② in a hurry; in haste

jísù 急速 hurriedly; hastily

jíxìng 急性 (medicine) an acute case

jíxū 急需 to need urgently

jíyú 急于 to be in a hurry or anxious to (finish the task, conclude the war, etc.); eager

jízào 急躁 rash and impatient

jízhěn 急诊 (medicine) emergency treatment

jízhěnshì 急诊室 emergency room; ER

jíbìng 疾病 diseases

jíshǒu 棘手 difficult to handle

jí 集 ① to assemble; to collect; to gather together; to concentrate ② a collection of works by one or more authors; to compile; to edit ③ a fair; a periodical market ④ achievements

jíhé 集合 to assemble; to gather together; to muster

jíhuì 集会 a meeting; a conference; an assemblage; an assembly

J

jíjié 集结 to concentrate (troops)

jíjǐn 集锦 a collection of homogeneous passages from various literary pieces

jíquán 集权 centralization of authority; concentration of power

jíshì 集市 a periodic market

jíshuǐqū 集水区 a drainage area or drainage basin; a catchment area or catchment basin

jítǐ 集体 collective

jítuán 集团 a bloc; a faction; a clique

jíyóu 集邮 philately; stamp collection

jízhōng 集中 ① to concentrate; to centralize ② to gather

jízī 集资 to raise funds; to collect money; to pool resources

jí 辑 ① friendly ② to collect; to compile; to gather

jídù 嫉妒 jealous; envy; jealousy

jí 籍 ① books; volumes; reading materials ② one's hometown or native place

jíguàn 籍贯 one's native place or hometown

jǐ 几 ① how many (or much) ② a few; some ③ which; when
⇨jī

jǐhé 几何 ① geometry ② how much

jǐ 己 ① self; one's own; oneself ② the sixth of the Ten Celestial Stems (tiāngān 天干)

jǐ 挤 ① to push; to jostle ② to wring; to squeeze; to twist; to press ③ to crowd; to throng; to pack

jǐmǎn 挤满 to pack (a place, car, etc.) to capacity

jǐ 给 ① to provide; provisions; to supply; supplies ② to award; to approve; to grant ③ sufficiency; affluence ④ glib; eloquent
⇨gěi

jǐfù 给付 to pay

jǐyǔ 给与 to give

jǐliang 脊梁 ① the back ② (construction) a ridgepole

jǐsuǐ 脊髓 the spinal cord

jǐzhuī 脊椎 the vertebrae

jì 计 ① a scheme; a plot; a trick ② a plan; a program; to discuss or plan ③ to calculate; to count ④ a mechanical measuring device

jìchéngchē 计程车 a taxi

jìhuà 计划 a plan; a program; to plan; to devise

jìjiào 计较 ① to haggle; to fuss about ② to negotiate ③ to care ④ to plan

jìsuàn 计算 ① to calculate; to count ② to consider

jìsuànjī 计算机 a calculating machine; a computer

jì 记 ① to remember; to call to mind; to keep in mind ② to record; to register ③ a book recording anecdotes, etc. ④ seals or chops; a sign; a mark

jìde 记得 to remember

jìhao 记号 a mark; a sign; a symbol

jìlù 记录 ① to record; to note down ② a note-taker ③ a record

jìqǔ 记取 to remember or bear in mind (this lesson, defeat, etc.)

jìxing 记性 memory

jìyì 记忆 memory or recollection

jìyìlì 记忆力 a retentive faculty

jìyìtǐ 记忆体 (computer) memory

jìzǎi/jìzài 记载 to record; an account

jìzhě 记者 a reporter; a journalist

jìzhěhuì 记者会 a press conference

jìzhù 记住 Remember!; to bear in mind

jì 纪 ① a historical record; annals; chronicles ② institutions; laws and regulations; discipline ③ a century ④ to arrange; to put in order ⑤ the age of a person ⑥ a geological period ⑦ a surname

jìlù 纪录 a record; to take notes

jìlùpiàn 纪录片 a documentary film

jìlǜ 纪律 discipline; laws and regulations

jìniàn 纪念 to remember; to commemorate

jìniànguǎn 纪念馆 a memorial hall; a museum in memory of somebody

jìniànpǐn 纪念品 a souvenir; a memento

jìniànrì 纪念日 a commemoration day; a memorial day; an anniversary

jìniàntáng 纪念堂 a memorial hall; a commemoration hall

jìyào 纪要 a recording of important facts; a summary

jìyuán 纪元 in the year of our Lord...; the Christian era

jìgōng 技工 a skilled worker

jìnéng 技能 skill; technical ability

jìqiǎo 技巧 ingenuity; dexterity; adroitness; skill

jìshī 技师 an engineer or a technician

jìshù 技术 techniques; technology; skill

jìshù rényuán 技术人员 technicians; technical personnel

jìshùxìng 技术性 technical; of a technical nature

jìyì 技艺 skill; art; craft

jì 系 to bind; to tie; to hang up ⇨xì

jì 忌 ① jealous; to envy ② to fear; a fear ③ to shun ④ to prohibit; (to) taboo ⑤ death anniversaries of one's parents, etc.

jì 际 ① a border or boundary; an edge ② in the middle; between; among ③ an opportunity; fortune or luck

jìnǚ 妓女 a prostitute; a whore

jì 季 ① a season; a quarter of a year ② the last (month of a season) ③ the youngest (of brothers) ④ a surname

jìdù 季度 a quarter (of a year)

jìfēng 季风 (meteorology) the monsoon

jìjié 季节 a season

jìjūn 季军 the second runner-up in a contest

jì 剂 ① a dose (of medicine) ② prepared medicines or drugs ③ to prepare (medicines and drugs)

jìliàng 剂量 (pharmaceutics) a dosage; a dose

jì/jī 迹 footprints; traces; tracks

jìxiàng/jīxiàng 迹象 signs; marks; indications

jì 既 ① since; as ② already ③ all

jìrán 既然 since (it is so, etc.); this being the case

jìshì 既是 since; this being the case

jì...yě... 既……也…… is... and...; not only...but also...

jì...yòu... 既……又…… is... and...; not only...but also...

jì 继 ① to continue; to carry on ② to follow; to inherit; to succeed to ③ then; afterwards

jìchéng 继承 to inherit; to succeed to

jìxù 继续 to continue; to last; to go on

jì 祭 ① to worship; to offer sacrifices to; to honor by a rite or service ② to wield

jìdiǎn 祭典 services or ceremonies of offering sacrifices

jìsì 祭祀 to worship; to offer sacrifices to; to honor by a service or rite

jì 寄 ① to send; to transmit; to mail ② to entrust; to consign; to commit; to deposit

jìtuō 寄托 to consign or commit (one's soul to God, emotions to writing, etc.)

jì/jí 寂 ① quiet; still; serene; peaceful; desolate ② the death of a Buddhist monk or nun

jìjìng/jíjìng 寂静 quiet; still

jìmò/jímò 寂寞 lonely; lonesome

jì/jī 绩 ① to spin; to twist ② merit; achievements; exploits; meritorious labor

jìxiào/jīxiào 绩效 results;

effects; achievements

jì 暨 to reach; to attain; to overtake

jiā 加 ① plus; to add ② to increase; to augment ③ to append

jiābān 加班 to work overtime

jiābèi 加倍 to double; to redouble

jiāgōng 加工 to process (goods)

jiāgōngyè 加工业 the processing industry

jiājǐn 加紧 to intensify; to step up

jiājù 加剧 to aggravate; to sharpen; to cause to become worse or more severe

jiākuài 加快 to speed up; to accelerate

jiāméng 加盟 to join an alliance, a fraternity, or a secret society

Jiānádà 加拿大 Canada

jiāqiáng 加强 to strengthen; to reinforce

jiārè 加热 to heat; to warm

jiārù 加入 ① to join; to accede to ② to add into

jiāshang 加上 to plus; to add

jiāshēn 加深 ① to deepen ② to become more severe

jiāsù 加速 to step up; to accelerate

jiāxīn 加薪 to give a pay raise

jiāyǐ 加以 ① used before a polysyllabic verb to indicate that the action is directed towards something or someone mentioned above ② in addition; moreover

jiāyóu 加油 ① to oil ② to refuel ③ to step up effort

jiāyóuzhàn 加油站 a gas station

jiāzhòng 加重 to increase work loads, burdens, etc.

jiā/jiá 夹 ① to be wedged between; to be sandwiched ② to squeeze; to press; to occupy both sides of ③ pincers ④ a folder to keep sheets of paper, etc. ⑤ to carry secretly ⑥ to mix; to mingle ⇨jiá

jiākè/jiákè 夹克 a jacket

jiāzá/jiázá 夹杂 mixed-up

jiāzi/jiázi 夹子 folders for keeping documents, papers, pictures, etc.; clips

jiā 佳 ① beautiful; good; fine ② auspicious ③ distinguished

jiājié 佳节 a festival; a carnival

jiārén 佳人 a beauty

jiāyáo 佳肴 a delicacy

jiāzuò 佳作 an excellent (literary) work

jiāsuǒ 枷锁 ① the cangue and lock ② (figuratively) bondage; shackles

jiā 家 ① home; house; household; family; of a household; domestic ② a specialist

jiācháng 家常 the daily life of a family; domestic trivia

jiāchù 家畜 livestock; domestic animals

jiādiàn yòngpǐn 家电用品 home appliances

jiāhuo 家伙 ① (comically) a character ② a tool

jiājiā-hùhù 家家户户 every family and household

jiājiào 家教 ① family education ② a tutor

jiājìng 家境 the financial condition of a family

jiājù 家具 furniture

jiāli 家里 ① a home ② my wife

jiāmén 家门 a family (viewed in the light of its social standing)

jiārén 家人 the members of one's family

jiāshì 家事 housekeeping; housework

jiāshǔ 家属 one's family or dependents

jiātíng 家庭 a home; a household

jiātíng zhǔfù 家庭主妇 a housewife

jiāwù 家务 household affairs; housework

jiāxiāng 家乡 one's hometown

jiāyòng 家用 domestic expenses

jiāyù-hùxiǎo 家喻户晓 well-known; widely known

jiāyuán 家园 hometown; native heath

J

jiāzhǎng 家长 the head of a family or household

jiāzú 家族 a family; a clan

jiāhuì 嘉惠 to benefit

jiājiǎng 嘉奖 to commend (as an encouragement)

jiāniánhuáhuì 嘉年华会 a carnival

jiá 夹 of two or more layers; lined (garments, etc.) ⇨jiā

jiá 颊 the cheeks

jiǎ 甲 ① the first of the Ten Celestial Stems ② armor; shell; crust ③ most outstanding ④ a measure of land in Taiwan (equal to 0.97 hectare)

jiǎbǎn 甲板 the deck (of a ship)

jiǎ 假 ① false; not real; phony; artificial; fake; bogus; sham ② supposing; if ⇨jià

jiǎdìng 假定 ① if; supposing ② a postulate

jiǎmào 假冒 ① to counterfeit ② to assume the identity of somebody else

jiǎrú 假如 if; in case; supposing

jiǎruò 假若 if; in case; supposing

jiǎshè 假设 a hypothesis; a supposition

jiǎshǐ 假使 if; in case; supposing

jiǎshuō 假说 a postulate; a hypothesis

jiǎxiǎng 假想 ① a hypothesis ② imaginary

jiǎxiàng 假象 false appearances

jiǎzhuāng 假装 to pretend; to assume the appearance of

jià 价 ① prices; cost; value ② (chemistry) valence

jiàgé 价格 prices

jiàmǎ 价码 the price of a commodity

jiàqián 价钱 prices

jiàzhí 价值 value

jià 驾 ① to ride; to drive; to pilot ② to yoke; to put the horses to the carriage ③ to excel; to surpass ④ vehicles ⑤ an honorific

epithet ⑥ to control; to reign or rule ⑦ the emperor

jiàchē 驾车 to drive a vehicle

jiàshǐ 驾驶 ① to drive (automobiles); to pilot (aircraft); to steer (boats) ② a driver

jiàshǐyuán 驾驶员 a driver; a pilot

jiàyù 驾驭 ① to drive (horse-drawn vehicles) ② to control; to tame

jià 架 ① a prop; a stand; a rack; a frame ② to prop up; to set up; to support ③ a framework or scaffold ④ to frame up (a charge, etc.); to fabricate ⑤ to lay something on ⑥ a quarrel

jiàgòu 架构 structure; framework

jiàshè 架设 to build over something

jiàzi 架子 ① a rack; a stand; a frame; a scaffold ② a skeleton; an outline

jià 假 a holiday ⇨jiǎ

jiàqī/jiàqí 假期 a vacation; a holiday

jiàrì 假日 a holiday

jiàtiáo 假条 ① an application for leave ② a leave permit

jià 嫁 ① (said of a woman) to get married; to marry a man ② to marry off a daughter ③ to impute (blame, a crime, etc.) to another

jiān 尖 sharp; acute; pointed; keen

jiānbīng 尖兵 (military) a point

jiānjiào 尖叫 to scream; to shriek

jiānruì 尖锐 ① sharp-pointed ② sharp; keen ③ shrill; piercing ④ intense; acute

jiānzi 尖子 ① the best of its kind; the pick of the bunch; the cream of the crop ② (in opera singing) a sudden rise in pitch

jiān 奸 ① crafty; wicked; villainous; cunning; evil ② selfish ③ disloyal ④ false ⑤ adultery; fornication; licentiousness ⑥ a

traitor; a villain

jiānmiè 歼灭 to annihilate; to wipe out

jiān 坚 ① strong and durable ② calm; steady; stable; determined ③ steadfastly ④ solid; firm ⑤ to dedicate to; to devote to ⑥ the strongest position or point of enemy troops ⑦ armor, etc.

jiānchí 坚持 to insist on; to persist in

jiāndìng 坚定 determined; steadfast; staunch

jiāngù 坚固 solid; firm; stable

jiānjué 坚决 firmly (opposed to, etc.)

jiānqiáng 坚强 strong; staunch

jiānrěn 坚忍 fortitude; firmness; dedication

jiānrèn 坚韧 great strength or durability

jiānshí 坚实 solid; strong; durable; substantial

jiānshǒu 坚守 ① to firmly stand by (one's promise, principle, etc.) ② to defend (a place) resolutely

jiānxìn 坚信 to have absolute faith; to believe firmly

jiānyìng 坚硬 hard and solid

jiānzhēn-bùqū 坚贞不屈 to remain loyal and unyielding

jiān 间 ① a measure word for rooms ② between two things; the space between; among ③ within a definite time or space
⇨jiàn

jiān 肩 ① shoulders ② to shoulder (responsibility, etc.); to sustain ③ to employ; to appoint

jiānbǎng 肩膀 ① the shoulder ② a sense of responsibility

jiānjù 艰巨 hard; arduous; laborious

jiānkǔ 艰苦 trying; hard; privation

jiānnán 艰难 difficulty; distress; hardship

jiānxiǎn 艰险 difficult and dangerous

jiānxīn 艰辛 hard; arduous; laborious

jiān 监 ① to supervise; to superintend; to oversee; to direct; to inspect ② to confine; to keep in custody; to imprison
⇨jiàn

jiānchá 监察 to supervise; to control; control

Jiānchá Yuàn 监察院 Control Yuan (one of the five major branches of the government of the Republic of China)

jiāndū 监督 to supervise; to superintend; to oversee

jiānjìn 监禁 ① to confine; to imprison ② custody; to guard

jiānláo 监牢 a prison; a jail

jiānshì 监视 ① to keep a watchful eye on ② to monitor

jiānshìqì 监视器 a watchdog; a monitor

jiānyù 监狱 a prison; a jail

jiān 兼 ① and; also; together with; both; equally; concurrently ② to unite in one; to connect; to annex

jiānchāi 兼差 to take two or more jobs concurrently; a part-time job

jiāngù 兼顾 to look after both sides

jiānrèn 兼任 to serve concurrently as

jiānzhí 兼职 to take two or more jobs concurrently; a part-time job

jiān/jiàn 渐 (said of the territory) to reach
⇨jiàn

jiān 煎 ① to fry in fat or oil ② to decoct ③ (figuratively) to torment; to kill

jiān'áo 煎熬 ① to decoct until almost dry ② to torture; to torment

jiǎn 拣 ① to pick up (something another has left behind, etc.) ② to select; to choose; to pick

jiǎn 茧 ① cocoons; a chrysalis ② a callus

Jiǎnpǔzhài 柬埔寨 Cambodia

jiǎn 捡 to pick up; to collect

jiǎn 检 ① a book label ② to sort ③ to inspect; to check up; to collate ④ a form; a pattern ⑤ to restrict; to regulate

jiǎncè 检测 to test; to examine

jiǎnchá 检查 to inspect; to examine; to test

jiǎnchá 检察 ① to inspect ② inspection

jiǎncháguān 检察官 a court prosecutor; a procurator

jiǎndìng 检定 ① to inspect and approve (or sanction) ② inspection

jiǎnjǔ 检举 to inform the authorities of an unlawful act, plot, etc.

jiǎntǎo 检讨 to review and discuss (past performances, etc.); to make self-examination

jiǎnxiū 检修 to examine and repair; to overhaul

jiǎnyàn 检验 to inspect and examine

jiǎn 减 to decrease; to reduce; to lessen; to diminish; to subtract; to cut

jiǎnchǎn 减产 to cut production or output

jiǎndī 减低 to decrease; to diminish; to reduce

jiǎnféi 减肥 to reduce (weight)

jiǎnhuǎn 减缓 to retard; to slow down

jiǎnqīng 减轻 to lighten; to lessen; to mitigate

jiǎnruò 减弱 to weaken; to subside

jiǎnshǎo 减少 to decrease; to diminish; to lessen; to reduce

jiǎnshuì 减税 to reduce, cut, or lower taxes

jiǎn 剪 ① to cut or clip with scissors; to shear; to trim ② scissors; clippers; shears ③ to annihilate; to destroy completely

jiǎncái 剪裁 to tailor clothing materials for a dress

jiǎncǎi 剪彩 to cut the ribbon

jiǎndāo 剪刀 scissors; clippers

jiǎnjiē 剪接 to edit or cut a film

jiǎntiē 剪贴 ① to clip and paste (something such as from a newspaper, etc.) in a scrapbook or on cards ② cutting out (as a school children's activity)

jiǎn 简 ① brief; succinct; terse; simple ② (in ancient China) a slip or tablet of bamboo for writing ③ a letter; a note ④ a surname

jiǎnbào 简报 a briefing

jiǎnbiàn 简便 simple and convenient

jiǎnchēng 简称 to be called or known as...for short

jiǎndān 简单 ① simple; brief ② ordinary

jiǎnduǎn 简短 brief; terse; succinct; short

jiǎnhuà 简化 to simplify; simplification

jiǎnjié 简洁 (said of a piece of writing) brief and to the point; succinct

jiǎnjiè 简介 a brief introduction; a synopsis

jiǎnlòu 简陋 simple and crude

jiǎnmíng 简明 brief and clear; concise

jiǎntǐzì 简体字 a simplified Chinese character

jiǎnyào 简要 brief and concise

jiǎnyì 简易 simple; easy

jiǎnzhí 简直 ① simply; outright; at all ② honest; unaffected

jiàn 见 ① to see; to perceive; to understand; to observe or examine ② to visit; to see; to call on or at; to meet ③ to receive (visitors, etc.); to come face to face with

jiàndào 见到 ① to meet; to see ② to perceive or think of

jiànjiě 见解 one's views, ideas or observations or opinions about something

jiànmiàn 见面 to come face to face; to see; to meet

jiànshi 见识 ① knowledge and experience; scope; sense ② to experience (something new)

J

jiànxiào 见效 effective; efficacious

jiànzhèng 见证 to bear witness

jiàn 件 a measure word for things, clothes, etc.

jiàn 间 ① a crevice; a leak; space in between ② to divide; a division of a house; to separate ③ to put a space between; to drive a wedge between; to part friends ④ to change; to substitute ⑤ to block up ⑥ (said of illness) to get a little better ⑦ occasionally ⇨jiān

jiàndié 间谍 a spy; a secret agent

jiàngé 间隔 ① separated; spaced at intervals ② distance; intervals

jiànjiē 间接 indirect; vicariously

jiàn 建 ① to establish; to build ② to propose; to suggest

jiànguó 建国 ① to found (or establish) a state ② to build up a country

jiànjiāo 建交 to establish diplomatic relations

jiànlì 建立 to establish; to build; to set up; to found

jiànshè 建设 to construct; to build; construction

jiànyì 建议 to propose; to suggest

jiànzào 建造 to build; to construct; to frame

jiànzhù / jiànzhú 建筑 ① to build; to construct ② a building or structure

jiànzhùshī / jiànzhúshī 建筑师 an architect

jiànzhùwù / jiànzhúwù 建筑物 a building; a structure

jiàn 贱 ① cheap; inexpensive; low-cost ② lowly; humble; inferior in position ③ lowdown; base; ignoble; despicable ④ to slight; to look down on ⑤ (a self-depreciatory term) my

jiàn 健 ① healthy; strong ② vigorous; capable ③ fond of; inclined to; liable to ④ to strengthen; to toughen

jiànkāng 健康 ① health ② healthy

jiànměi 健美 healthy and handsome

jiànquán 健全 in good condition

jiànshēn 健身 ① to exercise; to work out; to lift weights ② bodybuilding

jiànshēnfáng 健身房 a gymnasium; a gym

jiànxíng 健行 to hike; hiking

jiànzhuàng 健壮 healthy and robust

jiàn 监 a eunuch ⇨jiān

jiàn 舰 a warship; a man-of-war; a naval vessel

jiàn 渐 gradually; little by little; by degrees ⇨jiān

jiànjiàn 渐渐 gradually

jiàntà 践踏 ① to trample; to tread on ② to abuse

jiànzi 毽子 a shuttlecock

jiàn 溅 to splash; to sprinkle; to spray; to spill

jiàn 鉴 ① a mirror ② to mirror; to reflect ③ to study or examine; to scrutinize ④ an example serving as a rule or warning

jiànbié 鉴别 to distinguish (the genuine from an imitation); to judge or identify; to discriminate

jiàndìng 鉴定 to examine and determine; to judge; to make an appraisal

jiànyú 鉴于 in view of; seeing that

jiàn 键 a key (to a door or on a musical instrument, etc.)

jiànpán 键盘 a keyboard (on a piano, typewriter, etc.)

jiàn 箭 ① an arrow ② a sign which is like an arrow

jiāng 江 ① a large river ② the Changjiang (Yangzi) River

jiānghú 江湖 ① rivers and lakes ② all places in the country

jiānghu 江湖 ① sophisticated and shrewd ② practicing quackery; a quack ③ wandering; vagrant

Jiāngnán 江南 the entire area south of the Yangzi River (particularly referring to southern Jiangsu)

jiāng 将 ① (used with a verb expressing future action) going to; about to ② used with a noun functioning as a direct object ③ to nourish ⇨jiàng

jiāngjìn 将近 approximately; close to; nearly

jiāngjūn 将军 ① a general or admiral ② a call to indicate a checkmate (in Chinese chess) ③ to challenge

jiānglái 将来 the future; the days to come

jiāngyào 将要 going to or about to (do something); on the point of (doing something)

jiāng 姜 ① ginger ② a surname

jiāng 僵 ① to be inactive; stiff; rigid; numb ② to lie flat ③ to be at a stalemate; deadlocked

jiānghuà 僵化 ① heading toward a deadlock ② to become rigid; to ossify

jiāngjú 僵局 a deadlock; a stalemate

jiāngyìng 僵硬 rigid; stiff

jiāngjiè 疆界 borders; frontiers

jiǎng 讲 ① to speak; to talk ② to explain; to explicate ③ to pay particular attention to ④ to be particular about ④ as to; when it comes to ⑤ to have recourse to

jiǎnghuà 讲话 to talk; to speak; to address

jiǎngjià 讲价 to haggle over prices; to bargain

jiǎngjiě 讲解 to discuss and explain

jiǎngjiu 讲究 ① to be particular or elaborate (about something); to have regard for ② (said of dress, etc.) tasteful

jiǎngkè 讲课 to teach; to lecture

jiǎnglǐ 讲理 ① to have regard for reason ② to argue with someone in order to convince him that he is wrong

jiǎngqiú 讲求 ① to investigate; to study ② to strive for; to be elaborate about

jiǎngshī 讲师 a lecturer; an instructor

jiǎngshòu 讲授 to teach; to lecture; to instruct

jiǎngshù 讲述 to explain and discuss (subjects, problems, etc.)

jiǎngxí 讲习 short-term training or instruction

jiǎngyǎn 讲演 to speak or lecture; a speech

jiǎngyì 讲义 ① teacher's handouts at school; (mimeographed or printed) teaching materials ② commentaries on classics

jiǎngzuò 讲座 a series of lectures for teaching purposes, usually given at meetings, over the radio, television, or in journal installments

jiǎng 奖 ① to encourage; to exhort ② to praise; to commend ③ to cite or give a prize or reward (for a merit, etc.) ④ a prize or reward

jiǎngjīn 奖金 prize money; a bounty; a bonus

jiǎnglì 奖励 to encourage by rewards

jiǎngpǐn 奖品 prizes or rewards

jiǎngshǎng 奖赏 ① rewards in money, etc. ② to reward

jiǎngxuéjīn 奖学金 a scholarship; a fellowship

jiǎngzhāng 奖章 a medal

jiǎngzhù 奖助 to provide with financial assistance

jiǎngzhuàng 奖状 a citation of meritorious services, etc.

jiǎng 桨 an oar

Jiǎng 蒋 a surname

Jiǎng Jièshí 蒋介石 Chiang Kai-shek, 1887-1975, late President of the Republic of China (1948-1975)

jiàng 降 ① to descend ② to lower ③ to condescend; to deign ④ to drop; to decline

J

⇨xiáng

jiàngdào 降到 to step down to

jiàngdī 降低 to lower; to fall; to drop

jiàngjià 降价 to cut, lower, or reduce the price

jiànglín 降临 ① to come down; to fall ② to condescend (to visit)

jiàngluò 降落 ① to land; landing; descent; to descend ② to drop; to rain down

jiàng 将 a general; an admiral; a military leader of high rank
⇨jiāng

jiànglǐng 将领 high-ranking military officers; a general

jiàng 强 inflexible; obstinate; stubborn
⇨qiáng, qiǎng

jiàng 酱 ① soybean sauce; soy ② food in the form of paste; jam

jiàngyóu 酱油 soybean sauce; soy; soy sauce

jiāo 交 ① to submit; to hand in or over ② to meet ③ to exchange ④ to intersect

jiāochā 交叉 to cross each other; to intersect

jiāocuò 交错 to interlock

jiāodài 交代 ① to hand over responsibility ② to give an explanation

jiāodiǎn 交点 a point of intersection

jiāofù 交付 ① to hand over ② to make payment

jiāogē 交割 a business transaction

jiāogěi 交给 to hand to; to give to

jiāohù 交互 mutually; reciprocally

jiāohuàn 交换 to exchange

jiāohuò 交货 to deliver goods; delivery

jiāojí 交集 (said of different feelings) to be mixed

jiāojì 交际 social intercourse

jiāojiē 交接 ① to make contact with each other ② to adjoin each other ③ to hand over and to take over (duties)

jiāoliú 交流 to flow across each other

jiāoliúdào 交流道 (traffic) an interchange

jiāoqíng 交情 friendship

jiāoshè 交涉 to negotiate; negotiation

jiāoshǒu 交手 to exchange blows (in a fight)

jiāotán 交谈 to converse

jiāotì 交替 to alternate

jiāotōng 交通 ① traffic ② communication

Jiāotōng Bù 交通部 Ministry of Transportation and Communications

Jiāotōng Dàxué 交通大学 National Chiao Tung University

jiāowǎng 交往 to have friendly relations

jiāoxiǎngyuètuán 交响乐团 an orchestra

jiāoyì 交易 a trade; business transaction; to trade

jiāoyìsuǒ 交易所 a stock exchange; a bourse

jiāoyǒu 交友 to make friends

jiāozhī 交织 to interlace; to interweave

jiāo 郊 ① suburbs of a city ② a ceremony for offering sacrifices to Heaven and Earth

jiāoqū 郊区 suburban districts; suburbs; outskirts; a suburban area

jiāowài 郊外 suburbs

jiāoyóu 郊游 an outing; an excursion

jiāo 浇 ① to water (plants, flowers, etc.) ② to sprinkle water on

jiāoguàn 浇灌 to water (plants, etc.)

jiāo 娇 ① tender; delicate; beautiful; lovely ② spoiled; pampered; coddled

jiāoqì 娇气 delicate; not very healthy

jiāo'ào 骄傲 proud; haughty; disdainful

jiāo 胶 ① glue; gum ② resin; sap ③ anything sticky ④ rubber; plastics ⑤ to stick on or togeth-

jiāobǎn 胶版 an offset plate

jiāojuǎn 胶卷 unexposed film

jiāopiàn 胶片 film

jiāo 教 to teach; to guide
⇨jiào

jiāofǎ 教法 teaching methods; pedagogy

jiāoshū 教书 to teach (usually for a living)

jiāoxué 教学 to teach; to teach school

jiāo 焦 ① scorched or burned; charred ② the smell or stench of things burned ③ worried and anxious ④ a surname

jiāodiǎn 焦点 ① focus ② a burning point; a focal point

jiāojí 焦急 very anxious; in deep anxiety

jiāolǜ 焦虑 deeply worried and anxious

jiāotàn 焦炭 coke

jiāonóng 蕉农 banana growers

jiáo 嚼 (jué) to chew; to masticate; to munch

jiǎo 角 ① a tenth of a dollar; a ten-cent piece ② something in the shape of a horn ③ the horn of an animal ④ a direction; a corner ⑤ an angle ⑥ a cape; a promontory
⇨jué

jiǎodù 角度 ① an angle ② angular measure

jiǎoluò 角落 a corner; a nook

jiǎozhì/jiǎozhí 角质 horny; corneous

jiǎojiǎozhě 佼佼者 an outstanding person

jiǎohuá 狡猾 cunning; crafty; sly; wily; artful

jiǎozi 饺子 stuffed dumplings; ravioli

jiǎo 绞 ① to twist; to twine; to wring ② to hang (a criminal) ③ rudeness ④ to mix up

jiǎozhèng 矫正 to correct or rectify

jiǎo 脚 ① the feet ② the leg or base of something

jiǎoběn 脚本 the script of a play, an opera, etc.

jiǎobù 脚步 steps; paces; strides; footsteps

jiǎotàchē 脚踏车 a bicycle

jiǎo 搅 ① to stir; to mix ② to agitate; to disturb; to annoy

jiǎobàn 搅拌 to stir or churn; to mix

jiǎohuo 搅和 ① to mingle ② to confuse

jiǎo 缴 ① to surrender (articles); to submit ② to pay (taxes, tuition, etc.)

jiǎojiāo 缴交 to turn in; to hand over; to surrender; to submit

jiǎonà 缴纳 to pay (taxes, tuition, etc.)

jiào 叫 ① to be called or known as ② to cry; to shout; to scream; a shout or scream ③ to call; to summon ④ to cause

jiàohǎn 叫喊 to shout; to yell; to scream; to cry

jiàohǎo 叫好 to cheer; to applaud

jiàohuan 叫唤 ① to shout ② to call; to summon

jiàorǎng 叫嚷 to shout; to howl; to clamor

jiàozuò 叫做 to be called; to be known as

jiào 觉 a sleep; a nap
⇨jué

jiào 校 ① to compare ② to proofread; proofs ③ to revise (books, etc.); to collate
⇨xiào

jiàochē 轿车 a sedan (a kind of automobile)

jiào 较 ① to compare ② in a greater or lesser degree; more or less; earlier or later ③ to compete; to dispute ④ fairly; quite; relatively

jiàoliàng 较量 to compare (strength, etc.) in a contest

jiào 教 ① a religion ② an order; a directive ③ to educate ④ to urge; to incite; to bid; to instigate ⑤ to

instruct; instruction(s); to advise; advice ⑥ to have; to let; to make ⇨jiāo

jiàocái 教材 teaching materials

jiàodǎo 教导 ① to instruct ② guidance

jiàoguān 教官 a military instructor; a drill master

jiàohuà 教化 ① culture ② to bring enlightenment to the people by education

jiàohuì 教会 the church

jiàohuì 教诲 to teach and admonish

jiàokēshū 教科书 the textbook

jiàoliàn 教练 ① a coach (of athletes); an instructor ② to train

jiàoshī 教师 a teacher

jiàoshì 教室 a classroom

jiàoshòu 教授 a professor

jiàosuō 教唆 to instigate; to incite; to abet

jiàotáng 教堂 a church; a mosque

jiàotiáo 教条 a doctrine

jiàotú 教徒 a (religious) believer or follower

jiàowùchù 教务处 the office of the dean of studies

jiàowùzhǎng 教务长 the dean of studies (of a college or university)

jiàoxùn 教训 ① a lesson ② to admonish; teachings

jiàoyǎng 教养 to bring up; to rear

jiàoyù 教育 ① to educate ② education

Jiàoyù Bù 教育部 Ministry of Education

jiàoyù bùzhǎng 教育部长 a minister of education

Jiàoyù Jú 教育局 the bureau of education (under a special municipal government)

jiàoyù júzhǎng 教育局长 the director of the bureau of education (under a special municipal government)

Jiàoyù Tīng 教育厅 Department of Education (under a provincial government)

jiàoyuán 教员 a member of the teaching profession; a teacher

jiàozhí 教职 the occupation of teaching

jiàozhíyuán 教职员 the teaching and administrative staff of a school

jiàosù/xiàosù 酵素 an enzyme

jiē 阶 ① a way leading to the main hall ② a flight of steps or stairs ③ a grade or a rank ④ to rely on

jiēcéng 阶层 subdivisions within a class of people; a class of people

jiēduàn 阶段 a stage or phase

jiējí 阶级 a rank; a class (of people)

jiē 皆 all; every; entire

jiēshì 皆是 (they) all are

jiē 结 ① to stutter; to stammer ② tough; strong; durable

jiē/jié 结 to bear (fruit); to form (seed) ⇨jié

jiēguǒ/jiéguǒ 结果 (said of plants) to bear fruit ⇨jiéguǒ

jiēshi 结实 ① strong; sturdy ② tough; durable; solid

jiē 接 ① to receive; to accept ② to welcome; to meet ③ to join; to connect ④ to graft ⑤ to come close to; to make contact with ⑥ to succeed to

jiēbān 接班 to relieve another in work

jiēbānrén 接班人 a successor

jiēchù 接触 ① to make contact with ② (said of nations) to wage war against each other

jiēdài 接待 to receive (a guest); reception

jiēdào 接到 to receive

jiē'èr-liánsān 接二连三 one after another; continuously

jiēguǎn 接管 to take over (the management of)

jiējiàn 接见 to receive (a visitor, etc.)

jiējìn 接近 to come close; to

approach

jiēlì 接力 a relay

jiēlián 接连 repeatedly; to continue

jiēnà 接纳 to accept (a proposal, advice, etc.)

jiēqià 接洽 to contact, discuss, or negotiate

jiērèn 接任 to take over an office; to succeed

jiēshōu 接收 to take over; to receive

jiēshǒu 接手 to carry on the task of the predecessor

jiēshòu 接受 to accept (an invitation, an assignment, etc.)

jiēsòng 接送 ① to receive and send off (guests or visitors) ② transportation to and from a certain place

jiētì 接替 to relieve; to succeed (a predecessor)

jiēxù 接续 to continue; to connect

jiēzhe 接着 ① then; shortly afterward ② to follow; to add ③ to catch

jiēzhòng 接种 (medicine) to have an inoculation; to inoculate

jiē 揭 ① to unveil, uncover, or unearth; to expose ② announce; to publicize

jiēfā 揭发 to expose (a plot, scandal, etc.)

jiēkai 揭开 ① to pull apart or separate ② to uncover

jiēlù 揭露 to uncover or expose (another's secret, etc.)

jiēmù 揭幕 ① to raise or lift the curtain (of a meeting, exhibition, etc.); to unveil—to inaugurate

jiēshì 揭示 to announce; to reveal

jiēxiǎo 揭晓 to make public; to publish

jiē 街 a street; a road in a city; a thoroughfare

jiēdào 街道 streets; roads in a city or town

jiēfang 街坊 ① neighbors; the neighborhood ② neighborhood

jiētóu 街头 street corners; streets

jié 节 ① a node; a knot; a joint ② a passage; a paragraph; a section ③ a festival; a holiday ④ seasons ⑤ to curtail; to economize ⑥ to restrain; to control; to restrict ⑦ principles; integrity; fidelity; constancy; uprightness ⑧ (music) beats; rhythm; time

jiéjiǎn 节俭 to be frugal; to practice austerity; to economize

jiéjié 节节 successively; steadily

jiémù 节目 a program; items on a program

jiénéng 节能 to save energy

jiéqìng 节庆 a festival; a holiday

jiérì 节日 a festival; a holiday

jiéshěng 节省 to economize; to save

jiéyù 节育 birth control

jiéyuē 节约 to economize; to save

jiézhì 节制 to restrict; to hold down; to limit; to control

jiézòu 节奏 rhythm

jié 劫 ① to rob; to plunder; to take by force ② sufferings; misfortunes; disasters

jiéchí 劫持 ① to threaten ② to hijack

jiéchū 杰出 outstanding; extraordinary

jiézuò 杰作 a masterpiece

jiébái 洁白 clean and white; immaculate

jiéjìng 洁净 clean; untainted; stainless

jié 结 ① to tie; to knot; to weave ② a knot ③ to unite; to join; to connect ④ to congeal; coagulation ⑤ to form; to found; to constitute ⑥ a result; an outcome ⑦ to pay or settle (as an account, etc.) ⑧ a node
⇨jiē

jiégòu 结构 ① structure ② (said of a piece of writing) the arrangement of ideas; presentation

jiéguǒ 结果 ① in the end; finally ② the result, outcome, or consequence

J

⇨jiēguǒ

jiéhé 结合 ① to get united; to combine with ② to get married; to marry

jiéhébìng 结核病 tuberculosis

jiéhūn 结婚 marriage; to get married

jiéjiāo 结交 to associate with; to befriend; to make friends with

jiéjīng 结晶 to crystallize; crystallization; crystal

jiéjú 结局 the outcome; the result; the end

jiélùn 结论 the conclusion (of a meeting, argument, etc.)

jiéméng 结盟 to ally with; alignment

jiéshù 结束 to conclude; to end; to wind up

jiésuàn 结算 to settle accounts; settlement of accounts

jiéyè 结业 to graduate; to conclude or complete a training course

jiéyuán 结缘 to associate on good terms

jiézhàng 结账 to settle accounts; to pay up

jié 偈 hasty; scudding

jié 捷 ① to win; to triumph; the prizes of a victory ② swift; quick; rapid; agile

jiéjìng 捷径 a shortcut; a snap course

Jiékè 捷克 Czech

jiéyùn 捷运 rapid transit

jié 截 ① to cut; to section; to truncate ② to stop; to close; to end ③ to detain; to withhold ④ a slice; a division; a section

jiézhǐ 截止 to close (application, registration, etc.) upon reaching the deadline

jiézhì 截至 by (a specified time); up to

jiélì 竭力 to do one's best

jiě 姐 ① one's elder sister or sisters ② a general term for women, usually young

jiějie 姐姐 one's elder sister

jiěmèi 姐妹 sisters

jiě 解 ① to unfasten; to untie; to loosen ② to take off; to strip ③ to relieve (pain, etc.) ④ to relieve; to alleviate (pain, etc.) ⑤ to solve (difficult problems, etc.) ⑥ to explain; to clarify ⑦ ideas; views ⑧ to break up, separate, or disperse ⑨ to cut apart; to dissect ⑩ to dissolve ⑪ to discharge (water, etc.); to defecate

jiěchú 解除 ① to annul or cancel (a contract, agreement, etc.) ② to remove; to get rid of ③ to relieve (a person of his duties, etc.) ④ (law) to restore to the original status

jiědá 解答 ① explanations or answers to certain questions ② to answer or explain

jiěfàng 解放 to untie or set free; to liberate

jiěfàngjūn 解放军 liberation army; the People's Liberation Army (of the People's Republic of China)

jiěgù 解雇 to get fired; to fire; to dismiss; to discharge

jiějué 解决 ① to settle (a dispute, fight, etc.); to solve (a problem) ② to dispose of; to finish off

jiěkāi 解开 to untie; to unbind; to loosen; to undo

jiěkě 解渴 to quench thirst; to allay thirst

jiěpōu/jiěpǒu 解剖 ① anatomization; to dissect; dissection ② to analyze; analysis

jiěsàn 解散 to dismiss; to disband

jiěshì 解释 to explain; explanation

jiěshuō 解说 ① to explain ② to appease; to resolve (a dispute, etc.)

jiětǐ 解体 disintegration; dissolution

jiětuō 解脱 to extricate

jiěxī 解析 to analyze; analysis

jiěxīdù 解析度 (computer) resolution

jiěyán 解严 to announce martial law ended

jiěyuē 解约 to annul a contract or agreement

J

jiè 介 ① a shelled aquatic animal ② to lie between ③ great and honorable ④ to aid; to benefit ⑤ tiny

jiècí 介词 a preposition

jièmiàn 介面 (computer) an interface

jièrù 介入 to get involved; to interfere with

jièshào 介绍 to introduce (a person to another)

jièyú 介于 to lie in between

jiè 戒 ① to warn; to admonish; to caution ② to abstain from; to refrain from; to give up ③ to guard against; to avoid ④ a commandment; Buddhist monastic discipline

jièbèi 戒备 on guard (against enemy attacks, natural disasters, etc.)

jièyán 戒严 to impose a curfew

jièzhǐ 戒指 a ring (on a finger)

jiè 届 a measure word for periodic terms or events

jièmǎn 届满 (said of a term) to expire

jièshí 届时 at the appointed time

jiè 界 ① a boundary ② world ③ to limit; to demarcate; to define; to delimit

jièmiàn 界面 interface

jièxiàn 界限 ① a border ② to limit; to restrict

jièxiàn 界线 a boundary; a borderline

jiè 借 ① to lend ② to borrow ③ to avail oneself of; to make use of; to resort to ④ to make a pretext of ⑤ if; supposing

jièdài 借贷 ① to ask for a loan ② debit and credit sides

jièjiàn 借鉴 to learn a lesson from another person's experience

jièjìng 借镜 to learn a lesson from another person's experience

jièkǒu 借口 an excuse; a pretext

jièyòng 借用 to borrow

jièzhù 借助 to have the aid of; to draw support from

jiè 藉 to rely on; to lean on; on the strength of; to avail oneself

of; by means of

jīn 斤 a catty

jīn 今 ① present; recent; modern ② now; currently; presently; nowadays

jīnhòu 今后 hereafter; henceforward; from now on

jīnnián 今年 this year

jīnrì 今日 today

jīnshēng 今生 this present life

jīntiān 今天 today

jīnwǎn 今晚 tonight

jīnyè 今夜 tonight

jīn 金 ① gold ② metal ③ wealth; money ④ excellent; precious; fine ⑤ golden ⑥ durable ⑦ a surname

jīnbì 金币 gold coins

jīn'é 金额 the amount of money

jīnhuángsè 金黄色 bright yellow; golden

Jīnmén 金门 ① Kinmen (or Quemoy), an island opposite Xiamen in Fujian ② the Gate of Gold—(figuratively) the gate of the palace

Jīnniúzuò 金牛座 Taurus

jīnpái 金牌 a gold medal

jīnqián 金钱 money; cash; riches; wealth

jīnróng 金融 finance; banking; a monetary situation

jīnróng jīgòu 金融机构 a finance house

jīnróngkǎ 金融卡 a fiscard; an ATM card

jīnróng wēijī/jīnróng wéijī 金融危机 a monetary crisis; a financial panic

jīnsè 金色 golden

jīnshǔ 金属 metals

Jīnxīng 金星 (astronomy) Venus

jīnyú 金鱼 goldfish

jīnzhēn 金针 ① (Chinese medicine) an acupuncture needle ② a daylily

jīnzìtǎ 金字塔 a pyramid

jīnjīn-yǒuwèi 津津有味 ① (to do something) with great relish or interest; with gusto ② very tasty

jīntiē 津贴 an allowance; to sub-

sidize

jīn 筋 ① tendons; sinews; muscles ② veins that stand out under the skin ③ plant fibers resembling a tendon

jīngǔ 筋骨 ① bones and muscles—physique; build (of one's body) ② strength

jīn 禁 to endure; to bear; to withstand; to stand
⇨jìn

jīn 仅 ① only ② barely; scarcely; almost

jīnjǐn 仅仅 only; hardly enough; barely

jīnyǒu 仅有 to have only...; There is (or are) only....

jǐn 尽 ① to let (someone do it) ② the utmost; the extreme
⇨jìn

jǐnguǎn 尽管 ① even if; no matter ② not hesitate to

jǐnkuài 尽快 as quickly (or soon) as possible

jǐnliàng 尽量 as (much, soon, strong, etc.) as possible

jǐn 紧 ① tight; firm; fast; secure; taut; tense; close ② urgent; critical; pressing

jǐnbēng 紧绷 to stretch taut

jǐncòu 紧凑 ① compact ② (said of an entertainment program, a show, a composition, etc.) one climax after another

jǐnjí 紧急 urgent; critical

jǐnjiēzhe 紧接着 to follow close behind

jǐnmì 紧密 ① rigidly precise; rigorous ② compact and orderly ③ to close together ④ rapid and intense

jǐnpò 紧迫 urgent; pressing

jǐnqiào 紧俏 (said of consumer goods) in great demand but short supply

jǐnsuō 紧缩 to retrench; to curtail

jǐnzhāng 紧张 nervous; taut; tight; tension

jǐnbiāosài 锦标赛 a sports tournament; championship contests; championships

jǐnxiù 锦绣 ① fine brocade ② as beautiful as brocade

jǐn 谨 ① cautious; prudent; careful; attentive ② sincerely; reverent; deferential

jǐnshèn 谨慎 prudent; cautious

jìn 尽 ① to exhaust; to use up ② to put to the best use ③ to complete; to finish; to accomplish ④ all; entirely; totally; completely; wholly ⑤ the utmost
⇨jǐn

jìnlì 尽力 to make efforts; to exert oneself; to do one's best

jìnliàng 尽量 as much as possible

jìnqíng 尽情 to one's heart's content

jìntóu 尽头 the extremity; the end

jìnxīn 尽心 to devote all one's energies

jìn 进 ① to go ahead; to move forward; to proceed; to advance ② to improve; improvement; progress ③ to enter ④ to recommend; to introduce ⑤ to offer (advice, presents, etc.) ⑥ a generation ⑦ income ⑧ rooms in a house divided by a courtyard; a courtyard

jìnbù 进步 to improve; to progress; improvement; progress; progressive

jìnchǎng 进场 to get into an examination room, a sports arena, etc.

jìnchéng 进程 progress in a course of action

jìnchū 进出 ① to get in and out; incoming and outgoing ② (business) a turnover

jìnchūkǒu 进出口 ① imports and exports ② exits and entrances

jìndù 进度 (said of work) degree of progress

jìn'ér 进而 to proceed to the next step

jìngōng 进攻 to attack; attack; offensive

jìnhuà 进化 to evolve; evolution

jìnjūn 进军 to march (troops to

war); to advance (with armed forces)

jìnkǒu 进口 ① to import; importation ② an intake (for liquid or gaseous matters)

jìnlai 进来 to come in; to enter

jìnqǔ 进取 ① to forge ahead with effort; to advance ② to be aggressive, as in jockeying for position, etc.

jìnqu 进去 to get in; to enter; to go in

jìnrù 进入 to enter; to get in; to reach

jìnshí 进食 to eat; to take food

jìnxíng 进行 ① to proceed (with one's business, plan, etc.); to carry on ② to advance; to march forward

jìnxiū 进修 to advance in study; to engage in advanced studies

jìnyíbù 进一步 to take one step ahead; to move further ahead

jìnzhǎn 进展 progress; headway

jìnzhù 进驻 to march troops to a place and garrison it

jìn 近 ① near or close (in space) ② near or close (in time); immediate; recent ③ near or close (in abstract relation); intimate ④ to approach; to approximate

jìndài 近代 modern times; recent times

jìndàishǐ 近代史 modern history

jìnlái 近来 recently; lately

jìnnián 近年 in recent years

jìnqī/jìnqí 近期 in the near future

jìnrì 近日 recently; lately

jìnshì 近视 nearsightedness; myopia

jìnsì 近似 similar to; resembling

jìn/jìng 劲 ① vigor; energy; strength ② spirit ③ an air; manner
⇨jìng

jìntóu/jìngtóu 劲头 ① vigor; drive ② energy; strength ③ manner; expression ④ enthusiasm

jìnjí 晋级 promotion; to promote

jìnshēng 晋升 to rise in rank; to promote

jìn 浸 to dip; to immerse; to soak; to permeate; to percolate

jìn 禁 ① to prohibit; to forbid; to ban ② to confine; to imprison; to detain ③ a secret
⇨jīn

jìnjì 禁忌 ① a taboo; to taboo ② to avoid; to abstain from

jìnlìng 禁令 a prohibition; a ban

jìnqū 禁区 ① a forbidden region; a restricted zone ② a preserve

jìnzhǐ 禁止 to forbid; to prohibit; to ban

jīng 茎 a stalk; a stem

jīngdū 京都 ① the national capital ② Kyoto, Japan

Jīngjù 京剧 Beijing opera

jīng 经 ① to pass through or by ② the warp of a fabric; things running lengthwise ③ common or customary ways, rules, regulations, etc. ④ to plan; to arrange; to regulate; to rule; to manage; to deal in; to engage in ⑤ menses ⑥ human arteries, etc. ⑦ classic books; religious scriptures; books of significant value ⑧ longitude

jīngcháng 经常 frequently; often; constantly

jīngdiǎn 经典 ① religious scriptures ② classics

jīngfèi 经费 a budget; funds

jīngguò 经过 ① to pass by or through ② process; experience

jīngjì 经纪 ① to manage (a business) ② a manager; a broker

jīngjì 经济 ① economy; economic ② economical; to economize

Jīngjì Bù 经济部 the Ministry of Economic Affairs

jīngjì chéngzhǎnglǜ 经济成长率 the economic growth rate

jīngjìrén 经纪人 ① a manager (of entertainers, boxers, etc.) ② a broker; an agent

jīngjìxué 经济学 economics

jīnglǐ 经理 ① a manager (of a company) ② to manage, direct, regulate, etc.

J

jīnglǐ 经历 ① one's past experiences ② to undergo; to go through

jīngshāng 经商 to go into business

jīngshòu 经受 to undergo; to experience; to withstand; to stand; to weather

jīngshū 经书 classic books

jīngxiāo 经销 to sell as a consignee

jīngyàn 经验 experience; empirical

jīngyíng 经营 to operate or manage (a shop, a business, etc.)

jīngyóu 经由 by (a person); through or via (a place)

jīng 惊 ① to startle; to surprise; to amaze; to astound; to alarm; to flabbergast; to dumbfound; to terrify; to frighten ② afraid; frightened; scared; fearful; terrified ③ to marvel; to be surprised; to be amazed

jīngdòng 惊动 ① to astonish; to startle; to stir up; to alarm ② to bother; to disturb

jīnghuāng 惊慌 to lose one's head from terror; to be frightened and confused

jīnghuáng 惊惶 frightened; panic-stricken

jīngqí 惊奇 to be surprised; to be amazed; to marvel

jīngrén 惊人 surprising; astounding; astonishing; startling; amazing; sensational

jīngtàn 惊叹 to marvel; to exclaim

jīngxǐ 惊喜 pleasantly surprised

jīngxià 惊吓 to frighten; to scare; to alarm suddenly

jīngxiǎn 惊险 breathtaking; alarmingly dangerous; thrilling

jīngyà 惊讶 to marvel; to be surprised; to be amazed

jīngyì 惊异 to marvel; to be surprised; to be amazed

jīngpiàn 晶片 a chip

jīngyíng 晶莹 sparkling

jīng 睛 ① the pupil of the eye ② eyes

jīngjīng-yèyè 兢兢业业 cautious and attentive

jīng 精 ① fine and delicate; exquisite ② dedicated; intensive ③ keen; smart; sharp; clever ④ skilled; to specialize in ⑤ polished rice; unmixed rice ⑥ the essence; the essentials ⑦ very; completely; extremely ⑧ energy; spirits ⑨ the male sperm; semen ⑩ a goblin; a spirit; a demon

jīngcǎi 精彩 ① the highlight or climax (of a play, etc.); the most attractive or wonderful part (of something) ② Wonderful! Bravo! Excellent!

jīngchéng 精诚 purity and sincerity; earnest and sincere

jīngdǎ-xìsuàn 精打细算 calculate carefully and budget strictly

jīngguāng 精光 ① stark-naked; without a stitch on; completely nude ② nothing left; exhausted; completely gone

jīnghuá 精华 the essence; the essentials

jīngjiǎn 精简 to simplify

jīngjìn 精进 to devote oneself to improvement

jīnglì 精力 stamina; vitality; energy

jīnglíng 精灵 an elf; a fairy

jīngměi 精美 exquisite; delicate and beautiful

jīngmì 精密 minute or detailed; precise

jīngmíng 精明 keen or sharp; clever

jīngpǐn 精品 an exquisite article

jīngquè 精确 precise; accurate; precision; accuracy

jīngshén 精神 ① one's spirit ② mental

jīngshen 精神 lively; vigorous

jīngshénbìng 精神病 mental illness

jīngsuǐ 精髓 the marrow; the essence; the pith

jīngtōng 精通 well-versed in; good at; expert at

jīngxì 精细 ① fine (materials, etc.); delicate and painstaking (workmanship, handicraft, etc.); exquisite ② very careful and attentive

jīngxīn 精心 elaborate; attentive and circumspect; meticulous; to put all one's mind in

jīngxuǎn 精选 to pick the best; to hand-pick; to select

jīngyìqiújīng 精益求精 Second best is not good enough—to try for the best.

jīngzhì 精致 fine; exquisite; delicate

jīng 鲸 a whale

jīngyú 鲸鱼 a whale

jǐng 井 a well

jǐng 颈 the neck; the throat

jǐng 景 ① scenery; views ② prospects; circumstances; situations ③ (in motion pictures, stage shows, etc.) settings; background scenes ④ big and strong ⑤ great ⑥ high ⑦ bright and luminous ⑧ to admire; to respect ⑨ a surname

jǐngguān 景观 (geography) landscape

jǐngqì 景气 (economics) booming; prosperity

jǐngsè 景色 scenery; landscapes

jǐngwù 景物 scenery; landscapes

jǐngxiàng 景象 appearances; scenes; conditions; outlooks; sights

jǐngzhì 景致 scenes; views; a vista

jǐng 警 ① to guard; to keep watch ② to warn; to alert ③ an alarm ④ quick; alert ⑤ the police

jǐngbào 警报 an alert; an alarm; a warning

jǐngchá 警察 a policeman; a cop

Jǐngchá Jú 警察局 county (or city) police headquarters

jǐnggào 警告 ① to warn; to caution; to admonish ② a warning

jǐngjiè 警戒 ① to be on the alert ② to warn and admonish

jǐngjué 警觉 vigilant; alert; watchful

jǐngjuéxìng 警觉性 vigilance; alertness; watchfulness

jǐngtàn 警探 a police detective

jǐngtì 警惕 ① to be wary; to be alert; to be watchful ② a warning

jǐngwèi 警卫 ① to guard ② a guard

jǐngyuán 警员 a policeman; a cop

jǐngzhèng 警政 police administration

jìng 劲 strong; tough; powerful; sturdy
⇨jìn

jìng 径 ① a narrow path; a byway ② a shortcut ③ a diameter ④ direct; straight ⑤ already—implying a sense of surprise

jìng 净 ① clean; pure; to cleanse; to purify ② only; merely; nothing but ③ empty; vain ④ net (income, etc.) ⑤ a role in Chinese opera with a heavily painted face ⑥ completely; totally

jìnghuà 净化 to purify

jìngzhí 净值 net value

jìngluán 痉挛 convulsions; spasm; cramp; a jerk

jìng 竞 to compete; to vie

jìngbiāo 竞标 competitive bidding

jìngjì 竞技 a race; a contest; a tournament

jìngsài 竞赛 a race; a contest

jìngxuǎn 竞选 to campaign; to run for

jìngzhēng 竞争 to compete; to vie; competition

jìngzhēngzhě 竞争者 a competitor

jìng 竟 ① rather unexpectedly; somewhat to one's surprise; in a way thought to be rather unlikely ② to come to an end; to terminate; to go through the whole course; to finish; to complete

jìngrán 竟然 somewhat unexpectedly; somewhat to one's surprise

J

jìngshì 竟是 to turn out to be

jìng 敬 ① to respect; to revere; to honor; to esteem ② to present; to offer

jìng'ài 敬爱 to respect and love

jìng'éryuǎnzhī/jìng'éryuànzhī 敬而远之 to keep a person or a thing at a respectful distance; to keep a person or a thing at arm's length

jìngjiǔ 敬酒 to drink a toast; to toast

jìnglǐ 敬礼 to salute

jìngpèi 敬佩 to admire; to esteem; to respect

jìngyì 敬意 respects; regards

jìng 静 ① still; motionless; tranquility; quiet(ly); calm; silent ② peaceful; harmonious; serene ③ virtuous; chaste

jìngjìng 静静 quiet; silent

jìngqiāoqiāo/jìngqiǎoqiǎo 静悄悄 quietly; stealthily; very quiet

jìngtài 静态 a motionless state; the state of stillness; a stationary state

jìngzuò 静坐 to sit still with a peaceful mind; to sit still as a form of therapy

jìng 境 ① a boundary; a frontier; a border ② a place; an area ③ a state; a situation; circumstances

jìngdì 境地 ① a state; a condition; a position; a situation ② territory

jìngjiè 境界 ① a boundary ② a situation ③ a state (of mind); a realm

jìngnèi 境内 within the border; in the country

jìng 镜 ① a mirror ② lenses; spectacles; glasses ③ to mirror ④ to take warning (from a past failure)

jìngpiàn 镜片 a lens

jìngtóu 镜头 ① the lens of a camera ② a scene captured by the camera

jìngzi 镜子 ① a mirror ② a mirror (in a non-material sense) ③ a lens; glasses

jiǒngyì 迥异 a great difference; vastly different

jiūchán 纠缠 ① to tangle; to involve; entanglement ② to pester

jiūfēn 纠纷 disputes; quarrels; entanglements

jiūzhèng 纠正 to correct; to check; to discipline; to rectify

jiūjìng/jiùjìng 究竟 ① actually; exactly ② after all; finally ③ the very source; the outcome

jiū 揪 ① to clutch; to grasp with one's hand ② to pull; to drag ③ to pick on

jiǔ 九 nine; ninth

jiǔ 久 ① long ② for a long time ③ to detain someone long

jiǔ'érjiǔzhī 久而久之 over a long period of time

jiǔ 玖 an elaborate form of jiǔ 九, nine, used in checks, etc. to prevent fraud

jiǔ 酒 alcoholic drinks (brewed or distilled); wine; liquor; spirits

jiǔbā 酒吧 a bar (for alcoholic drinks)

jiǔdiàn 酒店 a tavern; a saloon

jiǔguǎn 酒馆 a tavern; a pub; a saloon; a bar

jiǔhuì 酒会 a cocktail party; a cocktail reception

jiǔjīng 酒精 alcohol

jiǔpíng 酒瓶 a bottle for alcoholic drinks

jiǔzuì 酒醉 drunk; intoxicated; tipsy

jiù 旧 ① old; past; former ② ancient; antique ③ longstanding

Jiùjīnshān 旧金山 San Francisco

jiù 救 ① to save; to relieve; to rescue; to aid; to help

jiùhùchē 救护车 an ambulance

jiùhuǒ 救火 ① to try to extinguish a fire ② firefighting

jiùjì 救济 to relieve (the suffering, the poor, etc.)

jiùmìng 救命 ① to save one's life ② Help!

jiùshēngtǐng 救生艇 a lifeboat

jiùyuán 救援 to help or aid (the distressed)

jiùzāi 救灾 to relieve victims of a disaster

jiùzhì 救治 to treat and cure (the sick); to remedy

jiùzhù 救助 to relieve or help (persons)

jiù 就 ① forthwith; right away ② exactly; precisely ③ namely ④ even if ⑤ to come or go to ⑥ to suit; to fit ⑦ to receive ⑧ to undergo ⑨ to assume ⑩ to follow

jiùcān 就餐 to eat; to dine

jiùcǐ 就此 then; thereupon; thereafter

jiùdì 就地 on the spot

jiùjìn 就近 at the nearest convenient place

jiù……láikàn 就……来看 from the viewpoint of...; from the perspective of...

jiù……láishuō 就……来说 as far as is concerned; where...is concerned

jiùrèn 就任 to take office

jiùshì 就是 ① exactly ② namely; that is ③ even if; even though ④ only; but

jiùshìshuō 就是说 that is to say; in other words; namely

jiùsuàn 就算 (colloquial) even though; even if; granted that

jiùxù 就绪 to be complete; to be all set; ready

jiùxué 就学 to go to school

jiùyào 就要 to be about to; to be going to

jiùyè 就业 to get employment; to get a job

jiùyī 就医 to receive or undergo medical treatment

jiùzhí 就职 assume office (usually high positions)

jiù 舅 ① a maternal uncle (one's mother's brother) ② a brother-in-law (one's wife's brother)

jiùfù 舅父 a maternal uncle

jiùjiu 舅舅 a maternal uncle (one's mother's brother)

jiùmǔ 舅母 a maternal aunt (one's mother's brother's wife)

jū 车 name of a chessman in a kind of Chinese chess ⇨chē

jūliú 拘留 to detain; detention

jūshù 拘束 ① to tie (someone) down; to restrain ② timid and awkward

jū 居 ① to dwell; to reside; to inhabit; to occupy ② an abode; a dwelling

jūduō 居多 to be the majority; mostly

jūjiā 居家 to lead one's life at home

jūmín 居民 residents or inhabitants

jūrán 居然 incredibly; to my surprise

jūshì 居室 ① a room or house for living in ② to cohabit

jūzhù 居住 to dwell; to inhabit; to live

jūgōng/júgōng 鞠躬 to bow; a bow

jú 局 ① an office; a bureau ② a situation; a state of affairs ③ an inning ④ a game

júbù 局部 having to do only with a part; partial; local

júmiàn 局面 an aspect; a situation

júshì 局势 an aspect; a situation

júxiàn 局限 to limit; to confine

júzhǎng 局长 the head or director of a government office or bureau

júhuā 菊花 a chrysanthemum

júzi 橘子 mandarin oranges; tangerines

jǔsàng 沮丧 despondent; crestfallen; downcast

jǔzhèn 矩阵 (mathematics) a matrix

jǔ 举 ① to lift; to raise ② to recommend; to commend; to praise ③ manner; deportment

jǔbàn 举办 to sponsor, organize,

J

or initiate

jǔdòng 举动 ① movement ② manner; behavior

jǔfán 举凡 generally speaking

jǔlì 举例 to give examples

jǔqǐ 举起 to lift; to raise

jǔshì 举世 all the world

jǔshì-wénmíng 举世闻名 to be known to the whole world; world-renowned

jǔshì-zhǔmù 举世瞩目 to attract worldwide attention

jǔshǒu 举手 to raise one's hand

jǔxíng 举行 to hold (examinations, rallies, parties, etc.); to take place

jǔzhǐ 举止 deportment; conduct

jǔzhòng 举重 weightlifting

jǔzú-qīngzhòng 举足轻重 so important is the role one plays in a matter that each step one takes may affect it in a significant way

jù 巨 ① great; big ② very

jùdà 巨大 giant (size); mammoth

jùrén 巨人 a giant

jùxīng 巨星 ① a giant star ② a superstar

jù 句 a sentence

jùzi 句子 a sentence

jù 拒 ① to refuse; to reject ② to defend; to ward off; to resist

jùjué 拒绝 to refuse

jù 具 ① an appliance, implement, utensil, tool, etc. ② complete; all complete

jùbèi 具备 ① to have (qualifications or advantages) ② all complete; all ready

jùtǐ 具体 concrete

jùyǒu 具有 to be provided with

jù 俱 to accompany

jùlèbù 俱乐部 a club

jùquán 俱全 to be available in all varieties

jù 剧 ① a drama; a theatrical work; a play ② intense; strenuous; acute; severe ③ to play

jùběn 剧本 a play; a scenario

jùchǎng 剧场 a theater

jùliè 剧烈 strenuous; intense; hard; fierce

jùqíng 剧情 the plot

jùtuán 剧团 an opera troupe; a troupe; a theatrical company

jùyuàn 剧院 a theater

jù 据 ① according to; on the basis of; on the grounds of ② to occupy; to take possession of ③ to seize ④ proof; evidence ⑤ a surname

jùbào 据报 according to reports

jùchēng 据称 according to reports, assertions, or claims

jùdiǎn 据点 a base (for operations or activities)

jùshuō 据说 It is said that....; according to hearsay

jùxī 据悉 It is reported that....

jù 距 ① distance ② a bird's spur

jùlí 距离 distance

jù 锯 ① a saw ② to saw; to cut with a saw ③ to amputate

jù 聚 to come or put together; to gather; to assemble; to collect

jùcān 聚餐 to get together for luncheon or dinner

jùhé 聚合 ① to gather; to assemble; to come together ② (chemistry) polymerization

jùhuì 聚会 to assemble; to gather

jùjí 聚集 to gather; to assemble

jùjīng-huìshén 聚精会神 to concentrate oneself

jùluò 聚落 a village; a town

juān 捐 ① tax; duty; charge; dues ② to donate; to contribute; to subscribe ③ to buy or purchase (an official rank) ④ to give up (one's life for a cause, etc.) ⑤ to remove

juānkuǎn 捐款 to donate money; donations

juānxiàn 捐献 to contribute; contributions

juānzèng 捐赠 to donate or contribute

juǎn 卷 ① to roll up ② to curl (hair, etc.); curly (hair) ③ to sweep off ④ a roll
⇨juàn

juǎnrù 卷入 to be drawn into

juàn 卷 ① painting which can be easily folded or rolled up ② a book ③ a test paper ④ files; filed documents
⇨**juǎn**

juàndài 倦怠 to be tired; worn out; languor

juàn 圈 an enclosure or a pen for keeping livestock
⇨**quān**

juàncūn 眷村 a military dependents' village

juànshǔ 眷属 dependents; family

jué 决 ① to decide; to conclude; to judge ② certain; definite ③ (said of a dike) to burst; to break ④ to execute a person

juébù 决不 never

juécè 决策 an adopted policy; a decision

juédìng 决定 to determine; to decide

juédìngxìng 决定性 decisive

juékǒu 决口 a rupture; an opening

juésài 决赛 the final (of a contest, race, etc.)

juésuàn 决算 a final financial statement

juéxīn 决心 to make up one's mind; to resolve

juéyì 决议 ① a resolution (reached at a meeting) ② to decide; to resolve

juéyì'àn 决议案 a resolution (reached at a meeting)

juézhàn 决战 a decisive battle; to fight a decisive battle

juéqiào 诀窍 the secret or knack of doing something

juézé 抉择 choice; to choose

jué 角 a dramatic role; a character

jué/jiǎo 角 to compete; to contest; to wrestle
⇨**jiǎo**

juésè 角色 a role; a character

juézhú/jiǎozhú 角逐 to contest (for a post, etc.)

jué 绝 ① extremely; utmost; ab-

solutely ② without match; peerless ③ to sever; to break off; to cut ④ to discontinue; to stop; to cease ⑤ to renounce; to decline ⑥ to run out of; exhausted; used up ⑦ without posterity ⑧ isolated; to separate ⑨ to destroy ⑩ leaving no leeway ⑪ a poem of four lines

juébù 绝不 never

juédàbùfēn 绝大部分 for the most part

juédàduōshù 绝大多数 the most; the overwhelming majority

juéduì 绝对 absolute(ly); definite(ly)

juéjì/juéjī 绝迹 to vanish completely

juéjiā 绝佳 extremely good; excellent

juéshí 绝食 to fast

juéwàng 绝望 hopeless; desperate; despair

juéyuán 绝缘 to insulate

juézhǒng 绝种 (said of species of animals, etc.) extinction; extinct

jué 觉 ① to tell; to feel ② to be conscious of; to sense ③ senses ④ to awaken; to realize; to discover
⇨**jiào**

juéchá 觉察 to discover; to realize; to detect; to be aware; sense

juéde 觉得 ① to feel ② to be conscious of; to realize; to sense ③ to think; to be of the opinion

juéwù 觉悟 to become aware; to realize

juéxǐng 觉醒 to wake up

jué 掘 to dig; to excavate; to make a hole or cave

juéshì 爵士 Sir (a title of nobility)

jūn 军 ① the military; forces; of national defense ② corps (as a military unit) ③ an armed service

jūnbèi 军备 armaments; arms

jūnduì 军队 troops; the armed forces

jūnfá 军阀 the militarist; the warlord

jūnfāng 军方 the military authorities

jūnguān 军官 (military) an officer

jūnhuǒ 军火 arms; munitions

jūnjiàn 军舰 a war vessel; a warship; a man-of-war

jūnrén 军人 a soldier; a serviceman

jūnshì 军事 military affairs

jūntuán 军团 ① an army (a unit consisting of a number of corps) ② any large unit of troops; a legion

jūnyī 军医 (military) a surgeon; a medic

jūnyòng 军用 for military use; military

jūnzhuāng 军装 a soldier's outfit; military uniform

jūn 均 ① equal; equally; even; level ② to be fair ③ all; also; too ④ a potter's wheel ⑤ an ancient musical instrument

jūnděng 均等 equality; equal; impartial; fair

jūnhéng 均衡 equality; balance; equilibrium

jūnyún 均匀 even (blending, etc.); uniform

jūn 龟 chapped; cracked
⇨guī

jūn 君 ① a sovereign; a monarch; a king; a lord ② you (used in addressing a male in formal speech)

jūnzǐ 君子 a perfect or true gentleman

jūn/jùn 菌 bacteria
⇨jùn

jùn 俊 ① talented; capable; superior; refined; smart; bright ② good-looking; handsome ③ big; huge

jùn 菌 mushroom
⇨jūn

K

kāfēi 咖啡 coffee

kāfēidiàn 咖啡店 a café; a coffee house; a coffee shop; a coffee bar

kāfēiguǎn 咖啡馆 a café; a coffee shop

kāfēitīng 咖啡厅 a café; a coffee shop

kǎ 卡 ① a card, as a visiting card; cardboard ② an abbreviated form for "calorie"
⇨qiǎ

kǎchē 卡车 a truck; a lorry

kǎdài 卡带 a cassette tape

kǎpiàn 卡片 a card; a calling card

kǎtōng 卡通 a cartoon; animation

kāi 开 ① to open ② to drive ③ to undo; to unfold; to wind off ④ to reveal; to disclose ⑤ to begin; to start ⑥ to found; to expand ⑦ to run (a shop or business) ⑧ to eliminate ⑨ to write down; to list ⑩ to state; to explain ⑪ to divide into ⑫ a carat

kāibàn 开办 to start or open (a shop, school, business, etc.)

kāicǎi 开采 to excavate; to mine

kāichē 开车 to drive a car

kāichú 开除 to dismiss; to fire

kāichuàng 开创 to found (a nation, big business, etc.); to start

kāidāo 开刀 ① to operate on (a patient); an operation ② to punish ③ to behead

kāidǎo 开导 to educate and enlighten

kāidiàn 开店 to open a shop; to run a store

kāidòng 开动 ① to start; to set in motion ② to be on the move

kāifā 开发 to develop; development (of natural resources, industry, etc.)

kāifā 开发 pay; hand out

kāifàn 开饭 time to eat

kāifàng 开放 ① to come into bloom ② to lift a ban ③ to open (to trade, traffic, etc.); to be open ④ to liberalize or hand over a government monopoly to private operations

kāigōng 开工 to go into operation; to start work; to begin a building project

kāiguān 开关 ① a switch or similar device to put on or shut off an electric current, etc. ② to open and close

kāiháng 开航 ① to open up for navigation ② to set sail

kāihù 开户 to open a bank account

kāihuā 开花 ① to flower; to blossom ② (said of shells) to burst

kāihuà 开化 civilized

kāihuì 开会 to hold a meeting; to attend a meeting or conference

kāikè 开课 ① to lecture on a new subject in the curriculum ② to start a class at the beginning of a new semester

kāikěn 开垦 to open up wasteland for farming

kāikǒu 开口 to open one's mouth; to speak

kāikuò 开阔 ① spacious; open; wide ② broad-minded

kāilǎng 开朗 ① open and clear ② broad-minded and outspoken

kāilù 开路 to pioneer; to cut the way, as in a jungle

kāimén 开门 to open the door

kāimíng 开明 enlightened; open-minded

kāimù 开幕 ① to raise the curtain ② to open; to begin a meeting

kāipán 开盘 (said of a market) the opening quotation

kāipì 开辟 to open up or develop (a new market, farm plot, etc.); to start

kāipiào 开票 ① to count ballots or votes ② to make out an invoice

kāiqǐ 开启 to open

kāishè 开设 to establish; to set up

kāishǐ 开始 to begin; to commence; to start

kāishuǐ 开水 boiled water

kāitiān-pìdì 开天辟地 ① to open or develop ② creation of the world

kāitóu 开头 in the beginning; from the start

kāituò 开拓 to open up, enlarge, or expand (new frontiers, territory, etc.)

kāiwánxiào 开玩笑 to play a joke; to joke

kāixiāo 开销 ① expenses; (an) expenditure ② to pay expenses

kāixīn 开心 ① happy; to have a great time ② to play a joke on; to amuse oneself at somebody's expense

kāixué 开学 The school starts.

kāiyǎn 开演 to start showing (a picture, etc.); (said of a play, movie, etc.) to begin; to start performing

kāiyè 开业 to start doing business; to start practicing (law, medicine, etc.)

kāiyèchē 开夜车 to burn the midnight oil; to stay up late at night

kāizhǎn 开展 to expand; to spread out; to develop

kāizhàn 开战 to declare war; to do battle

kāizhāng 开张 ① to open a shop; to start doing a business ② to expand, spread out, or develop

kāizhī 开支 expenses; (an) expenditure

kǎixuán 凯旋 to return in triumph

kǎimó 楷模 a model (for imitation)

kān 刊 ① a publication ② to publish ③ to hew; to cut

kāndēng 刊登 ① to publish ② to carry (an article)

kānwù 刊物 a periodical; a publication

kānzǎi/kānzài 刊载 ① to publish ② to carry (an article)

kān 看 ① to watch; to mind; to look after to guard; to keep under surveillance
⇨kàn

kānjiā 看家 ① to stay at home and look after the house ② stock-in-trade; one's trademark or skill ③ (money, etc.) saved for a rainy day

kānshǒu 看守 ① to watch or guard ② to detain

kānchá 勘察 to investigate; to inspect

kāntàn 勘探 exploration; prospecting

kān 堪 ① to sustain; to bear; to stand ② may; can

kǎn 砍 ① to chop; to hack; to fell (trees, etc.); to cut down ② to throw at

kǎnfá/kǎnfá 砍伐 to fell (trees, etc.)

kàn 看 ① to see; to look at; to observe; to watch; to read ② to visit; to call on ③ to examine; to consider; to think ④ to depend on ⑤ to present (tea, wine, etc.)
⇨kān

kànbìng 看病 ① to see a doctor ② to examine the patient

kànbuqǐ 看不起 to look down upon

kànchéng 看成 to look upon as; to regard as

kànchu 看出 to make out; to see

kàndài 看待 to treat (another, a child, friend, etc.); treatment

kàndào 看到 to see; to catch sight of

kàndeqǐ 看得起 to think highly of

kànfǎ 看法 an opinion; a viewpoint

kànguo 看过 ① to take a look at ② to make a perusal of ③ to have seen or read

kànhǎo 看好 to have a good prospect; to look promising

kànjian 看见 to see; to catch sight of

kànkan 看看 ① to take a look at ② to examine and survey ③ to visit or call on ④ to see the sights ⑤ to thumb through (a book, etc.)

kànlái 看来 it looks as if; evidently

kànqilai 看起来 to look like; to seem

kànshū 看书 to read a book

kànwàng 看望 to visit or call on

kànyàngzi 看样子 it seems; it looks as if

kànzuò 看作 to regard as; to consider to be

kāng 康 ① healthy ② peaceful ③ level, even, and smooth (road, etc.)

kāngfù 康复 recovery (from illness)

kāngkǎi 慷慨 ① generous ② (usually said of a hero) vehement; fervent

kāng 糠 ① husks of rice; rice bran or chaff ② of inferior quality; not sturdy; empty inside; things of no value ③ spongy

káng 扛 to lift (especially when only a single person is involved)

kàng 抗 ① to resist; to oppose ② to reject; to refute; to rebuke; to defy ③ high and virtuous ④ to raise; to set up ⑤ to hide; to conceal; to screen; to secrete

kànghàn 抗旱 drought-resistant; drought-resistance

kàngjī/kàngjí 抗击 to resist; to beat back

K

kàngjù 抗拒 to resist; to oppose

kàngtǐ 抗体 an antibody

kàngyì 抗议 to protest

kàngyuán 抗原 (medicine) an antigen

kàngzhàn 抗战 ① to fight the invading army ② the War of Resistance against Japan (1937-1945)

kàngzhēng 抗争 to contend; to oppose; to resist

kàng 炕 ① a brick bed warmed by a fire underneath (in North China) ② hot ③ dry; to dry

kǎo 考 ① to test; to examine ② to check; to investigate; to study

kǎochá 考察 to inspect; to examine

kǎochǎng 考场 an examination hall or site

kǎogǔ 考古 to study the life and culture of ancient people

kǎogǔxué 考古学 archeology

kǎogǔxuéjiā 考古学家 an archeologist

kǎohé 考核 to review or assess (a plan, proposal, etc.); to evaluate

kǎojì/kǎojì 考绩 to grade the service

kǎojuàn 考卷 an examination paper

kǎolǜ 考虑 to consider; to weigh; to think over

kǎoqǔ 考取 to pass an examination (for admission to employment, a school, etc.)

kǎoshang 考上 to pass an examination (for admission to employment, a school, etc.)

kǎosheng 考生 an examinee

kǎoshì 考试 an examination; a test; a quiz

kǎoyàn 考验 ① to test; to try ② a test; a trial

kǎobèi 拷贝 a copy

kǎo 烤 ① to roast; to bake; to toast ② to warm by a fire ③ scorching

kǎoròu 烤肉 ① to barbecue ② barbecue

kǎoxiāng 烤箱 an oven for baking

kào 靠 ① near to; bordering on; to keep to (the left or the right), as in driving ② to lean on ③ to rely on; to depend on ④ (Chinese opera) make-believe armor worn by actors

kàojìn 靠近 ① near to; in the neighborhood ② to approach; to draw nearer

kēzé 苛责 to criticize severely; to rebuke; to excoriate

kē 柯 ① a tall evergreen tree ② a surname

Kēdá 柯达 Kodak, a brand name

kē 科 ① a department ② a section ③ a class; a variety; a family (of plants or animals) ④ the action in Chinese opera ⑤ a subject in the civil service examination of former times ⑥ a branch of academic or vocational studies

kēhuàn 科幻 science fiction

kējì 科技 science and technology

kēmù 科目 ① subjects, courses, classifications of academic studies ② the civil examination system in former times

kēpǔ 科普 popular science

Kēwēitè 科威特 Kuwait

kēxué 科学 science

kēxuéjiā 科学家 scientists

kēxuéyuàn 科学院 an academy of sciences

kēyán 科研 scientific research

kēzhǎng 科长 a section chief in various government agencies

kē 棵 a measure word for plants

kē 颗 a drop or droplet; a grain; a pill; a measure word for bombs, bullets, etc.

kēlì 颗粒 a drop; a grain; a bead

kē 磕 to strike; to bump; to knock; to collide

ké 咳 to cough
⇨hāi

késou 咳嗽 to cough; a cough

kě 可 ① may; can; to be able to

② an auxiliary ③ but; however
④ a surname

kě'ài 可爱 lovable; likable

kěbùkěyǐ 可不可以 can; may
(used at the beginning of a question)

kěbúshì 可不是 really; sure
enough

kědá 可达 attainable; accessible; within reach

kěfǒu 可否 can; may (used at the
beginning of a question)

kěgē-kěqì 可歌可泣 (said of
bravery or fortitude in serving
the nation) very moving; very
touching

kěguān 可观 ① to be worth
seeing ② considerable (sum of
money, losses, etc.)

kěguì 可贵 valuable; praiseworthy

kějiàn 可见 ① to be perceived
② that can be seen

kěkào 可靠 reliable (sources,
etc.); dependable

kěkǒu 可口 tasty; pleasant to the
palate

Kěkǒu Kělè 可口可乐 Coca
Cola or Coke

kělè 可乐 Coke; cola

kělián 可怜 pitiful; pitiable;
poor; miserable

kěnéng 可能 probable; possible

kěnéngxìng 可能性 possibility;
probability

kěpà 可怕 dreadful; frightening;
terrible

kěqiǎo 可巧 by coincidence;
coincidently

kěshì 可是 ① but; however ② to
be (in a more emphatic sense); will
really be

kěwàng 可望 it is expected
to...; it is supposed to...

kěwèi 可谓 one may well say; it
may be called

kěwù 可恶 detestable; hateful

kěxī/kěxí 可惜 It's a pity that....

kěxǐ 可喜 gratifying; heartening

kěxiǎng'érzhī 可想而知 to be

obvious; one can well imagine

kěxiào 可笑 laughable; ridiculous

kěxíng 可行 feasible; can be
carried out

kěxíngxìng 可行性 feasibility

kěyǐ 可以 ① can; may ② Yes, you
can. ③ Okay. That will do.

kě 渴 ① thirsty ② to long; to
crave; to pine

kěwàng 渴望 to long for; to
crave for; to aspire after

kè 克 ① a gram ② to win; to overcome; to conquer ③ to restrain ④
to be able to ⑤ to limit

kèfú 克服 ① to overcome ② to put
up with

kèzhì 克制 to restrain; to control

kè 刻 ① a quarter (of an hour)
② to carve; to engrave; to cut ③
cruel; heartless; unfeeling; cutting; harshly; acrimonious; biting ④ moment

kèbǎn 刻板 ① to engrave (for
printing) ② monotonous; dull;
stereotyped

kèbó 刻薄 cold-hearted; acrimonious

kèhuà 刻画 to depict; to portray

kèkǔ 刻苦 ① assiduous; hardworking ② simple and frugal

kèyì 刻意 to do something with
intensive attention

kè 客 ① a guest ② a stranger; an
alien; a foreigner ③ a customer
④ foreign; strange; alien ⑤ an
adventurer ⑥ a surname

kèchē 客车 a passenger train
or bus

kèfáng 客房 a guest room

kèguān 客观 objective

kèhù 客户 a client

kèjī 客机 a passenger plane; an
airliner

Kèjiā 客家 (literally) "guest
families" which moved from
northern to southern China during periods of invasions by the
northern tribes in Chinese history—the Hakka people of South

K

China; the Hakkas

Kèjiāhuà 客家话 Hakka

kèmǎn 客满 (said of theater tickets, etc.) sold out; a full house

kèqi 客气 polite; courteous; sticking to the proprieties

kèrén 客人 a guest

kètīng 客厅 a parlor; a living room

kè 课 ① a class meeting ② a course (of study) ③ a lesson ④ to impose; to levy; to tax ⑤ a session at divination ⑥ to supervise

kèběn 课本 a textbook

kèchéng 课程 a curriculum

kèshí 课时 a class hour; a period

kèshuì 课税 to levy taxes; to impose taxes

kètáng 课堂 a classroom

kètí 课题 ① a task or problem (for students) ② a theme; a question for study

kèwài 课外 outside class; extra-curricular

kèwén 课文 the text or contents of a lesson

kèyè 课业 schoolwork; lessons

kèzhǎng 课长 a section chief

kěn 肯 to be willing; to approve of; to consent to; to permit; to agree

kěndìng 肯定 affirmative; positive; sure; definite

kěnqiè 恳切 very sincere; earnest

kěnqiú 恳求 to implore; to plead

kěn 啃 to bite; to gnaw; to nibble

kēng 坑 ① a pit; a hole in the ground ② to entrap

kēngshēng 吭声 to utter a sound or a word

kōng 空 ① empty; hollow; void ② to empty; to exhaust; to reduce to extremity ③ fictitious; unreal; impractical ④ vain and useless (efforts, etc.); ineffective; fruitless ⑤ high and vast ⑥ the sky; space ⑦ (Buddhism) sunyata; empty; void; vacant; nonexistent ⑧ merely; only

kōng/kòng 空 (on the stock exchange) bear; oversold position ⇨**kòng**

kōngdòng 空洞 ① vast and empty ② (said of writings, thought, etc.) shallow

kōngfúyuán 空服员 a flight attendant

kōnghuà 空话 empty talks; talks without content

kōngjiān 空间 space

kōngjūn 空军 the air force

kōngkuàng 空旷 expansive; vast and boundless

kōngnàn 空难 a plane crash or collision

kōngqì 空气 air or atmosphere (also used figuratively)

kōngqì wūrǎn 空气污染 air pollution

kōngqián 空前 unprecedented

kōngtán 空谈 empty talks; idle chatter

kōngtiáo 空调 air conditioning

kōngxiǎng 空想 ① an impractical thought or idea; a daydream ② to daydream

kōngxīn 空心 ① hollow ② nothing in mind

kōngxū 空虚 empty; void; emptiness

kōngyùn 空运 air freight; to transport by air

kōngzhàn 空战 an air battle

kōngzhōng 空中 in the air; in the sky

kōngzhōng bāshì 空中巴士 an air bus

kōngzhōng dàxué 空中大学 an open university

kōngzhōng xiǎojiě 空中小姐 a stewardess (of a passenger plane); an air hostess

kǒng 孔 ① a hole; an orifice; an opening; an aperture ② very; exceedingly ③ of or pertaining to Confucius or Confucianism ④ urgent; badly ⑤ a surname

kǒngquè 孔雀 a peacock

Kǒngzǐ 孔子 Confucius

kǒng 恐 ① to fear; to dread ② I

K

am afraid....

kǒngbù 恐怖 terror; horror; fear

kǒnghè 恐吓 to intimidate; to threaten; to menace; to blackmail

kǒnghuāng 恐慌 ① panic; panicky ② (economic) depression or crises

kǒngjù 恐惧 fear; dread; fright

kǒnglóng 恐龙 a dinosaur

kǒngpà 恐怕 ① perhaps; I think; maybe ② I'm afraid that....

kòng 空 ① leisure; free time; spare time ② blank (space); vacant; vacancy; to leave blank or vacant ③ spacious—implying a sense of awe ④ a chance; an opportunity ⑤ wanting; deficient; impoverished
⇨**kōng**

kòngbái 空白 a blank in a paper or form

kòngdì 空地 a vacant area; a vacant lot; vacancy

kòngr 空儿 ① leisure; spare time ② a vacant space; a gap ③ an opportunity

kòngxì 空隙 a crevice; a gap; a loophole

kòng 控 ① to control; control ② to accuse; to charge; to sue ③ to draw (a bow)

kònggào 控告 to accuse

kòngsù 控诉 ① to accuse before an authority ② to appeal to a higher court

kòngzhì 控制 to control; control; to dominate

kōu 抠 ① to raise ② to grope for ③ to inquire into; to delve into ④ to dig with fingers (or something pointed) ⑤ to be stingy

kǒu 口 ① the mouth ② a person ③ a certain article (as a cistern, a big jar, etc.) ④ an opening ⑤ a crack ⑥ the edge or blade of a knife ⑦ a gate (especially in the Great Wall or city walls)

kǒu'àn 口岸 a port

kǒubēi 口碑 public praise

kǒucái 口才 eloquence; eloquent

kǒudai 口袋 a pocket

kǒugǎn 口感 the taste or texture (of food)

kǒuhào 口号 ① a slogan ② (military) an oral command

kǒuhóng 口红 a lipstick

kǒujiǎo 口角 corner of the mouth

kǒujìng 口径 the caliber (of a gun, etc.)

kǒuqì 口气 ① the meaning (usually hidden) of words said ② the way of speaking

kǒuqiāng 口腔 the cavity of the mouth

kǒuqín 口琴 a harmonica

kǒushì 口试 an oral test

kǒushuǐ 口水 saliva

kǒutóu 口头 verbally; orally

kǒuwèi 口味 taste

kǒuwěn 口吻 a tone

kǒuyīn 口音 an accent (in speaking a peculiar language or dialect)

kǒuyǔ 口语 plain, spoken language ② to slander

kòu 扣 ① to tap; to strike; to rap; to pull ② to fasten; to button; to buckle ③ to cover on top ④ to deduct ⑤ to detain; to confine ⑥ to impound; to withhold ⑦ a button; a hook; a buckle

kòuchú 扣除 to deduct

kòudǐ 扣抵 to withhold money or goods from a debtor as payment of his debt

kū 枯 ① withered; dry ② dried wood ③ ill health; emaciated

kūzào 枯燥 ① uninteresting; dull ② dry

kū 哭 to weep; to cry; to sob; to wail; to whimper

kūqì 哭泣 to sob; to weep

kūlong 窟窿 holes

kǔ 苦 ① bitter ② painful; hard; difficult; laborious; miserable ③ strenuous; earnest; diligent ④ to abhor ⑤ to feel miserable about

kǔgōng 苦工 toil; hard labor

kǔnàn 苦难 privation; suffering; hardship

K

kǔnǎo 苦恼 misery; distress; trouble

kǔzhōng 苦衷 a reason for doing something not easily understood by others

kù 库 a storeroom; a granary ② a treasury

kùcún 库存 a stock; reserve

kùfáng 库房 a storeroom; a warehouse

kù 裤 drawers; trousers; pants

kùzi 裤子 pants

kù 酷 ① (said of intoxicants) strong ② (said of fragrance) very stimulating ③ cruel; brutal; harsh ④ exceedingly

kuā 夸 ① to exaggerate; to boast; to brag ② to praise ③ big; great ④ to show off

kuādà 夸大 to exaggerate

kuājiǎng 夸奖 to praise; to acclaim; to extol

kuāyào 夸耀 to flaunt; to show off

kuāzhāng 夸张 to exaggerate; to overstate

kuǎ 垮 ① to topple; to collapse ② to wear down ③ to put to rout ④ to fall (out of power)

kuà 跨 ① to take a stride; to stride ② to sit astride on; to straddle; to ride ③ to cut across; to go beyond; to extend across

kuàguó 跨国 transnational; international; multinational

kuàyuè 跨越 to stride over (a ditch, etc.)

kuài 会 to add; to compute ⇨huì

kuàijì 会计 ① accounting ② an accountant; a treasurer

kuàijìshī 会计师 C.A. (a chartered accountant); C.P.A. (a certified public accountant)

kuài 块 ① a lump; a piece; a cube ② a lump (or clod) of earth ③ a piece of (land, bread, etc.) ④ alone; to be all by oneself

kuài 快 ① quickly; fast; hasty; soon ② to hurry up; to make

haste ③ quick-witted; ingenious ④ sharp (blades, etc.); keen ⑤ pleasant; happy ⑥ nearly; near ⑦ honest; straightforward

kuàibào 快报 a dispatch; a bulletin

kuàicān 快餐 a quick meal; a snack

kuàidì 快递 express delivery

kuàigǎn 快感 a pleasant feeling

kuàihuo 快活 happy; joy

kuàijié 快捷 speedy; fast; nimble

kuàilè 快乐 happy; joy

kuàimén 快门 a camera shutter

kuàisù 快速 fast; quick; prompt

kuàiyào 快要 is nearly...; is about to...

kuàizi 筷子 chopsticks

kuān 宽 ① broad; wide; spacious; vast ② magnanimous; lenient; tolerant; liberal; forgiving; indulgent ③ well-off ④ to loosen; to widen

kuānchang 宽敞 spacious; roomy

kuāndà 宽大 lenient; magnanimous

kuāndù 宽度 width; breadth

kuānguǎng 宽广 vast; broad; spacious; wide

kuānkuò 宽阔 roomy; wide; spacious

kuānpín 宽频 broadband (as in internet connection)

kuānróng 宽容 to forgive; to pardon

kuānshù 宽恕 to forgive; to pardon

kuānsōng 宽松 loose and comfortable

kuǎn 款 ① a fund; a sum of money; money ② sincerity; sincere; sincerely ③ an article, an item, etc. (in a contract, treaty, etc.) ④ to entertain; to treat well ⑤ empty (words, etc.)

kuǎndài 款待 to entertain with courtesy and warmth; hospitality

kuǎnshì 款式 fashions; styles; patterns

K

kuǎnxiàng 款项 a sum of money; a fund; money

kuāng 筐 a rectangular chest or box woven from bamboo strips (or wicker); a shallow basket

kuáng 狂 ① crazy; mad; mentally deranged ② violent ③ unrestrained; uninhibited; wild ④ haughty

kuángfēng 狂风 a very strong wind; a fierce wind

kuánghuānjié 狂欢节 a carnival

kuángrè 狂热 ① fanatical; feverish ② a fad

kuángwàng 狂妄 extremely conceited

kuànggōng 旷工 to neglect work

kuàngkè 旷课 to cut school; to truant

kuàng 况 ① to compare; comparative ② situations; conditions ③ to visit; to call on

kuàngqiě 况且 moreover; besides; furthermore

kuàng 矿 ① a mineral; ore ② mining ③ a mine

kuàngcáng 矿藏 mineral reserves; mineral resources

kuàngchǎn 矿产 mineral resources

kuànggōng 矿工 a miner

kuàngjǐng 矿井 a mine; a pit

kuàngqū 矿区 a mining district; an ore field

kuàngshān 矿山 mountains containing mineral deposits; a mine

kuàngshí 矿石 a mineral; ore

kuàngwù 矿物 a mineral

kuàngyè 矿业 mining industry; mining

kuàng/kuāng 框 ① a frame ② the skeleton (of a lantern, etc.) ③ to frame

kuī 亏 ① to lose; to damage; to have a deficit ② to lack; to want; short; deficient ③ to treat unfair-ly; to be unfair to ④ fortunately; luckily ⑤ used in a mocking sense ⑥ the waning; to wane

kuīdài 亏待 to maltreat

kuīqiàn 亏欠 ① a deficit ② insufficiency ③ to owe

kuīsǔn 亏损 ① a deficit; a loss; to deplete ② enfeebled or weakened by illness

kuíhuā 葵花 a sunflower

kuìyáng 溃疡 an ulcer

kūnbù 昆布 kelp (*Laminaria japonica*)

kūnchóng 昆虫 insects

kǔn 捆 ① to bind; to tie up ② a bundle

kùn 困 ① fatigued; weary; tired ② difficult; hard ③ to trouble; to worry; to harass; to be stranded; to be hard-pressed ④ poor

kùnhuò 困惑 to perplex; to confuse

kùnjìng 困境 a predicament; straits

kùnkǔ 困苦 in great distress; poverty-stricken

kùnnan 困难 difficulty; hardship

kùnrǎo 困扰 to perplex; to confuse

kuò 扩 to enlarge; to magnify; to expand; to extend

kuòchōng 扩充 to expand; to enlarge

kuòdà 扩大 ① to enlarge; to expand ② to swell; to distend

kuòjiàn 扩建 to extend (a factory, mine, etc.)

kuòsàn 扩散 ① (physics) to diffuse; diffusion ② to scatter about

kuòyīnqì 扩音器 a megaphone; a loudspeaker

kuòzhǎn 扩展 to stretch; to extend; to spread

kuòzhāng 扩张 ① to extend; to spread; to expand ② to dilate; dilation

kuò 阔 ① broad; wide; width ② separated; widely apart ③ rich; loaded; wealthy; extravagant

K

L

lājī/lèsè 垃圾 garbage; refuse

lājīchǎng/lèsèchǎng 垃圾场 a garbage heap

lājīduī/lèsèduī 垃圾堆 a garbage heap

lā 拉 ① to pull; to drag; to hold; to draw ② to play ③ to lengthen; to elongate ④ to discharge (especially stool, urine, etc.)

Lādīng Měizhōu 拉丁美洲 Latin America

lādùzi 拉肚子 to suffer from diarrhea

lāhui 拉回 to pull back

lākai 拉开 ① to pull open; to draw aside ② to increase the distance between

lāpiào 拉票 to solicit votes; to canvass

lā la 啦 (onomatopoeia) the sound of water, rain, etc.
⇨la

lǎba 喇叭 ① a trumpet ② a loud-speaker

làyuè 腊月 the 12th month of the lunar year

làzhú 蜡烛 a candle

là 辣 ① pungent; piquant; hot ② vicious; ruthless ③ (said of smell or taste) to burn; to bite

làjiāo 辣椒 capsicum; chilli

làmèi 辣妹 a sexy girl

la 啦 a sentence-final particle
⇨lā

lái 来 ① to come; coming; to arrive ② to return; to come back; returning

láibīn 来宾 a guest; a visitor

láibují 来不及 unable to make it in time

láidào 来到 to arrive; to come

láide 来得 ① to be able to; competent ② to act or speak with great force ③ to happen; to come ④ to emerge (from a comparison) as;

to come out as

láideji 来得及 there is time for...

láidiàn 来电 ① an incoming telegram (telephone); your message ② to telephone; to send a telegram here

láifǎng 来访 to come to visit

láihuí 来回 coming and going; to come and go

láihuí-láiqù 来回来去 (dialect) back and forth; over and over again

láikè 来客 a visitor; a guest

láilì 来历 past history; origin; background

láilín 来临 to arrive; to approach; to come

láinián 来年 the next year; the years to come

láiwǎng 来往 coming and going

láiwǎng 来往 social intercourse or connection

láixìn 来信 ① your letter ② to send a letter here

láiyuán 来源 the source; the origin

láizì 来自 to come from; to derive from

lài 赖 ① to accuse without grounds or evidence; to put the blame on somebody else ② to repudiate (a debt); to disavow; to deny something which one has said or done ③ to postpone or procrastinate intentionally ④ no good; poor; bad ⑤ to rely on; to depend on ⑥ lazy ⑦ a surname

lánhuā 兰花 an orchid; a cymbidium

Lányǔ 兰屿 Lanyu, an islet off the coast of Southeastern Taiwan

lán 拦 to impede; to obstruct; to hinder; to block

lánjié 拦截 to intercept; to attack or stop on the way

lán 栏 ① a railing; a balustrade; a fence ② a pen for domesticated animals ③ column ④ (of a form) column with a list of items to be filled in ⑤ billboard

lángān 栏杆 ① a railing; a balustrade ② silk trimming for girls

lánwèi 栏位 (computer) field

lán 蓝 ① blue; indigo ② an indigo plant ③ a surname

lántú 蓝图 a blueprint; an outline of a project

lán 篮 a basket

lánbǎn 篮板 (basketball) a backboard

lánqiú 篮球 basketball

lánzi 篮子 baskets

lǎn 览 ① to look at ② to read

lǎnchē 缆车 a cable car

lǎn 懒 lazy; indolent; idle; inactive; listless

lǎnde 懒得 not to feel like (doing something); not disposed or too tired to do anything; not to be in the mood to; to be disinclined to

lǎnduò 懒惰 lazy; idle; indolent

lǎnsǎn 懒散 indolent; inactive

làn 烂 ① overripe; rotten; to rot; to fester ② cooked soft; well cooked ③ worn-out ④ bright; brilliant ⑤ to scald; to burn; to scorch ⑥ dissolute

làn 滥 ① to overflow; to flood; to inundate; inundation ② to do things without plans; reckless ③ to practice no self-restraint; to give way to unbridled license ④ to abuse (one's power, influence, etc.) ⑤ false; not true ⑥ superfluous words or expressions

lànyòng 滥用 ① to spend excessively ② to abuse

láng 狼 ① a wolf ② a heartless, cruel person; cruel and heartless; cunning and crafty ③ name of a constellation

lángbèi 狼狈 ① desperate ② in a difficult position ③ embarrassed ④ heartless and cruel persons

lǎngdú 朗读 to read aloud

lǎngsòng 朗诵 to read aloud

làng 浪 ① waves; billows; breakers ② dissolute; rash; debauched; unrestrained

làngcháo 浪潮 ① tide; waves ② (figuratively) tide; tendency

làngfèi 浪费 to waste; to lavish; waste

làngmàn 浪漫 ① debauched ② romantic

lāo 捞 ① to pull or drag out of the water ② to fish up; to get by improper means

láo 劳 ① to labor; to take the toil; to work ② to trouble; to worry; to bother ③ meritorious deeds; services

láo/lào 劳 to comfort or entertain (the tired)

láobǎo 劳保 labor insurance

láodòng 劳动 to toil; to labor

láodong 劳动 to trouble

láodònglì 劳动力 ① labor force; work force; manpower ② capacity or ability for physical labor

láogǎi 劳改 (said of criminals) to reform through forced labor

láogōng 劳工 laborers; workers

láojià 劳驾 to be sorry to have to trouble someone to do something

láolèi 劳累 to fatigue, tire, or exhaust

láolì 劳力 ① labor ② labor physically

láozī 劳资 labor and management

láo 牢 ① secure; stable; firm; fast ② a jail; a prison ③ a pen; a stable; a cage

láofáng 牢房 a prison cell

láogù 牢固 secure; firm

láojì 牢记 to keep firmly in mind

láosāo 牢骚 grumbling; complaint

láodao 唠叨 to nag; to din

lǎo 老 ① old; aged ② a prefix added to a surname to indicate familiarity and friendship ③ always ④ very ⑤ a prefix added to numbers to indicate the order of birth

⑥ the youngest ⑦ (said of meat, etc.) tough; overcooked ⑧ parents ⑨ to treat with the reverence to the aged ⑩ (said of color) dark

lǎobǎixìng 老百姓 the people; the common people

lǎobǎn 老板 ① a boss; a master ② a keeper; a proprietor

lǎobǎnniáng 老板娘 ① a proprietress; proprietor's wife ② boss's wife; a mistress

lǎobīng 老兵 an old soldier; a veteran

lǎochéng 老成 sophisticated; experienced

lǎodà 老大 ① old ② the eldest child ③ the leader of a gang ④ extremely; exceedingly

lǎodàniáng 老大娘 an aunty; a granny

lǎodàyé 老大爷 (in addressing an aged man) uncle; grandpa

lǎogōng 老公 ① an old man ② (slang) one's husband

lǎogong 老公 eunuch

lǎogōnggong 老公公 ① an old man ② a eunuch

lǎohàn 老汉 an old man

lǎohǔ 老虎 a tiger

lǎohuà 老化 aging

lǎojiā 老家 ① one's original home ② hell

lǎojiù 老旧 old-style; old-fashioned

lǎonián 老年 old age; old life; late years

lǎoniánrén 老年人 the aged; the old people

lǎopéngyou 老朋友 an old friend

lǎopo 老婆 (vulgar usage) wife

lǎorén 老人 an old person

lǎorenjia 老人家 ① old persons (a term of respect) ② parents

lǎoshī 老师 a teacher

lǎoshì 老是 always; all the time; constantly

lǎoshi 老实 honest; truthful

lǎoshishuō 老实说 to be honest; frankly,...

lǎoshǔ 老鼠 a rat; a mouse

lǎotàipó 老太婆 an old woman

lǎotàitai 老太太 an old lady

lǎotiān 老天 Heaven—divine justice

lǎotiānyé 老天爷 Heaven

lǎotóuzi 老头子 ① an old chap; an old fellow ② one's husband

lǎowài 老外 (slang) a foreigner

lǎoxiānsheng 老先生 ① (in addressing an aged man) venerable sir ② an old gentleman

lǎoxiāng 老乡 ① a fellow villager; a fellow townsman ② a term used to address a (male) stranger

lǎoye 老爷 ① sir ② an old man

lǎoyíbèi 老一辈 the older generation

lǎoyīng 老鹰 the eagle

Lǎozǐ 老子 Laozi, 604-531 B.C., a renowned philosopher and founder of Taoism

lǎozi 老子 ① one's father ② (a term used when one is angry) I

lǎolao 姥姥 ① one's maternal grandmother ② a midwife

lào 涝 to flood; floods

lào 落 ① to fall or drop (in prices, etc.) ② (said of a bird, etc.) to land; to perch ③ to get a net income; a surplus ⇨luò

lè 乐 ① happy; glad; joyful; joyous; cheerful; elated; content; pleased; delighted; willing ② pleasant; agreeable; enjoyable; pleasing; comfortable ⇨yuè

lèguān 乐观 optimistic

lèqù 乐趣 delight; pleasure; joy; fun

lèyì 乐意 ① willing ② pleased

lèyú 乐于 to like or love (doing something)

lèyuán 乐园 a paradise; Elysium

lè 勒 ① to force; to compel ② (calligraphy) a horizontal stroke ⇨lēi

lèsuǒ 勒索 to blackmail; to extort

le 了 ① a perfective marker ② a sentence-final particle

⇨liǎo

lēi 勒 to tighten
⇨lè

léi/lěi 累 ① a nuisance ② to fasten; to bind
⇨lèi, lěi

léi 雷 ① thunder ② a mine (an explosive)

léidá 雷达 a radar

léishè 雷射 a laser

léitóng 雷同 similar; identical; exactly the same

léiyǔ 雷雨 a thunderstorm

lěi 垒 ① to pile up ② a military wall; a rampart ③ a base

lěi 累 ① to accumulate through a length of time ② to pile up ③ to repeat; repeatedly; successively

lěi/lèi 累 ① to involve; involvement; to implicate ② a family burden
⇨léi, lèi

lěijī 累积 to accumulate; to pile up

lěijì 累计 to include previous figures in the calculation

lèi 泪 tears

lèishuǐ 泪水 tears

lèi 类 ① a species; a kind; a class; a race; a group; a category ② similar; alike ③ (now rarely) good; virtue

lèibié 类别 classification; categorization

lèisì 类似 to resemble; similar to; like

lèixíng 类型 a type; a category

lèi 累 ① tired; weary; fatigue ② to owe; to be in debt ③ (said of eyes) to strain
⇨léi, lěi

lěng 冷 ① cold ② cold in manner; frosty ③ (said of business, farming, etc.) off-season ④ unfrequented; deserted; out-of-the-way ⑤ strange; rare ⑥ receiving little attention; unwelcome

lěngdàn 冷淡 cold (expressions); indifferent (attitudes)

lěngdòng 冷冻 freezing

lěnghàn 冷汗 ① a cold sweat ② clammy perspiration

lěngjìng 冷静 calm or composed

lěngkù 冷酷 merciless; heartless

lěngmén 冷门 not popular or not in great demand

lěngmò 冷漠 indifferent; apathetic

lěngqì 冷气 ① air conditioning ② cold air

lěngqìjī 冷气机 an air conditioner

lěngqīng 冷清 desolate; lonely; deserted

lěngquè 冷却 to get cold; to cool off

lěngyǐn 冷饮 cold drinks

lěngzhàn 冷战 cold war

lěngzhan 冷战 to shiver with cold

lèng 愣 ① dumbfounded ② reckless; rash; irresponsible; rude ③ outspoken

lī 哩 to speak indistinctly
⇨lǐ, li

límǐ 厘米 centimeter

lí 离 ① to leave; to depart; to separate; separation ② to defy; to go against ③ distant from; apart from

líbié 离别 to say good-bye; to leave; to separate

líhūn 离婚 to divorce; a divorce

líjiā 离家 to leave home; to be away from home; to depart from home

líkāi 离开 to separate from; to leave; to depart; to keep away from

lípǔ 离谱 too far away from what is normal or acceptable

líqù 离去 to leave; to go away; to depart

lítí 离题 to depart from the topic

líxiū 离休 to retire (used for cadres who joined the communist party before October 1, 1949)

lízhí 离职 ① to leave or resign from one's office ② to retire from one's office

lí 梨 a pear

lí 犁 ① to till; to plow ② a plow

límíng 黎明 dawn; daybreak

líhuàn 罹患 to suffer from (a disease)

línàn 罹难 to fall victim to a disaster

línànzhě 罹难者 a victim

líba 篱笆 a bamboo fence

lǐ 礼 ① courtesy; propriety; decorum; politeness; civility; etiquette ② rites; ceremony ③ a gift; a present

lǐbài 礼拜 ① a week ② church service; worship

lǐbàirì 礼拜日 Sunday

lǐbàitiān 礼拜天 Sunday

lǐfú 礼服 ceremonial dress

lǐjié 礼节 etiquette

lǐmào 礼貌 etiquette; politeness; civility

lǐpǐn 礼品 a gift; a present

lǐtáng 礼堂 ① an auditorium ② a hall decorated for a wedding ceremony or funeral service

lǐwù 礼物 a gift; a present

lǐyí 礼仪 etiquette; protocol; decorum

lǐ 李 ① plums ② a surname

lǐ 里 ① a unit of linear measure about one third of a mile ② a neighborhood, or community, of 25 families (in ancient times); a neighborhood ③ within; inside ④ used to indicate time of day, night, a season, etc. ⑤ the lining of a dress or clothes
⇨lǐ

lǐbian 里边 inside

lǐchéng 里程 ① mileage ② the course of development; course

lǐmiàn 里面 inside; within

lǐtou 里头 inside

lǐzhǎng 里长 the head of a subdivision of the district, or borough, in a city or county

lǐ 哩 a mile
⇨lī, li

lǐ 浬 (a unit of distance used chiefly in navigation) a nautical mile; a geographic mile; a sea mile

lǐ 理 ① reason; logic; cause; truth; right ② law; principles; doctrine; theory; science ③ to arrange ④ to govern; to operate; to regulate; to manage; to run ⑤ to reply or answer; to respond ⑥ texture; grain (in wood, skin, etc.) ⑦ name of a religious sect

lǐcái 理财 to manage finances

lǐcǎi 理睬 to pay attention to; to heed

lǐfà/lǐfǎ 理发 to cut the hair; to have a haircut

lǐgōng 理工 science and engineering

lǐhuà 理化 ① physics and chemistry ② politics and education; to govern and educate

lǐhuì 理会 ① to understand; to comprehend ② to heed; to pay attention to

lǐjiě 理解 to comprehend; to understand

lǐlùn 理论 ① theory ② to argue

lǐniàn 理念 a rational concept; an idea

lǐpéi 理赔 (insurance) adjustment

lǐshì 理事 ① board directors (of a company) ② an administrator ③ to manage or administer affairs

lǐshìhuì 理事会 the board of directors

lǐshìzhǎng 理事长 the board chairman

lǐsuǒdāngrán 理所当然 as a matter of course; naturally

lǐxiǎng 理想 ① ideal ② ideas; thought

lǐxìng 理性 (philosophy) reason; rationality

lǐxué 理学 ① natural sciences ② a school of learning in the Song Dynasty devoted to the study of the classics with a rational approach

lǐyīng 理应 duty-bound to; ought to

lǐyóu 理由 reasons; grounds

lǐzhí-qìzhuàng 理直气壮 with confidence for one knows that he is in the right

lǐzhì 理智 intellect; reason

lì 力 ① strength; force; power; ability; vigor ② vigorously; earnestly ③ to do one's best

lìdiǎn 力点 a point of force (on a lever)

lìliang 力量 strength; force; power

lìqi 力气 ① physical strength or power ② an effort

lìqiú 力求 to do one's best to; to strive to

lìtú 力图 to try hard; to strive to

lìxíng 力行 to practice or perform energetically

lìxué 力学 ① to study with diligence or industry; to study hard ② (physics) mechanics

lìzhēng 力争 to struggle hard

lì 历 ① to pass; to elapse ② to undergo; to go through; to experience ③ things or duration that had come to pass ④ all previous (occasions, sessions); what has taken place ⑤ through; throughout; successive ⑥ to last (a certain period of time)

lìchéng 历程 process; course

lìdài 历代 successive generations; the dynasties in their successive order

lìjiè 历届 successive (or all) previous

lìjīng 历经 to have experienced, undergone, or encountered many times

lìlái 历来 hitherto; till now; heretofore

lìliàn 历练 to practice and experience

lìnián 历年 in the years past

lìshí 历时 to last (a certain period of time)

lìshǐ 历史 history

lìshǐxìng 历史性 historic

lìhai 厉害 ① fierceness; ferociousness ② very (ill, etc.); serious (damage, destruction, etc.)

lì 立 ① to stand ② to establish; to found; to build; to erect; to create; to start ③ to stand on one's own feet; to live ④ immediately; at once

lìchǎng 立场 a position; a stand; an attitude

lìfǎ 立法 to legislate; to make laws

lìfǎ wěiyuán 立法委员 a legislator; a law maker

Lìfǎ Yuàn 立法院 Legislative Yuan

lìfāng 立方 (mathematics) cube

lìfāngmǐ 立方米 a cubic meter

lìguó 立国 to found a state

lìjí 立即 at once; immediately; right away

lìjiāoqiáo 立交桥 an overpass

lìkè 立刻 at once; immediately; promptly; right away

Lìtáowǎn 立陶宛 Lithuania

lìtǐ 立体 ① three-dimensional ② a solid

lìxià 立下 to draw up (a legal document, etc.)

lìzhì 立志 to make up one's mind to pursue some object; to resolve

lìzú 立足 ① to have a foothold somewhere ② to base oneself upon

lì 丽 beautiful; elegant; fine; magnificent

lì 利 ① profit; benefit; advantage; gain ② sharp ③ to benefit; to serve

lìbì 利弊 advantages and disadvantages

lìhài 利害 interest and disinterest

lìhai 利害 sharp; shrewd

lìlǜ 利率 the interest rate

lìniào 利尿 diuresis

lìqì 利器 ① cutting instruments; cutlery ② a very useful and effective tool

lìrùn 利润 profit; gain; net profit

lìxí/lìxì 利息 interest

lìyì 利益 benefit; profit; advantage

lìyòng 利用 to utilize; to make use of

lìqīng 沥青 ① asphalt; pitch ② another name of resin

lì 例 ① an example; an instance ② a precedent ③ a regulation; a rule; a custom ④ regular; routine

lìrú 例如 for example; for instance; such as

lìwài 例外 an exception

lìxíng 例行 routine; regular

lìzi 例子 an example; an instance

lìshǔ 隶属 to be attached to

lìzhī 荔枝 a litchi

lìluo 俐落 well-executed

lìlín 莅临 to be present; to arrive

lìzi 栗子 a chestnut

lì 粒 ① a grain (of rice, etc.) ② a pill; a bead ③ to get grain to eat

lìzǐ 粒子 (physics) a particle

li/lǐ 里 a nominal suffix used to indicate location, time, domain, etc.
⇨lǐ

li 哩 a sentence particle which cannot be used in the interrogative sentence
⇨lǐ, lǐ

liǎ 俩 two; a pair; a couple
⇨liǎng

lián 连 ① to connect; to join; to unite ② in succession ③ a company (of soldiers) ④ together with ⑤ even; and; including ⑥ a surname

liándài 连带 joint (responsibility, obligation, etc.)

lián...dài... 连……带…… ① and; as well as ② and; while

lián...dōu... 连……都…… even...can (or cannot)...

liánduì 连队 (military) a company

liángǔn-dàipá 连滚带爬 to roll and crawl

liánjiē 连接 ① continuously ② to adjoin

liánjiēcí 连接词 (grammar) a conjunction

liánjié 连结 to connect; to join

liánlián 连连 ① continuously; unceasingly; again and again ② one after another

liánluò 连络 liaison; to make contact with

liánmáng 连忙 promptly; quickly; immediately; at once

liánmián 连绵 continuous; unbroken; uninterrupted

liánnián 连年 year after year

liánrèn 连任 to continue in one's office for another term; to be reappointed or reelected

liánrì 连日 for consecutive days

liánshǔ/liánshù 连署 to sign jointly; joint signatures

liánsuǒdiàn 连锁店 a chain store

liántóng 连同 together with; in addition to; along with

liánxì 连系 to keep in contact; contact

liánxiàn 连线 unbroken; continuous

liánxù 连续 successive; continuous; incessantly

liánxùjù 连续剧 (television) a soap opera; a drama series

liányè 连夜 all through the night

liánzhǎng 连长 a company commander

lián 帘 a loose hanging screen for a door or window, usually made of stringed beads, bamboo slabs, etc.; blinds; a curtain ② a flag as a shop sign

liánhuā 莲花 lotus blossoms or water lilies

liánzǐ 莲子 lotus seeds

lián 联 ① to unite; to ally; to connect; to join; to make an alliance ② allied (forces, etc.); joint (effort, etc.); mutual (guaranties, etc.) ③ a couplet

liánbāng 联邦 a federal union; a federal state

liánduì 联队 (said of the air force) a wing

liánhé 联合 to unite; to form an alliance of some kind; joint (effort, etc.)

Liánhéguó 联合国 United Nations

liánhéhuì 联合会 a federa-

L

tion; a union

liánhuān 联欢 to have a get-together

liánjūn 联军 allied forces

liánluò 联络 to communicate with; to contact

liánméng 联盟 an alliance; a union; to form an alliance, etc.

liánsài 联赛 league matches

liánshǒu 联手 to join hands (with someone); to gang up

liánxì 联系 ① to unite; to link; to relate ② to get in touch with

liánxiǎng 联想 association of ideas; to associate

liányì 联谊 activities for promoting fellowship

liányìhuì 联谊会 a party or an association for promoting fellowship

lián 廉 ① incorrupt; upright ② inexpensive; cheap ③ to examine; to inspect

liánjià 廉价 a low price

liánjié 廉洁 incorrupt; incorruptible

liánzhèng 廉政 to remove governmental corruption; honest and clean government

liándāo 镰刀 a sickle

liǎn 脸 the face (used both in its physical and figurative senses)

liǎnjiá 脸颊 cheeks

liǎnkǒng 脸孔 the face

liǎnpáng 脸庞 the shape of one's face; a facial configuration

liǎnpén 脸盆 a washing basin

liǎnpǔ 脸谱 (Chinese opera) face paintings indicating the personality, dispositions, etc. of the characters

liǎnsè 脸色 ① a complexion ② facial expression

liǎnshang 脸上 ① in (or on) the face ② face (in its figurative sense)

liàn 练 ① to practice; to train; to exercise ② skilled; experienced ③ to soften and whiten raw silk by boiling

liànbīng 练兵 to drill troops; to train troops

liànxí 练习 ① to train; to practice (so as to gain skill) ② exercises

liàn 炼 ① to smelt; to refine; to condense (milk); to temper (a metal) with fire ② (Chinese medicine) to keep herbs, etc. boiling for a long time ③ to train; to form character by hardship

liàngāng 炼钢 to refine steel; steelmaking

liànjīnshù 炼金术 alchemy

liàn 恋 ① to love (one of the other sex); to be in love ② to feel a persistent attachment (for a thing)

liàn'ài 恋爱 tender passions; to be in love

liànqíng 恋情 love between man and woman

liànrén 恋人 a sweetheart

liàn 链 a chain

liànzi 链子 a chain

liáng 良 ① good; fine; desirable ② instinctive; inborn; innate

liángduō 良多 very much; numerous; a great deal

liánghǎo 良好 good; fine; desirable

liángjī 良机 a good chance

liángxīn 良心 conscience

liángzhī 良知 ① instinct; innate knowledge ② an understanding friend

liángzhǒng 良种 ① (agriculture) a good variety with higher economic value ② (animal husbandry) a fine breed

liáng 凉 ① cool; chilly ② discouraged; disappointed ③ thin ④ name of one of the 16 states during the Eastern Jin

liángkuai 凉快 ① cool and comfortable ② to cool oneself

liángshuǐ 凉水 cold water

liáng 梁 ① beams of a house ② a ridge; a swelling ③ a bridge ④ Liang, name of a dynasty (502-

557 A.D.) ⑤ a state during the Epoch of Warring States, also known as Wei ⑥ a surname

liáng 量 to measure
⇨liàng

liáng 粮 ① grain; food; provisions; rations ② farm or land taxes

liángpiào 粮票 a food coupon; a grain coupon

liángshí 粮食 foodstuffs; provisions

liǎng 两 ① two; a pair; a couple ② a tael (a unit of weight) ③ both; either ④ (in ancient China) a piece of cloth, etc. of about 44 feet

liǎng'àn 两岸 ① both banks; both sides (of a river, etc.) ② both sides of Taiwan Straits; Mainland China and Taiwan

liǎngcè 两侧 two sides

liǎngjí 两极 the opposing poles

liǎngkǒuzi 两口子 husband and wife

liǎngpáng 两旁 both sides; two sides

liǎngshǒu 两手 dual tactics

liǎngxìng 两性 ① both sexes ② amphoteric

liǎng 俩 craft; ability
⇨liǎ

liàng 亮 ① bright; lustrous; brilliant; luminous; radiant; clear ② to display; to show

liàngguāng 亮光 bright light; flash

liàngxiàng 亮相 to pose for the audience's admiration on the stage

liàngjiě 谅解 to forgive; to be understanding

liàng 辆 a measure word for vehicles

liàng 量 ① quantity ② capacity ③ to estimate
⇨liáng

liàng 晾 ① to dry in the air; to air; to hang in the wind to dry ② to dry in the sun

liáokuò 辽阔 vast; distant

liáochéng 疗程 the course (or period) of treatment

liáofǎ 疗法 a cure; a therapy

liáoxiào 疗效 curative effect

liáoyǎng 疗养 to recuperate; to convalesce

liáoyǎngyuàn 疗养院 a sanatorium; a sanitarium

liáo 聊 ① to chat; a chat ② interest

liáotiānr 聊天儿 to chat; a chat

liáocǎo 潦草 ① (said of handwriting) hasty and careless; illegible ② perfunctory

liǎo 了 ① to finish; to end; to complete ② intelligent; remarkable ③ to understand
⇨le

liǎobuqǐ 了不起 Wonderful!

liǎojiě 了解 to understand; to comprehend

liào 料 ① to conjecture; to reckon; to estimate ② material; stuff; makings ③ to manage; to handle; to care ④ to consider; to calculate

liàolǐ 料理 ① to manage; to dispose of ② a dish

Liào 廖 a surname

liē/liě 咧 to babble
⇨liě

liě 咧 to stretch (the mouth) horizontally
⇨liē

liè 列 ① to arrange in a line; to line up ② to enumerate ③ a line; a series ④ to display

lièchē 列车 a train

lièguó 列国 the various states or nations

lièjǔ 列举 to enumerate

lièrù 列入 to be included in; to be incorporated in

lièwéi 列为 listed as

lièxí 列席 to be present (at a meeting as an observer)

liè 劣 inferior; mean; bad; of low quality

liè 烈 ① fiery; acute; vehement; fierce; strong; violent ② honest and virtuous; just and straightforward; chaste

lièhuǒ 烈火 a blazing fire; a fierce fire

lièjiǔ 烈酒 strong drink; a stiff drink

lièshì 烈士 martyrs

lièrén 猎人 a hunter; a huntsman

lièwù 猎物 game; a quarry

liè 裂 ① to crack; to break; a crack ② to split or divide up (profits, etc.); to rend; to sever

lín 邻 ① a neighbor ② neighborhood; a community ③ neighboring; adjoining; contiguous ④ a basic community unit which consists of a number of families in the same neighborhood

línguó 邻国 a neighboring country

línjìn 邻近 ① located nearby; located in the vicinity ② neighborhood

línjū 邻居 neighbors; people next door

línlǐ 邻里 neighborhood; a community

línzhǎng 邻长 the head of a basic community unit

lín 林 ① a forest; a grove; a copse ② circles; numerous; many; a great body of (capable persons, etc.) ③ a surname

línchǎng 林场 ① wooded land; a forest ② a logging station

línlì 林立 (literally) to stand like trees in a forest—a great many; a forest of (stacks, derricks, etc.)

línmù 林木 a forest; woods

línqū 林区 a forest zone; a forest region; a forest

línyè 林业 the forestry industry

lín 临 ① on the point of; near to; during; at; while ② to approach; to descend; to come to; to reach; to visit ③ to look down from above—preside over ④ to copy; to imitate ⑤ temporary; provisional ⑥ a surname

línchuáng 临床 clinical

línjìn 临近 close by; close to; close on

línshí 临时 for the time being; temporary; provisional

lín 淋 to soak with water; to drip ⇨**lìn**

línxuǎn 遴选 to choose or pick (a person); to select

lín 磷 phosphorus ⑥ water flowing between stones

lìn / lín 淋 to filter; to strain ⇨**lín**

línglì 伶俐 clever; intelligent; smart

líng 灵 ① clever; nimble; sharp; with quick reflexes ② good; excellent; efficacious; effective; to work ③ the spirit; the soul ④ wonderful; a wonder ⑤ mysterious; supernatural; divine ⑥ a fairy; an elf ⑦ anything pertaining to the deceased ⑧ witchcraft

línggǎn 灵感 ① inspiration ② the faculty of telepathy

línghún 灵魂 the soul; the spirit

línghuó 灵活 energetic, active, and clever; quick-witted; quick-minded; flexible; nimble

língmǐn 灵敏 adroitness; dexterity; sensitive; clever; skillful; active; acute; nimble

língqiǎo 灵巧 ① clever; ingenious; nimble ② cute; lovable

língyàn 灵验 ① (said of a prediction or prophecy) to come true with unbelievable accuracy ② (said of a drug, etc.) with uncanny or unbelievable efficacy

línglóng 玲珑 ① pleasing; delicate; cute; fine; regular ② bright ③ tinkling of jades

líng 铃 (jingling) bells

língchén 凌晨 the wee hours

língtīng 聆听 to listen to

líng 零 ① zero; nil; naught ② a fraction; fractional; remainder ③ a light rain; drizzle

língjiàn 零件 component parts; spare parts

língqián 零钱 small change; petty cash; odd change

língshí 零食 snacks; refresh-

ments

língshòu 零售 retail sales; to sell by retail

língsuì 零碎 fragments; fragmentary; fractions

língxià 零下 subzero

língxīng 零星 ① fragmented; fractional; not as a whole ② scattered

língyòngqián 零用钱 pocket money

líng 龄 age; years

líng / lìng 令 a ream (of paper) ⇨**lìng**

lǐng 岭 ① a mountain ② the ridge of a mountain; a mountain range

lǐng 领 ① to lead; to head; to guide ② to receive; to get ③ the neck ④ the collar; the neckband ⑤ to understand ⑥ (now rarely) to manage; to operate

lǐngdài 领带 ① a necktie ② to lead

lǐngdǎo 领导 ① to lead; leadership ② a guide

lǐngduì 领队 ① the leader of a group or team ② to lead a group

lǐnghuì 领会 to understand; to appreciate

lǐngqǔ 领取 to get; to receive

lǐngshì 领事 (diplomacy) a consul

lǐngtǔ 领土 territory

lǐngwù 领悟 to understand; to comprehend

lǐngxiān 领先 ① to lead; to walk ahead ② the lead; the first place or position

lǐngxiù 领袖 a leader; the leading figure

lǐngyù 领域 ① the territory of a nation ② a realm; a domain; a sphere; a field

lǐngzi 领子 the collar or neck of a garment

lìng 另 ① another; extra; in addition; besides ② to separate; separation (as of a couple); to divide

lìngwài 另外 besides; in addition

lìng 令 ① to cause; to make ② to order ③ a directive; an order

⇨**líng**

liū 溜 ① to slip; to slide ② to go secretly and quietly

⇨**liù**

liūbīng 溜冰 to skate; skating

liú 刘 ① a surname ② to kill

Liú Bāng 刘邦 Liu Bang, the founder of the Han Dynasty, whose reign lasted from 206 to 194 B.C.

liúlǎn 浏览 to glance over; to skim through

liú 留 ① to remain; to stay; to be at a standstill ② to leave ③ to preserve; to reserve ④ to ask somebody to stay ⑤ to detain; to obstruct; to keep; to delay

liúliàn 留恋 reluctant to leave; unwilling to part with

liúniàn 留念 as a keepsake or souvenir

liúshén 留神 to pay attention; to be careful

liúxià 留下 ① to leave ② to detain; to stop ③ to remain; to stay ④ to preserve

liúxīn 留心 to pay attention; to take heed

liúxué 留学 to study abroad

liúxuéshēng 留学生 a student studying abroad

liúyán 留言 ① a message ② to leave a message

liúyì 留意 to pay attention; to be careful; to be cautious

liú 流 ① to flow; to discharge ② to wander; to stray ③ a class; a rank ④ a branch; a division ⑤ unsettled; unfixed; mobile

liúchàng 流畅 (usually said of the style of writing) fluent; smooth

liúchéng 流程 ① technological process ② (mining) circuits

liúchuán 流传 to transmit or be transmitted, from person to person or from generation to generation; to spread

liúcìwǎng 流刺网 a drift net

liúdòng 流动 ① to be in flowing motion ② on the move ③ mobile;

L

itinerant

liúhàn 流汗 to perspire; to sweat

liúkòu 流寇 wandering bandits

liúlàng 流浪 to wander about; to rove

liúlì 流利 fluent

liúliàng 流量 (hydrology) flow capacity; discharge

liúlù 流露 to reveal unknowingly; to manifest

liúluò 流落 to become an outcast in a strange land

liúmáng 流氓 a hoodlum; a hooligan; a villain; a rascal

liúshī 流失 to run off; to be washed away

liúshì 流逝 (said of time) to elapse; to pass; passage

liúshuǐ 流水 flowing water; current

liútōng 流通 in circulation; to circulate; to ventilate

liúxīng 流星 (astronomy) a meteor

liúxíng 流行 ① to be in vogue; fashionable; prevalent ② (said of a contagious disease) to spread, rage, or be rampant

liúxíngxìng gǎnmào 流行性感冒 influenza; flu

liúxuè / liúxiě 流血 to shed blood; to bleed

liúyán 流言 idle talk; rumor; hearsay

liúyù 流域 drainage basin; drainage area

liúli 琉璃 ① glass ② porcelain ③ colored glaze ④ glossy gems

Liúqiú 琉球 Ryukyu

liúsuān 硫酸 sulfuric acid

liǔ 柳 ① a willow tree ② name of one of the 28 Constellations ③ (figuratively) a singsong house; the red-light district ④ a surname

liǔqín 柳琴 a plucked stringed instrument

liǔshù 柳树 a willow tree

liù 六 six

Liùfǎ Quánshū 六法全书 *The Complete Volume of Six Laws*

liù 陆 an elaborate form of liù 六 used in documents or checks to prevent forgery
⇨**lù**

liù 溜 ① rapids ② a row; a column ③ surroundings; neighborhood
⇨**liū**

lóng 龙 ① a dragon ② of the emperor; imperial ③ a huge extinct reptile ④ a surname

lóngjuǎnfēng 龙卷风 a tornado; a cyclone; a twister

Lóngshān Sì 龙山寺 Long Shan Temple, an old temple in Taipei, Taiwan

lóngtóu 龙头 ① a faucet; a tap; a cock ② the top successful candidate in the imperial examination under the former civil service examination system ③ the leader of a sect, secret society, etc.

lóngyǎn 龙眼 longan

lóng 聋 ① deaf; hard of hearing ② deaf—stupid and ignorant

lóng 笼 ① a cage; a coop ② a basket; a container
⇨**lǒng**

lóngzi 笼子 a cage; a coop

lóngzhòng 隆重 impressive, grand, and solemn

lǒng 拢 ① to gather; to collect; to tie ② to comb (hair) ③ to come alongside; to approach; to reach ④ to add up; to sum up ⑤ to lean ⑥ a special fingering in playing the lute

lǒngduàn 垄断 a monopoly; to monopolize

lǒng / lóng 笼 to include; to encompass
⇨**lóng**

lǒngzhào / lóngzhào 笼罩 to cover completely; to permeate; to shroud

lòng 弄 lane; alley
⇨**nòng**

lōu 搂 ① to hold up; to tuck up ② to squeeze or extort (money, etc.) ③ to gather up; to collect; to rake together

L

⇨lǒu

lóu 楼 ① a building of two stories or more; a tower ② floor; level

lóudào 楼道 a corridor; a passageway

lóufáng 楼房 a building of two stories or more

lóushang 楼上 upstairs

lóutī 楼梯 a staircase

lóuxià 楼下 downstairs

lǒu 搂 to hold in the arms; to embrace; to hug

⇨lǒu

lòu 漏 ① leak; to leak ② to slip or omit unintentionally; to neglect ③ to divulge; to disclose

lòudòng 漏洞 a shortcoming; a loophole

lòushuì 漏税 to evade tax payment

lòu 露 to appear; to emerge; to show

⇨lù

lòumiàn 露面 to show up; to appear in public; to show one's face; to make an appearance

lou 喽 a sentence-final particle

lú 卢 ① black ② a surname

Lúshān 庐山 Mt. Lu, a famous summer resort (in Jiangxi)

lú 炉 a stove; an oven; a fireplace; a hearth

lúzi 炉子 a stove; a furnace; a kiln

lù 陆 ① land; the shore; a continent ② by way of land; land transportation ③ a surname

⇨liù

lùdì 陆地 land

lùjūn 陆军 the army; the land force

lùxù 陆续 continuous; one by one; one after another

lù 录 ① to take down; to copy; to record ② a record ③ to accept (applicants)

lùfàngyǐngjī 录放影机 a videocassette recorder

lùqǔ 录取 to accept

lùxiàng 录像 videotape record-

ing

lùyīn 录音 ① to record ② recording

lùyīndài 录音带 a recording tape

lùyīnjī 录音机 a tape recorder; a recorder

lùyīnshì 录音室 a recording room

lùyǐng 录影 to videotape

lùyǐngdài 录影带 a videotape

lùyǐngjī 录影机 a video recorder

lùyòng 录用 to accept for employment

lùzhì 录制 to record

lù 鹿 a deer; a stag; a doe

lù 路 ① a way; a road; a path ② directions; courses ③ a sort; a kind; a gang ④ a way; means ⑤ a surname

lùbiāntān 路边摊 street vendors; sidewalk peddlers

lùbiāo 路标 a road sign; a signpost

lùchéng 路程 a journey; traveling distance

lùdēng 路灯 a streetlamp

lùduàn 路段 a section of a highway or railway

lùguò 路过 to pass by or through (a place)

lùjìng 路径 a way; a road; a route

lùkǒu 路口 an entrance to a road or street; a street intersection; a street crossing

lùmiàn 路面 a road surface

lùrén 路人 ① a wayfarer ② a stranger

lùshang 路上 on the way; along the way; en route

Lùtòushè 路透社 Reuters; Reuter's News Agency

lùtú 路途 a way; a road

lùxiàn 路线 a route; a road; a course

lùzi 路子 a way; a method; means; an approach

lù 露 ① uncovered; exposed; to show; to reveal; to betray ② dew

③ a cold, soothing, and aromatic drink; beverages distilled from flowers, fruit, or leaves
⇨lòu

lùtiān 露天 open-air; outdoor

lùyíng 露营 ① to camp; to bivouac ② an open-air camping; a jamboree; a camporee

lǘ 驴 an ass; a donkey

lǚ 旅 ① a traveler; a passenger ② to travel; to lodge ③ (military) a brigade; troops ④ a multitude; people

lǚchéng 旅程 the route a traveler takes from one place to another

lǚdiàn 旅店 a tavern; an inn

lǚfèi 旅费 traveling expenses

lǚguǎn 旅馆 a hotel; a hostel; an inn

lǚkè 旅客 a traveler; a passenger

lǚtú 旅途 on one's way (to a destination); during one's trip

lǚxíng 旅行 to travel

lǚxíngshè 旅行社 a travel agency; a travel bureau

lǚyóu 旅游 a tour; tourism

lǚyóuyè 旅游业 the tourist trade; tourism

lǚ 铝 aluminum

lǚ 屡 frequently; repeatedly; again and again

lǚcì 屡次 repeatedly; frequently

lǚlì 履历 one's personal history

lǚlìbiǎo 履历表 a biographic sketch

lǚxíng 履行 to fulfill or carry out

lǜshī 律师 a lawyer; a barrister

lǜ 率 ① (mathematics) ratio ② a suffix used to indicate a measure or rate ③ calculate
⇨shuài

lǜ 绿 green (color)

Lǜdǎo 绿岛 Green Island, off the southeastern Taiwan coast, the site of a reformatory camp

lǜdēng 绿灯 ① (transportation) the green light ② permission to go ahead with some project; the green light

lǜdì 绿地 space reserved for parks,

trees, or meadows in an urban community

lǜdòu 绿豆 mung beans

lǜhuà 绿化 to plant trees, build parks, or lay out lawns in deserts or urban areas

luǎn 卵 ① an egg; an ovum ② roe ③ the testicles

luàn 乱 ① chaos; confusion; distraction; anarchy ② out of order; out of sorts ③ confused; perplexed; agitated; disarranged; raveled ④ rebellion; revolt; insurrection

luànqībāzāo 乱七八糟 in confusion; topsy-turvy

lüè 掠 ① to take by force; to rob; to plunder; to pillage ② to brush; to pass lightly on the side; to sweep past ③ a long stroke to the left in Chinese calligraphy

lüèduó 掠夺 to seize or rob by force

lüè 略 ① approximate; rough; brief ② slight; small in extent ③ to scheme; to plan ④ strategy ⑤ to invade; to seize ⑥ to omit; to leave out ⑦ to survey the boundaries

lüèwēi/lüèwéi 略微 slightly; a little; somewhat

lūn 抡 ① to turn or spin with hands or arms ② to brandish ③ to squander

Lúndūn 伦敦 London

lúnlǐ 伦理 moral principles; ethics

lún 论 an alternative of lùn 论 for some phrases
⇨lùn

Lúnyǔ 论语 The Analects of Confucius, one of the Four Books

lún 沦 ripples; eddying water

lúnwéi 沦为 to become what is way below the social position one used to occupy

lúnxiàn 沦陷 occupied by or lost to the enemy

lún 轮 ① a wheel ② to recur; to alternate ③ to take turns; by turns; in relays ④ majestic; stately

lúnchuán 轮船 a steamship; a steamer

lúnkuò 轮廓 an outline; a silhouette

lúnliú 轮流 to take turns; by turns

lúntāi 轮胎 the tire (of a wheel)

lúnyǐ 轮椅 a wheelchair

lúnzi 轮子 a wheel

lùn 论 ① to discuss; to comment on; to talk about ② a theory; a dissertation; an essay ③ to debate; to dispute ④ to regard; to consider ⑤ in terms of; by ⇨lún

lùndiǎn 论点 the point at issue; an issue; a thesis

lùndiào 论调 the tone or argument (of a speech, etc.)

lùnshù 论述 to discuss; to expound

lùntán 论坛 the world of criticism; a tribune of opinions; a forum

lùnwén 论文 a treatise; a thesis; an essay

lùnzhèng 论证 demonstration; to expound and prove

luō 啰 to chatter
⇨luó

luōsuo 啰唆 vexingly verbose or wordy

luó 罗 ① thin, light silk ② a net; a' snare ③ to arrange over a wide space ④ a surname

Luódān 罗丹 Auguste Rodin, French sculptor (1840-1917)

Luófúgōng 罗浮宫 Louvre, a national museum in Paris

luóliè 罗列 to arrange for display; to spread out

Luómǎ 罗马 Rome

Luómǎníyà 罗马尼亚 Romania

luóbo 萝卜 a daikon radish; a carrot

luó 啰 ① noisiness ② a band of outlaws ③ used as a slightly argumentative final particle
⇨luō

luóji 逻辑 logic

luó 锣 a gong

luózi 骡子 a mule

luókuāng 箩筐 a large basket made of bamboo

luósī 螺丝 a male screw; an external screw; a screw

luósīdīng 螺丝钉 a male screw; an external screw; a screw

luǒtǐ 裸体 nude; naked; without a stitch on

luòtuo 骆驼 a camel

luò 落 ① to fall; to decline; to wither; weakened; fallen ② few and far-spaced; to stand apart; loose and scattered ③ to lose a village; a hamlet ⑤ to put (pen to paper) ⑥ to settle down ⑦ a pile; a heap
⇨lào

luòchā 落差 the drop in elevation

luòchéng 落成 completion (of a new building, etc.)

luòde 落得 to result in; as a result; to end in

luòdì 落地 ① to be born ② to fall to the ground

luòdìchuāng 落地窗 a French window

luòhòu 落后 to fall behind; to lag behind

luòpò 落魄 jobless and listless; down in one's luck; out of luck

luòshí 落实 ① to carry out ② practicable

luòwǎng 落网 (said of a criminal) to be caught; to be captured

luòwǔ 落伍 anachronistic; out of date

luòxia 落下 to fall down; to drop

luòxuǎn 落选 to fail in an election

luòyè 落叶 fallen leaves

L

M

mā 妈 ① one's mother ② a woman servant

māma 妈妈 mama; mother

Māzǔ 妈祖 Goddess of the Sea

má 麻 ① hemp; jute; ramie; sisal; flax ② sesame ③ numb; torpid ④ a tingle; to tingle ⑤ pockmarked ⑥ rough ⑦ pitted; spotty ⑧ measles ⑨ leprosy ⑩ to paralyze

mábì 麻痹 paralysis; palsy; numbness

mádài 麻袋 a jute bag; a hemp bag

máfan 麻烦 ① troublesome ② trouble ③ to bother

májiàng 麻将 mahjong, Chinese gambling game

mámù 麻木 paralyzed; numbed; palsied

máquè 麻雀 a sparrow

Máshěng Lǐgōng 麻省理工 Massachusetts Institute of Technology (MIT)

mázuì 麻醉 ① to anesthetize ② to dope; to drug

mǎ 马 a horse

mǎchē 马车 a carriage; a coach; a landau

mǎdá 马达 a motor

Mǎdájiāsījiā 马达加斯加 Madagascar

mǎhu 马虎 ① careless; perfunctory; sloppy; slovenly ② not very good; so-so

Mǎkè 马克 (formerly) a Deutsche mark

Mǎkèsī zhǔyì 马克思主义 Marxism; the system of economic and political thought developed by Karl Marx

mǎlāsōng 马拉松 marathon

Mǎláixīyà 马来西亚 Malaysia; Malaysian

Mǎláiyà 马来亚 Malaya; a state of Malaysia

mǎlì 马力 horsepower

mǎlíngshǔ 马铃薯 a potato

mǎlù 马路 a street; a highway; a road

Mǎnílā 马尼拉 Manila, capital of Philippines

mǎshàng 马上 ① right away; at once; immediately; without delay ② on horseback

mǎtǒng 马桶 ① a toilet ② a chamber pot; a closestool

mǎxì 马戏 a circus show; a circus

Mǎzǔ 马祖 the Mazu Islands

mǎ 吗 a character used in transliterating
⇨ma

mǎ 码 ① yard (a measure of length) ② a symbol; a code; a sign or thing indicating number

mǎtou 码头 a dock; a quay; a wharf; a pier

mǎyǐ 蚂蚁 an ant

mà 骂 to call names; to swear; to curse; to revile

ma 吗 a sentence-final particle used in questions
⇨mǎ

ma 嘛 as in lǎma 喇嘛—a lama (a priest of Lamaism)

mái 埋 ① to bury ② to secrete; to lie in wait
⇨mán

máifú 埋伏 an ambush; to ambush

máimò 埋没 to bury (one's talents, etc.)

máitóu 埋头 to bury oneself in; to immerse oneself in; to be absorbed in

mǎi 买 ① to buy; to purchase ② to win over (usually with a promise of favors in return)

mǎidān 买单 to pay the bill

mǎifāng 买方 the buyer

mǎijìn 买进 to buy

mǎimai 买卖 ① a line of business; trade ② to buy and sell

mǎirù 买入 to buy

mǎizhǔ 买主 the buyer

mài 迈 ① to stride; to step ② to surpass or exceed ③ to go on a long journey ④ old (age) ⑤ to pass

màijìn 迈进 to forge ahead

màixiàng 迈向 to march toward

màikèfēng 麦克风 a microphone

màizi 麦子 wheat; barley

mài 卖 ① to sell ② to betray; to harm another in order to benefit oneself ③ to show off; to flaunt

màiguó 卖国 to betray one's country; sedition or treason

màilì 卖力 to work hard willingly

màinong 卖弄 to flaunt; to show off

màizuò 卖座 ① (said of a theater, etc.) to draw large audiences ② (said of a restaurant, etc.) to attract large numbers of customers

màibó 脉搏 the pulse; pulsation

màiluò 脉络 things that are related and form a system of their own

mán 埋 as in **mányuàn** 埋怨—to grumble; to complain ⇨**mái**

mányuàn 埋怨 to blame; to grumble; to complain; complaint

mán 蛮 ① barbarous; savage; barbarians in the south ② quite; pretty; very; fairly

mánhèng 蛮横 barbarous; savage

mántou 馒头 steamed buns; steam bread

mán 瞒 ① to hide the truth; to fool others by lying; to deceive ② dim-sighted; poor vision

mǎn 满 ① proud; haughty ② full; filled completely; entirely; perfectly ④ to expire ⑤ plentiful; abundant ⑥ Manzhou

Mǎn Hàn quánxí 满汉全席 the complete Manzhou and Chinese

banquet, featuring numerous courses and delicacies, which lasts as long as one or two days

mǎnhuái 满怀 a heart full of (enthusiasm, sorrow, etc.)

mǎnqiāng 满腔 to have one's bosom filled with

Mǎnqīng 满清 the Qing Dynasty (1644-1911)

mǎnyì 满意 satisfied; content

mǎnyuè 满月 ① (of a baby) to be one month old ② a full moon

mǎnzú 满足 to satisfy or be satisfied; content

Màngǔ 曼谷 Bangkok, capital of Thailand

mànyán 蔓延 to spread; to creep

mànbù 漫步 to ramble; to stroll

màncháng 漫长 endless; infinite

mànhuà 漫画 a cartoon; a caricature

mànhuàjiā 漫画家 a cartoonist; a caricaturist

mànyóu 漫游 to travel about for pleasure

màn 慢 ① slow; sluggish ② negligent ③ haughty; rude; disrespectful; arrogant; supercilious ④ to postpone; to defer

mànman 慢慢 ① leisurely; slowly; unhurriedly; to take one's time ② by and by; gradually; little by little

mànpǎo 慢跑 to jog; jogging

mànyòng 慢用 to have an enjoyable meal

mànxìng 慢性 ① chronic (disease, etc.) ② slow (in taking effect)

mángguǒ 芒果 a mango

máng 忙 ① busy; short of time; fully occupied ② hurried; in haste; to make haste

mánglù 忙碌 ① busy; fully occupied ② hurriedly; in great haste

mángcóng 盲从 to follow blindly

mángdiǎn 盲点 (anatomy) a

blind spot; a scotoma

mángmù 盲目 ① blind ② lacking insight or understanding ③ reckless; aimless

mángrén 盲人 a blind person

mángmáng 茫茫 vast; boundless

mángrán 茫然 vague; blank; uncertain

māo 猫 the cat

máo 毛 ① ten cents; a dime ② hair; fur; feathers; down ③ very young; little ④ gross; untouched; unpolished ⑤ flurried; panic-stricken; scared; ⑥ vegetation ⑦ a surname

máobǐ 毛笔 a writing brush; a hair pencil

máobìng 毛病 ① fault; defects; shortcoming; blemish ② trouble; disorder ③ disease; illness

máofà/máofǎ 毛发 body hairs and hair

máojīn 毛巾 a towel

máotǎn 毛毯 a woolen blanket

máoxiàn 毛线 woolen yarn; knitting wool

máoyī 毛衣 woolen sweaters; sweaters

máodùn 矛盾 to contradict; contradiction; inconsistency

Máotáijiǔ 茅台酒 *Maotai*—a strong, colorless liquor produced in Maotai, Guizhou

màomì 茂密 growing densely

màoshèng 茂盛 luxuriant; flourishing; lush; exuberant

mào 冒 ① to put forth; to issue forth; to go up (as fire, smoke, etc.) ② to risk; to brave; to be exposed to (hardships) ③ incautious; imprudent; rash

màojìn 冒进 premature advance; rash advance

màopái 冒牌 a fake; an imitation

màoxiǎn 冒险 to take risks

màorán 贸然 rashly; blindly

màoyì 贸易 trade; to trade

mào 帽 ① a hat; a headwear ② a cap (of a fountain pen, screw, etc.)

màozi 帽子 ① a hat; a cap ② a label; a tag

mào 貌 ① a facial appearance; features ② a general appearance; a manner; form; bearing ③ to appear or pretend to be like ④ a ceremonious manner

me 么 as in **shénme** 什么—what

méi 没 ① none; nothing; no ② not yet; negative ⇨mò

méibànfǎ 没办法 to have no solution; to be powerless to solve a problem or issue

méicuò 没错 ① I'm quite sure. ② can't go wrong

méifázi/méifázi 没法子 no way out; no alternative (but...)

méiguānxi 没关系 It does not matter. Never mind.

méishénme 没什么 ① Nothing! Never mind! ② not difficult, bad, etc.

méishì 没事 ① without anything to do ② all right; O.K.

méishuōde 没说的 ① perfect; excellent ② no doubt; indisputable ③ needless to say

méiwèntí 没问题 no problem; surely

méixiǎngdào 没想到 unexpectedly; to have not thought about

méiyìsi 没意思 weary; bored

méiyòng 没用 useless; of no use

méiyǒu 没有 no; not; without

méizhé 没辙 Nothing can be done about it.

méigui 玫瑰 ① the rose (blossoms) ② black mica—a sparkling red gem

méiguizhěn 玫瑰疹 (medicine) rose rash

méi 枚 ① a measure word for coins, etc. ② the stalk; the trunk as opposed to branches ③ a gag for troops marching at night when silence means a lot

méi 眉 ① eyebrows ② the side ③ the top margin of a printed

page in a book ④ a rare surname

méimao 眉毛 the eyebrows

méitóu 眉头 the space between the eyebrows

méi 梅 ① prunes ② a surname

méihuā 梅花 ① plum blossoms ② a wintersweet

méihuālù 梅花鹿 sika; a spotted deer

méiyǔ 梅雨 the rainy season in early summer when plums are ripening

méijiè 媒介 ① a medium ② a go-between

méitǐ 媒体 a medium

méi 煤 ① coal; charcoal; coke ② carbon; soot

méiqì 煤气 gas (for lighting or heating)

méi 霉 ① mold; mildew; must ② germs; bacteria ③ fungi ④ dirty; dingy

méijūn/méijùn 霉菌 ① fungi; mold fungi ② germs; bacteria

měi 每 every; each; per

měidāng 每当 whenever; every time

měiféng 每逢 every time or whenever

měigé 每隔 every (three hours, five days, two feet, etc.)

měiměi 每每 repeatedly; often

měitiān 每天 every day; daily

měi 美 ① beautiful; pretty; fine; fair ② good; excellent; splendid; nice ③ to be pleased with oneself ④ to praise

měidé 美德 virtue

Měifāng 美方 the American side; on the part of the Americans

měigǎn 美感 the esthetic sense

měigōng 美工 ① art designing ② an art designer

měiguān 美观 pleasant to the eye

Měiguó 美国 the United States; the United States of America; America

Měiguórén 美国人 an American; the Americans

měihǎo 美好 exquisite; fine

měihuà 美化 to beautify

Měijí 美籍 of American nationality

Měijīn 美金 the (American) dollar

měijǐng 美景 beautiful scenery; beautiful landscape

Měijūn 美军 American troops; U.S. forces

měilì 美丽 beautiful; pretty; fair

měimǎn 美满 (said of a life, home, etc.) happy; sweet

měimiào 美妙 exquisite; very pleasant

měinǚ 美女 a beautiful woman; a beauty

měiróng 美容 to apply make-up or undergo plastic surgery

měiróngyuàn 美容院 a beauty parlor

měishí 美食 fine food; delicacies

měishù 美术 the fine arts

měishùguǎn 美术馆 an art museum (or gallery)

měiwèi 美味 delicious; tasty

měixué 美学 esthetics; aesthetics

Měiyǔ 美语 American English

Měiyuán 美元 the American dollar; the U.S. dollar

měizhōng-bùzú 美中不足 a flaw that mars perfection

Měizhōu 美洲 the Americas

měi 镁 magnesium

mèi 妹 a younger sister

mèimei 妹妹 a younger sister

mèilì 魅力 glamor; sexiness; attractiveness; spell; charm; charisma

mēn 闷 ① (said of weather, rooms, etc.) oppressive or suffocating; stuffy ② to cover the tea pot for a while when one makes tea with boiling water ③ to shut oneself or somebody indoors ④ (said of a sound) muffled
⇨mèn

M

ménrè 闷热 sticky; sultry; sweltering

mén 门 ① a door; a gateway ② a piece of (artillery); a (cannon) ③ a sect; a school ④ a class; a category ⑤ the key; the turning point ⑥ a clan; a family ⑦ a surname

méndāng-hùduì 门当户对 families of equal standing; well-matched

ménhù 门户 ① a family ② a strategic position ③ a sect; a bloc ④ a door

ménjìn 门禁 a checkpoint at the gate

ménkǎn 门槛 a threshold; a doorsill

ménkǒu 门口 a gate; a doorway; an entrance

ménpiào 门票 an admission ticket; an entrance ticket

ménshì 门市 to sell by retail; to sell over the counter

ménshìbù 门市部 a retail department; a sales department

ménzhěn 门诊 to treat patients at the OPD; the outpatient service

mèn 闷 melancholy; depressed; bored; in low spirits
⇨mēn

men/mén 们 an adjunct to a pronoun or noun to indicate plurality

méngyá 萌芽 ① the initial stage of something ② to sprout; to be in bud

méng 蒙 ① to cover (up); to wrap ② naive; childish ③ ignorant; gullible; stupid ④ to cheat; to deceive; to fool ⑤ to bear; to take
⇨Měng

méngjūn 盟军 allied troops; allied forces

měng 猛 ① bold; brave; fierce; violent ② sudden and quick (strikes, thrusts, etc.) ③ severe; strict; stringent ④ a surname

měngliè 猛烈 fierce; violent and savage

měngrán 猛然 suddenly; abruptly

Měng/Méng 蒙 short for Mongolia
⇨méng

Měnggǔ/Ménggǔ 蒙古 Mongolia; Mongolian

Mèngzǐ 孟子 Mencius

mèng 梦 ① a dream ② to dream ③ wishful thinking; wishful

mèngdào 梦到 to dream about

mènghuàn 梦幻 illusion; a dream; reverie

mèngjiàn 梦见 to dream

mèngjìng 梦境 dreamland

mèngxiǎng 梦想 ① a daydream ② to dream of

mèngyǎn 梦魇 a nightmare; a bad dream

mī 眯 to close one's eyes into narrow slits
⇨mí

míbǔ 弥补 to stop or fill up (a gap); to supplement

mímàn 弥漫 ① to be present all over; to fill the air ② brimming or overflowing water ③ to permeate

mí 迷 ① to enchant; to be crazy about; to charm; to fascinate ② a fiend; a fan ③ indistinct; vague; dim

mígōng 迷宫 a labyrinth; a maze

míhu 迷糊 ① muddle-headed ② unconscious; half awake and half asleep ③ dazzled ④ vague; dim; indistinct

míhuò 迷惑 ① to misguide; to delude; to confuse; to mislead ② confused; puzzled; bewildered

míliàn 迷恋 to be in blind love with; to be infatuated with; to be a slave of

mílù 迷路 to go astray; to get lost

míní 迷你 mini

mírén 迷人 charming; fascinating; enchanting

míshī 迷失 to get lost; to lose (one's way, etc.)

M

míxìn 迷信 to believe blindly; superstition

mí/mǐ 眯 a foreign body getting into the eye ⇨mī

mí 谜 a riddle; a puzzle; a conundrum; an enigma

míyǔ 谜语 a riddle; a conundrum

mǐ 米 ① meter (the fundamental unit of length in the metric system) ② hulled or husked rice; uncooked rice ③ a shelled or a husked seed

mǐfàn 米饭 cooked rice

mǐfěn 米粉 ① rice flour ② thin noodles made of rice flour

mǐkāng 米糠 rice bran; paddy chaff

Mǐlán 米兰 Milan, an industrial city in central Lombardy, in N Italy

mì 觅 to seek; to search or look for

mìjué 秘诀 a knack; secrets (of success, etc.); the key (to the solution of a problem)

mìmì 秘密 secret; confidential; hidden; clandestine

mìshū 秘书 a secretary

mìshūzhǎng 秘书长 a secretary-general

mì 密 ① dense; tight; thick ② close; intimate ③ secret; confidential; hidden

mìdù 密度 density

mìfēng 密封 to seal tightly or securely

mìjí 密集 concentrated; crowded together

mìmǎ 密码 a secret code

mìqiè 密切 (said of relations, contact, etc.) close or intimate

mì 蜜 ① honey; nectar (in a flower) ② sweet; syrupy; honeyed

mìfēng 蜜蜂 a honeybee; a bee

mián 眠 ① to sleep; sleep ② to hibernate; hibernation

miányán 绵延 to stretch over a long distance

miányáng 绵羊 sheep

mián 棉 cotton

miánbèi 棉被 a cotton quilt

miánhuā 棉花 cotton

miányī 棉衣 cotton clothes

miǎn 免 ① to dismiss (from office) ② to forego; to spare; to excuse; to exempt ③ to avoid; to escape; to evade

miǎnbuliǎo 免不了 unavoidable; to have to

miǎnchú 免除 ① to exempt ② to prevent

miǎnde 免得 to save (the trouble of); to avoid; so as not to

miǎnfèi 免费 free of charge; gratuitous

miǎnshuì 免税 free of duty; duty-free

miǎnyì 免疫 immunity

miǎnlì 勉励 to encourage; to urge

miǎnqiǎng 勉强 ① involuntarily; reluctantly ② barely ③ to force ④ unconvincing

Miǎndiàn 缅甸 Burma; Myanmar

miàn 面 ① the face of a person ② the surface; the top; the face ③ to indicate something flat ④ extent; range; scale; scope ⑤ to face or confront; to look ⑥ face-to-face; in or to one's face; personally; directly ⑦ (mathematics) a plane ⑧ a side; a direction; an aspect ⑨ flour ⑩ dough ⑪ noodles

miànbāo 面包 bread

miànbāochē 面包车 a minibus; a minivan

miànbāodiàn 面包店 a bakery

miànduì 面对 to face; to confront; opposite; facing

miànduìmiàn 面对面 face-to-face; vis-à-vis

miànfěn 面粉 flour

miànjī 面积 area

miànjù 面具 a mask

miànkǒng 面孔 the face (of a person)

miànlín 面临 to be faced with; to be confronted with; to be up against

miànmào 面貌 appearance;

face; looks

miànmiàn-jùdào 面面俱到 well considered in every respect

miànmù 面目 face; features; looks; appearance; countenance

miànqián 面前 before; in front of; in the presence of

miànróng 面容 countenance; face

miànshì 面试 an oral quiz; an audition; an interview

miàntán 面谈 to talk face-to-face; to take up a matter with somebody personally

miàntiáo 面条 noodles; spaghetti; vermicelli

miànzi 面子 ① honor; one's face (in the figurative sense) ② the outside or facing of a garment

miáo 苗 ① a sprout ② descendants; posterity ③ the Miao tribe in southwestern China ④ summer hunting ⑤ a surname ⑥ a beginning or omen

Miáolì 苗栗 Miaoli, a county in central Taiwan

miáo 描 ① to trace; to draw; to sketch ② to describe; to depict

miáohuì 描绘 to paint; to sketch; to describe

miáoshù 描述 to describe

miáoxiě 描写 to describe; to portray

miǎo 秒 ① (said of time or a degree) a second ② the beard of grain

miǎoxiǎo 渺小 very small; tiny; infinitesimal

miào 妙 ① wonderful; excellent ② very interesting; intriguing ③ clever; subtle; ingenious

miào 庙 a temple; a shrine

miàohuì 庙会 a fair held at the site of a temple when the faithful converge to worship the deity

miàoyǔ 庙宇 a temple; a shrine

miè 灭 ① to destroy; to ruin; to wipe out; to exterminate ② to put out; to extinguish; to go out

mièwáng 灭亡 to perish

mièshì 蔑视 to disdain; to slight; to flout or disregard (rules, etc.); to defy (orders, etc.)

mín 民 ① the people; the subject; the populace; the public ② civilians ③ a surname

mínbīng 民兵 ① a militiaman ② a militia force

mínfǎ 民法 the civil law; the civil code

míngē 民歌 a folk song; a ballad

mínguó 民国 ① a republic; a democracy ② the Republic of China, founded in 1912

mínháng 民航 civil aviation

Mínháng Jú 民航局 Civil Aeronautics Administration (CAA)

mínjiān 民间 among the people

Mínjìndǎng 民进党 Democratic Progressive Party (DPP)

mínshēng 民生 the people's livelihood

mínshì 民事 ① civil affairs ② agricultural affairs

mínsú 民俗 folkways

mínxuǎn 民选 popularly elected

mínyáo 民谣 a folk song

mínyì 民意 public opinion; popular sentiments

mínyì dàibiǎo 民意代表 people's representatives

mínyíng 民营 privately owned

mínyòng 民用 civil; for civil use

mínzhòng 民众 the people; the multitude; the masses; the populace

mínzhǔ 民主 democratic; democracy

mínzhǔ zhèngzhì 民主政治 democracy

mínzú 民族 a nation; a people

mínzúxìng 民族性 national character

mínzúxué 民族学 ethnology

Mǐnnányǔ 闽南语 the southern Fujian dialect

mǐngǎn 敏感 ① sensitive ② (medicine) allergic

mǐnjié 敏捷 agile; adroit; quick;

M

nimble

mǐnruì 敏锐 keen; sharp; sharp-witted; acute

míng 名 ① a name; a designation; a title; rank ② position; honor; fame; renown; reputation ③ famous; noted; distinguished; renowned; valuable; precious; noble; rare; great

míngcè 名册 a roster; a roll

míngchēng 名称 the name or designation (of a thing)

míngcí 名词 ① a noun ② a term

míngcì 名次 one's position or standing

míngdān 名单 a name list; a roster; a roll

míng'é 名额 the number of openings, or quota (for employees, students, etc.)

míngfùqíshí 名副其实 to be worthy of the name or reputation

míngguì 名贵 valuable; precious; rare

mínghào 名号 the name (of a person, a ship, etc.)

míngjiā 名家 ① a master (in a branch of art) ② the Nominalist school of philosophy ③ an illustrious family

míngjiàng 名将 a great general or admiral

mínglì 名利 fame and gain

míngpái 名牌 ① a famous brand ② a nameplate

míngpiàn 名片 a calling card

míngqi 名气 fame; reputation; renown

míngrén 名人 a celebrity; a notable

míngshēng 名声 fame; reputation; renown

míngshèng 名胜 a scenic spot; a resort

míngtang 名堂 ① a dignified name or designation ② a result that is worth mentioning

míngxià 名下 ① under (one's) account ② to (one's) account

míngyán 名言 a maxim; an adage

míngyī 名医 a famous doctor

míngyì 名义 ① the name ② the outward reason

míngyù 名誉 ① honor; reputation ② honorary

míngzi 名字 the name (of a person, etc.)

míng 明 ① next (day or year) ② light; bright; brilliant ③ clear; understandable; to clarify; to understand; obvious; evident ④ intelligent; clever ⑤ clear; bright ⑥ daybreak; dawn ⑦ eyesight; the seeing faculty ⑦ the Ming Dynasty (1368- 1644 A.D.) ⑧ aboveboard; honest ⑨ a surname

míngbai 明白 ① to understand; to know (a trick, secret, etc.) ② clever and bright ③ obvious

Míngcháo 明朝 the Ming Dynasty (1368-1644 A.D.)

Míngdài 明代 the Ming Dynasty

mínglǐ 明理 understanding; reasonable

míngliàng 明亮 bright (eyes, etc.); well-illuminated (rooms, etc.)

míngliǎo 明了 ① to understand ② clear and evident

míngmíng 明明 obviously; plainly

míngnián 明年 next year; the coming year

míngquè 明确 clear and definite; unequivocal

míngrì 明日 ① tomorrow ② one of these days; some day

míngtiān 明天 tomorrow

míngxiǎn 明显 evident; obvious; clear

míngxìnpiàn 明信片 a postcard; a postal card

míngxīng 明星 ① a famous performer or athlete ② a bright star

míngzhī 明知 to know perfectly well; to be fully aware

míngzhì 明智 sensible; sagacious; wise

míng 鸣 ① (said of birds) to sing; to chirp; to warble; (said of cocks) to crow ② the notes of birds ③ to make sounds; to sound

míngxiǎng 冥想 deep meditation

mìng 命 ① life ② a fate; destiny; a lot ③ the ordinances of Heaven ④ orders; a command

mìng'àn 命案 a case of murder or homicide

mìnglìng 命令 to order; to command

mìngmíng 命名 to name, christen, baptize, or dub

mìngtí 命题 ① to prepare examination questions ② a proposition (in logic)

mìngyùn 命运 a fate; destiny; a lot; fortune

mìngzhòng 命中 to hit the target

miùlùn 谬论 an absurd statement; a fallacious argument

mō 摸 ① to feel or touch lightly with fingers; to caress ② to grope ③ to try to find out; to seek after; ④ to try to get at

mōsuo 摸索 ① to do things slowly ② to grope (in the dark, the meaning of, etc.); to feel (in one's pocket, etc.)

mó 模 ① to imitate; to copy ② a model; a norm ③ blurred; indistinct
⇨mú

mófàn 模范 an example; a model

mófǎng 模仿 to imitate; to copy

móhu 模糊 ① dim; vague; ambiguous ② to obscure

mónǐ 模拟 to simulate; to imitate

móshì 模式 a model; a formula; a miniature; a pattern

mótèr 模特儿 ① a model (for artists, photographers, etc.) ② a manikin

móxíng 模型 a model; a formula; a miniature; a pattern

mó 膜 ① membrane ② a film; a thin coating ③ to kneel and wor-

ship

mócā 摩擦 ① to chafe; to scour ② friction

mótuōchē 摩托车 a motorcycle

mó 磨 ① to dawdle; to waste time; to while away ② to rub; to grind; to polish; to wear ③ sufferings; obstacles; setbacks
⇨mò

móliàn 磨炼 to train; to harden; to discipline

mógu 蘑菇 ① a variety of edible mushrooms ② to dawdle; to dilly-dally ③ to pester; to worry

mófǎ 魔法 witchcraft; wizardry; sorcery; magic

móguǐ 魔鬼 devils; demons; evil spirits

móshù 魔术 witchcraft; wizardry; sorcery; magic

mǒ 抹 ① to wipe; to rub; to mop ② to smear; to apply to ③ to obliterate; to blot out
⇨mò

mǒbù 抹布 a dish cloth; a cleaning rag

mǒhēi 抹黑 (informal) to blacken someone's name; to throw mud at; to bring shame on; to discredit; mudslinging

mǒshā 抹杀 to withhold recognition from; to obliterate; to blot out

mò 末 ① last; final ② unimportant; insignificant ③ the end; the tip

mòqī/mòqí 末期 the last stage; the terminal stage

mò 没 ① to sink; to submerge ② to overflow; to rise beyond ③ to disappear ④ to go into oblivion ⑤ none; exhausted ⑥ eliminated ⑦ completed; finished ⑧ to take property away from another; to confiscate ⑨ to die
⇨méi

mòluò 没落 ① to sink ② the decline (of an empire, etc.)

mòshōu 没收 to confiscate; confiscation

mò 抹 ① to plaster ② a tight undergarment ③ to turn ⇨mǒ

mòli 茉莉 white jasmine

mòshēng 陌生 unfamiliar; strange; inexperienced

mòshēngrén 陌生人 a stranger

mò 莫 ① not ② a surname

mòbù 莫不 there is no one that does not; there is no one that is not

mòdà 莫大 greatest; utmost

mòguòyú 莫过于 Nothing (or no one) is more...than...

mòmíng 莫名 inexpressible; indescribable

mòmíngqímiào 莫名其妙 ① incomprehensible; mysterious; baffling ② impossible (as in an impossible person)

Mòsīkē 莫斯科 Moscow

Mòzháté 莫札特 Wolfgang Amadeus Mozart, 1756-1791, Austrian composer

mòshì 漠视 ① to despise ② to ignore

mò 墨 ① a Chinese ink stick; ink ② calligraphy ③ black; dark ④ a black dye ⑤ literate; letters; learning ⑥ statutes; institutions

mòshuǐ 墨水 ① ink ② learning; letters

Mòxīgē 墨西哥 Mexico

mòmò 默默 ① quietly; silently ② secretly; in one's heart

mòqì 默契 a tacit understanding; an implicit agreement; a secret agreement

mò 磨 ① a mill ② to turn around ③ to grind (grain, etc.) ⇨mó

móu 牟 ① to seek ② to bellow (or low)

móu 谋 ① to scheme; to plan; to plot; to design ② a scheme; a stratagem; a conspiracy ③ to seek; to try to get ④ to consult ⑤ astute; resourceful

móuqiú 谋求 to try to get; to seek

móushā 谋杀 to murder

móushēng 谋生 to make a living; to get a livelihood

mǒu 某 ① a certain person or thing ② formerly used in place of "I"

mǒumǒu 某某 so-and-so; a certain person

mǒurén 某人 ① a certain person ② a pronoun used in place of one's own name

mǒuxiē 某些 certain (things, people, etc.)

mú/mó 模 a mold; a form; a matrix ⇨mó

mújù/mójù 模具 a mold; a matrix; a pattern; a die

múyàng/móyàng 模样 appearances; looks

múzǔ/mózǔ 模组 a module

mǔ 母 ① one's mother ② female ③ mother—(figuratively) the origin

mǔgōngsī 母公司 a parent company

mǔjī 母鸡 a hen

mǔnǚ 母女 mother and daughter

mǔqīn 母亲 mother

mǔtǐ 母体 the mother body

mǔxiào 母校 one's alma mater; Alma Mater

mǔyǔ 母语 ① one's native language ② a parent language

mǔzǐ 母子 ① mother and son ② principal and interest

mǔ 亩 a Chinese land measure (equal to 797 square yards)

mù 木 ① a tree; wood; timber ② made of wood; wooden ④ simple; honest ⑤ senseless; benumbed ⑥ a coffin

mùbǎn 木板 planks; boards

mùcái 木材 lumber; timber

mùguā 木瓜 a papaya

mùjiang 木匠 a carpenter; a woodworker

mùkè 木刻 wood engraving; a woodcut

mùliào 木料 wooden material;

N

wood; lumber

mù'ǒu 木偶 a puppet

mùtou 木头 ① wood ② a stupid fellow

mùwū 木屋 a log cabin

mùzhà 木栅 a stockade

mù 目 ① the eye ② a table of contents; a category

mùbiāo 目标 ① an objective; a target; to target ② an aim; a goal

mùdì 目的 a purpose; an objective; an end; an aim

mùdìdì 目的地 a destination

mùdǔ 目睹 to see directly; to witness

mùguāng 目光 insight; vision; sight

mùjī/mùjí 目击 to witness

mùlù 目录 ① contents ② a list; a catalogue

mùqián 目前 now; the present

mùzhōng-wúrén 目中无人 to be supercilious; to be overweening

mùyù 沐浴 ① to bathe ② to steep in or receive favor ③ to soak in

mù 牧 ① to pasture; to shepherd ② a pasture ③ to govern ④ a magistrate

mùchǎng 牧场 a pasture; a ranch

mùmín 牧民 to shepherd the people; to govern the people

mùqū 牧区 a pastoral area

mùshī 牧师 a preacher; a clergyman

mùyángrén 牧羊人 a shepherd

mùyè 牧业 animal husbandry; livestock industry

mù 募 ① to recruit or enlist (personnel) ② to raise (funds); to collect

mùjí 募集 to recruit; to raise; to collect

mùkuǎn 募款 to raise funds

mù 墓 a grave; a tomb; a mausoleum

mùdì 墓地 the site of a grave or tomb; a cemetery

mù 幕 ① a screen; a curtain ② a tent ③ an act ④ an adviser; staffs ⑤ to cover

mùhòu 幕后 behind the scenes; backstage

mùliáo 幕僚 staffs; secretaries; advisers

Mùníhēi 幕尼黑 ① Munich, Germany ② (figuratively) international appeasement

mùsīlín 穆斯林 a Muslim

N

ná 拿 ① to hold in one's hand; to grasp; to take ② to arrest; to apprehend; to capture ③ to use; to employ (a method, device, etc.) ④ with; in

náchu 拿出 to take out

ná...láishuō 拿……来说 to take...for example

nániē 拿捏 ① deliberately make things difficult for others ② to pretend to observe rules of propriety

Nápólún 拿破仑 Napoleon Bonaparte (1769-1821), a famous French military strategist and emperor

náqù 拿去 to take away

náshǒu 拿手 to be particularly good or dexterous at

nǎ 哪 (as interrogative) where; which
⇨na

nǎge 哪个 ① Which one? ② Who is it?

nǎli 哪里 where

nǎpà 哪怕 even if

nǎr 哪儿 where

nǎxiē 哪些 which; who; what

nà 那 ① that; those ② then; in that case

nàbiān 那边 that way or side; over there (often emphasizing "not here")

nàge 那个 ① that one ② embarrassing ③ funny ④ too much, too far, too hot, etc.

nàli 那里 that place; there; over there

nàme 那么 ① so; that; in that way ② then; such being the case ③ about; or so

nàr 那儿 that place; at that place; there; over there

nàshí 那时 at that time or moment; then

nàtiān 那天 that day

nàxiē 那些 those

nàyàng 那样 ① that case or manner ② that (indicating degree)

nà 呐 ① to shout ② to speak hesitatingly

nàhǎn 呐喊 to give a whoop, or to shout (in a battle, etc.)

nà 纳 ① to receive; to take; to accept; to admit; to adopt ② to offer as tribute ③ to enjoy; to feel ④ to patch old clothes ⑤ a surname

nàmènr 纳闷儿 ① to feel depressed ② to feel curious

nàrù 纳入 to bring into

nàshuì 纳税 to pay duties or taxes

na 哪 a sentence-final particle ⇨**nǎ**

nǎishì 乃是 ① but ② which is...; to be; really is (are)

nǎizhì 乃至 ① so that; so...as to; leading to ② hence; consequently

nǎi 奶 ① the breasts of a woman ② milk ③ grandma ④ to feed with milk; to breast-feed ⑤ a term of respect for married women

nǎichá 奶茶 tea with milk

nǎifěn 奶粉 milk powder

nǎinai 奶奶 ① a term of respect for older women ② grandma

nǎiyóu 奶油 butter

nài 耐 to bear; to endure; to stand; to resist

nàifán 耐烦 patient

nàilì 耐力 endurance; staying power; stamina

nàixīn 耐心 patience; perseverance

nàixìng 耐性 patience; perseverance

nàiyòng 耐用 durable; sturdy

nán 男 ① a human male; a man; a boy; a son ② a baron

nánfāng 男方 the bridegroom's family, relatives and friends collectively

nánháizi 男孩子 a boy

nánnǚ 男女 ① male and female; men and women; both sexes ② one's children ③ attendants; servants

nánpéngyou 男朋友 a boyfriend

nánpú 男仆 a male servant

nánrén 男人 a man

nánren 男人 a husband

nánshēng 男生 a boy

nánxìng 男性 ① the male sex ② the masculine gender

nánzǐ 男子 a man

nán 南 ① south; southward ② a type of ancient music played in the south of China ③ a surname

nánběi 南北 ① north and south ② from north to south ③ (in ancient China) a man

nánbian 南边 ① the south; the southern side ② the southern provinces of China

nánbù 南部 southern part; south

Nánchāng 南昌 Nanchang, capital of Jiangxi Province

nánfāng 南方 the south; the South

Nán Fēi 南非 South Africa

N

Nánjīng 南京 Nanjing

nánmiàn 南面 ① the south ② the throne facing south—the monarch

Nánshā Qúndǎo 南沙群岛 Nansha Qundao; the Spratly Islands

Nánsīlāfū 南斯拉夫 Yugoslavia

nánxià 南下 to go down south

Nán Yà 南亚 South Asia

Nányáng 南洋 ① the area which covers Southeast Asia and Indonesia ② the Chinese coastal region south of the Shandong ③ the South Seas

nán 难 ① difficult; not easy; hard ② unable; not in a position to ③ unpleasant; not good ⇨nàn

nándào 难道 Is it possible...? Do you really mean to say...?

nándé 难得 ① rare; hard to get; hard to come by ② fortunate; lucky ③ rarely; seldom

nándù 难度 degree of difficulty; difficulty

nánguài 难怪 ① no wonder that ② it's understandable that

nánguān 难关 an impasse; an obstacle or obstruction difficult to overcome; a difficult situation; a crisis

nánguò 难过 ① to feel uneasy; to feel bad; to feel sorry ② hard to endure or bear; uncomfortable ③ difficult; hard

nánkān 难堪 ① to embarrass; embarrassment ② intolerable; unbearable

nánkàn 难看 ① bad-looking; not pleasant to the eye; ugly; offensive; repulsive ② embarrassing; awkward

nánmiǎn 难免 can hardly avoid; inescapable

nánshòu 难受 ① to feel bad; to feel sorry ② unbearable; intolerable ③ to suffer pain; to feel unwell

nántí 难题 a hard nut to crack; a tough problem; a puzzle

nánwàng 难忘 difficult to forget; unforgettable

nányǐ 难以 difficult; hard to

nàn 难 ① disaster; calamity; misfortune ② to rebuke; to reprove; to reprimand ③ to discountenance ⇨nán

nànmín 难民 refugees

nángkuò/nánguā 囊括 to encompass; to include; to comprise

nǎohuǒ 恼火 to become irritated; annoyed

nǎo 脑 the brain

nǎodai 脑袋 the head

nǎohǎi 脑海 the mind

nǎojīn 脑筋 brains; mentality; mental capacity

nǎolì 脑力 brains; mental capability; mental exertion

nǎozi 脑子 ① the brain ② mental capability

nào 闹 ① to disturb; to agitate; to trouble ② to have or experience (disasters, sickness, etc.) ③ noisy; uproarious; stormy; clamorous

nàoqū 闹区 a market quarter; a business district; a downtown area

nàoshì 闹事 to cause trouble or uproar

nàoxiàohua 闹笑话 to arouse ridicule; to make oneself a laughingstock

nàozhewánr 闹着玩儿 to raise hell just for fun or joke

nàozhōng 闹钟 an alarm clock

ne 呢 a sentence-final particle indicating response to expectation ⇨ní

nèi 内 ① inside; within; inner; interior ② wife

nèibù 内部 the interior; the internal parts

nèidì 内地 the hinterland; the inland

nèigé 内阁 the cabinet

nèihán 内含 to contain

N

nèihán 内涵 (logic) intension; connotation

nèiháng 内行 a specialist; an expert

nèikē 内科 internal medicine

nèikù 内裤 underpants; briefs

nèilù 内陆 inland; interior

nèimù 内幕 an inside story

nèiróng 内容 ① content ② the meaning, theme, etc. of a literary work

nèiwài 内外 ① inside and outside ② domestic and foreign; home and abroad ③ around; about

nèixiáng 内详 the name and address of the sender enclosed

nèixiāo 内销 (said of local products) for domestic sale or market

nèixīn 内心 heart

nèiyī 内衣 underwear; undergarments

nèizài 内在 inherent; intrinsic; internal

nèizàng 内脏 internal organs; viscera

nèizhàn 内战 a civil war

nèizhèng 内政 internal (or domestic) affairs

Nèizhèng Bù 内政部 the Ministry of the Interior

nèn 嫩 ① tender; delicate ② young; immature ③ (of color) light

néng 能 ① can; to be able to ② capability; talent; competence ③ energy, as atomic energy

néngbùnéng 能不能 can or can't; may or may not

néngfǒu 能否 can or can't; may or may not

nénggàn 能干 capable; able; very competent and efficient

nénggē-shànwǔ 能歌善舞 (usually said of a woman) skilled in both singing and dancing

nénggòu 能够 able to; capable of; may; can

néngjiàndù 能见度 visibility

nénglì 能力 ① a faculty; ability;

capability ② power, as the power of the Almighty, etc.

néngliàng 能量 ① (physics) energy ② capabilities

néngnai 能耐 skill; ability; capability

néngshǒu 能手 a capable or competent person; an expert

néngyuán 能源 the sources of energy

ńg 嗯 the nasal sound used to express doubt
⇨ǹg, ňg

ňg 嗯 the nasal sound used when one is surprised or indifferent
⇨ńg, ǹg

ǹg 嗯 the nasal sound used when one makes a response or promise
⇨ńg, ňg

Níbó'ěr 尼泊尔 Nepal

nílóng 尼龙 (textile) nylon

Níluóhé 尼罗河 the Nile River; the Nile

ní 呢 ① a woolen fabric ② a murmur
⇨ne

ní 泥 ① mud; mire; earth; soil; clay ② mashed vegetables or fruit; paste ③ to paste; to plaster
⇨nì

nítǔ 泥土 mud; clay; earth; soil

nǐ 拟 ① to plan; to intend; to decide; to determine ② to draft; to draw up; to design ③ to imitate

nǐdìng 拟定 to draw up or map out (a plan); to draft

nǐ 你 you (singular)

nǐmen 你们 you (plural)

nì 泥 ① to be tied down by conventions, old practices; very conservative ② to request with sweet words ③ inapplicable
⇨ní

nìchēng 昵称 a term of endearment; a pet name

nì 逆 ① to oppose; to go against ② beforehand; in advance ③ inverse; converse; adverse

nìchā 逆差 (commerce) an ad-

N

verse balance of trade; a deficit

níjìng 逆境 adverse circumstances; adversity

nìliú 逆流 ① an adverse current ② against the current; against the stream; up the stream

nìzhuǎn 逆转 ① to deteriorate; to turn to the worse ② a reversal

nì 腻 ① fatty or greasy (food) ② smooth ③ dirty ④ bored; tired; weary

nián 年 ① a year ② one's age ③ a surname

niánchū 年初 the beginning of the year

niándài 年代 ① an age, era, generation, etc. ② years in a decade

niándǐ 年底 the end of a year

niándù 年度 a year fixed arbitrarily for convenience, a better administrative purpose, etc., as a fiscal year, a school year, etc.

niánfèn 年份 age; time

niánguān 年关 the end of a year when all accounts and debts must be settled

niánhuà 年画 drawings or pictures sold at Lunar New Year, usually on the subject of good luck

niánhuì 年会 an annual meeting or convention

niánjí 年级 (in school) a grade

niánjì 年纪 years; age

niánlǎo 年老 to get old; aged

niánlíng 年龄 age

niánnián 年年 every year; year after year

niánqīng 年青 young; juvenile

niánqīng 年轻 young; youthful; youth

niánshào 年少 young

niántóu 年头 ① times ② a year ③ the beginning of a year ④ a harvest

niánxiàn 年限 a service life

niánzhǎng 年长 old or aged; older

niánzhōng 年终 the end of a year

niánzī 年资 ① the years one

spends in an endeavor or job ② seniority

nián 粘 sticky; glutinous; adhesive
⇨zhān

nián 黏 ① to stick ② sticky; glutinous; gluey; adhesive; clammy; viscid

niǎn 捻 to twist with fingers; to toy with

niǎn 撵 ① to expel; to oust; to drive ② to catch up

niàn 廿 twenty

niàn 念 ① to read out aloud; to chant; to recite ② to study; to attend school ③ to think of; to miss; to remember ④ twenty

niànshū 念书 ① to read a book aloud ② to study ③ to receive an education

niàntou 念头 an idea; a thought

niáng 娘 ① mother ② girls or women

niángjia 娘家 one's wife's family

niàng 酿 ① to brew; to ferment ② to take shape or form slowly ③ wine

niǎo 鸟 a bird

niǎolèi 鸟类 birds

niào 尿 ① urine ② to urinate

niē 捏 ① to knead; to pinch; to squeeze or press with fingers ② to mold (mud, etc.) ③ to fabricate; to trump up; to make up

niēzào 捏造 to fabricate (evidence, etc.); to trump up (charges, etc.)

nín 您 a deferential form of "nǐ 你" (you)

níng 宁 peace; repose; serenity; tranquility
⇨nìng

níngjìng 宁静 quiet; tranquil; serene; placid; calm

níng/nǐng 拧 to twist; to pinch; to wring
⇨nìng, nìng

níngméng 柠檬 lemon

nínggù 凝固 (said of liquid) to

N

congeal; to solidify

níngjié 凝结 to condense; to curdle

níngjù 凝聚 ① to concentrate ② to curdle

níngshì 凝视 to gaze (lovingly)

níng 拧 ① to wrench; to twist; to screw ② wrong; mistaken ③ to differ; to disagree
⇨níng, nìng

Nìng 宁 a surname

nìng/níng 宁 would rather; had rather; would sooner
⇨níng

nìngkě/níngkě 宁可 would rather

nìngkěn/níngkěn 宁肯 would rather

nìngyuàn/níngyuàn 宁愿 would rather; would sooner

nìng 拧 pigheaded; stubborn
⇨níng, níng

niú 牛 ① an ox; cattle; a cow; a bull ② (said of a person) stubborn; headstrong ③ a surname

Niúdùn 牛顿 Sir Isaac Newton (1642-1727), English philosopher and mathematician

niúnǎi 牛奶 (cow's) milk

niúpái 牛排 steak; beefsteak

niúròu 牛肉 beef

niúròumiàn 牛肉面 noodles served with stewed beef

niúrǔ 牛乳 cow milk

niúzǎikù/niúzǐkù 牛仔裤 blue jeans; jeans

niǔ 扭 ① to wrench; to twist; to turn; to wring ② to seize; to grasp

niǔlì 扭力 (physics) torsion

niǔqū 扭曲 to twist

niǔzhuǎn 扭转 ① to turn round ② to turn (the tide of a war or contest) for the better ③ to wring; to wrench; to twist

niǔkòu 纽扣 a button

Niǔxīlán 纽西兰 New Zealand

Niǔyuē 纽约 New York

niǔ 钮 buttons

niǔkòu 钮扣 buttons

nóng 农 ① agriculture; farming ② to farm ③ a farmer; a peasant

nóngchǎnpǐn 农产品 farm products; agricultural products

nóngchǎng 农场 a farm

nóngcūn 农村 farm village

nóngdì 农地 agricultural fields; farmland

nóngfū 农夫 a husbandman; a farmer

nónghù 农户 a peasant family

nónghuì 农会 a farmers' association (or cooperative)

nóngjiā 农家 a farming family

nóngjù 农具 farm tools; agricultural implements

nónglì 农历 the lunar calendar

nónglín 农林 agriculture and forestry

nóngmào shìchǎng 农贸市场 agricultural trade market

nóngmín 农民 farmers; peasants; the farming population

nóngrén 农人 a farmer; a husbandman

nóngtián 农田 agricultural fields; farmland

nóngyào 农药 pesticide; agricultural chemicals

nóngyè 农业 agriculture; farming

nóngzuòwù 农作物 farm products; crops

nóng 浓 ① (said of drinks, liquids, etc.) thick; strong; heavy; concentrated ② (said of colors) deep; dark ③ dense ④ (said of a smell) strong; heavy

nóngdù 浓度 ① (chemistry) concentration ② density

nónghòu 浓厚 ① (said of material things) thick and dense ② (said of feelings, interest, etc.) deep; great

nóngyù 浓郁 strong; heavy; rich

nòng 弄 ① to handle; to do ② to play with ③ to make fun of; to mock
⇨lòng

nòngcuò 弄错 to make a mis-

O

take

nònghuài 弄坏 to bungle; to spoil

nòngxū-zuòjiǎ 弄虚作假 to practice fraud; to employ trickery; to resort to deception

núbì 奴婢 slaves; servants

núcai 奴才 ① a slave; a serf; a bondman ② a good-for-nothing; a useless fellow; a yes-man

núlì 奴隶 a serf; a slave

núyì 奴役 to enslave

nǔlì 努力 to make efforts; to strive

nù 怒 ① temper; anger; rage; angry; furious ② to put forth with vigor (as plants, etc.); to sprout; to spring up ③ forceful and vigorous

nùhǒu 怒吼 to roar; roars

nùhuǒ 怒火 flames of fury; fury

nùqì 怒气 anger; wrath; rage; fury

nǚ 女 ① a woman, a female ② a daughter; a girl; a maiden; a lady

nǚ'ér 女儿 ① one's daughter ② a girl

nǚfāng 女方 on the woman's part (when the other party concerned is a man)

nǚhái 女孩 a girl

nǚláng 女郎 a maiden; a young woman; a young girl

nǚpéngyou 女朋友 a girlfriend

nǚrén 女人 a woman

nǚshén 女神 a goddess

nǚshēng 女生 a girl

nǚshì 女士 Ms.; a lady

nǚwáng 女王 a queen regnant

nǚxìng 女性 female; the fair sex

nǚyǒu 女友 a girl friend

nǚzhǔjué 女主角 a leading lady; a heroine

nǚzǐ 女子 a woman; a girl

nuǎn 暖 warm or genial (weather)

nuǎnhuo 暖和 ① warm ② to warm up

nuǎnqì 暖气 warm vapor; warm air

nüèdài 虐待 to maltreat; to torture

nuó 挪 to move; to shift; to transfer

Nuówēi 挪威 Norway

Nuòbèi'ěr 诺贝尔 Alfred Bernard Nobel, 1833-1896, Swedish chemist

Nuòbèi'ěrjiǎng 诺贝尔奖 Nobel prizes

nuòyán 诺言 a promise; a pledge

nuòruò 懦弱 weak; cowardly

O

ō 噢 (an interjection) oh

ó 哦 (an interjection) oh; ah

ōu 欧 ① Europe; European ② to vomit ③ to beat ④ to sing ⑤ (electricity) ohm, the SI unit of electrical resistance ⑥ a surname

Ōu Měi 欧美 Europe and America

Ōuzhōu 欧洲 Europe

ōudǎ 殴打 to fisticuff

ǒutù 呕吐 to vomit; to disgorge

ǒu 偶 ① an idol; an image ② coincidentally; accidentally ③ once in a while; occasionally ④ not to be taken for granted ⑤ an even number ⑥ a counterpart ⑦ a mate; to mate ⑧ one's company; fellows; buddies

ǒu'ér 偶而 occasionally

ǒu'ér 偶尔 occasionally

ǒurán 偶然 ① by chance ② unexpectedly

ǒuxiàng 偶像 an idol; an image

P

pā 趴 ① to prostrate oneself; to lie face downwards ② to bend over

pá 扒 ① to gather up; to rake up ② to stew; to braise ③ to scratch; to claw
⇨bā

pá 爬 ① to creep; to crawl ② to climb; to clamber ③ to scratch ④ to lie face downwards

páshān 爬山 to climb mountains

páshang 爬上 to climb up

pà 怕 ① to fear; to dread; afraid; scared; apprehensive ② maybe; perhaps; I am afraid....; I suppose....

pāi 拍 ① to strike with the hand; to slap; to clap; to pat; to swat ② to fawn; to flatter ③ the time or beat of a piece of music

pāimǎpì 拍马屁 to flatter; to soft-soap; to curry favor

pāimài 拍卖 to auction off; an auction

pāipiàn 拍片 to shoot a film

pāishè 拍摄 to take (a picture)

pāizhào 拍照 to take a picture or photo

pāizi 拍子 (music) time; rhythm

pái 排 ① a row; a line; a rank ② to arrange; to put in order ③ (military) a platoon ④ to clear out ⑤ to expel; to exclude ⑥ to rehearse ⑦ a raft ⑧ to push

páichì 排斥 to discriminate against; to expel

páichú 排除 to get rid of; to remove

páidàng / páidǎng 排档 ① C a row of market stalls ② T a gear (in an automobile engine)

páiduì 排队 to line up; to stand in a queue

páiháng 排行 one's seniority among brothers and sisters

páijǐ 排挤 ① to expel somebody out of an inner circle or clique, etc. ② to push aside; to elbow out

páiliè 排列 to arrange in series, rows, etc.

páimíng 排名 to list names according to the order of seniority or position

páiqìguǎn 排气管 an exhaust pipe

páiqiú 排球 volleyball

páishuǐ 排水 to drain water; drainage

páishuǐgōu 排水沟 a discharge ditch; a drainage ditch

páizhǎng 排长 a platoon leader

páihuái 徘徊 ① to linger; to walk to and fro ② hesitating ③ to fluctuate

pái 牌 ① a bulletin board ② a tablet; a signboard; a plate ③ a card; a tag; a label ④ a trademark; a brand

páizi 牌子 ① a bulletin board ② a card; a label ③ a brand ④ a signboard; a plate

pài 派 ① a division; a school (of philosophy, art, etc.); a party ② a faction ③ to assign; to dispatch; to send ④ pie

pàibié 派别 ① factions ② schools

(of thought)

pàichūsuǒ 派出所 a police station

pàiqiǎn 派遣 to dispatch

pàitóu 派头 manner; air

pàixì 派系 ① factions (within a political party, etc.) ② affiliation with (a school or party)

pàiyuán 派员 to send a staffer or officer

pàizhù 派驻 to accredit

Pān 番 a county in Guangdong province
⇨fān

pān 攀 ① to hold to; to climb; to hang on; to clamber ② to involve

pāndēng 攀登 to climb; to scale

pānyán 攀岩 rock climbing

pán 盘 ① a tray; a plate; a dish ② to investigate; to interrogate ③ twisted; entangled; entwined; intricate; winding; to entangle; to entwine ④ (said of a chess match, etc.) a round

pánxuán 盘旋 to circle; to hover around

pánzi 盘子 a tray; a plate; a dish

pàn 判 to judge; to conclude

pànchǔ 判处 to sentence; to condemn

pàndìng 判定 to judge; to decide

pànduàn 判断 judgment, decision, or conclusion

pànjué 判决 a verdict; a sentence

pàn 拚 ① to go all out ② at the risk of ③ to reject

pànmìng 拚命 to risk one's life

pàn 盼 ① to hope; to expect ② to look ③ (descriptive of the black and white of the eyes) well defined

pànwàng 盼望 to hope; to wish

pànbiàn 叛变 a mutiny; to revolt

pànnì 叛逆 ① to revolt; sedition ② one who rebels against his country or superiors

pàntú 叛徒 a rebel; an insurgent

pàn 畔 ① a side; a bank ② a boundary between fields

pángdà 庞大 immense; huge; enormous

páng 旁 ① side ② by the side of; nearby ③ other; else

pángbiān 旁边 ① the side; by the side of ② nearby; in the vicinity of

pángrén 旁人 ① bystanders; onlookers; outsiders ② the others

pángtīng 旁听 to audit

páng/pāng 磅 the noise of stone crashing
⇨bàng

pángxiè 螃蟹 a crab

pàng 胖 obese; fat; corpulent

pàngzi 胖子 a fat or corpulent person; a fatty

pāo 抛 ① to throw; to cast; to hurl ② to abandon; to reject; to give up ③ to cast aside; to leave behind

pāoqì 抛弃 to abandon; to throw away; to give up

pāo 泡 ① loose and soft; spongy ② an amount of excrement or urine
⇨pào

páo 刨 to dig; to excavate

páo 炮 to refine medicinal herbs
⇨bāo, pào

pǎo 跑 ① to run ② to run away; to flee

pǎobù 跑步 to run; to jog

pǎochē 跑车 a racer; a sports car

pǎodào 跑道 ① a track ② a runway

pào 泡 ① bubbles; suds; froth; foam ② to steep; to soak; to dip; to infuse (tea, etc.) ③ a blister ④ (slang) to dawdle; to fool around (especially with women)
⇨pāo

pàocài 泡菜 vegetables preserved in salted water

pàochá 泡茶 to infuse tea; to make tea

pàomiàn 泡面 instant noodles

pàomò 泡沫 suds; foam; froth

pàoshuǐ 泡水 to soak in water

pàotāng 泡汤 ① (said of a dream) busted; (said of money) wasted;

(said of hope) dashed ② to take a bath in the hot spring

pào 炮 ① a catapult ② an artillery piece; a cannon; a gun
⇨bāo, páo

pàodàn 炮弹 a cannonball or shot; a shell

pàohuǒ 炮火 artillery fire; gunfire

péi 陪 ① to accompany; to keep company ② to assist

péibàn 陪伴 to keep company; to accompany

péitóng 陪同 to accompany

péixùn 培训 to train; to give training

péiyǎng 培养 ① to grow (plants) ② to raise (kids) ③ to foster

péiyù 培育 to raise; to breed

péi 赔 ① to compensate or indemnify; to make up for a loss due to one's fault; to pay for ② to offer (an apology) ③ to lose money

péicháng 赔偿 compensation; indemnity; to recompense; to make amends for

péikuǎn 赔款 an indemnity; a compensation; reparations

péiqián 赔钱 ① to make a pecuniary compensation ② to lose money in business

pèi 佩 ① to wear; to carry ② to admire; to adore

pèifu 佩服 to admire; to respect

pèi 配 ① to fit; to suit; to be a match for; to match; to equal ② to dispense (medicines); to prepare (according to a demand) ③ to pair; to match ④ to join in marriage ⑤ to mate ⑥ to exile ⑦ a spouse; a partner ⑧ subordinate; supplementary; supporting; attached ⑨ to deserve; to be worthy of

pèibèi 配备 ① an outfit; equipment ② to provide; to fit out

pèifā 配发 to distribute

pèifāng 配方 to dispense prescriptions

pèihé 配合 to be in tune with; to be adapted to

pèihé 配合 compatible

pèijǐ 配给 ① to distribute in rations; to allocate ② allocation

pèijiàn 配件 accessories

pèijué 配角 ① to appear with another leading player; to costar ② a supporting role; a minor role

pèi'ǒu 配偶 a spouse; a mate

pèisè 配色 to blend (or match) colors

pèitào 配套 to form a complete set

pèiyīn 配音 (movies) to dub; dubbing; to synchronize; synchronization

pèiyuè 配乐 to dub in background music; incidental music

pèizhì 配制 to prepare or concoct according to a recipe or prescription

pēn 喷 ① to spurt; to gush ② to spray; to sprinkle

pēnqī 喷漆 to spray paint (or lacquer)

pēnshè 喷射 (said of gas or liquid) to shoot out; to jet

pén 盆 a bowl; a basin; a tub

péndì 盆地 (geology) a basin

pēngjī 抨击 to criticize; to lash

pēngrèn 烹饪 to cook or prepare (food); cooking

pēngtiáo 烹调 to cook or prepare (food); cooking

péngyou 朋友 a friend

péng 彭 ① big ② longevity ③ proud

péng 棚 a tent; a shed; a (mat) awning

péngbó 蓬勃 booming; vigorously

Péng 澎 the Pescadores

péng/pēng 澎 the roaring of colliding billows

Pénghú 澎湖 the Penghus or the Pescadores, in the Taiwan Straits

péngzhàng 膨胀 inflation; bloated; to swell

pěng 捧 ① to hold something

P

in both hands ② to boost; to flatter; to treat as a VIP ③ to support, cheer, or render assistance by one's presence

pěngchǎng 捧场 to render support or assistance (by one's presence, endorsement, etc.)

pèng 碰 ① to collide; to hit; to touch; to bump ② to meet unexpectedly; to run into ③ to take one's chance

pèngdào 碰到 ① to meet someone unexpectedly ② to touch something

pèngdīngzi 碰钉子 to be rebuked

pèngjiàn 碰见 to meet or encounter someone unexpectedly; to run into

pèngshang 碰上 to bump into

pèngzhuàng 碰撞 to hit; to run into

pī 批 ① a whole batch (of things or people); a large quantity or number ② to comment; to judge; to criticize

pīfā 批发 wholesale

pīfù 批复 to reply (to a message from a subordinate), usually by writing on the paper carrying the message

pīgǎi 批改 to correct (students' papers)

pīpàn 批判 to appraise; to judge

pīpíng 批评 to criticize; criticism; comment

pīshì 批示 to instruct or direct (usually by writing on the paper carrying a message from a subordinate)

pīzhǔn 批准 to approve; to ratify

pǐ/pēi 坯 ① group of hills ② unfired pottery

pī 披 ① to throw on (a garment, etc.); to wear untidily ② to spread out; to disperse ③ to open (a book, scroll, etc.); to unroll ④ to thumb through or read casually

pīlù 披露 to reveal; to make known; to publish

pī 劈 ① to cleave; to split; to rive; to rend ② a wedge
⇨pǐ

pí 皮 ① skin; fur; hide; leather; rind; peltry; bark ② a thin sheet ③ naughty ④ a surname

píbāo 皮包 a handbag or purse

pícǎo 皮草 furs

pídài 皮带 a leather belt

pífū 皮肤 skin

pígé 皮革 leather

píjiāzi/píjiázi 皮夹子 a wallet

píxié 皮鞋 leather shoes

píyǐngxì 皮影戏 the shadow show

píbèi 疲惫 fatigued; tired; weary

pífá 疲乏 tired; exhausted

píjuàn 疲倦 tired; exhausted; weary

píláo 疲劳 fatigue; exhaustion; weariness

píruǎn 疲软 ① tired and feeble ② (said of commodities) to decrease in demand ③ (said of finance) to weaken

píjiǔ 啤酒 beer

pípa 琵琶 pipa

píqi 脾气 a temper or disposition

pǐ 匹 ① a bolt (of cloth) ② to match ③ equal

pǐ/pī 匹 a measure word for horses

pǐ 否 evil; bad
⇨fǒu

pǐzi 痞子 a rascal; a scoundrel

pǐ/pī 劈 to split; to chop
⇨pī

pì 屁 ① a fart ② the hip

pìgu 屁股 the hip; the buttocks; the rump; the bottom

pì 辟 ① to open up; to develop ② to rid; to do away with ③ to refute

pìrú 譬如 for instance; for example; to suppose

piān/piàn 片 ① a photograph ② a phonograph record
⇨piàn

piānzi/piànzi 片子 ① a film;

a movie ② a roll of film
⇨pìanzi

piān 扁 small
⇨pìan

piān 偏 ① an auxiliary verb indicating a sense of contrariness or determination ② leaning; inclined to one side ③ biased; not fair; prejudiced; partial

piānchā 偏差 errors; deviation

piānhào 偏好 a hobby

piānjiàn 偏见 prejudice; bias

piānpì 偏僻 out-of-the-way; secluded

piānpiān 偏偏 unfortunately it happened that...

piānshí 偏食 to eat certain dishes only

piānxiàng 偏向 to lean or to be inclined toward

piānyuǎn 偏远 remote; faraway

piānzhòng 偏重 ① to give undue emphasis to ② to have extraordinary faith in (somebody)

piān 篇 ① a measure word for compositions, poems, etc. ② a chapter; a section; a part ③ a page ④ books; volumes

piānfu 篇幅 ① the length (of a piece of writing) ② space (of a periodical or newspaper)

pián 便 cheap; inexpensive
⇨bìan

piányi 便宜 ① cheap; inexpensive ② to gain advantage

pìan 片 a piece; a slice; a fragment; a chip
⇨pìan

pìanduàn 片段 ① passages or fragments of a writing ② parts; fragments

pìankè 片刻 a little while; a moment

pìanmiàn 片面 ① unilateral ② one-sided

pìanmíng 片名 title of a motion picture

pìanzi 片子 a calling card
⇨pìanzi

pìan 骗 ① to cheat; to defraud;

to swindle; to deceive ② to get by fraud

pìanrén 骗人 to cheat others; to defraud others; to swindle others; to lie

pìanzi 骗子 a swindler; a cheat; a confidence man; a racketeer; an impostor

piāo 漂 to drift; to float; to be tossed about
⇨piǎo, pìao

piāo 飘 ① to blow (in the air); to waft; to move with the wind ② a cyclone; a whirling wind ③ to float; to drift

piāoyáng 飘扬 to be blown about in the wind; to flutter

piǎo 漂 to bleach
⇨piāo, pìao

pìao 票 ① a ticket ② a ballot ③ a bill; a note ④ a hostage ⑤ amateur performance

pìaofáng 票房 ① a box office; a ticket window ② a club of amateur Peking opera actors ③ box office—(figuratively) the power of a show or performer to attract an audience

pìaojià 票价 the price of a ticket

pìaojù 票据 bills; notes; receipts

pìaoxuǎn 票选 to elect by casting ballots

pìao 漂 pretty; nice; sleek
⇨piāo, piǎo

pìaoliang 漂亮 ① pretty; handsome ② brilliant; beautiful ③ wise in worldly ways

piē 撇 ① to cast away; to throw away; to abandon ② to skim
⇨piě

piē 瞥 to have a casual and short glance; to catch a glimpse of

piě 撇 ① (calligraphy) a stroke made in the lower left direction ② to purse the mouth (in contempt or to resist an impulse to cry)
⇨piē

pīn 拼 ① to join together; to incorporate; to put together; to make a whole ② to risk ③ to spell

(a word)

pīnbó 拼搏 to struggle hard; to go all out

pīncòu 拼凑 ① to put bits together to make a whole ② (machinery) to cannibalize ③ to raise money here and there

pīnmìng 拼命 ① to risk one's life ② with all one's might

pín 贫 ① poverty; poor; destitute; impoverished ② deficiency; deficient; lack ③ garrulous

pínfá 贫乏 wanting; destitute; insufficient

pínkǔ 贫苦 poor; destitute; poverty-stricken

pínkùn 贫困 impoverished; in straitened circumstances; poor

pínmín 贫民 poor people; a pauper

pínqióng 贫穷 penury; poor; needy; destitution; poverty; impoverishment

pínxuè/pínxiě 贫血 anaemia; anaemic

pín 频 ① incessant; successive; continuous; frequently or repeatedly ② frequency; urgent; precarious

píndào 频道 (television) a channel

pínfán 频繁 frequent; incessant; busy

pínlǜ 频率 frequency

pínpín 频频 incessantly; repeatedly; continuously

pǐn 品 ① to appraise; to rate ② an article; a commodity ③ a rank or grade in the government service in former times ④ personality; character ⑤ to find out

pǐncháng 品尝 to taste (food) in order to appraise, rate, or grade its worth

pǐndé 品德 personal character

pǐnwèi 品味 taste; a savor

pǐnxíng/pǐnxìng 品行 one's moral character and performance; behavior

pǐnzhì/pǐnzhí 品质 quality

pǐnzhǒng 品种 a species or variety

pìn/pìng 聘 ① to invite for service; to employ; to engage ② to be betrothed; to be engaged ③ to ask; to inquire

pìnqǐng/pìngqǐng 聘请 to engage; to appoint

pìnrèn/pìngrèn 聘任 to employ or engage for a post

pìnyòng/pìngyòng 聘用 to employ; to engage

pīngpāngqiú 乒乓球 table tennis

píng 平 ① level; even ② equal ③ peaceful ④ to conquer; to quell (a revolt); to calm down ⑤ to control; to regulate ⑥ (said of prices) to go back to normal after sharp rises ⑦ (sports) to make the same score ⑧ to pacify; to bring peace to ⑨ short for Beiping

píng'ān 平安 safe and sound; peace

píngcháng 平常 ① normal; natural ② usual(ly) ③ ordinary; so-so

píngdàn 平淡 commonplace; insipid; ordinary

píngděng 平等 equality; equal

píngdì 平地 ① a piece of level ground; the plain ② suddenly

píngfán 平凡 common; ordinary; usual

píngfǎn 平反 to reverse or redress a miscarriage of justice

píngfāng 平方 (mathematics) a square

píngfáng 平房 a one-storied house; a bungalow

pínghé 平和 ① mildly; mild ② name of a county in Fujian Province

pínghéng 平衡 equilibrium; balance

píngjiāodào 平交道 a level crossing

píngjìng 平静 quiet; calm

píngjūn 平均 the average

píngmiàn 平面 a plane or plane surface

píngmín 平民 a commoner; a civilian

píngrì 平日 on usual days; ordinarily

píngshí 平时 ordinarily; in normal times

píngshùn 平顺 ① smooth and orderly ② the name of a county in Shanxi Province

píngtái 平台 ① a flat-top building ② a stadium-like building ③ balcony, open porch, or portico

píngtǎn 平坦 level, even, and smooth (going, roads, etc.)

píngwěn 平稳 steady and smooth; stable

píngxī/píngxí 平息 to come to an end; to subside

píngxíng 平行 ① parallel ② of equal rank

píngyōng 平庸 commonplace; dull

píngyuán 平原 a plain; a steppe

píngzhěng 平整 ① to level ② neat; smooth

píng 评 ① to comment; to criticize; to review ② comments; reviews ③ to judge

píngbǐ 评比 to appraise through comparison; to compare and assess

píngdìng 评定 to examine, judge, and decide

píngfēn 评分 marks or points given by a judge

pínggū 评估 to evaluate; to estimate

píngjià 评价 ① to appraise ② an objective assessment of the worth or merit of a person, a piece of writing, etc.

píngliáng 评量 to weigh; to evaluate

pínglùn 评论 to comment; to review

píngshěn 评审 ① to examine and determine ② a judge

píngxuǎn 评选 to choose through public appraisal

píngyǔ 评语 comments; criticism

píng 凭 ① to rely upon ② to be based on; to go by; to base on; to take as a basis ③ to lean on ④ a basis; proof; evidence ⑤ no matter (what, how, etc.)

píngjiè 凭借 ① by means of ② to rely on ③ something on which one relies

píng 坪 ① a level piece of ground ② (in Japanese measurement) an area of 6 feet square

píngguǒ 苹果 an apple

Píngdōng 屏东 Pingtung county in Taiwan

píngzhàng 屏障 ① a barrier ② to shield; to guard

píng 瓶 a bottle; a pitcher; a jug; a vase

píngjǐng 瓶颈 ① a bottleneck ② bottle neck

píngzi 瓶子 a bottle

píngshuǐ-xiāngféng 萍水相逢 to meet by accident

pō 坡 a slope; a bank; a hillside

pō 泼 ① to pour; to sprinkle; to spill ② ferocious; fierce; spiteful; villainous

pō/pǒ 颇 somewhat

pójia 婆家 one's husband's family

pópo 婆婆 ① the mother of one's husband ② a term of respect for an old lady

pò 迫 ① pressing; urgent; imminent ② to press; to force; to compel ③ distressed; pressed

pòbùjídài 迫不及待 too impatient to wait

pòhài 迫害 to persecute; to oppress cruelly

pòqiè 迫切 urgent; pressing; imperative

pòshǐ 迫使 to force or compel (one to do a thing)

pò 破 ① dilapidated; destroyed; ruined ② to break ③ to defeat; to beat (the enemy); to capture (enemy territory) ④ to expose; exposed; (to see) through; to lay

bare ⑤ to spend (money, etc.) ⑥ to solve or break (a murder case, etc.); to analyze ⑦ to come to an end ⑧ paltry

pò'àn 破案 to break a criminal case; to solve a case

pòchǎn 破产 bankruptcy

pòchú 破除 to eliminate; to get rid of

pòhuài 破坏 to ruin; to destroy; to violate

pòhuò 破获 to break (into a secret hideout) and capture (criminals, loots, etc.)

pòjiù 破旧 shabby; worn-out; dilapidated

pòlàn 破烂 wastes or refuse; junk

pòlì 破例 to make an exception

pòliè 破裂 ① to break off; rupture; severance ② broken; cracked

pòsuì 破碎 ① to come to pieces ② broken (heart, hope, etc.)

pōuxī/pǒuxī 剖析 to analyze; to dissect

pū 扑 ① to throw oneself on; to spring at ② to flap; to flutter ③ to beat; to strike; to pound ④ to dash; to smash

pūkè 扑克 poker (a gambling game)

pūkèpái 扑克牌 playing cards

pūmiè 扑灭 to exterminate (vermins); to extinguish (a fire)

pū 铺 to lay in order; to spread; to arrange; to pave
⇨pù

púrén 仆人 a servant

púsà 菩萨 ① Bodhisattva ② Buddha

pútao 葡萄 grapes

pútáojiǔ 葡萄酒 grape wine; port wine; a vintage; wine

pútáotáng 葡萄糖 glucose

Pútáoyá 葡萄牙 Portugal

pǔshí/púshí 朴实 ① (said of dresses, style, etc.) simple; plain ② honest; sincere

pǔsù/púsù 朴素 (said of dresses, etc.) simple and plain

pǔ 普 universal; all; widespread; everywhere; general

pǔbiàn 普遍 universal; general; widespread

pǔchá 普查 a general survey

pǔjí 普及 ① universal; available to all ② to popularize; to disseminate

pǔtōng 普通 ordinary; common; plain

pǔtōnghuà 普通话 the common dialect of the Chinese language; Mandarin

pǔ 谱 ① a register; a table; a list ② (music) a score ③ to compose (a song) ④ a general idea; a rough

pǔqǔ 谱曲 to compose a song

pù 铺 ① a store; a shop; a grocery ② a plank bed
⇨pū

pùbù 瀑布 a waterfall; a cataract

pùguāng 曝光 (photography) exposure

pùlù 曝露 to expose to the open air

Q

qī 七 the number seven (Note: When qī 七 precedes a 4th-tone sound, its pronunciation should

be changed to the second tone, i.e. qí.)

qīzuǐ-bāshé 七嘴八舌 every-

body talking at the same time

qī 沏 ① to infuse ② (said of the flowing water) rapidly; turbulently

qī 妻 one's formal or legal wife

qīzǐ 妻子 one's wife and children

qīzi 妻子 one's wife

qī 柒 another form of 七 (seven), used in writing checks, etc. to prevent fraud

qīxī/qīxí 栖息 to rest; to stay; to perch

qīxīdì/qīxídì 栖息地 a habitat

qīcǎn 凄惨 tragic; heartrending

qīliáng 凄凉 dreary; desolate

qī/qí 期 ① periods; times ② a designated time; a time limit ③ to expect; to hope; to wait

qīdài/qídài 期待 to expect; to hope

qīhuò/qíhuò 期货 (economics) futures; goods to be delivered at a specified time; the future delivery

qījiān/qíjiān 期间 a period; a term

qīkān/qíkān 期刊 a periodical

qīmò/qímò 期末 at the end of a term or semester

qīmòkǎo/qímòkǎo 期末考 the terminal examination; the final examination of a school term; the final

qīwàng/qíwàng 期望 to expect; to hope

qīxiàn/qíxiàn 期限 a time limit; a deadline

qīxǔ/qíxǔ 期许 to expect; expectation

qīzhōng/qízhōng 期中 midterm; interim

qīfu 欺负 to insult; to oppress; to bully

qīpiàn 欺骗 to cheat; to deceive; to swindle

qīwǔ 欺侮 to insult or ridicule; to bully

qī 漆 ① varnish; lacquer ② to varnish; to lacquer; to paint ③ a

varnish tree; a lacquer tree ④ pitch-black

qīhēi 漆黑 pitch-dark; pitch-black

qí 齐 ① equal; uniform; to be on a level ② to set in order ③ name of a dynasty ④ name of an ancient feudal state ⑤ a surname

qíquán 齐全 everything complete; nothing missing; all in readiness

qí 其 ① a pronoun—he, she, it, they; his, her, its, their ② this; that; the

qícì 其次 secondly; besides

qíjiān 其间 in; among; in between; between

qíshí 其实 in fact; as a matter of fact

qítā 其他 the others; the rest

qíyú 其余 the others; the rest

qízhōng 其中 in; among; in the midst

qí 奇 ① strange; uncanny; occult; rare ② wonderful ③ to feel strange about
⇨jī

qíguài 奇怪 strange; unusual; odd

qíguān 奇观 a spectacular or wonderful sight or phenomenon

qíhuā-yìmù 奇花异木 exotic flowers and unusual trees

qíjì/qíjī 奇迹 miracles; wonders

qímiào 奇妙 wonderful; rare

qítè 奇特 unique; outstanding; strange

qíyì 奇异 strange; unusual; odd

qíshì 歧视 to act biasedly; to discriminate against

qídǎo 祈祷 to pray; to offer a prayer

qífú 祈福 to pray for blessings

qíqiú 祈求 to pray for; to appeal for

qí 骑 ① to ride (a horse, etc.); to sit astride on ② cavalry; a rider; a jockey

qímǎ 骑马 to ride a horse

Q

qíshì 骑士 ① a knight ② a horseback rider

qí 棋 ① any piece used in the game of chess ② chess or other similar games

qízǐ 棋子 chess pieces

qí 旗 ① a flag; a pennant; a banner; a streamer ② a sign; an insignia; an emblem ③ an administrative division of Mongolia and Qinghai ④ the Manchus

qíhào 旗号 an army signal; a flag

qípáo 旗袍 traditional costume for women, which is a close fitting dress with high neck and slit skirt

qízhì 旗帜 flags, pennants, streamers, etc.

qízi 旗子 a flag

qǐgài 乞丐 a beggar

qǐqiú 乞求 to beg for; to supplicate; to implore

qǐbù 岂不 Wouldn't it result in...? Isn't that...? Wouldn't it be...?

qǐyǒucǐlǐ 岂有此理 What kind of reasoning is that? How absurd!

qǐguǎn/qìguǎn 企管 business management

qǐhuà/qìhuà 企划 to design; to lay out; to plan

qǐtú/qìtú 企图 ① to intend; to attempt ② a plan

qǐtúxín/qìtúxín 企图心 enterprising spirit

qǐyè/qìyè 企业 an enterprise

qǐyèjiā/qìyèjiā 企业家 an entrepreneur

qǐ 启 ① to enlighten ② to begin; to start ③ to open ④ to inform; to state

qǐchéng 启程 to start on a journey; to set out

qǐdòng 启动 to start (a machine, etc.)

qǐfā 启发 to prompt mental development

qǐshì 启示 revelation

qǐshì 启事 a notice; an announcement (in writing)

qǐyòng 启用 to start using

qǐ 起 ① to rise; to get up; to stand up; to go up ② to happen; to take place ③ to begin; to start ④ to build; to establish ⑤ a measure word for incidents

qǐbù 起步 to start; to begin

qǐcǎo 起草 to prepare a draft; to draft

qǐchū 起初 at first; in the beginning; originally

qǐchuáng 起床 to get out of bed; to get up

qǐdiǎn 起点 a starting point

qǐfēi 起飞 to take off; a takeoff

qǐfú 起伏 ① to undulate; undulation ② ups and downs; the rise and fall

qǐhòng 起哄 to create disturbances

qǐhuǒ 起火 ① to catch fire; to be on fire ② to lose one's temper ③ to cook meals

qǐjiā 起家 ① the early background of a successful person ② to establish oneself in the world; to carve out a career

qǐjìn/qǐjìng 起劲 (said of actions, performances, etc.) showing much zeal; eager; energetic; vigorous; with gusto

qǐlai 起来 to stand up; to sit up; to rise; to get up

qǐmǎ 起码 at least

qǐsè 起色 ① a sign of improvement ② a sign of recovery

qǐshēn 起身 ① to set out; to leave; to get off ② to get up

qǐsù 起诉 (said of a prosecutor) to file a formal indictment

qǐyì 起义 to start an uprising (in a righteous revolution); to revolt

qǐyuán 起源 the origin; the source; the beginning

qì 气 ① to be angry; to be indignant; rage; anger ② to provoke; to goad; to make angry; to annoy ③ air; gas; vapor; the atmosphere ④ breath ⑤ bearing; manner ⑥

smells; odors ⑦ spirit; morale ⑧ influence ⑨ weather

qìchuǎn 气喘 ① to pant; to gasp ② asthma

qìdào 气道 (physiology) the respiratory tract

qìfēn 气氛 atmosphere; mood

qìfèn 气愤 to be angry, furious, enraged, or indignant

qìgài 气概 spirit; air; bearing; manner

qìgōng 气功 (Chinese boxing) a system of deep breathing exercises

qìguǎn 气管 trachea; windpipe

qìhòu 气候 ① climate; weather ② situations

qìlì 气力 strength; effort; energy

qìliú 气流 an airflow; an air current

qìmén 气门 a steam valve

qìpài 气派 a dignified air

qìpò 气魄 spirit; vigor; moral strength

qìqiú 气球 a balloon

qìshì 气势 vehemence; fervor

qìtǐ 气体 gas; the gaseous body; vapor

qìwèi 气味 smacks; smells; odors

qìwēn 气温 the temperature

qìxī/qìxí 气息 breath

qìxiàng 气象 ① weather; climates ② atmosphere

Qìxiàng Jú 气象局 a weather bureau

qìyā 气压 air pressure

qìzhì/qìzhí 气质 dispositions; temperament

qì 迄 up to; down to; so far; till

qìjīn 迄今 up to now; until now; so far; to this day

qì 弃 ① to discard; to cast aside ② to reject; to abandon; to desert ③ to forget ④ to throw away one's own life

qì'ér 弃儿 an abandoned child; a foundling

qìquán 弃权 (in voting) to ab-

stain; a waiver

qì 汽 gas; steam; vapor

qìchē 汽车 an automobile

qìchuán 汽船 a steamship; a steamboat; a steamer

qìshuǐ 汽水 soda water; soft drinks or soda pop

qìyóu 汽油 gasoline; gas

qìhé 契合 to be in agreement; harmony

qìjī 契机 ① (philosophy) a moment ② a turning point; a critical point of time

qìyuē 契约 a written contract or agreement

qì 砌 ① to lay (bricks, etc.); to pave; to raise in layers; to build ② steps

qì 器 ① an instrument; an implement; a utensil; a tool; a piece of apparatus ② magnanimity ③ talent; ability

qìcái 器材 implements and materials

qìguān 器官 the apparatus; the organs

qìjù 器具 tools; instruments

qìwù 器物 an implement; a tool; an instrument; a utensil

qìxiè 器械 a machine; machinery; an apparatus; an appliance

qiā 掐 ① to cut with fingernails; to nip; to pinch; to give a pinch ② to hold; to grasp; to clutch; to gather with the hand ③ to dig the nail into

qiǎ 卡 a clip; a fastener

qiǎ/kǎ 卡 ① to choke; to be choked ② to be squeezed in between; to be sandwiched ③ to block; to check ④ a customs barrier; a roadblock; a checkpoint ⇨kǎ

qià 洽 ① to negotiate; to consult ② harmony; agreement ③ to spread; to diffuse

qiàshāng 洽商 to discuss (details of a contract, etc.)

qiàtán 洽谈 to discuss or consult (problems) together

Q

qià 恰 proper; appropriate; suitable

qiàdàng 恰当 appropriate; fitting; apt; apposite

qiàdào-hǎochù 恰到好处 neither too much nor too little; just right

qiàhǎo 恰好 ① just; exactly ② by coincidence

qiàqià 恰恰 ① just; exactly ② the chirping of birds ③ by coincidence

qiàqiǎo 恰巧 by coincidence; by chance

qiàrúqífèn 恰如其分 just suited or becoming to one's importance

qiān 千 ① thousand ② many; numerous

qiānfāng-bǎijì 千方百计 a thousand schemes—by hook or by crook

qiānjūn-wànmǎ 千军万马 a large number of mounted and foot soldiers

qiānkè 千克 kilogram (kg)

qiānwǎ 千瓦 kilowatt (kW)

qiānwàn 千万 ① an expression used to emphasize an injunction ② a huge amount

qiān 迁 ① to move; to remove ② to change ③ to be banished

qiānjiù 迁就 to compromise

qiānxǐ 迁徙 to move; to remove

qiānyí 迁移 to move (to a new address)

qiān 牵 ① to lead along; to drag; to pull; to haul ② to involve; to affect ③ to control; to restrain

qiānchě 牵扯 complication (of a matter); to involve; to implicate

qiānlián 牵连 to drag (into trouble); to involve; to implicate

qiānshè 牵涉 to involve; to implicate

qiānyǐn 牵引 ① to draw ② to involve (in trouble)

qiānzhì 牵制 ① to restrain; to curb ② to divert (enemy attention)

qiān 铅 lead (a metal)

qiānbǐ 铅笔 a pencil; a lead pencil

qiānxū 谦虚 ① modest; unassuming; self-effacing ② to make modest remarks

qiānxùn 谦逊 humble; modest; unassuming

qiān 签 ① to sign one's name; to put down one's signature; to subscribe; to endorse ② bamboo slips used for drawing lots or divination ③ a label ④ a slip of bamboo engraved with signs to be used in gambling or divination; a lot ⑤ a label ⑥ a small sharp-pointed stick

qiāndìng 签订 to conclude and sign (a treaty, etc.)

qiānfā 签发 to sign and issue (a document, certificate, etc.)

qiānmíng 签名 to sign; a signature

qiānshī 签诗 a doggerel poem or quote foretelling one's fortune as denoted by a divination lot drawn by oneself

qiānshǔ/qiānshù 签署 to sign or initial (a document)

qiānyuē 签约 to sign a contract, treaty, etc.

qiānzhèng 签证 a visa; to visa

qiānzì 签字 a signature; to sign or initial

qián 前 ① front; forward; before ② previous; former; preceding; past; of earlier times ③ future ④ to advance; to proceed; to progress; to precede

qiánbèi 前辈 a senior

qiánbian 前边 ① the front ② ahead; in front

qiánchéng 前程 ① a future ② a career

qiánfāng 前方 ① the front (in war) ② the forward direction

qiánfēng 前锋 the vanguard; the van

qiánhòu 前后 ① the front and the rear; before and after ② (indicating time) around; about ③ from beginning to end; altogether

qiánjìn 前进 to advance; to proceed; to go forward; to progress

qiánjǐng 前景 ① a foreground ② the foreground of a painting ③ prospects; vistas; perspectives

qiánkē 前科 a previous criminal record

qiánliè 前列 the front row; the forefront; the van

qiánmiàn 前面 ① the front; the front side ② ahead; in front

qiánnián 前年 the year before last

qiánpū-hòujì 前仆后继 Behind the fallen is an endless column of successors.

qiánqī/qiánqí 前期 the earlier stage; the early days

qiánrén 前人 people of former times; forefathers; predecessors; people of the past

qiánrèn 前任 a predecessor

qiánrì 前日 the day before yesterday

qiánshēn 前身 the forerunner

qiánshì 前世 ① the previous generation ② the previous life

qiánsuǒwèiyǒu 前所未有 unprecedented

qiántí 前提 ① a premise ② a prerequisite

qiántiān 前天 the day before yesterday

qiántou 前头 ① in front; ahead ② before

qiántú 前途 the prospect

qiánwǎng 前往 to go to (a place); to visit

qiánwèi 前卫 ① front-line troops ② a forward ③ vanguard; avant-garde

qiánxī/qiánxì 前夕 the eve (of an event)

qiánxiàn 前线 the front line (in war); the front

qiányán 前言 a foreword; a preface

qiányuàn 前院 the front courtyard

qiánzhě 前者 the former

qiánchéng 虔诚 devout; piety; sincerity; pious

qián 钱 ① money; cash ② a unit of weight (equal to 1/10th of a tael) ③ a surname

qiánbāo 钱包 a wallet; a purse

qiáncái 钱财 wealth; riches

qiánzi 钳子 ① tweezers; pincers; forceps; tongs ② a convict; a prisoner

Qiánlóng 乾隆 reigning title of Emperor Gao Zong of the Qing Dynasty, whose reign lasted from 1736 to 1796

Q

qián 潜 ① to hide; to conceal ② to dive ③ hidden; secret; latent

qiáncáng 潜藏 to be in hiding

qiánfú 潜伏 ① to lie hidden ② latent; hidden

qiánlì 潜力 potential; hidden force

qiánnéng 潜能 potential energy; potentiality

qiánrù 潜入 ① to enter secretly; to slip in ② to dive into (water)

qiánshuǐ 潜水 to dive

qiánshuǐtǐng 潜水艇 a submarine

qiántǐng 潜艇 a submarine

qiányìshí/qiányìshì 潜意识 subconsciousness

qiánzài 潜在 latent

qiǎn 浅 ① shallow; superficial ② easy; simple ③ (color) light ④ (said of land) narrow and small

qiǎnbó 浅薄 superficial; shallow; meager

qiǎnxiǎn 浅显 apparent; obvious; easily understood

qiǎnzé 谴责 to reprimand; to reproach

qiàn 欠 ① to owe; to owe money ② deficient; lacking ③ to raise slightly (a part of the body) ④ to yawn

qiànquē 欠缺 ① to lack; deficient; short of ② shortcomings

qiàn/qiān 嵌 to inlay; to set in

qiànyì 歉意 regrets; apologies

qiāng 抢 head (winds); adverse ⇨qiǎng

qiāng 枪 ① a rifle; a pistol; a gun ② a spear; a lance; a javelin

qiāngbì 枪毙 to execute by shooting

qiāngxiè 枪械 weapons

qiāng 腔 ① the cavity—especially referring to the chest and belly ② a cavity in any vessel ③ a tune ④ an accent of one's pronunciation; a tone of one's voice ⑤ a manner

qiāngdiào 腔调 ① a tune; the melody of a tune ② an accent ③ a manner or style of behavior

qiáng 强 ① strong; powerful; vigorous ② better ③ violent ⇨jiàng, qiǎng

qiángbào 强暴 ① fierce; violent; ferocious; atrocious ② rape

qiángdà 强大 powerful and strong

qiángdào 强盗 a robber; a bandit

qiángdiào 强调 to emphasize; to stress

qiángdù 强度 intensity (of light, etc.)

qiánghuà 强化 to strengthen; to intensify

qiángjiān 强奸 to rape; to violate

qiángjiàn 强健 strong and healthy

qiángjìng 强劲 powerful; forceful

qiángliè 强烈 violent; strong; intense; severe; acute; keen

qiángquán 强权 brute force; might

qiángrén 强人 ① robbers ② a strongman

qiángrèn 强韧 strong; tough; tenacious

qiángshèng 强盛 strong and prosperous

qiángxíng 强行 to force

qiángyìng 强硬 ① hard; strong ② defiant

qiángzhì 强制 compulsory; to compel; to force

qiángzhuàng 强壮 strong; vigorous; virile; energetic; robust

qiáng 墙 a wall; a fence

qiángbì 墙壁 a wall (of a building)

qiángjiǎo 墙角 a corner between two walls

qiǎng 抢 ① to take by force; to snatch; to rob; to loot ② to do something in haste, as in an emergency; to rush ③ to try to beat others in a performance ⇨qiāng

qiǎng'àn 抢案 (law) a case of robbery

qiǎngduó 抢夺 to rob; to loot; to plunder

qiǎnggòu 抢购 to try to beat others in making purchases (as in time of war, etc.)

qiǎngjié 抢劫 to rob; robbery

qiǎngjiù 抢救 to make emergency rescue

qiǎng 强 ① to force ② to make an effort; to strive ⇨jiàng, qiáng

qiǎngpò 强迫 to force (one to do something)

qiǎngqiú 强求 to demand; to exact; to impose

qiāoqiāode/qiǎoqiǎode 悄悄地 stealthily; secretly; in a clandestine way

qiāojiā 跷家 (slang) to run away from home

qiāokè 跷课 (slang) to avoid attending classes

qiāo 锹 a spade; a shovel

qiāo 敲 ① to rap; to strike; to tap; to beat; to knock ② to extort; to blackmail; to overcharge ③ a truncheon

qiāozhuāng 乔装 to disguise oneself

qiáobāo 侨胞 overseas Chinese

qiáoshēng 侨生 children of overseas Chinese who attend schools in China

qiáo 桥 ① a bridge; any bridge-like structure ② beams of a structure ③ tall; high; elevated

qiáoliáng 桥梁 any material which forms the span of a bridge

qiáo 翘 ① long tail feathers ② to raise ③ outstanding
⇨**qiào**

qiáo 瞧 ① to see; to look at ② to steal a glance; to glance quickly

qiáobuqǐ 瞧不起 to look down upon; to despise

qiǎo 巧 ① clever; witty ② ingenious; artful ③ coincidence; coincidental ④ pretty; cute ⑤ a clever feat; a stunt

qiǎohé 巧合 a coincidence

qiǎokèlì 巧克力 chocolate

qiǎomiào 巧妙 ingenuity; ingenious; skillful

qiào/ké 壳 shells; husks; coverings

qiào 俏 ① like; similar; to resemble; to be like ② pretty and cute; good-looking ③ (commodities) enjoying brisk sale at higher prices; in great demand

qiàobì 峭壁 a precipice; a cliff

qiào 翘 to project upward; to stick up; to turn upward
⇨**qiáo**

qiē 切 to cut; to mince; to slice; to carve
⇨**qiè**

qiēchú 切除 ① to cut out; to resect ② excision; resection

qiēcuō 切磋 to improve oneself through discussions with another

qiēduàn 切断 to sever; to cut asunder

qiézi 茄子 an eggplant

qiě 且 ① moreover; still; further ② just; for the time being ③ both...and...

qiè 切 to be close to
⇨**qiē**

qièshēn 切身 personal (interests)

qièshí 切实 sure; certain

qièqǔ 窃取 to steal

qiètīng 窃听 to eavesdrop; eavesdropping

qièzéi 窃贼 a thief; a burglar

qīnpèi 钦佩 to admire; to respect

qīnfàn 侵犯 (law) to encroach upon other's rights; to violate; to invade

qīnhài 侵害 to infringe or encroach upon

qīnlüè 侵略 ① to invade ② aggression

qīnrù 侵入 to intrude

qīnshí 侵蚀 erosion; to encroach; to erode

qīnxí 侵袭 to attack stealthily

qīnzhàn 侵占 to take (the property, the land, etc. of another) illegally

qīn 亲 ① parents ② relatives ③ to love; intimate; near to; dear ④ personally; personal; in person; self ⑤ to kiss
⇨**qìng**

qīn'ài 亲爱 love; affection; dear

qīnbǐ 亲笔 one's own handwriting; to write personally

qīnhélì 亲和力 (chemistry) affinity ② affability; amiability

qīnjìn 亲近 to be near to or intimate with; to be close to

qīnkǒu 亲口 (said of words, etc.) right from one's own mouth; to state or tell personally

qīnlín 亲临 to arrive personally

qīnmì 亲密 intimate; intimacy; close

qīnpéng hǎoyǒu 亲朋好友 relatives and friends

qīnqi 亲戚 relatives

qīnqiè 亲切 intimately; cordially; kind

qīnrè 亲热 very dear; very intimate; very much in love

qīnrén 亲人 close relatives—as one's parents, brothers, spouse, children, etc.

qīnshēn 亲身 personally; in person

qīnshēng 亲生 ① to give birth to ② one's own (parents or chil-

qīnshǒu 亲手 personally; with one's own hands

qīnshǔ 亲属 relatives; family members

qīnwěn 亲吻 to kiss

qīnyǎn 亲眼 with one's own eyes; personally

qīnyǒu 亲友 friends and relatives

qīnzǐ 亲子 ① parents and children ② one's own son (as distinct from an adopted son)

qīnzì 亲自 personally; in person

qíncài 芹菜 celery

Qín Shǐhuáng 秦始皇 the First Emperor of Qin, 259-210 B.C.

qín 琴 ① a Chinese fretted instrument with seven or five strings somewhat similar to the zither ② a musical instrument

qín 禽 birds; fowls

qín 勤 ① diligent; industrious; sedulous; hardworking ② frequently; regularly

qínfèn 勤奋 diligent; assiduous; industrious

qíngōng-jiǎnxué 勤工俭学 a part-work and part-study system

qínjiǎn 勤俭 diligent and frugal

qínkěn 勤恳 diligent and conscientious; industrious and honest

qínláo 勤劳 to toil or labor sedulously

qǐnshì 寝室 a bedroom

qīng 青 ① green; blue; black ② green grass ③ not ripe ④ young; youth; youthful ⑤ the skin of bamboo ⑥ the white of an egg ⑦ short for Qinghai Province or Qingdao City

qīngcài 青菜 vegetables; the greens

qīngchūn 青春 ① one's youth; young adulthood ② age (in asking a youth)

qīngchūnqī/qīngchūnqí 青春期 adolescence; puberty; teens

qīngcuì 青翠 fresh green; verdant

qīnghuā 青花 ① fine stripes on an inkstone ② flowers design on porcelain

qīnglài 青睐 a look of joy; favor; preference

qīngnián 青年 youths; young people

qīngshàonián 青少年 teenagers; youngsters

qīngwā 青蛙 a frog

qīng 轻 ① light ② simple; easy; facile ③ mild; gentle; soft; tender; lightly ④ mean; base; lowly; unimportant ⑤ frivolous; flippant; fickle; rash; reckless ⑥ to slight; to neglect; to ignore

qīngbiàn 轻便 handy; convenient; light; portable

qīngbó 轻薄 ① frivolous; flippant ② disrespectful; irreverent ③ to insult

qīnggōngyè 轻工业 light industry

qīnghū 轻忽 to neglect; to slight; to ignore

qīngkuài 轻快 ① agile; brisk; spry; nimble; sprightly ② light-hearted ③ lively

qīngmiè 轻蔑 to despise; to disdain; to contemn; to slight

qīngqiǎo 轻巧 ① light and efficient; handy ② dexterous(ly)

qīngshāng 轻伤 a slight injury; a minor wound

qīngshì 轻视 to make light of; to slight

qīngsōng 轻松 ① to lighten; to relax ② easy; comfortable

qīngwēi/qīngwéi 轻微 light; slight; little

qīngyì 轻易 ① easy; facile; effortless ② reckless; rash

qīngyíng 轻盈 (said of a woman) nimble and shapely

qīng 氢 hydrogen

qīng 倾 ① to slant; to bend ② to collapse; to fall flat; to upset; to subvert ③ to pour out ④ to exhaust (one's wealth, etc.); to

qīngdào 倾倒 to dump

qīngsù 倾诉 to pour out (one's heart, troubles, etc.)

qīngtīng 倾听 to listen carefully

qīngxiàng 倾向 ① to be inclined to ② a tendency; a trend

qīngxiāo 倾销 a cutthroat sale; dumping

qīngxié 倾斜 ① to slant ② the angle formed by a stratum with the level; to slope

qīng 清 ① pure; clean; clear ② clear, simple, and easily understandable ③ to arrange; to place in order ④ to conclude; to terminate; to settle ⑤ to clean ⑥ virtuous; honest ⑦ the Qing Dynasty (1644-1911 A.D.)

qīngbái 清白 (said of a person's character, etc.) clean; innocent

qīngchá 清查 to check, investigate, survey thoroughly

Qīngcháo 清朝 the Qing Dynasty (1644-1911 A.D.)

qīngchè 清澈 limpid (water); crystal-clear

qīngchén 清晨 early in the morning; dawn

qīngchú 清除 ① to eliminate, rid of, clear away, liquidate, or remove ② to clean or tidy up (a house)

qīngchu 清楚 ① clear; without ambiguity ② to understand

qīngdān 清单 a detailed list of items which serves as a receipt, statement, etc.

qīngdàn 清淡 ① not enthusiastic; calm ② slack ③ (said of food) simple; without grease or heavy seasoning

qīnghán 清寒 ① poor but clean and honest ② (said of weather, etc.) cold and crisp ③ (said of moonlight) cold and bright

qīnghuá 清华 ① (literary style) outstanding and beautiful ② eminent and honest gentle-

men ③ moonlight ④ enchanting views

qīngjié 清洁 clean; sanitary

qīngjìng 清净 clean and pure

qīngjìng 清静 quiet (houses, surroundings, etc.)

qīnglǐ 清理 ① to settle (accounts, etc.); clearance (of sales, etc.) ② to arrange; to tidy up

qīnglián 清廉 clean, honest, and capable (officials, etc.)

qīngliáng 清凉 refreshing (weather, water, etc.); nice and cool

qīngsǎo 清扫 to clean up; to sweep

qīngshuǎng 清爽 ① sober ② quiet and comfortable ③ clear and easy to understand ④ to have everything (debts, etc.) settled; relieved

qīngshuǐ 清水 clear (or fresh) water

qīngsuàn 清算 ① to liquidate; liquidation ② to purge

qīngxī 清晰 ① loud and clear (in radio reception, talking, listening, etc.) ② clearly

qīngxǐ 清洗 to wash; to clean

qīngxīn 清新 refreshing (style, fashion, etc.); fresh

qīngxǐng 清醒 ① to come to; wide awake ② clear-minded; sober

qīngyísè 清一色 uniformly; homogeneous

qīngyōu 清幽 quiet and secluded

qīngzǎo 清早 early in the morning; dawn

qīngzhēnsì 清真寺 a mosque

qīngtíng 蜻蜓 a dragonfly

qíng 情 ① feelings; emotions; sentiments ② fact; detail; situation; condition ③ love; affection; passion ④ nature; reason

qíng'ài 情爱 love (between men and women)

qíngbào 情报 information; intelligence reports

qíngcāo 情操 ① sentiment (connoting highbrow and compli-

cated sentiment) ② noble thoughts and feelings

qíngdiào 情调 ① a mood; taste ② (psychology) affective feeling tone

qíngfù 情妇 a mistress; the other woman

qínggǎn 情感 emotions; feelings; affection

qínggē 情歌 a love song

qínghuái 情怀 a mood; feelings

qíngjié 情节 ① a plot (of a play, novel, etc.) ② details (of an affair or event); circumstances

qíngjié 情结 (psychology) a complex

qíngjǐng 情景 a scene; a sight

qíngjìng 情境 circumstances; a situation

qíngkuàng 情况 a situation; circumstances

qínglǐ 情理 reason; common sense

qínglǚ 情侣 lovers

qíngqù 情趣 sentiment; interest

qíngrén 情人 a paramour, sweetheart, or lover

Qíngrénjié 情人节 St. Valentine's Day

qíngshì 情势 a situation; the state of affairs

qíngshì 情事 the facts

qíngshū 情书 a love letter; a billet-doux

qíngtài 情态 ① a situation; a condition ② demeanor; spirit; a mood

qíngxíng 情形 a situation; circumstances; conditions

qíngxù 情绪 ① emotions; a mood ② depression; the sulks

qíngyì 情谊 friendship; amity

qíngyì 情意 feeling; sentiment; affection

qíngyù 情欲 passion; sensual or carnal desire; lust; eroticism

qíng 晴 ① (said of the weather) fine; fair; bright; clear ② when the rain stops

qínglǎng 晴朗 (said of the sky) fine and cloudless

qíngtiān 晴天 a fine day; a cloudless day

qǐng 请 ① to request; to ask; to beg ② please ③ to seek the service of; to engage

qǐngjià 请假 to ask for leave of absence

qǐngjiǎn 请柬 an invitation card

qǐngjiào 请教 to request advice; to consult

qǐngkè 请客 to invite guests; to give a party

qǐngqiú 请求 to request; to ask; to beg

qǐngshì 请示 to ask for instructions

qǐngtiě 请帖 an invitation card

qǐngwèn 请问 Please tell me....; May I ask you...?

qǐngyuàn 请愿 to petition

qìng 庆 ① festivity; blessing; felicity; joy ② to celebrate; to congratulate; to rejoice

qìngdiǎn 庆典 national festivities and celebration ceremonies

qìnghè 庆贺 to celebrate; to rejoice; to offer congratulations

qìngxìng 庆幸 to congratulate or rejoice oneself

qìngzhù 庆祝 to celebrate; celebration

qìng 亲 relatives by marriage ⇨qīn

qióng 穷 ① poor; impoverished; destitute ② the extreme; the farthest; an end ③ distress; affliction ④ thoroughly

qióngkǔ 穷苦 destitute; poverty; poverty-stricken

qióngrén 穷人 destitute people; the poor

qiūlíng 丘陵 mounds; craggy terrains; hills

qiū 邱 ① a hill ② name of a county in Shandong Province ③ a surname

qiū 秋 ① autumn; fall ② time; a period ③ a season ④ a year ⑤ a

harvest; ripening of grains

qiūjì 秋季 autumn (season)

qiūshōu 秋收 the autumn harvest

qiūtiān 秋天 autumn; fall

qiúfàn 囚犯 a prisoner; a convict; a jailbird

qiú 求 ① to ask for; to pray for; to beg ② demand ③ to seek ④ to covet; to desire

qiúhūn 求婚 to propose

qiújiù 求救 to seek relief; to ask for rescue

qiúxué 求学 to receive education; to study

qiúzhí 求职 positions wanted

qiúzhù 求助 to resort to; to seek help

qiú 球 ① a ball or anything shaped like a ball ② the globe; the earth

qiúchǎng 球场 a playground for ball games

qiúduì 球队 teams for playing ball games

qiúmí 球迷 fans of ball games

qiúpāi 球拍 rackets (for tennis, etc.)

qiúsài 球赛 a ball game

qiúxié 球鞋 tennis shoes; sneakers

qiúyuán 球员 a ballplayer

qū 区 ① a district; an area; a zone ② to distinguish; to discriminate ③ a border ④ little; few

qūbié 区别 to discriminate; to distinguish

qūfēn 区分 to set apart; to consider

qūgōngsuǒ 区公所 a district office

qūyù 区域 a district; a zone

qūyùxìng 区域性 regional

qū 曲 ① bent; crooked; twisted; winding ② little known; obscure ③ wrong; unjustifiable
⇨qǔ

qūxiàn 曲线 curved line; curve

qūzhé 曲折 ① bends; curves ② complicated

qūdòng 驱动 (machinery)

drive

qūzhú 驱逐 to drive out; to get rid of; to expel; to eliminate

qū 屈 ① to bend; to flex; to bow; to crook ② to humiliate; to humble ③ wrong; injustice ④ in the wrong ⑤ to be in an inferior or uncomfortable position ⑥ a surname

qūfú 屈服 to succumb, yield, or submit to (power, a threat, etc.); to give in

qū 趋 ① to go quickly; to hasten; to hurry ② to be inclined; to tend; to follow

qūshì 趋势 ① a trend; a tendency ② to go after men of power

qūxiàng 趋向 ① a tendency; a trend ② to tend to; to incline to

qú 渠 ① a drain; a channel; a ditch ② he; she

qúdào 渠道 ① an irrigation ditch ② a channel

qǔ 曲 ① a type of verse for singing, which emerged in the Southern Song and Jin Dynasties and became popular in the Yuan Dynasty ② a piece of music; a song
⇨qū

qǔzi 曲子 a number; a song; a tune; a melody

qǔ 取 ① to take; to receive; to fetch; to obtain; to take hold of ② to select; to choose ③ to summon; to recall

qǔcái 取材 to select material

qǔdài 取代 to replace; to substitute

qǔdé 取得 to gain; to acquire; to obtain

qǔdì 取缔 to prohibit; to punish the violator

qǔjǐng 取景 to find a view (to photograph, paint, etc.)

qǔjué 取决 It's up to (someone else to make the decision).

qǔshèng 取胜 to win a victory

qǔxiàng 取向 orientation

qǔxiāo 取消 to cancel; to nullify

qǔxiào 取笑 to laugh at; to make

fun of

qǔyàng 取样 sampling

qǔyuè 取悦 to please

qǔ 娶 to take a wife

qù 去 ① to go away; to depart ② an auxiliary verb ③ to get rid of; to remove ④ to be apart ⑤ past; gone ⑥ the fourth of the four tones in Chinese phonetics ⑦ (Beijing opera) to play the part of

qùchù 去处 ① whereabouts ② the place one is heading for ③ a place; a site

qùnián 去年 last year; the year past

qùshì 去世 to die; to leave the world

qù 趣 interest; fun; interesting; funny

qùwèi 趣味 fun; interest; taste

quān 圈 ① a circle; a ring ② a circle—a number of persons bound together by having the same interests ③ to circle ④ with a return to the starting point; round ⇨juàn

quāntào 圈套 a snare; a trap; a trick

quānzi 圈子 a circle

quán 权 ① power; authority; inherent rights; jurisdiction; influence ② an expedient way; expediency; alternative ③ temporarily; for the time being

quánlì 权力 power; authority

quánlì 权利 rights

quánshì 权势 power and influence

quánwēi 权威 ① an authority (in certain sphere of knowledge) ② power and prestige

quánxiàn 权限 limitation of power or authority

quányì 权益 rights and interests

quán 全 ① perfect ② complete; whole; total; intact; all; entire; absolute ③ to keep whole or intact

quánbù 全部 the whole; completely; total

quánchéng 全程 the whole course

quándōu 全都 all; altogether; everyone

quánguó 全国 the whole country or nation

quánguóxìng 全国性 nationwide; countrywide

quánhuì 全会 a plenary meeting; a plenary session; a plenum

quánjí 全集 the complete works of (Shakespeare, etc.)

quánjiā 全家 the whole family

quánjú 全局 the overall situation

quánlěidǎ 全垒打 a home run

quánlì 全力 (with) all-out effort

quánlìyǐfù 全力以赴 to spare no efforts

quánmiàn 全面 overall; comprehensive

quánmín 全民 the whole (or entire) people

quánpán 全盘 total; overall

quánqiú 全球 the globe; the world

quánrán 全然 completely (ignorant, etc.); totally

quánshēn 全身 the whole body

quánshù 全数 the whole amount; the total number; the sum total

quántǐ 全体 all; everybody

quánxīn-quányì 全心全意 wholeheartedly

quánshì 诠释 to interpret; to explain

quán 泉 ① a spring; a fountain ② money (archaic) ③ a surname

quányuán 泉源 a fountainhead; a springhead; a source; a wellspring

Quánzhōu 泉州 Quanzhou, Fujian Province

quán 拳 ① a fist ② sparring feats; various forms of boxing ③ strength

quánjí/quánjí 拳击 boxing; the boxing art

quántou 拳头 a fist

quányù 痊愈 to have been

cured; to have recovered from illness

quǎn 犬 a dog; a canine

quàn 劝 to exhort; to urge; to advise; to persuade

quàndǎo 劝导 to exhort and guide

quàngào 劝告 to advise; to counsel; to exhort

quànshuō 劝说 to persuade; to advise

quànzǔ 劝阻 to dissuade

quàn 券 ① a ticket ② a certificate ③ a bond

quē 缺 ① deficient; lacking; short; incomplete; defective ② a vacancy; an opening

quēdiǎn 缺点 a defect; a shortcoming; a flaw

quēfá 缺乏 to lack; to be short of

quēkǒu 缺口 ① a breach; a gap ② a notch

quēshǎo 缺少 to lack; to be short of

quēxí 缺席 to be absent (from a meeting, etc.)

quēxiàn 缺陷 a defect; a shortcoming; a handicap; inadequacy

qué 瘸 ① to be lame ② a cripple; a lame man

què 却 ① still; but; yet ② to refuse to accept ③ to retreat; to withdraw

quèshì 却是 nevertheless; in fact; the fact is...

què 确 ① sure; certain; secure; real; true; valid ② firm; firmly

quèbǎo 确保 to secure; to insure; to be sure to

quèdìng 确定 ① to decide; to fix; to settle; to determine ② certain; sure

quèlì 确立 to establish firmly

quèqiè 确切 accurate; exact; precise

quèrèn 确认 to certify; to affirm; to confirm

quèshí 确实 real; true; certain

quèxìn 确信 to be convinced; to believe firmly

quèzáo 确凿 accurate; precise

qún 裙 a skirt; a petticoat; an apron

qúnzi 裙子 a skirt

qún 群 a group; a multitude; a host; a crowd; a swarm; a large number

qúndǎo 群岛 an archipelago

qúnjū 群居 to live as a group; gregarious

qúnluò 群落 a community

qúntǐ 群体 a colony (of corals, etc.)

qúnzhòng 群众 a crowd; a mob

R

rán 然 ① yes; most certainly; permission; right; correct ② really; if so

rán'ér 然而 however; but; nevertheless

ránhòu 然后 then; afterward; later

rán 燃 to burn; to ignite; to light

ránliào 燃料 fuel

ránshāo 燃烧 to burn; to be on fire; to be in flames; combustion

rǎn 染 ① to dye ② to soil; to pollute ③ to get infected; to catch a disease; infectious ④ to have an affair with ⑤ (in Chinese painting and calligraphy) to make strokes

rǎnliào 染料 dyestuff; dye

rǎnsètǐ 染色体 (genetics) a

chromosome

răng 嚷 to shout; to cry; to call out loudly

ràng 让 ① to give way; to make a concession; to back down; to yield; to give ground ② to allow; to let; to permit ③ to turn over; to transfer; to surrender; to cede ④ to step aside; to make way; to let by

ràngbù 让步 to give way; to yield

ráo 饶 ① to forgive; to spare; to have mercy; to let somebody off ② to give something extra as a gift; to let somebody have something into the bargain ③ abundant; plentiful; full of; fertile ④ lenient; liberal ⑤ (now rarely) even though; in spite of the fact that; whatever

răo 扰 ① to disturb; to agitate; to harass ② to trespass on somebody's hospitality

răoluàn 扰乱 to disturb; to agitate

ráo 绕 ① to march round; to circle ② to go around; to make a detour

rě 若 as in bōrě 般若—(Buddhism) prajñā, wisdom
⇨**ruò**

rě 惹 ① to induce; to cause; to bring upon oneself; to incur ② to provoke; to rouse; to offend

rè 热 ① hot; heated; burning; to heat ② fever ③ earnest; ardent; zealous; enthusiastic; passionate

rè'ài 热爱 to love passionately

rècháo 热潮 ① great mass fervor ② an upsurge

rèchén 热忱 enthusiasm; sincerity; earnest

rèdài 热带 the tropics

règǒu 热狗 a hot dog

rèlèi-yíngkuàng／rèlèi-yíng-kuāng 热泪盈眶 tearful; eyes moistening

rèliàn 热恋 to be passionately in love

rèliàng 热量 the quantity of heat; calories

rèliè 热烈 fervent; passionate; vehement

rèluò 热络 on friendly terms; very intimate

rèmài 热卖 to be in great demand; to sell well; to have a ready market

rèmén 热门 something very much in vogue or fashion; a craze

rènao 热闹 ① bustling; populous; noisy ② prosperous; thriving ③ lively; merry

rèqíng 热情 passion; ardor; fervor

rèshuǐ 热水 hot water

rèshuǐpíng 热水瓶 a thermos (bottle)

rèxiàn 热线 ① (physics) a heat ray ② a hot line (the telephone line between the White House and the Kremlin)

rèxīn 热心 zealous; warmhearted

rèzhōng 热衷 ① to be keen on; to be fond of ② to crave for; to desire

rén 人 a human being; a person; people

réncái 人才 a man of ability; a talent

réncháo 人潮 a stream of people

réncì 人次 person-times

réndào 人道 philanthropy; humanitarianism

réndào zhǔyì 人道主义 humanism; humanitarianism

réngé 人格 character; personality

réngōng 人工 ① human labor ② man-made

rénhé 人和 popularity or harmony with the people, colleagues, constituents, etc.

rénhuò 人祸 a man-made disaster

rénjì guānxi 人际关系 human relations

rénjiā 人家 a human abode

rénjia 人家 ① other persons ② he, she, or they ③ I

rénjiān 人间 the world of mortals

rénjūn 人均 per person; per head

rénkǒu 人口 population

rénlèi 人类 man; mankind; the human race

rénlèixué 人类学 anthropology

rénlì 人力 human power or strength

rénmǎ 人马 ① general term for members of a collective ② troops (consisting of soldiers and horses)

rénmen 人们 people; men; the public

rénmín 人民 people

Rénmínbì 人民币 Renminbi (RMB); unit of money used in the People's Republic of China

rénmìng 人命 human life

rénqì 人气 popularities; public support

rénqíng 人情 human sentiment, emotion, or feeling

rénqíngwèi 人情味 friendliness; hospitality

rénquán 人权 human rights

rénqún 人群 a crowd, throng, or multitude (of people)

rénrén 人人 everybody

rénshēn 人身 ① (law) personal (liberty) ② human body

rénshēn 人参 ginseng

rénshēng 人生 human life; life

rénshì 人士 personages

rénshì 人世 the world

rénshì 人事 ① human affairs ② personnel affairs ③ human endeavors

rénshǒu 人手 ① manpower ② a human hand

rénshòu 人寿 one's span of life

rénshòu bǎoxiǎn 人寿保险 life insurance

rénshù 人数 a count (of people)

réntǐ 人体 a human body

réntóu 人头 ① the number of people ② relations with people

rénwéi 人为 man-made; artificial; imitation

rénwén 人文 ① humanities ② human affairs

rénwù 人物 ① a personage or figure ② people and things

rénxīn 人心 human heart, will, or feeling

rénxīn-huánghuáng 人心惶惶 jittery or panicky

rénxíngdào 人行道 a sidewalk; a footpath

rénxìng 人性 human nature

rénxing 人性 human feeling; reason

rénxuǎn 人选 candidates (for certain jobs)

rényǐngr 人影儿 a human shadow

rényuán 人员 the personnel; the staff

rényuánr 人缘儿 relations with others

rénzào 人造 man-made; artificial; imitation

rénzào wèixīng 人造卫星 a satellite

rénzhì/rénzhí 人质 a hostage

rén 仁 ① benevolence; humanity; mercy; kindness; charity ② kernel

rén'ài 仁爱 humanity; philanthropy

réncí 仁慈 charity; kindness

Rén 任 a surname
⇨rèn

rěn 忍 ① to endure; to bear; to tolerate; to put up with; to suffer ② merciless; truculence ③ to forbear; to repress

rěnbuzhù 忍不住 ① cannot stand it any more ② can not help (laughing, etc.)

rěnnài 忍耐 patience; forbearance; patient

rěnshòu 忍受 to endure; to bear; to suffer

rěntòng 忍痛 ① to bear pain

with dignity ② (to give up or sell something) reluctantly

rěnxīn 忍心 hard-hearted; to steel one's heart

rèn 认 ① to recognize; to know; to make out ② to admit; to acknowledge ③ to accept; to resign oneself to ④ to adopt ⑤ to promise to do something

rèncuò 认错 ① to admit a fault or mistake ② to make identification incorrectly

rènde 认得 to know; to recognize

rèndìng 认定 ① to conclude or decide; to believe firmly ② to set one's mind on

rèngòu 认购 to offer to buy; to subscribe

rèngǔ quánzhèng 认股权证 (accounting) stock warrants

rènkě 认可 to sanction; to approve

rènqīng 认清 to see or know clearly (which is which)

rènshi 认识 ① to know ② to understand

rèntóng 认同 to identify; identification

rènwéi 认为 to think that...; to consider that...

rènzhēn 认真 to be serious; to be earnest

rènzhèng 认证 attestation; authentication

rènzhī 认知 cognition

rèn 任 ① to employ (one for a job) ② to let (one act at will) ③ a duty ④ to bear (a burden) ⑤ an official post; office
⇨**Rén**

rènhé 任何 any; whatever

rènmìng 任命 to appoint; appointment

rènpíng 任凭 without restriction; (to allow someone to do something) at will

rènqī/rènqì 任期 the tenure of office

rènwu 任务 duty; responsibility

rènxìng 任性 doing as one pleases; unrestrained

rènyì 任意 arbitrary; at will

rènzhí 任职 to hold a post; to be in office

rènshēn 妊娠 to be pregnant; pregnancy

rēng 扔 ① to throw; to hurl ② to abandon; to discard

réng 仍 still; yet

réngjiù 仍旧 still; yet

réngrán 仍然 still; yet

réngshì 仍是 still is (what it used to be); still was (what it had been)

rì 日 ① the sun ② a day ③ day; daytime ④ Japan; Japanese ⑤ time ⑥ every day; daily

rìbào 日报 a daily newspaper

Rìběn 日本 Japan

rìcháng 日常 common; usually; ordinarily; daily

rìcháng shēnghuó 日常生活 daily life

rìchéng 日程 ① the agenda on a specific day (of a conference) ② an itinerary

rìchū 日出 sunrise

rìguāng 日光 sunshine; the light of the sun

rìguāngdēng 日光灯 a fluorescent lamp

rìhòu 日后 in the days to come; in the future

rìjì 日记 a diary

rìjiān 日间 at daytime; in the daytime

rìjiàn 日渐 with each passing day

Rìjūn 日军 Japanese troops

rìmiǎn 日冕 (astronomy) corona, a faintly luminous envelope outside of the sun's chromosphere

Rìnèiwǎ 日内瓦 Geneva, Switzerland

rìqī/rìqí 日期 date

rìqián 日前 a few days ago; recently

rìqū 日趋 gradually; day by day

rìquánshí 日全食 a total

eclipse of the sun

Rìwén 日文 Japanese (written language)

rìxīn-yuèyì 日新月异 continuous improvement; ever newer

rìyè 日夜 day and night

rìyì 日益 increasingly; day by day

rìyòng 日用 of daily use

rìyòngpǐn 日用品 daily necessities

Rìyǔ 日语 Japanese (spoken language)

Rìyuè Tán 日月潭 Sun Moon Lake, Taiwan

rìzhì 日志 a daily record

rìzi 日子 ① time; duration ② life; living

róng 荣 ① glory; honor ② luxuriant; lush; teeming

rónghuò 荣获 to get or win the honor

róngmín 荣民 retired servicemen; veterans

róngxìng 荣幸 honored; to have the honor of

róngyào 荣耀 glory; honor; splendor

róngyù 荣誉 honor

róng 绒 ① fine; furry; flossy ② any kind of woolen goods or fabric with soft nap ③ fine wool; woolen; velvety; velvet

róng 容 ① to contain; to hold ② to allow; to permit ③ to forgive; to pardon ④ to forbear; forbearance ⑤ a face; an expression; a countenance

róngjī 容积 ① volume; cubic capacity ② floor space

róngjīlǜ 容积率 floor space ratio

róngliàng 容量 the capacity

róngnà 容纳 ① to contain ② to tolerate

róngqì 容器 a container

róngrěn 容忍 to endure; to bear; to tolerate

róngxǔ 容许 to allow; to permit

róngyán 容颜 a facial appearance

róngyì 容易 ① easy ② apt to; liable to

róng 溶 ① to dissolve; to melt ② (said of rivers) having much water

rónghuà 溶化 to dissolve; to melt

róngjiě 溶解 to dissolve; to melt

róngyè 溶液 (chemistry) solution

róngshù 榕树 a banyan tree

róng 熔 to smelt; to weld or fuse metals

róng 融 ① to melt ② cheerful; happy; joyful ③ to melt into; to blend; to harmonize ④ very bright; glowing; burning

rónghé 融合 to blend; to fuse

rónghuà 融化 to melt; to fuse; to thaw

róngqià 融洽 (said especially of human relations) harmonious

róu 柔 ① soft and tender ② amiable; pliant; yielding; submissive; gentle; supple ③ the new grass budding in spring

róuhé 柔和 soft; gentle; amiable; tender

róuruǎn 柔软 soft; yielding; lithe

róu 揉 ① to rub; to knead ② to crumple by hand ③ to massage ④ to subdue; to make smooth or peaceful ⑤ mixed-up; confused

ròu 肉 ① flesh ② meat of animals; meat or pulp of fruits, etc. ③ physical; carnal ④ flesh and blood—dearest, as one's children ⑤ slow-motion

ròulèi 肉类 meats

ròumá 肉麻 a creepy feeling; disgusting

ròusōng 肉松 fried shredded meat; meat fluff

ròutǐ 肉体 flesh and blood; physical

rú 如 ① like; as ② if; supposing ③ as if ④ as good as; equal to ⑤ to follow (advice); to listen to ⑥ should; ought to ⑦ on or in (time)

rúcǐ 如此 thus; like this

rúguǒ 如果 if; supposing

rúguǒshuō 如果说 what if...

rúhé 如何 ① How (can we deal with...)? ② What do you think of it? How about it? ③ What to do now? How is it?

rújīn 如今 now; nowadays

rúqī/rúqí 如期 on time; punctually

rúshì 如是 ① (Buddhism) thus ② such

rútóng 如同 like (a dream, etc.)

rúxià 如下 as follows; as below

rúyì 如意 as one wishes

rúyuàn 如愿 ① if willing ② as one wishes

rúzuì-rúchī 如醉如痴 to be drunk with; to be crazy about

Rújiā 儒家 Confucianists; the Confucian school

rǔ 乳 ① breasts; the nipple ② milk ③ any milk-like liquid ④ the young of animals, birds, etc. ⑤ to give birth

rǔái 乳癌 breast cancer

rǔlào/rǔluò 乳酪 junket; curds

rǔniú 乳牛 the dairy cattle; a milch cow

rù 入 ① to enter; to come into ② to join; to come into the company of ③ to arrive at; to reach ④ to put in ⑤ receipts; income ⑥ to get out of sight; to disappear ⑦ to get (inside, picked, elected, etc.) ⑧ to agree with; to conform to ⑨ one of the four tones of a character

rùchǎngquàn 入场券 an admission ticket

rùgǔ 入股 to become a shareholder

rùjìng 入境 to enter a country

rùkǒu 入口 an entrance

rùmén 入门 to have an elementary knowledge of

rùqīn 入侵 to invade; to intrude

rùshì 入世 to take part in human society

rùshǒu 入手 to begin; to start; to put one's hand to

rùshuì 入睡 to go to sleep; to fall asleep

rùwéi 入围 to be selected as one of the few

rùxuǎn 入选 to be selected

rùxué 入学 to enter school

rùyù 入狱 to be imprisoned

ruǎn 软 ① soft; pliable; tender ② gentle; soft; mild ③ weak; cowardly ④ easily moved or influenced ⑤ poor in quality, ability, etc.

ruǎngǔ 软骨 (anatomy) a cartilage

ruǎnhuà 软化 ① to soften; to conciliate ② to soften

ruǎnjiàn 软件 (computer) software

ruǎnpiàn 软片 (photographic) film; roll film

ruǎnruò 软弱 weak; feeble; flabby

ruǎntǐ 软体 (computer) software

ruìlì 锐利 sharp; pointed

Ruìdiǎn 瑞典 Sweden

Ruìshì 瑞士 Switzerland

ruìxuě 瑞雪 ① a timely snow in late winter or early spring; a seasonable snow that will kill pests and that portends a bumper crop in the coming year ② a Chinese medicinal herb

rùn 闰 ① with surplus or leftover ② usurped; deputy or substitute ③ extra, inserted between others, as a day, or a month; to intercalate

rùnhuáyóu 润滑油 lubricating oil

rùnzé 润泽 ① moist and glossy ② to invigorate; to moisten

ruò 若 similar to; like
⇨ rě

ruòfēi 若非 unless; if not

ruògān 若干 some; a few; several

ruòshì 若是 if; suppose

ruòyào 若要 if...has (have) to...

ruò 弱 ① weak; fragile; feeble;

tender ② inferior ③ young ④ a little less than

ruòdiǎn 弱点 a weak point; a weakness

ruòzhě 弱者 the weak and the timid

S

sā 撒 ① to loosen; to unleash ② to relax; to ease ③ to exhibit; to display; to show
⇨**sǎ**

sāhuǎng 撒谎 to tell a lie; to lie

sǎ 洒 to splash; to sprinkle (liquids)

sǎ 撒 to scatter; to sprinkle; to disperse
⇨**sā**

sà 卅 thirty; 30th (of a month)

Sà'ěrwǎduō 萨尔瓦多 El Salvador

sāi 腮 the cheeks

sāi 塞 (usually used in the spoken language) a cork or stopper; to cork; to seal
⇨**sài, sè**

sāichē 塞车 a traffic jam; a traffic block

sài 塞 strategic points along the frontiers
⇨**sāi, sè**

Sàinàhé 塞纳河 the Seine River

sài 赛 ① to compete; to contest; to rival; to contend for superiority ② a race; a tournament; a match; a game ③ to surpass ④ a surname

sàichē 赛车 a car race; to race cars

sàipǎo 赛跑 to run a race on foot; a foot race

sān 三 three; third; thrice

sāndù kōngjiān 三度空间 three-dimensional space

sānfān-wǔcì 三番五次 time and again; over and over again;

repeatedly

sāngū-liùpó 三姑六婆 women whose professions are either illegitimate or disreputable such as 尼姑, 道姑, 卦姑, 牙婆, 媒婆, 师婆, 虔婆, 药婆, 稳婆 (a reference to despicable women in general)

sānhéyuàn 三合院 a Chinese courtyard with a mainroom and two side rooms on three sides

sānjiǎo 三角 ① trigonometry ② three angles

sānjiǎoxíng 三角形 a triangle

sānlúnchē 三轮车 a pedicab; a tricycle

sānmíngzhì 三明治 a sandwich

sānqīwǔ jiǎnzū 三七五减租 the 37.5% rental reduction policy, the first step taken in Taiwan's land reform program in 1949, under which the ceiling of farm rental was fixed at 37.5% of the crop yield

Sānxiá 三峡 the Three Gorges of the Changjiang (Yangzi) River

sǎn 伞 ① an umbrella ② a parachute

sǎn 散 ① loose; loosened ② idle; leisurely ③ powdered medicine
⇨**sàn**

sǎnwén 散文 prose

sàn 散 ① to scatter; to disperse ② to disseminate; to give out ③ to end; to be over; to stop
⇨**sǎn**

sànbù 散布 ① to scatter; to sprinkle ② to spread

sànbù 散步 to take a walk, a

stroll, or a ramble

sànfā 散发 ① to send out; to emit ② to distribute; to issue; to give out

sànrè 散热 to dissipate heat

sāngshì 丧事 funeral affairs

sāngshù 桑树 a mulberry tree

sǎngzi 嗓子 ① the throat ② one's voice

sàngshēng 丧生 to lose one's life

sàngshī 丧失 to lose; to be deprived of

sāodòng 骚动 disturbance; upheaval; unrest

sāorǎo 骚扰 to disturb; to harass; to agitate

sǎo 扫 ① to sweep with a broom; to clear away; to clean ② to wipe out; to weed out; to exterminate; to mop up ③ sweepingly; totally ④ to paint (the eyebrows, etc.)
⇨sào

sǎochú 扫除 ① to sweep up; to clean ② to eliminate

sǎodì 扫地 ① to sweep the floor ② (said of reputation) to soil

sǎohēi 扫黑 to crack down on crime

sǎomiáo 扫描 (electricity) scanning

sǎomiáoqì 扫描器 a scanner

sǎozi 嫂子 the wife of one's elder brother; a sister-in-law

sào 扫 a broom
⇨sǎo

sè 色 ① a color; a tinge; a tint; a hue ② facial expression; a look; an appearance ③ sensuality; lust; lewdness; carnal pleasure ④ worldly things ⑤ a kind; a sort
⇨shǎi

sècǎi 色彩 a tinge; a color; a hue; a tint

sèdiào 色调 a shade of color; a tone

sèqíng 色情 sexual passion; lust

sèsù 色素 pigment

sèxiàng 色相 ① (Buddhism) the outward appearance of a thing

② feminine charm

sèzé 色泽 a tinge; a color; a hue; a tint

sè 塞 (usually used in the written language) ① to block; to stop up; to clog ② to stuff; to squeeze in; to fill
⇨sāi, sài

sēnlín 森林 forest

sēng 僧 a Buddhist; a priest; a monk

shā 杀 ① to kill; to put to death; to slaughter ② to weaken; to deflate ③ to fight ④ extremely; exceedingly

shāhài 杀害 to murder; to kill

shājià 杀价 to reduce prices; to cut price down

shārén 杀人 to kill a person; to murder

shāshǒu 杀手 a hit man; a killer

shāsǐ 杀死 to kill; to slay; to murder

shā 沙 ① sand; tiny gravel or pebbles ② the land around water; a beach; a sandbank; a desert ③ (said of fruit, especially melons) overripe ④ hoarse—not glossy or smooth; granular ⑤ a kind of clay for making utensils, etc.

shāfā 沙发 a sofa

Shāguó 沙国 short for Saudi Arabia

shākēng 沙坑 a sand pit

shālā 沙拉 salad

shālāyóu 沙拉油 salad oil

shālóng 沙龙 a salon

shāmò 沙漠 a desert

shātān 沙滩 a sandbank; a sandy beach

shātǔ 沙土 sandy soil

Shāwūdì Ālābó 沙乌地阿拉伯 Saudi Arabia

shāyǎ 沙哑 (said of the voice) hoarse; husky

shāzhōu 沙洲 a shoal; a sand bar; a sandbank

shāzi 沙子 ① sand; grit ② small grains; pellets

shā 纱 ① yarn, as cotton yarn ② gauze; thin silk or cloth

shābù 纱布 ① gauze ② a bandage

shā 砂 ① sand; coarse sand; gravel ② coarse—not smooth ③ infinitesimal

Shāshìbǐyà 莎士比亚 William Shakespeare

shā 煞 ① to brake; to stop; to bring to a close ② to offset; to reduce; to mitigate ③ an auxiliary particle in old usage ④ to tighten; to bind
⇨shà

shāchē 煞车 ① to fasten goods on a truck or cart with ropes ② to brake

shāyú 鲨鱼 a shark

shá 啥 what

shǎ 傻 ① stupid; foolish; dumb ② naive ③ stunned; stupefied; terrified ④ to think or work mechanically

shǎguā 傻瓜 a fool; a silly; a blockhead

shǎzi 傻子 an idiot; a blockhead

shà 煞 ① a fierce god; a malignant deity; an evil spirit; a goblin ② very; much; extremely ③ to bring to an end; to conclude
⇨shā

shāi 筛 ① a sieve; a screen; a sifter; a strainer ② to sieve; to screen; to sift; to strain

shāixuǎn 筛选 screening; sieving; sifting

shāizi 筛子 a sieve; a sifter

shǎi 色 ① dice ② color
⇨sè

shài 晒 to expose to sunlight; to dry in the sun

shàitàiyáng 晒太阳 to be exposed to the sun

shān 山 a mountain; a hill

shāndì 山地 a mountainous region

shāndǐng 山顶 a mountaintop; a hilltop

Shāndōng 山东 Shandong Province

shāndòng 山洞 a cave; a tunnel; a grotto

shānfēng 山峰 a mountaintop

shāngāng 山冈 a ridge; a mountain ridge

shāngōu 山沟 a gully; a ravine; a valley

shāngǔ 山谷 a dale; a ravine; a gorge

shānhé 山河 mountains and rivers—(figuratively) the territory of a nation

shānjiǎo 山脚 the foot of a mountain

shānlín 山林 ① a mountain forest ② the place where a hermit lives

shānlǐng 山岭 the mountain range

shānlù 山路 a mountain path

shānmài 山脉 a mountain range; mountains

shānmù-jìyí 山牧季移 transhumance

shānpō 山坡 a mountainside; a hillside

shānqiū 山丘 mountains and hills

shānqū 山区 a mountain area

shānshuǐ 山水 ① mountains and rivers ② natural scenery; a landscape

shānshuǐhuà 山水画 a landscape painting

shāntóu 山头 a mountaintop; a hilltop

Shānxī 山西 Shanxi Province

shānyáng 山羊 a goat

shānyāo 山腰 the mid-slope of a mountain

shānyě 山野 mountain villages and the remote wilderness

shān 删 to delete; to take out; to erase

shānchú 删除 to delete; to strike out

shān 衫 a shirt; a garment; a gown

shānhú 珊瑚 coral

shān 扇 to fan; to instigate; to

incite
⇨shàn

shǎn 闪 ① to dodge; to evade; to avoid ② to flash; a flash, as of lightning; a very brief glimpse ③ to twist, strain, or sprain (one's back, etc.) ④ to cast away; to leave behind

shǎndiàn 闪电 ① lightning ② to lighten ③ with lightning speed

shǎnguāngdēng 闪光灯 a flashlight; a blinker

shǎnshǎn 闪闪 flickering; scintillating; to glint; to flash

shǎnshuò 闪烁 ① to twinkle; twinkling; to scintillate ② vague; evasive

shǎnyào 闪耀 to glint; to twinkle; to sparkle

Shàn 单 a surname
⇨chán, dān

shàn 扇 ① a fan ② a measure word for door or gate leaves
⇨shān

shànzi 扇子 a fan

shàn 善 ① good; virtuous; goodness; virtue ② to be good at; to be skilled in ③ to perfect; to make a success of ④ to remedy; to relieve ⑤ properly

shàn'è 善恶 good and evil; virtue and vice

shànhòu 善后 rehabilitation (after a disaster, a tragedy, etc.)

shànliáng 善良 (said of a person) kindhearted; well-disposed

shànxīn 善心 a compassionate heart; kindness

shànyì 善意 ① good or kindly intentions ② well-meaning

shànyòng 善用 to know well how to do...; to make good use of...

shànyú 善于 to be good at; to be skilled in

shàn 禅 to abdicate (the throne)
⇨chán

shàn 擅 ① unauthorized; arbitrary ② to monopolize; to take exclusive possession ③ to be

good at; to be expert in

shàncháng 擅长 to excel in; to be good at

shànzì 擅自 to do something without authorization

shāng 伤 ① a cut, wound, or injury ② to cut or injure ③ to hurt (feelings) ④ to make sick ⑤ grief; to grieve; distressed ⑥ to impede; an impediment

shānghài 伤害 to hurt; to injure; to harm

shānghén 伤痕 a scar; a bruise

shāngkǒu 伤口 a wound

shāngnǎojīn 伤脑筋 ① troublesome ② to beat one's brains; to have a nut to crack

shāngshì 伤势 the condition of an injury (or a wound)

shāngwáng 伤亡 casualties

shāngxīn 伤心 ① to hurt one's feelings; to break one's heart ② very sad

shāngyuán 伤员 wounded personnel; the wounded

shāng 商 ① commerce; trade; business ② a merchant, a trader; a businessman ③ (arithmetic) the quotient ④ to discuss; to exchange views; to confer

shāngbiāo 商标 a trademark

shāngchǎng 商场 a market place; a bazaar

shāngdiàn 商店 a store; a shop

shāngjiā 商家 a business firm

shāngliang 商量 to exchange opinions or views; to confer

shāngpǐn 商品 merchandise; goods

shāngquè 商榷 to discuss and consider

shāngrén 商人 a merchant; a businessman

shāngtán 商谈 to exchange views

shāngtǎo 商讨 a discussion; to discuss

shāngwù 商务 commercial affairs; business affairs

shāngxuéyuàn 商学院 the col-

lege of commerce

shāngyè 商业 commerce

shāngyì 商议 to discuss and debate

shǎngwu 晌午 (colloquial) mid-day; high noon

shǎng 赏 ① to reward; to award; to bestow; to grant; to give to an inferior ② a reward; an award ③ to appreciate; to enjoy; to admire ④ (a polite expression) to be given the honor of...

shǎngxīn-yuèmù 赏心悦目 to flatter the heart and please the eye—beautiful and restful

shǎngyuè 赏月 to enjoy moon-light

shàng 上 ① above ② upper; upward; up ③ top; summit; on ④ to ascend; to mount; to board ⑤ better; superior ⑥ previous; before ⑦ to go to court

shàngbān 上班 to go to office; to go on duty

shàngbānzú 上班族 white-collar workers

shàngbǎng 上榜 to have one's name included in the name list of successful candidates of an examination

shàngbào 上报 ① to report to a higher body; to report to one's boss ② to be published in news-papers

shàngbian 上边 ① the upper side ② up there

shàngcéng 上层 the upper layer, level, or stratum

shàngchǎng 上场 ① (drama) to go on stage; to enter ② (sports) to enter the court

shàngchē 上车 to get on or into (a car, bus, truck, or train)

shàngchuáng 上床 to go to bed

shàngdàng 上当 to be taken in

shàngděng 上等 first-class; superior quality

Shàngdì 上帝 God

shàngdiào 上吊 to commit sui-cide by hanging; to hang oneself

shàngfāng 上方 ① the place above ② the celestial realm

shàngfēng 上风 ① the upper hand; advantage ② windward

Shànghǎi 上海 Shanghai

shànghǎo 上好 superior; ex-cellent; the best

shàngjí 上级 higher-ups; superi-ors

shàngjiē 上街 ① to go into (or on) the street ② to go shopping

shàngjìn 上进 to make progress; to advance

shàngkè 上课 (said of students) to attend class; (said of teachers) to conduct class

shàngkōng 上空 in the sky; overhead

shànglái 上来 to begin; to get started

shànglai 上来 Come up! Come out!

shànglù 上路 ① to start a jour-ney ② (slang) good; well-behaved

shàngmén 上门 to visit

shàngmian 上面 ① the top; above ② the higher authorities

shàngqián 上前 to come for-ward

shàngqu 上去 to go up; to as-cend

shàngrèn 上任 ① to take up an official appointment ② a prede-cessor

shàngshān 上山 to go up a hill; to go to the mountains

shàngshēng 上升 to soar or rise

shàngshì 上市 (said of new products) to go on the market

shàngshù 上述 the aforemen-tioned

shàngsi 上司 a boss; a superior official

shàngsù 上诉 ① to appeal to a higher court ② to state one's case to a superior

shàngtái 上台 ① to go on the stage ② to assume office

shàngtiān 上天 ① Heaven; Providence; God ② to go up to the

sky

shàngtou 上头 ① the top; above; up ② the authorities

shàngwǎng 上网 to use the Internet; to surf the Net; to get on-line

shàngwǔ 上午 forenoon; a.m.

shàngxià 上下 ① above and below; up and down ② superior and inferior; ruler and subjects; senior and junior; high and low ③ about; more or less ④ heaven and earth ⑤ to go up and come down

shàngxiàn 上限 the upper limit

shàngxiào 上校 colonel (in the army, marine, and air force); captain (in the navy)

shàngxué 上学 to go to school

shàngxún 上旬 the first ten days of a month

shàngyǎn 上演 to perform; to stage (a play)

shàngyī 上衣 upper garments; jackets

shàngyǐn 上瘾 to become addicted to a certain drug or habit

shàngyìng 上映 to show (a movie)

shàngyóu 上游 ① the upper reaches (of a river) ② advanced position

shàngzhǎng 上涨 (said of commodity prices or flood waters) to rise

shàng 尚 to uphold; to honor; to esteem

shāo 捎 ① to carry; to take or bring along at one's convenience ② to brush over lightly ③ to wipe out

shāo 烧 ① to burn ② to boil; to heat ③ to roast; to stew ④ to run a fever; to have a temperature ⑤ a fever

shāobing 烧饼 a sesame seed cake

shāohuǐ 烧毁 to burn down; to destroy in fire

shāojiǔ 烧酒 white spirits

shāoxiāng 烧香 to burn joss sticks in worship

shāo 梢 ① the tip of a branch or things of similar shape ② the end of something—the result, etc. ③ the rudder

shāo 稍 ① slightly; a little; slight ② somewhat; rather ③ gradually

shāohòu 稍后 shortly (or soon) afterward

shāoshāo 稍稍 ① briefly ② gradually ③ just a little

shāowēi/shāowéi 稍微 slightly; a little; a bit

sháozi 勺子 a ladle; a spoon; a scoop

shǎo 少 ① small or little (in number, quantity, or duration) ② missing; lost ③ to be short of ⇨**shào**

shǎobuliǎo 少不了 ① indispensable; cannot do without ② unlikely to be lost

shǎojiàn 少见 seldom seen; unique; rare

shǎoliàng 少量 a small amount (or quantity); a little; a few

shǎoshù 少数 ① minority (a few; a small number (of)

shǎoshù mínzú 少数民族 ethnic minority

shǎoxǔ 少许 a little bit; a little; a sprinkling of

shào 少 ① young; youthful; junior; juvenile ⇨**shǎo**

shàonián 少年 ① a boy; a juvenile; a youth ② young

shàonǚ 少女 a young girl; a damsel

shàoxiào 少校 major (in the army, air force, and marine corps); lieutenant commander (in the navy)

shàoye 少爷 a young master (of a rich family); a young lord

shào 哨 ① a whistle ② an outpost; a guard station ③ to patrol

shàobīng 哨兵 a sentinel or sentry

shēchǐ 奢侈 luxury; wasteful; prodigal

shēwàng 奢望 to entertain hopes beyond one's ability to realize; a wild hope

shé 舌 the tongue

shétou 舌头 the tongue

shé 折 ① to lose money; to fail in business ② to break; to snap
⇨zhē, zhé

shé 蛇 a snake; a serpent

shě 舍 ① to throw away ② to reject; to give up; to abandon; to relinquish; to renounce; to part with; to forsake; to let go ③ to give alms
⇨shè

shěbude 舍不得 reluctant to give up, let go, etc.

shěde 舍得 to be willing to part with (a person, thing, etc.)

shěqì 舍弃 to give up or renounce

shè 设 ① to establish; to set up; to found ② to arrange; to plan or devise ③ to furnish; to provide ④ to lay out; to display

shèbèi 设备 ① equipment ② defense works

shèdìng 设定 (law) to establish legal relationship

shèfǎ 设法 to think up a method or a way

shèjì 设计 ① to design ② to map out a scheme

shèlì 设立 to establish; to set up

shèshī 设施 ① installations; facilities ② to plan and execute

shèxiǎng 设想 ① to have consideration for ② to imagine; to think

shèzhì 设置 ① to establish; to set up; to found ② establishment; installations

shè 社 ① an association; an organization; a corporation; an agency ② society; a community

shèhuì 社会 society; a community

Shèhuì Chù 社会处 the Department of Social Affairs

Shèhuì Jú 社会局 the bureau of social affairs (under a city or county government)

shèhuìxué 社会学 sociology

shèhuì zhǔyì 社会主义 socialism

shèjiāo 社交 social intercourse; sociality

shèlùn 社论 an editorial

shèqū 社区 a community

shètuán 社团 an association; a corporation

shèyuán 社员 a member

shèzhǎng 社长 the president or director (of an association, newspaper, etc.)

shè 舍 ① a house ② an inn ③ to halt; to stop; to rest ④ a self-depreciating possessive pronoun for the first person singular in formal speech
⇨shě

shè 射 ① to shoot ② to send out (light, heat, etc.) ③ archery

shèjí/shèjí 射击 to shoot; shooting

shèshǒu 射手 an archer; a shooter

shè 涉 ① to wade ② to cross ③ to experience ④ to involve; to entangle

shèjí 涉及 to involve; to relate to

shèwài 涉外 to be involved with foreign affairs or foreign nationals

shèxián 涉嫌 to be involved (in a crime)

shè 摄 ① to take in; to absorb; to attract ② to take a photograph (or a shot) of ③ to regulate ④ to represent

shèqǔ 摄取 to take in; to absorb

Shèshì 摄氏 Celsius

shèyǐng 摄影 photography; to take a photograph of

shèyǐngjī 摄影机 a camera

shèyǐngpéng 摄影棚 a sound stage; a (movie) studio

shèyǐngshī 摄影师 a photographer; a cameraman

S

shéi 谁 ① who ② anyone; someone

shēnbào 申报 to declare; to file (tax returns)

shēnqǐng 申请 application

shēnqǐngrén 申请人 an applicant

shēnqǐngshū 申请书 an application form; a written request

shēnshù 申述 to state; to explain in detail

shēnsù 申诉 to appeal; to lodge a complaint

shēn 伸 ① to stretch; to extend; to straighten ② to report

shēnchu 伸出 to stretch outward

shēnshǒu 伸手 to reach out one's hand

shēnzhǎn 伸展 to stretch; to spread out

shēnzhāng 伸张 to expand (power)

shēn 身 ① a body; a trunk ② one's own person; oneself ③ a child in the womb ④ in person; personally

shēnbiān 身边 ① at (or by) one's side ② (to have something) on one; with one

shēncái 身材 physique; physical build; figure

shēncháng 身长 ① the stature or height (of a person) ② the body length (of an animal)

shēnduàn 身段 ① physique; a figure ② postures (of a dancer).

shēnfen 身分 ① status; capacity; identity ② dignity

shēnfènzhèng 身分证 a citizenship card; an identity card; an ID card

shēngāo 身高 stature; height

shēnhòu 身后 after one's death

shēnjià 身价 one's social position or prestige

shēnjiào 身教 to teach by personal example

shēnqū 身躯 a body; stature

shēnshang 身上 ① on one's body ② (to have something) with one

shēnshǒu 身手 agility; dexterity; artistic skill

shēntǐ 身体 ① the body ② health

shēnxīn 身心 body and mind

shēnyǐng 身影 a person's silhouette; a form; a figure

shēnzi 身子 a body

shēnyín 呻吟 to groan; to moan

shēn 参 ① name of a star ② a ginseng
⇨cān

shēnshì 绅士 a gentleman; an esquire

shēn 深 ① deep; depth ② profound; mysterious; difficult ③ close; intimate ④ very

shēn'ào 深奥 deep; abstruse; profound

shēnchén 深沉 ① dark ② (said of a person) impenetrable; unfathomable; calm

shēnchù 深处 the deep, inner, or obscure part (of woods, heart, etc.)

shēndù 深度 ① depth (of a river, box, tank, etc.) ② profundity (of learning, etc.) ③ understanding (of the ways of the world); sophistication

shēngǎn 深感 to feel keenly or deeply

shēnhòu 深厚 ① long and close (friendship, relationship, etc.) ② profound (learning, training, etc.) ③ deep-seated; solid

shēnhuà 深化 to deepen

shēnkè 深刻 ① profound significance ② penetrating (views, comments, etc.)

shēnqiǎn 深浅 ① deep or shallow; depth ② (said of colors) deep or light ③ (good or evil) intentions

shēnqiè 深切 deeply; sincerely; intensely

shēnqíng 深情 deep affection or love

shēnrù 深入 (to research, study, delve, etc.) deeply or thoroughly into something; to reach or penetrate deep (into enemy territory)

shēnshān 深山 deep in the mountain

shēnshēn 深深 very deeply

shēnsī 深思 deep thought; contemplation; to think deeply

shēnxìn 深信 to believe strongly; firmly convinced

shēnyè 深夜 deep in the night

shēnyuǎn 深远 deep and far (in meaning, significance, etc.)

shēnzào 深造 to pursue advanced study

shēnzhī 深知 to know thoroughly; to realize fully

shēnzhòng 深重 very grave; extremely serious

shén 甚 what
⇨shèn

shénme 甚么 what

shénmede 甚么的 things like that; and so on

shén 神 ① gods; deities; immortals; spiritual beings ② soul; mind; spirit ③ appearances; looks; expressions; airs ④ supernatural; marvelous; wondrous; miraculous; mysterious; mystical ⑤ smart; clever

shénfu 神父 a Catholic father

shénhuà 神话 a myth; mythology

shénjīng 神经 nerve

shénmì 神秘 mysterious; mystical; mystery

shénmíng 神明 the gods; deities; divinities

shénqí 神奇 marvelous; miraculous

shénqì 神气 ① an expression; an air ② dignified; imposing ③ to put on airs

shénqíng 神情 an appearance; an air

shénsè 神色 a look; an expression

shénshèng 神圣 holy; sacred; divine

shéntài 神态 looks; appearances; facial expressions

shéntōng 神通 ubiquitous supernatural power, especially of the Buddha

shénxiān 神仙 an immortal; a celestial being

shénxiàng 神像 ① an image of a dead person ② an idol

Shěn 沈 a surname

shěn 审 ① to examine; to review; to investigate ② cautious

shěnchá 审查 to examine; to review

shěndìng 审定 to authorize (a publication, etc.)

shěnhé 审核 to examine and consider

shěnlǐ 审理 to try; to hear

shěnměi 审美 to be esthetic or artistic; to appreciate the beautiful; estheticism; appreciation of the beautiful

shěnpàn 审判 ① to try (a case or person in a law court) ② a trial

shěnpī 审批 to examine and approve

shěnshèn 审慎 cautious; careful

shěnxùn 审讯 to hold a hearing (on a legal case); to interrogate a prisoner

shěnyì 审议 consideration; deliberation

shěnmǔ 婶母 ① an aunt (the wife of one's father's younger brother) ② an address for one's aunt

shèn 肾 ① the kidneys ② the testicles

shènyán 肾炎 nephritis

shènzàng 肾脏 the kidneys

shèn 甚 ① to a great extent; to a high degree; very; exceedingly ② more than
⇨shén

shènduō 甚多 very much or many

shènwéi 甚为 very; much

shènzhì 甚至 even to the extent that...; even; to go so far as...

shènzhìyú 甚至于 though it may seem improbable (emphasizing the limit of what is possible or

S

probable); even; even to the extent that...; to go so far as...

shèn 渗 to permeate; to percolate; to infiltrate; to seep; to ooze

shènrù 渗入 ① to permeate; to seep into ② (said of influence, etc.) to penetrate

shèntòu 渗透 to seep through; to permeate

shènzhòng 慎重 cautious; careful; prudent; discreet

shēng 升 ① to rise; to raise; to ascend ② to advance; to promote ③ liter

shēnggāo 升高 to rise; to ascend

shēnghuá 升华 ① (chemistry) to sublime ② the rising of things to a higher level

shēngjí 升级 ① (said of an official) to be promoted ② (school) to advance to a higher grade

shēngqí 升旗 to hoist a flag

shēngqiān 升迁 promotion

shēngxué 升学 to enter a higher school

shēngzhí 升值 (economics) ① to revalue ② to appreciate

shēng 生 ① to breed; to bear; to beget; to produce ② to be born; to come into being or existence ③ unfamiliar; strange ④ unripe; raw; uncooked ⑤ to live; life; living; alive ⑥ a pupil; a student ⑦ savage; untamed; barbarian ⑧ the male character type in Chinese opera ⑨ creatures

shēngbìng 生病 to get sick; to fall ill

shēngchǎn 生产 ① to produce ② to give birth to

shēngchǎnlì 生产力 productivity

shēngchǎnlǜ 生产率 the production rate

shēngchǎnxiàn 生产线 production line

shēngcí 生词 a new word

shēngcún 生存 to survive; survival; existence

shēngdòng 生动 vivid; lively; lifelike

shēnghuó 生活 ① life ② to live

shēnghuǒ 生火 to make a fire; to build a fire

shēngjī 生机 ① liveliness ② the chance of survival

shēngjì 生计 livelihood; living

shēnglǐ 生理 physiological functions and processes; physiology

shēnglǐ shízhōng 生理时钟 biological clock

shēngmìng 生命 life

shēngmìnglì 生命力 vitality

shēngpà 生怕 very anxious; very apprehensive

shēngpíng 生平 ① one's brief biographical sketch ② in the course of life

shēngqì 生气 ① to get angry; to get mad ② vitality; liveliness

shēngqián 生前 before one's death

shēngqù 生趣 the pleasure of life

shēngrén 生人 ① a stranger ② a living person

shēngrì 生日 birthday

shēngshū 生疏 unfamiliar; unskilled

shēngsǐ 生死 life and death

shēngtài 生态 the relations and interactions between organisms and their environment, including other organisms

shēngwù 生物 ① a living thing ② biology

shēngwùxué 生物学 biology

shēngxiào 生肖 the relation of the year of one's birth to one of the 12 animals (the mouse, the ox, the tiger, the rabbit, the dragon, the snake, the horse, the sheep, the monkey, the fowl, the dog, and the pig)

shēngxiào 生效 to go into effect

shēngyá 生涯 ① a career; a life ② livelihood

shēngyì 生意 vitality

shēngyi 生意 business; trade

S

shēngyìng 生硬 awkward; stiff

shēngyù 生育 to give birth to; to bear

shēngzhǎng 生长 to grow; to develop; growth

shēngzhí 生殖 (biology) reproduction

shēngzhíqì 生殖器 reproductive organs; genitals

shēngzì 生字 a new word; an unfamiliar word

shēng 声 ① sound; voice; a tone ② music ③ language; a tongue ④ reputation; fame ⑤ to make known

shēngchēng 声称 to assert; to declare

shēngdiào 声调 ① tone; note ② the tone of a Chinese character

shēngguāng 声光 ① fame and conditions (of a person, etc.) ② (said of movies) sound and lighting

shēnglàng 声浪 the sound wave

shēngmíng 声明 to announce; to declare

shēngqǐng 声请 to make requests with reasons stated

shēngshì 声势 influence; fame; prestige and power

shēngwàng 声望 fame; reputation; prestige

shēngxiǎng 声响 ① sound; noise ② reputation

shēngyīn 声音 a sound; a voice

shēngyù 声誉 reputation; fame

shēngyuán 声援 to give moral support

shēngchù 牲畜 livestock

shēngkou 牲口 livestock

shēng 笙 a kind of panpipe with 13 reeds

shéngzi 绳子 a rope; a line; a cord

shěng 省 ① a province; provincial ② economical; frugal; to economize ③ to save; to omit; to reduce; to abridge
⇨xǐng

shěngdǎngbù 省党部 provin-

cial headquarters of a political party

shěngde 省得 ① lest ② to avoid; to save (trouble, etc.)

shěnghuì 省会 a provincial capital

shěnglüè 省略 to omit; to abridge; omission

shěngqián 省钱 to save money; economical

shěngshì 省事 ① to save trouble ② easy

shěngxià 省下 to save

shěngyìhuì 省议会 the provincial assembly

shěngyìyuán 省议员 a provincial assemblyman

shěngzhǎng 省长 the governor of a province in the early republican years

shěngzhèngfǔ 省政府 the provincial government

shěngzhǔxí 省主席 the governor of a province

shèng 圣 ① a sage ② sacred; holy

Shèngdàn 圣诞 Christmas

Shèngdànjié 圣诞节 Christmas; Christmas Day

shèngdì 圣地 a holy ground

Shèngjīng 圣经 the Bible

shènglíng 圣灵 the Holy Ghost; the Holy Spirit

shèngmǔ 圣母 ① the Virgin Mary; the Holy Mother ② an empress dowager

shèngrén 圣人 a sage; a saint

shèngxián 圣贤 sages and virtuous men; saints

shèng 胜 ① to win; to excel; to triumph; to surpass; to get the better of ② victory; success ③ (sports) a win ④ a scenic view; a place of natural beauty ⑤ excellent; distinctive; wonderful

shèng/shēng 胜 to be competent enough (for a task)

shèngdì 胜地 famous scenic spot

shèngfù 胜负 victory and defeat; the outcome (of a contest); success or failure

S

shèngguo 胜过 to excel; to surpass

shènglì 胜利 ① victory ② successfully

shèngrèn/shēngrèn 胜任 competent; qualified; equal to

shèng 乘 historical records ⇨chéng

shèng 盛 ① abundant; rich; exuberant; flourishing; prosperous ② (said of fire, storm, etc.) to rage ⇨chéng

shèngchǎn 盛产 to abound in; to be rich in

shèngdà 盛大 grand; magnificent; majestic

shènghuì 盛会 a grand gathering; a magnificent assembly

shèngkāi 盛开 in full bloom

shèngmíng 盛名 a glorious name; great reputation

shèngqíng 盛情 warm thoughtfulness; utmost sincerity

shèngxíng 盛行 to be popular or in vogue

shèngzhuāng 盛装 in full dress; in rich attire

shèng 剩 to remain; to be left over; in excess; residues; remainder; surplus; remains

shèngxia 剩下 the remainder; to be left over

shèngyú 剩余 the surplus

shī 尸 a corpse; a carcass

shītǐ 尸体 a corpse; remains

shī 失 ① to let slip; to neglect; to miss ② to lose ③ an omission; a mistake

shībài 失败 to fail; a failure; a defeat

shīdiào 失掉 to lose (a chance, confidence, etc.)

shīkòng 失控 out of control; runaway

shīlì 失利 to suffer a defeat (or setback)

shīliàn 失恋 to be jilted; to lose one's love

shīlíng 失灵 (said of a machine, instrument, etc.) to be out of order

shīluò 失落 to lose

shīmián 失眠 to suffer from insomnia; insomnia

shīmíng 失明 to become blind; blind

shīqù 失去 to lose

shīshì 失事 an accident; to meet with an accident

shīshǒu 失手 to break something or hurt somebody by accident; slip

shītiáo 失调 ① maladjustment ② to be careless about one's health, etc.

shīwàng 失望 disappointment

shīwù 失误 an error; an omission

shīxiào 失效 ① (law) to be invalidated; null and void ② (said of medicines, etc.) to lose potency or efficacy

shīxué 失学 to lack formal schooling or education

shīyè 失业 to lose one's job; jobless

shīyèlǜ 失业率 the rate of unemployment

shīyuē 失约 ① to break a date or an appointment ② to break one's promise

shīzhǔ 失主 (law) the owner of lost property or the victim of a robbery, burglary, etc.

shīzōng 失踪 missing

shī 师 ① a teacher; a tutor ② a division in the Chinese army ③ an army ④ a model; an example ⑤ to teach ⑥ to pattern or model after another ⑦ a specialist (of painting, music, etc.) ⑧ a local administrative chief

shīdà 师大 a normal university

shīfàn 师范 ① short for normal schools ② a master, tutor or teacher ③ to imitate; to emulate ④ worthy of being patterned after

shīfu 师父 ① tutors; masters; teachers ② a respectful term of address for monks, nuns, etc.

shīfu 师傅 ① (collectively) teach-

ers; masters; tutors ② the tutors of a king ③ a polite term of address for an artisan as a carpenter, cook, etc.

shīmǔ 师母 the wife of one's tutor, teacher, or master

shīshēng 师生 teachers and students

shīzhǎng 师长 ① one's teachers; faculty members ② a division commander

shīzī 师资 ① teachers ② the qualifications of a teacher

shī 诗 ① poetry; poems; poetic ② anything or quality as an offspring of pure imagination ③ short for *The Book of Odes* edited by Confucius

shīgē 诗歌 ① poems and songs collectively ② poetry

shīrén 诗人 a poet

shī 狮 the lion

shīzi 狮子 a lion

Shīzǐzuò 狮子座 (astronomy) Leo

shī 施 ① to act; to do; to make ② to apply ③ to bestow; to grant; to give (alms, etc.) ④ a surname

shīféi 施肥 to apply fertilizers

shīgōng 施工 to start construction or building

shījiā 施加 to exert; to bring to bear on

shīxíng 施行 ① (law) to enforce; to execute ② to perform

shīyǔ 施与 to give to the poor; to give to charity

shīzhǎn 施展 to display (one's feat, talent, skill, etc.)

shīzhèng 施政 (government) to administer; to govern

shīzhèng bàogào 施政报告 an administrative report (delivered by a head of state, province, etc. to the legislature, assembly, etc.)

shī 湿 damp; moist; wet; humid; to get wet

shīdì 湿地 a damp place; a marsh or swamp

shīdù 湿度 humidity

shīrùn 湿润 damp; to moisten

shí 十 ① ten; the tenth ② complete; completely; perfect; perfectly; extremely

shí'èrzhǐcháng 十二指肠 a duodenum

shífēn 十分 ① very ② completely ③ 10 points

shíquán-shíměi 十全十美 perfect; complete

shízìlùkǒu 十字路口 ① the junction of crossroads ② a point of decision

shízú 十足 extremely; completely

shí 石 ① rocks; stones; minerals, etc. ② a calculus, as a kidney calculus (commonly known as a kidney stone) ③ stone tablets ④ name of an ancient musical instrument ⑤ a surname

⇨**dàn**

shídiāo 石雕 ① stone carving ② carved stone

shígāo 石膏 gypsum; plaster

shíhuà 石化 to petrify

shíhuà gōngyè 石化工业 the petrochemical industries

shíhuī 石灰 lime

shíkuài 石块 a piece of stone or rock; a pebble; a boulder

shíqì 石器 stoneware; stone implements

shítián 石田 barren land; a field which is not arable

shítou 石头 stones; rocks

shíyóu 石油 crude oil; petroleum

shí 时 ① time; fixed time ② an era; an epoch; an age; a period ③ a season ④ hours ⑤ often; frequently ⑥ fashionable ⑦ proper and adequate ⑧ opportune (moments); opportunity ⑨ timely; seasonable ⑩ now...now...; sometimes...sometimes...

shíchā 时差 ① (astronomy) the equation of time ② the time difference of two places located on different longitudes or time zones

shícháng 时常 often; frequently

S

shídài 时代 an era; an epoch; a period

Shídài Zázhì 时代杂志 *Time* magazine

shí'ér 时而 from time to time; sometimes

shífēn/shífèn 时分 ① seasons; periods ② time

shíguāng 时光 time

shíhou 时候 time; hour; juncture; moment

shíjī 时机 opportunity

shíjiān 时间 ① time; the hour ② time—as opposed to space

shíjiānbiǎo 时间表 a timetable; a schedule

shíjié 时节 a period of the year; season

shíkè 时刻 ① time; hour ② always; constantly; continually

shímáo 时髦 fashionable; modern; up-to-date

shíqī/shíqí 时期 ① times; a period ② duration

shírì 时日 ① time ② an auspicious time ③ this day

shíshàng 时尚 a fad

shíshí 时时 often; frequently; continually

shíshì 时事 current events

shísù 时速 speed per hour

shíxià 时下 nowadays; in these days

shíxiào 时效 (law) prescription; the duration of validity

shízhōng 时钟 a clock

shízhuāng 时装 ① fashionable dresses ② (in show biz) modern dresses

shí/shì 识 ① to know, to recognize; to discern ② an opinion; a view ③ knowledge

shíbié/shìbié 识别 ① to discern; to distinguish ② identification

shí 实 ① real; true ② concrete; substantial ③ honest; faithful ④ practically ⑤ fact; reality ⑥ fruit; seed

shídì 实地 ① practically ② on the spot

shíhuà 实话 the truth

shíhuì 实惠 a real benefit; substantial

shíjì 实际 ① actual; real ② practical; realistic ③ reality; practice

shíjiàn 实践 to practice (a principle); to put in practice

shíkuàng 实况 factual conditions

shílì 实力 strength

shílì 实例 a living example; an example

shíqíng 实情 the real picture or real story (of a case)

shíshī 实施 to put (regulations, plans, etc.) into effect; to implement

shíshìqiúshì 实事求是 to work conscientiously or seriously; to make conscientious efforts to do things

shítǐ 实体 substance (as opposed to form)

shíwù 实物 goods or produce (as opposed to money)

shíxí 实习 to practice what one has been taught

shíxiàn 实现 to realize (a plan, etc.); (said of a dream, etc.) to come true

shíxíng 实行 to practice (a principle)

shíyàn 实验 ① to experiment; to test ② an experiment; a test

shíyànshì 实验室 a laboratory

shíyè 实业 industry; business

shíyòng 实用 ① practical use ② useful

shízài 实在 ① really; truly ② real; concrete

shízài 实在 well-done

shízhèng 实证 ① (Chinese medicine) a case of a physically strong patient running a high fever or suffering from such disorders as stasis of blood, constipation, etc. ② concrete evidence

shízhì/shízhì 实质 essence; substance

shí 拾 ① to pick up; to collect ② a formal form of the figure ten used to prevent fraud in a document or check ③ to put away ④ an armlet used by archers

shí 食 ① to eat ② food; meal ③ livelihood; living ④ (an old usage) salary; pay ⑤ eclipse

shípǐn 食品 foods; food items; foodstuffs

shípǔ 食谱 a cookbook; a collection of recipes

shítáng 食堂 a mess hall; the restaurant

shíwù 食物 eatables; provisions; foodstuffs

shíyòng 食用 ① edible ② living expenses

shíyù 食欲 appetite

shǐ 史 ① history; chronicles; annals ② a surname

shǐliào 史料 historical data

shǐqián shídài 史前时代 the prehistoric age

Shǐwǎjílán 史瓦济兰 Swaziland

shǐxué 史学 history (as a science)

shǐ 使 ① to use; to employ; to apply ② to make; to act ③ to indulge in ④ to send as diplomatic personnel; diplomatic envoys ⑤ an envoy; an emissary; a minister

shǐchū 使出 to exert

shǐdé 使得 ① all right; can be done or used ② to make; to cause

shǐhuan 使唤 ① to run errands for ② to order others to do something

shǐjié 使节 an envoy; an official mission abroad

shǐjìn / shǐjìng 使劲 to exert effort

shǐmìng 使命 a mission

shǐmìnggǎn 使命感 a sense of calling

shǐyòng 使用 to use; to employ

shǐ 始 ① to start; to begin; to be the first ② the beginning; the start; the first

shǐzhōng 始终 throughout; from beginning to end

shǐ 驶 ① (said of vehicles) to run; (said of vessels) to sail ② fast; fleeting

shǐ 屎 excrement

shì 士 ① a scholar; a man of learning; a gentleman ② a non-commissioned officer ③ a person ④ name of a chessman in Chinese chess

shìbīng 士兵 soldiers; privates; enlisted men

shìlín 士林 the intelligentsia; a scholastic community; literary circles

shìqì 士气 ① the morale of a fighting force ② the trends and temperaments of scholars in a given era

shì 氏 ① a family name; a surname ② the title of a government position in former times
⇨Zhī

shìzú 氏族 a family; a clan

shì 示 ① to show; to indicate ② to make known; to notify; a notice ③ to instruct ④ to demonstrate

shìfàn 示范 to set an example

shìwēi 示威 to demonstrate (by a mass meeting or parade)

shìyìtú 示意图 a sketch map

shì 世 ① the world ② a person's life span ③ a generation ④ an age

shìdài 世代 ① a generation ② from generation to generation ③ the times

shìjì 世纪 a century

shìjiān 世间 on earth; in the world

shìjiè 世界 the world

shìjièguān 世界观 a philosophical view (or concept) of the world; a world view

shìjiè mòrì 世界末日 the end of the world; doomsday

shìrén 世人 people of the world

shìshàng 世上 on earth; in the world

shìshì 世事 affairs of the world

shìsú 世俗 customs and traditions

shìnǚ 仕女 ① young men and women ② a painting portraying

S

beautiful women

shìchǎng 市 ① a market (place) ② a city

shìchǎng 市场 a market (place)

shìgōngsuǒ 市公所 a city or town office

shìjià 市价 market prices; the current price (of a commodity)

shìlì 市立 municipal

shìmiàn 市面 ① market conditions ② the sights and splendors in big cities

shìmín 市民 citizens

shìqū 市区 ① the area within the city limits ② the downtown area

shìróng 市容 the appearance of a city

shìyìhuì 市议会 a city council

shìzhǎng 市长 the mayor of a city

shìzhèn 市镇 small towns; towns

shìzhèng 市政 municipal administration

shìzhèngfǔ 市政府 a city government

shì 式 ① fashion; style ② a pattern; a type ③ a ceremony ④ a system

shìyàng 式样 ① a type; a model ② a mode; a style

shìde/sìde 似的 to give the impression that

shì 势 ① power; force; influence ② a tendency ③ the natural features ④ a situation ⑤ signs; gestures ⑥ male genitals

shìlì 势力 force; power; influence

shì 事 ① an affair; a matter; business ② a job; an occupation; a task ③ duties; functions ④ a service ⑤ a subject ⑥ to manage a business

shìbiàn 事变 an incident

shìgù 事故 an accident

shìhòu 事后 after an event; afterward

shìjì/shìjì 事迹 ① the accomplishments, exploits, etc. of a person during his or her life time

② a vestige

shìjiàn 事件 an incident; an event

shìlì 事例 an example; a precedent

shìqíng 事情 a matter

shìshí 事实 a fact; truth; reality

shìshíshang 事实上 in fact; in reality

shìtài 事态 the situation

shìwù 事务 business; work; general affairs

shìwù 事物 things; articles; objects

shìwùsuǒ 事务所 an office

shìxiān 事先 beforehand

shìxiàng 事项 an individual matter (as part of a whole); an item

shìyè 事业 ① an enterprise; a career

shìyí 事宜 ① affairs; matters ② the necessary arrangements

shìhòu 侍候 to wait upon; to serve

shì 饰 ① to ornament; to decorate; to polish (writing) ② ornamentation; decorations ③ to excuse oneself on a pretext, etc.; to fake ④ clothing and dresses ⑤ to whitewash; to deceive; to cover up ⑥ to play the role of; to act the part of

shì 试 ① to try; to test; to experiment ② to examine ③ to use ④ to sound out; to put up a trial balloon ⑤ to compare

shìbàn 试办 to do something on an experimental basis

shìfēi 试飞 to test a new airplane in flight; a trial flight

shìjuàn 试卷 a test paper; an examination paper

shìtí 试题 questions in a test or examination

shìtú 试图 to attempt; to try

shìxíng 试行 to try out something

shìyàn 试验 an experiment; to experiment

shìyòng 试用 to use on a trial basis

shìzhì 试制 to trial-produce; to trial-manufacture

shì 视 ① to look at; to observe;

to inspect; to see; to watch ② to consider or regard as; to take it for ③ to compare; to be equivalent to

shìchá 视察 to inspect

shìchuāng 视窗 (computer) window

shìjué 视觉 the sense of sight

shìlì 视力 the visual faculty; eyesight

shìtīng 视听 ① what one saw and heard ② public opinion ③ audiovisual

shìtú 视图 (machinery) a view

shìwéi 视为 to regard or consider as

shìxiàn 视线 ① the line of vision or sight—the straight line between an object and one's eyes ② eyesight

shìxùn huìyì 视讯会议 a videoconference; videoconferencing

shìyě 视野 the field of vision; visual field

shìmùyídài 拭目以待 to' wait for the result anxiously; to wait and see

shì 是 ① the verb to be (for all persons and numbers) ② yes; right; positive (as contrasted to negative)

shìbúshì 是不是 Is it true or not? Are you...? Is he...?

shìde 是的 yes; right; That's it.

shìfēi 是非 ① right and wrong; yes and no ② gossip; scandal ③ discord

shìfǒu 是否 Is it...? Are you...? Is he...?

shì 适 ① to go; to arrive at; to reach ② just right; exactly; appropriate; fit; just ③ comfortable; at ease with oneself ④ to follow; to be faithful to ⑤ only ⑥ by chance; accidentally ⑦ just now

shìdàng 适当 proper; appropriate; fit

shìdù 适度 appropriate; within limits

shìféng 适逢 at the very time (when something else took place)

shìhé 适合 suitable or suitable for; to fit

shìshí 适时 at the right time

shìyí 适宜 fit; suitable; proper

shìyìng 适应 to adapt; adaptation (to environment, etc.)

shìyòng 适用 fit or suitable for use

shìzhōng 适中 proper; adequate; appropriate

shì 室 ① a room; an apartment; a home ② wife

shìyǒu 室友 a roommate

shì 逝 ① to pass; to be gone; to depart ② to pass on; to die

shìshì 逝世 to pass away; to die

shì 释 ① to set free ② to explain; to interpret ③ to relieve ④ to disperse; to dispel ⑤ of Buddha or Buddhism

shìfàng 释放 to set free; to release

shìhào 嗜好 one's liking, hobby, or weakness for something

shìyán 誓言 a vow; an oath

shì 匙 a key
⇨chí

shōu 收 ① to draw together; to gather; to collect ② to end; to come to a close ③ to receive; to accept; to take ④ to contain ⑤ to retrieve; to take back

shōucáng 收藏 to collect and keep

shōucángjiā 收藏家 a collector

shōuchéng 收成 harvest

shōudào 收到 to receive; to obtain

shōufā 收发 to receive and send out (official papers, documents, etc.)

shōufèi 收费 to collect fees; to charge

shōufù 收复 to recover (lost territory)

shōugē 收割 to reap; to harvest

shōugòu 收购 to buy up; to purchase

shōuhuí 收回 to recover; to recall; to retrieve

S

shǒuhuò 收获 ① harvest; fruits (of efforts) ② to reap

shǒují 收集 collection; to collect; to gather

shǒujù 收据 a receipt

shǒukàn 收看 to watch (television)

shǒulù 收录 ① to employ; to recruit ② to include (in a list, etc.)

shǒumǎi 收买 ① to bribe ② to buy up ③ to win (support, people's hearts, etc. by less than honorable means)

shǒupán 收盘 the closing quotation (of a stock or commodity) for the day

shǒurù 收入 ① to take in; to include ② income; earnings; revenue; receipts

shǒushi 收拾 ① to clear away; to tidy ② to manage ③ to punish

shǒusuō 收缩 ① to shrink; to contract ② systole

shǒutīng 收听 to tune in; to listen to (the radio)

shǒuyì 收益 to get benefit; benefit

shǒuyīnjī 收音机 a radio receiving set; a radio

shǒuzhī 收支 income and expenditure

shǒu 手 ① hand; of the hand; having to do with the hand ② to have in one's hand; to hold ③ a skilled person; a person ④ action ⑤ personally

shǒubì 手臂 the arm from the wrist up

shǒubiǎo 手表 a wristwatch

shǒucè 手册 a handbook; a manual

shǒudiàntǒng 手电筒 a flashlight; an electric torch

shǒuduàn 手段 ① the means (as opposed to the end) ② a devious way of dealing with people

shǒufǎ 手法 workmanship; artistry; skill; technique

shǒugōng 手工 handwork; handiwork

shǒují 手机 a cellular phone

shǒujiǎo 手脚 ① hand and foot ② motion; action ③ tricks; juggles

shǒujīn 手巾 a towel

shǒujuàn 手绢 a handkerchief

shǒuliúdàn 手榴弹 a hand grenade

shǒupà 手帕 a handkerchief

shǒuqiāng 手枪 a pistol; a revolver; a gun

shǒushang 手上 in one's hands

shǒushì 手势 a gesture; a sign; to sign

shǒushù 手术 a surgical operation; surgery

shǒutào 手套 gloves; gauntlets; mittens

shǒuwàn 手腕 ① the wrist ② skill; tact; tricks; ability

shǒuxù 手续 procedures; red tape

shǒuxùfèi 手续费 service charges

shǒuyì 手艺 handicrafts; a trade

shǒuzhǎng 手掌 the palm (of the hand)

shǒuzhǐ 手指 ① a finger ② to point at something with the index finger

shǒuzú 手足 brothers

shǒu 守 ① to guard; to protect; to defend; to watch ② to wait ③ to keep (a secret, etc.) ④ to stick to; to maintain ⑤ to abide by

shǒufǎ 守法 to abide by the law

shǒuhù 守护 to guard; to protect

shǒujiù 守旧 sticking to old ways; conservative

shǒuwèi 守卫 ① to guard ② a guard

shǒu 首 ① the head ② the king; the emperor; the chief; the leader ③ a measure word for poems, songs, etc. ④ the first; the beginning

shǒuchuàng 首创 to found; to start; to initiate

shǒucì 首次 the first time

shǒudū 首都 the (national)

capital

Shǒu'ěr 首尔 Seoul, the capital of South Korea

shǒufǔ 首府 the capital city

shǒulǐng 首领 ① the leader; the chief ② head and neck

shǒunǎo rénwù 首脑人物 the chief; the boss; the key member; the mastermind

shǒuqūyìzhǐ 首屈一指 the foremost; second to none; the best

shǒushì 首饰 jewelry; ornaments; trinkets

shǒuxí 首席 the highest-ranking or highest-positioned; the senior

shǒuxiān 首先 the very first; at first; first of all

shǒuxiàng 首相 the prime minister; the premier

shǒuyào 首要 of the first importance; first of all; chief

shǒuyè 首页 the first page; page number one; the title page

shǒuzhǎng 首长 the chief; the leading cadre

shòumìng 寿命 the life span of a person

shòuxing 寿星 ① a reference to a person on his birthday ② the God of Longevity ③ Canopus

shòu 受 ① to receive; to accept; to get ② to take; to stand; to suffer; to tolerate; to endure ③ to be pleasant to the ears, etc.) ④ preceding a verb to form a passive voice

shòubuliǎo 受不了 cannot stand it

shòudào 受到 to be subjected to; to suffer

shòudeliǎo 受得了 to be able to endure

shòuhài 受害 to be victimized

shòuhàirén 受害人 the victim

shòuhuì 受惠 to be benefited

shòukǔ 受苦 to suffer (hardships)

shòulǐ 受理 to accept (a petition, complaint, etc.)

shòunàn 受难 to be in distress

shòupiàn 受骗 to be cheated or swindled; to be fooled; to be tricked

shòushāng 受伤 to be injured; to get hurt; to be wounded

shòuxíngrén 受刑人 a prisoner; one who is doing time

shòuxùn 受训 to receive training

shòuyì 受益 to benefit from; to benefit by

shòuyìrén 受益人 a beneficiary

shòuliè 狩猎 hunting; to hunt or trap game

shòu 授 ① to give; to hand over to; to confer (a degree, prize, etc.) ② to teach; to tutor ③ to give up (one's life, etc.)

shòukè 授课 to teach; to tutor

shòuquán 授权 ① to authorize ② to license

shòuyǔ 授予 to confer; to give

shòu 售 to sell

shòuhòu fúwù 售后服务 after-sales service

shòuhuò 售货 to sell goods

shòuhuòyuán 售货员 a salesman; a salesgirl; a salesclerk

shòujià 售价 the (retail) price (of a commodity)

shòu 瘦 thin; lean; slim; meager; scrawny; emaciated

shū 书 ① writings; a book ② a document; a certificate ③ a letter ④ to write ⑤ the style of the calligraphy; script

shūbāo 书包 a satchel; a school-bag

shūběn 书本 a book

shūdiàn 书店 a bookstore

shūfǎ 书法 calligraphy

shūfáng 书房 a study

shūhuà 书画 works of calligraphy and painting

shūjí 书籍 books

shūjì 书记 a clerk

shūjià 书架 a bookshelf; a book rack

shūjú 书局 a bookstore

shūkān 书刊 books and maga-

zines

shūmiàn 书面 written form of communication

shūmù 书目 a book catalog

shūxiě 书写 to write

shūxìn 书信 letters; correspondence

shūzhuō 书桌 a desk

shūqíng 抒情 to express one's feelings

shūkùn 纾困 to provide financial relief

shūshu/shúshu 叔叔 ① a younger brother of one's father ② a younger brother of one's husband

shū 殊 ① different; special; strange ② distinguished; outstanding ③ still; yet ④ exceed; over

shūróng 殊荣 special honors

shū 梳 ① to comb ② a comb; a coarse comb

shūzi 梳子 a comb

shūchàng 舒畅 ① pleasant; comfortable ② leisurely and harmonious

shūfu 舒服 comfortable; cozy; comfort

shūshì 舒适 comfortable; cozy; snug

shūzhǎn 舒展 to limber up; to unfold; to relax; to stretch

shū 疏 ① careless; neglectful ② unfamiliar; distant; unfriendly ③ thin; sparse; few ④ to channel; to remove obstructions ⑤ coarse ⑥ to present point by point ⑦ to explicate; to annotate

shūdǎo 疏导 ① to channel ② to enlighten

shūhu 疏忽 careless; remiss; negligent; oversight; to neglect

shūsàn 疏散 to disperse; dispersion

shūshī 疏失 remiss; at fault; negligent

shūyuǎn 疏远 (said of relations) not close

shū 输 ① to transport; to convey; to haul ② to be beaten; to lose (a

game, contest, etc.)

shūchū 输出 ① export (of goods); to export ② (computer) output

shūrù 输入 ① import (of goods); to import ② (computer) input

shūsòng 输送 to transport; to convey

shūxuè/shúxiě 输血 ① (medicine) blood transfusion ② to give aid and support; to give somebody a shot in the arm

shūcài 蔬菜 vegetables

shūguǒ 蔬果 vegetables and fruit

shúhuí 赎回 to recover by paying money; to redeem; to ransom

shú 塾 an anteroom or vestibule

shú/shóu 熟 ① cooked or well-done (as opposed to raw); prepared or processed ② ripe (fruit); to ripen ③ very familiar; well-versed; experienced; conversant ④ deep or sound (sleep) ⑤ careful or painstaking (survey, study, inspection, etc.)

shúliàn/shóuliàn 熟练 experienced, skilled, or dexterous

shúrén/shóurén 熟人 an old acquaintance

shúxī/shóuxī 熟悉 very familiar with

shúzhī/shóuzhī 熟知 well acquainted or familiar with; to know well

shǔ 暑 ① hot; heat; the heat of summer ② midsummer; summer

shǔjià 暑假 summer vacation

shǔqi/shǔqí 暑期 ① summer ② the summer vacation

shǔ 属 ① to belong to; to be subordinate to ② a category; a class; a kind
⇨zhǔ

shǔxià 属下 one's subordinate

shǔxìng 属性 an attribute

shǔyú 属于 to belong to

shǔ 署 a public office

shǔ/shù 署 ① to arrange ② to write down; to put down ③ to be

a deputy

shǔ 数 ① to count; to enumerate ② to count (as best, etc.); to be reckoned as exceptionally (good, bad, etc.).
⇨shù

shù 术 ① a skill; a feat ② a way or method to do something

shùyǔ 术语 professional jargon; terminology; technical terms

shù 束 ① a bunch; a bundle ② to bind ③ to control; to restrain; restraint

shùfù/shúfú 束缚 restrictions; to restrain; to bind up

shù 述 ① to give an account of; to explain; to expound ② to follow (precedents); to carry forward

shù 树 ① a tree ② to plant ③ to erect; to establish

shùgàn 树干 the trunk of a tree

shùlì 树立 to establish (a reputation, etc.)

shùlín 树林 a forest; woods

shùmiáo 树苗 a seedling; a sapling

shùmù 树木 a tree

shùyè 树叶 the leaf of a tree; foliage

shùzhī 树枝 the branch of a tree

shù 竖 ① to erect; to set up; to stand ② upright; perpendicular; vertical ③ petty officers in the palace ④ a downward, perpendicular stroke in calligraphy

shùlì 竖立 to erect

shù 数 ① number; quantity; amount; sum ② (mathematics) numbers ③ several; a few ④ a plan; an idea ⑤ fate; destiny ⑥ art
⇨shǔ

shùchuánjī 数传机 (computer) modulator-demodulator; modem

shù'é 数额 number; sum

shùjù 数据 data

shùjùjī 数据机 (computer) a modulator-demodulator; a modem

shùliàng 数量 quantity; amount

shùmù 数目 number; sum

shùwèi 数位 digital

shùwèi xiàngjī 数位相机 digital camera

shùxué 数学 mathematics

shùzhí 数值 numerical value

shùzì 数字 a numeral; a figure; a digit

shùkǒu 漱口 to gargle the throat

shùkǒushuǐ 漱口水 a gargle; a mouthwash

shuā 刷 ① to brush; to scrub; to clean; to daub ② to eliminate ③ a brush
⇨shuà

shuākǎ 刷卡 to pay by a credit card

shuāyá 刷牙 to brush the teeth

shuāzi 刷子 a brush

shuǎ 耍 to play; to sport

shuà/shuā 刷 to select; to pick out
⇨shuā

shuāi 衰 ① to decline; weakening; failing (health, etc.) ② declining or falling (nations, etc.)

shuāijié 衰竭 exhaustion; prostration

shuāilǎo 衰老 senile; senility

shuāiruò 衰弱 to debilitate; weak; sickly; not healthy

shuāituì 衰退 failing (energy, strength, etc.)

shuāi 摔 ① to throw to the ground; to fling; to break ② to fall down; to tumble; to lose one's balance ③ to get rid of; to shake off (a tail, etc.)

shuāidǎo 摔倒 ① (said of a person) to fall down ② (in wrestling, etc.) to fell the opponent or to throw the opponent to the ground

shuǎi 甩 ① to throw away; to discard; to cast away ② to leave (somebody) behind ③ to swing

shuài 帅 ① (slang) dashing; smart looking ② to lead; to command ③ commander-in-chief ④ to follow (with orders)

S

shuàigē 帅哥 a handsome guy

shuài 率 ① to lead (troops, a team, etc.); to command ② rash and hasty ③ simple and candid; frank; straightforward; to the point ④ (said of men) dashing ⇨lǜ

shuàilǐng 率领 to lead (troops, a team, etc.); to head (a mission, etc.)

shuàixiān 率先 to be the first; to take the lead

shuān 拴 ① to tie up; to fasten ② to drive a wedge between two parties

shuāng 双 ① a pair; a brace; a couple; persons or things that come in pairs ② two; both; even (as distinct from odd)

shuāngbāotāi 双胞胎 twins

shuāngbiān 双边 bilateral

shuāngchóng 双重 double; dual; twofold

shuāngdǎ 双打 to play in doubles (as tennis); doubles

shuāngfāng 双方 both parties or sides

shuāngshǒu 双手 the two hands; both hands

shuāng 霜 ① frost; hoarfrost ② white and powdery—like hoarfrost ③ coolness; indifference; grave ④ virtuous; pure and clean

shuǎng 爽 ① refreshing; bracing; pleasant; crisp; agreeable; brisk ② frank; straightforward; open-hearted ③ to feel well ④ to fail; to miss; to lose ⑤ to be in error

shuǎngkuai 爽快 ① straightforward; open-hearted ② readily and briskly ③ comfortable; pleasant

shuǐ 水 ① water ② a general term for seas, lakes, rivers, etc. ③ liquid; juice ④ flood disaster; flood ⑤ a surname

shuǐcǎi 水彩 watercolor

shuǐcǎihuà 水彩画 a watercolor painting; a watercolor

shuǐchǎn 水产 marine products

shuǐchí 水池 a pool; a pond

shuǐdào 水道 ① a watercourse; a waterway ② (by) water

shuǐdào 水稻 aquatic rice (as opposed to hill rice)

shuǐdiàn 水电 water and electricity

shuǐfèn 水分 moisture; water content

shuǐgōu 水沟 a ditch; a drain; a gutter

shuǐguǎn 水管 a water pipe

shuǐguǒ 水果 fruit

shuǐjiǎo 水饺 Chinese ravioli; boiled dumplings

shuǐjīng 水晶 crystal; crystallized quartz

shuǐkù 水库 a reservoir

shuǐlì 水力 water power

shuǐlì 水利 water conservancy

shuǐliàng 水量 water volume; amount of water

shuǐliú 水流 water current; water flow

shuǐmiàn 水面 the water surface; the water level

shuǐmòhuà 水墨画 a painting done with ink and water to bring out different shades of darkness

shuǐní 水泥 cement

shuǐniǎo 水鸟 water birds; waterfowls

shuǐniú 水牛 a water buffalo

shuǐpíng 水平 horizontal

shuǐshǒu 水手 a sailor; a mariner

shuǐtǔ 水土 ① the natural environment ② soil and water

shuǐwèi 水位 the water stage; the water level

shuǐyù 水域 waters; a water area

shuǐyuán 水源 ① the riverhead; the waterhead ② a source of water

shuǐzāi 水灾 flood disaster; floods

shuǐzhēngqì 水蒸气 water vapor; steam; vapor

shuǐzhì/shuǐzhì 水质 properties of particular specimens of

water

shuǐzhǔn 水准 a standard; a level

shuì 说 to persuade; to influence

⇨shuō

shuì 税 taxes; duties on commodities

shuì'é 税额 an amount of tax

shuìlǜ 税率 tax rates; duty rates

shuìshōu 税收 tax revenue

shuìwù 税务 tax administration; affairs pertaining to taxation

shuì 睡 to sleep; to rest with eyes closed

shuìjiào 睡觉 to sleep; to go to bed

shuìmián 睡眠 sleep

shuìzháo 睡着 to have fallen asleep

shùn 顺 ① to follow; to submit to; obedient ② in the same direction as ③ agreeable; favorable; comfortable ④ to arrange; to put in order ⑤ convenient; smooth ⑥ to take the opportunity to

shùnbiàn 顺便 at one's convenience; without taking extra trouble

shùnchàng 顺畅 smooth; unhindered

shùnlì 顺利 (going) smoothly; having no trouble; easy (going); encountering no difficulties

shùnshǒu 顺手 ① smooth (operation); easy (going) ② to do something without extra trouble ③ handy; conveniently

shùnxù 顺序 ① order; sequence ② according to right order

shùnxù-jiànjìn 顺序渐进 to follow in proper sequence and make gradual progress; to follow in order and advance step by step; to proceed in an orderly way and step by step

shùnyìng 顺应 to adjust

shùnjiān 瞬间 in an instant

shuō 说 ① to speak; to talk; to say ② to explain; to clarify ③ to scold ④ a theory ⑤ a description; a narration; a statement

⇨shuì

shuōbudìng 说不定 maybe; perhaps; probably

shuōchū 说出 to speak out; to reveal; to utter

shuōcí 说词 excuses; pretexts

shuōdào 说到 to speak of; to mention

shuōdào 说道 to say

shuōfǎ 说法 to preach Buddhism

shuōfa 说法 the way of reasoning; an argument

shuōfú/shuìfú 说服 to persuade; to convince

shuōhuà 说话 ① to speak; to talk; to say ② to tell stories ③ a chat; a talk ④ gossip; talk

shuōhuǎng 说谎 to tell a lie; to lie

shuōmíng 说明 ① to explain; to clarify; to expound ② expository writing

shuōmíngshū 说明书 a written explanation

shuōqǐ 说起 ① to start talking about; to bring up (a subject) ② with reference to; as for

shuōqilai 说起来 ① as a matter of fact; in fact ② to mention

shuōqíng 说情 to solicit a favor or to ask for mercy on behalf of others

shuōwán 说完 to finish speaking

shuōxiào 说笑 to joke; to talk and laugh

shuòshì 硕士 a holder of the master's degree

sī 司 ① to have charge of; to preside over ② a (government) department

sīfǎ 司法 judicature; judiciary

Sīfǎ Bù 司法部 the Judicial Departments

Sīfǎ Yuàn 司法院 the Judicial Yuan

sījī 司机 a driver; a chauffeur

sīlìng 司令 a commander

sīlìngbù 司令部 headquarters

sī 丝 ① silk ② very fine thread,

S

fiber, etc. as those making a spider's web ③ a general name of silk fabrics or goods ④ infinitesimal; a trace; a thread; a tiny bit ⑤ strings of musical instruments

sīháo 丝毫 the tiniest, slightest, or least bit

sīwà 丝袜 silk stockings; silk socks

sī 私 ① private; personal; person-to-person ② secret; clandestine ③ to have illicit relations or an affair with ④ contraband ⑤ prejudice; biased; to favor ⑥ selfish; selfishly ⑦ reproductive organs of both sexes

sīfángqián 私房钱 private savings

sīlì 私立 (usually said of schools, hospitals, etc.) established and operated by private funds

sīrén 私人 individual; personal; private

sīshēnghuó 私生活 one's private life

sīxià 私下 privately; secretly

sīxīn 私心 selfishness; favoritism

sīyíng 私营 privately-operated

sīyǒu 私有 privately-owned

sīyǒuzhì 私有制 private ownership of property

sīzì 私自 personally; privately

sī 思 ① to think; to contemplate; to consider ② memory; remembrance; to remember; to recall; to think of ③ to mourn; to grieve ④ to admire ⑤ to pine for ⑥ a final particle to sound off an expression

sīcháo 思潮 ① the prevailing trend of thought ② the changing tides of one's thought

sīkǎo 思考 to ponder; to think; contemplation

sīniàn 思念 to remember (old days, friends, etc.); to recall

sīqián-xiǎnghòu 思前想后 to ponder over (a matter, problem, situation, etc.)

sīsuǒ 思索 to study; to ponder over

sīwéi 思维 thought; thinking

sīxiǎng 思想 ① thought; ideas; mentality ② to think of; to recall

sīxù 思绪 a train of thought

sīwén 斯文 culture; men of letters; scholars; literati

sīwen 斯文 cultured; gentle; elegant; refined

sī 撕 to tear; to rip

sǐ 死 ① to die; to die for; dead; death ② used as an intensive or superlative; very; extremely ③ rigid, fixed, or unchangeable (regulations, etc.); immovable (drawers, etc.) ④ impassable; closed ⑤ obstinate or stubborn; persevering; resolute; resolutely ⑥ condemned (persons whose lives are numbered, as criminals on the death row) ⑦ inanimate; dull and stupid; inert; insensible; lifeless

sǐbǎn 死板 wooden (persons); rigid (regulations); fixed and unchangeable (methods, etc.)

sǐrén 死人 a dead person

sǐwáng 死亡 to die; death

sǐwánglǜ 死亡率 death rate; mortality

sǐxíng 死刑 a death penalty

sǐyīn 死因 the cause of death

sǐzhě 死者 the dead; the deceased

sì 四 ① four; fourth ② all around

sìchù 四处 everywhere; all around

Sìchuān 四川 Sichuan Province

sìfāng 四方 ① the four directions (east, west, north, and south) ② every direction; all sides; everywhere

sìjì 四季 the four seasons

sìmiàn-bāfāng 四面八方 on every side; all directions; all around

sìzhī 四肢 the four limbs

sìzhōuwéi 四周围 all around; on all sides

sì 寺 a temple; a mosque; a shrine; a monastery

sìmiào 寺庙 a temple

sìyuàn 寺院 temples

sì 似 ① to resemble; to seem ② like; as if

sìhū 似乎 it seems, appears, or looks as if or as though

sìshǐérfēi 似是而非 seemingly correct but really incorrect

sìxiào-fēixiào 似笑非笑 (One) looks smiling but (one) actually doesn't smile

sìfúqì 伺服器 (computer) server

sìliào 饲料 animal feed; fodder; forage

sìyǎng 饲养 to raise; to breed

sì 肆 ① to let loose; to indulge in; to behave without restraint ② to exhibit; to display ③ to execute a criminal and expose his corpse in the market ④ to extend; to expand ⑤ to assault; to attack suddenly ⑥ to use to the utmost; to exhaust ⑦ an elaborate form of four to prevent forgery

sōng 松 ① pines; firs ② loose; lax; slack ③ to relax ④ to loosen ⑤ soft; light

sōngshù 松树 a pine

sǒngyǒng 怂恿 to instigate; to incite

sǒng 耸 ① to alarm; to alert; to warn; to be sensational ② to rise up; to stretch up erect or at full length ③ to be born deaf ④ to urge; to egg on

sǒnglì 耸立 to tower aloft; to rise up steeply

Sòng 宋 ① the Song Dynasty (960-1279 A.D.); of or having to do with, the Song Dynasty ② a state in the Warring States period ③ a surname

Sòngcháo 宋朝 the Song Dynasty (960-1279 A.D.)

sòng 送 ① to send; to dispatch; to deliver; to convey ② to present; to give ③ to see someone off; to wish Godspeed to

sòngdào 送到 to send to; to deliver to

sònglǐ 送礼 to give presents; to send gifts

sòngxíng 送行 to see someone off; to give a send-off; to wish Godspeed to

sōu 搜 ① to search; to seek ② to inquire into; to investigate

sōuchá 搜查 to search (a house, a person, etc.)

sōují 搜集 to seek and gather; to collect (rare stamps, books, data, evidence against a suspect, etc.)

sōusuǒ 搜索 to search; to reconnoiter

sōuxún 搜寻 to search for; to seek and find

sōu/sāo 艘 a numerary adjunct for ships

sū 苏 ① purple perilla ② to revive; to come back to life; to resurrect ③ to awake ④ to rest ⑤ short for Jiangsu Province or Suzhou ⑥ a surname

Sū'é 苏俄 Soviet Russia

Sūgélādǐ 苏格拉底 Socrates, 469?-399 B.C., Athenian philosopher and teacher

Sūgélán 苏格兰 Scotland

Sūlián 苏联 the Soviet Union; the Union of Soviet Socialist Republic (USSR)

sūxǐng 苏醒 to come back to life; to revive; to come to

Sūzhōu 苏州 Suzhou, Jiangsu Province

sūyóu 酥油 butter

sú 俗 ① customs or customary ② vulgar; unrefined ③ common; popular ④ lay (as distinguished from clerical); worldly; secular ⑤ tasteless; trite

súchēng 俗称 commonly called...

súhuà 俗话 a common saying; a proverb

súhuàshuō 俗话说 as the proverb says; as the saying goes; as they say

súyǔ 俗语 a proverb; a popular saying; a common saying

sù 诉 ① to tell; to inform ② to accuse; to charge ③ to appeal ④ to resort to

S

sùkǔ 诉苦 to complain about one's grievances

sùshuō 诉说 to tell; to relate; to recount

sùsòng 诉讼 a lawsuit; to go to law; litigation

sùqīng 肃清 to wipe out or eliminate (rebels, etc.)

sù 素 ① white (color) ② plain; simple ③ vegetable food; a vegetarian diet ④ the original constitution of things; matter; elements ⑤ pure white silk ⑥ heretofore; up to the present ⑦ usually; generally ⑧ mourning

sùcái 素材 material; themes (of an artistic work) collected through daily experience

sùmiáo 素描 (said of writing or painting) a sketch

sùshí 素食 vegetarian food

sùyǎng 素养 one's general capacity and disposition as a result of long and regular self-discipline; accomplishments

sùzhì/sùzhí 素质 ① one's natural talent ② white

sù 速 quick; speed; speedy; prompt

sùchéng 速成 to attain goals within a short time

sùdù 速度 ① velocity; speed ② (music) a tempo

sùlǜ 速率 speed

sùshè 宿舍 a dormitory

sù 塑 ① to mold (in clay, etc.); to sculpt ② a figure; a model ③ plastics

sùjiāo 塑胶 plastics

sùjiāodài 塑胶袋 a plastic bag

sùliào 塑料 plastics; plastic materials

sùzào 塑造 to mold; to make by molding

sù 溯 ① to go upstream; to go against a stream ② to trace; to recall

suān 酸 ① sour; acid; tart ② stale; spoiled ③ sad; grieved; sorrowful ④ aching; a tingle; an ache ⑤ jealous; envious ⑥ stingy ⑦ (chemistry) acid

suàn 蒜 garlic

suàn 算 ① to count; to figure; to reckon; to compute; to calculate ② to infer; to guess; to foretell ③ to plan; to scheme

suànle 算了 ① Forget about it. ② settled; (said of a case) concluded

suànmìng 算命 to tell one's fortune

suànpán 算盘 an abacus

suànqilai 算起来 in total; all told

suànshì 算是 at last; finally

suànshù 算术 arithmetic

suànshù 算数 to count; to stand; to mean what one says

suànzhàng 算账 ① to settle an account ② to get even (with a person)

suī 虽 ① although; even though; even if; supposing ② only

suīrán 虽然 even though; although; in spite of; even if

suīshuō 虽说 even though; although

suí 随 ① to follow; to trace; to come after ② to accompany ③ to let (it go, be, etc.) ④ to resemble; to look like ⑤ to listen to; to submit to; to comply with

suíbiàn 随便 ① as you like; as you see fit; as you please ② casual; careless

suíchù 随处 everywhere; at all places

suídì 随地 anywhere; everywhere

suíhòu 随后 immediately afterward; right off; in no time at all; right after

suíjí 随即 right away; promptly; immediately; soon afterward

suíshēn 随身 to carry something with one; to take something with one; to carry about

suíshí 随时 at all times; anytime

suíshí-suídì 随时随地 at all times and places; anytime and anyplace; wherever and whenever

suíshǒu 随手 at hand; readily;

immediately

suítóng 随同 to follow or accompany; together with

suíyì 随意 according to your wish; as you like it; as you please

suíyuán 随缘 (Buddhism) ① one's activities resulting from the outer circumstances ② to do things in accordance with one's situation

suízhe 随着 along with; in the wake of; in pace with

suí/suì 遂 as in bànshēn-búsuí 半身不遂—hemiplegia ⇨suì

suì 岁 a year; age (of a person)

suìshu 岁数 age (of a person); years

suìyuè 岁月 times and seasons; time

suì 遂 ① to have one's will; to satisfy; to fulfill ② successful; to succeed ③ to proceed to; to reach ⇨suí

suì 碎 ① broken; smashed; torn; to break to pieces; to smash ② trivial; unimportant; trifling ③ garrulous; gabby

suìdào 隧道 a tunnel

suì 穗 ① fruits or grains in a cluster grown at the tip of a stem or stalk ② the ear of grain ③ another name of Guangzhou ④ a candle snuff; a candlewick

sūn 孙 ① a grandchild; a descendant ② a surname

sūnnǚ 孙女 a granddaughter

Sūn Yìxiān 孙逸仙 Dr. Sun Yatsen, Chinese political and revolutionary leader

sūnzi 孙子 ① a grandchild ② a grandson

sǔn 损 ① to detract; to damage; to injure; to destroy; harm; damage ② to lose; losses ③ to reduce; to decrease ④ weak; emaciated ⑤ to ridicule; to jeer at ⑥ (Chinese medicine) long-term emaciation

sǔnhài 损害 to impair; to injure; damage or loss

sǔnhào 损耗 to deplete; to exhaust (supply); to weaken (strength); loss

sǔnhuài 损坏 to damage; damage

sǔnrén-lìjǐ 损人利己 to harm others to benefit oneself

sǔnshāng 损伤 losses; to hurt (another's feelings, etc.)

sǔnshī 损失 losses; casualties

sǔnyì 损益 profit and loss; increase and decrease

sǔn 笋 bamboo shoots or sprouts

suō 缩 ① to contract; to shorten; to reduce; to decrease; to shrink ② to draw back; to recoil; to wince

suōduǎn 缩短 to shorten; to cut down; to shrink

suōjiǎn 缩减 to reduce; to lessen; to decrease

suōshuǐ 缩水 ① dehydration ② (said of fabrics) to shrink after washing

suōxiǎo 缩小 to reduce; to lessen; to shrink

suǒ 所 ① a place; a location; a position ② a building; an office ③ that which

suǒcháng 所长 one's specialty ⇨suǒzhǎng

suǒdé 所得 ① what one gets or receives ② income

suǒdéshuì 所得税 income tax

suǒshǔ 所属 subordinates; subordinate agencies

suǒwèi 所谓 so-called

suǒyǐ 所以 therefore; so; consequently

suǒyǐrán 所以然 reason; cause

suǒyǒu 所有 ① all; every ② to own ③ belongings

suǒyǒuquán 所有权 ownership

suǒyǒuzhì 所有制 the system of ownership

suǒzài 所在 ① a place; a location ② where one dwells

suǒzàidì 所在地 a seat

suǒzhǎng 所长 the head or director of an office ⇨suǒcháng

S

suǒ 索 ① a thick rope; a cable ② to search or inquire into ③ to demand; to ask; to exact ④ to decide to go ahead and do something without any more consideration

suǒpéi 索赔 to demand compensation; to claim

suǒqǔ 索取 to ask for

suǒxìng 索性 directly; to go all the way

suǒyǐn 索引 the index (of a book)

suǒnà 唢呐 a trumpet-like wind instrument

suǒsuì 琐碎 trifling; petty and varied

suǒ 锁 ① a lock ② fetters; chains ③ to lock ④ to confine ⑤ to lockstitch

suǒdìng 锁定 (computer) lockout

T

tā 他 ① he; him ② other; another ③ something else; somewhere else

tāmen 他们 they; them

tārén 他人 other people; somebody else

tā 它 it; that; this

tāmen 它们 they

tā 她 she

tāmen 她们 (referring to the feminine) they

tā 塌 ① to cave in; to fall in ruins; to collapse ② to sink; to droop

tāshi 塌实 ① steady and sure; dependable ② free from anxiety

tǎ 塔 ① a pagoda ② a tower ③ a lighthouse

tà 拓 to copy characters from an ancient tablet or tomb by rubbing over a paper placed on its surface ⇨tuò

tà 踏 ① to step upon; to tread upon; to trample ② to go to the spot (to make an investigation or survey)

tàqīng 踏青 to go hiking on a spring day; a spring outing

tāi 胎 ① a fetus; an embryo ② an unpolished, semiprocessed molding of something

tāi'ér 胎儿 a fetus; an unborn baby; an embryo

tāipán 胎盘 the placenta

tái 台 ① a raised platform ② a polite expression of addressing ③ a lookout; an observatory; a tower ④ a terrace; an elevated platform; a stage; a stand ⑤ short for Taiwan ⑥ a surname

Táiběi 台北 Taipei

Táibì 台币 Taiwan Currency

Táidōng 台东 ① Taitung City ② Taitung County

táifēng 台风 a typhoon; a hurricane

táijiē 台阶 ① steps leading up to a building ② brick or stone steps ③ a chance to extricate oneself from an awkward position

táimiàn 台面 (gambling) stakes

Táinán 台南 ① Tainan City ② Tainan County

Táishāng 台商 Taiwanese businessmen

Táiwān 台湾 Taiwan (Formosa)

Táiwān Dàxué 台湾大学 National Taiwan University

Táiwān Hǎixiá 台湾海峡 Taiwan Strait

Táiyín 台银 Bank of Taiwan

Táiyǔ 台语 Taiwanese (the language)

Táizhōng 台中 ① Taichung City ② Taichung County

tái 抬 to lift; to raise; to carry

táitóu 抬头 ① to raise one's head ② (said of the price) an upsurge; (said of fortune) a turn for the better ③ a bank's salutation for a client

tài 太 ① much; too; over; excessively; extremely; very ② very big or large ③ a term of respect, used in titles ④ a surname

tàijíquán 太极拳 tai chi chuan; shadowboxing

tàikōng 太空 space

tàikōngchuán 太空船 a spacecraft; a spaceship

tàikōngrén 太空人 an astronaut; a cosmonaut

tàikōngsuō 太空梭 a space shuttle; a shuttle

tàikōngzhàn 太空站 a space station

tàipíng 太平 peace; peaceful

Tàipíngyáng 太平洋 the Pacific Ocean

tàitai 太太 ① a madame ② one's wife

tàiyáng 太阳 the sun

tàiyángnéng 太阳能 solar energy

tàidu 态度 ① an attitude ② a manner

tàishì 态势 ① (military) a situation ② a posture

tài 泰 ① great; big ② quiet; calm; peace; ease ③ Thailand ④ good luck

Tàiguó 泰国 Thailand

tàirán 泰然 unperturbed

Tàishān 泰山 ① Mountain Tai (in Shandong) ② (figuratively) great importance ③ one's wife's father; father-in-law ④ Tarzan

tān 贪 ① to desire for more than one's rightful share ② to hope or wish for; to probe or search for

tānwū 贪污 corruption; graft

tānxīn 贪心 avarice; cupidity; greed

tān 摊 ① to spread; to open ② a pool of (water, mud, blood, etc.) ③ a booth; a stand; a stall to divide equally; to apportion

tānfàn 摊贩 a vendor or peddler

tānkāi 摊开 to spread out; to unfold

tānwèi 摊位 a stall or booth (especially a fixed one in a market)

tānzi 摊子 a stand; a booth; a stall

tān 滩 a beach; a sandbank; a shoal

tānhuàn 瘫痪 paralyzed; standstill

tán 坛 ① a platform for sacrificial rites; an altar ② a hall for important meetings and ceremonies in ancient China

tán 谈 ① to talk; to converse; to chat ② what is said or talked about; a talk

tándào 谈到 to speak of; to talk about; to refer to

tánhuà 谈话 a statement; a talk; a chat; to talk

tánlùn 谈论 to discuss; to talk about

tánpàn 谈判 negotiation; to negotiate

tánqǐ 谈起 to mention; to speak of

tántiān 谈天 to chat idly

tán 弹 ① to rebound ② to play ③ to impeach
⇨**dàn**

tánhé 弹劾 to impeach

tánhuáng 弹簧 a spring

tánqín 弹琴 to play (stringed instruments)

tánxìng 弹性 elasticity; resilience

tán 痰 phlegm; expectoration; sputum

tán 潭 ① deep water; a deep pool ② deep; profound

tǎnbái 坦白 frank; honest; to tell the truth

tǎnkè 坦克 (military) tank

T

tǎnkèchē 坦克车 a tank

tǎnrán 坦然 calm; unperturbed

tǎnzi 毯子 a blanket

tàn 叹 to sigh in wonderment or lamentation; to exclaim

tànqì 叹气 to sigh

tànwéiguānzhǐ 叹为观止 the most magnificent sight of all; an unrivaled sight

tàn 炭 ① charcoal ② coal

tàn 探 ① to find; to search; to prospect; to feel (in a pocket or bag) ② to spy; to investigate ③ a spy; a detective; a secret agent ④ to try; to venture; to tempt ⑤ to explore ⑥ to visit; to inquire about

tànbìng 探病 to visit the sick

tàncè 探测 to survey; to sound

tànjiū/tànjiù 探究 to investigate; to probe

tànqīn 探亲 to visit one's relatives

tànshì 探视 to visit (a patient, etc.)

tànsuǒ 探索 to probe; to search for; to look into

tàntǎo 探讨 to investigate; to study; to explore (possibilities, etc.); to approach (a problem, etc.); to discuss (causes or effects, etc.)

tàntóu-tànnǎo 探头探脑 to act stealthily

tànwàng 探望 ① to visit ② to look about

tànxiǎn 探险 to undertake an exploratory trip; exploration

tànzhēn 探针 (medicine) a probe

tànshuǐ huàhéwù 碳水化合物 carbohydrate

tāng 汤 ① soup; broth ② hot water ③ a surname

tāngchí 汤匙 a spoon

tāngyuán 汤圆 balls of glutinous rice

táng 唐 ① the Tang Dynasty ② a surname ③ abrupt; rude; preposterous; impertinent

Tángdài 唐代 the Tang Dynasty (618-907 A.D.)

tángsāncǎi 唐三彩 (archeology) the tri-colored glazed pottery of the Tang Dynasty

táng 堂 ① a hall; an office; a reception room ② a meeting place; a court of justice ③ a salutation for another's mother ④ relatives born of the same grandfather ⑤ venerable; grave; imposing

tángtáng 堂堂 ① dignified, venerable (appearances); impressive ② imposing; awe-inspiring; formidable

táng 塘 ① an embankment; a bund; a bank; a dike ② a square pool; a pond; a tank

táng 糖 sugar

tángguǒ 糖果 candy; sweets

tángniàobìng 糖尿病 diabetes

tǎngruò 倘若 if; in case

tǎng 躺 to be in a lying position; to lie down

tàng 烫 ① to scald; to burn ② very hot ③ to heat; to warm ④ to iron

tàng 趟 a measure word for a trip

tāo 掏 ① to take out; to pull out ② to dig; to scoop out

tāochu 掏出 to pull out or draw out

tāotāo-bùjué 滔滔不绝 talking fluently and endlessly

táo 逃 ① to run away; to flee; to fly; to abscond; to escape ② to dodge; to evade; to avoid; to shirk

táobì 逃避 to run away from; to shirk; to evade; to dodge

táohuāng 逃荒 to flee from a famine

táonàn 逃难 to seek refuge from calamities

táopǎo 逃跑 to run away; to flee; to escape

táoshēng 逃生 to flee for one's life

táoshuì 逃税 to avoid tax payment; tax evasion

táotuō 逃脱 to escape from; to free oneself from; to succeed in

escaping from

táoyì 逃逸 to break loose and get away; to escape

táozǒu 逃走 to run away; to flee; to escape

táo 桃 a peach

táohuā 桃花 the peach blossom

táozi 桃子 a peach

táo 陶 ① to make pottery or earthenware; pottery or earthenware ② happy; joyful ③ to move and influence a person ④ a surname

táocí 陶瓷 pottery and porcelain

táoqì 陶器 pottery; earthenware

táozuì 陶醉 to be intoxicated (with success, etc.); very happy; highly gratified

táoqì 淘气 naughty or annoying (children)

táotài 淘汰 ① to eliminate inferior contestants, goods, etc. ② elimination

tǎo 讨 ① to quell; to put down; to suppress ② to demand; to beg for; to get ③ to study; to examine into; to research ④ to denounce; to condemn ⑤ to marry (a wife or concubine) ⑥ (rarely) to govern; to administer

tǎohǎo 讨好 ① to curry favor; to please; to fawn on ② to be rewarded with a fruitful result

tǎojià-huánjià 讨价还价 to haggle over prices; to bargain

tǎojiào 讨教 May I ask for your advice?

tǎolùn 讨论 to discuss; discussion

tǎoyàn 讨厌 troublesome; nasty; to dislike

tào 套 ① a case; an envelope ② a suit (of clothes) ③ to wear or slip on (a sweater, etc.) ④ a trap ⑤ to harness ⑥ to pattern or model after ⑦ to trap or trick a person (into telling the truth) ⑧ convention; a formula

tàofáng 套房 a suite (of rooms)

tàoláo 套牢 lockup; to lock up

tàozhuāng 套装 an ensemble

tè 特 special; unique; peculiar; particular; extraordinary; unusual; outstanding; distinguished; exclusive

tèbié 特别 special; peculiar; particular

tèchǎn 特产 unique or special products (of a place)

tècǐ 特此 hereby

tèdì 特地 on purpose; specially

tèdiǎn 特点 characteristics; peculiarities

tèdìng 特定 ① specially designated ② specific; given

tèjì 特技 special skills; stunts; aerobatics

tèjià 特价 a specially reduced price

tèjiào 特教 special education (as for the blind, etc.)

tèpàiyuán 特派员 a correspondent (of a news agency, newspaper, etc.)

tèqū 特区 a special zone; a special district

tèquán 特权 privileges

tèsè 特色 special features; characteristics

tèshū 特殊 special; unusual; unique

tèwù 特务 a special military task

tèwu 特务 a secret agent

tèxiào 特效 special virtue or efficacy (of a medicine, etc.)

tèxiě 特写 ① a feature story (in a newspaper or magazine) ② a close-up (in a movie)

tèxìng 特性 characteristics; peculiarities

tèyì 特意 on purpose; intentionally

tèyǒu 特有 to have exclusively; unique; peculiar; special

tèyuē 特约 ① a special agreement or contract ② specially or exclusively engaged

tèzhēng 特征 distinctive features; characteristics

tèzhì/tèzhí 特质 special quali-

ties; characteristics; peculiarities

téng 疼 ① to ache; to hurt; pain; sore ② to dote on; to be fond of (a child)

téng'ài 疼爱 to be fond of (a child)

téngtòng 疼痛 to ache

téng 腾 ① to prance; to rear; to leap; to jump ② to go up; to rise; to fly; to soar ③ to turn over; to surrender; to transfer

téng 藤 a rattan; a vine

tīchú 剔除 to eliminate

tīcì 梯次 phases

tīxíng 梯形 (geometry) trapezoid

tī 踢 ① to kick ② to play (football)

tí 提 ① to lift by hand; to pull up ② to cause to rise or happen ③ to mention; to bring forward; to suggest ④ to obtain; to make delivery; to draw out ⑤ a rising stroke (in Chinese calligraphy)
⇨dī

tí'àn 提案 a motion; a proposal

tíbá 提拔 to promote (a person); to elevate

tíbāo 提包 a handbag; a valise

tíbō 提拨 ① to appropriate ② to remind

tíchàng 提倡 to promote (a cause, etc.); to advocate

tíchū 提出 to raise (a question, etc.); to put forth

tídào 提到 to mention

tígāng 提纲 an outline

tígāo 提高 to lift (morale, etc.); to raise (prices, etc.)

tígōng 提供 ① to offer (proposals, opinions, etc.); to provide (assistance, etc.) ② to sponsor (a TV or radio program, etc.)

tíjí 提及 to mention

tíjiāo 提交 to submit to another body for discussion

tíkuǎn 提款 to draw money from a bank

tíkuǎnjī 提款机 an automatic teller machine (ATM)

tíkuǎnkǎ 提款卡 an ATM card; a cash card

tíliàn 提炼 to refine (crude oil, etc.); to extract

tímíng 提名 to nominate

tíqǐ 提起 ① to lift up; to arouse (oneself to action, etc.) ② to mention

tíqián 提前 ① to give precedence or priority to ② (to complete a task, etc.) ahead of schedule

tíqǔ 提取 ① to draw (deposits from the bank) ② to pick up

tíshēng 提升 to promote (an officer, etc.); to elevate

tíshì 提示 ① to hint; a hint ② (drama) to prompt; to give a cue

tíwèn 提问 to ask a question

tíxǐng 提醒 to remind

tíyào 提要 ① a synopsis; a summary ② to bring forth the main points

tíyì 提议 to propose a proposal, suggestion, etc.

tízǎo 提早 ahead of schedule; in advance

tí 啼 (especially said of birds) to crow; to cry

tí 题 ① a subject; the title of a composition or speech ② a sign; a signal ③ the forehead ④ commentaries; notes ⑤ to sign; to write; to inscribe ⑥ the ornamental woodwork under the eaves of public buildings

tícái 题材 material constituting the main theme of an article, composition, etc.

tímù 题目 ① the subject or title of a composition or speech; a theme or heading ② a question or problem

tí 蹄 (zoology) a hoof ② the feet of beasts

tǐ 体 ① the body ② shape; form ③ an entity ④ a style; a fashion; a system ⑤ substance; essence ⑥ theory (as opposed to practice)

tǐcāo 体操 gymnastics; calisthenics

tǐgé 体格 physique

tǐhuì 体会 to understand through something beyond the intellect

tǐjī 体积 volume (of a solid)

tǐlì 体力 stamina; physical agility

tǐliàng 体谅 to be understanding or sympathetic toward; to be considerate of

tǐmiàn 体面 ① honor; dignity; face ② appearing good; looking elegant

tǐnéng 体能 stamina; physical agility

tǐpò 体魄 the human body as the source of strength

tǐrèn 体认 to perceive intuitively

tǐtiē 体贴 kind; considerate; thoughtful

tǐwēn 体温 body temperature

tǐxì 体系 a system; orderliness

tǐxiàn 体现 to embody; to incarnate; to reflect; to express

tǐxíng 体型 an external physical appearance; (physical) build

tǐyàn 体验 to experience firsthand; firsthand experience

tǐyù 体育 ① physical education ② athletics

tǐyùchǎng 体育场 a stadium; a playground

tǐyùguǎn 体育馆 a gymnasium

tǐzhì 体制 a system of rules; a system

tǐzhì/tǐzhí 体质 a bodily constitution; a physical makeup

tǐzhòng 体重 body weight

tì 剃 to shave

tì 替 ① to take the place of; to replace; to substitute ② for; on behalf of ③ to neglect

tìdài 替代 to replace; to substitute

tìhuàn 替换 to replace; to substitute

tiān 天 ① the sky; the heavens ② a day ③ seasons; weather ④ Nature; God; Heaven ⑤ nature; natural ⑥ father or husband ⑦ something indispensable

Tiān'ānmén 天安门 Tian An Men (the Gate of Heavenly Peace)

tiāncái 天才 a genius; natural talent

tiāncháng-dìjiǔ 天长地久 (literally) as old as heaven and earth—a very long time

tiānchuāng 天窗 a skylight

tiāndí 天敌 a natural enemy

tiāndì 天地 ① the world; the universe ② a field of activity ③ the upper and lower margins of a scroll ④ a world of difference

tiān'é 天鹅 a swan

tiānfèn 天分 natural endowments; talent

tiānfù 天赋 ① inherent and inborn ② natural endowments

tiānhòu 天候 weather

tiānhuābǎn 天花板 the ceiling (of a room)

tiānhuáng 天皇 ① the emperor of Japan; mikado ② the king of heaven

tiānkōng 天空 the sky; the firmament

tiānmìng 天命 ① a heavenly mandate ② fate ③ one's life span

tiānqì 天气 weather

tiānqiáo 天桥 an overhead bridge or elevated passage

tiānrán 天然 natural

tiānránqì 天然气 natural gas

tiānsè 天色 the color of the sky

tiānshang 天上 sky; in the sky

tiānshēng 天生 natural; to be born with; congenital; inborn

tiānshǐ 天使 ① an angel ② an emissary from the emperor

tiāntáng 天堂 heaven; a paradise

tiāntiān 天天 every day

tiānwén 天文 heavenly bodies; astronomy

tiānwénxué 天文学 astronomy

tiānxià 天下 the world

tiānxiàn 天线 an antenna (for radio, TV, etc.)

tiānxìng 天性 natural disposition

tiānzāi 天灾 a natural disaster

tiānzhēn 天真 naive; innocent

Tiānzhǔjiào 天主教 Catholicism

tiān 添 ① to add to; to increase; to replenish (stock, etc.) ② to have a baby

tiānjiā 添加 to add to; to increase

tián 田 ① agricultural land; cultivated land; a field; a rice field; farmland; cropland ② a surname

tiándì 田地 ① agricultural land ② position; condition; a plight

tiánjiān 田间 in the field

tiánjìng 田径 track and field

tiányě 田野 fields; cultivated lands

tiányuán 田园 fields and gardens

tián 甜 ① sweet; luscious ② agreeable; pleasant

tiándiǎn 甜点 sweet; dessert

tiánměi 甜美 ① sweet; luscious ② pleasant; refreshing

tiánmì 甜蜜 sweet as honey; honeyed; affectionate; fond; happy

tián 填 ① to fill up; to fill in; to stuff ② the sound of drumbeats

tiánbǔ 填补 to fill (vacancies, etc.); to make up a deficiency

tiánxiě 填写 to fill in (a blank, form, etc.)

tiǎn 舔 to lick; to taste

tiāo 挑 ① to select; to choose; to pick ② to carry things with a pole on one's shoulder; to shoulder ③ to pick by pitchfork
⇨tiǎo

tiāoti 挑剔 ① to be very particular in making selection ② to nitpick

tiāoxuǎn 挑选 to select; to choose

tiáo 条 ① an article, section, clause, etc. of an agreement, pact, treaty, law, etc. ② a measure word for long narrow things ③ in good order; (to present) one by one ④ stripes

tiáojiàn 条件 ① terms; conditions ② articles, clauses, etc. in an agreement, etc.

tiáokuǎn 条款 an article of laws;

a section, chapter, or clause of agreements, regulations, etc.

tiáolǐ 条理 ① reasonable; logical ② orderly; in good order

tiáolì 条例 rules, regulations, or laws

tiáomǎ 条码 (computer) a bar code

tiáowén 条文 the text of a treaty, regulation, law, etc.

tiáoyuē 条约 a treaty (between nations)

tiáozi 条子 ① a short letter; a note ② an order; a memo (often from a superior) ③ a summons for prostitutes

tiáo 调 ① to mix; to blend ② to regulate; to adjust ③ to mediate ④ to make fun of; to tease ⑤ balance; regular
⇨diào

tiáohé 调和 ① to mediate; to reconcile ② to harmonize ③ to adjust; to tune ④ to mix; to blend

tiáojì 调剂 ① to prepare drugs ② to adjust; to make adjustments

tiáojié 调节 ① to regulate; to adjust ② to moderate

tiáojiě 调解 to mediate; to patch up

tiáopí 调皮 ① naughty ② sly; treacherous; unruly; tricky

tiáowèipǐn 调味品 seasoning; spice; dressing material; condiment

tiáozhěng 调整 to adjust; to tune up

tiǎo 挑 ① to stir; to provoke; to arouse ② to dally; to make a pass at; to seduce
⇨tiāo

tiǎobō 挑拨 to instigate; to cause dispute

tiǎodòu 挑逗 to seduce; to arouse amorous desires

tiǎoxìn 挑衅 to provoke

tiǎozhàn 挑战 to challenge to a duel; a challenge

tiào 跳 ① to jump; to leap; to bounce; to spring ② to throb; to

pulsate; to beat ③ to skip (over); to make omissions

tiàocáo 跳槽 to abandon one occupation in favor of another; to get new employment

tiàodòng 跳动 to throb; to pulsate; to beat

tiàogāo 跳高 (sports) high jump (in track and field)

tiàopiào 跳票 a bounced check; a check that bounced

tiàoshéng 跳绳 rope skipping

tiàoshuǐ 跳水 to dive; to jump into the water; to dive from a diving board (or a springboard)

tiàotuō 跳脱 a bracelet

tiàowǔ 跳舞 to dance; dancing

tiàoxià 跳下 to jump down; to leap down

tiàoyuǎn 跳远 (sports) the broad jump; the long jump

tiàoyuè 跳跃 to jump; to leap; to hop

tiē 贴 ① to paste; to stick; to glue ② to keep close to; to nestle closely to ③ to make up the deficiency; to subsidize; subsidies; an allowance ④ proper; appropriate; comfortable ⑤ attached to

tiēqiè 贴切 proper or appropriate; apt

tiēshēn 贴身 ① personal servants ② closely attached, as children, undergarments, concubines, etc.

tiēxīn 贴心 intimate; close

tiě 铁 ① iron ② firm; indisputable; unyielding (like iron) ③ cruel; merciless; unfeeling ④ arms; weapons

tiědào 铁道 a railway; a railroad

tiěfànwǎn 铁饭碗 a very secure job

tiělù 铁路 a railroad; a railway

Tiělù Jú 铁路局 the Railway Administration

tīng 厅 ① a central or main room of a house ② a hall ③ a government agency

tīng 听 ① to hear; to listen ② to

obey; to follow ③ to wait for ④ a hall

tīng/tìng 听 ① to allow; to let ② to manage; to govern; to rule

tīngdào 听到 to hear of; to hear

tīnghuà 听话 ① to obey; obedient ② to wait for word or a reply

tīngjian 听见 to hear

tīngjiǎng 听讲 to listen to a talk; to attend a lecture

tīngjué 听觉 hearing; the sense of hearing

tīnglì 听力 ① hearing ② aural comprehension (in language teaching)

tīngqilai 听起来 to sound; to ring

tīngqǔ 听取 to listen (with due attention); to hear

tīngshuō 听说 ① It is reported that.... It is said that.... ② to obey

tīngxiě 听写 dictation; to dictate

tīngzhòng 听众 an audience; listeners

tíng 亭 ① a booth; a pavilion; a garden house or rest house ② slim and erect ③ exactly during

tíngzi 亭子 a pavilion

tíng 庭 ① a hall ② a yard ③ the imperial court ④ a court of justice

tíngyuán 庭园 a garden

tíngyuàn 庭院 a courtyard; a garden

tíng 停 ① to stop; to pause; to halt; to stay ② to suspend; to delay ③ percentage

tíngbǎi 停摆 to suspend work

tíngbó 停泊 to anchor; to berth; to dock

tíngchē 停车 to park a car

tíngchēchǎng 停车场 a parking lot

tíngchēwèi 停车位 a parking space

tíngdiàn 停电 ① blackout ② to cut off power supply

tíngdùn 停顿 to grind to a halt

tíngfàng 停放 to park; to place

tíngliú 停留 to stay

tíngzhǐ 停止 to stop; to cease

tíngzhì 停滞 ① to be held up ② indigestion

tǐng 挺 ① very ② to stand straight (or upright); to square; to straighten; rigid ③ to thrust forward (as one's breast) ④ to sustain; to endure; to stand; to hold out ⑤ to pull up ⑥ unyielding; tough ⑦ outstanding; remarkable ⑧ the number of machine guns

tǐngbá 挺拔 independent, eminent, and outstanding

tǐnglì 挺立 to stand upright; to stand erect

tǐng 艇 a long, narrow boat

tōng 通 ① to go, move, or flow unobstructed ② to let through; through ③ to lead to; to reach ④ open; passable ⑤ (said of a sentence) well-constructed; containing no fallacy ⑥ smooth; fluent ⑦ to communicate; to interchange ⑧ to understand thoroughly; to be versed in ⑨ thorough ⑩ common; popular ⑪ all; general; overall; throughout

tōngbào 通报 to notify

tōngcháng 通常 normally; usually; generally

tōngchē 通车 (said of roads, etc.) to be open (to vehicular traffic)

tōngchēng 通称 a popular name; popularly (or generally) known as...

tōngdào 通道 a passage; a way

tōngfēng 通风 ① to let the wind through; ventilation ② to let out news or secrets

tōnggào 通告 ① to notify ② a public notice; an announcement

tōngguān 通关 ① (while drinking in a group) engaging everyone else at the table in turn in a finger game ② customs clearance ③ to clear goods with the customs; to complete formalities at an immigration or customs check point at an airport or seaport

tōngguò 通过 ① to pass through ② (said of a motion or bill) to be passed ③ (said of a nomination or appointment) to be confirmed or approved

tōngháng 通航 air or sea navigation

tōnghóng 通红 red through and through; aglow; flaming red

tōnghuà 通话 to communicate by telephone or radio

tōnghuò-péngzhàng 通货膨胀 (economics) inflation

tōngjī/tōngqì 通缉 to order the arrest (of a criminal) by circular orders

tōnglù 通路 a thoroughfare; a passageway; a route

tōngshāng 通商 to have commercial intercourse; to trade

tōngshùn 通顺 (said of writings) fluent; smooth

tōngsú 通俗 popular; common

tōngtōng 通通 wholly; altogether

tōngxìn 通信 in correspondence with

tōngxíng 通行 ① to travel through (a road, etc.) ② common practice

tōngxùn 通讯 correspondence; communication

tōngxùnshè 通讯社 a news agency; a news service

tōngyòng 通用 ① (said of words or characters) interchangeable ② in common use ③ practicable; usable ④ (said of currency) in circulation

tōngzhī 通知 to inform; to notify; a notification

tóng 同 ① same; equal; identical; similar; common ② together ③ to share; to agree

tóngbàn 同伴 a companion

tóngbāo 同胞 a compatriot

tóngbù 同步 synchronism; to synchronize

tóngděng 同等 of the same rank or class

tónghào 同好 people with the same hobby

tónghuà 同化 to assimilate; assimilation

tóngjū 同居 to cohabit; a de facto marriage; a companionate marriage

tónglèi 同类 the same kind, class, or species

tóngliáo 同僚 colleagues

tóngméng 同盟 an alliance; a league

tóngnián 同年 of the same age

tóngqī/tóngqí 同期 ① of the same period ② of the same year, class, etc.

tóngqíng 同情 to sympathize

tóngrén 同仁 a colleague

tóngshí 同时 at the same time; simultaneously

tóngshì 同事 colleagues

tóngxiāng 同乡 the people from the same province, county, town, etc.

tóngxīn 同心 united at heart or in common purpose

tóngxíng 同行 to go together

tóngxìngliàn 同性恋 homosexuality

tóngxué 同学 a fellow student; a schoolmate

tóngyàng 同样 ① in the same way, manner, or fashion; likewise ② the same

tóngyè 同业 the people of the same trade or occupation

tóngyī 同一 the same

tóngyì 同意 to agree; to consent; to concur

tóngzhì 同志 a comrade

tóng 铜 copper; bronze; brass

tóngluó 铜锣 a copper gong

tóngxiàng 铜像 a bronze image; a bronze statue

tóng 童 ① a child; a minor; a virgin ② (said of land, etc.) bare; barren ③ a surname

tónggōng 童工 child labor; a child laborer

tónghuà 童话 nursery stories; fairy tales

tóngnián 童年 childhood; youth

tǒng 统 ① to govern; to rule; to control ② to unify; to unite ③ wholly; totally; all; completely; generally ④ succession; from generation to generation

tǒngchóu 统筹 to plan as a whole

tǒngjì 统计 ① statistics ② to count

tǒngtǒng 统统 wholly; completely; all

tǒngyī 统一 to unify; uniform; unitary

tǒngzhì 统制 ① a former military rank, equivalent to today's division commander ② to control; to govern and regulate; to exercise control (over)

tǒngzhì 统治 to reign; to rule; to govern

tǒng 捅 ① to poke; to stick ② to disclose; to let out ③ to offend; to provoke

tǒng 桶 a bucket; a tub; a pail; a barrel

tǒng 筒 a tube; a pipe; a cylinder

tòng 痛 ① painful; aching ② sorrowful; sad; bitter; poignant; bitterly ③ heartily; to one's heart's content

tòngchǔ 痛楚 pain; anguish

tònghèn 痛恨 to detest; to hate deeply

tòngkǔ 痛苦 painful; suffering; pain; anguish

tòngkuai 痛快 very happy; delighted

tòngxīn 痛心 heartbroken

tōu 偷 ① to steal; to filch; to burglarize; to pilfer ② to do something without others' knowledge; stealthily; surreptitiously

tōudù 偷渡 to stow away

tōulǎn 偷懒 to be lazy

tōuqiè 偷窃 to steal; to thieve

tōushuì 偷税 to evade tax payment

tōutōu 偷偷 stealthily; secretly; covertly

tóu 头 ① the head ② a measure word for cattle, etc. ③ the top; the first; first; the beginning ④ the two ends (of anything); a side; an aspect ⑤ the chief; the boss; the leader; the head (of a group) ⑥ (tou 头-) used as a suffix indicating positions or directions ⑦ (tou 头-) used as a suffix to certain verbs to indicate the worthiness

tóubù 头部 the head

tóudēng 头灯 (mining) a head lamp

tóuděngcāng 头等舱 a first-class cabin

tóudǐng 头顶 the top of one's head

tóufa 头发 hair on the head

tóujiǎng 头奖 the first prize

tóumù 头目 a chief; a leader; a ringleader; a chieftain

tóunǎo 头脑 ① brains; mind ② main threads; clues ③ the chief or boss

tóupí 头皮 the scalp

tóutòng 头痛 a headache

tóuxián 头衔 the official title of a person

tóuzi 头子 the leader (of bandits, rebels, etc.)

tóu 投 ① to throw; to pitch; to toss ② to project; to cast ③ to join; to submit to ④ to deliver (mail, etc.); to send (letters, etc.) ⑤ agreeable; congenial; harmonious; to fit in with; to cater to ⑥ to present as a gift ⑦ to lodge; to stay ⑧ to head (west, etc.)

tóubǎo 投保 to take out an insurance policy

tóubiāo 投标 to bid in a public tender

tóuchǎn 投产 to put into production

tóufàng 投放 ① to throw in ② to put (money) into circulation; to put (goods) on the market

tóugǎo 投稿 ① a contributed article ② to contribute an article

tóujī 投机 ① to speculate ② to see eye to eye

tóujī-dǎobǎ 投机倒把 to engage in speculation and profiteering

tóulán 投篮 (basketball) to shoot

tóupiào 投票 to cast a vote

tóurù 投入 ① to throw in ② to join (the army, revolutionaries, etc.) ③ to do something with concentration

tóushè 投射 ① to project; to shoot ② to harvest profit from speculation

tóushēn 投身 ① to give oneself to (the revolutionary cause, a military career, etc.) ② to find employment or shelter

tóushǒu 投手 (baseball) a pitcher

tóuxià 投下 ① to throw down; to drop ② to invest (capital)

tóuxiáng 投降 to surrender; to capitulate

tóuyǐng 投影 ① (mathematics) projection ② (art) cast shadow ③ to project

tóuzhì/tóuzhí 投掷 to throw (a discus, etc.)

tóuzī 投资 to invest; investment

tòu 透 ① to pass through; to penetrate ② thorough; quite; complete ③ to let out or through ④ to appear; to show

tòuchè 透彻 thorough; thoroughly; penetrating

tòuguò 透过 ① to pass through; to penetrate ② through the intermediary of

tòulù 透露 (said of something) to come to light; to divulge; to reveal; to let out

tòumíng 透明 transparent

tòumíngdù 透明度 transparency

tòushì 透视 ① to see through; to penetrate ② to observe what is behind a solid covering (by X-ray, etc.) ③ to gain a perspective of; perspective

tòuzhī 透支 to overdraw; to spend more than the budgeted

fund

tū/tú 凸 ① protuberant; convex ② to protrude; to jut

tū 秃 bald; bare

tū/tú 突 ① abrupt; sudden; unexpected; suddenly; unexpectedly ② to offend; to go against ③ to break through (enemy encirclement) ④ to project or jut out

tūchū/túchū 突出 ① to jut out ② outstanding; remarkable

tūjī/tújī 突击 to attack (or assault) suddenly; to raid

tūpò/túpò 突破 ① to break or smash (old records, etc.) ② to break through

tūrán/túrán 突然 suddenly; unexpectedly

tūwù/túwù 突兀 ① lofty and steep; high ② suddenly; abruptly; unexpectedly

tú 图 ① a picture; a map; a portrait; a chart; a diagram ② intention; aim; purpose ③ to plan; to scheme; to conspire ④ to seek; to pursue

tú'àn 图案 (fine arts) patterns

túbiǎo 图表 charts, diagrams, and tables—used in statistics

túhuà 图画 ① a drawing; a picture ② painting ③ to plot; to plan

túlì 图利 to desire to make money or profit

túpiàn 图片 pictures; photographs

túshì 图示 to indicate by a picture; the picture shows...

túshū 图书 maps, charts, and books

túshūguǎn 图书馆 a library

túshūshì 图书室 a reading room

túshuō 图说 books with illustrations; charts with notes; a manual with illustrative pictures

túténg 图腾 ① a totem ② (in old China) flags embroidered with the patterns of animals representing the various barbarian tribes

túxiàng 图像 an image; a picture

túxíng 图形 a graph; a figure

túyàng 图样 (architecture) a design

túzhāng 图章 a seal; a chop

túzhǐ 图纸 ① C a blueprint ② T drawing paper

tú 徒 ① disciples; followers; pupils; apprentices ② a crowd; a gang; a group of people ③ to go on foot ④ a punishment ⑤ only; merely; in vain ⑥ empty, as empty-handed ⑦ foot soldiers; infantry

túbù 徒步 to go on foot

túdì 徒弟 an apprentice; a disciple; a pupil

túrán 徒然 in vain; useless; meaningless

tú 途 a way; a road

tújìng 途径 a way; a road

túzhōng 途中 on the way; en route

tú 涂 ① to smear; to apply; to spread (ointment on a wound, etc.) ② to scribble; to scrawl ③ to erase; to blot out; to efface; to obliterate

túyā 涂鸦 ① to scribble ② graffiti

túshā 屠杀 to massacre

tǔ 土 ① earth; soil ② land; territory; domain ③ local; native; indigenous ④ unrefined; unenlightened ⑤ rustic; countrified ⑥ (raw) opium ⑦ an abbreviation for Turkey

tǔdì 土地 land

tǔdì 土地 local god of the land

tǔdòu 土豆 ① C potatoes ② T peanuts

Tǔ'ěrqí 土耳其 Turkey

tǔfēngwǔ 土风舞 folk dance

tǔmù 土木 civil engineering; construction projects

tǔrǎng 土壤 soil

Tǔxīng 土星 the planet Saturn

tǔzhù 土著 a native; an aborigine

tǔ 吐 to spit; to utter
⇨tù

tù 吐 to vomit; to throw up; to spew
⇨tǔ

tùzi 兔子 a hare; a rabbit

tuán 团 ① a sphere; something shaped like a ball ② a mass; a lump ③ a group; a party; a mission; an organization; a society ④ (infantry) a regiment, consisting of three battalions of foot soldiers ⑤ to unite

tuánjié 团结 union; solidarity; to unite

tuánjù 团聚 (said of a family, etc.) to congregate; a reunion; a gathering

tuántǐ 团体 an organization; group (action, etc.)

tuányuán 团员 a member

tuányuán 团圆 a union or reunion (especially of a family)

tuánzhǎng 团长 a regiment commander

tuī 推 ① to push; to shove ② to extend; to enlarge ③ to shirk; to shift (responsibility, etc.); to refuse ④ to elect; to recommend; to praise; to esteem ⑤ to move along; to change in succession (as seasons) ⑥ to look into; (to find out; to ponder; to infer; to deduce

tuīcè 推测 to infer; to deduce; to predict; to conjecture

tuīchén-chūxīn 推陈出新 to find new ways of doing things from old theories

tuīchí 推迟 to defer; to put off

tuīchóng 推崇 to respect; to praise highly

tuīchū 推出 ① to push out ② to present (a picture, a show, etc.)

tuīcí 推辞 to decline (an offer, invitation, etc.); to reject

tuīdòng 推动 to push (a sales project, etc.)

tuīfān 推翻 ① to overthrow (a government, etc.); to topple ② to stultify (a theory, principle, etc.)

tuīguǎng 推广 to propagate; to popularize

tuījiàn 推荐 to recommend (somebody for a job, etc.)

tuījìn 推进 to push forward; to advance

tuījǔ 推举 ① to recommend for a

post ② (weightlifting) to press

tuīkāi 推开 ① to push away ② to get away from (social activities, etc.)

tuīlái-tuīqù 推来推去 ① to pass the buck ② (to refuse to accept a present, assignment, etc.) by pushing it back and forth

tuīlǐ 推理 to reason (out); to infer

tuīlǐ xiǎoshuō 推理小说 detective stories

tuīlùn 推论 to infer; inference

tuīsuàn 推算 to calculate; to reckon

tuīxiāo 推销 to promote sales; to sell

tuīxiāoyuán 推销员 a salesman or saleswoman

tuīxíng 推行 to promote (a cause, movement, etc.)

tuīxuǎn 推选 to elect

tuífèi 颓废 ① ruined; weakened; decadent ② low-spirited; depressed

tuǐ 腿 the leg and the thigh

tuì 退 ① to retreat; to withdraw; to recede; to regress; to retrogress ② to send back; to give back; to return ③ to bow out; to retire ④ to recoil; to shrink

tuìbù 退步 ① to fall off; to regress; to retrogress; to fall backward; to suffer a relapse ② to retreat

tuìchū 退出 to withdraw or retreat (from a city or position)

tuìhuà 退化 to degenerate; to atrophy

tuìhuàn 退换 to return (merchandise) in exchange for another; to exchange a purchase

tuìhuí 退回 ① to return (a gift, defective merchandise, etc.); to send back ② to retreat; to turn back

tuìpiào 退票 ① (said of theaters, music halls, etc.) to refund; to return the ticket and get the money back ② (said of checks) to be dishonored; to bounce

tuìshāo 退烧 to reduce or remove fever

tuìwǔ 退伍 to retire or to be discharged from military service

tuìxiū 退休 to retire from active life

tuìxiūjīn 退休金 a retiring allowance; a pension

tuìxué 退学 to withdraw from a school; to drop out of a school

tūn 吞 to swallow; to engulf; to gulp

tūnshì 吞噬 ① (said of beasts) to swallow or devour (the prey) ② (said of fire, etc.) to devour; to engulf

tūntūn-tǔtǔ 吞吞吐吐 to hum and haw

tún 屯 ① to station (an army) ② to stockpile

tuō 托 ① to hold or lift, on the palm ② to entrust; to charge; to commission ③ a tray; a pad ④ to ask; to request ⑤ to consign ⑥ to use as an excuse or pretext ⑦ to send (messages, etc.) indirectly

tuō'érsuǒ 托儿所 a nursery school

tuōfú 托福 Thanks. (used in reply to others' congratulations on a success, a narrow escape, etc.)

tuō 拖 ① to drag along, after, or out ② to procrastinate; to drag out; to delay ③ to involve; to implicate

tuōlājī 拖拉机 a tractor

tuōlěi/tuōlèi 拖累 ① to involve or implicate ② a drag

tuōxié 拖鞋 slippers

tuōyán 拖延 to procrastinate; to delay

tuō 脱 ① to strip; to undress; to take off ② to abandon; to renounce; to cast off ③ to leave; to escape from; to get out of ④ to omit; omission; to miss out ⑤ to slip off

tuōlí 脱离 ① to break away ② away from; out of

tuōluò 脱落 to drop; to fall off

tuōshēn 脱身 to get away from; to escape

tuōshǒu 脱手 ① (said of goods or stock at hand) to sell out ② to slip off one's hands

tuōyīwǔ 脱衣舞 a striptease

tuōyǐng'érchū 脱颖而出 (in a race, competition, etc.) to overtake others or outscore rival teams

tuó 驮 to carry (a load) on the back

tuóluó 陀螺 a top

tuǒ 妥 ① firm; safe; secure ② appropriate ③ ready; set; to settle

tuǒdang 妥当 ① appropriate or secure ② ready

tuǒshàn 妥善 proper; appropriate

tuǒxié 妥协 ① a compromise; a reconciliation ② amity ③ appeasement (in international relations)

tuǒyuán 椭圆 (mathematics) an ellipse

tuò 拓 ① to expand; to aggrandize; to open up (new frontiers, etc.); to develop ② to push with hands
⇨**tà**

tuòzhǎn 拓展 to expand (business, etc.); to realize (great ambitions, etc.)

tuòmo 唾沫 saliva; spittle

T

W

wā 挖 ① to scoop out; to dig out ② to engrave with a knife; to cut or gouge

wājué 挖掘 to dig; to excavate

wā 哇 ① to vomit ② the sound of crying by a child
⇨wa

wā 蛙 a frog

wáwa 娃娃 a baby; a young child

wǎ 瓦 ① a tile ② earthenware; pottery ③ watt
⇨wà

wǎjiě 瓦解 to fall apart; to collapse; to disintegrate

wǎsī 瓦斯 gas; poisonous gas used in war

wà/wǎ 瓦 to cover a roof with tiles; to tile
⇨wǎ

wàzi 袜子 stockings; socks

wa 哇 a sentence-final particle
⇨wā

wāi 歪 ① aslant; askew; crooked; tilted; awry ② depraved; evil ③ to lie down on one side for a brief nap ④ to shirk one's responsibility and try to involve others

wāiqū 歪曲 to twist or confuse (things, facts, etc.) intentionally

wài 外 ① out; outside ② foreign; alien ③ diplomatic ④ besides ⑤ to alienate

wàibì 外币 foreign currency

wàibian 外边 ① out; outside ② faraway or distant places ③ a border region

wàibiǎo 外表 an outward appearance; an exterior

wàibīn 外宾 foreign visitors; foreign guests

wàibù 外部 the external of anything; outside

wàichū 外出 to go out

wàidì 外地 parts of the country other than where one is

wàidiàn 外电 dispatches from foreign news agencies

wàigōng 外公 one's maternal grandfather

wàiguān 外观 an outward appearance

wàiguó 外国 a foreign country

wàiguórén 外国人 a foreigner; an alien

wàiháng 外行 ① a greenhorn ② unskilled

wàihào 外号 a nickname

wàihuì 外汇 foreign exchange

wàijí 外籍 foreign nationality

wàijiā 外加 plus; in addition (to)

wàijiāo 外交 diplomacy; diplomatic

Wàijiāo Bù 外交部 Ministry of Foreign Affairs

wàijiāo bùzhǎng 外交部长 a minister of foreign affairs

wàijiè 外界 ① the outside ② outsiders ③ one's environment

wàikē 外科 surgery

wàiké 外壳 a shell; a case

wàilái 外来 outside; external; foreign

wàilì 外力 foreign influence; external pressure or influence

wàiliú 外流 to flow outward; the outflow

wàimào 外贸 foreign (or external) trade

wàimiàn 外面 an outward appearance

wàimian 外面 outside

wàipó 外婆 one's maternal grandmother

wàirén 外人 ① an outsider; a stranger ② a foreigner

wàishāng 外商 foreign businessmen

wàishěngrén 外省人 persons from another province

wàishì 外事 ① foreign affairs; external affairs ② affairs other than that of one's own home

wàitào 外套 an overcoat

wàitou 外头 outside

wàiwéi 外围 the perimeter

wàiwén 外文 a foreign language

wàixiàn 外线 ① exterior lines ② a person or persons making outside contact for a secret group ③ outside (telephone) connections

wàixiàng 外向 extroverted; outgoing

wàixiāo 外销 to export; export

wàixīngrén 外星人 an E.T. (extraterrestrial)

wàixíng 外形 an appearance; a contour

wàiyī 外衣 a coat; a jacket; outer clothing

wàiyǔ 外语 a foreign language

wàiyù 外遇 to have extramarital affairs

wàizài 外在 external; extrinsic

wàizhǎng 外长 a minister of foreign affairs

wàizī 外资 foreign capital

wàizǐ 外子 a reference to one's own husband

wàizǔfù 外祖父 one's maternal grandfather

wàizǔmǔ 外祖母 one's maternal grandmother

wān 弯 to bend; to curve

wānlù 弯路 a crooked road; a zigzag path

wānqū 弯曲 bent; curved

wānyāo 弯腰 to bend down; to stoop down

wān 湾 ① a bay; a gulf; a cove ② the bend of a stream ③ to anchor; to moor

wāndòu 豌豆 peas; garden peas

wán 丸 ① a pellet; a small ball; a pill ② an egg

wán 完 ① to finish; to complete; to bring to a conclusion ② to run out; to use up ③ whole; complete; perfect; intact

wánbèi 完备 complete with everything

wánbì 完毕 finished; completed

wánchéng 完成 to accomplish; to complete

wándàn 完蛋 (colloquial) ruined; busted

wángōng 完工 finished or completed

wánměi 完美 perfect

wánquán 完全 complete; entire

wánshàn 完善 immaculate perfect

wánzhěng 完整 complete; whole

wán 玩 ① to play (with); to toy with ② to find pleasure in; to amuse oneself with ③ to joke; to take things lightly ④ something to amuse oneself—as antiques, etc.

wánfǎ 玩法 to toy with laws; to take laws and regulations lightly

wánjù 玩具 a toy

wánnòng 玩弄 ① to toy with ② to juggle with ③ to fool; to play jokes on

wánshuǎ 玩耍 to play

wánxiào 玩笑 ① a joke; a jest ② to take something less seriously than it deserves

wányìr 玩意儿 ① a toy ② activities for entertainment or relaxation ③ a thing

wángù 顽固 ① stubborn; obstinate; headstrong ② ultraconservative

wánpí 顽皮 naughty or impish (children)

wánqiáng 顽强 stubborn; obstinacy; tenacious

wǎnrú 宛如 as if; as though; like

wǎn 挽 ① to draw (a bow, etc.); to pull ② to roll up (sleeves, etc.) ③ to seize ④ to restore

wǎnhuí 挽回 to try with effort to turn back an adverse tide; to retrieve

wǎnjiù 挽救 to save (a situation, a failing concern, etc.)

W

wǎn 晚 ① sunset; evening; night ② late ③ drawing toward the end ④ younger; junior

wǎn'ān 晚安 Good evening! Good night!

wǎnbào 晚报 an evening (or an afternoon) paper

wǎnbèi 晚辈 the younger generation; one's juniors

wǎncān 晚餐 dinner; supper

wǎnfàn 晚饭 dinner; supper

wǎnhuì 晚会 an evening gathering or meeting

wǎnjiān 晚间 evening; night

wǎnnián 晚年 old age; one's later (or remaining) years

wǎnqī/wǎnqí 晚期 the later period

wǎnshang 晚上 in the evening or night

wǎnyàn 晚宴 a dinner party

wǎnxī/wànxì 惋惜 to feel sorry for (a loss, etc.); to regret

wǎn 碗 a bowl (especially a small one)

wàn 万 ① ten thousand ② all; omni- ③ a very great number; myriad ④ very; extremely; absolutely ⑤ name of an ancient dance ⑥ a surname

wànfēn 万分 very; extremely

wàngǔ-chángqīng 万古长青 to remain fresh forever; to be everlasting

wànnéng 万能 omnipotent; almighty

wànsuì 万岁 (a slogan) Long live the....

wànwàn 万万 ① (used in the negative sense) extremely; absolutely ② a great many ③ 100 million

wànwù 万物 all things under the sun; all God's creation

wànyī 万一 ① one ten thousandth—a very tiny fraction ② just in case that; if by any chance ③ something not anticipated or happening accidentally

wànyǒu 万有 all matters in the world; all things under the sun; all creation

wāngyáng 汪洋 a vast expanse of water

wáng 亡 ① to perish ② to flee ③ lost; dead ④ the late

wángguó 亡国 ① a subjugated nation ② fall of a nation

wáng 王 ① a king; a ruler ② a prince, the highest rank of nobility ③ great; of a tremendous size ④ the strongest or most powerful ⑤ a salutation of respect ⑥ an audience with the ruler or emperor ⑦ a surname

wángcháo 王朝 a dynasty

wángfēi 王妃 ① a prince's wife ② a prince's concubine

wángguó 王国 a kingdom

wángzǐ 王子 a prince

wǎng 网 ① a net; a network; a web ② (figuratively) the dragnet; the arms of law ③ to bring together; to collect

wǎnglù 网路 a network; the Internet

wǎngluó 网罗 to bring together; to collect

wǎngluò 网络 the Internet

wǎngqiú 网球 tennis

wǎngyè 网页 webpage

wǎngyǒu 网友 a net friend; an online friend

wǎngzhàn 网站 website

wǎngzhǐ 网址 web address; website

wǎngzi 网子 a net

wǎng 往 ① to go toward; to depart; to be bound for ② formerly; past; bygone ③ an adverb indicating time or direction

wǎngcháng 往常 usually; heretofore; in the past

wǎngfǎn 往返 to come and go; to and fro

wǎnghòu 往后 ① backward ② hereafter

wǎnglái 往来 ① to go and return ② personal contact between two parties, etc.

W

wǎngnián 往年 in the years past

wǎngrì 往日 in the past

wǎngshì 往事 things that have come to pass

wǎngwǎng 往往 usually; often; frequently

wàngtú 妄图 to try (or attempt) boldly

wàngxiǎng 妄想 a daydream; to desire wildly

wàng 忘 ① to forget ② to omit; to miss (a line, etc.) ③ to neglect; to overlook

wàngdiào 忘掉 to forget

wàngjì 忘记 ① to fail to remember; to forget ② to neglect

wàngquè 忘却 to forget

wàng 旺 ① prosperous; to prosper; to flourish ② vigorous; prolific; productive ③ (said of light, fires, etc.) brilliant; bright or brightly

wàngjì 旺季 (said of business) a boom season; a busy season

wàngshèng 旺盛 ① prosperous; vigorous ② high (morale)

wàng 望 ① to view; to watch; to gaze into the distance ② to hope; to expect ③ the 15th day of each month of the lunar calendar ④ reputation; prestige ⑤ to call on; to visit

wàngyuǎnjìng 望远镜 a telescope

wēi/wéi 危 ① danger; dangerous; precarious; perilous ② restless; to fear; to be upset or afraid

wēihài/wéihài 危害 to endanger; to harm; to injure

wēijī/wéijī 危机 a crisis; a danger point; a critical point; a precarious moment

wēijí/wéijí 危急 urgent; (in) a state of emergency

wēixiǎn/wéixiǎn 危险 danger; dangerous; unsafe

Wēi'ěrsī 威尔斯 Wales, England

wēifēng 威风 ① power and prestige ② imposing; aweinspiring

wēilì 威力 ① the force that

inspires awe ② military force ③ the destructive force (of a typhoon, earthquake, nuclear device, etc.)

Wēinísī 威尼斯 Venice, a city in Italy

wēiquán 威权 an authority; power and prestige

wēiwàng 威望 prestige

wēixié 威胁 to threaten; a threat; intimidation

wēixìn 威信 ① one's dignity and credit; the prestige built up by keeping good faith ② the name of a county in Yunnan Province

wēi/wéi 微 ① small; minute; little; slight ② low; mean; humble ③ a polite expression for I, my, me ④ weak; sickly; feeble ⑤ subtle ⑥ obscure ⑦ hidden; concealed ⑧ to spy ⑨ if not; but for

wēibō/wéibō 微波 microwaves

wēibōlú/wéibōlú 微波炉 a microwave oven

wēibùzúdào / wéibùzúdào 微不足道 insignificant

wēichǔlǐqì/wéichǔlǐqì 微处理器 (computer) a microprocessor

wēifēng/wéifēng 微风 a breeze

wēiguān/wéiguān 微观 microscopic

wēimiào/wéimiào 微妙 subtle (positions); delicate (relations); obscure and mysterious (meanings, etc.)

Wēiruǎn/Wéiruǎn 微软 Microsoft

wēiruò/wéiruò 微弱 weak or feeble

wēishēngwù/wéishēngwù 微生物 microbes; microorganisms

wēiwēi/wéiwéi 微微 small; minute; diminutive

wēixiǎo/wéixiǎo 微小 ① very small; minute ② very low (voices, sounds, etc.)

W

wēixiào/wēixiào 微笑 to smile; a smile

wéi 为 ① to be ② to become ③ to serve as ④ to do; to act ⑤ to manage; to handle; to exercise; to administer; to govern ⇨wèi

wéinán 为难 ① troubled; in difficulties or a dilemma ② to make things difficult (for another)

wéiqī/wéiqī 为期 to serve as the date (for an occasion) or deadline

wéirén 为人 one's personality, temperament, or character; to behave; to conduct oneself

wéishēng 为生 to make a living

wéishǒu 为首 ① to be the head or leader ② headed by; led by

wéixiàn 为限 to serve as a limit; exclusively; not to exceed

wéizhǐ 为止 ① until; till; up to ② no further

wéizhǔ 为主 mainly; to be the most important

wéi 违 ① to go against; to defy; to disobey ② to be separated ③ to avoid ④ evil; fault

wéibèi 违背 to defy; to disobey; to disregard; to be contrary to

wéifǎ 违法 to be against the law; to be unlawful; to violate the law; to be illegal

wéifǎn 违反 to contradict; to disregard (the rules, etc.)

wéifàn 违犯 to violate (a rule or law)

wéiguī 违规 to be against regulations

wéiyuē 违约 a breach of contract; to break a contract or agreement

wéi 围 ① to surround; to enclose; to encircle; to hem in ② surroundings; environment ③ the circumference of a circle formed by a person's arms

wéigōng 围攻 to besiege; to beleaguer

wéijīn 围巾 a scarf; a muffler

wéiqí 围棋 the encirclement chess

wéiqiáng 围墙 an enclosing wall; a fence

wéirào 围绕 to surround; to encircle

wéigān 桅杆 the mast of a boat

wéi 唯 only

wéidú 唯独 only or alone; an exception

wéiwùlùn 唯物论 materialism

wéiwù zhǔyì 唯物主义 materialism

wéixīnlùn 唯心论 idealism

wéixīn zhǔyì 唯心主义 idealism

wéiyī 唯一 the only one, the only kind, etc.

wéiyǒu 唯有 only

wéi 惟 ① to think; to meditate ② only; alone ③ but; however

wéidú 惟独 only; alone

wéiyī 惟一 the only one

wéi 维 ① to tie; to hold fast; to secure ② to maintain; to safeguard ③ to unite; to hold together ④ long and slender—as fibers ⑤ an initial particle—only, but, etc. ⑥ a pattern or rule

wéichí 维持 to maintain; to keep; to guard and support; to sustain; preserve

wéihù 维护 to safeguard; to preserve; to uphold

wéishēngsù 维生素 vitamins

wéitāmìng 维他命 vitamins

wéixì 维系 to maintain; to keep

wéixiū 维修 to keep in (good) repair; to service; to maintain

Wéiyěnà 维也纳 Vienna

wěidà 伟大 great; extraordinary

wěizào 伪造 to forge; to falsify

wěizhuāng/wèizhuāng 伪装 disguise; camouflage

wěi 尾 ① the tail; the rear; the stern (of a ship); rear; back ②

last; final ③ remaining ④ a surname

wěiba 尾巴 a tail

wěiyì 尾翼 a tail surface; an
empennage

wěi 委 ① to depute; to deputize
② to send; to put in charge of; to
commission ③ to give up; to abandon ④ to be frustrated, weakened,
or tired ⑤ a grievance; a wrong ⑥
to stoop or lower oneself (in order
to avoid an open conflict, etc.)

wěiqu 委屈 ① a grievance;
complaints ② to be frustrated or
wronged ③ to take an office, etc.
far below one's ability ④ to put
someone to inconvenience

wěituō 委托 to commission; to
entrust

wěituōrén 委托人 a client

wěiyuán 委员 a member of a
committee

wěiyuánhuì 委员会 a com-
mittee; a council

wěisuō/wēisuō 萎缩 ① to dry
up and shrink; to shrink back ② to
atrophy

wèishēng 卫生 sanitation; sanitary; public health

Wèishēng Jú 卫生局 the
bureau of public health; the
bureau of sanitation

wèishēngsuǒ 卫生所 a public
health clinic

wèishēngzhǐ 卫生纸 tissue
paper; toilet paper

wèixīng 卫星 satellites

wèiyù 卫浴 things used for
hygiene and bathing (including
facilities, etc.)

wèi 为 for; for the good of; for
the sake of
⇨ wéi

wèihé 为何 why; for what reason

wèile 为了 for

wèishénme 为什么 What for?
Why?

wèi 未 ① not yet ② not ③ the
eighth of the Twelve Terrestrial
Branches ④ 1:00—3:00 p.m.

wèibì 未必 not always; not necessarily

wèicéng 未曾 never before

wèihūn 未婚 unmarried; single

wèihūnfū 未婚夫 one's fiancé

wèihūnqī 未婚妻 one's fiancée

wèilái 未来 future; in the future

wèimiǎn 未免 ① It must be
admitted that.... ② necessarily;
unavoidably

wèinéng 未能 to fail to; cannot

wèi 位 ① position; rank ② location

wèiyí 位移 (physics) displace-
ment

wèiyú 位于 situated at; located at

wèiyuán 位元 (computer) a bit

wèizhǐ 位址 (computer) address

wèizhì 位置 ① position (in
space); location ② position (in an
organization)

wèizi 位子 a seat

wèi 味 ① a taste; a flavor ② a
smell; an odor ③ a delicacy; a
dainty

wèidào 味道 ① a taste; a flavor
② a smell ③ a feeling

wèijīng 味精 monosodium glu-
tamate

wèi 畏 ① to stand in awe of; to
fear; to dread; to be afraid of ② to
revere; to respect

wèijù 畏惧 to dread; to be scared
of; to fear

wèi 胃 the stomach; the gizzard
(of birds and fowls)

wèikǒu 胃口 appetite

wèi 谓 ① to tell; to say ② to name;
to call; to designate ③ to think; to
be the opinion; to assume ④
meaning; sense

wèi 喂 ① hello; hey ② to feed;
to raise

wèiwèn 慰问 to show sympathy
by making inquiries

wēn 温 ① warm; lukewarm; to
warm ② to review; to revise ③
temperature ④ a surname

wēndài 温带 the Temperate Zone

W

wēndù 温度 temperature

wēndùjì 温度计 a thermometer

Wēngēhuá 温哥华 Vancouver, a city in Canada

wēnhé 温和 gentle; mild; temperate
⇨wēnhuo

wēnhuo 温和 warm
⇨wēnhé

wēnnuǎn 温暖 warm; warmth

wēnquán 温泉 a hot spring; a spa

wēnróu 温柔 warm and tender; sweet-natured

wēnshì 温室 a greenhouse

wēnxí 温习 to review (what has been learned)

wēnxīn 温馨 warm and fragrant

wēnxùn/wēnxún 温驯 meek; docile; tame

wēnyì 瘟疫 an epidemic; a plague; a pestilence

wén 文 ① a composition; an article ② language ③ literature; education; culture ④ civilian or civil (as opposed to military) ⑤ elegant; civil; polite; polished; mild; suave; cultured; urbane

wén/wèn 文 to cover up; to conceal; to gloss over

wénfǎ 文法 grammar

Wéngé 文革 short for the Great Cultural Revolution

wénhuà 文化 culture; civilization

wénhuǒ 文火 a slow fire (in cooking)

wénjiàn 文件 documents; legal papers

wénjiào 文教 culture and education

wénjù 文具 writing tools; stationery

wénmáng 文盲 an illiterate

wénmíng 文明 civilized; civilization

wénpíng 文凭 a diploma

wénrén 文人 ① a man of letters ② a man with a civilian background

wénshū 文书 ① documents; records ② an archivist

wéntán 文坛 the literary circles, world, or arena

wénwù 文物 cultural artifacts

wénxiàn 文献 records; documents

wénxué 文学 literature

wénxuéjiā 文学家 a literary man; a litterateur

wényǎ 文雅 graceful; refined; polished

wényán 文言 the literary language used in old China which is vastly different from the modern language; classical Chinese

wényì 文艺 literature (as one of the fine arts); belles-lettres

Wényì Fùxìng 文艺复兴 the Renaissance

wénzhāng 文章 an article; a composition

wénzì 文字 ① a letter; a character; written language ② writing

wén 纹 ① stripes; lines; streaks; veins ② ripples (of water) ③ (finger) prints ④ wrinkles (on the face) ⑤ to tattoo

wén 闻 ① to hear; to have heard ② to smell ③ to convey, forward, or transmit (a message, etc.) ④ to learn; learning; to understand ⑤ a surname

wénmíng 闻名 ① famous; distinguished ② to hear of someone's name

wén 蚊 a mosquito; a gnat

wénzi 蚊子 a mosquito; a gnat

wěn 吻 ① the lip ② to kiss; a kiss ③ the tone of one's speech

wěnluàn/wènluàn 紊乱 confused; tangled; chaotic

wěn 稳 ① stable; stability; steady; firm ② sure; certain ③ secure; security

wěndang 稳当 proper and secure

wěndìng 稳定 ① to stabilize ② stable; steady

wěngù 稳固 stable and firm;

W

secure

wěnjiàn 稳健 firm and steady

wěntuǒ 稳妥 secure and dependable; proper and secure

wèn 问 ① to ask; to inquire ② to ask after; to inquire after ③ to interrogate; to examine ④ to hold responsible

wèndá 问答 questions and answers; a dialogue

wènhǎo 问好 to ask about a person's health or welfare

wènhòu 问候 to ask about a person's health or welfare

wènjuàn 问卷 a questionnaire

wènshì 问世 (said of a new book or product) to come out

wèntí 问题 a problem; a question; an issue

wēng 翁 ① an old man ② a title of respect ③ a surname

wō 涡 a whirlpool; an eddy ⇨Guō

wō/wò 喔 the crowing of a cock; the cackling of fowls

wō 窝 ① a cave; a den; a nest ② an apartment; living quarters; a house ③ a hollow part of the human body; a pit ④ to bend; to crease ⑤ to hide; to harbor (a criminal, etc.)

wōnang 窝囊 ① stupid, cowardly and timid; good-for-nothing ② to feel vexed

wōniú/guāniú 蜗牛 a snail

wǒ 我 ① I; me; my ② we; our; us ③ self

wǒfāng 我方 our side; we

wǒguó 我国 our country

wǒmen 我们 we; us

wò 卧 ① to lie down; to rest; to sleep ② to lay or place across; to lie across

wòfáng 卧房 a bedroom

wòshì 卧室 a bedroom

wò 握 ① to hold fast; to grasp ② a handful

wòshǒu 握手 to shake hands

wūguī 乌龟 ① a turtle; a tortoise ② a cuckold

Wūkèlán 乌克兰 Ukraine, Russia

wūlóngchá 乌龙茶 oolong tea

wūtuōbāng 乌托邦 ① utopia—an ideal place or state ② Utopia

wūyā 乌鸦 a crow; a raven

wūyún 乌云 ① dark clouds ② (figuratively) a woman's black hair

wū 污 ① dirty; filthy ② to stain; to mar ③ corrupt

wūmiè 污蔑 to libel; to slander

wūrǎn 污染 to contaminate; to pollute

wūshuǐ 污水 sewage; filthy water

wūpó 巫婆 a witch

wū 呜 ① to weep; to sob ② to toot; to hoot; to zoom ③ Alas!

wūyè 呜咽 sobs; to sob; to weep

wūmiè 诬蔑 to libel; to slander

wūxiàn 诬陷 to incriminate falsely; to frame somebody

wū 屋 a house; a room; a shelter

wūdǐng 屋顶 a roof

wūyán 屋檐 the eaves

wūzhǔ 屋主 the owner of a house

wūzi 屋子 a house; a room

wú 无 ① negative; not; no; none ② without; destitute of; wanting; to lack; to have not ③ no matter what (or how); not yet

wúbǐ 无比 incomparable; peerless

wúbù 无不 all without exception

wúchǎn jiējí 无产阶级 the proletariat

wúcháng 无常 ① ever-changing; capricious; variable ② (Buddhism) anitya, impermanent ③ (Chinese mythology) name of a ghost or spirit that heralds a person's death ④ death

wúcháng 无偿 free; gratis; gratuitous

wúchǐ 无耻 shameless; brazen; impudent

wúcóng 无从 to have no place (or no way) to lay hands on or begin with

W

wúfǎ 无法 unable; incapable

wúfēi 无非 no other than; nothing but

wúgū 无辜 innocent; guiltless

wúguān 无关 irrelevant; to have nothing to do with

wúhuàkěshuō 无话可说 to have nothing to say

wúkěfènggào 无可奉告 no comment

wúkěnàihé 无可奈何 having no alternative; to have to

wúlǐ 无理 unreasonable

wúlì 无力 ① feeble; weak ② cannot afford

wúliáo 无聊 ① ennui; boredom ② nonsensical; silly

wúlùn 无论 ① no matter; whatever ② let alone; to say nothing of

wúlùn-rúhé 无论如何 anyway; in any case

wúnài 无奈 can't help it

wúnéng 无能 incompetent; incapable

wúnéngwéilì 无能为力 unable to help; can't do anything about it; powerless

wúqíng 无情 callous; heartless; ruthless

wúqíng-wúyì 无情无义 to be ruthless; to be emotionless and unrighteous

wúqióng 无穷 endless; boundless; limitless

wúshù 无数 ① countless; numerous ② an uncertain number of

wúsuǒwèi 无所谓 do not care

wúsuǒzuòwéi 无所作为 to attempt nothing and accomplish nothing

wúwēi-búzhì/wúwéi-búzhì 无微不至 very thoughtful; to be considerate in every way

wúwèi 无味 ① tasteless; dull (offers, etc.) ② unpalatable

wúxiàn 无限 limitless; boundless; infinite

wúxiàndiàn 无线电 radio; wireless

wúxiào 无效 ① ineffective; useless; to no avail ② invalid; null and void

wúxīn 无心 ① unintentional ② in no mood

wúxíng 无形 invisible

wúxū 无须 unnecessary; no need to

wúyí 无疑 without doubt; undoubtedly; unquestionably

wúyì 无异 not different from; tantamount to

wúyì 无意 to have no interest in; to have no intention (of doing something)

wúyòng 无用 useless; of no use

wúyuán 无缘 ① no opportunity or chance ② unable to

wúyuǎn-fújiè 无远弗届 No place is too far away to reached. (to reach everywhere)

wúzhī 无知 ignorant; (said of a child) innocent

wúrén 吾人 we

Wú 吴 ① name of a state in the Epoch of the Three Kingdoms ② name of a state in the Warring States period ③ a surname

Wú Fèng 吴凤 Wu Feng, (an official who, when head hunting was still common among the aborigines of Taiwan, ended the practice at the cost of his own life in 1768)

wútóng 梧桐 a firmiana

wǔ 五 five; fifth

wǔhuā-bāmén 五花八门 rich in variety

wǔjīn 五金 ① the five metals—gold, silver, copper, iron, and tin ② metals in general ③ hardware

wǔ 午 ① noon; high noon ② (in old Chinese time measurement) 11 a.m. to 1 p.m. ③ the seventh of the Twelve Terrestrial Branches (dìzhī 地支)

wǔcān 午餐 lunch; a midday meal

wǔfàn 午饭 lunch; a midday meal

W

wǔhòu 午后 afternoon

wǔyè 午夜 midnight

wǔ 伍 ① an elaborate form of **wǔ** 五 used in writing checks, etc. to prevent forgery ② five ③ to associate

wǔ 武 ① force; military ② warlike; martial

wǔgōng 武功 ① military achievements ② fighting skills

wǔlì 武力 military might; (by) force

wǔlín 武林 the circle of boxers

wǔqì 武器 weapons; arms

wǔshì 武士 ① a warrior ② a samurai ③ a knight or cavalier

wǔshù 武术 martial arts

wǔxiá 武侠 chivalry

wǔzhuāng 武装 ① armed; to arm; armament ② military uniform

wǔrǔ／wǔrù 侮辱 to insult; to humiliate ② an insult

wǔ 舞 ① to dance; to prance ② to brandish; to wave ③ to stir up

wǔbì 舞弊 misconduct, malpractice, or irregularities (of an official); to bribe

wǔchí 舞池 a dance floor

wǔdǎo／wǔdào 舞蹈 a dance

wǔhuì 舞会 a dancing party; a dance; a ball

wǔlóng 舞龙 a dragon dance

wǔnán 舞男 a gigolo

wǔqǔ 舞曲 dance music; a dance tune

wǔshī 舞狮 a lion dance

wǔtái 舞台 a stage (in a theater)

wǔtáijù 舞台剧 a stage play

wǔtīng 舞厅 a dance hall

wù 勿 do not; not; never; a negative word used in formal speech

wù 务 ① to attend to; to strive after; to be engaged in ② duty; business; affairs ③ must; necessary

wùbì 务必 must; by all means

wùshí 务实 to strive for thoroughness

wù 物 ① a thing; a matter; a being ② content; substance ③ the physical world; nature ④ other people

wùchǎn 物产 natural resources

wùjià 物价 commodity prices

wùjiàn 物件 articles; things

wùlǐ 物理 ① physics ② the law of nature

wùlì 物力 material means or resources

wùpǐn 物品 things; articles

wùtǐ 物体 (physics) a body; an object

wùzhì／wùzhí 物质 (physics) matter

wùzhǒng 物种 species

wùzī 物资 materials; supplies; goods

wù 误 ① an error; a mistake ② to miss ③ to delay ④ to harm; to injure ⑤ by accident

wùchā 误差 (mathematics) an error

wùdiǎn 误点 (said of trains, etc.) to be behind time

wùhuì 误会 to misunderstand; to misinterpret; to misconstrue; a misunderstanding

wùjiě 误解 to misunderstand; to misinterpret; to misconstrue; a misunderstanding

wù 恶 to hate; to detest; to dislike; to abhor; to loathe ⇨**è**

wù 悟 to become aware of; to realize; to awake to; to comprehend

wù 雾 fog; mist; vapor

X

xī/xì 夕 ① dusk; sunset; evening ② night ③ slant; oblique ④ to meet in the evening

xīyáng/xìyáng 夕阳 the setting sun

xī 西 west; the west; western ② Western; the West; European; American; Occidental; foreign

Xībānyá 西班牙 Spain

Xīběi 西北 northwest

Xīběi Hángkōng 西北航空 the Northwest Airlines

xībian 西边 west; west side

Xībólìyà 西伯利亚 Siberia

xībù 西部 ① the western part (of a territory) ② the West

xīcān 西餐 Western food; European or American meals

Xī Dé 西德 West Germany (East Germany and West Germany were united in 1990.)

xīfāng 西方 ① west; the West or Western ② a Buddhist paradise

xīfēng 西风 a west wind; a westerly; a wester

xīfú 西服 Western clothes, European or American attire

xīguā 西瓜 watermelons

xīhóngshì 西红柿 a tomato

Xīhú 西湖 the West Lake, name of various lakes in a number of provinces, the most famous one is at Hangzhou

xīmiàn 西面 west; west side

xīnán 西南 southwest

Xī Ōu 西欧 Western Europe

xīshì 西式 Western-style; Occidental style; European or American style

Xīxīlǐdǎo 西西里岛 Sicily, Italy

Xīyáng 西洋 the West; Western; European or American nations

xīyī 西医 Western medicine; doctors practicing Western medicine (as distinct from Chinese herb doctors)

xīyuán 西元 the Gregorian calendar, which begins with the year in which Christ was supposedly born; A.D.

Xīzàng 西藏 ① Tibet ② Tibetan

xīzhuāng 西装 Western-style clothes; a Western suit

xī 吸 ① to absorb; to imbibe; to suck in ② to attract; to draw ③ to inhale

xīdú 吸毒 to smoke opium; to take drugs

xīqǔ 吸取 ① to absorb (knowledge) ② to suck (liquid)

xīshí 吸食 to suck; to take in

xīshōu 吸收 ① to absorb; to take in ② to recruit or enlist

xīxuèguǐ/xīxiěguǐ 吸血鬼 a vampire

xīyān 吸烟 to smoke; smoking

xīyǐn 吸引 to attract; to draw

xīyǐnlì 吸引力 ① (physics) gravitation ② attraction

Xīlà 希腊 Greece; Greek

xīwàng 希望 a hope; a wish; expectations; to hope; to wish; to desire

xīrì/xírì 昔日 in former days (or times)

xī/xì 矽 silicon

Xīgǔ/Xìgǔ 矽谷 Silicon Valley

xīshēng 牺牲 ① sacrifice (offered to a deity) ② to sacrifice

xī/xí 息 ① a breath ② news; tidings ③ to stop; to end ④ interest (on money) ⑤ to rest

xīxī-xiāngguān/xíxí-xiāngguān 息息相关 related as closely as each breath is to the next

xī 悉 ① to know ② all; whole; total; entire

xī/xí 惜 ① to pity; to sympathize; to regret; to feel sorry for somebody ② to value highly; to have a

high opinion of (something); to show love or fondness for ③ to spare; to grudge

xī 稀 ① thin (liquids, etc.); watery; diluted ② rare; scarce; uncommon ③ scattered; sparse

xīfàn 稀饭 congee; gruel; porridge

xīshǎo 稀少 few; little; scarce; rare; sparse

xīshū 稀疏 scattered or dispersed; sparse

xīyǒu 稀有 rare; one in a million

xī 犀 ① (said of armor, weapons, etc.) sharp-edged and hard ② a rhinoceros

xījiǎo 犀角 ① a rhinoceros horn ② bone of the forehead

xīniú 犀牛 the rhinoceros

xī/xí 锡 tin

xī 溪 a mountain stream

xīliú 溪流 a brook

xīshuǐ 溪水 a mountain stream

xī/xí 熄 ① to extinguish (a fire); to put out (a light) ② to quash; to destroy; to obliterate

xīmiè/xímiè 熄灭 to extinguish (a fire); to put out (a light); to die out

xī 膝 the knee

xīgài 膝盖 the knee

xīpí 嬉皮 hippies

xīxì 嬉戏 to frolic; to play; to sport

xīshuài 蟋蟀 a cricket

xí 习 ① to learn; to familiarize oneself with; to receive training in ② habit; custom; practice ③ to follow; to repeat

xíguàn 习惯 habit; to be accustomed to

xísú 习俗 custom; practice

xítí 习题 problems to be worked out in the course of study; exercises

xíxìng 习性 temperament; dispositions

xí 席 ① a mat ② a feast ③ a seat ④ to take a seat ⑤ to rely on

xícì 席次 the order of seats

xíwèi 席位 a seat (at a conference, etc.)

xíjí/xíjí 袭击 ① a surprise attack ② to raid

xífù 媳妇 a daughter-in-law

xǐ 洗 ① to wash; to rinse; to cleanse; to clean; to clear ② to baptize
⇨Xiǎn

xǐdí 洗涤 to wash; to cleanse; to rinse

xǐjìng 洗净 to wash something until it's clean

xǐlǐ 洗礼 ① to baptize ② a severe test

xǐliǎn 洗脸 to wash one's face

xǐshèn 洗肾 dialysis or hemodialysis

xǐshǒujiān 洗手间 a toilet; a water closet; a lavatory

xǐyīfěn 洗衣粉 washing powder, laundry detergent

xǐyījī 洗衣机 a washing machine

xǐzǎo 洗澡 to take a bath

xǐ 喜 ① to like; to love; to be fond of ② joy; a joyful thing; a happy event ④ joyful; happy; delightful; pleasant; auspicious

xǐài 喜爱 to like; to love; to be fond of

xǐhào 喜好 to be fond of; to delight in

xǐhuan 喜欢 to like; to be fond of; to love

xǐjiǔ 喜酒 a wedding feast

xǐjù 喜剧 a comedy

xǐqì 喜气 joyful atmosphere or expression

xǐquè 喜鹊 the magpie

xǐshì 喜事 an occasion for joy (especially a wedding)

xǐxùn 喜讯 happy news; good news

xǐyuè 喜悦 joy; delight; gratification

xì 戏 ① a drama; a play; a show ② to jest; to have fun; to make fun ③ to play; to toy; to sport ④ a game

xìjù 戏剧 a drama; the theater

xìnòng 戏弄 to play a trick on; to tease

X

xìqǔ 戏曲 a drama; a play

xìshuǐ 戏水 to play in water

xìyuàn 戏院 a theater; a movie house

xì 系 ① (in a college or a university) a department or school ② a system; a line; a connecting link; a connection ③ (politics) a clique; a theoretic or party line ④ lineage; a genealogy ⑤ to relate to; to bear on ⑥ to belong to; to attach to; to connect with ⑦ to connect; to link; to join ⑧ to be concerned or anxious about ⇨jì

xìliè 系列 ① a row; a series ② a line or lineage

xìshù 系数 (mathematics) coefficient

xìtǒng 系统 a system; systematic

xìzhǔrèn 系主任 the head or chairman of a department (in a college)

xì 细 ① thin; slender; tall but lean; slim ② fine ③ tiny; small; little ④ petty; trifling; detailed ⑤ precise; exquisite; delicate (workmanship, etc.)

xìbāo 细胞 a cell

xìbù 细部 details (of a drawing); minute parts

xìjié 细节 minor points; trifles; details

xìjūn/xìjùn 细菌 bacteria; germs

xìnì 细腻 ① fine and delicate ② (in writings, dramas and movie directing) to take care of even the smallest points; not to overlook any details

xìxiǎo 细小 tiny; little; thin; petty

xìxīn 细心 careful; attentive; cautious; circumspective; to think of all aspects of something

xìzé 细则 bylaws

xìzhì 细致 ① fine and delicate; exquisite ② careful and thorough; meticulous; painstaking

xiā 虾 a shrimp

xiāmǐ 虾米 dried shrimps

xiā 瞎 ① blind; blindly ② rash; reckless; heedless; (to do things, etc.) without purpose or reason; at random; groundlessly ③ (dialect) to become tangled (said of thread, etc.)

xiá 峡 ① a gorge ② an isthmus ③ straits

xiágǔ 峡谷 (geography) a dale; a gorge

xiá'ài 狭隘 narrow-minded; parochial; narrow

xiáxiǎo 狭小 (said of rooms, etc.) narrow and small

xiáyì 狭义 the narrow sense

xiázhǎi 狭窄 narrow; cramped

xiácī 瑕疵 defects; flaws; blemishes

xiá 霞 colored, low-hanging clouds; rosy clouds

xià 下 ① to put down ② to lay ③ to fall ④ to descend ⑤ next ⑥ below; under ⑦ inferior; lower ⑧ to begin

xiàba 下巴 the chin

xiàbān 下班 to knock off; to get off work

xiàbǐ 下笔 to start writing

xiàbian 下边 as follows; following; below; under

xiàchang 下场 the conclusion; the end

xiàchē 下车 to get off (trains or vehicles, etc.)

xiàcì 下次 next time

xiàdá 下达 to transmit to (lower levels); to assign a task

xiàdiē/xiàdié 下跌 (said of price) to fall; to drop

xiàfāng 下方 ① south and west ② below; under ③ the earth

xiàfàng 下放 to transfer to a lower level

xiàjí 下级 ① lower levels ② subordinates

xiàjiàng 下降 to descend; to drop

xiàkè 下课 to get out of class; to finish class

xiàlai 下来 to come down

xiàliè 下列 ① as follows ② what are listed below

xiàlìng 下令 to give orders; to order

xiàluò 下落 whereabouts

xiàmiàn 下面 ① underneath ② following ③ lower levels; subordinates

xiàqí 下棋 to play chess

xiàqu 下去 ① to go down ② to go on

xiàrén 下人 a servant

xiàshān 下山 to go down a mountain

xiàshǒu 下手 ① to start doing something ② to commit a crime ③ a helper

xiàshuǐ 下水 to launch a boat

xiàshuǐdào 下水道 sewers; the sewerage system

xiàtà 下榻 to take up abode; to stay

xiàtái 下台 ① to get off stage ② to be relieved from office

xiàwǔ 下午 an afternoon

xiàwǔchá 下午茶 afternoon tea

xiàxiāng 下乡 to go to the country; to rusticate

xiàxuě 下雪 to snow

xiàxún 下旬 the last ten days of a month

xiàyóu 下游 downstream

xiàyǔ 下雨 to rain

xiàyǔtiān 下雨天 a rainy day

xiàzài 下载 (computer) to download

xià 吓 to frighten; to startle; to scare
⇨hè

xiàrén 吓人 ① to frighten people ② horrible; terrible

xiàyítiào 吓一跳 to be scared; to be frightened

xià 夏 ① summer ② big; spacious ③ a big house; a mansion ④ Cathay, the ancient name of China ⑤ a dynasty in Chinese history (2205-1782 B.C.)

xiàjì 夏季 the summer season

xiàlìngyíng 夏令营 summer camps

xiàrì 夏日 summer days

xiàtiān 夏天 summer; summer days

Xiàwēiyí 夏威夷 Hawaii

xiān 仙 ① a god; an immortal; a fairy ② a divine

xiāndān 仙丹 a panacea; a cure-all; an elixir

xiānjìng 仙境 ① a fairyland ② a place of exquisite natural beauty

xiānnǚ 仙女 a fairy

xiān 先 ① before; earlier; in advance ② first; foremost ③ the late...; the deceased... ④ one's forebears ⑤ the abbreviation for Mister or Sir

xiāndǎo 先导 ① to lead the way ② a model; a teacher ③ a guide

xiānfēng 先锋 a vanguard; a forerunner; the trailblazer

xiānhòu 先后 ① the order (of things narrated, placed, etc.) ② the ins and outs of an incident

xiānjìn 先进 predecessors; seniors

xiānqián 先前 before; previously

xiānqū 先驱 a vanguard; a forerunner; a pioneer

xiānsheng 先生 ① an honorable title for a teacher ② a name for the elderly and learned ③ Mister; Sir ④ a husband

xiāntiān 先天 ① natural physical endowments ② congenital; innate; inherent

xiānxíng 先行 ① to go ahead of the rest; to start off before the others ② beforehand; in advance

xiānwéi 纤维 fiber

xiānxì 纤细 fine; tiny; minute

xiān 掀 ① to lift with the hands; to raise ② to stir; to stir up; to cause; to rise

xiānqǐ 掀起 to stir up (a movement, etc.)

xiān 鲜 ① fresh; new ② delicious; tasty ③ bright; attractive
⇨xiǎn

X

xiānhóng 鲜红 bright red

xiānhuā 鲜花 fresh flowers

xiānmíng 鲜明 ① sharp; distinct ② bright-colored

xiānnǎi 鲜奶 fresh milk

xiānxuè / xiānxiě 鲜血 fresh blood; blood

xiānyàn 鲜艳 bright-colored; resplendent; attractively

xián 闲 ① a fence; a bar; a barrier ② to defend ③ familiar with; accustomed to ④ leisure; spare time ⑤ laws or regulations ⑥ a stable ⑦ quiet; tranquil; calm; placid

xiánhuà 闲话 ① to talk casually about; to chat about ② random or idle talk; gossip; complaint

xiánliáo 闲聊 ① to chat; to gossip ② a gossip; a chat

xiánhuì 贤惠 (usually said of women) virtuous and intelligent; good and wise

xián 弦 ① strings (of bows, etc.) ② the chord of an arc ③ the first or last quarter of a lunar month

xián 咸 saltish; salty; briny; salted

xián 衔 ① to hold in the mouth ② to harbor; to cherish ③ a bit (in a horse's mouth) ④ the title (of an official)

xiánjiē 衔接 to adjoin; to lie next to; to connect; to dovetail

xián 嫌 ① to detest; to dislike ② ill will; a grudge ③ to suspect; suspicion ④ to complain; to reject; to object

xiányí 嫌疑 suspicion; to suspect

xiányífàn 嫌疑犯 a suspect (of a crime, etc.)

xiǎn 显 ① to expose; to make known; to display; to show; to manifest ② high-positioned; eminent; prominent ③ well-known; renowned; famed; reputed ④ evident; manifest; clear ⑤ a prefix referring to one's forebears

xiǎnchū 显出 to appear; to show (in contrast)

xiǎnde 显得 to look; to seem; to appear

xiǎn'éryìjiàn 显而易见 evidently; apparently

xiǎnjiàn 显见 It is evident that....

xiǎnrán 显然 evident; clearly visible; obvious

xiǎnshì 显示 to indicate; to show; to reveal

xiǎnwēijìng / xiǎnwéijìng 显微镜 a microscope

xiǎnxiàn 显现 to appear; to reveal

xiǎnyǎn 显眼 conspicuous; striking; eye-catching

xiǎnzhù 显著 evident; clear; notable; eye-catching; marked; remarkable

Xiǎn 冼 a surname
⇨**xǐ**

xiǎn 险 ① dangerous; danger ② obstructed; difficult ③ a strategic pass ④ mean and crafty; cunning; sinister ⑤ nearly; almost

xiǎn 鲜 rare; few; seldom
⇨**xiān**

xiàn 县 a county; a prefecture

xiànchéng 县城 the seat of a county government; a county town

xiànyìhuì 县议会 a county council

xiànyìyuán 县议员 members of a district council

xiànzhǎng 县长 the chief county executive

xiànzhèngfǔ 县政府 a county government

xiàn 现 ① to emerge; to appear ② in time of need; extempore ③ current; now ④ cash ⑤ ready; available ⑥ actual

xiànchǎng 现场 the scene (of an incident); a site

xiànchéng 现成 ready; ready-made

xiàncún 现存 in stock; on hand; available

xiàndài 现代 modern; the present world

xiàndàihuà 现代化 to modernize; modernization

xiànjiēduàn 现阶段 the present stage

xiànjīn 现今 nowadays; at present; now

xiànjīn 现金 cash; ready money

xiànqián 现钱 ready money; cash

xiànrèn 现任 present (job or employment)

xiànshí 现实 ① reality ② pragmatic; real

xiànxiàng 现象 phenomena; appearances

xiànxíng 现行 existing; presently valid

xiànyǒu 现有 to have on hand; existing

xiànzài 现在 now; at present

xiànzhuàng 现状 things as they are; the status quo

xiàn 限 ① limits; restriction; to limit or restrict ② a boundary; a line ③ to specify; to fix

xiàndìng 限定 to limit

xiàndù 限度 limits; limitation; degree

xiànliàng 限量 limits; limitation

xiànqī/xiànqí 限期 ① a time limit; a deadline ② within a definite time

xiànyú 限于 (in writing, etc.) owing to the limitation of; due to (regulations, etc.)

xiànzhì 限制 limitations; to restrict

xiàn 线 ① a line ② threads ③ wires

xiànlù 线路 ① (electricity) a circuit ② a narrow path

xiànshàng 线上 (computer) on-line

xiànsuǒ 线索 a clue; a lead

xiàntiáo 线条 lines; streaks

xiànbīng 宪兵 military police; gendarmes

xiànfǎ 宪法 constitution (of a national government)

xiànzhèng 宪政 constitutional

government (or rule)

xiàn 陷 ① to sink; to fall; to submerge; to stick; to bog ② to frame (up); to harm another with trumped-up charges ③ to entrap; to beguile ④ to crush (the enemy position); to fall; to capture (a city, etc.) ⑤ a defect; a deficiency

xiànhài 陷害 to frame; to snare; to harm another with a trumped-up charge, slander, etc.

xiànjǐng 陷阱 a trap; a snare; a booby trap

xiànrù 陷入 to sink into; to fall into; to be entrapped

xiànr 馅儿 stuffing

xiànmù 羡慕 to envy; to covet

xiàn 献 ① to present; to forward; to offer; to dedicate; to donate ② to display; to show; to stage ③ to curry (favor, etc.); to flatter or cater to

xiànshēn 献身 to offer or dedicate oneself (to a cause, one's nation, etc.)

xiāng 乡 ① a village; the country, as contrasted with a city or town ② rural ③ one's native place or birthplace; one's village ④ a small administrative unit comprising several villages

xiāngcūn 乡村 a village; a country; a rural area

xiānggōngsuǒ 乡公所 a public office in charge of the administration of a group of villages

xiāngjiān 乡间 in the countryside; in the rural area

xiāngmín 乡民 villagers; countryfolk

xiāngqīn 乡亲 ① people hailing from the same area ② local people; villagers

xiāngtǔ 乡土 ① one's hometown or native place ② local geography and history

xiāngxia 乡下 countryside; a rural area

xiāngyuàn 乡愿 a hypocrite or an impostor in the countryside

xiāngzhǎng 乡长 ① elders in

X

a village ② the chief of a group of villages

xiāngzhèn 乡镇 a small town which is essentially a rural village

xiāng 相 each other; one another; mutually; reciprocal ⇨xiàng

xiāng'ài 相爱 to love each other

xiāngbǐ 相比 to compare with each other

xiāngchà/xiāngchā 相差 to differ

xiāngchǔ 相处 to spend time together; to live together

xiāngchuán 相传 ① (said of a report) to be transmitted from person to person ② to be passed or handed down from generation to generation

xiāngdāng 相当 ① equivalent; to correspond to ② considerable ③ appropriate; fit

xiāngděng 相等 equal; equivalent

xiāngduì 相对 ① opposite; face to face ② relative ③ corresponding

xiāngduìlùn 相对论 the theory of relativity

xiāngfǎn 相反 contrary; opposed to each other

xiāngfǎng 相仿 alike; similar

xiāngféng 相逢 to come across

xiāngfú 相符 to tally; to correspond

xiāngguān 相关 related; connected; to have to do with

xiānghù 相互 one another; mutually; reciprocally

xiāngjì 相继 in succession

xiāngjiāo 相交 ① to intersect ② to make friends with each other; to become associated with each other

xiāngjiào 相较 to compare with each other

xiāngjìn 相近 close (in amount, quality, degree, etc.); approximate

xiānglián 相连 connected; joined; linked

xiāngpèi 相配 to match well

xiāngqīn/xiàngqīn 相亲 an interview prior to marriage; to size up a prospective mate in an arranged meeting

xiāngqīn-xiāng'ài 相亲相爱 to be kind to each other and love each other

xiāngróng 相容 (computer) compatible

xiāngshí/xiāngshì 相识 ① to know each other ② an acquaintance

xiāngsì 相似 alike; similar

xiāngtōng 相通 to communicate with each other; to be interlinked

xiāngtóng 相同 ① the same ② similar

xiāngxiàng 相像 to resemble; to be similar

xiāngxìn 相信 to believe; to have faith in

xiāngyìng 相应 ① corresponding; relevant ② to support each other ③ (documentary usage) should

xiāngyù 相遇 to meet each other

xiāng 香 ① sweet-smelling; fragrant; aromatic; balmy ② tasty; delicious ③ fair; beautiful ④ spice; balm; incense

xiāngbīn 香槟 champagne

xiāngcháng 香肠 sausage

xiānggǎng 香港 Hong Kong (Hongkong)

xiānggǎngjiǎo 香港脚 athlete's foot

xiānggū 香菇 a kind of edible mushroom grown on wooden logs

xiāngjiāo 香蕉 a banana

xiāngliào 香料 spice; balm

xiāngqì 香气 a sweet smell; a pleasant odor; fragrance

xiāngshuǐ 香水 perfume; scent

xiāngwèi 香味 spicy taste; aromatic flavor

xiāngyān 香烟 ① cigarettes ② continuity of the family line ③ smoke of burning incense

xiāngzào 香皂 perfumed soap;

toilet soap

xiāng 箱 ① a box; a chest; a trunk ② the box or body of a carriage

xiāngzi 箱子 a box; a chest; a trunk

xiāng 镶 ① to fill in (a tooth, etc.); to mount; to inlay; to set (jewels, etc.) ② to edge; to border; to hem

xiāng 详 ① complete; detailed; details ② to know the details ③ please see...for details ④ to explain; to interpret

xiángjìn 详尽 detailed and complete

xiángqíng 详情 details of an event, etc.

xiángxì 详细 in every detail and particular

xiáng 降 ① to surrender; to submit to ② to conquer ⇨ jiàng

xiǎng 享 ① to enjoy; to receive ② to offer

xiǎngfú 享福 to enjoy happiness and prosperity

xiǎnglè 享乐 to seek pleasure; to make merry

xiǎngshòu 享受 to enjoy; to indulge oneself in

xiǎngyòng 享用 to enjoy the use of

xiǎngyǒu 享有 to possess; to have in possession

xiǎng 响 ① (said of sound) loud or high ② a report; a sound; an echo ③ to make a sound; to ring

xiǎngliàng 响亮 sonorous; loud and clear; stentorian

xiǎngshēng 响声 a sound; an echo; a noise

xiǎngyìng 响应 to echo in support; to respond favorably; to rise in support

xiǎngyàn 飨宴 a feast

xiǎng 想 ① to think; to consider; to suppose ② to hope; to expect ③ to plan ④ to remember with longing; to miss ⑤ to want; would like to

xiǎngbì 想必 presumably; probably

xiǎngbudào 想不到 to one's surprise; unexpectedly

xiǎngdào 想到 to think of; to remember

xiǎngfa 想法 an idea; an opinion; a view

xiǎngfāng-shèfǎ 想方设法 to try everything possible; to try every means; to try by hook or by crook

xiǎngkāi 想开 to have succeeded in getting over a loss or misfortune; to stop worrying

xiǎngniàn 想念 to miss (something or someone)

xiǎngqǐ 想起 to think of; to remember; to occur

xiǎngxiǎngkàn 想想看 to think about it

xiǎngxiàng 想象 to imagine; to fancy

xiǎngxiànglì 想象力 imagination

xiǎngyào 想要 to want to; to feel like

xiǎngyìxiǎng 想一想 to pause to think

xiàng 向 ① to turn; to face ② a direction; a trend ③ until now ④ a surname

xiàngdǎo 向导 a guide

xiànglái 向来 hitherto; heretofore; until now

xiàngliàng 向量 vector

xiàngwǎng 向往 ① to admire and try to imitate (a great person, etc.) ② to aspire; to long

xiàngxīnlì 向心力 centripetal force

xiàng 项 ① an item; an article; a matter; a kind; a class ② the back of a cap or crown ③ the back of the neck; the nape ④ funds; a sum of money ⑤ (mathematics) a term

xiàngliàn 项链 a necklace

xiàngmù 项目 an item; an article (in an agreement, etc.)

Xiàng Yǔ 项羽 Xiang Yu, a

great warrior who contested the throne with the founding emperor of the Western Han Dynasty and lost

xiàng 巷 a lane; an alley

xiàngkǒu 巷口 an entrance to a lane

xiàngzi 巷子 a lane; an alley

xiàng 相 ① to examine; to study; to read ② a countenance; facial features ③ the prime minister (in feudal times) ④ to assist; to help
⇨xiāng

xiàngjī 相机 a camera

xiàngpiàn 相片 a photograph; a photo

xiàngsheng 相声 a Chinese comic dialogue; a cross talk

xiàng 象 ① an elephant ② a phenomenon; the outward appearance or expression of anything—especially weather, heavenly bodies, etc.; shape; an image ③ a portrait; an image snapshot ④ ivory

xiàngqí 象棋 Chinese chess

xiàngzhēng 象征 ① to symbolize ② a symbol

xiàng 像 ① an image; a portrait ② to resemble; resemblance ③ like; as

xiàngshì 像是 to look like; to seem

xiàngyàng 像样 presentable; decent

xiàngjiāo 橡胶 rubber

xiàngpí 橡皮 ① an eraser ② rubber

xiāo 削 to peel; to pare with a knife
⇨xuē

xiāoyáo 逍遥 to loiter about; to saunter about

xiāo 消 ① to vanish; to disappear; to die out ② to disperse; to eliminate; to remove ③ to alleviate; to allay ④ to extinguish; to quench ⑤ to need; to take

xiāochú 消除 to eliminate; to get rid of

xiāodú 消毒 to disinfect; to sterilize

xiāofáng 消防 firefighting

xiāofángduì 消防队 a fire department; a fire brigade

xiāofèi 消费 consumption; to consume

xiāofèizhě 消费者 a consumer

xiāohào 消耗 to consume (or expend)

xiāohuà 消化 ① to digest (food); digestion ② to absorb mentally

xiāojí 消极 negative; pessimistic; passive

xiāojiě 消解 to clear up; to dispel

xiāomiè 消灭 ① to annihilate ② to die out

xiāoqiǎn 消遣 pastimes; diversions; recreation

xiāoshī 消失 to vanish; to disappear

xiāoshì 消逝 to die away; to vanish

xiāoxi 消息 news; tidings; information

xiāoxi rénshì 消息人士 a well-informed source

xiāo 萧 ① a common variety of artemisia ② reverent; respectful ③ quiet; lonely; desolate ④ a surname

xiāotiáo 萧条 ① (said of a place or situation) deserted; desolate ② (said of business) sluggish; depressed; slack

xiāo 销 ① to vanish; to dispel; to cancel ② to be marketed; to be circulated; to sell ③ to melt ④ pig iron; crude iron

xiāohuǐ 销毁 to destroy

xiāolù 销路 a sale; a market

xiāoshòu 销售 to sell (goods)

xiāoshòuliàng 销售量 sales volume

xiāosǎ 潇洒 (usually said of a man's manner) dashing and refined

xiǎo 小 ① small; little; tiny ② minor ③ young; junior ④ hum-

ble; mean ⑤ slight; unimportant; trivial

xiǎobiàn 小便 ① urine; urination ② to urinate; to make water

xiǎochī 小吃 a snack

xiǎodì 小弟 ① a little brother ② a little boy ③ a young male servant ④ (of males) a form of self-address used among friends or acquaintances

xiǎo'ér 小儿 ① an infant; a child ② my son (a self-depreciatory term)

xiǎo'érkē 小儿科 ① pediatrics ② (slang) parsimonious

xiǎo'érmábìzhèng 小儿麻痹症 poliomyelitis; polio

xiǎofàn 小贩 a vendor; a peddler

xiǎofèi 小费 a tip (given to a waiter, porter, etc.)

xiǎoguǐ 小鬼 ① the spirits serving the ruler of the lower world ② an imp; a mischievous child

xiǎoháir 小孩儿 a child

xiǎoháizi 小孩子 a child

xiǎohuǒzi 小伙子 a young fellow

xiǎojiě 小姐 a young (unmarried) lady

xiǎokàn 小看 to think little of; to slight

xiǎomài 小麦 wheat

xiǎomèi 小妹 ① a little sister ② a little girl ③ a young female servant ④ (of females) a form of self-address used among friends or acquaintances

xiǎomǐ 小米 millet

xiǎopéngyou 小朋友 children (a term expressing goodwill)

xiǎoqì 小器 ① narrow-minded ② niggardly

xiǎorén 小人 a mean person

xiǎoshí 小时 an hour

xiǎoshíhou 小时候 as a child; in childhood

xiǎoshù 小数 a decimal fraction; a decimal

xiǎoshùdiǎn 小数点 the decimal point

xiǎoshuō 小说 a novel; fiction

xiǎotíqín 小提琴 a violin

xiǎotōu 小偷 a thief; a burglar

xiǎotuǐ 小腿 the calf (of the leg)

xiǎoxīn 小心 careful; cautious

xiǎoxīn-yìyì 小心翼翼 very timidly; very gingerly

xiǎoxíng 小型 small-sized; miniature

xiǎoxué 小学 a primary school; an elementary school

xiǎoxuéshēng 小学生 a (primary school) pupil

xiǎozi 小子 a young fellow (usually with slight contempt)

xiǎozǔ 小组 a group formed for a specific purpose

xiǎode 晓得 to know; to be aware of

xiào 孝 filial piety; of or having to do with filial piety

xiàoshùn 孝顺 to show filial obedience or devotion for (one's parents)

xiàozǐ 孝子 ① a devoted child ② a bereaved son

xiàoxiàng 肖像 a portrait

xiào 校 ① a school ② field-grade (officers)
⇨jiào

xiàochē 校车 a school bus

xiàohuī 校徽 a school emblem; a badge

xiàomén 校门 a gate of a school or college

xiàoqìng 校庆 anniversary celebrations of a school

xiàoshè 校舍 school premises

xiàowù 校务 school administration

xiàoyǒu 校友 an alumnus or alumna

xiàoyuán 校园 the school ground; the campus

xiàozhǎng 校长 a principal; a schoolmaster

xiào 笑 ① to laugh; to smile; to grin; to giggle; to titter; to chuckle; to snicker ② to ridicule; to deride; to jeer

xiàohua 笑话 ① a joke ② a ridiculous error ③ to ridicule

xiàoróng 笑容 a smile

xiàoshēng 笑声 sound of laughter

xiàoxīxī 笑嘻嘻 to be all smiles; to look very happy

xiào 效 ① effect; effectiveness; efficacy ② to imitate; to mimic; to follow ③ to devote ④ to offer

xiàofǎ 效法 to take as a model; to imitate

xiàoguǒ 效果 effect; result

xiàoláo 效劳 to render service; to work for

xiàolì 效力 ① effect; efficacy ② to render service

xiàolǜ 效率 efficiency

xiàonéng 效能 effect

xiàoyì 效益 beneficial result; benefit

xiàoyìng 效应 (physics) effect

xiàoyòng 效用 usefulness; use; utility

xiàozhōng 效忠 to be loyal to; allegiance

xiē 些 a small quantity or number; a few; some

xiē 歇 ① to rest ② to sleep ③ to come to an end; to stop ④ to lodge

xiébàn 协办 to cooperate in doing something

xiédìng 协定 an agreement

xiéhuì 协会 an association; a society

xiélǐ 协理 ① an assistant manager ② an official rank in the Qing Dynasty

xiélì 协力 to exert together

xiéshāng 协商 to negotiate; to discuss

xiétiáo 协调 to coordinate; harmony

xiéyì 协议 ① an agreement ② to discuss

xiézhù 协助 to assist; to help mutually

xiézuò 协作 to cooperate; to coordinate

xiéxié 邪 ① evil; depraved; wicked;

mean; vicious ② pertaining to sorcery or demonism; abnormal

xié/xiá 挟 ① to clasp or hold under the arm ② to embrace; to bosom ③ to presume upon (one's influence, advantage, etc.) ④ to extort

xiéchí/xiáchí 挟持 ① to grasp someone on both sides by the arms ② to hold someone under duress

xié 斜 inclined; sloping; slanting; leaning; oblique; diagonal

xiépō 斜坡 a slope

xié/xī 携 ① to take; to carry ② to help; to lead

xiédài/xīdài 携带 to carry with oneself; to take along

xiéshǒu/xīshǒu 携手 ① to hold each other's hand ② to co-operate

xié 鞋 shoes; footwear

xiézi 鞋子 shoes

xiě 写 to write; to sketch; to draw; to represent

xiěshēng 写生 to draw or paint from nature; to sketch

xiěshí 写实 realistic (as distinct from romantic)

xiěxìn 写信 to write a letter

xiězhào 写照 an image; portrayal; a description

xiězhēn 写真 to draw or paint a portrait

xiězì 写字 to write

xiězuò 写作 writing

xiè 泄 ① to leak out; to reveal ② to vent ③ to scatter; to disperse

xièlòu 泄露 to leak out (information, secrets, etc.); to reveal or expose unintentionally

xièqì 泄气 ① to lose strength, momentum, etc. ② discouraging; disappointed ③ to give vent to one's pent-up resentment, frustration, etc.

xiè 泻 ① to drain; water flowing down ② diarrhea; to have loose bowels

xiè 卸 ① to get rid of; to remove

② to unload (cargoes, etc.) ③ to resign; to retire from office

xièrèn 卸任 to quit a public office

xièxiè 屑 ① chips; crumbs; bits; odds and ends; trifles ② to care; to mind

xiè 谢 ① to thank ② to decline ③ to fade; to wither ④ a surname

xièjué 谢绝 to decline (an offer, etc.)

xièyì 谢意 gratitude; appreciation

xièxie 谢谢 Thank you. Thanks.

xīn 心 ① the heart ② the mind ③ the core; the inside ④ intention; idea; ambition ⑤ conscience; moral nature ⑥ one of the constellations

xīn'ài 心爱 (things or persons) dear to one's heart

xīndé 心得 what one gains from intense study, meditation, or long practice

xīndòng 心动 ① palpitation or fluttering of the heart ② to become interested in something

xīnjìng 心境 a mood; a humor

xīnlǐ 心理 ① mentality; psychology ② thought and ideas ③ mental

xīnlǐxué 心理学 psychology

xīnlǐxuéjiā 心理学家 a psychologist

xīnlì 心力 the exercise of one's mental capabilities; mental power; the vigor of the mind

xīnli 心里 ① the region of the human body around the chest ② in one's heart; in one's mind; mentally

xīnmùzhōng 心目中 ① in one's heart or mind ② in one's memory

xīnqíng 心情 a mood; a humor

xīnruǎn 心软 soft-hearted; tender-hearted

xīnshēng 心声 ① spoken language ② the heart's desire; intentions

xīnshì 心事 something weighing on one's mind; a load on one's mind; worry

xīnsī 心思 ① ideas ② a mood ③ intentions

xīnsuān 心酸 heartsore; grief-stricken; to sadden

xīntài 心态 mentality

xīnténg 心疼 ① (literally) heart-ache ② to love dearly

xīntiào 心跳 ① heartbeat ② palpitation of the heart caused by fear

xīntóu 心头 ① the heart; the mind ② the heart of an animal

xīnxiǎng 心想 to think; to expect; to figure

xīnxiōng 心胸 ① will; ambition ② capacity for tolerance

xīnxuè/xīnxiě 心血 energy; painstaking care

xīnyǎnr 心眼儿 ① one's intention; conscience ② mind ③ cleverness or wits

xīnyí 心仪 to look upon someone as a model due to admiration

xīnyì 心意 ① ideas; intentions; opinions ② regard

xīnyuàn 心愿 ① a wish aspiration ② a promise to a god

xīnzàng 心脏 the heart (as an organ)

xīnzàngbìng 心脏病 heart disease

xīnzhì 心智 mentality

xīnzhōng 心中 in one's heart or mind

xīnkǔ 辛苦 ① to work hard; to go through hardships ② laborious; toilsome

xīnláo 辛劳 pains; toil

xīnqín 辛勤 hardworking; industrious; diligent

xīnsuān 辛酸 sad; bitter; miserable

xīnxīn-kǔkǔ 辛辛苦苦 laboriously; with great efforts; to take great pains

xīnshǎng 欣赏 to appreciate, enjoy, or admire

xīnwèi 欣慰 comforted; contented; satisfaction

xīnxīn-xiàngróng 欣欣向荣

① (said of flowers in spring) blossoming ② (said of business, financial situations, etc.) flourishing; thriving; prospering

xīn 锌 zinc

xīn 新 ① new; fresh; novel ② modern; recent ③ beginning; starting ④ the prefix "neo"

xīncháo 新潮 fashion; fashionable

xīnchén-dàixiè 新陈代谢 ① (biology) metabolism ② the new superseding the old

xīnchūn 新春 ① the early spring ② the Lunar New Year

xīnfáng 新房 ① a bridal chamber ② a new house

xīnhūn 新婚 newly married

Xīnjiāpō 新加坡 Singapore

Xīnjiāng 新疆 Xinjiang or Chinese Turkestan

xīnjìn 新近 recently; newly; lately

xīnjìn rényuán 新进人员 ① new employees of an organization ② a novice

xīnláng 新郎 a bridegroom

xīnnián 新年 New Year

xīnniáng 新娘 a bride

xīnqí 新奇 novel; new

xīnrén 新人 ① new employees ② a bride; a bride and a bridegroom ③ a new love ④ a man with modern thoughts

xīnrèn 新任 newly appointed

xīnshēng 新生 ① newborn ② a new student ③ a new life; rebirth

xīnshī 新诗 free verse written in the vernacular

xīnshì 新式 of a new style; modern

xīnshǒu 新手 a new hand (at a job); a greenhorn; a novice

Xīntáibì 新台币 New Taiwan Dollar (NT$)

xīnwén 新闻 news

xīnwéngǎo 新闻稿 a press release

xīnwénjiè 新闻界 the circle of journalists; the press circle

xīnxiān 新鲜 ① fresh ② new; original; novel

xīnxīng 新兴 newly risen; burgeoning

xīnxíng 新型 a new type; a new pattern

xīnxiù 新秀 a person who has begun to distinguish himself in a given field

xīnyǐng 新颖 novel; new; original

xīnzhī 新知 ① new friends ② new knowledge; new learning

Xīnzhú 新竹 a city in Taiwan

xīn 薪 ① salary; pay ② firewood; fuel; fagots

xīnjīn 薪金 one's salary or pay; wages

xīnshuǐ 薪水 salary; pay; wages

xìn 信 ① a letter ② believing; true ③ to believe or trust ④ honesty; truthfulness; faith; confidence; trust ⑤ news; a message; information; word ⑥ an envoy; an emissary; a messenger

xìndài 信贷 credit

xìnfēng 信封 an envelope

xìnhào 信号 a signal (with flags, lamps, etc.)

xìnjiàn 信件 mail or letters (collectively)

xìnlài 信赖 ① trust ② to trust

xìnniàn 信念 a belief; a conviction

xìnrèn 信任 ① to trust; to have faith in ② trust

xìntú 信徒 a believer (of a religion, etc.)

xìntuō 信托 ① trust ② to trust

xìnxī/xìnxí 信息 news; information; a message

xìnxiāng 信箱 a mailbox; a letter box

xìnxīn 信心 faith; confidence

xìnyǎng 信仰 belief; to believe in

xìnyòng 信用 credit

xìnyòng hézuòshè 信用合作社 a credit cooperative

xìnyòngkǎ 信用卡 a credit card

xìnyòngzhuàng 信用状 a letter of credit

xìnyù 信誉 credit and reputation

xīng 兴 ① to rise; to thrive; to prosper; to flourish ② to happen; to take place; to occur ③ to start; to begin; to launch; to initiate; to establish; to found; to open
⇨xìng

xīngbàn 兴办 to set up; to initiate

xīngfèn 兴奋 excited; stimulated; excitement

xīngjiàn 兴建 to establish; to build; to construct

xīnglóng 兴隆 prosperous; thriving; vigorous

xīngqǐ 兴起 to gain power; to rise

xīngwàng 兴旺 prosperous; thriving

xīng 星 ① any heavenly body that shines; stars, planets, satellites, etc. ② a spark or sparks ③ droplets; small particles of anything; very tiny ④ name of one of the constellations ⑤ a movie star

xīngchén 星辰 stars; heavenly bodies

xīngguāng 星光 starlight

xīngqī/xīngqí 星期 week

xīngqī èr/xīngqí èr 星期二 Tuesday

xīngqī liù/xīngqí liù 星期六 Saturday

xīngqī rì/xīngqí rì 星期日 Sunday

xīngqī sān/xīngqí sān 星期三 Wednesday

xīngqī sì/xīngqí sì 星期四 Thursday

xīngqī wǔ/xīngqí wǔ 星期五 Friday

xīngqī yī/xīngqí yī 星期一 Monday

xīngqiú 星球 planets; stars

xīngtuán 星团 (astronomy) a constellation

xīngxīng 星星 tiny spots

xīngxing 星星 stars, planets, and satellites

xīngyún 星云 (astronomy) a nebula

xīngzuò 星座 (astronomy) a constellation

xīngxīng 猩猩 a chimpanzee; an orangutan

xīng 腥 ① raw, undressed meat ② an offensive smell, especially of fish or blood

xíng 刑 penalty; punishment

xíngchǎng 刑场 an execution ground

xíngfǎ 刑法 criminal law; the criminal code

xíngshì 刑事 criminal; penal

xíng 行 ① to walk; to go on foot ② to move; to go; to travel ③ able; capable ④ to act; to do; to work ⑤ to publish ⑥ to be current; to prevail ⑦ all right; O.K.; enough ⑧ baggage for travel ⑨ a road; a path

xíng/xìng 行 one's behavior or conduct
⇨háng

xíngchē 行车 ① the movement of vehicles ② to drive a vehicle

xíngchéng 行程 ① a traveler's route or itinerary ② to embark on a journey ③ a march; a journey

xíngdòng 行动 to act; to move; to make a move

xíngdòng diànhuà 行动电话 the cellular telephone

xínghuì 行贿 to bribe; to offer a bribe

xíngjīng 行经 ① to pass (a place, store, etc.); to pass through ② (said of women) in the period

xíngjìng 行径 ① one's conduct or behavior; actions ② a path; a trail

xíngjūn 行军 ① the movement of an army; a march ② the deployment of military forces

xínglǐ 行李 baggage; luggage

xíngrén 行人 pedestrians; passersby

xíngshàn 行善 to do good deeds; to do charitable work

xíngshǐ 行使 to exercise (powers, etc.); to employ

xíngshǐ 行驶 to drive (cars); to sail or steer (boats)

xíngshì 行事 ① to proceed; to execute (usually a clandestine mission); to do something planned ② conduct or behavior ③ to deal with people

xíngwéi 行为 ① behavior; conduct ② (law) acts

xíngxiāo 行销 to sell; to effect sales; to be on sale

xíngxīng 行星 the planets

xíngzhèng 行政 government; administration of public affairs ② the executive branch of a government

xíngzhèng qūyù 行政区域 an administrative efficiency

Xíngzhèng Yuàn 行政院 Executive Yuan

xíngzōng 行踪 tracks or whereabouts of a person

xíngzǒu 行走 to walk

xíng 形 ① a form; a shape ② a complexion ③ a terrain; a contour ④ expression; to describe ⑤ in comparison ⑥ to show

xíngchéng 形成 to form; to take shape

xíng'érshàngxué 形而上学 metaphysics

xíngróng 形容 ① to describe ② shape; form

xíngróngcí 形容词 an adjective

xíngshì 形式 ① form ② formality ③ style

xíngshì 形势 ① a situation ② a terrain or contour

xíngtài 形态 an appearance; a form; a state

xíngtǐ 形体 the human body which has a form or shape

xíngxiàng 形象 ① a form; an image ② (fine arts) form as contrasted to substance

xíngxíng-sèsè 形形色色 of all shapes and colors; a great variety and diversity

xíngzhuàng 形状 the appearance or shape of a thing

xíng 型 ① an earthen mold for casting ② a model; a pattern; a standard ③ a statute; a law ④ a style; a fashion; a type

xínghào 型号 a model; a type

xíngtài 型态 a form; a shape; a pattern

xǐng 省 ① to examine (oneself, etc.); to reflect; to introspect ② to understand; to know ③ to visit (one's seniors, etc.) ④ to test; an examination ⑤ memory ⇨shěng

xǐng 醒 ① to recover from (drunkenness, a stupor, etc.) ② to awake; to wake up; to be roused ③ to be clear or cool in mind

xǐnglái 醒来 to wake up

xǐngmù 醒目 ① to catch the eye; to attract attention; eye-catching; refreshing ② awake; not asleep

xìng 兴 ① interest; enthusiasm ② cheerful; happy; gay; merry ⇨xīng

xìnggāo-cǎiliè 兴高采烈 cheerful; elated; in high spirits; jubilant

xìngqù 兴趣 interest

xìngzhì 兴致 interest; eagerness; enthusiasm

xìng 杏 ① an apricot ② almonds— apricot kernels ③ apricot flowers

xìng 幸 ① well-being and happiness ② fortunately; luckily; thanks to ③ to feel happy about; to favor

xìng'ér 幸而 luckily; fortunately; thanks to

xìngfú 幸福 happiness and well-being; bliss

xìnghǎo 幸好 luckily; fortunately

xìngkuī 幸亏 luckily; fortunately

xìngyùn 幸运 ① lucky ② good luck

xìng 性 ① nature; natural property; temper ② a quality or prop-

erty ③ sex

xìng'ài 性爱 sexual love

xìngbié 性别 the sex of a person—male or female

xìnggǎn 性感 sex appeal; sexy

xìnggé 性格 disposition; personality; character

xìngjiàoyù 性教育 sex education

xìngmìng 性命 a person's life

xìngnéng 性能 ① qualities and capabilities of machinery ② natural ability

xìngqíng 性情 disposition

xìngsāorǎo 性骚扰 sexual harassment

xìngxiàng 性向 disposition

xìngxíngwéi 性行为 sexual behavior

xìngyù 性欲 sexual desire or urge

xìngzhì/xìngzhí 性质 property; characteristics; nature

xìng 姓 ① surname; one's family name ② a clan; a family; people

xìngmíng 姓名 the full name of a person

xiōng 凶 ① evil; bad ② unlucky; unfortunate ③ famine ④ fear; fearsome ⑤ very; excessive; excess ⑥ fierce; violent; cruel; ferocious ⑦ truculent; inhuman

xiōng'è 凶恶 evil; wicked; malignant

xiōnghěn 凶狠 ferocious, truculent, savage, fierce, etc.

xiōngměng 凶猛 fierce; ferocious

xiōngshǒu 凶手 the murderer; the killer

xiōng 兄 ① one's elder brother ② a term used in addressing a senior of the same generation to show respect

xiōngdì 兄弟 brothers

xiōngdi 兄弟 ① one's younger brother ② a designation for juniors of the same generation among one's relatives ③ I (a modest term)

Xiōngyálì 匈牙利 Hungary

xiōngyǒng 汹涌 (said of water) turbulent; tumultuous

xiōng 胸 ① the chest; the breast; the bosom; the bust; the thorax ② the mind (as narrow-minded, etc.); one's capacity

xiōngbù 胸部 the chest

xiōnghuái 胸怀 ambition or aspiration; mind

xiōngkǒu 胸口 the middle of the chest

xiōngtáng 胸膛 the breast or bosom; the thorax

xióng 雄 ① male; masculine; virile ② a person or state having great power and influence ③ heroic; brave; strong; ambitious ④ to win; to triumph; victory

xiónghòu 雄厚 ample; plentiful; rich; abundant

xióngwěi 雄伟 grandeur; majestic; stately

xióngzhuàng 雄壮 virile; powerful; strong; majestic

xióng 熊 ① a bear ② shining bright ③ a surname

xióngdǎn 熊胆 the gall secretion of a bear (used in Chinese medicine)

xióngmāo 熊猫 a panda

xiū 休 ① rest; to rest ② to stop; to cease

xiūjià 休假 a holiday; to have a holiday

xiūqì 休憩 to have a rest; to rest

xiūxi 休息 to take a rest; rest

xiūxián 休闲 leisure; relaxation; ease

xiūyǎng 休养 to rest; to recuperate

xiū 修 ① to repair; to mend ② to construct; to build ③ to prune; to cut; to sharpen; to trim ④ to study; to cultivate ⑤ to adorn; to decorate ⑥ long; slender ⑦ to write; to compile; to edit

xiūbǔ 修补 to repair; to mend

xiūdìng 修订 to revise

xiūfù 修复 to complete a repair job

X

xiūgǎi 修改 to correct; to alter

xiūhǎo 修好 ① to cultivate friendship with other states, etc. ② to do good deeds in order to win blessings

xiūjiàn 修建 to repair and build

xiūlǐ 修理 ① to repair ② to torture

xiūnǚ 修女 a Catholic nun; a sister

xiūshì 修饰 to doll up

xiūxíng 修行 to practice Buddhist or Taoist rules

xiūyǎng 修养 ① to seek perfection in scholastic or ethical pursuits ② man's moral culture as the result of training

xiūzhèng 修正 to correct; to alter

xiūzhù/xiūzhú 修筑 to build; to construct

xiūchǐ 羞耻 a sense of shame

xiù 秀 ① beautiful; elegant; graceful; delicate; fine ② brilliant; excellent; competent; outstanding ③ (said of grain crops) to put forth new flowers or ears

xiùlì 秀丽 beautiful; elegant; graceful; fine

xiù 臭 ① scent; smells; odors ② to smell
⇨chòu

xiù 袖 ① the sleeve ② to hide or put things in sleeves

xiùzi 袖子 the sleeve

xiù 绣 ① to embroider ② embroidery

xiù 锈 rust

xiù 嗅 to smell; to scent; to sniff

xū 须 ① to have to; must; to need ② necessary; proper ③ probably ④ a beard ⑤ to stop at ⑥ a surname

xūyào 须要 to have to; must

xūzhī 须知 ① to have to know; should know ② that which is essential to know—common knowledge; to note

xū 虚 ① empty; hollow; void; unoccupied ② unreal; false; deceptive; unfounded; groundless ③ weak; feeble ④ abstract; shapeless

xūjiǎ 虚假 false; unreal; dishonest

xūnǐ 虚拟 to suppose; to assume; to imagine; fictitious

xūruò 虚弱 debility; weak; feeble

xūwěi/xūwèi 虚伪 spurious; insincere; hypocrisy

xūwú 虚无 nothingness; emptiness; nil; void

xūxīn 虚心 open-minded

xū 需 ① to need; to require; to demand ② expenses; provisions; needs; necessaries ③ hesitation; delay

xūqiú 需求 to need; to require; needs; demands

xūyào 需要 to need or require; needs or requirements

xú 徐 slow; calm; composed; gently

xúxú 徐徐 ① slow ② steady; relaxed and dignified

xǔ 许 ① perhaps; maybe ② to promise; to approve; to permit ③ (said of a young girl) to be betrothed ④ to praise; to commend ⑤ to expect

xǔduō 许多 many; numerous; much

xǔjiǔ 许久 for a long time

xǔkě 许可 to approve; to permit or allow

xǔyuàn 许愿 ① to make a vow (to a god) ② to promise somebody a reward

xǔxǔrúshēng 栩栩如生 (said of a portrait, etc.) true to life; lifelike; to the life

xù 序 ① a preface; a foreword ② order

xùliè 序列 a rank; order

xùmù 序幕 the prologue; the prelude

xùyán 序言 a preface; a foreword

xùshù 叙述 to tell; to narrate

xùtán 叙谈 to get together and chat; to chitchat

xù 畜 to rear or raise (livestock or children) ⇨chù

xùchǎnpǐn 畜产品 animal products

xùmù 畜牧 animal husbandry

xùjiǔ 酗酒 to indulge in excessive drinking

xù 续 ① to continue; to extend; to renew ② to add; to supply more

xùjí 续集 the sequel (of a movie, etc.)

xùdao 絮叨 tiresomely talkative; to nag

xù 蓄 ① to collect; to store; to save up; to reserve ② to cultivate (long hair or a beard); to grow ③ to raise; to rear; to breed ④ to wait; to expect

xùyì 蓄意 to harbor certain intentions or ideas; premeditated (murder, etc.)

xuānbù 宣布 to announce

xuānchēng 宣称 to claim; to assert

xuānchuán 宣传 to publicize; (sales) propaganda

xuāndǎo 宣导 to guide (the people) by creating a better understanding

xuāndú 宣读 to read out (a declaration, an announcement, etc.) in public

xuāngào 宣告 to announce; to declare

xuānpàn 宣判 to announce the verdict

xuānshì 宣示 to make publicly known

xuānshì 宣誓 to take an oath

xuānyán 宣言 a declaration; a manifesto

xuānyáng 宣扬 to publicize and exalt

xuánguān 玄关 ① the entrance to Buddhism ② the door of a house ③ a vestibule

xuán 悬 ① to hang or be hanged or hung; to suspend or be suspended ② to be in suspension; to be in suspense; unsettled; unsolved ③ unfounded; without a basis; unsupported ④ far apart ⑤ to be concerned for

xuánguà 悬挂 to hang (decorations)

xuánniàn 悬念 worry and concern for a friend or close family member far away

xuánshū 悬殊 very different

xuányá/xuányái 悬崖 a precipice

xuán 旋 ① to revolve; to circle; to spin; to move in an orbit ② to return; to turn back ⇨xuàn

xuánlǜ 旋律 melody

xuánzhuǎn 旋转 to turn round and round

xuǎn 选 ① to select; to choose; choice ② to elect; elections

xuǎnbá 选拔 to select

xuǎnchū 选出 to pick out; to select; to elect

xuǎndìng 选定 to decide on a selection

xuǎngòu 选购 to select and make purchase

xuǎnjí 选集 a collection of literary works

xuǎnjǔ 选举 to elect; to vote; elections

xuǎnmín 选民 the eligible voters among the citizenry; constituency

xuǎnpiào 选票 a ballot

xuǎnqǔ 选取 to select; to choose

xuǎnshǒu 选手 a member of a sports team or delegation representing a school, an area, or a country; a contestant

xuǎnxiū 选修 to take as an elective course

xuǎnyòng 选用 to select and appoint to a post

xuǎnzé 选择 a choice; to choose

xuǎnzhàn 选战 an election campaign

xuànyào 炫耀 ① to flaunt; to show off ② bright and brilliant

xuān 旋 ① a whirlwind; a whirl ② to heat wine ⇨xuàn

xuànfēng 旋风 a whirlwind

xuànrǎn 渲染 ① to color with paint ② to make exaggerated additions in a story or report; to play up

xuē/xuè 削 ① to cut; to pare; to shave; to whittle ② to deprive ⇨xiāo

xuējiǎn/xuèjiǎn 削减 to curtail; to cut down

xuēruò/xuèruò 削弱 to enfeeble; to weaken; to devitalize

xuēzi 靴子 boots

xué/xuè 穴 ① a cave; a den; a hole ② points in the human body where acupuncture can be applied ③ (Chinese boxing) points in the human body where nerve centers are supposed to be located, a strike at which may cause paralysis or even death

xué 学 ① to learn; to study; to imitate ② of or having to do with learning; academic

xuéfèi 学费 tuition

xuéfēn 学分 units, credits, or semester hours

xuéhǎo 学好 to learn from good examples; to emulate one's betters

xuéhuì 学会 ① a learned society; an institute ② to succeed in learning (a skill)

xuéjiè 学界 the academic circles

xuékē 学科 a subject; a course

xuélì 学历 educational background

xuénián 学年 an academic (or a school) year

xuépài 学派 a school (of thought)

xuéqī/xuéqí 学期 a (school) term; a semester

xuéqū 学区 a school district

xuérén 学人 a scholar

xuésheng 学生 a student; a pupil

xuéshēnghuì 学生会 a student union; a student association

xuéshí 学时 a class hour; period

xuéshí/xuéshì 学识 erudition; learning; scholarship

xuéshì 学士 a holder of the bachelor's degree

xuéshù 学术 learning; science

xuéshùjiè 学术界 academic circles

xuéshuō 学说 a theory

xuétóng 学童 a school child

xuétú 学徒 ① an apprentice ② a student

xuéwèi 学位 an academic degree

xuéwen 学问 learning; scholarship; erudition

xuéxí 学习 to learn; to study

xuéxiào 学校 a school

xuéyè 学业 schoolwork

xuéyuán 学员 a student (usually of a college or a training course)

xuéyuàn 学院 ① a college (in a university) ② an academy

xuézhǎng 学长 one's senior at school

xuézhě 学者 a scholar; a learned person

xuézhì 学制 an educational system

xuézǐ 学子 a student; a pupil

xuě 雪 ① snow ② pure white; bright ③ to clean; to wash or wipe away

xuěbái 雪白 snow-white

xuěhuā 雪花 a snowflake

xuějiā 雪茄 a cigar

xuělí 雪梨 ① Sidney, Australia ② a kind of pear

xuěrén 雪人 a snowman

xuè/xiě 血 ① blood ② blood relationship

xuèguǎn/xiěguǎn 血管 a blood vessel

xuèhàn/xiěhàn 血汗 blood and sweat—hard toil

xuèjì/xiějī 血迹 bloodstained; a bloodstain

X

xuèniào/xiěniào 血尿 (medicine) blood in the urine; hematuria

xuètǒng/xiětǒng 血统 blood relationship; a strain; lineage; consanguinity; pedigree

xuèxīng/xiěxīng 血腥 reeking of blood; bloody; sanguinary

xuèxíng/xiěxíng 血型 a blood type; a blood group

xuèyā/xiěyā 血压 blood pressure

xuèyè/xiěyè 血液 the blood

xuèyè xúnhuán/xiěyè xúnhuán 血液循环 blood circulation

xūn 熏 ① (said of smell) to assail nostrils ② to move or touch

xūn 薫 ① to cauterize ② to perfume; to embalm ③ to smoke; to fumigate

xún 寻 to seek; to search

xúncháng 寻常 usual; ordinary; common

xúnqiú 寻求 to seek

xúnzhǎo 寻找 to look for; to seek for

xúnhuí 巡回 to go the rounds; to tour

xúnlǐ 巡礼 ① a pilgrimage to a holy land ② an inspection or sightseeing tour

xúnluó 巡逻 to patrol

xúnshì 巡视 (said of ranking officials) to inspect

xún 询 ① to inquire ② to deliberate and plan

xúnwèn 询问 to inquire; to ask

xún 循 ① to follow; to comply with ② to postpone ③ in orderly fashion ④ (obsolete) to touch ⑤ to inspect

xúnhuán 循环 circulation

xùn 训 ① to lecture; to teach; to exhort ② (to serve as) a lesson ③ an old proverb, etc.

xùnliàn 训练 to drill; to train; training

xùn 讯 ① information; news ② to ask; to inquire; to question ③ to put on trial; to question in court; to interrogate

xùnxī/xùnxí 讯息 news; information; tidings

xùnsù 迅速 by leaps and bounds; quick; swift; rapid

xùn 逊 ① respectful and compliant; obedient ② to resign; resigning; to surrender; to abdicate; yielding ③ humble; modest

Y

yā 压 ① to press ② to crush ③ to control; to quell ④ (said of enemy troops, etc.) to close in; to press near ⑤ to hold (a document, etc.) without taking action; to pigeonhole ⑥ to excel; to surpass others

yākèlì 压克力 (chemistry) acrylic resin

yālì 压力 pressure

yāpò 压迫 ① to oppress; pressure; to force ② oppression, pressure

yāsuìqián 压岁钱 money given to children by elders on the Lunar New Year's Eve

yāsuō 压缩 to compress; to condense

yāyì 压抑 to curb; to repress

yāyùn 压韵 to rhyme

yāzhì 压制 ① to suppress (one's anger, etc.); to restrain (usually by force) ② (military) to neutralize (enemy fire by massive bom-

bardment)

yā 呀 a creaking sound
⇨ya

yā 押 ① to mortgage; to pawn; to pledge ② to detain or imprison (temporarily) ③ a signature ④ to escort

yājīn 押金 a cash pledge; a deposit

yāpiàn 鸦片 opium

yā 哑 a sentence-final particle
⇨yǎ

yā 鸭 a duck

yāzi 鸭子 a duck

yá 牙 ① teeth ② to bite ③ ivory articles

yáchǐ 牙齿 a tooth or teeth

yágāo 牙膏 toothpaste

yákē 牙科 dentistry

yáshuā 牙刷 a toothbrush

yáyī 牙医 a dentist

yá 芽 a sprout; a shoot; a bud

yá/yái 崖 ① a cliff; a precipice ② the brink; the verge ③ precipitous; high and steep; forbidding

yǎ 哑 ① dumb; mute ② hoarse; husky
⇨yā

yǎ 雅 ① refined; polished; sophisticated; not common or vulgar ② elegant; graceful ③ name of an ancient musical instrument ④ (now rarely) a wine vessel

yǎdiǎn 雅典 Athens, capital of Greece

yà 轧 to crush; to grind
⇨gá

yàjūn 亚军 the runner-up

Yàzhōu 亚洲 Asia

ya 呀 a sentence-final particle indicating reduced forcefulness
⇨yā

yān 咽 the throat; the larynx; the pharynx
⇨yàn, yè

yān 烟 ① smoke; fumes ② tobacco; a smoke; a cigarette ③ mist; vapor ④ opium

yāncǎo 烟草 tobacco

yāncōng 烟囱 a chimney; a

stovepipe

yānhuǒ 烟火 ① kitchen smoke which suggests presence of humans ② cooked food (as distinct from herbs and fruits which are supposed to be the food of immortals) ③ a signal fire or beacon ④ smoke and fire

yānhuo 烟火 fireworks

yānjuǎnr 烟卷儿 a cigarette

yānwù 烟雾 smoke; mist; vapor; smog

yān 淹 to submerge; to drown; to soak; to steep in; to flood

yānmò 淹没 ① drowned ② to waste a talent as if by submerging it

yán 延 ① to lengthen; to spread; to extend ② to delay; to defer ③ to prolong ④ to procrastinate

yáncháng 延长 to lengthen; to extend; to prolong

yánchí 延迟 to delay; to be delayed

yánhuǎn 延缓 to postpone; to put off; to defer

yánlǎn 延揽 to recruit the service of (talented men)

yánqī/yánqí 延期 to be postponed; to be put off

yánshēn 延伸 to extend; to stretch

yánwù 延误 to fail because of procrastination

yánxù 延续 to continue; to be continued

yán 严 ① tight ② stern; strict; severe; grim; inclement; inexorable; relentless; rigorous; rigid; grave; solemn ③ reverence ④ father ⑤ a surname

yángé 严格 strict; stringent; rigid; rigorous

yánhán 严寒 severe cold

yánjǐn 严谨 careful; cautious; well-knit

yánjìn 严禁 to prohibit or forbid strictly

yánjùn 严峻 stern; severe; rigorous; grim

yánkē 严苛 harsh

yánlì 严厉 strict; stringent; rigid; rigorous

yánmì 严密 rigid; rigorous; strict; exact

yánsù 严肃 serious-looking; serious

yánzhòng 严重 serious; severe; grave

yán 言 ① speech; words ② to say; to talk; to speak; to mean; to express ③ a language; a dialect

yáncí 言辞 words or expressions; statements; wording; diction

yánlùn 言论 speech

yánxíng 言行 words and deeds

yányǔ 言语 spoken language; speech; words

yán 岩 ① a large rock ② a mountain

yánshí 岩石 a rock; a crag

yánrè 炎热 (said of weather) very hot

yán 沿 ① to follow; to go along; along ② to hand down; to continue ③ successive; continuous ④ the edge; the brim

yán'àn 沿岸 along the coast of...; littoral

yánhǎi 沿海 ① along the coast ② offshore

yántú 沿途 along the way

yánxí 沿袭 to follow the old or traditional (practices, customs, precedents, etc.)

yányòng 沿用 to continue following the old practices, customs, etc.

yán 研 ① to go to the very source; to study; to investigate; to research; to examine ② to grind; to powder

yánjiū/yánjiù 研究 to study and research

yánjiūshēng/yánjiùshēng 研究生 a graduate student

yánjiūshì/yánjiùshì 研究室 a research laboratory

yánjiūsuǒ/yánjiùsuǒ 研究所 a research laboratory; a research institute; a graduate school

yánjiūyuán/yánjiùyuán 研究员 a researcher

yánjiūyuàn/yánjiùyuàn 研究院 a research institute

yántǎo 研讨 to study and discuss; to investigate and research

yántǎohuì 研讨会 a seminar; a symposium

yánxí 研习 to research and study

yánxíhuì 研习会 a study meeting or conference

yánzhì 研制 ① to manufacture; to develop ②(Chinese medicine) to prepare medicinal powder by grinding

yán 盐 common salt; salt

yánbā 盐巴 (dialect) salt; common salt

yánluówáng 阎罗王 ① the Ruler of Hades; the King of Hell ② a tyrant; one who is feared by all others

yánliào 颜料 dyestuffs; pigments

yánsè 颜色 color; hue; pigment ② countenance; facial expression ③ a lesson

yǎnrán 俨然 dignified-looking

yǎnshēng 衍生 to derive from

yǎn 掩 ① to cover; to hide; to conceal; to cover up ② to shut; to close

yǎngài 掩盖 to cover up; to conceal

yǎnhù 掩护 ① to cover (friendly troops on a special assignment) ② camouflage

yǎnshì 掩饰 to cover; to conceal

yǎn 眼 ① the eye ② a look; a glance ③ a tiny hole; an opening; an orifice; an aperture ④ a key point

yǎnguāng 眼光 sight; insight; vision; discerning ability; power of judgment

yǎnhuā-liáoluàn 眼花撩乱 (scenes so varied and confusing as) to dazzle the eyes

yǎnjiè 眼界 one's field of vision;

an outlook

yǎnjìng 眼镜 glasses; spectacles

yǎnjīng 眼睛 the eyes

yǎnkàn 眼看 ① imminent; soon ② to see something happening ③ to watch helplessly

yǎnkuàng/yǎnkuāng 眼眶 an orbit; an eye socket

yǎnlèi 眼泪 tears

yǎnlì 眼力 ① eyesight; vision ② discerning ability

yǎnpí 眼皮 eyelids

yǎnqián 眼前 ① right before one's eyes ② at this moment; now; at present

yǎnsè 眼色 the expression of one's eyes (indicating one's intention, wish, etc.); a hint or a cue given with the eyes

yǎnshén 眼神 expression of the eyes

yǎnxià 眼下 at present; currently; at the moment

yǎn 演 ① to perform for entertainment; to act; to play ② to expound ③ to exercise; to practice ④ to evolve; to develop

yǎnbiàn 演变 to develop and change; to evolve

yǎnchàng 演唱 to sing on stage

yǎnchū 演出 (said of entertainers) to perform; to present (a play)

yǎnhuà 演化 to develop and change; to evolve; evolution

yǎnjì 演技 acting

yǎnjiǎng 演讲 to deliver a speech; to orate

yǎnjìn 演进 to evolve; to develop

yǎnliàn 演练 drill

yǎnshuō 演说 to deliver a speech

yǎnsuàn 演算 to do mathematical problems

yǎnxí 演习 military exercises; maneuvers

yǎnxì 演戏 ① to act in a play ② to playact

yǎnyuán 演员 an actor or actress

yǎnzòu 演奏 (said of musicians) to perform

yǎnzòuhuì 演奏会 a concert; a recital

yànwù 厌恶 to loathe; to dislike

yàn 咽 to swallow; to gulp ⇨yān, yè

yàn 宴 to entertain; to feast

yànhuì 宴会 a banquet; a feast

yànqǐng 宴请 to entertain (to dinner)

yànxí 宴席 a banquet; a feast

yàn 验 ① to test; to examine; to analyze ② to produce an effect ③ to verify; to prove

yànshōu 验收 to accept (goods, buildings, etc.) after ascertaining that the quality or quantity meets requirements

yànzhèng 验证 to test and verify

yànwō 燕窝 swallow's nests found on seaside cliffs, etc., built of seaweed and a certain secretion by swallows, used as an ingredient for a highly valued Chinese dish

yànzi 燕子 a swallow

yāngqiú 央求 to beg; to entreat; to implore; to plead

yáng 扬 ① to raise ② to display; to expose; to make evident; to make known ③ to scatter; to spread ④ to praise; to acclaim ⑤ to wave; to flutter ⑥ high or raised (voice, cry, etc.) ⑦ (said of flames) blazing ⑧ to stir; to get excited ⑨ a surname

yángyán 扬言 to exaggerate; to declare in public

yáng 羊 a sheep; a goat

yángmáo 羊毛 wool

yángròu 羊肉 mutton

yángshuǐ 羊水 amniotic fluid

yáng 阳 ① the sun; solar; sunlight ② the north of a stream ③ the south of a hill ④ positive (electricity, etc.) ⑤ male; masculine ⑥ bright; brilliant ⑦ the male genitals ⑧ pertaining to

this world, as opposed to Hades

yángguāng 阳光 sunshine; sunlight; sunbeams

Yángmíngshān 阳明山 Mt. Yang-ming in Taiwan

yángsǎn 阳伞 a parasol; an umbrella

yángtái 阳台 a veranda or balcony

yáng 杨 ① a poplar ② a surname

yángshù 杨树 poplar tree

yáng 洋 ① foreign; Western; Occidental ② an ocean ③ imported

yángcōng 洋葱 an onion

yángyì 洋溢 to be filled with; to brim with

yángzhuāng 洋装 ① Western dress ② Western binding (for books)

yǎng 仰 ① to look up ② to adore, admire, or revere ③ to lean or rely upon ④ to swallow

yǎnglài 仰赖 to look to (somebody for help); to rely upon

yǎngmù 仰慕 to adore; to admire and respect

yǎngwàng 仰望 ① to look up at ② to respectfully seek guidance or help from; to look up to

yǎng 养 ① to grow; to raise; to breed; to rear; to bring up ② to support or keep (a family, etc.) ③ to give birth to ④ to nourish; to cultivate (one's mind, etc.) ⑤ to educate ⑥ to nurse (a wound or illness)

yǎng/yàng 养 to support one's parents

yǎngchéng 养成 to discipline and train; to cultivate (good habits, etc.)

yǎngfèn 养分 the amount of nutritious substance in a given food item; nutrition

yǎnghuo 养活 ① to support or keep (a family or somebody) ② to rear; to bring up

yǎnglǎo 养老 ① (said of persons) to retire and enjoy the fruit of

one's work in the past ② to provide for the aged

Yǎnglèduō 养乐多 the trademark of a yogurt preparation

yǎngliào 养料 nutrition; nutritious value

yǎngshēng 养生 to preserve one's health; to keep in good condition

yǎngyù 养育 to rear; to raise and educate

yǎngzhí 养殖 to breed (aquatics)

yǎngzhí yúyè 养殖渔业 pisciculture

yǎng 氧 oxygen

yǎnghuà 氧化 to oxidize or be oxidized; oxidation

yǎngqì 氧气 oxygen

yǎng 痒 to itch; to tickle

yàng 样 ① a sort; a kind; a variety ② a style; a pattern; a mode; a form ③ appearances; looks ④ a sample

yàngběn 样本 a sample

yàngpǐn 样品 a specimen; a sample (of a commodity)

yàngshì 样式 style; modes; patterns

yàngyàng 样样 each and every; all; every kind

yàngzi 样子 ① appearance; shape ② sample; model ③ tendency; likelihood ④ manner

yāoguài 妖怪 ① a monster or demon ② a Circe; a siren ③ a spirit transformed from a very old animal, tree, etc.

yāo 要 ① to ask for; to demand ② to engage; to make an agreement ③ to invite ④ to coerce; to threaten
⇨yào

yāoqiú 要求 ① to demand; to request ② a demand; a request

yāo 腰 ① the midriff; the waist ② the middle of something; the waist portion of a region ③ the kidneys

yāodài 腰带 ① a girdle; a waistband ② (anatomy) a pelvic girdle

yāo 邀 ① to invite; to ask; to request ② to intercept

yāojí 邀集 to invite to a gathering

yāoqǐng 邀请 to invite; invitation

yāoyuē 邀约 ① an engagement; an invitation ② to invite; to make an appointment

yáo 窑 ① a kiln; a brick furnace ② pottery ③ a pit in a coal mine; a coal shaft ④ a cave—for human dwelling ⑤ a brothel

yáoyán 谣言 unfounded report; rumor

yáo 摇 ① to wag; to shake; to wave; to rock ② (said of one's confidence, determination, etc.) to sway, wobble, shake ③ to scull; to row (a boat, etc.) ④ to agitate; to incite; to annoy

yáobǎi 摇摆 to swing to and fro; to oscillate; to vacillate

yáogǔnyuè 摇滚乐 rock-and-roll

yáohuang 摇晃 to shake (a bottle, etc.)

yáotóu 摇头 to shake one's head—in disapproval or out of sympathy

yáokòng 遥控 remote control; telecontrol

yáoyuǎn 遥远 far and remote

yǎo 咬 to bite; to gnaw

yào 药 ① medicine; remedy; a drug; pharmaceuticals ② to kill with poison; to poison

yàocái 药材 medicinal substance

yàofāng 药方 a (medicinal) prescription

yàofáng 药房 a druggist's store; a dispensary; a pharmacy

yàojì 药剂 medicine; remedy; a drug

yàojìshī 药剂师 a pharmacist; a druggist

yàojú 药局 a druggist's store; a dispensary; a pharmacy

yàopǐn 药品 pharmaceutical products; drugs

yàoshuǐ 药水 liquid medicine

yàowán 药丸 a pill medicine; a pill

yàowù 药物 drug; medicine

yào 要 ① must; should; ought to ② to want; to demand; to need; to require; to desire; to take ③ will; shall—to indicate the future tense ④ if; in case ⑤ necessary; important; essential; necessity ⑥ brief ⑦ to summarize; a summary; a generalization; a synopsis
⇨yāo

yàobù 要不 if not; otherwise; the other alternative being...;

yàobùrán 要不然 otherwise; or

yàobùshì 要不是 If it were not for...; but for....

yàobúyào 要不要 Do you want it? Do I have to...? Shall (I, he, etc.)...? Do yo want (me, him, etc.)...?

yàodiǎn 要点 the important or main points; the gist; the essential points

yàofàn 要犯 an important or dangerous criminal; a most-wanted criminal

yàohǎo 要好 ① to be friend ② to be in love with ③ to desire to excel

yàojiàn 要件 ① an important document; an urgent or confidential matter, etc. ② a prerequisite; a necessary condition

yàojǐn 要紧 important and urgent

yàolǐng 要领 essential points; essentials

yàome 要么 or; either...or

yàomìng 要命 ① very; extremely; awfully ② too much to endure

yàoshi 要是 if; in case

yàosù 要素 essentials; chief ingredients or elements or factors

yàoshi 钥匙 a key

yàoyǎn 耀眼 dazzling; to dazzle

yē/yé 耶 transliteration of English names

Yēdànjié/Yédànjié 耶诞节 Christmas

Yēsū Jīdū/Yēsū Jīdū 耶稣基督 Jesus Christ

yéye 爷爷 ① grandfather; grandpa ② sir

yě 也 ① and; also; besides; either; too ② still ③ even

yěhǎo 也好 That's fine.

yěshì 也是 also the same

yěxǔ 也许 perhaps; probably

yějīn 冶金 metallurgy

yěliàn 冶炼 to smelt

yě 野 ① wild; uncultured; undomesticated; coarse; barbarous; rude ② the people (as opposed to the government) ③ the countryside; fields; the wilderness

yěcān 野餐 a picnic; a barbecue

yěgǒu 野狗 a wild dog; a stray dog; a dog without an owner

yěmán 野蛮 ① barbarous; savage; uncivilized ② unreasonable; rude; brutal

yěniú 野牛 a wild ox; a bison; a buffalo

yěshēng 野生 wild; undomesticated

yěshòu 野兽 a wild beast; a brute

yěwài 野外 the outdoors; the open

yěxīn 野心 ① ambition; careerism ② greediness

yè 业 ① work; occupations; professions; vocations; callings; trades ② estate; property ③ already

yèjì/yèjī 业绩 the track record

yèwù 业务 business activities

yèyǐ 业已 to have already been

yèyú 业余 ① spare time ② amateur

yèzhǔ 业主 the proprietor; the owner

yè 叶 ① a leaf; a petal (of a flower) ② a leaf or two pages (of a book) ③ a period; an era or epoch ④ something light and tiny—as a small boat in a lake ⑤ a surname

yèpiàn 叶片 (botany) the leaf blade

yèzi 叶子 a leaf

yè 页 a page (in books, etc.); a sheet (of paper, etc.)

yè/yì 曳 to haul; to tug; to drag; to trail

yè 夜 ① night; dark(ness) ② a night trip; night traveling

yèbān 夜班 night shifts; night work

yèjiān 夜间 at night; in the night

yèjiānbù 夜间部 the night department (of a school, college, or university)

yèjǐng 夜景 night scenes (of a locality)

yèli 夜里 at night

yèsè 夜色 the dim light of night—moonlight

yèshì 夜市 business activities in night hours; markets devoted to nighttime business

yèwǎn 夜晚 at night; in the night

yèzǒnghuì 夜总会 a nightclub

yè 咽 to be choked; to weep or speak in a choked voice; to sob ⇨yān, yàn

yè 液 liquid; juices; secretions; sap

yèjīng 液晶 (physics) a liquid crystal

yètǐ 液体 liquid

yī 一 ① a; an; the ② one; unit ③ whole; all; throughout ④ single; alone ⑤ union; uniformity; uniform ⑥ to unify; to unite ⑦ once; as soon as ⑧ each; per; every time (Note: When yī precedes a 4th-tone sound, it is pronounced as yí. When the sound followed yī is a 1st-, 2nd-, or 3rd-tone sound, yī is pronounced as yì.)

yìbān 一般 common; general; commonly; generally

yìbān'éryán 一般而言 generally speaking; in general

yìbānláishuō 一般来说 generally speaking; in general

yìbānxìng 一般性 generality

yíbàn 一半 a half; half; in part

yíbèizi 一辈子 as long as one lives; a lifetime

Y

yìbiān 一边 ① on one side; by the side ② at the same time

yìbiān...yìbiān... 一边……一边…… ① on one side..., and on the other side... ② to do..., and...at the same time

yìbìng 一并 all; wholly; together with

yìbō-sānzhé 一波三折 hitting one snag after another

yíchànà 一刹那 in a moment

yìchéng-búbiàn 一成不变 fixed; unchangeable; invariable; inflexible

yídàzǎo 一大早 in the early morning

yídài 一带 the area (around a particular place)

yídàn 一旦 ① once; whenever ② a day

yídào 一道 ① together ② (problem, etc.) ③ on the same path

yìdiǎnr 一点儿 ① a little bit ② somewhat

yídìng 一定 certainly; surely; necessarily

yídù 一度 once; on one occasion; for a time

yíduàn 一段 ① one paragraph, passage or stanza ② a section; a length of...

yìfān 一番 ① a kind, type, style, etc. ② once ③ a (silver dollar)

yìfān-fēngshùn / yìfán-fēng- shùn 一帆风顺 to proceed smoothly without a hitch

yìfāngmiàn 一方面 ① one side ② on the one hand..., on the other hand...

yígài 一概 all; without exception; totally

yígài'érlùn 一概而论 discussed or regarded in the same frame of mind or in an indiscriminating manner

yìgān-èrjìng 一干二净 ① thoroughly cleaned-up ② completely

yígege 一个个 ① one by one ② each and every one

yígejìnr / yígejìngr 一个劲儿

full of zest or enthusiasm

yígòng 一共 altogether; in all; all told

yìgǔ 一股 ① a streak; a strand ② one share (in stockholding) ③ a band (of bandits) ④ a (strong smell) ⑤ full of (spirit, zest, etc.)

yíguàn 一贯 from beginning to end; consistent; unswerving

yìháng 一行 a row; a line; a single file
⇨yìxíng

yíhōng'érsàn / yìhōng'érsàn 一哄而散 (said of crowds) to disperse in a hubbub

yíhuìr / yìhuìr 一会儿 ① in a moment ② now...now...

yíhuìr...yíhuìr... / yìhuìr... 一会儿……一会儿 …… now...now...; one moment... next...

yíjìzhīcháng 一技之长 proficiency in a particular line (or field); professional skill

yī...jiù... 一……就…… no sooner...than...

yìjǔ 一举 with one action; at a blow; at one fell swoop

yìkǒuqì 一口气 ① in one breath; without stop ② breath

yíkuài 一块 a piece; a block

yíkuàir 一块儿 together; altogether

yìlái 一来 ① on the one hand ② as soon as (someone) arrives

yìlǎn-wúyú 一览无余 (literally) A single glance takes in all—a panoramic view.

yìlián 一连 ① successively ② a company

yìliánchuàn 一连串 a series of

yìliú 一流 ① first-rate ② of the same class

yílù 一路 all the way

yílù-píng'ān 一路平安 to have a safe journey; Bon voyage!

yílù-shùnfēng 一路顺风 to have a good trip; Bon voyage!

yílù 一律 without exception (or discrimination)

Y

yìmáo-bùbá 一毛不拔 very stingy; parsimonious

yímiàn 一面 one side; an aspect

yímiàn...yímiàn... 一面…… 一面…… ① on one side..., and on the other side... ② to do...and... at the same time

yìmú-yíyàng/yìmò-yíyàng 一模一样 exactly the same; identical

yìpáng 一旁 one side; on the sideline

yípiàn 一片 a denominative adjective for any object which is flat and thin

yìqí 一齐 at the same time

yìqǐ 一起 ① together ② in the same place

yíqiè 一切 all; everything

yìqún 一群 a group; a crowd; a herd; a pack; a flock

yírú 一如 to be the same as

yìshēn 一身 ① a suit ② the whole body; all over the body ③ a solitary person

yìshēng 一生 a lifetime

yìshí 一时 ① for a moment ② a period of time ③ accidentally

yìshǒu 一手 single-handedly

yìtǐ 一体 ① an organic (or integral) whole ② all people concerned; to a man

yìtiāndàowǎn 一天到晚 from morning till night; all day long

yìtóng 一同 together with; in the company of

yìtóu 一头 ① a head (covered with gray hair, dust, skin ailments, etc.) ② (said of cattle, hogs, mules, etc.) a head ③ a jerky motion of the head

yíwèi 一味 habitually; invariably

yíxìliè 一系列 a series of

yíxià 一下 once

yíxiàzi 一下子 ① at once ② at one stroke

yíxiàng 一向 ① hitherto ② consistently

yìxiē 一些 ① some; a few ② somewhat

yìxīn 一心 ① wholeheartedly ② at one

yìxíng 一行 a group of (officials, businessmen, etc. during a trip) ⇨yìháng

yíyàng 一样 ① alike; in the same manner ② an (object, item, or article)

yì...yě... 一……也…… merely

yìyī 一一 one by one; each separately

yízài 一再 repeatedly; again and again

yìzǎo 一早 in the early morning

yízhèn 一阵 a sudden gust (of wind, laughter, etc.)

yízhènzi 一阵子 for a while

yìzhí 一直 always; constantly

yízhì 一致 unanimously; one and all; consistent

yī 伊 ① he; she ② a surname

Yīlākè 伊拉克 Iraq

Yīlǎng 伊朗 Iran

Yīsīlánjiào 伊斯兰教 Islam; Islamism

yī 衣 ① clothing; dress; apparel; garments; attire ② a coating; a covering ③ skin or peel of fruits

yīfu 衣服 clothes; clothing; dress

yīguì 衣柜 a wardrobe; a chest of drawers for clothing

yīshang 衣裳 clothes; garments; clothing

yīwù 衣物 clothing and other articles of daily use

yīzhuó 衣着 clothing; attire; apparel; dress

yī 医 ① to cure or treat (diseases) ② a doctor; a physician; surgeon ③ medical science; medical service

yījiè 医界 the medical circles; the medical world

yīliáo 医疗 to cure or treat (a disease); medical treatment

yīshēng 医生 a doctor; a physician; a surgeon

yīshī 医师 a doctor; a physician;

a surgeon

yīshù 医术 medical skill; the art of healing

yīwù 医务 medical matters

yīwùshì 医务室 an infirmary; a medical office

yīxué 医学 medical science

yīxuéyuàn 医学院 a college of medicine

yīyào 医药 healing drugs; medicines

yīyuàn 医院 a hospital

yīzhì 医治 to cure (a disease); medical treatment; to doctor

yī 依 ① to depend on; to lean to ② to follow; to comply with; to consent; to yield to ③ to be tolerant to ④ to forgive ④ according to

yīcì 依次 in order (in proper sequence or position); one by one

yīfǎ 依法 according to law

yīfù 依附 ① to depend on ② to submit to

yījiù 依旧 as usual; as before

yījù 依据 according to; in accordance with

yīkào 依靠 to rely on; to depend on

yīlài 依赖 to depend on

yīrán 依然 as before; as usual; still

yīyī-bùshě 依依不舍 unwilling to part

yīzhào 依照 according to; in accordance with

yī 壹 an elaborate form of yī 一 — used mostly in accounting and especially in checks to prevent forgery or alterations

yíbiǎo 仪表 ① appearance and deportment ② a rule; a model

yíqì 仪器 (laboratory, medical, etc.) an instrument; an apparatus

yíshì 仪式 ceremonies; rites

yí 宜 ① right; fitting; proper; good ② should; ought to; had better ③ a matter ④ to fit; to suit; to put in order ⑤ a surname

yí 咦 (an interjection of surprise) well; why; hey

yí 姨 ① the sisters of one's wife ② the sisters of one's mother ③ a concubine

yífu 姨父 an uncle

yímā 姨妈 the married sisters of one's mother

yí 移 ① to shift; to move ② to change; to alter; to influence; to affect ③ to forward; to transmit; to transfer; to transplant; to convey ④ to give; to endow

yídòng 移动 to move; to shift; to change

yíjiāo 移交 to turn over

yímín 移民 ① to immigrate; immigration ② to emigrate; to settle people (in a new region, etc.); to colonize ③ an immigrant ④ an emigrant

yízhí 移植 ① to transplant ② grafting; transplanting

yízhuǎn 移转 to transfer (certain rights, holdings, etc.)

yí 遗 ① to leave over ② remnants; leftovers ③ anything left behind by the deceased; to bequeath; to hand down; a legacy ④ to lose; lost ⑤ things lost ⑥ to miss; an omission due to negligence ⑦ to abandon; to desert ⑧ to forget ⑨ to urinate ⑩ short for nocturnal emission

yíchǎn 遗产 ① property left behind by a deceased person ② a legacy

yíchǎnshuì 遗产税 legacy tax; inheritance tax

yíchuán 遗传 to inherit; hereditary; heredity

yíhàn 遗憾 to regret; regret; to feel sorry; regrettable

yíjī/yíjì 遗迹 relics; vestiges; traces

yíliú 遗留 to leave behind either intentionally or unintentionally

yíqì 遗弃 ① (law) to desert or to fail to support one's legal dependents ② to cast away; to abandon

yíshī 遗失 to lose; lost

yítǐ 遗体 ① the remains (of a deceased person); the corpse ② one's body (handed down by one's parents)

yíwàng 遗忘 to forget; to neglect

yíwù 遗物 things left behind by a dead person

yízhǐ 遗址 the old site of some building or a city which no longer exists

yízhì 遗志 the ideal or wish not carried out before one's death

yí 疑 ① doubtful; dubious; skeptical; doubt; to doubt; to question ② suspicious; to suspect ③ strange; incomprehensible; mysterious; questionable ④ sham; dummy; false

yíhuò 疑惑 to doubt; to suspect

yílǜ 疑虑 anxiety; misgivings

yínán 疑难 a question; a problem; a puzzle

yísì 疑似 could be; suspected to be

yíwèn 疑问 a question; doubt; uncertainty

yíxīn 疑心 ① to doubt ② suspicion

yǐ 乙 ① the second of the Ten Celestial Stems ② one ③ someone

yǐ 已 ① already ② to come to an end; to finish ③ to cease ④ used to indicate the past ⑤ a final particle to add emphasis

yǐjīng 已经 already

yǐrán 已然 to be already so

yǐ 以 by means of; because of

yǐbiàn 以便 so as to; in order to

yǐhòu 以后 after; afterward

yǐjí 以及 and; including; as well as

yǐlái 以来 since

yǐmiǎn 以免 in order to avoid; so as not to

yǐnèi 以内 within

yǐqián 以前 before

Yǐsèliè 以色列 Israel

yǐshàng 以上 above

yǐshēn-zuòzé 以身作则 to set examples by one's own action

yǐwài 以外 ① outside; beyond ② other than; besides

yǐwǎng 以往 in the past; formerly

yǐwéi 以为 to regard...as; to think; to consider

yǐxià 以下 below

yǐzhì 以至 ① up to; until ② so... that

yǐzhì 以致 so that; with the result that

yǐzhìyú 以至于 so that

yǐ 倚 ① to rely on; to depend on ② to lean toward; to rest on

yǐ 椅 a chair; a bench

yǐzi 椅子 a chair; a bench

yì 亿 ① a hundred million ② tranquility; repose ③ (according to) estimates

yìwàn 亿万 hundreds of millions; millions upon millions

yì 义 ① justice; righteousness ② generosity; charity; philanthropy; chivalry ③ meaning; connotations ④ artificial; unreal; false ⑤ a surname

Yìdàlì 义大利 Italy

yìgōng 义工 a volunteer worker

yìmài 义卖 a charity sale; a bazaar

yìwù 义务 duty; obligation

yì 艺 art; skill; talent; craft; dexterity

yìrén 艺人 an entertainer

yìshù 艺术 art

yìshùjiā 艺术家 an artist

yìshùpǐn 艺术品 a work of art; an object of art

yìwén 艺文 literature and fine arts

yì 忆 to remember; to bear in mind; to recall; to recollect

yì 议 ① to criticize; to comment; criticism; comment ② an opinion; a view ③ to discuss; to argue; to debate; to negotiate; to talk over ④ argumentative writing; argumentation; an essay; a treatise

yǐ'àn 议案 a bill; a proposal

Y

yìchéng 议程 an agenda

yìdìng 议定 to arrive at a decision after discussion or negotiation

yìdìngshū 议定书 a protocol

yìhuì 议会 a parliament; an assembly; a council

yìjià 议价 ① to negotiate over the price ② the negotiated price

yìlùn 议论 ① comments ② to discuss; to talk ③ argument; debate

yìtí 议题 a topic for discussion; a subject of debate

yìyuán 议员 a councilor; a parliamentarian

yìzhǎng 议长 the speaker, president, or chairman of an assembly, parliament, etc.

yìjí 亦即 that is; i.e.; namely; viz.

yì 异 ① different; difference ② peculiar; extraordinary; uncommon; strange; unusual ③ foreign; unfamiliar; unknown ④ to marvel; to wonder ⑤ to separate

yìcháng 异常 extraordinary; different; unusual; strange

yìdòng 异动 changes; a reshuffle

yìguó 异国 a foreign country

yìqū-tónggōng 异曲同工 The writings are different, but the excellence is the same.

yìwù 异物 ① a rare treasure; an extremely valuable object ② a peculiar thing; a strange thing; an uncommon thing ③ the dead

yìxiāng 异乡 a strange land; a foreign land

yìxìng 异性 ① of the other sex; the opposite sex ② of a different nature

yìyì 异议 dissent; objections

yì 抑 ① to restrain; to force to (do, perform, etc.) ② to press down; to repress ③ to bend or lower (one's head) ④ an exclamatory, roughly equivalent to "oh" or "alas" ⑤ to stop

yìhuò 抑或 besides; moreover; or

yìzhì 抑制 to restrain; to suppress; to repress

yì 役 ① military service ② to guard the frontier ③ to dispatch ④ to employ as a servant ⑤ to serve ⑥ to do

yìnán 役男 the male citizens between 18 and 45 who are eligible for military service

yì 译 to translate; translation

yìyuán 译员 an interpreter; a translator

yì 易 ① easy ② to exchange; to barter ③ to change (places, jobs, owners, etc.) ④ amiable; lenient ⑤ I Ching; the Book of Changes ⑥ a surname

yì 奕 ① gorgeous; elegant; good-looking ② worried; unsettled; anxious ③ in good order; in sequence

yìmiáo 疫苗 vaccine

yìqíng 疫情 information about an epidemic; an epidemic situation

yìzhù 挹注 to supplement; to draw from one to make up the deficits in another

yì 益 ① to increase; to add to; to augment ② benefit; profit; advantage

yìchu 益处 advantages; benefit; profit

yìrì 翌日 tomorrow

yì 意 ① meaning ② a hint; a suggestion ③ a thought; an idea; sentiments ④ intention; inclination ⑤ expectations

yìjiàn 意见 an opinion; a suggestion; a view

yìjìng 意境 a frame of mind; conception

yìliào 意料 expectations

yìniàn 意念 an idea

yìshí/yìshì 意识 consciousness

yìshídào/yìshìdào 意识到 to be conscious of; to realize

yìsi 意思 ① meaning ② intention; desire ③ interest

yìtú 意图 to intend to do some-

thing; intention

yìwài 意外 ① unexpected; accidental ② a surprise; an accident

yìwàixiǎn 意外险 accident insurance

yìwèi 意味 ① an impression ② to portend

yìwèizhe 意味着 to signify; to mean

yìxiǎng-búdào 意想不到 never thought of; unexpectedly

yìxiàng 意向 intentions; inclinations

yìxiàng 意象 an image; imagery; an idea; a concept

yìyì 意义 meaning; significance

yìyuàn 意愿 inclination; wish; volition

yìzhì 意志 volition; will; will power

yìlì 毅力 perseverance; indomitability

yìrán 毅然 firmly; courageously

yì 翼 ① wings ② fins ③ to protect; to patronize

yīn 因 ① cause; reason ② for; because of

yīncái-shījiào 因材施教 to teach according to the student's ability or aptitude

yīncǐ 因此 therefore; hence; thus

yīn'ér 因而 therefore; and so; thereupon

yīnguǒ 因果 ① cause and effect ② karma; preordained fate

yīnsù 因素 factors; elements

yīnwèi 因为 inasmuch as; since; because; as

yīnyìng 因应 to adjust; to react

yīnyuán 因缘 (Buddhism) primary and secondary causes; a chance; the chain of cause and effect

yīnzǐ 因子 (mathematics) a factor

yīn 阴 ① cloudy; dark ② secret ③ cunning and crafty ④ shady ⑤ negative (as opposite to positive, as electricity) ⑥ the back side ⑦ the north side of a mountain ⑧ the south side of a stream ⑨ reproductive organs of both sexes ⑩ Hades; Hell ⑪ feminine; female ⑫ time ⑬ a surname

yīn'àn 阴暗 dim; dark; gloomy; overcast

yīndào 阴道 ① the vagina ② a shaded road ③ the "subordinate ways"—the ways of subjects to the king, of children to parents and of wife to husband

yīnmái 阴霾 haze; thin mist

yīnmóu 阴谋 a plot; a secret scheme; a conspiracy

yīntiān 阴天 a cloudy day

yīnyǐng 阴影 shades; shadows

yīn 音 ① sound; voice ② (usually used in correspondence) news; information ③ a musical note ④ tone; accent; timbre

yīnfú 音符 (music) notes

yīnjié 音节 a syllable

yīnliàng 音量 the volume (of sound)

yīnsè 音色 timbre; tone color

yīnxiǎng 音响 ① sound; acoustics ② audio

yīnyuè 音乐 music

yīnyuèhuì 音乐会 a concert; a musical recital

yīnyuèjiā 音乐家 a musician

yīnyuèxì 音乐系 the department of music in college

yīnzhì/yīnzhí 音质 tonality; tone quality

yīn 殷 an alternative name for the latter half of the Shang Dynasty

yīnqiè 殷切 ardent; eager

yín 银 ① silver ② money; wealth ③ silvery

yínháng 银行 a bank

Yínhé 银河 the Milky Way; the Galaxy

yínmù 银幕 (motion-picture) screen

yínsè 银色 silvery

yínzi 银子 silver (as one of valuables)

yínhuì 淫秽 dirty (books, etc.); obscene

yǐn 引 ① to guide ② to quote ③ to cause ④ to pull ⑤ to retire ⑥ a unit of length (= 33⅓ meters) ⑦ to introduce

yǐnbào 引爆 to ignite; to detonate

yǐndǎo 引导 to guide; to lead

yǐnfā 引发 (chemistry) initiation

yǐnjìn 引进 ① to introduce from elsewhere ② to recommend

yǐnqǐ 引起 to cause; to give rise to

yǐnqíng 引擎 an engine

yǐnrén-rùshèng 引人入胜 ① to lead into wonderland ② (said of books) absorbing

yǐnrén-zhùmù 引人注目 noticeable; conspicuous

yǐnrù 引入 to lead into; to draw into

yǐnyán 引言 a preface; a foreword

yǐnyòng 引用 to quote

yǐnyòu 引诱 to induce; to lure; to entice; to tempt

yǐn 饮 ① to drink ② drinks ⇨yìn

yǐnchá 饮茶 ① (in Guangdong) to drink tea along with refreshments ② to drink tea

yǐnliào 饮料 beverages; drinks

yǐnshí 饮食 ① drink and food ② to drink and eat

yǐnshuǐ 饮水 ① drinking water ② to drink water

yǐnyòng 饮用 to drink

yǐn 隐 ① dark; obscure; not evident or obvious ② hidden; concealed; secret; mysterious ③ to retire; to reject public life; to live like a hermit ④ painful; grievous ⑤ a riddle ⑥ destitute; poor ⑦ to examine and study

yǐnbì 隐蔽 to conceal; to take cover; to cover up

yǐncáng 隐藏 to hide; to conceal

yǐnmán 隐瞒 to hide the truth; to cover up

yǐnshì 隐士 a retired scholar; a recluse

yǐnxíng yǎnjìng 隐形眼镜 contact lenses

yǐnyǐn 隐隐 indistinct; unclear; faint

yǐnyōu 隐忧 hidden or latent worries

yǐnyuē 隐约 indistinct; obscure; ambiguous; abstruse

yìn 印 ① to print; to stamp; to imprint ② a seal; a stamp; a chop ③ an imprint

yìnbiǎojī 印表机 a printer

Yìndù 印度 India

yìnhuā 印花 a revenue stamp

Yìnní 印尼 Indonesia

yìnrǎn 印染 printing and dyeing (of textiles)

yìnshuā 印刷 to print

yìnxiàng 印象 an impression; a mental image

yìnxiàngpài 印象派 the impressionist school (of the fine arts)

yìnzhāng 印章 a general name for stamps, seals, and chops

yìnzhèng 印证 to confirm; to corroborate

yìn 饮 to make animals drink ⇨yǐn

yīng 应 should; ought to; need

yīng/yìng 应 to assent to ⇨yìng

yīngdāng 应当 duty-bound; should; ought to

yīnggāi 应该 should; ought to; need

yīng 英 ① English; British ② a hero; an outstanding person ③ surpassing; outstanding; prominent; distinguished ④ fine; handsome ⑤ a surname

yīngbàng 英镑 the pound sterling

yīngcái 英才 a person of outstanding ability or talent

yīngcùn 英寸 (linear measure) inch

Yīnggélán 英格兰 England

Yīngguó 英国 Great Britain; Britain; the United Kingdom;

England

Yīngguórén 英国人 an Englishman; a Briton; the English; the British

yīngjùn 英俊 (said of a man) handsome

yīnglǐ 英里 (linear measure) mile

yīngmíng 英明 (said of leaders) intelligent; sagacious; perspicacious

Yīngwén 英文 the (written) English language; English

yīngxióng 英雄 a hero; a great man

yīngyǒng 英勇 brave; courageous

Yīngyǔ 英语 the (spoken) English language; English

yīng'ér 婴儿 a baby; an infant

yīnghuā 樱花 the oriental cherry

yīngtáo 樱桃 cherries

yīng 鹰 a hawk; an eagle; a falcon

yíng 迎 to receive; to greet; to meet; to welcome

yínghé 迎合 to cater to

yíngjiē 迎接 to receive; to greet; to welcome

yíngmiàn 迎面 right against one's face in the opposite direction

yíngkuī 盈亏 ① (said of the moon) waxing and waning ② profits and losses

yínglì 盈利 profit; gains; surpluses

yíngyú 盈余 profit; gains; surpluses

yíngguāngmù 萤光幕 a screen

yínghuǒchóng 萤火虫 a firefly; a glowworm

yíngmù 萤幕 a screen

yíng 营 ① military barracks; a camp; a battalion ② to manage; to administer; to handle; to operate; to run

yíngdì 营地 campsite; camping ground

yíngjiàn 营建 to manage or handle the construction of; to construct

yínglì 营利 to engage in making profit

yíngyǎng 营养 nutrition; nourishment

yíngyè 营业 to engage in business; business operation

yíngyè'é 营业额 the volume of business

yíngzào 营造 to construct; to build

yíngzi 蝇子 house fly (insect)

yíng 赢 ① to win ② to have a surplus ③ a surname

yíng 赢 ① to win; to beat ② gains; profits

yíngdé 赢得 to win (honor, a privilege, etc.)

yíngjiā 赢家 the winner

yǐng 影 ① a shadow; an image; a trace; a vague impression ③ to copy and imitate ④ to hide

yǐngběn 影本 a facsimile edition; a rubbing

yǐngjí 影集 ① a miniseries ② photograph (or picture, photo) album

yǐngmí 影迷 a movie fan

yǐngpiàn 影片 a motion picture; movies

yǐngshè 影射 ① to counterfeit (trademarks, etc.); to delude; to humbug ② to hint by suggestive remarks

yǐngtán 影坛 the movie circles; moviedom

yǐngxiǎng 影响 to affect; to influence

yǐngxiàng 影像 an image; a portrait

yǐngyìn 影印 ① photogravure ② xerography

yǐngyìnběn 影印本 a photolithographic edition; a photostatic copy

yǐngzhǎn 影展 a photographic exhibition; a film festival

yǐngzi 影子 ① a shadow ② (figuratively) a trace

Y

yìng 应 ① to respond to; to answer; to echo; to react to ② to comply with; to grant ③ to deal with; to cope with
⇨yīng

yìngbiàn 应变 ① to prepare oneself for change ② to adapt oneself to changes

yìngchou 应酬 ① social appointments ② to treat with courtesy

yìngduì 应对 ① to answer questions ② repartee

yìngfù 应付 ① to deal with; to cope with; to handle

yìngjí 应急 to meet an emergency

yìngyàn 应验 to come true; to be fulfilled

yìngyāo 应邀 at somebody's invitation

yìngyòng 应用 ① to utilize; to make use of ② for practical application

yìngzhēng 应征 ① to respond to a want ad ② to be recruited

yìng 映 ① to mirror; to reflect; a reflection ② to project (slides, pictures, etc.) ③ to shine; shining; to blind; blinding (glare, light, etc.)

yìng 硬 ① hard; stiff; solid; firm ② rigid; inflexible; obstinate; very insistent; unyielding ③ by force; to manage to do something in a forced manner ④ to solidify; to harden; to stiffen ⑤ (said of quality) good ⑥ able (person)

yìngdié 硬碟 (computer) a hard disk

yìngdù 硬度 hardness

yìngjiàn 硬件 (computer) hardware

yìngpán 硬盘 (computer) a hard disk

yìngtǐ 硬体 (computer) hardware

yō 唷 an exclamation expressing surprise or pain

yōng/yǒng 拥 ① to hug; to embrace; to hold ② to crowd; to throng; to swarm ③ to follow; to support

yōngbào/yǒngbào 拥抱 to embrace; to hug; to hold in one's arms

yōnghù/yǒnghù 拥护 to advocate; to support; to back

yōngjǐ/yǒngjǐ 拥挤 crowded; packed

yōngyǒu/yǒngyǒu 拥有 to have; to possess; to own

yōngsú 庸俗 vulgar; unrefined

yǒng 永 long in time; everlasting; eternal; permanent

yǒngchuí-bùxiǔ 永垂不朽 immortal (accomplishment, fame, etc.)

yǒnghéng 永恒 eternity; eternal; everlasting; perpetual

yǒngjiǔ 永久 permanent; perpetual; eternal; lasting

yǒngyuǎn 永远 forever; eternally; perpetually

yǒng 勇 ① brave; courageous; bold; valiant; intrepid; fearless ② bravery; courage ③ a soldier; a conscript

yǒnggǎn 勇敢 brave; courageous

yǒngqì 勇气 courage; bravery; valor

yǒngshì 勇士 a brave fighter; a warrior

yǒngyú 勇于 to be brave in; to have the courage to

yǒng 涌 ① to gush; to pour ② to rise

yǒngxiàn 涌现 to crop up (in one's mind)

yǒngyuè 踊跃 ① to leap ② enthusiastically

yòng 用 ① to use; to employ ② to exert ③ use ④ to need; need ⑤ finance ⑥ effect ⑦ to eat; to drink

yòngbuzháo 用不着 there is no need to

yòngchu 用处 a purpose

yòngdezháo 用得着 ① to need ② it is necessary to

yòngdì 用地 land for a specific use

yòngfǎ 用法 directions for using

yònggōng 用功 to study diligently; to study hard

yònghù 用户 a customer (of a utility); a user; a consumer

yòngjù 用具 a tool; an appliance; an implement

yònglì 用力 to exert oneself; to make an effort; to put forth one's strength

yòngpǐn 用品 articles for use

yòngrén 用人 to employ people

yòngren 用人 a servant

yòngshuǐ 用水 ① to use water ② water for a specific use

yòngtú 用途 a purpose

yòngwán 用完 to use up; to exhaust

yòngxīn 用心 ① to take care; to pay attention ② motive; intention

yòngyǐ 用以 in order to; so as to

yòngyì 用意 an intention; a purpose; an idea

yòngyǔ 用语 terminology; phraseology

yòngjīn 佣金 a bribe; a commission

yōu 优 ① good; excellent ② victory; winning ③ players (as in an opera) ④ soft

yōudài 优待 favorable treatment

yōudiǎn 优点 merits; good qualities; advantages

yōuhuì 优惠 preferential; favorable

yōuliáng 优良 fine; good

yōuliè 优劣 ① good and bad ② bright and dull ③ fit and unfit

yōuluòrǔ 优酪乳 yogurt; sour milk

yōuměi 优美 ① wonderful; graceful; fine ② anything that inspires a sense of joy

yōushèng 优胜 winning; superior

yōushì 优势 supremacy; superiority

yōuxiān 优先 priority; to take precedence

yōuxiù 优秀 outstanding; remarkable

yōuyǎ 优雅 graceful; elegant

yōuyì 优异 excellent; remarkable; brilliant

yōuyuè 优越 superior; outstanding

yōuzhì/yōuzhí 优质 high (or top) quality

yōuguān 攸关 to concern (reputation, life, etc.); a matter of (reputation, life and death, etc.)

yōu 忧 ① pensive; mournful; grieved; sad ② anxiety; to worry about; concerned about; anxious; apprehensive

yōulù 忧虑 worried; anxious

yōushāng 忧伤 worried and grieved

yōuxīn 忧心 a sad heart

yōuyù 忧郁 melancholy; depressed; dejected

yōufú 幽浮 UFO (unidentified flying object)

yōujìng 幽静 tranquil; placid; serene

yōumò 幽默 humorous; humor

yōujiǔ 悠久 long in time

yōuxián 悠闲 leisurely; unrestrained; unhurried

yóu 尤 ① especially or particularly ② a mistake; an error ③ to feel bitter against; to reproach; to blame ④ special or outstanding ⑤ a surname

yóuqí 尤其 above all; in particular; particularly; especially

yóu 由 ① by; through ② from ③ up to (someone to make a decision) ④ reason; cause; a source; derivation

yóucǐ 由此 hence; from this; therefore

yóucǐ-kějiàn 由此可见 thus it can be seen; this shows; that proves

yóulái 由来 ① derivation; a source ② so far; up to now

yóuyú 由于 because of; owing to; due to; as a result of

yóu 邮 ① a post office ② postal ③ to deliver mails, letters, etc. ④ a wayside station where couriers on government service change horses ⑤ a hut; a lodge in the field

yóubāo 邮包 a postal parcel

yóuchāi 邮差 a mailman; a postman

yóudiàn 邮电 postal and cable service

yóugòu 邮购 ① mail order ② to buy by mail order

yóujì 邮寄 to send by mail; to mail

yóujiàn 邮件 mail matter; postal items; the post; mail

yóujú 邮局 a post office

yóupiào 邮票 a postal stamp

yóuzhèng 邮政 postal administration; postal service; postal affairs

yóuzī 邮资 postal charges

yóu 犹 ① a kind of monkey ② a surname ③ strategy; scheme; plot

yóurú 犹如 just like

yóuyù 犹豫 undecided; to hesitate

yóu 油 ① a general name for oil, fat, grease, either animal or vegetable ② anything in liquid form which is inflammable, as gasoline, etc. ③ to oil ④ to varnish; to paint ⑤ greasy ⑥ sly; polished and over-experienced ⑦ luxuriant; prospering; flourishing

yóucài 油菜 rape

yóuhuà 油画 an oil painting

yóuliào 油料 petroleum, oil, and lubricant (POL)

yóumén 油门 ① a throttle ② an accelerator

yóunì 油腻 (said of food) greasy; oily

yóuqī 油漆 ① paint; varnish ② to paint

yóutián 油田 an oil field

yóutiáo 油条 ① fritters of twisted dough—a Chinese specialty usually for breakfast ② a suave, well-oiled person, long on experience but short on sincerity

yóuyān 油烟 soot; lampblack

yóuzhī 油脂 ① (chemistry) olein ② oil and grease; fats

yóu/yòu 铀 uranium

yóu 游 ① to swim; to float; to waft; to drift ② to wander about ③ part of a river ④ to travel; to go to a distance ⑤ freely wield (a sword), move (one's eyes), stretch (one's sight), etc.⑥ a surname

yóujī/yóují 游击 a hit-and-run attack

yóujīduì/yóujíduì 游击队 a guerrilla band; guerrillas

yóukè 游客 a traveler; a tourist

yóulǎn 游览 to visit; to tour; sightseeing

yóulǎnchē 游览车 a bus or train for tourists or sightseers

yóulè 游乐 to make merry; entertainment

yóulèchǎng 游乐场 an amusement park

yóumù 游牧 nomadic

yóuqì 游憩 to play and rest

yóurén 游人 a sightseer; a tourist; a visitor

yóuwán 游玩 to play; to recreate

yóuxì 游戏 to play; play

yóuxíng 游行 ① to parade; a parade ② to demonstrate (in protest)

yóuxué 游学 to study abroad; to pursue advanced study far away from home

yóuyǒng 游泳 swimming

yóuyǒngchí 游泳池 a swimming pool

yǒu 友 ① a friend; friendly; friendship ② fraternity; fraternal love ③ to befriend

yǒu'ài 友爱 friendship; fraternal love

yǒubāng 友邦 friendly nations; allies

yǒuhǎo 友好 friendly; amity

Y

(treaty, etc.)

yǒuqíng 友情 friendship

yǒurén 友人 friends

yǒushàn 友善 friendly

yǒuyì 友谊 friendship

yǒu 有 to have; to be present; to exist; there is

yǒudài 有待 ① to wait until ② to require or need (improvement, investigation, etc.)

yǒude 有的 ① some ② Yes, there is....; Yes, I have....

yǒudeshì 有的是 to be found everywhere; to have plenty of

yǒudiǎnr 有点儿 some; a little; somewhat

yǒuguān 有关 to concern

yǒuhài 有害 detrimental; harmful

yǒujī 有机 organic

yǒujià zhèngquàn 有价证券 securities; negotiable or marketable securities

yǒujiànyúcǐ 有鉴于此 in view of this

yǒujiào-wúlèi 有教无类 to provide education for all people without discrimination

yǒukòng 有空 to have time (for doing something)

yǒukǒu-wúxīn 有口无心 to say what one does not mean; to be sharp-tongued but not malicious

yǒulǐ 有理 reasonable justified

yǒulì 有力 strong

yǒulì 有利 profitable; advantageous; favorable; beneficial; helpful; conducive

yǒuliǎngxiàzi 有两下子 to have a real skill; to know one's stuff

yǒumíng 有名 famous; renowned; noted; well-known; illustrious; distinguished

yǒuqī túxíng / yǒuqī túxíng 有期徒刑 (law) imprisonment for a definite term (as opposed to life imprisonment)

yǒuqián 有钱 rich; wealthy; well-to-do

yǒuqíng 有情 ① affected by love; to have a tender feeling for one of the opposite sex ② (Buddhism) any creature

yǒuqù 有趣 interesting; amusing; fascinating

yǒurú 有如 just like; as if; as though

yǒushēng-yǒusè 有声有色 (said of a description or performance) vivid; impressive

yǒushí 有时 sometimes; now and then; occasionally

yǒushíhou 有时候 sometimes; now and then

yǒushì 有事 ① to be busy ② to meet with an accident

yǒusuǒ 有所 to some extent; somewhat

yǒuwéi 有为 capable of great achievements

yǒuxiàn 有限 limited; restricted; finite

yǒuxiàn 有线 wired; equipped with wires

yǒuxiàn diànshì 有线电视 cable TV

yǒuxiàn gōngsī 有限公司 a limited company; a limited liability company

yǒuxiào 有效 effective; effectual; valid

yǒuxiē 有些 ① some; a few ② somewhat

yǒuxīn 有心 to have a mind to

yǒuxīnrén 有心人 a person who has a mind to do something useful

yǒuxíng 有形 visible; tangible; concrete

yǒuyì 有益 advantageous; useful; profitable; beneficial

yǒuyì 有意 ① to intend; purposeful ② to be interested

yǒuyìdiǎn 有一点 a bit; a little

yǒuyìsi 有意思 interesting; exciting; enjoyable; amusing

yǒuyòng 有用 useful; practical; beneficial

yǒuyuán 有缘 linked by ties of fate

Y

yǒuzhùyú 有助于 to be conducive to

yòu 又 ① also; again; in addition to; and ② moreover; furthermore ③ and (used in a mixed fraction such as one and three fourths)

yòushì 又是 ① again ② also ③ still another ④ the same as

yòu 右 ① right (as opposed to left) ② west ③ to assist; to aid

yòubian 右边 the right-hand side

yòupài 右派 ① the right wing ② the rightists; the conservatives

yòuqīng 右倾 right-leaning; conservative

yòushǒu 右手 ① the right hand ② the right-hand side

yòu 幼 ① young; delicate ② to take care of the young

yòuchóng 幼虫 a larva

yòu'ér 幼儿 an infant; a baby

yòu'éryuán 幼儿园 kindergarten

yòunián 幼年 childhood

yòutóng 幼童 a young child

yòuzhì 幼稚 immature; naive

yòuzhìyuán 幼稚园 a kindergarten

yòu 诱 ① to guide; to lead ② to decoy; to tempt; to allure; to lure; to captivate

yòuhuò 诱惑 ① to entice; to lure; to allure; to tempt; to beguile ② to attract; attractive

yòuyīn 诱因 an inducement

yú 于 ① (a particle in literary use) in; at; by; to ② (a verb in literary use) to go or proceed; to take ③ in; on; at; by; from ④ than; then; to; with reference to ⑤ compared with ⑥ a surname

yúshì 于是 then; so; thus; thereafter

yú 余 ① remaining; the remnant or remainder; the rest ② a surplus; an overplus; an excess ③ a balance ④ a complement of a number or figure; odd ⑤ after ⑥ a surname

yúdì 余地 a spare space; an

alternative; elbowroom; leeway

yú'é 余额 ① a surplus amount; a balance ② vacancies to be filled

yú 鱼 fish

yúchí 鱼池 a fishpond

yúlèi 鱼类 fishes; Pisces

yúmiáo 鱼苗 fry (of fish)

yúwǎng 鱼网 a fishnet; a fishing net

yúwēn 鱼塭 a fish farm

yúlè 娱乐 amusement; entertainment; to amuse; to entertain

yú 渔 ① to fish ② to seize; to acquire forcibly

yúchǎng 渔场 fishing grounds

yúchuán 渔船 a fishing boat

yúfū 渔夫 a fisherman

yúgǎng 渔港 a fishing harbor

yúmín 渔民 fishermen

yúrén 渔人 a fisherman

yúwǎng 渔网 a fishing net

yúyè 渔业 fishery

yú 逾 ① to exceed; to pass over; more than ② to transgress ③ added

yúkuài 愉快 cheerful; happy; pleased; delighted

yúyuè 愉悦 joyful; glad; happy

yúshù 榆树 an elm; an elm tree

yú 虞 ① anxieties; worries ② to expect; to anticipate ③ to deceive; to cheat ④ name of a legendary dynasty ⑤ name of a state in the Epoch of Spring and Autumn ⑥ a Chinese family surname

yúchǔn 愚蠢 stupid; dull

yúmèi 愚昧 benighted; stupid; ignorant

yúlùn 舆论 public opinion

yǔ 与 ① and; with; together with ② to give; to impart
⇨yù

yǔcǐtóngshí 与此同时 at the same time

yǔqí...bùrú 与……不如 It's better to...than (rather than)...; ...rather than...

yǔzhòngbùtóng 与众不同 extraordinary; uncommon

Y

yǔ 予 to give

yǔyǐ 予以 to give; to offer

yǔzhòu 宇宙 the universe

yǔmáo 羽毛 a feather; a plume; down

yǔmáoqiú 羽毛球 badminton

yǔ 雨 rain; rainy

Yǔguǒ 雨果 Victor Marie Hugo (1802-1885), French poet, novelist and dramatist

yǔjì 雨季 the rainy season; the monsoon

yǔsǎn 雨伞 an umbrella

yǔshuǐ 雨水 ① rain water ② one of 24 climatic periods in the solar calendar, which falls on February 19 or 20

yǔtiān 雨天 a rainy day

yǔxié 雨鞋 rainshoes; galoshes

yǔyī 雨衣 a raincoat

yǔ 语 ① language; speech ② a word; a sentence ③ a saying; a proverb ④ a sign; a signal ⑤ to speak; to say; to talk

yǔdiào 语调 the tone of one's speech; intonation

yǔfǎ 语法 wording; grammar; syntax

yǔhuì 语汇 vocabulary

yǔqì 语气 ① the tone (of one's speech); the manner of speaking ② (grammar) mood

yǔwén 语文 language and literature

yǔyán 语言 a language; speech

yǔyánxué 语言学 linguistics; philology

yǔyì 语意 the meaning (of a word, etc.)

yǔyīn 语音 ① pronunciation ② a phone

yù 与 to take part in; to participate in
⇨ yǔ

yùhuì 与会 to participate in a conference

yù 玉 ① a precious stone—especially jade; a gem ② a polite expression for "your" ③ (said of a person, especially a woman)

pure; fair; beautiful ④ a designation of things belonging to a girl or young woman ⑤ a surname

yùmǐ 玉米 maize; Indian corn

yùqì 玉器 a jade article

Yùshān 玉山 ① Mt. Yü, the highest mountain peak in Taiwan ② elegant and majestic ③ name of a county in Jiangxi

yùtou 芋头 (botany) a taro

yù 育 ① to produce; to give birth to; to breed ② to raise; to bring up; to nourish; to nurse ③ to educate

yù 狱 ① jail; prison ② a lawsuit

yùgāng 浴缸 a bathtub

yùshì 浴室 a bathroom

yù 预 ① to prepare; to make ready; reserve (funds, troops, etc.) ② beforehand; previously; in advance ③ to take part in

yùbào 预报 a forecast; an advance notice

yùbèi 预备 to prepare; to get ready beforehand; preparatory

yùcè 预测 to predict; to make a forecast

yùdìng 预订 to reserve (seats, rooms, etc.)

yùdìng 预定 to set (a date, etc.); to be scheduled

yùfáng 预防 to prevent beforehand; to nip in the bud; to prepare against

yùgào 预告 to inform or notify beforehand; advance notice; to herald

yùgū 预估 to predict; to estimate

yùjì 预计 to estimate; to surmise; estimates; to calculate in advance

yùjiàn 预见 to anticipate; to envision; to foresee; foresight; prevision

yùliào 预料 to predict; to surmise; to anticipate; to expect

yùqì/yùqí 预期 to expect; to estimate; to anticipate

yùsài 预赛 a preliminary competition

yùshěn 预审 a preliminary trial;

Y

an inquest

yùsuàn 预算 an estimate; a budget; to calculate in advance

yùxí 预习 ① (said of students) to prepare lessons before class ② to rehearse or drill; a rehearsal or drill

yùxiān 预先 beforehand; in advance

yùyán 预言 ① prophecy; a prediction; a forecast ② to predict; to foretell

yùyuē 预约 a preliminary agreement; to make an appointment

yùzhù 预祝 to congratulate (victory or success) beforehand

yù 域 ① a frontier; a boundary ② a region; a country; an area ③ to live; to stay

yù 欲 ① to desire; to intend; to long for; to want ② wish; desire; expectation; longing; appetite; passion; lust; greed ③ about to; on the point of

yùwàng 欲望 desires; to long for; longings; an aspiration

yù 喻 ① to use a figure of speech; an illustration; a parable ② to know; to be acquainted with ③ to explain; to make clear; to tell the meaning of; to instruct ④ a surname

yù 寓 ① to live temporarily; to sojourn; to dwell ② to consign

yùyán 寓言 a fable; an allegory

yù 遇 ① to meet; to run into; to come across; to encounter ② to treat; treatment ③ opportunity; luck ④ meeting of minds; to win confidence (of a superior, king, etc.) ⑤ to rival; to match with

yùdào 遇到 to run into; to meet with; to encounter

yùhài 遇害 to be murdered or assassinated

yùjiàn 遇见 to meet with; to run into; to come across; to bump into

yù 愈 ① to recover (from illness); to heal; healed; cured ② to a greater degree; even more

yù...yù... 愈……愈…… the

more... the more...

yuān 冤 ① oppression; injustice; a grievance; a wrong ② feud; animosity; enmity ③ to cheat; to lie ④ to spend money recklessly ⑤ to make false accusations

yuānwang 冤枉 to wrong; to accuse a person with a false charge

yuānyuán 渊源 ① the source ② relationship

yuán 元 ① a dollar ② the head ③ the beginning; the first; original ④ the eldest; chief; big ⑤ the Yuan Dynasty

Yuándàn 元旦 New Year's Day

yuánjiàn 元件 (computer) an element

yuánlǎo 元老 an elder person who has held high positions for long period of time and is highly respected by the nation

yuánqì 元气 vitality and constitution

yuánshǒu 元首 ① the chief of state; the king; the president, etc. ② the beginning

yuánshuài 元帅 the commander in chief

yuánsù 元素 (chemistry) the elements

yuánxiāo 元宵 ① the Lantern Festival ② small rice-flour dumplings eaten on the Lantern Festival

Yuánxiāojié 元宵节 the Lantern Festival

yuányuè 元月 ① the first month of the lunar calendar ② January

yuán 园 ① a piece of ground used for growing flowers, fruit, or vegetables; a garden; a plantation ② a public garden, park, or recreation ground

yuándì 园地 ① a garden ② (in a periodical) a space reserved for publishing articles or letters from readers

yuánlín 园林 a park; a garden

yuányì 园艺 gardening; horticulture

yuányóuhuì 园游会 a garden

Y

party

yuán 员 ① a member (of an organization, etc.) ② a person engaged in some field of activity ③ outer limits (of land, space, etc.)

yuán'é 员额 the authorized size of a staff; the number of employees

yuángōng 员工 employees (collectively)

yuán 原 ① original; primary ② the source; the origin; the beginning ③ a steppe; a vast plain; a field ④ to excuse; to pardon

yuánbǎn 原版 the original print or edition

yuánběn 原本 ① the cause of an incident; the ins and outs of an incident ② the origin of something ③ the author's manuscript; the original draft

yuándiǎn 原点 (mathematics) origin; the point of origin

yuángào 原告 the plaintiff; the prosecutor

yuánjià 原价 ① the original price ② the production cost (of an article, etc.) ③ the price of an article paid by the retailer to the manufacturer or wholesaler

yuánlái 原来 originally or formerly

yuánlǐ 原理 a principle

yuánliàng 原谅 forgiveness; to forgive; to pardon

yuánliào 原料 raw materials

yuánmù 原木 a log

yuánshǐ 原始 ① primitive; backward ② a source

yuánwén 原文 the original text

yuánxiān 原先 in the beginning; originally

yuánxíng 原形 ① the original form or shape ② one's true colors; the real face or form

yuányě 原野 the field; a plain

yuányì 原意 ① original intentions ② original meaning

yuányīn 原因 a reason; a cause

yuányóu 原油 crude oil; crude

petroleum

yuányǒu 原有 to possess originally; (what) one had before; (what) was here or there originally

yuánzé 原则 a principle

yuánzéshàng 原则上 in principle

yuánzhùmín 原住民 an aborigine

yuánzhuàng 原状 ① the original condition ② the status quo

yuánzǐ 原子 an atom

yuánzǐbǐ 原子笔 a ball-point pen

yuánzǐdàn 原子弹 an atomic bomb

yuánzǐnéng 原子能 atomic energy

yuán 圆 ① round; circular; spherical ② a circle ③ satisfactory; tactful ④ a monetary unit ⑤ complete; to complete; to make plausible; to justify

yuánhuán 圆环 a rotary; a traffic circle

yuánmǎn 圆满 ① satisfactory ② rounded out ③ complete

yuánrùn 圆润 mellow and full

yuánxíng 圆形 round; spherical; circular

yuánzhūbǐ 圆珠笔 a ballpoint pen

yuán 援 ① to aid; to help; to reinforce; to rescue ② to take hold of; to pull by hand ③ to lead ④ to invoke (a law, precedent, etc.)

yuánshǒu 援手 ① to extend a helping hand ② a helper

yuánzhù 援助 to aid; aid; to help

yuán 缘 ① a cause; a reason ② a hem; a margin; an edge; a fringe ③ relationship by fate; predestined relationship

yuángù 缘故 a cause; a reason

yuánrén 猿人 the ape; anthropoid apes; a gorilla

yuán 源 a source; a head (of a stream)

yuánquán 源泉 an original

source; a fountainhead

yuántóu 源头 a head or a source (of a stream)

yuǎn 远 ① far; distant; remote ② deep; profound

yuǎn/yuàn 远 to keep at a distance; to keep away from; to avoid; to shun

yuǎnchù 远处 distant; located far away; distant places

yuǎndà 远大 very promising (person, etc.); (to look) far ahead

Yuǎndōng 远东 the Far East

yuǎnfāng 远方 a distant place; a remote place

yuǎnjiàn 远见 foresight; a far-sighted view; prescience

yuǎnjǐng 远景 ① a vista; a distant view; a long-range perspective ② (movies) a long shot

yuǎnlí 远离 ① to depart for a distant place ② to keep away at a great distance

yuǎnyáng yúyè 远洋渔业 deep-sea fishery; pelagic fishery

yuǎnzú 远足 an excursion; an outing

yuàn 怨 ① ill will; hatred; enmity; animus; resentment ② to resent; to complain; to blame (others); to impute

yuànyán 怨言 complaints; grumbles

yuàn 院 ① a courtyard; a yard ② a designation for certain government offices and public places ③ short for the Executive Yuan, Legislative Yuan, Examination Yuan, Judicial Yuan, or Control Yuan

yuànshì 院士 a member of Academia Sinica, or an academician

yuànzhǎng 院长 the dean of a college or court of law; the director of a hospital, museum, etc.

yuànzi 院子 a yard; a courtyard

yuàn 愿 ① to be willing; to be desirous of; to hope; to wish ② anything one wishes or desires;

an ambition or aspiration ③ a vow ④ to think

yuànwàng 愿望 one's wish or aspiration; what one's heart desires

yuànyì 愿意 ① to be willing ② to like; to want ③ to approve of

yuē 约 ① a date; an appointment or engagement; a rendezvous; to make an appointment; to date ② about; around; approximately; estimated ③ an agreement; a covenant; a contract; a treaty ④ brief(ly); simply ⑤ poor; poverty; hardship; straitened ⑥ (mathematics) to reduce ⑦ to bind; to restrain ⑧ vague(ly)

Yuēdàn 约旦 Jordan

yuēdìng 约定 to agree upon; to agree to

yuēhǎo 约好 to have appointed; to have arranged

yuēhuì 约会 an appointment or engagement; a date

yuēshù 约束 to bind or restrain; restraint; restriction

yuè 月 ① the moon ② the month

yuèbing 月饼 a moon cake

yuèdǐ 月底 the end of a month

yuèfèn 月份 the month; monthly

yuèguāng 月光 moonlight

yuèjīng 月经 menses; periods; monthlies

yuèkān 月刊 a monthly (publication)

yuèliang 月亮 the moon

yuèqiú 月球 the moon

yuètái 月台 a platform (at a railway station)

yuèxīn 月薪 a monthly salary

yuè 乐 ① music ② a surname ⇨lè

yuèduì 乐队 a band; an orchestra

yuèqì 乐器 a musical instrument

yuèqǔ 乐曲 a piece of music; a musical composition

yuètuán 乐团 ① a philharmonic society ② a philharmonic orchestra

yuè 阅 ① to review; to inspect; to examine; to observe ② to read; to go over (examination papers) ③ to experience

yuèdú 阅读 to read

yuèjuàn 阅卷 to grade examination papers

yuèlǎnshì 阅览室 a reading room

yuè'ěr 悦耳 pleasant to the ear; musical

yuè 跃 to jump; to leap; to bound; to spring

yuè 越 ① to skip; to climb over; to cross over; to go across ② to go beyond; to transgress ③ even more; the more ④ name of an ancient state ⑤ a surname

yuèdōng 越冬 to pass, spend, or survive the winter; to live through the winter

yuèguò 越过 ① to go across; to cross ② to exceed; to overstep

yuèláiyuè... 越来越…… more and more; increasingly more

Yuènán 越南 Vietnam

yuè...yuè... 越……越…… the more...the more...

Yuè 粤 ① Guangdong Province ② Guangdong and Guangxi Provinces

yūn 晕 ① to faint; to swoon ② giddy and dizzy ③ (usually used sarcastically) to do things without a purpose
⇨yùn

yún 云 ① clouds ② a cloud of; a large number of ③ short for Yunnan Province

yúncai 云彩 clouds illuminated by the rising or setting sun

Yúnnán 云南 Yunnan Province

yún 匀 uniform; even

yǔnxǔ 允许 to assent; to consent; to grant; to permit

yǔnshí 陨石 a meteorite

yùnfù 孕妇 a pregnant woman

yùnyù 孕育 to nourish; to foster

yùn 运 ① to transport; to ship

② to move; to revolve ③ to utilize; to make use of ④ one's luck or fortune

yùndòng 运动 ① sports; physical exercises ② motion; movement ③ a social movement; a campaign; a drive ④ to lobby

yùndòngchǎng 运动场 a playground; a stadium; a gymnasium; a sports arena

yùndònghuì 运动会 an athletic meet; a sports meeting; games

yùndòngyuán 运动员 an athlete; a sportsman

yùnhé 运河 ① a canal ② the Grand Canal in China

yùnqì 运气 (Chinese pugilism) dynamic tension of muscles

yùnqi 运气 luck or fortune

yùnqiú 运球 to dribble balls; dribbling

yùnshū 运输 transportation; to transport

yùnshūjī 运输机 a military transport; a cargo plane

yùnsòng 运送 to convey; to transport; to deliver; to ship

yùnsuàn 运算 (mathematics) an operation

yùnxíng 运行 to move in an orbit, as a planet or satellite

yùnyòng 运用 to employ; to make use of; to exercise

yùnzhuǎn 运转 ① to revolve; revolution ② to work; to operate; to run

yùn 晕 (meteorology) a halo; vapors; a mist

yùn/yūn 晕 dazzled; to feel faint or dizzy
⇨yūn

yùnniàng 酝酿 ① to brew (wine or liquor) ② (said of a storm, disturbance, etc.) to begin to form; to brew

yùnlǜ 韵律 rhythm; rhyme scheme; meter

yùncáng 蕴藏 to have in store; to be rich in

Y

Z

zā/zhá 扎 to bind; to tie; to fasten
⇨zhā, zhá

zá 杂 ① miscellaneous ② to mix; to blend; mixed; blended ③ motley; medley ④ petty and numerous

zácǎo 杂草 weeds

záhuòdiàn 杂货店 a sundry store; a grocery

zájì 杂技 a variety of juggling skills; a vaudeville; an acrobatic feat

zájiāo 杂交 ① (biology) to hybridize; to cross ② hybridization; crossbreed; a cross; interbreeding ③ promiscuity

záluàn 杂乱 confused and disorderly; to be jumbled

záwén 杂文 an essay

záyīn 杂音 noises; (recording) humming or other unwanted sounds

zázhì 杂志 a magazine; a periodical; a journal

zázhì/zázhí 杂质 impurities

zá 砸 ① to crash and break; to squash; to smash; to knock; to pound ② to mash; to beat to a pulp

zāi 灾 a disaster; a calamity; a catastrophe

zāihài 灾害 disasters; calamities

zāihuāng 灾荒 famine caused by floods or droughts

zāihuò 灾祸 disasters or calamities; catastrophes

zāinàn 灾难 disasters; calamities

zāiqíng 灾情 the extent of a disaster or calamity

zāiqū 灾区 the afflicted area; the disaster area

zāi 栽 ① to plant ② to care; to assist ③ to fall; to fail ④ young trees, saplings, or cuttings for planting

zāipéi 栽培 ① to plant and culti-

vate ② to educate people ③ to give special favor

zǎi 载 a year

zǎi/zài 载 to record; to publish
⇨zài

zǎi 宰 ① to slaughter ② to preside; to govern ③ a surname

zài 再 ① again; repeated ② still; further; then

zàicì 再次 once more; once again

zàidù 再度 once more; once again

zàijiàn 再见 good-bye; see you again

zàilái 再来 ① to come again ② to encore ③ to request for or order a repetition

zàisān 再三 time and again; repeatedly

zàishēng 再生 ① to be a second so-and-so (a well-known figure already dead) ② regeneration; to regenerate

zàishēngchǎn 再生产 reproduction

zàishuō 再说 furthermore; besides

zàizhě 再者 furthermore; in addition; by way of a postscript (P.S.)

zài 在 ① at; in; on; up to ② used to indicate a progressive tense ③ to be alive; living; to be present; to exist ④ to rest with; to consist in; to depend on

zàichǎng 在场 to be present

zàihu 在乎 ① to care; to mind ② to consist in; to depend on (whether...)

zàishì 在世 alive; in this world

zàiwài 在外 ① excluding ② outside

zàiyědǎng 在野党 the opposition party or parties

zàiyì 在意 to mind; to care about

zàiyú 在于 to lie in; to consist in; to be determined by; to depend on

zàizài 在在 everywhere

zàizhí 在职 to be at one's post

zàizuò 在座 to be present (at a gathering)

zài 载 ① (said of vehicles, vessels, etc.) to carry (loads); to load ② to fill
⇨zǎi

zàizhòng 载重 ① to carry heavy loads; heavily loaded ② carrying capacity

zán 咱 I, me (in North China dialect)

zánmen 咱们 (inclusive) we; you and I

zǎn 攒 to hoard; to save; to accumulate
⇨cuán

zàn/zhàn 暂 ① temporarily; for a short time; not lasting ② suddenly; abruptly

zànqiě/zhànqiě 暂且 for the time being

zànshí/zhànshí 暂时 for the time being; temporarily

zàntíng/zhàntíng 暂停 ① to stop, halt, or suspend temporarily ② a time-out

zànxíng/zhànxíng 暂行 temporary; provisional

zàn 赞 to commend; to eulogize; to praise; to applaud; to laud

zànchéng 赞成 to agree to; to be in favor of

zànměi 赞美 to praise; to eulogize; eulogy; laud; praise

zànshǎng 赞赏 to praise; to appreciate

zàntàn 赞叹 to sing the praises of

zàntóng 赞同 to consent to; to approve of; to agree

zànyáng 赞扬 to glorify; to exalt; to uphold; commendation; glorification

zànzhù 赞助 to sponsor; to patronize; support

zànzhùrén 赞助人 a patron; a sponsor

zāngwù 赃物 plunder; booty; loot; spoils

zāng 脏 dirty; filthy

zàng 葬 to bury, inter, or consign to a grave

zànglǐ 葬礼 a funeral or burial service

zàng 藏 ① Tibet; Tibetans ② a storage; a warehouse; a depository ③ a collective name for the Buddhist and Taoist scriptures
⇨cáng

zāo 遭 ① to meet with; to incur; to be victimized; to suffer ② times of binding or turning around, as with a rope ③ a time; a turn

zāodào 遭到 to suffer; to meet with; to encounter

zāoshòu 遭受 to incur (losses, etc.); to be subjected to

zāoyāng 遭殃 to meet with misfortune or disaster

zāoyù 遭遇 ① to meet with; to encounter ② vicissitudes in one's life

zāo 糟 ① (said of a plan, arrangement, etc.) to become a mess or in bad shape ② decayed; rotten; spoiled ③ not sturdy or strong ④ sediment or dregs of wine ⑤ to soak food items (as fish, meat, etc.) in wine or wine sediment ⑥ lousy

zāogāo 糟糕 What a mess! Too bad!

zāotà 糟蹋 ① to waste (talent, great ability, etc. on trifles); to degrade or debase ② to insult

záo 凿 ① to chisel or dig; to bore or pierce through ② a chisel ③ to make a forced interpretation of text

zǎo 早 ① early; earlier; soon; before-hand; previous; premature; in advance ② morning ③ ago; before ④ Good morning!

zǎo'ān 早安 Good morning!

zǎocān 早餐 breakfast

Z

zǎochǎn 早产 premature birth

zǎochen 早晨 daybreak; (early) morning; dawn

zǎodiǎn 早点 breakfast

zǎofàn 早饭 breakfast

zǎonián 早年 years ago; in bygone years

zǎoqī/zǎoqí 早期 the early stage

zǎorì 早日 at an earlier date; soon

zǎoshang 早上 early in the morning

zǎowǎn 早晚 ① morning and evening ② sooner or later

zǎoxiān 早先 some time ago; before

zǎoyǐ 早已 to have already...

zǎo 枣 jujube, commonly called date

zǎo 澡 to wash; to bathe

zào 灶 ① a cooking stove or furnace ② a place for cooking; a kitchen

zào 造 ① to create; to make ② to build ③ to make up; to invent ④ to manufacture; to produce ⑤ (law) a party concerned in the suit ⑥ an era; a period ⑦ to institute

zàochéng 造成 ① to complete; to build up; to compose ② to result in

zàofǎn 造反 to rebel; to rise up against; revolt; uprising

zàofǎng 造访 to pay a visit to; to call on

zàofú 造福 to bring benefit to; benefit

zàohuà 造化 Heaven; Mother Nature; the Creator

zàohua 造化 one's luck or fortune

zàojià 造价 building cost; manufacturing cost

zàojiù 造就 ① to educate; to bring up ② one's achievement or accomplishment

zàojù 造句 to make a sentence

zàolín 造林 afforestation; reforestation

zàoshì 造势 to spin

zàowùzhǔ 造物主 the Creator

zàoxíng 造型 ① a model; a mold ② modeling; moldmaking ③ (machinery) molding

zàoyīn 噪音 unpleasant noise; a din

zé zé 则 ① a law; a rule; a regulation; a standard; a norm; a criterion ② a numerary particle used before news reports, advertisements, etc.

zé zé 责 ① one's duty, responsibility, obligation, etc. ② to demand; to be strict with ③ to punish; punishment ④ to upbraid; to censure; to reprimand; to blame

zébèi 责备 to upbraid; to reprimand; to reproach

zéguài 责怪 to blame

zérèn 责任 ① duty; responsibility; an obligation ② responsibility for a fault; blame

zérèngǎn 责任感 a sense of responsibility

zérènzhì 责任制 a system set up at a company that determines which employees are responsible for which tasks

zé 择 to select; to choose; to pick out

zéi 贼 ① a thief; a burglar; a robber; a bandit ② a rebel; a traitor ③ to kill ④ pests on the farm ⑤ a term of reviling ⑥ clever; cunning; crafty

zěn 怎 why; how; what

zěnme 怎么 why; how; what

zěnmebàn 怎么办 How (or what) to do now?; What should (I, etc.) do?

zěnmehuì 怎么会 How could this be possible?; How could it be like this?; How could it happen?

zěnmele 怎么了 What happened?; What's wrong?

zěnmeshuō 怎么说 What do you say?; What (did he, etc.) say?

zěnmeyàng 怎么样 Why?; How?; What?

zěnmezhe 怎么着 ① What

zěnnéng 怎能 how can (he do this to me?); how could (you...?)

zěnyàng 怎样 how; in what way

zēng 曾 ① older or younger by three generations ② a surname
⇨céng

zēng 增 to add to; to increase; to grow; to enlarge

zēngchǎn 增产 to increase production

zēngduō 增多 to add to; to increase

zēngjiā 增加 to add to; to increase

zēngjìn 增进 to promote (friendship, etc.); to increase (knowledge, etc.)

zēngqiáng 增强 to strengthen; to enhance

zēngshè 增设 to establish a new organization, unit, etc.

zēngtiān 增添 to add to; to supplement

zēngyuán 增援 to send reinforcements

zēngzhǎng 增长 a rise; to grow

zēngzī 增资 to increase capitalization

zèng 赠 to send (gifts); to confer or bestow (titles); to give

zèngpǐn 赠品 a gift; a present

zèngsòng 赠送 to present; to give; to donate

zèngyǔ 赠与 to present; to give; to donate

zhā 扎 to pierce; to prick

zhā/zhá 扎 to stop; to station; to post
⇨zā, zhá

zhāshi 扎实 solid; firm

zhā/zé 咋 to shout blusteringly

Zhā 查 a surname
⇨chá

zhā 渣 dregs; lees; grounds; sediment

zhá 扎 to struggle; to strive
⇨zā, zhá

zhá 闸 ① a floodgate; a lock; a sluice ② a brake ③ a switch or similar devices

zhá 炸 to fry in oil or fat; to deep-fry
⇨zhà

zhájī 炸鸡 ① to fry chicken ② fried chicken

zhǎ 眨 to wink; to blink

zhà 乍 ① at first; for the first time ② suddenly; unexpectedly

zhàpiàn 诈骗 to swindle

zhàqī 诈欺 fraud; imposture; cheating

zhàlan 栅栏 a fence; a palisade; a railing

zhà 炸 ① to explode; to burst; to bomb ② to get mad
⇨zhá

zhàdàn 炸弹 a bomb

zhàyào 炸药 dynamite; explosives

zhà 榨 to press (for juice or oil); to extract; to squeeze; to wring

zhāi 摘 ① to take off (one's hat, etc.); to pluck; to pick ② to choose; to select ③ to jot down (notes) ④ to expose; to unveil (a conspiracy, etc.)

zhāiyào 摘要 ① an abstract ② to summarize

zháiyuàn 宅院 a house with a courtyard

zhǎi 窄 ① narrow; contracted; tight ② mean; narrow-minded

zhài 债 a debt; an obligation

zhàiquán 债权 rights of a creditor

zhàiquàn 债券 bonds issued by a government or debentures issued by a company

zhàiwù 债务 debt or obligation

zhài 寨 a stockade

zhān 占 to divine
⇨zhàn

zhān 沾 ① to moisten; to wet ② to tinge; to stain; to contaminate ③ to touch ④ to benefit from ⑤ to be imbued with; to be infected with

zhānguāng 沾光 to benefit from

Z

the support or influence of someone

zhān/nián 粘 to paste up; to
attach to; to stick up; to glue
⇨**nián**

zhānyǎng 瞻仰 ① to pay
respects to ② to look up to

zhǎn 斩 ① to cut ② to kill; to
behead

zhǎncǎo-chúgēn 斩草除根
to eliminate the cause of trouble
completely

zhǎndīng-jiétiě 斩钉截铁 to
speak or act, with determination
and courage

zhǎn 盏 ① a measure word for
lamps ② a small shallow container; a small cup

zhǎn 展 ① to open ② to stretch;
to extend ③ to unfold; to unroll
④ to expand; to dilate ⑤ to prolong ⑥ to visit

zhǎnchū 展出 to display or to
put on display at an exhibition

zhǎnkāi 展开 ① to spread out; to
unfold ② to start (an activity, task,
etc.)

zhǎnlǎn 展览 to exhibit; to display

zhǎnlǎnhuì 展览会 an exhibition or exposition

zhǎnshì 展示 to show; to display; to exhibit

zhǎnwàng 展望 the prospects of
an undertaking

zhǎnxiàn 展现 to present before
one's eyes; to develop

zhǎnxiāo 展销 to display and
sell

zhǎnxīn 崭新 brand-new

zhàn 占 ① to seize; to usurp; to
occupy; to take by force
⇨**zhān**

zhànjù 占据 to occupy; to take
possession of

zhànlíng 占领 to occupy; to capture

zhànyǒu 占有 ① to own; to have
② to occupy

zhàn 战 ① to contest; to fight; to

contend ② war; warfare; fighting;
battle ③ to shudder ④ a surname

zhànchǎng 战场 a battlefield

zhànchē 战车 ① a tank (an
armored vehicle) ② a chariot

zhàndòu 战斗 ① to fight; to
combat; to engage in a battle
② (military) action

zhàndòujī 战斗机 a fighter
plane; a fighter

Zhànguó 战国 the Warring
States (403–221 B.C.)

zhànhòu 战后 postwar; after
the war

zhànhuǒ 战火 flames of war

zhànjī 战机 ① an opportunity for
combat ② a fighter

zhànjì/zhànjī 战绩 military
successes (or exploits)

zhànluàn 战乱 chaos and social
upheavals brought about by war

zhànlüè 战略 strategy

zhànshén 战神 the god of war

zhànshèng 战胜 to conquer; to
win a victory

zhànshì 战士 a warrior; a fighting man

zhànshì 战事 war; hostilities

zhànshù 战术 tactics; the art of
war

zhànxiàn 战线 a battle line; a
battle front; the action front

zhànyì 战役 a (military) campaign; a battle

zhànyǒu 战友 a comrade in arms

zhànzhàn-jīngjīng 战战兢兢
trembling with fear; very cautious

zhànzhēng 战争 war

zhàn 站 ① to stand ② a station;
a stop; a center for rendering
certain services

zhàngǎng 站岗 to stand guard;
to stand sentry

zhànlì 站立 to stand

zhànqilai 站起来 to stand up;
to rise

zhàntái 站台 a platform (at a
railway station)

zhànzhǎng 站长 the head of
a station; a stationmaster

Z

zhànzhù 站住 (word of command) halt; to stop; to stand

zhàn 颤 to tremble; to shiver; to shudder
⇨chàn

zhāng 张 ① a sheet (of paper); a leaf (of a book) ② to open; to stretch; to extend ③ to display

zhāngkai 张开 to stretch open; to open

zhānglì 张力 tensile strength; tension

zhāngtiē 张贴 to paste up

zhāngwàng 张望 to look around; to look about

zhāng 章 ① a piece of writing; a chapter ② a system; a statute; an organized body ③ an emblem; a seal; old ④ to make clear; to make known ⑤ a pattern; an example ⑥ a surname

zhāngchéng 章程 a set of regulation; constitution

zhāngyú 章鱼 an octopus

Zhānghuà 彰化 Changhua, a county in central Taiwan

zhāngxiǎn 彰显 to manifest

zhāngláng 蟑螂 a cockroach; a roach

zhǎng 长 ① to grow ② to increase; to advance ③ a head; a chief; a leader; a commander; a chairman ④ senior; old ⑤ the eldest ⑥ to look; appear; to become
⇨cháng

zhǎngbèi 长辈 the senior generation; the older member of a family; an elder

zhǎngdà 长大 to grow up; to attain manhood; to mature

zhǎngguān 长官 one's superior in office, etc.; (a polite expression) officers or officials; a commanding officer

zhǎnglǎo 长老 ① a senior or an elder ② a presbyter ③ reverent address for a monk

zhǎngxiàng 长相 one's looks or appearances

zhǎngzhě 长者 a senior; an elder; a person of virtue

zhǎngzǐ 长子 the eldest son

zhǎng 涨 to go up or rise (as prices, water, etc.)
⇨zhàng

zhǎngfú 涨幅 (said of commodity prices, stocks, etc.) the rate of increase or rise

zhǎngjià 涨价 to raise prices; appreciation

zhǎng 掌 ① the palm of the hand; the sole of the foot; paws of an animal ② to slap with one's hand; to smack ③ to have charge of; to supervise; to control

zhǎngguǎn 掌管 to take charge of; to supervise

zhǎngshēng 掌声 clapping; applause

zhǎngwò 掌握 in one's grasp; within one's power

zhàng 丈 ① a unit of length (=3⅓ meters) ② an elder; a senior ③ to measure; to survey

zhàngfū 丈夫 a man

zhàngfu 丈夫 a husband

zhàng 仗 ① weaponry ② to lean upon; to rely upon; to depend on ③ battle; war

zhàng 帐 ① a curtain; a mosquito net ② a tent ③ a canopy above the bed

zhàngpeng 帐篷 a tent; a matshed

zhàng 账 accounts

zhàngdān 账单 a bill; a check

zhànghào 账号 ① an account ② account number

zhànghù 账户 a bank account

zhàngmù 账目 accounts; itemized bills

zhàng 胀 ① to expand; expansion ② swelling of the skin, etc. ③ full-stomached; glutted

zhàng 涨 to swell; to expand
⇨zhǎng

zhàng'ài 障碍 ① obstacles; barriers; obstructions ② a malfunction; a handicap

zhāo 招 ① to beckon with one's hand; to summon ② to raise (an

Z

army, capital, etc.); to recruit ③ to cause; to effect; to incite; to incur; to invite ④ to entice; to induce ⑤ to confess; to admit ⑥ a poster; a notice; a signboard ⑦ to welcome; to receive ⑧ a move; a trick; a device

zhāobiāo 招标 invitation to bid at a tender

zhāodài 招待 ① to serve; to entertain ② a reception ③ a receptionist

zhāodàihuì 招待会 a reception

zhāohu 招呼 ① to beckon; to call ② to take care of

zhāokǎo 招考 to advertise for employees or students through competitive examinations

zhāomù 招募 ① to enlist troops (usually mercenaries) ② to solicit (investment, capital, etc.)

zhāopai 招牌 ① the signboard of a store or any other business concern ② the reputation of a large business firm or a quality product

zhāopìn/zhāopìng 招聘 to advertise for office vacancies

zhāoshēng 招生 to enroll students

zhāoshōu 招收 to advertise for students, apprentices, etc.

zhāoshǒu 招手 to wave a hand

zhāo 着 a plan; a method

zhāo/zhuó 着 a move (on the chessboard, in action, plants, etc.) ⇨zháo, zhe, zhuó

zhāo 朝 ① morning ② a day ⇨cháo

zhāohuì 朝会 a morning rally (in schools)

zhāoqì 朝气 fresh spirit

zhāoqì-péngbó 朝气蓬勃 full of vigor and vitality

zhāosān-mùsì 朝三暮四 to be inconsistent

zháo 着 to catch fire

zháo/zhāo 着 to bear; to take; to catch a cold ⇨zhāo, zhe, zhuó

zháojí/zhāojí 着急 anxious or

worried

zháoliáng/zhāoliáng 着凉 to catch a cold

zháomí 着迷 to be fascinated

zhǎo 找 ① to seek; to look for; to search for; to find ② to return (change)

zhǎobudào 找不到 to search or look in vain

zhǎodào 找到 to have succeeded in finding

zhǎoqián 找钱 to give change

zhǎoxún 找寻 to search for; to look for

zhǎozé 沼泽 a marsh; a swamp

zhàojí 召集 ① to call to arms ② to convene (a meeting, etc.)

zhàojírén 召集人 a convener

zhàokāi 召开 to convene, to convoke

zhào 兆 ① a trillion (10^{12}); a billion ② to portend; to foretell ③ an omen ④ a sign (in fortune-telling)

Zhào 赵 ① name of an ancient feudal state ② a surname

Zhào Gāo 赵高 Zhao Gao, a powerful eunuch during the Qin （秦）Dynasty (221-206 B.C.)

zhào 照 ① to shine upon; to light or illumine ② according to; in accordance with; to pattern on or after ③ to photograph; to take a picture; to shoot ④ to compare, collate, survey, etc. ⑤ a certificate or license ⑥ to look after; to take care of ⑦ to notify or proclaim ⑧ sunshine ⑨ a picture

zhàocháng 照常 as usual

zhàogu 照顾 to patronize

zhàohuì 照会 diplomatic notes; memoranda

zhàojiù 照旧 as usual; as before

zhàolì 照例 to follow precedents or usual practices; as a rule

zhàoliào 照料 to take care of; to look after

zhàomíng 照明 (said of photography, etc.) lighting

zhàopiàn 照片 a photograph; a

snapshot

zhàoshè 照射 to shine or light upon; to radiate

zhàoxiàng 照相 to take a picture or photograph

zhàoxiàngjī 照相机 a camera

zhàoyàng 照样 ① as usual; in the old manner ② to pattern after; to copy

zhàoyào 照耀 to radiate; to light up; to shine

zhàoyìng 照应 to correlate

zhàoyìng 照应 to take care of; to look after

zhào 罩 ① to coop; to cover; to wrap ② a cover; a shade ③ a bamboo basket for catching fish ④ a mantle; a cloak

zhàoshì 肇事 to stir up trouble or disturbances

zhē 折 ① to turn upside down; to fall head over heels ② to pour all out
⇨shé, zhé

zhēteng 折腾 ① to toss about ② to waste ③ to turn upside down

zhē 遮 ① to intercept; to block ② to hide; to cover; to screen; to shade; to shield; to conceal; to shut out

zhēbì 遮蔽 to cover; to screen

zhé 折 ① to break; to snap ② to bend; to humble; to bow ③ to fold ④ to sell, barter, or exchange ⑤ to submit to; to be willing ⑥ a discount in the price ⑦ to tear into halves; to destroy
⇨shé, zhé

zhédié 折叠 to fold

zhéhé 折合 (said of two currencies, etc.) equivalent to

zhékòu 折扣 abatement; a discount in the price

zhémó 折磨 to submit to an ordeal; trials and afflictions

zhé 哲 ① a sage; a thinker; a philosopher ② wise; wisdom; sagacious

zhélǐ 哲理 a philosophical principle

zhéxué 哲学 philosophy

zhéxuéjiā 哲学家 a philosopher; a thinker

zhě 者 ① those who; he who ② a particle combining with some words to form adverbials

zhè 这 ① this (a pronoun) ② this (a demonstrative adjective); such

zhèbān 这般 such; like this

zhèbiān 这边 ① this side; here ② this side; our side

zhège 这个 ① this; this one ② h'm, hem, or hum (an interjection indicating indecision when the sound ge is dragged too long)

zhèhuìr/zhèhuǐr 这会儿 now; at the moment

zhèlǐ 这里 here; this place; where we are

zhème 这么 so; thus; (in) this way; like this

zhèmezhe 这么着 this way (an expression to introduce a suggestion; an instruction of how to do something, etc.); like this; so

zhèr 这儿 ① here ② now; then

zhèxiàzi 这下子 this way; so; thus

zhèxiē 这些 these

zhèyàng 这样 so; thus; like this

zhèyàngyìlái 这样一来 this way; so; thus

zhèyàngzi 这样子 so; thus; (in) this way

zhèzhènzi 这阵子 recent; recently

zhe 着 an adverbial particle
⇨zhāo, zháo, zhuó

zhēn 针 ① a needle; a pin; a probe ② a stitch

zhēnduì 针对 ① to aim directly at; to focus on ② in accordance with

zhēnjiǔ 针灸 acupuncture and moxibustion; acupuncture and cauterization

zhēntóu 针头 (medicine) a syringe needle

zhēnchá 侦查 to investigate

zhēnchá 侦察 reconnaissance;

Z

to reconnoiter

zhēnpò 侦破 to crack a criminal case

zhēntàn 侦探 ① a detective ② to investigate

zhēncáng 珍藏 to treasure

zhēnguì 珍贵 valuable; treasurable; precious

zhēnxī/zhēnxí 珍惜 to treasure

zhēnzhū 珍珠 a pearl

zhēn 真 ① true; real; factual; substantial; actual; truly ② the highest sincerity one is capable of

zhēn'ài 真爱 true love

zhēnchéng 真诚 sincere; genuine; true

zhēnde 真的 true; real; actually

zhēnkōng 真空 vacuum

zhēnlǐ 真理 ① truth ② righteousness

zhēnpí 真皮 ① dermis ② genuine leather

zhēnqiè 真切 ① true and concise; vivid ② (to see or hear) clearly

zhēnqíng 真情 ① actual happenings (of an incident, etc.) ② real affections

zhēnshí 真实 actual; true; real; factual

zhēnshì 真是 ① it's really...; it's definitely... ② (used to express displeasure) how

zhēnshìde 真是的 (used for expressing complaints or slight anger) really; honestly

zhēnxiàng 真相 the truth (about a happening, etc.)

zhēnxīn 真心 from the bottom of one's heart; sincere; wholehearted

zhēnzhèng 真正 ① genuine ② actually; real

zhēnxuǎn 甄选 to select (talented people, etc.)

zhēn 臻 the utmost; the best

zhěn 诊 to examine (diseases, ailments, etc.); to diagnose

zhěnduàn 诊断 to diagnose (a disease); a diagnosis

zhěnliáo 诊疗 to diagnose and treat

zhěnsuǒ 诊所 a clinic; a dispensary

zhěnzhì 诊治 to diagnose and treat

zhěn 枕 a pillow

zhěn/zhèn 枕 to use something as a pillow; to pillow

zhěntou 枕头 a pillow

zhěnzi 疹子 measles; carbuncles

zhèn 阵 ① a column or row of troops; the army; the rank and file ② anything that occurs in a certain duration or spell of time ③ to battle; to go to war

zhèndì 阵地 a (military) position

zhènróng 阵容 ① the appearance of military deployment; the layout of troops ② the lineup of a cabinet ③ the cast of a movie

zhènxiàn 阵线 line of battle

zhènyíng 阵营 a camp; an encampment

zhènzhèn 阵阵 intermittently; intermittent (rains, winds, pain, etc.); now and again; at intervals; repeatedly; by fits and starts; gusts

zhènzi 阵子 a spell of

zhèn 振 ① to arouse to action; to raise; to rise ② to shake; to flap as wings ③ to pull up; to save; to relieve ④ to restore order

zhèndòng 振动 (physics) vibration; to vibrate

zhènfèn 振奋 ① to arouse; to stimulate ② encouraging; exciting

zhènxīng 振兴 to promote or develop (industrial endeavor, etc.); to prosper

zhèn 朕 the royal we (used exclusively by the emperor or king to mean I)

zhèn 震 ① to shake; to tremble, as an earthquake ② to excite; to shock ③ terrified; scared ④ (now rarely) thunder; a thunderclap ⑤ the 4th of the Eight Diagrams

zhèndàng 震荡 to shake; to vibrate

zhèndòng 震动 ① to vibrate; to

Z

shake; to move ② to be shocked or shaken

zhènhàn 震撼 to shake; shaken

zhènjīng 震惊 greatly surprised

zhèn 镇 ① a town; a township ② to subdue; to suppress; to quell; to put down ③ to cool with water or ice ④ weight ⑤ whole ⑥ a garrison post

zhèndìng 镇定 self-composed; calm; cool

zhèngōngsuǒ 镇公所 a town hall; a town house

zhènjìng 镇静 self-composed; calm; cool

zhènyā 镇压 to suppress; to put down; suppression

zhènzhǎng 镇长 the town master; the head of a town

zhēng 正 the first in the lunar calendar
⇨zhèng

zhēngyuè 正月 the first month of the lunar year

zhēng 争 ① to contend; to struggle; to strive ② to fight; to dispute; to argue; to quarrel ③ short of; to lack; to be deficient in

zhēngbiàn 争辩 to argue; to debate; to dispute

zhēngchǎo 争吵 to quarrel; to wrangle

zhēngduān 争端 the cause of dispute or quarrel

zhēngduó 争夺 to struggle for; to contend for

zhēnglùn 争论 to dispute; to argue

zhēngqì 争气 don't let down; to try to win credit for

zhēngqǔ 争取 to win over; to compete for

zhēngxiān-kǒnghòu 争先恐后 anxious to be ahead of others

zhēngyì 争议 to dispute; to argue

zhēngzhí 争执 to argue or dispute obstinately

zhēng 征 ① to levy taxes; to collect taxes ② to attack; to conquer; to tame ③ to journey far away

④ to take; to snatch ⑤ to call to arms ⑥ to summon ⑦ to ask; to inquire ⑧ to request; to seek for ⑨ to prove; to evidence ⑩ a sign

zhēngfú 征服 to conquer; conquest

zhēngqiú 征求 to seek; to solicit (answers, etc.); to want (an office clerk, etc.)

zhēngshōu 征收 to collect (taxes, duty, etc.)

zhēngzhào 征召 to draft the capable and virtuous for public service

zhēngzhào 征兆 a symptom; an omen

zhēng 挣 to make efforts; to strive
⇨zhèng

zhēngzhá 挣扎 to struggle; a struggle; to strive

zhēngjié 症结 ① obstruction of the bowels ② a difficult point (of a problem); a bottleneck; a crux

zhēng 睁 to open the eyes

zhēngkāi 睁开 to open (the eyes)

zhēng 筝 ① a kite ② a plucked stringed instrument in some ways similar to the zither; guzheng

zhēng 蒸 ① steam; to steam; to cook by steaming ② to evaporate ③ twigs or slender branches as fuel ④ crowded; crowds; the masses

zhēngfā 蒸发 evaporation; to evaporate

zhēngqì 蒸汽 steam; vapor

zhěngjiù 拯救 ① deliverance ② to save; to rescue; to deliver

zhěng 整 ① whole; complete; entire; intact ② to tidy; to set in order; to adjust; to arrange; to repair; to make ready ③ orderly; systematic; neat; tidy ④ sharp; punctually

zhěngdùn 整顿 to put in order or to put to right a poorly managed organization, firm, etc.

zhěngfēng 整风 rectification of incorrect style of work

zhěnggè 整个 wholly; entire-

Z

ly; whole; entire

zhěnghé 整合 ① to integrate; integration ② (geology) conformity

zhěngjié 整洁 neat and clean

zhěnglǐ 整理 to arrange; to put in order; to adjust

zhěngqí 整齐 ① neat; tidy ② even

zhěngshù 整数 a whole number; an integer; a round sum

zhěngtǐ 整体 the whole

zhěngtiān 整天 the whole day; all day long

zhěngxíng 整形 orthopedics

zhěngxiū 整修 to rebuild; to renovate

zhěngzhěng 整整 exactly

zhèng 正 ① exactly; just; right ② the obverse side; the right side ③ appropriate; proper ④ straightforward and unbending; honest and virtuous ⑤ original (texts, etc.) ⑥ main; principal ⑦ just; unbiased ⑧ positively ⑨ formal ⑩ to rectify; to correct ⑪ pure; not contaminated ⑫ the person in charge; the person in command; the principal (as against the secondary) ⑬ sharp; punctually ⑭ to mete out punishment for a criminal ⇨zhēng

zhèngbǐ 正比 direct proportion

zhèngcháng 正常 normal; common; usually

zhèngdāng 正当 right at that time; just when ⇨zhèngdàng

zhèngdàng 正当 proper; justifiable; legitimate ⇨zhèngdāng

zhèngfāngxíng 正方形 (geometry) a square

zhèngguī 正规 regular; standard

zhènghǎo 正好 exactly (at the right moment); exactly right; it just happened that...

zhèngjīng 正经 (said of manners, conducts, etc.) very proper; respectable; serious

zhèngmiàn 正面 the right side; the obverse side; the head (of a coin)

zhèngqì 正气 righteousness

zhèngqiǎo 正巧 exactly; it happens that...; exactly when...; coincidence

zhèngquè 正确 accurate; correct; right; proper

zhèngshì 正式 formally; official

zhèngshì 正视 to look straight in the eye; to look at something without bias or distortion

zhèngshì 正是 ① yes, exactly so ② an expression introducing a common saying which ends a chapter in the old chinese novel

zhèngtǒng 正统 orthodox; authorized

zhèngyì 正义 righteousness; justice

zhèngzài 正在 ① a term used before a verb to form a progressive tense ② (said of a position) exactly at

zhèngzōng 正宗 orthodox

zhèng 证 ① evidence; proof; testimony ② to give evidence; to bear testimony; to bear witness; to prove; to testify ③ a certificate; a card ④ a symptom

zhèngjiàn 证件 papers supporting a claim; documentary proof; credentials

zhèngjù 证据 testimony; evidence; witness; proof

zhèngmíng 证明 to prove; to testify

zhèngquàn 证券 securities (bills, bonds, etc.); stocks and bonds

zhèngquàn jiāoyìsuǒ 证券交易所 the stock exchange

zhèngrén 证人 a witness

zhèngshí 证实 to prove; to testify

zhèngshū 证书 a certificate; a diploma; credentials

zhèng 郑 ① solemn; formal; serious ② a surname ③ name of an ancient state in what is today's Henan

Z

zhèngzhòng 郑重 ① solemn; serious ② cautious; careful

zhèng 政 ① government ② politics; political affairs ③ administration; management

zhèngbiàn 政变 a coup d'état; a coup

zhèngcè 政策 a policy

zhèngdǎng 政党 a political party

zhèngfǔ 政府 a government

zhèngjì/zhèngjī 政绩 administrative achievements (of a government, ruler, or magistrate)

zhèngjiàn 政见 political views; politics

zhèngjú 政局 the political situation or scene

zhèngkè 政客 a politician who places personal gain above public interests

zhèngquán 政权 regime; political power

zhèngwù 政务 affairs of the government

zhèngwù cìzhǎng 政务次长 a political vice-minister (as distinct from 常务次长, the administrative vice-minister)

zhèngwùguān 政务官 high-ranking government officials in charge of administrative affairs (as distinct from 事务官, who are executive officers)

zhèngxié 政协 political consultative conference

zhèngzhì 政治 ① politics ② government administration

zhèngzhìjiā 政治家 a statesman

Zhèngzhì Jú 政治局 the Political Bureau; the Politburo (of Communist parties)

zhèng 挣 ① to struggle (for one's life, etc.) ② to earn (money, etc.)

zhèng/zhēng 挣 to get free from
⇨zhēng

zhèng 症 ① disease; an ailment ② symptoms or manifestations of a disease

zhèngzhuàng 症状 symptoms or manifestations of a disease

zhīhòu 之后 after this; afterward

zhījiān 之间 between; among

zhīlèi 之类 and so on; and so forth

zhīnèi 之内 within; inside; including; included

zhīqián 之前 before this; before; prior to

zhīshàng 之上 above; over; on

zhīwài 之外 besides this; in addition

zhīxià 之下 below...

zhīyī 之一 one of...

zhīzhōng 之中 in...; among...

zhī 支 ① a term for indicating amount or number ② to support; to sustain ③ to prop up; to put up ④ to prick up; to raise ⑤ to send away; to put somebody off ⑥ to pay; to disburse; to defray ⑦ a branch; a subdivision ⑧ (textile) count ⑨ the Terrestrial Branches used in calculation with the Celestial Stems

zhībù 支部 ① branch headquarters (of a political party) ② the radical

zhīchēng 支撑 to prop up; to support

zhīchí 支持 to support; to sustain

zhīchū 支出 expense; expenditure

zhīfù 支付 to pay (what is owed); to defray

zhīpèi 支配 ① to dominate ② to manage

zhīpiào 支票 a cheque or check

zhīyìng 支应 ① to take charge of cash receipts and payments ② to look after; to take care of

zhīyuán 支援 to aid; to support; to assist

zhīzhù 支柱 a prop; a support; a stay

Zhī 氏 name of an ancient barbarian tribe
⇨shì

zhī 只 ① a measure word for a bird,

Z

goat, hand, etc. ② single; alone; one of a pair ③ odd (number) ⇨zhǐ

zhī 汁 juice; the natural fluid; sap

Zhījiāgē 芝加哥 Chicago, Illinois

zhīma 芝麻 sesame

zhī 枝 ① the branches of a tree; a branch ② limbs ③ to branch off

zhīyè 枝叶 ① branches and leaves ② complications and diversities ③ children; offspring

zhī 知 ① to know; to understand; to recognize; to be aware of ② knowledge ③ to acquaint; to be familiar with; to befriend ④ to control; to operate; to direct ⑤ to wait on

zhīdao 知道 to know; to realize; to understand

zhījǐ 知己 ① a close or intimate friend ② intimate ③ to know oneself

zhījué 知觉 ① consciousness ② perception

zhīmíng 知名 well-known

zhīmíngdù 知名度 name recognition; name familiarity

zhīnéng 知能 consciousness; a sense of awareness

zhīqíng 知情 to be aware of (usually referring to a secret, plot, etc.); to be in the know

zhīshi 知识 knowledge; learning; information

zhīshi fènzǐ 知识分子 intellectuals; the intelligentsia

zhīxìng 知性 intellect

zhīzú 知足 to be content with what one has had

zhītǐ 肢体 the body

zhī 织 to weave; to knit

zhīfáng 脂肪 the fat of animals or plants

zhīzhū 蜘蛛 a spider

zhī 执 ① to maintain or uphold (a principle, etc.); to hold on stubbornly to ② to hold; to grasp; to seize

zhífǎ 执法 to enforce (or execute) the law

zhíqín 执勤 to be on duty

zhíxíng 执行 to execute (an order); to carry out

zhíyì 执意 to stick to one's own view; to insist on

zhízhào 执照 a license; a permit

zhízhèng 执政 to be in power; to hold the reins of the government

zhízhèngdǎng 执政党 the party in power; the ruling party

zhízhuó 执着 inflexible; to persist in

zhí 直 ① straight; to straighten ② upright and honest; fair; unbiased ③ vertical; longitudinal; from top to bottom ④ continuous; uninterrupted ⑤ directly; firsthand ⑥ outspoken; frank; straightforward ⑦ stiff; numb ⑧ just; simply; only; merely ⑨ a vertical stroke (in Chinese characters)

zhíbō/zhíbò 直播 (agriculture) direct seeding

zhídá 直达 to go nonstop to; through

zhídào 直到 till; until ② up to

zhíjiē 直接 direct; firsthand; directly

zhíjìng 直径 ① a diameter ② a straight path

zhíjué 直觉 intuition

zhíshēngjī 直升机 a helicopter

zhíxiáshì 直辖市 a special municipality

zhíxiàn 直线 ① a straight line ② steep; sharp

zhíxiāo 直销 to sell directly or direct sale by a manufacturer instead of through an agent

zhízhì 直至 ① till; until ② up to

zhízi 侄子 a nephew

zhí 值 ① prices of commodities; value; cost; to cost; to be worth ② at the time of... ③ to meet; to happen

zhíbān 值班 to be on duty

zhídé 值得 to be worthy of; to deserve

zhíqián 值钱 valuable; expensive

zhí 职 ① a profession or a vocation; a career ② a post; a position ③ an office; official duties ④ to govern; to direct; to manage

zhíbàng 职棒 professional baseball

zhíchēng 职称 the name of a position one holds; the title of a technical or professional post (such as engineer, professor, lecturer, academician, etc.)

zhígōng 职工 ① officers and workers (in a plant, company, etc.) ② workers with permanent jobs

zhínéng 职能 a function

zhíquán 职权 authority for exercising or discharging one's duties

zhíwèi 职位 one's office; one's position in an office

zhíwù 职务 one's official duties or obligations

zhíyè 职业 a profession; a vocation; an occupation

zhíyè fùnǚ 职业妇女 career women

zhíyuán 职员 staff members or employees of a company, office, etc.

zhízé 职责 one's position and responsibility; charge

zhí 植 ① to plant; to set up; to erect ② plants; vegetation

zhíbèi 植被 (botany) vegetation; plant cover

zhíwù 植物 vegetable; plant; flora

zhímín 殖民 to colonize

zhímíndì 殖民地 a colony

zhímín zhǔyì 殖民主义 colonialism

zhǐ 止 ① to stop; to desist; to still ② to rest in; to stay ③ deportment ④ to detain ⑤ to prohibit ⑥ to come to; to arrive at ⑦ still; calm; stagnant ⑧ only

zhǐtòng 止痛 to stop pain; to kill pain

zhǐyú 止于 to stop at; this far and no further

zhǐ 只 ① only; merely ② but; yet ⇨zhī

zhǐbùguò 只不过 only; just; merely

zhǐdé 只得 to have to

zhǐgù 只顾 ① to care about only (the present, etc.); to be absorbed in—implying shortsightedness ② please don't hesitate to...

zhǐguǎn 只管 (do anything) as you wish; please don't hesitate to...

zhǐhǎo 只好 the only alternative is to...; to have to

zhǐnéng 只能 can only; to have no alternative but to

zhǐshì 只是 ① merely; only; just ② but; yet

zhǐyào 只要 ① to want only... ② all one has to do is to...

zhǐyǒu 只有 ① to have to (do or be) ② to have...only; only; alone

zhǐ 址 ① land on which to build a house; a location; a site ② a foundation

zhǐ 纸 paper

zhǐzhāng 纸张 paper; sheets of paper

zhǐ 指 ① to point; to direct ② to indicate; to refer to; to mean ③ to hope ④ the main theme ⑤ intentions ⑥ to depend on

zhǐbiāo 指标 ① an index sign ② (mathematics) characteristic

zhǐchu 指出 to refer to; to point out

zhǐdǎo 指导 ① to instruct; to direct; to guide ② direction or guidance

zhǐdiǎn 指点 to teach; to advise

zhǐdìng 指定 ① to appoint ② to indicate clearly and with certainty ③ to allot

zhǐhuī 指挥 to conduct or direct (an orchestra, etc.); to command (an army, etc.)

zhǐhuīguān 指挥官 the commander

Z

zhǐjia 指甲 a fingernail

zhǐjiào 指教 ① direction and guidance ② (a polite expression) your advice or counsel

zhǐkòng 指控 to accuse; to charge

zhǐlìng 指令 a directive

zhǐmíng 指明 to indicate clearly; to point out

zhǐnán 指南 a directory; a guidebook; a primer

zhǐnánzhēn 指南针 a compass

zhǐpài 指派 to appoint; to assign

zhǐshì 指示 ① instruction; indication ② to direct; to instruct

zhǐshǒu-huàjiǎo 指手画脚 to gesticulate profusely

zhǐshù 指数 an index; an exponent

zhǐtou 指头 a finger

zhǐwang 指望 to hope for; to expect

zhǐwén 指纹 a fingerprint

zhǐxiàng 指向 to point to; to direct to

zhǐyǐn 指引 to direct; to guide; guidance

zhǐzé 指责 to accuse; to censure

zhǐzhēn 指针 ① a guide; a manual ② an index

zhǐzhèng 指正 ① to correct ② (a polite expression) to present herewith for your correction

zhì 至 ① to arrive at; to reach (a destination) ② very; extremely; to indicate the superlative degree— the most

zhìduō 至多 at (the) most

zhìjīn 至今 until now; so far; up to the present time

zhìshàng 至上 ① the most revered ② to come first

zhìshǎo 至少 at least; the least

zhìyú 至于 ① as to; with regard to ② to the extent of

zhì 志 ① will; purpose ② an ideal; ambition; wish ③ to make up one's mind to pursue some object; to be bent on doing something ④ annals; records

zhìqì 志气 ambition; will

zhìqù 志趣 purpose and interest; inclination; a bent

zhìxiàng 志向 purpose; ambition

zhìyuàn 志愿 ① aspiration; ambition ② voluntary

zhì 制 ① a system ② to prevail; to overpower; to control ③ to establish; to institute; to set up ④ used before the signature in letter writing to indicate the writer is in mourning ⑤ to produce; to manufacture ⑥ to make; to create ⑥ to compose (writings, literature, etc.); literary works ⑦ to cut out garments and make them ⑧ a form; a model; a pattern

zhìcái 制裁 to chastise; to sanction

zhìchéng 制成 to have completed production or making; to have produced or manufactured

zhìdìng 制订 to work out; to formulate

zhìdìng 制定 to institute; to establish

zhìdù 制度 a system; an institution

zhìfú 制服 a uniform

zhìpiàn 制片 (movie) a producer

zhìpǐn 制品 products; manufactures

zhìyào 制药 pharmacy

zhìyuē 制约 to restrict; to condition

zhìzào 制造 to produce; to manufacture; to make; to create

zhìzàoshāng 制造商 a manufacturer

zhìzàoyè 制造业 the manufacturing industry

zhìzhǐ 制止 to stop; to prevent

zhìzuò 制作 to make; to produce; to manufacture

zhìzuòrén 制作人 a producer

zhì 质 a pledge; a hostage

zhì/zhí 质 ① matters; substances; elements ② one's disposition or temperament; qualities ③

simple; plain ④ to question ⑤ to confront

zhìbiàn/zhíbiàn 质变 (philosophy) change in substance; qualitative change

zhìliàng/zhíliàng 质量 ① (physics) mass ② quality

zhìpǔ/zhípú 质朴 simple and unadorned

zhìwèn/zhíwèn 质问 ① to interrogate ② to raise questions in order to resolve one's doubt

zhìxún/zhíxún 质询 to interpellate; interpellation

zhìyā 质押 to mortgage

zhìyí/zhíyí 质疑 to question; to query

zhìzǐ/zhízǐ 质子 (physics) a proton

zhì 治 ① to administer; to control; to govern; to manage; to rule ② to regulate; to harness (a river) ③ to treat (a disease) ④ to cure ⑤ to punish ⑤ to study ⑥ the seat of the local government ⑦ peaceful and orderly

zhì'ān 治安 public security

zhìběn 治本 to deal with (or cure) a trouble, etc. at the source

zhìbiāo 治标 to cope with the symptoms only

zhìbìng 治病 to treat a disease or ailment

zhìlǐ 治理 ① to administer; to manage; to govern ② to harness; to regulate

zhìliáo 治疗 to treat or cure (a disease); therapy

zhì 致 ① to send; to present; to convey; to transmit; to extend (thanks, etc.) ② to cause to come; to cause (injury, death, etc.) ③ to bring about; to occasion or result in ④ one's principle, interest, hobby, etc. ⑤ to achieve; to attain; to amass (fortune) ⑥ to retire; to resign

zhìcí 致辞 to address; to deliver a speech

zhìdiàn 致电 to send a telegram or cable

zhìfù 致富 to become rich

zhìjìng 致敬 to salute

zhìlì 致力 to devote or dedicate oneself to

zhìmìng 致命 ① to sacrifice one's life ② fatal; fatality

zhìshǐ 致使 to cause; to result in

zhìsǐ 致死 to cause death; to result in death

zhìyì 致意 to convey one's best wishes or regards

zhìxù 秩序 ① order ② arrangement

zhì/zhí 掷 to throw; to cast

zhì 智 ① talented; capable; intelligent; clever; wisdom; wit ② prudence ③ a surname

zhìhuì 智慧 wisdom; intelligence

zhìhuì-cáichǎnquán 智慧财产权 intellectual property rights

zhìlì 智力 intelligence

Zhìlì 智利 Chile

zhì 痣 a mole; nevus

zhìliú 滞留 ① to remain at a standstill ② to loiter; to detain

zhì 置 ① to put; to place ② to establish; to set ③ to procure; to purchase

zhìshēn 置身 to stay; to place oneself

zhōng 中 ① the middle; among; within; between ② China or Chinese; Sino-

zhōng/zhòng 中 fit for; suitable for
⇨ **zhòng**

zhōngbù 中部 the central part; the middle part

zhōngcān 中餐 ① Chinese meal ② a midday meal

zhōngchǎn jiējí 中产阶级 the middle class; bourgeois

zhōngděng 中等 middle-class; medium

Zhōngdōng 中东 the Middle East (Asia)

zhōngduàn 中断 suspension; interruption

zhōngfàn 中饭 lunch; luncheon

Z

zhōngfēng 中锋 the center (in basketball, soccer, military operations, etc.)

Zhōnggòng 中共 Communist Party of China

zhōnggǔ 中古 the Middle Ages; medieval

Zhōngguó 中国 ① China; Cathay ② the Middle Kingdom

Zhōngguóhuà 中国话 Chinese; the Chinese language

zhōnghé 中和 ① justice and peace ② (chemistry) to neutralize

Zhōnghuá 中华 (originally, the region along the Yellow River where the Chinese people thrived) the Chinese nation; the Chinese people

Zhōnghuá Mínguó 中华民国 Republic of China

Zhōnghuá Mínzú 中华民族 a name for the ethnic groups that constitute the Chinese nation; the Chinese nation

Zhōnghuá Rìbào 中华日报 China Daily News

zhōngjí 中级 middle rank; intermediate

zhōngjiān 中间 in the middle; in the center

zhōngjiè 中介 intermediary; medium

zhōnglì 中立 neutral; neutrality

zhōngnián 中年 middle age

Zhōngqiūjié 中秋节 the Mid-Autumn Festival or the Moon Festival

Zhōngshān 中山 the courtesy name of Dr. Sun Yat-sen (孙逸仙), father of the Republic of China (often used as name of roads, schools, etc.)

Zhōngshāntáng 中山堂 any building named after Dr. Sun Yat-sen (often used as a city hall, community center, etc.)

Zhōngshēngdài 中生代 the Mesozoic (Era)

Zhōngshì 中式 the Chinese style or fashion

zhōngtú 中途 midway; halfway;

on the way

zhōngwài 中外 Chinese and foreign

Zhōngwén 中文 the Chinese language

zhōngwǔ 中午 noon; high noon; midday

zhōngxīn 中心 ① center ② central point

zhōngxīng 中兴 revival (of a nation or family); rejuvenation; resurgence

zhōngxíng 中型 medium-sized; middle-sized

zhōngxué 中学 middle school; secondary school; high school

zhōngxún 中旬 the middle part of a month

zhōngyāng 中央 the center; the middle

Zhōngyāng Rìbào 中央日报 Central Daily News

Zhōngyāng Yánjiūyuàn / Zhōngyāng Yánjiùyuàn 中央研究院 Academia Sinica

Zhōngyāng Yínháng 中央银行 Central Bank of China

zhōngyào 中药 Chinese medicine (mostly herbs)

zhōngyè 中叶 the middle decades of a century; the middle period (of a dynasty, century, reign)

zhōngyī 中医 a Chinese herb doctor

zhōngyōng 中庸 mediocre

zhōngyóu 中游 ① middle reaches (of a river) ② the state of being middling

zhōngyuán 中原 ① the Central Plains—the downstream regions of the Yellow River ② the midst of a plain

zhōngzhèng 中正 just; fair; unbiased; impartial; not prejudiced

zhōng 忠 ① faithful; loyal; sincere; patriotic ② devoted; honest

zhōngchéng 忠诚 loyal; faithful; staunch

zhōnggào 忠告 honest or sincere

advice; sincere counsel

zhōngshí 忠实 ① loyal and faithful ② reliable or truthful (reports, etc.)

zhōngyì 忠义 ① faithful and virtuous ② people of loyalty and virtue

zhōngyú 忠于 to have faith in; to be honest with

zhōngzhēn 忠贞 loyal (subjects, etc.); patriotic

zhōng 终 ① the end; to come to the end; the conclusion ② finally; at last; in the end; after all ③ death; to die ④ whole; all

zhōngchǎng 终场 ① the conclusion of any matter; the end of a show, game, etc. ② the last test under the former civil service examination system

zhōngdiǎn 终点 ① the terminus; the final point; the end; a destination ② (sports) finish

zhōngduān 终端 (electricity) a terminal

zhōngduānjī 终端机 a terminal

zhōngjí 终极 the finality or end

zhōngjié 终结 the end, conclusion, termination, etc.

zhōngjiū/zhōngjiù 终究 after all; in the end; in the longrun

zhōngnián 终年 ① the whole year; throughout the year ② the age at which one dies

zhōngrì 终日 throughout the day

zhōngshēn 终身 the whole life

zhōngshēng 终生 the whole life

zhōngyú 终于 in the end; finally; at last

zhōngzhǐ 终止 to stop; to end

zhōng 钟 ① a kind of wine container ② to concentrate; to accumulate ③ a bell (which tolls as distinct from that which jingles) ④ a clock ⑤ a surname

zhōngbiǎo 钟表 a timepiece; a clock and a watch

zhōngdiǎn 钟点 ① hours ② a time for something to be done or to happen

zhōngtóu 钟头 an hour

zhōngxīn 衷心 cordial; heartfelt; wholehearted

zhǒng 肿 to swell; a swelling; a boil

zhǒngliú 肿瘤 (medicine) a tumor

zhǒngzhàng 肿胀 to swell; swelling

zhǒng 种 ① seeds of grain ② races (of human beings) ③ a species; a genus; a kind or sort ④ descendants; posterity ⇨ zhòng

zhǒnglèi 种类 a sort, kind, variety, or class

zhǒngzhǒng 种种 ① various kinds ② short cropped hair ③ simple and sincere (as rural people)

zhǒngzi / zhǒngzǐ 种子 a seed

zhǒngzú 种族 (said of people) a race or tribe

zhòng 中 ① to hit (the target); to attain (a goal) ② to be hit by; to be affected by ⇨ zhōng

zhòngdú 中毒 to be poisoned; toxicosis

zhòngfēng 中风 to suffer from a stroke of paralysis or apoplexy

zhòngjiǎng 中奖 to win a (lottery) prize

zhòngkěn 中肯 ① to the point; to hit the mark ② cogency

zhòngshǔ 中暑 to have a sunstroke

zhòngjiè 仲介 ① an agency; an agent ② an organization or a person offering information ③ an intermediary; go-between

zhòng 众 ① many; numerous ② a crowd; a multitude; all; the masses ③ public or popular (opinion, views, etc.)

zhòngduō 众多 numerous

zhòngrén 众人 all people; the multitude

zhòngshēng 众生 ① all living creatures ② beasts or animals

zhòngsuǒzhōuzhī 众所周知 universally known; as everyone

knows

Zhòngyì Yuàn 众议院 ①
House of Representatives ②
Chamber of Deputies

zhòng 种 ① to plant; to sow;
to cultivate ② to vaccinate
⇨**zhǒng**

zhòngdì 种地 to farm; to cultivate the land

zhòngtián 种田 to farm; to
till the land

zhòngzhí 种植 to plant

zhòng 重 ① heavy; weighty;
much ② serious; grave ③ important; significant ④ to weigh; weight
⑤ severe ⑥ difficult ⑦ to value;
to emphasize
⇨**chóng**

zhòngdà 重大 ① important; of
great consequence; significant
② serious; grave

zhòngdiǎn 重点 the point or
center of emphasis

zhònggōngyè 重工业 heavy
industry

zhòngjīnshǔ 重金属 heavy
metals

zhònglì 重力 gravity

zhòngliàng 重量 weight

zhòngshāng 重伤 a serious
injury

zhòngshì 重视 to pay much
attention to; to consider important

zhòngtóuxì 重头戏 ① a play
involving much singing and action
② a role involving much singing
and action

zhòngxīn 重心 the center of
gravity

zhòngxíng 重刑 severe punishment

zhòngyào 重要 important; significant; vital

zhòngyòng 重用 to give (someone) an important assignment

zhòngzhèn 重镇 key positions
(in military operations); an important city

zhōu 州 ① an administrative
district in ancient China ② a state

(in the USA) ③ a place surrounded
by water; an islet; a sand bar

zhōu 周 ① a circumference; a
circuit ② all around; everywhere
③ complete ④ the Zhou Dynasty
⑤ to aid; to provide for ⑥ a week;
a period ⑦ a cycle; a revolution;
to revolve ⑧ a surname

zhōubiān 周边 a periphery

zhōudào 周到 thorough; considerate

zhōukān 周刊 a weekly periodical; a weekly

zhōumì 周密 careful and thorough

zhōumò 周末 the weekend

zhōunián 周年 a full year; an
anniversary

zhōuqī/zhōuqí 周期 a period;
a cycle

zhōuwéi 周围 ① surroundings;
environment ② the circumference

zhōuxiáng 周详 complete and
detailed

zhōuyóu 周游 to make a tour
in search of adventures, enjoyments, etc.

zhōuzāo 周遭 around

zhōuzhé 周折 a complicated or
troublesome course of development

zhōuzhuǎn 周转 ① circulating
or revolving (funds) ② to have
enough to meet the need

zhōu 洲 ① an island in a river
② a continent

zhōu 粥 congee; rice gruel

zhóu 轴 ① an axis; a pivot; an
axle ② (said of mounted paintings
or calligraphic works) a scroll

zhòu 宙 infinite time; time without beginning or end; eternity

zhòuyè 昼夜 day and night

zhòu 皱 ① wrinkles; creases;
folds; rumples ② to wrinkle; to
fold; to contract; to crease; to
crumple

zhòuwén 皱纹 wrinkles; creases;
folds; rumples

zhū 朱 ① red; vermilion ② a

Z

surname

zhūluójì 侏罗纪 (geology) the Jurassic Period

zhū 珠 ① a pearl ② a bead; a drop ③ the pupil of the eye

zhūbǎo 珠宝 jewelry; pearls and valuables

zhūzi 珠子 pearls; beads

zhū 株 ① a measure word for plants ② roots that grow above the ground

zhū 诸 all; various

zhūduō 诸多 many; numerous

zhūrú 诸如 such as

zhūrúcǐlèi 诸如此类 various things like this

zhūwèi 诸位 Ladies and Gentlemen!

zhū 猪 a pig; a hog

zhūròu 猪肉 pork

zhú 竹 ① bamboo ② slips of bamboo for writing

zhúlín 竹林 a bamboo grove

zhúzi 竹子 bamboo

zhú 逐 ① to chase; to pursue; to follow ② to drive off; to banish; to exile; to expel ③ little by little; gradually

zhúbù 逐步 step by step; to proceed orderly

zhújiàn 逐渐 little by little; gradually; by degrees

zhúnián 逐年 year by year; year after year

zhúyī 逐一 one by one

zhǔ 主 ① a master; a leader; a chief; a host ② Jesus Christ; God; Lord ③ main; chief; primary; principal ④ to officiate at; to preside over; to take charge of

zhǔbàn 主办 to sponsor; to take charge of

zhǔbiān 主编 an editor in chief

zhǔchí 主持 to officiate at; to preside over

zhǔcóng/zhǔzòng 主从 ① the master and his servant ② the principal and the secondary

zhǔdǎo 主导 leading; dominant; guiding

zhǔdòng 主动 to take the initiative

zhǔfù 主妇 a housewife; a hostess

zhǔguān 主观 the subjective point of view

zhǔguǎn 主管 ① to take charge of ② the boss; the chief

zhǔjī 主机 ① the main engine ② (air force) the lead plane; the leader ③ the host computer

zhǔjiàn 主见 the ideas or thoughts of one's own

zhǔjiǎng 主讲 ① to lecture; to speak on a special subject ② the main speaker

zhǔjiào 主教 a bishop

zhǔjué 主角 the leading player; the leading character in a novel; a hero or heroine; a protagonist

zhǔlì 主力 the main force

zhǔliú 主流 ① the mainstream ② the essential or main aspect

zhǔquán 主权 ① sovereignty ② the right of autonomy

zhǔrén 主人 ① an owner ② a host ③ a master

zhǔrénwēng 主人翁 ① a respectful term for a host ② a master

zhǔrèn 主任 the head of an office

zhǔshí 主食 staple food

zhǔtí 主题 the main theme (of an essay); the gist

zhǔtǐ 主体 ① the main body or the most important part of something ② the subjective (as against the objective)

zhǔxí 主席 a chairman; a president

zhǔyǎn 主演 to star; to play the leading role in a play or a motion picture

zhǔyào 主要 essential; important; major

zhǔyì 主义 a principle; a doctrine

zhǔyi 主意 an idea; a suggestion

zhǔyīn 主因 the major (or principal) cause

zhǔyǔ 主语 (grammar) the subject

Z

of a sentence

zhǔzǎi 主宰 ① the man in charge ② a god ③ to dominate; to dictate

zhǔzhāng 主张 ① to advocate ② an opinion

zhǔzhǐ 主旨 the gist, substance, or purport

zhǔzhì 主治 ① the major function of a drug ② a physician in charge of a patient or patients

zhǔzhì yīshī 主治医师 a physician in charge of a case

zhǔzhóu 主轴 (machinery) the main shaft; the spindle

zhǔ 拄 ① to lean on (a stick, etc.) ② a post; a prop ③ to ridicule; to make sarcastic remarks

zhǔ 煮 to cook; to boil; to stew; to decoct

zhǔfèi 煮沸 to boil

zhǔ 属 to instruct ⇨shǔ

zhǔfù 嘱咐 to instruct or bid (a person to do something)

zhǔtuō 嘱托 to entrust (a person with a task); to request (a person to do something)

zhǔmù 嘱目 to be the focus of attention

zhùlì 伫立 to stand still; to stand motionless

zhù 助 to help; to aid; to assist; help; assistance

zhùgōng 助攻 (military) a holding (or secondery) attack

zhùjiào 助教 a teaching assistant; a TA

zhùlǐ 助理 ① an assistant ② to assist

zhùlì 助力 help; assistance

zhùshǒu 助手 an assistant; a helper; an aide

zhùzhǎng 助长 to encourage (a tendency); to promote the development of

zhù 住 ① to dwell; to inhabit; to live ② to stop ③ used after verb to complement its meaning

zhùchù 住处 a residence; a dwelling; lodging; a domicile

zhùfáng 住房 housing; lodgings

zhùhù 住户 a resident family

zhùjiā 住家 a residence; a home

zhùmín 住民 an inhabitant; a resident

zhùsù 住宿 to stay overnight; to lodge

zhùsuǒ 住所 a dwelling place; a home; a residence; a domicile

zhùyuàn 住院 to be hospitalized

zhùzhái 住宅 a residence; a dwelling; a house

zhùzháiqū 住宅区 a residential area, district, or quarter

zhùzhǐ 住址 address

zhù 注 ① to pour (liquid) ② to concentrate; to engross; preoccupation ③ an explanatory note; a footnote; a commentary or remark; to annotate ④ stakes (in gambling) ⑤ to register; to record or list

zhùcè 注册 to register; registration

zhùdìng 注定 to be doomed; to be destined

zhùjiě 注解 ① to annotate ② a footnote; an annotation

zhùmíng 注明 to explain or state clearly in writing

zhùmù 注目 to gaze at; to stare at

zhùrù 注入 to pour into; to empty into

zhùshè 注射 to inject; to get a shot

zhùshì 注视 to look attentively

zhùshì 注释 ① to annotate ② a footnote; an annotation

zhùyì 注意 to pay attention to; to watch

zhùyìlì 注意力 attention

zhùyīn 注音 to make phonetic transcriptions

zhùzhòng 注重 to lay stress on; to emphasize

zhù 驻 ① to halt ② to remain temporarily; to station (troops, diplomatic representatives, etc.)

Z

zhùzhā/zhùzhá 驻扎 (said of troops) to be stationed at

zhùzi 柱子 a pillar; a post

zhù 祝 ① to wish someone happiness; to pray for happiness ② to congratulate; to felicitate ③ to celebrate ④ a surname

zhùfú 祝福 ① to bless ② to wish happiness to

zhùhè 祝贺 to congratulate; to felicitate; congratulations

zhùyuàn 祝愿 to pray for something

zhùchēng 著称 famous; renowned; celebrated

zhùmíng 著名 famous; renowned; celebrated

zhùzuò 著作 ① a literary work ② to write

zhùzuòquán 著作权 copyright

zhùyá 蛀牙 decayed teeth; dental caries

zhù 铸 ① to melt or cast metal; to coin; to mint ② to make or commit (blunders, etc.) ③ to educate and influence (a person) ④ a surname

zhùzào 铸造 ① to melt or cast (metal) ② to educate ③ to mint (coins)

zhù/zhú 筑 to build (out of earth, rock, etc.)

zhuā 抓 ① to grasp; to seize; to take; to snatch; to make a snatch at; to catch ② to scratch ③ to arrest

zhuājǐn 抓紧 to grasp firmly

zhuāzhù 抓住 ① to grasp; to grip; to clutch ② to keep from going away; to hold ③ to grip somebody's attention

zhuǎzi 爪子 a claw; a paw; a talon

zhuān 专 ① exclusive; special ② to monopolize ③ to specialize ④ to concentrate; to focus

zhuān'àn 专案 a special case (to be dealt with separately)

zhuāncháng 专长 a special skill; a specialty

zhuānchéng 专程 a special trip

zhuānfǎng 专访 a report pro-

duced by a journalist after having paid a special visit to the person or persons concerned

zhuāngōng 专攻 to specialize in

zhuānguì 专柜 a special counter; a counter dealing in specific commodities

zhuānjī 专机 a plane designated for a special use

zhuānjí 专辑 an album (of songs, etc.)

zhuānjiā 专家 a specialist; an expert

zhuānjīng 专精 to concentrate one's efforts or energy on

zhuānkē 专科 a particular course or field of study

zhuānlán 专栏 a special column (in a newspaper or magazine)

zhuānlì 专利 a monopoly; a patent

zhuānlìquán 专利权 a patent; a patent right

zhuānmén 专门 ① a specialty; a special field ② exclusively

zhuānrén 专人 a person specially assigned for a task

zhuānrèn 专任 (of an employee) full time; full-time

zhuāntí 专题 a special subject

zhuānxiàn 专线 ① a special railway line ② a special telephone line

zhuānxīn 专心 to be concentrated on; to focus on

zhuānyè 专业 ① a special field of study; a specialty ② a specialized trade

zhuānyèhù 专业户 specialized household

zhuānyòng 专用 to use exclusively

zhuānyuán 专员 a specialist in the government

zhuānzhèng 专政 dictatorship

zhuānzhì 专制 tyrannical; despotic; autocratic

zhuānzhù 专注 to concentrate one's attention on

zhuān 砖 brick

zhuǎn 转 ① to turn ② to take a turn; to shift; to change ③ to transport; to convey; to transfer ④ indirect; roundabout ⑤ to roll ⑥ to migrate; to move ⇨**zhuàn**

zhuǎnbiàn 转变 ① to undergo changes; to change ② a change or shift (of attitude, thinking, etc.)

zhuǎnbō/zhuànbò 转播 to relay a broadcast or telecast

zhuǎndá 转达 to transmit through another person or office; to convey

zhuǎndòng 转动 to budge; to move

zhuǎngào 转告 to pass on (words); to communicate; to transmit

zhuǎnhuà 转化 ① to change; to transform ② to react chemically

zhuǎnhuàn 转换 transition; to change; to switch

zhuǎnjī 转机 a turning point (usually from bad to good); a favorable turn

zhuǎnjiāo 转交 to send or deliver through or in care of another person

zhuǎnràng 转让 to transfer (ownership, title, etc.)

zhuǎnrù 转入 to change over to; to shift to; to switch over to

zhuǎnshēn 转身 to turn the body; to turn round

zhuǎnshǒu 转手 ① to pass on; to sell on what one has bought ② a very brief period of time

zhuǎntóuzī 转投资 external investment

zhuǎnwān 转弯 to take a turn; to turn in another direction

zhuǎnxiàng 转向 (said of wind) to change directions

zhuǎnyǎn 转眼 a very brief period of time; in the twinkling of an eye; an instant

zhuǎnyè 转业 to change one's trade; to change one's career

zhuǎnyí 转移 to change in position or direction; to divert; to shift;

to turn; to transfer

zhuǎnzǎi/zhuǎnzài 转载 to reprint (articles published in another publication)

zhuǎnzhàng 转账 to transfer accounts (in banking)

zhuǎnzhé 转折 complications; twists and turns

zhuàn 传 a biography ⇨**chuán**

zhuànjì 传记 a biography

zhuàn 转 to turn round and round; to rotate; to revolve; to gyrate ⇨**zhuǎn**

zhuàn 赚 to earn; to make money; to gain

zhuànqián 赚钱 to earn money; to make a profit

zhuàn 撰 to write; to compose

zhuànxiě 撰写 to write; to compose

zhuāng 妆 ① to doll up; to adorn oneself; to apply makeup ② jewels, etc. for adornment ③ to disguise; to pretend

zhuāng 庄 ① a village; a hamlet ② a large farmhouse; a manor house ③ solemn; dignified; stately; august; sober; gravity ④ a market; a shop; a store; a bank ⑤ a surname

zhuāngjia 庄稼 crops; harvests

zhuāngyán 庄严 ① dignified; solemn; stately; august ② to adorn; to make solemn

zhuāngzhòng 庄重 dignified; solemn

Zhuāngzǐ 庄子 ① Zhuang Zhou, a contemporary of Mencius who advocated Taoism ② the works of Zhuang Zhou

zhuāngzi 庄子 the landlord's mansion; a manor house; a farm village

zhuāng 桩 ① a stake; a post; a pile ② a measure word for affairs

zhuāng 装 ① to fill in or up; to pack; to load ② to install (machines, equipment, etc.) ③ to adorn; to dress or make up; ornamental

dressing; to decorate (a room, etc.) ④ to disguise ⑤ to pretend; to feign ⑥ to store; to keep ⑦ clothes and personal effects

zhuāngbàn 装扮 ① adornment; make-up; to dress or doll up; attire ② to disguise

zhuāngbèi 装备 equipment or an outfit

zhuāngchuán 装船 to load cargoes aboard a freighter

zhuānghuáng 装潢 to decorate (a room, shop, etc.); decoration

zhuāngpèi 装配 to assemble (a machine)

zhuāngshè 装设 to install; to equip

zhuāngshì 装饰 ① to doll up; to deck; to make up ② to adorn; to embellish

zhuāngxiè 装卸 to load and unload

zhuāngyùn 装运 to pack and transport; to load and ship

zhuāngzhì 装置 ① an installation; a (mechanical) device; a unit; a plant ② to install (equipment, etc.)

zhuàng 壮 ① strong; robust; vigorous; sturdy ② to strengthen ③ portly; stout ④ big; great ⑤ the prime of one's life

zhuàngdà 壮大 ① big and strong; vigorous ② to expand

zhuàngguān 壮观 a grand sight; a great sight

zhuànglì 壮丽 splendorous

zhuàngliè 壮烈 courageous

zhuàngzhì 壮志 great aspiration; great ambition

zhuàng 状 ① a condition; a state; a situation ② appearance; look; shape; form ③ written appeal ④ a certificate ⑤ to describe; to narrate; description

zhuàngkuàng 状况 a situation; circumstances; conditions

zhuàngtài 状态 a situation; a state; a condition

zhuàngyǔ 状语 (linguistics) an adverbial modifier

zhuàngyuan 状元 ① the top successful candidate in the imperial examination ② the very best

zhuàng 撞 ① to bump; to run into; to collide; to dash ② to meet by chance

zhuàngjī/zhuàngjí 撞击 to ram; to dash

zhuàngqiú 撞球 ① billiards ② billiard balls

zhuī 追 ① to chase; to pursue; to follow; to trace ② to drive; to expel ③ to demand insistently; to dun for ④ to try to recover (stolen goods, etc.)

zhuībǔ 追捕 to pursue and apprehend; to chase

zhuīchá 追查 to investigate; to trace (by observing marks, tracks, bits of evidence, etc.)

zhuīdào 追悼 to commemorate (the dead)

zhuīgǎn 追赶 to pursue; to chase; to try to catch up with

zhuījiā 追加 to make an addition (to a document, etc.)

zhuījiū/zhuījiù 追究 ① to investigate (a fault, offense, etc.) and punish (the guilty) ② to try insistently to find out (the ultimate cause, etc.)

zhuīqiú 追求 ① to seek; to pursue; to go after ② to court (a woman); courtship

zhuīsuí 追随 to follow

zhuīwèn 追问 to question insistently

zhuīxún 追寻 to seek; to pursue

zhuīzhú 追逐 to chase; to pursue

zhuīzōng 追踪 ① to follow the examples of the predecessors ② to trace; to trail

zhǔn 准 ① to approve; to permit; to grant ② in accordance with ③ definitely; certainly ④ a rule; a criterion; a standard; accurate; accuracy ⑤ level; even ⑥ to aim; to sight ⑦ would-be (son-in-law, bride, etc.); to-be ⑧ (law) quasi

zhǔnbèi 准备 ① to prepare; to

Z

get ready ② to plan

zhǔnkǎozhèng 准考证 a ticket used to enter a testing center to take an exam (like for the SAT, GRE, MSAT, etc.)

zhǔnquè 准确 correct; accurate; precise

zhǔnshí 准时 punctual; punctuality

zhǔnxǔ 准许 to approve; to permit; to allow

zhǔnzé 准则 a rule; a standard; a criterion

zhuō 捉 ① to seize; to grasp; to catch; to hold ② to apprehend; to arrest

zhuō 桌 ① a table; a desk ② dishes for guests around the table ③ a tableful of guests

zhuōmiàn 桌面 the top of a table

zhuōqiú 桌球 table tennis; Ping-Pong

zhuōzi 桌子 a table; a desk

zhuózhuàng 茁壮 vigorous; strong

zhuóyuè 卓越 excellent; remarkable

zhuóliáng 酌量 to weigh and consider

zhuóqíng 酌情 to take circumstances into consideration; to make allowance

zhuó 啄 (said of a bird) to peck

zhuó 着 ① to wear (garments, etc.) ② to apply (color, etc.); to start

zhuó/zháo 着 to hit the bull's-eye; right to the point; very worthwhile
⇨zhāo, zháo, zhe

zhuóshí 着实 ① concrete and substantial; dependable ② really

zhuóshǒu 着手 to start doing something

zhuóxiǎng/zháoxiǎng 着想 for the sake of

zhuóyǎn/zháoyǎn 着眼 to watch; to eye with attention

zhuózhòng 着重 to emphasize; emphasis

zhuómó 琢磨 ① to cut and polish ② to study and improve
⇨zuómó

zīxún 咨询 to inquire; to consult

zī 姿 ① the manner; an air; carriage; bearing ② looks

zīshì 姿势 ① carriage; deportment; bearing ② (in photography) a pose

zītài 姿态 ① carriage; deportment; bearing ② a gesture

zī 资 ① money; wealth; property; means; capital ② one's qualifications, position, or record of service ③ natural endowments or gifts; one's disposition ④ to avail of ⑤ to aid or help; to assist; to subsidize; to support ⑥ to supply; to provide ⑦ expenses; fees; charges ⑧ to trust to

zīběn 资本 funds; capital

zīběnjiā 资本家 a capitalist

zīběn zhǔyì 资本主义 capitalism

zīchǎn 资产 ① property; real estate ② (accounting) assets

zīchǎn jiējí 资产阶级 the bourgeoisie; the middle class

zīfāng 资方 the management (of a shop, factory, etc.); capital

zīgé 资格 qualifications, requirements, or seniority of a person

zījīn 资金 funds; capital

zīlì 资历 qualifications and experiences (of an applicant, etc.); professional background

zīliào 资料 data

zīliàokù 资料库 (computer) data base; data bank

zīshēn 资深 senior; seniority

zīxùn 资讯 information

zīyuán 资源 resources; natural resources

zīzhèng 资政 a political advisor to the President of the Republic of China

zīzhù 资助 to help another with money

zīshāng 谘商 (psychology)

counseling

zīxún 咨询 to inquire and consult; to seek advice

zīshēng 孳生 to grow and multiply

zīrùn 滋润 ① to freshen; to enrich ② to moisten; moist

zīwèi 滋味 taste; flavor

zīzhǎng 滋长 to grow; to thrive

zǐ 子 ① a child; a son; an offspring ② a seed; an egg ③ the first of the twelve Terrestrial Branches ④ a rank of the nobility equivalent to a viscount ⑤ a designation used in speaking of or to a man in former times (somewhat similar to "mister")

zǐdàn 子弹 a bullet

zǐdì 子弟 young dependents; children

zǐgōng 子宫 the womb; the uterus

zǐgōngjǐng 子宫颈 the cervix (of the womb)

zǐgōngjǐng'ái 子宫颈癌 cervical cancer

zǐnǚ 子女 sons and daughters; children

zǐsūn 子孙 descendants; posterity

zǐ 仔 ① careful ② (said of animals or fowls) young

zǐxì 仔细 careful; punctilious; attentive

zǐ 姊 one's elder sister or sisters

zǐmèi 姊妹 sisters

zǐ 籽 seeds of plants

zǐ 紫 purple; violet

Zǐjìnchéng 紫禁城 the Forbidden City in Peking with four gates and a circumference of approximately four kilometers

zǐsè 紫色 purple; violet

zǐwàixiàn 紫外线 ultraviolet rays

zǐwēi/zǐwéi 紫薇 (botany) crape myrtle

zì 自 ① from ② self; personal; private; in person; personally ③ natural; naturally ④ a surname

zìbēi 自卑 to underestimate oneself

zìbìzhèng 自闭症 (psychiatry) autism

zìchēng 自称 to call oneself; to claim

zìcǐ 自此 from then on; henceforth

zìcóng 自从 since then; ever since

zìdòng 自动 ① voluntary; of one's own free will ② automatic

zìdònghuà 自动化 automation; to automate

zìfā 自发 to work without being prodded; to take the initiative; spontaneous

zìfèi 自费 to pay one's own expenses

zìfù-yíngkuī 自负盈亏 (said of an enterprise) to assume sole responsibility for its profits or losses

zìgǔ 自古 since ancient times

zìgǔyǐlái 自古以来 since ancient times

zìháo 自豪 to feel proud of; to take pride in

zìjǐ 自己 self; oneself; one's person

zìjiā 自家 (colloquial) oneself

zìjué 自觉 ① self-consciousness ② to feel something concerning oneself; aware

zìláishuǐ 自来水 running water; tap water

zìlì 自立 independent; self-supporting

zìlì-gēngshēng/zìlì-gèngshēng 自力更生 to achieve self-renewal with one's own effort; self-reliance

zìlǜ 自律 ① to control oneself; to exercise self-restraint or self-control; self-discipline ② (ethics) autonomy

zìmǎn 自满 complacency; to be satisfied with oneself

zìqiáng 自强 to goad oneself; to drive oneself hard; to strive for improvement or progress

Z

zìrán 自然 ① nature ② certainly; surely; of course ③ (in primary school) a subject or course of study concerning natural sciences

zìran 自然 at ease; natural

zìrán'érrán 自然而然 a matter of course

zìránjiè 自然界 the natural world, including animals, plants and minerals

zìrán kēxué 自然科学 natural sciences

zìrèn 自认 ① to believe ② to accept adversity with resignation

zìshā 自杀 to commit suicide; suicide

zìshēn 自身 oneself

zìshǐ-zhìzhōng 自始至终 from beginning to end

zìshì 自是 ① to consider oneself as right ② from then on; since then

zìsī 自私 selfish; selfishness

zìsī-zìlì 自私自利 selfish; selfishness

zìwèi 自卫 self-defense; to defend oneself

zìwǒ 自我 self; ego

zìxiāng-máodùn 自相矛盾 inconsistent

zìxìn 自信 self-confidence

zìxíng 自行 individually; personally; by oneself

zìxíngchē 自行车 a bicycle; a bike

zìxìng 自性 (Buddhism) one's original and unaltered nature

zìxiū 自修 to learn and practice by oneself

zìxué 自学 to study on one's own; to study independently; to teach oneself

zìyán-zìyǔ 自言自语 to talk to oneself

zìyòng 自用 ① to do something without consulting others; to have morbid faith in one's talent and capability ② for personal or private (property); for personal or private use

zìyóu 自由 ① freedom; liberty ② at ease ③ of one's own free will

zìyóuchē xiéhuì 自由车协会 an amateur cycling association

zìyóushì 自由式 (swimming) freestyle

zìyóu shìchǎng 自由市场 free market

zìyóu-zìzài 自由自在 carefree

zìyuàn 自愿 voluntary

zìzài 自在 freely

zìzai 自在 at ease (with oneself and the world)

zìzé 自责 to blame oneself; self-reproach

zìzhì 自制 ① self-restraint; self-discipline ② self-made; self-manufactured; to manufacture locally or by the plant concerned

zìzhì 自治 ① autonomy ② self-discipline

zìzhìqū 自治区 an autonomous region

zìzhǔ 自主 independent; autonomy

zìzhǔquán 自主权 sovereignty (of a state)

zìzhù 自助 self-help; to help oneself

zìzhuàn 自传 an autobiography

zìzūn 自尊 ① self-respect; self-esteem ② egotistic

zìzūnxīn 自尊心 a sense of self-respect; self-esteem

zì 字 ① a word; a character; a letter; a logograph ② (formerly) a name or style taken at the age of 20, by which one was sometimes called

zìdiǎn 字典 a dictionary; a lexicon; a thesaurus

zìfú 字符 (computer) character

zìmǔ 字母 an alphabet; a letter (of an alphabet)

zìmù 字幕 subtitle

zìtǐ 字体 (printing) a style of letter or character; a type

zìxíng 字形 the form of a (written or printed) character

Z

zìyǎn 字眼 a word; a character

zìyàng 字样 ① models of Chinese characters ② words or phrases used in a certain context

zōng 宗 ① a sect; a religion ② an ancestor; a clan ③ to believe in ④ a surname

zōngjiào 宗教 religion

zōngpài 宗派 ① branches of a clan or a religion ② schools of philosophy or academic learning

zōngzhǐ 宗旨 a purpose; an objective

zōng/zòng 综 ① synthesis ② to sum up ③ to arrange

zōnghé/zònghé 综合 synthesis; synthesize

zōngyì jiémù/zòngyì jiémù 综艺节目 a variety show

zōngsè 棕色 brown, the color of palm fibers

zōng 踪 ① a footprint; a track; traces; a vestige ② to follow the tracks of; to keep track of; to trail

zōngjì/zōngjì 踪迹 ① a track; traces; a vestige ② to keep track; to follow up clues

zōngyǐng 踪影 traces; a vestige

zǒng 总 ① to gather; to collect; to assemble; to unite ② chief; principal; central ③ all; general; overall; complete; total ④ always ⑤ at any rate; in any event

zǒngbiānjí 总编辑 an editor-in-chief

zǒngbù 总部 headquarters

zǒngcái 总裁 a director general, president, or governor (of a bank, political party, etc.)

zǒngdàilǐ 总代理 (business) a general agent

zǒngdeláishuō 总的来说 to sum up; in short; in a word

zǒngdé 总得 to have to; somehow

zǒngdū 总督 a viceroy; a governor-general

zǒng'é 总额 the total amount; the sum total

zǒng'éryánzhī 总而言之 in

short; in brief; in a word; in conclusion; to sum up

zǒnggōnghuì 总工会 a federation of labor unions

zǒnggòng 总共 altogether; in all; all told

zǒnghé 总和 the sum total; the total

zǒnghuì 总会 ① a conglomeration; an assemblage; a collection ② central committee or administrative body (of an association, etc.) ③ a club ④ bound to; inevitable; sure to happen

zǒngjì 总计 the sum total; the total; the grand total

zǒngjià 总价 the total (price)

zǒngjiān 总监 an inspector general; a chief inspector

zǒngjié 总结 ① summation; conclusion; finale ② to sum up

zǒngjīnglǐ 总经理 a general manager

zǒnglǐ 总理 ① a prime minister; a premier ② a president (of a political party, etc.)

zǒngshì 总是 always; without exception

zǒngshù 总数 the total amount; the sum total

zǒngsīlìng 总司令 a commander in chief

zǒngsuàn 总算 ① on the whole; in general ② finally

zǒngtǒng 总统 the president (of a state)

zǒngtǒng dàxuǎn 总统大选 a presidential election

zǒngtǒngfǔ 总统府 the presidential office

zǒngwù 总务 general affairs

zǒngzhī 总之 in short; in brief; in a word; in conclusion; to sum up

zònghéng/zōnghéng 纵横 ① the horizontal and the vertical; in length and breadth ② (during the Epoch of Warring States) the two opposing principles of a confederacy against Qin and a federation under Qin ③ to roam

Z

about without opposition ④ with great ease

zònghuǒ 纵火 to commit arson

zòngrán 纵然 even though; even if

zòngróng 纵容 to connive at

zòngshǐ 纵使 even though; even if

zòngzi 粽子 a glutinous rice dumpling; rice tamale

zǒu 走 ① to walk; to go on foot ② to leave; to go away; to depart ③ to visit ④ to let out or lose (unintentionally); to leak out ⑤ to go; to travel

zǒudào 走道 ① a pavement; a sidewalk ② a path; a footpath ③ an aisle

zǒudòng 走动 ① to take a walk; to go for a stroll ② to have intercourse; to visit

zǒufǎng 走访 ① to visit ② to interview; to have an interview with

zǒugǒu 走狗 a lackey; a tool

zǒuhòumén 走后门 to get in by the back door; to secure advantages through pull or influence

zǒukai 走开 Beat it! Get out of the way!

zǒuláng 走廊 a corridor; a hall; a veranda

zǒulòu 走漏 (said of secrets, plots, etc.) to leak out

zǒulù 走路 to walk; to go on foot

zǒusī 走私 to smuggle

zǒuxiàng 走向 ① the run; the trend ② (geology) strike ③ to move toward; to head for; to be on the way to

zǒuzou 走走 to take a walk; to take an airing

zòu 奏 ① to play (music or musical instruments) ② to report to the throne ③ to achieve; to produce; to perform

zòu 揍 ① to beat; to slug (somebody); to hit hard

zū 租 ① to rent; to lease; to let; to hire; to charter ② rent; rental ③ a tax; to tax

zūjiè 租界 a foreign settlement or concession

zūjīn 租金 rent or rental

zūlìn 租赁 to rent (a house, etc.); to lease

zūyòng 租用 to rent for use; to be tenanted

zú 足 ① the foot; the leg ② sufficient; full; enough; adequate ③ the base (of an object)

zúgòu 足够 enough; sufficient; full; ample

zújì/zújì 足迹 ① whereabouts ② a footprint; a footmark; a track

zúqiú 足球 football; soccer

zúyǐ 足以 sufficient to; enough to

zúzú 足足 full; no less than; as much as

zú 族 ① a tribe; a family ② a race (of people) ③ a class or group of things with common features

zúqún 族群 an ethnic group

zúrén 族人 fellow clansmen

zǔ 阻 ① to hinder; to obstruct; to impede; to blockade ② to separate; separated ③ to prevent; to stop; to prohibit ④ difficulty; to suffer ⑤ to rely on ⑥ a strategic pass

zǔài 阻碍 an obstacle or hindrance; to obstruct; obstruction; to impede

zǔdǎng 阻挡 to stop; to be in the way

zǔlán 阻拦 to stop; to prevent; to retard

zǔlì 阻力 the force of resistance

zǔnáo 阻挠 to obstruct; to thwart; obstruction

zǔsè 阻塞 ① to block up; to clog; to obstruct ② a jam; a block

zǔzhǐ 阻止 to stop or prevent; to prohibit or proscribe; to block

zǔ 组 ① a group; a team; a section; a department; an organization; a union ② to organize; to arrange; to unite; to form ③ tassels; a fringe; a girdle; a tape

zǔchéng 组成 to form; to constitute

Z

zǔhé 组合 ① to unite; to make up ② (mathematics) combinations ③ a company; a union

zǔjiàn 组件 (electricity) a package; a module

zǔzhǎng 组长 the chief of a department or section in a government agency

zǔzhī 组织 ① to organize; to constitute ② an organization; a formation ③ (biology) tissue; texture

zǔzhuāng 组装 to assemble; to put together

zǔfù 祖父 one's grandfather

zǔguó 祖国 one's homeland; one's fatherland

zǔmiào 祖庙 an ancestral shrine or temple

zǔmǔ 祖母 one's grandmother

zǔxiān 祖先 forefathers; ancestors; forebears

zǔzong 祖宗 forefathers; ancestors; forebears

zuān 钻 ① to pierce; to drill; to bore; to dig through; to penetrate ② to go through; to make one's way into ③ to study intensively; to dig into; to bury oneself in ④ to gain (profit, a position, etc.) through special favor, contact, relations, etc. ⑤ to bore or pierce a hole
⇨zuàn

zuānyán 钻研 to study or scrutinize thoroughly

zuàn 钻 ① a diamond; a jewel ② a gimlet; an awl or auger; a borer; a drill
⇨zuān

zuànjiè 钻戒 a diamond ring

zuànshí 钻石 a diamond

zuǐ 嘴 ① the mouth; the bill or beak (of a bird); the snout (of a pig, etc.) ② a nozzle

zuǐbā 嘴巴 the mouth

zuǐchún 嘴唇 the lips

zuì 最 extreme; superlative

zuìchū 最初 ① the first; the earliest ② at first; in the beginning

zuìduō 最多 the most; at most

zuìhǎo 最好 ① had better ② the best

zuìhòu 最后 the last; the ultimate; the final

zuìjiā 最佳 the best

zuìjìn 最近 ① the nearest; the closest ② recently; lately

zuìshǎo 最少 the least; the minimum

zuìzhōng 最终 the final; the last; the ultimate

zuì 罪 ① sin; crime; fault; vice; evil; guilt ② suffering; pain

zuì'è 罪恶 sin; crime; vice; evil; guilt

zuìfàn 罪犯 a criminal; an offender

zuìmíng 罪名 a charge (brought against a person)

zuìxíng 罪行 criminal acts; atrocities; offenses

zuìzhuàng 罪状 the nature of an offense or crime; a charge (brought against a person)

zuì 醉 ① drunk; intoxicated ② infatuated; charmed

zūn 尊 ① to honor; to respect; to venerate; to revere; to esteem ② honored; honorable; noble; esteemed; respectable

zūnguì 尊贵 noble; honorable; respectable

zūnjìng 尊敬 to respect; to revere; respect; reverence

zūnyán 尊严 dignity; honor; respectability

zūnzhòng 尊重 to venerate; to hold in reverence; to honor; to respect; to esteem; to uphold

zūnshǒu 遵守 to observe; to abide by; to keep (a promise)

zūnxún 遵循 to follow; to accord with; to obey; to go by

zūnzhào 遵照 to follow; to observe; to accord with; to obey

zuó 昨 yesterday; lately; past

zuórì 昨日 yesterday

zuótiān 昨天 yesterday

zuówǎn 昨晚 last night

Z

zuómo/zhuómó 琢磨 to ponder over; to consider ⇨zhuómó

zuǒ 左 ① the left side ② the east side ③ improper ④ to be demoted; to descend ⑤ inconvenience ④ erroneous; mistaken ⑦ unduly stubborn ⑧ to disregard

zuǒbian 左边 the left side; the left-hand side

zuǒcè 左侧 on the left side

zuǒshǒu 左手 the left hand

zuǒyòu 左右 ① left and right—nearby; at hand ② servants; aides ③ to sway

zuò 作 ① to do; to make ② the works (of a writer, etc.) ③ to write; to compose ④ to regard...as; to take...for ⑤ to rise up ⑥ to pretend; to affect

zuò'àn 作案 to commit a crime

zuòbì 作弊 to cheat (especially in examinations); to indulge in corrupt practices

zuòchéng 作成 to arrange or complete (a job); to help succeed (in an undertaking, etc.)

zuòfǎ 作法 a way of doing or handling things

zuòfèi 作废 to nullify; to cancel

zuòfēng 作风 one's way of doing things

zuòguài 作怪 mischievous; to act mischievously

zuòjiā 作家 a writer; an author

zuòpǐn 作品 the works

zuòqǔjiā 作曲家 a composer

zuòwéi 作为 ① conduct; behavior ② to accomplish ③ to serve as; to look upon as

zuòwén 作文 ① a composition ② to write a composition

zuòwù 作物 crops

zuòxī/zuòxí 作息 work and rest

zuòxiù 作秀 (informal) ① to appear in a stage show ② to grandstand

zuòyè 作业 students' homework

zuòyòng 作用 ① effect ② functions

zuòzhàn 作战 to go to battle; to fight against

zuòzhě 作者 a writer; an author

zuòzhèng 作证 to act as a witness in court

zuòzhǔ 作主 to take up responsibility for making a decision

zuò 坐 ① to sit; a seat ② to ride (on a bus, train, etc.) ③ (said of a building) to have its back towards ④ (said of a building) to fall back from pressure; to sink ⑤ to kneel ⑥ to get (profit, etc.) without work ⑦ to keep on; to persist in ⑧ to reach; to arrive at ⑨ (said of guns, etc.) to recoil; to kick

zuòbān 坐班 to keep office hours

zuòláo 坐牢 to be jailed or imprisoned

zuòxia 坐下 to sit down

zuòzhèn 坐镇 personally take charge of (an operation or mission)

zuò 座 a seat; a stand

zuòr 座儿 a seat

zuòtán 座谈 to have an informal discussion

zuòtánhuì 座谈会 a discussion meeting; a symposium

zuòwèi 座位 a seat

zuòyòumíng 座右铭 a motto

zuò 做 ① to work; to make; to do ② to act as ③ to pretend to be

zuò'ài 做爱 to make love

zuòcài 做菜 to cook; to prepare a meal

zuòdào 做到 to accomplish; to achieve

zuòfǎ 做法 way of doing a thing; practice

zuòfàn 做饭 to prepare food

zuògōng 做工 to work

zuòkè 做客 to be a guest

zuòmèng 做梦 ① to dream ② to daydream

zuòrén 做人 ① to conduct oneself; to behave

zuòshēngyi 做生意 to do busi-

ness transactions
zuòshì 做事 ① to handle affairs;

to do a deed; to act ② to work; to have a job

Z

Tips on Pronunciation

A Chinese syllable has three components: the initial, the final, and the tone. To help improve understanding, we use English pronunciation to represent the sounds of Mandarin. However, one must bear in mind that those English examples are provided only for better understanding; they are not exactly equivalent to sounds of Mandarin.

1. Initials:

There are 21 initials in total. The initials b, p, d, t, k, l, m, n, f, h, j are pronounced approximately like in English, while p, t, k should always be aspirated. However, some initials require more attention.

g	Always like g in "go," never like "orange."
s	Always like s in "see," never like "rose."
q	Like in "cheap," but with the lips spread.
x	Like in "sheet," but with the lips spread.
r	Like in "right," but with the lips spread.
z	Like in "kids."
c	Like in "cats."
zh[1]	Like in "jerk."
ch	Like in "church."
sh	Like in "shirt."

1 When you say zh, ch, sh, say it with the tip of your tongue curled back.

2. Finals:

There are 35 finals in total. Most of them are pronounced approximately like in English. They can be divided into 5 groups.

Simple vowels & diphthongs	a	Like in "f<u>a</u>ther."
	o	Like in "m<u>o</u>re."
	e	Like in "h<u>e</u>r," but stronger. [2]
	ai	Like in "<u>ai</u>sle."
	ei	Like in "<u>ei</u>ght."
	ao	Like in "h<u>ow</u>."
	ou	Like in "s<u>ou</u>l."
Simple vowels plus nasal endings	an	Simple vowel "a" + "n."
	en	Simple vowel "e" + "n."
	ang	Simple vowel "a" + "ng" like in "si<u>ng</u>."
	eng	Simple vowel "e" + "ng."
	ong	Like in "l<u>ong</u>."
Finals beginning with medial "i"	i	Like in "sk<u>i</u>." [3]
	ia, ie, iao, iou[4], in, ian, ing, iang, iong	Medial "i" + other finals.

	u	Like in "fl<u>u</u>te."
Finals beginning with medial "u"	ua, uo, uai, uei, uan, uen, uang, ueng	Medial "u" + other finals.
Finals beginning with medial "ü"	ü[5]	Say "i" as in "sk<u>i</u>." Maintain your tongue position, then round your lips and say "u" as in "flute."
	üe, üan, ün	Medial "ü" + other finals.

2 The pronunciation of simple vowel "e" differs from the compound vowel "e," like in "ei," "ie," or "uei," in which the "e" should be pronounced like in "l<u>e</u>t."

3 When "i" is preceded by zh, ch, sh, r, z, c, s, it is pronounced like in "s<u>i</u>r."

4 When "iou," "uei," "uen," is preceded by an initial, it should be changed into "iu," "ui," "un," e.g. "niu," "dui," "sun."

5 Only when "ü" is put together with the initial "n, l," the 2 dots should be retained, e.g. "n" + "ü" → "nü," but "x" + "ü" → "xu."

When finals beginning with a medial are not preceded by any initials, the medial should change its form, e.g. "i" → "yi," "ia" → "ya," "u" → "wu," "ua" → "wa," "ü" → "yu."

The finals in "s<u>un</u>" & "x<u>un</u>" or "z<u>u</u>" & "j<u>u</u>" look

the same, but will be pronounced differently.

3. Tones:

There are four tones in Mandarin Chinese. Tones refer to pitches of individual syllables. Usually, a syllable has a different meaning when it is pronounced with a different tone. The main four tones in Mandarin are marked as follows: − (1st), ́ (2nd), ̌ (3rd), ̀ (4th), and no mark to indicate the neutral tone. Marks are placed above the main vowel of a syllable, i.e. the one which is pronounced with the mouth widest open.

1st tone	high level	−	mā	妈	mother
2nd tone	middle rising	́	má	麻	hemp
3rd tone	falling rising	̌	mǎ	马	horse
4th tone	high falling	̀	mà	骂	scold

Introduction to Chinese Characters

The written form of the Chinese language consists of characters, which have a long standing history. The earliest known examples of Chinese writing were found on Neolithic pottery wares, which existed between 8000 and 5000 B.C. The primitive forms of Chinese writing closely resemble the later forms of writing, which became more abstract.

The total number of Chinese characters is estimated at more than 50,000, of which only about 5,000 are in common use, and about 2,000 are needed for daily life. Each character is placed in a square and stands for a meaningful syllable. The basic elements of writing characters include strokes, radicals, and the stroke order.

Basic Strokes of Chinese Characters

1. "、" — (diǎn) 点 a dot, e.g. 六, 言
2. "一" — (héng) 横, a horizontal stroke from left to right, e.g. 二, 三
3. "丨" — (shù) 竖, a vertical stroke from top to bottom, e.g. 中, 巾
4. "丿" — (piě) 撇, a slash down to the left, e.g. 人, 禾
5. "乀" — (nài) 捺, a slash down to the right, e.g. 果, 来

6. "ㇴ"— (tí) 提, a slash up to the right, e.g. 我, 海

7. "乛"— (héng gōu) 横钩, a horizontal stroke with a hook at the right end, e.g. 你, 字

8. "亅"— (shù gōu) 竖钩, a vertical stroke with a hook at the bottom to the left, e.g. 小, 事

9. "乀"— (xié gōu) 斜钩, a slash down to the right with a hook at the end, e.g. 我, 找

10. "ㄱ"— (héng zhé) 横折, a horizontal first and then turns to a vertical, e.g. 口, 国

11. "ㄴ"— (shù zhé) 竖折, a vertical first and then turns to a horizontal, e.g. 巨, 忙

12. "ㄋ"— (héng zhé gōu) 横折钩 a horizontal first and then turns to a vertical with a hook at the end, e.g. 包, 的

13. "ㄥ"— (shù zhé gōu) 竖折钩 a vertical first and then turns to a horizontal with a hook at the end, e.g. 吃, 九

Stroke Order of Writing Chinese Characters

1. Top to bottom as in "三": 一 → 二 → 三

2. Left to right as in "川": 丿 → 刂 → 川

3. Upper left corner to lower right corner as in "您": 亻 → 你 → 您

4. Outside to inside as in "月": 冂 → 月

5. When two or more strokes cross, horizontal strokes before perpendicular strokes as in "十": 一 → 十

6. Slash to the left before slash to the right as in "人": 丿 → 人

7. Center stroke before symmetrical wings as in "小": 亅 → 刂 → 小

8. Inside before sealing off the enclosure as in "回": 冂 → 回 → 回

Basic Composition of Chinese Characters

1. ☐	Only one part, for example: 人, 日, 月
2. ▤	One part on the top and the other in the bottom, equally occupy the square, e.g. 要, 雷, 票
3. ▤	One smaller part on the top and one larger part at the bottom, e.g. 买, 宜, 每
4. ▤	One larger part on the top and one smaller part at the bottom, e.g. 其, 且, 黑
5. ▤	Three parts equally occupy the square, e.g. 茶, 卖, 菜
6. ▤	One large part on the top and two smaller parts at the bottom, e.g. 药, 蒜, 筷
7. ▤	Two smaller parts on the top and one large part at the bottom, e.g. 想, 帮, 留
8. ▥	One part on the left and the other on the right, equally occupy the square, e.g. 期, 好, 找
9. ▥	One smaller part on the left and one larger part on the right, e.g. 仁, 块, 吃

10.		One larger part on the left and one smaller part on the right, e.g. 刻, 引, 到
11.		Three parts equally occupy the square, e.g. 谢, 渐, 随
12.		One large part on the left and two smaller parts on the right, e.g. 鞋, 临, 楷
13.		Two smaller parts on the left and one large part on the right, e.g. 封, 部, 影
14.		The lower right part surrounded by the upper left part, e.g. 床, 有, 房
15.		The lower left part surrounded by the upper right part, e.g. 可, 司, 句
16.		The upper right part surrounded by the lower left part, e.g. 这, 边, 还
17.		The upper right part surrounded by the lower bigger left part, e.g. 题, 起, 超
18.		One or more parts surrounded on three sides with only the right side open, e.g. 区, 匹, 匠
19.		One or more parts surrounded on three sides with only the bottom open, e.g. 间, 问, 风
20.		One or more parts surrounded on three sides with only the upper side open, e.g. 凶, 函, 幽

21. □ The outside part surrounds the inside part, e.g. 回, 因, 国

Radicals

Every character has a radical. The radicals are similar to the roots of English words. Therefore the radicals are helpful in recognizing, memorizing and reproducing characters.

There are a total of one hundred and eighty nine radicals in Chinese, of which some fifty are commonly used. These radicals are used either independently or as parts of more complex characters. They are meaning components — they generally succeed in giving a hint of the meaning of the character, such as "心 (xīn)" means "relating to thought and emotion," "言 / 讠(yán)" means "relating to speech," and "水(shuǐ)" means "relating to water." Most of the radicals are pictographs.

The radicals are also used to organize characters in Chinese dictionaries; therefore the knowledge of radicals can be advantageous in using a Chinese dictionary.

The Six Categories of Chinese Characters (六书 Liùshū)

The Six Categories (Pictograph 象形 xiàngxíng, Ideograph 指事 zhǐshì, Semantic Compound 会意 huìyì, Phonetic Compound 形声 xíngshēng,

Semantic Transfer 转注 zhuǎnzhù, and Phonetic Borrowing 假借 jiǎjiè) traditionally refer to the ways Chinese characters were originally composed or used. The first four types refer to the internal structures of characters, while the last two refer to how characters are used either semantically or phonetically. The following are examples of the first four types of Liùshū, which are the most common ways to compose Chinese characters.

1.   Pictograph 象形 xiàngxíng

Chinese pictographs, like Egyptian hieroglyphics, were the earliest form of writing and directly depicted actual objects, e.g.

彳 人 (rén, man), almost life-like drawing of a full human body.

⊙ 日 (rì, sun), which is a picture of the sun.

𝒫 月 (yuè, moon), which is a picture of the moon.

2.   Ideograph 指事 zhǐshì

Ideographic characters refer to objects or concepts not directly through an actual depiction but through the aid of a non-pictographic element. While pictographs are simplex, ideographs are in most cases complex as the letter incorporates a pictograph plus a referential indicator.

二 上 (shàng, above), which is a picture with an object above the horizon.

= 下 (xià, below), which is a picture with an object below the horizon.

人 大 (dà, big), a man full and maximally stretched.

朩 本 (běn, root), a line below a tree to refer to its

roots.

3.　Semantic Compound 会意 huìyì

　　　Semantic compounds are aggregate characters making use of mostly two pictographic and/or ideographic characters for the purpose of referring to new concepts or ideas. In this way, the meanings are implied.

囚 囚 (qiú, imprisonment), a man held in a cage.

休 休 (xiū, to rest), a man leaning against the tree.

从 从 (cóng, to follow), one man walking behind another.

林 林 (lín, woods), doubling the same item "tree" to represent a large quantity.

4.　Phonetic Compound 形声 xíngshēng

　　　Phonetic compound characters consist of two components, one of which, usually called a radical, indicates the semantic category the character belongs to, while the other, the phonetic element, refers to the sound, the pronunciation of the entire character. Of the characters still in use today, over 90% of them are phonetic compound characters.

河 河 (hé, river), 氵 means "water" and 可 pronounces kě.

草 草 (cǎo, grass), 艹 means "grass" and 早 pronounces zǎo.

味 味 (wèi, flavor), 口 means "mouth" and 未 pronounces wèi.

想 想 (xiǎng, think; miss), 心 means "heart" and 相 pronounces xiāng.

Essential Measure Words

量词	拼音	释义	例词
把	bǎ	a handful of; a bunch of	一把尺、一把刀、一把吉他、一把钥匙、一把伞、一把青菜、一把钞票、一把梳子、一把剪刀、一把眼泪、一把鼻涕
班	bān	1. a class; a group of 2. scheduled or regular runs (of the bus, etc.)	一班飞机、一班火车、一班公共汽车、一班学生
包	bāo	a package of; a sack of	一包香烟、一包米、一包面粉、一包零食、一包饼干、一包咖啡、一包糖
杯	bēi	a cup of; a glass of	一杯水、一杯咖啡、一杯茶、一杯果汁、一杯饮料、一杯可乐

本	běn	a book of	一本书、一本小说、一本笔记本、一本日记、一本课本、一本杂志、一本字典、一本漫画
笔	bǐ	a debt of; a sum of	一笔资料、一笔纪录、一笔生意、一笔交易、一笔开销、一笔款项、一笔钱
部	bù	a work of (novel, writing, etc.)	一部电影、一部小说、一部作品、一部电视剧、一部电脑、一部车
册	cè	a volume	一册故事书、一册教科书、一册账簿
层	céng	1. a layer; a story 2. a blanket of; a coat of	一层楼、一层阶梯、一层蛋糕、一层奶油、一层灰
场	chǎng	1. a measure word for a play, opera, movie, etc. 2. a bout of 3. a game of	一场表演、一场电影、一场游戏、一场比赛、一场雨、一场病、一场误会

匙	chí	a spoonful of	一匙糖、一匙盐巴、一匙汤、一匙油、一匙洗衣粉
出	chū	a measure word for plays	一出戏、一出舞台剧、一出电影、一出电视剧
串	chuàn	a string of; a cluster of	一串项链、一串珍珠、一串钥匙、一串鞭炮、一串葡萄、一串香蕉、一串烤肉
床	chuáng	a measure word for sheets, guilts	一床床单、一床棉被
次	cì	a measure word for occasions or events, such as experiences, etc.	一次经验、一次机会、一次失败、一次打击
打	dá	a dozen	一打鸡蛋、一打汽水、一打铅笔
袋	dài	a bag of; a sack of	一袋面粉、一袋米
道	dào	a beam of; a shaft of; a trail of	一道菜、一道伤口、一道光、一道彩虹、一道墙
滴	dī	a drop of	一滴眼泪、一滴血、一滴雨、一滴水

叠	dié	a pile of; a stack of; a wad of	一叠盘子、一叠钞票、一叠纸、一叠信、一叠账单
碟	dié	a plate of	一碟小菜、一碟花生
顶	dǐng	a measure word for hats, etc.	一顶假发、一顶帽子
栋	dòng	a measure word for houses, buildings, etc.	一栋房子、一栋别墅、一栋大楼、一栋公寓、一栋建筑物
段	duàn	a section of; a length of; a period of	一段文章、一段影片、一段旅程、一段感情、一段对话、一段时间、一段回忆
堆	duī	a pile of; a heap of	一堆土、一堆沙、一堆玩具、一堆雪、一堆石头、一堆垃圾
对	duì	a pair of; a couple of	一对耳环、一对戒指、一对手表、一对钢笔、一对花瓶、一对春联、一对情侣、一对夫妻、一对父子、一对儿女
队	duì	a group of; a troop of	一队球员、一队军队、一队士兵

顿	dùn	a measure word to indicate the number of times actions occur, such as meals, scoldings, etc.	一顿饭、一顿大餐、一顿打骂、一顿毒打
朵	duǒ	a measure word for flowers, etc.	一朵花、一朵玫瑰、一朵云
份	fèn	a copy of; a helping of; a piece of	一份餐点、一份早餐、一份礼物、一份报告、一份报纸、一份资料、一份情感、一份心意
封	fēng	a measure word for letters	一封信、一封讯息、一封情书
幅	fú	a measure word for pictures, scrolls, etc.	一幅画、一幅字帖、一幅海报
副	fù	1. a set of 2. a pack of; a pair of	一副眼镜、一副手套、一副扑克、一副碗筷、一副对联、一副德性、一副得意的样子
个	gè	a commonly used measure word	一个老师、一个人、一个故事、一个地方、一个钟头、一个杯子、一个苹果、一个鼻子、一个嘴巴

根	gēn	a piece of (string, rope, etc.); a bar of	一根头发、一根睫毛、一根火柴、一根手指、一根香蕉
罐	guàn	a can of; a jug of	一罐汽水、一罐饮料、一罐奶粉
锅	guō	a pot of	一锅饭、一锅粥、一锅热水、一锅热汤
行	háng	a line of	一行诗、一行字、一行泪
盒	hé	a box of	一盒饼干、一盒糖果、一盒巧克力、一盒火柴、一盒名片
壶	hú	a jug of	一壶茶、一壶水、一壶酒
户	hù	a household (a family)	一户人家、一户民宅
家	jiā	a measure word for families, enterprises, restaurants, hotels, etc.	一家餐厅、一家商店、一家电影院、一家超市、一家百货公司、一家公司、一家银行、一家人
架	jià	a measure word for airplanes, etc.	一架飞机、一架直升机、一架喷射机

间	jiān	a measure word for rooms	一间教堂、一间教室、一间办公室、一间房间
件	jiàn	a measure word for things, clothes, works, etc.	一件衣服、一件裤子、一件外套、一件工作、一件事、一件案件
节	jié	a measure word for class periods at school; a paragraph; a length of	一节课、一节新闻、一节车厢、一节甘蔗、一节竹子
局	jú	a game of; a round of	一局牌局、一局棋、一局球赛、一局比赛
句	jù	a line of; a word of	一句名言、一句话、一句成语、一句歌词
卷	juǎn juàn	a measure word for books, etc.; a roll of	一卷录音带、一卷录影带、一卷底片、一卷胶带、一卷竹简、一卷书
颗	kē	a measure word for the small round things, such as pills, etc.	一颗糖果、一颗药丸、一颗红豆、一颗子弹、一颗钻石、一颗心
棵	kē	a measure word for trees	一棵树、一棵植物

客	kè	a helping of; a portion of	一客牛排、一客套餐、一客冰品
口	kǒu	a measure word for people, cisterns, wells, etc.; a mouthful of	一口饮料、一口饭、一口井、一口人、一口气
块	kuài	a lump of; a piece of	一块肉、一块蛋糕、一块土地、一块木板、一块石头
捆	kǔn	a bale of; a wisp of	一捆木材、一捆稻草、一捆报纸、一捆书、一捆绳子
篮	lán	a basket of	一篮水果、一篮菜、一篮鸡蛋、一篮衣服
粒	lì	a grain (of rice, etc.)	一粒米、一粒饭、一粒豆子、一粒沙
辆	liàng	a measure word for vehicles	一辆车、一辆公共汽车、一辆出租车、一辆摩托车、一辆卡车
列	liè	a row of	一列火车、一列车厢、一列队伍

枚	méi	a measure word for coins, rockets, etc.	一枚硬币、一枚徽章、一枚邮票、一枚火箭、一枚炸弹
门	mén	a measure word for academic courses, subjects, or disciplines, etc.	一门学问、一门功课、一门学科、一门亲事
面	miàn	a measure word for things that are flat and smooth, such as mirrors, etc.	一面墙、一面镜子、一面黑板、一面旗子
名	míng	a measure word for people, especially one with profession or high social status	一名学生、一名教师、一名医生、一名护士、一名病患
排	pái	a line of	一排房屋、一排商店、一排座位、一排队伍、一排行道树
盘	pán	1. a plate of 2. (said of a chess match, etc.) a round of	一盘菜、一盘水果、一盘棋

盆	pén	1. a basin of 2. a pot of	一盆水、一盆花、一盆植物
批	pī	a batch of; an array of	一批货物、一批商品、一批乘客、一批旅客
匹	pǐ	1. a measure word for horses 2. a bolt of	一匹布、一匹马、一匹驴
篇	piān	a measure word for compositions, poems, etc	一篇文章、一篇散文、一篇小说、一篇演讲稿、一篇公告
片	piàn	1. a slice of 2. an area of	一片光盘、一片草地、一片树林、一片田野、一片花瓣、一片叶子、一片比萨、一片饼干、一片吐司、一片起司
瓶	píng	a bottle of	一瓶水、一瓶酒、一瓶汽水、一瓶果汁、一瓶香水
起	qǐ	a measure word for incidents	一起事故、一起火灾、一起意外、一起车祸、一起案件

群	qún	a group of; a crowd of; a flock of; a herd of	一群人、一群学生、一群小孩、一群绵羊、一群狗
扇	shàn	a measure word for door or gate leaves	一扇窗、一扇门
首	shǒu	a measure word for poems, songs, etc.	一首诗、一首曲子、一首歌、一首音乐
束	shù	a bundle of; a cluster of; a beam of	一束花、一束头发、一束光
双	shuāng	a pair of	一双鞋子、一双袜子、一双筷子、一双手套、一双手、一双眼睛、一双眉毛、一双儿女
艘	sōu	a measure word for ships	一艘船、一艘潜水艇、一艘游艇、一艘货轮、一艘邮轮、一艘巡洋舰
所	suǒ	a measure word for buildings	一所学校、一所机构、一所医院

台	tái	a measure word for machines, equipment, etc.	一台钢琴、一台冰箱、一台电脑、一台冷气机、一台电视机、一台洗衣机、一台音响、一台相机、一台录音机
堂	táng	a measure word for classes or periods	一堂课
套	tào	a suit of (clothes); a set of books, etc.	一套书、一套课程、一套餐具、一套洋装、一套西装、一套衣服
条	tiáo	a measure word for long narrow things; a bar of	一条项链、一条毛巾、一条马路、一条河、一条直线、一条鱼、一条龙、一条蛇
通	tōng tòng	a measure word for telegrams, documents, or to indicate the number of times a drum is beaten	一通电话、一通简讯、一通电报、一通鼓
桶	tǒng	a bucket of; a barrel of	一桶汽油、一桶水、一桶米

头	tóu	a measure word for cattle, etc.; a head of	一头牛、一头羊、一头象、一头狮子
团	tuán	a lump; a ball of	一团毛线、一团泥巴、一团火球、一团面团
碗	wǎn	a bowl of	一碗饭、一碗面、一碗汤、一碗水
位	wèi	a measure word for people (respective)	一位老师、一位学生、一位作家
箱	xiāng	a box of; a crate of	一箱珠宝、一箱衣服、一箱书、一箱饮料、一箱水果
项	xiàng	a measure word for tasks, requirements, decisions, etc.	一项比赛、一项运动、一项特技、一项建设、一项特征、一项规定
样	yàng	a sort of; a kind of; a type of	一样礼物、一样商品、一样菜、一样食材、一样水果
盏	zhǎn	a measure word for lamps or drinks	一盏灯、一盏酒

张	zhāng	a measure word for certain flat things, such as paper, paintings, etc.	一张纸、一张图片、一张卡片、一张照片、一张车票、一张桌子、一张椅子、一张嘴巴
只	zhī	a measure word for birds, goats, hands, etc.	一只狗、一只老虎、一只鸟、一只猫、一只耳环、一只袜子、一只手、一只耳朵、一只眼睛
支	zhī	a stick of; a contingent of	一支笔、一支蜡烛、一支口红、一支队伍、一支歌曲、一支球队
枝	zhī	a measure word for long thin piece of something; a branch of (flowers)	一枝花、一枝扫把、一枝笔

种	zhǒng	a kind of; a sort of	一种水果、一种动物、一种植物、一种颜色、一种说法、一种想法、一种方法、一种意见、一种心情、一种习惯
组	zǔ	a group of; a set of	一组密码、一组零件、一组家具、一组沙发、一组人员、一组乐队
座	zuò	a measure word for mountains, buildings, structures, etc.	一座山、一座湖、一座水池、一座桥、一座花园、一座灯塔、一座雕像、一座佛像

Numbers

1. Cardinal

○	一	二	三	四	五
0	1	2	3	4	5
líng	yī	èr	sān	sì	wǔ
NING	I	ar		SY	UO

六	七	八	九	十
6	7	8	9	10
liù	qī	bā	jiǔ	shí
Nu	chi	•		SR

百	千	万
100	1000	10000
bǎi	qiān	wàn
	chēn	

Chinese numbers are like building blocks

Saying Chinese numbers is a piece of cake. Learn the principles and you should be able to say any number you want. For example, 15 is "10+5 shíwǔ," 94 is "90+4 jiǔshísì," and 950 is "900+50 jiǔbǎi wǔshí."

Now try to say these numbers in Chinese.

numbers	your answers
20	
37	
88	
300	
532	
802	

The answers will be at the end of this chapter.

10,000≠ten thousand

Instead of "thousand" in English, "wàn (10,000/ten thousand)" is the basic unit of calculation for large sums in Chinese. Therefore, "a hundred thousand" should be "shíwàn" (10 × wàn), while a million is "bǎiwàn" (100 × wàn) and ten million is "qiānwàn" (1,000 × wàn). Another even larger unit called "yì (亿)" is required when calculating sums larger than a hundred million.

"èr" vs. "liǎng"

When followed by a measure word, "2" is pronounced as "liǎng," such as "liǎng ge rén (two persons)" or "liǎng zhāng piào (two tickets)." However the figure two is read "èr (2)" if no measure word goes immediately after it such as "èrshí (20)," "èrbǎi (200)," "èrqiān." In Taiwan, people say "liǎngbǎi (200)," "liǎngqiān (2000)" instead, but "liǎngshí (20)" is never allowed.

"4" is a big trouble

Some people find it is hard to distinguish between "4 (sì)" and "10 (shí)." In fact, they are similar to each other. If you mistake No.4 (sì hào) for No.10 (shí hào) when you are asking for directions, you most probably will get lost. Or when at a cashier, if you mistake "14 dollars (shísì kuàiqián)" for "40 dollars (sìshí kuàiqián)," then you definitely will suffer from a great loss.

By the way, you might find that in some buildings, especially in hospitals or hotels, there is no such thing as a fourth floor. This is because, the number 4, pronounced as "sì," sounds almost the same as "death (sǐ)," and no one would like to stay in a place that seems to say you are "doomed to die."

2. Ordinal

To form ordinals, all you have to do is to put the prefix "dì" in front of the cardinals. Therefore, "the first" should be "dì-yī."

第一 (dì-yī)	the first
第二 (dì-èr)	the second
第三 (dì-sān)	the third
第四 (dì-sì)	the fourth
第五 (dì-wǔ)	the fifth

The answers for the quiz in p.351

numbers	pinyin	characters
20	èrshí	二十
37	sānshíqī	三十七
88	bāshíbā	八十八
300	sānbǎi	三百
532	wǔbǎi sānshí'èr	五百三十二
802	bābǎi líng èr	八百零二

Practical Daily Usage
日常实用语句
Rìcháng Shíyòng Yǔjù

Asking for Directions 问路 wènlù

Excuse me, where is the railway station?
请问，火车站在哪里?
Qǐngwèn, huǒchēzhàn zài nǎli?

Excuse me, which direction is China Hotel?
请问，中国饭店怎么走?
Qǐngwèn, Zhōngguó Fàndiàn zěnme zǒu?

I'm lost.
我迷路了。
Wǒ mílù le.

Is there a post office near here?
这附近有邮局吗?
Zhè fùjìn yǒu yóujú ma?

Is this Zhongshan North Road?
这里是中山北路吗?
Zhèli shì Zhōngshān Běilù ma?

Bank 银行 yínháng

Can I withdraw cash using this credit card?
我能用这张信用卡领钱吗?
Wǒ néng yòng zhèi zhāng xìnyòngkǎ lǐngqián ma?

Can I exchange foreign currency (personal checks) here?
这里能兑换外币（私人支票）吗?
Zhèli néng duìhuàn wàibì (sīrén zhīpiào) ma?

Could you (please) tell me when the bank is open?
请告诉我银行的营业时间。
Qǐng gàosu wǒ yínháng de yíngyè shíjiān.

How much commission do you charge?
你们收多少手续费?
Nǐmen shōu duōshao shǒuxùfèi?

I would like to change some money.
我想兑换点儿钱。
Wǒ xiǎng duìhuàn diǎnr qián.

What is the exchange rate?
汇率是多少?
Huìlǜ shì duōshao?

Where are the ATMs?
哪里有自动柜员机?
Nǎli yǒu zìdòng guìyuánjī?

Communication 沟通 gōutōng

Can you translate this for me?
你能为我翻译一下吗?
Nǐ néng wèi wǒ fānyì yíxià ma?

Could you speak more slowly, please?
请你说慢一点儿。
Qǐng nǐ shuō màn yìdiǎnr.

Do you speak English?
你会说英语吗?
Nǐ huì shuō Yīngyǔ ma?

Do you understand?
你懂了吗?
Nǐ dǒngle ma?

Does anyone here speak English?
这儿有人会说英语吗?
Zhèr yǒu rén huì shuō Yīngyǔ ma?

How long have you been here?
你来多久了?
Nǐ lái duōjiǔ le?

I don't speak Chinese.
我不会说中文。
Wǒ bú huì shuō Zhōngwén.

I don't understand.
我不懂。
Wǒ bù dǒng.

I only speak a little Chinese.
我只会说一点儿中文。
Wǒ zhǐ huì shuō yìdiǎnr Zhōngwén.

Never mind.
没关系。
Méi guānxi.

No problem.
没问题。
Méi wèntí.

Not at all!
不客气!
Bú kèqi!

Please give me a hand.
请你帮我个忙。
Qǐng nǐ bāng wǒ ge máng.

Please write it down.
请你写下来。
Qǐng nǐ xiě xialai.

Sorry, could you please say that again?
对不起,请你再说一遍。
Duìbuqǐ, qǐng nǐ zài shuō yí biàn.

Thank you.
谢谢。
Xièxie.

What is today's date?
今天几月几号?
Jīntiān jǐ yuè jǐ hào?

What day is today?
今天星期几?
Jīntiān xīngqī jǐ?

What does this mean?
这是什么意思?
Zhè shì shénme yìsi?

What time is it?
现在几点?
Xiànzài jǐ diǎn?

Congratulations 祝贺 zhùhè

Congratulations!
恭喜!
Gōngxǐ!

Happy Birthday!
生日快乐!
Shēngrì kuàilè!

Happy New Year!
新年快乐!
Xīnnián kuàilè!

Have a nice weekend!
周末愉快!
Zhōumò yúkuài!

Have a safe trip!
一路顺风!
Yílù-shùnfēng!

I hope you have a good time!
祝你玩得愉快!
Zhù nǐ wán de yúkuài!

Greetings 招呼 zhāohu

Good-bye!
再见!
Zàijiàn!

Good morning!
早安!
Zǎo'ān!

Good night!
晚安!
Wǎn'ān!

Hello!
你好!
Nǐ hǎo!

Here's my name card.
这是我的名片。
Zhè shì wǒ de míngpiàn.

How have you been recently?
最近怎么样?
Zuìjìn zěnmeyàng?

It's nice to see you again.
很高兴再见到你。
Hěn gāoxìng zài jiàndào nǐ.

I've heard so much about you.
久仰。
Jiǔyǎng.

Long time no see!
好久不见!
Hǎo jiǔ bú jiàn!

Pleased to meet you.
很高兴认识你。
Hěn gāoxìng rènshi nǐ.

See you next time.
下次见。
Xiàcì jiàn.

Health 健康 jiànkāng

Can I have a medical certificate?
请给我开诊断书。
Qǐng gěi wǒ kāi zhěnduànshū.

Do you have anything for a cold?
我要治感冒的药。
Wǒ yào zhì gǎnmào de yào.

How do I take the medicine?
这个药怎么服用?
Zhèi ge yào zěnme fúyòng?

I caught a cold.
我感冒了。
Wǒ gǎnmào le.

I'd like to see an English-speaking doctor.
我要找个会说英语的医生。
Wǒ yào zhǎo ge huì shuō Yīngyǔ de yīshēng.

I don't feel well.
我觉得不舒服。
Wǒ juéde bù shūfu.

I feel dizzy.
我头晕。
Wǒ tóuyūn.

I feel sick.
我觉得想吐。
Wǒ juéde xiǎng tù.

I have a diarrhea.
我拉肚子。
Wǒ lādùzi.

I have a fever.
我发烧了。
Wǒ fāshāo le.

I have a pain here.
我这儿痛。
Wǒ zhèr tòng.

I have a sore throat (toothache).
我喉咙痛（牙痛）。
Wǒ hóulong tòng (yá tòng).

I have allergies to medicine.
我对药过敏。
Wǒ duì yào guòmǐn.

I want to register to see the doctor.
我要挂号。
Wǒ yào guàhào.

I've become ill.
我生病了。
Wǒ shēngbìng le.

I've been bitten by an insect.
我被虫子咬了。
Wǒ bèi chóngzi yǎo le.

Please explain what is wrong with me.
请告诉我是什么病。
Qǐng gàosu wǒ shì shénme bìng.

Where can I buy this medicine?
哪里能买到这个药？
Nǎli néng mǎidào zhèi ge yào?

Hotel 住宿 zhùsù

Are there any others?
还有没有别的房间？
Hái yǒu méiyǒu bié de fángjiān?

Could you have my baggage brought up?
请帮我把行李送来好吗？
Qǐng bāng wǒ bǎ xíngli sònglai hǎo ma?

Do you accept credit cards or traveler's checks?
可以使用信用卡或旅行支票吗？
Kěyǐ shǐyòng xìnyòngkǎ huò lǚxíng zhīpiào ma?

Do you give a discount for students?
学生有没有优惠？
Xuésheng yǒu méiyǒu yōuhuì?

Do you have a room available tonight?
今天晚上有没有房间？
Jīntiān wǎnshang yǒu méiyǒu fángjiān?

Do you have any off-season discount rate?
有没有淡季优惠？
Yǒu méiyǒu dànjì yōuhuì?

How much is it per night?
住一晚多少钱？
Zhù yì wǎn duōshao qián?

I'd like a wake-up call.
早上请打电话叫醒我。
Zǎoshang qǐng dǎ diànhuà jiàoxǐng wǒ.

I'd like a pot of mineral water.
我要矿泉水。
Wǒ yào kuàngquánshuǐ.

I'd like a single room (double room).
我要一间单人房（双人房）。
Wǒ yào yì jiān dānrénfáng (shuāngrénfáng).

I'd like to change to another room.
我想换一个房间。
Wǒ xiǎng huàn yí ge fángjiān.

I'd like to stay an extra night.
我想再住一晚。
Wǒ xiǎng zài zhù yì wǎn.

Is there a dining room?
这儿有没有餐厅?
Zhèr yǒu méiyǒu cāntīng?

Is there another hotel nearby?
附近还有其他旅馆吗?
Fùjìn hái yǒu qítā lǚguǎn ma?

May I see the room, please?
我可以看一看房间吗?
Wǒ kěyǐ kàn yí kàn fángjiān ma?

Please bring me some ice cubes and water.
请送冰块和水给我。
Qǐng sòng bīngkuài hé shuǐ gěi wǒ.

When is breakfast?
几点吃早餐?
Jǐ diǎn chī zǎocān?

Restaurants 餐厅 cāntīng

Can you recommend any dishes?
你可以推荐几道菜吗?
Nǐ kěyǐ tuījiàn jǐ dào cài ma?

Do you have an English menu?
你有英文菜单吗?
Nǐ yǒu Yīngwén càidān ma?

Don't add too much seasoning.
味道不要太重。
Wèidào búyào tài zhòng.

How much longer will our food be?
我们点的菜还要等多久？
Wǒmen diǎn de cài hái yào děng duōjiǔ?

I am a vegetarian.
我是吃素的。
Wǒ shì chīsù de.

I can't use chopsticks.
我不会用筷子。
Wǒ bú huì yòng kuàizi.

I like to eat Chinese food.
我喜欢吃中国菜。
Wǒ xǐhuan chī Zhōngguó cài.

It's all together.
我们的账一起算。
Wǒmen de zhàng yìqǐ suàn.

It's my treat.
我请你吃饭。
Wǒ qǐng nǐ chīfàn.

Just a cup of tea, please.
请给我一杯茶就好。
Qǐng gěi wǒ yì bēi chá jiù hǎo.

May I have the menu?
请给我菜单。
Qǐng gěi wǒ càidān.

No MSG, please.
请不要放味精。
Qǐng búyào fàng wèijīng.

This restaurant is full.
这家餐厅客满了。
Zhèi jiā cāntīng kèmǎn le.

Please don't make it spicy.
不要放辣。
Búyào fàng là.

Please give me a knife and fork.
请给我刀子和叉子。
Qǐng gěi wǒ dāozi hé chāzi.

That's not what I ordered.
我点的不是这个菜。
Wǒ diǎn de bú shì zhèi ge cài.

The check, please.
请给我账单。
Qǐng gěi wǒ zhàngdān.

The service in this restaurant is excellent.
这家餐厅的服务很好。
Zhèi jiā cāntīng de fúwù hěn hǎo.

We'd like a table in the nonsmoking section.
我们要非吸烟区的位子。
Wǒmen yào fēi xīyānqū de wèizi.

We'd like to pay separately.
我们要各付各的。
Wǒmen yào gè fù gè de.

What is this dish made of ?
这道菜是用什么做的?
Zhèi dào cài shì yòng shénme zuò de?

Do we need to leave a tip here?
要不要给小费?
Yào bú yào gěi xiǎofèi?

Would you like to make a reservation?
要不要订位?
Yào bú yào dìngwèi?

Shopping 买东西 mǎi dōngxi

Are you open in the evening?
你们晚上营业吗?
Nǐmen wǎnshang yíngyè ma?

Can I try it on?
我可以试穿吗?
Wǒ kěyǐ shìchuān ma?

Can you give me a discount?
能打折扣吗?
Néng dǎ zhékòu ma?

Can you reduce the price?
能便宜一点儿吗？
Néng piányi yìdiǎnr ma?

Could I have a receipt, please?
请给我收据。
Qǐng gěi wǒ shōujù.

Could you wrap it for me?
你能不能帮我包起来？
Nǐ néng bù néng bāng wǒ bāo qilai?

Do you accept credit cards?
可以用信用卡吗？
Kěyǐ yòng xìnyòngkǎ ma?

Do you accept traveler's checks?
你们收不收旅行支票？
Nǐmen shōu bù shōu lǚxíng zhīpiào?

Do you have another color (style)?
还有别的颜色（样式）吗？
Hái yǒu bié de yánsè (yàngshì) ma?

Do you have anything larger (smaller)?
有大（小）一点儿的吗？
Yǒu dà (xiǎo) yìdiǎnr de ma?

Do you have anything less expensive?
还有更便宜的吗？
Hái yǒu gèng piányi de ma?

How much is this?
这个多少钱？
Zhèi ge duōshao qián?

I'd like to change this, please.
我想要换这个。
Wǒ xiǎng yào huàn zhèi ge.

I'd like to think about it.
我再考虑一下。
Wǒ zài kǎolǜ yíxià.

I'm just looking.
我只是看看。
Wǒ zhǐshì kànkan.

It's too expensive.
太贵了。
Tài guì le.

Let's go shopping.
我们去逛街吧。
Wǒmen qù guàngjiē ba.

Welcome!
欢迎光临!
Huānyíng guānglín!

Where do I pay?
在哪儿付款?
Zài nǎr fùkuǎn?

Telephoning 打电话 dǎ diànhuà

Can I have your telephone number?
请告诉我你的电话号码。
Qǐng gàosu wǒ nǐ de diànhuà hàomǎ.

Can I make an international call from here?
这里能不能打国际电话?
Zhèli néng bù néng dǎ guójì diànhuà?

Could you ask him to call me back?
你可以请他回电吗?
Nǐ kěyǐ qǐng tā huídiàn ma?

Extension 123, please.
请转分机 123 。
Qǐng zhuǎn fēnjī 123.

He is not in now.
他现在不在。
Tā xiànzài bú zài.

Hold the line, please.
请不要挂电话。
Qǐng búyào guà diànhuà.

I can't hear you.
我听不清楚。
Wǒ tīng bù qīngchu.

I'd like a phone card, please.
请给我一张电话卡。
Qǐng gěi wǒ yì zhāng diànhuàkǎ.

I'll call back later.
我过一会儿再打。
Wǒ guò yíhuìr zài dǎ.

I would like to make a collect call.
我要打对方付费电话。
Wǒ yào dǎ duìfāng fùfèi diànhuà.

Just a minute, please.
请稍候。
Qǐng shāo hòu.

May I speak to Mr. Chen?
请问，陈先生在吗？
Qǐngwèn, Chén xiānsheng zài ma?

May I take your message?
你要留话吗？
Nǐ yào liúhuà ma?

Please call me.
请打电话给我。
Qǐng dǎ diànhuà gěi wǒ.

Please say it again. (Pardon?)
请你再说一次。
Qǐng nǐ zài shuō yí cì.

Please speak slowly.
请说慢一点儿。
Qǐng shuō màn yìdiǎnr.

Sorry, wrong number.
对不起，打错了。
Duìbuqǐ, dǎcuò le.

Speaking.
我就是。
Wǒ jiù shì.

Thank you, I'll phone back.
谢谢，我再打过去。
Xièxie, wǒ zài dǎ guòqu.

This is the Far East Company.
这里是远东公司。
Zhèlǐ shì Yuǎndōng Gōngsī.

When will he be back?
他什么时候回来?
Tā shénme shíhou huílai?

Where is the nearest phone booth?
最近的电话亭在哪儿?
Zuì jìn de diànhuàtíng zài nǎr?

Who is speaking, please?
请问你是哪位?
Qǐngwèn nǐ shì něi wèi?

Transportation 交通 jiāotōng

Are taxis expensive?
搭出租车 (计程车) 贵不贵?
Dā chūzūchē (jìchéngchē) guì bú guì?

Are there any seats left in the nonsmoking section?
禁烟区还有座位吗?
Jìnyānqū hái yǒu zuòwèi ma?

Are there any ships leaving for Shanghai tomorrow?
明天有开往上海的船班吗?
Míngtiān yǒu kāi wǎng Shànghǎi de chuánbān ma?

Could you call a taxi for me?
请帮我叫一辆出租车 (计程车)。
Qǐng bāng wǒ jiào yí liàng chūzūchē (jìchéngchē).

How do I switch lines (buses)?
我应该怎么换车?
Wǒ yīnggāi zěnme huàn chē?

How long does it take to get to the Taipei Main Station?
到台北车站要多久?
Dào Táiběi Chēzhàn yào duōjiǔ?

How long until the next bus?
下一班巴士 (公共汽车) 要多久?
Xià yì bān bāshì (gōnggòng qìchē) yào duōjiǔ?

How much is one ticket?
一张票多少钱？
Yì zhāng piào duōshao qián?

I would like to buy a round-trip ticket.
我要买来回票。
Wǒ yào mǎi láihuípiào.

I'd like a window seat, please.
我想要靠窗的座位。
Wǒ xiǎng yào kào chuāng de zuòwèi.

I'm going to take a plane there.
我会搭飞机去。
Wǒ huì dā fēijī qù.

Is this seat taken?
这个座位有人吗？
Zhèi ge zuòwèi yǒu rén ma?

Is there food for sale on the train?
火车上贩卖餐点吗？
Huǒchē shang fànmài cāndiǎn ma?

Please take me to the National Palace Museum.
请到故宫。
Qǐng dào Gùgōng.

Where can I buy a ticket?
到哪里买票？
Dào nǎli mǎi piào?

Where is the nearest subway station?
最近的地铁站在哪里？
Zuì jìn de dìtiězhàn zài nǎli?

Which stop is Tiananmen Square?
天安门是第几站？
Tiān'ānmén shì dì-jǐ zhàn?

Which track is my train on?
在第几月台搭车？
Zài dì-jǐ yuètái dā chē?

Pinyin
English-Chinese
Dictionary

拼音英汉辞典

User's Guide

- **Dictionary entries:** A total more than 12,000 words have been selected, with usefulness as the main criterion.

- **Word type:** Marked in italics. For example:

  arms *n.* 武器 wǔqì (weapons). — *v.* 武装 wǔzhuāng.

- **Chinese definition:** Each English entry is followed by concise Chinese definitions, which are arranged based on their frequency of use. In addition, when usage in mainland China and Taiwan differs, the mainland China usage is listed first, followed by a slash (/) and then the Taiwanese usage. For example:

  scheme *n.* ①计划 jìhuà (plan). ②阴谋 yīnmóu (conspiracy). ③图表 túbiǎo (diagram). ④设计 shèjì (design). — *v.* 计划 jìhuà (plan), 图谋 túmóu (connive).

  sauna *n.* 桑拿浴 sāngnáyù / 三温暖 sānwēnnuǎn.

- **Hanyu pinyin:** In order to help readers properly pronounce the words, each word is followed by its Hanyu Pinyin. When pronunciation differs across the strait, the Mainland pronunciation is listed first, followed by the Taiwanese pronunciation. For example:

  architecture *n.* 建筑 jiànzhù / jiànzhú.

- **English explanation:** In order to help readers fully grasp the meaning of each word, a clear and precise English explanation is added whenever there are several different meanings for the same word. There are two types of English explanation.

  The first, which is marked ( ), is the equivalent of an English definition for that word. The second, which is marked ⟨ ⟩, is a hint that will help readers distinguish between the different entries for a single word. For example:

  flourish *v.* ①繁盛 fánshèng (prosper). ②兴隆 xīnglóng (thrive). ③挥动 huīdòng (wave).

fresh *adj.* ①新鲜的 xīnxiān de ⟨food⟩. ②清新的 qīngxīn de ⟨air⟩. ③淡的 dàn de ⟨water⟩. ④新奇的 xīnqí de ⟨idea⟩.

- **Important expressions:** This dictionary contains a number of important and useful expressions, which are marked in bold and italics. For example:

shut *v.* 闭 bì, 关闭 guānbì. *~ off* 关掉 guāndiào. *~ up* 住 口 zhùkǒu, 闭嘴 bìzuǐ.

体 例 说 明

● **词　　条**：本辞典收录逾 12,000 个词条，以实用为主。
● **词　　性**：以斜体标示。例如：

> **arms** *n.* 武器 wǔqì (weapons). — *v.* 武装 wǔzhuāng.

● **中文义译**：为确切符合读者的实际应用需求，每个词条均提供重要简明之中文义译，按照其常用性排序，并同时列出两岸差异之说法，以「/」隔开，前者为大陆说法，后者为台湾说法。例如：

> **scheme** *n.* ①计画 jìhuà (plan). ②阴谋 yīnmóu (conspiracy). ③图表 túbiǎo (diagram). ④设计 shèjì (design). — *v.* 计画 jìhuà (plan), 图谋 túmóu (connive).

> **sauna** *n.* 桑拿浴 sāngnáyù / 三温暖 sānwēnnuǎn.

● **汉语拼音**：为帮助读者正确念出中文的发音，每个中文字均特别加注汉语拼音，并同时列出两岸差异之发音，以「/」隔开，前者为大陆音，后者为台湾音。例如：

> **architecture** *n.* 建筑 jiànzhù / jiànzhú.

● **英文注解**：为使读者在应用本辞典时能完全掌握正确词义，除单义词条外，所有有异义词条之中文义译均加注清晰可别的英文注解，有效帮助读者正确选用中文义译。本字典有两种英文注解形式，其一是 （ ），此为相当于该中文词义之英文解释；其二是 〈 〉，此为可供区别之重点提示。例如：

> **flourish** *v.* ①繁盛 fánshèng (prosper). ②兴隆 xīnglóng (thrive). ③挥动 huīdòng (wave).

> **fresh** *adj.* ①新鲜的 xīnxiān de 〈food〉. ②清新的 qīngxīn de 〈air〉. ③淡的 dàn de 〈water〉. ④新奇的 xīnqí de 〈idea〉.

● **重要短语**：本辞典所选录之重要片语，以粗斜体标示。例如：

> **shut** *v.* 闭 bì, 关闭 guānbì. **~ off** 关掉 guāndiào. **~ up** 住口 zhùkǒu, 闭嘴 bìzuǐ.

A

a *indef. art.* ①一 yī (one). ②某一 mǒuyī (some).

abacus *n.* 算盘 suànpán.

abandon *v.* ①抛弃 pāoqì (desert). ②放弃 fàngqì (give up).

abate *v.* ①减少 jiǎnshǎo (reduce). ②减轻 jiǎnqīng (lighten).

abbey *n.* 修道院 xiūdàoyuàn.

abbreviate *v.* ①缩写 suōxiě 〈title〉.②缩短 suōduǎn (shorten).

abdicate *v.* 让位 ràngwèi 〈power〉.

abdomen *n.* 腹部 fùbù.

abduct *v.* ①绑架 bǎngjià (kidnap).②拐走 guǎizǒu (entice away).

abhor *v.* 憎恶 zēngwù.

abide *v.* 忍受 rěnshòu (tolerate). ~ *by* 遵守 zūnshǒu (obey).

ability *n.* 能力 nénglì.

able *adj.* 能干的 nénggàn de, 有才能的 yǒu cáinéng de (competent).

abnormal *adj.* 反常的 fǎncháng de.

aboard *adv. & prep.* 在船上 zài chuánshang 〈ship〉, 在火车上 zài huǒchēshang 〈train〉, 在飞机上 zài fēijīshang 〈plane〉, 在巴士上 zài bāshìshang 〈bus〉.

abode *n.* 住所 zhùsuǒ.

abolish *v.* 废除 fèichú.

abominable *adj.* 可恶的 kěwù de (hateful).

aboriginal *adj.* 原始的 yuánshǐ de. — *n.* 土著 tǔzhù.

aborigine *n.* 原住民 yuánzhùmín.

abort *v.* ①堕胎 duòtāi 〈pregnancy〉.②停止 tíngzhǐ (end).

abortion *n.* 堕胎 duòtāi.

abound *v.* 充满 chōngmǎn.

about *prep.* ①关于 guānyú (concerning). ②大约 dàyuē (approximately).

above *prep.* ①在……之上 zài...zhī shàng (higher than). ②超过 chāoguò (more than). — *adv.* 在上 zài shàng (higher up).

abrade *v.* 磨损 mósǔn.

abreast *adv.* 并肩 bìngjiān (side by side).

abridge *v.* 删减 shānjiǎn.

abroad *adv.* 在国外 zài guówài.

abrupt *adj.* 突然的 tūrán de / túrán de.

abscess *n.* 脓肿 nóngzhǒng.

abscond *v.* 潜逃 qiántáo.

absence *n.* ①缺席 quēxí (nonattendance). ②缺乏 quēfá (lack).

absent *adj.* 缺席的 quēxí de.

absentee *n.* 缺席者 quēxízhě.

absent-minded *adj.* 心不在焉的 xīnbúzàiyān de.

absolute *adj.* 绝对的 juéduì de.

absolve *v.* 免除 miǎnchú (free from responsibility).

absorb *v.* 吸收 xīshōu.

absorption *n.* ①吸收 xīshōu

(taking in). ②专注 zhuānzhù (concentration).

abstain v. ①戒除 jièchú (refrain from). ②弃投票权 qì tóupiàoquán 〈vote〉.

abstention n. ①戒除 jièchú (refraining from). ②弃投票权 qì tóupiàoquán 〈vote〉.

abstinence n. ①禁欲 jìnyù 〈sex〉. ②戒酒 jièjiǔ 〈liquor〉.

abstract adj. 抽象的 chōuxiàng de (not concrete). — v. 提炼 tíliàn (pick out). — n. 摘要 zhāiyào (summary).

absurd adj. 荒谬的 huāngmiù de.

abundance n. 丰富 fēngfù (variety), 充足 chōngzú (plenty).

abundant adj. 丰富的 fēngfù de (plentiful), 充足的 chōngzú de (more than enough).

abuse v. ①滥用 lànyòng (misuse). ②虐待 nüèdài (ill-treat). — n. 虐待 nüèdài.

abyss n. 深渊 shēnyuān.

academic adj. 学术性的 xuéshùxìng de.

academy n. ①学院 xuéyuàn (school). ②学术界 xuéshùjiè (scholarly world).

accelerate v. 加速 jiāsù.

accelerator n. 油门 yóumén 〈pedal〉, 加速器 jiāsùqì 〈device〉.

accent n. ①重音 zhòngyīn 〈mark〉. ②腔调 qiāngdiào 〈pronunciation〉.

accentuate v. ①读重音 dú zhòngyīn (stress a syllable). ②强调 qiángdiào (stress a point).

accept v. 接受 jiēshòu.

access n. ①接近 jiējìn (approach). ②进入权利 jìnrù quánlì (right of entry). ③通路

tōnglù (way of approach).

accessory n. 配件 pèijiàn.

accident n. 意外事件 yìwài shìjiàn. by ~ 偶然 ǒurán.

acclaim n. & v. 欢呼 huānhū.

accommodate v. ①适应 shìyìng (adjust to). ②容纳 róngnà (have enough space for). ③供住宿 gōng zhùsù (offer a place to live).

accommodation n. 住宿 zhùsù.

accompany v. ①陪伴 péibàn (go with). ②伴奏 bànzòu 〈music〉.

accomplice n. 共犯 gòngfàn.

accomplish v. 完成 wánchéng (complete), 实现 shíxiàn (bring about).

accomplished adj. ①熟练的 shúliàn de / shóuliàn de (skilled). ②优秀的 yōuxiù de (good at).

accord v. 给与 jǐyǔ (give). — n. 协定 xiédìng (agreement). in ~ with 与…… 一致 yǔ...yízhì.

accordance n. 一致 yízhì. in ~ with 依照 yīzhào.

according adj. 一致的 yízhì de. ~ to 依照 yīzhào.

accordion n. 手风琴 shǒufēngqín.

account n. ①说明 shuōmíng (explanation). ②叙述 xùshù (narrative). ③账目 zhàngmù (bill). on ~ of 因为 yīnwèi. take into ~ 加以考虑 jiāyǐ kǎolǜ.

accountant n. 会计员 kuàijìyuán.

accredit v. 授权 shòuquán (authorize).

accumulate v. 堆积 duījī.

A

accuracy n. 正确性 zhèngquèxìng.

accurate adj. 正确的 zhèngquè de.

accusation n. 控告 kònggào.

accuse v. 指控 zhǐkòng.

accustom v. 习惯于 xíguàn yú.

ace n. ①幺点 yāodiǎn (cards). ②杰出者 jiéchūzhě, 好手 hǎoshǒu (expert). — interj. A~! 太棒了！Tài bàng le!

acetate n. 醋酸盐 cùsuānyán.

acetone n. 丙酮 bǐngtóng.

acetylene n. 乙炔 yǐquē / yǐjué.

ache n. & v. 疼痛 téngtòng.

achieve v. ①完成 wánchéng (carry out). ②获得 huòdé (gain). ③达到 dádào (reach a goal).

acid n. 酸 suān.

acidic adj. 酸性的 suānxìng de.

acknowledge v. 承认 chéngrèn.

acne n. 粉刺 fěncì.

acorn n. 橡实 xiàngshí.

acoustic adj. 听觉的 tīngjué de.

acquaint v. 使熟悉 shǐ shúxī / shǐ shóuxī (familiarize).

acquaintance n. 相识者 xiāngshízhě / xiāngshìzhě.

acquainted adj. 认识的 rènshi de.

acquire v. 获得 huòdé.

acquisition n. 获得 huòdé, 习得 xídé.

acquit v. 宣告无罪 xuāngào wúzuì (declare innocent).

acre n. 英亩 yīngmǔ.

acrid adj. 辛辣的 xīnlà de.

acrimonious adj. 尖刻的 jiānkè de.

acrobat n. 卖艺者 màiyìzhě (tumbler).

acronym n. 首字母缩略语 shǒu zìmǔ suōlüèyǔ.

acrophobia n. 惧高症 jùgāozhèng.

across prep. 横过 héngguò, 越过 yuèguò (crosswise). — adv. 在对面 zài duìmiàn.

act n. ①行为 xíngwéi (behavior). ②一幕 yí mù (theater). ③法案 fǎ'àn (law). — v. ①行动 xíngdòng (take action). ②表现 biǎoxiàn (represent). ③扮演 bànyǎn (play a part). ④假装 jiǎzhuāng (pretend).

action n. ①行动 xíngdòng (movement). ②作用 zuòyòng (function). take ~ 采取行动 cǎiqǔ xíngdòng.

activate v. 使产生活动 shǐ chǎnshēng huódòng (actuate).

active adj. ①积极的 jījí de, 活跃的 huóyuè de (energetic). ②主动的 zhǔdòng de (not passive). ③活动的 huódòng de (working).

activity n. 活动 huódòng.

actor n. 演员 yǎnyuán (performer).

actress n. 女演员 nǚ yǎnyuán.

actual adj. 真实的 zhēnshí de (genuine), 实际的 shíjì de (real).

actualize v. 实现 shíxiàn, 落实 luòshí.

acumen n. 敏锐 mǐnruì.

acupuncture n. 针灸 zhēnjiǔ.

acute adj. ①敏锐的 mǐnruì de (senses). ②尖锐的 jiānruì de (analysis). ③剧烈的 jùliè de (severe).

ad n. 广告 guǎnggào.

A.D. n. 公元 gōngyuán / 西元

A

xīyuán.

adamant *adj.* 坚持的 jiānchí de, 固执的 gùzhí de.

adapt *v.* ①适应 shìyìng (adjust). ②改编 gǎibiān 〈a book or a play〉.

add *v.* ①增加 zēngjiā (increase). ②加 jiā 〈mathematics〉. ~ *up* 合计 héjì.

addict *v.* 上瘾 shàngyǐn. — *n.* 上瘾者 shàngyǐnzhě.

addiction *n.* 耽溺 dānnì.

addition *n.* 附加物 fùjiāwù (attachment). *in ~* 此外 cǐwài.

additional *adj.* 附加的 fùjiā de.

address *n.* ①住址 zhùzhǐ 〈location〉. ②演讲 yǎnjiǎng (speech).

adept *adj.* 熟练的 shúliàn de / shóuliàn de.

adequate *adj.* 足够的 zúgòu de.

adhere *v.* ①黏着 niánzhuó (stick firmly). ②忠于 zhōngyú (abide by).

adjacent *adj.* 毗连的 pílián de.

adjective *n.* 形容词 xíngróngcí.

adjourn *v.* 休会 xiūhuì.

adjust *v.* ①调节 tiáojié (modify). ②适应 shìyìng (adapt to).

administer *v.* 管理 guǎnlǐ (manage).

administration *n.* ①管理 guǎnlǐ (management). ②行政机关 xíngzhèng jīguān 〈department〉. ③行政 xíngzhèng 〈procedure〉. ④政府 zhèngfǔ (state leadership).

admirable *adj.* 可钦佩的 kě qīnpèi de.

admiral *n.* 海军上将 hǎijūn shàngjiàng.

admiration *n.* 钦佩 qīnpèi, 赞赏 zànshǎng.

admire *v.* 钦佩 qīnpèi, 赞赏 zànshǎng.

admission *n.* ①入场许可 rùchǎng xǔkě (permission to enter). ②承认 chéngrèn (acknowledgment). ③供认 gòngrèn / gōngrèn (confession). ④入场费 rùchǎngfèi (entry fee).

admit *v.* ①承认 chéngrèn (acknowledge). ②供认 gòngrèn / gōngrèn (confess). ③容许入场 róngxǔ rùchǎng (let in).

admonish *v.* 警告 jǐnggào.

adolescence *n.* 青春期 qīngchūnqī / qīngchúnqī.

adopt *v.* ①采纳 cǎinà (use). ②收养 shōuyǎng 〈a child〉.

adorable *adj.* 可爱的 kě'ài de (cute), 令人喜爱的 lìng rén xǐ'ài de (pleasing).

adore *v.* 崇拜 chóngbài (worship).

adorn *v.* 装饰 zhuāngshì.

ADP 自动数据处理 zìdòng shùjù chǔlǐ (automatic data processing).

adrift *adj. & adv.* 漂流的 piāoliú de.

ADSL 非对称式数位用户线路 fēi duìchènshì shùwèi yònghù xiànlù / fēi duìchèngshì shùwèi yònghù xiànlù.

adult *adj.* 成人的 chéngrén de. — *n.* 成人 chéngrén.

adultery *n.* 通奸 tōngjiān.

advance *v.* ①前进 qiánjìn (move forward). ②进步 jìnbù (make progress). — *n.* ①前进 qiánjìn (movement). ②进步

jìnbù (progress). ③预付 yùfù (prepayment). *in ~* 预先 yùxiān.

advanced adj. ①进步的 jìnbù de (evolved). ②先进的 xiānjìn de (newest and best). ③高级的 gāojí de ⟨level⟩.

advantage n. ①利益 lìyì (benefit). ②优势 yōushì (supremacy). *take ~ of* 利用 lìyòng.

adventure n. ①冒险 màoxiǎn (risk). ②奇遇 qíyù (unusual event).

adverb n. 副词 fùcí.

adversary n. 对手 duìshǒu (competitor), 仇敌 chóudí (enemy).

adverse adj. ①反对的 fǎnduì de (opposing). ②不利的 búlì de (harmful).

advertise v. 登广告 dēng guǎnggào.

advertisement n. 广告 guǎnggào.

advertising n. 广告 guǎnggào. *~ agency* 广告公司 guǎnggào gōngsī.

advice n. 劝告 quàngào, 忠告 zhōnggào (counsel), 建议 jiànyì (suggestion).

advise v. ①忠告 zhōnggào (counsel), 建议 jiànyì (suggest). ②通知 tōngzhī (inform).

advisor n. ①顾问 gùwèn (consultant). ②指导教授 zhǐdǎo jiàoshòu ⟨academics⟩.

advocate n. 提倡者 tíchàngzhě. — v. 提倡 tíchàng.

aerial adj. ①空气的 kōngqì de (airy). ②航空的 hángkōng de (from the sky).

aerolite n. 陨石 yǔnshí.

affable adj. 和蔼可亲的 hé'ǎi-kěqīn de.

affair n. ①事情 shìqíng (matter). ②恋情 liànqíng (romance).

affect v. ①影响 yǐngxiǎng (influence). ②感动 gǎndòng (move deeply).

affected adj. 假装的 jiǎzhuāng de (pretentious).

affection n. 情爱 qíng'ài (fondness).

affectionate adj. 挚爱的 zhì'ài de.

affiliate v. 使加入 shǐ jiārù. *~ with* 与……有关系 yǔ... yǒu guānxi. — n. 关系企业 guānxi qǐyè / guānxì qìyè (related business).

affinity n. 密切关系 mìqiè guānxi (close connection). *have an ~ for* 喜好…… xǐhào....

affirm v. ①证实 zhèngshí (acknowledge). ②断言 duànyán (assert).

affirmative n. & adj. 肯定 (的) kěndìng (de).

affix v. 固定 gùdìng (fix). — n. 词缀 cízhuì ⟨grammar⟩.

affluence n. 富裕 fùyù.

affluent adj. 富裕的 fùyù de.

afford v. ①力足以 lì zúyǐ, 负担得起 fùdān de qǐ ⟨money⟩. ②承受 chéngshòu ⟨effort, time, emotion, etc.⟩.

affront n. & v. 侮辱 wǔrǔ / wǔrù.

afloat adj. & adv. 飘浮的 piāofú de (floating).

afraid adj. 害怕的 hàipà de (frightened), 担心 dānxīn (concerned).

Africa 非洲 Fēizhōu.

A

after prep. & conj. 在……之后 zài...zhīhòu. ~ **all** 毕竟 bìjìng. — adv. 之后 zhīhòu.

aftermath n. 余波 yúbō, 后果 hòuguǒ.

afternoon n. 下午 xiàwǔ.

afterward(s) adv. 后来 hòulái.

again adv. 再 zài, 又 yòu.

against prep. ①反对 fǎnduì (opposed to). ②对照 duìzhào (compared to). ③抵抗 dǐkàng (resistant to). ④靠 kào (leaning on).

age n. ①年龄 niánlíng (number of years old). ②时代 shídài (era).

agency n. ①代理商 dàilǐshāng 〈business〉. ②机关 jīguān (organization).

agenda n. 议程 yìchéng.

agent n. 代理人 dàilǐrén, 经纪人 jīngjìrén (representative).

aggravate v. ①恶化 èhuà (worsen). ②激怒 jīnù (annoy).

aggregate n. 集合 jíhé (mass).

aggression n. 侵略 qīnlüè (attack).

aggressive adj. ①攻击的 gōngjī de / gōngjí de, 侵略的 qīnlüè de (attacking). ②积极的 jījí de 〈not passive〉.

aghast adj. 吓呆的 xiàdāi de.

agile adj. 敏捷的 mǐnjié de.

agitate v. ①扰乱 rǎoluàn (disturb). ②搅动 jiǎodòng (shake).

ago adv. 以前 yǐqián.

agony n. 痛苦 tòngkǔ.

agrarian adj. 农地的 nóngdì de.

agree v. ①同意 tóngyì (approve). ②一致 yízhì (correspond).

agreeable adj. ①令人愉快的 lìng rén yúkuài de (pleasant). ②赞成的 zànchéng de (in favor of).

agreement n. ①一致 yízhì (consistency). ②同意 tóngyì (approval). ③协定 xiédìng (contract).

agriculture n. 农业 nóngyè.

aground adj. & adv. 搁浅的 gēqiǎn de.

ahead adv. 在前方 zài qiánfāng (in front).

aid v. 帮助 bāngzhù, 援助 yuánzhù. — n. 帮助 bāngzhù (help).

aide n. 助手 zhùshǒu (assistant).

AIDS n. 艾滋病 àizībìng / 爱滋病 àizībìng.

aim v. 瞄准 miáozhǔn (point). — n. ①瞄准 miáozhǔn (target). ②目的 mùdì (intention).

air n. ①空气 kōngqì (gas). ②天空 tiānkōng (the sky). on the ~ 广播中 guǎngbō zhōng / guǎngbò zhōng. ~ **bag** 气囊 qìnáng. ~ **bridge** 登机桥 dēngjīqiáo / 空桥 kōngqiáo. ~ **conditioner** 空调设备 kōngtiáo shèbèi.

aircraft n. 飞行器 fēixíngqì.

airline n. ①航线 hángxiàn (route). ②航空公司 hángkōng gōngsī 〈business〉.

airmail n. 航空邮件 hángkōng yóujiàn.

airplane n. 飞机 fēijī.

airport n. 飞机场 fēijīchǎng.

airsick adj. 晕机的 yùnjī de / yùnjī de.

aisle n. 通道 tōngdào.

ajar adj. & adv. 半开的 bànkāi

de.

akin *adj.* ①类似的 lèisì de (similar). ②近亲的 jìnqīn de (related).

alarm *n.* 警报 jǐngbào. ~ *clock* 闹钟 nàozhōng.

albatross *n.* 信天翁 xìntiānwēng.

albino *n.* 白化病者 báihuàbìng zhě.

album *n.* ①相簿 xiàngbù 〈photographs〉. ②唱片集 chàngpiànjí 〈music record〉. ③集邮册 jíyóucè 〈stamps〉.

alcohol *n.* ①酒精 jiǔjīng 〈chemical〉. ②酒 jiǔ 〈liquor〉.

alcoholic *n.* 酒鬼 jiǔguǐ.

ale *n.* 麦酒 màijiǔ.

alert *adj.* 警觉的 jǐngjué de, 敏捷的 mǐnjié de 〈watchful〉. — *n.* 警报 jǐngbào 〈alarm〉. — *v.* ①发警报 fā jǐngbào, 使警戒 shǐ jǐngjiè (warn). ②通知 tōngzhī (notify).

algae *n.* 海藻 hǎizǎo.

algebra *n.* 代数 dàishù.

alias *n. & adv.* 别名 biémíng, 化名 huàmíng.

alibi *n.* 不在场证明 bú zàichǎng zhèngmíng.

alien *n.* ①外国人 wàiguórén (foreigner). ②外星人 wàixīngrén (extraterrestrial).

alienate *v.* 使疏远 shǐ shūyuǎn.

alight *v.* 下车 xià chē (get off).

align *v.* 排列成行 páiliè chéng háng.

alike *adj. & adv.* 相似的 xiāngsì de (similar), 同样的 tóngyàng de (of the same kind).

alimony *n.* 赡养费 shànyǎngfèi.

alive *adj.* ①活的 huó de (living). ②现存的 xiàncún de (in existence).

alkali *n.* 碱 jiǎn.

all *adj.* 全部的 quánbù de. — *pron.* 所有 suǒyǒu. *not at* ~ 毫不 háobù. — *adv.* 全体 quántǐ. ~ *right* 好 hǎo, 没问题 méi wèntí.

Allah *n.* 安拉 Ānlā.

allegation *n.* 指控 zhǐkòng.

allege *v.* 宣称 xuānchēng.

allegiance *n.* 忠诚 zhōngchéng.

allegory *n.* ①讽喻 fěngyù / fèngyù (metaphor). ②寓言 yùyán (fable).

allergic *adj.* 过敏 guòmǐn. ~ *to* 对……过敏 duì...guòmǐn.

allergy *n.* 过敏症 guòmǐnzhèng.

alleviate *v.* 缓和 huǎnhé, 减轻 jiǎnqīng.

alley *n.* 巷弄 xiànglòng.

alliance *n.* 联盟 liánméng.

allied *adj.* 同盟的 tóngméng de.

alligator *n.* 短吻鳄 duǎnwěn'è.

allocate *v.* 分配 fēnpèi (distribute), 拨出 bōchū (share).

allot *v.* 分配 fēnpèi.

allow *v.* ①允许 yǔnxǔ (permit). ②承认 chéngrèn (admit).

allowance *n.* 零用钱 língyòngqián 〈money〉.

alloy *n.* 合金 héjīn.

allude *v.* 暗指 ànzhǐ.

allusion *n.* 暗示 ànshì.

ally *v.* 结盟 jiéméng. 盟友 méngyǒu 〈friend〉, 同盟 国 tóngméngguó 〈country〉.

almanac *n.* ①历书 lìshū

(calendar). ②年鉴 niánjiàn (yearbook).

almighty adj. 万能的 wànnéng de (omnipotent).

almond n. 杏仁 xìngrén.

almost adv. ①差不多 chàbuduō / chābuduō (approximately). ②几乎 jīhū (not quite).

alms n. 救济物 jiùjìwù.

aloe n. 芦荟 lúhuì.

aloft adj. & adv. 在高处的 zài gāochù de.

alone adj. 单独的 dāndú de. — 单单只……的 dāndān zhǐ....

along prep. 沿着 yánzhe.

aloof adv. 远离 yuǎnlí. — adj. 冷淡的 lěngdàn de, 疏远的 shūyuǎn de.

aloud adv. 出声 chūshēng.

alphabet n. 字母 zìmǔ.

Alps 阿尔卑斯山 Āʼěrbēisīshān.

already adv. 已经 yǐjīng.

also adv. 而且 érqiě, 也 yě.

altar n. 祭坛 jìtán ⟨platform⟩.

alter v. 变更 biàngēng.

alternate v. 轮流 lúnliú, 交替 jiāotì. — adj. 交替的 jiāotì de.

alternative n. ①二择一的 èr zé yī de (choose one between two). ②另类的 lìnglèi de ⟨different⟩. ~ medicine 非传统医学 fēi chuántǒng yīxué.

although conj. 虽然 suīrán.

altimeter n. 高度计 gāodùjì.

altitude n. 高度 gāodù.

alto n. ①女低音 nǚdīyīn ⟨female⟩. ②男高音 nángāoyīn ⟨male⟩.

altogether adv. ①完全地 wánquán de (completely). ②总共 zǒnggòng (on the whole).

altruism n. 利他主义 lìtā zhǔyì.

aluminum n. 铝 lǚ. ~ foil 铝箔 lǚbó.

alumna n. 女校友 nǚxiàoyǒu.

alumnus n. 男校友 nánxiàoyǒu.

always adv. ①总是 zǒngshì (at all times). ②永远 yǒngyuǎn (forever).

am v. 是 shì.

a.m. 上午 shàngwǔ.

amass v. 积聚 jījù.

amateur n. 业余者 yèyúzhě.

amaze v. 使吃惊 shǐ chījīng.

amazement n. 吃惊 chījīng, 惊奇 jīngqí.

amazing adj. 惊奇的 jīngqí de.

Amazon River 亚马孙河 Yàmǎsūnhé / 亚马逊河 Yàmǎxùnhé.

ambassador n. 大使 dàshǐ.

amber n. 琥珀 hǔpò.

ambiguity n. 暧昧 àimèi, 含糊 hánhu.

ambiguous adj. 含糊的 hánhu de, 暧昧的 àimèi de.

ambition n. 野心 yěxīn, 企图心 qǐtúxīn / qìtúxīn.

ambitious adj. 有野心的 yǒu yěxīn de.

amble v. 漫步 mànbù.

ambulance n. 救护车 jiùhùchē.

ambush n. 埋伏 máifú.

amenable adj. 顺从的 shùncóng de, 服从的 fúcóng de.

amend v. 修正 xiūzhèng.

amendment n. 修正案 xiūzhèng'àn.

amenity n. 令人舒适之事物

lìng rén shūshì zhī shìwù.

America n. ①美国 Měiguó (the U.S.). ②美洲大陆 Měizhōu Dàlù (continent).

amethyst n. 紫水晶 zǐshuǐjīng.

amiable adj. 和蔼可亲的 hé'ǎi-kěqīn de.

amicable adj. 友善的 yǒushàn de.

amid prep. 在……当中 zài...dāngzhōng.

amiss adj. & adv. 有问题的 yǒu wèntí de.

ammeter n. 安培计 ānpéijì.

ammonia n. ①氨 ān ⟨gas⟩. ②氨水 ānshuǐ ⟨liquid⟩.

ammunition n. 弹药 dànyào, 军火 jūnhuǒ.

amnesia n. 健忘症 jiànwàngzhèng.

amnesty n. 大赦 dàshè, 特赦 tèshè.

amoeba n. 阿米巴 āmǐbā, 变形虫 biànxíngchóng.

among prep. 在……中 zài...zhōng.

amorous adj. ①求爱的 qiú'ài de (seeking love). ②性爱的 xìng'ài de (sexual).

amount n. ①总数 zǒngshù (the total). ②数量 shùliàng (number), 分量 fènliang (quantity). — v. ①合计 héjì (add up to). ②相当于 xiāngdāng yú (be equal to).

ampere n. 安培 ānpéi.

amphetamine n. 安非他命 ānfēitāmìng.

amphibian n. 两栖动物 liǎngqī dòngwù.

amphitheater n. ①圆形剧场 yuánxíng jùchǎng (performance arena). ②竞技场

jìngjìchǎng (competitive area).

ample adj. ①高大的 gāodà de (large). ②充裕的 chōngyù de (sufficient).

amplify v. ①扩大 kuòdà (enlarge). ②加强 jiāqiáng (increase magnitude). ③夸张 kuāzhāng (exaggerate).

amputate v. 切除 qiēchú.

amulet n. 护身符 hùshēnfú.

amuse v. 娱乐 yúlè.

amusement n. 娱乐 yúlè. ~ **park** 游乐园 yóulèyuán.

amusing adj. 有趣的 yǒuqù de.

anachronism n. 时代错误 shídài cuòwù.

analogous adj. 相似的 xiāngsì de, 类似的 lèisì de.

analogy n. ①相似 xiāngsì (sameness). ②类推 lèituī (reason from likeness).

analysis n. 分析 fēnxī.

analyze v. 分析 fēnxī.

anarchism n. 无政府主义 wú zhèngfǔ zhǔyì.

anarchy n. ①无政府（状态）wúzhèngfǔ (zhuàngtài) (absence of government). ②混乱 hùnluàn (disorder).

anatomy n. 解剖（学）jiěpōu (xué) / jiěpǒu (xué).

ancestor n. 祖先 zǔxiān.

anchor n. ①锚 máo (mooring). ②主播 zhǔbō ⟨media⟩. — v. 抛锚 pāomáo, 泊船 bóchuán.

ancient adj. 古代的 gǔdài de (old).

and conj. 和 hé, 及 jí.

anecdote n. 轶事 yìshì.

anemia n. 贫血 pínxuè / pínxiě.

anesthesia n. 麻醉 mázuì.

A

anew *adv.* 再 zài, 重新 chóngxīn.

angel *n.* 天使 tiānshǐ.

anger *n.* 忿怒 fènnù.

angle *n.* ①角 jiǎo〈mathematics〉. ②角度 jiǎodù, 观点 guāndiǎn (point of view).

Anglican *n. & adj.* 英国国教 Yīngguó Guójiào.

angry *adj.* 生气的 shēngqì de, 忿怒的 fènnù de.

anguish *n.* 极度痛苦 jídù tòngkǔ, 苦闷 kǔmèn.

angular *adj.* 有尖角的 yǒu jiānjiǎo de (having angles).

animal *n.* 动物 dòngwù.

animate *v.* ①赋予生气 fùyǔ shēngqì (bring to life). ②制作动画 zhìzuò dònghuà (make cartoons). — *adj.* 生动的 shēngdòng de (alive).

animosity *n.* 仇恨 chóuhèn.

ankle *n.* 踝 huái.

annex *v.* 并吞 bìngtūn (take over). — *n.* 附属建筑 fùshǔ jiànzhù / fùshǔ jiànzhú.

annihilate *v.* 歼灭 jiānmiè.

anniversary *n.* 周年 zhōunián.

annotate *v.* 注解 zhùjiě.

announce *v.* 宣告 xuāngào, 发表 fābiǎo (proclaim).

announcer *n.* 播音员 bōyīnyuán / 播报员 bòbàoyuán.

annoy *v.* ①使……烦恼 shǐ...fánnǎo (cause aggravation). ②打扰 dǎrǎo (bother). ③骚扰 sāorǎo (harass).

annoying *adj.* ①麻烦的 máfan de (bothersome). ②讨厌的 tǎoyàn de (unpleasant).

annual *adj.* 年度的 niándù de.

annuity *n.* 年金 niánjīn, 养老金 yǎnglǎojīn.

annul *v.* 注销 zhùxiāo.

anode *n.* 阳极 yángjí, 正极 zhèngjí.

anoint *v.* 涂油 tú yóu.

anomalous *adj.* 例外的 lìwài de, 反常的 fǎncháng de.

anomaly *n.* 例外 lìwài, 反常 fǎncháng.

anonymous *adj.* 匿名的 nìmíng de.

anorak *n.* 防风夹克 fángfēng jiākè / fángfēng jiákè.

another *adj.* ①另一的 lìng yī de (a different). ②再一个 zài yí ge (one more).

answer *n. & v.* 答复 dáfù, 回答 huídá (reply). ~ *ing machine* 电话录音机 diànhuà lùyīnjī / 答录机 dálùjī.

ant *n.* 蚂蚁 mǎyǐ.

antarctic *adj.* 南极的 nánjí de.

Antarctica 南极洲 Nánjízhōu.

antecedent *n.* ①先行词 xiānxíngcí〈grammar〉. ②前事 qiánshì〈history〉.

antelope *n.* 羚羊 língyáng.

antenna *n.* ①触须 chùxū〈insect〉. ②天线 tiānxiàn〈electronics〉.

anthem *n.* 圣歌 shènggē (hymn), 赞美诗 zànměishī (eulogy). *national* ~ 国歌 guógē.

anthology *n.* 诗集 shījí (poetry), 文选 wénxuǎn〈prose〉.

anthropology *n.* 人类学 rénlèixué.

antibiotic *n.* 抗生素 kàngshēngsù.

antibody *n.* 抗体 kàngtǐ.

anticipate *v.* ①预期 yùqī / yùqí (expect). ②期待 qīdài /

qídài (look forward to). ③抢先 qiǎngxiān (do something first).

antidote n. 解毒剂 jiědújì.

antifreeze n. 防冻剂 fángdòngjì.

antiquary n. 古物专家 gǔwù zhuānjiā, 骨董商 gǔdǒngshāng.

antiquated adj. ①陈旧的 chénjiù de (out of date). ②废弃的 fèiqì de (no longer in use).

antique n. 古董 gǔdǒng.

antiquity n. ①古代 gǔdài (distant past). ②古迹 gǔjì / gǔjī ⟨building⟩, 古物 gǔwù ⟨objects⟩.

antisocial adj. 反社交行为的 fǎnshèjiāo xíngwéi de.

antithesis n. 对立 duìlì.

antler n. 鹿角 lùjiǎo.

antonym n. 反义字 fǎnyìzì.

anus n. 肛门 gāngmén.

anvil n. 铁砧 tiězhēn.

anxiety n. 忧虑 yōulǜ (distress), 不安 bù'ān (concern).

anxious adj. ①不安的 bù'ān de (concerned). ②渴望的 kěwàng de (eager).

any adj. & pron. 任何 rènhé.

anybody pron. 任何人 rènhé rén.

anyhow adv. 无论如何 wúlùn-rúhé.

anyone pron. 任何人 rènhé rén.

anything pron. 任何事物 rènhé shìwù.

anyway adv. 无论如何 wúlùn-rúhé.

anywhere adv. 任何地方 rènhé dìfang.

aorta n. 大动脉 dàdòngmài.

apart adv. 分开地 fēnkāi de, 分离地 fēnlí de. ~ *from* 除了 ……以外 chúle...yǐwài.

apartheid n. 种族隔离制

种族 gélí zhì.

apartment n. 公寓 gōngyù.

apathy n. 冷淡 lěngdàn, 漠不关心 mòbùguānxīn.

ape n. 猿 yuán. — v. 模仿 mófǎng (imitate).

aperture n. 小孔 xiǎokǒng.

apex n. 尖顶 jiāndǐng.

aphorism n. 格言 géyán, 警语 jǐngyǔ.

apiece adv. 每个 měi ge.

apologize v. 道歉 dàoqiàn.

apology n. 道歉 dàoqiàn.

apoplexy n. 中风 zhòngfēng.

apostle n. 使徒 shǐtú.

apostrophe n. ①省略符号 shěnglüè fúhào ⟨can't⟩. ②所有格符号 suǒyǒugé fúhào ⟨teacher's⟩.

appall v. 使惊骇 shǐ jīnghài.

apparatus n. 仪器 yíqì.

apparel n. 衣服 yīfu.

apparent adj. ①显然的 xiǎnrán de (obvious). ②外表的 wàibiǎo de (seeming).

apparition n. 鬼怪 guǐguài, 幽灵 yōulíng.

appeal n. & v. ①恳求 kěnqiú (ask earnestly). ②上诉 shàngsù (take a case to a higher court).

appear v. ①出现 chūxiàn (show up). ②显得 xiǎnde (seem).

appearance n. ①出现 chūxiàn (show up). ②外观 wàiguān (the way one looks).

appease v. 平息 píngxī / píngxí.

append v. 附加 fùjiā (add on), 增补 zēngbǔ (supplement).

appendicitis n. 盲肠炎 mángchángyán.

appendix n. ①附录 fùlù ⟨written work⟩. ②盲肠

A

mángcháng ⟨medical⟩.

appetite n. ①食欲 shíyù, 胃口 wèikǒu ⟨food⟩. ②欲望 yùwàng (desire).

appetizer n. 开胃菜 kāiwèicài.

applaud v. ①鼓掌 gǔzhǎng (clap). ②赞许 zànxǔ (approve of).

apple n. 苹果 píngguǒ.

appliance n. 器具 qìjù.

applicant n. 申请人 shēnqǐngrén.

application n. ①申请 shēnqǐng (request). ②申请书 shēnqǐngshū ⟨document⟩.

apply v. ①申请 shēnqǐng (ask for). ②敷涂 fūtú (rub). ③应用 yìngyòng (put into use).

appoint v. ①任命 rènmìng ⟨position⟩. ②指定 zhǐdìng ⟨time⟩.

appointment n. ①约会 yuēhuì (arrangement to meet). ②任命 rènmìng ⟨position⟩.

appreciate v. ①欣赏 xīnshǎng (enjoy). ②感激 gǎnjī (be grateful). ③重视 zhòngshì (value).

apprehend v. ①捕捉 bǔzhuō (arrest). ②了解 liǎojiě (understand).

apprehension n. 忧惧 yōujù (anxiety).

apprentice n. 学徒 xuétú.

approach v. 接近 jiējìn (come near). — n. ①接近 jiējìn (approximation). ②通路 tōnglù (access), 入口 rùkǒu (entrance). ③方法 fāngfǎ (method).

appropriate adj. 适当的 shìdàng de. — v. 占用 zhànyòng.

approval n. ①批准 pīzhǔn (permission). ②赞成 zànchéng (agreement).

approve v. ①批准 pīzhǔn (permit). ②赞成 zànchéng (agree).

approximate adj. 大概的 dàgài de.

April n. 四月 Sìyuè.

apron n. 围裙 wéiqún.

apt adj. ①聪敏的 cōngmǐn de (intelligent). ②适当的 shìdàng de (suitable). ③易于……的 yìyú...de (likely to).

aptitude n. 资质 zīzhì / zìzhì (capability). ~ test 性向测验 xìngxiàng cèyàn.

aquarium n. 水族馆 shuǐzúguǎn.

Aquarius 水瓶座 Shuǐpíngzuò.

aquatic adj. ①水生的 shuǐshēng de (living in water). ②水中的 shuǐzhōng de (underwater).

aqueduct n. 水道 shuǐdào.

Arab n. 阿拉伯人 Ālābórén.

Arabic n. 阿拉伯语 Ālābóyǔ ⟨language⟩.

arable adj. 可耕的 kě gēng de.

arbitrary adj. ①任意的 rènyì de (random). ②专横的 zhuānhèng de (dictatorial).

arbitrate v. 仲裁 zhòngcái, 公断 gōngduàn.

arc n. 弧 hú (curved line).

arcade n. 骑楼 qílóu, 拱廊 gǒngláng (gallery).

arch n. 拱门 gǒngmén.

archaeology n. 考古学 kǎogǔxué.

archaic adj. ①古代的 gǔdài de (ancient). ②废弃的 fèiqì de (no longer used). ③古文的 gǔwén de ⟨language⟩.

archbishop n. 总主教 zǒngzhǔjiào.

A

archer *n.* 射手 shèshǒu.

archipelago *n.* ①群岛 qúndǎo (group of small islands). ②多岛之海 duō dǎo zhī hǎi (sea with many islands).

architect *n.* 建筑师 jiànzhùshī / jiànzhúshī ⟨builder⟩.

architecture *n.* 建筑 jiànzhù / jiànzhú.

arduous *adj.* 艰苦的 jiānkǔ de.

are *v.* 是 shì.

area *n.* ①地区 dìqū (region). ②面积 miànjī ⟨surface measure⟩.

arena *n.* 竞技场 jìngjìchǎng.

argue *v.* ①争论 zhēnglùn (quarrel). ②主张 zhǔzhāng (hold a view).

argument *n.* 争论 zhēnglùn (disagreement).

arid *adj.* 干旱的 gānhàn de.

Aries 白羊座 Báiyángzuò.

arise *v.* ①出现 chūxiàn (appear). ②发生 fāshēng (happen).

aristocracy *n.* ①贵族 guìzú (nobility), 贵族阶级 guìzú jiējí (upper class). ②贵族政治 guìzú zhèngzhì (government by the highest social rank).

aristocrat *n.* 贵族 guìzú.

aristocratic *adj.* ①贵族的 guìzú de (of the nobility). ②高级的 gāojí de (high-class).

arithmetic *n.* 算术 suànshù.

ark *n.* 方舟 fāngzhōu.

arm *n.* 手臂 shǒubì.

armada *n.* 舰队 jiànduì.

armament *n.* 军备 jūnbèi.

armistice *n.* 休战 xiūzhàn.

armor *n.* 甲胄 jiǎzhòu.

arms *n.* 武器 wǔqì (weapons). — *v.* 武装 wǔzhuāng.

army *n.* ①军队 jūnduì (military). ②陆军 lùjūn ⟨branch of the military⟩.

aroma *n.* 芳香 fāngxiāng.

aromatherapy *n.* 芳香疗法 fāngxiāng liáofǎ.

around *adv. & prep.* ①在······附近 zài...fùjìn (in the neighborhood of). ②到处 dàochù (everywhere). ③大约 dàyuē (approximately).

arouse *v.* ①激发 jīfā, 引起 yǐnqǐ (incite). ②唤醒 huànxǐng (awaken).

arrange *v.* ①整理 zhěnglǐ (order). ②安排 ānpái (plan).

array *v.* ①列阵 lièzhèn (set in order). ②盛装 shèngzhuāng (dress). — *n.* ①阵容 zhènróng (order). ②展示 zhǎnshì (display).

arrears *n.* 拖延 tuōyán, 拖欠 tuōqiàn.

arrest *v.* ①逮捕 dàibǔ / dǎibǔ (seize by law). ②阻挡 zǔdǎng (stop).

arrival *n.* 到达 dàodá.

arrive *v.* 到达 dàodá, 来临 láilín.

arrogant *adj.* 傲慢的 àomàn de, 自大的 zìdà de.

arrow *n.* ①箭 jiàn ⟨weapon⟩. ②箭号 jiànhào ⟨sign⟩.

arsenal *n.* 兵工厂 bīnggōngchǎng.

arsenic *n.* 砷 shēn, 砒霜 pīshuāng.

arson *n.* 纵火 zònghuǒ.

art *n.* ①艺术 yìshù, 美术 měishù (creation). ②人工 réngōng (not of nature). ③技艺 jìyì (skill).

artery *n.* ①动脉 dòngmài ⟨medical⟩. ②干道 gàndào

A

(main road).

arthritis n. 关节炎 guānjiéyán

article n. ①文章 wénzhāng (written work). ②物件 wùjiàn (object). ③冠词 guàncí 〈grammar〉.

articulate adj. ①清晰的 qīngxī de (clear). ②有口才的 yǒu kǒucái de (well-spoken). — v. ①清晰地发音 qīngxī de fāyīn (pronounce clearly). ②明白地表达 míngbai de biǎodá (express clearly).

artificial adj. ①人工的 réngōng de (man-made). ②做作的 zuòzuo de (insincere).

artillery n. ①大炮 dàpào (big guns). ②炮兵 pàobīng 〈corps〉.

artisan n. 技工 jìgōng.

artist n. 艺术家 yìshùjiā.

artistic adj. 艺术性的 yìshùxìng de.

as adv. 一样 yíyàng (equally). — conj. ①当 dāng (when). ②因为 yīnwèi (because). ③像 xiàng (like). ~ if 好像 hǎoxiàng.

a.s.a.p., ASAP 尽快 jǐnkuài.

asbestos n. 石棉 shímián.

ascend v. ①攀登 pāndēng (climb). ②上升 shàngshēng (rise).

ascent n. ①攀登 pāndēng (climb). ②上升 shàngshēng (rise).

ascertain v. 确定 quèdìng.

ascribe v. ①归因于 guīyīn yú (attribute as the cause). ②认定为 rèndìng wéi (consider to).

aseptic adj. 无菌的 wújūn de / wújùn de.

ash n. 灰 huī, 灰烬 huījìn (ember).

ashamed adj. 羞耻的 xiūchǐ de, 惭愧的 cánkuì de.

ashore adj. & adv. 在岸上 zài àn shang.

ashtray n. 烟灰缸 yānhuīgāng.

Asia 亚洲 Yàzhōu.

Asian adj. 亚洲的 Yàzhōu de. — n. 亚洲人 Yàzhōurén.

aside adv. 向旁边 xiàng pángbiān (to the side), 在旁边 zài pángbiān (on the side).

ask v. ①问 wèn, 询问 xúnwèn (question). ②请求 qǐngqiú (request). ③邀请 yāoqǐng (invite).

askew adj. & adv. 歪斜的 wāixié de.

asleep adj. ①睡着的 shuìzháo de (sleeping). ②麻痹的 mábì de (numb).

asp n. 埃及毒蛇 āijí dúshé.

asparagus n. 芦笋 lúsǔn.

aspect n. ①方面 fāngmiàn (side). ②外貌 wàimào, 样子 yàngzi (appearance).

aspersion n. 诽谤 fěibàng, 中伤 zhòngshāng.

asphalt n. 沥青 lìqīng, 柏油 bǎiyóu / bóyóu.

asphyxia n. 窒息 zhìxí / zhìxí.

aspirate n. 气音 qìyīn.

aspiration n. 热望 rèwàng, 抱负 bàofù (desire).

aspire v. 热望 rèwàng, 有抱负 yǒu bàofù (desire).

aspirin n. 阿司匹林 āsīpǐlín / 阿斯匹林 āsīpǐlíng.

ass n. ①驴 lǘ (donkey). ②笨蛋 bèndàn (stupid person). ③屁股 pìgu 〈part of body〉.

assail v. 攻击 gōngjī / gōngjí.

assassin n. 刺客 cìkè.

assassinate v. 暗杀 ànshā.

assault n. & v. 突击 tūjī / tújí
(attack).

assemble v. ①集会 jíhuì, 集合
jíhé (gather together). ②装配
zhuāngpèi (put together).

assembly n. 集会 jíhuì
(gathering), 会议 huìyì (meeting).

assent n. & v. 同意 tóngyì,
赞成 zànchéng.

assert v. 断言 duànyán, 宣称
xuānchēng (declare firmly).

assess v. 估价 gūjià.

asset n. ①资产 zīchǎn, 财产
cáichǎn (property). ②有价值
物 yǒu jiàzhí wù (valuable quality or skill). *immovable ~s* 不动
产 búdòngchǎn. *personal ~s*
动产 dòngchǎn.

assiduous adj. 勤勉的
qínmiǎn de (diligent).

assign v. ①分配 fēnpèi, 分派
fēnpài (allocate). ②指派 zhǐpài,
指定 zhǐdìng (appoint). ③让渡
ràngdù (transfer).

assignment n. ①分配 fēnpèi,
分派 fēnpài (allocation).
②指派 zhǐpài, 指定 zhǐdìng
(appointment). ③任务 rènwu
(duty). ④作业 zuòyè (task), 功
课 gōngkè (homework).

assimilate v. ①吸收 xīshōu
(absorb). ②同化 tónghuà
(become part of).

assist v. 帮助 bāngzhù.

assistance n. 帮助 bāngzhù.

assistant n. 助理 zhùlǐ, 助手
zhùshǒu.

associate v. 联合 liánhé,
结交 jiéjiāo (join or connect).
— n. 同伴 tóngbàn
(companion), 同事 tóngshì
(co-worker).

association n. ①协会 xiéhuì
(committee). ②联合 liánhé
(connection).

assume v. ①假设 jiǎshè
(suppose). ②担任 dānrèn
(undertake).

assumption n. ①假设 jiǎshè
(supposition). ②担任 dānrèn
(undertaking).

assurance n. ①保证
bǎozhèng (promise). ②自信
zìxìn (confidence).

assure v. ①保证 bǎozhèng
(promise). ②确信 quèxìn
(make certain).

asterisk n. 星号 xīnghào.

astern adv. 在船尾 zài
chuánwěi ⟨of a ship⟩.

asthma n. 气喘 qìchuǎn.

astigmatism n. 散光
sǎnguāng.

astonish v. 使惊奇 shǐ jīngqí.

astound v. 使大惊 shǐ dàjīng.

astray adj. & adv. 迷途的
mítú de.

astride adv. & prep. 跨着
kuàzhe, 骑着 qízhe.

astrology n. 占星学
zhānxīngxué.

astronaut n. 宇航员
yǔhángyuán / 太空人
tàikōngrén.

astronomy n. 天文学
tiānwénxué.

astute adj. 聪明的 cōngming
de (intelligent), 敏锐的 mǐnruì
de (perceptive).

asylum n. 避难所 bìnànsuǒ,
收容院 shōuróngyuàn
(refuge).

at prep. 在…… zài….

atheism n. 无神论 wúshénlùn.

athlete n. 运动员
yùndòngyuán.

athletic adj. 运动的 yùndòng
de.

athletics n. 体育运动 tǐyù yùndòng.

Atlantic Ocean 大西洋 Dàxīyáng.

atlas n. 地图集 dìtújí.

ATM 自动柜员机 zìdòng guìyuánjī.

atmosphere n. ①大气 dàqì, 空气 kōngqì (air). ②氛围 fēnwéi / 气氛 qìfēn (ambience).

atoll n. 环礁 huánjiāo.

atom n. 原子 yuánzǐ. ~ *bomb* 原子弹 yuánzǐdàn.

atrocious adj. ①凶暴的 xiōngbào de (evil). ②糟透的 zāo tòu de (awful).

atrophy n. & v. 萎缩 wěisuō / wěisuō.

attach v. ①附上 fùshàng, 贴上 tiēshàng (fasten or join). ②相关联 xiāngguānlián (connect with). ③伴随 bànsuí (go with).

attaché n. 随员 suíyuán.

attachment n. 附着 fùzhuó, 附件 fùjiàn (accessory).

attack n. & v. 攻击 gōngjī / gōngjī.

attain v. 达到 dádào (reach), 得到 dédào (achieve).

attempt n. & v. 尝试 chángshì, 企图 qìtú / qìtú (try).

attend v. ①出席 chūxí (be present at). ②注意 zhùyì (pay attention to). ③侍候 shìhòu (wait upon), 照顾 zhàogù (look after).

attendant n. 侍者 shìzhě (servant), 服务生 fúwùshēng (waiter). — adj. 伴随的 bànsuí de (accompanying).

attention n. 注意 zhùyì.

attest v. 证明 zhèngmíng (proof), 宣誓 xuānshì (claim).

attic n. 阁楼 gélóu.

attire n. ①盛装 shèngzhuāng (formal wear). ②服装 fúzhuāng (clothing).

attitude n. 态度 tàidu (outlook), 姿态 zītài (position).

attorney n. 代理人 dàilǐrén (agent), 律师 lǜshī (lawyer).

attract v. 吸引 xīyǐn, 引诱 yǐnyòu.

attraction n. 吸引力 xīyǐnlì.

attractive adj. ①好看的 hǎokàn de (good-looking). ②有吸引力的 yǒu xīyǐnlì de (appealing).

attribute v. 归因于 guīyīn yú. — n. 特质 tèzhì / tèzhì (quality).

auburn n. & adj. 赤褐色 chìhésè / chìhésè.

auction n. 拍卖 pāimài.

audacious adj. ①大胆的 dàdàn de (brave). ②无耻的 wúchǐ de (impudent).

audacity n. 大胆无耻 dàdàn wúchǐ (impudence).

audible adj. 听得见的 tīngdejiàn de.

audience n. 听众 tīngzhòng 〈aural〉, 观众 guānzhòng 〈visual〉.

audiobook n. 有声书 yǒushēngshū.

audit v. 稽核 jīhé, 查账 cházhàng.

audition n. & v. 试听 shìtīng.

auditorium n. 讲堂 jiǎngtáng, 集会厅 jíhuìtīng.

augment v. 加大 jiā dà (enlarge), 增加 zēngjiā (increase).

August n. 八月 Bāyuè.

aunt n. ①阿姨 āyí (mother's sister, woman of mother's generation). ②伯母 bómǔ

(father's older brother's wife), 婶母 shěnmǔ (father's younger brother's wife). ③舅母 jiùmǔ (mother's brother's wife). ④姑 gūgu (father's sister).

auspice n. 主办 zhǔbàn, 赞助 zànzhù (support).

auspicious adj. 吉利的 jílì de.

austere adj. ①严肃的 yánsù de (severe). ②朴素的 pǔsù de / pǔsù de (simple and plain).

authentic adj. 真正的 zhēnzhèng de, 真实的 zhēnshí de.

author n. 作家 zuòjiā, 作者 zuòzhě.

authority n. ①权威 quánwēi (power). ②专家 zhuānjiā (expert). ③当权者 dāngquánzhě (one in power). ④当局 dāngjú (government).

authorize v. ①授权 shòuquán (empower). ②认可 rènkě (permit).

auto n. 汽车 qìchē.

autobiography n. 自传 zìzhuàn.

autocracy n. 独裁政治 dúcái zhèngzhì.

autocrat n. 独裁者 dúcáizhě.

autograph n. 亲笔签名 qīnbǐ qiānmíng.

automatic adj. ①自动的 zìdòng de (mechanical). ②不自觉的 bú zìjué de (without thought).

automation n. 自动操作 zìdòng cāozuò.

automobile n. 汽车 qìchē.

autonomous adj. 自治的 zìzhì de. ~ region 自治区 zìzhìqū.

autonomy n. 自治 zìzhì.

autopsy n. 验尸 yànshī.

autumn n. 秋季 qiūjì, 秋天 qiūtiān.

auxiliary adj. 辅助的 fǔzhù de. – n. 助动词 zhùdòngcí.

avail v. 应用 yìngyòng, 使用 shǐyòng (use). – n. 效用 xiàoyòng.

avalanche n. 雪崩 xuěbēng.

avarice n. 贪婪 tānlán.

avenge v. 报仇 bàochóu, 报复 bàofù.

avenue n. ①大道 dàdào (wide road). ②林荫大道 línyìn dàdào / línyìn dàdào (tree-lined road).

average n. & adj. ①平均 píngjūn (mean). ②一般 yìbān (normal).

avert v. 避开 bìkai.

aviary n. 鸟舍 niǎoshè.

aviation n. 航空 hángkōng.

avid adj. ①热心的 rèxīn de (eager). ②贪婪的 tānlán de (greedy).

avocado n. 鳄梨 èlí.

avoid v. 避免 bìmiǎn.

await v. 等候 děnghòu, 等待 děngdài.

awake v. ①醒 xǐng ⟨from sleep⟩. ②觉悟 juéwù (become conscious).

award n. & v. 奖赏 jiǎngshǎng.

aware adj. 察觉的 chájué de, 有感觉的 yǒu gǎnjué de (having a sense), 知道的 zhīdào de (knowing).

away adv. ①不在 búzài (not present). ②在远方 zài yuǎnfāng (at a distance). ③离去 líqù (separate). *right* ~ 立即 lìjí.

awe n. & v. 敬畏 jìngwèi.

awesome adj. 了不起的 liǎobuqǐ de (very great).

awful adj. ①可怕的 kěpà de (terrible). ②极坏的 jí huài de

(very bad).

awhile *adv.* 片刻 piànkè.

awkward *adj.* ①笨拙地 bènzhuō de / bènzhuó de (clumsy). ②不合用的 bù héyòng de (not good for use). ③尴尬的 gāngà de (embarrassing).

awl *n.* 锥子 zhuīzi.

awning *n.* 雨篷 yǔpéng.

ax, axe *n.* 斧 fǔ.

axiom *n.* ①公理 gōnglǐ ⟨mathematics⟩. ②原理 yuánlǐ (principle).

axis *n.* 轴 zhóu.

axle *n.* 轮轴 lúnzhóu.

azalea *n.* 杜鹃花 dùjuānhuā.

azure *n. & adj.* 青色 qīngsè.

B

B.A. 文学士 wénxuéshì.

babble *v.* ①唠叨 láodao (chatter). ②模糊不清地说 móhu bù qīng de shuō (make unclear sounds).

baboon *n.* 狒狒 fèifèi.

baby *n.* 婴儿 yīng'ér.

baby boom *n.* 婴儿潮 yīng'ércháo.

babysitter *n.* 保姆 bǎomǔ.

bachelor *n.* ①单身汉 dānshēnhàn (unmarried man). ②学士 xuéshì (university degree).

back *n.* ①背部 bèibù ⟨body part⟩. ②背面 bèimiàn (rear of object). — *v.* 支持 zhīchí (support). — *adj.* 背后的 bèihòu de, 后面的 hòumiàn de (in back). — *adv.* ①向后 xiànghòu, 后退 hòutuì (backward). ②在……后面 zài...hòumiàn (behind).

backbone *n.* 脊椎骨 jǐzhuīgǔ ⟨animal⟩.

background *n.* 背景 bèijǐng.

backward(s) *adj. & adv.*

①向后（的）xiànghòu (de) (behind). ②落后 luòhòu (underdeveloped). *~ (s) and forward(s)* 往返的 wǎngfǎn de.

backyard *n.* 后院 hòuyuàn.

bacon *n.* 熏猪肉 xūnzhūròu, 培根 péigēn.

bacteria *n.* 细菌 xìjūn / xìjùn.

bad *adj.* 坏的 huài de. *too ~* 可惜 kěxī / kěxí.

badge *n.* 徽章 huīzhāng.

badger *n.* 獾 huān ⟨animal⟩. — *v.* 烦扰 fánrǎo (bother).

badly *adv.* ①不好 bùhǎo (not well). ②非常 fēicháng (very much).

badminton *n.* 羽毛球 yǔmáoqiú.

baffle *v.* ①使困惑 shǐ kùnhuò (puzzle). ②阻挠 zǔnáo, 妨碍 fáng'ài (prevent).

bag *n.* 袋 dài, 袋子 dàizi, 手提包 shǒutíbāo.

bagel *n.* 硬面包 yìngmiànbāo, 培果 péiguǒ.

baggage *n.* 行李 xíngli.

bail *n.* 保释金 bǎoshìjīn (money). — *v.* 保释 bǎoshì.

bailiff *n.* 执行官 zhíxíngguān.

bait *n.* 饵 ěr. — *v.* ①下饵 xià'ěr ⟨fishing⟩. ②诱惑 yòuhuò (tempt).

bake *v.* 烘烤 hōngkǎo ⟨oven⟩.

baker *n.* 面包师 miànbāoshī.

bakery *n.* 面包店 miànbāodiàn.

baking powder *n.* 发酵粉 fājiàofěn / fāxiàofěn.

balance *n.* ①平衡 pínghéng (equilibrium). ②差额 chā'é (difference). ③天平 tiānpíng ⟨scales⟩. — *v.* 使平衡 shǐ pínghéng (equalize).

balcony *n.* ①阳台 yángtái ⟨building⟩. ②楼座 lóuzuò ⟨theater⟩.

bald *adj.* 秃头的 tūtóu de.

bale *n.* & *v.* 捆 kǔn.

ball *n.* ①球 qiú (sphere). ②舞会 wǔhuì (dance party). ~ *game* 球赛 qiúsài.

ballad *n.* ①情歌 qínggē (song). ②叙事诗 xùshìshī (poem).

ballast *n.* 压舱物 yācāngwù.

ballerina *n.* 女芭蕾舞者 nǚ bālěiwǔ zhě.

ballet *n.* 芭蕾舞 bālěiwǔ. ~ *dancer* 芭蕾舞者 bālěiwǔ zhě.

balloon *n.* 气球 qìqiú.

ballot *n.* 投票用纸 tóupiào yòng zhǐ.

ballpoint *n.* 圆珠笔 yuánzhūbǐ / 原子笔 yuánzǐbǐ.

balm *n.* ①香膏 xiānggāo ⟨liquid⟩. ②镇痛剂 zhèntòngjì (comfort).

bamboo *n.* 竹 zhú.

ban *v.* 禁止 jìnzhǐ. — *n.* 禁令 jìnlìng.

banal *adj.* 乏味的 fáwèi de.

banana *n.* 香蕉 xiāngjiāo.

band *n.* ①带 dài, 绳 shéng (strip). ②乐队 yuèduì ⟨music⟩. ③一群 yì qún (group).

bandage *n.* 绷带 bēngdài. — *v.* 缚以绷带 fù yǐ bēngdài / fú yǐ bēngdài.

bandit *n.* 强盗 qiángdào, 土匪 tǔfěi.

bandy *v.* ①来回投掷 láihuí tóuzhì / láihuí tóuzhí (throw). ②争论 zhēnglùn (argue).

bang *n.* 猛然巨响 měngrán jùxiǎng (sudden noise).

bangle *n.* 手镯 shǒuzhuó ⟨hand⟩.

banish *v.* ①驱逐出境 qūzhú chūjìng (exile). ②消除 xiāochú (put away). ③摆脱 bǎituō (get rid of).

banister *n.* 栏杆 lángān.

banjo *n.* 五弦琴 wǔxiánqín.

bank *n.* ①银行 yínháng (financial institution). ②岸 àn, 堤 dī / tí (embankment). ③斜坡 xiépō (slope). ~ *account* 银行账户 yínháng zhànghù.

banker *n.* 银行家 yínhángjiā.

bankrupt *n.* 破产者 pòchǎnzhě. — *adj.* 破产的 pòchǎn de.

banner *n.* 旗帜 qízhì.

banquet *n.* 宴会 yànhuì.

banter *n.* & *v.* 嘲弄 cháonòng, 开玩笑 kāi wánxiào.

banyan *n.* 榕树 róngshù.

baptism *n.* 洗礼 xǐlǐ.

bar *n.* ①棒 bàng, 棍 gùn (stick). ②门闩 ménshuān ⟨door⟩. ③酒吧 jiǔbā (pub). — *v.* ①闩住 shuānzhù (block by putting a bar across). ②阻止 zǔzhǐ (prevent), 禁止 jìnzhǐ (prohibit).

B

barb n. 倒钩 dàogōu.

barbarian n. 野蛮人 yěmánrén. — adj. 野蛮的 yěmán de.

barbarous adj. ①残忍的 cánrěn de (cruel). ②野蛮的 yěmán de (uncivilized).

barbecue n. 烤肉 kǎoròu 〈meat〉. — v. 烧烤 shāokǎo 〈cook〉.

barber n. 理发师 lǐfàshī / lǐfǎshī.

barbershop n. 理发店 lǐfàdiàn / lǐfǎdiàn.

bare adj. ①赤裸的 chìluǒ de (uncovered, naked). ②起码的 qǐmǎ de (minimum). — v. 暴露 bàolù / pùlù (expose).

barely adv. 几乎没有 jīhū méiyǒu (hardly).

bargain n. ①交易 jiāoyì (deal). ②协议 xiéyì (agreement). ③便宜货 piányihuò, 廉价品 liánjiàpǐn 〈goods〉. — v. ①议价 yìjià, 杀价 shājià (haggle). ②协议 xiéyì (try to reach an agreement).

barge n. 平底货船 píngdǐ huòchuán, 驳船 bóchuán. — v. 鲁莽冲撞 lǔmǎng chōngzhuàng.

baritone n. 男中音 nánzhōngyīn.

bark n. ①狗吠声 gǒufèishēng 〈sound〉. ②树皮 shùpí 〈tree〉. — v. 狗吠 gǒufèi.

barley n. 大麦 dàmài.

barn n. 谷仓 gǔcāng.

barometer n. 气压计 qìyājì, 晴雨表 qíngyǔbiǎo.

baron n. 男爵 nánjué.

barracks n. 兵营 bīngyíng 〈for soldiers〉.

barrage n. ①猛烈炮火 měngliè pàohuǒ (heavy gunfire). ②炮轰 pàohōng 〈of speech〉.

barrel n. ①大桶 dàtǒng 〈container〉. ②枪管 qiāngguǎn 〈gun〉.

barren adj. 贫瘠的 pínjí de.

barricade n. & v. 障碍 zhàng'ài, 路障 lùzhàng.

barrier n. ①栅栏 zhàlan (fence). ②障碍 zhàng'ài (hindrance).

barrister n. 律师 lùshī.

barter n. & v. 以物易物 yǐwù-yìwù.

base n. ①根基 gēnjī (foundation). ②基地 jīdì 〈armed forces〉. ③垒 lěi 〈ball games〉. — adj. 卑鄙的 bēibì de (not honorable). — v. 以……为基础 yǐ...wéi jīchǔ. ~ **on** 基于 jīyú.

baseball n. 棒球 bàngqiú.

basement n. 地下室 dìxiàshì.

bash n. & v. 重击 zhòngjī / zhòngjí.

bashful adj. 害羞的 hàixiū de.

basic adj. 基本的 jīběn de, 基础的 jīchǔ de (fundamental). — n. 基础 jīchǔ (foundation).

basically adv. 基本上 jīběnshang.

basin n. ①盆 pén 〈bowl〉. ②水坑 shuǐkēng (pool). ③流域 liúyù, 盆地 péndì 〈drainage area〉.

basis n. 基础 jīchǔ (foundation), 根据 gēnjù (evidence). **on the ~ of...** 根据 gēnjù....

bask v. ①取暖 qǔnuǎn (enjoy warmth), 晒太阳 shàitàiyáng (sunbathe). ②陶醉 táozuì (enjoy).

basket n. 篮 lán, 篮子 lánzi.

basketball n. 篮球 lánqiú.

bass adj. 低音的 dīyīn de.
— n. ①男低音 nándīyīn
(lowest male voice). ②鲈鱼
lúyú 〈fish〉.

bassoon n. 巴松管
bāsōngguǎn.

bastard n. 私生子 sīshēngzǐ
(illegitimate child).

baste v. 烧烤时涂油脂
shāokǎo shí tú yóuzhī.

bastion n. 棱堡 léngbǎo.

bat n. ①棒 bàng (club), 球拍
qiúpāi 〈ball games〉. ②蝙蝠
biānfú 〈animal〉.

batch n. ①一炉 yì lú 〈food〉.
②一批 yì pī, 一群 yì qún
(group).

bath n. ①沐浴 mùyù (wash).
②澡盆 zǎopén (bathtub).
③浴室 yùshì (bathroom).

bathe v. ①沐浴 mùyù, 洗澡
xǐzǎo (take a bath). ②水洗
shuǐxǐ (wash).

bathing suit n. 泳衣 yǒngyī.

bathrobe n. 浴袍 yùpáo.

bathroom n. 浴室 yùshì.

bathtub n. 浴缸 yùgāng.

baton n. ①指挥棒 zhǐhuībàng
〈orchestra〉. ②警棍 jǐnggùn
〈police〉.

battalion n. 营 yíng.

batter v. ①捣坏 dǎohuài (wear
out). ②连击 liánjí / liánjī (beat).
— n. ①面糊 miànhù / miànhú
(mixture). ②打击手 dǎjíshǒu /
dǎjīshǒu 〈ball games〉.

battery n. ①电池 diànchí
(electric cells). ②炮兵连
pàobīnglián 〈army unit〉.

battle n. ①战争 zhànzhēng,
战役 zhànyì (war). ②争斗
zhēngdòu (fight).

battlement n. 城垛 chéngduǒ.

bauble n. 美丽但无用之饰品
měilì dàn wúyòng zhī shìpǐn
(small item of litte value).

bawl n. & v. 大喊 dàhǎn (yell),
哭叫 kūjiào (cry).

bay n. 海湾 hǎiwān (coast).
~ **window** 凸窗 tūchuāng /
túchuāng.

bayonet n. 刺刀 cìdāo.

bazaar n. 市集 shìjí
(shopping center), 传统市场
chuántǒng shìchǎng (traditional market).

BBS 电子公告板系统 diànzǐ
gōnggàobǎn xìtǒng / 电子布
告栏系统 diànzǐ bùgàolán
xìtǒng (Bulletin Board System).

B.C. 西元前 xīyuán qián.

be v. 是 shì.

beach n. 海滩 hǎitān (seaside),
沙滩 shātān (sandy bank).

beacon n. ①灯塔 dēngtǎ
(lighthouse). ②烽火 fēnghuǒ
(signal fire). ③信号 xìnhào
(marker).

bead n. 念珠 niànzhū.

beak n. 鸟嘴 niǎozuǐ.

beam n. ①横梁 héngliáng
(heavy bar). ②船舷 chuánxián
〈ship〉. ③光线 guāngxiàn 〈light〉.

bean n. 豆 dòu.

bear v. ①背 bēi, 负载 fùzài
(carry). ②生产 shēngchǎn,
生育 shēngyù (give birth to).
③容忍 róngrěn (tolerate).
— n. ①熊 xióng 〈animal〉.
②空头 kōngtóu / kòngtóu
〈stock market〉.

beard n. 胡须 húxū.

bearing n. ①举止 jǔzhǐ, 态度
tàidu (attitude). ②关系 guānxi,
意义 yìyì (relation). ③姿态
zītài (manner).

beast *n.* 兽 shòu, 动物 dòngwù.

beat *v.* ①打 dǎ (strike). ②击败 jíbài / jíbài (defeat). ③规律鼓动 guīlǜ gǔdòng (pulse). — *n.* ①敲打 qiāodǎ (drum). ②节拍 jiépāi (rhythm).

beaten *adj.* 被打败的 bèi dǎbài de (defeated).

beautician *n.* 美容师 měiróngshī.

beautiful *adj.* 美丽的 měilì de.

beautify *v.* 美化 měihuà.

beauty *n.* ①美 měi, 美貌 měimào (prettiness). ②美人 měirén (pretty person).

beaver *n.* 海狸 hǎilí.

because *conj.* 因为 yīnwèi.

beckon *v.* 招手示意 zhāoshǒu shìyì.

become *v.* ①变为 biànwéi (change into), 成为 chéngwéi (come to be). ②适合 shìhé, 相称 xiāngchèn / xiāngchèng (fit).

bed *n.* ①床 chuáng (furniture). ②基底 jīdǐ (base).

bedding *n.* 寝具 qǐnjù.

bedlam *n.* 喧扰 xuānrǎo.

bedroom *n.* 卧房 wòfáng.

bedsore *n.* 褥疮 rùchuāng.

bedtime *n.* 就寝时间 jiùqǐn shíjiān.

bee *n.* 蜜蜂 mìfēng.

beech *n.* 山毛榉 shānmáojǔ.

beef *n.* 牛肉 niúròu.

beefsteak *n.* 牛排 niúpái.

beehive *n.* 蜂窝 fēngwō.

beer *n.* 啤酒 píjiǔ.

beet *n.* 甜菜 tiáncài.

beetle *n.* 甲虫 jiǎchóng.

befall *v.* 降临 jiànglín, 发生 fāshēng.

befit *v.* 适合 shìhé.

before *adv. & prep. & conj.* ①以前 yǐqián (in the past). ②在……之前 zài...zhīqián (earlier than). ③在……的面前 zài...de miànqián (in front of).

beforehand *adv.* 事前 shìqián.

befriend *v.* 待之如友 dài zhī rú yǒu.

beg *v.* ①恳求 kěnqiú (favors). ②乞讨 qǐtǎo (money).

beggar *n.* 乞丐 qǐgài.

begin *v.* 开始 kāishǐ (start), 始于 shǐyú (originate with).

beginner *n.* ①初学者 chūxuézhě (for learning). ②初始者 chūshǐzhě (for starting).

beginning *n.* 开始 kāishǐ (start), 起源 qǐyuán (origin).

begrudge *v.* ①嫉妒 jídù (envy). ②舍不得 shěbude (give unwillingly).

behalf *n.* on ~ of 为了……（的利益）wèile...(de lìyì) (in the interest of), 作……的代表 zuò...de dàibiǎo (as somebody's representative).

behave *v.* 行为 xíngwéi, 举动 jǔdòng (act).

behavior *n.* 行为 xíngwéi (way of acting), 态度 tàidu (attitude).

behead *v.* 斩首 zhǎnshǒu.

behind *adv. & prep.* ①在后 zài hòu (in back of). ②落后 luòhòu (not progressive). ③较迟 jiàochí (late). ~ the times 落伍 luòwǔ

beige *n. & adj.* 棕灰色 zōnghuīsè.

being *n.* ①生命 shēngmìng (living thing). ②存在 cúnzài (existence).

belated *adj.* 误期的 wùqī de / wùqí de, 太迟的 tài chí de

(coming too late).

belch n. & v. 打嗝 dǎgé.

belfry n. 钟楼 zhōnglóu.

belief n. ①信念 xìnniàn, 信仰 xìnyǎng (religious faith). ②信任 xìnrèn, 相信 xiāngxìn (trust).

believe v. ①相信 xiāngxìn (trust). ②认为 rènwéi (think).

belittle v. 轻视 qīngshì, 贬低 biǎndī.

bell n. 铃 líng, 钟 zhōng.

bell-bottoms n. 喇叭裤 lǎbakù.

belligerent adj. ①好战的 hàozhàn de (war-mongering). ②交战的 jiāozhàn de (at war). ③好斗的 hàodòu de (aggressive).

bellow v. ①怒吼 nùhǒu, 咆哮 páoxiào / páoxiāo (yell). ②吼叫 hǒujiào (cow).

belly n. ①腹部 fùbù (abdomen). ②胃 wèi (stomach).

belong v. 属于 shǔyú, 归于 guīyú.

belongings n. 财产 cáichǎn, 所有物 suǒyǒuwù.

beloved adj. 所爱的 suǒ'ài de. — n. 所爱的人 suǒ'ài de rén ⟨a person⟩, 亲爱的朋友们 qīn'ài de péngyoumen ⟨address⟩.

below prep. 在……之下 zài...zhīxià (in a lower position). — adv. 在下面 zài xiàmiàn (at a lower place).

belt n. ①带 dài, 皮带 pídài ⟨clothing⟩. ②传送带 chuánsòngdài (conveyor).

bemoan v. 恸哭 tòngkū, 悲悼 bēidào.

bemused adj. 困惑的 kùnhuò de (perplexed).

bench n. ①长凳 chángdèng (long seat). ②工作台 gōngzuòtái (long worktable).

bend v. 使弯曲 shǐ wānqū (curve). — n. ①弯曲 wānqū (angle). ②转弯 zhuǎnwān (turn).

beneath adv. & prep. 在……下 zài...xià (under).

benediction n. 祝福 zhùfú, 祝祷 zhùdǎo.

beneficial adj. 有益的 yǒuyì de.

beneficiary n. 受益人 shòuyìrén.

benefit n. ①利益 lìyì (advantage). ②恩惠 ēnhuì (good deed). — v. 有益于 yǒuyì yú, 对……有利 duì...yǒulì.

benevolent adj. 慈善的 císhàn de.

benign adj. ①和蔼的 hé'ǎi de ⟨person⟩. ②良性的 liángxìng de ⟨disease⟩.

bent v. 弯曲的 wānqū de (not straight). — n. ①倾向 qīngxiàng (tendency). ②爱好 àihào (hobby).

bequeath v. 遗赠 yízèng / wèizèng.

bequest n. 遗赠 yízèng / wèizèng, 遗产 yíchǎn.

bereave v. 剥夺 bōduó.

bereaved adj. 丧亲的 sàngqīn de.

bereft adj. 丧失的 sàngshī de.

beriberi n. 脚气病 jiǎoqìbìng.

berry n. 浆果 jiāngguǒ.

berth n. ①卧铺 wòpù (place to sleep). ②船停泊处 chuán tíngbó chù (place to anchor).

beset v. ①围攻 wéigōng, 包围 bāowéi (surround and attack). ②困扰 kùnrǎo (trouble).

B

B

beside *prep.* ①在旁 zài páng (next to). ②和……比较 hé... bǐjiào (compared to).

besides *adv. & prep.* 而且 érqiě, 此外 cǐwài (also).

besiege *v.* ①围攻 wéigōng (surround and attack). ②困扰 kùnrǎo (trouble).

best *adj.* 最佳的 zuì jiā de, 最好的 zuì hǎo de. ~ *man* 男傧相 nánbīnxiàng, 伴郎 bànláng. — *n.* 最好 zuìhǎo. *at* ~ 充其量 chōngqíliàng. *ma ke the* ~ *of* 尽力而为 jìnlì-érwéi.

bestial *adj.* 像野兽的 xiàng yěshòu de (brutish).

best-known *adj.* 最出名的 zuì chūmíng de.

bestow *v.* 给予 jǐyǔ (give), 赠与 zèngyǔ (confer).

bet *v.* 打赌 dǎdǔ. *You* ~! 当然！ Dāngrán! — *n.* 赌注 dǔzhù.

betray *v.* ①出卖 chūmài (sell out). ②泄露 xièlòu (disclose).

betrothed *adj.* 已订婚的 yǐ dìnghūn de.

better *adj. & adv.* ①更好的 gèng hǎo de (more excellent). ②较佳的 jiào jiā de ⟨illness⟩. *had* ~ 最好 zuìhǎo.

between *adv. & prep.* 在…… 之间 zài...zhī jiān.

bevel *n.* ①斜面 xiémiàn (surface). ②斜角 xiéjiǎo (edge). — *v.* 使成斜角 shǐ chéng xiéjiǎo.

beveled *adj.* 斜面的 xiémiàn de ⟨surface⟩, 斜角的 xiéjiǎo de ⟨angle⟩.

beverage *n.* 饮料 yǐnliào.

bevy *n.* 一群 yì qún.

beware *v.* 留意 liúyì, 提防

dīfang / tífáng.

bewilder *v.* 使迷惑 shǐ míhuò.

bewitch *v.* ①施魔法 shǐ mófǎ, 迷惑 míhuò (work magic on). ②迷人 mírén (charm).

beyond *prep.* ①在……的那 边 zài...de nàbian (on the far side of). ②之后 zhīhòu (after). ③超过 chāoguò (exceeding).

bias *n.* ①偏见 piānjiàn, 成见 chéngjiàn (prejudice). ②斜线 xiéxiàn (diagonal).

bib *n.* 围兜 wéidōu.

Bible *n.* 圣经 Shèngjīng.

bibliography *n.* ①参考书目 cānkǎo shūmù (list of refer-ences). ②书志 shūzhì ⟨history of books⟩. ③作品目录 zuòpǐn mùlù (list of writings).

bicker *n. & v.* 争吵 zhēngchǎo.

bicycle *n.* 自行车 zìxíngchē. ~ *path* 自行车道 zìxíngchēdào.

bid *v.* ①出价 chūjià (offer as a price). ②命令 mìnglìng, 吩咐 fēnfù (command). — *n.* 出价 chūjià (an offered price).

biennial *n. & adj.* 两年一次 liǎng nián yí cì.

bifocals *n.* 远近视两用眼镜 yuǎn-jìnshì liǎngyòng yǎnjìng.

big *adj.* ①大的 dà de (large). ②重要的 zhòngyào de (important).

bigamy *n.* 重婚 chónghūn.

bigot *n.* 顽信者 wánxìnzhě, 偏执者 piānzhízhě.

bike *n.* ①自行车 zìxíngchē ⟨without motor⟩. ②轻型摩 托车 qīngxíng mótuōchē (motorbike).

bilateral *adj.* 两边的 liǎngbiān de, 双方的 shuāngfāng de.

bile *n.* 胆汁 dǎnzhī ⟨liquid⟩.

bilingual *adj.* 双语的 shuāngyǔ de.

bill *n.* ①账单 zhàngdān (list of charges). ②钞票 chāopiào (banknote). ③广告单 guǎnggàodān (printed notice). ④草案 cǎo'àn (draft of law). ⑤鸟嘴 niǎozuǐ (beak).

billet *n.* 兵营舍 bīngyíngshè (soldiers). — *v.* 安排兵舍 ānpái bīngshè.

billiards *n.* 台球 táiqiú / 撞球 zhuàngqiú.

billion *n.* 十亿 shíyì.

billow *n.* ①巨浪 jùlàng (large wave). — *v.* ①汹涌 xiōngyǒng (swell in waves). ②扬起 yángqǐ (swell out).

bimbo *n.* 漂亮而没大脑的女郎 piàoliang ér méi dànǎo de nǚláng.

bin *n.* 大箱 dàxiāng.

binary *adj.* 双重的 shuāngchóng de. — *n.* 双子星 shuāngzǐxīng (stars).

bind *v.* ①缚 fù / 缚 kǔn (tie together). ②包扎 bāozā / bāozhá (bandage). ③凝聚 níngjù (hold together). ④约束 yuēshù (compel).

bingo *n.* 宾戈 bīngē / 宾果游戏 bīnguǒ yóuxì.

biochemistry *n.* 生物化学 shēngwù huàxué, 生化 shēng-huà.

biography *n.* 传记 zhuànjì.

biology *n.* 生物学 shēngwùxué.

birch *n.* 桦树 huàshù.

bird *n.* 鸟 niǎo.

bird flu *n.* 禽流感 qínliúgǎn.

bird-strick *n.* 鸟击 niǎojī / niǎojí.

bird-watching *n.* 鸟类观察 niǎolèi guānchá.

birth *n.* ①出生 chūshēng, 出世 chūshì, 诞生 dànshēng (being born). ②出身 chūshēn, 家世 jiāshì (family origin).

birthday *n.* 生日 shēngrì.

birthmark *n.* 胎记 tāijì.

birthplace *n.* 出生地 chūshēngdì.

biscuit *n.* 饼干 bǐnggān.

bisect *v.* 一分为二 yī fēnwéi èr.

bisexual *adj.* 雌雄同体的 cíxióng-tóngtǐ de / cíxióng--tóngtǐ de (hermaphrodite). — *n.* 双性恋 shuāngxìngliàn.

bishop *n.* 主教 zhǔjiào.

bison *n.* 野牛 yěniú.

bit *n.* 一小块 yì xiǎo kuài (small piece), 一点点 yìdiǎndiǎn (small amount). *not a* ~ 毫不 háobù.

bitch *n.* ①母狗 mǔgǒu (female dog). ②贱女人 jiànnǚrén (bad woman).

bite *n.* ①咬 yǎo (act of biting). ②一口 yì kǒu (a mouthful). ③咬伤 yǎoshāng (bite wound). — *v.* ①咬 yǎo, 叮 dīng (sting). ②抓紧 zhuājǐn (grip). ③刺痛 cìtòng (cause pain).

bitter *adj.* ①苦的 kǔ de (taste). ②痛苦的 tòngkǔ de (sorrowful).

bitterness *n.* 苦 kǔ.

bizarre *adj.* 古怪的 gǔguài de.

black *adj.* ①黑色的 hēisè de (color). ②暗淡的 àndàn de (dark). — *n.* ①黑色 hēisè (color). ②黑人 hēirén (race). ~ *eye* 黑眼圈 hēiyǎnquān. ~ *hole* 黑洞 hēidòng. ~ *market* 黑市 hēishì.

~ tea 红茶 hóngchá.

blackboard n. 黑板 hēibǎn.

blacken v. ①变黑 biànhēi (become black), 变暗 biàn'àn (become dark). ②毁谤 huǐbàng (speak badly of).

blackguard n. 流氓 liúmáng, 无赖 wúlài.

blackmail n. & v. 勒索 lèsuǒ, 敲诈 qiāozhà.

blackout n. ①停电 tíngdiàn (power outage). ②昏厥 hūnjué (fainting spell).

blacksmith n. 铁匠 tiějiàng.

bladder n. 膀胱 pángguāng.

blade n. ①刀刃 dāorèn 〈knife〉. ②细叶片 xìyèpiàn 〈grass〉.

blame n. & v. 谴责 qiǎnzé, 归咎 guījiù.

bland adj. ①无味道的 wú wèidào de (tasteless). ②枯燥 无味的 kūzào-wúwèi de (boring).

blank n. ①空白 kòngbái 〈paper〉. ②空白 kòngbái, 空虚 kōngxū (emptiness). — adj. ①空白的 kòngbái de 〈paper〉. ②面无表情的 miànwú- -biǎoqíng de (expressionless).

blanket n. 毛毯 máotǎn.

blare n. & v. 高鸣 gāomíng, 大叫 dàjiào.

blasphemy n. 亵渎 xièdú.

blast n. ①一阵疾风 yí zhèn jífēng (violent gust of wind). ②吹奏声 chuīzòushēng (sound of instrument). ③爆炸 bàozhà (explosion). — v. ①炸开 zhàkāi (break open by explo- sion). ②摧毁 cuīhuǐ (destroy).

blatant adj. 乖张的 guāizhāng de.

blaze n. 火焰 huǒyàn (fire), 强光 qiángguāng (bright

light). — v. ①燃烧 ránshāo (burn). ②发强光 fā qiángguāng (shine brightly).

blazer n. 男性上衣 nánxìng shàngyī.

bleach v. 变白 biànbái, 漂白 piǎobái. — n. 漂白剂 piǎobáijì.

bleak adj. ①荒凉的 huāngliáng de (bare). ②寒冷 的 hánlěng de (cold).

bleat n. 牛羊叫声 niúyáng jiàoshēng.

bleed v. ①流血 liúxuè / liúxiě (emit blood). ②放血 fàngxiě (draw blood from).

blemish n. ①污点 wūdiǎn, 瑕疵 xiácī (spot). ②缺点 quēdiǎn (failing). — v. 玷污 diànwū.

blend v. ①调合 tiáohé (combine). ②混合 hùnhé, 混杂 hùnzá (mix). — n. 混合 （物） hùnhé (wù).

bless v. 祝福 zhùfú (wish good to).

blessing n. ①祝福 zhùfú, 祈福 qífú (grace). ②可喜的事 kě xǐ de shì (piece of luck).

blight n. 枯萎病 kūwěibìng / kūwēibìng. — v. ①使枯萎 shǐ kūwěi / shǐ kūwēi (drying up). ②摧残 cuīcán (destroy).

blind adj. ①瞎的 xiā de (unable to see). ②盲目的 mángmù de (unaware).

~ person 盲人 mángrén. — v. ①使失明 shǐ shīmíng (make somebody unable to see). ②使盲目 shǐ mángmù (make somebody unaware).

blindfold v. 蒙住眼睛 méngzhù yǎnjing.

blink v. ①眨眼 zhǎyǎn (wink). ②闪烁 shǎnshuò (twinkle).

bliss n. 极大的幸福 jí dà de xìngfú.

blister n. 水疱 shuǐpào, 脓疱 nóngpào ⟨skin⟩. — v. 生水疱 shēng shuǐpào.

blitz n. 闪电战 shǎndiànzhàn.

blizzard n. 暴风雪 bàofēngxuě.

bloc n. 集团 jítuán.

block n. ①一块 yí kuài (a piece of). ②阻碍 zǔ'ài, 障碍 zhàng'ài (obstacle). ③街区 jiēqū (area bordered by streets). — v. ①阻塞 zǔsè (plug up). ②阻碍 zǔ'ài (obstruct).

blockade n. & v. 封锁 fēngsuǒ.

blockage n. ①阻碍 zǔ'ài (state of being blocked). ②障碍物 zhàng'àiwù ⟨object⟩.

blog n. 博客 bókè / 部落格 bùluògé.

blond(e) adj. 金发的 jīnfà de / jīnfà de. — n. 金发的人 jīnfà de rén / jīnfà de rén.

blood n. ①血 xuè / xiě, 血液 xuèyè / xiěyè ⟨body⟩. ②血统 xuètǒng / xiětǒng (family relationship). **~ bank** 血库 xuèkù / xiěkù. **~ group** 血型 xuèxíng / xiěxíng.

bloody adj. ①血污的 xuèwū de / xiěwū de (covered with blood). ②血腥的 xuèxīng de / xiěxīng de (wounding and killing).

bloom n. ①花 huā (flower). ②花开 huākāi (blossom). ③壮盛时期 zhuàngshèng shíqí / zhuàngshèng shíqí (the best period). — v. 花开 huākāi (produce flowers).

blossom n. 花 huā, 花丛 huācóng. — v. 开花 kāihuā.

blot n. ①污痕 wūhén, 墨迹 mòjì / mòjī (stain). ②污点 wūdiǎn, 瑕疵 xiácī (blemish). — v. 沾上墨迹 zhānshang mòjì / zhānshàng mòjī (spoil).

blotch n. 大污渍 dà wūzì, 大斑点 dà bāndiǎn ⟨skin, paper, material, etc.⟩.

blouse n. 罩衫 zhàoshān, 上衣 shàngyī.

blow n. ①打 dǎ (punch). ②打击 dǎjī / dǎjí (shock). — v. ①吹 chuī ⟨air⟩. ②吹动 chuīdòng, 吹掉 chuīdiào ⟨move⟩. ③充气 chōngqì (fill with air). ④吹奏 chuīzòu ⟨trumpet⟩. **~ up** ①爆炸 bàozhà (explode). ②发脾气 fā píqi (get angry).

blow-dry v. 吹干 chuīgān.

blow-dryer n. 吹风机 chuīfēngjī.

blue n. & adj. 蓝色 lánsè. **~ chip** 绩优股 jìyōugǔ / jīyōugǔ. **~ jeans** 牛仔裤 niúzǎikù / niúzǐkù.

blue-collar adj. 蓝领的 lánlǐng de.

blueprint n. 蓝图 lántú.

bluff n. 虚张声势 xūzhāng-shēngshì.

blunder n. 大错 dà cuò. — v. ①犯错 fàncuò (make a mistake). ②盲动 mángdòng (move about uncertainly).

blunt adj. ①钝的 dùn de (not sharp). ②直率的 zhíshuài de (straightforward).

blur v. 使模糊 shǐ móhu (become unclear). — n. 模糊的事物 móhu de shìwù.

blurry adj. 模糊的 móhu de.

blurt v. 脱口而出 tuōkǒu'ér-chū.

blush n. & v. 脸红 liǎnhóng, 羞愧 xiūkuì.

B

bluster n. & v. ①狂吹 kuángchuī (blow). ②咆哮 páoxiào / páoxiāo (vent anger). ③恫吓 dònghè (threat).

boa constrictor n. 蟒蛇 mǎngshé.

boar n. ①野猪 yězhū (wild). ②雄猪 xióngzhū (male pig).

board n. ①木板 mùbǎn (thin plank). ②理事会 lǐshìhuì, 董事会 dǒngshìhuì (committee). ③膳食 shànshí (food). — v. ①搭乘 dāchéng (get on). ②用板盖住 yòng bǎn gàizhù (cover with). ③寄宿 jìsù (lodge).

boast v. 自夸 zìkuā, 夸耀 kuāyào, 吹牛 chuīniú.

boat n. 船 chuán, 小船 xiǎo chuán.

bob v. 上下疾动 shàngxià jídòng (move up and down). — n. 短发 duǎnfǎ / duǎnfà 〈hair〉.

bode v. 预示 yùshì, 预兆 yùzhào.

bodice n. 紧身胸衣 jǐnshēn xiōngyī.

body n. ①身体 shēntǐ, 躯体 qūtǐ (whole of a person, animal). ②躯干 qūgàn (torso). ③主要部分 zhǔyào bùfen (the main part). ~ *language* 肢体语言 zhītǐ yǔyán.

bodyguard n. 保镖 bǎobiāo.

bog n. 沼泽 zhǎozé.

bogey n. 高标准杆一杆 gāo biāozhǔngǎn yì gǎn.

bogus adj. 假的 jiǎ de, 伪造的 wěizào de / wèizào de.

boil n. & v. ①煮沸 zhǔfèi, 沸腾 fèiténg (heat a liquid). ②烹煮 pēngzhǔ (cook).

boiler n. 锅炉 guōlú, 烧水器 shāoshuǐqì 〈device〉.

boisterous adj. 喧闹的 xuānnào de (loud).

bold adj. ①大胆的 dàdǎn de (brave). ②无礼的 wúlǐ de (impudent).

bolster n. 长枕 chángzhěn, 长垫 chángdiàn.

bolt n. ①门闩 ménshuān 〈for door〉. ②螺栓 luóshuān 〈for joining parts〉. — v. ①闩住 shuānzhù (bar a door). ②逃走 táozǒu (flee). ~ *down* 囵囵吞入 húlún tūnrù (devour).

bomb n. 炸弹 zhàdàn. — v. 轰炸 hōngzhà.

bombard v. 炮轰 pàohōng.

bomber n. ①轰炸机 hōngzhàjī 〈aircraft〉. ②轰炸员 hōngzhàyuán 〈person〉.

bond n. ①束缚 shùfù / shùfú (restraint). ②契约 qìyuē (contract). ③债券 zhàiquàn 〈finance〉.

bondage n. ①奴隶 núlì (slavery). ②束缚 shùfù / shùfú (restraint).

bone n. 骨 gǔ, 骨头 gǔtou / gútou.

bonfire n. 户外升火 hùwài shēnghuǒ.

bonnet n. 软帽 ruǎnmào 〈hat〉.

bonus n. 红利 hónglì, 奖金 jiǎngjīn.

bony adj. 多骨的 duōgǔ de.

book n. 书 shū, 卷册 juàncè 〈text〉. — v. ①预定 yùdìng (reserve). ②登记 dēngjì (register).

booking n. 预约 yùyuē (reservation).

bookkeeper n. 簿记员 bùjìyuán.

bookkeeping n. 簿记 bùjì.

booklet *n.* 小册子 xiǎocèzi.

bookmark *n.* 书签 shūqiān.

bookshelf *n.* 书架 shūjià, 书橱 shūchú.

bookshop *n.* 书店 shūdiàn.

bookstore *n.* 书店 shūdiàn.

bookworm *n.* 书虫 shūchóng, 书呆子 shūdāizi.

boom *n. & v.* ①突起景气 tū qǐ jǐngqì / 突起景气 tú qǔ jǐngqī (time of prosperity). ②隆隆声 lónglóngshēng (deep resonant sound).

boor *n.* 粗鲁的人 cūlǔ de rén.

boost *v.* 提高 tígāo (lift), 加强 jiāqiáng (strengthen), 鼓吹 gǔchuī (promote).

boot *n.* 长靴 chángxuē, 靴子 xuēzi.

booth *n.* ①摊位 tānwèi (stall). ②小隔间 xiǎogéjiān (shed).
telephone ~ 电话间 diànhuàjiān / 电话亭 diànhuàtíng.
voting ~ 投票处 tóupiàochù.

border *n.* ①边缘 biānyuán (edge). ②边境 biānjìng, 边界 biānjiè (frontier). – *v.* 接邻 jiēlín, 连接 liánjiē.

bore *v.* ①钻孔 zuānkǒng (drill). ②使感到无聊 shǐ gǎndào wúliáo (make people bored).

bored *adj.* 感到无聊的 gǎndào wúliáo de.

boring *adj.* 无聊的 wúliáo de.

born *adj.* 天生的 tiānshēng de (natural).

borrow *v.* 借 jiè.

bosom *n.* ①胸 xiōng (breast). ②胸怀 xiōnghuái, 内心 nèixīn (heart).

boss *n.* 老板 lǎobǎn.

BOT 建造、运作、移转 jiànzào, yùnzuò, yízhuǎn

(Build Operate Transfer).

botany *n.* 植物学 zhíwùxué.

botch *v.* 拙劣地做 zhuōliè de zuò / 拙劣的做 zhuóliè de zuò.

both *adj. & adv. & pron.* 二者 的 èr zhě de.

bother *n. & v.* 麻烦 máfan, 烦扰 fánrǎo.

bottle *n.* 瓶 píng, 瓶子 píngzi.

bottom *n.* ①底 dǐ, 底部 dǐbù (lowest part). ②尾部 wěibù, 尽头 jìntóu (ending). ③根基 gēnjī, 基础 jīchǔ (base). ④屁股 pìgu ⟨body part⟩.
Bottoms up! 干杯 Gānbēi!

bough *n.* 大树枝 dà shùzhī.

bounce *n. & v.* ①反弹 fǎntán (rebound). ②跳起 tiàoqǐ (leap suddenly).

bound *adj.* ①被缚的 bèifù de / bèifú de (fastened by). ②有义 务的 yǒu yìwù de (having a duty). – *v.* 跳跃 tiàoyuè, 弹起 tánqǐ ⟨jump⟩.

boundary *n.* 界线 jièxiàn, 境界 jìngjiè.

boundless *adj.* 无限的 wúxiàn de.

bounteous *adj.* 丰富的 fēngfù de (plentiful).

bounty *n.* ①慷慨 kāngkǎi (generosity). ②津贴 jìntiē (reward).

bouquet *n.* 花束 huāshù.

bourgeois *n.* 中产阶级 zhōngchǎn jiējí.

bow *v.* ①鞠躬 jūgōng / júgōng (bend forward). ②屈服 qūfú (yield). – *n.* ①弓 gōng ⟨weapon⟩. ②蝶形结 diéxíng língjié (knot). ③琴弓 qíngōng ⟨for playing instruments⟩.

bowel *n.* 肠 cháng ⟨organ⟩.

bowl *n.* 碗 wǎn, 钵 bō ⟨dish⟩.

B

bowling n. 保龄球 bǎolíngqiú. ~ *alley* 保龄球场 bǎolíngqiúchǎng.

box n. ①箱 xiāng, 盒 hé (case). ②包厢 bāoxiāng (small private room).

boxer n. 拳击手 quánjīshǒu / quánjíshǒu.

boxing n. 拳击 quánjī / quánjí.

boy n. 男孩 nánhái. ~ *scout* 童子军 tóngzǐjūn.

boycott n. & v. 杯葛 bēigé, 抵制 dǐzhì.

boyfriend n. 男朋友 nánpéngyou.

boyhood n. 童年 tóngnián, 少年时代 shàonián shídài.

bra n. 胸罩 xiōngzhào.

brace n. ①支撑 zhīchēng, 支架 zhījià (support). ②曲柄 qūbǐng (tool). ③齿列矫正器 chǐliè jiǎozhèngqì (teeth). — v. 支撑 zhīchēng (support). ~ *yourself*, ~ *up* 振作 zhènzuò.

bracelet n. 手镯 shǒuzhuó.

bracket n. ①方括弧 fāngkuòhú / fāngguāhú (a mark [ ]). ②托架 tuōjià (support for something).

brackish adj. 略有盐味的 lüè yǒu yánwèi de.

brag n. & v. 自夸 zìkuā.

braid n. ①辫子 biànzi, 发辫 fàbiàn / fǎbiàn (hair). ②穗带 suìdài (clothing).

Braille n. 盲人点字法 Mángrén diǎnzìfǎ.

brain n. ①脑 nǎo (body part). ②智慧 zhìhuì, 智力 zhìlì (intellect). ~ *drain* 人才外流 réncái wàiliú.

braise v. 炖 dùn.

brake v. & n. 煞车 shāchē.

bramble n. 荆棘 jīngjí, 灌木 guànmù.

bran n. 糠 kāng, 麦麸 màifū.

branch n. ①树枝 shùzhī (tree). ②支流 zhīliú (tributary), 支线 zhīxiàn (secondary line). ③分店 fēndiàn (chain store). — v. 分支 fēnzhī.

brand n. ①商标 shāngbiāo, 牌子 páizi (trademark). ②烙印 làoyìn (mark). — v. 烙印 làoyìn (mark by burning).

brandish n. & v. 挥动 huīdòng.

brandy n. 白兰地 báilándì.

brass n. ①黄铜 huángtóng (alloy). ②铜管乐器 tóngguǎn yuèqì (instrument). ~ *band* 管乐队 guǎnyuèduì.

bravado n. 虚张声势 xūzhāng-shēngshì.

brave adj. 勇敢的 yǒnggǎn de.

bravo interj. 好! Hǎo!

brawl n. & v. 打架 dǎjià (fight).

brazen adj. ①无耻的 wúchǐ de (shameless). ②黄铜的 huángtóng de (like brass).

breach n. ①违反 wéifǎn (transgression). ②不睦 búmù, 不和 bùhé (alienation).

bread n. 面包 miànbāo.

breadth n. ①宽度 kuāndù (width). ②宽宏大量 kuānhóng-dàliàng (considering others). ③范围 fànwéi (scope).

break v. ①打破 dǎpò (come to pieces). ②违反 wéifǎn (transgress). ③弄坏 nònghuài, 破坏 pòhuài (ruin). ~ *in* 打断 dǎduàn, 介入 jièrù (interrupt). ~ *up* 脱离 tuōlí (separate).

breakdown n. ①病倒 bìngdǎo, 崩溃 bēngkuì (psychological). ②损坏

sǔnhuài, 故障 gùzhàng
〈mechanical〉.

breakfast *n.* 早餐 zǎocān.

breakthrough *n.* ①突破
tūpò / túpò 〈advance〉. ②重大
发现 zhòngdà fāxiàn 〈new
discovery〉.

breakup *n.* ①解散 jiěsàn,
瓦解 wǎjiě 〈collapse〉. ②分手
fēnshǒu, 绝交 juéjiāo 〈part
company〉. ③终止 zhōngzhǐ
〈end〉.

breast *n.* 胸部 xiōngbù, 乳房
rǔfáng.

breath *n.* 呼吸 hūxī.
catch one's ~ 松一口气 sōng yì
kǒu qì. *out of* ~ 喘不过气来
chuǎnbúguò qì lái.

breathe *v.* 呼吸 hūxī.

breed *v.* ①生育 shēngyù 〈give
birth to〉. ②饲养 sìyǎng, 养育
yǎngyù 〈raise〉. — *n.* 品种
pǐnzhǒng.

breeze *n.* 微风 wēifēng /
wéifēng.

brevity *n.* ①短暂 duǎnzàn /
duǎnzhàn 〈short duration〉.
②简洁 jiǎnjié, 简短 jiǎnduǎn
〈concision〉.

brew *v.* ①酿造 niàngzào
〈make drinks〉. ②图谋 túmóu,
酝酿 yùnniàng 〈be forming〉.
— *n.* 酿造 niàngzào 〈beer〉.

bribe *n. & v.* 贿赂 huìlù.

brick *n.* 砖 zhuān.

bride *n.* 新娘 xīnniáng.

bridegroom *n.* 新郎 xīnláng.

bridesmaid *n.* 女傧相
nǚbīnxiàng, 伴娘 bànniáng.

bridge *n.* ①桥 qiáo 〈crossing〉.
②舰桥 jiànqiáo 〈part of ship〉.
③桥牌 qiáopái 〈card game〉.
— *v.* 架桥 jiàqiáo.

bridle *n.* 马勒 mǎlè.

brief *adj.* 简洁的 jiǎnjié de
〈succinct〉, 简短的 jiǎnduǎn de
〈short〉. — *n.* 摘要 zhāiyào
〈summary〉. *in* ~ 简言之
jiǎnyánzhī.

briefcase *n.* 公事包
gōngshìbāo.

bright *adj.* ①光亮的
guāngliàng de 〈shining〉.
②聪明的 cōngmíng de 〈smart〉.
③愉快的 yúkuài de 〈cheerful〉.

brighten *v.* ①使光亮 shǐ
guāngliàng 〈become bright〉.
②使愉快 shǐ yúkuài 〈make
cheerful〉.

brilliant *adj.* ①灿烂的
cànlàn de, 光辉的 guānghuī
de 〈splendid〉. ②聪明的
cōngmíng de, 有才气的 yǒu
cáiqì de 〈smart〉.

brim *n.* 边 biān, 边缘
biānyuán 〈cup, bowl〉.

brine *n.* 盐水 yánshuǐ.

bring *v.* 带来 dàilái 〈carry〉.
~ *about* 导致 dǎozhì. ~ *up*
①养育 yǎngyù 〈raise〉. ②提到
tídào 〈mention〉.

brink *n.* 边缘 biānyuán.

brisk *adj.* 敏捷的 mǐnjié de,
轻快的 qīngkuài de.

bristle *n.* 鬃 zōng. — *v.* 竖立
shùlì.

brittle *adj.* 脆的 cuì de, 易碎
的 yìsuì de 〈fragile〉.

broad *adj.* ①宽的 kuān de
〈wide〉. ②辽阔的 liáokuò de
〈vast〉. ③广泛的 guǎngfàn de
〈wide-ranging〉.

broadband *n.* 宽频 kuānpín.

broadcast *v.* ①广播 guǎngbō /
guǎngbò 〈media〉. ②传布
chuánbù, 散播 sànbō / sànbò
〈make widely known〉.

broaden *v.* 扩大 kuòdà.

B

broadside n. 舷侧 xiáncè ⟨ship⟩.

broccoli n. 花椰菜 huāyēcài / huāyécài.

brochure n. 小册子 xiǎocèzi.

broil v. 烧烤 shāokǎo.

broken adj. ①坏掉的 huàidiào de ⟨no longer functional⟩. ②破裂的 pòliè de ⟨in pieces⟩. ③故障的 gùzhàng de ⟨damaged⟩.

broker n. 经纪人 jīngjìrén.

bronchitis n. 支气管炎 zhīqìguǎnyán.

bronze n. ①青铜 qīngtóng ⟨material⟩. ②青铜器 qīngtóngqì ⟨artwork⟩.

brooch n. 胸针 xiōngzhēn.

brood n. ①一窝孵雏 yì wō fūchú ⟨bird⟩. ②一家小孩 yì jiā xiǎohái ⟨human⟩.

brook n. 溪流 xīliú, 小河 xiǎohé. — v. 容忍 róngrěn ⟨tolerate⟩.

broom n. 扫帚 sàozhou.

broth n. 清汤 qīngtāng.

brother n. ①哥哥 gēge ⟨elder⟩. ②弟弟 dìdi ⟨younger⟩. ~ s 兄弟 xiōngdì ⟨male siblings⟩.

brotherhood n. ①兄弟关系 xiōngdì guānxi, 手足之情 shǒuzúzhīqíng ⟨relationship of brothers⟩. ②协会 xiéhuì, 团体 tuántǐ ⟨association⟩.

brow n. ①眉 méi, 眉毛 méimao ⟨eyebrow⟩. ②额 é ⟨forehead⟩.

brown n. & adj. 棕色 zōngsè. ~ sugar 红糖 hóngtáng.

browse v. 浏览书籍 liúlǎn shūjí ⟨skim⟩.

bruise v. 瘀伤 yūshāng.

brunch n. 早午餐 zǎowǔcān.

brush n. 刷子 shuāzi

⟨implement⟩. ②小冲突 xiǎo chōngtū / xiǎo chōngtú ⟨short fight⟩. ③丛林 cónglín ⟨bushes⟩. — v. 刷 shuā ⟨clean⟩, 涂 tú, 擦 cā ⟨apply to⟩.

brusque adj. 唐突的 tángtū de / tángtú de, 粗率的 cūshuài de.

brutal adj. 野蛮的 yěmán de ⟨barbaric⟩, 残忍的 cánrěn de ⟨cruel⟩.

brute n. ①野兽 yěshòu ⟨beast⟩. ②残暴者 cánbàozhě ⟨bully⟩.

bubble n. 泡沫 pàomò, 气泡 qìpào ⟨air⟩. — v. 起泡 qǐpào ⟨rise in⟩.

bubble gum n. 泡泡糖 pàopàotáng, 口香糖 kǒuxiāngtáng.

buck n. ①雄鹿 xiónglù ⟨male deer⟩. ②一美元 yì měiyuán ⟨one dollar⟩. — v. 摔落 shuāiluò.

bucket n. 水桶 shuǐtǒng.

buckle n. 扣环 kòuhuán. — v. 扣住 kòuzhù.

bud n. ①芽 yá, 花蕾 huālěi ⟨plant⟩. ②哥儿们 gērmen ⟨friend⟩. — v. 发芽 fāyá.

Buddhism n. 佛教 Fójiào.

Buddhist n. 佛教徒 Fójiàotú.

buddy n. ①哥俩 gēliǎ, 伙伴 huǒbàn ⟨partner⟩. ②老兄 lǎoxiōng ⟨fellow⟩.

budge v. 稍微移动 shāowēi yídòng / shāowéi yídòng.

budget n. 预算 yùsuàn. — v. 编预算 biān yùsuàn.

buff n. 浅黄褐色皮革 qiǎnhuánghèsè pígé / qiǎnhuánghésè pígé ⟨leather⟩. — v. 擦拭 cāshì.

buffalo n. 水牛 shuǐniú ⟨water buffalo⟩, 美国野牛

Měiguó yěniú (bison).

buffer *n.* 缓冲器 huǎnchōngqì.

buffet *n.* 自助餐 zìzhùcān. ~ *table* 餐台 cāntái.

buffoon *n.* 丑角 chǒujué, 小丑 xiǎochǒu.

bug *n.* 小虫 xiǎochóng.

bugle *n.* 喇叭 lǎba, 军号 jūnhào.

build *v.* ①建筑 jiànzhù / jiànzhú, 建造 jiànzào ⟨a house, etc.⟩. ②建立 jiànlì ⟨a company, etc.⟩. ~ *up* ①累积 lěijī (accumulate). ②增加 zēngjiā (increase). ③加强 jiāqiáng (strengthen). — *n.* 身材 shēncái, 体格 tǐgé.

builder *n.* 建筑业者 jiànzhù yèzhě / jiànzhú yèzhě ⟨build houses⟩. ②建立者 jiànlìzhě ⟨bring into development⟩.

building *n.* 建筑物 jiànzhùwù / jiànzhúwù.

bulb *n.* ①球茎 qiújīng ⟨plant⟩. ②电灯泡 diàndēngpào ⟨lamp⟩.

bulge *v.* 膨胀 péngzhàng, 胀大 zhàngdà.

bulk *n.* ①体积 tǐjī ⟨volume⟩. ②大部分 dàbùfen (most).

bulky *adj.* 庞大笨重的 pángdà bènzhòng de.

bull *n.* ①公牛 gōngniú ⟨animal⟩. ②多头 duōtóu ⟨stock market⟩.

bullet *n.* 子弹 zǐdàn. ~ *train* 子弹列车 zǐdàn lièchē.

bulletin *n.* ①告示 gàoshì, 公报 gōngbào (announcement). ②小型杂志 xiǎoxíng zázhì (newsletter).

bullion *n.* 金块 jīnkuài (gold), 银块 yínkuài (silver).

bully *n.* 恶霸 èbà. — *v.* 欺负

qīfu, 威胁 wēixié.

bulwark *n.* ①壁垒 bìlěi, 堡垒 bǎolěi (wall built for defense). ②船舷 chuánxián ⟨ship⟩.

bump *v.* 碰 pèng. ~ *into* 碰到 pèngdào (meet by accident).

bumper *n.* 保险杆 bǎoxiǎngǎn. — *adj.* 丰盛的 fēngshèng de.

bumpkin *n.* 乡巴佬 xiāngbālǎo.

bun *n.* 小圆甜面包 xiǎo yuán tián miànbāo.

bunch *n.* ①串 chuàn ⟨grapes⟩. ②束 shù ⟨flowers⟩. ③堆 duī ⟨objects⟩. — *v.* 扎成束 zāchéng shù / zháchéng shù.

bundle *n.* 束 shù, 捆 kǔn, 包裹 bāoguǒ. — *v.* 包捆 bāokǔn, 扎 zā / zhá (wrap together).

bungalow *n.* 平房 píngfáng (one-story house).

bungee jumping *n.* 蹦极跳 bèngjítiào / 高空弹跳 gāokōng tántiào.

bungle *n. & v.* 搞砸 gǎozá.

bunk *n.* ①铺位 pùwèi (bed). ②废话 fèihuà (nonsense).

bunker *n.* ①沙坑 shākēng (a place filled with sand). ②地堡 dìbǎo (underground shelter).

bunny *n.* 兔宝宝 tùbǎobao (rabbit).

buoy *n.* 浮标 fúbiāo, 浮筒 fútǒng. — *v.* ①使浮起 shǐ fúqǐ (keep floating). ②支持 zhīchí (support).

burden *n.* 负荷 fùhè, 重担 zhòngdàn (heavy load). — *v.* 给……负担 gěi...fùdān, 麻烦 máfan (trouble).

burdock *n.* 牛蒡 niúbàng.

bureau *n.* ①局 jú, 处 chù, 署

B

shǔ (government department).
②办公处 bàngōngchù
(office).

bureaucracy n. 官僚政治
guānliáo zhèngzhì.

bureaucrat n. 官方人员
guānfāng rényuán (civil
servant), 官僚 guānliáo
(negative connotation).

burglar n. 窃贼 qièzéi
(housebreaker).

burial n. 埋葬 máizàng ⟨act⟩,
葬礼 zànglǐ ⟨ceremony⟩.

burly adj. 魁梧的 kuíwú de.

burn v. 燃烧 ránshāo, 烧焦
shāojiāo. ~ **down** 烧尽 shāojìn.

burnish v. 擦亮 cāliàng.

burrow n. 地洞 dìdòng,
洞穴 dòngxué / dòngxuè.

bursar n. 会计员 kuàijìyuán.

burst n. & v. 爆炸 bàozhà
(explosion).

bury v. ①埋葬 máizàng (put
into the ground). ②掩藏
yǎncáng (hide away).

bus n. 公共汽车 gōnggòng
qìchē, 巴士 bāshì.

bush n. 灌木 guànmù ⟨plant⟩.

business n. ①生意 shēngyi,
买卖 mǎimai (trade). ②商店
shāngdiàn (a shop), 公司
gōngsī (a firm). ③职务 zhíwù,
职责 zhízé (task).

mind one's own ~ 不管闲事
bùguǎn xiánshì.

none of your ~ 不关你的事
bù guān nǐ de shì, 少管闲事
shǎoguǎn-xiánshì.

~ card 名片 míngpiàn.

~ hours 上班时间 shàngbān
shíjiān.

businessman/woman n.
商人 shāngrén, 生意人
shēngyirén.

business park n. 高科技工
业园区 gāokējì gōngyè
yuánqū.

bust n. ①半身雕塑像 bànshēn
diāosùxiàng (sculpture). ②胸部
xiōngbù (chest).

bustle v. 匆忙 cōngmáng
(hurry), 喧扰 xuānrǎo (rush
about). — n. 热闹 rènao.

busy adj. ①忙碌的 mánglù de
(occupied). ②热闹的 rènao de
(bustling).

but conj. 但是 dànshì, 然而
rán'ér.

butcher n. ①肉贩 ròufàn (one
who sells meat). ②屠夫 túfū
(one who slaughters animals for
food). — v. 屠杀 túshā.

butler n. 仆役长 púyìzhǎng.

butt n. ①柄 bǐng ⟨tools or
weapons⟩. ②烟蒂 yāndì
⟨cigarette⟩. ③笑柄 xiàobǐng
⟨person⟩. — v. 以头撞 yǐ tóu
zhuàng (hit with the head).

butter n. 奶油 nǎiyóu.

peanut ~ 花生酱
huāshēngjiàng.

butterfly n. 蝴蝶 húdié.

buttock n. 臀 tún, 屁股 pìgu.

button n. 钮扣 niǔkòu. — v.
扣 kòu.

buttress n. 扶墙 fúqiáng, 拱
壁 gǒngbì.

buxom adj. 丰满的 fēngmǎn
de.

buy v. ①买 mǎi (purchase).
②换得 huàndé (to be
exchangeable for).

buyer n. 买主 mǎizhǔ,
采购者 cǎigòuzhě.

buzz n. 嗡嗡声
wēngwēngshēng.

by prep. ①在……近旁
zài...jìnpáng (near). ②借以

jièyǐ (by means of). ③沿着
yánzhe (along). ④经由
jīngyóu, 经过 jīngguò (past).
⑤不晚于…… bù wǎn yú...
(not later than).

bye-bye *interj.* 再会 zàihuì,
再见 zàijiàn.

bylaw *n.* ①地方法规 dìfāng
fǎguī ⟨local ordinance⟩. ②组织
章程 zǔzhī zhāngchéng

⟨organization⟩.

bypass *n.* 旁道 pángdào, 外
环道 wàihuándào (road).

bypath *n.* 小路 xiǎolù.

by-product *n.* 副产品
fùchǎnpǐn ⟨object⟩.

bystander *n.* 旁观者
pángguānzhě.

byway *n.* 小路 xiǎolù.

C

C

cab *n.* 出租汽车 chūzū qìchē /
计程车 jìchéngchē (taxi).

cabaret *n.* 歌舞表演 gēwǔ
biǎoyǎn.

cabbage *n.* 甘蓝菜 gānláncài.

cabin *n.* ①小屋 xiǎowū (hut).
②船舱 chuáncāng ⟨ship⟩. ③机
舱 jīcāng ⟨airplane⟩.

cabinet *n.* ①橱 chú, 柜 guì
⟨furniture⟩. ②内阁 nèigé
⟨government⟩.

cable *n.* ①电缆 diànlǎn ⟨wires⟩.
②电报 diànbào ⟨communi-
cation⟩. ~ *car* 缆车 lǎnchē.
~ *television* 有线电视 yǒuxiàn
diànshì.

cactus *n.* 仙人掌 xiānrénzhǎng.

CAD 计算机辅助设计
jìsuànjī fǔzhù shèjì / 电脑辅
助设计 diànnǎo fǔzhù shèjì
(computer-aided design).

Caesarean section 剖腹生
产 pōufù shēngchǎn / 剖腹
shēngchǎn.

café *n.* ①餐厅 cāntīng (small
restaurant). ②咖啡店 kāfēidiàn

(coffee shop).

cafeteria *n.* 自助餐厅 zìzhù
cāntīng.

caffeine *n.* 咖啡因 kāfēiyīn.

cage *n.* 笼 lóng. — *v.* 监禁
jiānjìn.

cajole *v.* 哄骗 hǒngpiàn.

cake *n.* 糕 gāo, 蛋糕 dàngāo.
a piece of ~ 易如反掌 yìrúfǎn-
zhǎng.

calamity *n.* 不幸事件 búxìng
shìjiàn, 灾难 zāinàn.

calcium *n.* 钙 gài.

calculate *v.* ①计算 jìsuàn
(compute). ②预计 yùjì (predict).

calculation *n.* ①计算 jìsuàn
(count). ②预计 yùjì (prediction).

calculator *n.* 计算机 jìsuànjī.

calculus *n.* 微积分学
wēijīfēnxué / wéijīfēnxué.

calendar *n.* 日历 rìlì.

calf *n.* ①小牛 xiǎoniú (young
cow). ②小腿 xiǎotuǐ ⟨leg⟩.

caliber *n.* ①口径 kǒujìng
(diameter of a bullet). ②才干
cáigàn (quality of a person).

C

call v. ①喊 hǎn, 叫 jiào (cry out).
②召唤 zhàohuàn (summon).
③打电话 dǎ diànhuà (phone).
n. 呼声 hūshēng (voice).
~ *waiting* 电话插播 diànhuà
chābō / diànhuà chābō.

calligraphy n. 书法 shūfǎ.

callous adj. ①起茧的 qǐjiǎn de
⟨skin⟩. ②无情的 wúqíng de
⟨emotionally cold⟩.

callow adj. 乳臭未干 rǔxiù-
-wèigān.

callus n. 茧 jiǎn.

calm adj. ①安静的 ānjìng de
⟨quiet⟩. ②宁静的 níngjìng de
⟨tranquil⟩. — n. 平静 píngjìng.
— v. ①安慰 ānwèi ⟨comfort⟩.
②使平静 shǐ píngjìng ⟨quiet⟩.

calorie n. 卡路里 kǎlùlǐ.

camel n. 骆驼 luòtuo.

camera n. 照相机 zhàoxiàngjī
⟨photos⟩, 摄影机 shèyǐngjī
⟨video⟩.

camouflage n. & v. 掩饰
yǎnshì ⟨cover up⟩, 伪装
wěizhuāng / wèizhuāng
⟨pretend⟩.

camp n. ①露营 lùyíng
⟨encampment⟩. ②营地 yíngdì
⟨place⟩. — v. 露营 lùyíng.

campaign n. ①战役 zhànyì
⟨battle⟩. ②运动 yùndòng
⟨movement⟩. ③竞选 jìngxuǎn
⟨election⟩. — v. 从事运动
cóngshì yùndòng ⟨movement⟩,
竞选 jìngxuǎn ⟨election⟩.

campfire n. 营火 yínghuǒ.

campus n. 校园 xiàoyuán, 校
区 xiàoqū.

can aux. v. ①能 néng, 会 huì
⟨be able⟩. ②可以 kěyǐ ⟨may⟩.
— n. 罐头 guàntou ⟨container⟩.

canal n. 运河 yùnhé.

canary n. 金丝雀 jīnsīquè

⟨bird⟩. ~ *yellow* 淡黄色
dànhuángsè.

cancel v. 取消 qǔxiāo ⟨abolish⟩,
删去 shānqù ⟨delete⟩.

cancer n. 癌 ái ⟨disease⟩.
Cancer 巨蟹座 Jùxièzuò.

candid adj. 坦白的 tǎnbái de,
正直的 zhèngzhí de.

candidate n. 候选人
hòuxuǎnrén.

candle n. 蜡烛 làzhú.

candor n. 坦白 tǎnbái
⟨frankness⟩.

candy n. 糖果 tángguǒ.

cane n. ①茎 jīng ⟨stem⟩. ②手杖
shǒuzhàng ⟨walking stick⟩.
— v. 鞭笞 biānchī ⟨beat⟩.

canister n. 金属罐
jīnshǔguàn.

canned adj. ①装罐的
zhuāngguàn de ⟨in a can⟩.
②陈腔滥调的 chénqiāng-
-làndiào de ⟨clichéd⟩.

cannibal n. 食人肉者 shí
rénròu zhě.

cannon n. 大炮 dàpào, 加农
炮 jiānóngpào.

canoe n. 独木舟 dúmùzhōu.
— v. 乘独木舟 chéng
dúmùzhōu.

canon n. ①教规 jiàoguī
⟨church⟩. ②准则 zhǔnzé
⟨principle⟩.

canteen n. ①水壶 shuǐhú
⟨water container⟩. ②福利社
fúlìshè ⟨bar⟩.

canvas n. ①帆布 fānbù /
fánbù ⟨material⟩. ②画布
huàbù ⟨for painting⟩.

canvass n. & v. ①拉票 lāpiào
⟨for votes⟩. ②招徕 zhāolái ⟨for
clients⟩. ③调查 diàochá
⟨survey⟩.

canyon n. 峡谷 xiágǔ.

cap n. ①便帽 biànmào (hat). ②盖子 gàizi (lid). ③上限 shàngxiàn (limit).

capability n. 能力 nénglì.

capable adj. 有能力的 yǒu nénglì de, 能干的 nénggàn de.

capacity n. 容量 róngliàng.

cape n. 岬 jiǎ.

capillary n. 毛细管 máoxìguǎn 〈tube〉, 微血管 wēixuèguǎn / wéixiěguǎn (blood vessel).

capital n. ①首都 shǒudū (chief city). ②资金 zījīn (assets). — adj. ①主要的 zhǔyào de (chief). ②上等的 shàngděng de (excellent). ~ *letter* 大写字母 dàxiě zìmǔ. ~ *punishment* 死刑 sǐxíng.

capitalism n. 资本主义 zīběn zhǔyì.

capitalize v. ①资本化 zīběnhuà (change into money). ②大写 dàxiě (write with a capital letter). ~ *on* 趁机利用 chènjī lìyòng.

capitulate v. 有条件投降 yǒu tiáojiàn tóuxiáng.

cappuccino n. 卡布奇诺 kǎbùqínuò.

caprice n. 反复无常 fǎnfù--wúcháng.

Capricorn 山羊座 Shānyángzuò.

capsize v. 翻覆 fānfù.

capsule n. ①胶囊 jiāonáng 〈medicine〉. ②太空舱 tàikōngcāng (spaceship). ③荚 jiá 〈plants〉.

captain n. ①队长 duìzhǎng 〈team〉. ②船长 chuánzhǎng 〈ship〉. ③陆军上尉 lùjūn shàngwèi 〈army officer〉.

④海军上校 hǎijūn shàngxiào 〈naval officer〉.

caption n. ①标题 biāotí (heading). ②插图说明 chātú shuōmíng 〈picture〉. ③电影字幕 diànyǐng zìmù (subtitles).

captivate v. 迷惑 míhuò.

captive n. 俘虏 fúlǔ. — adj. 被捕的 bèi bǔ de (captured).

capture n. & v. ①捕捉 bǔzhuō (apprehension). ②占领 zhànlǐng (conquest).

car n. 车 chē, 汽车 qìchē (automobile).

car phone n. 汽车无线电话 qìchē wúxiàn diànhuà.

caramel n. ①焦糖 jiāotáng (burnt sugar). ②牛奶糖 niúnǎitáng 〈candy〉.

carat n. 克拉 kèlā.

caravan n. 商队 shāngduì, 车队 chēduì.

carbohydrate n. 醣 táng, 碳水化合物 tànshuǐ huàhéwù.

carbon n. 碳 tàn. ~ *paper* 复写纸 fùxiězhǐ.

carcass n. 动物尸体 dòngwù shītǐ 〈animal〉.

carcinogen n. 致癌物 zhì'áiwù.

card n. ①卡片 kǎpiàn (stiff paper). ②卡 kǎ (member). ③名片 míngpiàn (business card). ④明信片 míngxìnpiàn (postcard).

cardboard n. 硬纸板 yìngzhǐbǎn.

cardigan n. 羊毛衫 yángmáoshān.

cardinal adj. ①首要的 shǒuyào de, 基本的 jīběn de (fundamental). ②鲜红色的 xiānhóngsè de (deep scarlet). — n. ①枢机主教 shūjī zhǔjiào

〈Catholic church〉. ②鲜红色 xiānhóngsè 〈vermillion〉.

cardiogram n. 心电图 xīndiàntú.

care n. ①照顾 zhàogù 〈protection〉. ②忧虑 yōulù 〈worry〉. *take ~ of* 照顾 zhàogù 〈people〉. ②处理 chǔlǐ 〈things〉. *with ~* 小心 xiǎoxīn. — v. ①在乎 zàihu 〈feel that something matters〉. ②关心 guānxīn 〈be concerned about〉. *~ for* 喜欢 xǐhuan, 爱好 àihào 〈like〉.

career n. ①事业 shìyè 〈business〉. ②职业 zhíyè 〈job〉. ③生涯 shēngyá 〈life history〉.

careful adj. 谨慎的 jǐnshèn de, 小心的 xiǎoxīn de.

careless adj. 粗心的 cūxīn de 〈negligent〉.

caress n. & v. 爱抚 àifǔ.

cargo n. 货物 huòwù.

Caribbean Sea 加勒比海 Jiālèbǐhǎi.

caricature n. 讽刺漫画 fěngcì mànhuà / fèngcì mànhuà.

carnage n. 大屠杀 dàtúshā.

carnal adj. 肉体的 ròutǐ de 〈of flesh〉, 性欲的 xìngyù de 〈sexual〉.

carnation n. 康乃馨 kāngnǎixīn.

carnival n. 嘉年华会 jiāniánhuáhuì.

carnivore n. 肉食动物 ròushí dòngwù.

carol n. 欢乐颂 huānlèsòng 〈song〉.

carp v. 吹毛求疵 chuīmáo-qiúcī. — n. 鲤鱼 lǐyú 〈fish〉.

carpenter n. 木匠 mùjiang.

carpet n. 地毯 dìtǎn. — v. 铺

地毯 pū dìtǎn.

carriage n. 四轮马车 sì lún mǎchē.

carrier n. ①运送人 yùnsòngrén 〈person〉. ②运输业者 yùnshū yèzhě 〈company〉. ③带菌者 dàijūnzhě / dàijùnzhě 〈disease〉.

carrot n. 胡萝卜 húluóbo.

carry v. ①携带 xiédài / xīdài 〈bring〉. ②搬运 bānyùn 〈convey〉. ③传达 chuándá, 传播 chuánbō / chuánbò 〈spread〉. *~ on* 继续 jìxù. *~ out* 完成 wánchéng.

cart n. ①手拉车 shǒulāchē 〈pushcart〉. ②轻便货车 qīngbiàn huòchē 〈small light vehicle〉.

cartilage n. 软骨 ruǎngǔ.

carton n. 厚纸盒 hòu zhǐhé.

cartoon n. ①漫画 mànhuà 〈drawing〉. ②动画片 dònghuàpiàn / 卡通影片 kǎtōng yǐngpiàn 〈animation〉.

cartridge n. ①弹药筒 dànyàotǒng 〈ammunition〉. ②软片卷筒 ruǎnpiàn juǎntǒng 〈case〉.

carve v. ①雕刻 diāokè 〈chisel〉. ②切 qiē 〈cut〉.

case n. ①事 shì 〈event〉, 例 lì 〈example〉, 案子 ànzi 〈project〉. ②情形 qíngxing 〈situation〉. ③案件 ànjiàn, 诉讼 sùsòng 〈lawsuit〉. ④箱 xiāng, 盒 hé 〈box〉. *~ study* 个案研究 gè'àn yánjiū / gè'àn yánjiù. *in any ~* 无论如何 wúlùn-rúhé. *in that ~* 既然如此 jìrán-rúcǐ. *just in ~* 万一 wànyī.

cash n. 现金 xiànjīn. *~ register* 现金出纳机 xiànjīn chūnàjī / 收银机 shōuyínjī. — v. 现现

duìxiàn.

cashier n. 出纳员 chūnàyuán.

cashmere n. 开斯米羊毛 kāisīmǐ yángmáo.

casino n. 赌场 dǔchǎng.

cask n. 桶 tǒng.

casket n. ①棺材 guāncái (coffin). ②小珠宝箱 xiǎo zhūbǎoxiāng ⟨jewelry⟩.

casserole n. 砂锅 shāguō.

cassette n. 卡式匣 kǎshìxiá, 卡带 kǎdài ⟨tape⟩, 录音带 lùyīndài ⟨sound⟩, 录像带 lùxiàngdài / 录影带 lùyǐngdài ⟨video⟩.

cassock n. 神职长袍 shénzhí chángpáo.

cast v. ①投 tóu, 掷 zhì / zhí ⟨throw⟩. ②铸造 zhùzào ⟨mold⟩. ③派演 pàiyǎn ⟨actor⟩. — n. ①投 tóu, 掷 zhì / zhí ⟨throwing⟩. ②铸成物 zhùchéngwù ⟨sculpture⟩. ③演员阵容 yǎnyuán zhènróng ⟨group of actors⟩.

caste n. ①世袭阶级 shìxí jiējí ⟨Hinduism⟩. ②社会阶级 shèhuì jiējí ⟨social class⟩.

castigate v. 严惩 yánchéng, 痛斥 tòngchì.

castle n. 城堡 chéngbǎo.

castrate v. 阉割 yāngē.

casual adj. ①偶然的 ǒurán de ⟨accidental⟩. ②非正式的 fēi zhèngshì de ⟨informal⟩.

casualty n. 伤亡者 shāngwángzhě ⟨dead or injured person⟩.

cat n. 猫 māo.

CAT scan 电脑断层摄影术 diànnǎo duàncéng shèyǐngshù.

catacomb n. 陵寝 língqǐn.

catalog(ue) n. 目录 mùlù, 型录 xínglù.

catalyst n. 触媒 chùméi ⟨a gent for change⟩, 催化剂 cuīhuàjì ⟨chemical⟩.

catapult n. ①弹弓 dàngōng ⟨slingshot⟩. ②弹射器 tánshèqì ⟨apparatus⟩.

cataract n. ①白内障 báinèizhàng ⟨disease⟩. ②大瀑布 dà pùbù ⟨waterfall⟩.

catastrophe n. 大灾祸 dà zāihuò.

catch v. ①捕捉 bǔzhuō ⟨hold⟩. ②赶上 gǎnshang ⟨be in time for⟩. ③罹患 líhuàn ⟨become infected with⟩. — n. ①接球 jiēqiú ⟨ball⟩. ②捕获物 bǔhuòwù ⟨something caught⟩. ③锁环 suǒhuán ⟨lock⟩.

catcher n. 捕手 bǔshǒu ⟨baseball⟩.

categorical adj. ①无条件的 wú tiáojiàn de ⟨unconditional⟩. ②绝对的 juéduì de ⟨absolute⟩.

categorize v. 分类 fēnlèi.

category n. 类 lèi, 种类 zhǒnglèi.

caterpillar n. 毛虫 máochóng.

cathedral n. 总教堂 zǒngjiàotáng, 大教堂 dàjiàotáng.

cathode n. 阴极 yīnjí.

Catholic adj. 天主教的 Tiānzhǔjiào de.

cattle n. 牛 niú.

cauliflower n. 花椰菜 huāyēcài / huāyécài.

cause n. ①原因 yuányīn, 理由 lǐyóu ⟨reason⟩. ②目标 mùbiāo ⟨aim⟩. — v. ①引起 yǐnqǐ ⟨arouse⟩. ②致使 zhìshǐ ⟨compel⟩.

causeway n. 堤道 dīdào / tídào.

C

caustic adj. ①腐蚀性的 fǔshíxìng de (corrosive). ②刻薄的 kèbó de (harsh).

caution n. ①小心 xiǎoxīn, 谨慎 jǐnshèn (attention). ②警告 jǐnggào (warning).

cautious adj. 小心的 xiǎoxīn de, 谨慎的 jǐnshèn de.

cavalry n. 骑兵队 qíbīngduì.

cave n. 洞穴 dòngxué / dòngxuè, 山洞 shāndòng. — v. 陷落 xiànluò. ~ in 塌陷 tāxiàn.

cavern n. 巨穴 jùxué / jùxuè.

caviar n. 鱼子酱 yúzǐjiàng.

cavity n. ①洞 dòng, 凹处 āochù (hole). ②蛀牙 zhùyá (teeth).

cayenne pepper n. 辣椒 làjiāo.

CD 光盘 guāngpán / 光碟 guāngdié (compact disc).

CD-ROM 唯读光盘 wéidú guāngpán / 唯读光碟 wéidú guāngdié (compact disc read-only memory).

cease v. 停止 tíngzhǐ, 终止 zhōngzhǐ.

cedar n. 西洋杉 xīyángshān.

ceiling n. ①天花板 tiānhuābǎn ⟨of a room⟩. ②最高限度 zuìgāo xiàndù (highest limit).

celebrate v. ①庆祝 qìngzhù (commemorate). ②称赞 chēngzàn (praise).

celebration n. ①庆祝 qìngzhù ⟨act⟩. ②庆祝活动 qìngzhù huódòng, 庆典 qìngdiǎn ⟨occasion⟩.

celebrity n. ①名人 míngrén (famous person). ②名誉 míngyù (fame).

celery n. 芹菜 qíncài.

celestial adj. 天空的 tiānkōng de, 天上的 tiānshang de.

celibate n. 独身者 dúshēnzhě. — adj. 独身的 dúshēn de.

cell n. ①小室 xiǎo shì (small room). ②小囚房 xiǎo qiúfáng ⟨prison⟩. ③细胞 xìbāo ⟨biology⟩.

cellar n. 地下室 dìxiàshì, 地窖 dìjiào.

cello n. 大提琴 dàtíqín.

cellphone n. 行动电话 xíngdòng diànhuà.

cellular adj. 细胞状的 xìbāozhuàng de. ~ phone 行动电话 xíngdòng diànhuà.

Celsius adj. 摄氏的 Shèshì de.

cement n. 士敏土 shìmǐntǔ / 水泥 shuǐní.

cemetery n. 墓地 mùdì.

censor n. 检查员 jiǎncháyuán. — v. 检查 jiǎnchá.

censure n. & v. 非难 fēinàn, 谴责 qiǎnzé.

census n. 户口调查 hùkǒu diàochá.

cent n. 分 fēn.

centenarian n. 百岁人瑞 bǎisuì rénruì.

centenary n. 百年纪念 bǎinián jìniàn (100th anniversary).

center n. 中心 zhōngxīn, 中央 zhōngyāng.

centigrade adj. 摄氏的 shèshì de.

centimeter n. 公分 gōngfēn.

centipede n. 蜈蚣 wúgōng.

central adj. ①中心的 zhōngxīn de, 中央的 zhōngyāng de (at the center). ②主要的 zhǔyào de (main).

centralize v. 集中 jízhōng.

centrifugal adj. 离心的 líxīn de.

century n. 世纪 shìjì.

ceramic adj. 陶器的 táoqì de, 制陶的 zhìtáo de.

cereal n. ①谷类 gǔlèi (grain). ②谷类食品 gǔlèi shípǐn (food made from grain).

ceremony n. 典礼 diǎnlǐ, 仪式 yíshì.

certain adj. ①确信的 quèxìn de (sure). ②某 mǒu (one), 某些 mǒuxiē (some). ③确实的 quèshí de (absolute). make ~ 确定 quèdìng.

certainly adv. ①确定地 quèdìng de (absolutely), 的确 díquè (really). ②当然 dāngrán (of course).

certainty n. ①确实 quèshí (assurance). ②既成事实 jìchéngshìshí (a fact).

certificate n. 证明书 zhèngmíngshū.

certify v. 证明 zhèngmíng (prove).

chafe n. & v. 擦伤 cāshāng, 擦痛 cātòng.

chaff n. 谷壳 gǔké, 糠 kāng.

chain n. ①链 liàn (link). ②一连串 yìliánchuàn, 一系列 yíxìliè (series). ~ store 连锁店 liánsuǒdiàn. — v. 以链锁住 yǐ liàn suǒzhù.

chair n. ①椅子 yǐzi (furniture). ②主席席位 zhǔxí xíwèi, 主委 zhǔwěi (position).

chairman n. 主席 zhǔxí.

chairperson n. 主席 zhǔxí.

chalk n. 粉笔 fěnbǐ. — v. 用粉笔写 yòng fěnbǐ xiě.

challenge n. & v. 挑战 tiǎozhàn.

chamber n. ①房间 fángjiān, 寝室 qǐnshì (room). ②议事厅 yìshìtīng, 议会 yìhuì (government building). ~ music 室内乐 shìnèiyuè.

chameleon n. 变色龙 biànsèlóng, 蜥蜴 xīyì.

champagne n. 香槟酒 xiāngbīnjiǔ.

champion n. ①冠军 guànjūn (winner). ②拥护者 yōnghùzhě / yǒnghùzhě (backer). — v. 拥护 yōnghù / yǒnghù.

chance n. ①机会 jīhuì (opportunity). ②冒险 màoxiǎn (risk). by ~ 偶然地 ǒurán de. — adj. 偶然的 ǒurán de.

chancellor n. ①首相 shǒuxiàng, 总理 zǒnglǐ (prime minister). ②大臣 dàchén (official of high rank).

change v. ①改变 gǎibiàn (vary). ②更换 gēnghuàn (alter). ③兑换 duìhuàn (exchange). ④转换 zhuǎnhuàn (shift). — n. ①变化 biànhuà (alteration). ②零钱 língqián (coins).

changeable adj. 易变的 yìbiàn de (easy to change), 可变的 kěbiàn de (unsettled).

channel n. ①海峡 hǎixiá (waterway). ②河床 héchuáng (bed of a river). ③航道 hángdào, 运河 yùnhé (canal). ④频道 píndào (station). ⑤途径 tújìng, 管道 guǎndào (means).

chant n. ①圣歌 shènggē (religion). ②口号 kǒuhào (slogan).

chaos n. 混乱 hùnluàn, 失序 shīxù.

chap v. 皲裂 zhòuliè. — n. 家伙 jiāhuo, 小伙子 xiǎohuǒzi.

chapel n. 礼拜堂 lǐbàitáng.

chaplain n. ①牧师 mùshī

C

C

(priest). ②教诲师 jiàohuìshī 〈prison〉.

chapter *n.* ①章 zhāng, 篇 piān (part). ②段落 duànluò (period).

char *v.* 烧焦 shāojiāo.

character *n.* ①特性 tèxìng, 特征 tèzhēng (distinctiveness). ②性格 xìnggé, 品性 pǐnxìng (personality). ③角色 juésè (role). ④文字 wénzì (letter).

characteristic *adj.* 典型的 diǎnxíng de. — *n.* 特征 tèzhēng, 特质 tèzhí / tèzhí.

charade *n.* 猜字游戏 cāizì yóuxì.

charcoal *n.* 木炭 mùtàn.

charge *n.* & *v.* ①索价 suǒjià (asking for price). ②控告 kònggào, 指控 zhǐkòng (accusation). ③充电 chōngdiàn (putting electricity into). ④突击 tūjí / túji (attack).

chariot *n.* 双轮战车 shuānglún zhànchē.

charisma *n.* 魅力 mèilì.

charity *n.* ①博爱 bó'ài, 慈悲 cíbēi (kindness). ②慈善团体 císhàn tuántǐ, 慈善机构 císhàn jīgòu 〈organization〉.

charlatan *n.* ①江湖郎中 jiānghú lángzhōng, 庸医 yōngyī (quack). ②骗子 piànzi (cheat).

charm *n.* ①魅力 mèilì, 魔力 mólì (attractiveness). ②咒语 zhòuyǔ, 魔咒 mózhòu 〈magic〉. — *v.* ①迷住 mízhù (attract). ②施魔咒 shī mózhòu (use magic on).

charming *adj.* 迷人的 mírén de.

chart *n.* ①图表 túbiǎo (diagram). ②航海图 hánghǎitú

(map of sea). — *v.* 制图 zhìtú (map).

charter *n.* ①特许状 tèxǔzhuàng 〈license〉. ②宪章 xiànzhāng (document). — *v.* 包租 bāozū (rent).

chase *n.* & *v.* ①追捕 zhuībǔ, 追赶 zhuīgǎn (running after). ②追 zhuī, 追求 zhuīqiú (pursuit).

chasm *n.* 裂痕 lièhén.

chassis *n.* 底盘 dǐpán.

chaste *adj.* 贞节的 zhēnjié de, 纯洁的 chúnjié de.

chasten *v.* ①惩戒 chéngjiè (punish). ②抑制 yìzhì (constrain).

chastise *v.* 惩罚 chéngfá.

chastity *n.* 纯洁 chúnjié, 贞洁 zhēnjié.

chat *n.* & *v.* 闲谈 xiántán.

chat room *n.* 聊天室 liáotiānshì.

chateau *n.* 城堡 chéngbǎo.

chatter *n.* & *v.* ①喋喋不休 diédié-bùxiū (talking quickly). ②啁啾 zhōujiū 〈sounds of birds〉.

chauffeur *n.* 司机 sījī.

chauvinism *n.* 沙文主义 shāwén zhǔyì.

cheap *adj.* ①便宜的 piányi de (inexpensive). ②廉价的 liánjià de (worthless).

cheat *v.* ①欺骗 qīpiàn (deceive). ②作弊 zuòbì 〈test〉. — *n.* 骗子 piànzi (con man).

check *v.* ①检查 jiǎnchá, 核对 héduì (examine). ②阻止 zǔzhǐ, 抑制 yìzhì (block). ~ *in* 办理登记 bànlǐ dēngjì. ~ *out* 结账离去 jiézhàng líqù. — *n.* ①阻止 zǔzhǐ (stop). ②支票 zhīpiào 〈for payment〉. ③方格花式 fānggé huāshì 〈pattern〉. ④账

单 zhàngdān (bill), 收据 shōujù (receipt).

checked *adj.* 有格子的 yǒu gézi de.

checkmate *v.* 将死 jiāngsǐ, 攻王棋 gōng wángqí ⟨chess⟩.

cheek *n.* 颊 jiá, 面颊 miànjiá.

cheer *n.* ①喝采 hècǎi (applause). ②喜悦 xǐyuè, 愉快 yúkuài (happiness). — *v.* 欢呼 huānhū, 喝采 hècǎi (applaud).

cheerful *adj.* 快乐的 kuàilè de, 高兴的 gāoxìng de.

cheese *n.* 乳酪 rǔlào / rǔluò, 起司 qǐsī.

chef *n.* 主厨 zhǔchú.

chemical *adj.* 化学的 huàxué de. — *n.* 化学药品 huàxué yàopǐn.

chemical weapon *n.* 化学武器 huàxué wǔqì.

chemist *n.* 化学家 huàxuéjiā.

chemistry *n.* 化学 huàxué.

cheque *n.* 支票 zhīpiào.

cherish *v.* ①珍惜 zhēnxī / zhēnxí (care for tenderly). ②怀着 huáizhe (remember tenderly).

cherry *n.* ①樱桃 yīngtáo ⟨fruit⟩. ②樱桃树 yīngtáoshù ⟨tree⟩.

chess *n.* 西洋棋 xīyángqí.

chest *n.* ①胸部 xiōngbù (breast). ②箱子 xiāngzi (box).

chestnut *n.* ①栗树 lìshù ⟨tree⟩. ②栗褐色 lìhèsè / lìhésè (brown). ③栗子 lìzi ⟨nut⟩.

chew *v.* 咀嚼 jǔjué. ~ *ing gum* 口香糖 kǒuxiāngtáng.

chic *n. & adj.* 高雅 gāoyǎ.

chick *n.* ①雏鸡 chújī (chicken). ②女孩子 nǚháizi (girl).

chicken *n.* ①鸡 jī ⟨animal⟩. ②鸡肉 jīròu ⟨meat⟩. ~ *pox* 水痘 shuǐdòu.

chicory *n.* 菊苣 jújù.

chief *n.* 领袖 lǐngxiù, 首领 shǒulǐng. — *adj.* 主要的 zhǔyào de.

chiefly *adv.* 主要地 zhǔyào de, 首要地 shǒuyào de.

chieftain *n.* 酋长 qiúzhǎng.

child *n.* ①小孩 xiǎohái (young person). ②子女 zǐnǚ (son and daughter).

childhood *n.* 童年 tóngnián.

childish *adj.* 幼稚的 yòuzhì de (immature), 孩子气的 háiziqì de (childlike).

chill *n.* ①寒意 hányì, 寒冷 hánlěng (coldness). ②寒栗 hánlì (shivering). — *v.* 使寒冷 shǐ hánlěng (make cold).

chilly *adj.* ①寒冷的 hánlěng de (cold). ②冷淡的 lěngdàn de (aloof).

chime *n.* 一套乐钟 yí tào yuèzhōng. — *v.* 鸣钟 míng zhōng (ring).

chimney *n.* ①烟囱 yāncōng (smokestack). ②玻璃灯罩 bōli dēngzhào (glass tube).

chimpanzee *n.* 黑猩猩 hēixīngxing.

chin *n.* 下颌 xiàhàn, 下巴 xiàba.

china *n.* 瓷器 cíqì.

Chinatown *n.* 中国城 Zhōngguóchéng, 唐人街 Tángrénjiē.

Chinese *n. & adj.* ①中国人 Zhōngguórén ⟨people⟩. ②中文 Zhōngwén ⟨language⟩.

chip *n.* ①碎片 suìpiàn, 木屑 mùxiè (small piece). ②缺口 quēkǒu (crack). ③芯片 xīnpiàn / 晶片 jīngpiàn ⟨computer⟩. — *v.* ①切成薄片 qiēchéng báopiàn / qiēchéng bópiàn

(cut). ②碎裂 suìliè (break).

chirp n. & v. 吱喳叫 zīzhājiào / zhīzhājiào, 唧唧声 jījīshēng / jíjīshēng.

chisel n. 凿子 záozi. — v. 凿刻 záokè.

chivalry n. 骑士制度 qíshì zhìdù, 骑士精神 qíshì jīngshén.

chlorine n. 氯 lǜ.

chocolate n. 巧克力 qiǎokèlì.

choice n. 选择 xuǎnzé.

choir n. 唱诗班 chàngshībān.

choke v. ①使窒息 shǐ zhìxī / shǐ zhìxí (throttle). ②窒息 zhìxī / zhìxí (be unable to breathe). ③阻塞 zǔsè (block).

cholera n. 霍乱 huòluàn.

cholesterol n. 胆固醇 dǎngùchún.

choose v. 选择 xuǎnzé, 挑选 tiāoxuǎn.

chop v. 砍 kǎn, 切 qiē. — n. 图章 túzhāng (seal).

choppy adj. 波浪起伏的 bōlàng qǐfú de.

chopstick n. 筷子 kuàizi.

choral adj. 合唱团的 héchàngtuán de, 唱诗班的 chàngshībān de.

chord n. 和弦 héxián.

chore n. 杂务 záwù, 零工 línggōng.

choreography n. 舞蹈术 wǔdǎoshù / wǔdàoshù.

chorus n. 合唱团 héchàngtuán. — v. 合颂 hésòng.

Christ n. 基督 Jīdū.

christen v. 施洗礼 shīxǐlǐ.

Christian adj. 基督教的 Jīdūjiào de. — n. 基督徒 Jīdūtú.

Christianity n. 基督教 Jīdūjiào.

Christmas n. 圣诞节 Shèngdànjié.

chromium n. 铬 gè.

chromosome n. 染色体 rǎnsètǐ.

chronic adj. 慢性的 mànxìng de, 长期的 chángqī de / chángqí de.

chronicle n. 编年史 biānniánshǐ, 年代记 niándàijì.

chronology n. ①年表 niánbiǎo (list). ②年代学 niándàixué (science).

chrysalis n. 蛹 yǒng (pupa).

chrysanthemum n. 菊花 júhuā.

chubby adj. 圆胖的 yuánpàng de.

chuck v. ①抛掷 pāozhì / pāozhí (throw). ②轻抚 qīngfǔ (touch).

chuckle n. & v. 低声轻笑 dīshēng qīngxiào.

chum n. 密友 mìyǒu.

chump n. ①厚木块 hòu mùkuài (wood). ②傻瓜 shǎguā (fool).

chunk n. 厚块 hòukuài.

church n. ①教堂 jiàotáng (building). ②礼拜 lǐbài (service).

churn n. 搅乳器 jiǎorǔqì. — v. 搅拌 jiǎobàn.

chute n. ①斜槽 xiécáo (sloped passage). ②急流 jíliú (rapid fall of water).

cigar n. 雪茄烟 xuějiāyān.

cigarette n. 香烟 xiāngyān.

cinder n. ①煤渣 méizhā (coal). ②余烬 yújìn (ash).

cinema n. ①电影院 diànyǐngyuàn (theater). ②电影 diànyǐng (films).

cinnamon n. 肉桂 ròuguì.

cipher n. ①零 líng (zero). ②不重要者 bú zhòngyào zhě (nobody). ③暗号 ànhào, 密码 mìmǎ (code). — v. 译成暗号 yìchéng ànhào.

circle n. ①圆 yuán ⟨shape⟩. ②周期 zhōuqī / zhōuqí, 循环 xúnhuán (a chain of events). — v. ①绕行 ràoxíng (move around). ②环绕 huánrào (encircle).

circuit n. ①巡回 xúnhuí (journey). ②电路 diànlù ⟨electricity⟩.

circular adj. ①圆的 yuán de (round). ②循环的 xúnhuán de (cyclic). — n. 传单 chuándān.

circulate v. ①循环 xúnhuán (move). ②传布 chuánbù (publicize).

circulation n. ①循环 xúnhuán ⟨movement⟩. ②传布 chuánbù (broadcasting). ③销路 xiāolù, 发行量 fāxíngliàng (distribution).

circumcise v. 割包皮 gē bāopí.

circumference n. 圆周 yuánzhōu.

circumnavigate v. 环游 huányóu.

circumstance n. 情形 qíngxing, 情况 qíngkuàng.

circus n. 马戏团 mǎxìtuán.

cistern n. 水槽 shuǐcáo, 贮水池 zhùshuǐchí / zhǔshuǐchí (tank).

cite v. ①引用 yǐnyòng, 引述 yǐnshù (quote). ②引证 yǐnzhèng (refer to as proof).

citizen n. ①公民 gōngmín ⟨country⟩. ②市民 shìmín ⟨city⟩.

city n. 城市 chéngshì, 都市

dūshì.

city hall n. 市政厅 shìzhèngtīng, 市政府 shìzhèngfǔ.

civic adj. 市民的 shìmín de ⟨city⟩, 公民的 gōngmín de ⟨country⟩.

civil adj. ①公民的 gōngmín de, 市民的 shìmín de (communal). ②平民的 píngmín de (civilian). ③礼貌的 lǐmào de (polite).

civilian n. 平民 píngmín.

civilization n. 文明 wénmíng.

civilize v. 教化 jiàohuà, 开化 kāihuà.

claim n. & v. ①声称 shēngchēng, 主张 zhǔzhāng (say). ②要求 yāoqiú, 请求 qǐngqiú (ask for).

clairvoyant n. 透视者 tòushìzhě. — adj. 有透视力的 yǒu tòushìlì de (perceptive).

clam n. 蛤 gé, 蚌 bàng.

clamber n. & v. 攀登 pāndēng.

clammy adj. 湿冷黏糊的 shīlěng niánhu de.

clamor n. & v. 叫嚣 jiàoxiāo, 喧闹 xuānnào.

clamp n. 钳子 qiánzi, 夹子 jiāzi / jiázi. — v. 用钳子夹住 yòng qiánzi jiāzhù / yòng qiánzi jiázhù.

clan n. 宗族 zōngzú (group), 部落 bùluò (tribe).

clandestine adj. 秘密的 mìmì de (secret), 暗中的 ànzhōng de (hidden).

clang n. 叮当声 dīngdāngshēng. — v. 发叮当声 fā dīngdāngshēng.

clap n. 轰声 hōngshēng. — v. 拍手 pāishǒu, 鼓掌 gǔzhǎng

C

(applaud).

claret n. 红葡萄酒 hóngpútáo jiǔ.

clarify v. 澄清 chéngqīng (clear up), 阐明 chǎnmíng (expound).

clarinet n. 竖笛 shùdí.

clarity n. 清晰 qīngxī, 澄清 chéngqīng.

clash n. & v. ①冲突 chōngtū / chōngtú (conflict). ②撞击声 zhuàngjīshēng / zhuàngjíshēng 〈sound〉.

clasp n. ①扣子 kòuzi, 钩子 gōuzi (buckle). ②紧握 jǐnwò, 紧抱 jǐnbào (firm hold). — v. ①紧握 jǐnwò (grasp). ②紧抱 jǐnbào (hold). ③扣住 kòuzhù, 钩住 gōuzhù (fasten).

class n. ①班 bān (group). ②课 kè (lesson). ③类 lèi, 种类 zhǒnglèi (category). ④阶级 jiējí (status).

classic adj. ①古典的 gǔdiǎn de (classical). ②经典的 jīngdiǎn de (time-honored). — n. 一流 作品 yīliú zuòpǐn (masterpiece).

classical adj. 古典的 gǔdiǎn de, 古典派的 gǔdiǎnpài de. ~ music 古典音乐 gǔdiǎn yīnyuè.

classify v. 分类 fēnlèi (categorize), 分等级 fēn děngjí (break into levels).

classmate n. 同学 tóngxué.

classroom n. 教室 jiàoshì.

clatter n. & v. 劈啪声 pīpāshēng, 哗啦声 huālāshēng.

clause n. ①条款 tiáokuǎn (provision). ②子句 zǐjù 〈grammar〉.

claw n. 爪 zhuǎ. — v. 用爪撕 yòng zhuǎ sī.

clay n. 黏土 niántǔ.

clean adj. ①干净的 gānjìng de, 清洁的 qīngjié de (not dirty). ②清白的 qīngbái de (pure). — v. 清洁 qīngjié, 打扫 dǎsǎo.

cleaning n. 清洁 qīngjié, 打扫 dǎsǎo.

cleanse v. 使清洁 shǐ qīngjié, 使纯洁 shǐ chúnjié.

clear adj. ①清楚的 qīngchu de, 清晰的 qīngxī de, 明白的 míngbai de (unambiguous). ②明亮的 míngliàng de (bright). ③晴朗的 qínglǎng de (cloudless). — v. 清除 qīngchú, 清理 qīnglǐ.

clearing n. 开垦地 kāikěndì 〈land〉. ~ house 票据交换所 piàojù jiāohuànsuǒ.

clearly adv. ①清楚地 qīngchu de (distinctly). ②显然地 xiǎnrán de (evidently).

cleave v. 劈开 pīkai, 裂开 lièkai (split).

clef n. 谱号 pǔhào.

clemency n. 仁慈 réncí.

clergy n. 牧师 mùshī, 教士 jiàoshì.

clergyman n. 牧师 mùshī, 教士 jiàoshì.

clerical adj. ①牧师的 mùshī de 〈clergy〉. ②书记的 shūjì de (secretarial).

clerk n. ①办事员 bànshìyuán 〈office〉. ②店员 diànyuán 〈shop〉.

clever adj. ①聪明的 cōngmíng de (intelligent). ②灵巧的 língqiǎo de (skillful).

cliché n. 陈腔滥调 chén-qiāng-làndiào.

click n. & v. 滴答声 dīdāshēng.

client n. ①顾客 gùkè, 客户 kèhù 〈business〉. ②委托人

clientele n. 顾客 gùkè.

cliff n. 悬崖 xuányá / xuányái.

climate n. 气候 qìhòu.

climax n. ①顶点 dǐngdiǎn, 极点 jídiǎn (high point). ②高潮 gāocháo (best part).

climb v. 攀登 pāndēng, 攀爬 pānpá.

cling v. ①紧抱 jǐnbào (hold). ②紧贴着 jǐntiēzhe (stick).

clinic n. 诊所 zhěnsuǒ.

clinician n. 临床医生 línchuáng yīshēng.

clink n. 叮当声 dīngdāngshēng.

clip n. 剪 jiǎn, 修剪 xiūjiǎn (cut). — v. 夹子 jiāzi / jiázi (fastener).

clique n. 派系 pàixì.

cloak n. 斗篷 dǒupeng (clothing). — v. 遮盖 zhēgài, 掩盖 yǎngài.

cloakroom n. 衣帽间 yīmàojiān.

clock n. 时钟 shízhōng.
 around the ~ 二十四小时连续地 èrshísì xiǎoshí liánxù de.

clockwise adj. & adv. 顺时针方向的 shùnshízhēn fāngxiàng de.

clod n. 土块 tǔkuài, 泥块 níkuài.

clog n. 木屐 mùjī. — v. 塞住 sāizhù (block).

cloister n. 修道院 xiūdàoyuàn (monastery). — v. 隐居 yǐnjū.

close v. ①关 guān, 闭 bì (shut). ②结束 jiéshù (end). — adj. ①接近的 jiējìn de (near). ②亲近的 qīnjìn de, 亲密的 qīnmì de (dear).

closed adj. 关闭的 guānbì de.

closely adv. ①紧密地 jǐnmì de (compactly). ②接近地 jiējìn de

(nearly).

closet n. 橱柜 chúguì.

closure n. ①关闭 guānbì (shut). ②终止 zhōngzhǐ (end).

clot n. 凝块 níngkuài. — v. 凝结 níngjié.

cloth n. 布 bù, 布块 bùkuài.

clothes n. 衣服 yīfu.

clothing n. 衣服 yīfu.

cloud n. 云 yún.

cloudless adj. 无云的 wú yún de, 晴朗的 qínglǎng de.

cloudy adj. ①有云的 yǒu yún de, 阴天的 yīntiān de (sunless). ②朦胧的 ménglóng de, 晦暗的 huìàn de (blurred).

clover n. 苜蓿 mùxu / mùsù.

clown n. 丑角 chǒujué, 小丑 xiǎochǒu (circus).

club n. ①俱乐部 jùlèbù (society). ②梅花 méihuā (cards).

cluck n. & v. 咯咯声 gēgēshēng.

clue n. 线索 xiànsuǒ.

clump n. ①草丛 cǎocóng (grass), 树丛 shùcóng (trees).

clumsy adj. 笨拙的 bènzhuō de / bènzhuó de.

cluster n. 串 chuàn, 簇 cù. — v. 群聚 qúnjù, 丛生 cóngshēng.

clutch v. 抓牢 zhuāláo. — n. ①紧抓 jǐnzhuā (grasp). ②离合器 líhéqì (machine).

clutches v. 紧握 jǐnwò (grasp).

clutter v. 弄乱 nòngluàn, 乱堆 luànduī. — n. 混乱 hùnluàn.

coach n. ①四轮马车 sì lún mǎchē (horse-drawn). ②客车厢 kèchēxiāng (railway carriage). ③教练 jiàoliàn (trainer). — v. 训练 xùnliàn, 指导 zhǐdǎo.

coagulate v. 凝结 níngjié.

coal n. 煤 méi, 煤炭 méitàn.

C

C

~ *mine* 煤矿 méikuàng.

coalesce v. 联合 liánhé, 结合 jiéhé.

coalition n. ①联合 liánhé (combination). ②联盟 liánméng (alliance).

coarse adj. ①粗糙的 cūcāo de (rough). ②粗劣的 cūliè de (low quality). ③粗俗的 cūsú de (boorish).

coast n. 海岸 hǎi'àn, 沿海地区 yánhǎi dìqū. — v. ①滑行 huáxíng (slide). ②沿岸航行 yán àn hángxíng 〈sail〉.

coat n. 外衣 wàiyī, 外套 wàitào. — v. 涂覆 túfù.

coating n. 被覆层 bèifùcéng.

coax v. 劝哄 quànhǒng.

cobblestone n. 圆石块 yuánshíkuài, 鹅卵石 éluǎnshí.

cobra n. 眼镜蛇 yǎnjìngshé.

cobweb n. 蜘蛛网 zhīzhūwǎng.

cocaine n. 可卡因 kěkǎyīn / 古柯硷 gǔkējiǎn.

cock n. ①公鸡 gōngjī (rooster). ②雄鸟 xióngniǎo (male bird). — v. ①竖起 shùqǐ (turn upwards). ②扣扳机 kòu bānjī 〈gun〉.

cockpit n. 驾驶舱 jiàshǐcāng.

cockroach n. 蟑螂 zhāngláng.

cockscomb n. 鸡冠 jīguān.

cocktail n. 鸡尾酒 jīwěijiǔ.

cocoa n. 可可粉 kěkěfěn.

coconut n. 椰子 yēzi / yézi.

cocoon n. 蚕茧 cánjiǎn.

cod n. 鳕鱼 xuěyú.

coddle v. 溺爱 nì'ài (pamper).

code n. ①法典 fǎdiǎn, 法规 fǎguī 〈law〉. ②规则 guīzé (rules). ③密码 mìmǎ (secret signs).

coed n. 女生 nǚshēng.

coerce v. 强迫 qiǎngpò.

coexist v. 共存 gòngcún.

coffee n. 咖啡 kāfēi.

coffer n. 保险箱 bǎoxiǎnxiāng.

coffin n. 棺材 guāncái, 枢 jiù.

cog n. 轮齿 lúnchǐ.

cognac n. 白兰地酒 báilándìjiǔ, 干邑酒 gānyìjiǔ.

cohabit v. 同居 tóngjū.

cohere v. ①黏着 niánzhuó (stick). ②连贯 liánguàn (remain united).

coherent adj. ①一贯的 yíguàn de (consistent). ②清楚的 qīngchu de (clear).

cohesion n. ①附着 fùzhuó, 黏着 niánzhuó (sticking). ②凝聚 níngjù, 团结 tuánjié 〈people〉. ③凝结 níngjié 〈objects〉.

coil v. 盘绕 pánrào 〈wind〉, 卷起 juǎnqǐ (roll). — n. ①卷 juǎn (roll). ②线圈 xiànquān 〈electric wire〉.

coin n. 硬币 yìngbì, 铜板 tóngbǎn. — v. ①铸（硬币）zhù 〈yìngbì〉 (mint). ②创造 chuàngzào (invent).

coincide v. ①同时发生 tóngshí fāshēng (happen at the same time). ②符合 fúhé, 一致 yízhì (be in agreement).

coincidence n. 巧合 qiǎohé (accident).

coke n. 焦炭 jiāotàn.

cold adj. ①寒冷的 hánlěng de (chilly). ②冷漠的 lěngmò de (unemotional). — n. ①寒冷 hánlěng 〈weather〉. ②感冒 gǎnmào 〈sickness〉. *catch a* ~ 着凉 zháoliáng / zhāoliáng, 感冒 gǎnmào.

cold-blooded adj. ①冷血的 lěngxuè de / lěngxiě de 〈biology〉. ②残忍的 cánrěn de.

C

无情的 wúqíng de (cruel).

collaborate *v.* ①合作 hézuò (work together). ②通敌 tōngdí (aid the enemy).

collapse *n. & v.* 倒塌 dǎotā (fall down), 崩溃 bēngkuì (come to ruin).

collar *n.* ①衣领 yīlǐng (clothes). ②项圈 xiàngquān (animals).

colleague *n.* 同事 tóngshì, 同僚 tóngliáo.

collect *v.* 收集 shōují, 搜集 sōují (gather together).

collection *n.* ①搜集品 sōujípǐn, 收藏品 shōucángpǐn (objects). ②收集 shōují (act of collecting).

collective *adj.* 集体的 jítǐ de, 共有的 gòngyǒu de.

college *n.* 学院 xuéyuàn, 大学 dàxué.

collide *v.* ①碰撞 pèngzhuàng (strike together). ②冲突 chōngtū / chōngtú, 抵触 dǐchù (be opposed).

collision *n.* ①相撞 xiāngzhuàng (crash). ②冲突 chōngtū / chōngtú, 抵触 dǐchù (conflict).

colloquial *adj.* 口语的 kǒuyǔ de, 会话的 huìhuà de.

cologne *n.* 科隆香水 kēlóng xiāngshuǐ / 古龙水 gǔlóngshuǐ.

colon *n.* ①冒号 màohào (punctuation). ②结肠 jiécháng (intestine).

colonel *n.* 上校 shàngxiào.

colonial *adj.* 殖民地的 zhímíndì de.

colonist *n.* 殖民者 zhímínzhě.

colonnade *n.* 柱廊 zhùláng.

colony *n.* ①殖民地 zhímíndì (area). ②殖民 zhímín, 移民群

体 yímín qúntǐ (people).

color *n.* 颜色 yánsè. — *v.* 染色 rǎnsè (dye), 着色 zhuósè (paint).

colorful *adj.* 鲜艳的 xiānyàn de, 多彩的 duōcǎi de (full of color).

colossal *adj.* 巨大的 jùdà de.

colt *n.* 小雄马 xiǎo xióngmǎ.

column *n.* ①圆柱 yuánzhù (pillar). ②专栏 zhuānlán (article).

columnist *n.* 专栏作家 zhuānlán zuòjiā.

coma *n.* 昏迷 hūnmí.

comb *n.* 梳子 shūzi. — *v.* 梳发 shūfà / shūfǎ.

combat *n. & v.* 战斗 zhàndòu.

combatant *adj.* 战斗的 zhàndòu de. — *n.* 战斗员 zhàndòuyuán.

combination *n.* 联合 liánhé, 合并 hébìng.

combine *v.* 联合 liánhé, 结合 jiéhé.

combustible *adj.* 易燃的 yìrán de.

combustion *n.* 燃烧 ránshāo.

come *v.* ①来 lái (move towards). ②到 dào, 到达 dàodá (arrive). ~ *about* 发生 fāshēng (occur). ~ *across* 偶然遇到 ǒurán yùdào (happen upon). ~ *back* 回来 huílai. ~ *from* 来自 láizì.

comedian *n.* 喜剧演员 xǐjù yǎnyuán (actor), 丑角 chǒujué (comic).

comedy *n.* 喜剧 xǐjù.

comet *n.* 彗星 huìxīng.

comfort *v.* 安慰 ānwèi (console). — *n.* 舒适 shūshì (amenity).

comfortable *adj.* 舒服的 shūfu de, 舒适的 shūshì de.

comic *adj.* ①喜剧的 xǐjù de 〈comedy〉. ②滑稽的 huájī de (funny).

coming *n.* 到来 dàolái (arrival). — *adj.* 即将到来的 jíjiāng dàolái de (upcoming).

comma *n.* 逗点 dòudiǎn.

command *n. & v.* ①命令 mìnglìng, 指挥 zhǐhuī 〈order〉. ②控制 kòngzhì (control).

commander *n.* ①司令官 sīlìngguān, 指挥官 zhǐhuīguān (commanding officer). ②海军中校 hǎijūn zhōngxiào 〈navy〉.

commandment *n.* 戒律 jièlǜ.

commando *n.* 突击队 tūjíduì / tújíduì.

commemorate *v.* 纪念 jìniàn, 庆祝 qìngzhù.

commence *v.* 开始 kāishǐ.

commend *v.* 称赞 chēngzàn, 赞扬 zànyáng.

comment *n. & v.* ①说法 shuōfǎ (remark). ②批评 pīpíng, 评论 pínglùn (criticism). ③评注 píngzhù, 注释 zhùshì (annotation).

commentary *n.* 注解 zhùjiě (explanatory notes).

commerce *n.* 商业 shāngyè, 贸易 màoyì.

commercial *adj.* 商业的 shāngyè de. — *n.* 广告 guǎnggào.

commiserate *v.* 同情 tóngqíng, 怜悯 liánmǐn.

commission *n.* ①委员会 wěiyuánhuì (committee). ②佣金 yòngjīn 〈sales〉. — *v.* 委托 wěituō, 委任 wěirèn (give authority to).

commit *v.* ①犯（罪）fàn (zuì) 〈crime〉, 犯（错）fàn (cuò) 〈error〉. ②委托 wěituō, 交付

jiāofù (entrust).

committee *n.* 委员会 wěiyuánhuì.

commodity *n.* 商品 shāngpǐn, 物品 wùpǐn.

common *adj.* ①共同的 gòngtóng de, 公共的 gōnggòng de (public). ②普通的 pǔtōng de (ordinary). ③常见的 chángjiàn de (usual).

commonly *adv.* 普通地 pǔtōng de, 一般地 yìbān de.

commonplace *adj.* 平凡的 píngfán de.

commonwealth *n.* 联邦 liánbāng (confederation), 共和国 gònghéguó (republic).

commotion *n.* 暴动 bàodòng.

communal *adj.* 公用的 gōngyòng de, 公有的 gōngyǒu de.

commune *v.* ①与……亲近 yǔ...qīnjìn (be in close touch with). ②密谈 mìtán (talk with in an intimate way). — *n.* 公社 gōngshè (community).

communicate *v.* ①传达 chuándá, 传送 chuánsòng (convey). ②沟通 gōutōng, 通讯 tōngxùn (exchange information). ③传染 chuánrǎn (infect).

communication *n.* ①传达 chuándá (transmission). ②沟通 gōutōng (exchange).

communion *n.* ①圣餐 shèngcān 〈Christian ritual〉. ②交流 jiāoliú (exchange).

communiqué *n.* 公报 gōngbào.

communism *n.* 共产主义 gòngchǎn zhǔyì.

community *n.* ①住宅小区 zhùzhái xiǎo qū / 社区 shèqū

C

(neighborhood). ②团体 tuántǐ (group). ③共有 gòngyǒu (sharing).

commute v. ①通勤 tōngqín (travel). ②折算 zhésuàn (exchange). ③减轻 jiǎnqīng (lighten).

compact adj. ①塞紧的 sāijǐn de, 紧密的 jǐnmì de (closely packed). ②简洁的 jiǎnjié de, 简明的 jiǎnmíng de (brief). — n. ①契约 qìyuē (agreement). ②小型汽车 xiǎoxíng qìchē (small car). ③小粉盒 xiǎo fěnhé (container). ~ disc 激光唱片 jīguāng chàngpiàn / 雷射唱片 léishè chàngpiàn.

~ disc player 激光唱机 jīguāng chàngjī / 雷射唱盘 léishè chàngpán.

companion n. 同伴 tóngbàn, 伙伴 huǒbàn.

companionship n. 友谊 yǒuyì, 交情 jiāoqíng.

company n. ①公司 gōngsī (business). ②访客 fǎngkè, 宾客 bīnkè (visitors). ③陪伴 péibàn, 同伴 tóngbàn (companion). ④友谊 yǒuyì (fellowship). ⑤一群 yì qún, 一队 yí duì (group).

comparable adj. 可比较的 kě bǐjiào de (similar), 可比拟的 kě bǐnǐ de (as good as).

comparative adj. 比较的 bǐjiào de. — n. 比较级 bǐjiàojí.

compare v. ①比较 bǐjiào (contrast). ②比拟 bǐnǐ, 比喻 bǐyù (draw a parallel).

comparison n. 比较 bǐjiào.

compartment n. 小隔间 xiǎo géjiān (small room), 车室 chēshì (carriage).

compass n. 指南针

zhǐnánzhēn, 罗盘 luópán. — v. 绕行 ràoxíng.

compassion n. 同情 tóngqíng.

compatible adj. 相容的 xiāngróng de, 符合的 fúhé de.

compatriot n. 同胞 tóngbāo.

compel v. 迫使 pòshǐ.

compensate v. 赔偿 péicháng, 补偿 bǔcháng.

compensation n. 赔偿 péicháng, 补偿 bǔcháng.

compete v. ①竞争 jìngzhēng (business). ②比赛 bǐsài (contest).

competence n. 能力 nénglì.

competent adj. 能干的 nénggàn de (capable), 胜任的 shèngrèn de / shēngrèn de (sufficiently skilled).

competition n. ①竞争 jìngzhēng (rivalry). ②比赛 bǐsài (contest).

competitor n. 竞争者 jìngzhēngzhě, 敌手 díshǒu.

compilation n. 编辑 biānjí, 编纂 biānzuǎn.

compile v. 编纂 biānzuǎn, 编辑 biānjí.

complain v. 抱怨 bàoyuàn.

complaint n. ①抱怨 bàoyuàn (grievance). ②疾病 jíbìng (illness).

complement n. ①补充物 bǔchōngwù (supplement). ②足量 zúliàng, 全数 quánshù (aggregate). ~ v. 补充 bǔchōng.

complete adj. 完整的 wánzhěng de, 完全的 wánquán de. — v. 完成 wánchéng (finish).

completely adv. 完全地 wánquán de.

completion n. 完成

C

wánchéng.

complex adj. ①复杂的 fùzá de (complicated). ②合成的 héchéng de (compound).

complexion n. ①面色 miànsè, 肤色 fūsè (skin coloring), 外观 wàiguān (appearance). ②形势 xíngshì (situation).

compliance n. 顺从 shùncóng.

complicate v. 使复杂 shǐ fùzá, 使麻烦 shǐ máfan.

complicated adj. 复杂的 fùzá de.

complicity n. 共犯 gòngfàn, 同谋 tóngmóu.

compliment n. & v. 赞美 zànměi (praise), 恭维 gōngwéi (flattery).

comply v. 顺从 shùncóng, 遵从 zūncóng.

component adj. 组成的 zǔchéng de. — n. 成分 chéngfèn (ingredient), 因素 yīnsù (factor).

compose v. ①组成 zǔchéng, 构成 gòuchéng (constitute). ②著作 zhùzuò, 创作 chuàngzuò (create).

composer n. 作曲家 zuòqǔjiā.

composite adj. 混合的 hùnhé de. — n. 合成物 héchéngwù.

composition n. ①成分 chéngfèn (contents). ②著作 zhùzuò, 作品 zuòpǐn (piece). ③作文 zuòwén (essay).

compositor n. 排字工人 páizì gōngrén.

composure n. 镇静 zhènjìng.

compound adj. 合成的 héchéng de, 复合的 fùhé de. — n. 复合物 fùhéwù, 混合物 hùnhéwù (combination). — v.

组成 zǔchéng, 合成 héchéng.

comprehend v. 了解 liǎojiě (understand), 领悟 lǐngwù (realize).

comprehensible adj. 可理解的 kě lǐjiě de.

comprehensive adj. 广泛的 guǎngfàn de, 全面的 quánmiàn de.

compress v. 压缩 yāsuō (press together). — n. 压布 yābù, 绷带 bēngdài.

comprise v. ①包括 bāokuò / bāoguā, 包含 bāohán (include). ②组成 zǔchéng, 构成 gòuchéng (constitute).

compromise v. ①妥协 tuǒxié, 和解 héjiě (make concession). ②危及 wēijí / wéijí (threaten), 连累 liánlěi / liánlèi (discredit). — n. 妥协 tuǒxié, 和解 héjiě.

compulsion n. 强迫 qiǎngpò, 强制 qiángzhì / qiǎngzhì.

compulsory adj. 强制的 qiángzhì de / qiǎngzhì de, 义务的 yìwù de (obligatory).

compunction n. 良心的责备 liángxīn de zébèi, 懊悔 àohuí.

computer n. 计算机 jìsuànjī / 电脑 diànnǎo. ~ *graphics* 电脑绘图 diànnǎo huìtú. ~ *screen* 电脑屏幕 diànnǎo píngmù / 电脑萤幕 diànnǎo yíngmù. ~ *virus* 电脑病毒 diànnǎo bìngdú.

comrade n. ①同伴 tóngbàn, 朋友 péngyou (companion). ②同志 tóngzhì ⟨of a political party⟩.

con n. & adv. 反对 fǎnduì (against). — v. 欺骗 qīpiàn (trick). *pros* and ~s 正反两面 zhèngfǎn liǎngmiàn.

concave adj. 凹的 āo de, 凹

面的 āomiàn de.

conceal v. 隐藏 yǐncáng, 隐匿 yǐnnì.

concede v. ①承认 chéngrèn (admit). ②让与 ràngyǔ (give in), 让步 ràngbù (yield), 容许 róngxǔ (allow).

conceit n. 自负 zìfù, 自大 zìdà.

conceive v. ①怀孕 huáiyùn (become pregnant). ②构思 gòusī (think of).

concentrate v. ①专心 zhuānxīn (be attentive). ②集中 jízhōng (accumulate). ③浓缩 nóngsuō (condense).

concentration n. ①专心 zhuānxīn (attention). ②集中 jízhōng (gathering). ~ camp 集中营 jízhōngyíng.

concept n. 概念 gàiniàn.

conception n. ①概念 gàiniàn (concept). ②构思 gòusī, 构想 gòuxiǎng (idea).

concern v. ①与……有关 yǔ...yǒuguān (related to). ②关心 guānxīn (care about), 注意 zhùyì (notice). ③担心 dānxīn, 忧虑 yōulǜ (worry about). — n. ①关心 guānxīn (care). ②企业 qǐyè / qìyè, 事业 shìyè (business). ③担心 dānxīn, 忧虑 yōulǜ (anxiety). ④关心的事 guānxīn de shì ⟨affair⟩.

concert n. 音乐会 yīnyuèhuì, 演奏会 yǎnzòuhuì.

concerto n. 协奏曲 xiézòuqǔ.

concession n. ①让步 ràngbù (yielding). ②特许权 tèxǔquán (special right).

conciliate v. ①调解 tiáojiě (mediate). ②抚慰 fǔwèi (soothe).

concise adj. 简明的 jiǎnmíng de, 简洁的 jiǎnjié de.

conclude v. ①终结 zhōngjié, 结束 jiéshù (end). ②作出结论 zuòchū jiélùn (make judgment).

conclusion n. ①终结 zhōngjié, 结束 jiéshù (end). ②结论 jiélùn (judgment).

concoct v. ①调制 tiáozhì (make by mixing). ②编造 biānzào, 虚构 xūgòu (invent).

concord n. 和谐 héxié, 协调 xiétiáo.

concourse n. ①汇集 huìjí (crowd). ②大厅 dàtīng (building).

concrete adj. 具体的 jùtǐ de. — n. 混凝土 hùnníngtǔ. — v. 铺混凝土 pū hùnníngtǔ.

concur v. ①同意 tóngyì (agree). ②同时发生 tóngshí fāshēng (happen at the same time).

condemn v. ①谴责 qiǎnzé, 责难 zénàn (blame). ②宣告有罪 xuāngào yǒuzuì (convict).

condense v. ①浓缩 nóngsuō (reduce). ②使简洁 shǐ jiǎnjié, 简述 jiǎnshù (abbreviate). ③凝结 níngjié (become liquid).

condescend v. 屈尊 qūzūn, 俯就 fǔjiù.

condition n. ①状况 zhuàngkuàng, 情形 qíngxing (state). ②条件 tiáojiàn (stipulation). ③健康情形 jiànkāng qíngxing (health). ④身分地位 shēnfen dìwèi (position in society).

condolence n. 慰问 wèiwèn, 吊唁 diàoyàn.

condom n. 避孕套 bìyùntào / 保险套 bǎoxiǎntào.

condone v. 宽恕 kuānshù, 饶恕 ráoshù.

conduct n. ①行为 xíngwéi, 品

C

行 pǐnxíng / pínxìng (behavior).
②处理 chǔlǐ, 经营 jīngyíng
(management). — v. ①引导
yǐndǎo, 指引 zhǐyǐn (lead).
②指挥 zhǐhuī (be in charge of).

conductor n. ①车掌
chēzhǎng, 售票员
shòupiàoyuán (bus or tram).
②指挥 zhǐhuī (orchestra).
③导体 dǎotǐ (electricity).

cone n. ①圆锥形 yuánzhuīxíng
(shape). ②球果 qiúguǒ (tree).

confection n. 糖果 tángguǒ,
蜜饯 mìjiàn.

confederacy n. 联盟
liánméng, 邦联 bānglián
(alliance).

confederate adj. 同盟的
tóngméng de, 联盟的
liánméng de. — n. ①同盟
tóngméng, 联盟 liánméng
(ally). ②同谋 tóngmóu, 共犯
gòngfàn (accomplice).

confer v. ①赐予 cìyǔ / sìyǔ,
授予 shòuyǔ (give). ②商量
shāngliang (consult).

conference n. 会谈 huìtán,
会议 huìyì.

confess v. ①承认 chéngrèn,
供认 gòngrèn / gōngrèn
(admit). ②忏悔 chànhuǐ
(tell one's sins).

confession n. ①供认 gòngrèn
/ gōngrèn (admission), 承认
chéngrèn (acknowledgment).
②忏悔 chànhuǐ (repentance).

confetti n. 五彩碎纸 wǔcǎi
suìzhǐ.

confidant n. 密友 mìyǒu, 知
己 zhījǐ.

confide v. 倾诉 qīngsù (tell).

confidence n. ①信赖 xìnlài
(trust). ②自信 zìxìn (assurance).

confident adj. 自信的 zìxìn

de, 肯定的 kěndìng de.

confidential adj. 机密的 jīmì
de (secret).

confine v. ①监禁 jiānjìn (cage).
②限制 xiànzhì (restrict).

confines n. 疆界 jiāngjiè.

confirm v. ①证实 zhèngshí
(give proof of). ②确认 quèrèn
(verify).

confiscate v. 没收 mòshōu,
充公 chōnggōng.

conflict n. & v. ①争斗
zhēngdòu (fight). ②冲突
chōngtú / chòngtú
(disagreement).

conform v. 顺应 shùnyìng.

confound v. ①使困惑 shǐ
kùnhuò, 使迷惑 shǐ míhuò
(confuse and amaze). ②混淆
hùnxiáo / hùnyáo (mix up).

confront v. 面对 miànduì, 面
临 miànlín.

Confucius n. 孔子 Kǒngzǐ.

confuse v. ①使困惑 shǐ
kùnhuò (baffle). ②使混乱 shǐ
hùnluàn (cause disorder).
③混淆 hùnxiáo / hùnyáo (fail
to distinguish).

confusion n. ①困惑 kùnhuò
(perplexity). ②混乱 hùnluàn
(disorder).

congeal v. 冻结 dòngjié, 凝结
níngjié.

congenial adj. 意气相投的
yìqì-xiāngtóu de.

congenital adj. 天生的
tiānshēng de, 先天的 xiāntiān
de.

conglomerate v. 使成团形
shǐ chéng tuánxíng. — adj. 集
聚的 jùjù de. — n. ①集成物
jíchéngwù (material). ②企业集
团 qǐyè jítuán / qìyè jítuán
(large business firm).

congratulate v. 庆贺 qìnghè, 祝贺 zhùhè.

congratulation n. ①贺词 hècí 〈words〉. ②祝贺 zhùhè 〈expression of joy〉.

congregate v. 集合 jíhé, 聚集 jùjí.

congress n. ①会议 huìyì 〈meeting〉. ②国会 guóhuì, 议会 yìhuì 〈law-making body〉.

Congress n. 美国国会 Měiguó guóhuì.

congruent adj. ①一致的 yízhì de 〈agreeable〉. ②全等的 quánděng de 〈equal size and shape〉.

congruous adj. 适合的 shìhé de, 调合的 tiáohé de.

conifer n. 针叶树 zhēnyèshù.

conjecture n. & v. 推测 tuīcè, 猜想 cāixiǎng.

conjugal adj. 婚姻的 hūnyīn de, 夫妻的 fūqī de.

conjugate v. 列出（动词）变化 lièchū (dòngcí) biànhuà 〈grammar〉.

conjunction n. ①连接词 liánjiēcí 〈grammar〉. ②连结 liánjié 〈connection〉.

conjunctivitis n. 结膜炎 jiémóyán.

conjure v. ①变魔术 biàn móshù 〈do magic〉. ②施魔法 shī mófǎ 〈bewitch〉.

connect v. ①连接 liánjiē 〈join〉. ②联想 liánxiǎng 〈associate〉.

connection n. ①连接 liánjiē 〈contact〉. ②关系 guānxi 〈relation〉.

connive v. 纵容 zòngróng, 默许 mòxǔ.

connoisseur n. 鉴赏家 jiànshǎngjiā.

connotation n. 暗示 ànshì,

意味 yìwèi.

conquer v. 击败 jībài / jíbài, 征服 zhēngfú.

conquest n. ①征服 zhēngfú 〈conquering〉. ②战利品 zhànlìpǐn 〈booty〉. ③占领地 zhànlǐngdì 〈conquered territory〉.

conscience n. 良心 liángxīn.

conscientious adj. 有良心的 yǒu liángxīn de, 认真的 rènzhēn de, 尽责的 jìnzé de.

conscious adj. 察觉的 chájué de, 有意识的 yǒu yìshí de / yǒu yìshì de.

conscript adj. 征召入伍的 zhēngzhào rùwǔ de. — n. 征兵 zhēngbīng, 征召 zhēngzhào.

consecrate v. 奉为神圣 fèngwéi shénshèng, 奉献 fèngxiàn.

consecutive adj. 连续的 liánxù de.

consensus n. 共识 gòngshí / gòngshì.

consent n. & v. 同意 tóngyì, 答应 dāyìng.

consequence n. ①结果 jiéguǒ 〈result〉, 后果 hòuguǒ 〈aftermath〉. ②影响 yǐngxiǎng 〈effect〉.

consequent adj. 因而发生的 yīn'ér fāshēng de 〈resulting〉.

consequential adj. 因而发生的 yīn'ér fāshēng de 〈resulting〉.

consequently adv. 因此 yīncǐ, 所以 suǒyǐ.

conservation n. 保护 bǎohù, 保存 bǎocún.

conservative adj. 保守的 bǎoshǒu de. — n. 保守者 bǎoshǒuzhě, 保守派 bǎoshǒupài.

conservatory n. 温室 wēnshì 〈greenhouse〉.

C

conserve v. ①保存 bǎocún (preserve). ②节约 jiéyuē (save). — n. 蜜饯 mìjiàn.

consider v. ①考虑 kǎolǜ, 思考 sīkǎo (think about). ②顾虑 gùlǜ, 顾及 gùjí (take into account). ③认为 rènwéi, 视为 shìwéi (regard as).

considerable adj. ①可观的 kěguān de (worthy of note). ②相当大的 xiāngdāng dà de (large). ③相当多的 xiāngdāng duō de (many).

considerate adj. 体谅的 tǐliàng de, 体贴的 tǐtiē de.

consideration n. ①考虑 kǎolǜ, 思考 sīkǎo (deliberation). ②体谅 tǐliàng, 顾虑 gùlǜ (being considerate).

considering prep. 就……而论 jiù……ér lùn.

consign v. ①移交 yíjiāo (hand over). ②委托 wěituō (commit). ③寄运 jìyùn (send).

consist v. ~ of 由……组成 yóu...zǔchéng, 包括 bāokuò / bāoguā.

consistency n. ①一致 yízhì, 一贯 yíguàn (coherence). ②浓度 nóngdù (degree of firmness).

consistent adj. 前后一贯的 qiánhòu yíguàn de (invariable), 一致的 yízhì de (compatible).

consolation n. ①安慰 ānwèi (comfort). ②安慰物 ānwèiwù (something which consoles).

console v. 安慰 ānwèi.

consolidate v. ①巩固 gǒnggù, 强化 qiánghuà (strengthen). ②合并 hébìng (combine).

consonant n. 子音 zǐyīn. — adj. 和谐的 héxié de, 协调的 xiétiáo de.

consort n. 配偶 pèiǒu.

conspicuous adj. ①显著的 xiǎnzhù de, 明显的 míngxiǎn de (obvious). ②引起注目的 yǐnqǐ zhùmù de (inciting attention).

conspiracy n. 阴谋 yīnmóu.

conspire v. 共谋 gòngmóu, 阴谋 yīnmóu (plan secretly to do wrong).

constable n. 警察 jǐngchá.

constant adj. ①不断的 búduàn de (continuous). ②不变的 búbiàn de, 永恒的 yǒnghéng de (eternal).

constellation n. 星座 xīngzuò.

consternation n. 惊愕 jīng'è, 惊惶失措 jīnghuáng-shīcuò.

constipation n. 便秘 biànmì.

constituency n. 选民 xuǎnmín.

constituent adj. 组成的 zǔchéng de, 构成的 gòuchéng de (component). — n. ①成分 chéngfèn, 要素 yàosù (ingredient). ②选民 xuǎnmín (voter).

constitute v. ①构成 gòuchéng, 组成 zǔchéng (compose). ②设立 shèlì, 成立 chénglì (establish).

constitution n. ①宪法 xiànfǎ 〈law〉. ②体格 tǐgé (health). ③构成 gòuchéng, 组织 zǔzhī (structure).

constitutional adj. 宪法的 xiànfǎ de.

constrain v. ①强制 qiángzhì / qiǎngzhì, 强迫 qiǎngpò (force). ②束缚 shùfù / shùfú, 抑制 yìzhì (restrain).

constrict v. 压缩 yāsuō, 收缩 shōusuō.

construct *v.* 构造 gòuzào, 建造 jiànzào.

construction *n.* ①建造 jiànzào, 构造 gòuzào (act of constructing). ②建筑物 jiànzhùwù / jiànzhúwù (building). ~ **site** 工地 gōngdì.

consul *n.* 领事 lǐngshì.

consult *v.* ①请教 qǐngjiào, 咨询 zīxún (ask for information or advice). ②查阅 cháyuè (look up). ③商量 shāngliang (discuss).

consultant *n.* 顾问 gùwèn.

consultation *n.* ①请教 qǐngjiào, 咨询 zīxún (asking for advice). ②商议 shāngyì (discussion).

consume *v.* ①消耗 xiāohào (use up). ②吃光 chīguāng (devour). ③烧毁 shāohuǐ (destroy by fire).

consumer *n.* 消费者 xiāofèizhě.

consummate *v.* 完成 wánchéng. — *adj.* 完全的 wánquán de.

consumption *n.* ①消耗 xiāohào (using up). ②消耗量 xiāohàoliàng (amount consumed).

contact *n.* ①联系 liánxì, 联络 liánluò (being in touch). ②联络人 liánluòrén (person to get in touch with). ~**s** 关系 guānxi (connections). *come in ~ with* 接触 jiēchù. ~ **lenses** 隐形眼镜 yǐnxíng yǎnjìng. — *v.* 跟……联络 gēn...liánluò.

contagion *n.* 接触传染 jiēchù chuánrǎn.

contain *v.* ①包含 bāohán, 容纳 róngnà (hold). ②控制 kòngzhì, 抑制 yìzhì (control).

contaminate *v.* 沾污 zhānwū (pollute), 弄脏 nòngzāng (make dirty).

contemplate *v.* ①注视 zhùshì (gaze). ②沉思 chénsī, 默想 mòxiǎng (consider). ③预期 yùqí / yùqì, 打算 dǎsuàn (intend).

contemporary *n. & adj.* 同时代 tóng shídài.

contempt *n.* 轻视 qīngshì, 轻蔑 qīngmiè.

contend *v.* 争斗 zhēngdòu, 竞争 jìngzhēng.

content *v.* 使满足 shǐ mǎnzú. — *adj.* 满足的 mǎnzú de. — *n.* 内容 nèiróng (what's inside).

contention *n.* ①争论 zhēnglùn (argument). ②主张 zhǔzhāng, 论点 lùndiǎn (view).

contentment *n.* 满足 mǎnzú.

contest *n.* 竞争 jìngzhēng, 比赛 bǐsài (competition). — *v.* 争论 zhēnglùn (argue).

context *n.* 上下文 shàngxiàwén.

continent *n.* 大陆 dàlù (mainland), 洲 zhōu (land).

continental *adj.* 大陆的 dàlù de.

contingent *n.* 分遣队 fēnqiǎnduì (group). — *adj.* 视情况而定的 shì qíngkuàng ér dìng de (depending on).

continual *adj.* 连续的 liánxù de, 不断的 búduàn de.

continue *v.* ①继续 jìxù (go on). ②持续 chíxù (remain). ③再继续 zài jìxù, 恢复 huīfù (restart).

continuous *adj.* 不断的 búduàn de (uninterrupted), 连续的 liánxù de (connected).

contort *v.* 扭歪 niǔwāi (twist),

C

歪曲 wāiqū (bend).

contour *n.* 轮廓 lúnkuò (shape), 外形 wàixíng (outline).

contraband *n.* 违禁品 wéijìnpǐn (goods).

contract *v.* ①收缩 shōusuō, 缩小 suōxiǎo (condense). ②订约 dìngyuē (sign an agreement). ③感染 gǎnrǎn (become infected by). — *n.* 合同 hétong, 契约 qìyuē (agreement).

contradict *v.* ①反驳 fǎnbó (speak against). ②抵触 dǐchù (be contrary to).

contradiction *n.* 矛盾 máodùn.

contralto *n.* 女低音 nǚdīyīn.

contraption *n.* 新奇玩意 xīnqí wányì.

contrary *adj.* ①相反的 xiāngfǎn de (contradictory). ②逆向的 nìxiàng de (adverse). ③倔强的 juéjiàng de, 刚愎的 gāngbì de (stubborn).

contrast *n.* ①对比 duìbǐ, 对照 duìzhào (comparison). ②差别 chābié (difference). — *v.* ①对比 duìbǐ, 对照 duìzhào (compare). ②分别 fēnbié (differentiate).

contribute *v.* ①捐助 juānzhù (donate). ②促成 cùchéng, 有助于 yǒu zhù yú (assist). ③提供 tígōng (provide).

contribution *n.* ①捐助 juānzhù, 贡献 gòngxiàn (donation). ②捐助物 juānzhùwù (donated goods).

contrive *v.* ①发明 fāmíng, 设计 shèjì (invent). ②设法 shèfǎ, 图谋 túmóu (plan).

control *n.* ①控制 kòngzhì, 操纵 cāozòng (rule). ②抑制 yìzhì, 克制 kèzhì (restrain).

③管理 guǎnlǐ, 支配 zhīpèi (administer). ④核对 héduì (check).

controversy *n.* 争论 zhēnglùn.

convalesce *v.* 病后康复 bìng hòu kāngfù.

convene *v.* 集会 jíhuì, 召集 zhàojí.

convenience *n.* ①方便 fāngbiàn, 便利 biànlì (being convenient). ②便利的事物 biànlì de shìwù (amenity).

convenient *adj.* 方便的 fāngbiàn de, 便利的 biànlì de.

convent *n.* 修道院 xiūdàoyuàn.

convention *n.* ①集会 jíhuì, 会议 huìyì (assembly). ②条约 tiáoyuē, 协定 xiédìng (agreement). ③惯例 guànlì, 习俗 xísú (custom).

conventional *adj.* 传统的 chuántǒng de, 惯例的 guànlì de (customary).

converge *v.* 集中于一点 jízhōng yú yì diǎn, 汇合 huìhé (meet at a point).

conversation *n.* 会话 huìhuà.

converse *v.* 谈话 tánhuà (talk). — *adj.* 倒转的 dàozhuǎn de, 相反的 xiāngfǎn de (opposite).

conversion *n.* ①变换 biànhuàn (change). ②信仰改变 xìnyǎng gǎibiàn, 皈依 guīyī (change of beliefs).

convert *v.* ①转变 zhuǎnbiàn, 变换 biànhuàn (change). ②改变信仰 gǎibiàn xìnyǎng, 皈依 guīyī (change beliefs).

convex *adj.* 凸状的 tūzhuàng de / tūzhuàng de.

convey *v.* ①运送 yùnsòng, 运输 yùnshū (carry). ②传达

chuándá (communicate).

convict v. 宣判有罪 xuānpàn yǒuzuì. — n. 罪犯 zuìfàn.

conviction n. ①坚信 jiānxìn (assurance). ②信念 xìnniàn (belief). ③定罪 dìngzuì (act of convicting).

convince v. 说服 shuōfú / shuìfú, 使信服 shǐ xìnfú.

convocation n. 召集 zhàojí, 集会 jíhuì.

convoy v. 护送 hùsòng, 护卫 hùwèi. — n. ①护送 hùsòng 〈act〉. ②护送队 hùsòngduì 〈group〉.

convulse v. ①剧烈震动 jùliè zhèndòng 〈shake〉. ②痉挛 jìngluán 〈illness〉.

coo n. 咕咕声 gūgūshēng.

cook n. 厨师 chúshī. — v. 烹调 pēngtiáo, 煮 zhǔ.

cookie n. 饼干 bǐnggān.

cooking n. 烹调 pēngtiáo.

cool adj. ①凉的 liáng de (moderately cold). ②冷静的 lěngjìng de (calm). ③冷淡的 lěngdàn de (aloof). ④酷 kù (trendy). — v. 使变凉 shǐ biàn liáng (make cool). ~ down 使冷静 shǐ lěngjìng, 使平静 shǐ píngjìng (calm).

coop n. 鸡舍 jīshè, 鸡笼 jīlóng. coop up 关入笼内 guānrù lóng nèi.

co-op n. 合作社 hézuòshè.

cooperate v. 合作 hézuò.

cooperation n. 合作 hézuò.

cooperative adj. 合作的 hézuò de. — n. 合作社 hézuòshè.

coordinate adj. 同等的 tóngděng de (equal), 对等的 duìděng de 〈grammar〉. — n. ①同等的人或物 tóngděng de

rén huò wù 〈people or things〉. ②座标 zuòbiāo 〈map〉. — v. ①调和 tiáohé, 协调 xiétiáo (go together). ②安排 ānpái (arrange).

cop n. 警察 jǐngchá 〈officer〉.

cope v. 对付 duìfu, 应付 yìngfù. ~ with 应付 yìngfù, 处理 chǔlǐ.

copious adj. 丰富的 fēngfù de.

copper n. ①铜 tóng 〈metal〉. ②铜币 tóngbì 〈coin〉.

copse n. 矮树丛 ǎishùcóng.

copy n. ①复本 fùběn, 复制品 fùzhìpǐn (duplicate). ②一册 yí cè, 一本 yì běn (volume). — v. ①抄写 chāoxiě (make a copy of). ②模仿 mófǎng (imitate).

copyright n. 版权 bǎnquán, 著作权 zhùzuòquán.

coral n. ①珊瑚 shānhú 〈object〉. ②珊瑚色 shānhúsè 〈color〉. — adj. 珊瑚制的 shānhú zhì de. ~ reef 珊瑚礁 shānhújiāo.

cord n. ①细绳 xìshéng 〈string〉. ②小电线 xiǎo diànxiàn 〈cable〉. ③腱 jiàn, 索状组织 suǒzhuàng zǔzhī 〈body part〉.

cordial n. 甘露酒 gānlùjiǔ. — adj. 客气的 kèqi de (polite), 热心的 rèxīn de (enthusiastic).

cordon n. 警戒线 jǐngjièxiàn, 哨兵线 shàobīngxiàn 〈military〉.

corduroy n. 灯心绒 dēngxīnróng.

core n. ①果核 guǒhé 〈fruit〉. ②核心 héxīn (center).

cork n. ①软木 ruǎnmù 〈wood〉. ②软木塞 ruǎnmùsāi (plug).

corn n. ①玉米 yùmǐ (maize). ②鸡眼 jīyǎn 〈skin problem〉. ~ chip 玉米片 yùmǐpiàn.

C

C

cornea n. 眼角膜 yǎnjiǎomó.

corner n. ①角 jiǎo (angle). ②角落 jiǎoluò (nook). ③转角处 zhuǎnjiǎochù (turn).

cornet n. 短号 duǎnhào.

coronary adj. 冠状的 guānzhuàng de. — n. 心脏病发作 xīnzàngbìng fāzuò (heart attack).

coronation n. 加冕礼 jiāmiǎnlǐ.

coroner n. 法医 fǎyī, 验尸官 yànshīguān.

coronet n. 冠冕 guānmiǎn (crown).

corporal adj. 肉体的 ròutǐ de. — n. 下士 xiàshì.

corporate adj. ①法人的 fǎrén de, 社团的 shètuán de (business). ②团体的 tuántǐ de, 共有的 gòngyǒu de (collective).

corporation n. ①法人 fǎrén, 法人团体 fǎrén tuántǐ (organization). ②市政当局 shìzhèng dāngjú (local government). ③股份有限公司 gǔfèn yǒuxiàn gōngsī (company).

corps n. ①部队 bùduì (army). ②军团 jūntuán (divisions of military force).

corpse n. 尸体 shītǐ.

corpuscle n. 血球 xuèqiú / xiěqiú.

correct adj. ①对的 duì de (right), 正确的 zhèngquè de (accurate). ②适当的 shìdàng de (appropriate).

correction n. 改正 gǎizhèng, 修正 xiūzhèng.

correlate v. 相关连 xiāngguānlián.

correspond v. ①与……一致 yǔ...yízhì (harmonize). ②通信

tōngxìn (exchange letters). ③相似 xiāngsì, 相当 xiāngdāng (be similar).

correspondence n. ①通信 tōngxìn (letter-writing). ②符合 fúhé, 一致 yízhì (agreement).

correspondent n. ①通信者 tōngxìnzhě (one who exchanges letters). ②通讯员 tōngxùnyuán, 记者 jìzhě (reporter).

corridor n. 走廊 zǒuláng, 回廊 huíláng.

corroborate v. 证实 zhèngshí.

corrode v. 腐蚀 fǔshí, 侵蚀 qīnshí.

corrugate v. 起皱纹 qǐ zhòuwén.

corrupt adj. ①贪污的 tānwū de (bribable). ②腐败的 fǔbài de (rotten). ③不洁的 bùjié de (impure). — v. ①贿赂 huìlù (bribe). ②腐化 fǔhuà (make corrupt).

corset n. 束腹 shùfù.

cosmetic n. 化妆品 huàzhuāngpǐn. — adj. 化妆用的 huàzhuāng yòng de.

cosmic adj. 宇宙的 yǔzhòu de.

cosmonaut n. 宇航员 yǔhángyuán / 太空人 tàikōngrén.

cosmopolitan adj. 世界性的 shìjièxìng de (from all over the world), 世界主义的 shìjiè zhǔyì de (doctrine).

cosmos n. 宇宙 yǔzhòu.

cost n. ①费用 fèiyòng (expenditure). ②价格 jiàgé (price). — v. ①价值 jiàzhí (be valued at). ②花费 huāfèi (expend).

costume n. ①服装 fúzhuāng

(clothes). ②舞台装 wǔtáizhuāng ⟨actor⟩.

cosy *adj.* 温暖舒适的 wēnnuǎn shūshì de.

cot *n.* 婴儿床 yīng'érchuáng.

cottage *n.* 小屋 xiǎowū, 村舍 cūnshè.

cotton *n.* 棉 mián, 棉花 miánhuā.

couch *n.* ①长沙发 chángshāfā (sofa). ②卧椅 wòyǐ (a bed-like seat). — *v.* 表达 biǎodá (express).

cougar *n.* 美洲狮 měizhōushī.

cough *v.* 咳嗽 késou.

council *n.* ①会议 huìyì (assembly). ②委员会 wěiyuánhuì (committee). *city ~* 市议会 shìyìhuì.

counsel *n.* ①建议 jiànyì, 劝告 quàngào (advice). ②商量 shāngliang, 商议 shāngyì (consultation). ③律师 lǜshī, 法律顾问 fǎlǜ gùwèn (lawyer). — *v.* 建议 jiànyì, 劝告 quàngào.

counselor *n.* 顾问 gùwèn (consultant).

count *v.* ①数 shǔ (name the numbers). ②算 suàn (add up). ③考虑在内 kǎolǜ zàinèi, 包括 bāokuò / bāoguā (include). ④有价值 yǒu jiàzhí, 有意义 yǒu yìyì (be important). *~ down* 倒读秒 dàodúmiǎo, 倒数计秒 dàoshǔ-jìmiǎo / 倒数计时 dàoshǔ-jìshí.

countable *adj.* 可数的 kěshǔ de.

countenance *n.* 面容 miànróng (appearance), 表情 biǎoqíng (expression).

counter *n.* ①柜台 guìtái (desk). ②筹码 chóumǎ (chip).

— *adj. & adv.* 相反的 xiāngfǎn de.

counteract *v.* 抵消 díxiāo.

counterbalance *n.* ①平衡锤 pínghéngchuí ⟨weight⟩. ②平衡力 pínghénglì ⟨force⟩. — *v.* 使平衡 shǐ pínghéng.

counterfeit *adj.* 赝造的 yànzào de, 假冒的 jiǎmào de. — *n.* 赝品 yànpǐn, 伪造品 wěizàopǐn / wěizàopǐn.

counterfoil *n.* 存根 cúngēn, 存据 cúnjù.

countermand *v.* 撤回 chèhuí, 取消 qǔxiāo.

counterpart *n.* 相对的人 xiāngduì de rén ⟨person⟩, 相对的物 xiāngduì de wù ⟨thing⟩.

countersign *v.* 连署 liánshǔ / liánshù, 副署 fùshǔ / fùshù.

countless *adj.* 无数的 wúshù de.

country *n.* ①国家 guójiā (nation). ②乡村 xiāngcūn (countryside).

countryman *n.* ①同胞 tóngbāo (compatriot). ②乡下人 xiāngxiàrén ⟨countryside⟩.

countryside *n.* 乡间 xiāngjiān, 乡下 xiāngxia.

county *n.* 郡 jùn, 县 xiàn.

coup *n.* ①政变 zhèngbiàn ⟨political takeover⟩. ②奏效的策略 zòuxiào de cèlüè (achievement).

couple *n.* ①一对 yí duì (a pair). ②夫妇 fūfù (husband and wife). ③情侣 qínglǚ (lovers). — *v.* 连接 liánjiē (join).

couplet *n.* 对句 duìjù, 对联 duìlián.

coupon *n.* 优待券 yōudàiquàn.

courage *n.* 勇气 yǒngqì, 胆量 dǎnliàng.

courier *n.* 信差 xìnchāi, 快递员 kuàidìyuán (messenger).

course *n.* ①过程 guòchéng, 进程 jìnchéng (process). ②路线 lùxiàn (path). ③课程 kèchéng (curriculum). ④高尔夫球场 gāo'ěrfū qiúchǎng 〈golf〉. ⑤一道菜 yí dào cài (meal). — *v.* 运行 yùnxíng, 流动 liúdòng (flow).

court *n.* ①法院 fǎyuàn, 法庭 fǎtíng 〈law〉. ②宫廷 gōngtíng, 朝廷 cháotíng (palace). ③庭院 tíngyuàn (courtyard). ④球场 qiúchǎng 〈ball games〉. — *v.* ①讨好 tǎohǎo, 奉承 fèngchéng (ingratiate). ②求爱 qiú'ài, 追求 zhuīqiú (try to win someone's affections).

courteous *adj.* 有礼貌的 yǒu lǐmào de, 谦恭的 qiāngōng de.

courtesy *n.* 礼貌 lǐmào, 谦恭 qiāngōng (good manners).

courtier *n.* 朝臣 cháochén.

court-martial *n.* 军事法庭 jūnshì fǎtíng. — *v.* 以军法审判 yǐ jūnfǎ shěnpàn.

courtship *n.* 求爱 qiú'ài, 求爱时期 qiú'ài shíqī / qiú'ài shíqí.

courtyard *n.* 庭院 tíngyuàn.

cousin *n.* ①堂哥 tánggē (father's brother's son, elder), 堂弟 tángdì (father's brother's son, younger). ②堂姐 tángjiě (father's brother's daughter, elder), 堂妹 tángmèi (father's brother's daughter, younger). ③表哥 biǎogē (father's sister's son; mother's brother's or sister's son, elder), 表弟 biǎodì (father's sister's son, younger; mother's brother's or sister's son, younger). ④表姐 biǎojiě (father's sister's daughter, elder;

mother's brother's or sister's daughter, elder), 表妹 biǎomèi (father's sister's daughter, younger; mother's brother's or sister's daughter, younger).

cove *n.* 小海湾 xiǎo hǎiwān.

cover *v.* ①盖 gài, 覆盖 fùgài (overlay). ②足够涵盖 zúgòu hángài (be enough for). ③包括 bāokuò / bāoguā (contain). ④掩护 yǎnhù (protect). — *n.* ①遮盖物 zhēgàiwù (covering). ②封面 fēngmiàn 〈for papers or a book〉. ③盖子 gàizi (cap).

cover story *n.* 封面故事 fēngmiàn gùshì.

covert *adj.* 暗地的 àndì de.

cow *n.* 牛 niú, 母牛 mǔniú.

coward *n.* 懦夫 nuòfū. — *adj.* 胆怯的 dǎnqiè de / dǎnquè de.

cower *v.* 畏缩 wèisuō.

coy *adj.* 腼腆的 miǎntiǎn de, 忸怩的 niǔní de.

CPR 心肺复苏术 Xīnfèi Fùsūshù (cardiopulmonary resuscitation).

crab *n.* 蟹 xiè, 蟹肉 xièròu.

crack *n.* ①裂缝 lièfèng (split). ②劈啪声 pīpāshēng 〈sound〉. — *v.* ①发爆裂声 fā bàolièshēng (make sound). ②破裂 pòliè, 裂开 lièkai (break). ③解开 jiěkai, 解答 jiědá (solve).

cracker *n.* 薄脆饼干 báocuì bǐnggān / bócuì bǐnggān (biscuit). *fire ~* 鞭炮 biānpào.

crackle *v.* 发劈啪声 fā pīpāshēng. — *n.* 爆裂声 bàolièshēng.

crackpot *n.* 狂想者 kuángxiǎngzhě.

cradle *n.* ①摇篮 yáolán (small bed for a baby). ②发源地 fāyuándì (place of origin).

C

craft n. ①手艺 shǒuyì, 手工艺 shǒugōngyì (skilled work). ②技术 jìshù, 技巧 jìqiǎo (skill). ③船 chuán (boat), 飞机 fēijī (airplane), 太空船 tàikōngchuán (spaceship).

craftsman n. 工匠 gōngjiàng.

crag n. 峭壁 qiàobì, 危岩 wēiyán / wéiyán.

cram v. 填塞 tiánsè, 塞满 sāimǎn (fill). ②强记应考 qiǎngjì yìngkǎo 〈study〉. ~ **school** 补习班 bǔxíbān.

cramp n. 抽筋 chōujīn, 痉挛 jìngluán.

cranberry n. 小红莓 xiǎohóngméi, 蔓越莓 mànyuèméi.

crane n. ①鹤 hè 〈bird〉. ②起重机 qǐzhòngjī 〈machine〉.

cranium n. 头盖骨 tóugàigǔ.

crank n. ①曲柄 qūbǐng 〈apparatus〉. ②易怒者 yìnùzhě 〈bad-tempered〉, 古怪者 gǔguàizhě (nut).

crash n. ①坠毁 zhuìhuǐ, 猛撞 měngzhuàng (collision). ②崩溃 bēngkuì, 垮台 kuǎtái (collapse). ③猛然轰声 měngrán hōng shēng 〈sound〉. — v. ①撞毁 zhuànghuǐ, 坠毁 zhuìhuǐ (collide). ②猛撞 měngzhuàng, 碰撞 pèngzhuàng (strike). ③破产 pòchǎn, 崩溃 bēngkuì (come to ruin).

crass adj. ①粗俗的 cūsú de, 粗鲁的 cūlǔ de (coarse). ②愚蠢的 yúchǔn de (stupid).

crate n. 板条箱 bǎntiáoxiāng.

crater n. ①火山口 huǒshānkǒu (mouth of a volcano). ②弹坑 dànkēng (hole made by a bomb).

cravat n. 领结 lǐngjié.

crave v. 渴望 kěwàng (desire),

恳求 kěnqiú (beg for).

crawl n. & v. ①爬行 páxíng, 爬爬 pá pá (creep). ②徐行 xúxíng (moving slowly).

crayfish n. 小龙虾 xiǎolóngxiā.

crayon n. 蜡笔 làbǐ.

craze n. 狂热 kuángrè.

crazy adj. ①疯狂的 fēngkuáng de (mad). ②狂热的 kuángrè de (excited).

creak v. 发喀吱声 fā kāzhīshēng. — n. 喀吱声 kāzhīshēng.

cream n. ①乳脂 rǔzhī 〈milk〉. ②乳霜 rǔshuāng (ointment). ③精华 jīnghuá (best part).

crease n. 摺痕 zhéhén, 皱摺 zhòuzhé. — v. 弄皱 nòngzhòu.

create v. 创造 chuàngzào, 创作 chuàngzuò (make), 制造 zhìzào (produce).

creation n. 创造 chuàngzào, 创作 chuàngzuò, 创造物 chuàngzàowù.

creative adj. 有创造力的 yǒu chuàngzàolì de.

creator n. ①创造者 chuàngzàozhě (maker). ②上帝 Shàngdì (God).

creature n. ①生物 shēngwù (living being). ②人 rén (person). ③动物 dòngwù (animal).

credentials n. ①资历 zīlì (professional background). ②证明书 zhèngmíngshū (documentation).

credible adj. 可信的 kěxìn de, 可靠的 kěkào de.

credit n. ①信用 xìnyòng 〈financial〉. ②学分 xuéfēn 〈school〉. ③相信 xiāngxìn, 信任 xìnrèn (trust). ④名誉 míngyù, 名望 míngwàng (reputation).

— v. ①相信 xiāngxìn, 信赖 xìnlài (trust). ②带来荣誉 dàilái róngyù (bring about honor). ③把……记入贷方 bǎ...jìrù dàifāng (monetary account). ~ card 信用卡 xìnyòngkǎ.

creditor n. 债权人 zhàiquánrén, 贷方 dàifāng.

creed n. 教条 jiàotiáo, 信条 xìntiáo.

creek n. 小溪 xiǎoxī.

creep n. & v. 爬行 páxíng (crawl), 缓慢移动 huǎnmàn yídòng (moving slowly).

creeper n. 爬虫 páchóng, 爬行动物 páxíng dòngwù.

creepy adj. 毛骨悚然的 máogǔ-sǒngrán de.

cremate v. 火葬 huǒzàng.

crepe n. ①绉纱 zhòushā (fabric with a wrinkled surface). ②可丽饼 kělìbǐng. ~ paper 绉纹纸 zhòuwénzhǐ.

crescendo adv. 渐强的 jiànqiáng de, 渐响的 jiànxiǎng de.

crescent n. 新月形 xīnyuèxíng. — adj. 新月形的 xīnyuèxíng de. ~ moon 新月 xīnyuè.

cress n. 水芹 shuǐqín.

crest n. ①鸟冠 niǎoguān (comb). ②山顶 shāndǐng (apex). ③饰章 shìzhāng (badge).

crevasse n. 裂缝 lièfèng.

crevice n. 裂缝 lièfèng, 罅隙 xiàxì.

crew n. ①工作人员 gōngzuò rényuán (workers). ②水手 shuǐshǒu ⟨ship⟩. ③机员 jīyuán ⟨airplane⟩.

crib n. 婴儿床 yīng'érchuáng (baby's bed). — v. 剽窃 piāoqiè / piàoqiè, 抄袭 chāoxí (copy).

cricket n. ①蟋蟀 xīshuài

⟨insect⟩. ②板球 bǎnqiú ⟨game⟩.

crime n. 罪 zuì, 罪行 zuìxíng / zuìxìng.

criminal n. 犯罪者 fànzuìzhě, 犯人 fànrén. — adj. 犯罪的 fànzuì de, 犯法的 fànfǎ de.

crimson n. & adj. 深红色 shēnhóngsè.

cringe v. ①畏缩 wèisuō (flinch). ②奉承 fèngchéng, 谄媚 chǎnmèi (toady).

crinkle v. 绉 zhòu (produce crinkles). — n. 绉纹 zhòuwén (wrinkle).

cripple n. 残障者 cánzhàngzhě. — v. 使残废 shǐ cánfèi.

crisis n. ①危机 wēijī / wéijī (time of great danger). ②转折点 zhuǎnzhédiǎn / 转捩点 zhuǎnlièdiǎn (turning-point).

crisp adj. ①脆的 cuì de (crunchy). ②干冷的 gānlěng de (cold and dry). ③清新的 qīngxīn de (fresh).

crisscross adj. 十字形的 shízìxíng de. — v. 成十字形 chéng shízìxíng.

criterion n. ①标准 biāozhǔn, 规范 guīfàn (standard). ②条件 tiáojiàn (condition).

critic n. 评论家 pínglùnjiā ⟨person⟩.

critical adj. ①批评的 pīpíng de (criticizing). ②吹毛求疵的 chuīmáo-qiúcī de (fault-finding). ③有判断力的 yǒu pànduànlì de (analytical). ④危急的 wēijí de / wéijí de (in crisis), 关键性的 guānjiànxìng de (at a turning point).

criticism n. 批评 pīpíng.

criticize v. 批评 pīpíng (find fault), 责难 zénàn (blame).

croak n. 嘶哑声 sīyǎshēng.
— v. 嘶哑 sīyǎ.

crock n. ①瓦罐 wǎguàn (pot).
②碎瓦片 suìwǎpiàn (broken
pieces). ③废话 fèihuà
(nonsense).

crockery n. 陶器 táoqì, 瓦器
wǎqì.

crocodile n. 鳄鱼 èyú.

crocus n. 番红花 fānhónghuā.

croissant n. 羊角面包
yángjiǎo miànbāo / 牛角面包
niújiǎo miànbāo.

crook n. ①恶棍 ègùn, 流氓
liúmáng (criminal). ②骗子
piànzi (cheat). ③弯柄手杖
wānbǐng shǒuzhàng (stick).

crooked adj. 弯曲的 wānqū
de (bent).

crop n. ①农作物 nóngzuòwù
(agricultural plants). ②收成
shōuchéng (harvest). — v. ①吃
草 chīcǎo, 啃啮 kěnniè (bite
off). ②剪短 jiǎnduǎn (cut).

croquet n. 槌球游戏 chuíqiú
yóuxì.

cross n. ①十字形 shízìxíng
〈shape〉. ②十字架 shízìjià (an
upright post). — v. 横越过
héngyuèguò, 穿过 chuānguò
(go across). — adj. ①横的
héng de, 横过的 héngguò de
(passing across). ②易怒的 yì
nù de, 坏脾气的 huài píqi de
(bad-tempered).

crossbow n. 石弓 shígōng.

crossbreed v. 杂交 zájiāo.
— n. 杂种 zázhǒng, 混种
hùnzhǒng.

cross-country adj. 越野的
yuèyě de.

cross-examine v. 盘问
pánwèn.

crossing n. ①平交道

píngjiāodào 〈railway〉. ②十字
路口 shízì lùkǒu (intersection).

cross-legged adj. & adv. 盘
着腿的 pánzhe tuǐ de, 翘着腿
的 qiáozhe tuǐ de.

crossroad n. 十字路口 shízìlùkǒu, 交叉路 jiāochālù.

crouch n. & v. 蹲伏 dūnfú.

crow v. ①鸡叫 jījiào 〈rooster〉.
②自鸣得意 zìmíng-déyì
(boast). — n. ①乌鸦 wūyā
〈bird〉. ②鸡叫 jījiào 〈cock〉.

crowbar n. 铁橇 tiěqiāo, 橇
棍 qiāogùn.

crowd n. 群众 qúnzhòng, 人
群 rénqún. — v. 挤满 jǐmǎn,
拥挤 yōngjǐ / yǒngjǐ.

crowded adj. 拥挤的 yōngjǐ
de / yǒngjǐ de.

crown n. ①王冠 wángguān,
皇冠 huángguān (headwear).
②顶部 dǐngbù (apex). — v.
①加冕 jiāmiǎn (enthrone).
②加荣誉于 jiā róngyù yú
(reward with).

crucial adj. 决定性的
juédìngxìng de, 极重要的 jí
zhòngyào de.

crucifix n. 耶稣受难像 Yēsū
shòunàn xiàng / Yésū
shòunàn xiàng.

crude adj. ①未提炼的 wèi
tíliàn de, 未加工的 wèi
jiāgōng de (natural state). ②粗
鲁的 cūlǔ de (rude). ③粗劣的
cūliè de (amateurish).

cruel adj. 残忍的 cánrěn de,
残酷的 cánkù de.

cruelty n. 残酷 cánkù.

cruise n. & v. 巡航 xúnháng.

crumb n. 面包屑 miànbāoxiè
〈bread〉.

crumble v. 弄碎 nòngsuì.

crumple v. 变皱 biànzhòu,

压皱 yāzhòu.

crunch v. 嘎扎地响 gāzhā de xiǎng.

crusade n. ① C~s 十字军 shízìjūn (the Crusade). ②改革运动 gǎigé yùndòng (reform movement).

crush v. 压碎 yāsuì, 压坏 yāhuài.

crust n. ①面包皮 miànbāopí ⟨bread⟩. ②地壳 dìqiào / dìké ⟨earth⟩.

crustacean n. 甲壳类动物 jiǎqiàolèi dòngwù / jiǎkélèi dòngwù.

crusty adj. ①有硬壳的 yǒu yìngké de (having a hard crust). ②粗暴的 cūbào de, 易怒的 yìnù de (grumpy).

crutch n. 拐杖 guǎizhàng.

crux n. 问题症结 wèntí zhēngjié.

cry v. ①喊叫 hǎnjiào (yell). ②哭泣 kūqì (weep). ③叫 jiào, 啼 tí ⟨animal⟩.

crypt n. 地下墓穴 dìxià mùxué / dìxià mùxué.

crystal n. 水晶 shuǐjīng.
— adj. 水晶制的 shuǐjīng zhì de.

cub n. ①幼兽 yòushòu (young animal). ②小伙子 xiǎohuǒzi, 年轻人 niánqīngrén (young man). ③生手 shēngshǒu, 学徒 xuétú (apprentice).

cube n. 立方体 lìfāngtǐ.

cubicle n. 小寝室 xiǎo qǐnshì.

cuckoo n. 布谷鸟 bùgǔniǎo.

cucumber n. 胡瓜 húguā, 黄瓜 huángguā.

cud n. 反刍的食物 fǎnchú de shíwù.

cuddle v. 爱抚 àifǔ, 抚抱 fǔbào.

cudgel n. 短棒 duǎnbàng.
— v. 以棍棒打 yǐ gùnbàng dǎ.

cue n. 提示 tíshì, 暗示 ànshì.

cuff n. 袖口 xiùkǒu.

cuisine n. 烹饪 pēngrèn (cooking).

culminate v. 达到顶点 dádào dǐngdiǎn.

culprit n. 犯人 fànrén, 罪人 zuìrén.

cult n. ①教派 jiàopài ⟨religious⟩. ②崇拜 chóngbài (worship).

cultivate v. ①耕种 gēngzhòng ⟨farm⟩. ②培养 péiyǎng (foster), 栽培 zāipéi, 养殖 yǎngzhí (grow).

cultural adj. 文化的 wénhuà de, 人文的 rénwén de.

culture n. ①文化 wénhuà (art). ②文明 wénmíng (civilization). ③教养 jiàoyǎng (education).

culvert n. 排水沟 páishuǐgōu, 下水道 xiàshuǐdào.

cunning adj. 狡猾的 jiǎohuá de.

cup n. ①杯 bēi, 杯子 bēizi ⟨container⟩. ②奖杯 jiǎngbēi ⟨prize⟩.

cupboard n. 碗橱 wǎnchú.

cur n. ①恶犬 èquǎn ⟨dog⟩. ②无赖 wúlài, 下流的人 xiàliú de rén ⟨man⟩.

curable adj. 可治疗的 kě zhìliáo de.

curative adj. 有疗效的 yǒu liáoxiào de.

curator n. 展览负责人 zhǎnlǎn fùzérén.

curb n. ①人行道 rénxíngdào (sidewalk). ②边栏 biānlán (edge). ③抑制 yìzhì (restrain).
— v. 抑制 yìzhì (restraint).

curd n. 凝乳 níngrǔ.

curdle v. ①凝结 níngjié (form curds). ②变质 biànzhì / biànzhí (spoil).

cure v. 医治 yīzhì, 治愈 zhìyù. — n. 治疗 zhìliáo 〈act〉, 疗法 liáofǎ 〈method〉.

cured adj. 痊愈的 quányù de.

curfew n. 宵禁 xiāojìn.

curiosity n. 好奇心 hàoqíxīn, 好奇 hàoqí.

curious adj. ①好奇的 hàoqí de (inquistive). ②奇怪的 qíguài de (strange).

curl v. 卷曲 juǎnqū. — n. ①卷曲 juǎnqū 〈shape〉. ②卷发 juǎnfà / juǎnfǎ 〈hair〉.

currant n. 小葡萄干 xiǎo pútáogān.

currency n. ①通货 tōnghuò, 货币 huòbì (money). ②流通 liútōng, 通用 tōngyòng (popular use).

current n. ①水流 shuǐliú 〈water〉. ②气流 qìliú 〈air〉. ③电流 diànliú 〈electricity〉. — adj. ①流通的 liútōng de, 通行的 tōngxíng de (widespread). ②现行的 xiànxíng de (in effect). ③流行的 liúxíng de (fashionable).

curriculum n. 课程 kèchéng.

curry n. 咖喱 gālí / kālí, 咖喱食品 gālí shípǐn / kālí shípǐn. ~ **favor** 拍马屁 pāimǎpì, 谄媚 chǎnmèi.

curse v. 诅咒 zǔzhòu, 咒骂 zhòumà. — n. ①诅咒 zǔzhòu, 咒骂 zhòumà 〈words〉. ②祸源 huòyuán, 祸根 huògēn (cause of misfortune).

cursor n. 光标 guāngbiāo / 游标 yóubiāo 〈computer〉.

curt adj. 草率无礼的 cǎoshuài wúlí de.

curtail v. 缩短 suōduǎn (shorten).

curtain n. ①窗帘 chuānglián 〈window〉. ②帐幕 zhàngmù, 帷幕 wéimù 〈stage〉.

curtsy n. 屈膝礼 qūxīlǐ.

curve n. 曲线 qūxiàn 〈line〉, 弯曲 wānqū (bend). — v. 弯曲 wānqū.

cushion n. 垫子 diànzi, 坐垫 zuòdiàn (pillow).

custard n. 牛奶蛋糕 niúnǎi dàngāo (cake), 布丁 bùdīng (pudding).

custody n. ①监护 jiānhù (guardianship). ②监禁 jiānjìn (captivity). ③保管 bǎoguǎn, 保护 bǎohù (care).

custom n. ①风俗 fēngsú, 习俗 xísú, 惯例 guànlì (convention). ②关税 guānshuì (import duties).

customary adj. 习惯的 xíguàn de (habitual), 习俗的 xísú de (traditional).

customer n. 顾客 gùkè.

customs n. ①海关 hǎiguān 〈government institution〉. ②关税 guānshuì 〈taxes〉.

cut v. ①割 gē (sever), 切 qiē (slice), 剪 jiǎn (clip). ②缩减 suōjiǎn (abbreviate). ~ **in** 中断 zhōngduàn. ~ **and paste** 剪贴 jiǎntiē.

cute adj. 可爱的 kě'ài de.

cutlet n. 薄肉片 báoròupiàn / bóròupiàn.

cutter n. ①切割器具 qiēgē qìjù 〈tool〉. ②小汽艇 xiǎo qìtǐng 〈vessel〉.

cutthroat n. 凶手 xiōngshǒu, 谋杀者 móushāzhě. — adj. 凶狠的 xiōnghěn de, 残暴的

C

cánbào de (ruthless).

cutting n. 剪报 jiǎnbào.
— adj. 尖刻的 jiānkè de, 锋利的 fēnglì de.

cuttlefish n. 乌贼 wūzéi, 墨鱼 mòyú.

cyberbank n. 网络银行 wǎngluò yínháng / 网络银行 wǎnglù yínháng.

cybercafé n. 网路咖啡店 wǎnglù kāfēidiàn, 网吧 wǎngbā / 网咖 wǎngkā.

cyberspace n. 网络世界 wǎngluò shìjiè / 网路世界 wǎnglù shìjiè.

cycle n. 周期 zhōuqī / zhōuqí, 循环 xúnhuán (series). — v. 骑

脚踏车 qí jiǎotàchē (ride a bicycle).

cyclone n. 旋风 xuànfēng, 飓风 jùfēng (hurricane).

cylinder n. ①圆筒 yuántǒng (a hollow tube). ②汽缸 qìgāng (piston).

cymbal n. 钹 bá.

cynic n. 愤世嫉俗者 fènshì-jísú zhě.

cynical adj. ①讥笑的 jīxiào de, 讽刺的 fěngcì de / fèngcì de (sarcastic). ②愤世嫉俗的 fènshì-jísú de (world-weary).

cypress n. 柏树 bǎishù / bóshù.

czar n. 沙皇 shāhuáng (tsar).

D

dab v. 涂敷 túfū. — n. ①轻拍 qīngpāi (pat). ②少量 shǎoliàng (small amount).

dabble v. 涉猎 shèliè (be involved in).

dad n. 爸爸 bàba.

daddy n. 爸爸 bàba.

daffodil n. 黄水仙 huángshuǐxiān.

dagger n. 短剑 duǎnjiàn, 匕首 bǐshǒu (knife).

daily adj. & adv. 每日的 měirì de, 日常的 rìcháng de. — n. 日报 rìbào.

dainty adj. ①高雅的 gāoyǎ de (delicate). ②讲究的 jiǎngjiu de (choosy).

dairy n. ①乳品厂 rǔpǐnchǎng 〈factory〉. ②酪农场

làonóngchǎng / luònóngchǎng 〈farm〉. ③乳品店 rǔpǐndiàn 〈store〉. — adj. 牛奶的 niúnǎi de.

dais n. 坛 tán, 高台 gāotái.

daisy n. 雏菊 chújú.

dale n. 山谷 shāngǔ.

dam n. 水坝 shuǐbà. — v. ①筑水坝 zhù shuǐbà / zhú shuǐbà (close off a river). ②阻止 zǔzhǐ (block).

damage n. & v. 损害 sǔnhài (injury), 损失 sǔnshī (loss).

dame n. 夫人 fūrén.

damn n. & v. 咒骂 zhòumà (curse). — interj. 该死! Gāisǐ!

damp adj. 潮湿的 cháoshī de. — n. 湿气 shīqì.

dampen v. ①使潮湿 shǐ cháoshī (make damp). ②使沮

丧 shǐ jǔsàng (make sad).

dance v. 跳舞 tiàowǔ. — n. 跳舞 tiàowǔ, 舞蹈 wǔdǎo / wǔdào. **~ hall** 舞厅 wǔtīng.

dancing n. 跳舞 tiàowǔ.

dandelion n. 蒲公英 púgōngyīng.

dandruff n. 头皮屑 tóupíxiè.

danger n. 危险 wēixiǎn / wéixiǎn.

dangerous adj. 危险的 wēixiǎn de / wéixiǎn de.

dangle v. 摇摆 yáobǎi, 摇晃 yáohuang (hang loosely).

dank adj. 阴湿的 yīnshī de.

dare v. ①敢 gǎn, 胆敢 dǎngǎn (be brave enough to). ②激 jī (challenge).

daring n. & adj. 勇敢 yǒnggǎn, 大胆 dàdǎn.

dark adj. 黑暗的 hēi'àn de (without light). **~ horse** 黑马 hēimǎ. — n. 黑暗 hēi'àn (darkness).

darken v. 使黑暗 shǐ hēi'àn.

darkroom n. 暗房 ànfáng.

darling n. 亲爱的人 qīn'ài de rén. — adj. 亲爱的 qīn'ài de (dearly loved).

dart n. 镖枪 biāoqiāng. — v. 急冲 jíchōng, 突进 tūjìn / tújìn (rush).

dash v. ①掷 zhì / zhí, 猛掷 měngzhì / měngzhí (throw violently). ②猛撞 měngzhuàng (rush into). ③使挫败 shǐ cuòbài (discourage). — n. ①突进 tūjìn / tújìn (sprint). ②少量 shǎoliàng (small amount). ③破折号 pòzhéhào (mark).

dashboard n. 仪表板 yíbiǎobǎn.

data n. 资料 zīliào. **~ base** 数据库 shùjùkù / 资料库 zīliàokù.

date n. ①日期 rìqī / rìqí (day). ②约会 yuēhuì (appointment). ③枣子 zǎozi (fruit). **out of ~** 过时的 guòshí de. — v. 记载日期 jìzǎi rìqī / jìzài rìqí.

daughter n. 女儿 nǚ'ér.

daughter-in-law n. 儿媳妇 érxífù.

daunt v. 使畏惧 shǐ wèijù, 使气馁 shǐ qìněi (dismay).

dawdle v. 浪费光阴 làngfèi guāngyīn, 闲荡 xiándàng.

dawn n. ①黎明 límíng (daybreak). ②开端 kāiduān (beginning). — v. 破晓 pòxiǎo.

day n. 白天 báitiān (daytime), 一天 yìtiān (one day).

daybreak n. 破晓 pòxiǎo, 黎明 límíng.

daydream n. 白日梦 báirìmèng, 幻想 huànxiǎng. — v. 作白日梦 zuò báirìmèng.

daylight n. ①日光 rìguāng (light of day). ②白昼 báizhòu (daytime).

daytime n. 白天 báitiān, 白昼 báizhòu.

daze v. 使晕眩 shǐ yùnxuàn / shǐ yūnxuàn, 使眩惑 shǐ xuànhuò.

dazzle v. 使目眩 shǐ mùxuàn, 使眩惑 shǐ xuànhuò. — n. 眩目强光 xuànmù qiángguāng.

dead adj. ①死的 sǐ de, 无生命的 wú shēngmìng de (not alive). ②麻木的 mámù de (numb). ③失灵的 shīlíng de, 无效的 wúxiào de (not working). ④无生气的 wú shēngqì de (boring). — n. 死人 sǐrén.

deaden v. 使减弱 shǐ jiǎnruò.

deadline n. 最后期限 zuìhòu qīxiàn / zuìhòu qíxiàn, 截止时间 jiézhǐ shíjiān, 截止日期

jiézhǐ rìqí / jiézhǐ rìqí.

deadlock n. 僵局 jiāngjú (standstill).

deadly adj. 致命的 zhìmìng de (fatal). — adv. 如死地 rú sǐ de (like death).

deaf adj. 聋的 lóng de.

deal v. ①分配 fēnpèi (give out). ②发牌 fāpái (allot cards). — n. ①交易 jiāoyì 〈business〉. ②量 liàng, 分量 fēnliàng (amount). ③发牌 fāpái 〈card〉.
a great ~ of 大量的 dàliàng de.

dealer n. ①商人 shāngrén (trader). ②发牌者 fāpáizhě (a person who deals cards).

dean n. ①院长 yuànzhǎng, 系主任 xìzhǔrèn 〈university〉. ②主持牧师 zhǔchí mùshī 〈clergy〉.

dear adj. ①亲爱的 qīn'ài de (much loved). ②昂贵的 ángguì de (expensive). — n. 亲爱的人 qīn'ài de rén.

dearth n. 缺乏 quēfá, 缺少 quēshǎo (scarcity).

death n. 死亡 sǐwáng.

debase v. 降低 jiàngdī (lower value), 贬低 biǎndī (degrade).

debate n. & v. 讨论 tǎolùn, 辩论 biànlùn (argue about).

debauch v. 使堕落 shǐ duòluò, 使放荡 shǐ fàngdàng (behave badly).

debauchery n. 放荡 fàngdàng.

debilitate v. 使衰弱 shǐ shuāiruò.

debit n. 借方 jièfāng. — v. 登入借方 dēngrù jièfāng.

debris n. ①瓦砾 wǎlì (remains). ②垃圾 lājī / lèsè (garbage).

debt n. ①债务 zhàiwù, 负债 fùzhài (money owed). ②恩情

ēnqíng (gratitude).

debut n. ①初进社交界 chū jìn shèjiāojiè 〈young person〉. ②初次登台 chūcì dēngtái 〈actor〉.

decade n. 十年 shí nián.

decadence n. 衰落 shuāiluò, 颓废 tuífèi.

decaf n. 不含咖啡因的咖啡 bù hán kāfēiyīn de kāfēi.

decant v. 慢慢倒出 mànman dàochū 〈pour〉.

decapitate v. 斩首 zhǎnshǒu, 砍头 kǎntóu.

decay n. & v. ①腐败 fǔbài, 腐烂 fǔlàn (rot). ②衰弱 shuāiruò, 衰落 shuāiluò (go bad).

decease n. 死亡 sǐwáng.

deceased n. 死者 sǐzhě.

deceit n. 欺骗 qīpiàn, 诈骗 zhàpiàn.

deceive v. 欺骗 qīpiàn, 诈骗 zhàpiàn.

decelerate v. 减速 jiǎnsù, 减缓 jiǎnhuǎn.

December n. 十二月 Shí'èryuè.

decency n. 合宜 héyí, 得体 détǐ.

deception n. 欺骗 qīpiàn, 诈骗 zhàpiàn.

decibel n. 分贝 fēnbèi 〈physics〉.

decide v. 决定 juédìng.

deciduous adj. 落叶的 luòyè de 〈plant〉.

decimal adj. 十进的 shíjìn de. — n. ①十进位制 shíjìnwèizhì 〈system〉. ②小数点 xiǎoshùdiǎn 〈point〉.

decimate v. 大量毁灭 dàliàng huǐmiè.

decipher v. 解码 jiěmǎ, 解谜 jiěmí.

decision n. ①决定 juédìng

D

(choice). ②判决 pànjué (judgment).

deck n. 甲板 jiǎbǎn ⟨floor⟩.

declaration n. 宣言 xuānyán, 声明 shēngmíng.

declare v. ①公告 gōnggào, 宣告 xuāngào (announce). ②声明 shēngmíng, 声称 shēngchēng (assert). ③申报 shēnbào ⟨Customs⟩.

decline v. ①谢绝 xièjué (refuse). ②衰落 shuāiluò, 衰微 shuāiwēi / shuāiwéi (become weaker). — n. 衰落 shuāiluò, 衰弱 shuāiruò.

decode v. 解码 jiěmǎ.

decompose v. ①分解 fēnjiě ⟨into parts⟩. ②腐烂 fǔlàn (decay).

decontaminate v. ①消除污染 xiāochú wūrǎn (clean). ②消毒 xiāodú (disinfect).

decorate v. ①装饰 zhuāngshì, 布置 bùzhì (beautify). ②授勋 shòuxūn (honor).

decoration n. ①装饰 zhuāngshì (decorating). ②装饰品 zhuāngshìpǐn (adornment). ③勋章 xūnzhāng (medal).

decoy n. 诱饵 yòu'ěr (bait). — v. 引诱 yǐnyòu.

decrease n. & v. 减少 jiǎnshǎo.

decree n. ①法令 fǎlìng, 政令 zhènglìng (law). ②判决 pànjué (judgment). — v. 颁令 bānlìng, 规定 guīdìng.

decrepit adj. 衰老的 shuāilǎo de.

dedicate v. 奉献 fèngxiàn, 贡献 gòngxiàn (devote).

deduce v. 推论 tuīlùn, 演绎 yǎnyì (reach a conclusion).

deduct v. 扣除 kòuchú (take off), 减除 jiǎnchú (reduce).

deduction n. ①扣除 kòuchú ⟨taxes⟩. ②扣除额 kòuchú'é (amount deducted). ③推论 tuīlùn ⟨logic⟩.

deed n. ①行为 xíngwéi (behavior), 事迹 shìjì / shíjì (act). ②契约 qìyuē, 契书 qìshū (contract).

deep adj. ①深的 shēn de (not shallow). ②深刻的 shēnkè de (profound). ③专心的 zhuānxīn de (concentrating). ④深奥的 shēn'ào de (abstruse). ⑤浓厚的 nónghòu de (thick). ⑥深的 shēn de, 浓的 nóng de ⟨color⟩. ⑦低沉的 dīchén de ⟨voice⟩. — adv. 深深地 shēnshēn de.

deepen v. 加深 jiāshēn, 变深 biànshēn.

deer n. 鹿 lù.

deface v. 毁伤 huǐshāng (harm), 损毁 sǔnhuǐ (spoil the surface).

defame v. 诽谤 fěibàng, 中伤 zhòngshāng.

default n. & v. ①不履行 bù lǚxíng ⟨contract⟩. ②不还债 bù huánzhài ⟨debt⟩.

defeat n. & v. ①击败 jībài / jíbài (beating). ②受挫 shòucuò, 失败 shībài (frustration).

defect n. 缺点 quēdiǎn, 缺陷 quēxiàn, 短处 duǎnchù.

defective adj. 有缺点的 yǒu quēdiǎn de (imperfect), 不健全的 bú jiànquán de (incomplete).

defend v. ①防御 fángyù, 保护 bǎohù (protect). ②辩护 biànhù (justify).

defendant n. 被告 bèigào.

defense n. ①防御 fángyù (protection). ②辩护 biànhù

(justification).

defensive adj. ①防御的 fángyù de (protective). ②辩解 的 biànjiě de (apologetic).

defer v. ①延缓 yánhuǎn, 延期 yánqī / yánqī (delay). ②遵从 zūncóng (obey).

defiance n. ①违抗 wéikàng (disobedience). ②挑战 tiǎozhàn (challenge).

deficient adj. 不足的 bùzú de, 缺乏的 quēfá de (lacking).

deficit n. 赤字 chìzì (budget), 不足额 bù zú'é (amount).

defile v. ①弄脏 nòngzāng (make dirty). ②玷污 diànwū (make impure).

define v. ①下定义 xià dìngyì (name), 阐释 chǎnshì (explain). ②立界限 lì jièxiàn (boundary).

definite adj. ①明确的 míngquè de, 确定的 quèdìng de (set). ②清楚的 qīngchu de, 清晰的 qīngxī de (clear).

definition n. ①定义 dìngyì (explanation). ②清晰度 qīngxīdù (clarity).

definitive adj. ①最后的 zuìhòu de, 确定的 quèdìng de (final). ②权威性的 quánwēixìng de (authoritative).

deflate v. 放出空气 fàngchū kōngqì (let out air).

deflation n. 通货紧缩 tōnghuò jǐnsuō.

deflect v. 使偏斜 shǐ piānxié, 使转向 shǐ zhuǎnxiàng.

deform v. ①使变形 shǐ biànxíng (put out of shape). ②使残废 shǐ cánfèi (distort).

deformed adj. 畸形 jīxíng.

defraud v. 骗取 piànqǔ, 诈取 zhàqǔ.

defrost v. 除冰 chúbīng, 除霜

chúshuāng (remove ice).

deft adj. 灵巧的 língqiǎo de (skillful), 熟练的 shúliàn de / shóuliàn de (practiced).

defunct adj. ①死的 sǐ de (dead). ②不存在的 bù cúnzài de (no longer existing).

defy v. ①公然反抗 gōngrán fǎnkàng (resist openly). ②不服 从 bù fúcóng, 违抗 wéikàng (disobey). ③挑逗 tiǎo, 激 jī (challenge).

degenerate v. ①退步 tuìbù, 堕落 duòluò (deteriorate). ②退 化 tuìhuà (biological phenomena).

degrade v. 降级 jiàngjí (demote).

degree n. ①程度 chéngdù, 等 级 děngjí (level). ②度 dù, 度数 dùshù (unit of measurement). ③阶级 jiējí, 地位 dìwèi (rank). ④学位 xuéwèi (university).

dehydrate v. 脱水 tuōshuǐ, 使 干燥 shǐ gānzào.

deign v. 屈尊 qūzūn, 俯就 fǔjiù.

deity n. ①神性 shénxìng (divine nature). ②神 shén (spirit).

dejected adj. 沮丧的 jǔsàng de.

delay v. ①耽搁 dāng, 延迟 yánchí (make late). ②延期 yánqī / yánqī (put off).

delectable adj. ①令人愉快的 lìng rén yúkuài de (delightful). ②可口的 kěkǒu de (delicious).

delegate n. 代表 dàibiǎo. — v. ①委派……为代表 wěipài... wéi dàibiǎo (appoint). ②委托 wěituō (entrust).

delegation n. 代表团 dàibiǎotuán (group).

delete v. 删除 shānchú, 去除 qùchú.

deliberate adj. ①故意的 gùyì de (intentional). ②深思熟虑的 shēnsī-shúlǜ de / shēnsī-shóulǜ de (carefully considered). ③从容不迫的 cóngróng-búpò de / cōngróng-búpò de (unhurried and cautious). — v. 考虑 kǎolǜ.

delicacy n. ①精致 jīngzhì, 优美 yōuměi (daintiness). ②微妙 wēimiào / wéimiào (subtlety). ③灵敏 língmǐn (sensitivity). ④美食 měishí, 佳肴 jiāyáo (good food).

delicate adj. ①易损的 yìsǔn de, 脆弱的 cuìruò de (easily broken). ②微妙的 wēimiào de / wéimiào de, 灵巧的 língqiǎo de (sensitive). ③精密的 jīngmì de (precise).

delicious adj. 美味的 měiwèi de, 好吃的 hǎochī de.

delight n. 欣喜 xīnxǐ, 愉快 yúkuài (joy). — v. 使愉快 shǐ yúkuài.

delighted adj. 愉快的 yúkuài de.

delightful adj. 令人愉快的 lìng rén yúkuài de (very pleasant).

delinquent adj. 失职的 shīzhí de (failing to perform a duty). — n. 犯罪少年 fànzuì shàonián.

delirious adj. 狂乱的 kuángluàn de (wild), 狂言呓语的 kuángyán yìyǔ de (incoherent).

delirium n. 精神错乱 jīngshén cuòluàn, 呓语 yìyǔ.

deliver v. ①递送 dìsòng (hand over). ②陈述 chénshù, 发表 fābiǎo (speech).

delivery n. ①递送 dìsòng

(delivering). ②演说技巧 yǎnshuō jìqiǎo (skill in giving a speech). ③分娩 fēnmiǎn (childbirth).

Delta n. 希腊字母 Xīlà zìmǔ (Greek letter).

delta n. 三角洲 sānjiǎozhōu (mouth of a river).

delude v. 欺骗 qīpiàn (cheat), 迷惑 míhuò (confuse).

deluge n. ①大水灾 dà shuǐzāi (great flood). ②大量涌至 dàliàng yǒng zhì (coming in a heavy flood).

delusion n. 幻想 huànxiǎng (false belief).

deluxe adj. 豪华的 háohuá de.

delve v. 钻研 zuānyán (search deeply).

demand n. & v. ①要求 yāoqiú (request). ②需求 xūqiú, 需要 xūyào (need).

demarcate v. 定界线 dìng jièxiàn, 划界 huàjiè (mark the limits of).

demeanor n. 行为 xíngwéi (behavior), 态度 tàidu (attitude).

demented adj. 疯狂的 fēngkuáng de, 发狂的 fākuáng de (crazy).

democracy n. ①民主主义 mínzhǔ zhǔyì ⟨idea⟩. ②民主政治 mínzhǔ zhèngzhì ⟨system⟩. ③民主国家 mínzhǔ guójiā ⟨nation⟩.

democrat n. ①民主主义者 mínzhǔ zhǔyì zhě ⟨advocate⟩. ②民主党人 mínzhǔdǎng rén ⟨party member⟩.

demolish v. ①拆除 chāichú, 破坏 pòhuài (destroy). ②推翻 tuīfān (tear down).

demon n. 恶魔 èmó.

demonstrate v. ①示范 shìfàn

D

(show). ②证明 zhèngmíng
(prove). ③表明 biǎomíng
(make known). ④示威 shìwēi
(oppose publicly).

demonstrative adj. 感情流
露的 gǎnqíng liúlù de
(showing feelings openly).

demoralize v. 使士气低落
shǐ shìqì dīluò (dishearten).

demure adj. ①假正经的
jiǎzhèngjing de (hypocritical).
②严谨的 yánjǐn de, 端庄的
duānzhuāng de (serious).

denial n. ①否认 fǒurèn (not
admitting). ②拒绝 jùjué (refusal).

denomination n. ①名称
míngchēng (name). ②单位
dānwèi (unit). ③宗派 zōngpài,
派别 pàibié (religious sect).

denominator n. 分母 fēnmǔ.

denote v. 表示 biǎoshì
(express), 意谓 yìwèi (hint at).

denounce v. 指责 zhǐzé, 谴责
qiǎnzé (blame).

dense adj. ①浓密的 nóngmì
de (liquid or air). ②稠密的
chóumì de (people). ③愚钝的
yúdùn de (stupid).

density n. ①密度 mìdù
⟨physics⟩. ②浓密 nóngmì
⟨consistency⟩.

dent n. 凹陷 āoxiàn, 凹痕
āohén. — v. 使凹陷 shǐ āoxiàn.

dental adj. 牙齿的 yáchǐ de.

dentist n. 牙医 yáyī.

denunciation n. ①谴责
qiǎnzé (reproval). ②告发
gàofā (declaring untrue).

deny v. ①否认 fǒurèn (declare
untrue). ②拒绝 jùjué (refuse).

deodorant n. 防臭剂
fángchòujì.

depart v. 出发 chūfā (start out),
离开 líkāi (leave).

department n. ①部门 bùmén
(division). ②系 xì, 科 kē
⟨university⟩. ~ **store** 百货公司
bǎihuò gōngsī.

departure n. 出发 chūfā, 离
去 líqù (the act of leaving).

depend v. ①依赖 yīlài, 依靠
yīkào (rely on). ②信赖 xìnlài
(trust).

dependence n. ①依赖 yīlài,
倚靠 yīkào (reliance). ②信赖
xìnlài, 信任 xìnrèn (trust).

dependent adj. ①依赖的 yīlài
de (depending). ②视……而定
shì...ér dìng, 取决于……
qǔjué yú... (conditional on).
— n. 眷属 juànshǔ, 被扶养人
bèi fúyǎngrén ⟨relative⟩.

depict v. 描绘 miáohuì
(describe), 描写 miáoxiě
(capture).

deplete v. ①用尽 yòngjìn, 耗
尽 hàojìn (use up). ②使空虚
shǐ kōngxū (weaken).

deplore v. 悲痛 bēitòng, 哀叹
āitàn.

deport v. 驱逐出境 qūzhú
chūjìng.

depose v. ①罢黜 bàchù, 免职
miǎnzhí (dethrone). ②作证
zuòzhèng (give evidence).

deposit v. ①存放 cúnfàng,
置放 zhìfàng (place). ②储存
chǔcún / chúcún, 存入 cúnrù
(save). ③淤积 yūjī, 沉淀
chéndiàn (precipitate). ④付定
金 fù dìngjīn (pay down payment). — n. ①沉淀物
chéndiànwù (precipitate). ②定
金 dìngjīn, 押金 yājīn (down
payment). ③存款 cúnkuǎn
(savings).

depot n. ①仓库 cāngkù, 库房
kùfáng (storehouse). ②火车站

huǒchēzhàn ⟨train⟩, 公车站 gōngchēzhàn ⟨bus⟩.

depraved adj. 堕落的 duòluò de, 败坏的 bàihuài de.

depreciate v. 贬值 biǎnzhí (fall in value).

depress v. ①使沮丧 shǐ jǔsàng (discourage). ②使萧条 shǐ xiāotiáo (make less active).

depression n. ①忧郁 yōuyù, 沮丧 jǔsàng (dejection). ②不景气 bù jǐngqì, 萧条 xiāotiáo (decline). ③洼穴 wāxué / wāxuè, 坑 kēng (indentation). ④忧郁症 yōuyùzhèng ⟨disease⟩. ⑤低气压 dīqìyā (low pressure).

deprive v. 剥夺 bōduó, 使丧失 shǐ sàngshī (take away from).

deprived adj. ①贫困的 pínkùn de (poor). ②被剥夺的 bèi bōduó de (be taken away).

depth n. 深 shēn, 深度 shēndù.

deputy n. 代理人 dàilǐrén, 代表 dàibiǎo.

derail v. 使出轨 shǐ chūguǐ.

derivation n. ①起源 qǐyuán, 由来 yóulái (origin). ②字源 zìyuán (origin of a word).

derive v. ①获得 huòdé, 得到 dédào (get). ②源于 yuányú, 引出 yǐnchu (originate from).

descend v. 下降 xiàjiàng, 落下 luòxia (go down).

descent n. ①斜坡 xiépō (decline). ②血统 xuètǒng / xiětǒng (ancestry).

describe v. ①叙述 xùshù (depict). ②描写 miáoxiě, 描绘 miáohuì (portray).

description n. 叙述 xùshù, 描述 miáoshù (depiction).

desecrate v. 亵渎 xièdú, 污辱 wūrǔ / wūrù.

desegregate v. 取消种族隔离 qǔxiāo zhǒngzú gélí.

desert n. & adj. 沙漠 shāmò. — v. ①放弃 fàngqì, 抛弃 pāoqì (abandon). ②潜逃 qiántáo (run away from).

deserve v. 应得 yīngdé, 应受 yīngshòu.

design n. ①设计 shèjì ⟨drawing⟩. ②图案 tú'àn (pattern). ③目的 mùdì, 企图 qǐtú / qìtú (intention). — v. ①设计 shèjì (draw). ②打算 dǎsuàn, 计画 jìhuà (plan).

designate v. ①指示 zhǐshì, 指明 zhǐmíng (point out). ②指派 zhǐpài, 指定 zhǐdìng (appoint).

desirable adj. 合意的 héyì de, 渴望的 kěwàng de.

desire v. ①想要 xiǎngyào, 渴望 kěwàng (wish). ②要求 yāoqiú, 请求 qǐngqiú (request).

desk n. 书桌 shūzhuō.

desolate adj. ①荒芜的 huāngwú de, 荒废的 huāngfèi de (deserted). ②孤寂的 gūjì de / gūjí de (friendless). — v. ①使荒凉 shǐ huāngliáng (make desolate). ②使孤寂 shǐ gūjì / shǐ gūjí (make lonely).

despair n. & v. 失望 shīwàng, 绝望 juéwàng.

desperate adj. ①绝望的 juéwàng de (hopeless). ②危急的 wēijí de / wéijí de, 严重的 yánzhòng de (serious).

despise v. 轻视 qīngshì, 蔑视 mièshì.

despite prep. 不管 bùguǎn, 尽管 jǐnguǎn.

despot n. 独裁者 dúcáizhě, 暴君 bàojūn.

dessert n. 甜点 tiándiǎn.

destination n. 目的地 mùdìdì.

destiny n. 命运 mìngyùn.

destitute adj. 贫困的 pínkùn de.

destroy v. 破坏 pòhuài, 毁坏 huǐhuài (ruin).

destruction n. 破坏 pòhuài, 毁坏 huǐhuài.

detach v. 分开 fēnkai, 解开 jiěkai.

detail n. 细节 xìjié, 详情 xiángqíng.

detain v. ①耽误 dānwù, 耽搁 dāngē (keep waiting). ②拘留 jūliú (hold in custody).

detect v. 发现 fāxiàn, 查出 cháchu.

detective n. 侦探 zhēntàn.

detention n. 拘留 jūliú, 留置 liúzhì.

deter v. 阻止 zǔzhǐ, 阻吓 zǔhè.

detergent n. 清洁剂 qīngjiéjì.

deteriorate v. 变坏 biànhuài, 恶化 èhuà.

determination n. 决心 juéxīn, 决定 juédìng (firm intention).

determine v. 决定 juédìng, 下决心 xià juéxīn.

determined adj. 坚决的 jiānjué de.

deterrent adj. 阻碍的 zǔài de. — n. 阻碍物 zǔàiwù.

detest v. 憎恶 zēngwù, 痛恨 tònghèn.

dethrone v. 废黜 fèichù, 罢黜 bàchù.

detonate v. 爆炸 bàozhà, 爆裂 bàoliè.

detour n. 迂回道 yūhuídào.

detract v. 减损 jiǎnsǔn.

detriment n. 损害 sǔnhài, 伤害 shānghài.

devastate v. 使荒废 shǐ huāngfèi.

develop v. ①发展 fāzhǎn (grow), 培育 péiyù (nurture). ②开发 kāifā (make use of). ③冲洗 chōngxǐ ⟨film⟩.

developed adj. 已发展的 yǐ fāzhǎn de. ~ countries 发达国家 fādá guójiā / 已开发国家 yǐ kāifā guójiā.

development n. 发展 fāzhǎn (growth), 开发 kāifā ⟨potential⟩.

deviate v. 偏离 piānlí.

device n. ①装置 zhuāngzhì, 设备 shèbèi (apparatus). ②策略 cèlüè, 诡计 guǐjì (gimmick).

devil n. 恶魔 èmó, 魔鬼 móguǐ.

devious adj. ①迂回的 yūhuí de (circuitous). ②不诚实的 bù chéngshí de (deceitful).

devise v. 设计 shèjì, 策画 cèhuà, 发明 fāmíng (plan or invent).

devote v. 奉献于 fèngxiàn yú, 专心于 zhuānxīn yú.

devoted adj. 忠实的 zhōngshí de.

devotion n. ①奉献 fèngxiàn, 致力 zhìlì (contribution). ②热爱 rè'ài (strong love).

devour v. ①狼吞虎咽 lángtūn-hǔyàn ⟨eat⟩. ②毁灭 huǐmiè (destroy).

devout adj. 虔敬的 qiánjìng de, 忠诚的 zhōngchéng de.

dew n. 露 lù, 露珠 lùzhū.

diabetes n. 糖尿病 tángniàobìng.

diabolic adj. 恶魔的 èmó de, 凶残的 xiōngcán de.

diagnose v. 诊断 zhěnduàn.

diagonal n. & adj. ①对角线 duìjiǎoxiàn ⟨line⟩. ②斜纹

diagram 77 **dilute**

xiéwén 〈pattern〉.

diagram n. 图解 tújiě.

dial n. ①针盘 zhēnpán 〈marked face〉. ②号码盘 hàomǎpán 〈phone〉. — v. 拨电话 bō diànhuà.

dialect n. 方言 fāngyán.

dialogue n. 对话 duìhuà.

diameter n. 直径 zhíjìng.

diamond n. ①钻石 zuànshí 〈stone〉. ②菱形 língxíng 〈shape〉. ③方块 fāngkuài 〈cards〉.

diaper n. 尿布 niàobù.

diarrhea n. 腹泻 fùxiè, 拉肚子 lādùzi.

diary n. 日记 rìjì.

dice n. 色子 shǎizi, 骰子 tóuzi.

dictate v. ①口述 kǒushù 〈read〉. ②命令 mìnglìng 〈give orders〉.

dictation n. ①口述 kǒushù 〈reading〉. ②听写 tīngxiě 〈write down another's speech〉.

dictator n. 独裁者 dúcáizhě.

dictionary n. 字典 zìdiǎn, 辞典 cídiǎn.

die v. ①死 sǐ, 死亡 sǐwáng 〈pass away〉. ②枯萎 kūwěi / kūwēi 〈wither〉.

diesel n. 柴油 cháiyóu.

diet n. 饮食 yǐnshí, 食物 shíwù 〈food〉. — v. 节食 jiéshí.

differ v. ①相异 xiāngyì, 不同 bùtóng 〈be different〉. ②意见相左 yìjiàn xiāngzuǒ, 不合 bùhé 〈disagree〉.

difference n. ①差别 chābié, 差异 chāyì, 不同 bùtóng 〈discrepancy〉. ②意见相左 yìjiàn xiāngzuǒ, 不合 bùhé 〈disagreement〉.

different adj. 不同的 bùtóng de, 相异的 xiāngyì de.

differentiate v. 区分 qūfēn,

辨别 biànbié.

difficult adj. 困难的 kùnnán de 〈hard〉, 费力的 fèilì de 〈tiring〉.

difficulty n. 困难 kùnnán.

diffuse v. 扩散 kuòsàn, 广布 guǎngbù. — adj. ①散布的 sànbù de, 扩散的 kuòsàn de 〈spread out〉. ②冗长的 rǒngcháng de 〈using too many words〉.

dig v. ①挖掘 wājué, 挖 wā 〈burrow〉. ②戳 chuō, 刺 cì 〈poke〉. — n. 戳 chuō, 刺 cì.

digest v. ①消化 xiāohuà 〈food〉. ②了解 liǎojiě 〈information〉.

digestion n. 消化力 xiāohuàlì.

digit n. ①数字 shùzì 〈number〉. ②手指 shǒuzhǐ 〈finger〉. ③足趾 zúzhǐ 〈toe〉.

dignified adj. 高贵的 gāoguì de, 尊严的 zūnyán de.

dignity n. ①高贵 gāoguì, 高尚 gāoshàng 〈nobleness〉. ②威严 wēiyán, 尊严 zūnyán 〈calm stateliness〉.

digress v. 离题 lítí.

dike n. ①堤 dī / tí 〈embankment〉, 水坝 shuǐbà 〈dam〉. ②沟 gōu, 渠 qú 〈ditch〉.

dilapidated adj. 倒塌的 dǎotā de, 残破的 cánpò de.

dilate v. 使膨胀 shǐ péngzhàng, 使扩大 shǐ kuòdà 〈enlarge〉.

dilemma n. 进退两难 jìntuìliǎngnán.

diligence n. 勤勉 qínmiǎn, 勤奋 qínfèn.

dilute v. 稀释 xīshì, 冲淡 chōngdàn. — adj. 稀释的 xīshì de, 淡的 dàn de.

D

dim adj. 微暗的 wēi'àn de / wéi'àn de (not bright), 模糊的 móhu de (not clear). — v. 使暗 淡 shǐ àndàn.

dime n. 一角硬币 yìjiǎo yìngbì.

dimension n. 尺寸 chǐcùn, 大 小 dàxiǎo.

diminish v. 减少 jiǎnshǎo, 缩 小 suōxiǎo.

diminutive adj. 小的 xiǎo de, 特别小的 tèbié xiǎo de.

dimple n. 酒涡 jiǔwō. — v. 出 现酒涡 chūxiàn jiǔwō.

din n. 喧哗声 xuānhuáshēng, 嘈杂声 cáozáshēng. — v. 喧 哗 xuānhuá, 吵闹 chǎonào.

dine v. 用餐 yòngcān, 吃饭 chīfàn.

dinghy n. 小艇 xiǎotǐng.

dingy adj. 肮脏的 āngzāng de.

dining room n. 饭厅 fàntīng.

Dinky n. 丁克族 Dīngkèzú / 顶克族 Dǐngkèzú.

dinner n. ①晚餐 wǎncān (evening meal). ②宴会 yànhuì, 餐宴 cānyàn (banquet).

dinosaur n. 恐龙 kǒnglóng.

DINS 顶士族 Dǐngshìzú (Double Income, No Sex.)

diocese n. 教区 jiàoqū.

dip v. ①沾 zhān (douse). ②掏 取 jū / jú, 汲取 jíqǔ (put and take out). ③下降 xiàjiàng, 下沉 xiàchén (descend). — n. 斜坡 xiépō (slope).

diploma n. 文凭 wénpíng, 毕 业证书 bìyè zhèngshū.

diplomacy n. ①外交 wàijiāo 〈international relations〉. ②外交 手腕 wàijiāo shǒuwàn (diplomatic skill).

diplomat n. 外交官

wàijiāoguān.

diplomatic adj. ①外交的 wàijiāo de (of diplomacy). ②有外交手腕的 yǒu wàijiāo shǒuwàn de (tactful).

dire adj. ①可怕的 kěpà de (terrible). ②迫切的 pòqiè de (urgent).

direct v. ①指示 zhǐshì, 指引 zhǐyǐn (guide). ②指导 zhǐdǎo, 管理 guǎnlǐ (administer). — adj. ①直的 zhí de (straight). ②直接的 zhíjiē de (straight-forward).

direction n. ①方向 fāngxiàng (way). ②指导 zhǐdǎo, 指示 zhǐshì (guidance).

directly adv. 直接地 zhíjiē de.

director n. ①指导者 zhǐdǎozhě (leader). ②董事 dǒngshì 〈business〉. ③导演 dǎoyǎn 〈movies〉.

directory n. 通讯录 tōngxùnlù (a book of names).

dirt n. ①泥土 nítǔ (soil). ②污垢 wūgòu (unclean matter). ③闲话 xiánhuà, 八卦 bāguà (gossip).

dirty adj. 脏的 zāng de, 不洁 的 bù jié de. ~ **trick** 卑鄙的行 为 bēibǐ de xíngwéi. — v. 弄脏 nòngzāng.

disability n. 无能力 wú nénglì 〈law〉.

disable v. 使无能 shǐ wúnéng, 使残废 shǐ cánfèi (make incapable).

disadvantage n. ①不利 búlì (unfavorable condition). ②缺点 quēdiǎn (weakness).

disagree v. 不同意 bù tóngyì, 意见不合 yìjiàn bùhé.

disappear v. 消失 xiāoshī.

disappoint v. 使失望 shǐ shīwàng.

disappointment n. 失望 shīwàng.

disapproval n. 反对 fǎnduì, 不赞成 bú zànchéng.

disapprove v. 不准许 bù zhǔnxǔ.

disarm v. 缴械 jiǎoxiè, 解除 武装 jiěchú wǔzhuāng.

disarray n. 杂乱 záluàn, 无秩 序 wú zhìxù.

disaster n. 灾祸 zāihuò, 大灾 难 dà zāinàn.

disband v. 解散 jiěsàn.

disbelieve v. 不相信 bù xiāngxìn, 怀疑 huáiyí.

discard v. 抛弃 pāoqì, 放弃 fàngqì.

discern v. 察觉 chájué (discover), 辨识 biànshí / biànshì (distinguish).

discharge n. & v. ①排出 páichū (send out). ②发射 fāshè ⟨guns⟩. ③解雇 jiěgù, 开除 kāichú ⟨employees⟩. ④释放 shìfàng (let off). ⑤卸货 xièhuò (unload). ⑥执行 zhíxíng ⟨of one's duty⟩. ⑦偿还 chánghuán ⟨of one's debts⟩.

disciple n. 门徒 méntú, 弟子 dìzǐ.

discipline n. ①纪律 jìlǜ (order). ②训练 xùnliàn (training). — v. ①训练 xùnliàn (train). ②惩罚 chéngfá (punish).

disclaim v. 否认 fǒurèn.

disclose v. 揭发 jiēfā (reveal), 泄露 xièlòu (make known).

disco n. 迪斯科舞厅 dísīkē wǔtīng / 迪斯可舞厅 dísīkě wǔtīng.

discolor v. (使) 变色 (shǐ) biànsè, (使) 褪色 (shǐ) tuìshǎi / (shǐ) tùnsè.

discomfort n. 不舒适 bù shūshì, 不安 bù'ān.

disconcert v. ①使不安 shǐ bù'ān (feel anxiety). ②扰乱 rǎoluàn (upset).

disconnect v. 使分离 shǐ fēnlí, 切断 qiēduàn.

disconsolate adj. 忧闷的 yōumèn de, 哀伤的 āishāng de.

discontent n. 不满 bùmǎn.

discontinue v. 停止 tíngzhǐ, 终止 zhōngzhǐ.

discord n. ①不一致 bù yízhì (disagreement). ②争论 zhēnglùn (argument). ③不和谐 bù héxié ⟨sound⟩.

discordant adj. 不和谐的 bù héxié de, 嘈杂的 cáozá de.

discount v. 打折扣 dǎzhékòu, 贴现 tiēxiàn. — n. 折扣 zhékòu, 减价 jiǎnjià.

discourage v. ①使气馁 shǐ qìněi, 使沮丧 shǐ jǔsàng (dishearten). ②劝阻 quànzǔ (deter).

discourteous adj. 失礼的 shīlǐ de, 粗鲁的 cūlǔ de.

discover v. 发现 fāxiàn.

discovery n. 发现 fāxiàn.

discredit v. ①使耻辱 shǐ diànrǔ / shǐ diànrù, 使不名誉 shǐ bù míngyù (defame). ②怀 疑 huáiyí, 不信任 bú xìnrèn (disbelieve). — n. ①耻辱 chǐrǔ / chǐrù, 不名誉 bù míngyù (disgrace). ②不信任 bú xìnrèn (loss of belief).

discreet adj. 谨慎的 jǐnshèn de, 慎重的 shènzhòng de.

discretion n. ①谨慎 jǐnshèn (being discreet). ②自由选择 zìyóu xuǎnzé, 自由决定 zìyóu juédìng (freedom to act).

discriminate v. ①区别 qūbié, 辨别 biànbié (distin-

guish). ②歧视 qíshì, 差别待遇 chābié dàiyù (be biased).

discus n. 铁饼 tiěbǐng.

discuss v. 讨论 tǎolùn, 议论 yìlùn.

discussion n. 讨论 tǎolùn, 议论 yìlùn.

disdain n. & v. 轻视 qīngshì, 轻蔑 qīngmiè.

disease n. 疾病 jíbìng.

disembark v. 登岸 dēng'àn, 登陆 dēnglù.

disengage v. ①释放 shìfàng, 解脱 jiětuō (release). ②使解开 shǐ jiěkai, 使脱离 shǐ tuōlí (loosen).

disentangle v. ①解开 jiěkai (unknot). ②松开 sōngkāi (release).

disfigure v. 毁容 huǐróng, 损 毁外观 sǔnhuǐ wàiguān.

disgrace n. & v. 不名誉 bù míngyù, 丢脸 diūliǎn, 耻辱 chǐrǔ / chǐrù.

disgruntled adj. 不高兴的 bù gāoxìng de, 不满的 bùmǎn de.

disguise n. & v. 假装 jiǎzhuāng, 伪装 wěizhuāng / wèizhuāng.

disgust n. 厌恶 yànwù, 憎恶 zēngwù. — v. 使厌恶 shǐ yànwù.

disgusting adj. 令人厌恶的 lìng rén yànwù de, 令人作呕 的 lìng rén zuò'ǒu de.

dish n. ①碟 dié, 盘 pán (plate). ②食物 shíwù, 菜肴 càiyáo (food).

dishearten v. 使沮丧 shǐ jǔsàng, 使气馁 shǐ qìněi.

disheveled adj. 蓬乱的 péngluàn de.

dishonest adj. 不诚实的 bù

chéngshí de.

dishonor n. 不名誉 bù míngyù, 耻辱 chǐrǔ / chǐrù. — v. ①侮辱 wǔrǔ / wǔrù, 使蒙 羞 shǐ méngxiū (disgrace). ②拒付 jùfù (bank).

disillusion n. & v. 醒悟 xǐngwù.

disinfect v. 消毒 xiāodú, 杀菌 shājūn / shājùn.

disinfectant n. 消毒剂 xiāodújì.

disinherit v. 剥夺继承权 bōduó jìchéngquán.

disintegrate v. 崩溃 bēngkuì (collapse), 瓦解 wǎjiě (lose unity).

disinterested adj. 公正的 gōngzhèng de (impartial).

disk n. ①圆盘 yuánpán (flat plate). ②磁盘 cípán / 磁碟片 cídiépiàn (computer).

~ **drive** 磁盘驱动器 cípán qūdòngqì / 磁碟机 cídiéjī (computer).

dislike n. & v. 嫌恶 xiánwù, 厌恶 yànwù.

dislocate v. 使脱臼 shǐ tuōjiù (bone).

dislodge v. 逐出 zhúchū (remove), 移出 yíchū (move).

disloyal adj. 不忠的 bùzhōng de, 不贞的 bùzhēn de, 背叛 的 bèipàn de.

dismal adj. 忧郁的 yōuyù de, 愁闷的 chóumèn de.

dismantle v. 拆除 chāichú, 拆卸 chāixiè.

dismay n. & v. 惊慌 jīnghuāng, 恐惧 kǒngjù (fear), 沮丧 jǔsàng (hopelessness).

dismember v. ①肢解 zhījiě (cut apart). ②瓜分 guāfēn, 分 割 fēngē (divide up).

dismiss v. ①解散 jiěsàn (let go). ②解雇 jiěgù, 开除 kāichú (fire). ③撇开 piēkāi (put away).

dismount v. 下马 xiàmǎ (get down).

disobey v. 违抗 wéikàng, 不服从 bù fúcóng.

disorder n. ①混乱 hùnluàn, 紊乱 wěnluàn / wènluàn (confusion). ②骚动 sāodòng, 骚乱 sāoluàn (riot). ③疾病 jíbìng (disease).

disorganize v. 破坏 pòhuài, 扰乱 rǎoluàn.

disown v. 否认有关系 fǒurèn yǒu guānxi.

dispatch v. ①发送 fāsòng (send off). ②一下子就完成（工作）yíxiàzi jiù wánchéng (gōngzuò) (finish quickly). ③处决 chǔjué (kill). — n. ①打发 dǎfa (dispatching), 发发 fā (sending). ②电讯 diànxùn (message).

dispel v. 驱散 qūsàn.

dispense v. 施予 shīyǔ (give), 分配 fēnpèi (allocate). ②配药 pèiyào ⟨medicine⟩.

disperse v. 使分散 shǐ fēnsàn, 使解散 shǐ jiěsàn. — v. 分散 fēnsàn, 散开 sànkai.

displace v. 取代 qǔdài, 替代 tìdài, 置换 zhìhuàn (replace).

display n. & v. ①陈列 chénliè, 展示 zhǎnshì (show). ②显露 xiǎnlù, 表现 biǎoxiàn (become visible).

displease v. 惹……生气 rě... shēngqì, 使不悦 shǐ búyuè.

disposable adj. 用后可丢弃的 yòng hòu kě diūqì de. ~ *chopsticks* 卫生筷 wèishēngkuài / 免洗筷 miǎnxǐkuài.

disposal n. 安排 ānpái, 处置 chǔzhì.

dispose v. ①处理 chǔlǐ, 处置 chǔzhì (deal with). ②布置 bùzhì, 安排 ānpái (arrange).

dispossess v. 强夺 qiángduó, 霸占 bàzhàn.

disprove v. 驳斥 bóchì, 反证 fǎnzhèng.

dispute n. & v. ①争论 zhēnglùn, 争吵 zhēngchǎo (argument). ②反驳 fǎnbó (disagreement).

disqualify v. 取消资格 qǔxiāo zīgé.

disregard n. & v. 忽视 hūshì, 不理 bùlǐ.

disrepair n. 失修 shīxiū.

disrepute n. 不名誉 bù míngyù, 坏名声 huài míngshēng.

disrespect n. 不敬 bújìng, 无礼 wúlǐ.

disrupt v. ①分裂 fēnliè, 瓦解 wǎjiě (break up). ②中断 zhōngduàn (disturb).

dissatisfy v. 使不满 shǐ bùmǎn.

dissect v. ①解剖 jiěpōu / jiěpǒu (cut up). ②详细研究 xiángxì yánjiū / xiángxì yánjiù, 剖析 pōuxī / pǒuxī (analyze).

disseminate v. 传播 chuánbō / chuánbò, 散布 sànbù.

dissent n. & v. 反对 fǎnduì, 有异议 yǒu yìyì.

dissertation n. 论文 lùnwén.

dissociate v. 分离 fēnlí, 分开 fēnkāi.

dissolve v. ①溶解 róngjiě (become liquid). ②解散 jiěsàn, 解除 jiěchú (break up).

dissuade v. 劝阻 quànzǔ.

distance n. 距离 jùlí. ~ *learning* 远距离教育 yuǎnjùlí

jiàoyú / 远距教学 yuǎnjù jiàoxué.

distant adj. ①遥远的 yáoyuǎn de (far). ②冷淡的 lěngdàn de, 疏远的 shūyuǎn de (aloof).

distaste n. 嫌恶 xiánwù, 憎厌 zēngyàn.

distill v. 蒸馏 zhēngliú / zhēngliù.

distinct adj. ①清楚的 qīngchu de, 清晰的 qīngxī de (clear). ②分别的 fēnbié de, 不同的 bùtóng de (different).

distinction n. ①区别 qūbié, 差别 chābié (difference). ②优越 yōuyuè, 卓越 zhuóyuè (excellence). ③特征 tèzhēng, 特性 tèxìng (quality of being unusual).

distinguish v. ①区别 qūbié, 辨别 biànbié (differentiate). ②看出来 kànchūlai (recognize).

distinguished adj. 著名的 zhùmíng de (well-known), 卓越的 zhuóyuè de (excellent).

distort v. ①使变形 shǐ biànxíng, 扭曲 niǔqū (twist). ②曲解 qūjiě, 歪曲 wāiqū (falsify).

distract v. ①使分心 shǐ fēnxīn (divide attention). ②使心烦 shǐ xīnfán, 使困扰 shǐ kùnrǎo (trouble).

distraught adj. 精神错乱的 jīngshén cuòluàn de.

distress n. 痛苦 tòngkǔ, 忧伤 yōushāng (anguish). — v. 使痛苦 shǐ tòngkǔ, 使苦恼 shǐ kǔnǎo.

distribute v. ①分发 fēnfā, 分配 fēnpèi (allocate). ②散布 sànbù, 分布 fēnbù (spread out).

distribution n. ①分发 fēnfā,

分配 fēnpèi (allocation). ②散布 sànbù, 分布 fēnbù (spreading).

district n. 地区 dìqū, 区域 qūyù.

distrust n. & v. 不信任 bú xìnrèn, 怀疑 huáiyí.

disturb v. ①打扰 dǎrǎo, 骚扰 sāorǎo (bother). ②弄乱 nòngluàn, 扰乱 rǎoluàn (disorder).

ditch n. 壕沟 háogōu, 沟渠 gōuqú. — v. ①挖沟 wā háogōu (make a ditch). ②丢弃 diūqì, 舍弃 shěqì (abandon).

ditto n. 同上 tóngshàng, 同前 tóngqián.

ditty n. 小曲 xiǎoqǔ, 歌谣 gēyáo.

dive n. & v. ①俯冲 fǔchōng, 骤降 zhòujiàng / zòujiàng (go down steeply and speedily). ②跳水 tiàoshuǐ (water).

diver n. 潜水者 qiánshuǐzhě.

diverge v. ①分岔 fēnchà 〈roads〉. ②分歧 fēnqí 〈opinions〉.

diverse adj. 不同的 bùtóng de (different), 多元化的 duōyuánhuà de (varied).

diversify v. 多样化 duōyànghuà.

diversion n. ①娱乐 yúlè, 消遣 xiāoqiǎn (amusement). ②转移 zhuǎnyí, 转向 zhuǎnxiàng (turning).

divert v. ①使转向 shǐ zhuǎnxiàng (change direction). ②消遣 xiāoqiǎn, 娱乐 yúlè (amuse).

divide v. ①分开 fēnkai, 划分 huàfēn (separate). ②分配 fēnpèi (allocate). ③除 chú 〈mathematics〉. ④分类 fēnlèi (categorize).

dividend n. ①股息 gǔxī / gǔxí ⟨stocks⟩. ②被除数 bèichúshù ⟨mathematics⟩.

divine adj. ①神的 shén de (God-like). ②极好的 jí hǎo de (excellent).

divinity n. ①神性 shénxìng (state of being divine). ②神学 shénxué (religious studies).

division n. ①分配 fēnpèi, 划分 huàfēn (allocation). ②不和 bùhé (disagreement). ③分界线 fēnjièxiàn (boundary). ④部门 bùmén, 组 zǔ (department). ⑤除法 chúfǎ ⟨mathematics⟩.

divorce n. & v. ①离婚 líhūn (ending of a marriage). ②分离 fēnlí, 分裂 fēnliè (separation).

divulge v. 泄露 xièlòu.

DIY 自己动手做 zìjǐ dòngshǒu zuò.

dizzy adj. 晕眩的 yùnxuàn de / yūnxuàn de, 头昏眼花的 tóuhūn-yǎnhuā de.

do v. ①做 zuò (carry out). ②完成 wánchéng (finish).

docile adj. 温顺的 wēnshùn de, 驯良的 xùnliáng de / xúnliáng de.

dock n. 船坞 chuánwù, 码头 mǎtou.

doctor n. ①医生 yīshēng ⟨medical⟩. ②博士 bóshì (Ph.D.).

doctrine n. 教条 jiàotiáo, 教义 jiàoyì ⟨religion⟩, 学说 xuéshuō (theory).

document n. 文件 wénjiàn, 公文 gōngwén (paper), 证件 zhèngjiàn (proof).

documentary adj. 文件的 wénjiàn de. — n. 纪录片 jìlùpiàn.

dodge n. & v. 躲开 duǒkai, 闪

避 shǎnbì.

doe n. ①雌鹿 cílù / cílù ⟨deer⟩. ②雌兔 cítù / cítù ⟨rabbit⟩.

dog n. 狗 gǒu, 犬 quǎn.

dogged adj. 顽强的 wánqiáng de, 固执的 gùzhí de.

dogma n. 教条 jiàotiáo, 教义 jiàoyì (belief).

dole v. 救济 jiùjì, 布施 bùshī. — n. ①救济 jiùjì, 布施 bùshī (giving out). ②救济品 jiùjìpǐn, 布施物 bùshīwù (something doled out).

doll n. 洋娃娃 yángwáwa, 玩偶 wán'ǒu.

dollar n. 元 yuán, 圆 yuán.

dolphin n. 海豚 hǎitún.

domain n. ①领土 lǐngtǔ, 版图 bǎntú (territory). ②领域 lǐngyù, 范围 fànwéi (sphere).

dome n. 圆顶 yuándǐng, 圆盖 yuángài.

domestic adj. ①家庭的 jiātíng de (family). ②国内的 guónèi de (native). ③人工饲养的 réngōng sìyǎng de ⟨not wild⟩.

dominant adj. ①支配的 zhīpèi de (dominating). ②较强的 jiào qiáng de (stronger).

dominate v. 统治 tǒngzhì, 支配 zhīpèi (control).

domineer v. 擅权 shànquán, 跋扈 báhù.

dominion n. ①统治权 tǒngzhìquán, 支配权 zhīpèiquán (authority). ②领土 lǐngtǔ, 版图 bǎntú (territory).

domino n. (pl.) 骨牌 gǔpái ⟨game⟩. ~ effect 多米诺骨牌效应 duōmǐnuò gǔpái xiàoyìng / 骨牌效应 gǔpái xiàoyìng.

donate v. 捐赠 juānzèng.

donkey n. 驴 lú.

donor n. 捐赠者 juānzèngzhě.

donut n. 甜甜圈 tiántiánquān.

doom n. ①命运 mìngyùn, 注定 zhùdìng (fate). ②死亡 sǐwáng, 劫数 jiéshù (death).

door n. 门 mén, 户 hù (gate).

doorstep n. 门阶 ménjiē.

doorway n. 门口 ménkǒu, 出入口 chūrùkǒu.

dope n. ①麻药 máyào, 大麻 dàmá (marijuana). ②笨蛋 bèndàn (idiot). — v. 下麻药 xià máyào.

dormant adj. ①冬眠的 dōngmián de (sleeping). ②潜伏的 qiánfú de (inactive).

dormitory n. 宿舍 sùshè.

dosage n. 剂量 jìliàng.

dose n. 一剂 yí jì, 一服 yì fú.

dossier n. 档案 dàng'àn / dǎng'àn.

dot n. 小点 xiǎodiǎn.

double adj. 双倍的 shuāngbèi de, 加倍的 jiābèi de (twice as much). ~ *bed* 双人床 shuāngrénchuáng. — n. 两倍 liǎngbèi. — v. 使加倍 shǐ jiābèi.

doubt v. 怀疑 huáiyí.

doubtless adv. 无疑地 wúyí de.

dough n. 生面团 shēng miàntuán.

dove n. 鸽子 gēzi (pigeon).

dowager n. 富孀 fùshuāng (rich widow).

down adv. & prep. ①往下地 wǎngxià de (from high to low). ②在下面 zài xiàmiàn (in a lower position). — adj. ①向下的 xiàngxià de (from high to low). ②消沉的 xiāochén de (depressed).

downcast adj. 沮丧的 jǔsàng de (depressed).

downfall n. 衰败 shuāibài

(ruin).

downgrade v. 降级 jiàngjí.

download v. 下载 xiàzài 〈computer〉.

downpour n. 大雨 dàyǔ.

downright adj. ①率直的 shuàizhí de (frank). ②完全的 wánquán de (thorough).

downsize v. 小型化 xiǎoxínghuà, 缩小 suōxiǎo.

downstairs adj. & adv. 楼下的 lóuxià de. — n. 楼下 lóuxià.

downtown n. & adj. 闹区 nàoqū, 商业区 shāngyèqū.

downward adj. & adv. 向下的 xiàngxià de, 下降的 xiàjiàng de.

dowry n. 嫁妆 jiàzhuāng.

doze n. & v. 小睡 xiǎoshuì, 打瞌睡 dǎkēshuì.

dozen n. 一打 yì dá / yì dǎ.

drab n. & adj. ①单调 dāndiào (dull). ②土褐色 tǔhèsè / tǔhésè 〈color〉.

draft n. ①草稿 cǎogǎo (rough version). ②汇票 huìpiào 〈bank〉. ~ *beer* 扎啤 zhāpí / 生啤酒 shēngpíjiǔ. — v. ①草拟 cǎonǐ, 起草 qǐcǎo, 画草图 huà cǎotú (outline). ②征募 zhēngmù (conscript).

drag v. 拖曳 tuōyè / tuōyì, 拉拉 lālā (pull along). ~ *out* 拖延 tuōyán.

dragon n. 龙 lóng.

dragonfly n. 蜻蜓 qīngtíng.

drain v. ①排干 páigān, 排水 páishuǐ (dry out). ②消耗 xiāohào (consume). — n. ①排水管 páishuǐguǎn (pipe), 下水道 xiàshuǐdào (ditch). ②消耗 xiāohào (use up).

drama n. 戏剧 xìjù (play), 剧本 jùběn (script).

drastic adj. 猛烈的 měngliè de, 彻底的 chèdǐ de.

draw v. ①拉 lā, 曳 yè / yì (drag). ②吸引 xīyǐn (attract). ③画 huà, 描绘 miáohuì 〈art〉.

drawback n. 缺点 quēdiǎn.

drawer n. 抽屉 chōuti.

drawing n. 绘图 huìtú 〈art〉, 制图 zhìtú 〈technical〉.

dread n. & v. 畏惧 wèijù, 害怕 hàipà.

dreadful adj. ①可怕的 kěpà de (terrible). ②令人讨厌的 lìng rén tǎoyàn de (unpleasant).

dream n. 梦 mèng. — v. 做梦 zuòmèng, 梦想 mèngxiǎng.

dreary adj. 阴郁的 yīnyù de (depressing), 沉闷的 chénmèn de (dull).

dress n. 服装 fúzhuāng, 衣服 yīfu. — v. 穿衣服 chuān yīfu (put clothes on). **~ up** 打扮 dǎbàn.

dressing n. ①绷带 bēngdài (bandage). ②调味料 tiáowèiliào, 调味酱 tiáowèijiàng (topping).

dressmaker n. 裁缝师 cáiféngshī.

dribble v. ①滴下 dīxia (drip). 垂涎 chuíxián (drool). ②运球 yùnqiú 〈ball〉.

drier n. ①烘干机 hōnggānjī 〈machine〉. ②干燥剂 gānzàojì 〈chemical〉.

drift n. ①吹积 chuījī (accumulation). ②大意 dàyì (gist).

drill n. ①练习 liànxí, 训练 xùnliàn (exercise). ②钻子 zuànzi 〈tool〉. — v. ①练习 liànxí, 训练 xùnliàn (train). ②钻 zuān, 钻孔 zuānkǒng

(penetrate).

drink v. ①喝 hē, 饮 yǐn (swallow). ②饮酒 yǐnjiǔ 〈alcohol〉. — n. ①饮料 yǐnliào (beverage). ②酒 jiǔ (alcoholic drinks).

drip v. 滴落 dīluò, 滴下 dīxia.

drive v. ①开车 kāichē (operate a vehicle). ②迫使 pòshǐ, 驱使 qūshǐ (compel). ③驱逐 qūzhú, 赶 gǎn (force to go away). — n. ①驾车出游 jiàchē chūyóu, 开车兜风 kāichē dōufēng (journey). ②精力 jīnglì, 力量 lìliang (energy).

driver n. 驾驶 jiàshǐ.
~'s license 驾驶执照 jiàshǐ zhízhào.

drizzle v. 下毛毛雨 xià máomaoyǔ. — n. 毛毛雨 máomaoyǔ.

drone n. ①雄蜂 xióngfēng (male bee). ②嗡嗡声 wēngwēngshēng 〈sound〉.

droop v. ①低垂 dīchuí (bend). ②枯萎 kūwěi / kūwēi 〈flowers〉.

drop n. ①滴 dī, 水滴 shuǐdī, 雨滴 yǔdī (drip). ②下降 xiàjiàng, 落下 luòxia (fall). — v. ①滴下 dīxia, 落下 luòxia (fall). ②下降 xiàjiàng, 下跌 xiàdiē / xiàdié (lower). ③开除 kāichú, 退学 tuìxué (eliminate). ④放弃 fàngqì, 抛弃 pāoqì (abandon).

drought n. 旱灾 hànzāi.

drown v. ①溺毙 nìbì, 淹死 yānsǐ (die in water). ②泛滥 fànlàn (flood). ③淹没 yānmò, 盖过 gàiguò (be louder than).

drowsy adj. 想睡的 xiǎng shuì de, 昏昏欲睡的 hūnhūn-yùshuì de.

drudge n. 做苦工者 zuò

D

kǔgōng zhě. — v. 做苦工 zuò kǔgōng.

drug n. ①药物 yàowù, 药 yào (medicine). ②麻醉药 mázuìyào (narcotic).

druggie n. 毒瘾者 dúyǐnzhě.

drugstore n. 药房 yàofáng (pharmacy), 杂货店 záhuòdiàn (variety store).

drum n. 鼓 gǔ. — v. 击鼓 jī gǔ / jí gǔ, 打鼓 dǎgǔ.

drumbeat n. 鼓声 gǔshēng.

drunk adj. 醉的 zuì de, 酒醉 的 jiǔzuì de (tipsy). — n. 酒醉 者 jiǔzuìzhě.

drunkard n. 醉汉 zuìhàn, 酒 鬼 jiǔguǐ.

drunken adj. 酒醉的 jiǔzuì de.

dry adj. ①干的 gān de, 干燥 的 gānzào de (without water). ②无甜味的 wú tiánwèi de (not sweet). ③枯燥的 kūzào de (boring). — v. 使干燥 shǐ gānzào, 弄干 nònggān.

dual adj. 二重的 èrchóng de, 双重的 shuāngchóng de.

dub v. ①取绰号 qǔ chuòhào (give a nickname) ②重新配音 chóngxīn pèiyīn (re-record).

dubious adj. ①怀疑的 huáiyí de (doubtful). ②可疑的 kěyí de (suspect).

duchess n. 公爵夫人 gōngjué fūrén.

duck n. 鸭子 yāzi.

duct n. 输送管 shūsòngguǎn, 导管 dǎoguǎn.

dud n. & adj. 不中用 bù-zhōngyòng, 无用 wúyòng.

due adj. ①应付给的 yīng fùgěi de (owing). ②适当的 shìdàng de (proper). ③到期的 dàoqī de / dàoqí de (expired). — n. ①应得物 yīngdéwù (deserts).

②(pl.) 费用 fèiyòng, 应付款 yīngfùkuǎn (fees).

duel n. & v. 决斗 juédòu.

duet n. 二重奏 èrchóngzòu 〈music〉.

duke n. 公爵 gōngjué.

dull adj. ①晦暗的 huǐàn de (dim). ②阴沉的 yīnchén de (cloudy). ③迟钝的 chídùn de, 笨的 bèn de (stupid). ④钝的 dùn de, 不锐利的 bú ruìlì de (unsharpened). ⑤乏味的 fáwèi de, 无聊的 wúliáo de (boring). — v. 变钝 biàndùn, 使迟钝 shǐ chídùn.

dumb adj. ①哑的 yǎ de (unable to speak). ②沉默的 chénmò de, 无言的 wúyán de (silent). ③笨的 bèn de (stupid).

dumbfound v. 使哑然 shǐ yǎrán, 使惊愕 shǐ jīng'è.

dummy n. ①人像模型 rénxiàng móxíng 〈figure〉. ②笨 蛋 bèndàn (idiot).

dump v. ①倾倒 qīngdào, 丢弃 diūqì (discard). ②倾销 qīngxiāo (sell at low prices).

dumpling n. 蒸煮面团 zhēngzhǔ miàntuán 〈dough〉, 水饺 shuǐjiǎo 〈Chinese food〉.

dumpy adj. ①矮胖的 ǎipàng de (short and fat). ②破烂肮脏 的 pòlàn āngzàng de (shabby and dingy).

dunce n. 迟钝者 chídùnzhě, 蠢材 chǔncái.

dune n. 沙丘 shāqiū.

dungeon n. 地牢 dìláo 〈prison〉.

dupe v. 欺骗 qīpiàn. — n. 受骗 者 shòupiànzhě.

duplicate adj. 复制的 fùzhì de (exactly like another). — n. 复制品 fùzhìpǐn, 副本 fùběn. — v. 复制 fùzhì, 复写 fùxiě

(copy exactly).

durable *adj.* 耐久的 nàijiǔ de, 耐用的 nàiyòng de.

duration *n.* 持续期间 chíxù qījiān / chíxù qījiān.

duress *n.* 强迫 qiǎngpò, 胁迫 xiépò (coercion).

during *prep.* 在……期间 zài ...qījiān / zài...qījiān.

dusk *n.* 黄昏 huánghūn, 傍晚 bàngwǎn / bāngwǎn. — *adj.* 昏暗的 hūn'àn de.

dusky *adj.* 微暗的 wēi'àn de / wéi'àn de, 略黑的 lüèhēi de (darkish).

dust *n.* 灰尘 huīchén. — *v.* ①拂去灰尘 fúqù huīchén (remove dust from). ②撒粉于 sǎfěn yú (sprinkle powder on).

dusty *adj.* 多灰尘的 duō huīchén de (covered with dust).

Dutch *adj.* 荷兰的 Hélán de. **go ~** 各付各的 gè fù gè de. — *n.* 荷兰人 Hélánrén.

duty *n.* ①义务 yìwù, 责任 zérèn (responsibility). ②职责 zhízé (task). ③税 shuì (tax).

DVD 数字式多功能光盘 shùzìshì duō gōngnéng guāngpán, 数码影碟 shùmǎ yǐngdié / 数位多功能影音光碟 shùwèi duō gōngnéng yǐngyīn guāngdié (Digital Versatile Disc).

dwarf *n.* 侏儒 zhūrú (midget). — *adj.* 矮小的 ǎixiǎo de.

dwell *v.* 居住 jūzhù. **~ on** 细想 xìxiǎng, 详述 xiángshù.

dwelling *n.* 住宅 zhùzhái (house).

dwindle *v.* 减少 jiǎnshǎo, 缩减 suōjiǎn.

dye *n.* 染料 rǎnliào. — *v.* 染 rǎn, 染色 rǎnsè.

dynamic *adj.* ①动力的 dònglì de ⟨physics⟩. ②精力充沛的 jīnglì chōngpèi de, 有动力的 yǒu dònglì de (energetic).

dynamite *n.* 炸药 zhàyào.

dynasty *n.* 朝代 cháodài, 王朝 wángcháo.

dysentery *n.* 痢疾 lìjí.

E

each *adj.* 每 měi, 每个 měi ge. — *pron.* 各自 gèzì, 每个 měi ge.

eager *adj.* ①热切的 rèqiè de (enthusiastic). ②渴望的 kěwàng de (hopeful).

eagle *n.* 鹰 yīng.

ear *n.* ①耳 ěr, 耳朵 ěrduo ⟨organ⟩. ②听觉 tīngjué, 听力 tīnglì (hearing).

earl *n.* 伯爵 bójué.

Earl Grey tea 伯爵茶 Bójuéchá.

early *adv.* 早 zǎo. — *adj.* 早 zǎo (before the expected time), 初期的 chūqī de / chúqí de ⟨a period of time⟩.

earn *v.* ①赚 zhuàn (gain). ②博得 bódé, 获得 huòdé (win).

earnest *adj.* ①认真的

rènzhēn de (conscientious).
②诚挚的 chéngzhì de (honest).

earnings n. 赚的钱 zhuàn de qián, 收入 shōurù (income), 工资 gōngzī (wages).

earphone n. 耳机 ěrjī.

earring n. 耳环 ěrhuán.

earth n. ① E= 地球 dìqiú 〈planet〉. ②陆地 lùdì, 大地 dàdì 〈land〉. ③泥土 nítǔ 〈soil〉.

earthenware n. 陶器 táoqì.

earthquake n. 地震 dìzhèn.

earthworm n. 蚯蚓 qiūyǐn.

ease n. ①舒适 shūshì, 安逸 ānyì 〈comfort〉. ②轻易 qīngyì, 不费力 bú fèilì 〈easiness〉. *at ~* 自在 zìzài. *with ~* 不费力 bú fèilì. — v. ①减轻 jiǎnqīng, 减缓 jiǎnhuǎn (lessen). ②放松 fàngsōng (relax). ③使舒适 shǐ shūshì, 使安心 shǐ ānxīn (put at ease).

easel n. 画架 huàjià.

easily adv. 容易地 róngyì de.

east n. ①东 dōng 〈direction〉. ②东方 dōngfāng (eastern region). ③东边 dōngbian, 东部 dōngbù (eastern part). *Far E ~* 远东 Yuǎndōng. *Middle E ~* 中东 Zhōngdōng. — adv. 东 dōng, 向东 xiàng dōng, 往东 wǎng dōng. — adj. ①东 dōng de (of the east). ②东方的 dōngfāng de (of the eastern region). ③东部的 dōngbù de (of the eastern part).

Easter n. 复活节 Fùhuójié.

eastern adj. 东方的 dōngfāng de. *~ hemisphere* 东半球 dōngbànqiú.

eastward adj. & adv. 向东的 xiàng dōng de.

easy adj. ①容易的 róngyì de (effortless). ②轻松的 qīngsōng de, 舒服的 shūfu de (comfortable). *take it ~* 放轻松 fàng qīngsōng.

easygoing adj. 随和的 suíhe de.

eat v. 吃 chī.

eatable adj. 可吃的 kě chī de.

eaves n. 屋檐 wūyán.

eavesdrop v. 偷听 tōutīng.

ebb n. & v. ①退潮 tuìcháo (flow back). ②衰退 shuāituì (weaken).

ebony n. 乌木 wūmù, 黑檀 hēitán 〈plant〉. — adj. 乌黑的 wūhēi de 〈color〉.

eccentric adj. 反常的 fǎncháng de (unusual), 古怪的 gǔguài de (strange). — n. 古怪的人 gǔguài de rén 〈person〉.

echo n. 回声 huíshēng, 回音 huíyīn. — v. 发出回音 fāchū huíyīn (resound).

eclipse n. ①日蚀 rìshí 〈solar〉, 月蚀 yuèshí 〈lunar〉. ②瑕掩 xiáyǎn 〈fame〉.

eco-awareness n. 环保意识 huánbǎo yìshí / huánbǎo yìshí.

eco-car n. 环保汽车 huánbǎo qìchē.

ecology n. ①生态 shēngtài (ecosystem). ②生态学 shēngtàixué 〈science〉.

economic adj. ①经济的 jīngjì de (having to do with economy). ②经济学的 jīngjìxué de (of economics).

economical adj. 经济的 jīngjì de, 俭约的 jiǎnyuē de.

economics n. 经济学 jīngjìxué.

economize v. 节约 jiéyuē.

economy n. 经济 jīngjì (economic affairs). *~ class* 经济舱 jīngjìcāng.

ecstasy *n.* ①狂喜 kuángxǐ (joy). ②E~ 〈一种〉迷幻药 (yì zhǒng) míhuànyào (an illegal drug).

eddy *n.* 漩涡 xuánwō (whirlpool). — *v.* 回旋 huíxuán.

edge *n.* ①边缘 biānyuán (periphery). ②边境 biānjìng (boundary). ③刀刃 dāorèn (blade). — *v.* ①加边 jiābiān (fringe). ②侧进 cèjìn (side).

edible *adj.* 可食的 kě shí de.

edit *v.* 编辑 biānjí, 校订 jiàodìng.

edition *n.* 版本 bǎnběn.

editor *n.* 编者 biānzhě, 编辑 biānjí.

editorial *adj.* 编辑的 biānjí de. — *n.* 社论 shèlùn.

educate *v.* 教育 jiàoyù, 教 jiāo.

education *n.* 教育 jiàoyù.

eel *n.* 鳗鱼 mányú, 鳝鱼 shànyú.

eerie, eery *adj.* 阴森可怕的 yīnsēn kěpà de.

effect *n.* ①影响 yǐngxiǎng, 效果 xiàoguǒ (result). ②印象 yìnxiàng, 感觉 gǎnjué (impression).

effective *adj.* 有效的 yǒuxiào de (serves its purpose), 生效的 shēngxiào de (goes into effect).

effeminate *adj.* 娘娘腔的 niángniángqiāng de.

effervesce *v.* 冒泡沫 mào pàomò.

efficiency *n.* 效率 xiàolǜ.

efficient *adj.* 有效率的 yǒu xiàolǜ de.

effigy *n.* 肖像 xiàoxiàng.

effort *n.* ①努力 nǔlì (hard work). ②成果 chéngguǒ

(accomplishment).

e.g. 例如 lìrú.

egg *n.* 蛋 dàn.

egghead *n.* 书呆子 shūdāizi.

eggplant *n.* 茄子 qiézi.

eggshell *n.* 蛋壳 dànké.

ego *n.* 自我 zìwǒ.

egocentric *adj.* 自我中心的 zìwǒ zhōngxīn de, 利己主义的 lìjǐ zhǔyì de.

egoism *n.* 自我主义 zìwǒ zhǔyì, 利己主义 lìjǐ zhǔyì.

egotism *n.* 自负 zìfù, 自我吹嘘 zìwǒ chuīxū.

eight *n. & adj.* 八 bā.

eighteen *n. & adj.* 十八 shíbā.

eighteenth *n. & adj.* 第十八 dì-shíbā.

eighth *n. & adj.* 第八 dì-bā.

eightieth *n. & adj.* 第八十 dì-bāshí.

eighty *n. & adj.* 八十 bāshí.

either *adj & pron.* 二者之一的 èr zhě zhī yī de (one of two choices), 任一的 rènyī de (any). — *conj.* ~ …*or*… 不是… …就是… búshì...jiùshì.... — *adv.* 也（不）yě (bù).

eject *v.* ①逐出 zhúchū, 放逐 fàngzhú (exile). ②发射 fāshè, 放出 fàngchū (discharge). ③退出 tuìchū 〈disk, tape〉.

elaborate *adj.* 精心制造的 jīngxīn zhìzào de (complicated). — *v.* 详尽说明 xiángjìn shuōmíng.

elapse *v.* 逝去 shìqù.

elastic *adj.* 有弹性的 yǒu tánxìng de (flexible). — *n.* 松紧带 sōngjǐndài, 橡皮筋 xiàngpíjīn.

elbow *n.* 手肘 shǒuzhǒu 〈arm〉.

elder *adj.* 年长的 niánzhǎng de, 年纪较大的 niánjì jiào dà de.

E

— n. 年长者 niánzhǎngzhě, 前辈 qiánbèi.

eldest adj. 最年长的 zuì niánzhǎng de.

elect v. ①选举 xuǎnjǔ, 选 xuǎn (vote for). ②选择 xuǎnzé (choose).

election n. 选举 xuǎnjǔ.

elector n. 选举人 xuǎnjǔrén.

electorate n. 选民 xuǎnmín 〈people〉, 选举团 xuǎnjǔtuán 〈committee〉.

electric adj. 电的 diàn de. ~ *power* 电力 diànlì.

electrical adj. 电的 diàn de.

electricity n. 电 diàn, 电流 diànliú.

electrocute v. ①施以电刑 shī yǐ diànxíng 〈put to death〉. ②触电致死 chùdiàn zhìsǐ 〈kill accidentally〉.

electrolysis n. 电解 diànjiě.

electromagnet n. 电磁石 diàncíshí.

electron n. 电子 diànzǐ.

electronic adj. 电子的 diànzǐ de. ~ *publishing* 电子出版 diànzǐ chūbǎn.
~ *shopping* 电子购物 diànzǐ gòuwù.
~ *transfer* 电子转账 diànzǐ zhuǎnzhàng.

electronics n. ①电子工业 diànzǐ gōngyè 〈industry〉. ②电子工程学 diànzǐ gōngchéngxué (the study of electronics).

electroplate n. & v. 电镀 diàndù.

electrotherapy n. 电疗 diànliáo.

elegant adj. 优雅的 yōuyǎ de, 高雅的 gāoyǎ de.

elegy n. 挽歌 wǎngē.

element n. ①要素 yàosù, 成分 chéngfèn (part). ②元素 yuánsù (substance).

elementary adj. 初步的 chūbù de (beginning level), 基本的 jīběn de (basic). ~ *school* 小学 xiǎoxué.

elephant n. 象 xiàng.

elevate v. 举起 jǔqǐ, 提高 tígāo.

elevation n. ①上升 shàngshēng, 提高 tígāo (act of elevating). ②高度 gāodù (height), 海拔 hǎibá (height above sea level).

elevator n. 电梯 diàntī 〈passenger〉, 升降机 shēngjiàngjī 〈freight〉.

eleven n. & adj. 十一 shíyī.

eleventh n. & adj. 第十一 dì-shíyī.

elicit v. 诱出 yòuchū, 引出 yǐnchu.

eligible adj. 合格的 hégé de.

eliminate v. ①除去 chúqù, 消除 xiāochú (remove). ②消灭 xiāomiè (wipe out), 干掉 gàndiào (kill).

elite n. 精英 jīngyīng, 杰出人物 jiéchū rénwù.

elk n. 麋鹿 mílù.

ellipse n. 椭圆 tuǒyuán 〈mathematics〉.

elm n. 榆树 yúshù.

elongate v. 延长 yáncháng, 延伸 yánshēn.

elope v. 私奔 sībēn.

eloquent adj. 雄辩的 xióngbiàn de, 口若悬河的 kǒuruòxuánhé de.

El Niño n. 厄尔尼诺现象 È'ěrnínuò xiànxiàng / 圣婴现象 shèngyīng xiànxiàng.

else adj. 别的 bié de, 其他的

qítā de. — *adv.* ①此外 cǐwài (in addition). ②否则 fǒuzé (otherwise).

elsewhere *adv.* 在别处 zài biéchù.

elude *v.* 逃避 táobì, 躲避 duǒbì (escape from).

emaciated *adj.* 消瘦的 xiāoshòu de (thin), 憔悴的 qiáocuì de (feeble).

e-mail *n.* 电子信函 diànzǐ xìnhán / 电子邮件 diànzǐ yóujiàn (electronic mail).

emancipate *v.* 解放 jiěfàng.

embalm *v.* 使尸体防腐 shǐ shītǐ fángfǔ.

embargo *n.* & *v.* 禁运 jìnyùn.

embark *v.* ①乘船 chéngchuán (board a ship). ②着手 zhuóshǒu (start).

embarrass *v.* 使困窘 shǐ kùnjiǒng, 使尴尬 shǐ gāngà.

embarrassing *adj.* 困窘的 kùnjiǒng de, 尴尬的 gāngà de.

embarrassment *n.* 困窘 kùnjiǒng, 尴尬 gāngà.

embassy *n.* 大使馆 dàshǐguǎn.

embellish *v.* ①装饰 zhuāngshì (adorn), 美化 měihuà (beautify).

ember *n.* 余烬 yújìn.

embezzle *v.* 盗用 dàoyòng, 侵吞 qīntūn.

emblem *n.* ①象征 xiàngzhēng (symbol). ②纹章 wénzhāng, 徽章 huīzhāng (badge).

embody *v.* 具体表现 jùtǐ biǎoxiàn (exemplify), 使具体化 shǐ jùtǐhuà (make physical).

embrace *v.* ①拥抱 yōngbào / yǒngbào (hold). ②接受

jiēshòu (accept). ③包含 bāohán (include). — *n.* 拥抱 yōngbào / yǒngbào.

embroider *v.* 刺绣 cìxiù.

embryo *n.* ①胚胎 pēitāi ⟨animals⟩. ②胚芽 pēiyá ⟨plants⟩.

emend *v.* 校订 jiàodìng, 修正 xiūzhèng.

emerald *n.* ①翡翠 fěicuì ⟨stone⟩. ②翠绿色 cuìlǜsè ⟨color⟩.

emerge *v.* ①出现 chūxiàn, 露出 lòuchū (come out). ②显露 xiǎnlù (become known).

emergency *n.* 紧急事件 jǐnjí shìjiàn. ~ *room* 急诊室 jízhěnshì.

emigrant *n.* 移民 yímín.

emigrate *v.* 移民 yímín.

eminent *adj.* ①闻名的 wénmíng de (famous). ②显著的 xiǎnzhù de (noticeable). ③优良的 yōuliáng de (excellent).

emission *n.* ①放射物 fàngshèwù (particle). ②放射 fàngshè (release).

emit *v.* 放射 fàngshè.

emotion *n.* 情绪 qíngxù, 感情 gǎnqíng.

emotional *adj.* ①感动的 gǎndòng de (moved). ②情绪的 qíngxù de (prone to overreaction).

emperor *n.* 皇帝 huángdì.

emphasis *n.* ①强调 qiángdiào (stress). ②加重语气 jiāzhòng yǔqì ⟨pronunciation⟩.

emphasize *v.* ①强调 qiángdiào (stress). ②重读 zhòngdú ⟨pronunciation⟩.

emphatic *adj.* ①强调的 qiángdiào de (using emphasis). ②坚持的 jiānchí de (insistent).

E

empire n. 帝国 dìguó.

empirical adj. ①凭经验的 píng jīngyàn de (based in experience). ②经验主义的 jīngyàn zhǔyì de (provable through experimentation).

employ v. ①雇用 gùyòng (hire). ②使用 shǐyòng (make use of).

employee n. 受雇者 shòugùzhě, 雇员 gùyuán.

employer n. 雇主 gùzhǔ.

employment n. ①职业 zhíyè (occupation). ②受雇 shòugù, 就业 jiùyè (the fact of being hired).

empress n. 皇后 huánghòu, 女皇 nǚhuáng.

empty adj. 空的 kōng de. — v. 变空 biàn kōng.

emulate v. ①努力赶上 nǔlì gǎnshang (try to do as well as). ②仿效 fǎngxiào (admire and seek to copy).

emulsion n. 乳状液 rǔzhuàngyè, 乳剂 rǔjì.

enable v. 使能够 shǐ nénggòu.

enamel n. 瓷釉 cíyòu, 珐琅 fàláng. — v. 涂瓷釉 tú cíyòu.

enchant v. ①使迷醉 shǐ mízuì (lure). ②施魔法于 shī mófǎ yú (use magic on).

encircle v. 环绕 huánrào, 包围 bāowéi.

enclose v. ①围起 wéiqǐ (surround). ②附寄 fùjì (put inside).

encore interj. 再表演一次 zài biǎoyǎn yí cì.

encounter n. & v. ①邂逅 xièhòu, 碰到 pèngdào (meeting unexpectedly). ②遭遇 zāoyù (being faced by).

encourage v. 鼓励 gǔlì.

encouragement n. 鼓励 gǔlì.

encroach v. 侵占 qīnzhàn.

encyclopedia n. 百科全书 bǎikē quánshū.

end n. ①尽头 jìntóu, 末端 mòduān (last part). ②结局 jiéjú, 结束 jiéshù (cessation). ③目的 mùdì (aim). ④死亡 sǐwáng (death). — v. 结束 jiéshù, 终止 zhōngzhǐ.

endanger v. 使危险 shǐ wēixiǎn / shǐ wéixiǎn, 危及 wēijí / wéijí.

endear v. 使受钟爱 shǐ shòu zhōng'ài.

endeavor n. & v. 努力 nǔlì, 尽力 jìnlì.

endemic adj. 地方性的 dìfāngxìng de (native). — n. 地方性疾病 dìfāngxìng jíbìng (disease).

ending n. 终止 zhōngzhǐ, 结局 jiéjú.

endless adj. 无尽的 wújìn de.

endorse v. ①认可 rènkě, 赞同 zàntóng (approve). ②签署 qiānshǔ / qiānshù (sign).

endow v. 捐赠 juānzèng (donate).

endurance n. ①忍耐 rěnnài (forbearance). ②忍受力 rěnshòulì (tolerance).

endure v. ①忍耐 rěnnài (bear), 忍受 rěnshòu (tolerate).

enemy n. 敌人 dírén.

energetic adj. ①精力充沛的 jīnglì chōngpèi de (high-spirited). ②积极的 jījí de (active).

energy n. ①精力 jīnglì, 活力 huólì (liveliness). ②能量 néngliàng (power).

enforce v. ①执行 zhíxíng

(carry out). ②强迫 qiǎngpò, 强制 qiǎngzhì / qiǎngzhì (force). ③增强 zēngqiáng (reinforce).

engage v. ①雇用 gùyòng (employ). ②忙于 máng yú (occupy). ③允诺 yǔnnuò, 保证 bǎozhèng (promise). ④与……交战 yǔ...jiāozhàn (fight with).

engaged adj. ①已订婚的 yǐ dìnghūn de (betrothed). ②被占用的 bèi zhànyòng de (being used). ③忙碌的 mánglù de (busy).

engagement n. ①订婚 dìnghūn (betrothal). ②约会 yuēhuì (appointment). ③交战 jiāozhàn (battle).

engine n. 引擎 yǐnqíng.

engineer n. 工程师 gōngchéngshī.

engineering n. 工程学 gōngchéngxué.

English n. & adj. ①英国人 Yīngguórén 〈people〉. ②英语 Yīngyǔ, 英文 Yīngwén 〈language〉.

engrave v. 雕刻 diāokè.

engross v. 使全神贯注 shǐ quánshén-guànzhù (occupy).

engulf v. 吞噬 tūnshì, 吞入 tūnrù.

enigma n. 谜 mí.

enjoy v. 享受 xiǎngshòu, 欣赏 xīnshǎng.

enlarge v. 扩大 kuòdà.

enlighten v. 启发 qǐfā, 开导 kāidǎo (instruct).

enlist v. ①使入伍 shǐ rùwǔ, 征募 zhēngmù (conscript). ②获得 huòdé, 取得 qǔdé (obtain).

enormous adj. 极大的 jí dà de, 巨大的 jùdà de.

enough adj. & adv. 足够的 zúgòu de. — interj. 够了！

Gòu le!

enquire v. 询问 xúnwèn.

enrich v. ①使充实 shǐ chōngshí (improve). ②使富足 shǐ fùzú (make rich).

enroll v. 登记 dēngjì.

ensign n. ①旗 qí (flag). ②海军少尉 hǎijūn shàowèi 〈navy〉.

enslave v. 奴役 núyì.

ensue v. 随后发生 suíhòu fāshēng.

ensure v. 保证 bǎozhèng, 确保 quèbǎo.

entail v. 使必须 shǐ bìxū (necessitate).

entangle v. 使纠缠 shǐ jiūchán, 牵连 qiānlián.

enter v. ①进入 jìnrù (come in). ②参加 cānjiā (engage in).

enterprise n. ①企业 qǐyè / qìyè, 事业 shìyè (business). ②进取心 jìnqǔxīn (willingness to do difficult things).

entertain v. ①娱乐 yúlè (amuse). ②招待 zhāodài (give a party).

entertainment n. 娱乐 yúlè.

enthrall v. 迷住 mízhù, 迷惑 míhuò.

enthusiasm n. 热心 rèxīn, 热衷 rèzhōng.

enthusiastic adj. 热心的 rèxīn de, 热衷的 rèzhōng de.

entice v. 诱惑 yòuhuò, 怂恿 sǒngyǒng.

entire adj. 整个的 zhěngge de, 全部的 quánbù de.

entirely adv. 全部地 quánbù de, 完全地 wánquán de (completely).

entitle v. ①定名为 dìngmíng wéi (name). ②使有权利 shǐ yǒu quánlì (empower).

entity n. 实体 shítǐ.

E

entrails n. 内脏 nèizàng.

entrance n. ①入口 rùkǒu (place where one enters), 门口 ménkǒu (doorway). ②进入 jìnrù (the act of entering).

entreat v. 恳求 kěnqiú.

entrenched adj. 确立的 quèlì de, 根深蒂固的 gēnshēn-dìgù de (firmly established).

entrepreneur n. 企业家 qǐyèjiā / qìyèjiā.

entrust v. 委托 wěituō, 托付 tuōfù.

entry n. ①进入 jìnrù (entering), 入口 rùkǒu (entrance). ②条目 tiáomù (item). ③参赛者 cānsàizhě (competitor).

enumerate v. ①列举 lièjǔ (list one by one). ②数 shǔ (count).

enunciate v. ①发音 fāyīn (pronounce). ②很清楚地表达 hěn qīngchu de biǎodá (express clearly).

envelop v. 包围 bāowéi (surround), 笼罩 lǒngzhào / lóngzhào (permeate).

envelope n. 信封 xìnfēng.

enviable adj. 令人羡慕的 lìng rén xiànmù de.

envious adj. 羡慕的 xiànmù de.

environment n. 环境 huánjìng.

environmental adj. ①环境的 huánjìng de (having to do with the environment). ②环保的 huánbǎo de (environmentalist).

environmentalism n. 环保主义 huánbǎo zhǔyì (theory), 环保意识 huánbǎo yìshí / huánbǎo yìshì (awareness).

envisage v. 想象 xiǎngxiàng, 设想 shèxiǎng (imagine).

envoy n. 使者 shǐzhě, 特使

特使 tèshǐ, 公使 gōngshǐ.

envy n. & v. 羡慕 xiànmù.

enzyme n. 酵素 jiàosù / xiàosù.

epic n. 史诗 shǐshī.

epidemic n. 传染病 chuánrǎnbìng. — adj. 流行性的 liúxíngxìng de.

epilepsy n. 癫痫症 diānxiánzhèng.

epilogue n. ①结尾 jiéwěi (a literary work). ②收场白 shōuchǎngbái (a play).

episode n. 插曲 chāqǔ.

epitaph n. 墓志铭 mùzhìmíng.

epithet n. 称号 chēnghào.

epitome n. 缩影 suōyǐng.

epoch n. 纪元 jìyuán, 时代 shídài.

EQ 情绪智商 qíngxù zhìshāng / 情绪商数 qíngxù shāngshù (emotional quotient).

equal adj. 相等的 xiāngděng de, 平等的 píngděng de. — n. 对手 duìshǒu. — v. 等于 děngyú.

equality n. 相等 xiāngděng, 平等 píngděng.

equally adv. 相等地 xiāngděng de, 同样地 tóngyàng de.

equate v. 视为相等 shìwéi xiāngděng.

equation n. 等式 děngshì, 方程式 fāngchéngshì.

equator n. 赤道 chìdào.

equestrian adj. 骑马的 qímǎ de.

equilibrium n. 平衡 pínghéng, 均衡 jūnhéng.

equinox n. 春分 chūnfēn (spring), 秋分 qiūfēn (autumn).

equip v. 装备 zhuāngbèi.

equipment n. 设备 shèbèi, 装备 zhuāngbèi.

equity n. 公平 gōngpíng, 公正 gōngzhèng.

equivalent adj. 同等的 tóngděng de.

equivocal adj. 模棱两可的 móléng-liǎngkě de.

ER 急诊室 jízhěnshì (emergency room).

era n. 时代 shídài, 纪元 jìyuán.

eradicate v. 根除 gēnchú, 消灭 xiāomiè.

erase v. 擦掉 cādiào, 抹去 mǒqù.

eraser n. 橡皮擦 xiàngpícā.

erect adj. 直立的 zhílì de. — v. ①建筑 jiànzhù / jiànzhú, 建立 jiànlì (build).②竖立 shùlì (stand upright).

erode v. 侵蚀 qīnshí, 腐蚀 fǔshí.

erotic adj. 性爱的 xìng'ài de, 情色的 qíngsè de.

err v. 犯错 fàncuò.

errand n. 差事 chāishì.

erratic adj. ①乖僻的 guāipì de, 古怪的 gǔguài de (eccentric). ②反复无常的 fǎnfù-wúcháng de (changeable without reason).

error n. ①错误 cuòwù, 过失 guòshī (mistake). ②误差 wùchā (mathematics).

erudite adj. 博学的 bóxué de.

erupt v. 爆发 bàofā.

escalate v. 逐渐上升 zhújiàn shàngshēng.

escalator n. 滚梯 gǔntī, 自动扶梯 zìdòng fútī / 电扶梯 diànfútī.

escapade n. 恣意作为 zìyì zuòwéi.

escape v. ①逃脱 táotuō, 逃走 táozǒu (flee). ②漏出 lòuchū (leak). ③逃避 táobì (avoid).

escarpment n. 悬崖 xuányá / xuányái, 绝壁 juébì.

escort n. ①护花使者 hùhuā shǐzhě ⟨date⟩.②护送者 hùsòngzhě (guard). ③护卫队 hùwèiduì (entourage). — v. 护送 hùsòng.

Eskimo n. 爱斯基摩人 Àisījīmórén.

esophagus n. 食道 shídào.

esoteric adj. 奥秘的 àomì de.

especially adv. 尤其是 yóuqí shì.

espionage n. 间谍活动 jiàndié huódòng.

espresso n. 浓缩咖啡 nóngsuō kāfēi.

essay n. 文章 wénzhāng.

essence n. 本质 běnzhì / běnzhí (nature), 精髓 jīngsuǐ (key part).

essential adj. ①必要的 bìyào de (necessary). ②本质的 běnzhì de / běnzhí de (basic).

establish v. ①建立 jiànlì, 设立 shèlì (set up). ②确立 quèlì, 确定 quèdìng (confirm).

establishment n. ①建立 jiànlì (creation). ②组织 zǔzhī, 机构 jīgòu (organization).

estate n. ①房地产 fángdìchǎn (real estate). ②财产 cáichǎn (belongings). ③遗产 yíchǎn (inheritance).

esteem v. 尊敬 zūnjìng, 尊重 zūnzhòng (respect). — n. 尊重 zūnzhòng, 尊敬 zūnjìng.

estimate n. & v. 估计 gūjì, 评估 pínggū.

estuary n. 入海口 rùhǎikǒu.

et cetera adv. 等等 děngděng (etc.).

etch v. 蚀刻 shíkè.

eternal adj. 永恒的 yǒnghéng

E

de, 永远的 yǒngyuǎn de (lasting), 不变的 búbiàn de (unchanging).

eternity n. ①永恒 yǒnghéng (infinity). ②来生 láishēng (the afterlife).

ether n. 醚 mí.

ethical adj. 伦理的 lúnlǐ de (having to do with ethics), 道德 的 dàodé de (moral).

ethics n. 道德学 dàodéxué, 伦理学 lúnlǐxué.

ethnic adj. 种族的 zhǒngzú de, 人种的 rénzhǒng de.

etiquette n. 礼节 lǐjié, 礼仪 lǐyí.

etymology n. 语源 yǔyuán, 语源学 yǔyuánxué.

EU 欧盟 Ōuméng (European Union).

eucalyptus n. 桉树 ānshù / ànshù, 尤加利树 yóujiālìshù.

eunuch n. 太监 tàijiàn, 阉人 yānrén.

euphemism n. 委婉语 wěiwǎnyǔ.

Euro n. 欧元 Ōuyuán.

Europe n. 欧洲 Ōuzhōu.

European adj. 欧洲的 Ōuzhōu de. — n. 欧洲人 Ōuzhōurén.

euthanasia n. 慈悲杀人 cíbēi shārén, 尊严死 zūnyánsǐ / 安乐死 ānlèsǐ.

evacuate v. ①撤离 chèlí (withdraw from). ②疏散 shūsàn (remove from).

evade v. ①逃避 táobì (escape from), 躲避 duǒbì (hide from). ②规避 guībì (avoid).

evaluate v. 评价 píngjià, 估计 gūjì.

evangelic adj. 福音的 fúyīn de.

evangelist n. 传福音者 chuán fúyīn zhě.

evaporate v. 蒸发 zhēngfā.

eve n. 前夕 qiánxī / qiánxì.

even adj. ①平坦的 píngtǎn de (flat). ②均匀的 jūnyún de, 规律的 guīlǜ de (regular). ③相等的 xiāngděng de (equal). ④沉稳的 chénwěn de (calm). ⑤偶数的 ǒushù de (number). — v. ①使平坦 shǐ píngtǎn (flatten). ②使相等 shǐ xiāngděng (equalize). — adv. 甚至 shènzhì, 即使 jíshǐ, 连 lián. ~ if 就算是 jiùsuàn shì, 即使 jíshǐ. ~ so 虽然如此 suīrán rúcǐ.

evening n. 傍晚 bàngwǎn / bāngwǎn, 晚间 wǎnjiān.

event n. ①事件 shìjiàn (affair). ②项目 xiàngmù (sports).

eventual adj. 结果的 jiéguǒ de, 最后的 zuìhòu de.

eventually adv. 最后 zuìhòu, 终于 zhōngyú.

ever adv. ①曾经 céngjīng (once). ②始终 shǐzhōng, 从来 cónglái (at all times). ~ since 自从 zìcóng. for ~ 永远 yǒngyuǎn.

evergreen adj. 常绿的 chánglǜ de, 长青的 chángqīng de.

everlasting adj. 永远的 yǒngyuǎn de, 永恒的 yǒnghéng de.

evermore adv. 永久 yǒngjiǔ.

every adj. ①每 měi, 每一 měi yī (each). ②所有的 suǒyǒu de (all).

everybody pron. 每个人 měi ge rén.

everyday adj. 日常的 rìcháng de.

everything pron. 每件事物 měi jiàn shìwù.

everywhere *adv.* 到处 dàochù, 每个地方 měi ge dìfang.

evict *v.* 逐出 zhúchū (force out).

evidence *n.* 证据 zhèngjù (proof), 迹象 jìxiàng / jīxiàng (sign).

evident *adj.* 明显的 míngxiǎn de, 显然的 xiǎnrán de.

evidently *adv.* 显然地 xiǎnrán de.

evil *adj.* 邪恶的 xié'è de, 罪恶的 zuì'è de. — *n.* 邪恶 xié'è, 罪恶 zuì'è.

evocative *adj.* 唤起的 huànqǐ de.

evoke *v.* 唤起 huànqǐ, 引起 yǐnqǐ.

evolution *n.* ①进化 jìnhuà, 发展 fāzhǎn (development). ②进化论 jìnhuàlùn (theory of evolution).

evolve *v.* 进化 jìnhuà, 展开 zhǎnkāi.

ewe *n.* 母羊 mǔyáng.

exact *adj.* 正确的 zhèngquè de, 精确的 jīngquè de (precise). — *v.* 强行索取 qiángxíng suǒqǔ (press for).

exactly *adv.* ①正确地 zhèngquè de, 精确地 jīngquè de (precisely). ②正好 zhènghǎo, 刚好 gānghǎo (just).

exaggerate *v.* 夸张 kuāzhāng, 夸大 kuādà.

exam *n.* 考试 kǎoshì.

examination *n.* ①检查 jiǎnchá (an act of examining). ②考试 kǎoshì (test). ③审问 shěnwèn (questioning).

examine *v.* ①检查 jiǎnchá (look at closely). ②考试 kǎoshì (test). ③审问 shěnwèn (question).

examiner *n.* 主考者 zhǔkǎozhě, 考官 kǎoguān.

example *n.* ①例子 lìzi, 实例 shílì (instance). ②样本 yàngběn (sample). *for ~* 例如 lìrú, 比如 bǐrú, 譬如说 pìrú shuō, 比方 说 bǐfāng shuō.

exasperate *v.* 激怒 jīnù (annoy).

excavate *v.* 挖掘 wājué, 挖出 wāchū.

exceed *v.* 超过 chāoguò, 超出 chāochū.

excel *v.* ①擅长于 shàncháng yú (be good at). ②优于 yōuyú, 胜过 shèngguò (be better than).

excellence *n.* 杰出 jiéchū, 卓越 zhuóyuè.

excellent *adj.* 卓越的 zhuóyuè de, 极好的 jí hǎo de, 优秀的 yōuxiù de.

except *prep.* 除……之外 chú...zhīwài.

exception *n.* 例外 lìwài.

exceptional *adj.* 特别的 tèbié de, 突出的 tūchū de / túchū de.

excerpt *n.* 摘录 zhāilù.

excess *n.* 超过 chāoguò, 过度 guòdù. *in ~ of* 超过 chāoguò.

excessively *adv.* 过度 guòdù.

exchange *v.* 交换 jiāohuàn, 调换 diàohuàn. — *n.* ①交换 jiāohuàn (replacement). ②交易 jiāoyì (bargain). ③兑换 duìhuàn ⟨money⟩. ④交易所 jiāoyìsuǒ ⟨place⟩. *~ rate* 汇率 huìlǜ.

exchequer *n.* 国库 guókù.

excise *n.* 国产税 guóchǎnshuì ⟨tax⟩. — *v.* 割除 gēchú (cut out), 删除 shānchú (remove).

excite *v.* ①使兴奋 shǐ xīngfèn, 使激动 shǐ jīdòng (stimulate).

②引起 yǐnqǐ (incite).

excited adj. 兴奋的 xīngfèn de, 激动的 jīdòng de.

excitement n. 兴奋 xīngfèn, 刺激 cìjī.

exciting adj. 令人兴奋的 lìng rén xīngfèn de.

exclaim v. 呼喊 hūhǎn, 惊叫 jīngjiào.

exclamation n. 呼喊 hūhǎn, 惊叫 jīngjiào. ~ mark 惊叹号 jīngtànhào.

exclude v. ①排斥 páichì (discriminate against). ②拒绝 jùjué (reject). ③排除 páichú (remove).

exclusion n. ①排斥 páichì (discrimination). ②排除 páichú (removal).

exclusive adj. ①限制严格的 xiànzhì yángé de (limited). ②高级的 gāojí de (classy). ③排他性的 páitāxìng de (rejecting outsiders).

excommunicate v. 逐出教会 zhúchū jiàohuì.

excrement n. 排泄物 páixièwù, 粪便 fènbiàn.

excrete v. 排泄 páixiè.

excursion n. 远足 yuǎnzú, 短程旅行 duǎnchéng lǚxíng.

excuse v. ①原谅 yuánliàng (forgive). ②免责 miǎnzé, 免刑 miǎnxíng (absolve). — n. 借口 jièkǒu, 托辞 tuōcí.

execute v. ①执行 zhíxíng, 实施 shíshī (carry out). ②处决 chǔjué (put to death). ③使生效 shǐ shēngxiào (contract).

execution n. ①执行 zhíxíng, 实施 shíshī (carrying out). ②处死 chǔsǐ (putting to death). ③签章生效 qiānzhāng shēngxiào (contract).

executive adj. ①执行的

zhíxíng de, 实行的 shíxíng de (being executed). ②行政的 xíngzhèng de (administrative). — n. ①行政官 xíngzhèngguān (administrator). ②经理 jīnglǐ, 主管 zhǔguǎn (manager).

executor n. 遗嘱执行人 yízhǔ zhíxíngrén.

exemplify v. 举例说明 jǔlì shuōmíng, 作为实例 zuòwéi shílì.

exempt v. 免除 miǎnchú, 豁免 huòmiǎn. — adj. 被免除的 bèi miǎnchú de.

exercise n. ①运动 yùndòng (sport). ②练习 liànxí (practice). ③习题 xítí, 作业 zuòyè (homework). ④演习 yǎnxí (training). ⑤运用 yùnyòng (use). — v. ①运动 yùndòng (work out). ②训练 xùnliàn (train).

exert v. 运用 yùnyòng (use).

exhale v. 呼出 hūchū.

exhaust v. 用尽 yòngjìn, 耗尽 hàojìn (use up). — n. 废气 fèiqì ⟨gas⟩.

exhausted adj. 精疲力尽的 jīngpí-lìjìn de.

exhaustion n. ①疲惫不堪 píbèi-bùkān (tiredness). ②耗尽 hàojìn (using up).

exhibit v. ①展览 zhǎnlǎn, 陈列 chénliè (display). ②表现 biǎoxiàn, 显示 xiǎnshì (demonstrate). — n. 展览品 zhǎnlǎnpǐn.

exhibition n. ①展览 zhǎnlǎn (exhibit). ②展览会 zhǎnlǎnhuì (show). ③表现 biǎoxiàn (demonstration).

exhilarate v. 使高兴 shǐ gāoxìng, 使兴奋 shǐ xīngfèn.

exhort v. 力劝 lìquàn, 劝告

quàngào.

exile v. 放逐 fàngzhú. — n. ① 放逐 fàngzhú (being in exile). ② 被放逐者 bèi fàngzhú zhě (person who is exiled).

exist v. ① 存在 cúnzài (be). ② 生存 shēngcún (live).

existence n. ① 存在 cúnzài (being). ② 生存 shēngcún (living).

exit n. ① 出口 chūkǒu (way out). ② 离去 líqù (departure). ③ 退场 tuìchǎng ⟨theater⟩. — v. 出去 chūqù, 退出 tuìchū.

exit poll 票站调查 piàozhàn diàochá / 选情调查 xuǎnqíng diàochá.

exonerate v. 免罪 miǎnzuì, 免责 miǎnzé.

exorbitant adj. 过多的 guòduō de, 过分的 guòfèn de.

exorcize v. 驱邪 qūxié.

exotic adj. ① 外国的 wàiguó de, 异国的 yìguó de (foreign). ② 珍奇的 zhēnqí de, 奇异的 qíyì de (strange).

expand v. ① 扩张 kuòzhāng, 扩大 kuòdà (broaden). ② 展开 zhǎnkāi, 扩展 kuòzhǎn (spread out).

expanse n. 广阔 guǎngkuò.

expansion n. 扩张 kuòzhāng, 扩大 kuòdà.

expatriate v. ① 放逐国外 fàngzhú guówài (exile). ② 移居国外 yíjū guówài (live abroad). — n. ① 流亡者 liúwángzhě (person who is exiled). ② 移居国外者 yíjū guówài zhě (one who resides abroad).

expect v. ① 预期 yùqī / yùqí (anticipate), ② 期待 qīdài / qídài

(hope for). ② 要求 yāoqiú (demand). ③ 认为 rènwéi (believe).

expectation n. 预期 yùqī / yùqí (anticipation), 期望 qīwàng / qíwàng, 期待 qīdài / qídài (hope).

expedient n. 权宜之计 quányízhìjì. — adj. 有用的 yǒuyòng de (useful), 有效的 yǒuxiào de (effective).

expedition n. ① 远征 yuǎnzhēng, 探险 tànxiǎn (voyage). ② 远征队 yuǎnzhēngduì (voyagers).

expel v. 驱逐 qūzhú.

expend v. 花费 huāfèi.

expenditure n. 花费 huāfèi, 开支 kāizhī.

expense n. 花费 huāfèi, 支出 zhīchū.

expensive adj. 贵的 guì de, 昂贵的 ángguì de.

experience n. & v. 经验 jīngyàn, 经历 jīnglì.

experienced adj. 有经验的 yǒu jīngyàn de.

experiment n. & v. 实验 shíyàn, 试验 shìyàn.

expert n. 专家 zhuānjiā. — adj. 老练的 lǎoliàn de, 熟练的 shúliàn de / shóuliàn de.

expertise n. 专门技术 zhuānmén jìshù.

expire v. ① 到期 dàoqī / dàoqí, 期满 qīmǎn / qímǎn (become invalid). ② 死亡 sǐwáng (die).

explain v. ① 解释 jiěshì, 说明 shuōmíng (clarify). ② 辩解 biànjiě (justify).

explanation n. ① 解释 jiěshì, 说明 shuōmíng (clarification). ② 辩解 biànjiě (justification).

E

explicit *adj.* 明确的 míngquè de, 清楚的 qīngchu de.

explode *v.* ①爆炸 bàozhà (blow up). ②推翻 tuīfān (destroy).

exploit *n.* 英勇行为 yīngyǒng xíngwéi (brave actions). 功绩 gōngjì / gōngjī (contribution). — *v.* ①利用 lìyòng (use something), 开发 kāifā (develop an area). ②剥削 bōxuē / bōxuè (take advantage of).

exploration *n.* ①探险 tànxiǎn (adventure), 探测 tàncè (probe). ②探讨 tàntǎo (examination).

explore *v.* ①探测 tàncè (probe), 探险 tànxiǎn (adventure). ②探讨 tàntǎo (examine).

explosion *n.* 爆发 bàofā, 爆炸 bàozhà.

explosive *adj.* 爆炸的 bàozhà de. — *n.* 爆炸物 bàozhàwù, 炸药 zhàyào.

export *v.* 输出 shūchū, 出口 chūkǒu. — *n.* ①输出 shūchū, 出口 chūkǒu (exporting). ②输出品 shūchūpǐn (exported product).

expose *v.* ①暴露 bàolù / pùlù (reveal). ②揭穿 jiēchuān (bring to light). ③曝光 bàoguāng / pùguāng (come to light). ④显露 xiǎnlù (show). ⑤接触 jiēchù (come in contact). ⑥展览 zhǎnlǎn, 陈列 chénliè (display).

exposition *n.* ①博览会 bólǎnhuì, 展览会 zhǎnlǎnhuì (exhibition). ②说明 shuōmíng (explanation).

exposure *n.* ①暴露 bàolù / pùlù (uncovering). ②揭穿 jiēchuān (being revealed). ③曝

光 bàoguāng / pùguāng 〈film〉. ④展览 zhǎnlǎn (displaying).

expound *v.* 详述 xiángshù, 详加说明 xiángjiā shuōmíng.

express *v.* ①表达 biǎodá, 表示 biǎoshì (convey). ②速递 sùdì / 快递 kuàidì (express delivery). — *adj.* ①清楚的 qīngchu de, 明确的 míngquè de (explicit). ②快速的 kuàisù de (fast). — *n.* 快车 kuàichē.

expression *n.* ①表达 biǎodá, 表示 biǎoshì (way of conveying). ②措辞 cuòcí (phrase). ③表情 biǎoqíng (facial expression).

expulsion *n.* 驱逐 qūzhú.

exquisite *adj.* ①精致的 jīngzhì de (fine), 优美的 yōuměi de (beautiful). ②剧烈的 jùliè de (severe). ③敏锐的 mǐnruì de (keen).

extend *v.* ①延长 yáncháng (prolong), 延期 yánqī / yánqí (postpone). ②扩大 kuòdà (enlarge). ③伸展 shēnzhǎn, 伸长 shēncháng (stretch out).

extension *n.* ①延长 yáncháng, 伸展 shēnzhǎn (prolongation). ②扩充 kuòchōng (addition). ③延期 yánqī / yánqí (postponement).

extensive *adj.* 广阔的 guǎngkuò de, 广泛的 guǎngfàn de.

extent *n.* ①程度 chéngdù (degree). ②长度 chángdù (length), 范围 fànwéi (scope).

exterior *n. & adj.* 外部 wàibù (outer part), 外表 wàibiǎo (appearance).

exterminate *v.* 消灭 xiāomiè.

external *adj.* ①外面的

wàimian de, 外部的 wàibù de
(outside). ②外来的 wàilái de
(not inherent). ③外国的
wàiguó de (foreign).

extinct *adj.* ①熄灭的 xīmiè de /
xímiè de (extinguished). ②灭
种的 mièzhǒng de (died out).

extinguish *v.* ①熄灭 xīmiè /
xímiè (put out). ②消灭 xiāomiè
(exterminate).

extort *v.* 勒索 lèsuǒ, 敲诈
qiāozhà.

extra *adj.* 额外的 éwài de.

extract *v.* ①拔取 báqǔ (take
out). ②引述 yǐnshù, 摘录
zhāilù (quote). ③榨取 zhàqǔ
(obtain by crushing). — *n.* ①浓
汁 nóngzhī, 提取物 tíqǔwù
(liquid extracted). ②引语 yǐnyǔ,
摘录 zhāilù (citation).

extraordinary *adj.* 特别的
tèbié de.

extravagance *n.* ①奢侈
shēchǐ (luxury). ②浪费 làngfèi
(wastefulness). ③放纵
fàngzòng (over-indulgence).

extravagant *adj.* ①奢侈的
shēchǐ de (luxurious). ②浪费
的 làngfèi de (wasteful). ③过

分的 guòfèn de (excessive).

extreme *adj.* ①极度的 jídù
de, 极端的 jíduān de (utmost).
②尽头的 jìntóu de, 最远的
zuì yuǎn de (farthest). ③偏激
的 piānjī de (exaggerated).
— *n.* 末端 mòduān, 极端
jíduān.

extremely *adv.* ①非常
fēicháng (very). ②极端地
jíduān de (too).

extremity *n.* ①末端 mòduān
(end). ②极度 jídù (extreme
degree).

exuberant *adj.* ①充满活力的
chōngmǎn huólì de (excited).
②茂盛的 màoshèng de (luxu-
riant).

exude *v.* 渗出 shènchu, 流出
liúchu (flow out).

eye *n.* ①眼睛 yǎnjing ⟨body
part⟩. ②眼光 yǎnguāng (taste).
an ~ for an ~ 以牙还牙 yǐyá-
-huányá.

eyeball *n.* 眼球 yǎnqiú.

eyebrow *n.* 眉毛 méimao.

eyelash *n.* 睫毛 jiémáo.

eyelid *n.* 眼脸 yǎnjiǎn.

eyesight *n.* 视力 shìlì.

F

ε**F**$\cup$

fable *n.* 寓言 yùyán.

fabric *n.* 织物 zhīwù.

fabricate *v.* ①建造 jiànzào
(construct). ②捏造 niēzào (lie),
虚构 xūgòu (invent).

fabulous *adj.* ①极好的 jí hǎo
de (excellent). ②惊人的

jīngrén de (unbelievable).

facade *n.* ①假象 jiǎxiàng
(pretense). ②建物正面 jiànwù
zhèngmiàn (front of building).

face *n.* ①脸 liǎn ⟨body part⟩.
②表面 biǎomiàn (surface),
面 miàn (facet). ③表情

biǎoqíng (expression). ④面子
miànzi (pride). *lose ~* 丢脸
diūliǎn. — *v.* ①面向……
miànxiàng... (be across from).
②面对 miànduì (confront), 面
临 miànlín (encounter). *~ -off*
对抗 duìkàng.

facet *n.* ①小平面 xiǎo
píngmiàn, 面 miàn (side).
②方面 fāngmiàn (aspect).

facetious *adj.* 轻浮的 qīngfú
de, 爱开不当玩笑的 ài kāi
búdàng wánxiào de.

facial *adj.* 面部的 miànbù de,
脸部的 liǎnbù de. — *n.* 做脸
zuòliǎn.

facile *adj.* ①轻而易举的 qīng-
éryìjǔ de (easily done). ②肤浅
的 fūqiǎn de (superficial).

facilitate *v.* 使便利 shǐ biànlì.

facility *n.* ①设备 shèbèi
(equipment). ②容易 róngyì
(ease). ③才能 cáinéng (ability).

facsimile *n.* ①模拟 mónǐ, 复制
fùzhì (copy). ②传真
chuánzhēn (fax).

fact *n.* 事实 shìshí, 真相
zhēnxiàng. *in ~* 其实 qíshí.

faction *n.* 派系 pàixì, 小派别
xiǎo pàibié.

factional *adj.* 派系的 pàixì de.

factor *n.* ①因素 yīnsù
(component). ②因数 yīnshù
〈mathematics〉.

factory *n.* 工厂 gōngchǎng,
制造处 zhìzàochù.

factual *adj.* 事实的 shìshí de.

faculty *n.* ①才能 cáinéng, 能
力 nénglì (ability). ②全体教职
员 quántǐ jiàozhíyuán 〈group〉.

fade *v.* ①褪色 tuìshǎi / tùnsè
(lose color). ②凋谢 diāowěi /
diāowēi, 衰落 shuāiluò
(wither).

Fahrenheit *n.* 华氏温度计
Huáshì wēndùjì.

fail *v.* ①失败 shībài (be
unsuccessful). ②不足 bùzú (be
insufficient). ③不及格 bù jígé
(not fulfill standard). ④使失望
shǐ shīwàng (disappoint).

failing *n.* 缺点 quēdiǎn.

failure *n.* ①失败 shībài (the
fact of failing). ②失败者
shībàizhě 〈person〉.

faint *adj.* ①模糊不清的 móhu
bùqīng de (unclear). ②昏晕的
hūnyūn de (dizzy). — *n. & v.*
昏厥 hūnjué.

fair *adj.* ①公平的 gōngpíng
de, 正直的 zhèngzhí de (just).
②美好的 měihǎo de (fine).
③晴朗的 qínglǎng de 〈weather〉.
— *n.* ①市集 shìjí (market). ②博
览会 bólǎnhuì (exhibition).

fairly *adv.* ①公平地 gōngpíng
de (justly). ②相当地
xiāngdāng de (rather).

fairy *n.* 小仙子 xiǎo xiānzǐ.
~ tale 童话故事 tónghuà gùshi.

faith *n.* ①信任 xìnrèn, 相信
xiāngxìn (trust). ②信仰 xìnyǎng
(religious belief).

faithful *adj.* 忠实的 zhōngshí
de (loyal), 诚信的 chéngxìn
de (honest).

fake *n.* ①赝品 yànpǐn, 伪造品
wěizàopǐn / wèizàopǐn (duplicate). ②骗子 piànzi (cheat).
— *v.* 伪造 wěizào / wèizào
(forge), 假装 jiǎzhuāng (pretend). — *adj.* 假的 jiǎ de.

falcon *n.* 猎鹰 lièyīng.

fall *v.* ①落下 luòxia, 倒下
dǎoxia (drop). ②下降 xiàjiàng
(decrease). ③陷落 xiànluò
(surrender). ④堕落 duòluò
(degenerate). *~ apart* 崩溃

bēngkuì. ~ *asleep* 睡着 shuìzháo.

~ *for* ①听信 tīngxìn (be fooled).
②迷恋 míliàn (fall in love).

~ *in love* 爱上 àishang.

~ *out with...* 跟...吵架 gēn...
chǎojià. ~ *through* 失败 shībài.

— n. 秋季 qiūjì, 秋天 qiūtiān.

fallacy n. 错误 cuòwù, 谬见
miùjiàn.

fallen adj. ①落下的 luòxia de
(down). ②死亡的 sǐwáng de
(dead).

fallible adj. 会犯错的 huì
fàncuò de.

fallow n. & adj. 休耕 xiūgēng.

false adj. ①假的 jiǎ de (untrue).
②错的 cuò de (erroneous).

falsify v. 伪造 wěizào /
wèizào.

falter v. 蹒跚 pánshān /
mánshān (stagger).

fame n. 名气 míngqì, 声誉
shēngyù.

familiar adj. ①认识的 rènshi
de (acquainted). ②熟悉的
shúxī de / shóuxī de (close).
③亲密的 qīnmì de (intimate).
④常见的 chángjiàn de
(common).

family n. 家庭 jiātíng (household), 家人 jiārén (relatives).

famine n. 饥荒 jīhuāng.

famish v. 挨饿 áiè / āiè.

famous adj. 有名的 yǒumíng
de, 著名的 zhùmíng de.

fan n. ①风扇 fēngshàn (blow-
er). ②迷 mí (enthusiast).

fanatic n. 狂热者 kuángrèzhě.

fanciful adj. 异想天开的
yìxiǎng-tiānkāi de.

fancy n. ①想象力 xiǎngxiànglì
(imagination). ②看法 kànfǎ, 念
头 niàntou (idea). — v. ①想象
xiǎngxiàng (imagine). ②喜欢

xǐhuan (like). — adj. ①精选的
jīngxuǎn de (elaborate). ②花哨
的 huāshao de / 花俏的
huāqiào de (not plain).

fang n. 尖牙 jiānyá.

fantabulous adj. 棒极了的
bàng jí le de.

fantastic adj. ①奇特的 qítè
de (strange). ②很棒的 hěn
bàng de (excellent). ③幻想的
huànxiǎng de (imaginary).

fantasy n. 想象 xiǎngxiàng,
幻想 huànxiǎng.

far adj. 远的 yuǎn de (distant).
— adv. 久远地 jiǔyuǎn de
(remotely). *so* ~ 到目前为止
dào mùqián wéizhǐ. *the F- East*
远东 Yuǎndōng.

faraway adj. 久远的 jiǔyuǎn
de.

farce n. 闹剧 nàojù 〈play〉.

fare n. ①票价 piàojià, 车费
chēfèi (ticket price). ② 食物
shíwù (food).

farewell interj. 再会! zàihuì!
— adj. 告别的 gàobié de.

farm n. 农田 nóngtián, 农场
nóngchǎng. — v. 耕田
gēngtián.

farmer n. 农夫 nóngfū.

farmhouse n. 农舍 nóngshè.

farther adj. 较远的 jiào yuǎn
de (more distant). — adv. 较远
地 jiào yuǎn de (further).

farthest adj. & adv. 最远的
zuì yuǎn de.

fascinate v. ①使着迷 shǐ
zháomí (charm). ②蛊惑 gǔhuò
(bewitch).

Fascism n. 法西斯主义
Fǎxīsī zhǔyì.

fashion n. ①流行 liúxíng (popularity). ②时髦 shímáo (style).
③作风 zuòfēng (manner).

fashionable adj. 时髦的 shímáo de (stylish), 流行的 liúxíng de (popular).

fast adj. ①快的 kuài de (quick). ②牢固的 láogù de (attached). ③耐久的 nàijiǔ de (lasting). ~ **lane** 快车道 kuàichēdào. ~ **track** 捷径 jiéjìng.

fasten v. 系牢 jìláo (attach).

fast-food adj. 速食的 sùshí de.

fastidious adj. 吹毛求疵的 chuīmáo-qiúcī de, 讲究细节的 jiǎngjiū xìjié de.

fat adj. 肥的 féi de (obese), 胖的 pàng de (plump). — n. 脂肪 zhīfáng ⟨biology⟩, 肥肉 féiròu (fatty meat). ~ **farm** 减肥中心 jiǎnféi zhōngxīn.

fatal adj. 致命的 zhìmìng de.

fatalism n. 宿命论 sùmìnglùn.

fatality n. ①灾祸 zāihuò (accident). ②死亡 sǐwáng (death). ③宿命 sùmìng (fate).

fate n. ①命运 mìngyùn (destiny). ②结局 jiéjú (end).

father n. 父亲 fùqīn, 爸爸 bàba.

Father's Day 父亲节 Fùqīnjié.

father-in-law n. 公公 gōnggong (husband's father), 岳父 yuèfù (wife's father).

fatigue n. 疲劳 píláo. — v. 使疲劳 shǐ píláo.

fatuous adj. 愚昧的 yúmèi de (stupid).

faucet n. 水龙头 shuǐlóngtóu.

fault n. ①缺点 quēdiǎn (defect). ②错误 cuòwù, 过失 guòshī (error). ③断层 duàncéng ⟨geology⟩. — v. 责怪 zéguài (blame).

favor n. & v. ①赞成 zànchéng (approval). ②偏爱 piān'ài (preference). **do... a** ~ 帮……（一个）忙 bāng...(yí ge) máng.

favorable adj. ①赞成的 zànchéng de (approving). ②良好的 liánghǎo de (good).

favorite adj. 最喜爱的 zuì xǐ'ài de. — n. 最爱 zuì ài.

fawn v. 巴结 bājie, 奉承 fèngcheng (flatter).

fax n. & v. 传真 chuánzhēn. ~ **machine** 传真机 chuánzhēnjī.

fear n. 惧怕 jùpà, 恐惧感 kǒngjùgǎn.

fearful adj. ①害怕的 hàipà de (afraid). ②可怕的 kěpà de (frightening).

fearless adj. 无畏的 wúwèi de.

feasible adj. ①可行的 kěxíng de (possible). ②适宜的 shìyí de (suitable).

feasibility n. 可行性 kěxíngxìng.

feast n. ①宴会 yànhuì (meal). ②节庆 jiéqìng (festival).

feat n. 功绩 gōngjì / gōngjī.

feather n. 羽毛 yǔmáo.

feature n. ①面貌 miànmào ⟨face⟩. ②特征 tèzhēng, 特色 tèsè (characteristic). ③特写 tèxiě ⟨article⟩.

February n. 二月 Èryuè.

federal adj. 联邦的 liánbāng de.

fee n. 费 fèi.

feeble adj. 微弱的 wēiruò de / wéiruò de.

feed v. 喂食 wèishí, 饲养 sìyǎng (nourish).

feedback n. 反馈 fǎnkuì / 回馈 huíkuì.

F

feel v. ①感觉 gǎnjué, 觉得 juéde (consider). ②触摸 chùmō (touch), 感觉到 gǎnjué dào (experience).

feeler n. 触角 chùjiǎo, 触须 chùxū (antenna).

feeling n. ①感觉 gǎnjué (awareness). ②感情 gǎnqíng (passion). ③情绪 qíngxù (emotion). ④感受力 gǎnshòulì (responsiveness).

feet n. 脚 jiǎo.

feint n. & v. 佯攻 yánggōng (pretended attack).

feline adj. 似猫的 sì māo de (like a cat). — n. 猫科动物 māokē dòngwù.

fellow n. ①人 rén, 家伙 jiāhuo (man). ②同伴 tóngbàn (companion), 同事 tóngshì (co-worker).

fellowship n. ①交情 jiāoqíng (companionship). ②补助金 bǔzhùjīn (grant). ③会员 huì, 团体 tuántǐ (group). ④会员资格 huìyuán zīgé (membership).

female n. 女性 nǚxìng (human), 雌性 cíxìng / cìxìng (animal). — adj. 女性的 nǚxìng de (human), 雌的 cí de / cì de (animal).

feminine adj. ①女性化的 nǚxìnghuà de (women). ②阴性的 yīnxìng de (linguistics).

feminism n. 女性主义 nǚxìng zhǔyì, 女权主义 nǚquán zhǔyì, 男女平等主义 nánnǚ píngděng zhǔyì.

fen n. 沼泽 zhǎozé.

fence n. 栅栏 zhàlan, 篱笆 líba.

fencing n. 剑术 jiànshù.

fender n. 挡泥板 dǎngníbǎn.

feng shui n. 风水 fēngshuǐ.

ferment v. 发酵 fājiào / fāxiào, 酝酿 yùnniàng.

fern n. 羊齿植物 yángchǐ zhíwù.

ferocious adj. 凶猛的 xiōngměng de.

ferret n. 雪貂 xuědiāo (animal). — v. 搜索 sōusuǒ (search for).

ferry n. 渡船 dùchuán (ferry-boat). — v. 运送 yùnsòng.

fertile adj. 肥沃的 féiwò de, 多产的 duōchǎn de (productive).

fertilize v. 施肥 shīféi (soil).

fertilizer n. 肥料 féiliào.

fervent adj. 热情的 rèqíng de, 热烈的 rèliè de.

fervor n. 热情 rèqíng, 热烈 rèliè.

fester v. 化脓 huànóng, 溃烂 kuìlàn.

festival n. 节日 jiérì, 庆典 qìngdiǎn.

fetch v. ①取来 qǔlai (bring). ②售得 shòudé (sell for). ③接来 jiēlai (people).

fetid adj. 恶臭的 èchòu de.

fetish n. ①满足性欲之物 mǎnzú xìngyù zhī wù (in psychology). ②受崇拜之神物 shòu chóngbài zhī shénwù (magical figurine).

fetter n. & v. ①脚镣 jiǎoliào / jiǎoliáo (chain). ②束缚 shùfù / shùfú (restraint).

feud n. 世仇 shìchóu, 不和 bùhé.

feudal adj. 封建的 fēngjiàn de.

feudalism n. 封建主义 fēngjiàn zhǔyì.

fever n. ①发烧 fāshāo (high temperature). ②热病 rèbìng (disease). ③狂热 kuángrè

(excited state).

few *n. & pron.* 很少 hěn shǎo, 几个 jǐge, 一些 yìxiē.

fiancé *n.* 未婚夫 wèihūnfū.

fiancée *n.* 未婚妻 wèihūnqī.

fib *n.* 小谎 xiǎohuǎng.

fiber *n.* 纤维 xiānwéi.

fickle *adj.* 多变的 duōbiàn de.

fiction *n.* ①虚构故事 xūgòu gùshì (story). ②小说 xiǎoshuō (novel).

fiddle *n.* 小提琴 xiǎotíqín.

fidelity *n.* 忠诚 zhōngchéng (loyalty).

fidget *v.* 坐立不安 zuòlì- -bù'ān.

field *n.* ①田地 tiándì, 田野 tiányě (land). ②领域 língyù (domain). ③场地 chǎngdì (area).

fiend *n.* 恶魔 èmó (devil).

fierce *adj.* 凶猛的 xiōngměng de.

fiery *adj.* ①燃烧的 ránshāo de (flaming). ②暴躁的 bàozào de, 激怒的 jīnù de (angry).

fifteen *n. & adj.* 十五 shíwǔ.

fifteenth *n. & adj.* 第十五 dì-shíwǔ.

fifth *n. & adj.* 第五 dì-wǔ.

fiftieth *n. & adj.* 第五十 dì- -wǔshí.

fifty *n. & adj.* 五十 wǔshí.

fig *n.* 无花果 wúhuāguǒ ⟨plant⟩.

fight *v.* ①吵架 chǎojià (quarrel). ②打架 dǎjià (battle). ③打仗 dǎzhàng, 与……战争 yǔ...zhànzhēng (be at war with). ④抗争 kàngzhēng (oppose). ~ *for...* 为……奋斗 wèi... fèndòu.

fighter *n.* ①拳击手 quánjíshǒu / quánjíshǒu

(boxer). ②斗士 dòushì, 战士 zhànshì ⟨person⟩. ③战斗机 zhàndòujī ⟨aircraft⟩.

figment *n.* 虚构之事 xūgòu zhī shì.

figurative *adj.* 比喻的 bǐyù de.

figure *n.* ①数字 shùzì (numeral). ②身材 shēncái (body shape). ③人物 rénwù (person). ④图形 túxíng, 图表 túbiǎo (diagram). — *v.* ①认为 rènwéi (think), 觉得 juéde (feel). ②扮演 bànyǎn (play a role). ~ *out* 了解 liǎojiě (understand). *It* ~ *s!* 难怪! Nánguài!

filament *n.* ①线 xiàn (thread). ②灯丝 dēngsī (wire in bulb).

file *n.* ①卷宗 juànzōng, 档案 dàng'àn / dǎng'àn (folder). ②锉刀 cuòdāo ⟨tool⟩. — *v.* 归档 guīdàng / guīdǎng.

fill *v.* ①充满 chōngmǎn, 装满 zhuāngmǎn (make full). ②递补 dìbǔ ⟨position⟩. ③供应 gōngyìng (supply). ~ *in,* ~ *out* 填写 tiánxiě.

film *n.* ①胶卷 jiāojuǎn / 软片 ruǎnpiàn ⟨photography⟩. ②电影 diànyǐng (movie). ③薄层 báocéng / bócéng (layer).

film-maker *n.* 电影制作人 diànyǐng zhìzuòrén.

filter *n.* 过滤器 guòlǜqì.

filth *n.* 污秽 wūhuì.

fin *n.* 鳍 qí.

final *adj.* 最后的 zuìhòu de. — *n.* 期末考试 qīmò kǎoshì / qīmò kǎoshì (end-of-term test), 决赛 juésài (competition).

finally *adv.* 最后 zuìhòu (at the end), 终于 zhōngyú (at last).

finance *n.* 财政 cáizhèng ⟨economic regulations⟩, 财务

cáiwù 〈wealth〉, 金融 jīnróng
(having to do with money).
Ministry of F~ 财政部
Cáizhèngbù.

finances *n.* 财务 cáiwù
(wealth), 经济情况 jīngjì
qíngkuàng (economic situation).

financial *adj.* 财政的
cáizhèng de, 财务的 cáiwù de.

find *v.* ①找到 zhǎodào (seek
out). ②发现 fāxiàn (discover).
③发觉 fājué (observe), 得知
dézhī (learn).

fine *adj.* ①美好的 měihǎo de
(beautiful). ②精巧的 jīngqiǎo
de (delicate). ③安好的 ānhǎo
de (well). ④晴朗的 qínglǎng
de (weather). ⑤细的 xì de
(slender). — *n.* 罚金 fájīn. — *v.*
处以罚金 chǔyǐ fájīn, 罚款
fákuǎn.

finery *n.* 华服 huáfú.

finger *n.* 手指 shǒuzhǐ.

fingerprint *n.* 指纹 zhǐwén.

finish *n. & v.* 结束 jiéshù
(end), 完成 wánchéng
(completion).

finite *adj.* 有限的 yǒuxiàn de.

fir *n.* 枞树 cōngshù.

fire *n.* ①火 huǒ (flame). ②火灾
huǒzāi 〈calamity〉. ③炉火 lúhuǒ
(in fireplace). ~ *door* 防火门
fánghuǒmén. ~ *engine* 消防车
xiāofángchē. ~ *extinguisher*
灭火器 mièhuǒqì. ~ *hydrant*
消防栓 xiāofángshuān.
— *v.* ①射击 shèjī / shèjī, 开枪
kāiqiāng (shoot). ②解雇 jiěgù
(dismiss). ③纵火 zònghuǒ
(set on fire).

firecracker *n.* 爆竹 bàozhú,
鞭炮 biānpào.

firefighter *n.* 消防队员
xiāofáng duìyuán.

firefly *n.* 萤火虫
yínghuǒchóng.

fireman *n.* 消防队员
xiāofáng duìyuán.

fireplace *n.* 壁炉 bìlú.

fireproof *adj.* 防火的 fánghuǒ
de.

fireworks *n.* 烟火 yānhuo.

firm *adj.* 坚固的 jiāngù de,
坚定的 jiāndìng de (rigid).
— *n.* 商店 shāngdiàn (store),
公司 gōngsī (company).

first *adj.* 第一的 dì-yī de, 最初
的 zuìchū de (initial). ~ *name*
名 míng. ~ *person* 第一人称
dì-yī rénchēng. — *n.* 第一个
dì-yī ge (initial), 第一名 dì-yī
míng 〈contest〉. — *adv.* 首先
shǒuxiān, 第一 dì-yī. ~ *of all*
首先 shǒuxiān. *at* ~ 当初
dāngchū, 最初 zuìchū.

first-class *adj.* 头等的
tóuděng de.

fiscal *adj.* 财政的 cáizhèng de.

fish *n.* 鱼 yú 〈animal〉, 鱼肉
yúròu 〈meat〉. — *v.* 钓鱼
diàoyú, 捕鱼 bǔyú.

fisherman *n.* 渔夫 yúfū 〈job〉,
钓客 diàokè 〈fun〉.

fishing *n.* 钓鱼 diàoyú, 捕鱼
bǔyú.

fission *n.* 分裂 fēnliè.

fist *n.* 拳 quán, 拳头 quántou.

fit *v.* 适合 shìhé, 适合于 shìhé
yú. — *adj.* ①适宜的 shìyí de,
合适的 héshì de (suitable).
②适当的 shìdàng de, 对的
duì de (proper). ③健康的
jiànkāng de (healthy).

fitting *adj.* 适当的 shìdàng
de, 适合的 shìhé de. — *n.*
①试穿 shìchuān 〈clothing〉.
②配件 pèijiàn, 装备 zhuāngbèi
(small standardized part).

F

five n. & adj. 五 wǔ.

fix v. ①修理 xiūlǐ (repair). ②固定 gùdìng (regularize). ③确定 quèdìng, 决定 juédìng (determine). ④使牢固 shǐ láogù (secure).

fixed adj. 牢固的 láogù de (secure), 固定的 gùdìng de (regular).

fizz n. & v. 嘶嘶声 sīsīshēng.

flabby adj. 松软的 sōngruǎn de, 松弛的 sōngchí de.

flag n. 旗 qí, 旗子 qízi.

flagpole n. 旗杆 qígān.

flagrant adj. 穷凶极恶的 qióngxiōng-jí'è de (very bad). ②无耻的 wúchǐ de (shameless).

flair n. 特色 tèsè (style).

flake n. 薄片 báopiàn / bópiàn. — v. 成片剥落 chéngpiàn bōluò.

flamboyant adj. ①灿烂的 cànlàn de (colorful). ②炫耀的 xuànyào de (showy).

flame n. 火焰 huǒyàn. — v. 发出火焰 fāchū huǒyàn (flare up), 燃烧 ránshāo (burn).

flamingo n. 火鹤 huǒhè ⟨bird⟩.

flank n. ①侧面 cèmiàn (side). ②侧腹 cèfù ⟨body part⟩.

flannel n. 法兰绒 fǎlánróng.

flap v. 拍打 pāidǎ, 扑拍 pūpāi, 鼓翼 gǔyì.

flare n. & v. 火焰摇曳 huǒyàn yáoyè / huǒyàn yáoyì (flame), 闪光 shǎnguāng (flicker).

flash n. ①闪光 shǎnguāng, 闪烁 shǎnshuò (glare). ②闪光灯 shǎnguāngdēng ⟨photograph⟩. — v. ①闪光 shǎnguāng (flicker). ②突然出现 tūrán chūxiàn / túrán chūxiàn, 闪现 shǎnxiàn (appear suddenly).

flashback n. 倒叙 dàoxù.

flashlight n. 手电筒 shǒudiàntǒng.

flask n. 扁瓶 biǎnpíng (flat bottle).

flat adj. ①平的 píng de, 平坦的 píngtǎn de (level). ②单调的 dāndiào de (dull). ③扁的 biǎn de (with little thickness). ④无气的 wú qì de ⟨tire⟩. — n. 公寓 gōngyù, 楼房 lóufáng (apartment).

flatten v. (使)平坦 (shǐ) píngtǎn, 变平 biànpíng.

flatter v. 谄媚 chǎnmèi, 取悦 qǔyuè.

flattery n. 谄媚 chǎnmèi.

flaunt n. & v. 炫耀 xuànyào.

flavor n. 味道 wèidào. — v. 调味 tiáowèi.

flaw n. ①裂缝 lièfèng (crack). ②缺点 quēdiǎn (defect), 瑕疵 xiácī (blemish).

flax n. 亚麻 yàmá.

flea n. 跳蚤 tiàozǎo.

fleck n. 斑点 bāndiǎn.

flee v. 逃走 táozǒu (escape), 逃避 táobì (evade).

fleece n. 羊毛 yángmáo (wool). — v. 剪羊毛 jiǎn yángmáo (shear).

fleet n. 舰队 jiànduì.

fleeting adj. 疾逝的 jíshì de.

flesh n. ①肉 ròu (meat). ②骨肉 gǔròu (one's own children). **~ and blood** ①血肉之躯 xuèròuzhīqū / xiěròuzhīqū (human beings). ②骨肉 gǔròu (family). **in the ~** 本人 běnrén.

flexible adj. ①有弹性的 yǒu tánxìng de (adjustable). ②易弯曲的 yì wānqū de (bendable).

flick n. & v. 轻打 qīngdǎ, 轻弹 qīngtán.

F

flicker v. 闪烁 shǎnshuò, 摇曳 yáoyè / yáoyì. — n. 闪动 shǎndòng.

flier n. ①飞行员 fēixíngyuán (airman). ②传单 chuándān 〈advertisement〉.

flight n. ①飞行 fēixíng (flying). ②航程 hángchéng (journey).

flimsy adj. 脆弱的 cuìruò de (not strong), 轻而薄的 qīng ér báo de / qīng ér bó de (light and thin).

flinch n. & v. 畏缩 wèisuō.

fling v. 投 tóu, 掷 zhì / zhí 〈throw〉.

flint n. 打火石 dǎhuǒshí, 燧石 suìshí.

flip v. ①弹抛 tánpāo, 轻弹 qīngtán 〈into the air〉. ②翻 fān 〈turn over〉.

flippant adj. 无礼的 wúlǐ de.

flirt v. 调情 tiáoqíng. — n. 调情者 tiáoqíngzhě, 卖弄风骚者 màinong fēngsāo zhě.

float v. 漂流 piāoliú, 漂浮 piāofú 〈drift〉. — n. 浮标 fúbiāo 〈buoy〉.

flock n. 群 qún 〈group〉. — v. 群集 qúnjí.

flog v. 重打 zhòngdǎ, 鞭笞 biānchī.

flood n. 洪水 hóngshuǐ, 水灾 shuǐzāi. — v. 泛滥 fànlàn, 淹没 yānmò 〈overflow〉.

floor n. ①地板 dìbǎn 〈ground〉. ②楼层 lóucéng 〈story〉.

flop v. ①啪嗒地跳动 pādā de tiàodòng 〈move clumsily〉. ②猛落 měngluò 〈fall〉. ③失败 shībài 〈fail〉.

floppy adj. 松软的 sōngruǎn de. ~ disk 软盘 ruǎnpán / 磁碟片 cídiépiàn.

floral adj. 花的 huā de.

florist n. 花店 huādiàn 〈store〉, 花商 huāshāng 〈person〉.

flotilla n. 小舰队 xiǎo jiànduì.

flounder v. 挣扎 zhēngzhá 〈struggle〉. 鲽鱼 diéyú, 比目鱼 bǐmùyú.

flour n. 面粉 miànfěn.

flourish v. ①繁盛 fánshèng 〈prosper〉. ②兴隆 xīnglóng 〈thrive〉. ③挥动 huīdòng 〈wave〉.

flout v. 轻视 qīngshì.

flow n. & v. 流动 liúdòng.

flowchart n. 流程图 liúchéngtú.

flower n. 花 huā. — v. 开花 kāihuā.

flu n. 流行性感冒 liúxíngxìng gǎnmào.

fluctuate v. 动摇 dòngyáo, 波动 bōdòng, 变动 biàndòng.

fluent adj. 流利的 liúlì de, 流畅的 liúchàng de.

fluff n. 软毛 ruǎnmáo, 绒毛 róngmáo 〈soft, feathery stuff〉. — v. 使松软 shǐ sōngruǎn.

fluid n. 液体 yètǐ, 流体 liútǐ. — adj. ①流动的 liúdòng de 〈flowing〉. ②易变的 yì biàn de 〈easily changed〉.

flunk v. 不及格 bù jígé.

fluorescence n. 萤光 yíngguāng.

fluorescent adj. 萤光的 yíngguāng de.

flurry n. ①疾风 jífēng 〈wind〉. ②骤雨 zhòuyǔ / zòuyǔ 〈rain〉. ③小雪 xiǎoxuě 〈snow〉. ④骚动 sāodòng 〈activity〉.

flush v. ①发红 fāhóng, 脸红 liǎnhóng 〈blush〉. ②冲洗 chōngxǐ 〈wash out〉. ③惊起 jīngqǐ 〈drive out〉. — n. 同花 tónghuā 〈cards〉.

F

fluster v. 使慌乱 shǐ huāngluàn.

flustered adj. 手忙脚乱的 shǒumáng-jiǎoluàn de.

flute n. 笛 dí.

flutter n. & v. 鼓翼 gǔyì, 拍翅 pāichì (flap).

fly v. ①飞 fēi, 飞行 fēixíng (move through the air). ②搭飞机 dā fēijī (go by airplane). ③空运 kōngyùn (transport by air). ④飘扬 piāoyáng (flutter). ⑤飞奔 fēibēn (move quickly). — n. 苍蝇 cāngying (housefly).

foal n. ①小马 xiǎomǎ ⟨horse⟩. ②小驴 xiǎolǘ ⟨ass⟩.

foam n. 泡沫 pàomò (bubble). — v. 起泡 qǐpào.

focus n. 焦点 jiāodiǎn (focal point or central point), 焦距 jiāojù (focal length). — v. 集中焦点于…… jízhōng jiāodiǎn yú....

fodder n. 刍料 chúliào.

foe n. 敌人 dírén, 仇人 chóurén.

fog n. 雾 wù (mist).

foggy adj. 有浓雾的 yǒu nóngwù de.

foil v. 阻挠 zǔnáo (prevent), 打败 dǎbài (defeat). — n. ①箔 bó ⟨metal⟩. ②陪衬 péichèn ⟨contrast⟩.

fold n. & v. 摺叠 zhédié (bend).

folder n. 文件夹 wénjiànjiā / wénjiànjiá.

foliage n. 树叶 shùyè (leaves).

folk n. ①民族 mínzú (ethnic group). ②人们 rénmen (people). — adj. 民间的 mínjiān de.

~ *customs* 民俗 mínsú.

~ *dance* 土风舞 tǔfēngwǔ.

~ *hero* 民族英雄 mínzú

yīngxióng. ~ *song* 民谣 mínyáo.

follow v. ①跟随 gēnsuí, 跟着 gēnzhe (go after). ②接着 jiēzhe, 继之而来 jìzhī'érlái (succeed). ③遵循 zūnxún (obey). ④理解 lǐjiě (comprehend).

follower n. 追随者 zhuīsuízhě, 门徒 méntú (pupil).

following n. 拥护者 yōnghùzhě / yǒnghùzhě. — adj. 下列的 xiàliè de (listed below), 下一(个) xià yí (ge) (next). ~ *day* 第二天 dì-èr tiān.

follow-up n. 追踪调查 zhuīzōng diàochá (trace). — adj. 后续的 hòuxù de.

folly n. 愚笨 yúbèn.

fond adj. 喜爱的 xǐ'ài de (like).

fondle v. 爱抚 àifǔ.

font n. ①洗礼盆 xǐlǐpén ⟨baptismal⟩. ②字型 zìxíng ⟨type⟩.

food n. 食物 shíwù. ~ *bank* 食物赈贫站 shíwù zhènpínzhàn.

foodie n. 美食家 měishíjiā.

fool n. ①愚人 yúrén (silly person). ②小丑 xiǎochǒu (clown). — v. 愚弄 yúnòng (trick), 欺骗 qīpiàn (cheat). ~ *around* ①开玩笑 kāiwánxiào (joke). ②鬼混 guǐhùn, 乱来 luànlái (mess around). ③玩弄 wánnòng (tease).

foolish adj. 愚蠢的 yúchǔn de, 笨的 bèn de.

foot n. ①足 zú, 脚 jiǎo ⟨of person, animals⟩. ②呎 chǐ (measure of length). ③基部 jībù (base). *on* ~ 徒步 túbù, 步行 bùxíng.

football n. ①足球 zúqiú (soccer). ②美式足球 měishì zúqiú (American football).

F

footlights n. 脚灯 jiǎodēng.

footnote n. 注脚 zhùjiǎo, 注释 zhùshì.

footpath n. 小径 xiǎojìng, 人行道 rénxíngdào.

footprint n. 足迹 zújì / zújī, 脚印 jiǎoyìn.

footstep n. ①脚步声 jiǎobùshēng 〈sound〉. ②步伐 bùbù (a step). ③足迹 zújì / zújī (footprint).

footstool n. 脚凳 jiǎodèng.

for prep. ①为 wèi, 为了 wèile (on behalf of). ②替 tì (in place of). ③因为 yīnwèi, 由于 yóuyú (because of). ④对 duì, 对……来说 duì…láishuō (with respect to). ⑤赞成 zànchéng (in favor of).

forage n. 饲料 sìliào. — v. 搜寻 sōuxún.

forbear v. 抑制 yìzhì, 忍住 rěnzhù (refrain).

forbid v. 禁止 jìnzhǐ (prohibit).

forbidden adj. 被禁止的 bèi jìnzhǐ de.

force n. ①力 lì, 力量 lìliang (strength). ②势力 shìlì, 影响力 yǐngxiǎnglì (power). ③军队 jūnduì 〈army〉. — v. 强迫 qiǎngpò (compel).

forceps n. 钳子 qiánzi, 镊子 nièzi.

ford n. 浅滩 qiǎntān. — v. 涉过 shèguò.

forearm n. 前臂 qiánbì.

forecast n. & v. 预测 yùcè, 预告 yùgào.

forefather n. 祖先 zǔxiān.

forefinger n. 食指 shízhǐ.

forefront n. 最前部 zuì qiánbù.

foregoing adj. 之前的 zhīqián de.

foreground n. 前景 qiánjǐng.

forehead n. 前额 qián'é.

foreign adj. 外国的 wàiguó de (of another country), 外来的 wàilái de (coming from outside).

foreigner n. 外国人 wàiguórén.

foreman n. 工头 gōngtóu, 领班 lǐngbān.

foremost adj. ①最好的 zuìhǎo de (best). ②首要的 shǒuyào de (most important). ③最先的 zuìxiān de (first).

forerunner n. 先驱 xiānqū.

foresee v. 预知 yùzhī, 预见 yùjiàn.

foresight n. 先见之明 xiānjiànzhīmíng, 远见 yuǎnjiàn.

forest n. 森林 sēnlín.

forestall v. 先发制人地阻止 xiānfā-zhìrén de zǔzhǐ.

foretell v. 预言 yùyán.

forethought n. 深谋远虑 shēnmóu-yuǎnlǜ.

forever adv. 永远地 yǒngyuǎn de.

forewarn v. 预先警告 yùxiān jǐnggào.

foreword n. 前言 qiányán, 序 xù.

forfeit v. ①被没收 bèi mòshōu (be taken away). ②丧失 sàngshī (lose). n. 没收物 mòshōuwù.

forge n. ①铁工厂 tiěgōngchǎng (smithy). ②锻铁炉 duàntiělú (furnace). — v. ①锻打 duàndǎ (hammer out). ②伪造 wěizào / wèizào, 假造 jiǎzào (counterfeit).

forget v. 忘记 wàngjì, 遗忘 yíwàng.

forgive v. 原谅 yuánliàng.

forgo v. 弃绝 qìjué, 放弃 fàngqì.

fork n. 叉 chā, 叉子 chāzi. — v. ①叉起 chāqǐ 〈utensil〉.

F

②分岔 fēnchà (split).

forlorn *adj.* ①被遗弃的 bèi yíqì de (deserted). ②可怜的 kělián de (pitiable). ③绝望的 juéwàng de (hopeless).

form *n.* ①形状 xíngzhuàng (appearance). ②形式 xíngshì (shape). — *v.* ①形成 xíngchéng (take shape). ②组成 zǔchéng (make).

formal *adj.* 正式的 zhèngshì de.

formation *n.* ①形成 xíngchéng, 构成 gòuchéng (structure). ②排列 páiliè (order).

former *adj.* ①从前的 cóngqián de, 以前的 yǐqián de (earlier). ②前者的 qiánzhě de (previous).

formerly *adv.* 以前 yǐqián, 从前 cóngqián.

formidable *adj.* 令人畏惧的 lìng rén wèijù de.

formula *n.* ①公式 gōngshì (rule). ②配方 pèifāng ⟨substance⟩.

formulaic *adj.* 公式化的 gōngshìhuà de.

formulate *v.* 明确陈述 míngquè chénshù (express clearly).

forsake *v.* 遗弃 yíqì, 抛弃 pāoqì.

fort *n.* 堡垒 bǎolěi, 要塞 yàosài.

forth *adv.* ①向前 xiàngqián (forward). ②外出 wàichū (out).

forthcoming *adj.* ①即将出现的 jíjiāng chūxiàn de (imminent). ②现成的 xiànchéng de, 准备好的 zhǔnbèi hǎo de (ready). ③愿意回答的 yuànyì huídá de (willing to answer).

forthwith *adv.* 立刻 lìkè.

fortieth *n. & adj.* 第四十 dì-

-sìshí.

fortification *n.* 堡垒 bǎolěi, 要塞 yàosài.

fortify *v.* ①设防 shèfáng (protect). ②加强 jiāqiáng (strengthen).

fortnight *n.* 两星期 liǎng xīngqī / liǎng xīngqí, 双周 shuāngzhōu.

fortress *n.* 堡垒 bǎolěi, 要塞 yàosài.

fortunate *adj.* 幸运的 xìngyùn de.

fortunately *adv.* 幸好 xìnghǎo, 好在 hǎozài.

fortune *n.* ①命运 mìngyùn (fate). ②幸运 xìngyùn (luck). ③财富 cáifù (wealth).

fortuneteller *n.* 算命者 suànmìngzhě.

forty *n. & adj.* 四十 sìshí.

forum *n.* ①座谈会 zuòtánhuì (meeting). ②论坛 lùntán ⟨open discussion⟩.

forward *adv.* 向前 xiàngqián. — *adj.* 向前的 xiàngqián de (front). — *v.* ①转送 zhuǎnsòng, 传递 chuándì (pass on). ②促进 cùjìn (advance). — *n.* 前锋 qiánfēng ⟨sports⟩.

fossil *n.* 化石 huàshí ⟨rock⟩.

foster *v.* ①培养 péiyǎng (cultivate). ②助长 zhùzhǎng (promote). ③抚育 fǔyù (bring up).

foul *adj.* ①污秽的 wūhuì de (dirty). ②令人厌恶的 lìng rén yànwù de (disgusting). ③不正的 bú zhèng de (unfair). ④犯规的 fànguī de ⟨sports⟩.

found *v.* 建立 jiànlì, 创设 chuàngshè.

foundation *n.* ①基础 jīchǔ, 根基 gēnjī (basis). ②地基 dìjī

(base). ③建立 jiànlì, 创办 chuàngbàn (establishment). ④基金会 jījīnhuì 〈organization〉.

founder *n.* 创办者 chuàngbànzhě, 建立者 jiànlìzhě.

foundry *n.* 铸造厂 zhùzàochǎng.

fountain *n.* 喷水池 pēnshuǐchí.

four *n. & adj.* 四 sì, 四个 sì ge.

fourteen *n.* 十四 shísì.

fourteenth *n. & adj.* 第十四 dì-shísì.

fourth *n. & adj.* 第四 dì-sì.

fowl *n.* 禽类 qínlèi.

fox *n.* 狐狸 húli 〈animal〉.

fraction *n.* ①部分 bùfen, 碎片 suìpiàn 〈piece〉. ②分数 fēnshù 〈mathematics〉.

fracture *n. & v.* 破裂 pòliè, 折断 zhéduàn 〈break〉. ②骨折 gǔzhé 〈medical〉.

fragile *adj.* 易碎的 yì suì de.

fragment *n.* 碎片 suìpiàn.

fragrant *adj.* 芳香的 fāngxiāng de.

frail *adj.* ①脆弱的 cuìruò de 〈flimsy〉. ②意志薄弱的 yìzhì bóruò de 〈wavering〉.

frame *n.* ①框 kuàng / kuāng, 框架 kuàngjià / kuāngjià 〈border〉. ②体格 tǐgé 〈shape〉. ③镜头 jìngtóu 〈film〉. ④骨架 gǔjià 〈skeleton〉. — *v.* ①架构 jiàgòu, 拟定 nǐdìng 〈plan〉. ②诬陷 wūxiàn 〈crime〉.

framework *n.* ①骨架 gǔjià 〈frame〉. ②组织 zǔzhī 〈organization〉, 体系 tǐxì 〈system〉. ③思想脉络 sīxiǎng màiluò 〈frame of reference〉.

franchise *n.* ①选举权 xuǎnjǔquán 〈right to vote〉. ②特

权 tèquán 〈privilege〉. ③经销权 jīngxiāoquán 〈right to deal〉. ④加盟体 jiāméngtǐ 〈business〉.

frank *adj.* 坦白的 tǎnbái de, 率直的 shuàizhí de.

frantic *adj.* 发狂似的 fākuáng shì de / fākuáng sì de.

fraternal *adj.* ①兄弟的 xiōngdì de 〈having to do with brothers〉. ②友善的 yǒushàn de 〈friendly〉.

fraternity *n.* ①兄弟会 xiōngdìhuì 〈society of men〉. ②手足之情 shǒuzúzhīqíng 〈brotherhood〉.

fraud *n.* 诈欺 zhàqī, 欺骗 qīpiàn.

fraught *adj.* 充满的 chōngmǎn de 〈filled with〉.

fray *n.* 争吵 zhēngchǎo, 喧哗 xuānhuá 〈quarrel〉.

freak *n.* 怪物 guàiwù, 畸形 jīxíng 〈abnormal feature〉. — *adj.* 怪异的 guàiyì de.

freckle *n.* 雀斑 quèbān.

free *adj.* ①自由的 zìyóu de 〈at liberty〉. ②无拘束的 wú jūshù de 〈not bound〉. ③免费的 miǎnfèi de 〈without charge〉. ④空闲的 kòngxián de 〈unoccupied〉. ~ *speech* 言论自由 yánlùn zìyóu. ~ *will* 自由意志 zìyóu yìzhì. — *v.* 释放 shìfàng, 使自由 shǐ zìyóu.

freedom *n.* 自由 zìyóu.

Freemason *n.* 共济会会员 Gòngjìhuì huìyuán.

freeway *n.* 高速公路 gāosù gōnglù.

freewill *adj.* 自愿的 zìyuàn de.

freeze *v.* ①结冰 jiébīng 〈become ice〉. ②冻僵 dòngjiāng 〈chill〉. ③冷冻 lěngdòng 〈refrigerate〉. ④冻结 dòngjié

F

(fix).

freight n. ①货物 huòwù (cargo). ②运费 yùnfèi (money).

French n. & adj. ①法国人 Fǎguórén 〈people〉. ②法语 Fǎyǔ 〈language〉. ~ *fries* 炸土豆条 zhá tǔdòutiáo / 薯条 shǔtiáo. ~ *kiss* 法式接吻 fǎshì jiēwěn.

frenzy n. 狂乱 kuángluàn.

frequency n. 频率 pínlǜ, 次数 cìshù.

frequent adj. 频繁的 pínfán de, 屡次的 lǚcì de.

fresco n. 壁画 bìhuà.

fresh adj. ①新鲜的 xīnxiān de 〈food〉. ②清新的 qīngxīn de 〈air〉. ③淡的 dàn de 〈water〉. ④新奇的 xīnqí de 〈idea〉.

freshman n. 新生 xīnshēng 〈student〉, 新鲜人 xīnxiānrén 〈society〉.

fret v. 烦躁 fánzào.

friar n. 修道士 xiūdàoshì.

friction n. ①摩擦 mócā 〈rubbing〉. ②冲突 chōngtū / chōngtú, 不和 bùhé 〈conflict〉.

Friday n. 星期五 Xīngqíwǔ / Xīngqíwǔ.

fridge n. 冰箱 bīngxiāng.

friend n. 朋友 péngyou, 友人 yǒurén 〈companion〉.

friendly adj. 友善的 yǒushàn de 〈well-disposed〉, 亲切的 qīnqiè de 〈affectionate〉.

friendship n. 友谊 yǒuyì, 友情 yǒuqíng.

fright n. 惊骇 jīnghài, 恐怖 kǒngbù.

frighten v. 惊吓 jīngxià, 使害怕 shǐ hàipà.

frightful adj. 可怕的 kěpà de.

frigid adj. ①严寒的 yánhán

de 〈very cold〉. ②冷淡的 lěngdàn de 〈unfriendly〉.

frill n. 褶边 zhěbiān / zhébiān 〈folds〉.

fringe n. ①穗 suì, 须边 xūbiān 〈border〉. ②边缘 biānyuán 〈edge〉.

frisk v. 搜身 sōushēn 〈search〉.

frisky adj. 欢跃的 huānyuè de.

fritter v. 慢慢耗费 mànman hàofèi 〈waste〉. — n. 油条 yóutiáo, 油煎饼 yóujiānbǐng.

frivolous adj. ①不重要的 bú zhòngyào de 〈unimportant〉. ②轻浮的 qīngfú de 〈not serious〉.

frock n. ①僧袍 sēngpáo 〈monk〉. ②长袍 chángpáo 〈gown〉.

frog n. 蛙 wā, 青蛙 qīngwā.

frolic n. & v. 嬉戏 xīxì, 作乐 zuòlè 〈play〉.

from prep. ①从 cóng, 自 zì 〈time, place〉. ②离 lí 〈distance〉.

front n. ①前部 qiánbù, 前面 qiánmiàn 〈forefront〉. ②前线 qiánxiàn 〈battle area〉. ③锋面 fēngmiàn 〈weather〉. *in* ~ *of* 在……的前面 zài...de qiánmiàn.

frontage n. 正面 zhèngmiàn.

frontier n. 边界 biānjiè, 边境 biānjìng 〈border〉.

frost n. 霜 shuāng.

frostbite n. 冻伤 dòngshāng, 冻疮 dòngchuāng.

froth n. 泡沫 pàomò 〈bubbles〉. — v. 起泡沫 qǐ pàomò.

frown n. & v. 皱眉 zhòuméi.

frozen adj. 结冰的 jiébīng de, 冻僵的 dòngjiāng de.

frozen embryo n. 冷冻胚胎 lěngdòng pēitāi.

frugal adj. 节俭的 jiéjiǎn de.

fruit n. 水果 shuǐguǒ, 果实

guǒshí.

fruitful *adj.* ①结果实的 jiē guǒshí de, 丰收的 fēngshōu de (abundant). ②有成果的 yǒu chéngguǒ de, 有利的 yǒulì de (profitable).

fruitless *adj.* 无效的 wúxiào de (useless).

frustrate *v.* 使受挫 shǐ shòucuò (make frustrated), 使失败 shǐ shībài (cause to fail).

frustrated *adj.* 有挫折感的 yǒu cuòzhégǎn de.

fry *v.* 油煎 yóujiān ⟨skillet⟩, 油炸 yóuzhá (deep fry), 炒 chǎo (stir-fry).

FTP 档案传输协定 dàng'àn chuánshū xiédìng / dǎng'àn chuánshū xiédìng ⟨computer⟩.

fudge *n.* 牛奶软糖 niúnǎi ruǎntáng.

fuel *n.* 燃料 ránliào.

fugitive *n.* 亡命之徒 wángmìngzhītú, 逃亡者 táowángzhě ⟨person⟩. — *adj.* 逃亡的 táowáng de.

fulfil *v.* ①履行 lǚxíng, 完成 wánchéng (accomplish). ②满足 mǎnzú (satisfy).

full *adj.* 满的 mǎn de, 装满的 zhuāngmǎn de (filled).
~-figured 丰满的 fēngmǎn de. *~ moon* 满月 mǎnyuè.

full-time *adj.* 全职的 quánzhí de, 专任的 zhuānrèn de.

fully *adv.* 完全地 wánquán de, 充分地 chōngfèn de (completely).

fumble *n. & v.* 笨拙地处理 bènzhuō de chǔlǐ / bènzhuó de chǔlǐ (mishandle).

fume *n. (pl.)* 难闻的烟 nánwén de yān ⟨smoke⟩. — *v.* ①发出烟气 fāchū yānqì (emit

smoke). ②发怒 fānù (be angry).

fun *n.* 乐趣 lèqù (enjoyment). *make ~ of* 开……的玩笑 kāi...de wánxiào. — *adj.* 好玩的 hǎowán de, 有趣的 yǒuqù de.

function *n.* ①作用 zuòyòng, 功能 gōngnéng (purpose). ②职责 zhízé (duty). — *v.* 运转 yùnzhuǎn.

fund *n.* ①基金 jījīn, 专款 zhuānkuǎn ⟨money⟩. ②蕴藏 yùncáng ⟨things⟩.

fundamental *adj.* 基本的 jīběn de (basic), 重要的 zhòngyào de (important). — *n.* 基本原理 jīběn yuánlǐ, 基本法则 jīběn fǎzé.

funeral *n.* 葬礼 zànglǐ, 丧礼 sānglǐ.

fungus *n.* 菌类 jūnlèi / jùnlèi.

funnel *n.* ①漏斗 lòudǒu ⟨for liquids⟩. ②烟囱 yāncōng ⟨for gases⟩.

funny *adj.* ①有趣的 yǒuqù de, 好玩的 hǎowán de (humorous). ②滑稽古怪的 huájī gǔguài de (strange). ③好笑的 hǎoxiào de (laughable).

fur *n.* 毛皮 máopí.

furious *adj.* 狂怒的 kuángnù de.

furl *v.* 卷起 juǎnqǐ.

furnace *n.* 火炉 huǒlú, 熔炉 rónglú.

furnish *v.* ①提供 tígōng, 供应 gōngyìng (provide). ②家具布置 jiājù bùzhì ⟨furniture⟩.

furniture *n.* 家具 jiājù.

furrow *n.* 犁沟 lígōu.

furry *adj.* 毛皮制的 máopí zhì de.

further *adj.* 较远的 jiào yuǎn de (more distant). — *adv.* 较远

地 jiào yuǎn de (farther). — v. 促进 cùjìn, 推展 tuīzhǎn.

furthermore adv. 此外 cǐwài, 再者 zàizhě.

furtive adj. 鬼鬼祟祟的 guǐguǐsuìsuì de.

fury n. 盛怒 shèngnù.

fuse n. ①保险丝 bǎoxiǎnsī (wire). ②导火线 dǎohuǒxiàn, 引信 yǐnxìn ⟨bomb⟩. ~ **box** 电源保险丝箱 diànyuán bǎoxiǎnsī xiāng. — v. 熔化 rónghuà.

fuselage n. 机身 jīshēn.

fusible adj. 易熔的 yì róng de.

fusion n. 熔合 rónghé, 融解 róngjiě.

fuss n. & v. ①大惊小怪 dà-jīng-xiǎoguài, 小题大做 xiǎo-tí-dàzuò. ②忙乱 mángluàn ⟨hurry⟩.

futile adj. 徒劳的 túláo de, 无用的 wúyòng de.

future n. 将来 jiānglái, 未来 wèilái. — adj. 未来的 wèilái de.

fuzz n. 绒毛 róngmáo, 细毛 xìmáo.

fuzzy logic 模糊理论 móhu lǐlùn, 模糊逻辑 móhu luóji.

G

G8 八大工业国 bā dà gōngyèguó.

gadget n. 小巧的机械 xiǎoqiǎo de jīxiè.

gag v. 塞住口 sāizhù kǒu ⟨plug⟩.

gaily adv. 欢乐地 huānlè de ⟨happily⟩.

gain v. ①获得 huòdé (obtain). ②增加 zēngjiā (increase). ③促进 cùjìn, 进步 jìnbù (improve). — n. 利益 lìyì, 利润 lìrùn (profit).

gait n. 步态 bùtài, 步法 bùfǎ.

gala n. 欢庆 huānqìng.

galaxy n. 银河 yínhé.

gale n. 强风 qiángfēng (windstorm).

gallant adj. 英勇的 yīngyǒng de (brave).

gallery n. ①陈列馆 chénlièguǎn, 画廊 huàláng ⟨art⟩. ②观众 guānzhòng ⟨sports⟩.

gallon n. 加仑 jiālún.

gallop n. 飞跑 fēipǎo.

gamble n. & v. 赌博 dǔbó.

gambler n. 赌徒 dǔtú.

game n. ①游戏 yóuxì (amusement). ②比赛 bǐsài (contest). ~ **plan** 行动计划 xíngdòng jìhuà. ~ **show** 有奖游戏节目 yǒu jiǎng yóuxì jiémù.

gang n. 一群 yì qún, 一帮 yì bāng ⟨gangster⟩.

gangster n. 歹徒 dǎitú.

gap n. 缝隙 fèngxì, 裂缝 lièfèng (break).

gape n. & v. 张嘴注视 zhāngzuǐ zhùshì (stare with an open mouth).

garage n. ①车库 chēkù ⟨for parking⟩. ②修车厂 xiūchēchǎng ⟨for repairing⟩.

garbage n. 垃圾 lājī / lèsè. ~ **can** 垃圾箱 lājīxiāng / lèsèxiāng. ~ **truck** 垃圾车 lājīchē / lèsèchē.

garble v. 窜改 cuàngǎi.

garden n. 花园 huāyuán, 庭园 tíngyuán ⟨flower⟩.

gardener n. 园丁 yuándīng.

gargle v. 漱口 shùkǒu.

garish adj. 俗丽的 súlì de, 炫耀的 xuànyào de.

garlic n. 蒜 suàn, 大蒜 dàsuàn.

garment n. 衣服 yīfu.

garrulous adj. 爱说闲话的 ài shuō xiánhuà de ⟨talkative⟩.

gas n. ①气体 qìtǐ ⟨vapor⟩. ②瓦斯 wǎsī ⟨fuel⟩. ~ **station** 加油站 jiāyóuzhàn.

gaseous adj. 气体的 qìtǐ de.

gash n. 切痕 qiēhén, 伤痕 shānghén.

gasoline n. 汽油 qìyóu.

gasp v. 喘气 chuǎnqì ⟨breathe quickly⟩.

gastric adj. 胃的 wèi de. ~ **ulcer** 胃溃扬 wèikuìyáng.

gate n. ①门 mén, 大门 dàmén ⟨door⟩. ②登机门 dēngjīmén ⟨planes⟩.

gather v. ①聚集 jùjí, 集合 jíhé ⟨assemble⟩. ②采集 cǎijí ⟨collect⟩.

gathering n. 聚集 jùjí, 集合 jíhé.

gaudy adj. 俗丽的 súlì de.

gauge n. 计量器 jìliàngqì ⟨measuring tool⟩. — v. 计量 jìliàng / jìliáng, 测量 cèliáng ⟨measure⟩.

gaunt adj. 瘦削的 shòuxuē de / shòuxuè de ⟨extremely thin⟩.

gauze n. 纱布 shābù, 薄纱 báoshā / bóshā.

gay adj. ①愉快的 yúkuài de ⟨merry⟩. ②同性恋的 tóngxìngliàn de ⟨homosexual⟩. — n. 同性恋 tóngxìngliàn.

gaze n. & v. 凝视 níngshì, 注视 zhùshì.

gear n. ①齿轮 chǐlún ⟨wheel⟩. ②工具 gōngjù, 用具 yòngjù ⟨tool⟩.

geek n. 呆子 dāizi.

gelatin n. 胶 jiāo, 胶质 jiāozhì / jiāozhí.

gem n. 宝石 bǎoshí, 珠宝 zhūbǎo ⟨jewel⟩.

Gemini 双子座 Shuāngzǐzuò.

gender n. ①性别 xìngbié ⟨sex⟩. ②性 xìng ⟨grammar⟩.

gene n. 基因 jīyīn.

genealogy n. 系谱学 xìpǔxué ⟨study of family history⟩.

general adj. ①一般的 yìbān de ⟨common⟩. ②概括的 gàikuò de / gàiguā de, 总的 zǒng de ⟨overall⟩. — n. 将军 jiāngjūn, 上将 shàngjiàng ⟨officer⟩. ~ **election** 大选 dàxuǎn.

generalize v. 归纳 guīnà, 概括 gàikuò / gàiguā ⟨summarize⟩.

generally adv. ①通常地 tōngcháng de ⟨usually⟩. ②广泛地 guǎngfàn de ⟨widely⟩.

generate v. 产生 chǎnshēng, 造成 zàochéng ⟨cause⟩.

generation n. ①一代 yídài, 世代 shìdài ⟨a stage in family descent⟩. ②同时代的人 tóngshídài de rén ⟨people in the same period⟩. ~ **gap** 代沟 dàigōu.

generator n. 发电机 fādiànjī.

generic adj. 属的 shǔ de,

类的 lèi de (of a genus).

generosity n. 慷慨 kāngkǎi, 宽大 kuāndà.

generous adj. 慷慨的 kāngkǎi de, 大方的 dàfāng de.

genetic engineering n. 基因工程 jīyīn gōngchéng.

genetics n. 遗传学 yíchuánxué.

genial adj. 和蔼的 hé'ǎi de, 亲切的 qīnqiè de.

genius n. 天才 tiāncái (talent), 天赋 tiānfù (gift).

genocide n. 大屠杀 dàtúshā.

gentle adj. 温和的 wēnhé de, 文雅的 wényǎ de.

gentleman n. 绅士 shēnshì, 君子 jūnzǐ.

genuine adj. ①真正的 zhēnzhèng de (real). ②真诚的 zhēnchéng de (sincere).

geography n. 地理学 dìlǐxué ⟨science⟩.

geology n. 地质学 dìzhìxué / dìzhíxué.

geometric adj. 几何学的 jǐhéxué de.

geometry n. 几何学 jǐhéxué.

germ n. 细菌 xìjūn / xìjùn, 病菌 bìngjūn / bìngjùn (bacteria).

German n. & adj. ①德国人 Déguórén ⟨people⟩. ②德语 Déyǔ ⟨language⟩.

germinate v. 使发芽 shǐ fāyá (sprout).

gesture n. 手势 shǒushì.

get v. ①获得 huòdé, 得到 dédào (obtain). ②拿到 nádào, 捉住 zhuōzhù (fetch). ③了解 liǎojiě, 明白 míngbai (comprehend). ~ *through* 通过 tōngguò. ~ *together* 相聚 xiāngjù. ~ *up* 起床 qǐchuáng.

ghost n. 鬼 guǐ, 灵魂 línghún (spirit).

ghostbuster n. 驱鬼者 qūguǐzhě.

giant n. 巨人 jùrén (colossus). — adj. 巨大的 jùdà de (huge).

gift n. 礼物 lǐwù (present).

gifted adj. 有天赋的 yǒu tiānfù de (very talented).

gigantic adj. 巨大的 jùdà de.

giggle n. & v. 傻笑 shǎxiào, 咯咯地笑 gēgē de xiào.

gill n. 鳃 sāi ⟨fish⟩.

gimmick n. 花招 huāzhāo, 噱头 xuétóu / xuētóu.

gin n. 杜松子酒 dùsōngzǐjiǔ.

ginger n. 姜 jiāng ⟨plant⟩.

gingerly adj. & adv. 小心谨慎的 xiǎoxīn jǐnshèn de.

giraffe n. 长颈鹿 chángjǐnglù.

girl n. 女孩 nǚhái, 少女 shàonǚ.

girlfriend n. 女朋友 nǚpéngyou.

gist n. 要旨 yàozhǐ, 要点 yàodiǎn.

give v. ①给予 jǐyǔ (grant). ②供给 gōngjǐ (offer). ~ *in* 屈服 qūfú. ~ *up* 放弃 fàngqì.

glacier n. 冰河 bīnghé.

glad adj. 高兴的 gāoxìng de, 快乐的 kuàilè de (pleased and happy).

gladiator n. 斗士 dòushì.

glamour n. 魅力 mèilì (attractiveness).

glance n. 一瞥 yìpiē (look). — v. 瞥见 piējiàn (look).

gland n. 腺 xiàn.

glare n. & v. ①眩光 xuànguāng (strong light). ②怒视 nùshì (fierce look).

glass n. ①玻璃 bōlí ⟨substance⟩. ②玻璃杯 bōlíbēi (cup).

gleam n. & v. 闪光 shǎnguāng

(flash).

glee n. 欢乐 huānlè (merriment).

glib adj. 油腔滑调的 yóuqiāng-huádiào de (smooth-spoken).

glide v. 滑行 huáxíng (slide).

glimmer n. 微光 wēiguāng / wéiguāng (gleam). — v. 发微光 fā wēiguāng / fā wéiguāng.

glimpse n. 一瞥 yìpiē. — v. 瞥见 piējiàn.

glitter n. & v. 闪烁 shǎnshuò.

gloat v. 洋洋得意地看着 yángyáng-déyì de kànzhe (brag).

global adj. 全球的 quánqiú de (universal). ~ *village* 地球村 dìqiúcūn. ~ *warming* 全球暖化 quánqiú nuǎnhuà.

globalization n. 全球化 quánqiúhuà.

globalize v. 全球化 quánqiúhuà.

globe n. 地球 dìqiú (the earth).

gloom n. 幽暗 yōu'àn, 阴暗 yīn'àn (semidarkness).

gloomy adj. 忧郁的 yōuyù de (sad).

glorify v. ①赞美 zànměi (praise). ②加荣耀于 jiā róngyào yú (make glorious).

glorious adj. 光荣的 guāngróng de, 辉煌的 huīhuáng de (possessing glory).

glory n. ①光荣 guāngróng (honor). ②赞美 zànměi (adoration). ③壮丽 zhuànglì (great beauty).

gloss n. & v. 光泽 guāngzé.

glossary n. 字汇 zìhuì, 词汇 cíhuì (vocabulary), 字汇表 zìhuìbiǎo, 词汇表 cíhuìbiǎo (wordlist).

glove n. 手套 shǒutào.

glow n. & v. 容光焕发 róngguāng-huànfā (flush).

glucose n. 葡萄糖 pútáotáng.

glue n. 胶 jiāo. — v. 黏 nián.

go v. 去 qù, 行走 xíngzǒu (move).
~ *abroad* 出国 chūguó.
~ *ahead* 向前进 xiàng qián jìn, 做下去 zuòxiaqu. ~ *into* 进入 jìnrù. ~ *on* 继续 jìxù. ~ *out* 外出 wàichū. ~ *through* 经历 jīnglì.

goal n. ①目标 mùbiāo (target). ②球门 qiúmén (football).

goat n. 山羊 shānyáng.

god n. 上帝 shàngdì, 神 shén (divine being).

goddess n. 女神 nǚshén.

godfather n. 教父 jiàofù (religion).

goggles n. 护目镜 hùmùjìng, 挡风眼镜 dǎngfēng yǎnjìng.

gold n. 金 jīn, 黄金 huángjīn. ~ *card* 金卡 jīnkǎ.

golden adj. ①黄金的 huángjīn de (metal). ②金色的 jīnsè de (color).

golf n. 高尔夫球 gāo'ěrfūqiú.

gondola n. 平底船 píngdǐchuán (boat).

gone adj. ①消失的 xiāoshī de (past). ②死去的 sǐqù de (dead).

good adj. 好的 hǎo de (fine).
~ *afternoon* 午安 wǔ'ān.
~ *evening* 晚安 wǎn'ān.
~ *morning* 早安 zǎo'ān.
~ *night* 晚安 wǎn'ān.

good-bye n. & interj. 再见 zàijiàn.

good-for-nothing adj. 无用的 wúyòng de. — n. 无用之人 wúyòng zhī rén.

good-looking adj. 貌美的 màoměi de, 漂亮的 piàoliang de.

good-natured adj. 和蔼的

G

hé'ǎi de.

goodness n. 良善 liángshàn (quality of being good).

goods n. 货物 huòwù, 商品 shāngpǐn, 东西 dōngxi (things).

goodwill n. 善意 shànyì, 好意 hǎoyì.

goose n. 鹅 é ⟨bird⟩.

gorge n. 峡谷 xiágǔ. — v. 塞饱 sāibǎo, 狼吞虎咽 lángtūn-hǔyàn (stuff).

gorgeous adj. 华丽的 huálì de (splendid).

gorilla n. 猩猩 xīngxing.

gory adj. 染血的 rǎnxuè de / rǎnxiě de.

gosh interj. 天哪！Tiānna! 哎呀！Āiyā!

gospel n. 福音 fúyīn.

gossip n. 闲话 xiánhuà (chatter). — v. 说闲话 shuō xiánhuà.

gourmet n. 美食家 měishíjiā.

govern v. ①治理 zhìlǐ, 管理 guǎnlǐ (be in charge of). ②控制 kòngzhì (control).

government n. ①政府 zhèngfǔ (administration). ②管理 guǎnlǐ (management).

governor n. 州长 zhōuzhǎng ⟨of a state⟩.

gown n. 长袍 chángpáo.

grab n. & v. 攫 jué, 掠夺 lüèduó (snatch).

grace n. 优雅 yōuyǎ (elegance).

graceful adj. ①优雅的 yōuyǎ de ⟨shape or movement⟩. ②温文儒雅的 wēnwén-rúyǎ de ⟨manner⟩.

gracious adj. ①优雅的 yōuyǎ de (elegant). ②仁慈的 réncí de (merciful).

grade n. ①等级 děngjí (level).

②年级 niánjí (class). ③成绩 chéngjī / chéngjì, 分数 fēnshù (mark).

gradient n. 坡度 pōdù, 斜度 xiédù.

gradual adj. 逐渐的 zhújiàn de.

graduate v. 毕业 bìyè ⟨finish⟩. — n. 毕业生 bìyèshēng.

graduate school n. 研究生院 yánjiūshēngyuàn / 研究所 yánjiūsuǒ.

graduation n. 毕业 bìyè.

grain n. 谷物 gǔwù, 谷类 gǔlèi (seed).

gram n. 克 kè ⟨weight⟩.

grammar n. 文法 wénfǎ.

granary n. 谷仓 gǔcāng.

grand adj. 宏伟的 hóngwěi de (magnificent), 重大的 zhòngdà de (enormous).

G- Canyon 大峡谷 Dàxiágǔ. **~ jury** 大陪审团 dà péishěntuán. **~ piano** 平台型钢琴 píngtáixíng gāngqín.

grandchild n. 孙子 sūnzi.

granddaughter n. 孙女 sūnnǚ.

grandeur n. 宏伟壮丽 hóngwěi zhuànglì (spectacle).

grandfather n. 祖父 zǔfù.

grandiose adj. 浮华不实的 fúhuá-bùshí de.

grandmother n. 祖母 zǔmǔ.

grandson n. 孙子 sūnzi.

grant v. ①授与 shòuyǔ, 赠与 zèngyǔ (give). ②允许 yǔnxǔ, 答应 dāyìng (allow).

grape n. 葡萄 pútao.

grapefruit n. 葡萄柚 pútáoyòu.

graph n. 图表 túbiǎo.

graphic adj. ①生动的

shēngdòng de (vivid). ②绘画的 huìhuà de ⟨drawing⟩. ~ **arts** 平面艺术 píngmiàn yìshù.

grasp v. 紧握 jǐnwò, 抓住 zhuāzhù ⟨catch⟩.

grass n. 草 cǎo.

grasshopper n. 蚱蜢 zhàměng.

grateful adj. 感谢的 gǎnxiè de.

gratitude n. 感谢 gǎnxiè, 感激 gǎnjī.

gratuity n. 小费 xiǎofèi ⟨tip⟩.

gravel n. 碎石 suìshí.

gravestone n. 墓碑 mùbēi.

graveyard n. 墓地 mùdì.

gravity n. ①地心引力 dìxīnyǐnlì, 引力 yǐnlì, 重力 zhònglì ⟨gravitation⟩. ②严重 yánzhòng, 重大 zhòngdà ⟨seriousness⟩. ③严肃 yánsù, 庄重 zhuāngzhòng ⟨solemnity⟩.

gravy n. 肉汤 ròutāng, 卤汁 lǔzhī ⟨sauce⟩.

gray n. & adj. 灰色 huīsè.

graze v. ①吃青草 chī qīngcǎo ⟨eat grass⟩. ②擦过 cāguò ⟨brush⟩.

grease n. 油脂 yóuzhī.

great adj. ①大的 dà de ⟨large⟩. ②伟大的 wěidà de ⟨remarkable⟩. ③极好的 jí hǎo de ⟨excellent⟩.

greed n. 贪婪 tānlán.

greedy adj. 贪婪的 tānlán de ⟨avaricious⟩.

Greek n. & adj. ①希腊人 Xīlàrén ⟨people⟩. ②希腊文 Xīlàwén ⟨language⟩.

green n. & adj. 绿色 lǜsè. ~ **bean** 四季豆 sìjìdòu.

greenhouse n. 温室 wēnshì. ~ **effect** 温室效应 wēnshì xiàoyìng.

greet v. 欢迎 huānyíng, 打招呼 dǎ zhāohu.

greeting n. 问候 wènhòu ⟨regards⟩.

greyhound n. ①灵猩 língtí ⟨animal⟩. ②(G~) 灰狗巴士 huīgǒu bāshì ⟨bus⟩.

gregarious adj. 社交的 shèjiāo de, 好交际的 hào jiāojì de ⟨sociable⟩.

grenade n. 手榴弹 shǒuliúdàn.

grid n. 格子 gézi.

grief n. 悲伤 bēishāng.

grievance n. 委屈 wěiqu, 不平 bùpíng.

grieve v. 使悲伤 shǐ bēishāng, 痛苦 tòngkǔ.

grill n. ①烤架 kǎojià ⟨device⟩. ②烧烤食品 shāokǎo shípǐn ⟨food⟩. — v. 烧 shāo, 烤 kǎo ⟨cook⟩.

grim adj. 严厉的 yánlì de.

grimace n. 愁眉苦脸 chóuméi-kǔliǎn, 鬼脸 guǐliǎn.

grime n. 污秽 wūhuì.

grin n. 露齿笑 lòu chǐ xiào.

grind v. 磨碎 mósuì, 研磨 yánmó ⟨crush⟩.

grip n. & v. 紧握 jǐnwò.

groan n. & v. 呻吟 shēnyín.

grocer n. 杂货商 záhuòshāng.

grocery n. 杂货店 záhuòdiàn.

groggy adj. ①眩晕虚弱的 xuànyùn xūruò de / xuànyūn xūruò de ⟨weak⟩. ②不稳的 bùwěn de ⟨unsteady⟩.

groom n. 新郎 xīnláng ⟨bridegroom⟩.

groomsman n. 男傧相 nánbīnxiàng.

gross adj. ①总的 zǒng de ⟨total⟩. ②重大错误的 zhòngdà cuòwù de ⟨extremely bad⟩. — n. 毛收入 máoshōurù ⟨income⟩. — v. 总共赚入

G

zǒnggòng zhuàn rù.

grotesque *adj.* 古怪的 gǔguài de, 怪诞的 guàidàn de.

ground *n.* 地dì, 土地 tǔdì (land).

groundless *adj.* 无根据的 wú gēnjù de.

group *n.* 群 qún, 组 zǔ, 团体 tuántǐ (set).

grow *v.* ①生长 shēngzhǎng, 成长 chéngzhǎng (develop). ②增长 zēngzhǎng (increase). ③种植 zhòngzhí ⟨plant⟩. ~ *up* 长大 zhǎngdà.

growl *v.* 作低吠声 zuò dīfèishēng.

grown-up *n.* 成人 chéngrén.

growth *n.* ①生长 shēngzhǎng (development). ②增长 zēngzhǎng (increase).

gruesome *adj.* 毛骨悚然的 máogǔ-sǒngrán de (horrible).

grumble *v.* 发牢骚 fā láosāo.

grunt *n. & v.* 咕噜声 gūlūshēng.

guarantee *n. & v.* 保证 bǎozhèng.

guarantor *n.* 保证人 bǎozhèngrén.

guard *v.* 看守 kānshǒu. — *n.* ①守卫者 shǒuwèizhě, 卫兵 wèibīng ⟨watchman⟩. ②警戒 jǐngjiè ⟨lookout⟩.

guardian *n.* 监护人 jiānhùrén.

guerrilla *n.* 游击队 yóujīduì / yóujíduì.

guess *n. & v.* 猜想 cāixiǎng.

guest *n.* 客人 kèrén, 旅客 lǚkè.

guidance *n.* 指导 zhǐdǎo.

guide *v.* 引导 yǐndǎo, 指导 zhǐdǎo (lead).

guidebook *n.* 旅游指南 lǚyóu zhǐnán.

guilt *n.* 罪 zuì, 罪行 zuìxíng / zuìxíng (guiltiness).

guilty *adj.* ①有罪的 yǒuzuì de ⟨not innocent⟩. ②有罪恶感的 yǒu zuì'ègǎn de (ashamed).

guitar *n.* 吉他 jítā.

gulf *n.* 海湾 hǎiwān (bay).

gull *n.* 海鸥 hǎi'ōu ⟨bird⟩.

gulp *v.* 吞饮 tūnyǐn (swallow hastily).

gum *n.* ①树胶 shùjiāo ⟨tree⟩. ②口香糖 kǒuxiāngtáng ⟨for chewing⟩.

gun *n.* 枪 qiāng.

gunpowder *n.* 火药 huǒyào.

gust *n.* 一阵强风 yízhèn qiángfēng.

guts *n.* ①内脏 nèizàng (bowels). ②勇气 yǒngqì (courage).

gutter *n.* 排水沟 páishuǐgōu.

guy *n.* 人 rén, 家伙 jiāhuo.

guzzle *v.* 豪饮 háoyǐn.

gym *n.* 体育馆 tǐyùguǎn (gymnasium).

gymnasium *n.* 健身房 jiànshēnfáng, 体育馆 tǐyùguǎn.

gymnast *n.* 体育家 tǐyùjiā ⟨expert⟩, 体操运动员 tǐcāo yùndòngyuán ⟨gymnastics⟩.

gymnastics *n.* 体操 tǐcāo.

gynecology *n.* 妇科医学 fùkē yīxué ⟨medical⟩.

gyrate *v.* 旋转 xuánzhuǎn (revolve).

gyroscope *n.* 回转仪 huízhuǎnyí, 陀螺仪 tuóluóyí.

G

EHch

habit *n.* 习惯 xíguàn.

habitation *n.* ①居住 jūzhù (living in). ②住所 zhùsuǒ (place to live in).

habitual *adj.* 惯常的 guàncháng de.

hack *v.* 乱砍 luànkǎn, 劈 pī.

hacker *n.* 黑客 hēikè / 电脑骇客 diànnǎo hàikè ⟨computer⟩.

hag *n.* 老丑婆 lǎo chǒu pó (ugly woman).

haggard *adj.* 憔悴的 qiáocuì de ⟨person⟩.

haggle *n. & v.* 讨价还价 tǎojià-huánjià (bargaining).

hail *n.* 冰雹 bīngbáo (frozen raindrops).

hair *n.* 发 fà / fǎ, 头发 tóufa, 毛 máo, 毛发 máofà / máofǎ.

haircut *n.* 理发 lǐfà / lǐfǎ, 剪发 jiǎnfà / jiǎnfǎ.

hairdo *n.* 发型 fàxíng / fǎxíng.

hairdresser *n.* 理发师 lǐfàshī / lǐfǎshī.

hairstyle *n.* 发型 fàxíng / fǎxíng.

hairy *adj.* 多毛的 duō máo de.

halcyon *adj.* 平静的 píngjìng de, 太平的 tàipíng de.

hale *adj.* 强壮的 qiángzhuàng de.

half *n.* 一半 yíbàn, 二分之一 èr fēn zhī yī. — *adj.* 一半的 yíbàn de.

halfway *adj. & adv.* 半路的 bànlù de, 中途的 zhōngtú de.

hall *n.* ①会堂 huìtáng (auditorium). ②走廊 zǒuláng (corridor). ③大厅 dàtīng (large room).

Halloween *n.* 万圣节前夕 Wànshèngjié qiánxī / Wànshèngjié qiánxì.

hallucination *n.* 幻觉 huànjué.

halt *n. & v.* ①中止 zhōngzhǐ (end). ②停止前进 tíngzhǐ qiánjìn (stop).

ham *n.* 火腿 huǒtuǐ.

hamburger *n.* 汉堡包 hànbǎobāo / 汉堡 hànbǎo.

hammer *n.* 锤 chuí, 铁锤 tiěchuí. — *v.* 锤打 chuídǎ.

hammock *n.* 吊床 diàochuáng.

hand *n.* 手 shǒu (fist). — *v.* 交给 jiāogěi, 传递 chuándì.

handbag *n.* 手提包 shǒutíbāo.

handbook *n.* 手册 shǒucè (pamphlet), 指南 zhǐnán (guidebook).

handcuff *n.* 手铐 shǒukào.

handful *n.* 一撮 yì cuō / yí cuò, 一把 yì bǎ ⟨amount⟩.

handicap *n.* 障碍 zhàng'ài ⟨disability⟩.

handicraft *n.* 手艺 shǒuyì, 手工艺 shǒugōngyì.

handkerchief *n.* 手帕 shǒupà.

handle *n.* 把手 bǎshǒu ⟨part⟩. — *v.* 处理 chǔlǐ (take care of), 控制 kòngzhì (control).

handsome *adj.* ①好看的 hǎo kàn de (good-looking). ②英俊的 yīngjùn de ⟨man⟩.

handwriting *n.* 笔迹 bǐjì / bǐjī, 手迹 shǒujì / shǒujī.

H

handy *adj.* 便利的 biànlì de (convenient).

hang *v.* ①挂 guà, 吊 diào 〈place〉。②绞死 jiǎosǐ〈execute〉。

hanger *n.* 挂钩 guàgōu 〈hook〉，衣架 yījià〈clothes〉。

hangman *n.* 刽子手 guìzishǒu / kuàizishǒu.

haphazard *n.* 偶然 ǒurán.

happen *v.* 发生 fāshēng (take place).

happening *n.* 事件 shìjiàn.

happily *adv.* ①快乐地 kuàilè de，幸福地 xìngfú de〈happy〉。②幸好 xìnghǎo，幸运地 xìngyùn de (fortunately).

happiness *n.* 快乐 kuàilè, 幸福 xìngfú.

happy *adj.* 快乐的 kuàilè de (good spirits)，幸福的 xìngfú de (contentment).

harass *v.* 骚扰 sāorǎo (disturb)，困扰 kùnrǎo (bother).

harassment *n.* 骚扰 sāorǎo.

harbor *n.* 港 gǎng, 港口 gǎngkǒu.

hard *adj.* ①坚硬的 jiānyìng de (solid)。②辛苦的 xīnkǔ de, 困难的 kùnnán de (difficult)。③艰苦的 jiānkǔ de (painful)。④剧烈的 jùliè de (strong)。~ **disk** 硬盘 yìngpán / 硬碟 yìngdié.

harden *v.* 使坚硬 shǐ jiānyìng.

hardhearted *adj.* 无情的 wúqíng de.

hardly *adv.* 几乎不 jīhū bù (almost not).

hardship *n.* 艰苦 jiānkǔ.

hardware *n.* ①武器 wǔqì (weapon)。②硬件 yìngjiàn / 硬体 yìngtǐ〈computer〉。

hardy *adj.* ①吃苦耐劳的 chīkǔ-nàiláo de〈man〉。②耐寒的 nàihán de〈plants〉。

hare *n.* 野兔 yětù.

harm *n. & v.* 损害 sǔnhài (damage)，伤害 shānghài (hurt).

harmful *adj.* 有害的 yǒuhài de.

harmless *adj.* 无害的 wúhài de.

harmonica *n.* 口琴 kǒuqín.

harmonious *adj.* ①调和的 tiáohé de, 协调的 xiétiáo dé (amicable)。②悦耳的 yuè'ěr de (melodious).

harmonize *v.* 调和 tiáohé, 和谐 héxié (balance).

harmony *n.* ①调和 tiáohé, 和谐 héxié (balance)。②和声 héshēng〈music〉。

harp *n.* 竖琴 shùqín.

harsh *adj.* ①粗糙的 cūcāo de (rough)。②刺耳的 cì'ěr de (croaking)。③刺眼的 cìyǎn de (dazzling)。④苛刻的 kēkè de (severe).

harvest *n.* ①收获 shōuhuò (gathering in)。②结果 jiéguǒ (result)。— *v.* 收获 shōuhuò (gather).

haste *n.* 匆忙 cōngmáng, 急忙 jímáng〈hurried〉。

hasten *v.* 催促 cuīcù, 使赶快 shǐ gǎnkuài.

hasty *adj.* ①匆忙的 cōngmáng de (hurried)。②草率的 cǎoshuài de (rushed).

hat *n.* 帽子 màozi.

hatch *v.* ①孵 fū, 孵化 fūhuà (brood)。②计画 jìhuà, 设计 shèjì (plan)。— *n.* 舱口 cāngkǒu, 舱门 cāngmén〈ship〉。

hate *n. & v.* 憎恶 zēngwù, 痛

恨 tònghèn (loathing).

~ *mail* 攻击性信件 gōngjīxìng xìnjiàn / gōngjīxìng xìnjiàn, 黑函 hēihán.

hatred n. 憎恶 zēngwù, 痛恨 tònghèn (loathing).

haul v. 拖 tuō, 拉 lā (pull or drag). — n. 用力拖 yònglì tuō (dragging).

haunt v. 常去 chángqù (visit frequently).

have v. 有 yǒu, 具有 jùyǒu (possess). ~ *to* 不得不 bùdé bù.

haven n. 避难所 bìnànsuǒ ⟨safe⟩.

hawk n. 隼 sǔn / zhǔn, 鹰 yīng ⟨bird⟩.

hawker n. 小贩 xiǎofàn.

hay n. 干草 gāncǎo, 秣 mò.

hazard n. 冒险 màoxiǎn, 危险 wēixiǎn / wéixiǎn (danger).

hazardous adj. 冒险的 màoxiǎn de (dangerous).

haze n. 阴霾 yīnmái (thin mist).

hazel n. ①榛 zhēn ⟨tree⟩. ②淡褐色 dànhèsè / dànhésè ⟨color⟩.

hazy adj. 有雾的 yǒuwù de.

H-bomb n. 氢弹 qīngdàn.

he pron. 他 tā.

head n. ①头 tóu, 头部 tóubù ⟨part of body⟩. ②领袖 lǐngxiù, 首长 shǒuzhǎng, 主管 zhǔguǎn (chief). — v. ①为首 wéishǒu, 领导 lǐngdǎo (be in charge of). ②朝……前进 cháo...qiánjìn (head for).

headache n. 头痛 tóutòng.

heading n. 标题 biāotí.

head-hunt v. 猎人头 liè réntóu.

headlight n. 前灯 qiándēng.

headline n. 标题 biāotí ⟨newspaper⟩.

headmaster n. 校长 xiàozhǎng.

headquarters n. 总部 zǒngbù.

headstrong adj. 顽固的 wángù de (stubborn).

headway n. 进步 jìnbù, 进展 jìnzhǎn (progress).

heal v. 治愈 zhìyù (make well again).

health n. 健康 jiànkāng ⟨body or mind⟩.

healthful adj. 有益健康的 yǒuyì jiànkāng de.

healthy adj. 健康的 jiànkāng de ⟨person⟩, 有益健康的 yǒuyì jiànkāng de ⟨food⟩.

heap n. ①堆 duī (pile). ②大量 dàliàng, 许多 xǔduō (mass). — v. 堆积 duījī.

hear v. 听见 tīngjian, 听到 tīngdào.

hearing n. 听力 tīnglì, 听觉 tīngjué (ability to hear). ~ *aid* 助听器 zhùtīngqì.

hearsay n. 谣传 yáochuán.

hearse n. 灵车 língchē.

heart n. ①心脏 xīnzàng ⟨part of body⟩. ②心 xīn, 感情 gǎnqíng ⟨feeling⟩. ③红心 hóngxīn ⟨cards⟩.

heartbreak n. 伤心 shāngxīn, 悲痛 bēitòng.

hearth n. 炉床 lúchuáng.

hearty adj. ①热诚的 rèchéng de (warm). ②强壮的 qiángzhuàng de (strong). ③丰盛的 fēngshèng de (large).

heat n. ①热 rè (hot). ②暖气 nuǎnqì (warm air). — v. 加热 jiārè (warm up).

heater n. 加热器 jiārèqì, 暖炉 nuǎnlú.

heave v. ①举起 jǔqǐ (lift).

H

②投 tóu, 掷 zhì / zhí (throw).

heaven n. ①天堂 tiāntáng 〈religion〉. ②天空 tiānkōng (sky).

heavenly adj. ①美丽的 měilì de (beautiful). ②愉悦的 yúyuè de (delightful). ③天空的 tiānkōng de 〈sky〉.

heavy adj. ①重 zhòng (weighty). ②大量的 dàliàng de (amount). ~ *industry* 重工业 zhònggōngyè.

Hebrew n. & adj. ①希伯来人 Xībóláirén 〈people〉. ②希伯来 语 Xībóláiyǔ 〈language〉.

heckle v. 诘问 jiéwèn (bother).

hedge n. 树篱 shùlí (bushes). — v. ①以树篱围 yǐ shùlí wéi 〈garden〉. ②骑墙 qíqiáng (go with the tide).

heed n. & v. 注意 zhùyì, 留意 liúyì.

heel n. 后跟 hòugēn.

height n. 高 gāo, 高度 gāodù.

heir n. 继承人 jìchéngrén.

heirloom n. 祖传物 zǔchuánwù, 家传之宝 chuánjiāzhībǎo.

helicopter n. 直升机 zhíshēngjī.

helium n. 氦 hài.

hell n. ①地狱 dìyù 〈religion〉. ②苦境 kǔjìng (suffering).

hello n. & v. & interj. 喂! Wèi! 哈啰! Hāluo!

helmet n. 头盔 tóukuī.

help v. ①帮忙 bāngmáng, 帮助 bāngzhù (aid). ②减轻 jiǎnqīng, 减缓 jiǎnhuǎn (lessen). — n. 帮助 bāngzhù.

helper n. 助手 zhùshǒu.

helpful adj. 有帮助的 yǒu bāngzhù de.

helping n. 一份 yífèn.

helpless adj. 无助的 wúzhù de, 无能为力的 wúnéngwéilì de.

hem n. 褶边 zhěbiān / zhébiān.

hemisphere n. 半球 bànqiú.

hemorrhoids n. 痔疮 zhìchuāng.

hemp n. ①麻 má 〈plant〉. ②大麻 dàmá (marijuana).

hen n. 母鸡 mǔjī 〈chicken〉.

hence adv. 因此 yīncǐ, 所以 suǒyǐ (therefore).

henceforth adv. 今后 jīnhòu, 从此 cóngcǐ.

henchman n. 亲信 qīnxìn.

her pron. 她 tā, 她的 tā de.

herb n. 药草 yàocǎo (medicine).

herd n. 兽群 shòuqún 〈animals〉. — v. 群集 qúnjí (group together).

here adv. 在这里 zài zhèlǐ (in, at).

hereafter adv. 此后 cǐhòu (from now on). — n. 将来 jiānglái.

hereby adv. 借此 jiècǐ.

hereditary adj. ①遗传的 yíchuán de 〈of body〉. ②世袭 的 shìxí de 〈of position〉.

heredity n. 遗传 yíchuán.

herein adv. 在此 zài cǐ, 鉴于 jiàn yú.

hereof adv. 关于此点 guānyú cǐ diǎn.

heresy n. 异说 yìshuō.

heretic n. 异教徒 yìjiàotú.

heritage n. 遗产 yíchǎn.

hermit n. 隐者 yǐnzhě, 隐士 yǐnshì (recluse).

hernia n. 疝气 shànqì 〈medical〉.

hero n. 英雄 yīngxióng (great man).

heroic adj. 英勇的 yīngyǒng de (very brave).

heroin n. 海洛因 hǎiluòyīn 〈drug〉.

heroism n. 英勇事迹 yīngyǒng shìjī / yīngyǒng shìjì.

herpes n. 疱疹 pàozhěn 〈medical〉.

herring n. 鲱鱼 fēiyú / fēiyú.

hers pron. 她的 tā de.

herself pron. 她自己 tā zìjǐ.

hesitant adj. 犹豫的 yóuyù de, 迟疑的 chíyí de 〈uncertain〉.

hesitate v. 犹豫 yóuyù, 迟疑 chíyí (undecided).

hesitation n. 踌躇 chóuchú, 迟疑 chíyí (state of hesitating).

heterogeneous adj. 异种的 yìzhǒng de, 不同类的 bù tónglèi de 〈different〉.

hexagon n. 六角形 liùjiǎoxíng.

hey interj. 喂！Wèi！

heyday n. 全盛时期 quánshèng shíqī / quánshèng shíqí.

hi interj. 喂！Wèi！嗨！Hāi！

hibernate v. 冬眠 dōngmián.

hiccup n. & v. 打嗝 dǎgé.

hidden adj. ①隐藏的 yǐncáng de 〈hide〉. ②秘密的 mìmì de 〈secret〉.

hide v. ①隐藏 yǐncáng, 藏 cáng (keep out of sight). ②隐瞒 yǐnmán (keep secret). — n. 兽皮 shòupí (animal's skin).

hide-and-seek n. 捉迷藏 zhuōmícáng.

hideous adj. 丑恶的 chǒu'è de, 可憎的 kězēng de.

hierarchy n. ①阶级组织 jiējí zǔzhī (organization). ②阶级制度 jiējí zhìdù (system).

high adj. ①高的 gāo de (tall). ②主要的 zhǔyào de, 重大的 zhòngdà de (chief). — adv. 高 gāo, 高度地 gāodù de.

~ *blood pressure* 高血压 gāoxuèyā / gāoxiěyā. ~ *school* 中学 zhōngxué.

highland n. 高地 gāodì, 高原 gāoyuán.

highlight v. 使显著 shǐ xiǎnzhù, 强调 qiángdiào (emphasize).

highly adv. 高度地 gāodù de, 非常 fēicháng (very).

Highness n. 殿下 diànxià 〈title〉.

high-pitched adj. 声调高的 shēngdiào gāo de.

high-pressure adj. 高压的 gāoyā de, 强迫的 qiǎngpò de.

high tech n. & adj. 高技术 gāojìshù / 高科技 gāokējì.

highway n. 公路 gōnglù.

hijack v. 劫持 jiéchí 〈airplane〉.

hike n. & v. 健行 jiànxíng, 远足 yuǎnzú, 徒步旅行 túbù lǚxíng.

hiking n. 健行 jiànxíng, 远足 yuǎnzú, 徒步旅行 túbù lǚxíng.

hilarious adj. ①欢乐的 huānlè de (happy). ②爆笑的 bàoxiào de 〈joke〉.

hill n. 丘陵 qiūlíng, 小山 xiǎoshān.

hillside n. 山坡 shānpō.

him pron. 他 tā.

himself pron. 他自己 tā zìjǐ.

hinder v. 妨碍 fáng'ài, 阻止 zǔzhǐ.

Hindu n. & adj. ①印度教教徒 Yìndùjiào jiàotú 〈of Hinduism〉. ②印度人 Yìndùrén 〈people〉.

Hinduism n. 印度教 Yìndùjiào.

hinge n. ①铰链 jiǎoliàn 〈metal part〉. ②枢纽 shūniǔ 〈key〉.

H

hint n. & v. 暗示 ànshì, 提示 tíshì ⟨indirect statement⟩.

hip n. 臀 tún.

hippo n. 河马 hémǎ.

hippopotamus n. 河马 hémǎ.

hire v. ①租用 zūyòng ⟨things⟩. ②雇用 gùyòng ⟨person⟩.

his pron. 他的 tā de.

hiss v. ①发嘶嘶声 fā sīsīshēng ⟨sound⟩. ②发嘘声 fā xūshēng ⟨jeer⟩.

historian n. 历史学家 lìshǐxué jiā.

historic adj. 史上著名的 shǐshang zhùmíng de, 历史性的 lìshǐxìng de.

historical adj. 历史的 lìshǐ de, 基于历史的 jīyú lìshǐ de.

history n. 历史 lìshǐ.

hit v. ①击中 jīzhòng / jízhòng, 打中 dǎzhòng ⟨strike⟩. ②打击 dǎjī / dǎjí ⟨affect⟩. — n. ①打击 dǎjī / dǎjí ⟨blow⟩. ②成功 chénggōng ⟨success⟩.

hitch v. 系住 jìzhù ⟨fasten⟩.

hitchhike v. 搭便车 dā biànchē.

hive n. 蜂房 fēngfáng.

hoard v. 贮藏 zhùcáng / zhǔcáng. — n. 贮藏物 zhùcángwù / zhǔcángwù.

hoarse adj. 嘶哑的 sīyǎ de.

hoax n. 骗人的把戏 piànrén de bǎxì, 骗局 piànjú.

hobby n. 嗜好 shìhào.

hockey n. ①曲棍球 qūgùnqiú ⟨field⟩. ②冰上曲棍球 bīng shang qūgùnqiú ⟨ice⟩.

hog n. ①猪 zhū ⟨pig⟩. ②贪婪者 tānlánzhě ⟨person⟩.

hoist v. 举起 jǔqǐ, 升高 shēnggāo ⟨lift⟩. — n. 起重机 qǐzhòngjī ⟨apparatus⟩.

hold v. ①握住 wòzhù, 抓住 zhuāzhù ⟨grip⟩. ②拥有 yōngyǒu / yǒngyǒu ⟨possess⟩. ③举行 jǔxíng ⟨take place⟩. ④容纳 róngnà, 装 zhuāng ⟨contain⟩. ⑤保持 bǎochí ⟨keep in⟩. — n. ①握 wò, 持 chí ⟨grip⟩. ②掌握 zhǎngwò, 支配 zhīpèi ⟨control⟩.

holder n. 持有人 chíyǒurén.

holding n. ①所有物 suǒyǒuwù ⟨belongings⟩. ②持有股份 chíyǒu gǔfèn ⟨shares in a business⟩.

holdup n. ①耽搁 dānge ⟨delay⟩. ②拦路抢劫 lánlù qiǎngjié ⟨rob⟩.

hole n. 洞 dòng, 洞穴 dòngxué / dòngxuè ⟨cavity⟩.

holiday n. 假日 jiàrì, 休假 xiūjià. ~ center 渡假村 dùjiàcūn.

hollow adj. ①空的 kōng de ⟨empty⟩. ②空虚的 kōngxū de, 虚假的 xūjiǎ de ⟨insubstantial⟩. — n. 洞 dòng, 凹陷 āoxiàn.

Holocaust n. 大屠杀 Dàtúshā ⟨World War II⟩.

holy adj. ①神圣的 shénshèng de ⟨regarded as sacred⟩. ②圣洁的 shèngjié de ⟨moral and pure⟩.

homage n. 尊崇 zūnchóng, 敬意 jìngyì.

home n. ①家 jiā, 家庭 jiātíng ⟨place where one lives⟩. ②家乡 jiāxiāng ⟨native land⟩. ~ shopping 电视购物 diànshì gòuwù.

homeless adj. 无家可归的 wújiā-kěguī de.

homely adj. ①不漂亮的 bú piàoliang de ⟨not pretty⟩, 平凡的 píngfán de ⟨plain⟩.

homemade adj. 自制的 zìzhì de.

homepage n. 主网页 zhǔwǎngyè

zhǔwǎngyè, 首页 shǒuyè 〈computer〉.

homesick adj. 思乡的 sīxiāng de, 想家的 xiǎngjiā de.

homework n. 家庭作业 jiātíng zuòyè.

homosexual adj. 同性恋的 tóngxìngliàn de. — n. 同性恋者 tóngxìngliàn zhě.

honest adj. 诚实的 chéngshí de (truthful), 正直的 zhèngzhí de (not cheating).

honestly adv. 诚实地 chéngshí de, 坦白地 tǎnbái de.

honesty n. 诚实 chéngshí, 正直 zhèngzhí.

honey n. 蜂蜜 fēngmì (sweet substance).

honeymoon n. 蜜月 mìyuè. — v. 度蜜月 dù mìyuè.

honor n. ①荣幸 róngxìng (regard). ②荣誉 róngyù (reputation). — v. 使荣耀 shǐ róngyào (show great respect for).

honorable adj. 可敬的 kějìng de, 高尚的 gāoshàng de (admirable).

honorary adj. 名誉上的 míngyùshang de.

hood n. 头巾 tóujīn 〈covering〉, 兜帽 dōumào 〈hat〉.

hoof n. 蹄 tí 〈animals〉.

hook n. 钩 gōu, 钓钩 diàogōu. — v. 钩住 gōuzhù 〈hold〉.

hoop n. 箍 gū, 环箍 huángū (circular band). — v. 加箍于 jiā gū yú.

hop v. 单脚跳跃 dānjiǎo tiàoyuè. — n. 跳跃 tiàoyuè (short jump).

hope n. & v. 希望 xīwàng (wish).

hopeless adj. 没有希望的 méiyǒu xīwàng de.

hopeful adj. 有希望的 yǒu xīwàng de.

horizon n. 地平线 dìpíngxiàn, 水平线 shuǐpíngxiàn.

horizontal adj. 地平的 dìpíng de, 水平的 shuǐpíng de.

hormone n. 荷尔蒙 hé'ěrméng.

horn n. ①角 jiǎo (antler). ②号角 hàojiǎo, 喇叭 lǎba 〈instrument〉.

horoscope n. 天宫图 tiāngōngtú, 占星 zhānxīng.

horrible adj. 可怕的 kěpà de, 恐怖的 kǒngbù de (terrible).

horrid adj. 可怕的 kěpà de, 可厌的 kěyàn de.

horrify v. 使恐怖 shǐ kǒngbù, 使战栗 shǐ zhànlì (terrify).

horror n. ①恐怖 kǒngbù, 恐惧 kǒngjù (fear). ②厌恶 yànwù (dislike).

horsepower n. 马力 mǎlì.

horseshoe n. 蹄铁 títiě.

horsewhip n. 马鞭 mǎbiān.

hose n. ①长统袜 chángtǒngwà (stockings). ②橡皮管 xiàngpíguǎn, 软管 ruǎnguǎn (tube).

hospitable adj. 好客的 hàokè de.

hospital n. 医院 yīyuàn.

hospitality n. 好客 hàokè, 款待 kuǎndài.

host n. ①主人 zhǔrén 〈of a group〉. ②主持人 zhǔchírén 〈of a show〉.

hostage n. 人质 rénzhì 〈person〉.

hostel n. 旅社 lǚshè.

hostess n. 女主人 nǚzhǔrén.

hostile adj. 敌对的 díduì de, 怀敌意的 huái díyì de

〈unfriendly〉.

hostility n. 敌意 díyì, 敌对 díduì 〈being hostile〉.

hot adj. ①热的 rè de 〈warm〉. ②辛辣的 xīnlà de 〈spicy〉. ③暴躁的 bàozào de 〈angry〉.

hotel n. 旅馆 lǚguǎn.

hour n. 小时 xiǎoshí, 钟头 zhōngtóu 〈time〉.

house n. 房屋 fángwū, 住宅 zhùzhái 〈building〉. — v. 供给住所 gōngjǐ zhùsuǒ 〈provide accommodation〉.

household adj. 家庭的 jiātíng de, 家属的 jiāshǔ de.

housekeeper n. 管家 guǎnjiā.

housemaid n. 女佣 nǚyòng.

housewife n. 主妇 zhǔfù.

housework n. 家事 jiāshì.

housing n. 供给住宅 gōngjǐ zhùzhái.

how adv. 如何 rúhé, 怎样 zěnyàng 〈in what way〉.

however adv. 无论如何 wúlùnrúhé. — conj. 然而 rán'ér.

howl v. 嗥叫 háo, 咆哮 páoxiào / páoxiāo.

Huanghe River 黄河 Huánghé.

hug v. 紧抱 jǐnbào, 拥抱 yōngbào / yǒngbào 〈to hold close〉.

huge adj. 巨大的 jùdà de.

hum v. 嗡嗡叫 wēngwēngjiào. — n. 嗡嗡声 wēngwēngshēng 〈indistinct murmur〉.

human adj. 人的 rén de, 人类的 rénlèi de. — n. 人 rén, 人类 rénlèi.

humane adj. 仁慈的 réncí de 〈having kindness〉.

humanism n. 人文主义 rénwén zhǔyì, 人道主义

réndào zhǔyì.

humanity n. ①人性 rénxìng 〈human nature〉. ②人道 réndào 〈mercy〉.

humble adj. 谦虚的 qiānxū de.

humid adj. 潮湿的 cháoshī de.

humiliate v. 羞辱 xiūrǔ / xiūrù, 使丢脸 shǐ diūliǎn.

humility n. 谦恭 qiāngōng.

humor n. ①幽默 yōumò 〈sense of fun〉. ②情绪 qíngxù, 心情 xīnqíng 〈mood〉.

humorist n. 幽默作家 yōumò zuòjiā 〈writer〉.

humorous adj. 幽默的 yōumò de.

hump n. ①隆肉 lóngròu 〈lump〉. ②圆丘 yuánqiū 〈mound〉.

humpback n. 驼背 tuóbèi.

hundred n. & adj. 一百 yìbǎi.

hunger n. ①饥饿 jī'è 〈starvation〉. ②渴望 kěwàng 〈desire〉.

hungry adj. 饥饿的 jī'è de 〈starving〉.

hunt n. & v. ①狩猎 shòuliè 〈chase〉. ②搜索 sōusuǒ, 追捕 zhuībǔ 〈search for〉.

hunter n. 猎人 lièrén 〈people〉.

hurdle n. 栏 lán, 跳栏 tiàolán 〈athletics〉.

hurl v. 用力投掷 yònglì tóuzhì / yònglì tóuzhí 〈throw violently〉.

hurricane n. 飓风 jùfēng.

hurry v. 催促 cuīcù. — n. 匆忙 cōngmáng.

hurt v. 使疼痛 shǐ téngtòng 〈pain〉, 使受伤 shǐ shòushāng 〈injury〉. — n. 疼痛 téngtòng 〈pain〉, 伤害 shānghài 〈injury〉.

husband n. 丈夫 zhàngfu.

hush v. 安静 ānjìng.

husk *n.* 外壳 wàiké ⟨grain⟩.
— *v.* 去壳 qùké.

husky *adj.* ①壳的 ké de
⟨husk⟩. ②沙哑的 shāyǎ de
⟨sound⟩.

hustle *v.* ①驱赶 qūgǎn, 催促
cuīcù ⟨hurry⟩. ②推挤 tuījǐ
⟨push⟩.

hut *n.* 小屋 xiǎowū, 茅舍
máoshè ⟨small roughly-built
house⟩.

hutch *n.* 笼子 lóngzi ⟨cage⟩.

hybrid *n.* 杂种 zázhǒng, 混种
hùnzhǒng ⟨parents of different
species⟩.

hydrant *n.* 消防栓
xiāofángshuān.

hydroelectric *adj.* 水力发电
的 shuǐlì fādiàn de.

hydrogen *n.* 氢 qīng
⟨chemistry⟩.

hygiene *n.* 卫生学
wèishēngxué.

hymn *n.* 赞美诗 zànměishī.

hypermedia *n.* 超媒体
chāoméitǐ.

hyphen *n.* 连字号 liánzìhào.

hypnosis *n.* 催眠 cuīmián.

hypnotism *n.* 催眠术
cuīmiánshù.

hypocrisy *n.* 伪善 wěishàn /
wèishàn.

hypocrite *n.* 伪君子 wěijūnzǐ
/ wèijūnzǐ.

hypothesis *n.* 假说 jiǎshuō,
假设 jiǎshè.

hysteria *n.* 歇斯底里症
xiēsīdǐlǐ zhèng ⟨wild uncontrol-
lable emotion⟩.

I

I *pron.* 我 wǒ.

ice *n.* 冰 bīng ⟨frozen water⟩.
~ *cream* 冰淇淋 bīngqílín.
~ *hockey* 冰上曲棍球
bīng shang qūgùnqiú.
~ *skates* 冰鞋 bīngxié / 溜冰鞋
liūbīngxié.

iceberg *n.* 冰山 bīngshān.

icebox *n.* 冰箱 bīngxiāng.

icing *n.* 糖衣 tángyī ⟨frosting⟩.

icon *n.* ①圣像 shèngxiàng
⟨picture⟩. ②图像 túxiàng, 图标
túbiāo ⟨computer⟩.

icy *adj.* 冰的 bīng de ⟨very cold⟩.

idea *n.* 想法 xiǎngfǎ ⟨thought⟩,
观念 guānniàn ⟨concept⟩, 主意
zhǔyi ⟨plan⟩.

ideal *n.* 理想 lǐxiǎng. — *adj.*
①理想的 lǐxiǎng de ⟨perfect⟩.
②想象中的 xiǎngxiàngzhōng
de ⟨imaginary⟩.

idealistic *adj.* 理想主义的
lǐxiǎng zhǔyì de.

idealize *v.* 理想化 lǐxiǎnghuà.

identical *adj.* 同一的 tóngyī
de ⟨the same⟩, 相同的
xiāngtóng de ⟨exactly alike⟩.

identification *n.* 认明
rènmíng, 识别 shíbié / shìbié.
~ *card* 身分证 shēnfènzhèng.

identify *v.* 认明 rènmíng,
识别 shíbié / shìbié.

identity n. 身分 shēnfen.

ideology n. 意识形态 yìshí xíngtài / yìshì xíngtài.

idiom n. 成语 chéngyǔ, 惯用语 guànyòngyǔ.

idiot n. 白痴 báichī, 傻瓜 shǎguā, 笨蛋 bèndàn.

idle adj. ①闲散的 xiánsǎn de (not busy). ②懒惰的 lǎnduò de (lazy).

idol n. 偶像 ǒuxiàng.

idolize v. 偶像化 ǒuxiànghuà.

if conj. 如果 rúguǒ, 假如 jiǎrú (supposing).

ignite v. 点火 diǎnhuǒ, 着火 zháohuǒ.

ignorance n. 无知 wúzhī, 愚昧 yúmèi.

ignorant adj. 无知的 wúzhī de, 愚昧的 yúmèi de.

ignore v. 忽视 hūshì (neglect).

ill adj. 生病的 shēngbìng de.

illegal adj. 违法的 wéifǎ de.

illegible adj. 难读的 nándú de, 难认的 nánrèn de (difficult to read).

illegitimate adj. ①违法的 wéifǎ de (illegal). ②私生的 sīshēng de ⟨birth⟩.

illicit adj. 不法的 bùfǎ de, 被禁止的 bèi jìnzhǐ de (unlawful).

illiteracy n. 文盲 wénmáng.

illiterate adj. 文盲的 wénmáng de.

illness n. 疾病 jíbìng.

illogical adj. 不合逻辑的 bùhé luójí de.

illuminate v. ①照明 zhàomíng, 照耀 zhàoyào (brighten). ②阐释 chǎnshì (clarify).

illusion n. 幻影 huànyǐng.

illustrate v. ①加插图 jiā

chātú (picture). ②举例说明 jǔlì shuōmíng (explain).

illustration n. ①插图 chātú, 图解 tújiě (picture). ②实例 shílì (example).

illustrious adj. 著名的 zhùmíng de (famous).

image n. ①像 xiàng, 肖像 xiàoxiàng (statue). ②意象 yìxiàng, 形象 xíngxiàng (mental picture).

imaginable adj. 可想象的 kě xiǎngxiàng de.

imaginary adj. 想象的 xiǎngxiàng de.

imagination n. 想象力 xiǎngxiànglì ⟨ability⟩, 想象 xiǎngxiàng ⟨act⟩.

imagine v. 想象 xiǎngxiàng.

imbalance n. 不平衡 bù pínghéng.

imitate v. 模仿 mófǎng (mimic), 效法 xiàofǎ (be like).

imitation n. ①模仿 mófǎng (copy). ②仿造品 fǎngzàopǐn (duplicate).

immaculate adj. 纯洁的 chúnjié de (pure).

immaterial adj. ①不重要的 bú zhòngyào de (insignificant). ②非物质的 fēi wùzhì de / fēi wùzhí de, 精神上的 jīngshénshang de (spiritual).

immature adj. 未成熟的 wèi chéngshú de / wèi chéngshóu de.

immediate adj. ①立即的 lìjí de, 立刻的 lìkè de (instant). ②邻近的 línjìn de (near).

immense adj. 巨大的 jùdà de, 广大的 guǎngdà de.

immerse v. 使浸没 shǐ jìnmò (sink).

immigrant n. 移民 yímín.

immigrate v. 移居入境 yíjū rùjìng.

immigration n. 移民 yímín.

imminent adj. 急迫的 jípò de, 危急的 wēijí de / wéijí de.

immobile adj. 不能移动的 bùnéng yídòng de.

immoral adj. 不道德的 bú dàodé de.

immortal adj. 不死的 bù sǐ de, 不朽的 bùxiǔ de.

immovable adj. 不可移动的 bùkě yídòng de.

immune adj. 免疫的 miǎnyì de.

immunity n. 免疫性 miǎnyìxìng.

immunize v. 使免疫 shǐ miǎnyì.

impact n. ①冲击 chōngjī / chōngjí (collision). ②影响 yǐngxiǎng (strong effect).

impair v. 损害 sǔnhài, 削弱 xuēruò / xuèruò.

impale v. 刺穿 cìchuān.

impartial adj. 公正的 gōngzhèng de.

impartiality n. 公正 gōngzhèng.

impassable adj. 不能通行的 bùnéng tōngxíng de.

impassioned adj. 热情的 rèqíng de (passionate).

impassive adj. 无感情的 wú gǎnqíng de (without emotion).

impatient adj. 不耐烦的 búnàifán de.

impeach v. 弹劾 tánhé (accuse).

impede v. 妨碍 fáng'ài, 阻碍 zǔ'ài.

impel v. 推进 tuījìn (propel).

imperative adj. ①必要的

bìyào de (necessary). ②紧急的 jǐnjí de, 急迫的 jípò de (urgent). — n. 祈使法 qíshǐfǎ ⟨grammar⟩.

imperfect adj. 不完全的 bù wánquán de, 有缺点的 yǒu quēdiǎn de.

imperial adj. 帝国的 dìguó de, 皇帝的 huángdì de.

imperialism n. 帝国主义 dìguó zhǔyì.

impersonal adj. 不具人格的 bú jù réngé de.

impersonate v. 扮演 bànyǎn (pretend to be), 模仿 mófǎng (intentionally copy).

implant v. 灌输 guànshū (put in deeply).

implement n. 器具 qìjù, 工具 gōngjù. — v. 实施 shíshī, 履行 lǚxíng (carry out).

implicate v. ①牵涉 qiānshè, 涉及 shèjí (involve). ②暗示 ànshì (imply).

implication n. ①牵涉 qiānshè, 涉及 shèjí (involvement). ②暗示 ànshì (hint).

implicit adj. 暗示的 ànshì de (implied).

imply v. 暗示 ànshì.

impolite adj. 无礼的 wúlǐ de, 不客气的 búkèqi de.

import n. & v. 输入 shūrù, 进口 jìnkǒu.

importance n. 重要 zhòngyào, 重要性 zhòngyàoxìng.

important adj. 重要的 zhòngyào de, 重大的 zhòngdà de.

impose v. 把……强加于 bǎ... qiángjiā yú (place on).

imposition n. 负担 fùdān (burden).

I

impossible *adj.* 不可能的 bù kěnéng de (not possible).

impostor *n.* 骗子 piànzi.

impotent *adj.* ①无力的 wúlì de, 衰弱的 shuāiruò de (weak). ②阳痿的 yángwěi de 〈medical〉.

impound *v.* 扣押 kòuyā, 充公 chōnggōng.

impoverish *v.* 使贫困 shǐ pínkùn (make poor).

impress *v.* 使印象深刻 shǐ yìnxiàng shēnkè (influence deeply).

impression *n.* 印象 yìnxiàng.

impressive *adj.* 印象深刻的 yìnxiàng shēnkè de.

imprint *n.* ①印迹 yìnjì / yìnjī, 印记 yìnjì (print). ②出版说明 chūbǎn shuōmíng 〈publication〉.

imprison *v.* 下狱 xiàyù, 禁锢 jìngù.

improbable *adj.* 未必然的 wèi bìrán de (not likely to happen).

impromptu *adj. & adv.* 临时 的 línshí de, 即席的 jíxí de. — *n.* 即席演说 jíxí yǎnshuō 〈speech〉.

improper *adj.* ①不适当的 bú shìdàng de (inappropriate). ②错误的 cuòwù de (incorrect).

improve *v.* 改善 gǎishàn, 改进 gǎijìn.

improvement *n.* 改善 gǎishàn, 改进 gǎijìn.

improvise *v.* 即席创作 jíxí chuàngzuò.

impulsive *adj.* 冲动的 chōngdòng de.

impure *adj.* 脏的 zāng de, 不 纯洁的 bù chúnjié de.

impurity *n.* 不洁 bùjié.

in *adv. & prep.* 在……内 zài... nèi, 在……情况下 zài... qíngkuàng xià.

inability *n.* 无能力 wú nénglì, 无才能 wú cáinéng.

inaccessible *adj.* 难亲近的 nán qīnjìn de, 难接近的 nán jiējìn de.

inaccuracy *n.* 错误 cuòwù (mistake).

inaccurate *adj.* 不准确的 bù zhǔnquè de, 错误的 cuòwù de.

inadequate *adj.* 不充分的 bù chōngfèn de (insufficient).

inanimate *adj.* ①无生命的 wú shēngmìng de (lifeless). ②无生气的 wú shēngqì de (boring).

inapplicable *adj.* 不适用的 bú shìyòng de.

inappropriate *adj.* 不适宜 的 bú shìyí de.

inapt *adj.* 不恰当的 bú qiàdàng de (unsuitable).

inaudible *adj.* 听不见的 tīngbujiàn de.

inborn *adj.* 天生的 tiānshēng de.

incalculable *adj.* 数不尽的 shǔbujìn de.

incapable *adj.* 无能力的 wú nénglì de.

incapacitate *v.* 使无能力 shǐ wú nénglì, 使无资格 shǐ wú zígé (disable).

incarcerate *v.* 监禁 jiānjìn (shut in a prison).

incense *n.* 香 xiāng, 香料 xiāngliào. — *v.* 激怒 jīnù (make angry).

incentive *n.* 刺激 cìjī, 诱因 yòuyīn.

incessant *adj.* 不断的 búduàn

de, 继续的 jìxù de.

incest *n.* 乱伦 luànlún.

inch *n.* 吋 cùn.

incident *n.* 事件 shìjiàn (event).

incidental *adj.* 附带的 fùdài de (minor).

incinerate *v.* 烧成灰 shāo chéng huī, 焚化 fénhuà.

inclination *n.* 倾向 qīngxiàng.

incline *v.* 倾向于 qīngxiàng yú (tend towards). — *n.* 倾斜 qīngxié (slope).

include *v.* 包括 bāokuò / bāoguā, 包含 bāohán.

inclusive *adj.* 包括的 bāokuò de / bāoguā de, 包含的 bāohán de.

incoherent *adj.* 无连贯的 wú liánguàn de.

income *n.* 收入 shōurù, 所得 suǒdé. ~ *tax* 所得税 suǒdéshuì.

incomparable *adj.* 无比的 wúbǐ de, 不可比拟的 bùkě bǐnǐ de.

incompatible *adj.* 不相容的 bù xiāngróng de.

incompetent *adj.* 无能力的 wú nénglì de (not able), 不合格的 bù hégé de (not qualified).

incomplete *adj.* 不完全的 bù wánquán de.

incomprehensible *adj.* 不能理解的 bùnéng lǐjiě de.

inconceivable *adj.* 难以想象的 nányǐ xiǎngxiàng de (can't be imagined).

inconclusive *adj.* 非决定性的 fēi juédìngxìng de.

inconsequential *adj.* 不重要的 bú zhòngyào de (of no significance).

inconsiderable *adj.* 不足道

的 bùzúdào de (insignificant), 不重要的 bú zhòngyào de (unimportant).

inconsiderate *adj.* 不体贴的 bù tǐtiē de.

inconsistent *adj.* 矛盾的 máodùn de, 不一致的 bù yízhì de (not in harmony).

inconstant *adj.* 反复无常的 fǎnfù-wúcháng de (changeable).

inconvenience *n.* 不便 búbiàn.

inconvenient *adj.* 不便的 búbiàn de.

inconvertible *adj.* 不能兑换的 bùnéng duìhuàn de (currency).

incorporate *v.* 合并 hébìng, 并入 bìngrù (merge).

incorrect *adj.* 错误的 cuòwù de.

increase *v.* 增加 zēngjiā.

incredible *adj.* 难以置信的 nányǐ-zhìxìn de.

increment *n.* 增加 zēngjiā (increase).

incur *v.* 招致 zhāozhì, 招惹 zhāorě.

incurable *adj.* 无可救药的 wúkějiùyào de, 不能治疗的 bùnéng zhìliáo de.

incursion *n.* 袭击 xíjí / xíjí, 入侵 rùqīn (raid).

indebted *adj.* ①感激的 gǎnjī de (grateful). ②负债的 fùzhài de (money).

indecent *adj.* ①不适当的 bú shìdàng de (improper). ②不道德的 bú dàodé de (immodest).

indeed *adv.* 的确 díquè, 实在 shízài (really). — *interj.* 真的! Zhēnde!

indefinite *adj.* ①不确定的 bú quèdìng de (unclear). ②无限制

的 wú xiànzhì de (unlimited).

indemnify v. 使免于蒙受损失 shǐ miǎn yú méngshòu sǔnshī ‹protect›.

indemnity n. 赔款 péikuǎn, 赔偿 péicháng.

indent v. ①成锯齿状 chéng jùchǐzhuàng (make notches). ②缩排 suōpái ‹papers›.

independence n. 独立 dúlì, 自主 zìzhǔ.

independent adj. 独立的 dúlì de, 自主的 zìzhǔ de.

indescribable adj. 难以形容的 nányǐxíngróng de.

indestructible adj. 不能破坏的 bùnéng pòhuài de.

index n. ①索引 suǒyǐn (alphabetical list). ②指标 zhǐbiāo (sign). ③食指 shízhǐ (finger).

Indian n. & adj. ①印度人 Yìndùrén ‹of India›. ②印第安人 Yìndì'ānrén (American Indian). ③印第安语 Yìndì'ānyǔ (American Indian language). the ~ Ocean 印度洋 Yìndùyáng.

indicate v. 指示 zhǐshì, 指出 zhǐchū.

indication n. 指示 zhǐshì, 象征 xiàngzhēng.

indicative adj. 指示的 zhǐshì de.

indicator n. 指示器 zhǐshìqì.

indict v. 起诉 qǐsù, 控告 kònggào (accuse).

indifference n. 不关心 bù guānxīn.

indifferent adj. 不关心的 bù guānxīn de, 没兴趣的 méi xìngqù de.

indigenous adj. 土著的 tǔzhù de, 本土的 běntǔ de.

indigestible adj. 难消化的

nán xiāohuà de.

indigestion n. 消化不良 xiāohuà-bùliáng.

indignity n. 侮辱 wǔrǔ / wǔrù, 轻蔑 qīngmiè.

indirect adj. 间接的 jiànjiē de.

indiscriminate adj. 未加区别的 wèi jiā qūbié de.

indispensable adj. 不可缺的 bùkě quē de, 必要的 bìyào de.

indisputable adj. 不容争辩的 bùróng zhēngbiàn de.

indissoluble adj. 不能溶解的 bùnéng róngjiě de.

indistinct adj. 不清楚的 bù qīngchu de, 模糊的 móhu de (unclear).

individual n. 个人 gèrén, 个体 gètǐ. — adj. ①个别的 gèbié de, 个人的 gèrén de (personal). ②独特的 dútè de (characteristic).

Indochina n. 中南半岛 Zhōngnán Bàndǎo.

indoor adj. 室内的 shìnèi de.

indoors adv. 在室内 zài shìnèi.

induce v. ①引诱 yǐnyòu, 劝诱 quànyòu (persuade). ②招致 zhāozhì (cause).

indulge v. 放任 fàngrèn, 纵容 zòngróng.

industrial adj. 工业的 gōngyè de.

industrialize v. 工业化 gōngyèhuà.

industrious adj. 勤勉的 qínmiǎn de.

industry n. ①工业 gōngyè ‹production›. ②勤勉 qínmiǎn (diligence).

inebriate v. 使醉 shǐ zuì (make drunk). — n. 醉汉 zuìhàn, 酒鬼 jiǔguǐ (alcoholic).

ineffective adj. 无效的

wúxiào de.

ineffectual *adj.* 无效果的 wú xiàoguǒ de, 无益的 wúyì de (futile).

inefficient *adj.* 无效率的 wú xiàolǜ de.

inelegant *adj.* 不雅的 bùyǎ de.

ineligible *adj.* 没有资格的 méiyǒu zīgé de.

inept *adj.* 不合适的 bù héshì de (unfit).

inequality *n.* 不平等 bù píngděng.

inevitable *adj.* 不可避免的 bùkě bìmiǎn de.

inexact *adj.* 不精确的 bù jīngquè de.

inexcusable *adj.* 不能原谅的 bùnéng yuánliàng de.

inexpensive *adj.* 价廉的 jiàlián de.

inexperience *n.* 无经验 wú jīngyàn.

infamous *adj.* 不名誉的 bù míngyù de.

infamy *n.* 不名誉 bù míngyù, 丑名 chǒumíng.

infancy *n.* 幼年 yòunián.

infant *n.* 婴儿 yīng'ér. — *adj.* 婴儿的 yīng'ér de.

infantry *n.* 步兵 bùbīng ⟨army⟩.

infatuate *v.* 使迷恋 shǐ míliàn.

infect *v.* 传染 chuánrǎn, 感染 gǎnrǎn ⟨disease⟩.

infection *n.* 传染 chuánrǎn, 传染病 chuánrǎnbìng.

infectious *adj.* 传染性的 chuánrǎnxìng de.

infer *v.* 推论 tuīlùn.

inferior *adj.* 下级的 xiàjí de (low in rank), 较低的 jiàodī de (lower).

inferiority *n.* 下级 xiàjí, 低劣

dīliè. ~ *complex* 自卑感 zìbēigǎn.

infest *v.* 扰乱 rǎoluàn, 蹂躏 róulìn ⟨pests⟩.

infinite *adj.* 无限的 wúxiàn de (without limits).

infinitive *n. & adj.* 不定词 búdìngcí ⟨grammar⟩.

infinity *n.* 无限 wúxiàn, 无穷 wúqióng.

inflame *v.* ①激怒 jīnù, 煽动 shāndòng (provoke). ②发炎 fāyán, 红肿 hóngzhǒng ⟨medical⟩.

inflammable *adj.* 易燃的 yìrán de (burnable).

inflammation *n.* 发炎 fāyán.

inflate *v.* 充气 chōngqì (fill with air), 使膨胀 shǐ péngzhàng (swell).

inflation *n.* ①通货膨胀 tōnghuò-péngzhàng ⟨currency⟩. ②膨胀 péngzhàng (increase).

inflection *n.* ①音调变化 yīndiào biànhuà ⟨tone⟩. ②语尾变化 yǔwěi biànhuà ⟨grammar⟩.

inflexible *adj.* ①坚定的 jiāndìng de (uncompromising). ②不可弯曲的 bùkě wānqū de (unbending).

inflict *v.* 使遭受 shǐ zāoshòu, 施罚 shīfá.

infliction *n.* 施罚 shīfá.

inflow *n.* 流入 liúrù.

influence *n.* 影响 yǐngxiǎng, 势力 shìlì.

influential *adj.* 有影响力的 yǒu yǐngxiǎnglì de.

influenza *n.* 流行性感冒 liúxíngxìng gǎnmào ⟨medical⟩.

inform *v.* 通知 tōngzhī, 通报 tōngbào (give information).

informal *adj.* 非正式的 fēi zhèngshì de.

information *n.* ①消息 xiāoxi (news). ②情报 qíngbào, 知识 zhīshi (data). ③信息 xìnxī / 资讯 zīxùn ⟨computer⟩.

~ *center* 问讯处 wènxùnchù / 询问处 xúnwènchù.

infringe *v.* 侵犯 qīnfàn, 侵害 qīnhài.

infuriate *v.* 激怒 jīnù.

ingratitude *n.* 忘恩负义 wàng'ēn-fùyì.

ingredient *n.* 成分 chéngfèn.

inhabit *v.* 居住于 jūzhù yú.

inhabitant *n.* 居民 jūmín.

inhale *v.* 吸入 xīrù.

inharmonious *adj.* 不和谐的 bù héxié de.

inherent *adj.* 与生俱来的 yǔshēngjùlái de.

inherit *v.* 继承 jìchéng.

inheritance *n.* ①继承 jìchéng (succession). ②遗产 yíchǎn (heritage).

inhibit *v.* 抑制 yìzhì, 阻止 zǔzhǐ.

inhospitable *adj.* 冷淡的 lěngdàn de, 不好客的 bú hàokè de (not friendly).

inhuman *adj.* 不人道的 bù réndào de, 残忍的 cánrěn de (cruel).

inhumane *adj.* 不人道的 bù réndào de, 残忍的 cánrěn de (cruel).

initial *adj.* 最初的 zuìchū de.
— *n.* 起首字母 qǐshǒu zìmǔ.

initiate *v.* 创始 chuàngshǐ, 开始 kāishǐ.

initiative *n.* ①初步 chūbù (the first act). ②创造力 chuàngzàolì (inventiveness). ③创制权 chuàngzhìquán ⟨election⟩.

inject *v.* 注射 zhùshè (put into).

injunction *n.* 命令 mìnglìng, 禁止令 jìnzhǐlìng ⟨law⟩, 禁制令 jìnzhìlìng ⟨court⟩.

injure *v.* 伤害 shānghài, 损害 sǔnhài.

injury *n.* 伤害 shānghài, 损害 sǔnhài (harm).

injustice *n.* 不公正 bù gōngzhèng, 不公平 bù gōngpíng.

ink *n.* 墨水 mòshuǐ.

~ *jet printer* 喷墨打印机 pēnmò dǎyìnjī / 针孔喷墨印表机 zhēnkǒng pēnmò yìnbiǎojī ⟨computer⟩.

inland *adj.* 内陆的 nèilù de, 内地的 nèidì de (interior).

in-law *n.* 姻亲 yīnqīn.

inlet *n.* 水湾 shuǐwān, 海口 hǎikǒu, 入口 rùkǒu.

in-line skates 滚轴溜冰鞋 gǔnzhóu liūbīngxié / 直排轮溜冰鞋 zhípáilún liūbīngxié.

inmate *n.* 被收容者 bèi shōuróng zhě.

inn *n.* 客栈 kèzhàn, 小酒馆 xiǎo jiǔguǎn.

innate *adj.* 天生的 tiānshēng de.

inner *adj.* 内部的 nèibù de, 内在的 nèizài de.

inning *n.* 一局 yì jú ⟨baseball⟩.

innkeeper *n.* 旅馆主人 lǚguǎn zhǔrén.

innocence *n.* 清白 qīngbái, 无罪 wúzuì ⟨not guilty⟩.

innocent *adj.* ①无罪的 wúzuì de (not guilty). ②天真的 tiānzhēn de (naive).

innovate *v.* 革新 géxīn, 创新 chuàngxīn, 改革 gǎigé.

innumerable *adj.* 无数的 wúshù de.

inopportune *adj.* 不合时宜的 bùhé-shíyí de.

inorganic *adj.* 无机的 wújī de 〈chemistry〉.

input *n.* 输入 shūrù 〈computer〉.

inquire *v.* 询问 xúnwèn, 查问 cháwèn.

inquiry *n.* ①询问 xúnwèn, 查阅 cháyuè 〈inquiring〉. ②调查 diàochá 〈investigation〉.

inquisition *n.* 审讯 shěnxùn, 调查 diàochá.

inquisitive *adj.* 好问的 hàowèn de, 好奇的 hàoqí de.

insane *adj.* 患精神病的 huàn jīngshénbìng de, 发狂的 fākuáng de 〈mentally ill〉.

inscription *n.* 铭刻 míngkè, 刻字 kèzì.

insect *n.* 昆虫 kūnchóng.

insecure *adj.* ①缺乏自信的 quēfá zìxìn de 〈not cofident〉. ②随时不保的 suíshí bù bǎo de 〈lost〉. ③不安全的 bù ānquán de 〈not safe〉.

insensible *adj.* ①无知觉的 wú zhījué de 〈unconscious〉. ②未察觉的 wèi chájué de 〈unaware〉.

insensitive *adj.* 无感觉的 wú gǎnjué de 〈lack of feeling〉. 不敏感的 bù mǐngǎn de 〈obtuse〉.

inseparable *adj.* 不能分离的 bùnéng fēnlí de.

insert *v.* 插入 chārù.

inside *n.* 内部 nèibù, 内侧 nèicè. — *adj. & adv.* 在内部 zài nèibù, 在……里面 zài... lǐmiàn.

insight *n.* 洞察 dòngchá, 见识 jiànshi.

insignificant *adj.* 不重要的 bú zhòngyào de.

insincere *adj.* 不诚恳的 bù chéngkěn de.

insinuate *v.* 暗指 ànzhǐ, 暗讽 ànfěng / ànfèng.

insipid *adj.* ①乏味的 fáwèi de 〈dull〉. ②无味的 wúwèi de 〈flavorless〉.

insist *v.* ①坚持 jiānchí 〈emphasize〉. ②主张 zhǔzhāng 〈declare〉.

insolent *adj.* 无礼的 wúlǐ de 〈rude〉. 傲慢的 àomàn de 〈arrogant〉.

insoluble *adj.* ①不能溶解的 bùnéng róngjiě de 〈not able to dissolve〉. ②不能解决的 bùnéng jiějué de 〈unsolvable〉.

insomnia *n.* 失眠 shīmián.

inspect *v.* 检查 jiǎnchá, 视察 shìchá.

inspection *n.* 检查 jiǎnchá.

inspector *n.* 检查员 jiǎncháyuán.

inspiration *n.* ①灵感 línggǎn 〈creativity〉. ②激励 jīlì 〈spur〉.

inspire *v.* ①激励 jīlì, 鼓舞 gǔwǔ 〈animate〉. ②给灵感 gěi línggǎn 〈fill with creativity〉.

instability *n.* 不稳定 bù wěndìng.

install *v.* ①安装 ānzhuāng, 设置 shèzhì 〈set up〉. ②使就职 shǐ jiùzhí 〈position〉. ③安置 ānzhì 〈place〉.

installment *n.* ①分期付款 fēnqī fùkuǎn / fēnqí fùkuǎn 〈payment〉. ②分册 fēncè, 一册 yí cè 〈book〉.

instance *n.* 例子 lìzi, 例证 lìzhèng. *for* ~ 例如 lìrú.

instant *n.* 立即 lìjí. — *adj.* ①立刻的 lìkè de 〈immediate〉. ②紧急的 jǐnjí de 〈urgent〉.
~ *noodles* 方便面

fāngbiànmiàn / 速食面 sùshímiàn, 泡面 pàomiàn.

instantly adv. 立刻 lìkè.

instead adv. 代替 dàitì.

instep n. 脚背 jiǎobèi.

instinct n. 本能 běnnéng.

instinctive adj. 本能的 běnnéng de, 天生的 tiānshēng de.

institute v. 创立 chuànglì (establish). — n. 学会 xuéhuì, 研究所 yánjiùsuǒ / yánjiùsuǒ.

institution n. ①机构 jīgòu, 社团 shètuán (organization). ②惯例 guànlì (convention).

instruct v. ①教导 jiàodǎo, 教授 jiàoshòu (teach). ②指示 zhǐshì (command).

instruction n. ①指导 zhǐdǎo (leadership), 教导 jiàodǎo (teaching). ②指示 zhǐshì, 命令 mìnglìng (command).

instructive adj. 教育性的 jiàoyùxìng de.

instrument n. ①仪器 yíqì, 器具 qìjù (apparatus). ②乐器 yuèqì (music).

insufficient adj. 不充足的 bù chōngzú de.

insulate v. 隔离 gélí, 使孤立 shǐ gūlì (isolate).

insult n. & v. 侮辱 wǔrǔ / wǔrù (isolate).

insurance n. 保险 bǎoxiǎn (contract).

insure v. 保险 bǎoxiǎn.

intact adj. 未触动的 wèi chùdòng de (untouched), 完整的 wánzhěng de (complete).

intake n. ①摄取量 shèqǔliàng (amount). ②入口 rùkǒu (opening).

integral adj. ①整体的 zhěngtǐ de, 完整的 wánzhěng de (whole). ②必要的 bìyào de,

关键的 guānjiàn de (key).

integrate v. 整合 zhěnghé, 结合 jiéhé, 合并 hébìng (combine).

integrity n. 完整 wánzhěng (completeness).

intellect n. 智力 zhìlì, 理解力 lǐjiělì (intelligence).

intellectual adj. 智力的 zhìlì de (of the intellect). — n. 知识分子 zhīshi fènzǐ.

~ property rights 知识产权 zhīshi chǎnquán / 智慧财产权 zhìhuì cáichǎnquán.

intelligence n. ①智力 zhìlì, 理解力 lǐjiělì (intellect). ②情报 qíngbào, 消息 xiāoxi (information).

intelligent adj. 有才智的 yǒu cáizhì de, 有理解力的 yǒu lǐjiělì de.

intelligentsia n. 知识分子 zhīshi fènzǐ.

intelligible adj. 可理解的 kě lǐjiě de.

intend v. 意欲 yìyù, 想要 xiǎngyào, 企图 qìtú / qǐtú.

intense adj. ①强烈的 qiángliè de (ardent). ②剧烈的 jùliè de (fierce).

intensify v. 使强烈 shǐ qiángliè.

intensity n. 强度 qiángdù (degree).

intensive adj. ①彻底的 chèdǐ de, 深入的 shēnrù de (thorough). ②密集的 mìjí de, 集中的 jízhōng de (concentrated).

intent n. 意向 yìxiàng (law).

intention n. 意图 yìtú.

intentional adj. 有意的 yǒuyì de.

inter v. 埋葬 máizàng (bury).

interact v. 交互作用 jiāohù zuòyòng.

intercept v. ①中途拦截 zhōngtú lánjié (stop). ②截断 jiéduàn (cut off).

intercession n. 代人求情 dài rén qiúqíng.

interchange v. 交换 jiāohuàn, 更换 gēnghuàn, 替换 tìhuàn (exchange). — n. 立交桥 lìjiāoqiáo / 交流道 jiāoliúdào (highway).

interchangeable adj. 可交换的 kě jiāohuàn de.

intercom n. 对讲机 duìjiǎngjī.

intercourse n. ①交际 jiāojì, 交流 jiāoliú (exchange). ②性交 xìngjiāo (sex).

interest n. ①关心 guānxīn (attention). ②兴趣 xìngqù, 嗜好 shìhào (hobby). ③利息 lìxī / lìxí (money). ~ **group** 利益团体 lìyì tuántǐ. ~ **rates** 利率 lìlǜ. — v. 使感兴趣 shǐ gǎn xìngqù, 引起兴趣 yǐnqǐ xìngqù.

interested adj. 感兴趣的 gǎn xìngqù de.

interesting adj. 有趣的 yǒuqù de.

interfere v. 妨碍 fáng'ài, 干涉 gānshè.

interference n. 妨碍 fáng'ài, 干涉 gānshè, 干扰 gānrǎo.

interior n. 内部 nèibù. — adj. 内部的 nèibù de.

interject v. 突然插入 tūrán chārù / túrán chārù.

interjection n. 感叹词 gǎntàncí (grammar).

interlock v. 互相连结 hùxiāng liánjié.

intermediary n. 中间人 zhōngjiānrén, 调解者 tiáojiězhě (mediator). — adj.

中间的 zhōngjiān de, 调解的 tiáojiě de.

intermediate adj. ①中间的 zhōngjiān de (middle). ②中级的 zhōngjí de (level).

intermission n. 间歇 jiànxiē.

intern n. 实习医生 shíxí yīshēng (doctor), 实习者 shíxízhě (other professions).

internal adj. 内部的 nèibù de.

international adj. 国际的 guójì de.

Internet n. 因特网 Yīntèwǎng, 国际互联网 Guójì hùliánwǎng / 网际网路 Wǎngjì wǎnglù (computer).

Internet café 网吧 Wǎngbā / 网路咖啡店 Wǎnglù kāfēidiàn, 网咖 Wǎngkā.

interpret v. ①解释 jiěshì, 阐明 chǎnmíng (explain). ②口译 kǒuyì (translate orally).

interpretation n. ①解释 jiěshì (explanation). ②口译 kǒuyì (translation).

interpreter n. 传译员 chuányìyuán.

interrogate v. 审问 shěnwèn, 讯问 xùnwèn.

interrogative adj. 疑问的 yíwèn de. — n. 疑问词 yíwèncí (grammar).

interrupt v. ①中断 zhōngduàn, 打断 dǎduàn (break in). ②妨碍 fáng'ài (obstruct).

intersect v. 交叉 jiāochā (cross).

intersection n. 交叉点 jiāochādiǎn, 交叉 jiāochā.

interval n. 间隔 jiàngé.

intervene v. 干涉 gānshè, 调停 tiáotíng.

interview n. & v. 会见 huìjiàn, 面谈 miàntán (meeting).

I

intestine n. 肠 cháng.

intimacy n. 亲密 qīnmì, 亲近 qīnjìn.

intimate adj. ①亲密的 qīnmì de, 亲近的 qīnjìn de (close). ②详细的 xiángxì de (detailed). — v. 暗示 ànshì (imply).

intimidate v. 恐吓 kǒnghè, 胁迫 xiépò (threaten).

into prep. 进入……之内 jìnrù……zhī nèi (inside).

intolerable adj. 无法忍受的 wúfǎ rěnshòu de (unbearable).

intolerant adj. 不容忍的 bù róngrěn de.

intonation n. 语调 yǔdiào, 音调 yīndiào 〈voice〉.

intoxicate v. ①使醉 shǐ zuì (cause to be drunk). ②使兴奋 shǐ xīngfèn (excite).

intranet n. 内联网 nèiliánwǎng / 内部网路 nèibù wǎnglù 〈computer〉.

intricate adj. 错综复杂的 cuòzōng-fùzá de / cuòzòng-fùzá de.

intrigue n. 阴谋 yīnmóu, 密谋 mìmóu. — v. ①密谋 mìmóu (plot). ②引起兴趣 yǐnqǐ xìngqù (interest).

introduce v. ①介绍 jièshào (acquaint). ②引进 yǐnjìn (bring in).

introduction n. ①介绍 jièshào 〈acquaint〉. ②前言 qiányán, 绪论 xùlùn (preface).

introductory adj. 导引的 dǎoyǐn de.

intuition n. 直觉 zhíjué, 第六感 dìliùgǎn.

intuitive adj. 直觉的 zhíjué de.

invade v. 侵略 qīnlüè, 入侵 rùqīn 〈attack〉.

invalid n. 病弱者 bìngruòzhě, 病人 bìngrén (weak person). — adj. 无效的 wúxiào de, 无用的 wúyòng de (not vaild).

invaluable adj. 无价的 wújià de, 极珍贵的 jí zhēnguì de.

invariable adj. 不变的 búbiàn de.

invasion n. 侵入 qīnrù, 侵犯 qīnfàn.

invent v. 发明 fāmíng (create or design).

invention n. 发明 fāmíng (creation).

inventory n. ①目录 mùlù, 货物清单 huòwù qīngdān (list). ②存货 cúnhuò 〈goods〉.

inverse adj. 倒转的 dàozhuǎn de, 颠倒的 diāndǎo de.

invert v. 倒转 dàozhuǎn, 颠倒 diāndǎo (reverse).

invertebrate n. 无脊椎动物 wú jǐzhuī dòngwù.

invest v. 投资 tóuzī.

investigate v. 调查 diàochá (examine), 研究 yánjiū / yánjiù (research).

investigation n. 调查 diàochá (examination), 研究 yánjiū / yánjiù (research).

investment n. 投资 tóuzī.

invigorate v. 赋予活力 fùyǔ huólì, 鼓舞 gǔwǔ.

invincible adj. 难以征服的 nányí zhēngfú de.

invisible adj. 看不见的 kànbújiàn de.

invitation n. 邀请 yāoqǐng (request).

invite v. ①邀请 yāoqǐng (ask). ②招致 zhāozhì, 引来 yǐnlái (attract).

invocation n. 祈求 qíqiú (prayer).

invoice *n. & v.* 发票 fāpiào.

involuntary *adj.* 非自愿的 fēi zìyuàn de.

involve *v.* ①包括 bāokuò / 包刮 bāoguā, 包含 bāohán 〈contain〉. ②牵涉 qiānshè, 涉及 shèjí 〈embroil〉.

inward *adj. & adv.* 向内的 xiàngnèi de, 在内的 zàinèi de.

iodine *n.* 碘 diǎn, 碘酒 diǎnjiǔ 〈chemistry〉.

IQ, I.Q. 智力商数 zhìlì shāngshù, 智商 zhìshāng 〈intelligence quotient〉.

irate *adj.* 发怒的 fānù de.

iris *n.* ①虹膜 hóngmó 〈eyes〉. ②鸢尾 yuānwěi 〈plant〉.

Irish *n. & adj.* ①爱尔兰人 Ài'ěrlánrén 〈people〉. ②爱尔兰语 Ài'ěrlányǔ 〈language〉.

iron *n.* ①铁 tiě 〈metal〉. ②熨斗 yùndǒu 〈for clothes〉. — *adj.* 铁的 tiě de. — *v.* 熨平 yùnpíng.

ironic *adj.* 讽刺的 fěngcì de / fěngcì de.

irony *n.* 讽刺 fěngcì / fěngcì.

irrational *adj.* 无理性的 wú lǐxìng de 〈unreasonable〉, 不合理的 bù hélǐ de 〈absurd〉.

irregular *adj.* 不规则的 bù guīzé de.

irrelevant *adj.* 不相关的 bù xiāngguān de.

irreligious *adj.* 反宗教的 fǎn zōngjiào de.

irreparable *adj.* 不能修补的 bùnéng xiūbǔ de.

irreplaceable *adj.* 不能替换的 bùnéng tìhuàn de.

irresistible *adj.* 不可抵抗的 bùkě dǐkàng de.

irresolute *adj.* 优柔寡断的 yōuróu-guǎduàn de.

irrespective *adj.* 不顾的 búgù de, 不论的 búlùn de.

irresponsible *adj.* 不负责任的 bú fù zérèn de.

irreverent *adj.* 不敬的 bújìng de.

irrevocable *adj.* 不能撤回的 bùnéng chèhuí de.

irrigate *v.* 灌溉 guàngài 〈supply with water〉.

irritable *adj.* 易怒的 yì nù de.

irritate *v.* 激怒 jīnù 〈make angry〉.

is *v.* 是 shì.

Islam *n.* ①回教 Huíjiào 〈religion〉. ②回教徒 Huíjiàotú 〈Muslims〉. ③回教世界 Huíjiào shìjiè 〈Muslim world〉.

island *n.* 岛 dǎo, 岛屿 dǎoyǔ.

islander *n.* 岛民 dǎomín.

isolate *v.* 孤立 gūlì, 隔离 gélí.

issue *v.* 发行 fāxíng 〈publish〉. — *n.* ①发行 fāxíng 〈publication〉. ②事项 shìxiàng, 要项 yàoxiàng 〈affair〉. ③结果 jiéguǒ 〈result〉. ④争论点 zhēnglùndiǎn 〈point〉.

it *pron.* 它 tā.

Italian *n. & adj.* ①意大利人 Yìdàlìrén / 义大利人 Yìdàlìrén 〈people〉. ②意大利语 Yìdàlìyǔ / 义大利语 Yìdàlìyǔ 〈language〉.

italic *adj.* 斜体的 xiétǐ de. — *n.* 斜体字 xiétǐzì.

itch *n.* 痒 yǎng 〈skin〉. — *v.* 发痒 fāyǎng 〈scratch〉.

item *n.* 项目 xiàngmù, 条 tiáo, 款 kuǎn.

itinerary *n.* 旅行记录 lǚxíng jìlù, 旅行计画 lǚxíng jìhuà.

its *pron.* 它的 tā de.

itself *pron.* 它自己 tā zìjǐ.

ivory *n.* 象牙 xiàngyá 〈ele-

phant's tusk).

ivy n. 常春藤 chángchūnténg.

J

chē

jab n. & v. 刺 cì, 戳 chuō.

jabber v. 含糊地说 hánhu de shuō. — n. 含糊不清的话 hánhu bùqīng de huà.

jack n. 千斤顶 qiānjīndǐng ‹device›.

jacket n. 夹克 jiākè / jiákè, 外套 wàitào.

jade n. 翡翠 fěicuì, 玉 yù.

jagged adj. 锯齿状的 jùchǐzhuàng de.

jaguar n. 美洲虎 měizhōuhǔ.

jail n. 监狱 jiānyù, 监牢 jiānláo.

jam v. ①推挤 tuījǐ ‹crowd›. ②拥塞 yōngsè / yǒngsè ‹block›. — n. 果酱 guǒjiàng ‹jelly›.

janitor n. 管理员 guǎnlǐyuán.

January n. 一月 Yīyuè.

Japanese n. & adj. ①日本人 Rìběnrén ‹people›. ②日语 Rìyǔ ‹language›.

jar n. 瓶 píng, 瓶子 píngzi, 罐子 guànzi ‹bottle›.

jargon n. 术语 shùyǔ, 行话 hánghuà.

jasmine n. 茉莉 mòlì.

jaundice n. 黄疸病 huángdǎnbìng ‹medical›.

jaunt n. & v. 游览 yóulǎn.

javelin n. 标枪 biāoqiāng.

jaw n. 颚 è.

jazz n. 爵士乐 juéshìyuè ‹music›.

jealous adj. 嫉妒的 jídù de (unhappy and angry).

jeans n. 牛仔裤 niúzǎikù / niúzǐkù.

jeep n. 吉普车 jípǔchē.

jeer n. & v. 嘲弄 cháonòng, 嘲笑 cháoxiào.

jelly n. ①果酱 guǒjiàng ‹spread on bread›. ②果冻 guǒdòng ‹solid›.

jellyfish n. 水母 shuǐmǔ, 海蜇 hǎizhé.

jeopardize v. 使危险 shǐ wēixiǎn / shǐ wéixiǎn, 危害 wēihài / wéihài.

jeopardy n. 危险 wēixiǎn / wéixiǎn.

jerk n. ①急拉 jílā (pull). ②抽动 chōudòng (twitch). ③混蛋 húndàn / hùndàn (idiot). — v. 急拉 jílā (pull suddenly).

jest n. 笑柄 xiàobǐng. — v. 嘲弄 cháonòng, 取笑 qǔxiào.

Jesus n. 耶稣 Yēsū / Yésū, 上帝 Shàngdì.

jet n. ①喷射 pēnshè (spout). ②喷口 pēnkǒu (nozzle). ③喷气式飞机 pēnqìshì fēijī / pēnshèjī ‹aircraft›. — v. 喷射 pēnshè, 喷出 pēnchū (gush).

Jew n. 犹太人 Yóutàirén.

Jewish adj. 犹太的 Yóutài de.

jewel n. 珠宝 zhūbǎo, 宝石 bǎoshí (gem).

jewelry n. 珠宝 zhūbǎo.

jiffy n. 一瞬间 yíshùnjiān, 马上 mǎshàng (in a moment).

jigsaw n. 拼图玩具 pīntú wánjù ⟨puzzle⟩.

jingle n. & v. 叮当响 dīngdāngxiǎng.

jinx v. 使倒霉 shǐ dǎoméi (give bad luck).

job n. 工作 gōngzuò, 职业 zhíyè (regular paid employment).

jockey n. 骑师 qíshī.

jog v. ①轻推 qīngtuī, 轻触 qīngchù (push slightly). ②唤起 huànqǐ (recall). ③慢跑 mànpǎo (run slowly). — n. 轻推 qīngtuī, 轻触 qīngchù.

join v. ①连接 liánjiē (connect). ②会合 huìhé (meet). ③加入 jiārù (participate in).

joint n. ①接头 jiētóu (place joined). ②关节 guānjié ⟨bones⟩. —adj. 共同的 gòngtóng de, 共有的 gòngyǒu de.

joke n. 笑话 xiàohuà, 玩笑 wánxiào. — v. ①说笑话 shuō xiàohuà, 开玩笑 kāiwánxiào ⟨humor⟩. ②取笑 qǔxiào (tease).

jolly adj. 愉快的 yúkuài de (cheerful).

jostle n. & v. 推撞 tuīzhuàng.

jot n. 少量 shǎoliàng. ~ **down** 摘要记下 zhāiyào jìxià.

journal n. ①日记 rìjì, 日志 rìzhì (diary). ②期刊 qīkān / qíkān (periodical).

journalism n. 新闻业 xīnwényè.

journalist n. 新闻工作者 xīnwén gōngzuò zhě, 新闻记者 xīnwén jìzhě.

journey n. 旅行 lǚxíng (trip), 旅程 lǚchéng (itinerary). — v. 旅行 lǚxíng.

jowl n. 颚 è, 下颚 xià'è.

joy n. 欢乐 huānlè, 喜悦 xǐyuè (great happiness).

joyful adj. 欢喜的 huānxǐ de, 喜悦的 xǐyuè de.

jubilant adj. 喜洋洋的 xǐyángyáng de (delighted).

Judaism n. 犹太教 Yóutàijiào.

judge n. ①法官 fǎguān ⟨court⟩. ②裁判 cáipàn ⟨contest⟩. v. ①裁判 cáipàn (decide). ②审判 shěnpàn (convict). ③判断 pànduàn (evaluate).

judgment n. ①判决 pànjué (conviction). ②判断 pànduàn, 判断力 pànduànlì (discretion).

judicial adj. 司法的 sīfǎ de.

judicious adj. 明智的 míngzhì de (wise), 深思远虑的 shēnsī-yuǎnlǜ de (well-considered).

judo n. 柔道 róudào.

jug n. 壶 hú, 水罐 shuǐguàn (pitcher).

juggle v. 变戏法 biàn xìfǎ, 要把戏 shuǎbǎxì.

juice n. 汁 zhī, 液 yè.

juicy adj. 多汁的 duōzhī de (having much juice).

jukebox n. 自动点唱机 zìdòng diǎnchàngjī.

July n. 七月 Qīyuè.

jumble v. 混杂 hùnzá, 混合 hùnhé (mix). — n. 一团糟 yìtuánzāo, 混杂 hùnzá ⟨mixed up⟩.

jumbo adj. 巨大的 jùdà de.

jump v. ①跳 tiào, 跳跃 tiàoyuè (leap). ②暴涨 bàozhǎng (rise). ③跳过 tiàoguo, 越过 yuèguo (hurdle).

jumper n. 跳跃者 tiàoyuèzhě ⟨person⟩.

jumpy adj. 神经质的

J

shénjīngzhì de / shénjīngzhí de (nervous).

junction n. 交叉点 jiāochādiǎn (intersection), 连接处 liánjiēchù (connection).

June n. 六月 Liùyuè.

jungle n. 丛林 cónglín (a thick tropical forest).

junior adj. ①年幼的 niányòu de (younger). ②资浅的 zīqiǎn de (lower). — n. 年幼者 niányòuzhě, 少年 shàonián.
~ *high school* 初级中学 chūjí zhōngxué.

junk n. 破烂 pòlàn, 废物 fèiwù (unwanted things).
~ *food* 垃圾食物 lājī shíwù / lèsè shíwù, 零食 língshí.
~ *mail* 垃圾邮件 lājī yóujiàn / lèsè yóujiàn.

junkie n. 有毒瘾者 yǒu dúyǐn zhě, 毒虫 dúchóng.

juridical adj. 法律上的 fǎlǜshang de, 审判上的

shěnpànshang de.

jurisdiction n. 司法权 sīfǎquán <law>, 管辖权 guǎnxiáquán <area of control>.

juror n. 陪审员 péishěnyuán.

jury n. 陪审团 péishěntuán (group of jurors).

just adj. 公正的 gōngzhèng de, 公平的 gōngpíng de (fair). — adv. ①正好 zhènghǎo, 正要 zhèngyào (exactly). ②刚才 gāngcái (very recently). ③只是 zhǐshì (only).

justice n. 公平 gōngpíng, 正义 zhèngyì (fairness).

justifiable adj. 有理由的 yǒu lǐyóu de.

justify v. 证明正当 zhèngmíng zhèngdàng, 为……辩护 wèi...biànhù (give a good reason for).

juvenile adj. 少年的 shàonián de (young). — n. 少年 shàonián (youth).

K

kale n. 甘蓝 gānlán.

kaleidoscope n. 万花筒 wànhuātǒng <tube>.

kangaroo n. 袋鼠 dàishǔ.

karaoke n. 卡拉 OK kǎlā OK.

karate n. 空手道 kōngshǒudào.

keel n. 龙骨 lónggǔ <bar>. — v. 倾倒 qīngdǎo (fall over sideways).

keen adj. ①锋利的 fēnglì de, 尖锐的 jiānruì de (sharp). ②敏

锐的 mǐnruì de (perceptive).

keep v. ①保存 bǎocún, 保持 bǎochí (hold). ②持续 chíxù (continue). ③维持 wéichí (maintain). ④照顾 zhàogù, 保管 bǎoguǎn (care for). ⑤保留 bǎoliú (retain).

keepsake n. 纪念品 jìniànpǐn.

keg n. 小桶 xiǎo tǒng.

kennel n. 狗屋 gǒuwū, 狗窝 gǒuwō (house for dog).

kerchief n. 头巾 tóujīn.

kernel n. ①核仁 hérén (core). ②核心 héxīn, 要点 yàodiǎn (point).

ketchup n. 番茄酱 fānqiéjiàng.

kettle n. 壶 hú, 锅 guō (a metal container).

key n. ①钥匙 yàoshi (opener). ②解答 jiědá (answer), 关键 guānjiàn (essential point). ③键 jiàn (piano). ~ *word* 关键语 guānjiànyǔ.

keyboard n. 键盘 jiànpán.

keyhole n. 钥匙孔 yàoshikǒng.

khaki n. & adj. ①卡其布 kǎqíbù (cloth). ②卡其色 kǎqísè (color).

kick n. & v. 踢 tī (strike with the foot).

kid n. ①小孩 xiǎohái, 孩子 háizi (child). ②小山羊 xiǎo shānyáng (goat). — v. 戏弄 xìnòng (deceive).

kidnap v. 绑架 bǎngjià.

kidney n. 肾 shèn.

kill v. ①杀 shā, 杀死 shāsǐ (slaughter). ②摧毁 cuīhuǐ, 破坏 pòhuài (destroy). ③消磨 xiāomó (time).

kilogram n. 公斤 gōngjīn.

kilometer n. 公里 gōnglǐ.

kilowatt n. 千瓦 qiānwǎ.

kilt n. 褶式短裙 zhěshì duǎnqún / zhéshì duǎnqún.

kimono n. ①和服 héfú (coat-like garment worn in Japan). ②晨服 chénfú (loose dressing gown).

kin n. 家族 jiāzú (family), 亲属 qīnshǔ (relatives).

kind adj. 亲切的 qīnqiè de (friendly), 仁慈的 réncí de (nice). — n. 种 zhǒng, 类 lèi (type).

kindergarten n. 幼儿园

yòu'éryuán / 幼稚园 yòuzhìyuán.

kindhearted adj. 仁慈的 réncí de.

kindle v. 点燃 diǎnrán, 燃烧 ránshāo.

kindly adj. 亲切的 qīnqiè de (friendly), 仁慈的 réncí de (nice).

kindness n. 亲切 qīnqiè (friendliness), 仁慈 réncí (behavior).

kindred n. 家族 jiāzú (family), 亲属 qīnshǔ (one's relatives).

king n. 国王 guówáng (monarchy), 君主 jūnzhǔ (ruler).

kingdom n. 王国 wángguó (empire).

king-size(d) adj. 特大的 tèdà de (bigger than usual).

kink n. 扭结 niǔjié (twist).

kiosk n. ①贩卖亭 fànmàitíng (stand). ②电话亭 diànhuàtíng (telephone booth).

kiss n. & v. 吻 wěn, 接吻 jiēwěn.

kit n. 一套用具 yítào yòngjù (a set of tools).

kitchen n. 厨房 chúfáng.

kite n. 风筝 fēngzheng (toy).

kitten n. 小猫 xiǎomāo.

kiwi n. 猕猴桃 míhóutáo / 奇异果 qíyìguǒ (fruit).

knack n. 窍门 qiàomén, 技巧 jìqiǎo (skill).

knapsack n. 背包 bēibāo, 背袋 bēidài.

knead v. ①揉 róu (clay). ②按摩 ànmó (muscle).

knee n. 膝 xī.

kneel v. 跪下 guìxia, 屈膝 qūxī.

knell n. 丧钟声 sāngzhōngshēng.

knickknack n. 小衣饰 xiǎo

K

yīshì.

knife *n.* 刀 dāo, 小刀 xiǎodāo (cutting blade). — *v.* 用刀切 yòng dāo qiē.

knight *n.* ①骑士 qíshì 〈soldier〉. ②爵士 juéshì 〈title〉.

knit *v.* 编织 biānzhī.

knob *n.* ①把手 bǎshou (handle). ②节 jié, 瘤 liú (protuberance).

knock *v.* 敲 qiāo 〈door〉, 撞 zhuàng (hit hard). — *n.* 敲打声 qiāodǎshēng (a pounding noise).

knockout *n.* 打败 dǎbài, 击倒 jīdǎo / jídǎo.

knot *n.* 结 jié 〈rope〉. — *v.* 打结 dǎjié (tie in a knot).

know *v.* ①知道 zhīdao (have learned). ②认识 rènshi (be familiar with).

knowledge *n.* 知识 zhīshi, 学识 xuéshí / xuéshì (learning).

knuckle *n.* 指关节 zhǐ guānjié (finger joint).

koala *n.* 树袋熊 shùdàixióng / 无尾熊 wúwěixióng.

Korean *n. & adj.* ①韩国人 Hánguórén 〈people〉. ②韩国语 Hánguóyǔ 〈language〉.

kowtow *v.* 磕头 kētóu.

kungfu *n.* 中国功夫 Zhōngguó gōngfu, 中国武术 Zhōngguó wǔshù.

L εʋŏ

lab *n.* 实验室 shíyànshì.

label *n.* 标签 biāoqiān. — *v.* 贴标签 tiē biāoqiān, 标记 biāojì (tag).

labor *n.* ①劳力 láolì (manual work), 工作 gōngzuò (work). ②劳工 láogōng (workers).

laboratory *n.* 实验室 shíyànshì.

laborer *n.* 劳工 láogōng.

laborious *adj.* 辛劳的 xīnláo de (tiresome), 艰难的 jiānnán de (difficult).

lack *n. & v.* 缺乏 quēfá, 不足 bùzú.

lad *n.* 少年 shàonián (youth).

ladder *n.* 梯 tī (stairs).

laden *adj.* 载满的 zàimǎn de.

ladle *n.* 长柄勺 chángbǐngsháo.

lady *n.* 夫人 fūrén, 贵妇 guìfù (women), 淑女 shūnǚ / shúnǚ 〈well-bred〉.

lag *v.* 落后 luòhòu, 延迟 yánchí (delay).

lagoon *n.* 潟湖 xìhú 〈shallow〉.

lair *n.* 巢穴 cháoxué / cháoxuè.

laity *n.* ①一般信徒 yìbān xìntú 〈religion〉. ②外行人 wàihángrén, 门外汉 ménwàihàn 〈nonprofessional〉.

lake *n.* 湖 hú.

lama *n.* 喇嘛 lǎma.

lamb *n.* 羔羊 gāoyáng.

lame *adj.* 跛足的 bǒzú de (crippled). — *v.* 使跛 shǐ bǒ.

lament *v.* 哀悼 āidào. — *n.* ①哀悼 āidào (wailing). ②哀歌 āigē, 挽诗 wǎnshī (dirge).

lamp n. 灯 dēng.

land n. ①陆地 lùdì (earth). ②田地 tiándì (farm). ③国土 guótǔ (country). — v. 使着陆 shǐ zhuólù, 降落 jiàngluò (alight).

landing n. 登陆 dēnglù, 降落 jiàngluò (alighting).

landlady n. 女房东 nǚfángdōng.

landlord n. ①房东 fángdōng ⟨house⟩. ②地主 dìzhǔ ⟨land⟩. ③主人 zhǔrén ⟨hotel⟩.

landmark n. 陆标 lùbiāo, 界标 jièbiāo ⟨building⟩.

landscape n. ①风景 fēngjǐng (scenery). ②风景画 fēngjǐnghuà ⟨picture⟩.

landslide n. 山崩 shānbēng.

lane n. 小路 xiǎolù, 小径 xiǎojìng, 巷道 xiàngdào (path).

language n. ①语言 yǔyán ⟨speech⟩. ②术语 shùyǔ (jargon).

lank adj. 细直的 xìzhí de (thin and straight).

lanky adj. 瘦长的 shòucháng de (thin).

lantern n. 灯笼 dēnglong ⟨container⟩.

lap n. 大腿上侧 dàtuǐ shàngcè. — v. 舐食 shìshí (lick).

lapidary n. 宝石匠 bǎoshíjiàng.

lapse n. & v. ①失误 shīwù, 差错 chācuò (error). ②堕落 duòluò (backsliding).

laptop n. 膝上型计算机 xīshangxíng jìsuànjī, 笔记本电脑 bǐjìběn diànnǎo / 笔记型电脑 bǐjìxíng diànnǎo.

larceny n. 窃盗 qièdào.

lard n. 猪油 zhūyóu.

large adj. 大的 dà de (big).

largely adv. 主要地 zhǔyào de (mainly), 大部分地

大部分的 dàbùfen de (mostly).

lark n. ①云雀 yúnquè ⟨bird⟩. ②玩乐 wánlè ⟨for fun⟩.

larva n. 幼虫 yòuchóng.

laryngitis n. 喉炎 hóuyán.

laser n. 激光 jīguāng / 雷射 léishè ⟨physics⟩. ~ *printer* 激光打印机 jīguāng dǎyìnjī / 雷射印表机 léishè yìnbiǎojī.

lash n. ①皮条 pítiáo (whip). ②鞭打 biāndǎ (whipping). ③睫毛 jiémáo (eyelash). — v. ①鞭打 biāndǎ (whip). ②抨击 pēngjī / pēngjí (criticize).

lass n. 少女 shàonǚ (girl).

last adj. ①最后的 zuìhòu de (final). ②上次的 shàngcì de (most recent). ~ *name* 姓 xìng. — adv. 最后地 zuìhòu de (finally). — v. 延续 yánxù, 持续 chíxù (continue).

lasting adj. 持久的 chíjiǔ de, 永久的 yǒngjiǔ de (enduring).

latch n. 门闩 ménshuān (bar). — v. 栓上 shuānshang.

late adj. ①迟到的 chídào de, 晚的 wǎn de (delayed). ②已故的 yǐgù de (dead). ~ *movie* 夜场电影 yèchǎng diànyǐng / 午夜场 wǔyèchǎng.

lately adv. 近来 jìnlái, 最近 zuìjìn.

latent adj. 潜在的 qiánzài de, 潜伏的 qiánfú de.

later adj. 更迟的 gèngchí de, 更后的 gènghòu de.

latest adj. 最近的 zuìjìn de, 最新的 zuìxīn de.

lathe n. 车床 chēchuáng.

lather n. 肥皂泡沫 féizào pàomò ⟨soap⟩.

Latin n. & adj. 拉丁文 Lādīngwén. ~ *America* 拉丁美洲 Lādīng Měizhōu.

L

latitude n. 纬度 wěidù.

latte n. 拿铁 nátiě.

latter adj. 后者的 hòuzhě de, 后半的 hòubàn de (later).

lattice n. 格子 gézi.

laud v. 赞美 zànměi.

laugh n. & v. 笑 xiào.

laughter n. 笑 xiào, 笑声 xiàoshēng.

launch v. ①下水 xiàshuǐ (set off). ②发射 fāshè (blast off). ③开始 kāishǐ, 展开 zhǎnkāi (begin). — n. ①下水 xiàshuǐ 〈ship〉. ②发射 fāshè 〈rocket〉.

launder v. 洗熨 xǐyùn (wash).

laundry n. ①洗衣店 xǐyīdiàn 〈store〉. ②待洗衣物 dài xǐ yīwù (washing).

laureate n. 桂冠诗人 guìguān shīrén (poet laureate).

laurel n. ①月桂树 yuèguìshù 〈tree〉. ②荣誉 róngyù (honor).

lava n. 熔岩 róngyán.

lavatory n. 洗手间 xǐshǒujiān, 厕所 cèsuǒ.

lavender n. 薰衣草 xūnyīcǎo 〈plant〉.

lavish adj. ①丰富的 fēngfù de (bountiful). ②浪费的 làngfèi de (wasteful). — v. 浪费 làngfèi.

law n. 法律 fǎlǜ (rule).

lawful adj. 合法的 héfǎ de (legal).

lawmaker n. 立法者 lìfǎzhě.

lawn n. 草地 cǎodì (grass).

lawsuit n. 诉讼 sùsòng.

lawyer n. 律师 lǜshī.

lax adj. ①宽松的 kuānsōng de (loose). ②散漫的 sǎnmàn de / sànmàn de (careless).

laxative adj. 通便的 tōngbiàn de. — n. 泻药 xièyào.

lay v. ①置放 zhìfàng, 安放 ānfàng (put down). ②铺设 pūshè (cover). ③产卵 chǎnluǎn 〈eggs〉. — adj. ①世俗的 shìsú de 〈religion〉. ②外行的 wàiháng de (amateur).

layer n. 层 céng (thickness).

layman n. ①俗人 súrén 〈religion〉. ②外行人 wàihángrén (amateur).

layout n. 设计 shèjì (design).

lazy adj. 懒惰的 lǎnduò de (indolent).

lead v. ①引导 yǐndǎo (conduct). ②率领 shuàilǐng (command). ③领先 lǐngxiān (head). — n. 铅 qiān 〈metal〉.

leader n. 领袖 lǐngxiù (chief).

leadership n. ①领导地位 lǐngdǎo dìwèi 〈status〉. ②领导能力 lǐngdǎo nénglì (ability).

leading adj. 主要的 zhǔyào de, 一流的 yīliú de.

leaf n. ①叶 yè 〈plant〉. ②书页 shūyè 〈paper〉.

leaflet n. ①小叶 xiǎoyè (small leaf). ②传单 chuándān (printed sheet).

league n. 联合 liánhé, 同盟 tóngméng 〈group〉, 联盟 liánméng (confederation).

leak n. 漏洞 lòudòng, 漏隙 lòuxì (hole). — v. ①漏出 lòuchū, 渗漏 shènlòu (drip). ②泄露 xièlòu (make known).

leakage n. 漏 lòu.

lean v. ①倾斜 qīngxié (incline). ②靠 kào, 倚靠 yǐkào (support). ③依靠 yīkào (rely for support).

leap n. 跳跃 tiàoyuè (jump).

learn v. ①学习 xuéxí (be taught). ②得知 dézhī (find out).

learning n. 学识 xuéshí / xuéshì, 学问 xuéwen (knowledge).

lease n. 租约 zūyuē 〈contract〉. — v. 租用 zūyòng 〈rent〉.

leash n. 皮带 pídài.

least adj. & pron. 最小的 zuìxiǎo de, 最少的 zuìshǎo de. — adv. 最少 zuìshǎo.

leather n. 皮革 pígé 〈hide〉.

leave v. ①离开 líkāi 〈go away〉. ②遗留 yíliú, 留下 liúxia 〈bequeath〉. ③辞去 cíqù 〈quit〉. ④保留 bǎoliú 〈remain〉. — n. ①许可 xǔkě 〈permission〉. ②请假 qǐngjià 〈absence〉.

leaven n. 酵母 jiàomǔ / xiàomǔ 〈yeast〉. — v. 使发酵 shǐ fājiào / shǐ fāxiào 〈ferment〉.

lecture n. & v. ①演讲 yǎnjiǎng, 讲课 jiǎngkè 〈speech〉. ②训诫 xùnjiè 〈reprimand〉.

ledge n. 架 jià, 台 tái 〈a narrow flat shelf〉.

leech n. 水蛭 shuǐzhì. — v. 榨取 zhàqǔ.

leek n. 韭葱 jiǔcōng.

leer n. & v. ①斜视 xiéshì, 睨视 nìshì 〈sideways look〉. ②色眯眯地看 sèmīmī de kàn 〈thought of sex〉.

left adj. 左方的 zuǒfāng de. — n. 左方 zuǒfāng, 左侧 zuǒcè 〈side〉. — adv. 向左 xiàngzuǒ.

leftist n. 左派 zuǒpài.

leg n. 腿 tuǐ, 脚 jiǎo 〈limb〉.

legacy n. 遗产 yíchǎn 〈law〉.

legal adj. ①法律的 fǎlǜ de 〈judicial〉. ②合法的 héfǎ de 〈lawful〉.

legalize v. 使合法 shǐ héfǎ, 合法化 héfǎhuà.

legend n. 传说 chuánshuō, 传奇 chuánqí 〈myth〉.

legible adj. 可辨读的 kě biàndú de 〈readable〉.

legislate v. 立法 lìfǎ.

legislation n. 立法 lìfǎ 〈lawmaking〉.

legislative adj. 立法的 lìfǎ de.

legislator n. 立法者 lìfǎzhě.

legislature n. 立法机关 lìfǎ jīguān, 议会 yìhuì.

legitimate adj. 合法的 héfǎ de 〈legal〉, 正当的 zhèngdàng de 〈upright〉.

leisure n. & adj. 闲暇 xiánxiá, 空闲 kòngxián.

leisurely adj. & adv. 闲暇的 xiánxiá de.

lemon n. 柠檬 níngméng 〈fruit〉.

lemonade n. 柠檬水 níngméngshuǐ.

lend v. 借出 jièchū, 借与 jièyǔ 〈loan〉.

length n. 长度 chángdù, 长 cháng 〈measurement〉.

lengthen v. 加长 jiācháng, 变长 biàncháng.

lengthy adj. 长的 cháng de.

lenient adj. 宽大的 kuāndà de 〈generous〉, 温和的 wēnhé de 〈easy-going〉.

lens n. ①透镜 tòujìng 〈glass〉. ②水晶体 shuǐjīngtǐ 〈eye〉.

Lent n. 四旬斋 Sìxúnzhāi.

Leo n. 狮子座 Shīzizuò.

leopard n. 豹 bào.

leper n. 麻风病人 máfēngbìngrén 〈someone who has leprosy〉.

leprosy n. 麻风病 máfēngbìng.

lesbian n. & adj. 女同性恋 nǚtóngxìngliàn.

less adj. 较少的 jiàoshǎo de 〈amount〉, 较小的 jiàoxiǎo de 〈size, degree〉. — adv. 较少 jiàoshǎo 〈amount〉, 较小 jiàoxiǎo 〈size, degree〉.

lessen v. 减少 jiǎnshǎo, 缩小

L

suōxiǎo.

lesser adj. 较少的 jiàoshǎo de 〈amount〉, 较小的 jiàoxiǎo de 〈size, degree〉.

lesson n. ①课业 kèyè, 课 kè 〈class〉. ②教训 jiàoxun 〈reprimand〉.

lest conj. 唯恐 wéikǒng, 以免 yǐmiǎn 〈for fear that〉.

let v. ①让 ràng 〈allow〉. ②出租 chūzū 〈rent〉.

lethal adj. 致命的 zhìmìng de.

letter n. ①字母 zìmǔ 〈character〉. ②书信 shūxìn 〈message〉. ~ of credit 信用证 xìnyòngzhèng / 信用状 xìnyòngzhuàng.

lettuce n. 莴苣 wōju.

leukemia n. 血癌 xuě'ái / xiě'ái, 白血病 báixuèbìng / báixiěbìng.

levee n. 堤防 dīfáng / tífáng.

level adj. ①水平的 shuǐpíng de 〈flat〉. ②同等的 tóngděng de, 平等的 píngděng de 〈equal〉. — n. ①水平 shuǐpíng / 水准 shuǐzhǔn 〈standard〉. ②水平面 shuǐpíngmiàn 〈height〉. ③等级 děngjí 〈degree〉. ④程度 chéngdù 〈grade〉. ⑤楼 lóu, 层 céng 〈floor〉.

lever n. 杠杆 gànggǎn.

levy n. & v. 征税 zhēngshuì 〈tax〉.

lewd adj. 淫荡的 yíndàng de, 好色的 hàosè de 〈suggesting thoughts of sex〉.

lexicon n. 辞典 cídiǎn, 字典 zìdiǎn 〈dictionary〉.

liable adj. ①易患的 yì huàn de 〈likely〉. ②应负责的 yīng fùzé de 〈responsible〉.

liaison n. ①联络 liánluò 〈communication〉. ②外遇

wàiyù 〈affair〉.

liar n. 说谎者 shuōhuǎngzhě.

libel n. 诽谤 fěibàng 〈law〉.

liberal adj. ①慷慨的 kāngkǎi de 〈bountiful〉. ②宽厚的 kuānhòu de 〈broad-minded〉. ③自由主义的 zìyóu zhǔyì de 〈politics〉. — n. 自由主义者 zìyóu zhǔyì zhě 〈person〉.

liberate v. 释放 shìfàng 〈set free〉.

liberty n. 自由 zìyóu 〈freedom〉.

librarian n. 图书馆员 túshūguǎn yuán.

library n. 图书馆 túshūguǎn.

license n. ①执照 zhízhào 〈certificate〉. ②许可 xǔkě 〈permission〉. — v. 许可 xǔkě, 特许 tèxǔ 〈give permission〉.

lick n. & v. 舔 shì.

licorice n. ①甘草 gāncǎo 〈herb〉. ②甘草糖 gāncǎotáng 〈candy〉.

lid n. ①盖子 gàizi 〈cover〉. ②眼皮 yǎnpí 〈eyelid〉.

lie n. 谎言 huǎngyán 〈untrue statement〉. — v. ①说谎 shuō-huǎng, 撒谎 sāhuǎng 〈falsify〉. ②卧 wò, 躺 tǎng 〈recline〉.

lieutenant n. ①中尉 zhōngwèi 〈army〉. ②上尉 shàngwèi 〈navy〉.

life n. ①生命 shēngmìng 〈being〉. ②一生 yìshēng 〈all one's life〉. ~ insurance 人寿保险 rénshòu bǎoxiǎn. ~ style 生活方式 shēnghuó fāngshì.

lifeboat n. 救生艇 jiùshēngtǐng.

lifeguard n. 救生人员 jiùshēng rényuán.

lifeless adj. 无生命的 wú shēngmìng de 〈dead〉.

lifelong adj. 终身的

L

zhōngshēn de.

lifetime n. 一生 yìshēng, 终身 zhōngshēn.

lift v. 举起 jǔqi (raise). — n. ①举起 jǔqi (lifting). ②电梯 diàntī (elevator).

ligament n. 韧带 rèndài.

light n. ①光 guāng, 光线 guāngxiàn (ray). ②灯 dēng (lamp). — v. ①点燃 diǎnrán (ignite). ②使明亮 shǐ míngliàng (brighten). — adj. 轻的 qīng de (weight).

lighten v. ①使光明 shǐ guāngmíng, 照亮 zhàoliàng (brighten). ②使轻 shǐ qīng (weight).

lighter n. 打火机 dǎhuǒjī (cigarette).

lighthouse n. 灯塔 dēngtǎ.

lightning n. 闪电 shǎndiàn. ~ **bug** 萤火虫 yínghuǒchóng. ~ **rod** 避雷针 bìléizhēn.

likable adj. 可爱的 kě'ài de (cute), 受人喜欢的 shòu rén xǐhuan de (friendly).

like prep. 像……一样 xiàng... yíyàng (similar to). — adj. 同样的 tóngyàng de, 相似的 xiāngsì de. — v. 喜欢 xǐhuan (enjoy).

likelihood n. 可能性 kěnéngxìng.

likely adj. 可能的 kěnéng de (possible). — adv. 大概 dàgài, 也许 yěxǔ.

liken v. 比喻 bǐyù.

likeness n. 相似 xiāngsì (resemblance).

likewise adv. 同样地 tóngyàng de (similarly).

liking n. 爱好 àihào.

lilac n. 紫丁香 zǐdīngxiāng. — adj. 淡紫色的 dànzǐsè de.

lily n. 百合花 bǎihéhuā.

limb n. ①四肢 sìzhī ⟨body⟩. ②大枝 dàzhī ⟨tree⟩.

limber adj. 柔软的 róuruǎn de. — v. 变柔软 biàn róuruǎn.

lime n. ①石灰 shíhuī ⟨substance⟩. ②酸橙 suānchéng / 莱姆 láimǔ ⟨fruit⟩.

limit n. ①界限 jièxiàn (boundary). ②极限 jíxiàn (maximum). — v. 限制 xiànzhì (confine).

limitation n. 限制 xiànzhì, 有限 yǒuxiàn (confinement).

limited adj. 有限的 yǒuxiàn de (confined).

limousine n. 高级轿车 gāojí jiàochē ⟨car⟩.

limp adj. ①柔软的 róuruǎn de (soft). ②没有劲的 méiyǒu jìn de / 没有力 jìng de (weak).

linden n. 菩提树 pútíshù.

line n. ①线 xiàn, 直线 zhíxiàn (long narrow mark). ②列 liè, 排 pái (row). ③路线 lùxiàn (route). — v. 画线 huàxiàn (mark with lines). ~ **up** 排队 páiduì (form rows).

lineage n. 家系 jiāxì, 血统 xuètǒng / xiětǒng.

lineal adj. 直系的 zhíxì de, 正统的 zhèngtǒng de (in direct descending line).

linear adj. 线的 xiàn de (aligned).

linen n. 亚麻布 yàmábù ⟨cloth⟩.

liner n. 班轮 bānlún, 邮轮 yóulún ⟨ship⟩.

linger v. 徘徊 páihuái, 逗留 dòuliú (tarry).

linguist n. 语言学家 yǔyánxué jiā (philologist).

linguistic adj. 语言的 yǔyán de, 语言学的 yǔyánxué de.

L

lining n. 衬里 chènlǐ.

link v. 连结 liánjié (connect).

links n. 高尔夫球场 gāo'ěrfū qiúchǎng (golf course).

linoleum n. 油毡 yóuzhān, 油布 yóubù.

lion n. 狮子 shīzi.

lip n. 唇 chún 〈mouth〉.

lipstick n. 唇膏 chúngāo, 口红 kǒuhóng.

liquefy v. 液化 yèhuà.

liquid n. 液体 yètǐ (fluid). — adj. 液体的 yètǐ de (fluid). ~ crystal display 液晶显示器 yèjīng xiǎnshìqì.

liquidate v. 偿付 chángfù, 清算 qīngsuàn (pay).

liquor n. 酒 jiǔ, 酒类 jiǔlèi (alcohol).

lisp n. 口齿不清的发音 kǒuchǐ-bùqīng de fāyīn (unclear speech). — v. 含糊发音 hánhu fāyīn.

list n. 一览表 yìlǎnbiǎo. — v. 列表 lièbiǎo 〈catalog〉.

listen v. 倾听 qīngtīng, 听 tīng (hear).

listless adj. 无精打采的 wújīngdǎcǎi de (languid).

lite beer n. 低热量啤酒 dīrèliàng píjiǔ.

liter n. 公升 gōngshēng.

literacy n. 识字 shízì / shìzì.

literal adj. 文字上的 wénzìshang de (verbatim).

literary adj. 文学的 wénxué de (of literature).

literate adj. ①能读写的 néng dúxiě de, 识字的 shízì de / shìzì de (able to read). ②受过良好教育的 shòuguo liánghǎo jiàoyù de (well-educated).

literature n. 文学 wénxué (writings).

litigate v. 诉讼 sùsòng (contest in law).

litter n. 废弃物 fèiqì wù, 垃圾 lājī / lèsè (rubbish). — v. 使杂乱 shǐ záluàn, 弄乱 nòngluàn (scatter).

little adj. 少的 shǎo de 〈amount〉, 小的 xiǎo de 〈size〉. — adv. 很少 hěn shǎo (rarely). — n. 少许 shǎoxǔ.

live v. ①居住 jūzhù (dwell). ②活 huó, 生存 shēngcún (stay alive). ③生活 shēnghuó (remain alive). — adj. ①活的 huó de, 有生命的 yǒu shēngmìng de (living). ②当前的 dāngqián de (current).

livelihood n. 生计 shēngjì.

lively adj. ①活泼的 huópō de (vigorous). ②有生气的 yǒu shēngqì de, 生动的 shēngdòng de (active). ③轻快的 qīngkuài de (spirited).

liver n. 肝脏 gānzàng 〈organ〉.

livestock n. 家畜 jiāchù 〈animals〉.

livid adj. ①青黑色的 qīnghēisè de (black and blue). ②愤怒的 fènnù de (very angry).

living adj. ①活的 huó de (alive). ②现存的 xiàncún de (existing). ③逼真的 bīzhēn de (lifelike). — n. 生计 shēngjì, 生存 shēngcún (livelihood). earn one's ~ 谋生 móushēng.

lizard n. ①蜥蜴 xīyì 〈reptile〉. ②壁虎 bìhǔ (gecko).

llama n. 骆马 luòmǎ.

load n. 负荷 fùhè, 载量 zàiliàng (weight). — v. 装载 zhuāngzài (pack).

loaf n. 一条面包 yìtiáo miànbāo 〈bread〉. — v. 游手

L

好闲 yóushǒu-hàoxián.

loan n. ①贷款 dàikuǎn ⟨money⟩. ②借出 jièchū ⟨lending⟩.

loath adj. 厌恶的 yànwù de (hateful), 极不愿意的 jí bú yuànyì de (unwilling).

loathe v. 厌恶 yànwù.

lobby n. 大厅 dàtīng, 接待室 jiēdàishì (hall). — v. 游说 yóushuì.

lobe n. 耳垂 ěrchuí (earlobe).

lobster n. 龙虾 lóngxiā.

local adj. ①地方的 dìfāng de, 本地的 běndì de ⟨district⟩. ② 局部的 júbù de ⟨part⟩. — n. 本地居民 běndì jūmín.

locality n. 所在地 suǒzàidì, 现场 xiànchǎng.

locate v. 位于 wèiyú (situate).

location n. 位置 wèizhì, 场所 chǎngsuǒ (place).

lock n. ①锁 suǒ ⟨door⟩. ②水闸 shuǐzhá ⟨water⟩. — v. 锁 suǒ (latch).

locker n. 橱柜 chúguì.

locomotion n. 移动 yídòng (movement).

locomotive n. 火车头 huǒchētóu. — adj. 移动的 yídòng de (moving).

locust n. 蝗虫 huángchóng.

lodge v. ①提供住宿 tígōng zhùsù (shelter). ②住宿 zhùsù (stay). — n. 小旅馆 xiǎo lǚguǎn (hotel).

lodging n. 寄宿处 jìsùchù (place to stay).

loft n. 顶楼 dǐnglóu (attic).

lofty adj. 高的 gāo de, 高耸的 gāosǒng de (high).

log n. ①圆木 yuánmù ⟨wood⟩. ②航海日志 hánghǎi rìzhì ⟨record⟩.

logic n. 逻辑 luóji ⟨process⟩, 理则学 lǐzéxué ⟨field of study⟩.

logo n. 商标 shāngbiāo.

loin n. ①(pl.) 腰部 yāobù (waist). ②腰肉 yāoròu ⟨meat⟩. ③耻骨区 chǐgǔqū (sex organs).

loiter v. 闲荡 xiándàng, 徘徊 páihuái (hang around).

lollipop n. 棒棒糖 bàngbàngtáng.

lone adj. 孤寂的 gūjì de / gūjí de (alone).

lonely adj. 孤单的 gūdān de, 寂寞的 jìmò de / jímò de.

lonesome adj. 寂寞的 jìmò de / jímò de.

long adj. ①长的 cháng de (lengthy). ②长久的 chángjiǔ de (lasting). — adv. 长久地 chángjiǔ de.

long-distance adj. 长途的 chángtú de.

longevity n. 长寿 chángshòu (long life).

longing n. & adj. 渴望 kěwàng.

longitude n. 经度 jīngdù.

look v. ①看 kàn (see). ②看似 kànsì (seem). ③面向 miànxiàng (face). ~ **after** 照料 zhàoliào. ~ **down on** 瞧不起 qiáobuqǐ. ~ **for** 寻找 xúnzhǎo. ~ **out** 当心 dāngxīn. — n. ①看 kàn (glance). ②表情 biǎoqíng (expression). ③容貌 róngmào (appearance).

loom n. 织布机 zhībùjī.

loop n. 圈环 quānhuán (circle). — v. 使成圈环 shǐ chéng quānhuán (make into a loop).

loophole n. 漏洞 lòudòng.

loose adj. ①松的 sōng de (loosened). ②自由的 zìyóu de (free). ③宽松的 kuānsōng de (slack). ④散漫的 sǎnmàn de /

sànmàn de, 不精确的 bù jīngquè de (ill-defined).

loosen v. ①解开 jiěkai (release). ②松开 sōngkāi (become loose).

loot n. 掠夺品 lüèduópín (spoil). — v. 掠夺 lüèduó.

lop v. 砍伐 kǎnfá / kǎnfā.

Lord n. 上帝 Shàngdì (God).

lord n. 贵族 guìzú (noble).

lore n. 学问 xuéwen, 传说的知识 chuánshuō de zhīshi (tale).

lorry n. 卡车 kǎchē.

lose v. ①失去 shīqù, 遗失 yíshī (fail to find). ②损失 sǔnshī (waste). ③输掉 shūdiào (be defeated). ④迷失 míshī (be lost).

loss n. 损失 sǔnshī (gone from one's possession).

lost adj. ①失去的 shīqù de (forfeited). ②迷路的 mílù de (disorientated).

lot n. ①许多 xǔduō, 很多 hěn duō (many). ②一块地 yíkuài dì (piece of land). ③签 qiān (decision by chance). ④命运 mìngyùn, 运气 yùnqi (fortune).

lottery n. 彩券 cǎiquàn (raffle).

lotto n. 乐透 lètòu.

lotus n. 莲花 liánhuā ⟨flower⟩.

loud adj. 大声的 dàshēng de, 吵闹的 chǎonào de (noisy).

loudspeaker n. 扩音器 kuòyīnqì ⟨apparatus⟩.

lounge v. 闲散度日 xiánsàn dùrì (pass time idly). — n. 会客室 huìkèshì.

louse n. 虱 shī ⟨insect⟩.

lousy adj. ①糟透的 zāotòu de (bad). ②多虱的 duō shī de (lice-infested).

lout n. 粗鄙之人 cūbǐ zhī rén.

lovable adj. 可爱的 kě'ài de.

love n. ①爱 ài, 爱情 àiqíng (fondness). ②爱人 àirén, 情人 qíngrén (lover). ~ affair 恋情 liànqíng. — v. 爱 ài (adore).

lovely adj. 可爱的 kě'ài de (charming).

lover n. 爱人 àirén, 情人 qíngrén (love).

low adj. ①低的 dī de (not high). ②微贱的 wēijiàn de / wéijiàn de (abject). ③低级的 dījí de (vulgar).

lower v. 降低 jiàngdī, 降下 jiàngxià (reduce).

lowly adj. 低的 dī de, 卑下的 bēixià de (humble).

loyal adj. 忠诚的 zhōngchéng de, 忠实的 zhōngshí de.

loyalty n. 忠诚 zhōngchéng.

lozenge n. ①菱形 língxíng ⟨shape⟩. ②药片 yàopiàn ⟨medicine⟩.

lubricant n. 润滑油 rùnhuáyóu.

lubricate v. 加润滑油 jiā rùnhuáyóu, 润滑 rùnhuá.

lucid adj. 明白的 míngbai de, 清楚的 qīngchu de.

Lucifer n. 金星 Jīnxīng (Venus).

luck n. 运气 yùnqi, 幸运 xìngyùn.

lucky adj. 幸运的 xìngyùn de (fortunate).

lucrative adj. 可获利的 kě huòlì de (profitable).

ludicrous adj. 可笑的 kěxiào de (laughable), 滑稽的 huájī de (ridiculous).

lug v. 猛拉 měnglā, 拖拉 tuōlā (drag).

luggage n. 行李 xíngli.

lukewarm adj. 温热的 wēnrè de (slightly warm).

L

lull v. 使平静 shǐ píngjìng, 使缓和 shǐ huǎnhé (soothe). — n. 间歇 jiànxiē (break).

lullaby n. 摇篮曲 yáolánqǔ, 催眠曲 cuīmiánqǔ.

lumber n. 木材 mùcái (wood).

luminous adj. 发光的 fāguāng de (bright).

lump n. ①小块 xiǎokuài (mass). ②肿块 zhǒngkuài (bulge). — v. ①使结成块状 shǐ jiéchéng kuàizhuàng (form into lumps). ②混为一谈 hùnwéiyìtán 〈place together〉.

lunacy n. 疯癫 fēngdiān (madness).

lunar adj. ①月亮的 yuèliang de 〈moon〉. ②阴历的 yīnlì de 〈calendar〉.

lunatic n. 疯子 fēngzi, 精神病者 jīngshénbìng zhě. — adj. 疯狂的 fēngkuáng de.

lunch n. 午餐 wǔcān (midday meal). ~ box 盒饭 héfàn / 便当 biàndāng. — v. 吃午餐 chī wǔcān.

luncheon n. 午餐 wǔcān.

lung n. 肺 fèi.

lunge n. ①刺 cì (stab). ②前冲 qiánchōng (rush).

lurch n. & v. 倾斜 qīngxié, 摇晃 yáohuang (stumble).

lure n. ①魅力 mèilì, 诱惑力 yòuhuòlì (attraction). ②诱饵 yòu'ěr (bait). — v. 诱惑 yòuhuò.

lurid adj. ①色彩浓烈的 sècǎi nóngliè de (strongly colored). ②惊人的 jīngrén de, 骇人的 hàirén de (sensational).

lurk v. 潜伏 qiánfú (hide).

lush adj. ①茂盛的 màoshèng de (luxuriant). ②奢侈的 shēchǐ de (luxurious).

lust n. 色欲 sèyù, 欲望 yùwàng (desire). — v. 渴望 kěwàng (desire).

luster n. 光彩 guāngcǎi, 光泽 guāngzé (brightness).

lute n. 琵琶 pípa.

luxuriant adj. 茂盛的 màoshèng de, 肥沃的 féiwò de (fertile).

luxurious adj. 奢侈的 shēchǐ de (wasteful), 豪华的 háohuá de (very fine and expensive).

luxury n. 奢侈 shēchǐ (extravagance).

lying n. 说谎 shuōhuǎng.

lymph n. 淋巴 línbā 〈physiology〉.

lyric n. ①抒情诗 shūqíngshī 〈poem〉. ②(pl.) 歌词 gēcí 〈words〉. — adj. 抒情的 shūqíng de.

M

macabre adj. 阴森的 yīnsēn de, 可怕的 kěpà de.

macaroni n. 通心粉 tōngxīnfěn, 通心面 tōngxīnmiàn.

mace n. 权杖 quánzhàng

M

(staff).

machine n. 机械 jīxiè, 机器 jīqì.

machinery n. 机器 jīqì.

mackerel n. 鲭鱼 qīngyú.

mad adj. ①疯狂的 fēngkuáng de, 精神异常的 jīngshén--yìcháng de (insane). ②愤怒的 fènnù de (angry). ③狂热的 kuángrè de (enthusiastic).

madam n. 女士 nǚshì, 夫人 fūrén.

madden v. ①使发狂 shǐ fākuáng (craze). ②使愤怒 shǐ fènnù (anger).

madness n. 疯狂 fēngkuáng (crazy), 精神错乱 jīngshén cuòluàn (lunacy).

Madonna n. 圣母玛利亚 Shèngmǔ Mǎlìyà.

madrigal n. 抒情短诗 shūqíng duǎnshī (short love poem).

Mafia n. 黑手党 Hēishǒudǎng.

mag n. 杂志 zázhì (magazine).

magazine n. ①杂志 zázhì (journal). ②火药库 huǒyàokù (ammunition).

magenta n. 紫红色 zǐhóngsè 〈color〉.

maggot n. 蛆 qū (larva).

magic n. 魔法 mófǎ 〈by witches〉. 魔术 móshù 〈by conjurors〉. adj. 魔术的 móshù de.

magician n. 魔术师 móshùshī.

magnate n. 巨子 jùzǐ, 大亨 dàhēng.

magnet n. 磁铁 cítiě (lode-stone).

magnetic adj. ①有吸引力的 yǒu xīyǐnlì de (attractive). ②有磁性的 yǒu cíxìng de 〈magnet〉.

magnetism n. 磁性 cíxìng.

magnificent adj. 壮丽的 zhuànglì de, 宏伟的 hóngwěi de.

magnify v. ①放大 fàngdà (enlarge). ②夸张 kuāzhāng (exaggerate).

magnitude n. ①大小 dàxiǎo (size). ②重要性 zhòngyàoxìng (importance).

magpie n. ①鹊 què 〈bird〉. ②饶舌者 ráoshézhě 〈person〉.

mahogany n. ①桃花心木 táohuāxīnmù 〈wood〉. ②红褐色 hónghèsè / hónghésè 〈color〉.

maid n. 女仆 nǚpú (servant).

maiden n. 未婚少女 wèihūn shàonǚ. — adj. 未婚的 wèihūn de (unmarried).

mail n. 邮件 yóujiàn, 信件 xìnjiàn (letters). — v. 邮寄 yóujì.

mailbox n. 信箱 xìnxiāng, 邮筒 yóutǒng.

mailman n. 邮差 yóuchāi.

maim v. 使残废 shǐ cánfèi.

main adj. 主要的 zhǔyào de, 重要的 zhòngyào de (chief). — n. 主干线 zhǔgànxiàn, 总管道 zǒngguǎndào (chief pipe). *in the ~* 大致上 dàzhìshang.

mainland n. 大陆 dàlù.

mainly adv. 主要地 zhǔyào de, 大部分 dàbùfen (chiefly).

maintain v. ①维持 wéichí, 保持 bǎochí (keep up). ②保养 bǎoyǎng (keep in good condition). ③供养 gōngyǎng / gòngyǎng (support). ④坚持 jiānchí (insist).

maintenance n. 维持 wéichí, 保养 bǎoyǎng (preservation).

maize n. 玉蜀黍 yùshǔshǔ.

M

majestic *adj.* 庄严的 zhuāngyán de.

majesty *n.* ①庄严 zhuāngyán, 威严 wēiyán (stateliness). ②高贵 gāoguì (nobility). ③陛下 bìxià (royalty).

major *adj.* ①较大的 jiàodà de (bigger), 较多的 jiàoduō de (greater). ②主要的 zhǔyào de (chief). — *n.* ①主修科 zhǔxiūkē (subject). ②少校 shàoxiào 〈army〉.

majority *n.* 多数 duōshù, 大部分 dàbùfen (the bulk).

make *v.* ①做 zuò, 制造 zhìzào (produce). ②使 shǐ (oblige). ③获得 huòdé, 赚 zhuàn (gain). ~ *up* ①组成 zǔchéng (constitute). ②捏造 niēzào (fabricate). ③化妆 huàzhuāng 〈with cosmetics〉.

maker *n.* 制造者 zhìzàozhě (manufacturer).

make-up *n.* ①化妆品 huàzhuāngpǐn (cosmetics). ②组成 zǔchéng (composition).

malady *n.* 疾病 jíbìng (disease).

malaria *n.* 疟疾 nüèjí 〈medical〉.

male *n.* ①男人 nánrén (man). ②雄性 xióngxìng 〈animal〉. — *adj.* ①男性的 nánxìng de (of men). ②雄性的 xióngxìng de 〈animal〉.

malevolence *n.* 恶意 èyì.

malfunction *n.* 故障 gùzhàng.

malice *n.* 恶意 èyì, 怨恨 yuànhèn (spite).

malicious *adj.* 恶意的 èyì de.

malignant *adj.* ①致命的 zhìmìng de, 恶性的 èxìng de (fatal). ②怀恶意的 huái èyì de (malevolent).

malleable *adj.* 可锻的 kě duàn de (moldable).

mallet *n.* 木槌 mùchuí (hammer).

malnutrition *n.* 营养不良 yíngyǎng bùliáng.

malt *n.* 麦芽 màiyá (grain).

maltreat *v.* 虐待 nüèdài (torture), 苛待 kēdài (treat poorly).

mama *n.* 妈妈 māma.

mammal *n.* 哺乳动物 bǔrǔ dòngwù.

mammoth *n.* 长毛巨象 chángmáo jùxiàng. — *adj.* 巨大的 jùdà de (enormous).

man *n.* ①人 rén (human being). ②男人 nánrén (male).

manacle *n.* 手铐 shǒukào. — *v.* 上手铐 shàng shǒukào (handcuff), 束缚 shùfù / shùfú (fetter).

manage *v.* ①管理 guǎnlǐ, 经营 jīngyíng (administer). ②处理 chǔlǐ (handle). ③完成 wánchéng (accomplish).

management *n.* ①管理 guǎnlǐ, 经营 jīngyíng (administering). ②管理人员 guǎnlǐ rényuán (administrator), 资方 zīfāng 〈as opposed to labor〉.

manager *n.* 经理 jīnglǐ.

Mandarin *n.* 汉语 Hànyǔ (Chinese).

mandate *n.* ①命令 mìnglìng, 训令 xùnlìng (order). ②委任 wěirèn, 委托 wěituō (authorization).

mandolin *n.* 曼陀林琴 màntuólínqín.

mane *n.* 鬃 zōng.

maneuver *n. & v.* ①策略 cèlüè, 计谋 jìmóu (plan). ②调

M

动 diàodòng (move). ③演习 yǎnxí 〈military〉.

manger n. 马槽 mǎcáo.

mangle v. 撕裂 sīliè (destroy).

mango n. 芒果 mángguǒ.

manhood n. 成年 chéngnián (adulthood).

mania n. ①癫狂 diānkuáng (insanity). ②狂热 kuángrè, 热中 rèzhōng (enthusiasm).

manicure n. & v. 修指甲 xiūzhǐjia.

manifest v. ①显示 xiǎnshì, 表明 biǎomíng (show clearly). ②显露 xiǎnlù (reveal). — n. 载货清单 zàihuò qīngdān 〈checklist〉.

manifesto n. 宣言 xuānyán.

manifold adj. 多种的 duōzhǒng de, 多方面的 duōfāngmiàn de (various). — v. 复写 fùxiě.

manipulate v. ①把持 bǎchí, 操纵 cāozòng (control). ②应付 yìngfù (handle), 使用 shǐyòng (manage).

mankind n. 人类 rénlèi (humanity).

manly adj. ①勇敢的 yǒnggǎn de (brave). ②男子汉的 nánzǐhàn de (masculine).

man-made adj. 人造的 rénzào de.

manner n. ①方法 fāngfǎ, 方式 fāngshì (way). ②态度 tàidu (attitude). ③礼貌 lǐmào (politeness). ④习俗 xísú (custom). ⑤种类 zhǒnglèi (kind).

mannerism n. 独特风格 dútè fēnggé 〈style〉.

mansion n. 大厦 dàshà / dàxià, 宅邸 zháidí (residence).

manslaughter n. 杀人 shārén.

mantis n. 螳螂 tángláng.

mantle n. 斗篷 dǒupeng, 披风 pīfēng (cloak).

manual adj. ①手的 shǒu de 〈hands〉. ②手工的 shǒugōng de (done by hand). — n. 手册 shǒucè, 简介 jiǎnjiè (handbook).

manufacture v. 制造 zhìzào, 生产 shēngchǎn (make). — n. ①制造 zhìzào (making). ②制造品 zhìzàopǐn (product).

manufacturer n. 制造商 zhìzàoshāng.

manure n. 肥料 féiliào, 粪肥 fènféi.

manuscript n. 手稿 shǒugǎo, 原稿 yuángǎo.

many adj. 许多的 xǔduō de.

map n. 地图 dìtú (chart). — v. 绘地图 huì dìtú.

maple n. ①枫树 fēngshù 〈tree〉. ②枫木 fēngmù 〈wood〉.

mar v. 损毁 sǔnhuǐ (damage), 伤害 shānghài (hurt).

marathon n. 马拉松 mǎlāsōng.

maraud v. 抢掠 qiǎnglüè.

marble n. 大理石 dàlíshí 〈limestone〉.

march v. 行军 xíngjūn, 行进 xíngjìn (parade). — n. ①行军 xíngjūn 〈troops〉. ②进行曲 jìnxíngqǔ 〈music〉.

March n. 三月 Sānyuè.

mare n. 母马 mǔmǎ.

margarine n. 人造奶油 rénzào nǎiyóu.

margin n. ①边 biān, 边界 biānjiè (edge). ②页边 yèbiān, 空白 kòngbái (space). ③余地 yúdì (extra).

marigold n. 金盏花 jīnzhǎnhuā.

M

marijuana n. 大麻 dàmá.

marina n. 游艇港 yóutǐnggǎng.

marine adj. ①海的 hǎi de (of the sea). ②海军的 hǎijūn de 〈navy〉. — n. ①水兵 shuǐbīng (soldier). ②船只 chuánzhī (ship). ③舰队 jiànduì (fleet).

mariner n. 水手 shuǐshǒu, 船员 chuányuán.

marital adj. 婚姻的 hūnyīn de.

maritime adj. ①海的 hǎi de (of the sea). ②沿海的 yánhǎi de (near the sea).

mark n. ①符号 fúhào, 记号 jìhào (sign). ②污点 wūdiǎn, 痕迹 hénjì / hénjī (stain). ③标志 biāozhì, 特征 tèzhēng (figure). ④分数 fēnshù (grade). — v. ①做记号 zuò jìhào (put a mark on). ②标示 biāoshì (indicate). ③评分 píngfēn (grade).

marker n. 麦克笔 màikèbǐ 〈pen〉.

market n. 市场 shìchǎng, 商场 shāngchǎng (mart). — v. 在市场上买卖 zài shìchǎng shang mǎimai, 交易 jiāoyì.

marketing n. 买卖 mǎimai (sales), 行销 xíngxiāo (promotion).

marketplace n. 市场 shìchǎng, 市集 shìjí.

marksman n. 射手 shèshǒu.

marmalade n. 柑橘果酱 gānjú guǒjiàng.

maroon n. & adj. 栗色 lìsè, 茶色 chásè (brownish red).

marquis n. 侯爵 hóujué.

marriage n. ①婚姻 hūnyīn, 结婚 jiéhūn (matrimony). ②婚礼 hūnlǐ (wedding).

marrow n. 骨髓 gǔsuǐ 〈bone〉.

marry v. ①结婚 jiéhūn 〈matrimony〉. ②使结合 shǐ jiéhé (join).

Mars n. 火星 Huǒxīng.

marsh n. 沼泽 zhǎozé, 湿地 shīdì.

marshal n. ①高级军官 gāojí jūnguān 〈official〉. ②司仪 sīyí (for public events). — v. 整理 zhěnglǐ, 使排列 shǐ páiliè (arrange).

marten n. 貂 diāo.

martial adj. ①战争的 zhànzhēng de (of war). ②军事的 jūnshì de (of military). ③好战的 hàozhàn de (warlike). ~ **art** 武术 wǔshù. ~ **law** 戒严令 jièyánlìng.

martyr n. 殉道者 xùndàozhě, 烈士 lièshì (victim).

marvel n. 惊异之事物 jīngyì zhī shìwù (remarkable thing). — v. 惊异 jīngyì.

Marxism n. 马克思主义 Mǎkèsī zhǔyì / 马克斯主义 Mǎkèsī zhǔyì.

mascara n. 睫毛膏 jiémáo gāo.

mascot n. 吉人 jírén, 福星 fúxīng.

masculine adj. ①男性的 nánxìng de (male). ②有男子气概的 yǒu nánzǐ qìgài de (manly).

mask n. 面具 miànjù (disguise). — v. 戴面具 dài miànjù.

masochism n. 受虐狂 shòunüèkuáng.

mason n. 泥水匠 níshuǐjiàng.

masquerade n. 化装舞会 huàzhuāng wǔhuì (masked ball). — v. 伪装 wěizhuāng /

M

wèizhuāng.

mass *n.* ①块 kuài, 团 tuán (bulk). ②大量 dàliàng, 多数 duōshù (lot). ~ *media* 大众媒体 dàzhòng méitǐ.

~ *transportation* 公交 gōngjiāo / 大众运输 dàzhòng yùnshū.

Mass *n.* 弥撒 Mísa.

massacre *n. & v.* 大屠杀 dàtúshā.

massage *n. & v.* 按摩 ànmó.

masseur *n.* 按摩师 ànmóshī.

massive *adj.* 又大又重的 yòu dà yòu zhòng de (large and heavy).

mast *n.* 桅 wéi 〈boat〉.

master *n.* ①主人 zhǔrén (owner). ②男教师 nánjiàoshī (teacher). ③船长 chuánzhǎng (captain). — *v.* 精通 jīngtōng.

Master Card *n.* 万事达卡 Wànshìdákǎ.

masterful *adj.* 专横的 zhuānhèng de (imperious).

masterly *adj.* 巧妙的 qiǎomiào de.

masterpiece *n.* 杰作 jiézuò, 名著 míngzhù.

mastery *n.* ①支配 zhīpèi, 控制 kòngzhì (control). ②精通 jīngtōng (great skill).

mat *n.* 席子 xízi, 垫子 diànzi (cushion).

matador *n.* 斗牛士 dòuniúshì.

match *n.* ①火柴 huǒchái (fire). ②相配 xiāngpèi (fit).

matchmaker *n.* 媒人 méirén.

mate *n.* ①配偶 pèi'ǒu (spouse). ②伙伴 huǒbàn (companion).

material *n.* ①材料 cáiliào, 原料 yuánliào (substance). ②料子 liàozi 〈cloth〉. ③资料 zīliào (information). — *adj.* ①物质的 wùzhì de / wùzhí de (of substance). ②肉体的 ròutǐ de (of the body).

materialism *n.* 唯物论 wéiwùlùn.

materialize *v.* 具体化 jùtǐhuà (make concrete).

maternal *adj.* 母亲的 mǔqīn de, 母系的 mǔxì de.

maternity *n.* 母性 mǔxìng.

math *n.* 数学 shùxué.

mathematical *adj.* 数学的 shùxué de.

mathematician *n.* 数学家 shùxuéjiā.

mathematics *n.* 数学 shùxué.

matriculate *v.* 准许入学 zhǔnxǔ rùxué.

matrimony *n.* 结婚 jiéhūn, 婚姻 hūnyīn.

matron *n.* ①已婚妇女 yǐhūn fùnǚ (married woman). ②女舍监 nǚshèjiān 〈of dormitory〉. ③护士长 hùshizhǎng (nursing officer).

matter *n.* ①事情 shìqing (affair). ②物质 wùzhì / wùzhí (material). *as a* ~ *of fact* 事实上 shìshíshàng. *no* ~ 无论 wúlùn. — *v.* 关系重要 guānxi zhòngyào.

matting *n.* 席 xí.

mattress *n.* 床垫 chuángdiàn.

mature *adj.* ①成熟的 chéngshú de / chéngshóu de (full-grown). ②到期的 dàoqī de / dàoqí de (due).

mauve *n. & adj.* 淡紫色 dànzǐsè.

maxim *n.* 格言 géyán (proverb).

M

maximize v. 使达最大限度 shǐ dá zuìdà xiàndù.

maximum n. 最大限度 zuìdà xiàndù (level), 最大量 zuì dàliàng (amount). — adj. 最高 的 zuìgāo de, 最大的 zuìdà de.

may aux. v. ①可能 kěnéng (might). ②可以 kěyǐ (can).

May n. 五月 Wǔyuè.

maybe adv. 可能 kěnéng, 大 概 dàgài.

mayonnaise n. 蛋黄酱 dànhuángjiàng, 美乃滋 měinǎizī.

mayor n. 市长 shìzhǎng.

maze n. ①迷宫 mígōng (labyrinth). ②迷惘 míwǎng (confusion).

me pron. 我 wǒ.

meadow n. 草地 cǎodì, 草原 cǎoyuán (grassland).

meager adj. ①瘦的 shòu de (thin). ②贫弱的 pínruò de (scanty).

meal n. 餐 cān, 食物 shíwù.

mean v. ①意谓 yìwèi (symbolize). ②打算 dǎsuàn, 意 欲 yìyù (intend). — adj. ①低劣 的 dīliè de (lowly). ②吝啬的 lìnsè de, 自私的 zìsī de (self-ish). ③卑贱的 bēijiàn de (poor). ④中庸 zhōngyōng de, 平均的 píngjūn de (average).

meander v. 蜿蜒而流 wānyán'érliú (wander).

meaning n. 意义 yìyì. — adj. 有意义的 yǒu yìyì de.

meantime adv. 同时 tóngshí.

meanwhile n. & adv. 同时 tóngshí.

measles n. 麻疹 mázhěn.

measure v. 量 liáng, 测 cè

(calculate). — n. ①标准 biāozhǔn, 单位 dānwèi (standard). ②议案 yì'àn (bill).

measurement n. 量度 liángdù / liángduò.

meat n. 肉 ròu, 肉类 ròulèi (flesh).

mechanic n. 机匠 jījiàng, 技 师 jìshī.

mechanical adj. 机械的 jīxiè de, 机械制的 jīxiè zhì de (of machinery).

mechanism n. 机械装置 jīxiè zhuāngzhì (machine part).

mechanize v. 机械化 jīxièhuà.

medal n. 奖牌 jiǎngpái, 奖章 jiǎngzhāng.

meddle v. 干预 gānyù.

media n. 媒体 méitǐ, 媒介 méijiè.

mediate v. 仲裁 zhòngcái, 调 停 tiáotíng.

medical adj. 医学的 yīxué de, 医药的 yīyào de.

medicate v. 以药物治疗 yǐ yàowù zhìliáo.

medicinal adj. 有药效的 yǒu yàoxiào de.

medicine n. ①药 yào, 药物 yàowù (medication). ②医学 yīxué (healing).

medieval adj. 中世纪的 zhōngshìjì de.

mediocre adj. 平凡的 píngfán de (average).

meditate v. ①沉思 chénsī (reflect). 冥思 míngsī (religion).

Mediterranean Sea 地中 海 Dìzhōnghǎi.

medium adj. 中间的 zhōngjiān de, 中庸的 zhōngyōng de. — n. ①中间 zhōngjiān, 中庸 zhōngyōng

M

(average). ②媒介物 méijièwù, 媒体 méitǐ (media).

meek *adj.* 温顺的 wēnshùn de, 谦和的 qiānhé de (humble).

meet *v.* ①遇到 yùdào (encounter), 会面 huìmiàn (see in person). ②迎接 yíngjiē (pick up). ③会合 huìhé (gather). ④交会 jiāohuì (cross). ⑤满足 mǎnzú (satisfy).

meeting *n.* ①会议 huìyì (assembly). ②碰上 pèngshang (encounter). ③约会 yuēhuì (appointment). ④交会 jiāohuì (crossing).

megaphone *n.* 扩音器 kuòyīnqì.

melancholia *n.* 忧郁症 yōuyùzhèng.

melancholy *n. & adj.* 忧郁 yōuyù.

mellow *adj.* 柔和的 róuhé de (soft).

melodious *adj.* 悦耳的 yuè'ěr de.

melodrama *n.* 通俗剧 tōngsújù 〈play〉.

melody *n.* 旋律 xuánlǜ.

melon *n.* 瓜 guā.

melt *v.* 融化 rónghuà, 溶解 róngjiě (dissolve).

member *n.* ①会员 huìyuán, 社员 shèyuán (associate). ②肢体 zhītǐ (limb).

membership *n.* 会员资格 huìyuán zīgé (admission).

membrane *n.* 膜 mó, 薄膜 bómó.

memento *n.* 纪念品 jìniànpǐn.

memo *n.* 备忘录 bèiwànglù.

memoir *n.* 传记 zhuànjì (biography).

memorable *adj.* 值得纪念的 zhídé jìniàn de.

memorandum *n.* 备忘录 bèiwànglù (note).

memorial *n.* 纪念物 jìniànwù (monument). — *adj.* 纪念的 jìniàn de, 追悼的 zhuīdào de.

memorize *v.* 记忆 jìyì, 背诵 bèisòng.

memory *n.* ①记忆 jìyì (remembrance). ②怀念 huáiniàn (recollection).

men *n.* 男人们 nánrénmen.

menace *n. & v.* 威吓 wēihè, 胁迫 xiépò.

mend *v.* ①修补 xiūbǔ, 修理 xiūlǐ (repair). ②改进 gǎijìn, 改善 gǎishàn (improve).

menial *n.* 奴仆 núpú, 佣人 yōngrén.

menopause *n.* 停经期 tíngjīngqī / tíngjīngqí, 更年期 gēngniánqī / gēngniánqí.

menses *n.* 月经 yuèjīng.

mental *adj.* ①心理的 xīnlǐ de (psychological). ②智力的 zhìlì de (intellectual).

mentality *n.* ①智力 zhìlì (intelligence). ②心理状态 xīnlǐ zhuàngtài (attitude).

mention *n. & v.* 提及 tíjí, 谈起 tánqǐ. *Don't ~ it.* 不客气 búkèqì.

menu *n.* 菜单 càidān (bill of fare).

mercantile *adj.* 商业的 shāngyè de.

mercenary *n.* 佣兵 yōngbīng.

merchandise *n.* 商品 shāngpǐn, 货物 huòwù. — *v.* 交易 jiāoyì, 买卖 mǎimai (deal).

merchant *n.* 商人 shāngrén.

merciful *adj.* 仁慈的 réncí de.

merciless *adj.* 残忍的 cánrěn de.

M

mercury *n.* ①水银 shuǐyín, 汞 gǒng (quicksilver). ②(M-) 水星 Shuǐxīng 〈planet〉.

mercy *n.* 慈悲 cíbēi, 怜悯 liánmǐn (kindness).

mere *adj.* 只 zhǐ, 仅仅 jǐnjǐn, 不过是 búguòshì.

merely *adv.* 仅仅 jǐnjǐn.

merge *v.* 合并 hébìng.

meridian *n.* 子午线 zǐwǔxiàn (longitude).

merit *n.* 优点 yōudiǎn (good point), 功绩 gōngjì / gōngjī 〈reward〉.

mermaid *n.* 人鱼 rényú, 美人鱼 měirényú.

merry *adj.* 快乐的 kuàilè de, 愉快的 yúkuài de.

merry-go-round *n.* 旋转木马 xuánzhuǎn mùmǎ.

mesh *n.* 网孔 wǎngkǒng. — *v.* 以网捕捉 yǐ wǎng bǔzhuō (snare).

mess *n.* 乱七八糟 luànqībā-zāo (untidy objects). — *v.* 使紊乱 shǐ wěnluàn / shǐ wěnluàn, 弄糟 nòngzāo (clutter). ~ *up* 弄乱 nòngluàn, 弄糟 nòngzāo.

message *n.* ①消息 xiāoxi, 音讯 yīnxùn (information). ②含意 hányì (significance).

messenger *n.* 信差 xìnchāi, 使者 shǐzhě.

metabolism *n.* 新陈代谢 xīnchén-dàixiè.

metal *n.* 金属 jīnshǔ 〈substance〉.

metallic *adj.* 金属的 jīnshǔ de.

metaphor *n.* 隐喻 yǐnyù, 暗喻 ànyù.

meteor *n.* 流星 liúxīng.

meteorite *n.* 陨石 yǔnshí.

meteorology *n.* 气象学 qìxiàngxué.

meter *n.* 公尺 gōngchǐ, 米 mǐ 〈measure〉.

method *n.* ①方法 fāngfǎ (way). ②条理 tiáolǐ, 顺序 shùnxù (orderliness).

methodical *adj.* 有条理的 yǒu tiáolǐ de, 有秩序的 yǒu zhìxù de.

methodology *n.* 方法论 fāngfǎlùn.

metropolis *n.* ①大都市 dàdūshì, 都会 dūhuì (city). ②首都 shǒudū, 首府 shǒufǔ (capital).

metropolitan *adj.* ①大都市的 dàdūshì de (of a city). ②首都的 shǒudū de (of a capital). — *n.* 都会居民 dūhuì jūmín.

Mexican *n. & adj.* ①墨西哥人 Mòxīgērén (people). ②墨西哥语 Mòxīgēyǔ (language).

mica *n.* 云母 yúnmǔ.

microbe *n.* 微生物 wēishēngwù / wéishēngwù, 细菌 xìjùn / xíjùn (bacterium).

microbiology *n.* 微生物学 wēishēngwùxué / wéishēngwùxué.

microchip *n.* 微晶片 wēijīngpiàn / wéijīngpiàn 〈electricity〉.

microcircuit *n.* 积体电路 jītǐ diànlù.

microcomputer *n.* 微电脑 wēidiànnǎo / wéidiànnǎo.

microcosm *n.* 小宇宙 xiǎo yǔzhòu, 缩影 suōyǐng.

microfilm *n.* 缩影胶卷 suōyǐng jiāojuǎn.

microorganism *n.* 微生物 wēishēngwù / wéishēngwù.

microphone *n.* 麦克风 màikèfēng.

microscope *n.* 显微镜

M

xiǎnwēijìng / xiǎnwéijìng.

mid *adj.* 中间的 zhōngjiān de, 中央的 zhōngyāng de.

midday *n. & adj.* 正午 zhèngwǔ.

middle *adj.* 中间的 zhōngjiān de (central). — *n.* 中间 zhōngjiān (center). *the M- East* 中东 Zhōngdōng.

middle-aged *adj.* 中年的 zhōngnián de.

middle-class *adj.* 中产阶级 的 zhōngchǎn jiējí de.

midge *n.* 小虫 xiǎochóng.

midget *n.* 侏儒 zhūrú, 矮人 ǎirén.

midland *n. & adj.* 内陆 nèilù.

mid-life crisis 中年危机 zhōngnián wēijī / zhōngnián wéijī.

midnight *n. & adj.* 午夜 wǔyè. *~ snack* 夜餐 yècān / 宵 夜 xiāoyè.

midst *n.* 中间 zhōngjiān.

midsummer *n.* 仲夏 zhòngxià.

midterm *adj.* 学期中的 xuéqī zhōng de / xuéqí zhōng de. — *n.* 期中考试 qīzhōng kǎoshì / qízhōng kǎoshì (test).

midway *adj. & adv.* 中途的 zhōngtú de.

midwife *n.* 助产士 zhùchǎnshì, 接生婆 jiēshēngpó.

mien *n.* 风采 fēngcǎi, 态度 tàidu.

might *aux. v.* 可能 kěnéng (be able). — *n.* 力气 lìqi, 力量 lìliang (strength).

mighty *adj.* ①强有力的 qiáng yǒulì de (strong). ②巨大的 jùdà de (enormous).

migraine *n.* 偏头痛 piāntóutòng.

migrant *n.* 候鸟 hòuniǎo ⟨bird⟩, 迁居者 qiānjūzhě ⟨people⟩.

migrate *v.* 迁移 qiānyí, 移居 yíjū.

migration *n.* 迁移 qiānyí, 移 动 yídòng.

mild *adj.* ①温和的 wēnhé de, 宽大的 kuāndà de ⟨gentle⟩. ②温暖的 wēnnuǎn de ⟨warm⟩. ③适口的 shìkǒu de ⟨taste⟩.

mildew *n.* 霉 méi.

mile *n.* 哩 lǐ, 英里 yīnglǐ.

mileage *n.* 哩数 lǐshù, 哩程 líchéng.

milestone *n.* 哩程标 líchéngbiāo.

militant *adj.* 好战的 hàozhàn de, 好斗争的 hào dòuzhēng de.

militarism *n.* 军国主义 jūnguó zhǔyì.

military *adj.* 军事的 jūnshì de. — *n.* ①军队 jūnduì ⟨troops⟩. ②军人 jūnrén ⟨soldier⟩.

militia *n.* 民兵部队 mínbīng bùduì, 国民兵 guómínbīng.

milk *n.* 牛奶 niúnǎi. — *v.* 挤乳 jǐ rǔ.

milky *adj.* 乳白色的 rǔbáisè de.

mill *n.* ①碾磨机 niǎnmójī ⟨machine⟩. ②制造厂 zhìzàochǎng ⟨factory⟩.

millennium *n.* ①千禧年 qiānxǐnián / qiānxǐnián ⟨the Bible⟩. ②一千年 yìqiān nián ⟨period⟩.

millet *n.* 粟 sù, 稷 jì.

million *n.* 百万 bǎiwàn (1,000,000).

millionaire *n.* 百万富翁 bǎiwàn fùwēng.

M

mime *n.* 哑剧 yǎjù / 默剧 mòjù (pantomine).

mimeograph *n.* 油印机 yóuyìnjī.

mimic *v.* 模仿 mófǎng (copy).

mimosa *n.* 含羞草 hánxiūcǎo 〈plant〉.

mince *v.* 切碎 qiēsuì, 剁碎 duòsuì (chop).

mind *n.* ①脑力 nǎolì, 理解力 lǐjiělì (brain). ②心 xīn, 心意 xīnyì, 想法 xiǎngfa (opinion). *make up one's ~* 决心 juéxīn. — *v.* 注意 zhùyì, 留心 liúxīn (notice).

minded *adj.* 有意的 yǒuyì de.

mindful *adj.* 注意的 zhùyì de, 留意的 liúyì de.

mindless *adj.* 不留心的 bù liúxīn de (heedless).

mine *pron.* 我的 wǒ de. — *n.* ①矿 kuàng, 矿坑 kuàngkēng (coal). ②地雷 dìléi 〈weapon〉.

miner *n.* 矿工 kuànggōng 〈worker〉.

mineral *n.* 矿物 kuàngwù 〈substance〉. *~ water* 矿泉水 kuàngquánshuǐ.

mineralogy *n.* 矿物学 kuàngwùxué.

mingle *v.* 混合 hùnhé.

mini *n.* 迷你 mínǐ, 小型 xiǎoxíng (miniature).

miniature *n.* 小模型 xiǎo móxíng. — *adj.* 小型的 xiǎoxíng de.

minimize *v.* 极小化 jíxiǎohuà 〈reduce〉.

minimum *n.* 最低限度 zuìdī xiàndù, 最小量 zuì xiǎoliàng. — *adj.* 最小的 zuìxiǎo de, 最低的 zuìdī de (least).

mining *n.* 采矿 cǎikuàng

〈mine〉.

minister *n.* ①牧师 mùshī (clergyman). ②部长 bùzhǎng (head). ③公使 gōngshǐ (ambassador).

ministry *n.* ①部 bù 〈government〉. ②内阁 nèigé (cabinet). ③牧师 mùshī (clergyman).

mink *n.* ①貂 diāo 〈animal〉. ②貂皮 diāopí (fur skin).

minor *adj.* 较小的 jiàoxiǎo de, 较次要的 jiào cìyào de 〈smaller〉. — *n.* ①未成年者 wèichéngnián zhě 〈of age〉. ②副修科目 fùxiū kēmù 〈subject〉.

minority *n.* ①少数 shǎoshù (smaller number). ②未成年 wèichéngnián 〈age〉. ③少数民族 shǎoshù mínzú 〈nationality〉.

minstrel *n.* 吟游诗人 yínyóu shīrén.

mint *n.* ①薄荷 bòhe 〈plant〉. ②造币厂 zàobìchǎng 〈coin〉. — *v.* 铸币 zhùbì 〈coin〉.

minus *adj.* 减的 jiǎn de, 负的 fù de. — *n.* 负数 fùshù.

minute *n.* 分 fēn, 分钟 fēnzhōng 〈time〉. *wait a ~* 稍等 shāoděng. — *adj.* 细微的 xìwēi de / xìwéi de.

miracle *n.* 奇迹 qíjì / qíjī (wonder).

mirage *n.* 海市蜃楼 hǎishì-shènlóu.

mire *n.* 泥泞 nínìng, 泥沼 nízhǎo. — *v.* 陷入泥泞 xiànrù nínìng (bog).

mirror *n.* 镜子 jìngzi. — *v.* 反映 fǎnyìng.

mirth *n.* 欢乐 huānlè, 欢笑 huānxiào.

misadventure *n.* 不幸

M

búxìng.

misappropriate v. 侵占 qīnzhàn, 盗用 dàoyòng.

misbehave v. 行为不端 xíngwéi bùduān.

miscalculate v. 误算 wùsuàn.

miscarriage n. 流产 liúchǎn ⟨pregnancy⟩.

miscarry v. 流产 liúchǎn ⟨pregnancy⟩.

miscellaneous adj. 繁杂的 fánzá de, 各种的 gèzhǒng de.

miscellany n. 混杂 hùnzá ⟨mixture⟩.

mischance n. 不幸 búxìng, 恶运 èyùn.

mischief n. ①伤害 shānghài, 危害 wēihài / wéihài ⟨damage⟩. ②恶作剧 èzuòjù, 戏谑 xìxuè / xìnüè ⟨foolish⟩.

mischievous adj. 有害的 yǒuhài de ⟨harmful⟩.

misconceive v. 误解 wùjiě.

misconduct n. 行为不检 xíngwéi bùjiǎn ⟨misbehavior⟩.

misdeed n. 恶行 èxíng / èxìng.

miser n. 守财奴 shǒucáinú, 吝啬鬼 lìnsèguǐ.

miserable adj. 悲惨的 bēicǎn de, 痛苦的 tòngkǔ de ⟨wretched⟩.

misery n. 悲惨 bēicǎn, 痛苦 tòngkǔ.

misfire n. & v. ①失败 shībài ⟨plan⟩. ②不着火 bù zháohuǒ, 不发火 bù fāhuǒ ⟨gun or engine⟩.

misfit n. 不适应者 bú shìyìng zhě.

misfortune n. 不幸 búxìng.

misgiving n. 疑虑 yílǜ, 不安 bù'ān.

misguided adj. 被误导的 bèi

wùdǎo de.

mishap n. 灾祸 zāihuò.

misjudge v. 误判 wùpàn.

mislead v. 误导 wùdǎo.

mismanage v. 处置失当 chǔzhì shīdàng.

misprint n. & v. 印错 yìncuò, 误印 wùyìn.

misquote v. 误引 wùyǐn.

misrepresent v. 误传 wùchuán, 误述 wùshù.

miss v. ①漏失 lòushī, 错过 cuòguò ⟨lose⟩. ②失误 shīwù, 不中 búzhòng ⟨fail⟩. ③想念 xiǎngniàn, 怀念 huáiniàn ⟨long for⟩. — n. 错失 cuòshī, 未中 wèizhòng ⟨failure to hit⟩.

Miss n. 小姐 xiǎojiě ⟨maiden⟩.

missile n. 飞弹 fēidàn ⟨projectile⟩.

missing adj. 不见的 bújiàn de, 失踪的 shīzōng de ⟨lost⟩.

mission n. ①使命 shǐmìng, 任务 rènwu ⟨task⟩. ②使节团 shǐjiétuán, 代表团 dàibiǎotuán ⟨representatives⟩.

missionary n. 传教士 chuánjiàoshì. — adj. 传教的 chuánjiào de ⟨religion⟩.

misspell v. 拼错 pīncuò.

misspend v. 虚度 xūdù, 浪费 làngfèi.

mist n. 雾 wù. — v. 起雾 qǐ wù.

mistake n. 错误 cuòwù, 误会 wùhuì. — v. 误会 wùhuì, 弄错 nòngcuò.

mister n. ⋯⋯先生 ...xiānsheng.

mistress n. 情妇 qíngfù ⟨lover⟩.

mistrust n. & v. 怀疑 huáiyí.

misty adj. 有雾的 yǒu wù de.

misunderstand v. 误解 wùjiě.

M

misuse n. & v. ①误用 wùyòng, 滥用 lànyòng (careless use). ②虐待 nüèdài (abuse).

mitigate v. 减轻 jiǎnqīng, 使缓和 shǐ huǎnhé.

mitt n. 棒球手套 bàngqiú shǒutào 〈glove〉.

mix n. & v. 混合 hùnhé 〈combination〉.

mixed adj. 混合的 hùnhé de (mingled).

mixture n. 混合物 hùnhéwù.

moan n. & v. 呻吟 shēnyín (groan).

moat n. 壕沟 háogōu.

mob n. ①群众 qúnzhòng, 民众 mínzhòng (crowd). ②暴徒 bàotú, 暴民 bàomín (rioter).

mobile adj. 移动的 yídòng de (movable).

mobilize v. 动员 dòngyuán.

mock n. & v. 嘲弄 cháonòng, 嘲笑 cháoxiào (ridicule).

mockery n. 嘲弄 cháonòng (ridicule).

mode n. ①方式 fāngshì (way). ②样式 yàngshì (form).

model n. ①模型 móxíng (scale). ②模范 mófàn (example). ③款式 kuǎnshì (style).

moderate adj. 适度的 shìdù de, 有节制的 yǒu jiézhì de (restrained).

moderator n. 仲裁者 zhòngcáizhě, 调停者 tiáotíngzhě (mediator).

modern adj. 现代的 xiàndài de (present). — n. 现代人 xiàndàirén.

modernism n. 现代主义 xiàndài zhǔyì.

modernize v. 现代化 xiàndàihuà.

modest adj. ①谦虚的 qiānxū de (humble). ②高雅的 gāoyǎ de (decent).

modesty n. 谦虚 qiānxū, 谦逊 qiānxùn (unobtrusiveness).

modify v. 修改 xiūgǎi, 修正 xiūzhèng (change).

modulate v. 调节 tiáojié (adjust).

mohair n. 毛海 máohǎi, 安哥拉山羊毛 āngēlā shānyángmáo.

moist adj. 潮湿的 cháoshī de (wet).

moisten v. 使潮湿 shǐ cháoshī, 弄湿 nòngshī.

moisture n. 湿气 shīqì (humidity).

molar n. 臼齿 jiùchǐ.

mold n. ①模型 móxíng, 模子 múzi / mòzi (shape). ②霉 méi 〈spore〉. — v. 模铸 múzhù / mòzhù (shape into).

molder v. 崩坏 bēnghuài.

moldy adj. 发霉的 fāméi de.

mole n. ①痣 zhì (spot). ②鼹鼠 yǎnshǔ 〈animal〉.

molecule n. 分子 fēnzǐ 〈particle〉.

molest v. 干扰 gānrǎo, 妨害 fánghài (disturb). 骚扰 sāorǎo (harass).

mollify v. 安慰 ānwèi, 缓和 huǎnhé (soothe).

molt n. & v. 换毛 huànmáo, 蜕皮 tuìpí.

mom n. 妈妈 māma.

moment n. ①瞬间 shùnjiān, 片刻 piànkè 〈time〉. ②重要 zhòngyào (importance).

momentary adj. 瞬间的 shùnjiān de.

momentous adj. 极重要的 jí zhòngyào de.

M

momentum *n.* 动量 dòngliàng, 动力 dònglì 〈physics〉.

monarch *n.* 君主 jūnzhǔ, 国王 guówáng.

monarchic *adj.* 君主的 jūnzhǔ de.

monarchy *n.* 君主政体 jūnzhǔ zhèngtǐ 〈empire〉.

monastery *n.* 修道院 xiūdàoyuàn, 僧院 sēngyuàn.

monastic *adj.* 修道院的 xiūdàoyuàn de 〈of monasteries〉.

Monday *n.* 星期一 Xīngqīyī / Xīngqíyī.

monetary *adj.* 货币的 huòbì de.

money *n.* 金钱 jīnqián, 货币 huòbì 〈currency〉. *make* ~ 赚钱 zhuànqián.

Mongolian *n.* ①蒙古人 Měnggǔrén / Ménggǔrén 〈people〉. ②蒙古语 Měnggǔyǔ / Ménggǔyǔ 〈language〉.

mongoos(e) *n.* 獴 měng / méng.

mongrel *n.* 杂种狗 zázhǒnggǒu 〈dogs〉. — *adj.* 杂种的 zázhǒng de.

monitor *n.* ①班长 bānzhǎng 〈of school〉. ②监视员 jiānshìyuán, 监听员 jiāntīngyuán 〈person〉. ③监视器 jiānshìqì, 监听器 jiāntīngqì 〈machine〉. — *v.* 监视 jiānshì 〈watch〉, 监听 jiāntīng 〈listen to〉.

monk *n.* 修道士 xiūdàoshì 〈Christianity〉, 僧侣 sēnglǚ 〈Buddhism〉.

monkey *n.* 猴子 hóuzi, 猿 yuán 〈simian〉.

monogamy *n.* 一夫一妻 yìfū-yìqī.

monologue *n.* 独白 dúbái 〈soliloquy〉.

monopolize *v.* 垄断 lǒngduàn.

monopoly *n.* ①独占 dúzhàn 〈sole possession〉. ②专卖 zhuānmài 〈sole right to trade〉.

monorail *n.* 单轨 dānguǐ.

monosyllable *n.* 单音节字 dān yīnjié zì.

monotheism *n.* 一神论 yìshénlùn.

monotone *n.* 单调 dāndiào.

monotonous *adj.* 单调的 dāndiào de 〈boring〉.

monsoon *n.* 季风 jìfēng 〈wind〉.

monster *n.* 怪物 guàiwù 〈creature〉.

monstrous *adj.* ①巨大的 jùdà de 〈huge〉. ②恐怖的 kǒngbù de, 凶恶的 xiōng'è de 〈horrible〉.

month *n.* 月 yuè.

monthly *adj.* 每月的 měi yuè de. — *n.* 月刊 yuèkān.

monument *n.* 纪念碑 jìniànbēi 〈memorial〉.

mood *n.* 心情 xīnqíng, 情绪 qíngxù.

moody *adj.* 心情不定的 xīnqíng búdìng de 〈uneven emotions〉, 忧郁的 yōuyù de 〈gloomy〉.

moon *n.* 月亮 yuèliang 〈heavenly body〉. ~ *cake* 中秋月饼 zhōngqiū yuèbǐng.

moonlight *n. & adj.* 月光 yuèguāng.

moor *n.* 旷野 kuàngyě, 荒地 huāngdì 〈wilderness〉.

moose *n.* 麋 mí.

mop *n.* 拖把 tuōbǎ 〈for cleaning〉. — *v.* 洗擦 xǐcā 〈scrub〉.

M

mope *v.* 抑郁不乐 yìyù-búlè.

moral *adj.* ①道德的 dàodé de (ethical). ②有道德的 yǒu dàodé de (virtuous). — *n.* ①教训 jiàoxun, 寓意 yùyì (lesson). ②道德 dàodé (ethic).

morale *n.* 士气 shìqì.

morality *n.* 道德 dàodé, 美德 měidé (virtue).

morass *n.* 沼地 zhǎodì, 泥沼 nízhǎo (marsh).

morbid *adj.* ①疾病的 jíbìng de, 病态的 bìngtài de (sick). ②不健康的 bú jiànkāng de, 不正常的 bú zhèngcháng de (unhealthy).

more *adj. & adv. & pron.* 更多的 gèngduō de ⟨quantity⟩, 更大的 gèngdà de ⟨size⟩.

moreover *adv.* 而且 érqiě, 此外 cǐwài.

morgue *n.* 陈尸所 chénshīsuǒ (mortuary).

Mormon *n.* 摩门教徒 Móménjiàotú.

morning *n.* 早晨 zǎochén, 上午 shàngwǔ.

morning-glory *n.* 牵牛花 qiānniúhuā.

moron *n.* 低能者 dīnéngzhě.

morose *adj.* 忧郁的 yōuyù de (gloomy).

morphia *n.* 吗啡 mǎfēi.

morphine *n.* 吗啡 mǎfēi.

morrow *n.* 翌日 yìrì, 明天 míngtiān (the next day).

morsel *n.* ①一口 yìkǒu (bite). ②少量 shǎoliàng (small amount).

mortal *adj.* ①人类的 rénlèi de, 凡人的 fánrén de (human). ②会死的 huì sǐ de ⟨human⟩. ③致命的 zhìmìng de (fatal).

mortar *n.* ①灰泥 huīní ⟨cement⟩. ②迫击炮 pòjīpào / pòjípào ⟨gun⟩.

mortgage *n. & v.* 抵押 dǐyā (deposit).

mortify *v.* 使屈辱 shǐ qūrǔ / shǐ qūrù (cause shame).

mortuary *n.* 停尸间 tíngshījiān, 太平间 tàipíngjiān.

mosaic *n.* 镶嵌 xiāngqiàn / xiāngqiān, 嵌工 qiàngōng / qiāngōng (inlay).

mosque *n.* 回教寺院 Huíjiào sìyuàn.

mosquito *n.* 蚊子 wénzi.

moss *n.* 苔 tái, 藓 xiǎn.

most *adj. & pron.* ①最多的 zuìduō de, 最大的 zuìdà de (greatest in number). ②大多数的 dàduōshù de (majority). — *adv.* 最 zuì.

mostly *adv.* ①主要地 zhǔyào de (mainly). ②通常 tōngcháng (usually).

motel *n.* 汽车旅馆 qìchē lǚguǎn.

moth *n.* 蛾 é (insect).

mothball *n.* 樟脑丸 zhāngnǎowán.

motherboard *n.* 主机板 zhǔjībǎn ⟨computer⟩.

mother *n.* 母亲 mǔqīn, 妈妈 māma (female parent). **~ country** 祖国 zǔguó. **~ tongue** 母语 mǔyǔ.

mother-in-law *n.* 婆婆 pópo (husband's mother), 岳母 yuèmǔ (wife's mother).

Mother's Day *n.* 母亲节 Mǔqīnjié.

motif *n.* 主题 zhǔtí, 主旨 zhǔzhǐ.

motion *n.* ①动作 dòngzuò (movement). ②动议 dòngyì

M

(proposal). — v. 示意 shìyì.

motivate v. 引起动机 yǐnqǐ dòngjī (encourage), 激发 jīfā (inspire).

motive n. 动机 dòngjī (intention).

motor n. ①马达 mǎdá, 发动机 fādòngjī (machine). ②汽车 qìchē (car).

motorbike n. 轻型机车 qīngxíng jīchē.

motorcycle n. 机车 jīchē.

motto n. 箴言 zhēnyán, 座右铭 zuòyòumíng (maxim).

mound n. 土堆 tǔduī, 堤 dī / tí (dike).

mount v. ①登上 dēngshang (ascend). ②骑乘 qíchéng (ride). — n. 山 shān (mountain).

mountain n. 山 shān, 山脉 shānmài (peak).

mountaineer n. 登山者 dēngshānzhě (climber).

mourn v. 哀悼 āidào, 悲伤 bēishāng (feel sorrow).

mournful adj. 哀悼的 āidào de, 悲伤的 bēishāng de.

mourning n. 哀悼 āidào, 悲伤 bēishāng (grief).

mouse n. ①鼠 shǔ (rat). ②胆小者 dǎnxiǎozhě (timid person). ③鼠标 shǔbiāo / 滑鼠 huáshǔ (computer).

mousse n. ①慕丝 mùsī (hair). ②奶油冻甜点 nǎiyóudòng tiándiǎn (dessert).

mouth n. ①嘴 zuǐ, 口 kǒu (face). ②出入口 chūrùkǒu (opening). ③河口 hékǒu (river).

mouthful n. 一口 yìkǒu, 少量 shǎoliàng (quantity).

moveable adj. 可移动的 kě yídòng de (mobile).

move v. ①移动 yídòng (change

position). ②感动 gǎndòng (affect the emotions). ③搬家 bānjiā, 迁动 qiāndòng (change residence). ④提议 tíyì (suggest).

movement n. ①行动 xíngdòng, 活动 huódòng (action). ②运动 yùndòng (by group).

movie n. 电影 diànyǐng, 影片 yǐngpiàn (film).

mow v. 割 gē, 刈 yì (cut).

MP3 电脑压缩档案 diànnǎo yāsuō dǎng'àn / diànnǎo yāsuō dǎng'àn.

Mr. n. 先生 xiānsheng.
~ *Right* 如意郎君 rúyì lángjūn.

Mrs. n. 太太 tàitai, 夫人 fūrén.

Ms. n. 女士 nǚshì.

Mt. Everest 埃弗勒斯峰 Āifúlèsīfēng.

much adj. 很多的 hěn duō de (a large quantity). — adv. ①多 duō, 极 jí (more). ②非常 fēicháng (greatly).

muck n. 粪肥 fènféi.

mucus n. 黏液 niányè.

mud n. 泥 ní (mire).

muddle n. & v. 混乱 hùnluàn.

muddy adj. 泥泞的 nínìng de (miry).

mudguard n. 挡泥板 dǎngníbǎn.

muff n. 暖手筒 nuǎnshǒutǒng (warm material).

muffin n. 松饼 sōngbǐng.

muffle v. 裹包 guǒbāo, 包围 bāowéi (wrap), 蒙住 méngzhù (silence).

mug n. 马克杯 mǎkèbēi (beaker).

Muhammad n. 穆罕默德 Mùhǎnmòdé.

mulberry n. 桑树 sāngshù (tree), 桑葚 sāngshèn (fruit).

M

mule n. 骡 luó 〈animal〉.

mull v. 仔细考虑 zǐxì kǎolù.

multifarious adj. 多种的 duōzhǒng de, 各式各样的 gèshì-gèyàng de.

multilateral adj. 多边的 duōbiān de (involving two or more participants). ~ **trade** 多边贸易 duōbiān màoyì.

multimedia n. 多介质 duōjièzhì / 多媒体 duōméitǐ.

multiple adj. 复合的 fùhé de, 复式的 fùshì de (numerous). — n. 倍数 bèishù 〈mathematics〉.

multiplication n. ①增多 zēngduō, 倍加 bèijiā (multiplying). ②乘法 chéngfǎ 〈mathematics〉.

multiply v. ①增加 zēngjiā (increase). ②乘 chéng 〈mathematics〉.

multitude n. ①众多 zhòngduō (large number). ②群众 qúnzhòng (crowd).

mum adj. 沉默的 chénmò de.

mumble v. 喃喃自语 nánnán-zìyǔ (murmur).

mummy n. 木乃伊 mùnǎiyī.

mumps n. 腮腺炎 sāixiànyán.

munch v. 用力咀嚼 yònglì jǔjué.

mundane adj. 世俗的 shìsú de, 现世的 xiànshì de (secular).

municipal adj. 都市的 dūshì de, 市政的 shìzhèng de (civic).

munition n. 军火 jūnhuǒ, 军需品 jūnxūpǐn.

mural n. 壁画 bìhuà.

murder n. & v. 谋杀 móushā.

murderer n. 凶手 xiōngshǒu, 谋杀犯 móushāfàn.

murky adj. 黑暗的 hēi'àn de, 阴暗的 yīn'àn de (dark).

murmur n. ①潺潺声 chánchánshēng 〈of stream〉. ②呢喃声 nínánshēng 〈of words〉.

muscle n. 肌肉 jīròu 〈tissue〉.

muscular adj. 肌肉的 jīròu de (of muscles).

muse v. 沉思 chénsī, 冥想 míngxiǎng.

museum n. 博物馆 bówùguǎn.

mushroom n. 蘑菇 mógu, 蕈 xùn (fungus).

music n. 音乐 yīnyuè 〈sound〉, 乐曲 yuèqǔ 〈composition〉.

musical adj. 音乐的 yīnyuè de (of music). — n. 音乐剧 yīnyuèjù.

musician n. 音乐家 yīnyuèjiā 〈person〉.

musk n. 麝香 shèxiāng.

muskrat n. 麝鼠 shèshǔ.

Muslim n. & adj. 回教徒 Huíjiàotú.

muslin n. 薄棉布 báomiánbù / bómiánbù.

must aux. v. 必须 bìxū.

mustache n. 髭 zī, 须 xū.

mustard n. ①芥菜 jiècài 〈plant〉. ②芥末 jièmo 〈condiment〉.

muster n. & v. 集合 jíhé, 召集 zhàojí (gathering).

musty adj. 发霉的 fāméi de, 陈腐的 chénfǔ de (moldy).

mutation n. ①变化 biànhuà (change). ②突变 tūbiàn / túbiàn 〈genes〉.

mute adj. ①沉默的 chénmò de (silent). ②哑的 yǎ de (dumb). — n. 哑巴 yǎba (person unable to speak).

mutilate v. 使残废 shǐ cánfèi.

mutiny n. & v. 叛变 pànbiàn, 兵变 bīngbiàn.

mutter v. 喃喃低语 nánnán-

M

N

-dīyǔ.

mutton *n.* 羊肉 yángròu.

mutual *adj.* 相互的 xiānghù de, 共同的 gòngtóng de (reciprocal). ~ *fund* 共同基金 gòngtóng jījīn.

muzzle *n.* ①口鼻 kǒubí ⟨animal⟩. ②枪口 qiāngkǒu, 炮口 pàokǒu ⟨gun⟩. — *v.* 封口 fēngkǒu.

my *pron.* 我的 wǒ de.

myopia *n.* 近视 jìnshì ⟨medical⟩.

myriad *n.* 无数 wúshù (extremely large number).

myself *pron.* 我自己 wǒ zìjǐ.

mystery *n.* 神秘 shénmì, 奥妙 àomiào (secret).

mystic *n.* 神秘主义者 shénmì zhǔyì zhě.

mystify *v.* 使迷惑 shǐ míhuò.

myth *n.* ①神话 shénhuà (legend). ②虚构故事 xūgòu gùshì (fiction).

mythology *n.* 神话学 shénhuàxué.

N

nag *v.* 唠叨 láodao.

nail *n.* ①指甲 zhǐjia ⟨finger⟩. ②钉子 dīngzi (stud). — *v.* 钉牢 dìngláo.

naive *adj.* 天真的 tiānzhēn de.

naked *adj.* 赤裸的 chìluǒ de.

name *n.* ①名字 míngzi (given name). ②名称 míngchēng (title). ③姓名 xìngmíng (full name). — *v.* 命名 mìngmíng, 取名 qǔmíng.

namely *adv.* 就是 jiùshì, 即 jí.

nanny *n.* 奶妈 nǎimā, 保姆 bǎomǔ.

nap *n. & v.* 小睡 xiǎoshuì.

nape *n.* 颈背 jǐngbèi.

napkin *n.* 餐巾 cānjīn.

narcissus *n.* 水仙花 shuǐxiānhuā.

narcotic *n.* 麻醉剂 mázuìjì. — *adj.* 麻醉的 mázuì de.

narrate *v.* ①叙述 xùshù (relate). ②说明 shuōmíng (explain).

narration *n.* 记叙文 jìxùwén.

narrative *n.* ①故事 gùshì (story). ②叙述 xùshù (storytelling).

narrow *adj.* 窄的 zhǎi de. — *v.* 变窄 biànzhǎi, 使狭小 shǐ xiáxiǎo.

narrow-minded *adj.* 气量小的 qìliàng xiǎo de, 小心眼 xiǎoxīnyǎn de.

nasal *adj.* ①鼻的 bí de ⟨of nose⟩. ②鼻音的 bíyīn de ⟨of sound⟩. — *n.* 鼻音 bíyīn ⟨sound⟩.

nasty *adj.* ①为难的 wéinán de (mean). ②肮脏的 āngzāng de (dirty).

nation *n.* ①国家 guójiā (country). ②国民 guómín (citizens). ③民族 mínzú ⟨ethnicity⟩.

national *adj.* ①国家的 guójiā de ⟨country⟩. ②国民的 guómín

de 〈citizens〉. ③民族的 mínzú de 〈ethnicity〉.

nationalism n. 国家主义 guójiā zhǔyì, 爱国主义 àiguó zhǔyì.

nationality n. 国籍 guójí (citizenship).

nationalize v. ①使国有 shǐ guóyǒu (owned by state). ②国家化 guójiāhuà (become a country).

nationalized adj. 国有的 guóyǒu de 〈property〉.

native n. 本地人 běndìrén. — adj. 本地的 běndì de, 本土的 běntǔ de (local).

nativity n. 诞生 dànshēng (birth).

natural adj. ①自然的 zìrán de (to be expected). ②天赋的 tiānfù de (inherent). ③天然的 tiānrán de (not artificial).

naturally adv. ①自然地 zìrán de (of its own accord). ②天然地 tiānrán de (not artificially).

nature n. ①自然 zìrán (wildlife). ②天性 tiānxìng, 特质 tèzhì / tèzhí (characteristics).

naughty adj. 顽皮的 wánpí de.

nausea n. 作呕 zuò'ǒu.

nauseous adj. 恶心的 ěxīn de.

nautical adj. 船舶的 chuánbó de (of ships), 航海的 hánghǎi de (of navigation).

naval adj. 海军的 hǎijūn de.

navel n. 肚脐 dùqí.

navigate v. 航行 hángxíng (sail).

navigation n. 航海 hánghǎi, 航行 hángxíng.

navy n. 海军 hǎijūn. ~ **blue** 深蓝色 shēnlánsè. — adj. ①近的

jìn de (close), 离……很近 lí…… hěn jìn (close to...). ②亲密的 qīnmì de (intimate). — prep. 接近 jiējìn. — v. 靠近 kàojìn, 接近 jiējìn.

nearby adj. 附近的 fùjìn de.

nearly adv. 几乎 jīhū, 差不多 chàbuduō / chābuduō (almost).

nearsighted adj. 近视的 jìnshì de.

neat adj. 整洁的 zhěngjié de (clean).

necessarily adv. 必定 bìdìng, 必然 bìrán.

necessary adj. 必要的 bìyào de.

necessitate v. 使必要 shǐ bìyào.

necessity n. 必要 bìyào (requirement), 急需 jíxū (urgent need).

neck n. 颈 jǐng, 脖子 bózi 〈body〉.

necklace n. 项链 xiàngliàn.

necktie n. 领带 lǐngdài.

need n. 需要 xūyào. — v. 需要 xūyào.

needle n. 针 zhēn.

needless adj. 不需要的 bù xūyào de.

needy adj. 贫穷的 pínqióng de.

negation n. 否定 fǒudìng.

negative adj. ①否定的 fǒudìng de (contrary). ②消极的 xiāojí de (pessimistic). ③负面的 fùmiàn de (the bad side of something).

neglect v. 忽略 hūlüè, 疏忽 shūhu.

negligence n. 疏忽 shūhu.

negligible adj. 微不足道的 wēibùzúdào de / wēibùzúdào de.

N

negotiable *adj.* 可磋商的 kě cuōshāng de.

negotiate *v.* 磋商 cuōshāng, 协商 xiéshāng (discuss), 谈判 tánpàn, 交涉 jiāoshè ⟨diplomacy, trade, etc.⟩.

negotiation *n.* 磋商 cuōshāng, 协商 xiéshāng (discussion), 谈判 tánpàn, 交涉 jiāoshè ⟨diplomacy, trade, etc.⟩.

neighbor *n.* 邻居 línjū.

neighborhood *n.* 附近 fùjìn, 邻近 línjìn.

neighboring *adj.* 附近的 fùjìn de, 邻近的 línjìn de.

neither *adv.* 既不……也不…… jìbù...yěbù....

neon *n.* ①氖 nǎi ⟨gas⟩. ②霓虹灯 níhóngdēng ⟨light⟩.

nephew *n.* 侄儿 zhí'ér (brother's son), 外甥 wàisheng (sister's son).

nepotism *n.* 裙带关系 qúndài guānxi.

nerve *n.* ①神经 shénjīng (part of body). ②勇气 yǒngqì, 胆量 dǎnliàng (courage).

nervous *adj.* ①紧张的 jǐnzhāng de (anxious). ②神经的 shénjīng de (nervous).

nest *n.* 窠 kē (burrow). — *v.* 筑巢 zhùcháo / zhúcháo.

nestle *v.* ①舒适地躺下 shūshì de tǎngxia (lie down). ②依偎 yīwēi (cuddle).

net *n.* 网 wǎng, 网状物 wǎngzhuàngwù (netting). — *v.* 用网捕 yòng wǎng bǔ. — *adj.* 净值的 jìngzhí de. ~ *price* 实价 shíjià. ~ *profit* 净利 jìnglì. ~ *weight* 净重 jìngzhòng.

nettle *n.* 荨麻 xúnmá ⟨plant⟩.

~ *rash* 荨麻疹 xúnmázhěn.

network *n.* 网状组织 wǎngzhuàng zǔzhī, 网络 wǎngluò / 网路 wǎnglù.

neurology *n.* 神经学 shénjīngxué.

neurosis *n.* 神经病 shénjīngbìng.

neurotic *adj.* 神经病的 shénjīngbìng de (crazy), 神经过敏的 shénjīng guòmǐn de (overly sensitive). — *n.* 神经病患 shénjīng bìnghuàn.

neuter *adj.* ①无性的 wúxìng de ⟨gender⟩. ②中性的 zhōngxìng de ⟨grammar⟩. — *v.* 去势 qùshì, 阉割 yāngē.

neutral *adj.* 中立的 zhōnglì de.

neutron *n.* 中子 zhōngzǐ.

never *adv.* 从未 cóngwèi (never yet), 永不 yǒngbù, 决不 juébù (at no time).

nevertheless *adv.* 尽管如此 jǐnguǎn rúcǐ, 然而 rán'ér.

new *adj.* 新的 xīn de. *N- Year* 新年 xīnnián. *N- Year's Day* 元旦 Yuándàn. *N- Year's Eve* 除夕 Chúxī / Chúxì.

newborn *adj.* 刚出生的 gāng chūshēng de, 新生的 xīnshēng de.

news *n.* ①新闻 xīnwén (report). ②消息 xiāoxi (information).

newscast *n.* 新闻广播 xīnwén guǎngbō / xīnwén guǎngbò.

newsgroup *n.* 讨论群组 tǎolùn qúnzǔ.

newsletter *n.* 简讯 jiǎnxùn, 通讯 tōngxùn.

newspaper *n.* 报纸 bàozhǐ.

newsstand *n.* 书报摊 shūbàotān.

N

next adj. ①下一个 xià yí ge
(next one). ②其次的 qícì de ‹in
a list›. — adv. 接下来 jiēxialai
(afterwards), 下次 xiàcì (next
time). — prep. 在……旁边
zài...pángbiān.

nibble n. & v. 一点一点地吃
yìdiǎn yìdiǎn de chī.

nice adj. ①好的 hǎo de (good).
②友善的 yǒushàn de
(friendly). ③优雅的 yōuyǎ de
(elegant).

niche n. ①壁龛 bìkān (alcove).
②适合之处 shìhé zhī chù
(suitable place).

nick n. 刻痕 kèhén (small cut).

nickel n. ①镍 niè (Ni). ②镍币
nièbì ‹coin›.

nickname n. 绰号 chuòhào,
昵称 nìchēng.

nicotine n. 尼古丁 nígǔdīng.

niece n. 侄女 zhínǚ (brother's
daughter), 外甥女
wàishengnǚ (sister's
daughter).

niggard n. 小气鬼 xiǎoqiguǐ.
— adj. 吝啬的 lìnsè de, 小气
的 xiǎoqi de (stingy).

night n. 夜晚 yèwǎn.
~ **blindness** 夜盲 yèmáng.
~ **school** 夜校 yèxiào.

nightcap n. ①睡帽 shuìmào
‹hat›. ②睡前酒 shuìqiánjiǔ
‹drink›.

nightclub n. 夜总会
yèzǒnghuì.

nightgown n. 长睡衣 cháng
shuìyī, 睡袍 shuìpáo.

nightingale n. 夜莺 yèyīng
‹bird›.

nightlife n. 夜生活
yèshēnghuó.

nightmare n. 梦魇 mèngyǎn,
恶梦 èmèng.

nil n. 无 wú, 零 líng.

nimble adj. 敏捷的 mǐnjié de,
轻快的 qīngkuài de (agile).

nine n. & adj. 九 jiǔ.

nineteen n. & adj. 十九 shíjiǔ.

nineteenth n. & adj. 第十九
dì-shíjiǔ.

ninetieth n. & adj. 第九十
dì-jiǔshí.

ninety n. & adj. 九十 jiǔshí.

ninja n. 忍者 rěnzhě.

ninth n. & adj. 第九 dì-jiǔ.

nip v. ①咬 yǎo (bite). ②刺骨
cìgǔ (chill).

nipple n. 乳头 rǔtóu (teat).

nit n. 卵 luǎn.

nitrogen n. 氮 dàn
‹chemistry›.

nitwit n. 蠢人 chǔnrén (fool).

no adj. ①没有 méiyǒu (lack).
②不 bù, 不是 bú shì
‹disagreement›.

nobility n. ①高贵 gāoguì
(dignity). ②贵族 guìzú (nobleman).

noble adj. ①贵族的 guìzú de
(royal). ②高贵的 gāoguì de
(dignified). ③高尚的 gāoshàng
de, 伟大的 wěidà de (heroic).

nobleman n. 贵族 guìzú.

nobody pron. 无人 wú rén.
— n. 平凡的人 píngfán de
rén, 小人物 xiǎorénwù.

nocturnal adj. 夜间的 yèjiān
de (nightly).

nod n. & v. ①点头 diǎntóu
(bow). ②打盹 dǎdǔn (doze).

noise n. 噪音 zàoyīn, 吵闹声
chǎonàoshēng (unpleasant
sound).

noisy adj. 吵闹的 chǎonào de.

nomad n. 游牧民族 yóumù
mínzú ‹people›, 流浪者
liúlàngzhě (wanderer).

N

nominal adj. ①名义上的 míngyìshang de, 挂名的 guàmíng de (in name only). ②极微薄的 jí wēibó de / jí wéibó de (small).

nominate v. 提名 tímíng (propose).

nomination n. 提名 tímíng.

nominee n. 被提名者 bèi tímíng zhě.

noncommissioned adj. 无任命状的 wú rènmìngzhuàng de.

none pron. ①毫无 háowú (not any). ②无一人 wú yì rén (no one).

nonentity n. 小人物 xiǎorénwù (unimportant person).

nonprofit adj. 非营利的 fēi yínglì de.

nonsense n. 无意义的话 wú yìyì de huà, 废话 fèihuà 〈meaningless〉, 胡说 húshuō 〈untrue〉.

nonsmoking adj. 禁烟的 jìnyān de.

nonstop adj. & adv. 直达的 zhídá de.

noodle n. ①面条 miàntiáo 〈food〉. ②傻瓜 shǎguā 〈person〉.

nook n. ①角落 jiǎoluò (corner). ②隐蔽处 yǐnbìchù (sheltered spot).

noon n. 中午 zhōngwǔ, 正午 zhèngwǔ. — adj. 中午的 zhōngwǔ de.

noose n. 活结 huójié (slipknot).

nor conj. 也不 yě bù.

norm n. 标准 biāozhǔn, 规范 guīfàn.

normal adj. 正常的 zhèngcháng de, 一般的 yìbān de, 标准的 biāozhǔn de.

normalization n. 正常化 zhèngchánghuà, 标准化 biāozhǔnhuà.

north n. ①北 běi 〈direction〉. ②北方 běifāng (northern region). ③北边 běibian, 北部 běibù (northern part). — adv. 北 běi, 向北 xiàng běi, 往北 wǎng běi. — adj. ①北 běi (of the north). ②北方的 běifāng de (of the northern region). ③北部的 běibù de (of the northern part).

North America 北美洲 Běiměizhōu.

North Pole 北极 Běijí.

northern adj. 北方的 běifāng de. ~ **hemisphere** 北半球 běibànqiú.

northward adv. 向北地 xiàng běi de.

nose n. 鼻子 bízi 〈organ〉.

nostalgia n. ①乡愁 xiāngchóu (homesickness). ②怀旧 huáijiù (long for the past).

nostril n. 鼻孔 bíkǒng.

nosy adj. 好管闲事的 hào guǎn xiánshì de.

not adv. 不 bù.

notable adj. ①值得注意的 zhíde zhùyì de, 显著的 xiǎnzhù de (remarkable). ②著名的 zhùmíng de (well-known).

notary n. 公证人 gōngzhèngrén.

note n. ①备忘录 bèiwànglù, 笔记 bǐjì (memo). ②注释 zhùshì (annotation). ③音符 yīnfú 〈music〉. — v. ①注意 zhùyì (notice). ②记录 jìlù, 写下 xiěxia (write down).

notebook n. ①笔记本 bǐjìběn (book). ②笔记本电脑 bǐjìběn diànnǎo / 笔记型电脑 bǐjìxíng

diànnǎo ⟨computer⟩.

noted *adj.* 著名的 zhùmíng de, 显著的 xiǎnzhù de (famous).

nothing *n.* 什么都没有 shénme dōu méiyǒu, 无 wú.

notice *n. & v.* ①注意 zhùyì (attention). ②通知 tōngzhī (information).

notify *v.* 通知 tōngzhī.

notion *n.* ①观念 guānniàn, 概念 gàiniàn (concept). ②意见 yìjiàn, 想法 xiǎngfa (idea).

notoriety *n.* 恶名 èmíng.

notorious *adj.* 恶名昭彰的 èmíng-zhāozhāng de.

notwithstanding *conj.* 虽然 suīrán.

nougat *n.* 牛轧糖 niúzhátáng ⟨candy⟩.

noun *n.* 名词 míngcí ⟨grammar⟩.

nourish *v.* ①滋养 zīyǎng (provide nutrition). ②培养 péiyǎng (develop).

novel *adj.* 新奇的 xīnqí de. — *n.* 小说 xiǎoshuō.

novelist *n.* 小说家 xiǎoshuōjiā.

novelty *n.* 新奇 xīnqí (newness).

November *n.* 十一月 Shíyīyuè.

novice *n.* 生手 shēngshǒu, 初学者 chūxuézhě (beginner).

now *adv.* 现在 xiànzài, 目前 mùqián.

nowadays *n. & adv.* 现今 xiànjīn, 时下 shíxià.

nowhere *adv.* 无处 wúchù.

noxious *adj.* ①有毒的 yǒu dú de (poisonous). ②有害的 yǒu hài de (harmful).

nozzle *n.* 管嘴 guǎnzuǐ

⟨opening⟩, 喷气口 pēnqìkǒu ⟨spout⟩.

nuance *n.* 细微差异 xìwēi chāyì / xìwéi chāyì.

nuclear *adj.* 核的 hé de.
~ *energy* 核能 hénéng.
~ *power station* 核电站 hédiànzhàn / 核能电厂 hénéng diànchǎng.

nucleus *n.* 核心 héxīn, 中心 zhōngxīn.

nude *adj.* 裸体的 luǒtǐ de (naked). — *n.* 裸体画像 luǒtǐ huàxiàng ⟨arts⟩.

nudge *v.* 轻推 qīngtuī.

nudity *n.* 裸体 luǒtǐ.

nuisance *n.* 讨厌的人或事 tǎoyàn de rén huò shì.

null *adj.* 无效的 wúxiào de (of no effect).

numb *adj.* 麻木的 mámù de. — *v.* 使麻木 shǐ mámù.

number *n.* ①数 shù, 数字 shùzì (numeral). ②号码 hàomǎ ⟨serial number⟩. ③一期 yì qī / yì qí ⟨publications⟩. ④数目 shùmù (amount). *phone* ~ 电话号码 diànhuà hàomǎ.

numeral *n. & adj.* 数字 shùzì.

numerous *adj.* 极多的 jí duō de, 无数的 wúshù de.

nun *n.* 修女 xiūnǚ ⟨Catholic⟩, 尼姑 nígū ⟨Buddhist⟩.

nunnery *n.* 女修道院 nǚxiūdàoyuàn ⟨Catholic⟩, 尼姑庵 nígū'ān ⟨Buddhist⟩.

nurse *n.* ①护士 hùshi ⟨hospital⟩. ②保姆 bǎomǔ (nanny). — *v.* ①看护 kānhù, 照顾 zhàogù (look after). ②哺乳 bǔrǔ (breastfeed).

nursery *n.* ①育儿室 yù'érshì ⟨children⟩. ②苗圃 miáopǔ ⟨plant⟩.

nurture *n. & v.* 养育 yǎngyù, 教养 jiàoyǎng (bringing-up).

nut *n.* ①核果 héguǒ, 坚果 jiānguǒ ⟨food⟩. ②疯子 fēngzi ⟨person⟩.

nutcracker *n.* 胡桃钳 hútáoqián ⟨tool⟩.

nutmeg *n.* 荳蔻 dòukòu.

nutrient *n.* 营养素 yíngyǎngsù.

nutrition *n.* 营养 yíngyǎng.

nutritious *adj.* 营养的 yíngyǎng de.

nuts *adj.* 疯的 fēng de, 笨的 bèn de.

nylon *n.* 尼龙 nílóng ⟨fiber⟩.

O

oak *n.* 橡树 xiàngshù.

oar *n.* 桨 jiǎng.

oasis *n.* 绿洲 lǜzhōu.

oath *n.* 誓约 shìyuē, 誓言 shìyán (promise). **take an ~** 发誓 fāshì.

oatmeal *n.* 麦片 màipiàn.

obedience *n.* 顺从 shùncóng, 服从 fúcóng.

obedient *adj.* 顺从的 shùncóng de, 听话的 tīnghuà de.

obese *adj.* 非常胖的 fēicháng pàng de.

obey *v.* 顺从 shùncóng, 服从 fúcóng.

obituary *n.* 讣闻 fùwén.

object *n.* ①东西 dōngxi (thing). ②目的 mùdì (goal). ③对象 duìxiàng (recipient). ④受词 shòucí ⟨grammar⟩. — *v.* 反对 fǎnduì (protest).

objection *n.* 反对 fǎnduì.

objective *n.* 目标 mùbiāo, 目的 mùdì (goal). — *adj.* 客观的 kèguān de (unbiased).

obligation *n.* 义务 yìwù (duty), 责任 zérèn (responsibility).

obligatory *adj.* ①义务的 yìwù de (required). ②必要的 bìyào de (necessary).

oblige *v.* ①强制 qiángzhì / qiǎngzhì, 逼迫 bīpò (force). ②施予恩惠 shīyǔ ēnhuì (do a favor).

oblique *adj.* ①斜的 xié de (slanting). ②间接的 jiànjiē de (indirect).

obliterate *v.* 消灭 xiāomiè (eliminate), 涂掉 túdiào (erase).

oblivious *adj.* 不在意的 bú zàiyì de.

oblong *n. & adj.* 长方形 chángfāngxíng.

obnoxious *adj.* 使人讨厌的 shǐ rén tǎoyàn de.

oboe *n.* 双簧管 shuānghuángguǎn.

obscene *adj.* 猥亵的 wěixiè de.

obscure *adj.* ①不清楚的 bù qīngchu de (unclear), 朦胧的 ménglóng de (vague). ②无名的 wúmíng de (unknown). ③暧昧的 àimèi de (ambiguous), 难解的 nánjiě de (complex).

obsequious *adj.* 谄媚的 chǎnmèi de

observant *adj.* 善于观察的 shànyú guānchá de.

observation *n.* ①观察 guānchá (notice). ②评论 pínglùn (comment).

observatory *n.* 天文台 tiānwéntái ⟨astronomy⟩、气象台 qìxiàngtái ⟨weather⟩.

observe *v.* ①观察 guānchá (notice). ②评论 pínglùn (remark). ③庆祝 qìngzhù, 纪念 jìniàn (celebrate). ④遵守 zūnshǒu (obey).

observer *n.* 观察者 guāncházhě.

obsess *v.* 常萦绕于心中 cháng yíngrào yú xīnzhōng, 着迷 zháomí.

obsolete *adj.* 作废的 zuòfèi de (useless), 被取代的 bèi qǔdài de (replaced).

obstacle *n.* 障碍 zhàng'ài.

obstetrics *n.* 产科医学 chǎnkē yīxué.

obstinate *adj.* 顽固的 wángù de, 固执的 gùzhí de.

obstruct *v.* 阻碍 zǔ'ài, 妨碍 fáng'ài.

obtain *v.* 得到 dédào, 获得 huòdé (get).

obtuse *adj.* ①钝的 dùn de, 迟钝的 chídùn de (stupid). ②钝角的 dùnjiǎo de ⟨geometry⟩.

obvious *adj.* 显然的 xiǎnrán de, 明显的 míngxiǎn de.

occasion *n.* ①场合 chǎnghé (a time and place). ②大事 dàshì (important event). ③时机 shíjī (chance). ④理由 lǐyóu (excuse).

occasionally *adv.* 偶尔 ǒu'ěr,

有时候 yǒushíhou.

occupant *n.* ①占有者 zhànyǒuzhě (possession). ②居住者 jūzhùzhě, 居民 jūmín (residence).

occupation *n.* ①占有 zhànyǒu (possession). ②职业 zhíyè (job).

occupational *adj.* 职业的 zhíyè de (vocational). *~ disease* 职业病 zhíyèbìng.

occupy *v.* ①占有 zhànyǒu, 占据 zhànjù (possess). ②居住于 jūzhù yú (live in). *be ~ied with* 忙着 mángzhe.

occur *v.* 发生 fāshēng (happen), 出现 chūxiàn (appear).

occurrence *n.* ①事情 shìqing, 事件 shìjiàn (event). ②发生 fāshēng (happening).

ocean *n.* 海洋 hǎiyáng.

Oceania 大洋洲 Dàyángzhōu.

oceanography *n.* 海洋学 hǎiyángxué.

o'clock *adv.* 点钟 diǎnzhōng.

octagon *n.* 八角形 bājiǎoxíng.

October *n.* 十月 Shíyuè.

octopus *n.* 章鱼 zhāngyú.

odd *adj.* ①奇数的 jīshù de ⟨numbers⟩. ②古怪的 gǔguài de (abnormal).

oddity *n.* 古怪 gǔguài ⟨situation⟩, 怪物 guàiwù ⟨thing or person⟩.

odds *n.* 可能性 kěnéngxìng (probability).

odious *adj.* 可恶的 kěwù de.

odor *n.* 气味 qìwèi, 味道 wèidào.

of *prep.* ……的 ...de.

off *adj.* 关的 guān de ⟨machine⟩. *get ~* 下 xià ⟨disembark⟩. *on and ~* 断断续续地 duànduàn-xùxù de (intermit-

O

tently). **take ~** 脱 tuō, 脱下 tuōxià 〈clothing〉.

take something ~ 拿掉 nádiào (remove from).

turn something ~ 关 guān 〈machine〉.

offend v. ①冒犯 màofàn (annoy). ②犯法 fànfǎ (transgress).

offender n. 违犯者 wéifànzhě.

offense n. ①犯罪 fànzuì (crime). ②冒犯 màofàn (annoyance). ③攻击 gōngjī / gōngjí (attack).

offensive adj. 冒犯的 màofàn de (annoying).

offer v. ①提供 tígōng (provide). ②奉献 fèngxiàn (present). ③出价 chūjià (price).

office n. ①办公室 bàngōngshì 〈room〉. ②职务 zhíwù (duty).

officer n. ①军官 jūnguān 〈military〉. ②官员 guānyuán (official). ③警官 jǐngguān (policeman).

official n. 官员 guānyuán, 公务员 gōngwùyuán. — adj. 公务的 gōngwù de, 职务的 zhíwù de (authorized).

officially adv. 官方地 guānfāng de 〈government〉, 正式地 zhèngshì de (formal).

offshore adj. 近海的 jìnhǎi de.

offspring n. 子孙 zǐsūn.

often adv. 常常 chángcháng.

oil n. ①油 yóu (fat). ②石油 shíyóu (petroleum).

oily adj. 油的 yóu de (fat).

ointment n. 软膏 ruǎngāo, 油膏 yóugāo.

OK adj. & adv. 好 hǎo, 可以 kěyǐ.

old adj. ①老的 lǎo de 〈person〉. ②旧的 jiù de 〈thing〉. ③古老的 gǔlǎo de 〈era〉.

old-fashioned adj. 过时的 guòshí de, 旧式的 jiùshì de.

olive n. 橄榄 gǎnlǎn 〈fruit〉. **~ oil** 橄榄油 gǎnlǎnyóu. — adj. 橄榄色的 gǎnlǎnsè de 〈color〉.

Olympic Games 奥林匹克运动会 Àolínpǐkè Yùndònghuì / Àolínpǐkè Yùndònghuì.

Olympics n. 奥运会 Àoyùnhuì.

omelet n. 煎蛋卷 jiān dànjuǎn.

omen n. 征兆 zhēngzhào, 预示 yùshì.

ominous adj. 恶兆的 èzhào de, 不吉的 bù jí de.

omit v. 省略 shěnglüè (leave out), 删除 shānchú (eliminate).

on prep. 在……之上 zài...zhī shàng. — adj. 开的 kāi de 〈machine〉.

once adv. ①一次 yícì (one time). ②曾经 céngjīng (in the past). — n. 一次 yícì. **at ~** 立刻 lìkè. — conj. 一旦……就 yídàn... jiù (as soon as).

one n. 一 yī. **~ another** 互相 hùxiāng. **~ by ~** 一个一个的 yíge yíge de. — adj. 单一的 dānyī de (single), 某一的 mǒu yī de (some one).

onerous adj. 讨厌的 tǎoyàn de, 可恶的 kěwù de.

one's pron. ①某人的 mǒurén de (someone's). ②自己的 zìjǐ de (one's own).

oneself pron. 自己 zìjǐ.

ongoing adj. ①继续中的 jìxù zhōng de, 进行中的 jìnxíng zhōng de (in process). ②长期 chángqī / chángqí (long-term).

onion n. 洋葱 yángcōng.

onlooker n. 旁观者 pángguānzhě.

only adj. 唯一的 wéiyī de (sole). — adv. 唯一 wéiyī (solely). *not ~... but also* 不但……而且 búdàn...érqiě. — conj. 不过 búguò, 只 zhǐ 〈amount〉.

onset n. 刚开始 gāng kāishǐ (the very beginning).

onshore adj. & adv. 向陆地 xiàng lùdì.

onslaught n. 猛攻 měnggōng.

on-the-spot adj. 现场的 xiànchǎng de.

onto prep. 到……之上 dào...zhī shàng.

onward adv. 向前 xiàngqián.

ooze v. 渗出 shènchu (leak). — n. 淤泥 yūní, 稀泥 xīní (slimy mud).

opaque adj. ①不透明的 bú tòumíng de 〈visual〉. ②不清楚的 bù qīngchǔ de, 暧昧的 àimèi de 〈situation〉.

open adj. ①打开的 dǎkāi de (not closed). ②公开的 gōngkāi de (public). — n. 户外 hùwài (outdoors). — v. 打开 dǎkāi (unclose).

opening n. ①洞 dòng, 开口 kāikǒu (hole). ②开始 kāishǐ (beginning). ③空缺 kòngquē (vacancy).

openly adv. ①公开地 gōngkāi de (publicly). ②公然地 gōngrán de (without disguise).

open-minded adj. 无偏见的 wú piānjiàn de (unprejudiced).

opera n. 歌剧 gējù.

operate v. ①运转 yùnzhuǎn 〈machine〉. ②操作 cāozuò (use). ③动手术 dòng shǒushù 〈surgery〉.

operation n. ①运转 yùnzhuǎn (working). ②操作 cāozuò (action). ③手术 shǒushù (surgery). ④军事行动 jūnshì xíngdòng 〈military〉.

operator n. ①操作员 cāozuòyuán 〈machine〉. ②接线生 jiēxiànshēng 〈telephone〉.

opinion n. 意见 yìjiàn, 看法 kànfǎ. *in my ~* 在我看来 zài wǒ kànlai.

opium n. 鸦片 yāpiàn.

opponent n. 对手 duìshǒu, 反对者 fǎnduìzhě.

opportune adj. 合时宜的 hé shíyí de.

opportunity n. 机会 jīhuì.

oppose v. 反对 fǎnduì, 与……对立 yǔ...duìlì.

opposite adj. ①相反的 xiāngfǎn de (opposed). ②相对的 xiāngduì de (contrasting). — n. 相对事物 xiāngduì shìwù.

opposition n. ①反对 fǎnduì (disapproval). ②反对党 fǎnduìdǎng 〈political party〉. ③对手 duìshǒu (opponent).

oppress v. 压迫 yāpò (repress).

oppression n. 压迫 yāpò.

optical adj. ①眼的 yǎn de 〈eyes〉. ②光学的 guāngxué de 〈vision〉.

optics n. 光学 guāngxué.

optimism n. 乐观主义 lèguān zhǔyì.

optimist n. 乐观主义者 lèguān zhǔyì zhě.

optimistic adj. 乐观的 lèguān de.

option n. 选择 xuǎnzé

(choice).

optional *adj.* ①可选择的 kě xuǎnzé de (can be chosen). ②不必要的 bú bìyào de (not required).

opulence *n.* 富裕 fùyù, 丰富 fēngfù.

opus *n.* 作品 zuòpǐn (a work).

or *conj.* ①或者 huòzhě. ②还是 háishi. ~ *else* 否则 fǒuzé, 要不然 yàobùrán.

oral *adj.* ①口头的 kǒutóu de, 口语的 kǒuyǔ de (spoken). ②口腔的 kǒuqiāng de (regarding the mouth).

orange *n.* 柳橙 liǔchéng ⟨fruit⟩. ②橘色 júsè, 橙色 chéngsè ⟨color⟩.

orator *n.* 演说者 yǎnshuōzhě.

orbit *n.* 轨道 guǐdào (circuit).

orchard *n.* 果园 guǒyuán.

orchestra *n.* 管弦乐队 guǎnxián yuèduì.

orchid *n.* 兰花 lánhuā.

ordain *v.* 任命神职 rènmìng shénzhí ⟨priest⟩.

ordeal *n.* 严酷考验 yánkù kǎoyàn (trial).

order *n.* ①顺序 shùnxù, 次序 cìxù (sequence). ②命令 mìnglìng (command). ③秩序 zhìxù, 规律 guīlǜ (rules). *an ~ for goods* 订单 dìngdān. *in ~ to* 为了…… wèile.... — *v.* 命令 mìnglìng (command). ~ *food* 点菜 diǎn cài. ~ *goods* 订购 dìnggòu, 订货 dìnghuò.

orderly *adj.* ①有秩序的 yǒu zhìxù de (organized). ②顺从的 shùncóng de (controlled).

ordinal *adj.* 顺序的 shùnxù de (showing order in series).

ordinary *adj.* 普通的 pǔtōng de, 一般的 yìbān de.

organ *n.* ①器官 qìguān ⟨of body⟩. ②风琴 fēngqín ⟨instrument⟩.

organic *adj.* 有机的 yǒujī de (living). ~ *food* 有机食品 yǒujī shípǐn.

organism *n.* 有机体 yǒujītǐ (a living being).

organization *n.* 机构 jīgòu, 组织 zǔzhī (institution).

organize *v.* 组织 zǔzhī (form).

orgy *n.* 性派对 xìngpàiduì.

orient *v.* 定方位 dìng fāngwèi (orientate).

Orient *n.* 东方 Dōngfāng.

Oriental *adj.* 东方的 Dōngfāng de.

Oriental *n.* 东方人 Dōngfāngrén.

orientation *n.* ①方向 fāngxiàng (direction). ②新人辅导 xīnrén fǔdǎo ⟨instruction⟩.

orifice *n.* 穴 xué / xuè, 洞 dòng.

origin *n.* ①起源 qǐyuán (beginning). ②出身 chūshēn (ancestry).

original *adj.* ①最初的 zuìchū de (earliest). ②有创作性的 yǒu chuàngzuòxìng de (creative). ③原创的 yuánchuàng de (genuine). — *n.* ①原物 yuánwù, 原作品 yuánzuòpǐn ⟨object⟩. ②原文 yuánwén ⟨writing⟩.

originality *n.* 创造力 chuàngzàolì.

originally *adv.* 原来 yuánlái, 最初 zuìchū (initially).

originate *v.* 创始 chuàngshǐ,

发明 fāmíng. ~ *from* 来自 láizì.

ornament *n.* 装饰品 zhuāngshìpǐn.

ornamental *adj.* 装饰的 zhuāngshì de.

orphan *n.* 孤儿 gū'ér.

orphanage *n.* 孤儿院 gū'éryuàn.

orthodox *adj.* ①正教的 zhèngjiào de ⟨religion⟩. ②公认的 gōngrèn de (approved).

orthopedics *n.* 整形手术 zhěngxíng shǒushù.

oscillate *v.* 摆动 bǎidòng, 振荡 zhèndàng (vibrate).

ostensible *adj.* ①表面的 biǎomiàn de (seeming). ②所谓的 suǒwèi de (so-called).

ostentatious *adj.* 炫耀的 xuànyào de.

osteoporosis *n.* 骨质疏松症 gǔzhì shūsōngzhèng / gǔzhí shūsōngzhèng.

ostrich *n.* 鸵鸟 tuóniǎo.

other *adj.* 其他的 qítā de, 别的 bié de.

otherwise *adv.* 用别的方法 yòng bié de fāngfǎ (using other means), 在其他方面 zài qítā fāngmiàn ⟨differently⟩. — *conj.* 否则 fǒuzé, 要不然 yàobùrán.

otter *n.* 水獭 shuǐtǎ / shuǐtà.

ought *aux. v.* 应该 yīnggāi (should).

ounce *n.* 盎司 àngsī.

our *pron.* 我们的 wǒmen de.

ours *pron.* 我们的 wǒmen de.

ourselves *pron.* 我们自己 wǒmen zìjǐ ⟨reflexive⟩.

oust *v.* ①逐出 zhúchū (expel). ②免职 miǎnzhí (unseat).

out *adj.* 在外 zàiwài. *to be ~* 不在 búzài (not present).

~. *adv.* 外出 wàichū.

— *prep.* 在……外 zài...wài.

~ *of something* 在……之外 zài...zhī wài.

outbid *v.* 出高价 chū gāojià.

outbreak *n.* 爆发 bàofā (outburst).

outburst *n.* 爆发 bàofā, 迸发 bèngfā.

outcast *n.* 被逐出者 bèi zhúchū zhě.

outcome *n.* 结果 jiéguǒ.

outdo *v.* 胜过 shèngguo.

outdoor *adj.* 户外的 hùwài de.

outdoors *adv.* 在户外 zài hùwài, 在外面 zài wàimian. — *n.* 户外 hùwài.

outer *adj.* 外面的 wàimian de. ~ *space* 外层空间 wàicéng kōngjiān / 外太空 wàitàikōng.

outfit *n.* 全套装备 quántào zhuāngbèi.

outgoing *adj.* ①友善的 yǒushàn de (friendly). ②外出的 wàichū de, 离去的 líqù de (going out).

outgrow *v.* 长得较大 zhǎng de jiào dà.

outing *n.* 远足 yuǎnzú.

outlandish *adj.* 奇异的 qíyì de (strange).

outlaw *n.* 不法之徒 bùfǎzhītú, 歹徒 dǎitú (criminal).

outlet *n.* ①出口 chūkǒu (way out). ②发泄方法 fāxiè fāngfǎ (emotional release).

outline *n.* 轮廓 lúnkuò (silhouette), 大纲 dàgāng (summary). — *v.* 概括 gàikuò / gàiguā.

outlook *n.* ①观点 guāndiǎn (viewpoint). ②展望 zhǎnwàng (future prospect).

O

outlying adj. 偏僻的 piānpì de (remote).

out-of-date adj. 过时的 guòshí de.

outpatient adj. 门诊的 ménzhěn de.

outpost n. 前哨 qiánshào.

output n. 输出 shūchū, 产量 chǎnliàng (production).

outrage n. ①粗暴 cūbào (atrocity). ②愤怒 fènnù (anger).

outrageous adj. ①粗暴的 cūbào de (atrocious). ②荒谬的 huāngmiù de (ridiculous).

outright adv. ①率直地 shuàizhí de (openly). ②直接的 zhíjiē de, 干脆 gāncuì (straightforward).

outside n. 外面 wàimian, 外侧 wàicè. — adj. 在外面的 zài wàimian de. — adv. 在外 zàiwài.

outsider n. 局外人 júwàirén.

outsize n. 特大号 tèdàhào.

outskirts n. 郊外 jiāowài.

outspoken adj. 直言的 zhíyán de.

outstanding adj. ①杰出的 jiéchū de, 引人注目的 yǐnrén--zhùmù de (great). ②未付的 wèifù de (unpaid).

outstretched adj. ①伸开的 shēnkāi de ⟨thing⟩. ②直躺的 zhítǎng de ⟨person⟩.

outstrip v. 超越 chāoyuè, 胜过 shèngguo.

outward(s) adj. 向外的 xiàngwài de. — adv. 向外 xiàngwài.

outweigh v. 比……重 bǐ... zhòng.

outwit v. 智取 zhìqǔ.

oval n. & adj. 卵形 luǎnxíng, 椭圆形 tuǒyuánxíng.

ovation n. 热烈喝采 rèliè hēcǎi.

oven n. 烤炉 kǎolú, 烤箱 kǎoxiāng.

over adv. & prep. 在……之上 zài...zhī shàng (above). — adj. 结束的 jiéshù de (finished).

overall adj. ①全面的 quánmiàn de, 全部的 quánbù de (complete). ②大体上 dàtǐshang (in general).

overboard adv. 落水 luòshuǐ.

overcast adj. 阴暗的 yīn'àn de.

overcharge v. 索价过高 suǒjià guò gāo.

overcoat n. 大衣 dàyī, 外套 wàitào.

overcome v. 克服 kèfú (conquer).

overdo v. ①过分 guòfèn, 过火 guòhuǒ (do excessively). ②煮太久 zhǔ tàijiǔ (overcook).

overdraft n. 透支 tòuzhī.

overdraw v. 透支 tòuzhī (make an overdraft).

overdue adj. 过期的 guòqī de / guòqí de.

overgrown adj. 成长过度的 chéngzhǎng guòdù de (having grown too large), 长满的 zhǎng mǎn de (covered).

overhang n. 突出物 tūchūwù / túchūwù.

overhaul v. 修改 xiūgǎi.

overhead adv. 在上面 zài shàngmian. — adj. 上面的 shàngmian de. — n. 支出 zhīchū (expense).

overhear v. 无意中听到 wúyìzhōng tīngdào.

overheat v. 过度加热 guòdù jiārè.

overlap v. 重叠 chóngdié, 重复 chóngfù.

overload *v.* 超负载 chāo fùzài (overburden).

overlook *v.* ①看漏 kànlòu, 忽略 hūlüè (ignore). ②俯视 fǔshì, 俯瞰 fǔkàn (look on to).

overnight *adj.* 夜间的 yèjiān de. — *adv.* ①一夜之间 yíyè zhījiān 〈in a short time〉. ②整夜地 zhěngyè de (for the night).

overpower *v.* 打败 dǎbài, 压倒 yādǎo (overcome).

overrate *v.* 高估 gāogū.

override *v.* 藐视 miǎoshì (ignore), 否决 fǒujué (do the opposite of).

overrule *v.* 推翻 tuīfān, 驳回 bóhuí (disallow).

overrun *v.* ①蔓延 mànyán (spread over). ②侵占 qīnzhàn, 蹂躏 róulìn (invade).

oversea(s) *adv.* 在海外 zài hǎiwài, 在外国 zài wàiguó.

oversee *v.* 监督 jiāndū.

overseer *n.* 监督者 jiāndūzhě.

oversight *n.* ①疏忽 shūhu, 失察 shīchá (neglect). ②监督权 jiāndūquán (right to oversee).

oversleep *v.* 睡过头 shuìguòtóu.

overstep *v.* 超越 chāoyuè.

overt *adj.* 公开的 gōngkāi de.

overtake *v.* 赶上 gǎnshang, 追及 zhuījí (catch).

overthrow *v.* 推翻 tuīfān

(overturn).

overtime *n.* 加班时间 jiābān shíjiān.

overture *n.* ①提议 tíyì (proposal). ②序曲 xùqǔ 〈music〉.

overturn *v.* 倾覆 qīngfù, 推翻 tuīfān.

overweight *adj.* 超重的 chāozhòng de. — *n.* 超重 chāozhòng.

overwhelm *v.* 压倒 yādǎo.

overwork *v.* 工作过度 gōngzuò guòdù.

overwrought *adj.* 过度紧张的 guòdù jǐnzhāng de (too nervous).

ovum *n.* 卵 luǎn, 卵细胞 luǎnxìbāo.

owe *v.* 欠 qiàn, 欠债 qiànzhài.

owing *adj.* 亏欠的 kuīqiàn de (unpaid).

owl *n.* 猫头鹰 māotóuyīng.

own *adj.* 自己的 zìjǐ de (belonging to oneself). — *v.* 拥有 yōngyǒu / yǒngyǒu (possess).

owner *n.* 所有者 suǒyǒuzhě.

ownership *n.* 所有权 suǒyǒuquán.

ox *n.* 公牛 gōngniú.

oxygen *n.* 氧气 yǎngqì.

oyster *n.* 牡蛎 mǔlì, 蚝 háo.

ozone *n.* 臭氧 chòuyǎng.
  ~ *layer* 臭氧层 chòuyǎngcéng.

O

P

pace *n.* ①步 bù (step). ②速度 sùdù (rate). ③步调 bùdiào (tempo).

Pacific Ocean 太平洋 Tàipíngyáng.

pacifism *n.* 和平主义 hépíng zhǔyì.

pacify *v.* 抚慰 fǔwèi (comfort), 使平静 shǐ píngjìng (calm).

pack *n.* ①包裹 bāoguǒ (bundle). ②背包 bēibāo (bag). ③一群 yìqún (group). — *v.* ①包装 bāozhuāng, 打包 dǎbāo (bundle). ②塞满 sāimǎn (cram).

package *n.* 包裹 bāoguǒ (parcel).

packed *adj.* 拥挤的 yōngjǐ de / yǒngjǐ de.

packing *n.* 包装材料 bāozhuāng cáiliào, 填料 tiánliào (wadding).

pact *n.* 协定 xiédìng (agreement), 公约 gōngyuē (accord).

pad *n.* ①垫 diàn, 软垫 ruǎndiàn (cushion). ②便条纸 biàntiáozhǐ, 拍纸簿 pāizhǐbù (notebook). — *v.* 填塞 tiánsāi (stuff).

paddle *v.* ①用桨划 yòng jiǎng huá (row). ②拍打 pāidǎ (hit).

paddock *n.* 小牧场 xiǎo mùchǎng, 围场 wéichǎng.

paddy *n.* ①水稻 shuǐdào (rice). ②稻田 dàotián (field).

padlock *n.* 挂锁 guàsuǒ.

pagan *n.* 异教徒 yìjiàotú. — *adj.* 异教的 yìjiào de.

page *n.* 页 yè.

pageant *n.* ①历史剧 lìshǐjù (historical play). ②游行 yóuxíng, 庆典 qìngdiǎn (celebration).

pagoda *n.* 宝塔 bǎotǎ, 浮屠 fútú.

pail *n.* 桶 tǒng.

pain *n.* ①痛苦 tòngkǔ, 疼痛 téngtòng (ache). ②辛苦 xīnkǔ (trouble).

painful *adj.* 痛苦的 tòngkǔ de.

painkiller *n.* 止痛药 zhǐtòngyào.

paint *n.* 油漆 yóuqī (for walls), 颜料 yánliào (pigment). — *v.* ①油漆 yóuqī (wall). ②绘画 huìhuà (picture).

painter *n.* ①画家 huàjiā (artist). ②油漆匠 yóuqījiàng (workman).

painting *n.* 画 huà, 绘画 huìhuà.

pair *n.* 一对 yíduì (living things), 一双 yìshuāng (inanimate objects).

pajamas *n.* 睡衣 shuìyī.

pal *n.* 朋友 péngyou, 伙伴 huǒbàn.

palace *n.* 宫殿 gōngdiàn, 皇宫 huánggōng.

palatable *adj.* 可口的 kěkǒu de, 味美的 wèiměi de (delicious).

pale *adj.* ①苍白的 cāngbái de (bloodless). ②暗淡的 àndàn de (dim).

palette *n.* 调色盘 tiáosèpán.

pall *n.* ①柩衣 jiùyī (mantle). ②

幕罩 mùzhào (covering).

pallid adj. 苍白的 cāngbái de (pale).

palm n. ①手掌 shǒuzhǎng (hand). ②棕榈 zōnglǘ (tree).

palmistry n. 手相术 shǒuxiàngshù.

palpable adj. 可触知的 kě chùzhī de (tangible), 明显的 míngxiǎn de (clear).

palpitate v. 悸动 jìdòng, 跳动 tiàodòng.

palpitation n. 心悸 xīnjì.

paltry adj. 无价值的 wú jiàzhí de, 微不足道的 wēibùzúdào de / wéibùzúdào de (trifling).

pamper v. 纵容 zòngróng.

pamphlet n. 小册子 xiǎocèzi.

pan n. 平底锅 píngdǐguō.

panacea n. 万灵药 wànlíngyào.

pancake n. 薄煎饼 báojiānbǐng / bójiānbǐng.

pancreas n. 胰脏 yízàng.

panda n. 猫熊 māoxióng.

pandemonium n. 大混乱 dà hùnluàn (chaos).

pane n. 窗玻璃 chuāngbōli.

panel n. ①方格 fānggé (oblong piece). ②讨论小组 tǎolùn xiǎozǔ, 座谈小组 zuòtán xiǎozǔ (group).

pang n. 剧痛 jùtòng.

panic n. 恐慌 kǒnghuāng. — adj. 恐慌的 kǒnghuāng de. — v. 使恐慌 shǐ kǒnghuāng.

panorama n. 全景 quánjǐng.

pansy n. 三色堇 sānsèjǐn.

pant n. 喘息 chuǎnxí / chuǎnxí, 喘气 chuǎnqì. — v. 喘息 chuǎnxí / chuǎnxí, 喘气 chuǎnqì (gasp).

panther n. 豹 bào.

panties n. 短衬裤 duǎn chènkù.

pantomime n. 哑剧 yǎjù / 默剧 mòjù.

pantry n. ①餐具室 cānjùshì (dishes). ②食品室 shípǐnshì (food).

pants n. 裤子 kùzi.

paparazzi n. 狗仔队 gǒuzǎiduì / gǒuzǎiduì.

paper n. ①纸 zhǐ (material). ②(pl.) 文件 wénjiàn (document). ③报纸 bàozhǐ (newspaper). ④论文 lùnwén (thesis), 报告 bàogào (report). — v. 糊纸 hú zhǐ.

paperback n. 平装本 píngzhuāngběn.

paperweight n. 书镇 shūzhèn.

paperwork n. 文书工作 wénshū gōngzuò.

paprika n. ①干辣椒 gānlàjiāo (pepper). ②辣椒粉 làjiāofěn (powder).

par n. ①标准 biāozhǔn, 常态 chángtài (average). ②同等 tóngděng, 同价 tóngjià (parity). ③标准杆数 biāozhǔn gǎnshù (golf).

parable n. 寓言 yùyán, 譬语 pìyù.

parachute n. 降落伞 jiàngluòsǎn.

parachutist n. 伞兵 sǎnbīng.

parade n. ①游行 yóuxíng (procession). ②阅兵 yuèbīng (military). — v. ①游行 yóuxíng (march). ②夸耀 kuāyào (display).

paradigm n. 模范 mófàn, 范典 fàndiǎn.

paradise n. 天堂 tiāntáng (heaven), 乐园 lèyuán (fantasy land).

paradox n. 似非而是的议论 sìfēi'érshì de yìlùn, 自相矛盾的话 zìxiāng-máodùn de huà.

paraffin n. 石蜡 shílà.

paragraph n. 段 duàn, 节 jié, 段落 duànluò.

parallel adj. 平行的 píngxíng de. — v. 与……平行 yǔ... píngxíng.

paralysis n. 麻痹 mábì, 瘫痪 tānhuàn.

paralytic adj. 麻痹的 mábì de, 瘫痪的 tānhuàn de.

paralyze v. 使麻痹 shǐ mábì, 使瘫痪 shǐ tānhuàn.

paramount adj. 最高的 zuìgāo de, 卓越的 zhuóyuè de.

paranoia n. 偏执狂 piānzhíkuáng, 妄想症 wàngxiǎngzhèng.

paranoid adj. 偏执狂的 piānzhíkuáng de. — n. 偏执狂患者 piānzhíkuáng huànzhě.

paraphernalia n. 小用品 xiǎo yòngpǐn, 小用具 xiǎo yòngjù (article).

paraphrase n. & v. 意译 yìyì.

parasite n. 寄生虫 jìshēngchóng.

parasol n. 阳伞 yángsǎn 〈umbrella〉.

paratrooper n. 伞兵 sǎnbīng.

paratroops n. 伞兵部队 sǎnbīng bùduì.

parcel n. 包裹 bāoguǒ, 小包 xiǎobāo (package). — v. 分配 fēnpèi.

parch v. 烘干 hōnggān, 烤干 kǎogān (toast under dry heat).

parchment n. 羊皮纸 yángpízhǐ.

pardon n. & v. ①宽恕 kuānshù, 原谅 yuánliàng

(forgiveness). ②赦免 shèmiǎn (absolution).

pare v. ①剥 bāo / bō, 削皮 xiāopí (peel). ②削减 xuējiǎn / xuèjiǎn (cut).

parent n. 父或母 fù huò mǔ.

parents n. 父母亲 fùmǔqīn, 双亲 shuāngqīn (father and mother).

parentage n. 出身 chūshēn, 家世 jiāshì.

parenthesis n. 括弧 kuòhú / guāhú.

parish n. 教区 jiàoqū.

park n. ①公园 gōngyuán (public garden). ②运动场 yùndòngchǎng (sports ground). — v. 停车 tíngchē.

parking n. 停车 tíngchē (car). ~ **lot** 停车场 tíngchēchǎng.

parley n. & v. 谈判 tánpàn.

parliament n. 国会 guóhuì, 议院 yìyuàn.

parlor n. 客厅 kètīng, 会客室 huìkèshì.

parody n. 讽刺诗文 fěngcì shīwén / fèngcì shīwén.

parole n. & v. 假释 jiǎshì.

parrot n. 鹦鹉 yīngwǔ.

parry v. 避开 bìkai, 挡开 dǎngkai.

parse v. 分析 fēnxī.

parsimonious adj. 吝啬的 lìnsè de.

parsley n. 荷兰芹 hélánqín, 西洋芹 xīyángqín.

parson n. 教区牧师 jiàoqū mùshī.

part n. ①部分 bùfen (portion). ②角色 juésè (role). ③台词 táicí (lines). ④地区 dìqū (area). — v. 分开 fēnkai (separate from).

partake v. ①参与 cānyù (par-

ticipate). ②分担 fēndān, 分享 fēnxiǎng (share).

partial *adj.* ①部分的 bùfen de (incomplete). ②偏袒的 piāntǎn de (not fair). ③偏爱的 piān'ài de (favoring).

partially *adv.* ①部分地 bùfen de (partly). ②偏袒地 piāntǎn de (prejudicially).

participant *n.* 参与者 cānyùzhě.

participate *v.* 参与 cānyù (take part), 参加 cānjiā (join).

participle *n.* 分词 fēncí.

particle *n.* ①微粒 wēilì / wéilì, 粒子 lìzǐ (small grains), 分子 fēnzǐ (small piece). ②质词 zhìcí / zhící, 冠词 guàncí ⟨grammar⟩.

particular *adj.* ①独特的 dútè de (distinct). ②特别的 tèbié de (special). ③挑剔的 tiāoti de (choosy). — *n.* 细节 xìjié (detail).

particularly *adv.* 特别地 tèbié de.

partisan *n.* 有偏见的 yǒu piānjiàn de.

partition *n.* 分割 fēngē, 瓜分 guāfēn (separation).

partly *adv.* 部分地 bùfen de.

partner *n.* 伙伴 huǒbàn (companion), 合伙人 héhuǒrén ⟨business⟩.

partnership *n.* 合伙 héhuǒ.

partridge *n.* 山鹑 shānchún, 鹧鸪 zhègū.

part-time *adj.* 兼任的 jiānrèn de.

party *n.* ①聚会 jùhuì, 宴会 yànhuì (social gathering). ②政党 zhèngdǎng ⟨politics⟩.

pass *v.* ①经过 jīngguò, 通过 tōngguò (go by). ②传给

chuángěi (hand over). ③及格 jígé (approve). — *n.* 通行证 tōngxíngzhèng (permit).

passable *adj.* ①可接受的 kě jiēshòu de (acceptable). ②可通过的 kě tōngguò de (unblocked).

passage *n.* ①通道 tōngdào, 走廊 zǒuláng (hallway). ②航行 hángxíng (voyage).

passenger *n.* 乘客 chéngkè, 旅客 lǚkè.

passion *n.* 热情 rèqíng.

passionate *adj.* 热情的 rèqíng de.

passive *adj.* 被动的 bèidòng de.

passport *n.* 护照 hùzhào.

password *n.* ①密码 mìmǎ ⟨machine⟩. ②口令 kǒulìng (secret word).

past *adj.* 过去的 guòqù de (past time).

pasta *n.* 面团 miàntuán.

paste *n.* 浆糊 jiànghu.

pastel *n.* 蜡笔 làbǐ.

pastime *n.* 娱乐 yúlè, 消遣 xiāoqiǎn.

pastor *n.* 牧师 mùshī.

pastry *n.* 糕饼 gāobǐng.

pasture *n.* 牧场 mùchǎng, 牧草地 mùcǎodì.

pasty *adj.* ①糊状的 húzhuàng de (like paste). ②苍白的 cāngbái de (pale).

pat *v.* 轻拍 qīngpāi.

patch *v.* 补绽 bǔzhàn. — *v.* 补缀 bǔzhuì.

patent *adj.* 专利的 zhuānlì de. — *n.* 专利 zhuānlì. — *v.* 取得专利 qǔdé zhuānlì.

paternal *adj.* 父亲的 fùqīn de, 父系 fùxì de.

paternity *n.* 父系 fùxì. ~ *leave*

陪产假 péichǎnjià.

path *n.* 小径 xiǎojìng, 小路 xiǎolù.

pathetic *adj.* 悲惨的 bēicǎn de.

pathology *n.* 病理学 bìnglíxué.

pathos *n.* 悲哀 bēi'āi.

patience *n.* 耐心 nàixīn.

patient *adj.* 有耐心的 yǒu nàixīn de. — *n.* 病人 bìngrén.

patriarch *n.* 元老 yuánlǎo, 族长 zúzhǎng.

patriot *n.* 爱国者 àiguózhě.

patriotic *adj.* 爱国的 àiguó de.

patriotism *n.* 爱国心 àiguóxīn.

patrol *n.* ①巡逻 xúnluó ⟨watch⟩. ②巡逻者 xúnluózhě ⟨watchman⟩. — *v.* 巡逻 xúnluó.

patron *n.* ①资助人 zīzhùrén ⟨sponsor⟩. ②顾客 gùkè ⟨customer⟩.

patronize *v.* ①光顾 guānggù, 惠顾 huìgù ⟨shop⟩. ②高高在上 gāogāo-zàishàng ⟨talk down to⟩. ③资助 zīzhù, 赞助 zànzhù ⟨support⟩.

patter *n.* 急速轻拍声 jísù qīngpāishēng.

pattern *n.* ①花样 huāyàng, 样式 yàngshì ⟨design⟩. ②模范 mófàn, 样本 yàngběn ⟨model⟩.

paunch *n.* 大肚子 dàdùzi.

pause *n.* 中止 zhōngzhǐ.

pave *v.* 铺 pū.

pavement *n.* 人行道 rénxíngdào.

pavilion *n.* 亭 tíng, 阁 gé.

paw *n.* 足掌 zúzhǎng, 爪 zhuǎ.

pawn *v.* 典当 diǎndàng, 质押 zhìyā.

pawnshop *n.* 当铺 dàngpù.

pay *v.* 付 fù, 支付 zhīfù. — *n.* 报酬 bàochou.

payable *adj.* ①可支付的 kě zhīfù de ⟨may be paid⟩. ②应支付的 yīng zhīfù de ⟨must be paid⟩.

payday *n.* 发薪日 fāxīnrì.

payee *n.* 收款人 shōukuǎnrén.

payer *n.* 付款人 fùkuǎnrén.

payment *n.* ①支付 zhīfù ⟨paying⟩. ②支付金额 zhīfù jīn'é ⟨amount of money⟩.

PC 个人机 gèrénjī / 个人电脑 gèrén diànnǎo ⟨personal computer⟩.

PDA 个人数字助理 gèrén shùzì zhùlǐ / 个人数位助理 gèrén shùwèi zhùlǐ ⟨personal digital assistant⟩.

pea *n.* 豌豆 wāndòu.

peace *n.* 和平 hépíng.

peaceful *adj.* 和平的 hépíng de.

peacemaker *n.* 调停人 tiáotíngrén.

peach *n.* ①桃子 táozi ⟨fruit⟩. ②桃树 táoshù ⟨tree⟩.

peacock *n.* 孔雀 kǒngquè.

peak *n.* 山顶 shāndǐng, 山峰 shānfēng.

peanut *n.* 花生 huāshēng.

pear *n.* ①梨 lí ⟨fruit⟩. ②梨树 líshù ⟨tree⟩.

pearl *n.* 珍珠 zhēnzhū.

peasant *n.* 农夫 nóngfū, 佃农 diànnóng.

peasantry *n.* 农夫 nóngfū.

peat *n.* 泥煤 níméi ⟨turf⟩.

pebble *n.* 小圆石 xiǎo yuánshí, 卵石 luǎnshí.

peck *v.* 啄 zhuó.

peculiar *adj.* ①特有的 tèyǒu de ⟨special⟩. ②奇怪的 qíguài de, 奇异的 qíyì de ⟨strange⟩.

peculiarity n. ①特性 tèxìng, 特色 tèsè (characteristic). ②怪癖 guàipǐ, 怪异 guàiyì (oddity).

pecuniary adj. 金钱上的 jīnqiánshang de.

pedagogy n. 教育学 jiàoyùxué.

pedal n. 踏板 tàbǎn.

pedant n. 迂腐学儒 yūfǔ xuérú.

pedantic adj. 迂儒的 yūrú de, 卖弄学问的 màinong xuéwen de.

peddle v. 沿街叫卖 yánjiē jiàomài (hawk).

peddler n. 小贩 xiǎofàn.

pedestal n. 基座 jīzuò.

pedestrian n. 步行者 bùxíngzhě, 行人 xíngrén.

pediatrics n. 小儿科 xiǎo'érkē.

pedigree n. 系谱 xìpǔ, 家系 jiāxì.

peek n. & v. 偷看 tōukàn.

peel n. 果皮 guǒpí. – v. 剥皮 bāopí / bōpí.

peep n. & v. 偷看 tōukàn, 窥视 kuīshì (peek).

peer n. 同辈 tóngbèi, 同侪 tóngchái. ~ *pressure* 同侪压力 tóngchái yālì. – v. 凝视 níngshì.

peevish adj. 脾气暴躁的 píqi bàozào de.

peg n. 木钉 mùdìng. – v. 钉住 dìngzhù.

pelican n. 鹈鹕 tíhú.

pellet n. ①小球 xiǎoqiú (small ball). ②小弹丸 xiǎo dànwán 〈gun〉. ③药丸 yàowán (pill).

pelt n. 毛皮 máopí.

pelvis n. 骨盆 gǔpén.

pen n. 笔 bǐ. ~ *pal* 笔友 bǐyǒu.

penal adj. 刑罚的 xíngfá de.

penalize v. 处罚 chǔfá.

penalty n. ①刑罚 xíngfá (punishment). ②罚金 fájīn (fine). ③判罚 pànfá 〈sports〉.

penance n. 忏悔 chànhuǐ, 赎罪 shúzuì.

pencil n. 铅笔 qiānbǐ.

pendant n. 垂饰 chuíshì.

pending adj. ①未决定的 wèi juédìng de (not yet decided). ②待解决的 dài jiějué de (not yet settled).

pendulum n. 钟摆 zhōngbǎi.

penetrate v. ①穿透 chuāntòu (bore through). ②渗透 shèntòu (spread through). ③洞察 dòngchá (see through). ④渗入 shènrù (infiltrate).

penguin n. 企鹅 qǐ'é / qì'é.

penicillin n. 盘尼西林 pánníxīlín.

peninsula n. 半岛 bàndǎo.

penis n. 阴茎 yīnjīng.

penitence n. 忏悔 chànhuǐ.

penknife n. 小刀 xiǎodāo.

penniless adj. 身无分文的 shēnwúfēnwén de.

penny n. ①便士 biànshì 〈British coin〉. ②一分 yì fēn (cent).

pension n. 养老金 yǎnglǎojīn (subsidy), 退休金 tuìxiūjīn (retirement pay).

pensive adj. 沉思的 chénsī de.

pentagon n. 五角形 wǔjiǎoxíng.

penthouse n. 阁楼 gélóu, 顶楼公寓 dǐnglóu gōngyù.

people n. ①人们 rénmen (persons). ②民族 mínzú (race).

pepper n. 胡椒 hújiāo.

peppermint n. 薄荷 bòhe.

P

per *prep.* 每 měi.

perceive *v.* 感觉 gǎnjué (feel), 察觉 chájué (see).

percent *n.* 百分比 bǎifēnbǐ.

percentage *n.* 百分率 bǎifēnlǜ.

perceptible *adj.* ①可察觉的 kě chájué de (noticeable). ②明显的 míngxiǎn de.

perception *n.* 感觉 gǎnjué, 知觉 zhījué.

perceptive *adj.* 知觉的 zhījué de.

perch *n.* 栖木 qīmù ⟨branch⟩. — *v.* 栖息 qīxī / qíxī (rest).

percolate *v.* 过滤 guòlǜ.

percussion *n.* 冲击 chōngjī / chōngjí, 碰撞 pèngzhuàng.

perdition *n.* 地狱 dìyù (hell).

perennial *adj.* 永久的 yǒngjiǔ de. — *n.* 多年生植物 duōniánshēng zhíwù.

perfect *adj.* ①完美的 wánměi de, 理想的 lǐxiǎng de (faultless). ②完全的 wánquán de (complete).

perfection *n.* ①完美 wánměi (faultlessness). ②完全 wánquán (completeness).

perfectly *adv.* 完全地 wánquán de (completely).

perforate *v.* 穿孔 chuānkǒng, 打洞 dǎdòng.

perform *v.* ①实行 shíxíng, 履行 lǚxíng (carry out). ②表演 biǎoyǎn (act).

performance *n.* ①表演 biǎoyǎn (acting). ②实行 shíxíng, 履行 lǚxíng (carrying out).

performer *n.* 表演者 biǎoyǎnzhě, 演出者 yǎnchūzhě.

perfume *n.* ①香味 xiāngwèi (fragrant smell). ②香水 xiāngshuǐ ⟨liquid⟩.

perhaps *adv.* 或许 huòxǔ, 可能 kěnéng.

peril *n.* 危险 wēixiǎn / wéixiǎn.

perimeter *n.* 周边 zhōubiān, 周围 zhōuwéi (periphery).

period *n.* ①时期 shíqī / shíqí, 期间 qījiān / qíjiān ⟨time⟩. ②句点 jùdiǎn (full stop).

periodical *n.* 期刊 qīkān / qíkān. — *adj.* 定期的 dìngqī de / dìngqí de.

periphery *n.* 周围 zhōuwéi.

periscope *n.* 潜望镜 qiánwàngjìng.

perish *v.* 死 sǐ, 死亡 sǐwáng (die).

peritonitis *n.* 腹膜炎 fùmóyán.

perjure *v.* 做伪证 zuò wěizhèng / zuò wèizhèng ⟨law⟩.

perm *n. & v.* 烫发 tàngfà / tàngfǎ.

permanence *n.* 永恒 yǒnghéng, 永久 yǒngjiǔ.

permanent *adj.* 永久的 yǒngjiǔ de.

permeate *v.* 弥漫 mímàn, 渗透 shèntòu.

permissible *adj.* 可容许的 kě róngxǔ de.

permission *n.* 许可 xǔkě, 允许 yǔnxǔ.

permissive *adj.* ①纵容的 zòngróng de (allowing too much freedom). ②准许的 zhǔnxǔ de (permissible).

permit *v.* 允许 yǔnxǔ, 准许 zhǔnxǔ. — *n.* 许可证 xǔkězhèng.

pernicious *adj.* 有害的 yǒuhài de.

perpendicular *adj.* ①垂直的 chuízhí de (vertical). ②成直

perpetrate v. 犯罪 fànzuì, 作恶 zuò'è.

perpetual adj. ①不断的 búduàn de (continual). ②永久的 yǒngjiǔ de (permanent).

perpetuate v. 使永久 shǐ yǒngjiǔ.

perpetuity n. 永久 yǒngjiǔ (eternity).

perplex v. 使迷惑 shǐ míhuò.

persecute v. 迫害 pòhài.

perseverance n. 坚忍 jiānrěn.

persevere v. 坚忍 jiānrěn, 坚持 jiānchí.

persimmon n. ①柿子 shìzi ⟨fruit⟩. ②柿子树 shìzishù ⟨tree⟩.

persist v. 坚持 jiānchí, 固执 gùzhí.

persistent adj. 坚持的 jiānchí de (persevering), 固执的 gùzhí de (stubborn).

person n. 人 rén.

personal adj. ①个人的 gèrén de, 私人的 sīrén de (private). ②本人的 běnrén de, 亲自的 qīnzì de (in person).

~ *computer* 个人计 gèrénjì / 个人电脑 gèrén diànnǎo.

personality n. ①个性 gèxìng, 性格 xìnggé (character). ②名人 míngrén (celebrity).

personally adv. 亲自地 qīnzì de.

personify v. 拟人化 nǐrénhuà.

personnel n. (pl.) 全体人员 quántǐ rényuán.

perspective n. ①透视法 tòushìfǎ ⟨art⟩. ②远景 yuǎnjǐng (outlook).

perspire v. 流汗 liúhàn.

persuade v. 说服 shuōfú / shuìfú, 劝服 quànfú.

persuasion n. ①说服 shuōfú / shuìfú (persuading). ②确信 quèxìn (belief).

persuasive adj. 有说服力的 yǒu shuōfúlì de / yǒu shuìfúlì de.

pert adj. ①冒失的 màoshī de, 鲁莽的 lǔmǎng de (impertinent). ②活泼的 huópō de (lively).

pertain v. ①有关 yǒuguān (be connected with). ②属于 shǔyú (belong to).

pertinent adj. ①有关的 yǒuguān de (relevant to). ②适切的 shìqiè de (to the point).

perturb v. 扰乱 rǎoluàn, 使不安 shǐ bù'ān.

pervade v. 弥漫 mímàn, 遍及 biànjí.

perverse adj. 乖张的 guāizhāng de, 倔强的 juéjiàng de.

perversion n. ①曲解 qūjiě (distortion). ②倒错 dàocuò (abnormality).

perversity n. 乖僻 guāipì, 倔强 juéjiàng.

pervert v. ①曲解 qūjiě (distort). ②使堕落 shǐ duòluò (go astray). — n. 变态 biàntài.

pessimism n. 悲观 bēiguān.

pessimist n. 悲观者 bēiguānzhě.

pest n. ①令人讨厌者 lìng rén tǎoyàn zhě (annoyance). ②害虫 hàichóng ⟨insect⟩.

pester v. 烦扰 fánrǎo.

pesticide n. 杀虫剂 shāchóngjì.

pet n. 伴侣动物 bànlǚ dòngwù, 安慰动物 ānwèi

dòngwù / 宠物 chǒngwù 〈animal〉. — v. 爱抚 àifǔ.

petal n. 花瓣 huābàn.

petition n. 请愿 qǐngyuàn, 陈情 chénqíng.

petrify v. ①使石化 shǐ shíhuà (change into stone). ②吓呆 xiàdāi (terrify).

petrol n. 汽油 qìyóu.

petroleum n. 石油 shíyóu.

petticoat n. 衬裙 chènqún.

petty adj. ①不重要的 bú zhòngyào de (unimportant). ②心胸狭窄的 xīnxiōng-xiázhǎi de (small-minded).

petulant adj. 易怒的 yìnù de.

pew n. 教堂长凳 jiàotáng chángdèng.

phantom n. ①幽灵 yōulíng (ghost). ②幻影 huànyǐng (illusion).

Pharaoh n. 法老 Fǎlǎo.

pharmacology n. 药物学 yàowùxué.

pharmacy n. 药房 yàofáng.

phase n. 阶段 jiēduàn, 时期 shíqī / shíqí (stage).

pheasant n. 雉 zhì.

phenomenal adj. 惊人的 jīngrén de (extraordinary).

phenomenon n. ①现象 xiànxiàng (event). ②特殊的人 tèshū de rén (very unusual person).

philosopher n. 哲学家 zhéxuéjiā.

philosophical adj. ①哲学的 zhéxué de (of philosophy). ②冷静的 lěngjìng de (calm).

philosophy n. 哲学 zhéxué, 哲理 zhélǐ.

phlegm n. 痰 tán.

phlegmatic adj. 迟钝的 chídùn de.

phobia n. 恐惧 kǒngjù.

phone n. 电话 diànhuà. ~ **card** 电话卡 diànhuàkǎ. — v. 打电话 dǎ diànhuà.

phone booth n. 公共电话亭 gōnggòng diànhuàtíng.

phoneme n. 音素 yīnsù.

phonetic adj. 语音的 yǔyīn de.

phonetics n. 语音学 yǔyīnxué.

phoney adj. 假的 jiǎ de (fake), 伪造的 wěizào de / wěizào de (false). — n. 赝品 yànpǐn.

phosphorescence n. 磷光 língguāng.

phosphorus n. 磷 lín.

photo n. 照片 zhàopiàn, 相片 xiàngpiàn.

photocopy n. 影印本 yǐngyìnběn. — v. 影印 yǐngyìn.

photogenic adj. 上镜头的 shàng jìngtóu de.

photograph n. 照片 zhàopiàn, 相片 xiàngpiàn. — v. 照相 zhàoxiàng 〈still〉, 摄影 shèyǐng 〈movies〉.

photographer n. 摄影家 shèyǐngjiā.

photography n. 摄影术 shèyǐngshù.

phrase n. ①片语 piànyǔ 〈grammar〉. ②措辞 cuòcí (expression).

physical adj. ①身体的 shēntǐ de (bodily). ②物质的 wùzhì de / wùzhì de (material).

physician n. 内科医生 nèikē yīshēng.

physicist n. 物理学家 wùlǐxué jiā.

physics n. 物理学 wùlǐxué.

physiology n. 生理学 shēnglǐxué.

physique *n.* 体格 tǐgé.

pianist *n.* 钢琴家 gāngqínjiā, 钢琴师 gāngqínshī.

piano *n.* 钢琴 gāngqín.

pick *v.* ①挑选 tiāoxuǎn (select). ②采 cǎi, 摘 zhāi (pluck).

picket *n.* ①尖桩 jiānzhuāng (stake). ②哨兵 shàobīng, 步哨 bùshào (soldier). — *v.* 站哨 纠察 zhànshào jiūchá (demonstrate).

pickle *n.* 腌汁 yānzhī (brine). — *v.* 腌 yān.

pickpocket *n.* 扒手 páshǒu.

picnic *n.* 野餐 yěcān.

pictorial *adj.* 图画的 túhuà de.

picture *n.* ①画 huà, 图画 túhuà (painting). ②照片 zhàopiàn (photograph). — *v.* ①描绘 miáohuì (portray). ②想象 xiǎngxiàng (imagine).

picturesque *adj.* 如画的 rúhuà de (charming).

pidgin *n.* 洋泾浜语 yángjīngbāngyǔ.

pie *n.* 馅饼 xiànbǐng, 派 pài.

piece *n.* ①片 piàn (slice), 块 kuài (chip). ②部分 bùfen (part). ③一首 yìshǒu (music). ④一篇 yìpiān (article).

piecemeal *adv.* ①逐渐地 zhújiàn de (little by little). ②零碎地 língsuì de, 片断地 piànduàn de (piece by piece).

pier *n.* 码头 mǎtou.

pierce *v.* 戳入 chuōrù, 刺 cì (penetrate).

piety *n.* 虔敬 qiánjìng, 虔诚 qiánchéng.

pig *n.* 猪 zhū.

pigeon *n.* 鸽子 gēzi.

pigment *n.* ①颜料 yánliào (colored powder). ②色素 sèsù (natural coloring matter).

pike *n.* 矛 máo (long-handled spear).

pile *n.* ①一堆 yìduī (heap). ②桩 zhuāng (post). — *v.* 堆积 duījī, 堆起 duīqǐ (heap).

pilfer *v.* 扒窃 páqiè, 偷窃 tōuqiè.

pilgrim *n.* 朝圣者 cháoshèngzhě.

pilgrimage *n.* 朝圣旅程 cháoshèng lǚchéng.

pill *n.* 药丸 yàowán.

pillage *n. & v.* 掠夺 lüèduó, 劫掠 jiélüè.

pillar *n.* 柱子 zhùzi (staff).

pillow *n.* 枕头 zhěntou.

pillowcase *n.* 枕头套 zhěntoutào.

pilot *n.* ①驾驶员 jiàshǐyuán (airman). ②领航员 línghángyuán (navigator). — *v.* 领航 língháng (navigate).

pimple *n.* 粉刺 fěncì, 青春痘 qīngchūndòu.

pin *n.* 大头针 dàtóuzhēn, 别针 biézhēn (tack).

pincers *n. (pl.)* 钳子 qiánzi (pliers).

pinch *n.* 捏 niē, 夹 jiā / jiá (nip).

pine *n.* ①松树 sōngshù (tree). ②松木 sōngmù (wood).

pineapple *n.* 凤梨 fènglí.

pinhole *n.* 针孔 zhēnkǒng.

pinion *n.* 翼 yì, 翅膀 chìbǎng (wing). — *v.* 束缚 shùfù / shúfù.

pink *n. & adj.* 粉红色 fěnhóngsè.

pinnacle *n.* ①尖顶 jiāndǐng, 尖峰 jiānfēng (peak). ②尖塔 jiāntǎ (spire).

pinpoint *n.* 针尖 zhēnjiān (point of a pin).

pint *n.* 品脱 pǐntuō.

P

pioneer *n.* 拓荒者 tuòhuāngzhě (first settler), 先锋 xiānfēng (forerunner). — *v.* 开拓 kāituò, 作先锋 zuò xiānfēng.

pious *adj.* 虔诚的 qiánchéng de.

pipe *n.* ①管 guǎn (tube). ②烟斗 yāndǒu 〈for smoking〉.

piquant *adj.* ①开胃的 kāiwèi de (tasty). ②辛辣的 xīnlà de (spicy). ③有趣的 yǒuqù de (interesting).

piracy *n.* ①海上抢劫 hǎishang qiǎngjié 〈ships〉. ②盗版 dàobǎn 〈software〉.

pirate *n.* 海盗 hǎidào (freebooter). — *v.* 盗印 dàoyìn (print illegally), 侵害著作权 qīnhài zhùzuòquán (infringe on copyright).

Pisces 双鱼座 Shuāngyúzuò.

pistol *n.* 手枪 shǒuqiāng.

piston *n.* 活塞 huósāi.

pit *n.* 坑 kēng (hole).

pitch *v.* ①扎营 zhāyíng / zháyíng (tent). ②投掷 tóuzhì / tóuzhí (throw). — *n.* ①投掷 tóuzhì / tóuzhí (throwing). ②倾斜度 qīngxiédù (slope).

pitcher *n.* ①水罐 shuǐguàn (jug). ②投手 tóushǒu 〈baseball〉.

piteous *adj.* 可怜的 kělián de.

pitfall *n.* 陷阱 xiànjǐng, 圈套 quāntào (trap).

pith *n.* 髓 suǐ.

pitiable *adj.* 可怜的 kělián de.

pitiful *adj.* 可怜的 kělián de.

pitiless *adj.* 无情的 wúqíng de, 无怜悯心的 wú liánmǐnxīn de.

pittance *n.* 微薄收入 wēibó shōurù / wéibó shōurù.

pity *n.* 怜悯 liánmǐn, 同情 tóngqíng.

pivot *n.* 旋轴 xuánzhóu, 枢轴 shūzhóu (swivel). — *v.* 以轴为中心旋转 yǐ zhóu wéi zhōngxīn xuánzhuǎn.

pixy *n.* 小精灵 xiǎo jīnglíng.

pizza *n.* 皮杂饼 pízábǐng / 披萨 pīsà, 意大利薄馅饼 yìdàlì báo xiànbǐng / 义大利薄馅饼 yìdàlì bó xiànbǐng.

placard *n.* 招贴 zhāotiē.

placate *v.* 抚慰 fǔwèi.

place *n.* ①地方 dìfang (area), 场所 chǎngsuǒ (location). ②地点 dìdiǎn (point). — *v.* 放 fàng, 置放 zhìfàng (put).

placenta *n.* 胎盘 tāipán.

placid *adj.* ①平静的 píngjìng de (calm). ②温和的 wēnhé de (even-tempered).

plague *n.* 瘟疫 wēnyì.

plaid *n.* 格子呢 géziní.

plain *adj.* ①清楚的 qīngchu de, 明白的 míngbai de (clear). ②平淡的 píngdàn de, 简单的 jiǎndān de (ordinary).

plaint *n.* 悲叹 bēitàn, 诉苦 sùkǔ (lament).

plaintiff *n.* 原告 yuángào.

plait *n.* 发辫 fàbiàn / fǎbiàn (braid). — *v.* 编成辫 biānchéng biàn (braid).

plan *n.* ①计画 jìhuà, 方案 fāng'àn (project). ②设计图 shèjìtú (diagram). — *v.* ①计画 jìhuà, 打算 dǎsuàn (intend). ②设计 shèjì (design).

plane *n.* ①飞机 fēijī (airplane). ②平面 píngmiàn (level).

planet *n.* 行星 xíngxīng.

planetarium *n.* 天文馆 tiānwénguǎn 〈building〉.

plank *n.* 厚板 hòubǎn (board).

plankton *n.* 浮游生物 fúyóu

shēngwù.

plant n. ①植物 zhíwù〈living〉.
②工厂 gōngchǎng (factory).
— v. 栽种 zāizhòng, 种植
zhòngzhí (sow).

plantation n. ①农场
nóngchǎng (farm). ②植林地
zhílíndì (for trees).

plaque n. 匾额 biǎn'é, 牌匾
páibiǎn.

plaster n. 灰泥 huīní.

plastic adj. 塑料的 sùliào de /
塑胶的 sùjiāo de. — n. 塑料
sùliào / 塑胶 sùjiāo.

plate n. 盘 pán, 碟 dié (dish).

plateau n. 高原 gāoyuán, 高
地 gāodì (tableland).

platform n. ①讲台 jiǎngtái
(podium). ②月台 yuètái (station).

platinum n. 白金 báijīn.
— adj. 白金的 báijīn de.

platitude n. 陈腔滥调
chénqiāng-làndiào.

platoon n. 排 pái, 小队
xiǎoduì.

plausible adj. 似合理的 sì
hélǐ de (reasonable).

play n. ①游戏 yóuxì, 游玩
yóuwán (amusement). ②戏剧
xìjù (drama). — v. ①玩 wán
(have fun). ②扮演 bànyǎn
(act). ③弹奏 tánzòu, 演奏
yǎnzòu (perform). ④比赛 bǐsài
(compete).

playboy n. 花花公子 huāhuā-
-gōngzǐ.

playful adj. 好嬉戏的 hào
xìxì de.

playground n. 游乐场
yóulèchǎng.

playmate n. 玩伴 wánbàn,
游伴 yóubàn.

plea n. ①辩解 biànjiě, 抗辩

kàngbiàn (appeal). ②恳求
kěnqiú (request).

plead v. ①辩护 biànhù
(appeal). ②恳求 kěnqiú
(request).

pleasant adj. 愉快的 yúkuài
de.

pleasantry n. 幽默 yōumò,
诙谐 huīxié (humorous
remark).

please v. ①使高兴 shǐ
gāoxìng, 取悦 qǔyuè (amuse).
②请 qǐng (request politely).

pleasure n. ①快乐 kuàilè
(enjoyment). ②乐趣 lèqù
(amusement).

pleat n. 褶 zhě / zhé. — v.
打褶 dǎzhě / dǎzhé.

pledge n. ①抵押品 dǐyāpǐn
(surety). ②誓言 shìyán, 誓约
shìyuē (vow). — v. 发誓 fāshì,
保证 bǎozhèng (guarantee).

plentiful adj. 丰富的 fēngfù
de, 充分的 chōngfèn de.

plenty n. 丰富 fēngfù, 充分
chōngfèn (fullness).

pliable adj. ①易曲的 yì qū de
(bendable). ②易受影响的 yì
shòu yǐngxiǎng de (easily led).

pliers n. 钳子 qiánzi.

plight n. 处境 chǔjìng, 情况
qíngkuàng.

plod v. ①蹒跚而行 pánshān-
érxíng / mánshān'érxíng,
重步行走 zhòngbù xíngzǒu
(trudge). ②孜孜从事 zīzī-
cóngshì (work).

plot n. ①阴谋 yīnmóu (plan).
②情节 qíngjié〈story〉. ③小块
地 xiǎokuài dì (small piece of
land). — v. ①图谋 túmóu, 密
谋 mìmóu (collude). ②制……
之图 zhì...zhī tú (chart).

plow n. 犁 lí.

ploy *n.* 策略 cèlüè.

pluck *v.* ①摘 zhāi, 采 cǎi (pick). ②拉 lā (pull).

plug *n.* ①塞子 sāizi (stopper). ②插头 chātóu ⟨electrical⟩. — *v.* 塞住 sāizhù ⟨block⟩.

plum *n.* ①李树 lǐshù, 梅树 méishù ⟨tree⟩. ②李子 lǐzi, 梅子 méizi ⟨fruit⟩.

plumage *n.* 羽毛 yǔmáo (feathers).

plumb *n.* 铅锤 qiānchuí. — *adj.* ①垂直的 chuízhí de (vertical). ②完全的 wánquán de (absolute).

plumber *n.* 铅管工人 qiānguǎn gōngrén.

plummet *n.* 铅锤 qiānchuí. — *v.* 垂直落下 chuízhí luòxia.

plump *adj.* 圆胖的 yuánpàng de.

plunder *v.* 掠夺 lüèduó. — *n.* 掠夺物 lüèduówù.

plunge *v.* ①跳进 tiàojin (fall into). ②投入 tóurù, 陷入 xiànrù (put into).

plural *adj.* 复数的 fùshù de. — *n.* 复数 fùshù ⟨grammar⟩.

plus *prep.* 加 jiā, 加上 jiāshang.

plush *n.* 丝绒 sīróng.

plutonium *n.* 钚bù.

ply *v.* ①定期来回 dìngqī láihuí / dìngqī láihuí (go back and forth regularly). ②经营 jīngyíng, 从事 cóngshì (work).

plywood *n.* 三夹板 sānjiābǎn / sānjiábǎn, 胶板 hébǎn.

p.m., P.M. *adj. & adv.* 下午 xiàwǔ, 午后 wǔhòu.

pneumonia *n.* 肺炎 fèiyán.

pock *n.* 痘痕 dòuhén, 麻子 mázi, 痘疱 dòupào.

pocket *n.* 口袋 kǒudài, 衣袋

yīdài.

pod *n.* 豆荚 dòujiá (beans).

poem *n.* 诗 shī, 韵文 yùnwén.

poet *n.* 诗人 shīrén. **~ laureate** 桂冠诗人 guìguān shīrén.

poetic *adj.* 诗的 shī de, 诗意 的 shīyì de.

poetry *n.* 诗 shī, 诗歌 shīgē.

poignant *adj.* ①痛切的 tòngqiè de (painful). ②深刻的 shēnkè de (deeply moving).

point *n.* ①尖端 jiānduān (sharp end). ②点 diǎn (dot). ③地点 dìdiǎn (place). ④要点 yàodiǎn (main idea). ⑤特点 tèdiǎn (quality). **~ of view** 见解 jiànjiě, 看法 kànfǎ. — *v.* 指 zhǐ, 指出 zhǐchū (indicate).

point-blank *adj. & adv.* ①近 距离射击的 jìn jùlí shèjí de / jìn jùlí shèjí de ⟨shot⟩. ②率直 的 shuàizhí de (direct).

pointed *adj.* ①尖的 jiān de (sharp). ②尖锐的 jiānruì de (biting).

pointer *n.* ①指示棒 zhǐshìbàng ⟨stick⟩. ②指针 zhǐzhēn (indicator).

pointless *adj.* 无意义的 wú yìyì de (meaningless).

poise *n.* 镇定 zhèndìng (calmness).

poison *n.* 毒物 dúwù, 毒药 dúyào. — *v.* 下毒 xiàdú, 毒害 dúhài.

poisonous *adj.* 有毒的 yǒudú de.

poke *v.* 刺 cì, 戳 chuō (thrust).

poker *n.* 扑克牌戏 pūkèpáixì. **~ face** 扑克脸 pūkèliǎn.

polar *adj.* ①近北极的 jìn běijí de ⟨north⟩. ②近南极的 jìn nánjí de ⟨south⟩.

pole *n.* ①北极 běijí ⟨north⟩.

②南极 nánjí 〈south〉. ③磁极 cíjí 〈magnet〉. ④电极 diànjí 〈electrical〉. ⑤竿 gān, 柱 zhù, 杆 gǎn 〈long stick〉.

police n. 警察 jǐngchá. **~ officer** 警员 jǐngyuán, 警官 jǐngguān.

policeman n. 警察 jǐngchá.

policewoman n. 女警 nǔjǐng.

policy n. ①政策 zhèngcè 〈strategy〉. ②保险单 bǎoxiǎndān 〈insurance〉.

polish v. 擦亮 cāliàng 〈rubbing〉, 磨光 móguāng 〈grinding〉. — n. ①光泽 guāngzé, 光滑 guānghuá 〈brightness〉. ②优雅 yōuyǎ 〈elegance〉.

Polish adj. 波兰的 Bōlán de. — n. 波兰语 Bōlányǔ.

polite adj. 有礼貌的 yǒu lǐmào de.

political adj. 政治的 zhèngzhì de.

politician n. 政治家 zhèngzhìjiā 〈profession〉, 政客 zhèngkè 〈negative connotation〉.

politics n. ①政治 zhèngzhì 〈art〉. ②政治学 zhèngzhìxué 〈science〉. ③政见 zhèngjiàn 〈views〉.

polka n. 波卡舞 bōkǎwǔ.

poll n. ①投票 tóupiào 〈ballot〉. ②民意调查 mínyì diàochá 〈survey〉.

pollen n. 花粉 huāfěn.

pollute v. 污染 wūrǎn.

pollution n. 污染 wūrǎn.

polo n. 马球 mǎqiú.

polygamy n. 一夫多妻 yìfū-duōqī.

polygon n. 多角形 duōjiǎoxíng, 多边形 duōbiānxíng.

polytheism n. 多神论 duōshénlùn.

pomade n. 发油 fàyóu / fǎyóu.

pomegranate n. 石榴 shíliu.

pompous adj. 自大的 zìdà de.

poncho n. 斗篷 dǒupeng.

pond n. 池塘 chítáng.

ponder v. 仔细考虑 zǐxì kǎolǜ, 沉思 chénsī.

ponderous adj. ①笨重的 bènzhòng de 〈heavy〉. ②慢吞吞的 màntūntūn de 〈slow〉.

pony n. 小马 xiǎomǎ.

ponytail n. 马尾 mǎwěi.

pool n. ①池 chí, 水塘 shuǐtáng 〈pond〉. ②游泳池 yóuyǒngchí 〈swimming pool〉. ③总赌注 zǒngdǔzhù 〈gambling〉.

poolroom n. 撞球场 zhuàngqiúchǎng.

poor adj. ①贫穷的 pínqióng de 〈having no money〉. ②可怜的 kělián de 〈pathetic〉. ③坏的 huài de, 差的 chà de / chā de 〈bad〉. ④贫瘠的 pínjí de 〈barren〉.

pop v. 发短促爆裂声 fā duǎncù bàolièshēng 〈explode lightly〉. — n. 短促爆裂声 duǎncù bàolièshēng 〈sound〉. — adj. 流行的 liúxíng de. **~ art** 普普艺术 pǔpǔ yìshù.

popcorn n. 爆米花 bàomǐhuā.

pope n. 教皇 jiàohuáng / 教宗 jiàozōng.

poplar n. 白杨 báiyáng.

poppy n. 罂粟 yīngsù.

populace n. 平民 píngmín, 民众 mínzhòng 〈common people〉.

popular adj. ①受欢迎的 shòu huānyíng de 〈accepted〉. ②流行的 liúxíng de 〈fashion-

able).

popularity *n.* 流行程度 liúxíng chéngdù.

popularize *v.* 使流行 shǐ liúxíng (make fashionable), 使普遍 shǐ pǔbiàn (broaden appeal of).

populate *v.* 居住于 jūzhù yú.

population *n.* 人口 rénkǒu.

populous *adj.* 人口稠密的 rénkǒu chóumì de.

porcelain *n.* 瓷器 cíqì.

porch *n.* 门廊 ménláng.

pore *n.* 毛孔 máokǒng.

pork *n.* 猪肉 zhūròu.

pornography *n.* 色情文字 sèqíng wénzì 〈writing〉, 色情照片 sèqíng zhàopiàn 〈picture〉.

porous *adj.* 多孔的 duōkǒng de, 有细孔的 yǒu xìkǒng de.

porpoise *n.* 海豚 hǎitún.

porridge *n.* 麦片粥 màipiànzhōu.

port *n.* 港口 gǎngkǒu, 埠 bù.

portable *adj.* 可携带的 kě xiédài de / kě xídài de.

portal *n.* 入口 rùkǒu 〈door〉.

portend *v.* 预示 yùshì.

porter *n.* ①搬运工 bānyùngōng, 挑夫 tiāofū 〈carrier〉. ②门房 ménfáng 〈door-keeper〉.

portfolio *n.* ①公事包 gōngshìbāo, 档案夹 dàng'ànjiā / dǎng'ànjiá 〈holder〉. ②档案文件 dàng'àn wénjiàn / dǎng'àn wénjiàn 〈folder〉.

porthole *n.* 舷窗 xiánchuāng.

portico *n.* 门廊 ménláng.

portion *n.* 部分 bùfen. — *v.* 分配 fēnpèi.

portly *adj.* 壮硕的 zhuàngshuò de.

portrait *n.* ①肖像 xiàoxiàng 〈drawing〉. ②描写 miáoxiě 〈description〉.

portray *v.* 描绘 miáohuì, 描写 miáoxiě 〈represent〉.

Portuguese *n. & adj.* ①葡萄牙人 Pútáoyárén 〈people〉. ②葡萄牙语 Pútáoyáyǔ 〈language〉.

pose *n.* ①姿势 zīshì 〈posture〉. ②装模作样 zhuāngmú-zuò-yàng / zhuāngmó-zuòyàng 〈act〉. — *v.* ①摆姿势 bǎi zīshì 〈model〉. ②提出 tíchū 〈ask〉.

posh *adj.* 豪华的 háohuá de.

position *n.* ①位置 wèizhì 〈location〉. ②工作 gōngzuò, 职位 zhíwèi 〈job〉. ③地位 dìwèi 〈rank〉. ④姿势 zīshì 〈pose〉.

positive *adj.* ①确定的 quèdìng de, 确实的 quèshí de 〈affirmative〉. ②明确的 míngquè de 〈explicit〉. ③积极的 jījí de, 有助益的 yǒu zhùyì de 〈beneficial〉. — *n.* ①阳极 yángjí 〈electricity〉. ②正数 zhèngshù 〈mathematics〉.

possess *v.* 拥有 yōngyǒu / yǒngyǒu.

possession *n.* 所有物 suǒyǒuwù.

possessive *adj.* ①有占有欲的 yǒu zhànyǒuyù de 〈domineering〉. ②所有格的 suǒyǒugé de 〈grammar〉.

possibility *n.* 可能 kěnéng 〈option〉, 可能性 kěnéngxìng 〈probability〉.

possible *adj.* 可能的 kěnéng de.

possibly *adv.* 或许 huòxǔ.

post *n.* ①邮件 yóujiàn 〈mail〉.

P

②邮政 yóuzhèng (postal service). ③柱 zhù, 桩 zhuāng (pole). ④哨站 shàozhàn, 岗位 gǎngwèi (sentry). ⑤职位 zhíwèi, 工作 gōngzuò (job). ~ *office* 邮局 yóujú. — *v.* ①邮寄 yóují (mail). ②张贴 zhāngtiē (stick up). ③公告 gōnggào, 公布 gōngbù (announce).

postage *n.* 邮资 yóuzī.

postcard *n.* 明信片 míngxìnpiàn.

poster *n.* 海报 hǎibào, 大幅广告 dàfú guǎnggào (placard).

posterior *adj.* 在后的 zàihòu de. — *n.* 臀部 túnbù.

posterity *n.* 后代 hòudài.

postgraduate *n.* 研究生 yánjiūshēng / yánjiùshēng.

posthumous *adj.* 死后的 sǐhòu de.

postman *n.* 邮差 yóuchāi.

postmark *n.* 邮戳 yóuchuō.

postmaster *n.* 邮政局长 yóuzhèng júzhǎng.

postmodernism *n.* 后现代主义 hòuxiàndài zhǔyì.

postmortem *adj.* 死后的 sǐhòu de. — *n.* 验尸 yànshī.

postpone *v.* 延期 yánqī / yánqí.

postscript *n.* 附笔 fùbǐ, 后记 hòujì.

posture *n.* ①姿势 zīshì ⟨physical⟩. ②态度 tàidu ⟨mental⟩. — *v.* 摆出姿势 bǎichu zīshì.

postwar *adj.* 战后的 zhànhòu de.

pot *n.* 壶 hú ⟨tea⟩, 盆 pén ⟨flowers⟩, 锅 guō ⟨cooking⟩.

potassium *n.* 钾 jiǎ.

potato *n.* 土豆 tǔdòu / 马铃薯 mǎlíngshǔ, 洋芋 yángyù.

potent *adj.* ①有效的 yǒuxiào de (effective). ②有力的 yǒulì de (powerful).

potential *adj.* 有可能性的 yǒu kěnéngxìng de, 潜在的 qiánzài de.

potter *n.* 陶工 táogōng.

pottery *n.* 陶器 táoqì.

pouch *n.* 小袋 xiǎodài.

poultice *n.* 膏药 gāoyào.

poultry *n.* 家禽 jiāqín.

pounce *v.* 扑过去 pūguoqu.

pound *n.* ①磅 bàng ⟨weight⟩. ②镑 bàng ⟨money⟩. ③兽栏 shòulán (enclosure). — *v.* 连续重击 liánxù zhòngjī / liánxù zhòngjí (strike).

pour *v.* 倒 dào, 灌 guàn.

poverty *n.* 贫穷 pínqióng (state of being poor).

powder *n.* 粉 fěn, 粉末 fěnmò. — *v.* ①使成粉 shǐ chéng fěn (reduce to powder). ②撒粉 sǎ fěn (put powder on).

power *n.* ①力 lì, 力量 lìliang (strength). ②能力 nénglì (ability). ③权力 quánlì, 势力 shìlì (authority).

powerboat *n.* 汽艇 qìtǐng.

powerful *adj.* 有力的 yǒulì de, 强的 qiáng de.

powerless *adj.* ①无力的 wúlì de ⟨strength⟩. ②无权的 wúquán de (without authority).

practical *adj.* ①实际的 shíjì de (realistic). ②实用的 shíyòng de (useful). ③应用的 yìngyòng de (applied). ~ *joke* 恶作剧 èzuòjù.

practically *adv.* ①实际上 shíjìshang, 事实上 shìshíshang (virtually). ②几乎 jīhū (almost).

practice n. ①练习 liànxí (exercise). ②习惯 xíguàn (habit). ③实行 shíxíng (application). — v. ①练习 liànxí, 训练 xùnliàn (exercise). ②实行 shíxíng (carry out).

pragmatic adj. 实用主义的 shíyòng zhǔyì de (practical).

pragmatics n. 语用学 yǔyòngxué.

prairie n. 大草原 dà cǎoyuán (plain).

praise n. & v. 赞美 zànměi, 称赞 chēngzàn.

praiseworthy adj. 值得赞美的 zhíde zànměi de.

prank n. 恶作剧 èzuòjù.

prattle v. 闲谈 xiántán (chatter).

pray v. 祈祷 qídǎo ⟨hope⟩, 祷告 dǎogào ⟨religion⟩.

prayer n. 祈祷 qídǎo.

preach v. 传教 chuánjiào, 讲道 jiǎngdào ⟨in church⟩.

preacher n. 传道者 chuándàozhě.

precarious adj. ①危险的 wēixiǎn de / wéixiǎn de (dangerous). ②不确定的 bú quèdìng de (uncertain).

precaution n. 预防 yùfáng.

precede v. 在前 zài qián.

precedence n. ①在先 zàixiān ⟨time⟩. ②上位 shàngwèi, 优先权 yōuxiānquán ⟨of importance⟩.

precedent n. 先例 xiānlì.

preceding adj. 在前的 zàiqián de, 在先的 zàixiān de.

precept n. 箴言 zhēnyán.

precinct n. 区域 qūyù (district).

precious adj. 珍贵的 zhēnguì de (valuable).

precipice n. 悬崖 xuányá / xuányái.

precipitate v. ①突然引起 tūrán yǐnqǐ / túrán yǐnqǐ (cause). ②加速……发生 jiāsù...fāshēng (hasten).

precis n. 大纲 dàgāng, 摘要 zhāiyào.

precise adj. ①精确的 jīngquè de (accurate). ②严谨的 yánjǐn de (careful).

precision n. & adj. 精密 jīngmì.

preclude v. 阻止 zǔzhǐ, 排除 páichú (exclude).

precocious adj. 早熟的 zǎoshú de / zǎoshóu de.

predatory adj. 掠夺的 lüèduó de.

predecessor n. ①前任 qiánrèn ⟨position⟩. ②祖先 zǔxiān (ancestor).

predicament n. 苦境 kǔjìng.

predicate n. 述语 shùyǔ ⟨grammar⟩.

predict v. 预言 yùyán, 预料 yùliào.

prediction n. 预言 yùyán.

predilection n. 偏爱 piān'ài, 偏好 piānhào.

predispose v. 偏向于 piānxiàng yú (incline to).

predominant adj. ①有优势的 yǒu yōushì de (prevailing). ②主要的 zhǔyào de (chief).

predominate v. 支配 zhīpèi, 控制 kòngzhì, 占优势 zhàn yōushì.

preeminent adj. 卓越的 zhuóyuè de.

prefabricate v. 预制 yùzhì.

preface n. 序言 xùyán.

prefect n. 长官 zhǎngguān.

prefecture n. 县 xiàn.

prefer v. 较喜欢 jiào xǐhuan, 偏好 piānhào (favor).

preferable adj. 较合意的 jiào héyì de.

preference n. 偏好 piānhào (favoritism).

preferential adj. ①优先的 yōuxiān de (privileged). ②优惠的 yōuhuì de (favorable).

prefix n. 字首 zìshǒu.

pregnancy n. 怀孕 huáiyùn.

prehistoric adj. 史前的 shǐqián de.

prejudge v. 贸然判断 màorán pànduàn.

prejudice n. 偏见 piānjiàn. — v. 使存偏见 shǐ cún piānjiàn (influence unfairly).

preliminary adj. 初步的 chūbù de.

prelude n. 前奏曲 qiánzòuqǔ, 序曲 xùqǔ 〈music〉.

premarital adj. 婚前的 hūnqián de.

premature adj. 过早的 guòzǎo de (too early), 未成熟的 wèi chéngshú de / wèi chéngshóu de (not mature).

premeditate v. 预谋 yùmóu.

premier n. 内阁总理 nèigé zǒnglǐ, 首相 shǒuxiàng. — adj. 首要的 shǒuyào de, 第一的 dì-yī de.

premiere n. 首演 shǒuyǎn.

premise n. 前提 qiántí.

premium n. ①额外费用 éwài fèiyòng (additional payment). ②保险费 bǎoxiǎnfèi 〈insurance〉.

premonition n. 预感 yùgǎn.

preoccupation n. 全神贯注 quánshén-guànzhù, 专心 zhuānxīn (concentration).

preparation n. 准备

zhǔnbèi, 预备 yùbèi (preparing).

preparatory adj. 预备的 yùbèi de. ~ school 大学预科 dàxué yùkē.

prepare v. ①预备 yùbèi, 准备 zhǔnbèi (arrange). ②为……铺路 wèi...pūlù (smooth the way for).

preposition n. 介系词 jièxìcí.

preposterous adj. 荒谬的 huāngmiù de (absurd).

prescribe v. ①开药方 kāi yàofāng 〈medicine〉. ②规定 guīdìng, 指定 zhǐdìng (assign).

prescription n. 药方 yàofāng, 处方 chǔfāng.

prescriptive adj. 规定的 guīdìng de.

presence n. ①在场出席 zàichǎng chūxí (attendance). ②风采 fēngcǎi 〈personality〉.

present v. ①给 gěi, 赠 zèng (give). ②介绍 jièshào (introduce). — n. 礼物 lǐwù. — adj. ①在场的 zàichǎng de (in attendance). ②现在的 xiànzài de (current).

presentation n. ①介绍 jièshào (introducing). ②演出 yǎnchū (acting).

presently adv. ①不久地 bùjiǔ de (soon). ②现在 xiànzài, 目前 mùqián (now).

preservation n. 保存 bǎocún.

preservative n. 防腐剂 fángfǔjì.

preserve v. 保存 bǎocún 〈food〉, 保持 bǎochí (maintain), 保护 bǎohù (protect). — n. ①自然保护区 zìrán bǎohùqū 〈place〉. ②(pl.) 果酱 guǒjiàng (jam).

preside v. ①主持 zhǔchí, 当主席 dāng zhǔxí (be in charge). ②管理 guǎnlǐ (govern).

presidency n. ①职位 zhíwèi (position). ②任期 rènqī / rènqí (term).

president n. ①总统 zǒngtǒng 〈of country〉. ②主席 zhǔxí, 会长 huìzhǎng 〈of a group〉. ③总裁 zǒngcái, 董事长 dǒngshìzhǎng 〈of a company〉.

press v. ①按 àn (push). ②熨烫 yùntàng (iron). ③迫 pò, 逼 bī (force). ④催促 cuīcù (urge). — n. ①压榨机 yāzhàjī 〈machine〉. ②印刷 yìnshuā (printing). ③新闻界 xīnwénjiè 〈newspapers〉. ~ conference 记者会 jìzhěhuì.

pressure n. 压力 yālì.

prestige n. 声望 shēngwàng.

presumable adj. 可假定的 kě jiǎdìng de.

presume v. 推测 tuīcè, 假定 jiǎdìng (suppose).

presumption n. 推测 tuīcè, 假定 jiǎdìng (supposition).

presuppose v. ①事先推定 shìxiān tuīdìng (assume). ②以……为前提 yǐ……wéi qiántí (prerequisite).

pretend v. 假装 jiǎzhuāng (claim).

pretension n. ①主张 zhǔzhāng (claim). ②自负 zìfù (conceit).

pretentious adj. ①自负的 zìfù de (pompous). ②炫耀的 xuànyào de (ostentatious).

pretext n. 借口 jièkǒu.

pretty adj. 漂亮的 piàoliang de (beautiful). — adv. 相当 xiāngdāng.

prevail v. ①盛行 shèngxíng (be widespread). ②战胜 zhànshèng (win).

prevailing adj. 盛行的 shèngxíng de (prevalent).

prevalent adj. 流行的 liúxíng de, 普遍的 pǔbiàn de.

prevent v. ①防止 fángzhǐ, 预防 yùfáng (avoid). ②阻碍 zǔài (hinder).

prevention n. 预防 yùfáng.

preventive adj. 预防的 yùfáng de.

preview n. 试映 shìyìng (see ahead of time), 预告片 yùgàopiàn (trailer).

previous adj. 在前的 zàiqián de, 先前的 xiānqián de (prior).

prey n. 被捕食的动物 bèi bǔshí de dòngwù.

price n. 价格 jiàgé (amount of money), 代价 dàijià (other cost). — v. 定价 dìngjià (set the cost).

priceless adj. 无价的 wújià de.

prick n. 尖刺 jiāncì. — v. ①刺 cì (stab). ②刺痛 cìtòng (hurt).

pride n. ①自尊 zìzūn (dignity). ②骄傲 jiāo'ào (arrogance).

priest n. 教士 jiàoshì, 牧师 mùshī.

primarily adv. 主要地 zhǔyào de.

primary adj. 首要的 shǒuyào de, 主要的 zhǔyào de. ~ school 小学 xiǎoxué.

prime adj. ①主要的 zhǔyào de, 首要的 shǒuyào de (primary). ②最上等的 zuì shàngděng de (best).

primer n. 入门书 rùménshū 〈book〉.

primitive adj. ①原始的 yuánshǐ de (ancient). ②最初的 zuìchū de (basic).

prince n. 王子 wángzǐ.

princess *n.* 公主 gōngzhǔ.

principal *adj.* 主要的 zhǔyào de ⟨chief⟩. — *n.* 校长 xiàozhǎng.

principle *n.* ①原则 yuánzé ⟨rule⟩. ②原理 yuánlǐ ⟨basics⟩. ③主义 zhǔyì ⟨belief⟩.

print *v.* ①印刷 yìnshuā ⟨on paper⟩. ②出版 chūbǎn ⟨publish⟩. — *n.* ①印刷 yìnshuā ⟨printing⟩. ②痕迹 hénjī / hénjì ⟨imprint⟩. ③印刷字体 yìnshuā zìtǐ ⟨characters⟩. *out of ~* 绝版 juébǎn.

printer *n.* ①印刷业者 yìnshuāyè zhě ⟨firm⟩. ②排版 工人 páibǎn gōngrén ⟨worker⟩. ③印刷机 yìnshuājī ⟨machine⟩. ④打印机 dǎyìnjī / 印表机 yìnbiǎojī ⟨for computers⟩.

printing *n.* ①印刷 yìnshuā ⟨act of printing⟩. ②印刷物 yìnshuāwù ⟨books⟩.

prior *adj.* 在前的 zàiqián de.

priority *n.* 优先权 yōuxiānquán.

prism *n.* ①棱镜 léngjìng ⟨glass⟩. ②棱柱体 léngzhùtǐ ⟨shape⟩.

prison *n.* 监狱 jiānyù, 牢房 láofáng.

prisoner *n.* 囚犯 qiúfàn, 犯人 fànrén.

privacy *n.* ①隐私权 yǐnsīquán, 隐私 yǐnsī ⟨secrecy⟩. ②独处 dúchǔ ⟨being alone⟩.

private *adj.* ①私人的 sīrén de ⟨not public⟩, 私有的 sīyǒu de ⟨personal⟩. ②秘密的 mìmì de ⟨secret⟩. — *n.* 士兵 shìbīng ⟨soldier⟩.

privilege *n.* 特权 tèquán.

prize *n.* 奖品 jiǎngpǐn ⟨reward⟩. — *v.* 珍视 zhēnshì ⟨value⟩.

prizefight *n.* 职业拳赛 zhíyè quánsài ⟨boxing match⟩.

pro *adv.* 赞成地 zànchéng de. — *n.* ①赞成者 zànchéngzhě ⟨supporter⟩. ②专业人员 zhuānyè rényuán ⟨professional⟩.

probability *n.* 可能性 kěnéngxìng.

probably *adv.* 可能 kěnéng, 大概 dàgài.

probation *n.* ①试用期 shìyòngqī / shìyòngqí ⟨trial period⟩. ②缓刑 huǎnxíng ⟨law⟩.

probe *v.* ①探查 tànchá ⟨examine⟩. ②探求 tànqiú ⟨investigate⟩.

problem *n.* 问题 wèntí.

procedure *n.* 程序 chéngxù.

proceed *v.* ①继续进行 jìxù jìnxíng ⟨continue⟩. ②开始进行 kāishǐ jìnxíng, 着手 zhuóshǒu ⟨start doing⟩.

proceeding *n.* ①(*pl.*) 记录 jìlù ⟨records⟩. ②(*pl.*) 诉讼程序 sùsòng chéngxù ⟨lawsuit⟩.

proceeds *n.* 营业额 yíngyè'é, 收益 shōuyì.

process *n.* ①过程 guòchéng ⟨course⟩. ②方法 fāngfǎ ⟨method⟩. ③进展 jìnzhǎn ⟨progress⟩. — *v.* 加工 jiāgōng ⟨treat⟩.

proclaim *v.* 宣布 xuānbù.

proclamation *n.* 宣布 xuānbù, 声明 shēngmíng ⟨announcement⟩.

proclivity *n.* 倾向 qīngxiàng, 癖性 pǐxìng.

procrastinate *v.* 拖延 tuōyán, 耽搁 dāngē.

prod *v.* 刺 cì, 戳 chuō ⟨poke⟩.

prodigal *adj.* 浪费的 làngfèi de.

prodigious *adj.* ①庞大的 pángdà de ⟨enormous⟩. ②惊人

的 jīngrén de (amazing).

prodigy n. ①奇才 qícái (genius). ②神童 shéntóng 〈child〉.

produce v. ①生产 shēngchǎn (make). ②拿出 náchu (bring out).

producer n. ①生产者 shēngchǎnzhě (manufacturer). ②制作人 zhìzuòrén 〈film〉.

product n. ①产品 chǎnpǐn, 产物 chǎnwù (goods). ②结果 jiéguǒ (result).

production n. ①生产 shēngchǎn (producing). ②产量 chǎnliàng (quantity). ~ *line* 流水线 liúshuǐxiàn / 生产线 shēngchǎnxiàn.

productive adj. ①生产的 shēngchǎn de, 肥沃的 féiwò de (fertile). ②产生利益的 chǎnshēng lìyì de (beneficial).

profane adj. 亵渎的 xièdú de (blasphemous).

profanity n. 亵渎 xièdú.

profess v. 声称 shēngchēng.

profession n. 职业 zhíyè (occupation).

professional adj. 专业的 zhuānyè de. — n. ①专家 zhuānjiā, 专业人员 zhuānyè rényuán (expert). ②职业选手 zhíyè xuǎnshǒu 〈sports〉.

professor n. 教授 jiàoshòu.

proficient adj. 熟练的 shúliàn de / shóuliàn de (well-practiced), 精通的 jīngtōng de (knowing well).

profile n. ①侧面像 cèmiànxiàng (side view). ②轮廓 lúnkuò (outline). ③人物简介 rénwù jiǎnjiè (biography).

profit n. 利益 lìyì, 利润 lìrùn. — v. ①对……有利 duì...yǒulì (benefit). ②获利 huòlì (earn money).

profitable adj. 有利益的 yǒu lìyì de.

profligate adj. ①浪费的 làngfèi de (wasteful). ②放荡的 fàngdàng de (shamelessly immoral).

profound adj. ①深的 shēn de 〈depth〉. ②深刻的 shēnkè de 〈knowledge〉.

profuse adj. 丰富的 fēngfù de (plentiful).

program n. ①节目 jiémù 〈performance〉. ②计划 jìhuà (plan). ③程式 chéngshì 〈computer〉.

progress n. ①进步 jìnbù (advance). ②前进 qiánjìn (forward movement).

progression n. 进展 jìnzhǎn (the action of progressing).

progressive adj. ①进步的 jìnbù de (advancing). ②前进的 qiánjìn de (moving forward).

prohibit v. ①禁止 jìnzhǐ (forbid). ②阻止 zǔzhǐ (prevent).

prohibitive adj. ①禁止的 jìnzhǐ de (not allowed). ②高昂的 gāo'áng de 〈of price〉.

project n. 计划 jìhuà, 方案 fāng'àn. — v. 投射 tóushè (cause a shadow).

projectile n. 发射物 fāshèwù.

projection n. 投射 tóushè, 放映 fàngyìng (projecting).

projector n. 放映机 fàngyìngjī.

proletariat n. 无产阶级 wúchǎn jiējí.

proliferate v. 繁殖 fánzhí (multiply).

prolific adj. 多产的 duōchǎn de (fruitful).

prologue n. 序言 xùyán,

开场白 kāichǎngbái.

prolong v. 延长 yáncháng.

prom n. 舞会 wǔhuì.

prominent adj. ①卓越的 zhuóyuè de (distinguished). ②突起的 tūqǐ de / túqǐ de (jutting out).

promiscuous adj. 滥交的 lànjiāo de ⟨sex⟩.

promise n. ①诺言 nuòyán (assurance). ②前途 qiántú (potential). – v. ①承诺 chéngnuò (assure). ②有……希望 yǒu...xīwàng, 有可能 yǒu kěnéng (give hope).

promote v. ①擢升 zhuóshēng, 提升 tíshēng (elevate). ②促进 cùjìn (move something forward). ③宣传促销 xuānchuán cùxiāo (market).

promotion n. ①升迁 shēngqiān (elevation). ②促进 cùjìn ⟨move something forward⟩. ③促销 cùxiāo (marketing).

prompt adj. ①立刻的 lìkè de (immediate). ②迅速的 xùnsù de (quick).

prone adj. ①易于……的 yì yú...de (inclined). ②俯卧的 fǔwò de (face down).

pronoun n. 代名词 dàimíngcí.

pronounce v. ①发音 fāyīn (utter). ②宣称 xuānchēng (announce).

pronunciation n. 发音 fāyīn.

proof n. 证明 zhèngmíng.

proofread v. 校对 jiàoduì. — n. 支撑 zhīchēng, 支持 zhīchí. — n. 支撑物 zhīchēngwù.

prop v. 支撑 zhīchēng, 支持 zhīchí. — n. 支撑物 zhīchēngwù.

propaganda n. 宣传 xuānchuán.

propagate v. ①繁殖 fánzhí

(reproduce). ②传播 chuánbō / chuánbò, 宣传 xuānchuán (spread).

propel v. 推进 tuījìn.

propeller n. 推进器 tuījìnqì.

proper adj. ①适当的 shìdàng de (appropriate). ②得体的 détǐ de (acceptable).

properly adv. 适当地 shìdàng de.

property n. ①财产 cáichǎn (possessions). ②特性 tèxìng (quality).

prophecy n. 预言 yùyán.

prophesy v. 预言 yùyán, 预告 yùgào.

prophet n. 预言家 yùyánjiā, 先知 xiānzhī.

proportion n. ①比例 bǐlì (ratio). ②部分 bùfen (part). ③均衡 jūnhéng (balance).

proportionate adj. 成比例的 chéng bǐlì de.

proposal n. ①建议 jiànyì, 提议 tíyì (suggestion). ②求婚 qiúhūn (offer of marriage).

propose v. ①提议 tíyì, 建议 jiànyì (suggest). ②求婚 qiúhūn ⟨marriage⟩.

proposition n. 提议 tíyì.

proprietor n. 所有者 suǒyǒuzhě.

propriety n. ①适当 shìdàng (appropriateness). ②得体 détǐ (good manners).

proscribe v. 禁止 jìnzhǐ (forbid).

prose n. 散文 sǎnwén.

prosecute v. 因……而起诉 yīn...ér qǐsù, 控告 kònggào (accuse).

prosecution n. 起诉 qǐsù, 控告 kònggào.

prosecutor n. 检察官

jiǎncháguān (official).

prospect n. ①展望 zhǎnwàng (expectation). ②景象 jǐngxiàng (scene).

prospective adj. 预期的 yùqī de / yùqí de.

prospectus n. 说明书 shuōmíngshū.

prosper v. 繁荣 fánróng.

prosperity n. 繁荣 fánróng.

prosperous adj. 繁盛的 fánshèng de.

prostitute n. 娼妓 chāngjì.

prostitution n. 卖淫 màiyín.

prostrate v. 使…倒下 shǐ...dǎoxia. — adj. ①俯卧的 fǔwò de (prone). ②被征服的 bèi zhēngfú de (overcome).

protagonist n. ①主角 zhǔjué (chief character). ②倡导者 chàngdǎozhě (leader).

protect v. 保护 bǎohù.

protection n. 保护 bǎohù.

protective adj. 保护的 bǎohù de.

protector n. 保护者 bǎohùzhě.

protectorate n. 保护国 bǎohùguó.

protein n. 蛋白质 dànbáizhì / dànbáizhí.

protest n. 抗议 kàngyì (demonstration), 反对 fǎnduì (objection). — v. 抗议 kàngyì.

Protestant n. & adj. 新教徒 Xīnjiàotú.

protocol n. ①议定书 yìdìngshū (agreement). ②外交礼节 wàijiāo lǐjié (etiquette).

proton n. 质子 zhìzǐ / zhízǐ.

prototype n. 原型 yuánxíng.

protract v. 延长 yáncháng.

protrude v. 伸出 shēnchu, 凸出 tūchū / túchū.

protuberant adj. 隆起的 lóngqǐ de, 凸出的 tūchū de / túchū de (bulging).

proud adj. ①以……为荣 yǐ...wéiróng (satisfied with). ②骄傲的 jiāo'ào de (arrogant).

prove v. 证明 zhèngmíng (show to be true).

proverb n. 谚语 yànyǔ, 格言 géyán.

provide v. 提供 tígōng, 供给 gōngjǐ (supply).

provided conj. 假若 jiǎruò.

providence n. 天意 tiānyì (destiny).

provident adj. 有先见的 yǒu xiānjiàn de (far-sighted).

providential adj. 幸运的 xìngyùn de (lucky).

province n. 省 shěng.

provincial adj. 省的 shěng de.

provision n. ①准备 zhǔnbèi (preparation). ②(pl.) 粮食 liángshí (food). ③条款 tiáokuǎn (law).

provisional adj. 临时的 línshí de.

proviso n. 但书 dànshū, 条件 tiáojiàn.

provocation n. 激怒 jīnù.

provocative adj. 挑拨性的 tiǎobōxìng de, 煽动的 shāndòng de.

provoke v. ①激怒 jīnù (make angry). ②引起 yǐnqǐ (arouse).

prowl v. 潜行 qiánxíng.

proximity n. 接近 jiējìn.

proxy n. ①代理 dàilǐ (authority). ②代理人 dàilǐrén (deputy). ③委托书 wěituōshū (document).

prude n. 故作拘谨的人 gùzuò jūjǐn de rén.

prudent adj. 谨慎的 jǐnshèn de.

prune v. 修剪 xiūjiǎn. — n. 干梅子 gān méizi.

psalm n. 赞美歌 zànměigē.

pseudonym n. 假名 jiǎmíng (false name), 笔名 bǐmíng (pen name).

psychedelic adj. 产生幻觉的 chǎnshēng huànjué de.

psychiatry n. 精神医学 jīngshén yīxué.

psychoanalysis n. 精神分析 jīngshén fēnxī.

psychological adj. 心理的 xīnlǐ de.

psychologist n. 心理学家 xīnlǐxué jiā.

psychology n. 心理学 xīnlǐxué.

psychotherapy n. 心理疗法 xīnlǐ liáofǎ.

pub n. 酒馆 jiǔguǎn.

puberty n. 青春期 qīngchūnqī / qīngchūnqí.

public adj. ①公众的 gōngzhòng de (of people in general). ②公开的 gōngkāi de (open). — n. 大众 dàzhòng (populace).

publication n. ①出版 chūbǎn (issuing). ②出版品 chūbǎnpǐn (book).

publicity n. 宣传 xuānchuán.

publicly adv. 公开地 gōngkāi de.

publish v. ①出版 chūbǎn 〈printing〉. ②发表 fābiǎo, 公开 gōngkāi (make publicly known).

pucker n. 皱 zhòu, 褶 zhě / zhé.

pudding n. 布丁 bùdīng.

puddle n. 水坑 shuǐkēng.

puff v. ①吹气 chuīqì, 喷 pēn (blow). ②喘息 chuǎnxī / chuǎnxí (pant). ③膨胀 péngzhàng (inflate). — n. ①吹 chuī, 喷 pēn 〈breath or wind〉. ②粉扑 fěnpū 〈powder〉.

pull v. ①拉 lā, 拖 tuō (drag). ②拔 bá (pull out). — n. 拉 lā (tug).

pulley n. 滑轮 huálún.

pullover n. 套头毛衣 tàotóu máoyī.

pulp n. ①果肉 guǒròu 〈fruit〉. ②纸浆 zhǐjiāng 〈for making paper〉.

pulpit n. 讲坛 jiǎngtán.

pulsate v. 脉动 màidòng, 跳动 tiàodòng (beat).

pulse n. ①脉搏 màibó (beat). ②拍子 pāizi (rhythm).

pulverize v. 磨成粉 mó chéng fěn, 捣碎 dǎosuì.

puma n. 美洲狮 měizhōushī.

pump n. 唧筒 jītǒng / jítǒng, 抽水机 chōushuǐjī. — v. 用抽水机汲水 yòng chōushuǐjī jíshuǐ (drain).

pumpkin n. 南瓜 nánguā.

pun n. 双关语 shuāngguānyǔ.

punch v. ①以拳击 yǐ quán jī / yǐ quán jí (hit with the fist). ②打洞 dǎdòng (pierce). — n. ①打孔器 dǎkǒngqì 〈tool〉. ②击 jī / jí, 打 dǎ (strike).

punctual adj. 守时的 shǒushí de.

punctuate v. ①加标点于 jiā biāodiǎn yú (put punctuation marks). ②打断 dǎduàn (interrupt).

punctuation n. 标点 biāodiǎn. ~ **marks** 标点符号 biāodiǎn fúhào.

puncture n. 孔 kǒng. — v. 穿

孔 chuānkǒng (pierce).

pungent adj. 刺激性的 cìjīxìng de, 辛辣的 xīnlà de.

punish v. 处罚 chǔfá, 惩罚 chéngfá.

punishment n. ①罚 fá, 刑罚 xíngfá (penalty). ②严厉的对待 yánlì de duìdài (rough treatment).

punt n. 平底小船 píngdǐ xiǎochuán.

puny adj. 弱的 ruò de.

pup n. 小狗 xiǎogǒu (puppy).

pupil n. 学生 xuésheng.

puppet n. ①木偶 mù'ǒu (doll). ②傀儡 kuǐlěi (person or group).

puppy n. 小狗 xiǎogǒu.

purchase v. 购买 gòumǎi (buy). — n. 购买 gòumǎi.

pure adj. ①纯粹的 chúncuì de (neat). ②纯净的 chúnjìng de (clean). ③纯洁的 chúnjié de (innocent). ④完全的 wánquán de (complete).

purely adv. ①完全地 wánquán de (completely). ②纯粹地 chúncuì de (merely).

purgative n. 泻药 xièyào.

purgatory n. 炼狱 liànyù.

purge v. ①清除 qīngchú (expel). ②洗涤 xǐdí (clean).

purify v. ①使清净 shǐ qīngjìng (clean). ②纯化 chúnhuà (clarify).

purity n. 纯洁 chúnjié.

purple n. 紫色 zǐsè. — adj. 紫色的 zǐsè de.

purpose n. ①目的 mùdì (intention). ②决心 juéxīn (determination).

purse n. 钱袋 qiándài, 钱包 qiánbāo.

pursue v. ①追捕 zhuībǔ, 追赶 zhuīgǎn (chase). ②追求 zhuīqiú (aim for).

pursuit n. ①追捕 zhuībǔ (chase). ②追求 zhuīqiú (going for). ③消遣 xiāoqiǎn (interest).

purvey v. 供应 gōngyìng.

pus n. 脓 nóng.

push v. ①推 tuī (press). ②催促 cuīcù (urge on).

pussy n. 猫咪 māomī (cat).

put v. ①放 fàng, 安置 ānzhì (place). ②提出 tíchu (express). *~ down* 放下 fàngxia. *~ on* 穿 chuān (clothes), 戴 dài (accessory).

putrefy v. 使腐败 shǐ fǔbài.

putrid adj. 腐烂的 fǔlàn de (rotten).

putty n. 油灰 yóuhuī.

puzzle n. ①难题 nántí (question). ②谜 mí (riddle). — v. ①困惑 kùnhuò (confuse). ②苦思 kǔsī (think).

pylon n. ①铁塔 tiětǎ (for power cable). ②指示塔 zhǐshìtǎ (in airports).

pyramid n. ①金字塔 jīnzìtǎ (Egypt). ②角锥 jiǎozhuī (shape).

python n. 蟒 mǎng, 巨蛇 jùshé.

Q

quack *n.* 鸭叫声 yājiàoshēng ⟨sound⟩. — *v.* 鸭叫声 yājiào.

quadrangle *n.* 四边形 sìbiānxíng, 方形 fāngxíng ⟨shape⟩.

quadrille *n.* 方块舞 fāngkuàiwǔ.

quadruple *adj.* 四倍的 sìbèi de (four times).

quagmire *n.* ①泥沼 nízhǎo (bog). ②困境 kùnjìng (difficulty).

quail *n.* 鹌鹑 ānchún ⟨bird⟩.

quaint *adj.* 古怪的 gǔguài de.

quake *v.* 震动 zhèndòng, 战栗 zhànlì.

qualification *n.* ①资格 zīgé (competence). ②限制 xiànzhì (limitation).

qualified *adj.* ①有资格的 yǒu zīgé de (appropriate). ②受限制的 shòu xiànzhì de (limited).

qualify *v.* ①给与……的资格 jǐyǔ...de zīgé (authorize). ②取得……的资格 qǔdé...de zīgé (become eligible). ③限制 xiànzhì (limit).

quality *n.* ①品质 pǐnzhì / pǐnzhí (goodness). ②特质 tèzhì / tèzhí (characteristic).

qualm *n.* 不安 bù'ān, 疑惧 yíjù (uncertainty).

quandary *n.* 困惑 kùnhuò, 窘境 jiǒngjìng.

quantitative *adj.* 可量化的 kě liànghuà de.

quantity *n.* 量 liàng.

quarantine *n.* & *v.* 隔离检疫 gélí jiǎnyì.

quarrel *n.* 争吵 zhēngchǎo, 口角 kǒujiǎo. — *v.* 争吵 zhēngchǎo (argue).

quarrelsome *adj.* 爱争吵的 ài zhēngchǎo de.

quarry *n.* 采石场 cǎishíchǎng ⟨place⟩. — *v.* 采石 cǎishí.

quart *n.* 夸脱 kuātuō.

quarter *n.* ①四分之一 sì fēn zhī yī (¼). ②一刻钟 yíkèzhōng (15 minutes). ③二角五分 èr jiǎo wǔ fēn (25 cents). ④区域 qūyù (area).

quarterly *adj.* 每季的 měijì de. — *adv.* 每季地 měijì de. — *n.* 季刊 jìkān.

quartet *n.* 四重唱 sìchóngchàng ⟨singers⟩, 四重奏 sìchóngzòu ⟨instruments⟩.

quartz *n.* 石英石 shíyīngshí.

quash *v.* 镇压 zhènyā (suppress).

quaver *v.* 震颤 zhènchàn / zhènzhàn.

quay *n.* 码头 mǎtou.

queasy *adj.* 作呕的 zuò'ǒu de, 不舒服的 bù shūfu de.

queen *n.* 女王 nǚwáng, 皇后 huánghòu.

queer *adj.* ①奇怪的 qíguài de, 古怪的 gǔguài de (bizarre). ②可疑的 kěyí de (suspicious). — *n.* 同性恋者 tóngxìngliàn zhě.

quell *v.* 压制 yāzhì.

quench *v.* ①熄灭 xīmiè / xímiè (extinguish). ②解渴 jiěkě (relieve thirst).

query n. 问题 wèntí. — v. 质问 zhìwèn / zhíwèn, 询问 xúnwèn (question).

quest n. 探寻 tànxún.

question n. 疑问 yíwèn, 问题 wèntí. ~ **mark** 问号 wènhào. — v. 质问 zhìwèn / zhíwèn.

questionable adj. 有问题的 yǒu wèntí de, 可疑的 kěyí de.

questionnaire n. 问卷 wènjuàn.

queue n. 一行队伍 yìháng duìwǔ.

quick adj. ①迅速的 xùnsù de (fast). ②即刻的 jíkè de (immediate). ③机伶的 jīling de (clever).

quicken v. 加速 jiāsù.

quickly adv. 快地 kuài de, 迅速地 xùnsù de.

quicksand n. 流沙 liúshā 〈sand〉.

quicksilver n. 水银 shuǐyín, 汞 gǒng.

quiet adj. ①安静的 ānjìng de (noiseless). ②平静的 píngjìng de (calm). ③温和的 wēnhé de (soft). — v. 使安静 shǐ ānjìng.

quietly adv. 安静地 ānjìng de.

quilt n. 棉被 miánbèi.

quinine n. 奎宁 kuíníng.

quintet n. 五重唱 wǔchóngchàng 〈singers〉, 五重奏 wǔchóngzòu 〈instruments〉.

quip n. 妙语 miàoyǔ, 警语 jǐngyǔ.

quit v. ①离去 líqù (leave). ②辞去 cíqù (resign).

quite adv. ①完全 wánquán (entirely). ②相当 xiāngdāng (fairly).

quiver n. & v. 颤抖 chàndǒu / zhàndǒu.

quiz v. 对……测验 duì... cèyàn, 考试 kǎoshì. — n. 小考 xiǎokǎo.

quota n. 配额 pèi'é, 限额 xiàn'é.

quotation n. ①引用文 yǐnyòngwén (citation). ②估价 gūjià (estimated price). ~ **marks** 引号 yǐnhào.

quote v. ①引用 yǐnyòng (cite). ②报（价）bào (jià) (offer a price).

quotient n. 商数 shāngshù.

R

rabbit n. 兔子 tùzi.

rabble n. 暴民 bàomín (disorderly crowd).

rabid adj. ①狂暴的 kuángbào de (furious). ②患狂犬病的 huàn kuángquǎnbìng de.

rabies n. 狂犬病 kuángquǎnbìng.

raccoon n. 浣熊 huànxióng / wǎnxióng.

race n. ①竞赛 jìngsài (contest). ②种族 zhǒngzú (people).

racial adj. 种族的 zhǒngzú de.

racism n. 种族歧视 zhǒngzú qíshì.

rack n. 挂物架 guàwùjià.

racket n. ①球拍 qiúpāi 〈tennis〉. ②喧哗 xuānhuá 〈noise〉. ③诈骗 zhàpiàn 〈swindle〉.

radar n. 雷达 léidá.

radiance n. 光辉 guānghuī, 光亮 guāngliàng.

radiant adj. ①光亮的 guāngliàng de 〈bright〉. ②容光焕发的 róngguāng-huànfā de 〈happy〉.

radiate v. 发射 fāshè.

radiation n. 辐射 fúshè.

radiator n. ①电热器 diànrèqì 〈heater〉. ②冷却器 lěngquèqì 〈engine〉.

radical adj. ①根本的 gēnběn de 〈fundamental〉. ②激进的 jījìn de 〈extreme〉. — n. 激进分子 jījìn fènzǐ.

radio n. ①无线电广播 wúxiàndiàn guǎngbō / wúxiàndiàn guǎngbō 〈broadcasting〉. ②收音机 shōuyīnjī 〈device〉. ~ **station** 无线电台 wúxiàn diàntái.

radioactive adj. 放射性的 fàngshèxìng de.

radioactivity n. 放射性 fàngshèxìng.

radish n. 萝卜 luóbo.

radium n. 镭 léi.

radius n. 半径 bànjìng.

raffle n. & v. 抽奖 chōujiǎng.

raft n. 筏 fá.

rag n. 破布 pòbù.

rage n. 盛怒 shèngnù. — v. 发怒 fānnù.

ragged adj. ①褴褛的 lánlǚ de, 破烂的 pòlàn de 〈tattered〉. ②凹凸不平的 āotū-bùpíng de / āotú-bùpíng de 〈uneven〉.

raid n. & v. 袭击 xíjī / xíjí 〈attack〉.

rail n. ①铁轨 tiěguǐ 〈track〉.

②栏杆 lángān 〈fence〉.

railing n. 栏杆 lángān.

railroad n. 铁路 tiělù, 铁道 tiědào.

rain n. 雨 yǔ. — v. 下雨 xiàyǔ.

rainbow n. 彩虹 cǎihóng.

raincoat n. 雨衣 yǔyī.

rainfall n. 降雨量 jiàngyǔliàng.

rainy adj. 多雨的 duōyǔ de.

raise v. ①举起 jǔqǐ 〈lift up〉. ②提高 tígāo 〈make higher〉. ③擢升 zhuóshēng 〈promote〉. ④养育 yǎngyù 〈bring up〉. ⑤招募 zhāomù 〈collect〉.

raisin n. 葡萄干 pútáogān 〈food〉.

rake n. 耙子 pázi. — v. 耙 pá.

rally v. ①召集 zhàojí 〈assemble〉. ②重振 chóngzhèn 〈recover〉. — n. 集会 jíhuì 〈meeting〉.

ram n. 公羊 gōngyáng. — v. 撞 zhuàng, 撞入 zhuàngrù 〈crash into〉.

ramble v. ①漫步 mànbù 〈stroll〉. ②漫谈 màntán 〈wander〉.

rambling adj. ①杂乱的 záluàn de 〈straggling〉. ②漫谈的 màntán de 〈aimless〉.

ramp n. 坡道 pōdào 〈slope〉.

rampage v. 乱冲 luànchōng.

rampant adj. 猖獗的 chāngjué de 〈widespread〉.

rampart n. 堡垒 bǎolěi, 壁垒 bìlěi 〈defensive wall〉.

ramshackle adj. 要倒塌的 yào dǎotā de 〈almost collapsing〉.

ranch n. 大牧场 dà mùchǎng, 大农场 dà nóngchǎng.

rancid adj. 腐臭的 fǔchòu de.

random adj. 无目的的 wú mùdì de, 随便的 suíbiàn de.

R

range n. ①范围 fànwéi (extent). ②射程 shèchéng 〈distance〉. ③靶场 bǎchǎng (shooting practice area). ④分布地区 fēnbù dìqū 〈area〉. — v. 在……范围之内 zài...fànwéi zhī nèi (be within).

rank n. ①阶级 jiējí (class). ②行列 hángliè (row). — v. ①使排列 shǐ páiliè (line). ②位居…… wèijū…, 列于…… liè yú... (place in order). — adj. 恶臭的 èchòu de (smelling).

rankle v. 使人心痛 shǐ rén xīntòng.

ransack v. ①遍搜 biànsōu (search). ②洗劫 xǐjié (rob).

ransom n. 赎金 shújīn.

rant v. 怒吼 nùhǒu, 咆哮 páoxiào / páoxiào.

rap v. 轻敲 qīngqiāo (knock). — n. ①敲击 qiāojī / qiāojí (knocking). ②饶舌音乐 ráoshé yīnyuè 〈music〉.

rape n. & v. 强奸 qiángjiān, 强暴 qiángbào.

rapid adj. 迅速的 xùnsù de, 快的 kuài de (fast). — n. 急流 jíliú.

rapt adj. 全神贯注的 quánshén-guànzhù de, 入神的 rùshén de (deep in thought).

rapture n. 欣喜若狂 xīnxǐ-ruòkuáng.

rare adj. 罕有的 hǎnyǒu de (uncommon). ~ **animal** 珍稀动物 zhēnxī dòngwù / 稀有动物 xīyǒu dòngwù.

rarity n. 罕有的事物 hǎnyǒu de shìwù.

rascal n. 流氓 liúmáng, 恶棍 ègùn.

rash adj. 卤莽的 lǔmǎng de, 轻率的 qīngshuài de. — n. 疹

zhěn.

raspberry n. 覆盆子 fùpénzǐ.

rat n. ①鼠 shǔ (mouse). ②卑鄙小人 bēibǐ xiǎorén (despicable person). ③叛徒 pàntú (betrayer). — v. 背叛 bèipàn (betray).

rate n. ①比率 bǐlǜ (ratio). ②速度 sùdù (speed). — v. 评估 pínggū (evaluate).

rather adv. 宁可 nìngkě / níngkě.

ratify v. ①批准 pīzhǔn (approve). ②确认 quèrèn (confirm).

rating n. 等级 děngjí (ranking).

ratio n. 比率 bǐlǜ 〈mathematics〉.

ration n. 配给量 pèijǐliàng, 配额 pèi'é (allotted quantity). — v. 配给 pèijǐ.

rational adj. ①理智的 lǐzhì de (sensible). ②合理的 hélǐ de (reasonable).

rationalism n. 理性主义 lǐxìng zhǔyì.

rationalize v. 合理化 hélǐhuà.

rattle v. 发嘎嘎声 fā gāgāshēng (make short, sharp sounds). — n. 嘎嘎声 gāgāshēng 〈noise〉.

raucous adj. ①沙哑的 shāyǎ de (hoarse). ②吵闹的 chǎonào de (noisy).

ravage n. & v. ①毁坏 huǐhuài (destruction). ②掠夺 lüèduó (robbery).

rave v. ①咆哮 páoxiào / páoxiào, 怒吼 nùhǒu (roar). ②过度赞扬 guòdù zànyáng (praise). — n. ①狂欢聚会 kuánghuān jùhuì (party). ②激赏 jīshǎng (praise).

raven n. 渡鸟 dùniǎo 〈bird〉.

ravenous adj. 饥饿的 jīè de (very hungry), 贪婪的 tānlán de (greedy).

ravine n. 峡谷 xiágǔ.

ravish v. ①迷住 mízhù (charm). ②强奸 qiángjiān (rape).

raw adj. ①生的 shēng de (uncooked). ②未加工的 wèi jiāgōng de (untreated). ③擦破皮的 cā pòpí de (chafed).

ray n. ①光线 guāngxiàn (beam). ②射线 shèxiàn (radiant light).

rayon n. 人造丝 rénzàosī.

razor n. 剃刀 tìdāo, 剃须刀 tìxūdāo / 刮胡刀 guāhúdāo.

reach v. ①到达 dàodá (arrive at). ②与……连络 yǔ...liánluò (contact).

react v. 反应 fǎnyìng (act).

reaction n. 反应 fǎnyìng.

reactor n. 原子炉 yuánzǐlú, 反应炉 fǎnyìnglú.

read v. ①读 dú, 阅读 yuèdú (study). ②朗读 lǎngdú (read aloud).

reader n. ①读者 dúzhě 〈person〉. ②读本 dúběn 〈book〉.

readily adj. ①简单地 jiǎndān de (easily). ②欣然 xīnrán (willingly).

reading n. ①读物 dúwù 〈book〉. ②见解 jiànjiě, 解读 jiědú (interpretation).

ready adj. ①预备好的 yùbèi hǎo de (prepared). ②愿意的 yuànyì de (willing).

ready-made adj. 现成的 xiànchéng de.

real adj. ①真的 zhēn de, 真实的 zhēnshí de (genuine). ②实际的 shíjì de (actual).
~ *estate* 不动产 búdòngchǎn.

really adv. 真实地 zhēnshí de, 真正地 zhēnzhèng de.

realism n. 现实主义 xiànshí zhǔyì, 写实主义 xiěshí zhǔyì.

realistic adj. ①逼真的 bīzhēn de, 写实的 xiěshí de (lifelike). ②实际的 shíjì de (practical).

reality n. 真实 zhēnshí.

realize v. ①了解 liǎojiě (comprehend). ②实现 shíxiàn (accomplish).

realm n. ①王国 wángguó (kingdom). ②领域 lǐngyù (field).

reap v. ①收割 shōugē (cut). ②获得 huòdé (get).

rear n. 后方 hòufāng, 背后 bèihòu. — adj. 后部的 hòubù de. — v. ①养育 yǎngyù (bring up). ②饲养 sìyǎng (feed).

reason n. ①理由 lǐyóu, 原因 yuányīn (cause). ②理性 lǐxìng (reasonableness).

reasonable adj. ①讲道理的 jiǎng dàolǐ de (sensible). ②合理的 hélǐ de (acceptable). ③公道的 gōngdào de (fair).

reassure v. 使安心 shǐ ānxīn.

rebate n. 折扣 zhékòu. — v. 给折扣 gěi zhékòu.

rebel n. 叛徒 pàntú, 谋反者 móufǎnzhě. — v. 反叛 fǎnpàn, 谋反 móufǎn.

rebellion n. 叛乱 pànluàn, 反叛 fǎnpàn.

rebirth n. 再生 zàishēng, 复活 fùhuó.

rebound n. & v. 弹回 tánhuí, 跳 tiào.

rebuff n. & v. 断然拒绝 duànrán jùjué.

rebuke n. 指责 zhǐzé, 谴责 qiǎnzé.

recall v. ①召回 zhàohuí (call

R

back). ②忆起 yìqǐ, 回忆 huíyì (remember).

recant v. 撤回 chèhuí, 取消 qǔxiāo.

recede v. 后退 hòutuì.

receipt n. 收据 shōujù.

receive v. ①收到 shōudào, 接受 jiēshòu ⟨get⟩. ②款待 kuǎndài ⟨greet⟩.

receiver n. ①收受者 shōushòuzhě ⟨person⟩. ②听筒 tīngtǒng ⟨of telephone⟩.

recent adj. 最近的 zuìjìn de.

recently adv. 近来 jìnlái.

receptacle n. 容器 róngqì.

reception n. ①接待 jiēdài ⟨greeting⟩. ②欢迎会 huānyínghuì ⟨party⟩.

receptionist n. 接待员 jiēdàiyuán.

receptive adj. 能接纳的 néng jiēnà de.

recess n. ①休会期 xiūhuìqī / xiūhuìqí, 休业期 xiūyèqī / xiūyèqí ⟨adjournment⟩. ②壁凹 bì'āo ⟨alcove⟩.

recession n. 萧条 xiāotiáo, 衰退 shuāituì ⟨economy⟩.

recipe n. 食谱 shípǔ ⟨cooking⟩.

recipient n. 接受者 jiēshòuzhě.

reciprocal adj. 相互的 xiānghù de, 互惠的 hùhuì de.

recital n. 独奏会 dúzòuhuì ⟨concert⟩.

recitation n. 朗诵 lǎngsòng ⟨declamation⟩.

recite v. 朗诵 lǎngsòng.

reckless adj. 卤莽的 lǔmǎng de, 不顾后果的 búgù hòuguǒ de.

reckon v. 计算 jìsuàn.

reclaim v. ①要求归还 yāoqiú guīhuán, 收回 shōuhuí

(recover). ②开垦 kāikěn (make usable).

recline v. 斜倚 xiéyǐ.

recluse n. 隐士 yǐnshì.

recognition n. ①认得 rènde, 认出 rènchu, 辨认 biànrèn (identification). ②承认 chéngrèn (admition).

recognize v. ①认得 rènde, 认出 rènchu, 辨认 biànrèn (identify). ②承认 chéngrèn (admit).

recoil v. 退却 tuìquè, 退缩 tuìsuō (draw back).

recollect v. 记起 jìqǐ, 忆起 yìqǐ.

recommend v. ①推荐 tuījiàn (speak in favor). ②劝告 quàngào (advise).

recommendation n. ①推荐 tuījiàn ⟨act⟩. ②推荐书 tuījiànshū ⟨statement⟩.

recompense v. ①赔偿 péicháng (make up for). ②报答 bàodá (reward).

reconcile v. 调解 tiáojiě.

reconnaissance n. 侦察 zhēnchá.

reconstruct v. 重建 chóngjiàn.

record v. ①纪录 jìlù (write down). ②录存 lùcún (preserve). — n. ①记录 jìlù (written statement). ②唱片 chàngpiàn (album). ③纪录 jìlù ⟨performance⟩.

recorder n. 录音机 lùyīnjī.

recount v. ①重数 chóngshǔ, 重新计算 chóngxīn jìsuàn (count again). ②描述 miáoshù (describe).

recoup v. 补偿 bǔcháng (make up).

recourse n. 求助 qiúzhù.

recover v. ①恢复 huīfù (get back). ②复元 fùyuán (get well again).

recovery n. ①恢复 huīfù (restoration). ②复元 fùyuán (healing).

recreation n. 娱乐 yúlè, 消遣 xiāoqiǎn.

recriminate v. 反控 fǎnkòng.

recruit n. ①新兵 xīnbīng (soldier). ②新加入者 xīn jiārù zhě (new member). — v. 招募 zhāomù.

rectangle n. 长方形 chángfāngxíng.

rectify v. 改正 gǎizhèng, 纠正 jiūzhèng (put right).

rectitude n. 正直 zhèngzhí (honesty).

rectum n. 直肠 zhícháng.

recuperate v. 恢复健康 huīfù jiànkāng (recover from illness).

recur v. 重现 chóngxiàn (happen again).

recycle v. 循环利用 xúnhuán lìyòng, 再使用 zài shǐyòng.

red n. & adj. 红色 hóngsè.

redeem v. ①赎回 shúhuí (buy back). ②挽回 wǎnhuí, 弥补 míbǔ (get back).

redemption n. ①赎回 shúhuí (buying back). ②救赎 jiùshú (rescue).

red-hot adj. 炽热的 chìrè de.

redress v. 改正 gǎizhèng, 纠正 jiūzhèng.

reduce v. ①减少 jiǎnshǎo, 降低 jiàngdī (decrease). ②浓缩 nóngsuō (condense).

reduction n. 减少 jiǎnshǎo 〈quantity〉, 降低 jiàngdī 〈level〉.

redundant adj. 多余的 duōyú de, 冗赘的 rǒngzhuì de.

reed n. 芦苇 lúwěi.

reef n. 暗礁 ànjiāo.

reek n. ①恶臭 èchòu 〈smell〉. ②浓烟 nóngyān 〈thick smoke〉. — v. 发出强烈臭气 fāchū qiángliè chòuqì.

reel n. ①纺车 fǎngchē, 卷轴 juǎnzhóu (bobbin). ②一卷 yìjuǎn 〈for a film〉. — v. 绕 rào (move).

reelect v. 重选 chóngxuǎn.

reestablish v. 重建 chóngjiàn.

referee n. ①仲裁者 zhòngcáizhě (arbitrator). ②裁判员 cáipànyuán (judge in a game).

reference n. ①参考 cānkǎo (something to consult). ②参考书 cānkǎoshū 〈book〉.

referendum n. 公民投票 gōngmín tóupiào.

refer to 提到 tídào, 谈到 tándào (speak of).

refill v. 再注满 zài zhùmǎn.

refine v. ①精制 jīngzhì, 提炼 tíliàn (purify). ②使文雅 shǐ wényǎ (cultivate).

reflect v. ①反射 fǎnshè (throw back). ②反映 fǎnyìng (echo).

reflection n. ①反射 fǎnshè (image). ②反映 fǎnyìng (echo).

reflex adj. 反射的 fǎnshè de. — n. 反射作用 fǎnshè zuòyòng.

reform v. 改革 gǎigé.

reformation n. 改革 gǎigé, 改良 gǎiliáng.

refract v. 使光屈折 shǐ guāng qūzhé.

refrain v. 抑制 yìzhì (control), 避免 bìmiǎn (avoid).

refresh v. ①提神 tíshén

R

(energize). ②唤起 huànqǐ
(remind).

refreshing adj. 提神的
tíshén de.

refreshment n. 提神
tíshén ⟨refresh⟩. ②点心
diǎnxin ⟨food or drink⟩.

refrigerate v. 冷藏
lěngcáng, 冷冻 lěngdòng.

refrigerator n. 冰箱
bīngxiāng.

refuge n. 避难所 bìnànsuǒ.

refugee n. 逃难者
táonànzhě.

refund n. & v. 退款 tuìkuǎn,
偿还 chánghuán.

refusal n. 拒绝 jùjué
(rejection).

refuse v. 拒绝 jùjué. — n. 垃
圾 lājī / lèsè.

regain v. 复得 fùdé (get back),
恢复 huīfù (recover).

regard v. ①视……为……
shì...wéi... (consider). ②注视
zhùshì (look at).

regardless adj. & adv.
无论如何 wúlùn-rúhé.

regency n. 摄政 shèzhèng.

regenerate v. 改造 gǎizào,
革新 géxīn. — adj. 改造过的
gǎizàoguo de.

regent n. 摄政者
shèzhèngzhě.

regime n. 政体 zhèngtǐ.

regiment n. 军团 jūntuán.

region n. 地区 dìqū, 区域
qūyù.

register n. 登记簿 dēngjìbù.
— v. 登记 dēngjì ⟨hotel⟩,
注册 zhùcè ⟨classes⟩.

registrar n. 注册员
zhùcèyuán.

registry n. 登记处 dēngjìchù,
注册处 zhùcèchù.

regret n. & v. ①抱歉 bàoqiàn
(regretfulness). ②遗憾 yíhàn
⟨pity⟩.

regular adj. ①定期的 dìngqī
de / dìngqí de, 有规律的 yǒu
guīlǜ de (consistent). ②有条理
的 yǒu tiáolǐ de (orderly).

regulate v. ①管制 guǎnzhì
(control). ②调节 tiáojié
(adjust).

regulation n. 规定 guīdìng,
规则 guīzé.

rehabilitate v. ①恢复 huīfù,
修复 xiūfù (restore). ②复职
fùzhí, 复权 fùquán (help
recover).

rehearsal n. 排演 páiyǎn
(practice).

rehearse v. 排演 páiyǎn
(practice).

reign n. ①朝代 cháodài, 王朝
wángcháo (dynasty). ②统治
tǒngzhì (rule). — v. 统治
tǒngzhì (rule).

reimburse v. 偿还
chánghuán.

rein n. 缰绳 jiāngshéng ⟨strap⟩.
— v. 驾驭 jiàyù, 控制 kòngzhì.

reindeer n. 驯鹿 xùnlù /
xúnlù.

reinforce v. 增强 zēngqiáng
(strengthen), 增援 zēngyuán
⟨troops⟩, 强调 qiángdiào
(emphasize).

reinstate v. 复职 fùzhí
⟨position⟩, 复权 fùquán ⟨power⟩.

reiterate v. 反复地说 fǎnfù
de shuō.

reject v. ①拒绝 jùjué (refuse).
②驳回 bóhuí (repel).

rejoice v. 欣喜 xīnxǐ, 高兴
gāoxìng.

rejuvenate v. 恢复青春
huīfù qīngchūn, 返老还童

fǎnlǎo-huántóng.

relapse v. 恶化 èhuà, 复发 fùfā.

relate v. ①叙述 xùshù (narrate). ②有关系 yǒu guānxi (be relevant).

related adj. 有关的 yǒuguān de.

relation n. ①关系 guānxi (connection). ②亲戚 qīnqi (relative).

relationship n. 关系 guānxi.

relative n. 亲戚 qīnqi.

relax v. 放松 fàngsōng.

relay n. ①接替人员 jiētì rényuán (shift). ②转播 zhuǎnbō / zhuǎnbò (broadcast). ③接力赛跑 jiēlì sàipǎo (race). — v. 传递 chuándì (transmit).

release n. & v. ①释放 shìfàng (set free). ②准许发表 zhǔnxǔ fābiǎo (make available).

relegate v. ①降级 jiàngjí, 贬黜 biǎnchù (demote). ②移交 yíjiāo (hand over).

relent v. 变温和 biàn wēnhé.

relevant adj. 有关的 yǒuguān de.

reliable adj. 可靠的 kěkào de, 可信赖的 kě xìnlài de.

reliance n. 信赖 xìnlài, 信任 xìnrèn.

relic n. 遗物 yíwù, 遗迹 yíjì / yíjī.

relief n. ①减轻 jiǎnqīng (alleviation). ②救济 jiùjì (aid).

relieve v. ①减轻 jiǎnqīng (lessen). ②解救 jiějiù, 援助 yuánzhù (aid).

religion n. 宗教 zōngjiào.

religious adj. 宗教的 zōngjiào de.

relinquish v. ①放弃 fàngqì (give up). ②放手 fàngshǒu (release).

relish n. ①嗜好 shìhào (liking). ②调味料 tiáowèiliào (sauce), 开胃菜 kāiwèicài (pickle). — v. 享受 xiǎngshòu, 喜好 xǐhào.

reluctant adj. 不甘愿的 bù gānyuàn de, 勉强的 miǎnqiǎng de.

rely v. 依赖 yīlài.

remain v. ①留下 liúxia (stay). ②剩下 shèngxia (be left).

remainder n. 残余 cányú.

remark n. ①评论 pínglùn (comment). ②注意 zhùyì (notice).

remarkable adj. 值得注意的 zhídé zhùyì de (worth noticing), 非凡的 fēifán de (extraordinary).

remedy v. ①治疗 zhìliáo (cure). ②纠正 jiūzhèng (correct). — n. 治疗 zhìliáo.

remember v. 记得 jìde.

remembrance n. ①记忆 jìyì (memory). ②纪念物 jìniànwù (souvenir).

remind v. 提醒 tíxǐng.

reminisce v. 追忆 zhuīyì.

reminiscence n. 追忆 zhuīyì (recall).

remiss adj. 疏忽的 shūhu de.

remission n. ①宽恕 kuānshù (forgiveness). ②和缓 héhuǎn (lessening).

remit v. 汇寄 huìjì (money).

remittance n. 汇款 huìkuǎn.

remnant n. 残余 cányú.

remonstrate v. 抗议 kàngyì (protest).

remorse n. 懊悔 àohuǐ, 悔恨 huǐhèn.

R

remote *adj.* ①遥远的 yáoyuǎn de (distant). ②冷淡的 lěngdàn de (aloof).

removal *n.* ①撤移 bānyí (transfer). ②免职 miǎnzhí (dismissal).

remove *v.* ①除去 chúqù (get rid of). ②移动 yídòng (transfer).

remunerate *v.* 报酬 bàochóu, 酬劳 chóuláo.

renaissance *n.* 新生 xīnshēng, 复兴 fùxīng. *the R-* 文艺复兴 Wényì fùxīng.

render *v.* ①给与 jǐyǔ, 报答 bàodá (give). ②演出 yǎnchū (perform). ③使……成为 shǐ...chéngwéi (make). ④翻译 fānyì (translate).

rendezvous *n.* ①约会 yuēhuì (appointment). ②会合地 huìhédì (place to meet).

rendition *n.* 演出 yǎnchū, 演奏 yǎnzòu (performance).

renegade *n.* 变节者 biànjiézhě, 叛徒 pàntú.

renew *v.* 更新 gēngxīn (update). 再开始 zài kāishǐ (start again).

renounce *v.* ①放弃 fàngqì (give up). ②与……断绝关系 yǔ...duànjué guānxi (refuse to associate with).

renovate *v.* 革新 géxīn, 变新 biànxīn (make new again).

renown *n.* 名望 míngwàng, 声誉 shēngyù.

rent *n.* 租金 zūjīn (rental).

renunciation *n.* 放弃 fàngqì (giving up).

reorganize *v.* 改组 gǎizǔ, 重组 chóngzǔ.

repair *n. & v.* ①修理 xiūlǐ 〈fix〉. ②修补 xiūbǔ 〈sew up〉.

reparation *n.* ①补偿 bǔcháng 〈damage〉. ②赔偿 péicháng 〈war damages〉.

repatriate *v.* 遣返 qiǎnfǎn.

repay *v.* ①付还 fùhuán (pay back). ②报答 bàodá (reward).

repeal *n. & v.* ①撤销 chèxiāo (withdrawal). ②废止 fèizhǐ (cancellation).

repeat *v.* ①复述 fùshù (say again). ②重复 chóngfù (do again).

repeatedly *adv.* 重复地 chóngfù de.

repel *v.* ①逐退 zhútuì (drive away). ②使不悦 shǐ búyuè (offend). ③排斥 páichì (keep out).

repent *v.* 后悔 hòuhuǐ.

repercussion *n.* 影响 yǐngxiǎng (effect).

repertoire *n.* 戏目 xìmù 〈drama〉, 曲目 qǔmù 〈music〉.

repertory *n.* 戏目 xìmù, 曲目 qǔmù.

repetition *n.* 重复 chóngfù, 反复 fǎnfù.

replace *v.* ①放回原处 fànghuí yuánchù (put back). ②代替 dàitì (take the place of).

replenish *v.* 再装满 zài zhuāngmǎn (refill), 补充 bǔchōng (recharge).

replica *n.* 复制品 fùzhìpǐn.

reply *n. & v.* 回答 huídá, 答复 dáfù.

report *n.* ①报导 bàodǎo 〈account〉. ②报告 bàogào 〈written〉. — *v.* ①报告 bàogào (give an account of). ②报到 bàodào (go to somebody). ③揭发 jiēfā (complain).

reporter *n.* 记者 jìzhě.

repose *n.* ①休息 xiūxi (rest).

②安静 ānjìng (quietness). — v.
休息 xiūxi.

represent v. ①表示 biǎoshì,
象征 xiàngzhēng (embody).
②代表 dàibiǎo (speak on behalf).

representation n. 代表
dàibiǎo.

representative n. 代表
dàibiǎo.

repress v. 压制 yāzhì, 压抑
yāyì.

reprieve n. & v. 延缓处决
yánhuǎn chǔjué.

reprimand n. & v. 惩戒
chéngjiè, 严斥 yánchì.

reprisal n. 报复 bàofù.

reproach n. & v. 谴责
qiǎnzé, 斥责 chìzé.

reproduce v. ①复制 fùzhì
(copy). ②生殖 shēngzhí
(procreate).

reproduction n. ①复制 fùzhì
(copying), 复制品 fùzhìpǐn (a
copy). ②生殖 shēngzhí
(procreation).

reprove v. 谴责 qiǎnzé.

reptile n. 爬行动物 páxíng
dòngwù.

republic n. 共和国
gònghéguó.

republican adj. 共和国的
gònghéguó de (of a republic).
— n. 共和党党员 gònghédǎng
dǎngyuán (party member).

repudiate v. 拒绝 jùjué
(refuse).

repulse v. 驱逐 qūzhú.

reputation n. 名誉 míngyù,
声望 shēngwàng.

repute n. 名誉 míngyù.

request n. & v. 请求 qǐngqiú,
要求 yāoqiú.

require v. ①需要 xūyào
(need). ②要求 yāoqiú

(demand).

requirement n. 必要事物
bìyào shìwù 〈thing〉, 必备条件
bìbèi tiáojiàn 〈qualification〉.

requisite adj. 需要的 xūyào
de, 必要的 bìyào de.

requite v. 回报 huíbào, 报答
bàodá (repay).

rescind v. 废止 fèizhǐ.

rescue n. & v. 解救 jiějiù, 救
出 jiùchu, 救援 jiùyuán.

research n. 研究 yánjiū /
yánjiù.

resemblance n. 相似
xiāngsì.

resemble v. 相似 xiāngsì.

resent v. 愤恨 fènhèn.

reservation n. ①预订 yùdìng
(booking). ②保留 bǎoliú
(doubt). ③保留地 bǎoliúdì
(protected area).

reserve v. ①留下 liúxia (keep).
②预约 yùyuē (book). — n.
①贮藏 zhùcáng / zhǔcáng
(stores). ②保留地 bǎoliúdì
(protected area).

reservoir n. 贮水池
zhùshuǐchí / zhǔshuǐchí, 水库
shuǐkù.

reside v. 居住 jūzhù (live).

residence n. 住宅 zhùzhái,
住处 zhùchù (dwelling).

resident n. 居民 jūmín.

residential adj. 住宅的
zhùzhái de.

residual adj. 残余的 cányú de.

residue n. 残余 cányú.

resign v. 辞职 cízhí (quit).

resignation n. ①辞职 cízhí
(resigning). ②辞呈 cíchéng
(letter to resign).

resin n. 树脂 shùzhī, 松脂
sōngzhī.

resist v. ①抵抗 dǐkàng

R

(oppose). ②防止 fángzhǐ (prevent).

resistance n. 抵抗 dǐkàng (opposition), 抵抗力 dǐkànglì 〈force〉.

resistor n. 电阻器 diànzǔqì.

resolute adj. 坚决的 jiānjué de, 断然的 duànrán de.

resolution n. ①决心 juéxīn, 坚决 jiānjué (determination). ②决议 juéyì (decision).

resolve v. ①决定 juédìng, 下决心 xiàjuéxīn (decide). ②解决 jiějué (have an answer to).

resonance n. 回响 huíxiǎng, 共鸣 gòngmíng.

resort n. 度假胜地 dùjiàshèngdì. — v. 采取 cǎiqǔ, 诉诸 sùzhū (adopt).

resound v. 回响 huíxiǎng, 共鸣 gòngmíng (echo).

resource n. (pl.) 资源 zīyuán.

respect n. ①尊敬 zūnjìng, 尊重 zūnzhòng (admiration). ②方面 fāngmiàn (aspect).

respectable adj. ①高尚的 gāoshàng de (decent). ②可观的 kěguān de (considerable). ③端庄的 duānzhuāng de (modest).

respectful adj. 恭敬的 gōngjìng de.

respective adj. 个别的 gèbié de.

respectively adv. 个别地 gèbié de, 各自地 gèzì de.

respiration n. 呼吸 hūxī.

respite n. 休息 xiūxi (rest), 中止 zhōngzhǐ (pause).

resplendent adj. 灿烂的 cànlàn de, 华丽的 huálì de.

respond v. ①回答 huídá (answer). ②回应 huíyìng (act in answer).

response n. 回答 huídá (answer), 回应 huíyìng (reaction).

responsibility n. 责任 zérèn 〈general〉, 职责 zhízé 〈work〉.

responsible adj. 负责的 fù zérèn de.

responsive adj. 有反应的 yǒu fǎnyìng de.

rest n. 休息 xiūxi (break). ~ **room** 厕所 cèsuǒ, 洗手间 xǐshǒujiān. ~ **stop** 休息站 xiūxizhàn. — v. 休息 xiūxi.

restaurant n. 餐厅 cāntīng, 餐馆 cānguǎn, 饭店 fàndiàn.

restless adj. ①不安静的 bù ānjìng de, 好动的 hàodòng de (agitated). ②无法休息的 wúfǎ xiūxi de (sleepless).

restoration n. ①修复 xiūfù (restoring). ②恢复 huīfù (bringing back).

restore v. ①修复 xiūfù (fix). ②归还 guīhuán (give back). ③恢复 huīfù (put in original condition).

restrain v. 克制 kèzhì, 抑制 yìzhì.

restraint n. 克制 kèzhì, 抑制 yìzhì.

restrict v. 限制 xiànzhì.

restriction n. 限制 xiànzhì.

result n. 结果 jiéguǒ 〈effect〉.

resume v. 再开始 zài kāishǐ (start again), 继续 jìxù (continue).

résumé n. 履历 lǚlì.

resurrect v. ①使复活 shǐ fùhuó (bring back to life). ②复兴 fùxīng (revive).

retail n. & v. 零售 língshòu.

retailer n. 零售商 língshòushāng.

retain v. ①保持 bǎochí (hold), 保留 bǎoliú (keep). ②记得 jìde

(remember).

retaliate v. 报复 bàofù.

retard v. 延迟 yánchí.

retarded adj. 智能迟缓的 zhìnéng chíhuǎn de.

retention n. 保留 bǎoliú (retaining).

reticent adj. 沉默的 chénmò de.

retina n. 视网膜 shìwǎngmó.

retire v. 退休 tuìxiū (stop working).

retirement n. 退休 tuìxiū.

retort v. 回嘴 huízuǐ (answer back), 反驳 fǎnbó (refute).

retrace v. 折回 zhéhuí (go back over).

retract v. ①缩回 suōhuí (pull back). ②收回 shōuhuí (withdraw).

retreat n. & v. 撤退 chètuì (withdrawal).

retribution n. 报应 bàoyìng.

retrieve v. 寻回 xúnhuí.

retrogressive adj. 后退的 hòutuì de, 退化的 tuìhuà de.

retrospect n. 回顾 huígù, 回溯 huísù.

return v. ①回来 huílai (come back). ②回归 huíguī (go back). ③归还 guīhuán (give back). — n. ①回来 huílai (coming back). ②盈利 yínglì (profit).

reunion n. 重聚 chóngjù (get together again), 团圆 tuányuán 〈of family, friends, etc.〉.

reveal v. ①显露 xiǎnlù (display). ②泄露 xièlòu (make known).

revelation n. 泄露 xièlòu.

revenge n. & v. 报仇 bàochóu, 报复 bàofù (vengeance).

revenue n. 收入 shōurù (income), 岁收 suìshōu 〈taxes〉.

revere v. 尊敬 zūnjìng.

reverence n. 尊敬 zūnjìng.

reversal n. 反转 fǎnzhuǎn, 逆转 nìzhuǎn.

reverse v. 反转 fǎnzhuǎn (go back), 颠倒 diāndǎo (turn over). — adj. 相反的 xiāngfǎn de. — v. ①反转 fǎnzhuǎn, 颠倒 diāndǎo (turn round). ②逆行 nìxíng (go backwards). ③取消 qǔxiāo (cancel).

revert v. 恢复原状 huīfù yuánzhuàng.

review v. ①复习 fùxí 〈of school work〉. ②评论 pínglùn 〈for publication〉. ③复审 fùshěn (re-examine).

revise v. 修订 xiūdìng, 校订 jiàodìng.

revision n. 修订 xiūdìng, 校订 jiàodìng.

revival n. 振兴 zhènxīng.

revive v. 振兴 zhènxīng.

revoke v. 取消 qǔxiāo.

revolt v. ①背叛 bèipàn (rebel). ②使厌恶 shǐ yànwù (disgust). — n. 背叛 bèipàn (rebellion).

revolution n. ①革命 gémìng (reformation). ②周期 zhōuqī / zhōuqí (circuit).

revolutionary adj. 革命性的 gémìngxìng de.

revolve v. 旋转 xuánzhuǎn (go around in a circle).

revolver n. 左轮手枪 zuǒlún shǒuqiāng.

reward n. & v. 报酬 bàochóu.

rewrite v. 重写 chóngxiě (write again), 改写 gǎixiě (correct).

R

rhapsody n. 狂想曲 kuángxiǎngqǔ.

rhetoric n. 修辞学 xiūcíxué.

rheumatism n. 风湿症 fēngshīzhèng.

rhinoceros n. 犀牛 xīniú.

rhyme v. 押韵 yāyùn. — n. ①韵 yùn (rhythm). ②诗 shī, 韵文 yùnwén (poem).

rhythm n. 韵律 yùnlǜ, 节奏 jiézòu.

rib n. 肋骨 lèigǔ / lègǔ (bone).

ribbon n. 丝带 sīdài (long, narrow strip).

rice n. 米 mǐ (uncooked), 饭 fàn (cooked).

rich adj. ①有钱的 yǒuqián de, 富有的 fùyǒu de (wealthy). ②富足的 fùzú de (abundant). ③肥沃的 féiwò de (fruitful).

rickets n. 佝偻病 yǔlǚbìng / yǔlóubìng.

rid v. 免除 miǎnchú.

riddance n. 除去 chúqù.

riddle n. 谜语 míyǔ, 谜 mí.

ride v. 骑 qí (bike, horse), 乘 chéng (be carried on). — n. 乘坐 chéngzuò.

rider n. ①骑乘者 qíchéngzhě (person). ②附文 fùwén, 附件 fùjiàn (statement).

ridge n. ①山脊 shānjǐ (hill). ②屋脊 wūjǐ (house).

ridicule n. & v. 讪笑 shànxiào, 嘲弄 cháonòng.

ridiculous adj. 荒谬的 huāngmiù de.

rife adj. ①流行的 liúxíng de (widespread). ②众多的 zhòngduō de (full of).

rifle n. 来福枪 láifúqiāng, 步枪 bùqiāng.

rig n. ①装备 zhuāngbèi (equipment). ②服装 fúzhuāng

(clothing). — v. 装索具于 zhuāng suǒjù yú.

right adj. ①正确的 zhèngquè de (correct). ②公正的 gōngzhèng de (just). ③右方的 yòufāng de (right-hand).

~ wing 右派 yòupài. — n. 权利 quánlì.

righteous adj. 正义的 zhèngyì de (morally right).

rigid adj. ①僵硬的 jiāngyìng de (stiff). ②严格的 yángé de (strict).

rim n. 边缘 biānyuán.

rind n. ①树皮 shùpí (of trees). ②果皮 guǒpí (of fruits).

ring n. ①环 huán, 圈 quān (circle). ②戒指 jièzhǐ (for finger). ③铃声 língshēng (sound). — v. 响 xiǎng (sound).

rink n. 旱冰场 hànbīngchǎng / 溜冰场 liūbīngchǎng.

rinse v. 清洗 qīngxǐ, 洗濯 xǐzhuó.

riot n. 暴动 bàodòng (violent disturbance). — v. 暴动 bàodòng, 骚动 sāodòng.

rip v. 撕开 sīkāi, 扯裂 chěliè.

ripe adj. 成熟的 chéngshú de / chéngshóu de.

ripen v. 使成熟 shǐ chéngshú / shǐ chéngshóu.

ripple n. 涟漪 liányī (very small wave). — v. 起涟漪 qǐ liányī.

rise v. ①站起 zhànqǐ (stand up). ②升起 shēngqǐ (advance in rank). ③起床 qǐchuáng (get up). ④上升 shàngshēng, 涨 zhǎng (increase). — n. ①往上的斜坡 wǎngshàng de xiépō (ascent). ②上升 shàngshēng, 增高 zēnggāo (increase).

risk n. 危险 wēixiǎn / wéixiǎn.

— v. 冒……危险 mào...
wēixiǎn / mào...wéixiǎn.

risky adj. 冒险的 màoxiǎn de.

rite n. 仪式 yíshì.

ritual n. 仪式 yíshì.

rival n. 竞争者 jìngzhēngzhě
(competitor), 对手 duìshǒu
(opponent), 敌手 díshǒu
(enemy). — v. 与……竞争
yǔ...jìngzhēng.

river n. 河 hé, 江 jiāng.

rivet n. 铆钉 mǎodīng.

rivulet n. 溪流 xīliú, 小河
xiǎohé.

road n. 路 lù, 道路 dàolù.

roam v. 闲逛 xiánguàng, 漫游
mànyóu.

roar v. 吼叫 hǒujiào. — n. 吼
hǒu.

roast v. 烤 kǎo (grill). — n. 烤
肉 kǎoròu ⟨meat⟩. — adj. 烘烤
的 hōngkǎo de.

rob v. 抢劫 qiǎngjié.

robber n. 强盗 qiángdào.

robbery n. 抢劫 qiǎngjié.

robe n. 长外袍 chángwàipáo.

robin n. 知更鸟 zhīgēngniǎo.

robot n. 机器人 jīqìrén.

robust adj. 强壮的
qiángzhuàng de.

rock n. 岩石 yánshí, 石块
shíkuài (stone). — v. 摇摆
yáobǎi, 摇动 yáodòng (sway).
~ *and roll* 摇滚乐 yáogǔnyuè.

rocket n. 火箭 huǒjiàn. — v.
向上直冲 xiàngshàng
zhíchōng.

rocky adj. 多岩石的 duō
yánshí de.

rod n. 杆 gǎn, 棒 bàng.

rogue n. 流氓 liúmáng, 恶棍
è'gùn.

role n. 角色 juésè (character).

roll v. ①滚 gǔn, 转 zhuàn
(move round). ②卷 juǎn (curl).
③辗平 niǎnpíng (flatten). — n.
①一卷 yìjuǎn (scroll). ②名册
míngcè, 名单 míngdān (list).

roller n. 滚轴 gǔnzhóu (cylinder), 滚轮 gǔnlún (wheel).
~ *coaster* 云霄飞车 yúnxiāo
fēichē. ~ *skate* 旱冰鞋
hànbīngxié / 溜冰鞋
liūbīngxié.

romance n. ①爱情故事
àiqíng gùshi ⟨story⟩. ②传奇小
说 chuánqí xiǎoshuō
⟨adventure⟩. ③情事 qíngshì
(love interest).

romantic adj. ①浪漫的
làngmàn de (dream-like). ②浪
漫派的 làngmànpài de ⟨of art,
music, etc.⟩.

roof n. 屋顶 wūdǐng ⟨building⟩,
顶部 dǐngbù (top).

rookie n. 生手 shēngshǒu, 新
手 xīnshǒu (beginner), 新兵
xīnbīng (recruit).

room n. ①房间 fángjiān
⟨in a house⟩. ②空间 kōngjiān
(space).

roommate n. 同屋 tóngwū /
室友 shìyǒu.

roost v. 栖息 qīxī / qīxí. — n.
栖木 qīmù.

rooster n. 公鸡 gōngjī.

root n. ①根 gēn, 根部 gēnbù
⟨plant⟩. ②根源 gēnyuán
(source). ③字根 zìgēn
⟨grammar⟩. ④根数 gēnshù
⟨mathematics⟩.

rope n. 绳 shéng.

rosary n. 念珠 niànzhū.

rose n. ①玫瑰 méiguī ⟨flower⟩.
②玫瑰色 méiguīsè ⟨color⟩.

rostrum n. 讲坛 jiǎngtán.

rosy adj. ①玫瑰色的 méiguīsè
de (reddish). ②光明的

R

guāngmíng de (bright).

rot v. 腐烂 fǔlàn, 腐坏 fǔhuài (decay). — n. 腐烂 fǔlàn, 腐坏 fǔhuài (rottenness).

rotary adj. 旋转的 xuánzhuǎn de.

rotate v. ①旋转 xuánzhuǎn (turn). ②循环 xúnhuán (recur in order).

rotation n. ①旋转 xuánzhuǎn (revolution). ②轮流 lúnliú (taking turns).

rotten adj. ①腐烂的 fǔlàn de 〈food〉. ②腐朽的 fǔxiǔ de 〈wood〉. ③坏的 huài de (bad).

rough adj. ①粗糙的 cūcāo de (coarse), 凹凸不平的 āotū--bùpíng de / āotū-bùpíng de (not even). ②粗鲁的 cūlǔ de (impolite). ③概略的 gàilüè de (approximate). ④粗厉的 cūlì de (rasping). ⑤艰苦的 jiānkǔ de (difficult).

roughen v. 使崎岖不平 shǐ qíqū bùpíng, 变粗糙 biàn cūcāo.

roughly adv. 概略地 gàilüè de.

round adj. 圆的 yuán de (circular). — n. 回合 huíhé, 局 jú 〈game〉.

rouse v. 唤醒 huànxǐng (waken).

rout v. 击溃 jīkuì / jíkuì (defeat completely). — n. 溃败 kuìbài.

route n. 路线 lùxiàn.

routine n. & adj. 例行公事 lìxíng gōngshì, 惯例 guànlì (regular activity).

rove v. 漫游 mànyóu.

row n. 列 liè, 排 pái (line). — v. 划船 huáchuán.

rowdy adj. 粗暴的 cūbào de.

royal adj. 王室的 wángshì de, 皇家的 huángjiā de.

royalty n. 皇族 huángzú, 皇室 huángshì (royal family).

R.S.V.P. 敬请答复 jìngqǐng dáfù.

rub v. 摩擦 mócā.

rubber n. 橡胶 xiàngjiāo, 橡皮 xiàngpí (substance). ~ **band** 橡皮筋 xiàngpíjīn.

rubbish n. ①废物 fèiwù, 垃圾 lājī / lèsè (waste). ②废话 fèihuà (nonsense).

rubble n. 碎石 suìshí, 瓦砾 wǎlì.

ruby n. ①红宝石 hóngbǎoshí 〈stone〉. ②深红色 shēnhóngsè 〈color〉.

rudder n. 船舵 chuánduò.

ruddy adj. 红润的 hóngrùn de.

rude adj. ①无礼貌的 wú lǐmào de, 粗鲁的 cūlǔ de (impolite). ②粗暴的 cūbào de, 猛烈的 měngliè de (violent).

rudimentary adj. 初期的 chūqī de / chūqí de (elementary).

rue v. 悔恨 huǐhèn.

ruffian n. 凶汉 xiōnghàn, 恶棍 ègùn.

ruffle v. ①使皱 shǐ zhòu (ripple). ②弄乱 nòngluàn (mess up). ③惹……生气 rě...shēngqì (annoy).

rug n. 地毯 dìtǎn (thick floor mat).

rugby n. 橄榄球 gǎnlǎnqiú.

rugged adj. 崎岖的 qíqū de (rocky).

ruin n. ①毁灭 huǐmiè (collapse). ②废墟 fèixū (debris). — v. 摧毁 cuīhuǐ, 破坏 pòhuài (destroy).

rule n. ①规则 guīzé (regulation). ②统治 tǒngzhì (govern-

ment), 管理 guǎnlǐ (management). ③惯例 guànlì (habit). — v. 统治 tǒngzhì (govern).

ruler n. ①统治者 tǒngzhìzhě (governor). ②尺 chǐ 〈for measuring〉.

rum n. 莱姆酒 láimǔjiǔ.

rumble n. & v. 隆隆声 lónglóngshēng 〈sound〉.

rumor n. 谣言 yáoyán (gossip). — v. 谣传 yáochuán.

rump n. 臀部 túnbù.

run v. ①跑 pǎo (race). ②行驶 xíngshǐ 〈car〉. ③运转 yùnzhuǎn (work). ④流 liú (flow). ⑤经营 jīngyíng 〈business〉. — n. 跑 pǎo (race).

runaway n. 逃亡者 táowángzhě.

runner n. 奔跑者 bēnpǎozhě (someone who runs).

running adj. ①连续的 liánxù de (consecutive). ②流动的 liúdòng de (flowing).

runway n. 跑道 pǎodào (air strip).

rupture n. & v. 破裂 pòliè (burst), 决裂 juéliè (breaking).

rural adj. 乡村的 xiāngcūn de.

rush v. ①冲进 chōngjìn (bolt). ②急促行事 jícù xíngshì (act quickly). — n. ①匆促 cōngcù (haste). ②冲进 chōngjìn (act of rushing).

Russian n. & adj. ①俄国人 Éguórén 〈people〉. ②俄语 Éyǔ 〈language〉.

rust n. 锈 xiù. — v. 生锈 shēngxiù (get rusty).

rustic adj. ①乡村的 xiāngcūn de (rural). ②单纯的 dānchún de (simple).

rustle n. & v. 沙沙声 shāshāshēng 〈sound〉.

rusty adj. ①生锈的 shēngxiù de (oxidized). ②荒疏的 huāngshū de (unused).

rut n. 车辙 chēzhé / chēchè (track made by wheels).

ruthless adj. 无情的 wúqíng de (cold), 残忍的 cánrěn de (cruel).

rye n. 裸麦 luǒmài, 黑麦 hēimài.

S

Sabbath n. 安息日 Ānxīrì / Ānxírì.

saber n. 军刀 jūndāo.

sable n. 貂 diāo.

sabotage n. & v. 阴谋破坏 yīnmóu pòhuài.

sachet n. 香囊 xiāngnáng.

sack n. 袋子 dàizi. — v. ①解雇

jiěgù (fire). ②劫掠 jiélüè (plunder).

sacrament n. 圣礼 shènglǐ. S~ 圣餐 Shèngcān (Communion).

sacred adj. 神圣的 shénshèng de.

sacrifice n. ①祭品 jìpǐn

(offering). ②牺牲 xīshēng (giving up). — v. ①祭祀 jìsì (offer). ②牺牲 xīshēng (give up).

sacrilege n. 亵渎 xièdú, 渎神 dúshén.

sad adj. ①悲伤的 bēishāng de, 难过的 nánguò de (sorrowful). ②令人悲伤的 lìng rén bēishāng de (distressing).

sadden v. 使悲伤 shǐ bēishāng.

saddle n. 鞍 ān. — v. 给…… 装鞍 gěi...zhuāng'ān.

sadness n. 悲伤 bēishāng, 难过 nánguò.

safe adj. ①安全的 ānquán de (secure). ②平安的 píng'ān de (peaceful). ③小心的 xiǎoxīn de (cautious).

safeguard n. & v. 保护 bǎohù, 防护 fánghù.

safety n. 安全 ānquán (security). ~ **belt** 安全带 ānquándài.

sag v. 压陷 yāxiàn, 下坠 xiàzhuì.

saga n. ①长篇故事 chángpiān gùshi (long story). ②英勇事迹 yīngyǒng shìjì / yīngyǒng shìjì (hero's journey).

sage adj. 贤明的 xiánmíng de. — n. 圣人 shèngrén.

Sagittarius 射手座 Shèshǒuzuò.

Sahara 撒哈拉沙漠 Sāhālā shāmò.

sail n. ①帆 fān / fán (foresail). ②航行 hángxíng (voyage). — v. ①航行 hángxíng (travel). ②驾驶 jiàshǐ (navigate).

sailboat n. 帆船 fānchuán / fánchuán.

sailing n. ①航行 hángxíng

(voyage). ②航海术 hánghǎishù (skill).

sailor n. ①船员 chuányuán (crew). ②水手 shuǐshǒu (seaman).

saint n. ①圣徒 shèngtú (religion). ②圣人 shèngrén (sage).

sake n. 缘故 yuángù. *for the ~ of* ... 为了…… wèile....

salad n. 色拉 sèlā / 沙拉 shālā, 生菜食品 shēngcài shípǐn.

salary n. 薪资 xīnzī.

sale n. 销售 xiāoshòu, 销路 xiāolù. *for ~* 出售 chūshòu. *on ~* 打折 dǎzhé.

salesman n. 推销员 tuīxiāoyuán, 业务员 yèwùyuán, 售货员 shòuhuòyuán.

saliva n. 唾液 tuòyè.

sallow adj. 病黄色的 bìnghuángsè de (sickly yellow), 气色差的 qìsè chà de / qìsè chā de (looking unwell).

salmon n. 鲑鱼 guīyú.

salon n. ①会客厅 huìkètīng (room). ②美术展览会 měishù zhǎnlǎnhuì, 画廊 huàláng (art gallery). ③艺文聚会 yìwén jùhuì (artistic gathering). ④美发沙龙 měifà shālóng / měifà shālóng (hair).

saloon n. 酒馆 jiǔguǎn, 酒吧 jiǔbā (bar).

salt n. 盐 yán.

salty adj. 咸的 xián de.

salubrious adj. 有益健康的 yǒuyì jiànkāng de, 怡人的 yírén de.

salutary adj. ①有益的 yǒuyì de (beneficial). ②健康的 jiànkāng de (healthy)

salutation n. 致意 zhìyì, 招呼 zhāohu.

salute v. ①致敬 zhìjìng, 敬礼 jìnglǐ (show honor). ②致意 zhìyì, 招呼 zhāohu (greet).

salvage n. 灾难救援 zāinàn jiùyuán. — v. ①灾难救援 zāinàn jiùyuán (damaged building). ②挽救 wǎnjiù (failed situation).

salvation n. ①拯救 zhěngjiù (redemption). ②救助 jiùzhù (help). *the S- Army* 救世军 Jiùshìjūn.

salve n. 软膏 ruǎngāo, 药膏 yàogāo (ointment).

same adj. 相同的 xiāngtóng de, 同样的 tóngyàng de.

sample n. 样本 yàngběn, 样品 yàngpǐn.

sanatorium n. 疗养院 liáoyǎngyuàn.

sanction n. & v. ①认可 rènkě, 批准 pīzhǔn (permission). ②制裁 zhìcái (penalty).

sanctity n. 神圣 shénshèng.

sanctuary n. ①圣所 shèngsuǒ (holy place). ②保护区 bǎohùqū (wildlife reserve). ③避难所 bìnànsuǒ (shelter).

sand n. 沙 shā.

sandal n. 凉鞋 liángxié.

sandglass n. 沙漏 shālòu.

sandwich n. 三明治 sānmíngzhì.

sandy adj. 含沙的 hánshā de.

sane adj. ①神志清醒的 shénzhì qīngxǐng de (not mad). ②明智的 míngzhì de (sensible).

sanguine adj. 乐天的 lètiān de (optimistic).

sanitary adj. 卫生的 wèishēng de. ~ *napkin* 卫生棉 wèishēngmián.

sanitation n. ①卫生 wèishēng, 公共卫生 gōnggòng wèishēng (hygiene). ②卫生设备 wèishēng shèbèi (equipment).

sanity n. 心智健全 xīnzhì jiànquán, 神志清醒 shénzhì qīngxǐng.

Santa Claus n. 圣诞老人 Shèngdàn Lǎorén.

sap n. 树液 shùyè (plant). — v. 削弱 xuēruò / xuèruò, 耗竭 hàojié.

sapphire n. 蓝宝石 lánbǎoshí.

sarcasm n. 讽刺 fěngcì / fèngcì, 讥讽 jīfěng / jīfèng.

sarcastic adj. 讽刺的 fěngcì de / fèngcì de, 讥讽的 jīfěng de / jīfèng de.

sardine n. 沙丁鱼 shādīngyú.

sash n. ①带 dài, 饰带 shìdài (clothing). ②窗框 chuāngkuàng / chuāngkuāng (window).

Satan n. 撒旦 Sādàn, 恶魔 Èmó.

satchel n. 小皮包 xiǎo píbāo, 小书包 xiǎo shūbāo.

satellite n. ①卫星 wèixīng (planet). ②人造卫星 rénzào wèixīng (man-made device). ~ *television* 卫星电视 wèixīng diànshì.

satin n. 缎 duàn.

satire n. 讽刺诗文 fěngcì shīwén / fèngcì shīwén.

satisfaction n. 满足 mǎnzú, 满意 mǎnyì.

satisfactory adj. 令人满意的 lìng rén mǎnyì de.

satisfied adj. 满足的 mǎnzú de, 满意的 mǎnyì de.

satisfy v. 使满足 shǐ mǎnzú, 使满意 shǐ mǎnyì.

S

saturate v. ①浸透 jìntòu (drench). ②饱和 bǎohé (fill completely).

Saturday n. 星期六 Xīngqīliù / Xīngqíliù.

Saturn n. 土星 Tǔxīng.

sauce n. 调味汁 tiáowèizhī, 调味酱 tiáowèijiàng.

saucepan n. 炖锅 dùnguō.

saucer n. 茶盘 chápán, 碟子 diézi.

sauna n. 桑拿浴 sāngnáyù / 三温暖 sānwēnnuǎn.

saunter v. 闲逛 xiánguàng, 漫步 mànbù.

sausage n. 腊肠 làcháng, 香肠 xiāngcháng.

savage adj. ①野蛮的 yěmán de (barbaric). ②残酷的 cánkù de (cruel), 凶猛的 xiōngměng de (fierce). — n. 野蛮人 yěmánrén.

savannah n. 大草原 dà cǎoyuán.

save v. ①拯救 zhěngjiù, 援救 yuánjiù (rescue). ②储蓄 chǔxù / chúxù, 存 cún (collect). ③节省 jiéshěng (lessen).

saving n. ①节省 jiéshěng (amount saved). ②(pl.) 储蓄 chǔxù / chúxù (money saved up).

savior n. 拯救者 zhěngjiùzhě.

savor v. ①享受 xiǎngshòu (enjoy). ②品尝 pǐncháng ⟨flavor⟩.

savory adj. 美味的 měiwèi de, 可口的 kěkǒu de (pleasant to taste).

saw n. 锯子 jùzi. — v. 锯开 jùkai.

saxophone n. 萨克斯管 sàkèsīguǎn / 萨克斯风 sàkèsīfēng.

say v. 说 shuō, 讲 jiǎng.

saying n. 谚语 yànyǔ, 格言 géyán.

scab n. 疤 bā, 痂 jiā.

scabbard n. 剑鞘 jiànqiào.

scaffold n. ①鹰架 yīngjià ⟨for building⟩. ②断头台 duàntóutái, 绞台 jiǎotái ⟨gallows⟩.

scaffolding n. 鹰架 yīngjià.

scald v. 烫伤 tàngshāng.

scale n. ①天秤 tiānchèng / 天枰 tiānpíng (balance). ②鳞 lín ⟨fish⟩. ③比例尺 bǐlìchǐ ⟨map⟩. ④刻度 kèdù (marks for measuring). ⑤音阶 yīnjiē ⟨music⟩.

scallop n. 扇贝 shànbèi.

scalp n. 头皮 tóupí. — v. 剥头皮 bāo tóupí / 剝头皮 bō tóupí.

scamper v. 蹦蹦跳跳地跑 bèngbèng-tiàotiào de pǎo.

scan v. ①细察 xìchá, 审视 shěnshì (examine). ②浏览 liúlǎn (glance at). ③扫描 sǎomiáo ⟨copy⟩.

scandal n. ①丑闻 chǒuwén (disgrace). ②诽谤 fěibàng (slander).

scanner n. 扫描仪 sǎomiáoyí / 扫描器 sǎomiáoqì.

scanty adj. 不足的 bùzú de, 少量的 shǎoliàng de.

scapegoat n. 代罪羔羊 dàizuì-gāoyáng.

scar n. 伤痕 shānghén, 疤 bā. — v. 留下伤痕 liúxia shānghén.

scarce adj. 缺乏的 quēfá de, 不足的 bùzú de.

scarcely adv. 几乎不 jīhū bù, 仅仅 jǐnjǐn.

scarcity n. 缺乏 quēfá, 不足 bùzú.

scare v. 惊吓 jīngxià, 惊恐

jīngkǒng. — n. 惊恐 jīngkǒng.

scared *adj.* 受惊的 shòujīng de, 害怕的 hàipà de.

scarecrow *n.* 稻草人 dàocǎorén.

scarf *n.* 围巾 wéijīn.

scarlet *n.* 深红 shēnhóng. — *adj.* 深红的 shēnhóng de. ~ *fever* 猩红热 xīnghóngrè.

scathing *adj.* 严苛的 yánkē de (severe).

scatter *v.* ①驱散 qūsàn (dispel). ②散播 sànbō / sànbō (spread).

scavenger *n.* 清道夫 qīngdàofū.

scenario *n.* 剧情 jùqíng, 剧本 jùběn.

scene *n.* ①现场 xiànchǎng (location). ②风景 fēngjǐng, 景色 jǐngsè (landscape). ③一幕 yímù (episode). ④场景 chǎngjǐng, 布景 bùjǐng (backdrop).

scenery *n.* ①风景 fēngjǐng, 景色 jǐngsè (landscape). ②舞台布景 wǔtái bùjǐng (backdrop).

scent *n.* ①香味 xiāngwèi (fragrance). ②气味 qìwèi (smell). ③香水 xiāngshuǐ (perfume). — *v.* 嗅出 xiùchu (smell).

schedule *n.* 表 biǎo, 时刻表 shíkèbiǎo (timetable), 行程表 xíngchéngbiǎo (agenda). — *v.* 将……列表 jiāng...lièbiǎo (put in schedule), 安排 ānpái (arrange).

scheme *n.* ①计画 jìhuà (plan). ②阴谋 yīnmóu (conspiracy). ③图表 túbiǎo (diagram). ④设计 shèjì (design). — *v.* 计画 jìhuà (plan), 图谋 túmóu (connive).

schizophrenia *n.* 精神分裂症 jīngshén fēnliè zhèng.

scholar *n.* 学者 xuézhě (learned person).

scholarship *n.* ①奖学金 jiǎngxuéjīn (award). ②学识 xuéshí / xuéshì, 学问 xuéwen (knowledge).

school *n.* 学校 xuéxiào 〈institution〉. ~ *bus* 校车 xiàochē. ~ *of thought* 学派 xuépài.

schooling *n.* 学校教育 xuéxiào jiàoyù.

schoolmate *n.* 同学 tóngxué.

schoolteacher *n.* 教师 jiàoshī.

sciatica *n.* 坐骨神经痛 zuògǔ shénjīng tòng.

science *n.* 科学 kēxué. ~ *fiction* 科幻小说 kēhuàn xiǎoshuō. ~ *park* 科学园区 kēxué yuánqū.

scientific *adj.* 科学的 kēxué de.

scientist *n.* 科学家 kēxuéjiā.

scintillate *v.* 发出火花 fāchū huǒhuā, 闪烁 shǎnshuò (twinkle).

scissors *n.* 剪刀 jiǎndāo.

scoff *n. & v.* 嘲笑 cháoxiào.

scold *v.* 责骂 zémà.

scoop *n.* ①勺子 sháozi (ladle). ②独家新闻 dújiā xīnwén 〈news〉. — *v.* 铲起 chǎnqǐ, 舀出 yǎochu.

scooter *n.* 摩托车 mótuōchē (motor scooter).

scope *n.* ①范围 fànwéi (range). ②眼界 yǎnjiè, 视野 shìyě (outlook).

scorch *v.* 烧焦 shāojiāo.

score *n.* ①得分 défēn (number of points). ②画线 huàxiàn, 记

S

号 jìhào (mark). ③账 zhàng,
欠款 qiànkuǎn (debt). ④分数
fēnshù, 成绩 chéngjì / chéngjī
(grade). — v. ①得分 défēn
(gain points). ②画线 huàxiàn,
作记号 zuò jìhào (mark).

scorn n. & v. 轻视 qīngshì,
轻蔑 qīngmiè, 蔑视 mièshì.

scornful adj. 轻蔑的 qīngmiè
de, 不屑的 búxiè de.

Scorpio 天蝎座 Tiānxiēzuò.

scorpion n. 蝎子 xiēzi.

scoundrel n. 无赖 wúlài, 恶
汉 èhàn.

scour v. ①擦亮 cāliàng (rub).
②洗涤 xǐdí (clean). ③遍寻
biànxún (search).

scourge n. ①鞭 biān (whip).
②天谴 tiānqiǎn ⟨suffering⟩.
— v. ①鞭笞 biānchí (whip).
②惩罚 chéngfá (punish).

scout n. 侦察兵 zhēnchábīng
(lookout). *Boy S~s* 童子军
Tóngzǐjūn. — v. 侦察 zhēnchá.

scowl n. & v. 皱眉表示
zhòuméi biǎoshì.

scramble v. ①攀缘 pānyuán,
爬行 páxíng (climb). ②争夺
zhēngduó (compete). *~d eggs*
炒蛋 chǎodàn. — n. ①攀缘
pānyuán, 爬行 páxíng (climb).
②争夺 zhēngduó (struggle).

scrap n. ①小片 xiǎopiàn, 小
块 xiǎokuài (piece). ②废物
fèiwù (waste). — v. 丢弃 diūqì
(throw away), 放弃 fàngqì
(abandon).

scrape v. ①擦伤 cāshāng
⟨injure⟩. ②擦净 cājìng (clean).
— n. ①摩擦声 mócāshēng
⟨sound⟩. ②麻烦 máfan
(trouble).

scratch v. 抓 zhuā, 搔 sāo.
— n. ①刮痕 guāhén (mark).

②抓伤 zhuāshāng (graze).

scrawl n. & v. 潦草书写
liáocǎo shūxiě, 涂鸦 túyā.

scream n. & v. 尖声叫喊
jiānshēng jiàohǎn.

screech n. 尖叫声
jiānjiàoshēng. — v. 尖叫
jiānjiào (cry out).

screen n. ①幕 mù, 屏 píng, 帘
lián, 帐 zhàng (curtain). ②银幕
yínmù ⟨movies⟩. ③屏幕 píngmù,
萤屏 yíngpíng / 萤幕 yíngmù
⟨TV⟩. — v. ①遮蔽 zhēbì, 掩护
yǎnhù (protect). ②审查
shěnchá (examine).

screenplay n. 电影脚本
diànyǐng jiǎoběn.

screw n. ①螺丝钉 luósīdīng
⟨nail⟩. ②螺旋桨 luóxuánjiǎng
(propeller). — v. ①钉住
dìngzhù (fasten). ②扭转
niǔzhuǎn, 旋转 xuánzhuǎn
(twist).

screwdriver n. 螺丝起子
luósīqǐzi.

scribble n. & v. ①潦草书写
liáocǎo shūxiě ⟨writing⟩. ②涂
鸦 túyā ⟨drawing⟩.

script n. ①笔迹 bǐjì / bǐjī, 手迹
shǒujì / shǒujī ⟨handwriting⟩.
②脚本 jiǎoběn (screenplay).

scripture n. ①经典 jīngdiǎn
⟨religion⟩. ② *the S~* 圣经
Shèngjīng (Bible).

scroll n. 纸卷 zhǐjuàn, 卷轴
juànzhóu.

scrub v. 擦洗 cāxǐ. — n. 灌木
丛 guànmùcóng ⟨bushes⟩.

scruff n. 颈背 jǐngbèi.

scruple n. 顾忌 gùjì.

scrupulous adj. 多虑的
duōlù de, 小心翼翼的
xiǎoxīn-yìyì de.

scrutiny n. 细察 xìchá, 详审

xiángshěn.

scuba n. 水肺 shuǐfèi.

scuffle n. & v. 混战 hùnzhàn, 扭打 niǔdǎ.

sculpt v. 雕刻 diāokè.

sculptor n. 雕刻家 diāokèjiā.

sculpture n. ①雕刻 diāokè 〈art form〉. ②雕像 diāoxiàng 〈art object〉.

scum n. 泡沫 pàomò, 浮渣 fúzhā.

scurrilous adj. 谩骂的 mànmà de, 辱骂的 rǔmà de / rùmà de.

scurry v. 急促奔走 jícù bēnzǒu.

scurvy n. 坏血症 huàixuèzhèng / huàixiězhèng.

scythe n. 大镰刀 dà liándāo.

sea n. 海 hǎi, 海洋 hǎiyáng.

seacoast n. 海岸 hǎi'àn.

seal n. ①海豹 hǎibào 〈animal〉. ②印章 yìnzhāng 〈stamp〉, 印信 yìnxìn 〈confirmation〉. ③封印 fēngyìn 〈attached to an envelope〉. — v. ①封住 fēngzhù 〈fasten〉. ②盖印于 gàiyìn yú 〈stamp〉.

seam n. 接缝 jiēfèng.

seaman n. 船员 chuányuán.

seamstress n. 女裁缝 nǚcáiféng.

search n. & v. 寻觅 xúnmì, 搜索 sōusuǒ 〈looking for〉.

~ *engine* 搜索引擎 sōusuǒ yǐnqíng / 搜寻引擎 sōuxún yǐnqíng.

searchlight n. 探照灯 tànzhàodēng.

seashore n. 海岸 hǎi'àn.

seaside n. 海边 hǎibiān.

season n. 季 jì, 季节 jìjié.

seasoning n. 调味品 tiáowèipǐn.

seat n. 座 zuò, 位置 zuòwèi.

~ *belt* 安全带 ānquándài.

seaweed n. 海藻 hǎizǎo.

secede v. 退出 tuìchū.

seclude v. 退隐 tuìyǐn, 隔离 gélí.

seclusion n. 退隐 tuìyǐn, 隔离 gélí.

second adj. 第二的 dì-èr de. — n. ①第二 dì-èr 〈after the first〉. ②秒 miǎo 〈time〉.

secondary adj. 其次的 qícì de, 第二的 dì-èr de.

~ *school* 中等学校 zhōngděng xuéxiào.

secondhand adj. 二手的 èrshǒu de, 用过的 yòngguo de. ~ *smoke* 二手烟 èrshǒuyān.

secret adj. 秘密的 mìmì de. — n. 秘密 mìmì.

secretary n. ①秘书 mìshū, 书记 shūjì 〈employee〉. ②大臣 dàchén, 部长 bùzhǎng 〈minister〉.

secrete v. 分泌 fēnmì 〈produce〉.

secretly adv. 秘密地 mìmì de.

sect n. 宗派 zōngpài.

section n. ①段 duàn, 片段 piànduàn, 部分 bùfen 〈part〉. ②区域 qūyù 〈area〉. ③部门 bùmén 〈department〉.

sector n. ①区域 qūyù 〈area〉. ②扇形 shànxíng 〈geometry〉.

secular adj. 世俗的 shìsú de.

secure adj. ①安全的 ānquán de 〈safe〉. ②牢固的 láogù de 〈fixed〉. ③稳定的 wěndìng de 〈stable〉. — v. ①获得 huòdé 〈obtain〉. ②使安全 shǐ ānquán 〈make safe〉. ③紧闭 jǐnbì, 关紧 guānjǐn 〈fasten〉.

security n. ①安全 ānquán 〈safety〉. ②安全措施 ānquán

S

cuòshī 〈measures〉. ~ *deposit* 抵押品 dǐyāpǐn.

sedate *adj.* 静肃的 jìngsù de.

sedative *n.* 镇定剂 zhèndìngjì.

sedentary *adj.* 惯坐的 guànzuò de, 久坐的 jiǔzuò de.

sediment *n.* 沉淀物 chéndiànwù.

seduce *v.* 诱惑 yòuhuò.

seduction *n.* 引诱 yǐnyòu, 诱惑 yòuhuò.

see *v.* ①看见 kànjiàn (behold). ②了解 liǎojiě (comprehend). ③会面 huìmiàn (meet). ④考虑 kǎolù, 想想 xiǎngxiang (consider).

seed *n.* 种子 zhǒngzi / zhǒngzǐ.

seek *v.* 寻找 xúnzhǎo, 追寻 zhuīxún.

seem *v.* 似乎 sìhū, 看似 kànsì.

seemly *adj.* 适当的 shìdàng de, 端庄的 duānzhuāng de.

seep *v.* 渗出 shènchu.

seesaw *n.* 跷跷板 qiāoqiāobǎn.

seethe *v.* 激昂 jī'áng, 激动 jīdòng (excite).

segment *n.* 部分 bùfen, 片断 piànduàn.

segregate *v.* 隔离 gélí.

seismic *adj.* 地震的 dìzhèn de.

seize *v.* ①抓住 zhuāzhù, 握住 wòzhù (grab). ②捕获 bǔhuò, 捉住 zhuōzhù (capture). ③攻占 gōngzhàn (invade). ④扣押 kòuyā, 没收 mòshōu (confiscate). ⑤夺取 duóqǔ (take).

seizure *n.* ①扣押 kòuyā, 没收 mòshōu (confiscation). ②发作 fāzuò 〈illness〉. ③夺取 duóqǔ (taking).

seldom *adv.* 很少 hěn shǎo,

不常 bùcháng.

select *v.* 选择 xuǎnzé, 挑选 tiāoxuǎn.

selection *n.* 选择 xuǎnzé, 挑选 tiāoxuǎn.

self *n.* 自身 zìshēn, 自己 zìjǐ.

self-aware *adj.* 自觉的 zìjué de.

self-conscious *adj.* ①忸怩的 niǔní de, 不自然的 bú zìrán de (shy). ②自觉的 zìjué de 〈self-aware〉.

self-contained *adj.* ①寡言的 guǎyán de (reserved). ②配备齐全的 pèibèi qíquán de 〈complete〉. ③独立的 dúlì de (independent), 自足的 zìzú de (self-sufficient).

self-control *n.* 自制 zìzhì.

self-denial *n.* 自制 zìzhì.

selfish *adj.* 自私的 zìsī de.

self-respect *n.* 自重 zìzhòng, 自尊 zìzūn.

self-service *n.* 自助 zìzhù.

self-sufficient *adj.* 自足的 zìzú de.

sell *v.* 卖 mài, 出售 chūshòu.

seller *n.* 卖方 màifāng, 售者 shòuzhě.

semantic *adj.* 语意的 yǔyì de.

semantics *n.* 语意学 yǔyìxué.

semblance *n.* ①外观 wàiguān, 外表 wàibiǎo (appearance). ②类似 lèisì (resemblance).

semen *n.* 精液 jīngyè.

semester *n.* 学期 xuéqī / xuéqí.

semicolon *n.* 分号 fēnhào.

seminar *n.* 研讨会 yántǎohuì, 讲习会 jiǎngxíhuì.

semiofficial *adj.* 半官方的 bànguānfāng de.

senate *n.* 上议院

shàngyìyuàn, 参议院 cānyìyuàn.

senator n. 参议员 cānyìyuán.

send v. ①寄送 jìsòng (mail). ②派 pài, 遣 qiǎn (dispatch). ③发出 fāchū (emit), 发射 fāshè (discharge).

senile adj. 衰老的 shuāilǎo de.

senior adj. ①年长的 niánzhǎng de (older). ②前辈的 qiánbèi de, 资深的 zīshēn de (superior). — n. ①年长者 niánzhǎngzhě (elder). ②前辈 qiánbèi, 上级 shàngjí (superior).

seniority n. 工龄 gōnglíng / 年资 niánzī.

sensation n. ①感觉 gǎnjué, 知觉 zhījué (feeling). ②轰动 hōngdòng (excitement).

sense n. ①意义 yìyì (meaning). ②感觉 gǎnjué, 知觉 zhījué (feeling). ③理智 lǐzhì (judgment). ④意识 yìshí / yìshì, 概念 gàiniàn (understanding). ~ of humor 幽默感 yōumògǎn. common ~ 常识 chángshí / chángshì. make ~ 合理 hélǐ, 有道理 yǒu dàolǐ. — v. 感觉 gǎnjué, 意识到 yìshí dào / yìshì dào.

senseless adj. ①无知觉的 wú zhījué de (unconscious). ②无意义的 wú yìyì de (meaningless). ③愚蠢的 yúchǔn de (foolish).

sensible adj. ①明智的 míngzhì de, 有理性的 yǒu lǐxìng de (reasonable). ②可察觉的 kě chájué de (perceptible).

sensitive adj. 敏感的 mǐngǎn de.

sensitivity n. ①敏感度 mǐngǎndù, 灵敏度 língmǐndù 〈person〉. ②感光度

gǎnguāngdù 〈film〉.

sensual adj. 肉欲的 ròuyù de.

sensuous adj. 感官的 gǎnguān de.

sentence n. ①句 jù, 句子 jùzi 〈language〉. ②判决 pànjué, 宣判 xuānpàn 〈law〉. — v. 宣判 xuānpàn.

sentiment n. ①感情 gǎnqíng (feeling). ②意见 yìjiàn, 观点 guāndiǎn (opinion). ③伤感 shānggǎn (tender feelings).

sentimental adj. 多愁善感的 duōchóu-shàngǎn de, 多情的 duōqíng de.

sentry n. 哨兵 shàobīng.

separate v. 分离 fēnlí, 分开 fēnkai. — adj. 分开的 fēnkai de.

separation n. 分离 fēnlí, 分开 fēnkai.

September n. 九月 Jiǔyuè.

sequel n. ①续集 xùjí, 续篇 xùpiān (continuation). ②结果 jiéguǒ, 结局 jiéjú (outcome).

sequence n. ①顺序 shùnxù (order). ②连续 liánxù (succession).

serenade n. 小夜曲 xiǎoyèqǔ.

serene adj. 宁静的 níngjìng de.

serf n. 农奴 nóngnú.

sergeant n. ①中士 zhōngshì, 士官 shìguān 〈military〉. ②巡佐 xúnzuǒ, 警官 jǐngguān 〈police〉.

serial n. 连载作品 liánzǎi zuòpǐn / liánzài zuòpǐn. — adj. 连续的 liánxù de.

series n. ①系列 xìliè, 一连串 yìliánchuàn (succession). ②连续剧 liánxùjù (soap opera).

serious adj. ①严肃的 yánsù de (stern). ②认真的 rènzhēn

de (earnest). ③严重的 yánzhòng de (severe).

sermon n. 说教 shuōjiào, 训诫 xùnjiè, 讲道 jiǎngdào.

serpent n. 蛇 shé.

serum n. 血浆 xuèjiāng / xiějiāng, 血清 xuèqīng / xiěqīng.

servant n. 仆人 púrén. *civil* ~ 公务员 gōngwùyuán.

serve v. ①服务 fúwù (assist). ②任职 rènzhí 〈job〉, 服役 fúyì 〈military〉. ③把……端上桌 bǎ...duānshang zhuō 〈food etc.〉.

server n. ①服务器 fúwùqì / 伺服器 sìfúqì 〈computer〉. ②服务者 fúwùzhě 〈person〉.

service n. ①服务 fúwù (something done for others). ②勤务 qínwù (public duties), 兵役 bīngyì (military duties). ③公职 gōngzhí (government employment). ④公共事业 gōnggòng shìyè (public business). ⑤礼拜式 lǐbàishì, 仪式 yíshì (ceremony). ⑥保养 bǎoyǎng (maintenance).

servile adj. 屈从的 qūcóng de.

session n. ①会议 huìyì (meeting). ②会期 huìqī / huìqí (period).

set v. ①放置 fàngzhì (put). ②调整 tiáozhěng (adjust). ③订定 dìngdìng (fix). ④沉落 chénluò (go down). ⑤凝固 nínggù (become solid). ⑥固定 gùdìng (make firm). ~ *about* 着手 zhuóshǒu, 开始 kāishǐ. ~ *up* 设定 shèdìng, 设立 shèlì, 创立 chuànglì.

setback n. 挫折 cuòzhé.

settee n. 长椅 chángyǐ.

setting n. ①环境 huánjìng

(environment). ②布景 bùjìng (backdrop). ③沉落 chénluò (going down). ④置放 zhìfàng (putting).

settle v. ①安置 ānzhì (place). ②安顿 āndùn (set up home). ③安坐 ānzuò (sit down). ④平息 píngxī / píngxí, 平静 píngjìng (calm down). ⑤解决 jiějué (resolve). ⑥付清 fùqīng (pay). ⑦沉落 chénluò (sink).

settlement n. ①殖民地 zhímíndì (colony). ②殖民 zhímín (colonists). ③解决 jiějué (settling). ④清偿 qīngcháng 〈debt etc.〉.

settler n. 殖民者 zhímínzhě (colonist), 移居者 yíjūzhě (immigrant).

seven n. & adj. 七 qī.

seventeen n. & adj. 十七 shíqī.

seventeenth n. & adj. 第十七 dì-shíqī.

seventh n. & adj. 第七 dì-qī.

seventieth n. & adj. 第七十 dì-qīshí.

seventy n. & adj. 七十 qīshí.

sever v. 切断 qiēduàn.

several adj. 几个的 jǐ ge de.

severe adj. ①严厉的 yánlì de (strict). ②剧烈的 jùliè de (violent). ③艰难的 jiānnán de (harsh).

sew v. 缝合 fénghé, 缝纫 féngrèn.

sewage n. 污水 wūshuǐ.

sewer n. 下水道 xiàshuǐdào, 阴沟 yīngōu (drain).

sewerage n. 下水道设备 xiàshuǐdào shèbèi.

sewing n. 缝纫 féngrèn.

sex n. ①性 xìng, 性别 xìngbié (gender). ②性行为 xìngxíngwéi

(sexual activity). *have* ~ 做爱 zuò'ài, 有性行为 yǒu xìngxíngwéi.

sexual *adj.* 性的 xìng de. ~ *harassment* 性骚扰 xìngsāorǎo.

sexy *adj.* 性感的 xìnggǎn de.

shabby *adj.* ①褴褛的 lánlǚ de, 破旧的 pòjiù de (in poor condition). ②卑鄙的 bēibǐ de (mean).

shack *n.* 小木屋 xiǎo mùwū.

shackle *n.* 手铐 shǒukào, 脚镣 jiǎoliào / jiǎoliào.

shade *n.* ①荫 yīn / yìn, 阴 yīn (shadow). ②遮阳 zhēyáng, 蔽日物 bìrìwù (covering). ③色度 sèdù ⟨color⟩. — *v.* ①遮蔽 zhēbì (conceal). ②使暗 shǐ àn (darken).

shadow *n.* 影子 yǐngzi, 阴影 yīnyǐng (shade). — *v.* ①使阴暗 shǐ yīn'àn (darken), 投影于……上 tóuyǐng yú...shàng. ②跟踪 gēnzōng (follow).

shadowy *adj.* 阴影的 yīnyǐng de.

shady *adj.* ①荫凉的 yìnliáng de (cool), 多阴影的 duō yīnyǐng de. ②可疑的 kěyí de (suspicious).

shaft *n.* ①箭干 jiàngàn, 矛柄 máobǐng (arrow). ②光线 guāngxiàn (beam).

shaggy *adj.* 毛茸茸的 máoróngróng de.

shake *v.* ①摇动 yáodòng (move). ②动摇 dòngyáo (weaken). ~ *hands* 握手 wòshǒu. — *n.* 摇动 yáodòng, 震动 zhèndòng.

shaky *adj.* 摇动的 yáodòng de, 不稳的 bù wěn de.

shall *aux. v.* ①将 jiāng (will).

②应该 yīnggāi (ought to).

shallow *adj.* ①浅的 qiǎn de ⟨water⟩. ②肤浅的 fūqiǎn de (superficial).

sham *n.* ①假装 jiǎzhuāng (pretence). ②赝品 yànpǐn (fake). — *adj.* 假的 jiǎ de, 假装的 jiǎzhuāng de.

shamble *v.* 蹒跚而行 pánshān'érxíng / mánshān-érxíng.

shambles *n.* 凌乱 língluàn.

shame *n.* 耻辱 chǐrǔ / chǐrù, 羞愧 xiūkuì.

shameful *adj.* 可耻的 kěchǐ de.

shameless *adj.* 无耻的 wúchǐ de.

shampoo *v.* 洗发 xǐfà / xǐfǎ. — *n.* 洗发精 xǐfàjīng / xǐfǎjīng ⟨soap⟩.

shank *n.* 胫 jìng, 胫骨 jìnggǔ, 小腿 xiǎotuǐ.

shanty *n.* 简陋小屋 jiǎnlòu xiǎo wū.

shape *n.* 形状 xíngzhuàng (form), 样子 yàngzi (appearance). — *v.* 使成形 shǐ chéngxíng.

share *n.* ①部分 bùfen, 份 fèn (portion). ②股份 gǔfèn (stock). — *v.* ①分享 fēnxiǎng (enjoy together), 分担 fēndān (divide a burden). ②共有 gòngyǒu (jointly own).

shareholder *n.* 股东 gǔdōng.

shark *n.* 鲨 shā, 鲛 jiāo.

sharp *adj.* ①锐利的 ruìlì de (cutting). ②急转的 jízhuǎn de ⟨direction⟩. ③剧烈的 jùliè de (severe). ④敏锐的 mǐnruì de (sensitive). ⑤精明的 jīngmíng de (clever). ⑥鲜明的 xiānmíng de (clear).

S

sharpen v. 使尖锐 shǐ jiānruì, 削 xiāo.

shatter v. 粉碎 fěnsuì.

shave v. 刮胡子 guāhúzi, 剃 tì.

shawl n. 披肩 pījiān, 围巾 wéijīn.

she pron. 她 tā.

sheaf n. 束 shù, 捆 kǔn.

shear v. 修剪 xiūjiǎn (cut).

shears n. 大剪刀 dà jiǎndāo.

sheath n. 鞘 qiào.

shed n. 小屋 xiǎo wū ⟨storing⟩, 家畜棚 jiāchùpéng ⟨cattle⟩. — v. 脱落 tuōluò ⟨fur⟩.

sheep n. 绵羊 miányáng.

sheer adj. ①纯粹的 chúncuì de, 全然的 quánrán de (pure). ②透明的 tòumíng de (transparent).

sheet n. 被单 bèidān, 床单 chuángdān.

shelf n. 架子 jiàzi.

shell n. ①壳 ké (outer). ②炮弹 pàodàn (ammunition).

shellfish n. 贝壳类 bèiké lèi.

shelter n. ①避难所 bìnànsuǒ (refuge), 遮蔽物 zhēbìwù (covering). ②庇护 bìhù, 遮蔽 zhēbì (protection). — v. ①庇护 bìhù (protect). ②掩护 yǎnhù (accommodate).

shelve v. ①放在架上 fàng zài jià shàng (put on). ②搁置 gēzhì (put off).

shepherd n. 牧羊人 mùyángrén. — v. ①带领 dàilǐng, 引导 yǐndǎo (lead). ②看守 kānshǒu (watch).

sheriff n. 警长 jǐngzhǎng.

sherry n. 雪利酒 xuělìjiǔ.

shield n. ①盾 dùn (buckler). ②防御物 fángyùwù (protection). — v. 保护 bǎohù, 防护 fánghù.

shift v. 变换 biànhuàn. — n. ①变换 biànhuàn (change). ②轮值 lúnzhí, 换班 huànbān ⟨work⟩.

shimmer v. 闪闪发光 shǎnshǎn-fāguāng. — n. 闪光 shǎnguāng.

shine v. ①发光 fāguāng, 发亮光 fāliàng (give off light). ②擦亮 cāliàng (polish). — n. ①光亮 guāngliàng (brightness). ②擦亮 cāliàng (polished appearance).

shiny adj. 发光的 fāguāng de.

ship n. 船 chuán. — v. 以船运送 yǐ chuán yùnsòng.

shipper n. 装运货物者 zhuāngyùn huòwù zhě.

shipping n. 船运 chuányùn (transporting).

shipwreck n. 船难 chuánnàn, 海难 hǎinàn.

shipyard n. 造船厂 zàochuánchǎng.

shirt n. 衬衫 chènshān.

shiver n. & v. 颤抖 chàndǒu / zhàndǒu.

shoal n. ①鱼群 yúqún (school of fish). ②浅滩 qiǎntān, 沙洲 shāzhōu (sandbank).

shock n. ①震惊 zhènjīng (surprising). ②震动 zhèndòng (disturbance). ③冲击 chōngjī / chōngjí (impact). ④休克 xiūkè ⟨medical⟩. — v. ①惊人 jīngrén, 震惊 zhènjīng (surprise). ②震动 zhèndòng (shake up). ③触电 chùdiàn ⟨electrical⟩.

shocking adj. ①惊人的 jīngrén de (surprising). ②糟糕的 zāogāo de, 很坏的 hěn huài de (in a terrible state).

shoe n. 鞋 xié.

shoemaker n. 鞋匠 xiéjiang.

shoestring n. 鞋带 xiédài.

S

shoot v. ①射击 shèjī / shèjí, 发射 fāshè (fire). ②射杀 shèshā (kill). — n. 芽 yá, 嫩枝 nènzhī (plant).

shop n. ①店 diàn, 店铺 diànpù (store). ②工厂 gōngchǎng (workshop). — v. 买东西 mǎi dōngxi, 购物 gòuwù (buy).

shopkeeper n. 店主 diànzhǔ.

shoplifter n. 扒手 páshǒu, 窃物者 qièwùzhě.

shopper n. 购物者 gòuwùzhě.

shopping n. 购物 gòuwù. ~ *mall* 购物商场 gòuwù shāngchǎng.

shore n. 岸 àn ⟨land⟩, 海岸 hǎi'àn ⟨sea⟩, 河岸 hé'àn ⟨river⟩.

short adj. ①短的 duǎn de (not long). ②矮的 ǎi de (not tall). ③简短的 jiǎnduǎn de (brief). ④不足的 bùzú de (lacking).

shortage n. 缺乏 quēfá, 不足 bùzú.

shortcoming n. 缺点 quēdiǎn, 短处 duǎnchù.

shortcut n. 捷径 jiéjìng.

shorten v. 使短 shǐ duǎn, 缩短 suōduǎn.

shorthand n. 速记法 sùjìfǎ.

short-handed adj. 人手不足的 rénshǒu bùzú de.

shortly adv. ①不久 bùjiǔ (soon). ②简略地 jiǎnlüè de (briefly).

shortsighted adj. ①短视的 duǎnshì de ⟨opinion⟩. ②近视的 jìnshì de ⟨eyes⟩.

shot n. ①子弹 zǐdàn, 炮弹 pàodàn (bullet). ②射手 shèshǒu (marksman). ③发射 fāshè, 射击 shèjī / shèjí (firing). *give it a ~* 尝试 chángshì.

should aux. v. 应该 yīnggāi.

shoulder n. 肩 jiān, 肩膀 jiānbǎng. ~ *pad* 垫肩 diànjiān. — v. 肩负 jiānfù.

shout n. & v. 喊 hǎn, 叫 jiào.

shove n. & v. 推挤 tuījǐ.

shovel n. 铲 chǎn. — v. 铲起 chǎnqi.

show v. ①展示 zhǎnshì (exhibit). ②显露 xiǎnlù (make visible). ③指出 zhǐchu (point out). ④证明 zhèngmíng (prove). ⑤做给……看 zuògěi...kàn (demonstrate). ~ *off* 夸耀 kuāyào. ~ *up* 出现 chūxiàn. — n. ①节目 jiémù (program). ②展览 zhǎnlǎn (exhibition). ③演出 yǎnchū, 表演 biǎoyǎn (performance). ④展现 zhǎnxiàn, 表示 biǎoshì (expression).

shower n. ①淋浴 línyù ⟨bath⟩. ②阵雨 zhènyǔ ⟨rain⟩. — v. ①淋浴 línyù (bathe). ②下阵雨 xià zhènyǔ (rain).

showroom n. 展示室 zhǎnshìshì.

shred n. 碎片 suìpiàn, 细条 xìtiáo. — v. 撕成碎片 sī chéng suìpiàn, 切成细条 qiē chéng xìtiáo.

shrewd adj. 精明的 jīngmíng de.

shriek n. & v. 尖叫 jiānjiào.

shrill adj. 尖声的 jiānshēng de.

shrimp n. 虾 xiā.

shrine n. ①圣殿 shèngdiàn, 祠堂 cítáng ⟨holy place⟩. ②神龛 shénkān ⟨tomb or casket⟩.

shrink n. & v. 缩小 suōxiǎo, 收缩 shōusuō (becoming smaller). ~ *back* 畏缩 wèisuō.

shroud n. 寿衣 shòuyī (burial garment).

S

shrub n. 灌木 guànmù.

shrug n. & v. 耸肩 sǒngjiān.

shudder n. & v. 战栗 zhànlì,
发抖 fādǒu.

shuffle v. ①曳足而行 yèzú'érxíng / yìzú'érxíng ⟨walk⟩. ②洗
牌 xǐpái ⟨card⟩.

shun v. ①避开 bìkai ⟨avoid⟩.
②排斥 páichì ⟨ostracize⟩.

shunt v. 转轨 zhuǎnguǐ ⟨train⟩.

shut v. 闭 bì, 关闭 guānbì.
~ *off* 关掉 guāndiào. ~ *up* 住
口 zhùkǒu, 闭嘴 bìzuǐ.

shutter n. ①百叶窗
bǎiyèchuāng ⟨window⟩. ②快门
kuàimén ⟨camera⟩.

shuttle n. 梭 suō. — v. 往返
移动 wǎngfǎn yídòng.

shuttlecock n. 羽毛球
yǔmáoqiú.

shy adj. 害羞的 hàixiū de, 羞
怯的 xiūqiè de / xiūquè de.

sibling n. 手足 shǒuzú, 兄弟
姊妹 xiōngdì zǐmèi.

sick adj. ①有病的 yǒubìng de,
不舒服的 bù shūfu de ⟨ill⟩.
②作呕的 zuò'ǒu de ⟨nauseous⟩.
③厌恶的 yànwù de ⟨upset by⟩.
~ *of something* 厌烦 yànfán.

sickle n. 镰刀 liándāo.

sickly adj. ①多病的 duōbìng
de, 不健康的 bú jiànkāng de
⟨often ill⟩. ②苍白的 cāngbái
de, 憔悴的 qiáocuì de ⟨pale⟩.
③令人作呕的 lìngrén-zuò'ǒu
de ⟨nauseating⟩.

sickness n. 患病 huànbìng.

side n. ①面 miàn ⟨face⟩. ②边
biān ⟨border⟩. ③方面 fāngmiàn
⟨aspect⟩.

sideboard n. 餐具橱 cānjùchú.

sidewalk n. 人行道
rénxíngdào.

siege n. & v. 围攻 wéigōng.

sieve n. 筛 shāi.

sift v. 筛 shāi, 过滤 guòlǜ.

sigh n. & v. 叹息 tànxī / tànxí.

sight n. ①视力 shìlì ⟨eyesight⟩.
②视野 shìyě ⟨view⟩. ③风景
fēngjǐng, 名胜 míngshèng
⟨scenery⟩.

sightsee v. 观光 guānguāng.

sightseer n. 观光客
guānguāngkè.

sign n. ①记号 jìhào, 符号
fúhào ⟨mark⟩. ②手势 shǒushì
⟨gesture⟩. ③迹象 jìxiàng /
jīxiàng, 征兆 zhēngzhào
⟨forewarning⟩. ④告示 gàoshì,
标志 biāozhì ⟨notice⟩. — v.
①签字 qiānzì, 签名 qiānmíng
⟨endorse⟩. ②以手势示意 yǐ
shǒushì shìyì ⟨gesture⟩.

signal n. 信号 xìnhào. — v. 发
信号 fā xìnhào. — adj. 显着的
xiǎnzhù de.

signatory n. 签名者
qiānmíngzhě.

signature n. 签字 qiānzì,
签名 qiānmíng, 署名 shǔmíng /
shùmíng.

significance n. ①意义 yìyì
⟨meaning⟩. ②重要(性)
zhòngyào (xìng) ⟨importance⟩.

significant adj. ①有意义的
yǒu yìyì de ⟨meaningful⟩. ②重
要的 zhòngyào de ⟨important⟩.

signify v. 表示 biǎoshì ⟨mean⟩.

silence n. ①寂静 jìjìng / jíjìng
⟨stillness⟩. ②沉默 chénmò
⟨muteness⟩. — v. 使沉默 shǐ
chénmò.

silent adj. ①寂静的 jìjìng de /
jíjìng de, 无声的 wúshēng de
⟨still⟩. ②沉默的 chénmò de
⟨mute⟩.

silicon n. 硅 guī / 矽 xì.
S~ Valley 硅谷 Guīgǔ / 矽谷

Xìgǔ.

silk n. 丝 sī, 蚕丝 cánsī.

silly adj. 愚蠢的 yúchǔn de.

silt n. 淤泥 yūní.

silver n. 银 yín 〈metal〉. ~ ware 银器 yínqì.

silversmith n. 银匠 yínjiàng.

similar adj. 类似的 lèisì de, 同样的 tóngyàng de.

similarity n. 类似 lèisì, 相似 xiāngsì.

similarly adv. 类似地 lèisì de.

simile n. 直喻 zhíyù, 明喻 míngyù.

simmer v. 慢煮 mànzhǔ, 炖 dùn.

simper v. 假笑 jiǎxiào 〈not sincere〉, 傻笑 shǎxiào 〈silly〉.

simple adj. ①简单的 jiǎndān de (not complicated). ②朴实的 pǔshí de / púshí de (plain). ③单纯的 dānchún de (innocent).

simplicity n. ①简单 jiǎndān (being simple). ②纯真 chúnzhēn (innocence).

simplify v. 使简化 shǐ jiǎnhuà (make easier), 使单纯 shǐ dānchún (make less complicated).

simply adv. ①简单地 jiǎndān de (in a simple way). ②简直 jiǎnzhí (really). ③仅 jǐn (just).

simulate v. ①模仿 mófǎng (imitate). ②假装 jiǎzhuāng (pretend), 伪装 wěizhuāng / wèizhuāng (fake).

simulator n. 模拟装置 móní zhuāngzhì.

simultaneous adj. 同时发生的 tóngshí fāshēng de.

sin n. 罪 zuì, 罪恶 zuì'è.

since prep. 从 cóng (from), 自……以后 zì...yǐhòu.
— conj. ①自……以后 zì

yǐhòu (after). ②既然 jìrán (as). ③因为 yīnwèi (because).

sincere adj. ①真实的 zhēnshí de, 诚实的 chéngshí de (honest). ②诚挚的 chéngzhì de (genuine).

sincerity n. 真实 zhēnshí, 诚恳 chéngkěn.

sinew n. 腱 jiàn.

sing v. 唱 chàng, 歌唱 gēchàng.

singer n. 歌手 gēshǒu.

single adj. ①单一的 dānyī de (one), 惟一的 wéiyī de (only). ②单身的 dānshēn de (not married). ③单人用的 dānrén yòng de (used for one person).
~ parent 单亲 dānqīn.
~ parent family 半边家庭 bànbiān jiātíng / 单亲家庭 dānqīn jiātíng. ~ room 单人房 dānrénfáng.

singular adj. ①单数的 dānshù de 〈grammar〉. ②奇特的 qítè de (uncommon). — n. 单数 dānshù.

sinister adj. ①有恶意的 yǒu èyì de (malevolent). ②邪恶的 xié'è de (evil). ③不祥的 bùxiáng de (inauspicious).

sink v. ①沉落 chénluò (go down). ②沉没 chénmò (founder). ③下降 xiàjiàng (become lower).

sinner n. 罪人 zuìrén.

sip v. 啜饮 chuòyǐn.

siphon n. 虹吸管 hóngxīguǎn.

sir n. 先生 xiānsheng (mister).

siren n. 海妖 hǎiyāo.

sister n. ①姐姐 jiějie 〈elder〉. ②妹妹 mèimei 〈younger〉. ③修女 xiūnǚ (nun). ~s 姐妹 jiěmèi (female siblings).

sit v. 坐 zuò.

S

site *n.* 位置 wèizhì, 地点 dìdiǎn.

situated *adj.* 坐落于……的 zuòluò yú...de.

situation *n.* ①情形 qíngxing, 情况 qíngkuàng (condition). ②职位 zhíwèi (employment). ③场所 chǎngsuǒ (location).

six *n. & adj.* 六 liù.

sixteen *n. & adj.* 十六 shíliù.

sixteenth *n. & adj.* 第十六 dì-shíliù.

sixth *n. & adj.* 第六 dì-liù.

sixtieth *n. & adj.* 第六十 dì--liùshí.

sixty *n. & adj.* 六十 liùshí.

size *n.* 大小 dàxiǎo, 尺寸 chǐcùn. **~ up** 估量 gūliáng / gūliàng.

sizzle *n. & v.* 嘶嘶声 sīsīshēng.

skate *n.* 冰刀 bīngdāo. *roller ~* 旱冰鞋 hànbīngxié / 溜冰鞋 liūbīngxié. *ice ~* 冰鞋 bīngxié / 溜冰鞋 liūbīngxié. — *v.* 溜冰 liūbīng.

skateboard *n.* 滑板 huábǎn.

skeleton *n.* 骨骼 gǔgé.

sketch *n.* ①草图 cǎotú, 素描 sùmiáo (drawing). ②短剧 duǎnjù (short play). — *v.* ①素描 sùmiáo (draw). ②记述……的概略 jìshù...de gàilüè (outline).

ski *n.* 滑雪板 huáxuěbǎn. — *v.* 滑雪 huáxuě.

skid *v.* 滑向一侧 huá xiàng yícè.

skiff *n.* 小艇 xiǎotǐng.

skillful *adj.* 熟练的 shúliàn de / shóuliàn de, 有技巧的 yǒu jìqiǎo de.

skill *n.* 技巧 jìqiǎo, 技能 jìnéng.

skim *v.* ①略读 lüèdú (read quickly). ②掠过 lüèguo (move

lightly).

skin *n.* ①皮肤 pífū (human). ②毛皮 máopí (animal). — *v.* 剥皮 bāopí / bōpí.

skip *v.* ①跳跃 tiàoyuè (jump). ②略过 lüèguo (pass over). ③跳读 tiàodú (reading).

skirt *n.* 裙子 qúnzi.

skunk *n.* 臭鼬 chòuyòu.

sky *n.* 天空 tiānkōng, 天 tiān.

skylark *n.* 云雀 yúnquè.

skylight *n.* 天窗 tiānchuāng.

skyscraper *n.* 摩天楼 mótiānlóu.

slab *n.* 厚板 hòubǎn.

slack *adj.* ①松弛的 sōngchí de (loose). ②懈怠的 xièdài de (idle). ③不活跃的 bù huóyuè de (inactive).

slacken *v.* ①使松弛 shǐ sōngchí (make looser). ②使缓慢 shǐ huǎnmàn (make slower).

slam *v.* 砰然关闭 pēngrán guānbì (shut). — *n.* 砰然声 pēngránshēng.

slander *n. & v.* 诽谤 fěibàng.

slang *n.* 俚语 lǐyǔ.

slant *v.* 倾斜 qīngxié.

slap *v.* ①掌击 zhǎngjī / zhǎngjí, 掴 guó. — *v.* 掌掴 zhǎngguó, 打 dǎ. — 巴掌 dǎ...bāzhǎng.

slat *n.* 细长薄板 xìcháng báobǎn / xìcháng bóbǎn.

slate *n.* 石板 shíbǎn (rock).

slaughter *n. & v.* 屠杀 túshā, 杀戮 shālù.

slave *n.* 奴隶 núlì.

slavery *n.* ①奴役 núyì (enslavement). ②奴隶身分 núlì shēnfen (being a slave).

slavish *adj.* 奴性的 núxìng de.

slay *v.* 杀戮 shālù (kill violently).

sled *n.* 雪橇 xuěqiāo, 雪车

S

xuěchē. — v. 乘雪橇 chéng xuěqiāo.

sleep v. 睡 shuì. — n. 睡眠 shuìmián.

sleepy adj. ①困的 kùn de, 想睡的 xiǎngshuì de (ready to sleep). ②不活泼的 bù huópō de (inactive).

sleet n. 霰 xiàn. — v. 降霰 jiàngxiàn.

sleeve n. 袖 xiù.

sleigh n. 雪车 xuěchē, 雪橇 xuěqiāo. — v. 乘雪橇 chéng xuěqiāo.

slender adj. ①纤细的 xiānxì de (slight). ②薄弱的 bóruò de (feeble).

slice n. 片 piàn, 薄片 báopiàn / bópiàn.

slick adj. 光滑的 guānghuá de (slippery).

slide v. 滑行 huáxíng, 滑动 huádòng. — n. ①溜滑梯 liūhuátī (chute). ②幻灯片 huàndēngpiàn (film).

slight adj. ①少许的 shǎoxǔ de, 微小的 wēixiǎo de / wéixiǎo de (imperceptible). ②瘦弱的 shòuruò de (thin).

slightly adv. 轻微地 qīngwēi de / qīngwéi de, 稍微 shāowēi / shāowéi.

slim adj. ①苗条的 miáotiao de, 细长的 xìcháng de (slender). ②微少的 wēishǎo de / wéishǎo de (small).

slime n. 黏土 niántǔ.

sling n. 吊索 diàosuǒ, 吊带 diàodài. — v. 投掷 tóuzhì / tóuzhí.

slink v. 潜行 qiánxíng, 潜逃 qiántáo.

slip v. ①滑倒 huádǎo (fall). ②犯错 fàncuò (make a mis-

take). ~ **away** 溜走 liūzǒu.

slipper n. 拖鞋 tuōxié.

slippery adj. ①滑的 huá de ⟨surface⟩. ②狡猾的 jiǎohuá de (devious).

slit v. 割裂 gēliè. — n. 裂缝 lièfèng.

slither v. 滑动 huádòng.

slogan n. 标语 biāoyǔ, 口号 kǒuhào.

slope v. 倾斜 qīngxié. — n. 倾斜 qīngxié, 斜坡 xiépō.

sloppy adj. ①邋遢的 lāta de (slovenly). ②泥泞的 nínìng de (muddy).

slot n. ①狭缝 xiáfèng (narrow opening). ②投币口 tóubìkǒu ⟨coin⟩.

sloth n. 怠惰 dàiduò.

slouch v. 弯腰驼背地走 wānyāo tuóbèi de zǒu.

slovenly adj. & adv. 邋遢的 lāta de.

slow adj. ①缓慢的 huǎnmàn de (not fast). ②迟钝的 chídùn de (obtuse).

slowly adv. 缓慢地 huǎnmàn de.

sludge n. 污泥 wūní.

slug n. 蛞蝓 kuòyú ⟨animal⟩.

sluggish adj. 行动迟缓的 xíngdòng chíhuǎn de (slow moving).

sluice n. ①水门 shuǐmén (gate). ②排水道 páishuǐdào (channel).

slum n. 贫民窟 pínmínkū.

slumber n. 睡眠 shuìmián. — v. 安睡 ānshuì.

slump v. ①猛然落下 měngrán luòxià (drop heavily). ②暴跌 bàodiē / bàodié ⟨price⟩.

slur v. 含糊说出 hánhu shuōchū (pronounce unclearly).

slut n. 放荡女子 fàngdàng

S

sly adj. ①狡猾的 jiǎohuá de, 诡秘的 guǐmì de (deceitful). ②顽皮的 wánpí de, 淘气的 táoqì de (mischievous).

small adj. 小的 xiǎo de.

smart v. 感到剧痛 gǎndào jùtòng ⟨hurt⟩. — adj. ①聪明的 cōngmíng de (clever). ②轻快的 qīngkuài de (quick).

smash v. ①捣碎 dǎosuì, 使破碎 shǐ pòsuì (break). ②碰撞 pèngzhuàng (hit).

smear v. ①涂 tú, 敷 fū (cover with). ②弄脏 nòngzāng, 涂污 túwū (make dirty).

smell v. ①闻 wén, 嗅 xiù (scent). ②发出气味 fāchū qìwèi (stink). — n. 味道 wèidào.

smile n. & v. 微笑 wēixiào / wéixiào.

smirk n. & v. 冷笑 lěngxiào, 得意地笑 déyì de xiào.

smock n. 罩衫 zhàoshān.

smog n. 烟雾 yānwù.

smoke n. 烟 yān, 烟雾 yānwù (fumes). — v. ①吸烟 xīyān ⟨cigarette⟩. ②冒烟 màoyān (fume).

smooth adj. ①平滑的 pínghuá de (flat). ②平静的 píngjìng de (calm). ③流畅的 liúchàng de (flowing). — v. ①使平滑 shǐ pínghuá (flatten). ②使平顺 shǐ píngshùn (make steady).

smother v. ①使窒息 shǐ zhìxī / shǐ zhìxí (choke). ②闷熄 mēnxī / mēnxí ⟨fire⟩.

smudge n. 污点 wūdiǎn, 污迹 wūjì / wūjì.

smug adj. 沾沾自喜的 zhānzhān-zìxǐ de.

smuggle v. 走私 zǒusī.

smut n. 猥亵书刊 wěixiè shūkān (pornographic materials).

snack n. 点心 diǎnxin, 小吃 xiǎochī.

snail n. 蜗牛 wōniú / guāniú.

snake n. 蛇 shé.

snap v. ①啪一声折断 pā yì shēng zhéduàn (crack). ②咬 yǎo (bite). — adj. 突然的 tūrán de / túrán de (sudden).

snapshot n. 快照 kuàizhào.

snare n. 罗网 luówǎng, 陷阱 xiànjǐng. — v. 诱捕 yòubǔ.

snarl v. 咆哮 páoxiào / páoxiào, 怒吼 nùhǒu (growl).

snatch v. 抢去 qiǎngqù, 夺去 duóqù.

sneak v. 偷偷进入 tōutōu jìnrù, 潜行 qiánxíng (go stealthily).

sneakily adv. 偷偷地 tōutōu de.

sneer v. 轻蔑 qīngmiè, 嘲笑 cháoxiào.

sneeze v. 打喷嚏 dǎpèntì. — n. 喷嚏 pēntì.

snicker n. & v. 暗笑 ànxiào, 窃笑 qièxiào.

sniff v. ①闻 wén, 嗅 xiù (smell). ②以鼻吸气 yǐ bí xīqì (breathe in noisily).

snigger n. & v. 暗笑 ànxiào, 窃笑 qièxiào.

snip v. 剪断 jiǎnduàn.

snipe n. 鹬 yù ⟨bird⟩. — v. 伏击 fújī / fújí, 狙击 jūjī / jūjí.

snippet n. 片段 piànduàn.

snivel v. 啜泣 chuòqì.

snob n. 势利小人 shìlì xiǎorén.

snoop v. 窥察 kuīchá.

snooze n. & v. 小睡 xiǎoshuì.

snore v. 打鼾 dǎhān. — n. 鼾声 hānshēng.

snort v. 嗤之以鼻 chīzhīyǐbí.

snow n. 雪 xuě. — v. 下雪 xiàxuě.

snowboard n. 滑雪板 huáxuěbǎn.

snowflake n. 雪花 xuěhuā.

snowstorm n. 暴风雪 bàofēngxuě.

snow-white adj. 雪白的 xuěbái de.

snowy adj. 多雪的 duōxuě de.

snub n. & v. 怠慢 dàimàn, 冷落 lěngluò.

snuff v. 用鼻吸 yòng bí xī. — n. 鼻烟 bíyān.

snug adj. 舒适的 shūshì de, 温暖的 wēnnuǎn de (comfortable).

so adv. 如此 rúcǐ. — conj. 所以 suǒyǐ.

soak v. 浸湿 jìnshī, 浸透 jìntòu.

soap n. 肥皂 féizào.

soar v. 高飞 gāofēi.

sob v. 啜泣 chuòqì.

sober adj. ①清醒的 qīngxǐng de (clear-headed). ②有节制的 yǒu jiézhì de (abstemious). ③严肃的 yánsù de (solemn).

so-called adj. 所谓的 suǒwèi de.

soccer n. 足球 zúqiú.

sociable adj. 好交际的 hào jiāojì de, 社交的 shèjiāo de.

social adj. ①群居的 qúnjū de 〈group〉.②社会的 shèhuì de 〈community〉. — n. 联谊会 liányìhuì.

socialism n. 社会主义 shèhuì zhǔyì.

socialist n. 社会主义者 shèhuì zhǔyì zhě.

society n. 社会 shèhuì.

sociology n. 社会学 shèhuìxué.

sock n. 短袜 duǎnwà.

socket n. 插座 chāzuò.

soda n. 苏打水 sūdáshuǐ / sūdǎshuǐ, 汽水 qìshuǐ.

sodium n. 钠 nà.

sofa n. 沙发 shāfā.

soft adj. ①柔软的 róuruǎn de (not hard).②温和的 wēnhé de (mild). ③柔和的 róuhé de 〈of light〉.

softball n. 垒球 lěiqiú.

soften v. 使柔软 shǐ róuruǎn.

software n. 软件 ruǎnjiàn / 软体 ruǎntǐ. ~ package 软件包 ruǎnjiànbāo / 套装软体 tàozhuāng ruǎntǐ.

soggy adj. 湿透的 shītòu de.

soil n. 土壤 tǔrǎng, 土 tǔ.

solar adj. 太阳的 tàiyáng de.

solder n. 焊料 hànliào. — v. 焊接 hànjiē.

soldier n. 军人 jūnrén, 士兵 shìbīng.

sole n. 唯一的 wéiyī de.

solely adv. ①独一地 dúyī de (alone). ②仅仅 jǐnjǐn (only).

solemn adj. 严肃的 yánsù de (serious), 庄重的 zhuāngzhòng de (grand).

solicit v. 恳求 kěnqiú, 请求 qǐngqiú.

solicitor n. 律师 lǜshī.

solid adj. ①坚实的 jiānshí de (dense). ②立体的 lìtǐ de (cubic). ③切实的 qièshí de (concrete). ④固体的 gùtǐ de 〈form〉.

solidify v. ①使凝固 shǐ nínggù (harden). ②使团结 shǐ tuánjié (become united).

solitary adj. ①唯一的 wéiyī de (only). ②僻远的 pìyuǎn de

S

(remote). ③孤独的 gūdú de (alone).

solitude n. ①孤独 gūdú (loneliness). ②荒僻 huāngpì (remoteness).

solo n. 独唱 dúchàng 〈singing〉, 独奏 dúzòu 〈performance〉. — adj. 单独的 dāndú de.

soluble adj. 可溶解的 kě róngjiě de.

solution n. ①解决 jiějué, 解答 jiědá (resolution). ②溶解 róngjiě (mixture).

solve v. 解答 jiědá, 解决 jiějué.

solvent adj. ①能偿债的 néng chángzhài de 〈credit〉. ②有溶解力的 yǒu róngjiělì de (able to dissolve).

somber adj. ①幽暗的 yōu'àn de (dark). ②忧郁的 yōuyù de (cheerless).

some adj. 一些 yìxiē.

somebody pron. 某人 mǒurén.

someday adv. 有一天 yǒuyìtiān.

somehow adv. 以某种方法 yǐ mǒuzhǒng fāngfǎ.

someone pron. 某人 mǒurén.

somersault n. 筋斗 jīndǒu. — v. 翻筋斗 fānjīndǒu.

something pron. 某事 mǒushì, 某物 mǒuwù.

sometime adv. 某时 mǒushí.

sometimes adv. 有时 yǒushí.

somewhat adv. & pron. 稍微 shāowēi / shāoéi.

somewhere adv. 在某处 zài mǒuchù.

son n. 儿子 érzi.

sonar n. 声纳 shēngnà.

sonata n. 奏鸣曲 zòumíngqǔ.

song n. 歌 gē, 歌曲 gēqǔ.

sonnet n. 十四行诗 shísìhángshī.

soon adv. ①不久 bùjiǔ (not long). ②早 zǎo, 快 kuài (early).

soot n. 煤烟 méiyān.

soothe v. 安慰 ānwèi, 抚慰 fǔwèi.

sophisticated adj. 世故的 shìgù de, 老练的 lǎoliàn de.

sophomore n. 二年级学生 èr niánjí xuésheng.

soppy adj. 浸透的 jìntòu de, 湿透的 shītòu de (very wet).

soprano n. 女高音 nǚgāoyīn.

sorcerer n. 男巫 nánwū.

sorcery n. 巫术 wūshù.

sordid adj. ①污秽的 wūhuì de (dirty). ②卑鄙的 bēibǐ de (contemptible).

sore adj. ①疼痛的 téngtòng de (painful). ②伤心的 shāngxīn de (sorrowful). — n. 痛处 tòngchù.

sorrow n. 悲伤 bēishāng.

sorrowful adj. 悲伤的 bēishāng de.

sorry adj. ①感到抱歉的 gǎndào bàoqiàn de (pitiful). ②难过的 nánguò de (grieved).

sort n. 种 zhǒng, 类 lèi. — v. 分类 fēnlèi.

so-so adj. & adv. 马马虎虎 mǎma-hūhū.

soul n. 灵魂 línghún.

sound n. 声音 shēngyīn. — v. ①发出声音 fāchū shēngyīn (make sound). ②听起来 tīngqilai (seem when heard).

soundproof adj. 隔音的 géyīn de.

soup n. 汤 tāng, 羹 gēng.

sour adj. ①酸的 suān de (acidic). ②乖戾的 guāilì de (bad-tempered).

source n. ①来源 láiyuán

S

(origin). ②水源 shuǐyuán
〈water〉.

south n. ①南 nán 〈direction〉.
②南方 nánfāng 〈southern
region〉. ③南边 nánbiān, 南部
nánbù (southern part). — adv.
南 nán, 向南 xiàng nán, 往南
wǎng nán. — adj. ①南 nán
(of the south). ②南方的
nánfāng de (of the southern
region). ③南部的 nánbù de
(of the southern part).

South America 南美洲
Nán Měizhōu.

southeast adj. 东南的
dōngnán de.

southern adj. 南方的
nánfāng de.

South Pole n. 南极 Nánjí.

southward adj. & adv. 向南
的 xiàng nán de.

southwest adj. 西南的 xīnán
de.

souvenir n. 纪念品 jìniànpǐn.

sovereign n. 元首 yuánshǒu,
统治者 tǒngzhìzhě (king or
queen). — adj. ①最高的
zuìgāo de (supreme). ②有主
权的 yǒu zhǔquán de (self-
governing).

sow v. 播种 bōzhǒng /
bòzhǒng. — n. 母猪 mǔzhū.

soybean n. 大豆 dàdòu, 黄豆
huángdòu.

soy sauce n. 酱油 jiàngyóu.

spa n. 温泉 wēnquán, 矿泉
kuàngquán.

space n. ①太空 tàikōng
〈astronomy〉. ②空间 kōngjiān
(emptiness). ~ **station** 宇宙站
yǔzhòuzhàn, 航天站
hángtiānzhàn / 太空站
tàikōngzhàn.

spaceship n. 宇宙飞船

yǔzhòu fēichuán / 太空船
tàikōngchuán.

spacious adj. 广阔的
guǎngkuò de.

spade n. ①铲子 chǎnzi 〈tool〉.
②黑桃 hēitáo 〈cards〉. — v. 铲
chǎn.

spaghetti n. 意大利面
yìdàlìmiàn / 义大利面
yìdàlìmiàn.

span n. ①一掌距 yì zhǎngjù
〈distance〉. ②一段时间
yíduàn shíjiān 〈time〉.

Spanish n. & adj. ①西班牙人
Xībānyárén 〈people〉. ②西班牙
语 Xībānyáyǔ 〈language〉.

spank v. 拍打 pāidǎ.

spanner n. 螺旋钳
luóxuánqián, 扳手 bānshou.

spar v. 拳斗 quándòu.

spare v. ①赦免 shèmiǎn, 饶恕
ráoshù (forgive). ②节省使用
jiéshěng shǐyòng (use in small
quantities). — adj. ①剩余的
shèngyú de, 多余的 duōyú de
(additional). ②备用的 bèiyòng
de (in reserve).

spark n. 火花 huǒhuā, 火星
huǒxīng. — v. ①发出火花
fāchū huǒhuā 〈fire〉. ②引发
yǐnfā (set off).

sparkle v. 发出火花 fāchū
huǒhuā, 闪烁 shǎnshuò.
— n. 火花 huǒhuā, 闪烁
shǎnshuò.

sparrow n. 麻雀 máquè.

sparse adj. 稀少的 xīshǎo de.

spasm n. 痉挛 jìngluán.

spawn n. 卵 luǎn. — v. 产卵
chǎnluǎn.

speak v. 说话 shuōhuà, 讲
jiǎng.

speaker n. 说话者
shuōhuàzhě.

spear n. 矛 máo, 枪 qiāng.

special adj. 特殊的 tèshū de, 特别的 tèbié de.

specialist n. 专家 zhuānjiā.

specialty n. ①专长 zhuāncháng (expertise). ②特性 tèxìng (quality).

species n. 种 zhǒng, 种类 zhǒnglèi.

specific adj. ①明确的 míngquè de (definite). ②特定的 tèdìng de (particular).

specification n. 详述 xiángshù.

specify v. 列举 lièjǔ.

specimen n. 样品 yàngpǐn (sample), 标本 biāoběn (example).

speck n. 斑点 bāndiǎn, 瑕疵 xiácī.

speckle n. 小点 xiǎodiǎn, 斑点 bāndiǎn.

spectacle n. ①奇观 qíguān, 景象 jǐngxiàng (sight). ②展览物 zhǎnlǎnwù (display).

spectacular adj. 壮观的 zhuàngguān de.

spectator n. 观众 guānzhòng, 旁观者 pángguānzhě.

spectrum n. 光谱 guāngpǔ.

speculate v. ①推测 tuīcè (make a guess). ②投机 tóujī (stocks).

speculation n. ①推测 tuīcè (making guesses). ②投机买卖 tóujī mǎimai (of stocks).

speech n. 演说 yǎnshuō.

speed n. 速度 sùdù. — v. 加速前进 jiāsù qiánjìn.

spell v. 拼字 pīnzì. — n. 符咒 fúzhòu (magic).

spelling n. 拼字 pīnzì.

spend v. ①花费 huāfèi (money). ②度过 dùguo (time).

sperm n. 精液 jīngyè.

sphere n. ①球 qiú, 球形 qiúxíng (shape). ②范围 fànwéi, 领域 lǐngyù (range).

spice n. 香料 xiāngliào, 调味品 tiáowèipǐn.

spicy adj. 辛辣的 xīnlà de.

spider n. 蜘蛛 zhīzhū.

spike n. 长钉 chángdīng, 大钉 dàdīng. — v. ①以大钉钉牢 yǐ dàdīng dìngláo (nail). ②暗加毒物于……中 àn jiā dúwù yú...zhōng (add drugs).

spill v. 泼出 pōchu, 溢出 yìchu.

spin v. ①纺织 fǎngzhī (thread). ②旋转 xuánzhuǎn (rotate).

spinach n. 菠菜 bōcài.

spindle n. ①纺锤 fǎngchuí (rod). ②轴 zhóu (pin).

spine n. 脊椎骨 jǐzhuīgǔ.

spinster n. 年长的未婚女性 niánzhǎng de wèihūn nǚxìng.

spiral n. & adj. 螺旋形 luóxuánxíng.

spire n. 塔尖 tǎjiān.

spirit n. ①精神 jīngshén, 心灵 xīnlíng (mind). ②灵魂 línghún (soul). ③幽灵 yōulíng, 精灵 jīnglíng (ghost). ④元气 yuánqì (liveliness).

spiritual adj. 精神上的 jīngshénshang de.

spit v. 吐唾液 tù tuòyè. — n. 唾液 tuòyè.

spite n. 恶意 èyì.

splash v. 溅 jiàn, 泼水 pōshuǐ. — n. 溅水声 jǐjiànshēng.

splendid adj. ①壮丽的 zhuànglì de, 辉煌的 huīhuáng de (glorious). ②很好的 hěn hǎo de (excellent).

splendor n. 壮丽 zhuànglì, 辉煌 huīhuáng.

splint n. 夹板 jiābǎn / jiābǎn.

split v. ①劈开 pīkai, 裂开 lièkai (break). ②分开 fēnkai, 分裂 fēnliè (divide). — n. ①裂开 lièkai (break). ②分裂 fēnliè (division).

spoil v. ①破坏 pòhuài (ruin). ②宠坏 chǒnghuài (coddle). ③腐坏 fǔhuài (rot).

spoken adj. 口头的 kǒutóu de.

spokesman n. 发言人 fāyánrén, 代言人 dàiyánrén.

sponge n. 海绵 hǎimián. — v. 用海绵吸干 yòng hǎimián xīgān.

sponsor n. ①保证人 bǎozhèngrén (guarantor). ②赞助人 zànzhùrén (supporter). — v. 赞助 zànzhù.

spontaneous adj. 自然的 zìrán de, 自发的 zìfā de.

spool n. 线轴 xiànzhóu.

spoon n. 匙 chí, 调羹 tiáogēng.

sporadic adj. 零星的 língxīng de, 偶尔的 ǒu'ěr de.

spore n. 孢子 bāozǐ.

sport n. 运动 yùndòng, 户外活动 hùwài huódòng.

sportsman n. 运动员 yùndòngyuán.

spot n. ①污点 wūdiǎn (stain). ②斑点 bāndiǎn 〈mark〉. ③地点 dìdiǎn (place).

spotlight n. 聚光灯 jùguāngdēng.

spouse n. 配偶 pèi'ǒu.

spout v. ①喷出 pēnchu (erupt). ②滔滔不绝地说 tāotāo-bùjué de shuō 〈speak〉. — n. 管嘴 guǎnzuǐ, 喷水口 pēnshuǐkǒu.

sprain n. & v. 扭伤 niǔshāng.

sprawl v. ①伸开手足而卧或坐 shēnkai shǒuzú ér wò huò

zuò 〈lie〉. ②蔓延 mànyán, 展开 zhǎnkai (spread).

spray n. ①水沫 shuǐmò 〈water〉. ②喷雾器 pēnwùqì 〈paint〉. — v. 喷洒 pēnsǎ.

spread v. ①铺 pū, 展开 zhǎnkai (lay out). ②涂敷 túfū (apply). ③延伸 yánshēn, 扩散 kuòsàn (broaden). ④散布 sànbù, 传播 chuánbō / chuánbō (scatter).

spring v. 跳跃 tiàoyuè (jump). — n. ①春季 chūnjì 〈season〉. ②弹簧 tánhuáng, 发条 fātiáo 〈device〉. ③跳跃 tiàoyuè 〈movement〉. ④泉源 quányuán 〈water〉.

sprinkle v. 洒 sǎ, 撒 sǎ. — n. 毛毛雨 máomaoyǔ.

sprint v. 全速冲刺 quánsù chōngcì.

sprout v. 发芽 fāyá. — n. 芽 yá.

spur n. ①激励 jīlì (encouragement). ②刺马钉 cìmǎdīng 〈horse〉. — v. ①激励 jīlì (encourage). ②以刺马钉刺 yǐ cìmǎdīng cì 〈horse〉.

spurious adj. 伪造的 wěizào de / wèizào de, 假的 jiǎ de (not genuine).

spurn v. 不屑地赶走 búxiè de gǎnzǒu.

spurt v. 喷出 pēnchu, 涌出 yǒngchu.

spy n. 间谍 jiàndié. — v. ①侦察 zhēnchá, 暗中调查 ànzhōng diàochá (be a spy). ②发现 fāxiàn (discover).

squabble n. & v. 小争吵 xiǎozhēngchǎo.

squad n. 小队 xiǎoduì 〈people〉, 班 bān 〈soldiers〉.

squadron n. ①骑兵中队 qíbīng zhōngduì 〈cavalry〉.

S

②中队 zhōngduì〈military〉.

squalid adj. 污秽的 wūhuì de.

squall v. 大哭 dàkū, 大叫 dàjiào. — n. ①狂风 kuángfēng〈wind〉. ②大哭 dàkū, 大叫 dàjiào〈cry〉.

squander v. 浪费 làngfèi.

square n. ①正方形 zhèngfāngxíng〈shape〉. ②广场 guǎngchǎng〈plaza〉. — adj. ①正方形的 zhèngfāngxíng de〈shape〉. ②直角的 zhíjiǎo de〈right-angled〉. ③公平的 gōngpíng de, 正直的 zhèngzhí de〈honest〉. — v. 使成方形 shǐ chéng fāngxíng.

squash v. ①压烂 yālàn, 压碎 yāsuì〈crush〉. ②挤入 jǐrù〈crowd〉. ③镇压 zhènyā〈repress〉. — n. ①压碎声 yāsuìshēng〈sound〉. ②南瓜 nánguā〈gourd〉.

squat v. 蹲踞 dūnjù.

squawk n. & v. 咯咯叫声 gēgē jiàoshēng〈bird〉.

squeak n. & v. 尖锐声 jiānruìshēng.

squeal n. & v. 尖叫声 jiānjiàoshēng.

squeamish adj. 有洁癖的 yǒu jiépǐ de.

squeeze v. 压榨 yāzhà, 挤压 jǐyā.

squid n. 乌贼 wūzéi, 鱿鱼 yóuyú.

squirm v. 蠕动 rúdòng, 扭曲 niǔqū.

squirrel n. 松鼠 sōngshǔ.

squirt v. 喷出 pēnchu.

stab n. & v. 刺 cì, 戳 chuō, 刺伤 cìshāng.

stability n. 稳定 wěndìng, 稳固 wěngù.

stabilize v. 使稳定 shǐ

wěndìng.

stable adj. 稳定的 wěndìng de.

stack n. 堆堆 duī〈pile〉.

stadium n. 体育场 tǐyùchǎng.

staff n. ①棒 bàng, 杖 zhàng〈stick〉. ②竿 gān〈pole〉. ③全体职员 quántǐ zhíyuán〈assistants〉.

stag n. 雄鹿 xiónglù〈male deer〉.

stage n. ①舞台 wǔtái〈platform〉. ②阶段 jiēduàn〈period〉.

stagger v. ①蹒跚 pánshān / mánshān, 摇晃 yáohuang〈falter〉. ②使吃惊 shǐ chījīng〈amaze〉.

stagnant adj. 不流动的 bù liúdòng de.

stagnate v. 停滞 tíngzhì.

staid adj. 沉着的 chénzhuó de.

stain n. 污点 wūdiǎn, 瑕疵 xiácī〈blemish〉. — v. 染污 rǎnwū〈blemish〉.

stair n. 楼梯 lóutī, 阶梯 jiētī.

staircase n. 楼梯 lóutī.

stake n. ①桩 zhuāng〈stick〉. ②赌注 dǔzhù〈bet〉.

stale adj. 不新鲜的 bù xīnxiān de〈no longer fresh〉.

stalk n. 茎 jīng. — v. 潜行 qiánxíng.

stall n. ①厩 jiù〈compartment〉. ②货摊 huòtān〈stand〉. — v. ①失速 shīsù〈speed〉. ②拖延 tuōyán〈delay〉.

stammer v. 口吃 kǒuchī / kǒují, 结巴地说 jiēba de shuō. — n. 口吃 kǒuchī / kǒují.

stamp v. ①跺 duò, 踏 tà〈foot〉. ②盖印于 gàiyìn yú〈imprint〉. — n. ①印章 yìnzhāng〈seal〉. ②邮票 yóupiào〈letter〉.

stance n. ①姿势 zīshì〈posture〉. ②态度 tàidu〈attitude〉. ③立场

lìchǎng (position).

stand v. ①站立 zhànlì (rise).
②竖起 shùqǐ (erect). ③不变
búbiàn (remain valid). ④忍受
rěnshòu (endure). — n. ①台架
táijià (support). ②摊 tān (stall).

standard n. 标准 biāozhǔn
⟨level⟩. — adj. 标准的
biāozhǔn de.

standing n. ①身分 shēnfen,
地位 dìwèi (position). ②持续
chíxù (continuance). — adj.
持续的 chíxù de (continuing).

standpoint n. 立场 lìchǎng,
观点 guāndiǎn.

stanza n. 一节 yìjié.

staple n. ①钉书针
dìngshūzhēn ⟨stapler⟩. ②主要
物产 zhǔyào wùchǎn
⟨product⟩.

stapler n. 钉书机 dìngshūjī.

star n. ①星 xīng ⟨astronomy⟩.
②星形 xīngxíng (pentagram).
③明星 míngxīng ⟨performer⟩.

starch n. ①淀粉 diànfěn
(carbohydrate). ②浆 jiāng
⟨clothes⟩.

stare v. 凝视 níngshì, 瞪眼
dèngyǎn.

starfish n. 海星 hǎixīng.

stark adj. ①僵硬的 jiāngyìng
de (stiff). ②全然的 quánrán
de (complete).

starry adj. 多星的 duōxīng de.

start v. 开始 kāishǐ (begin).
~ **out** 出发 chūfā (depart).
— n. 开始 kāishǐ, 着手
zhuóshǒu.

startle v. 使吃惊 shǐ chījīng.

startling adj. 令人吃惊的
lìng rén chījīng de.

starvation n. 饥饿 jī'è.

starve v. 饥饿 jī'è, 使挨饿
shǐ ái'è / shǐ āi'è.

state n. ①状态 zhuàngtài, 情
形 qíngxing (condition). ②国
家 guójiā (country). ③州 zhōu
(political unit). — v. 述说
shùshuō.

stately adj. 庄严的
zhuāngyán de.

statement n. 陈述 chénshù,
声明 shēngmíng.

statesman n. 政治家
zhèngzhìjiā.

static adj. 静止的 jìngzhǐ de,
静态的 jìngtài de. — n. 静电
jìngdiàn.

station n. ①岗位 gǎngwèi
(position). ②署 shǔ, 局 jú
(office). ③车站 chēzhàn
(stopping-place). ④电台
diàntái (channel).

stationary adj. 不动的 bú
dòng de, 固定的 gùdìng de.

stationery n. 文具 wénjù.

statistics n. 统计 tǒngjì.

statue n. 雕像 diāoxiàng.

stature n. ①身高 shēngāo,
身材 shēncái ⟨physical⟩. ②地
位 dìwèi ⟨status⟩.

status n. ①地位 dìwèi, 身分
shēnfen (position). ②状态
zhuàngtài (condition).

statute n. 法规 fǎguī, 法令
fǎlìng.

stay v. ①停留 tíngliú (remain).
②居住 jūzhù (be housed).
③延缓 yánhuǎn (postpone).

STD 性传播疾病 xìng
chuánbō jíbìng / 性病 xìngbìng
(Sexually Transmitted Disease).

steadfast adj. 坚定的
jiāndìng de, 不变的 búbiàn
de.

steadily adv. 稳健地 wěnjiàn
de.

steady adj. ①稳定的 wěndìng

S

de (stable). ②有规律的 yǒu guīlǜ de (unvarying).

steak n. 牛排 niúpái, 肉片 ròupiàn.

steal v. 偷 tōu, 窃取 qièqǔ.

steam n. 蒸气 zhēngqì, 水气 shuǐqì. — v. 蒸 zhēng.

steamboat n. 汽船 qìchuán.

steel n. 钢 gāng.

steep adj. ①陡峭的 dǒuqiào de (precipitous). ②过分的 guòfèn de (exorbitant). — v. 浸 渍于 jìnzì yú.

steeple n. 尖塔 jiāntǎ.

steer v. 驾驶 jiàshǐ, 掌舵 zhǎngduò.

stem n. 茎 jīng (stalk).

stench n. 臭气 chòuqì, 恶臭 èchòu.

step n. ①步 bù, 一步 yíbù (pace). ②步骤 bùzhòu / bùzòu (stage). — v. 踏 tà.

stepfather n. 继父 jìfù.

stepmother n. 继母 jìmǔ.

stereo n. 音响 yīnxiǎng.

stereotype n. ①刻板形象 kèbǎn xíngxiàng (common perception), 老套 lǎotào (fixed in form). ②铅版印刷 qiānbǎn yìnshuā ⟨printing⟩.

sterile adj. ①不肥沃的 bù féiwò de, 贫瘠的 pínjí de (barren). ②无菌的 wújūn de / wújùn de (germ-free).

sterilization n. 结扎 jiézā / jiézhá.

sterilize v. ①杀菌 shājūn / shājùn ⟨clean⟩. ②使不育 shǐ bùyù (castrate).

stern adj. ①严格的 yángé de (strict). ②严厉的 yánlì de (severe). — n. 船尾 chuánwěi.

stethoscope n. 听诊器 tīngzhěnqì.

stew v. 炖 dùn, 焖 mèn. — n. 炖菜 dùncài.

steward n. ①服务员 fúwùyuán (attendant). ②管家 guǎnjiā, 执事 zhíshì ⟨of a large house⟩.

stewardess n. ①女服务员 nǚ-fúwùyuán (attendant). ②女管家 nǚguǎnjiā ⟨of a house⟩.

stick n. ①棒 bàng, 棍 gùn (bar). ②木条 mùtiáo, 柴枝 cháizhī (branch). — v. ①刺 cì, 戳 chuō (dig). ②黏贴 niántiē (adhere).

sticker n. 黏贴标签 niántiē biāoqiān, 贴纸 tiēzhǐ ⟨paper⟩.

sticky adj. ①黏的 nián de (adhesive). ②湿热的 shīrè de (damp).

stiff adj. ①硬的 yìng de (firm). ②紧的 jǐn de (tight). ③困难的 kùnnán de, 棘手的 jíshǒu de (difficult). ④生硬的 shēngyìng de, 呆板的 dāibǎn de (clumsy). ⑤严厉的 yánlì de (strict).

stiffen v. ①变硬 biàn yìng (harden). ②使坚强 shǐ jiānqiáng (become strong).

stifle v. ①使窒息 shǐ zhìxì / shǐ zhìxí (smother). ②抑制 yìzhì (repress).

still adj. ①静寂的 jìngjì de / jìngjí de (noiseless). ②不动的 bú dòng de (unmoving). ③不 起泡的 bù qǐpào de (calm). — v. 使安静 shǐ ānjìng. — adv. 仍 réng, 仍然 réngrán, 还 hái (even so).

stimulant n. ①兴奋剂 xīngfènjì ⟨drug⟩. ②刺激物 cìjīwù (stimulus).

stimulate v. 刺激 cìjī, 鼓舞 gǔwǔ.

stimulus n. 刺激 cìjī, 激励 jīlì.

sting n. & v. ①刺 cì (prick). ②刺痛 cìtòng (stab).

stingy adj. 吝啬的 lìnsè de, 小气的 xiǎoqi de (miserly).

stink n. 臭味 chòuwèi. — v. 发臭味 fā chòuwèi (give a strong bad smell).

stipulate v. 规定 guīdìng, 约定 yuēdìng.

stipulation n. 条件 tiáojiàn (condition).

stir v. ①搅拌 jiǎobàn (mix). ②移动 yídòng (move). ③激发 jīfā (inspire).

stitch n. 一针 yìzhēn. — v. 缝 féng.

stock n. ①股票 gǔpiào, 公债 gōngzhài (shares). ②贮存 zhùcún / zhùcáng, 积蓄 jīxù (hoard). ③存货 cúnhuò, 现货 xiànhuò 〈goods〉. ④家畜 jiāchù 〈animals〉. — v. 备置 bèizhì, 采办 cǎibàn (keep a stock of).

stockbroker n. 证券经纪人 zhèngquàn jīngjìrén.

stocking n. 长袜 chángwà.

stoke v. 加燃料于 jiā ránliào yú (fill with coal).

stomach n. 胃 wèi.

stone n. ①石头 shítou, 石 shí (rock). ②纪念碑 jìniànbēi (memorial). ③宝石 bǎoshí (gem).

stony adj. ①石的 shí de (rocky). ②铁石心肠的 tiěshí--xīncháng de (heartless).

stool n. 凳 dèng, 凳子 dèngzi.

stoop v. 弯腰 wānyāo, 俯身 fǔshēn (lean over).

stop v. ①使停止 shǐ tíngzhǐ (cease). ②停止 tíngzhǐ (come to rest). ③阻止 zǔzhǐ (block).

④塞住 sāizhù (plug). ⑤停留 tíngliú (stay). — n. ①停止 tíngzhǐ (halt). ②停留处 tíngliúchù (resting-place). ③停留 tíngliú (stay). ④车站 chēzhàn (station).

stopper n. 塞子 sāizi, 阻塞物 zǔsèwù.

storage n. ①仓库 cāngkù (warehouse). ②贮藏 zhùcáng / zhǔcáng (storing).

store n. ①商店 shāngdiàn (shop). ②贮藏 zhùcáng / zhǔcáng (accumulation).

storehouse n. 仓库 cāngkù.

storekeeper n. 店主 diànzhǔ.

stork n. 鹳 guàn.

storm n. ①暴风雨 bàofēngyǔ 〈weather〉. ②骚动 sāodòng (outburst). — v. ①起风暴 qǐ fēngbào 〈weather〉. ②猛攻 měnggōng.

stormy adj. 有暴风的 yǒu bàofēng de 〈weather〉.

story n. ①故事 gùshi (tale). ②新闻报导 xīnwén bàodǎo (report). ③层 céng, 楼 lóu (floor).

stout adj. ①坚决的 jiānjué de (fearless). ②粗壮的 cūzhuàng de, 结实的 jiēshí de (thick).

stove n. 火炉 huǒlú, 暖炉 nuǎnlú.

stow v. 存放 cúnfàng, 堆置 duīzhì.

straight adj. ①直的 zhí de (aligned). ②整齐的 zhěngqí de (neat). ③连续的 liánxù de (continuous). ④坦白的 tǎnbái de, 正直的 zhèngzhí de (honest).

straighten v. 使直 shǐ zhí, 变直 biàn zhí.

straightforward adj. 正直

的 zhèngzhí de.

strain v. ①拉紧 lājǐn (pull).
②尽全力 jìn quánlì (endeavor).
③过劳 guòláo (exhaust). ④曲
解 qūjiě (twist from the truth).
⑤过滤 guòlǜ (filter). — n. ①过
度负担 guòdù fùdān, 辛苦
xīnkǔ (hardship). ②拉紧 lājǐn
(being stretched).

strait n. 海峡 hǎixiá.

strand n. ①绳股 shénggǔ
(rope). ②滨 bīn, 岸 àn (shore).
— v. 搁浅 gēqiǎn (run aground).

strange adj. ①奇异的 qíyì de,
奇怪的 qíguài de (abnormal).
②陌生的 mòshēng de
(unfamiliar).

stranger n. 陌生人
mòshēngrén.

strangle v. 勒死 lēisǐ, 使窒息
shǐ zhìxí / shǐ zhìxí.

strap n. 带 dài, 皮带 pídài
(strip). — v. 用带捆 yòng dài
kǔn (bind).

strategic adj. 战略上的
zhànlüèshang de.

strategy n. 策略 cèlüè, 战略
zhànlüè.

stratum n. 地层 dìcéng, 岩层
yáncéng (rock).

straw n. ①稻草 dàocǎo (dry
grass). ②吸管 xīguǎn (for
drinking).

strawberry n. 草莓 cǎoméi.

stray v. ①迷路 mílù (get lost).
②游荡 yóudàng (wander).

streak n. ①条纹 tiáowén
(line). ②性情 xìngqíng (quality).

stream n. ①溪 xī (river). ②流
动 liúdòng (flow).

street n. 街 jiē, 街道 jiēdào.

strength n. 力 lì, 力量 lìliang.

strengthen v. 加强 jiāqiáng,
变强 biàn qiáng.

strenuous adj. 费力的 fèilì de
(exhausting).

stress n. ①压力 yālì, 压迫
yāpò (tension). ②强调
qiángdiào (emphasis). ③重音
zhòngyīn (accent). — v. ①强调
qiángdiào, 着重 zhuózhòng
(emphasize). ②重读 zhòngdú
(words). ③加压力于 jiā yālì yú
(pressure).

stretch n. & v. 伸展 shēnzhǎn,
延伸 yánshēn (extension).

stretcher n. 担架 dānjià.

stricken adj. 受侵袭的 shòu
qīnxí de.

strict adj. ①严格的 yángé de,
严厉的 yánlì de (firm). ②精确
的 jīngquè de (accurate).

stride v. 大步行走 dàbù
xíngzǒu. — n. 大步 dàbù.

strike v. ①打 dǎ, 击 jī / jí, 敲
qiāo (hit). ②敲响 qiāoxiǎng
(chime). ③罢工 bàgōng (stop
work). ④取下 qǔxia (take down).
— n. ①罢工 bàgōng (stopping
of work). ②好球 hǎoqiú (ball).

striking adj. 显著的 xiǎnzhù
de, 引人注意的 yǐn rén zhùyì
de (attracting attention).

string n. ①线 xiàn, 细绳
xìshéng (cord). ②一串
yíchuàn, 一列 yíliè (series).
③弦 xián (instrument).

strip v. ①剥去 bāoqu / bōqu,
脱去 tuōqu (take off). ②夺去
duóqu (take away). ③裸露
luǒlù (bare yourself). — n. 狭长
片条 xiácháng piàntiáo.

stripe n. 条纹 tiáowén.

striped adj. 有条纹的 yǒu
tiáowén de.

strive v. ①努力 nǔlì, 奋斗
fèndòu (try). ②斗争 dòuzhēng
(struggle).

S

stroke n. ①打击 dǎjī / dǎjí (hit). ②笔画 bǐhuà 〈writing〉. ③中风 zhòngfēng 〈sickness〉. ④一动 yídòng 〈single movement〉.

stroll n. & v. 漫步 mànbù, 遨游 áoyóu 〈ramble〉.

strong adj. ①强的 qiáng de, 强壮的 qiángzhuàng de 〈power〉. ②浓的 nóng de 〈taste〉. ③有力的 yǒulì de 〈cogent〉.

structure n. ①构造 gòuzào, 结构 jiégòu 〈organization〉. ②建筑物 jiànzhùwù / jiànzhúwù 〈building〉.

struggle n. & v. ①挣扎 zhēngzhá 〈strive〉. ②努力 nǔlì 〈endeavor〉.

strut v. 高视阔步 gāoshì-kuòbù. — n. 支柱 zhīzhù, 撑木 chēngmù.

stubble n. ①残株 cánzhū 〈butt〉. ②短须 duǎnxū 〈beard〉.

stubborn adj. 顽固的 wángù de, 固执的 gùzhí de 〈determined〉.

stud n. ①饰钉 shìdìng 〈nail〉. ②种马 zhǒngmǎ 〈horse〉.

student n. 学生 xuésheng.

studio n. ①画室 huàshì, 工作室 gōngzuòshì 〈workroom〉. ②摄影棚 shèyǐngpéng 〈filming〉. ③播音室 bōyīnshì / bòyīnshì 〈broadcast〉. ④公寓套房 gōngyù tàofáng 〈apartment〉.

studious adj. 用功的 yònggōng de, 好学的 hàoxué de 〈fond of studying〉.

study n. & v. 读书 dúshū, 研究 yánjiū / yánjiù, 学习 xuéxí.

stuff n. 材料 cáiliào, 原料 yuánliào. — v. 填塞 tiánsè.

stuffing n. 填塞物 tiánsèwù.

stuffy adj. 通风不良的 tōngfēng bùliáng de.

stumble v. ①绊倒 bàndǎo 〈blunder〉. ②结巴 jiēba 〈stammer〉.

stump n. 残干 cángàn 〈tree〉. — v. 困惑 kùnhuò, 难倒 nándǎo 〈baffle〉.

stun v. ①使昏晕 shǐ hūnyūn 〈daze〉. ②使目瞪口呆 shǐ mù-dèng-kǒudāi, 使吃惊 shǐ chījīng 〈shock〉.

stunt v. 阻碍生长 zǔài shēngzhǎng. — n. ①特技 tèjì 〈skill〉. ②恶作剧 èzuòjù 〈trick〉.

stupendous adj. 惊人的 jīngrén de.

stupid adj. 愚蠢的 yúchǔn de.

stupor n. 昏迷 hūnmí, 恍惚 huǎnghū.

sturdy adj. 强健的 qiángjiàn de 〈strong〉, 坚决的 jiānjué de 〈firm〉.

stutter v. 口吃 kǒuchī / kǒují, 结巴 jiēba.

style n. ①风格 fēnggé 〈idiosyncrasy〉. ②样式 yàngshì 〈type〉. ③优雅 yōuyǎ 〈elegance〉. ④文体 wéntǐ 〈manner of writing〉.

stylish adj. 优雅的 yōuyǎ de 〈elegant〉, 时髦的 shímáo de 〈fashionable〉.

Styrofoam n. 保丽龙 Bǎolìlóng.

subconscious n. & adj. 潜意识 qiányìshí / qiányìshì, 下意识 xiàyìshí / xiàyìshì.

subdivide v. 再分 zàifēn, 细分 xìfēn.

subdue v. ①克服 kèfú, 征服 zhēngfú 〈overcome〉. ②抑制 yìzhì, 克制 kèzhì 〈repress〉.

subject n. ①主题 zhǔtí 〈theme〉. ②科目 kēmù 〈course〉.

S

— *adj.* 受制于……的 shòuzhì yú...de (captive). ~ *to* 易患……的 yìhuàn...de.
— *v.* 使蒙受 shǐ méngshòu (expose).

subjective *adj.* ①主观的 zhǔguān de (emotional). ②主词的 zhǔcí de ⟨grammar⟩.

sublime *adj.* 崇高的 chónggāo de, 高尚的 gāoshàng de (extremely good).

submarine *n.* 潜水艇 qiánshuǐtǐng.

submerge *v.* 浸入水中 jìnrù shuǐzhōng.

submission *n.* 服从 fúcóng, 屈服 qūfú (obedience).

submit *v.* ①服从 fúcóng (surrender). ②提出 tíchu (give in). ③主张 zhǔzhāng, 建议 jiànyì (suggest).

subordinate *adj.* 下级的 xiàjí de ⟨rank⟩, 次要的 cìyào de (less important). — *n.* 属下 shǔxià.

subscribe *v.* ①捐助 juānzhù, 认捐 rènjuān (pay money regularly). ②订阅 dìngyuè (buy regularly). ③同意 tóngyì (agree with).

subscription *n.* ①捐助款 juānzhùkuǎn (contribution). ②订阅金 dìngyuèjīn (fee).

subsequent *adj.* 随后的 suíhòu de, 接下来的 jiēxialai de.

subservient *adj.* 阿谀的 ēyú de.

subside *v.* ①退落 tuìluò, 消退 xiāotuì (decline). ②下沉 xiàchén, 下陷 xiàxiàn (sink).

subsidiary *adj.* ①辅助的 fǔzhù de, 次要的 cìyào de (ancillary). ②附属的 fùshǔ de (affiliated).

subsidize *v.* 补助 bǔzhù, 津贴 jīntiē.

subsidy *n.* 补助金 bǔzhùjīn, 津贴 jīntiē.

substance *n.* ①物质 wùzhì / wùzhí (material). ②实质 shízhì / shízhí, 意义 yìyì (meaning).

substantial *adj.* ①坚固的 jiāngù de (solid). ②相当大的 xiāngdāng dà de (considerable). ③有实体的 yǒu shítǐ de (real).

substantiate *v.* ①使具体化 shǐ jùtǐhuà (make concrete). ②证实 zhèngshí, 证明 zhèngmíng (prove).

substitute *n.* 代理人 dàilǐrén ⟨person⟩, 代替物 dàitìwù ⟨thing⟩. — *v.* 代替 dàitì.

subterranean *adj.* 地下的 dìxià de (under the ground).

subtitle *n.* ①副标题 fùbiāotí (secondary title). ②字幕 zìmù (caption).

subtle *adj.* ①精致的 jīngzhì de, 微妙的 wēimiào de / wéimiào de (delicate). ②敏锐的 mǐnruì de (clever). ③淡薄的 dànbó de (mild).

subtract *v.* 减去 jiǎnqù.

suburb *n.* 市郊 shìjiāo, 郊区 jiāoqū.

subvert *v.* 颠覆 diānfù, 毁灭 huǐmiè.

subway *n.* 地下铁 dìxiàtiě.

succeed *v.* ①成功 chénggōng (be successful). ②完成 wánchéng (complete). ③继承 jìchéng, 继任 jìrèn (come after).

success *n.* ①成功 chénggōng (accomplishment). ②成功者 chénggōngzhě ⟨person⟩. ③成功的事物 chénggōng de

shìwù 〈thing〉.

successful adj. 成功的 chénggōng de.

succession n. ①连续 liánxù (continuity). ②继承 jìchéng 〈property〉.

successive adj. 连续的 liánxù de.

successor n. 继任者 jìrènzhě, 后继者 hòujìzhě.

succinct adj. 简明的 jiǎnmíng de.

succulent adj. 多汁液的 duō zhīyè de (juicy).

succumb v. ①屈从 qūcóng (yield). ②死 sǐ (die).

such adj. 如此的 rúcǐ de, 这样的 zhèyàng de (of an extreme degree). ~ **as** 诸如…… zhūrú ....

suck v. ①吸入 xīrù (draw up). ②吸吮 xīshǔn (hold in the mouth). ③吸收 xīshōu (absorb).

suckle v. 哺乳 bǔrǔ, 喂奶 wèinǎi.

sudden adj. 突然的 tūrán de / túrán de, 忽然的 hūrán de.

suddenly adv. 突然地 tūrán de / túrán de.

suds n. 肥皂泡沫 féizào pàomò.

sue v. ①起诉 qǐsù, 控告 kònggào (indict). ②请求 qǐngqiú (beg).

suffer v. ①忍受 rěnshòu (bear). ②遭受 zāoshòu (experience). ③受惩罚 shòu chéngfá (be punished). ④受苦 shòukǔ (feel pain).

suffering n. 痛苦 tòngkǔ, 苦难 kǔnàn (pain).

suffice v. 足够 zúgòu (to be enough).

sufficient adj. 足够的 zúgòu

de, 充分的 chōngfèn de.

suffix n. 字尾 zìwěi, 语尾词 yǔwěicí.

suffocate v. 窒息 zhìxī / zhíxí, 闷死 mēnsǐ.

sugar n. 糖 táng.

suggest v. ①提议 tíyì, 建议 jiànyì (propose). ②暗示 ànshì (hint).

suggestion n. 建议 jiànyì.

suicide n. ①自杀 zìshā 〈act〉. ②自杀者 zìshāzhě 〈person〉.

suit n. ①一套 yítào 〈clothes〉. ②一副 yífù 〈card〉. ③诉讼 sùsòng 〈law〉. — v. ①适合于 shìhé yú (be a good match). ②合身 héshēn (fit in).

suitable adj. 适合的 shìhé de, 恰当的 qiàdàng de.

suitcase n. 手提箱 shǒutíxiāng.

suite n. 套房 tàofáng.

sulfur n. 硫磺 liúhuáng.

sulk n. & v. 愠怒 yùnnù, 不高兴 bù gāoxìng.

sullen adj. ①闷闷不乐的 mènmèn-búlè de (cheerless). ②阴沉的 yīnchén de (dark).

sultry adj. 闷热的 mēnrè de (hot and humid).

sum n. ①合计 héjì, 总合 zǒnghé (total amount). ②金额 jīn'é (amount of money). — v. 总计 zǒngjì.

summarize v. 摘要 zhāiyào, 概述 gàishù.

summary n. 摘要 zhāiyào. — adj. ①简明的 jiǎnmíng de (brief). ②迅速的 xùnsù de (hasty).

summer n. 夏季 xiàjì, 夏天 xiàtiān.

summit n. ①顶点 dǐngdiǎn, 巅峰 diānfēng (top). ②高层会

议 gāocéng huìyì ⟨meeting⟩.

summon v. ①传唤 chuánhuàn, 召唤 zhàohuàn ⟨command⟩. ②召集 zhàojí ⟨assemble⟩.

summons n. 传票 chuánpiào.

sumo n. 相扑 xiāngpū.

sun n. 日 rì, 太阳 tàiyáng ⟨star⟩. **~ block** 防晒乳 fángshàirǔ.

sunburn n. 晒伤 shàishāng ⟨sore⟩.

Sunday n. 星期日 Xīngqīrì / Xīngqírì.

sunken adj. 下陷的 xiàxiàn de.

sunlight n. 日光 rìguāng.

sunny adj. ①阳光充足的 yángguāng chōngzú de ⟨bright⟩. ②愉快的 yúkuài de, 开朗的 kāilǎng de ⟨cheerful⟩.

sunrise n. 日出 rìchū.

sunset n. 日落 rìluò.

sunshine n. 阳光 yángguāng.

sunstroke n. 中暑 zhòngshǔ.

suntan n. 日晒的肤色 rìshài de fūsè.

superb adj. ①宏伟的 hóngwěi de ⟨grand⟩. ②极好的 jí hǎo de, 第一流的 dì-yī liú de ⟨wonderful⟩.

superficial adj. ①表面的 biǎomiàn de, 外表的 wàibiǎo de ⟨on the surface⟩. ②肤浅的 fūqiǎn de ⟨without depth⟩.

superfluous adj. 多余的 duōyú de, 不必要的 bú bìyào de.

superior adj. ①上级的 shàngjí de ⟨senior⟩. ②优良的 yōuliáng de ⟨better⟩. ③有优越感的 yǒu yōuyuègǎn de ⟨arrogant⟩. — n. 上司 shàngsī, 长官 zhǎngguān.

superiority n. 优越 yōuyuè.

superlative adj. ①最高的

zuìgāo de ⟨the highest degree⟩. ②最高级的 zuì gāojí de ⟨grammar⟩.

superman n. 超人 chāorén.

supermarket n. 超级市场 chāojí shìchǎng.

supernatural adj. 超自然的 chāozìrán de.

supersede v. 替代 tìdài, 代换 dàihuàn.

supersonic adj. 超音速的 chāoyīnsù de. **~ waves** 超声波 chāoshēngbō / 超音波 chāoyīnbō.

superstition n. 迷信 míxìn.

superstitious adj. 迷信的 míxìn de.

supervise v. 监督 jiāndū, 管理 guǎnlǐ.

supervisor n. 监督者 jiāndūzhě, 管理者 guǎnlǐzhě.

supper n. 晚餐 wǎncān.

supplement n. 附录 fùlù, 补充 bǔchōng.

supplementary adj. 补充的 bǔchōng de, 附加的 fùjiā de.

supplicate v. 恳求 kěnqiú.

supply v. 供给 gōngjǐ ⟨provide for⟩. — n. 供应品 gōngyìngpǐn.

support n. & v. ①支持 zhīchí ⟨hold up⟩. ②维持 wéichí ⟨maintenance⟩, 抚养 fǔyǎng ⟨bringing-up⟩. ③支援 zhīyuán ⟨aid⟩.

suppose v. ①假定 jiǎdìng, 认为 rènwéi ⟨assume⟩. ②想象 xiǎngxiàng ⟨imagine⟩.

suppress v. ①镇压 zhènyā, 抑制 yìzhì ⟨repress⟩. ②压抑 yāyì ⟨restrain⟩. ③隐瞒 yǐnmán ⟨conceal⟩.

supreme adj. 至高的 zhìgāo de, 无上的 wúshàng de.

surcharge n. 额外价价 éwài

suǒjià.

sure *adj.* ①确信的 quèxìn de (assured). ②必定会的 bìdìng huì de (certain). ③确实的 quèshí de (accurate). — *adv.* 确实地 quèshí de, 的确 díquè, 当然 dāngrán.

surely *adv.* 确实地 quèshí de.

surf *v.* 冲浪 chōnglàng. — *n.* 碎浪 suìlàng.

surface *n.* 表面 biǎomiàn, 外表 wàibiǎo. — *v.* ①浮出水面 fúchu shuǐmiàn (rise). ②出现 chūxiàn (appear).

surge *v.* ①汹涌而至 xiōngyǒng'érzhì ⟨waves⟩. ②蜂拥而来 fēngyōng'érlái / fēngyǒng'érlái ⟨people⟩. — *n.* ①巨浪 jùlàng, 波涛 bōtāo / bōtáo ⟨waves⟩. ②汹涌 xiōngyǒng (rush).

surgeon *n.* 外科医生 wàikē yīshēng.

surgery *n.* ①外科手术 wàikē shǒushù (operation). ②手术室 shǒushùshì (operating room).

surly *adj.* 乖戾的 guāilì de, 粗暴的 cūbào de.

surmise *n. & v.* 臆测 yìcè, 推测 tuīcè.

surname *n.* 姓 xìng.

surpass *v.* 超越 chāoyuè, 凌驾 língjià, 胜过 shèngguò.

surplus *n.* 剩余 shèngyú, 盈余 yíngyú.

surprise *n.* 惊奇 jīngqí, 惊讶 jīngyà (astonishment). — *v.* 使惊奇 shǐ jīngqí, 使惊讶 shǐ jīngyà (cause shock to).

surprising *adj.* 令人惊奇地 lìng rén jīngqí de, 令人吃惊的 lìng rén chījīng de.

surrender *v.* ①投降 tóuxiáng ⟨war⟩. ②放弃 fàngqì (give up).

— *n.* ①投降 tóuxiáng (capitulation). ②放弃 fàngqì (giving up).

surreptitious *adj.* 秘密的 mìmì de, 偷偷的 tōutōu de (done secretly).

surround *v.* 环绕 huánrào, 包围 bāowéi.

surroundings *n.* 环境 huánjìng.

survey *v.* ①调查 diàochá (investigate). ②测量 cèliáng (measure).

survival *n.* 生存 shēngcún, 存活 cúnhuó, 继续存在 jìxù cúnzài.

survive *v.* 存活 cúnhuó, 生存 shēngcún.

survivor *n.* 生还者 shēnghuánzhě, 生存者 shēngcúnzhě.

susceptible *adj.* 敏感的 mǐngǎn de (sensitive), 易受影响的 yì shòu yǐngxiǎng de (impressionable).

suspect *v.* 猜想 cāixiǎng, 怀疑 huáiyí (distrust). — *n.* 嫌疑犯 xiányífàn. — *adj.* 可疑的 kěyí de.

suspend *v.* ①悬挂 xuánguà (hang). ②使暂停 shǐ zàntíng / shǐ zhàntíng (adjourn).

suspenders *n.* 吊裤带 diàokùdài (trousers).

suspense *n.* 悬而未决 xuán-érwèijué (indecisiveness).

suspicion *n.* 怀疑 huáiyí (doubt), 嫌疑 xiányí (mistrust).

suspicious *adj.* ①可疑的 kěyí de (doubtful). ②猜疑的 cāiyí de (suspected).

sustain *v.* ①支持 zhīchí, 维持 wéichí (support). ②蒙受 méngshòu (suffer). ③认可

S

sustenance n. 食物 shíwù (food).

swab n. ①拖把 tuōbǎ (mop). ②棉花棒 miánhuābàng ⟨Q-tip⟩. — v. 擦净 cājìng ⟨clean⟩.

swagger n. & v. 昂首阔步 ángshǒu-kuòbù ⟨walk⟩.

swallow v. 吞 tūn, 咽 yàn. — n. 燕子 yànzi.

swamp n. 沼泽 zhǎozé.

swan n. 天鹅 tiān'é.

swarm n. 群 qún. — v. 群集 qúnjí.

swarthy adj. 黝黑的 yǒuhēi de.

sway v. 摇摆 yáobǎi (swing from side to side).

swear v. 发誓 fāshì, 宣誓 xuānshì.

sweat n. 汗 hàn, 出汗 chūhàn. — v. 出汗 chūhàn.

sweater n. 毛衣 máoyī.

sweep v. ①扫 sǎo, 打扫 dǎsǎo ⟨clean⟩. ②掠过 lüèguo (move quickly).

sweet adj. ①甜的 tián de (sugary). ②柔和的 róuhé de (harmonious). ③甜美的 tiánměi de, 吸引人的 xīyǐn rén de (lovable). — n. 甜食 tiánshí ⟨candy⟩.

sweeten v. 变甜 biàn tián.

sweetheart n. 恋人 liànrén, 爱人 àirén ⟨lover⟩.

swell v. 膨胀 péngzhàng (expand), 增大 zēngdà (increase). — n. 大浪 dàlàng ⟨waves⟩.

swerve v. 突然转向 tūrán zhuǎnxiàng / túrán zhuǎnxiàng.

swift adj. & adv. 迅速的 xùnsù de (quick). ②即刻的

jíkè de (prompt).

swim v. 游泳 yóuyǒng.

swindle n. & v. 欺骗 qīpiàn.

swing v. ①摇摆 yáobǎi (sway). ②回转 huízhuǎn (turn around). ③荡秋千 dàng qiūqiān (swing on). — n. ①摇摆 yáobǎi (sway). ②秋千 qiūqiān (seat held by ropes).

swirl v. 打漩涡 dǎ xuánwō (spin). — n. 漩涡 xuánwō ⟨water⟩.

switch n. ①开关 kāiguān ⟨electric circuit⟩. ②转变 zhuǎnbiàn (shift).

switchboard n. ①配电盘 pèidiànpán ⟨electrical⟩. ②电话总机 diànhuà zǒngjī ⟨telephone⟩.

swivel n. 转环 zhuǎnhuán.

swollen adj. 肿的 zhǒng de, 胀的 zhàng de.

swoon v. 昏厥 hūnjué, 晕倒 yūndǎo (faint).

sword n. 剑 jiàn, 刀 dāo.

sworn adj. 宣誓过的 xuānshìguo de.

sycamore n. 大枫树 dàfēngshù.

syllable n. 音节 yīnjié.

syllabus n. 大纲 dàgāng.

symbol n. ①象征 xiàngzhēng (sign). ②符号 fúhào (mark).

symbolic adj. ①象征(性)的 xiàngzhēng(xìng) de ⟨sign⟩. ②符号的 fúhào de ⟨mark⟩.

symbolize v. 象征 xiàngzhēng.

symmetry n. 对称 duìchèn / duìchèng, 匀称 yúnchèn / yúnchèng.

sympathetic adj. 有同情心的 yǒu tóngqíngxīn de.

sympathize v. 同情

tóngqíng.

sympathy *n.* 同情 tóngqíng.

symphony *n.* 交响乐团 jiāoxiǎngyuètuán ⟨orchestra⟩, 交响曲 jiāoxiǎngqǔ ⟨music⟩.

symposium *n.* 专题论文会 zhuāntí lùnwénhuì.

symptom *n.* 征候 zhēnghòu, 征兆 zhēngzhào.

synagogue *n.* 犹太教的会堂 yóutàijiào de huìtáng.

synonym *n.* 同义字 tóngyìzì, 相似字 xiāngsìzì.

synonymous *adj.* 同义的 tóngyì de.

syntax *n.* 句法 jùfǎ.

synthesis *n.* 综合 zōnghé / zònghé, 合成 héchéng.

syringe *n.* 注射器 zhùshèqì.

syrup *n.* 糖浆 tángjiāng.

system *n.* ①系统 xìtǒng ⟨network⟩. ②制度 zhìdù ⟨institution⟩. ③方法 fāngfǎ ⟨method⟩.

systematic *adj.* 有系统的 yǒu xìtǒng de.

T

tab *n.* ①垂饰 chuíshì ⟨small strip⟩. ②账单 zhàngdān ⟨bill⟩.

table *n.* ①桌子 zhuōzi, 餐桌 cānzhuō ⟨furniture⟩. ②表 biǎo ⟨list⟩.

tablecloth *n.* 桌布 zhuōbù.

tablespoon *n.* 大汤匙 dà tāngchí.

tablet *n.* ①药片 yàopiàn ⟨pill⟩. ②碑 bēi ⟨stone⟩.

taboo *n.* 禁忌 jìnjì.

tacit *adj.* 心照不宣的 xīnzhào-bùxuān de.
~ *agreement* 默契 mòqì.

tack *n.* ①图钉 túdīng, 大头钉 dàtóudīng ⟨nail⟩. ②方向 fāngxiàng, 方针 fāngzhēn ⟨direction⟩. – *v.* 以大头钉钉住 yǐ dàtóudīng dìngzhù ⟨nail⟩. ~ *on* 加上 jiāshang, 附上 fùshang.

tackle *n.* 用具 yòngjù ⟨equipment⟩. *fishing* ~ 渔具 yújù.

– *v.* ①抱住 bàozhù ⟨seize⟩. ②抢球 qiǎngqiú ⟨football⟩. ③处理 chǔlǐ ⟨take care of⟩.

tact *n.* 得体 détǐ.

tactic *n.* 策略 cèlüè, 战略 zhànlüè.

tactical *adj.* 战术的 zhànshù de.

tactics *n.* 战术 zhànshù ⟨battle⟩.

tadpole *n.* 蝌蚪 kēdǒu.

tag *n.* 标签 biāoqiān ⟨label⟩. – *v.* 加上标签 jiāshang biāoqiān.

tail *n.* 尾巴 wěiba ⟨animal⟩, 后部 hòubù ⟨tail-end⟩. – *v.* 尾随 wěisuí ⟨follow⟩.

taillight *n.* 尾灯 wěidēng.

tailor *n.* 裁缝师 cáiféngshī.

take *v.* ①拿 ná ⟨grasp⟩, 握 wò ⟨grasp⟩, 取 qǔ ⟨attain⟩. ②捕 bǔ, 捉 zhuō ⟨capture⟩. ③带 dài ⟨bring⟩. ④吃 chī, 喝 hē, 服用

tale *n.* 故事 gùshì (story or report).

talent *n.* 才能 cáinéng (capability), 天分 tiānfèn (natural ability).

talented *adj.* 有才能的 yǒu cáinéng de, 有天分的 yǒu tiānfèn de.

talk *n.* 演讲 yǎnjiǎng (speech). — *v.* ①说话 shuōhuà, 讲话 jiǎnghuà (speak). ②闲聊 xiánliáo, 闲谈 xiántán (chat). ③讨论 tǎolùn (discuss).

talkative *adj.* 好说话的 hào shuōhuà de, 多嘴的 duōzuǐ de.

tall *adj.* 高的 gāo de.

talon *n.* 爪 zhǎo.

tame *v.* ①驯服 xùnfú / xúnfú ⟨animal⟩. ②克服 kèfú ⟨difficult⟩. — *adj.* ①驯服的 xùnfú de / xúnfú de (domesticated). ②单调的 dāndiào de, 乏味的 fáwèi de (boring).

tamper *v.* 干预 gānyù (interfere with something).

tan *v.* 晒黑 shàihēi (get a suntan). — *adj.* 黄褐色的 huánghèsè de / huánghésè de.

tang *n.* 强烈的味道 qiángliè de wèidào (sharp taste).

tangerine *n.* 柑橘 gānjú.

tangible *adj.* ①可触的 kěchù de (touchable). ②明确的 míngquè de (definite).

tangle *n. & v.* 缠结 chánjié.

tango *n.* 探戈舞 tàngēwǔ.

tank *n.* ①槽 cáo (container). ②战车 zhànchē, 坦克车 tǎnkèchē (armored vehicle).

tankard *n.* 大酒杯 dà jiǔbēi.

tanker *n.* ①油轮 yóulún ⟨ship⟩. ②油罐车 yóuguànchē ⟨vehicle⟩.

tanner *n.* 制革者 zhìgézhě.

tantalize *v.* 吊胃口 diào-wèikǒu, 逗惑 dòuhuò.

tantrum *n.* 发脾气 fāpíqi.

Taoism *n.* 道教 Dàojiào.

tap *v.* 轻敲 qīngqiāo, 轻拍 qīngpāi. — *n.* ①水龙头 shuǐlóngtóu (faucet). ②轻敲 qīngqiāo, 轻拍 qīngpāi (a light touch).

tape *n.* ①带子 dàizi, 胶带 jiāodài (band). ②录音带 lùyīndài ⟨audio⟩. ③录像带 / 录影带 lùyǐngdài ⟨video⟩. — *v.* ①捆住 kǔnzhù (tie). ②录音 lùyīn ⟨audio⟩. ③录像 lùxiàng / 录影 lùyǐng ⟨video⟩.

tapestry *n.* 绣帷 xiùwéi.

tar *n.* 柏油 bǎiyóu / bóyóu, 沥青 lìqīng.

tardy *adj.* ①缓慢的 huǎnmàn de (slow). ②晚到的 wǎndào de (late).

target *n.* ①靶 bǎ, 目标 mùbiāo (goal). ②对象 duìxiàng (object).

tariff *n.* ①关税 guānshuì (customs). ②价目表 jiàmùbiǎo (price list).

tarnish *v.* 失去光泽 shīqù guāngzé.

taro *n.* 芋 yù, 芋头 yùtou.

tarpaulin *n.* 防水布 fángshuǐbù (waterproof canvas).

tart *n.* 果子馅饼 guǒzi xiànbǐng ⟨food⟩. — *adj.* 酸的

fúyòng (eat or drink). ⑤乘 chéng, 坐 zuò ⟨transportation⟩. ⑥接受 jiēshòu (accept). ⑦采用 cǎiyòng (use). ⑧选修 xuǎnxiū ⟨course⟩. ⑨选择 xuǎnzé (choose).

suān de (sour).

tartan *n.* 格子呢 géziní.

task *n.* 工作 gōngzuò (work), 任务 rènwu (responsibility).

tassel *n.* 流苏 liúsū, 穗 suì.

taste *n.* ①味道 wèidào (flavor). ②味觉 wèijué (sensory). ③品味 pǐnwèi (appreciation). – *v.* 品尝 pǐncháng.

tasty *adj.* 味美的 wèiměi de (delicious).

tattoo *n.* ①纹身 wénshēn, 刺青 cìqīng (image on skin). ②归营号 guīyínghào (military signal).

taunt *n. & v.* 嘲笑 cháoxiào (tease), 嘲骂 cháomà (insult).

Taurus 金牛座 Jīnniúzuò.

taut *adj.* ①拉紧的 lājǐn de (tight). ②紧张的 jǐnzhāng de (tense).

tavern *n.* 酒店 jiǔdiàn (pub), 客栈 kèzhàn (inn).

tawny *adj.* 黄褐色的 huánghèsè de / huánghésè de.

tax *n.* 税 shuì (money). – *v.* 课税 kèshuì (require to pay tax).

taxation *n.* ①税制 shuìzhì (legal system). ②税收 shuìshōu (tax revenue).

taxi *n.* 出租车 chūzūchē / 计程车 jìchéngchē.

tea *n.* ①茶 chá (drink). ②茶叶 cháyè (leaves). ③下午茶 xiàwǔchá (meal).

teach *v.* 教 jiāo, 教书 jiāoshū.

teacher *n.* 教师 jiàoshī.

teaching *n.* ①教书 jiāoshū (instruction). ②教义 jiàoyì, 教训 jiàoxùn (doctrine).

teak *n.* 柚木 yòumù.

team *n.* 队 duì, 组 zǔ.

tear *n.* 泪 lèi, 眼泪 yǎnlèi (weeping). – *v.* 撕 sī, 撕裂

sīliè (rip).

tease *v.* 揶揄 yéyú, 嘲弄 cháonòng.

teaspoon *n.* 茶匙 cháchí.

teat *n.* 乳头 rǔtóu.

technical *adj.* ①工艺的 gōngyì de (craft), 技术上的 jìshùshang de (skill). ②专门的 zhuānmén de (specialized).

technician *n.* 技术人员 jìshù rényuán, 技工 jìgōng.

technique *n.* 技术 jìshù, 技巧 jìqiǎo (skill).

technology *n.* 科技 kējì (science), 工业技术 gōngyè jìshù (industry).

tedious *adj.* 冗长乏味的 rǒngcháng fáwèi de.

teenage *adj.* 十几岁的 shíjǐsuì de.

teenager *n.* 青少年 qīngshàonián.

teens *n.* 十几岁的年龄 shíjǐsuì de niánlíng.

teeth *n.* 牙齿 yáchǐ. *brush the ~* 刷牙 shuāyá.

teetotalism *n.* 禁酒主义 jìnjiǔ zhǔyì.

telegram *n.* 电报 diànbào.

telegraph *n.* ①电报机 diànbàojī (apparatus). ②电报 diànbào (telegram). – *v.* 发电报 fā diànbào.

telephone *n.* 电话 diànhuà. – *v.* 打电话 (给) dǎ diànhuà (gěi).

telescope *n.* 望远镜 wàngyuǎnjìng.

televise *v.* 由电视播送 yóu diànshì bōsòng / yóu diànshì bòsòng.

television *n.* 电视 diànshì (TV).

telex *n.* 电报 diànbào. *v.* – 电

传联系 diànchuán liánxì.

tell v. ①告诉 gàosu (advise).
②分辨 fēnbiàn, 辨别 biànbié
(distinguish).

temper n. ①脾气 píqi, 性情
xìngqing (disposition). ②心情
xīnqíng (mood). ③硬度 yìngdù
(degree of hardness). — v. 缓和
huǎnhé (alleviate), 调节
tiáojié (adjust).

temperament n. 气质 qìzhì /
qìzhí, 性情 xìngqing
(disposition).

temperate adj. ①有节制的
yǒu jiézhì de (moderate). ②温
和的 wēnhé de (climate).

temperature n. ①温度
wēndù (degree of heat). ②体温
tǐwēn (body). take one's ~ 量体
温 liáng tǐwēn.

tempest n. 暴风雨
bàofēngyǔ.

temple n. 庙 miào, 寺 sì, 神殿
shéndiàn (non-Christian reli-
gions).

tempo n. 拍子 pāizi (music),
速度 sùdù (speed).

temporal adj. 世俗的 shìsú
de (worldly).

temporary adj. 暂时的
zànshí de / zhànshí de.

tempt v. 引诱 yǐnyòu (arouse a
desire).

tempter n. 引诱者 yǐnyòuzhě.

ten n. & adj. 十 shí.

tenable adj. ①可防守的 kě
fángshǒu de (defensible).
②合理的 hélǐ de (reasonable).

tenancy n. 租赁 zūlìn.

tenant n. 房客 fángkè, 承租者
chéngzūzhě.

tend v. 倾向 qīngxiàng, 朝向
cháoxiàng.

tendency n. 倾向 qīngxiàng,

趋势 qūshì (trend).

tender adj. ①柔嫩的 róunèn
de (meat). ②柔软的 róuruǎn
de (soft). ③温柔的 wēnróu de
(gentle). ④柔和的 róuhé de
(mild). — v. ①提出 tíchu, 提供
tígōng (offer). ②投标 tóubiāo
(bid on).

tendon n. 腱 jiàn.

tennis n. 网球 wǎngqiú.

tenor n. ①男高音 nángāoyīn
(music). ②要旨 yàozhǐ (drift).
③风格 fēnggé (style).

tense adj. ①拉紧的 lājǐn de
(tight). ②紧张的 jǐnzhāng de
(nervous). — n. 时式 shíshì, 时
态 shítài.

tension n. ①拉紧 lājǐn (tight-
ness). ②紧张 jǐnzhāng
(nervousness).

tent n. 帐篷 zhàngpeng, 帷幕
wéimù.

tentacle n. 触角 chùjiǎo, 触须
chùxū (animal).

tentative adj. 试验性质的
shìyàn xìngzhì de / shíyàn
xìngzhí de.

tenth n. & adj. 第十 dì-shí.

tepid adj. ①微热的 wēirè de /
wēirè de (lukewarm). ②不大热
烈的 bú dà rèliè de (apathetic).

term n. ①期间 qījiān / qíjiān
(duration). ②学期 xuéqī /
xuéqí (semester). ③术语 shùyǔ
(technical name). ④条件
tiáojiàn (condition). ⑤措词
cuòcí (words).

terminal adj. 最终的
zuìzhōng de (last). — n. ①终
端机 zhōngduānjī (computer).
②航站 hángzhàn (airport).

terminate v. 终结 zhōngjié,
结束 jiéshù.

terminology n. 术语 shùyǔ,

专门名词 zhuānmén míngcí.

terminus n. 终点 zhōngdiǎn (the end), 终站 zhōngzhàn 〈station〉.

termite n. 白蚁 báiyǐ.

terrace n. 平台 píngtái 〈house〉.

terrain n. 地域 dìyù 〈region〉, 地形 dìxíng (topography).

terrestrial adj. 地球上的 dìqiúshang de 〈of the Earth〉, 陆地的 lùdì de 〈of the land〉.

terrible adj. ①可怕的 kěpà de, 令人恐惧的 lìng rén kǒngjù de (frightening). ②糟糕的 zāogāo de (very bad).

terribly adv. ①非常地 fēicháng de (extremely). ②糟糕地 zāogāo de (in a very bad way).

terrific adj. ①极好的 jí hǎo de (very good). ②非常的 fēicháng de (extreme).

terrify v. 使害怕 shǐ hàipà, 使恐怖 shǐ kǒngbù.

territorial adj. 领土的 lǐngtǔ de.

territory n. 领土 lǐngtǔ (possessed land), 地域 dìyù (area).

terror n. 恐惧 kǒngjù.

terrorism n. 恐怖主义 kǒngbù zhǔyì.

terrorist n. 恐怖分子 kǒngbù fènzǐ.

terse adj. 简洁的 jiǎnjié de.

test n. ①考验 kǎoyàn (trial). ②测验 cèyàn, 考试 kǎoshì 〈school〉. ③试验 shìyàn (experiment). — v. 试验 shìyàn, 考验 kǎoyàn (experiment), 检验 jiǎnyàn 〈medical purposes〉.

testament n. ①证明 zhèngmíng (proof). ②遗嘱 yízhǔ (will).

testicle n. 睾丸 gāowán.

testify v. 作证 zuòzhèng.

testimonial n. ①证明书 zhèngmíngshū 〈prove〉. ②推荐书 tuījiànshū (reference).

testimony n. ①证言 zhèngyán (statement). ②证据 zhèngjù (evidence).

test tube n. 试管 shìguǎn.

text n. 本文 běnwén (piece of writing), 原文 yuánwén (original version).

textbook n. 教科书 jiàokēshū, 课本 kèběn.

textile n. 织物 zhīwù.

texture n. 质地 zhìdì / zhídì 〈surface〉.

than conj. 比…… bǐ... (comparison).

thank v. 感谢 gǎnxiè, 道谢 dàoxiè.

thankful adj. 感谢的 gǎnxiè de.

Thanksgiving n. 感恩节 Gǎn'ēnjié.

that adj. & pron. 那 nà, 那个 nàge. — adv. 那么 nàme.

thaw n. & v. 融解 róngjiě.

the def. art. 这 zhè (this), 那 nà (that).

theater n. ①戏院 xìyuàn, 剧场 jùchǎng 〈building〉. ②戏剧 xìjù (drama).

their pron. 他们的 tāmen de.

theirs pron. 他们的 tāmen de.

theism n. 有神论 yǒushénlùn.

them pron. 他们 tāmen.

thematic adj. 主题的 zhǔtí de.

theme n. 主题 zhǔtí, 题目 tímù.

themselves pron. 他们自己 tāmen zìjǐ.

T

then adv. ①当时 dāngshí (at that time). ②然后 ránhòu (afterward). ③那么 nàme (therefore). ④并且 bìngqiě (also).

theology n. 神学 shénxué.

theoretical adj. 理论的 lǐlùn de.

theoretically adv. 理论上 lǐlùnshang (in principle).

theory n. 学说 xuéshuō, 理论 lǐlùn.

therapist n. 心理医生 xīnlǐ yīshēng.

therapy n. 疗法 liáofǎ, 治疗 zhìliáo (cure).

there adv. 那里 nàlǐ.

thereafter adv. 从此 cóngcǐ, 其后 qíhòu.

thereby adv. 借以 jièyǐ.

therefore adv. 所以 suǒyǐ, 因此 yīncǐ.

thermal adj. 热的 rè de (hot).

thermometer n. 温度计 wēndùjì, 寒暑表 hánshǔbiǎo.

thermos n. 热水瓶 rèshuǐpíng.

these adj. & pron. 这些 zhèxiē.

thesis n. ①论点 lùndiǎn (argument). ②论文 lùnwén (treatise).

they pron. 他们 tāmen.

thick adj. ①厚的 hòu de (not thin). ②密集的 mìjí de (dense). ③浓稠的 nóngchóu de (heavy).

thicken v. 变厚 biàn hòu.

thicket n. 灌木丛 guànmùcóng.

thickness n. 厚度 hòudù.

thief n. 贼 zéi, 小偷 xiǎotōu.

thigh n. 大腿 dàtuǐ.

thimble n. 顶针 dǐngzhēn.

thin adj. ①薄的 báo de / bó de (not thick). ②瘦的 shòu de

(slim). ③稀薄的 xībó de〈air〉. ④淡的 dàn de (weak).

thing n. ①东西 dōngxi (object). ②事情 shìqing (affair).

think v. ①思索 sīsuǒ, 想 xiǎng, 考虑 kǎolǜ (consider). ②认为 rènwéi (be of the opinion that), 觉得 juéde (feel).

thinking adj. 有思考力的 yǒu sīkǎolì de (thoughtful). — n. 思想 sīxiǎng, 思考 sīkǎo (thoughts), 见解 jiànjiě (opinion).

third n. & adj. 第三 dì-sān.

thirst n. 口渴 kǒukě.

thirsty adj. 口渴的 kǒukě de.

thirteen n. & adj. 十三 shísān.

thirteenth n. & adj. 第十三 dì-shísān.

thirtieth n. & adj. 第三十 dì-sānshí.

thirty n. & adj. 三十 sānshí.

this pron. 这 zhè, 这个 zhège.

thistle n. 蓟 jì.

thong n. 皮条 pítiáo, 皮带 pídài.

thorn n. 荆棘 jīngjí.

thorough adj. 完全的 wánquán de, 彻底的 chèdǐ de.

thoroughfare n. 通道 tōngdào.

those adj. & pron. 那些 nàxiē.

thou pron. 你 nǐ.

though conj. 虽然 suīrán, 纵使 zòngshǐ.

thought n. ①看法 kànfǎ, 想法 xiǎngfa (opinion). ②主意 zhǔyì (idea). ③思想 sīxiǎng (philosophy). ④思考 sīkǎo (thinking).

thoughtful adj. 深思的 shēnsī de (thinking deeply).

thoughtless adj. ①不关心他人的 bù guānxīn tārén de, 不体贴的 bù tǐtiē de (inconsiderate). ②欠考虑的 qiàn kǎolǜ de, 轻率的 qīngshuài de (careless).

thousand n. & adj. 千 qiān.

thrash v. ①打谷 dǎgǔ (thresh). ②鞭打 biāndǎ (beat). ③击败 jībài / jíbài (defeat).

thread n. 线 xiàn (sewing).

threat n. 恐吓 kǒnghè, 威胁 wēixié.

three n. & adj. 三 sān.

thresh v. 打谷 dǎgǔ.

threshold n. 门槛 ménkǎn.

thrift n. 节俭 jiéjiǎn.

thrifty adj. 节俭的 jiéjiǎn de.

thrill n. & v. 震颤 zhènchàn / zhènzhàn (tremor).

thrive v. 繁盛 fánshèng, 兴盛 xīngshèng.

throat n. 喉咙 hóulóng.

throb n. & v. 跳动 tiàodòng.

throes n. 阵痛 zhèntòng.

throne n. 王位 wángwèi ⟨political position⟩, 宝座 bǎozuò ⟨seat⟩.

throng n. 群众 qúnzhòng. — v. 蜂拥 fēngyōng / fēngyǒng, 挤满 jǐmǎn.

throttle n. 节流阀 jiéliúfá ⟨valve⟩. — v. 勒死 lēisǐ (strangle).

through prep. ①经过 jīngguò, 通过 tōngguò (pass by). ②遍及 biànjí (throughout). ③借 jiè, 由 yóu (by means of). ④从头到尾 cóngtóu-dàowěi (beginning to end).

throughout prep. 遍及 biànjí.

throw v. 投 tóu, 掷 zhì / zhí.

thrush n. 画眉鸟 huàméiniǎo.

thrust v. 用力推 yònglì tuī (push strongly). ~ *into* 插入 chārù.

thud n. 重击声 zhòngjīshēng / zhòngjíshēng (sound).

thug n. 恶棍 ègùn, 凶徒 xiōngtú.

thumb n. 拇指 mǔzhǐ.

thump v. 重击 zhòngjī / zhòngjí (beat heavily).

thunder n. 雷 léi ⟨lightning⟩, 雷声 léishēng ⟨sound⟩. — v. 打雷 dǎléi.

thunderbolt n. 雷电 léidiàn.

thunderclap n. 雷响 léixiǎng (crash of thunder).

Thursday n. 星期四 Xīngqīsì / Xīngqísì.

thus adv. 如此 rúcǐ, 于是 yúshì.

thwart v. 阻挠 zǔnáo.

thyme n. 百里香 bǎilǐxiāng.

tick n. 滴答声 dīdāshēng ⟨sound⟩. — v. 滴答响 dīdā xiǎng.

ticket n. ①票 piào, 车票 chēpiào ⟨transportation⟩. ②入场券 rùchǎngquàn, 门票 ménpiào ⟨entertainment⟩.

tickle v. ①呵痒 hēyǎng (touch or stroke). ②逗乐 dòulè, 使高兴 shǐ gāoxìng (fun).

ticklish adj. 怕痒的 pàyǎng de.

tide n. 潮 cháo, 潮汐 cháoxī / cháoxì.

tidings n. 消息 xiāoxi.

tidy adj. 整洁的 zhěngjié de. — v. 使整洁 shǐ zhěngjié.

tie v. ①系 jì, 绑 bǎng (fasten). ②与……得同分 yǔ...dé tóngfēn (be equal). — n. 领带 lǐngdài ⟨clothing⟩.

tiger n. 虎 hǔ, 老虎 lǎohǔ.

tight adj. ①紧的 jǐn de (fixed).

②紧密的 jǐnmì de (inflexible).
— adv. 紧紧地 jǐnjǐn de.

tighten v. 变紧 biàn jǐn.

tights n. 紧身衣 jǐnshēnyī.

tile n. 瓦 wǎ, 瓷砖 cízhuān.

till prep. & conj. 直到 zhídào.
— v. 耕种 gēngzhòng.

tilt v. 倾斜 qīngxié (slant).

timber n. 木材 mùcái (wood).

time n. ①时间 shíjiān ⟨hour⟩.
②时代 shídài (era). ③次数
cìshù (occasion). — v. 计时
jìshí.

timely adj. 适时的 shìshí de.

timer n. ①计时器 jìshíqì
⟨device⟩. ②计时员 jìshíyuán
⟨person⟩.

timetable n. 时刻表 shíkèbiǎo.

timid adj. 胆小的 dǎnxiǎo de,
胆怯的 dǎnqiè de / dǎnquè de.

tin n. 锡 xī / xí.

tincture n. 酊 dīng.

tinfoil n. 锡箔 xībó / xíbó.

tingle v. 感到刺痛 gǎndào
cìtòng. — n. 刺痛 cìtòng.

tinkle v. 发叮当声 fā
dīngdāngshēng. — n. 叮当声
dīngdāngshēng.

tint n. 色泽 sèzé ⟨color⟩, 浓淡
nóngdàn ⟨hue⟩. — v. 着色
zhuóshè.

tiny adj. 极小的 jí xiǎo de.

tip n. ①尖 jiān, 尖端 jiānduān
(sharp end). ②顶端 dǐngduān
(top). ③小费 xiǎofèi ⟨money⟩.
④指示 zhǐshì, 暗示 ànshì
(hint). — v. ①倾斜 qīngxié
(incline). ②给小费 gěi xiǎofèi
⟨money⟩. ③给暗示 gěi ànshì
(hint).

tipsy adj. 微醺的 wēixūn de /
wéixūn de.

tiptoe n. 脚尖 jiǎojiān. — v.
踮着脚走 diǎnzhejiǎo zǒu /

diǎnzhejiǎo zǒu.

tire v. 疲倦 píjuàn, 厌倦
yànjuàn. — n. 轮胎 lúntāi.

tired adj. 疲倦的 píjuàn de
⟨energy⟩, 厌倦的 yànjuàn de
⟨interest⟩.

tiresome adj. 令人厌倦的
lìng rén yànjuàn de (tedious),
无聊的 wúliáo de (boring).

tissue n. ①组织 zǔzhī ⟨biology⟩.
②薄纸 báozhǐ / bózhǐ, 面纸
miànzhǐ (tissue-paper).

title n. ①标题 biāotí, 名称
míngchēng (name). ②头衔
tóuxián (position).

titter n. & v. 窃笑 qièxiào.

to prep. ①向 xiàng, 对 duì, 往
wǎng (in the direction of).
②到 dào, 达 dá (towards a
destination).

toad n. 蟾蜍 chánchú ⟨frog⟩.

toast n. 烤土司 kǎo tǔsī. — v.
①烤 kǎo (grill). ②举杯祝贺
jǔbēi zhùhè (drink a toast to).

tobacco n. 烟草 yāncǎo.

today n. & adv. 今天 jīntiān.

toddle v. 蹒跚行走 pánshān
xíngzǒu / mánshān xíngzǒu.

toddler n. 刚学走路的幼儿
gāng xué zǒulù de yòu'ér.

toe n. 脚趾 jiǎozhǐ.

together adv. 一起 yìqǐ, 共同
gòngtóng.

toil n. & v. 辛劳 xīnláo, 辛苦工
作 xīnkǔ gōngzuò.

toilet n. ①浴室 yùshì
(bathroom). ②盥洗室
guànxǐshì, 厕所 cèsuǒ
(lavatory). ③马桶 mǎtǒng
⟨structure⟩.

token n. ①表征 biǎozhēng, 象
征 xiàngzhēng (symbol). ②代
币 dàibì (coin).

tolerance n. 宽容 kuānróng

(acceptance), 容忍度 róngrěndù (endurance).

tolerant *adj.* 宽容的 kuānróng de, 容忍的 róngrěn de.

tolerate *v.* 容忍 róngrěn.

toleration *n.* 容忍 róngrěn.

toll *v.* 鸣钟 míng zhōng (ring). — *n.* 通行费 tōngxíngfèi (charge).

tollway *n.* 收费高速公路 shōufèi gāosù gōnglù.

tomato *n.* 西红柿 xīhóngshì / 番茄 fānqié.

tomb *n.* 坟墓 fénmù.

tomboy *n.* 行为似男孩的女孩 xíngwéi sì nánhái de nǚhái, 男人婆 nánrénpó.

tomcat *n.* 雄猫 xióngmāo.

tomorrow *n. & adv.* 明天 míngtiān.

ton *n.* 吨 dūn / dùn.

tone *n.* ①声音 shēngyīn, 音调 yīndiào (sound). ②气氛 qìfēn (atmosphere). ③色调 sèdiào (color). ④语调 yǔdiào, 语气 yǔqì (manner).

tongs *n.* 钳 qián.

tongue *n.* ①舌 shé, 舌头 shétou (organ). ②语言 yǔyán (language).

tonic *n.* 滋补品 zībǔpǐn, 补药 bǔyào (medicine).

tonight *n. & adv.* 今夜 jīnyè, 今晚 jīnwǎn.

tonnage *n.* 吨位 dūnwèi / dùnwèi.

tonsil *n.* 扁桃腺 biǎntáoxiàn.

too *adv.* ①也 yě (also). ②太 tài, 过于 guòyú (overly).

tool *n.* 工具 gōngjù, 器具 qìjù.

tooth *n.* 牙齿 yáchǐ.

toothache *n.* 牙痛 yátòng.

toothbrush *n.* 牙刷 yáshuā.

toothpaste *n.* 牙膏 yágāo.

toothpick *n.* 牙签 yáqiān.

top *n.* 顶 dǐng, 最高点 zuì gāodiǎn, 上端 shàngduān. — *adj.* ①最高的 zuìgāo de (tallest). ②最好的 zuìhǎo de (best).

topic *n.* 话题 huàtí, 题目 tímù.

topple *v.* ①翻倒 fāndǎo (fall over), 摇摇欲坠 yáoyáo-yù-zhuì (be unsteady and fall). ②推翻 tuīfān (power).

torch *n.* 火炬 huǒjù, 火把 huǒbǎ.

torment *v.* 使痛苦 shǐ tòngkǔ. — *n.* 痛苦 tòngkǔ.

tornado *n.* 龙卷风 lóngjuǎnfēng.

torpedo *n.* 鱼雷 yúléi.

torpid *adj.* 麻痹的 mábì de (paralytic).

torpor *n.* 麻痹 mábì.

torrent *n.* 急流 jíliú.

torrid *adj.* ①炎热的 yánrè de (hot). ②激情的 jīqíng de (passionate).

tortoise *n.* 龟 guī, 乌龟 wūguī.

torture *n. & v.* 拷问 kǎowèn, 折磨 zhémó.

toss *v.* ①掷 zhì / zhí, 抛 pāo (cast). ②摇荡 yáodàng (swing).

total *adj.* ①全部的 quánbù de, 总的 zǒng de (entire). ②完全的 wánquán de (complete). — *n.* 合计 héjì, 总数 zǒngshù.

totalitarian *n.* 极权主义者 jíquán zhǔyì zhě.

totality *n.* 总数 zǒngshù (sum).

totally *adv.* 完全地 wánquán de.

totter *v.* 蹒跚 pánshān / mánshān, 摇摇欲坠 yáoyáo-yùzhuì (stagger).

touch *v.* ①触摸 chùmō, 触及 chùjí (emotion). ②感动

găndòng (move). ③达到 dádào (reach). — n. ①接触 jiēchù (contact). ②触觉 chùjué 〈sense〉.

touching adj. 动人的 dòngrén de, 令人感动的 lìng rén găndòng de.

touch screen n. 触摸式萤幕 chùmōshì yíngmù.

tough adj. ①坚韧的 jiānrèn de 〈firm〉. ②困难的 kùnnán de, 棘手的 jíshŏu de 〈difficult〉. ③粗暴的 cūbào de 〈violent〉.

tour n. & v. 旅行 lǚxíng 〈journey〉.

tourism n. ①观光 guānguāng 〈sightseeing〉. ②观光事业 guānguāng shìyè 〈business〉.

tourist n. 观光客 guānguāngkè, 游客 yóukè.

tournament n. 比赛 bǐsài, 竞赛 jìngsài.

town n. & v. 拖 tuō, 曳 yè / yì.

toward prep. 向 xiàng, 对 duì, 向着 xiàngzhe 〈in the direction of〉.

towel n. 毛巾 máojīn.

tower n. 塔 tă 〈tall narrow structure〉.

town n. 城镇 chéngzhèn, 市镇 shìzhèn.

toxic adj. 有毒的 yŏudú de.

toxin n. 毒素 dúsù.

toy n. 玩具 wánjù.

trace n. ①痕迹 hénjì / hénjī, 踪迹 zōngjì / zōngjī 〈vestige〉. ②微量 wēiliàng 〈little bit〉. — v. ①追踪 zhuīzōng 〈track〉. ②追溯 zhuīsù 〈seek out〉. ③描绘 miáohuì 〈sketch〉.

trachoma n. 砂眼 shāyăn.

track n. ①痕迹 hénjì / hénjī

〈vestige〉. ②路径 lùjìng 〈path〉. ③轨道 guǐdào 〈rail〉. ④径赛运动 jìngsài yùndòng 〈racetrack〉. — v. 追踪 zhuīzōng 〈follow〉.

tract n. ①区域 qūyù 〈area〉. ②小册子 xiăocèzi 〈written work〉.

traction n. 牵引 qiānyǐn, 拖曳 tuōyè / tuōyì.

tractor n. 牵引机 qiānyǐnjī.

trade n. ①贸易 màoyì 〈commerce〉. ②职业 zhíyè 〈profession〉. — v. 交易 jiāoyì, 做生意 zuòshēngyi.

trademark n. 商标 shāngbiāo.

trader n. 商人 shāngrén.

tradition n. 传统 chuántŏng, 惯例 guànlì 〈convention〉.

traffic n. 交通 jiāotōng, 运输 yùnshū 〈vehicles〉. ~ **light** 红绿灯 hónglǜdēng.

tragedy n. 悲剧 bēijù.

tragic adj. 悲剧的 bēijù de.

trail v. ①拖 tuō, 拉 lā 〈drag〉. ②尾随 wěisuí 〈follow〉. — n. ①痕迹 hénjì / hénjī, 踪迹 zōngjì / zōngjī 〈vestige〉. ②道路 dàolù, 小径 xiăojìng 〈path〉.

trailer n. 拖车 tuōchē 〈truck〉.

train n. ①火车 huŏchē 〈railway〉. ②连续 liánxù 〈sequence〉. ③行列 hángliè 〈row〉. — v. ①训练 xùnliàn 〈instruct〉. ②瞄准 miáozhŭn 〈aim〉. ③练习 liànxí 〈exercise〉.

trainer n. 训练者 xùnliànzhě.

training n. 训练 xùnliàn.

trait n. 特性 tèxìng, 特色 tèsè.

traitor n. 叛徒 pàntú, 反叛者 fănpànzhě.

tram n. 电车 diànchē 〈public passenger vehicle〉.

tramp v. ①沉重地行走 chénzhòng de xíngzǒu (walk with heavy steps). ②步行 bùxíng (walk). — n. ①徒步 旅行 túbù lǚxíng (long walk). ②飘泊者 piāobózhě (wanderer).

trample v. 践踏 jiàntà, 蹂躏 róulìn.

trampoline n. 跳床 tiàochuáng.

trance n. ①恍惚 huǎnghū (dreamy state). ②电子舞曲 diànzǐ wǔqǔ ⟨dance music⟩.

tranquil adj. 平静的 píngjìng de, 宁静的 níngjìng de.

tranquilize v. 使宁静 shǐ níngjìng.

transact v. 办理 bànlǐ, 处理 chǔlǐ.

transaction n. ①办理 bànlǐ (conduct). ②交易 jiāoyì (deal).

transcend v. ①超越 chāoyuè (surpass). ②胜过 shèngguò (be better than).

transcribe v. ①誊写 téngxiě, 抄写 chāoxiě (copy). ②录制 lùzhì (record).

transcript n. ①副本 fùběn, 誊本 téngběn. ②成绩单 chéngjìdān / chéngjīdān ⟨student⟩.

transfer v. ①移动 yídòng, 调动 diàodòng (move). ②让渡 ràngdù, 转让 zhuǎnràng (hand over). ③调任 diàorèn ⟨job⟩.

transform v. 使变形 shǐ biànxíng, 使改观 shǐ gǎiguān (change shape).

transformation n. ①变形 biànxíng, 改观 gǎiguān (transfiguration). ②变压 biànyā ⟨electrical⟩.

transformer n. 变压器 biànyāqì.

transfuse v. 输血 shūxuè / shūxiě ⟨blood⟩.

transgress v. ①逾越 yúyuè (go beyond). ②违犯 wéifàn ⟨law⟩.

transistor n. 电晶体 diànjīngtǐ ⟨electricity⟩.

transit n. ①运送 yùnsòng (transport). ②通过 tōngguò (traveling through).

transition n. 转移 zhuǎnyí, 变迁 biànqiān (change).

transitive adj. 及物的 jíwù de ⟨grammar⟩.

translate v. 翻译 fānyì.

translation n. ①翻译 fānyì (translating). ②译文 yìwén, 译本 yìběn (translated version).

translator n. 翻译家 fānyìjiā, 译者 yìzhě.

transmission n. ①传送 chuánsòng, 传达 chuándá (conveyance). ②播送 bōsòng / bòsòng (broadcast). ③传动系 统 chuándòng xìtǒng ⟨engine⟩.

transmit v. ①传送 chuánsòng, 传达 chuándá (move). ②传导 chuándǎo (communicate). ③传染 chuánrǎn (infect).

transparent adj. ①透明的 tòumíng de (clear). ②显然的 xiǎnrán de (obvious).

transplant v. ①移植 yízhí ⟨organs, plant⟩. ②迁移 qiānyí (move).

transport v. 运输 yùnshū, 运送 yùnsòng.

transportation n. 运输 yùnshū.

transpose v. 更换位置

gēnghuàn wèizhì ⟨change places⟩.

transverse *adj.* 横亘的 hénggèn de, 横断的 héngduàn de.

trap *n.* 陷阱 xiànjǐng ⟨device⟩, 圈套 quāntào ⟨plan⟩. — *v.* 诱捕 yòubǔ, 设陷阱 shè xiànjǐng, 计陷 jìxiàn.

trash *n.* 垃圾 lājī / lèsè, 废物 fèiwù.

trauma *n.* ①外伤 wàishāng, 创伤 chuāngshāng ⟨external injury⟩. ②精神创伤 jīngshén chuāngshāng ⟨emotional injury⟩.

travel *n. & v.* 旅行 lǚxíng, 旅游 lǚyóu.

traveler *n.* 旅行者 lǚxíngzhě ⟨tourist⟩.

traverse *v.* ①横过 héngguò, 横亘 hénggèn ⟨extend across⟩. ②穿过 chuānguò ⟨travel across⟩.

trawl *n.* 拖网 tuōwǎng ⟨large net⟩. — *v.* 以拖网捕鱼 yǐ tuōwǎng bǔyú.

tray *n.* 盘 pán, 碟 dié.

treacherous *adj.* 不忠的 bùzhōng de ⟨disloyal⟩, 叛逆的 pànnì de ⟨traitorous⟩.

treacle *n.* 糖蜜 tángmì.

tread *v.* ①行走 xíngzǒu ⟨walk⟩, 踩踏 cǎità ⟨step⟩. ②践踏 jiàntà ⟨trample⟩.

treadle *n.* 踏板 tàbǎn.

treason *n.* 叛逆 pànnì ⟨ruler⟩, 叛国 pànguó ⟨country⟩.

treasure *n.* 财宝 cáibǎo, 贵重品 guìzhòngpǐn. — *v.* 珍爱 zhēn'ài ⟨cherish⟩, 珍惜 zhēnxī / zhēnxí ⟨value⟩, 重视 zhòngshì ⟨see as important⟩.

treasurer *n.* 会计 kuàijì.

treasury *n.* ①金库 jīnkù, 宝库

宝库 bǎokù ⟨location⟩. ②基金 jījīn ⟨fund⟩. ③(T~) 财政部 cáizhèngbù ⟨government⟩.

treat *v.* ①对待 duìdài ⟨behave toward⟩. ②视为 shìwéi ⟨consider⟩. ③治疗 zhìliáo ⟨cure⟩. ④款待 kuǎndài, 请客 qǐngkè ⟨pay for⟩. ⑤处理 chǔlǐ ⟨deal with⟩.

treatise *n.* 论文 lùnwén.

treatment *n.* ①看待 kàndài, 对待 duìdài ⟨dealing with⟩. ②治疗 zhìliáo ⟨cure⟩. ③疗法 liáofǎ ⟨way⟩.

treaty *n.* 条约 tiáoyuē ⟨written agreement⟩.

treble *adj.* 三倍的 sān bèi de ⟨three times⟩. *n.* 最高音部 zuì gāoyīn bù ⟨music⟩.

tree *n.* 树 shù, 树木 shùmù.

tremble *n. & v.* 战栗 zhànlì, 发抖 fādǒu ⟨quiver⟩.

tremendous *adj.* ①惊人的 jīngrén de ⟨surprising⟩. ②巨大的 jùdà de ⟨big⟩. ③很棒的 hěn bàng de ⟨excellent⟩.

tremor *n.* 颤抖 chàndǒu / zhàndǒu ⟨slight shaking⟩.

trench *n.* 战壕 zhànháo, 沟 gōu.

trend *n. & v.* 趋势 qūshì, 倾向 qīngxiàng.

trepidation *n.* 惊恐 jīngkǒng ⟨great fear⟩.

trespass *v.* 侵入 qīnrù ⟨intrude⟩, 侵犯 qīnfàn ⟨violate⟩.

trestle *n.* 支架 zhījià ⟨table-top⟩.

trial *n.* ①审判 shěnpàn ⟨court⟩. ②试验 shìyàn, 考验 kǎoyàn ⟨test⟩. ③试用 shìyòng ⟨job⟩.

triangle *n.* 三角形 sānjiǎoxíng ⟨geometry⟩.

triangular adj. 三角形的 sānjiǎoxíng de.

tribe n. 种族 zhǒngzú ⟨race⟩, 部落 bùluò ⟨clan⟩.

tribunal n. 法庭 fǎtíng ⟨court⟩.

tributary n. & adj. 支流 zhīliú ⟨river⟩.

tribute n. ①贡品 gòngpǐn ⟨contribution⟩. ②赞辞 zàncí ⟨commendation⟩.

trick n. ①诡计 guǐjì, 欺诈 qīzhà ⟨trickery⟩. ②把戏 bǎxì, 戏法 xìfǎ ⟨conjuring magic⟩. ③恶作剧 èzuòjù ⟨joke⟩. — v. 欺骗 qīpiàn ⟨deceive⟩.

trickery n. 欺骗 qīpiàn.

trickle v. 滴流 dīliú, 慢慢地流 mànmàn de liú. — n. 细流 xìliú ⟨flow⟩.

tricycle n. 三轮车 sānlúnchē.

trifle n. ①琐事 suǒshì ⟨thing⟩. ②少量 shǎoliàng ⟨amount⟩.

trigger n. 扳机 bānjī ⟨gun⟩.

trill v. 以颤音唱 yǐ chànyīn chàng / yǐ zhànyīn chàng ⟨sing⟩. — n. 颤音 chànyīn / zhànyīn ⟨musical effect⟩.

trillion n. 兆 zhào ⟨a million million⟩.

trilogy n. 三部曲 sānbùqǔ.

trim v. 修整 xiūzhěng ⟨cut⟩. — adj. 整齐的 zhěngqí de ⟨neat and tidy⟩.

trinity n. 三合一 sān hé yī. the T~ 三位一体 Sān wèi yìtǐ.

trinket n. 小饰物 xiǎo shìwù ⟨small ornament⟩.

trip n. 旅行 lǚxíng, 远足 yuǎnzú ⟨journey⟩. — v. 跌倒 diēdǎo / diédǎo ⟨fall⟩.

triple n. & adj. 三倍 sān bèi ⟨three times⟩.

triplicate n. 一式三份 yí shì sān fèn ⟨document⟩.

tripod n. 三脚架 sānjiǎojià.

triumph n. 胜利 shènglì. — v. 获胜 huòshèng.

triumphant adj. 胜利的 shènglì de ⟨victorious⟩, 成功的 chénggōng de ⟨successful⟩.

trivial adj. ①不重要的 bú zhòngyào de ⟨unimportant⟩. ②琐碎的 suǒsuì de ⟨trifling⟩.

trolley n. ①电车 diànchē ⟨tram⟩. ②手推车 shǒutuīchē ⟨handcart⟩.

trombone n. 伸缩喇叭 shēnsuō lǎba.

troop n. ①群 qún ⟨group⟩. ②军队 jūnduì ⟨military⟩.

trophy n. 战利品 zhànlìpǐn ⟨hunting, war⟩.

tropic n. ①回归线 huíguīxiàn ⟨line⟩. ②热带 rèdài ⟨area⟩.

tropical adj. 热带的 rèdài de.

trot v. 快步走 kuàibùzǒu, 小跑 xiǎopǎo. — n. 疾走 jízǒu.

trouble n. 麻烦 máfan, 使烦恼 shǐ fánnǎo. — n. ①麻烦 máfan ⟨bother⟩. ②烦恼 fánnǎo ⟨worry⟩.

troublesome adj. 麻烦的 máfan de, 使人苦恼的 shǐ rén kǔnǎo de.

trough n. ①饲料槽 sìliàocáo ⟨food⟩. ②水槽 shuǐcáo ⟨liquid⟩.

troupe n. 班 bān, 团 tuán.

trousers n. 裤子 kùzi.

trout n. 鳟鱼 zūnyú.

trowel n. ①镘子 mànzi ⟨flat-bladed⟩. ②小铲子 xiǎo chǎnzi ⟨scoop⟩.

truant n. 逃学者 táoxuézhě ⟨school⟩.

truce n. 休战 xiūzhàn ⟨war⟩.

truck n. 卡车 kǎchē, 货车 huòchē ⟨carrying goods⟩.

T

truculent adj. 凶猛的 xiōngměng de, 好斗的 hàodòu de.

true adj. ①真实的 zhēnshí de (real). ②真正的 zhēnzhèng de (actual). ③忠实的 zhōngshí de (faithful).

truly adv. ①真实地 zhēnshí de (really). ②诚心地 chéngxīn de (sincerely). ③事实上 shìshíshang (actually).

trump n. 王牌 wángpái ⟨card games⟩. v. 出王牌获胜 chū wángpái huòshèng ⟨beat⟩.

trumpet n. 喇叭 lǎba ⟨instrument⟩.

trunk n. ①树干 shùgàn ⟨tree⟩. ②身躯 shēnqū ⟨body⟩. ③象鼻 xiàngbí ⟨nose⟩. ④大衣箱 dà yīxiāng ⟨large case⟩.

trust n. ①信赖 xìnlài (reliance). ②信托 xìntuō ⟨legal relation⟩. ③责任 zérèn ⟨responsibility⟩. ④托拉斯 tuōlāsī ⟨firm⟩. v. ①信赖 xìnlài, 信任 xìnrèn (rely on). ②委托 wěituō (entrust).

trustee n. 受托人 shòutuōrén.

trustworthy adj. 可信赖的 kě xìnlài de, 可靠的 kěkào de.

truth n. ①真实 zhēnshí ⟨facts⟩. ②真实性 zhēnshíxìng (accuracy). ③真理 zhēnlǐ (reality).

try v. ①尝试 chángshì (attempt). ②试验 shìyàn (examine). ③审问 shěnwèn ⟨law⟩.

tub n. 桶 tǒng, 盆 pén.

tubby adj. 圆胖的 yuánpàng de (short and fat).

tube n. ①管 guǎn, 筒 tǒng (pipe). ②(T~)地下铁道 dìxià tiědào ⟨subway⟩. ③真空管 zhēnkōngguǎn (valve).

tuberculosis n. 结核病 jiéhébìng, 肺结核 fèijiéhé.

tuck v. 摺起 zhéqǐ, 卷起 juǎnqǐ (fold). n. 褶 zhě / zhé, 裥 jiǎn ⟨skirt⟩.

Tuesday n. 星期二 Xīngqī'èr / Xīngqī'èr.

tuft n. 一束 yíshù, 一簇 yícù (bunch).

tug v. 用力拉 yònglì lā, 拖曳 tuōyè / tuōyì (pull).

tuition n. 学费 xuéfèi ⟨fee⟩.

tulip n. 郁金香 yùjīnxiāng.

tumble v. ①跌倒 diēdǎo / diédǎo, 跌落 diēluò / diéluò (fall). ②使跌倒 shǐ diēdǎo / shǐ diédǎo, 使跌落 shǐ diēluò / shǐ diéluò (cause to fall).

tumbler n. ①平底玻璃杯 píngdǐ bōlibēi (glass). ②杂技演员 zájì yǎnyuán (acrobat).

tumor n. 肿瘤 zhǒngliú.

tumult n. 喧嚣 xuānxiāo, 骚动 sāodòng.

tuna n. 鲔鱼 wěiyú.

tune n. 曲调 qǔdiào (melody). — v. 调音 tiáoyīn ⟨adjust⟩.

tunnel n. 隧道 suìdào, 地道 dìdào (underground passage).

turbine n. 涡轮机 wōlúnjī.

turbot n. 比目鱼 bǐmùyú, 鲽鱼 diéyú.

turbulence n. 乱流 luànliú ⟨air⟩.

turbulent adj. ①狂暴的 kuángbào de (violent). ②混乱 的 hùnluàn de (disorderly). ③骚动的 sāodòng de (riotous).

turf n. ①草地 cǎodì, 草皮 cǎopí ⟨grass⟩. ②地盘 dìpán.

turkey n. 火鸡 huǒjī.

turmoil n. 混乱 hùnluàn, 骚动 sāodòng.

turn v. ①旋转 xuánzhuǎn (rotate). ②转向 zhuǎnxiàng (change direction). ③转动 zhuǎndòng (twist). ④变成 biànchéng (become). ~ *off* 关闭 guānbì. ~ *on* 打开 dǎkāi.

turning n. 转弯处 zhuǎnwānchù. ~ *point* 转折点 zhuǎnzhédiǎn / 转捩点 zhuǎnlièdiǎn.

turnip n. 萝卜 luóbo.

turnover n. 营业额 yíngyè'é ⟨business⟩.

turnstile n. 十字旋转门 shízì xuánzhuǎnmén.

turpentine n. 松节油 sōngjiéyóu.

turquoise n. ①绿宝石 lǜbǎoshí ⟨stone⟩. ②青绿色 qīnglǜsè ⟨color⟩.

turret n. ①炮塔 pàotǎ ⟨gun⟩. ②小塔 xiǎotǎ, 角楼 jiǎolóu (small tower).

turtle n. 龟 guī, 海龟 hǎiguī.

tusk n. 长牙 chángyá.

tut n. & interj. 嘘! xū, 啧! zé.

tutor n. ①家庭教师 jiātíng jiàoshī ⟨home⟩. ②个人导师 gèrén dǎoshī ⟨school⟩.

twang n. ①弦声 xiánshēng ⟨instrument⟩. ②鼻音 bíyīn (speaking).

tweak n. & v. 拧 níng / nǐng, 扭 niǔ.

tweed n. 呢料 níliào.

tweezers n. 镊子 nièzi.

twelfth n. & adj. 第十二 dì-shí'èr.

twelve n. & adj. 十二 shí'èr.

twentieth n. & adj. 第二十 dì-èrshí.

twenty n. & adj. 二十 èrshí.

twice adv. 两次 liǎngcì ⟨number⟩, 两倍 liǎngbèi ⟨amount⟩.

twig n. 小枝 xiǎozhī, 嫩枝 nènzhī.

twilight n. ①曙光 shǔguāng / 晨曦 shǔguāng ⟨before sunrise⟩. ②薄暮 bómù ⟨before sunset⟩.

twill n. 斜纹布 xiéwénbù (cotton).

twin n. 孪生子之一 luánshēngzǐ zhī yī — adj. 孪生的 luánshēng de ⟨pair of children⟩.

twins n. 双胞胎 shuāngbāotāi.

twine n. 细绳 xìshéng ⟨string⟩.

twinkle n. & v. 闪烁 shǎnshuò ⟨flash⟩.

twirl n. & v. ①旋转 xuánzhuǎn (spin). ②扭转 niǔzhuǎn (twist).

twist v. ①搓 cuō, 捻 niǎn, 编 biān (coil). ②缠绕 chánrào (entangle). ③扭 niǔ, 拧 níng / nǐng (wrench). ④曲解 qūjiě (alter). n. ①扭 niǔ, 拧 níng / nǐng (wrench). ②曲折 qūzhé (bend).

twitch v. 抽动 chōudòng, 痉挛 jìngluán (jerk).

twitter n. & v. 鸟鸣 niǎomíng, 吱吱地叫 zhīzhī de jiào (chirp).

two n. & adj. 二 èr.

tycoon n. 巨子 jùzǐ, 大亨 dàhēng.

tympanitis n. 中耳炎 zhōng'ěryán.

type n. ①型 xíng, 类型 lèixíng, 种类 zhǒnglèi (kind). ②典型 diǎnxíng (example). ③字体 zìtǐ (font). v. 打字 dǎzì.

typewriter n. 打字机 dǎzìjī.

typhoid n. & adj. 伤寒 shānghán.

typhoon n. 台风 táifēng.

typhus *n.* 斑疹伤寒 bānzhěn shānghán.

typical *adj.* 典型的 diǎnxíng de.

typically *adv.* 典型地 diǎnxíng de.

typist *n.* 打字员 dǎzìyuán.

tyrannical *adj.* 暴虐的 bàonüè de.

tyranny *n.* 暴政 bàozhèng 〈government〉.

tyrant *n.* 暴君 bàojūn.

U

udder *n.* 乳房 rǔfáng.

UFO *n.* 不明飞行物体 bùmíng fēixíng wùtǐ, 幽浮 yōufú, 飞碟 fēidié.

ugly *adj.* 难看的 nánkàn de, 丑陋的 chǒulòu de.

ulcer *n.* 溃疡 kuìyáng.

ultimate *adj.* ①最后的 zuìhòu de, 终极的 zhōngjí de (final). ②根本的 gēnběn de (basic).

ultimatum *n.* 最后通牒 zuìhòu tōngdié.

ultrafiche *n.* 超微缩胶片 chāowēisuō jiāopiàn / chāowēisuō jiāopiàn.

ultraviolet *adj.* 紫外线的 zǐwàixiàn de.

umbrella *n.* 伞 sǎn, 雨伞 yǔsǎn.

umpire *n.* 裁判 cáipàn, 仲裁者 zhòngcáizhě.

unable *adj.* 不能的 bùnéng de.

unaccountable *adj.* 无法解释的 wúfǎ jiěshì de (inexplicable).

unaffected *adj.* ①未受影响的 wèi shòu yǐngxiǎng de (not influenced). ②无矫饰的 wú jiǎoshì de (natural).

unanimous *adj.* 全体一致的 quántǐ yízhì de.

unarmed *adj.* 无武装的 wú wǔzhuāng de.

unassuming *adj.* 谦虚的 qiānxū de.

unattended *adj.* ①无伴的 wúbàn de (unaccompanied). ②无人照料的 wú rén zhàoliào de (not taken care of).

unavoidable *adj.* 不得已的 bùdéyǐ de, 无可避免的 wú kě bìmiǎn de.

unaware *adj.* 未察觉的 wèi chájué de, 不知不觉的 bùzhī-bùjué de.

unbearable *adj.* 无法忍受的 wúfǎ rěnshòu de.

unbelief *n.* 不信 búxìn.

unbelievable *adj.* ①难以置信的 nányízhìxìn de (hard to believe). ②不可思议的 bùkě-sīyì de (outrageous).

unbroken *adj.* 未破损的 wèi pòsǔn de.

uncalled-for *adj.* ①不必要的 bú bìyào de (unnecessary). ②不当的 búdàng de (improper).

uncanny *adj.* ①神秘的

shénmì de (mysterious). ②怪
异的 guàiyì de (unnatural).

uncertain *adj.* ①不确定的
bú quèdìng de (not ascertained).
②不清楚的 bù qīngchu de
(unclear).

unchangeable *adj.* 不变的
bùbiàn de.

uncharitable *adj.* 不慈悲的
bù cíbēi de.

uncle *n.* ①叔叔 shūshu /
shúshu, 叔父 shūfù / shúfù
(father's younger brother). ②伯父
bófù, 伯伯 bóbo (father's older
brother). ③舅父 jiùfù, 舅舅
jiùjiu (mother's brother).

uncomfortable *adj.* 不舒服
的 bù shūfu de.

uncommon *adj.* 稀有的
xīyǒu de, 不寻常的 bù
xúncháng de.

uncompromising *adj.* 不妥
协的 bù tuǒxié de.

unconcerned *adj.* 不关心的
bù guānxīn de.

unconscious *adj.* 不知不觉
的 bùzhī-bùjué de, 无意识的
wú yìshí de / wú yìshì de.

uncouth *adj.* ①粗鲁的 cūlǔ
de (rude). ②笨拙的 bènzhuō
de / bènzhuó de (awkward).

uncover *v.* 打开覆盖 dǎkāi
fùgài.

undecided *adj.* 未决定的 wèi
juédìng de.

undeniable *adj.* 无可否认的
wú kě fǒurèn de.

under *prep.* ①在……之下
zài...zhī xià (below). ②少于
shǎo yú (less than). — *adv.*
在下面 zài xiàmian.

underbid *v.* 喊价低于 hǎnjià
dī yú.

underclothes *n.* 内衣裤

nèiyīkù.

undercurrent *n.* 潜流
qiánliú, 暗流 ànliú.

underdog *n.* 居劣势者 jū
lièshì zhě.

underestimate *v.* 低估 dīgū.

undergo *v.* 遭受 zāoshòu.

undergraduate *n.* 大学生
dàxuéshēng.

underground *adj. & adv.* 在
地下的 zài dìxià de (below
the surface). — *n.* 地下铁
dìxiàtiě (subway).

undergrowth *n.* 矮树丛
ǎishùcóng.

underline *v.* ①在下面画线
zài xiàmian huà xiàn (draw a
line under...). ②强调
qiángdiào (emphasize).

undermine *v.* 逐渐损坏
zhújiàn sǔnhuài (weaken).

underneath *prep.* 在……的
下面 zài...de xiàmian.
— *adv.* 在下面 zài xiàmian.

underpass *n.* 地下道
dìxiàdào ⟨underground⟩, 下层
道 xiàcéng dào ⟨lower level⟩.

undersell *v.* 低价出售 dījià
chūshòu.

understand *v.* 懂 dǒng, 了解
liǎojiě.

understanding *n.* ①理解力
lǐjiě lì ⟨ability⟩. ②谅解 liàngjiě
(sympathy). ③协议 xiéyì
(agreement).

understudy *n.* 候补演员
hòubǔ yǎnyuán.

undertake *v.* ①承担
chéngdān, 担负 dānfù (accept
responsibility for). ②从事
cóngshì (participate in), 着手
zhuóshǒu (start).

undertaker *n.* 殡葬业者
bìnzàngyè zhě.

undertaking *n.* 事业 shìyè (enterprise).

undervalue *v.* 低估 dīgū.

underwear *n.* 内裤 nèikù.

underworld *n.* ①地狱 dìyù (hell). ②地下社会 dìxià shèhuì (organized crime).

undeveloped *adj.* 未开发的 wèi kāifā de (land).

~ *countries* 不发达国家 bù fādá guójiā / 未开发国家 wèi kāifā guójiā.

undo *v.* ①解开 jiěkāi (unfasten). ②破坏 pòhuài (destroy). ③恢复原状 huīfù yuánzhuàng (reverse).

undoubted *adj.* 无疑的 wúyí de.

undress *v.* 脱去衣服 tuōqù yīfu.

undue *adj.* 不当的 búdàng de (inappropriate), 过分的 guòfèn de (excessive).

uneasy *adj.* ①不舒适的 bù shūshì de (uncomfortable). ②不自在的 bú zìzài de (awkward). ③不安的 bù'ān de (anxious).

unemployed *adj.* 失业的 shīyè de.

unemployment *n.* 失业 shīyè. ~ *rate* 失业率 shīyèlǜ.

unequal *adj.* 不相等的 bù xiāngděng de, 不平等的 bù píngděng de.

uneven *adj.* ①不平坦的 bù píngtǎn de (not smooth). ②参差不齐的 cēncī-bùqí de (unbalanced).

unexpected *adj.* 意外的 yìwài de.

unfair *adj.* 不公平的 bù gōngpíng de.

unfaithful *adj.* 不忠实的 bù zhōngshí de.

unfamiliar *adj.* 不熟悉的 bù shúxī de / bù shóuxī de.

~ *with...* 跟……不熟悉 gēn... bù shúxī / gēn...bù shóuxī.

unfasten *v.* 解开 jiěkāi.

unfavorable *adj.* 不利的 búlì de.

unfinished *adj.* 未完成的 wèi wánchéng de.

unfit *adj.* 不合适的 bù héshì de.

unfold *v.* ①打开 dǎkāi (open), 展开 zhǎnkāi (unfurl). ②表明 biǎomíng (reveal).

unforeseen *adj.* 预料不到的 yùliào bú dào de, 出乎意料的 chūhūyìliào de.

unforgettable *adj.* 难忘的 nánwàng de.

unfortunate *adj.* 不幸的 búxìng de.

unfriendly *adj.* 不友善的 bù yǒushàn de.

unfurl *v.* 展开 zhǎnkāi.

unfurnished *adj.* 不附家具 的 bú fù jiājù de.

ungrateful *adj.* 忘恩负义的 wàng'ēn-fùyì de.

unhappy *adj.* 不快乐的 bú kuàilè de.

unhealthy *adj.* 不健康的 bú jiànkāng de.

unicorn *n.* 独角兽 dújiǎoshòu.

uniform *adj.* 相同的 xiāngtóng de (the same), 不变 的 búbiàn de (unchanging). — *n.* 制服 zhìfú.

uniformity *n.* 一致性 yízhìxìng, 均一性 jūnyīxìng.

unify *v.* 统一 tǒngyī (combine), 使一致 shǐ yízhì (make uniform)

unilateral *adj.* 单方的 dānfāng de, 片面的 piànmiàn de.

unimportant *adj.* 不重要的 bú zhòngyào de.

union *n.* ①工会 gōnghuì (labor association). ②联合 liánhé, 结合 jiéhé (joining). ③婚姻 hūnyīn (marriage). ④同盟 tóngméng (alliance).

unique *adj.* 独特的 dútè de, 独一无二的 dúyī-wú'èr de.

unit *n.* ①单位 dānwèi 〈measurement〉. ②部队 bùduì (troop).

unite *v.* ①结合 jiéhé, 合并 hébìng, 联合 liánhé (combine). ②团结 tuánjié (cooperate).

united *adj.* ①联合的 liánhé de (joint). ②团结的 tuánjié de (cooperating).

unity *n.* ①单一 dānyī, 统一 tǒngyī (being united). ②和谐 héxié (agreement).

universal *adj.* ①全世界的 quánshìjiè de (world-wide). ②普遍的 pǔbiàn de (common). ③宇宙的 yǔzhòu de (cosmic).

universe *n.* 宇宙 yǔzhòu.

university *n.* 大学 dàxué.

unjust *adj.* 不公正的 bù gōngzhèng de.

unkind *adj.* 不厚道的 bú hòudào de.

unknown *adj.* 未知的 wèizhī de.

unlace *v.* 解开 jiěkai.

unlawful *adj.* 不合法的 bù héfǎ de, 违法的 wéifǎ de.

unless *conj.* 除非 chúfēi.

unlike *adj.* 不相似的 bù xiāngsì de.

unlikely *adj.* ①不像是真的 bú xiàng shì zhēn de (questionable). ②未必是的 wèibì shì de (not probable).

unlimited *adj.* 无限的 wúxiàn de.

unload *v.* 卸载 xièzài.

unlock *v.* 开锁 kāisuǒ.

unlucky *adj.* 不幸的 búxìng de.

unmarried *adj.* 未婚的 wèihūn de, 单身的 dānshēn de.

unmentionable *adj.* 不可提及的 bùkě tíjí de.

unmoved *adj.* 冷静的 lěngjìng de.

unnatural *adj.* ①不自然的 bú zìrán de (not natural). ②离谱的 lípǔ de, 夸张的 kuāzhāng de (stilted). ③邪恶的 xié'è de (evil).

unnecessary *adj.* 不必要的 bú bìyào de.

unnerve *v.* 使胆怯 shǐ dǎnqiè / shǐ dǎnquè.

unoccupied *adj.* ①空的 kōng de (vacant). ②空闲的 kòngxián de (free).

unofficial *adj.* 非正式的 fēi zhèngshì de (not formal), 非官方的 fēi guānfāng de (not authoritative).

unpack *v.* 拆箱 chāixiāng, 拆开 chāikai.

unparalleled *adj.* 无比的 wúbǐ de, 无以匹敌的 wúyǐ-pǐdí de.

unpleasant *adj.* ①使人不快的 shǐ rén búkuài de 〈situation〉. ②不友善的 bù yǒushàn de (unfriendly). ③令人讨厌的 lìng rén tǎoyàn de (annoying).

unpopular *adj.* ①不受欢迎

U

bú shòu huānyíng de (disliked). ②不流行的 bù liúxíng de (unfashionable).

unprecedented adj. 空前的 kōngqián de.

unpredictable adj. 不可预测的 bùkě yùcè de.

unprepared adj. 没有准备的 méiyǒu zhǔnbèi de.

unproductive adj. 无生产力的 wú shēngchǎnlì de.

unprofitable adj. 无利益的 wú lìyì de.

unqualified adj. 不合格的 bù hégé de.

unquestionable adj. 无疑的 wúyí de. 确定的 quèdìng de.

unravel v. 解开 jiěkai.

unreal adj. ①不真实的 bù zhēnshí de (not real). ②不可思议的 bùkě-sīyì de (surprising).

unreasonable adj. 不合理的 bù hélǐ de.

unrelenting adj. 无情的 wúqíng de, 严峻的 yánjùn de.

unreliable adj. 不可靠的 bù kěkào de, 不可信赖的 bùkě xìnlài de.

unreserved adj. ①未预订的 wèi yùdìng de (seat). ②坦率的 tǎnshuài de (open).

unrest n. 不安 bù'ān, 不宁 bùníng.

unripe adj. 未成熟的 wèi chéngshú de / wèi chéngshóu de.

unruly adj. ①难控制的 nán kòngzhì de (hard to control). ②顽皮的 wánpí de (naughty).

unsatisfactory adj. ①不能令人满意的 bùnéng lìng rén mǎnyì de (not satisfying). ②不合格的 bù hégé de (not

good enough).

unscathed adj. 未受伤害的 wèi shòu shānghài de.

unscrupulous adj. 不道德的 bú dàodé de, 无良知的 wú liángzhī de.

unseasonable adj. 不合季节的 bùhé jìjié de.

unseat v. 罢免 bàmiǎn, 去职 qùzhí.

unseen adj. 看不见的 kànbujiàn de.

unselfish adj. 不自私的 bú zìsī de.

unsettle v. 使不安 shǐ bù'ān (make anxious), 使动摇 shǐ dòngyáo (make unstable).

unsightly adj. 难看的 nánkàn de.

unsociable adj. 不善交际的 búshàn jiāojì de.

unsound adj. 不健康的 bú jiànkāng de (unhealthy).

unspeakable adj. 无法形容的 wúfǎ xíngróng de, 无法言喻的 wúfǎ-yányù de, 说不出的 shuōbuchū de.

unstable adj. 不稳定的 bù wěndìng de.

unsteady adj. 不坚定的 bù jiāndìng de.

unsuccessful adj. 未成功的 wèi chénggōng de.

unsuitable adj. 不合适的 bù héshì de.

unthinkable adj. 无法想象的 wúfǎ xiǎngxiàng de.

untidy adj. 邋遢的 lāta de, 凌乱的 língluàn de.

untie v. 解开 jiěkai.

until prep. & conj. 直到 zhídào.

untimely adj. & adv. 不合时宜的 bùhé-shíyí de.

untold adj. ①未说出的 wèi shuōchū de (kept secret). ②数不清的 shǔbuqīng de (countless).

untrue adj. 不真实的 bù zhēnshí de.

unusual adj. 异常的 yìcháng de.

unveil v. ①揭幕 jiēmù (inaugurate). ②揭露 jiēlù (reveal).

unwilling adj. 不愿意的 bú yuànyì de.

unwise adj. 不明智的 bù míngzhì de.

unworthy adj. 不值得的 bù zhíde de.

unwrap v. 解开 jiěkai, 打开 dǎkāi.

up adv. 往上 wǎngshàng, 向上 xiàngshàng. — prep. 朝上 cháoshàng (facing upward), 在……上面 zài...shàngmian (above). — adj. 上扬的 shàngyáng de.

update v. 成为最新的 chéngwéi zuìxīn de, 使更新的 shǐ gēngxīn de. — n. 最新消息 zuìxīn xiāoxi.

upgrade v. 使……升级 shǐ... shēngjí.

uphill adj. ①上坡的 shàngpō de (ascending). ②困难的 kùnnán de (difficult). — adv. 上坡地 shàngpō de, 向上地 xiàngshàng de.

uphold v. 支持 zhīchí (support), 赞成 zànchéng (approve of).

upholstery n. ①室内装潢业 shìnèi zhuānghuángyè ⟨business⟩. ②室内装潢品 shìnèi zhuānghuángpǐn ⟨materials⟩.

uplift v. 使振奋 shǐ zhènfèn (encourage).

upon prep. 在上 zài shàng.

upper adj. ①在上面的 zài shàngmian de (higher). ②上级的 shàngjí de (superior).

upright adj. ①直立的 zhílì de (vertical). ②诚实的 chéngshí de (honest), 有道德的 yǒu dàodé de (moral).

uproar n. 喧嚣 xuānxiāo, 骚动 sāodòng.

uproot v. 连根拔起 lián gēn báqǐ ⟨plant⟩.

upset v. ①打翻 dǎfān (overturn). ②使混乱 shǐ hùnluàn (disrupt). ③使烦乱 shǐ fánluàn (annoy). ④使悲伤 shǐ bēishāng (sadden).

upshot n. 结局 jiéjú, 结果 jiéguǒ.

upside-down adv. ①倒置地 dàozhì de (on its head). ②混乱地 hùnluàn de (disorderly).

upstairs adv. 在楼上 zài lóushang. — n. 楼上 lóushang.

upstart n. 暴发户 bàofāhù.

up-to-date adj. 最新的 zuìxīn de.

upward adj. & adv. 向上的 xiàngshàng de.

upwards adv. 向上地 xiàngshàng de.

uranium n. 铀 yóu / yòu.

Uranus n. 天王星 Tiānwángxīng.

urban adj. 都市的 dūshì de.

urbane adj. 有礼貌的 yǒu lǐmào de (polite).

urge v. ①驱策 qūcè (compel). ②催促 cuīcù (hurry), 力劝 lìquàn (persuade). ~ **on** 驱策 qūcè (encourage). — n. 欲望

yùwàng (desire).

urgent adj. 紧急的 jǐnjí de, 急迫的 jípò de.

urinate v. 小便 xiǎobiàn, 尿尿 niàoniào.

urine n. 尿 niào, 小便 xiǎobiàn.

urn n. ①骨灰坛 gǔhuītán 〈cremation〉. ②瓮 wèng 〈vase〉.

usage n. ①使用 shǐyòng, 用法 yòngfǎ 〈use〉. ②习惯 xíguàn, 惯例 guànlì 〈custom〉.

use v. 使用 shǐyòng, 利用 lìyòng 〈utilize〉.

used adj. ①惯于 guànyú 〈accustomed〉. ②用过的 yòngguo de, 二手的 èrshǒu de 〈second-hand〉.

useful adj. 有用的 yǒuyòng de.

useless adj. 无用的 wúyòng de.

usher n. 招待员 zhāodàiyuán.

usual adj. 通常的 tōngcháng de.

usually adv. 通常 tōngcháng.

usurer n. 放高利贷者 fàng gāolìdài zhě.

utensil n. 器皿 qìmǐn, 用具 yòngjù.

uterus n. 子宫 zǐgōng.

utility n. 效用 xiàoyòng 〈usefulness〉.

utilize v. 利用 lìyòng.

utmost adj. 最大的 zuìdà de 〈biggest〉, 极度的 jídù de 〈extreme〉. *do one's ~* 尽力而为 jìnlì'érwéi.

Utopia n. 乌托邦 wūtuōbāng, 理想国 lǐxiǎngguó.

utter adj. 完全的 wánquán de 〈complete〉. — v. 说出 shuōchū 〈make a sound〉.

utterly adv. 完全地 wánquán de.

UV 紫外线 zǐwàixiàn 〈ultraviolet〉.

V **V** úí

vacancy n. ①空缺 kòngquē 〈job〉. ②空房间 kōng fángjiān 〈room〉.

vacant adj. ①空的 kōng de 〈empty〉. ②空虚的 kōngxū de, 茫然的 mángrán de 〈absent-minded〉.

vacate v. ①空出 kòngchu 〈leave empty〉. ②搬出 bānchu 〈dwelling〉. ③让出 ràngchu 〈seat〉.

vacation n. 假期 jiàqī / jiàqí,

休假 xiūjià 〈holiday〉.

vaccinate v. 种痘 zhòngdòu, 接种疫苗 jiēzhòng yìmiáo.

vaccine n. 痘苗 dòumiáo, 疫苗 yìmiáo.

vacillate v. 犹疑不决 yóuyí-bùjué 〈waver〉.

vacuum n. 真空 zhēnkōng. *~ cleaner* 除尘器 chúchénqì / 吸尘器 xīchénqì. *~ tube* 真空管 zhēnkōngguǎn.

vacuum-packed adj. 真空

vagabond n. 流浪者 liúlàngzhě, 漂泊者 piāobózhě (tramp). — adj. 流浪的 liúlàng de, 漂泊的 piāobó de.

vagary n. 异想天开 yìxiǎng-tiānkāi ⟨thought⟩, 变幻莫测 biànhuàn-mòcè ⟨change⟩.

vagrant n. 流浪者 liúlàngzhě. — adj. 流浪的 liúlàng de, 游荡的 yóudàng de.

vague adj. ①模糊的 móhu de, 含混的 hánhùn de (dim). ②不明确的 bù míngquè de (uncertain).

vain adj. ①徒然的 túrán de, 无效的 wúxiào de (ineffectual). ②自负的 zìfù de (conceited).

valet n. 男仆 nánpú, 服务生 fúwùshēng.

valid adj. 有效的 yǒuxiào de (effective).

validity n. 有效性 yǒuxiàoxìng.

valley n. 谷 gǔ, 山谷 shāngǔ ⟨mountains⟩.

valor n. 英勇 yīngyǒng.

valuable adj. 有价值的 yǒu jiàzhí de, 贵重的 guìzhòng de. — n. 贵重物品 guìzhòng wùpǐn.

valuation n. 评价 píngjià, 估价 gūjià.

value n. 价值 jiàzhí (worth). — v. ①估价 gūjià (estimate). ②重视 zhòngshì (care for).

valve n. ①活门 huómén, 阀 fá (tap). ②瓣膜 bànmó ⟨in the heart⟩.

vampire n. 吸血鬼 xīxuèguǐ / xīxiěguǐ.

van n. 有盖货车 yǒu gài huòchē.

vanilla n. 香草 xiāngcǎo.

vanish v. 消失 xiāoshī.

vanity n. 自负 zìfù, 虚荣心 xūróngxīn.

vanquish v. 征服 zhēngfú, 击败 jībài / jíbài.

vantage n. 优势 yōushì (superiority). ~ **point** ①有利位置 yǒulì wèizhì ⟨position⟩. ②观点 guāndiǎn (viewpoint).

vapor n. 蒸气 zhēngqì, 烟雾 yānwù.

vaporize v. 蒸发 zhēngfā.

variable adj. 易变的 yìbiàn de, 可变的 kěbiàn de. — n. ①因素 yīnsù (factor). ②变数 biànshù ⟨mathematics⟩.

variant adj. 不同的 bùtóng de, 差异的 chāyì de. — n. 变体 biàntǐ, 异体 yìtǐ.

variation n. 变化 biànhuà, 改变 gǎibiàn (the act of varying).

varied adj. ①各样的 gèyàng de (diverse). ②富于变化的 fù yú biànhuà de (changing).

variety n. 变化 biànhuà (change), 多样 duōyàng (diversity).

various adj. 各样的 gèyàng de (diverse), 不同的 bùtóng de (different).

vary v. 改变 gǎibiàn, 变化 biànhuà.

vase n. 花瓶 huāpíng.

Vaseline n. 凡士林 fánshìlín.

vassal n. 家臣 jiāchén.

vast adj. 巨大的 jùdà de, 广大的 guǎngdà de.

vat n. 大桶 dàtǒng.

vault n. ①拱形圆屋顶 gǒngxíng yuánwūdǐng (arched roof). ②保险库 bǎoxiǎnkù ⟨safekeeping⟩.

V

③地下灵室 dìxià língshì
〈underground room〉. ④跳过
tiàoguo 〈jump〉. — v. 跳过
tiàoguo 〈jump〉. **pole ~** 撑竿跳
chēnggāntiào.

vaunt v. 夸耀 kuāyào.

VCR 录放影机 lùfàngyǐngjī
(video cassette recorder).

veal n. 小牛肉 xiǎoniúròu.

vegetable n. 蔬菜 shūcài.
— adj. 蔬菜的 shūcài de.

vegetarian n. 素食者
sùshízhě. — adj. 吃素的
chīsù de.

vegetation n. 植物 zhíwù.

vehement adj. 热烈的 rèliè
de, 激烈的 jīliè de.

vehicle n. 车辆 chēliàng (car),
交通工具 jiāotōng gōngjù
(transportation).

veil n. 面纱 miànshā, 面罩
miànzhào. — v. 以面罩遮掩
yǐ miànzhào zhēyǎn.

vein n. 静脉 jìngmài.

velocity n. 速度 sùdù.

velvet n. 天鹅绒 tiān'róng
〈material〉. — adj. 天鹅绒般的
tiān'róng bān de.

vend v. 兜售 dōushòu, 叫卖
jiàomài.

vendor n. 小贩 xiǎofàn
(peddler), 兜售者 dōushòuzhě
(seller).

venerable adj. 可敬的 kějìng
de.

venerate v. 尊敬 zūnjìng.

venereal adj. ①性交的
xìngjiāo de 〈sexual〉. ②性病的
xìngbìng de 〈disease〉.
~ disease 性病 xìngbìng.

vengeance n. 复仇 fùchóu,
报复 bàofù.

vengeful adj. 报复的 bàofù de.

venison n. 鹿肉 lùròu.

venom n. ①毒液 dúyè (poison). ②恶意 èyì (spite).

venomous adj. ①有毒的
yǒudú de (poisonous). ②恶毒
的 èdú de (spiteful).

vent n. 出口 chūkǒu, 通气孔
tōngqìkǒng (outlet). — v. 发
泄 fāxiè (relieve).

ventilate v. 使通风 shǐ
tōngfēng 〈air〉.

ventilation n. 通风 tōngfēng
〈air〉.

venture n. & v. 冒险 màoxiǎn.

venturesome adj. 冒险的
màoxiǎn de.

Venus n. 金星 Jīnxīng.

veranda n. 走廊 zǒuláng.

verb n. 动词 dòngcí.

verbal adj. ①言辞的 yáncí de
(lexical). ②口头的 kǒutóu de
(oral).

verbose adj. 冗长的
rǒngcháng de (wordy).

verdict n. ①陪审员的裁决
péishěnyuán de cáijué 〈jury〉.
②判断 pànduàn, 定论 dìnglùn
(judgment).

verge n. 边缘 biānyuán (edge).

verify v. ①证实 zhèngshí
(confirm). ②鉴定 jiàndìng
(ascertain).

verification n. 证实
zhèngshí.

veritable adj. 真正的
zhēnzhèng de, 确实的
quèshí de.

verity n. 真实性 zhēnshíxìng
(truth).

vermilion adj. 朱红的
zhūhóng de. — n. 朱红色
zhūhóngsè.

vermin n. ①害虫 hàichóng
〈insect〉. ②害兽 hàishòu 〈small
animal〉.

versatile adj. ①多才多艺的 duōcái-duōyì de 〈skill〉. ②多用途的 duō yòngtú de 〈uses〉.

verse n. ①诗 shī, 韵文 yùnwén (poetry, poem). ②诗节 shījié (stanza).

versed adj. 精通的 jīngtōng de.

version n. ①译文 yìwén, 译本 yìběn (translation). ②说法 shuōfa (description). ③版本 bǎnběn (form). ④形式 xíngshì (style).

versus prep. ……对…… ...duì....

vertebra n. 脊椎 jǐzhuī.

vertebrate n. 脊椎动物 jǐzhuī dòngwù.

vertical adj. 垂直的 chuízhí de. — n. 垂直线 chuízhíxiàn 〈line〉.

very adv. 很 hěn, 极 jí (extremely). — adj. 真正的 zhēnzhèng de (actual).

vessel n. ①容器 róngqì (container). ②船 chuán (ship).

vest n. 背心 bèixīn (waistcoat).

vestige n. 痕迹 hénjì / hénjī.

veteran n. ①退伍军人 tuìwǔ jūnrén, 老兵 lǎobīng (ex-serviceman). ②老手 lǎoshǒu (old hand).

veterinarian n. 兽医 shòuyī.

veterinary adj. 兽医的 shòuyī de.

veto n. ①否决权 fǒujuéquán 〈right〉. ②否决 fǒujué (refusal). — v. 使苦恼 shǐ kǔnǎo (trouble).

vexation n. 苦恼 kǔnǎo.

via prep. 经由 jīngyóu (through), 借 jiè (by).

viaduct n. 陆桥 lùqiáo, 高架桥 gāojiàqiáo.

vial n. 小瓶子 xiǎopíngzi.

vibrate v. 震动 zhèndòng.

vibration n. 震动 zhèndòng.

vice n. ①恶行 èxíng / èxíng (wickedness). ②缺点 quēdiǎn (fault). ③坏习惯 huài xíguàn (bad habit).

vice versa adv. 反之亦然 fǎnzhī yìrán.

vicinity n. 附近 fùjìn, 接近 jiējìn.

vicious adj. ①恶意的 èyì de (spiteful). ②有恶习的 yǒu èxí de (having bad habits). ③邪恶的 xié'è de (evil). ~ circle 恶性循环 èxìng xúnhuán. ~ game 电动玩具游戏 diàndòngwánjù yóuxì.

victim n. ①受害者 shòuhàizhě (one harmed). ②牺牲者 xīshēngzhě (casualty).

victor n. 胜利者 shènglìzhě.

victorious adj. 胜利的 shènglì de.

victory n. 胜利 shènglì.

video n. 电视屏 diànshì. — adj. 影像的 yǐngxiàng de.

videotape n. 录像带 lùxiàngdài / 录影带 lùyǐngdài. — v. 录像 lùxiàng / 录影 lùyǐng.

vie v. 竞争 jìngzhēng.

view n. ①景色 jǐngsè (scene). ②视野 shìyě, 眼界 yǎnjiè (range of sight). ③意见 yìjiàn (opinion). — v. ①观看 guānkàn (behold). ②把……看成 bǎ... kànchéng (regard as).

viewpoint n. 观点 guāndiǎn.

vigil n. 彻夜不眠 chèyè bù mián (sleeplessness).

vigilance n. 警戒 jǐngjiè.

vigor n. 活力 huólì, 精力 jīnglì

(energy).

vigorous *adj.* 精力充沛的 jīnglì-chōngpèi de (energetic).

vile *adj.* 恶劣的 èliè de (evil), 可耻的 kěchǐ de (shameful).

villa *n.* 别墅 biéshù.

village *n.* 村庄 cūnzhuāng.

villager *n.* 村民 cūnmín.

villain *n.* 恶徒 ètú (scoundrel).

vindicate *v.* 辩证 biànzhèng, 澄清 chéngqīng.

vindictive *adj.* 有复仇心的 yǒu fùchóuxīn de (vengeful).

vine *n.* 藤蔓植物 téngmàn zhíwù.

vinegar *n.* 醋 cù.

vineyard *n.* 葡萄园 pútáoyuán.

viola *n.* 中音提琴 zhōngyīntíqín.

violate *v.* ①违犯 wéifàn (transgress). ②侵害 qīnhài (injure). ③破坏 pòhuài (destroy). ④强暴 qiángbào (rape). ⑤亵渎 xièdú (disrespect).

violation *n.* 违犯 wéifàn (transgression).

violence *n.* ①猛烈 měngliè, 激烈 jīliè (vehemence). ②暴行 bàoxíng / bàoxìng, 暴力 bàolì (physical harm).

violent *adj.* ①猛烈的 měngliè de, 剧烈的 jùliè de (vehement). ②暴力的 bàolì de (harmful).

violet *n.* 紫罗兰 zǐluólán (plant).

violin *n.* 小提琴 xiǎotíqín.

viper *n.* 毒蛇 dúshé.

virgin *n.* 处女 chǔnǚ. — *adj.* 处女的 chǔnǚ de (vestal).

virginity *n.* 童贞 tóngzhēn (chastity).

Virgo 处女座 Chǔnǚzuò.

virtual *adj.* 实际上的 shíjìshang de (actual).

~ *reality* 虚拟现实 xūnǐ xiànshí / 虚拟实境 xūnǐ shíjìng.

virtue *n.* 德行 déxíng / déxìng, 美德 měidé (goodness).

virtuous *adj.* 美德的 měidé de.

virulent *adj.* ①有毒的 yǒudú de (poisonous). ②恶毒的 èdú de (spiteful).

virus *n.* 滤过性病毒 lǜguòxìng bìngdú.

visa *n.* 签证 qiānzhèng.

Visa Card 威士卡 Wēishìkǎ.

visage *n.* 面貌 miànmào.

vise *n.* 老虎钳 lǎohǔqián.

visible *adj.* 可见的 kějiàn de (can be seen).

vision *n.* ①视力 shìlì (eyesight). ②远见 yuǎnjiàn (foresight). ③幻影 huànyǐng, 幻象 huànxiàng (illusion). ④想象 xiǎngxiàng (imagination).

visionary *adj.* ①有远见的 yǒu yuǎnjiàn de (foresighted). ②幻想的 huànxiǎng de (illusory). — *n.* ①有远见者 yǒu yuǎnjiàn zhě ⟨foresight⟩. ②空想者 kōngxiǎngzhě ⟨lack reality⟩.

visit *n.* & *v.* 拜访 bàifǎng, 访问 fǎngwèn (call on), 参观 cānguān (tour).

visitor *n.* ①访客 fǎngkè, 宾客 bīnkè (guest). ②观光客 guānguāngkè (tourist).

visor *n.* 帽舌 màoshé ⟨hat⟩.

vista *n.* 远景 yuǎnjǐng (prospect).

visual *adj.* 视觉的 shìjué de (ocular), 看得见的 kàndejiàn de (visible).

vital adj. 生命的 shēngmìng de, 维持生命必需的 wéichí shēngmìng bìxū de 〈necessary〉.

vitality n. 生命力 shēngmìnglì, 活力 huólì 〈energy〉.

vitalize v. 赋以生命力 fù yǐ shēngmìnglì.

vitamin n. 维他命 wéitāmìng.

vivacious adj. 活泼愉快的 huópō yúkuài de.

vivid adj. ①鲜明的 xiānmíng de 〈bright〉. ②生动的 shēngdòng de 〈lifelike〉.

vocabulary n. 词汇 cíhuì 〈lexicon〉.

vocal adj. 声音的 shēngyīn de 〈of the voice〉, 有声音的 yǒu shēngyīn de 〈voiced〉.

vocalist n. 声乐家 shēngyuèjiā, 歌手 gēshǒu.

vocation n. 职业 zhíyè 〈occupation〉.

vocational adj. 职业的 zhíyè de. ~ **school** 技校 jìxiào / 职业学校 zhíyè xuéxiào.

vociferous adj. 吵闹的 chǎonào de.

vogue n. 流行 liúxíng, 时尚 shíshàng 〈fashion〉.

voice n. 声音 shēngyīn 〈sound〉. ~ **mail** 语音信箱 yǔyīn xìnxiāng.

void adj. ①无效的 wúxiào de 〈ineffectual〉. ②空的 kōng de, 空虚的 kōngxū de 〈empty〉.

volatile adj. ①挥发性的 huīfāxìng de 〈liquid〉. ②易变的 yìbiàn de 〈person〉.

volcano n. 火山 huǒshān.

volley n. 齐发 qífā, 连发 liánfā

〈missile〉.

volleyball n. 排球 páiqiú.

volt n. 伏特 fútè.

voltage n. 电压 diànyā.

voltmeter n. 伏特计 fútèjì, 电压表 diànyābiǎo.

volume n. ①卷 juàn, 册 cè 〈book〉. ②体积 tǐjī 〈capacity〉. ③音量 yīnliàng 〈sound〉.

voluminous adj. ①庞大的 pángdà de 〈large〉. ②大部头的 dàbùtóu de 〈book〉.

voluntary adj. 自愿的 zìyuàn de.

volunteer n. 志愿者 zhìyuànzhě, 义工 yìgōng. — v. 自愿做 zìyuàn zuò.

voluptuous adj. ①耽迷肉欲的 dānmí ròuyù de 〈sexual pleasure〉. ②肉感的 ròugǎn de 〈sexually attractive〉.

vomit v. 呕吐 ǒutù.

vote n. & v. 投票 tóupiào.

voter n. 投票者 tóupiàozhě.

vouch v. 担保 dānbǎo 〈guarantee〉.

voucher n. 收据 shōujù, 凭单 píngdān 〈receipt〉.

vow n. 誓言 shìyán. — v. 发誓 fāshì.

vowel n. 母音 mǔyīn.

voyage n. 航海 hánghǎi, 航行 hángxíng.

vulgar adj. ①粗俗的 cūsú de 〈impolite〉. ②通俗的 tōngsú de 〈common〉.

vulnerable adj. 易受伤害的 yì shòu shānghài de 〈weak〉.

vulture n. 兀鹰 wùyīng 〈bird〉.

V

W

wad *n.* 一卷 yìjuǎn (roll), 小块 xiǎokuài (small piece).

wadding *n.* 填料 tiánliào, 填塞物 tiánsèwù.

waddle *n. & v.* 蹒跚地走 pánshān de zǒu / mánshān de zǒu.

wade *v.* 跋涉 báshè, 步行渡过 bùxíng dùguò.

waffle *n.* 松饼 sōngbǐng.

waft *v.* 飘浮 piāofú.

wag *v.* 摇摆 yáobǎi, 摆动 bǎidòng.

wage *n.* 工资 gōngzī (pay). — *v.* 从事 cóngshì (engage in), 进行 jìnxíng (conduct). ~ *war* 打仗 dǎzhàng.

wager *n. & v.* 打赌 dǎdǔ.

wagon *n.* ①马车 mǎchē (horse-drawn carriage). ②运货车 yùnhuòchē (delivery vehicle).

wail *n. & v.* ①哭泣 kūqì (cry). ②悲叹 bēitàn (moan).

waist *n.* 腰 yāo.

waistband *n.* 腰带 yāodài.

wait *v.* ①等 děng, 等待 děngdài, 等候 děnghòu (halt). ②服侍 fúshì (serve). ~ *a minute* 等一下 děng yíxià.

waiter *n.* 侍者 shìzhě, 服务生 fúwùshēng.

waiting room *n.* 候车室 hòuchēshì.

waitress *n.* 女侍 nǚshì, 女服务生 nǚfúwùshēng.

wake *v.* 醒来 xǐnglái, 唤醒 huànxǐng.

wakeful *adj.* 醒着的 xǐngzhe de.

waken *v.* 醒来 xǐnglái, 唤醒 huànxǐng.

walk *v.* ①行走 xíngzǒu (on foot). ②散步 sànbù (take a stroll). — *n.* 散步 sànbù.

wall *n.* 墙 qiáng, 壁 bì.

wallet *n.* 皮夹 píjiā / píjiá, 钱包 qiánbāo.

wallow *v.* 打滚 dǎgǔn.

wallpaper *n.* 壁纸 bìzhǐ.

walnut *n.* ①胡桃 hútáo 〈nut〉. ②胡桃木 hútáomù 〈wood〉.

walrus *n.* 海象 hǎixiàng.

waltz *n.* 华尔兹舞 huá'ěrzīwǔ.

wand *n.* ①棒 bàng, 短杖 duǎnzhàng 〈stick〉. ②魔杖 mózhàng 〈conjurer〉.

wander *v.* ①漫游 mànyóu (roam freely). ②徘徊 páihuái (roam aimlessly).

wane *n. & v.* ①亏 kuī, 缺 quē 〈moon〉. ②减弱 jiǎnruò (decrease).

want *v.* ①想要 xiǎngyào (desire). ②需要 xūyào (need). — *n.* ①需要 xūyào (need). ②缺乏 quēfá (lack).

war *n.* 战争 zhànzhēng.

ward *n.* ①病房 bìngfáng 〈hospital〉. ②监房 jiānfáng 〈prison〉. ③被监护者 bèi jiānhù zhě (protected person).

warden *n.* 监护人 jiānhùrén, 管理人 guǎnlǐrén.

wardrobe *n.* ①衣柜 yīguì (closet). ②衣服 yīfu (clothing).

warehouse *n.* 仓库 cāngkù.

wares *n.* 商品 shāngpǐn.

warfare n. 战争 zhànzhēng.

warlike adj. 好战的 hàozhàn de (fond of war).

warm adj. 温暖的 wēnnuǎn de. — v. 使温暖 shǐ wēnnuǎn.

warmth n. 温暖 wēnnuǎn ⟨temperature⟩, 热情 rèqíng ⟨emotion⟩.

warn v. 警告 jǐnggào (caution).

warning n. 警告 jǐnggào.

warp v. 弯翘 wānqiào, 歪曲 wāiqū (twist).

warrant n. ①令状 lìngzhuàng ⟨document⟩. ②正当理由 zhèngdàng lǐyóu (justification). — v. ①保证 bǎozhèng (guarantee). ②使有正当性 shǐ yǒu zhèngdàngxìng (appear right). ③认为 rènwéi (think that).

warranted adj. 有道理的 yǒu dàolǐ de (sensible), 有正当理由的 yǒu zhèngdàng lǐyóu de (justified).

warrior n. 战士 zhànshì.

wart n. 疣 yóu.

wash n. & v. 洗 xǐ, 洗涤 xǐdí.

washer n. 洗衣机 xǐyījī.

washing n. 洗涤 xǐdí. ~ *machine* 洗衣机 xǐyījī.

washroom n. 厕所 cèsuǒ, 洗手间 xǐshǒujiān.

wasp n. 黄蜂 huángfēng.

wastage n. ①消耗 xiāohào (loss). ②消耗量 xiāohàoliàng (amount).

waste v. 浪费 làngfèi. — n. ①浪费 làngfèi (wasting). ②废物 fèiwù (trash). — adj. ①废弃的 fèiqì de (unwanted). ②荒芜的 huāngwú de (barren).

wastebasket n. 废纸篓 fèizhǐlǒu.

wasteful adj. 浪费的 làngfèi de.

watch v. ①看 kàn, 观看 guānkàn (look at). ②看守 kānshǒu (guard). ~ *after* 照顾 zhàogù (care for). ~ *out* 小心 xiǎoxīn. — n. ①表 biǎo (timer). ②看守 kānshǒu (act of watching).

watchful adj. 注意的 zhùyì de, 警戒的 jǐngjiè de.

watchmaker n. 表匠 biǎojiàng.

watchman n. 看守者 kānshǒuzhě.

watchword n. 口令 kǒulìng (password).

water n. 水 shuǐ. — v. 洒水 sǎshuǐ, 浇水 jiāoshuǐ (pour water on).

waterfall n. 瀑布 pùbù.

watermelon n. 西瓜 xīguā.

waterproof adj. 防水的 fángshuǐ de, 不透水的 bú tòushuǐ de.

watery adj. ①含水的 hánshuǐ de (containing water). ②淡的 dàn de (diluted-tasting). ③水汪汪的 shuǐwāngwāng de (tearful).

watt n. 瓦特 wǎtè.

wave n. ①波 bō, 波浪 bōlàng ⟨water⟩. ②波动 bōdòng (wave-like movement). ③波纹 bōwén, 波浪形 bōlàngxíng (curve). — v. ①波动 bōdòng (move). ②蜷曲 quánqū (curve). ③挥手 huīshǒu ⟨hand⟩.

waver v. ①摇曳 yáoyè / yáoyì (move unsteadily). ②犹豫 yóuyù (hesitate).

wax n. 蜡 là. — v. ①增大 zēngdà (increase). ②渐满 jiànmǎn ⟨moon⟩.

way n. ①路 lù (route). ②方向 fāngxiàng (direction). ③方法

W

fāngfǎ (method). ④风气 fēngqì (custom). *on the ~* 在路上 zài lùshang.

waylay *v.* 拦截 lánjié (intercept).

wayside *n. & adj.* 路边 lùbiān.

wayward *adj.* ①任性的 rènxìng de, 不负责任的 bú fù zérèn de (irresponsible). ②捉摸不定的 zhuōmō-bùdìng de (unpredictable).

we *pron.* 我们 wǒmen.

weak *adj.* ①虚弱的 xūruò de ⟨physical trait⟩. ②懦弱的 nuòruò de ⟨personality trait⟩. ③弱的 ruò de, 无力的 wúlì de (powerless). ④淡的 dàn de (watery).

weaken *v.* 使虚弱 shǐ xūruò, 变弱 biàn ruò.

weakness *n.* ①弱点 ruòdiǎn (defect). ②虚弱 xūruò (being weak). ③偏好 piānhào (fondness for).

wealth *n.* 财富 cáifù.

wealthy *adj.* 有钱的 yǒu qián de, 富裕的 fùyù de.

wean *v.* 使断乳 shǐ duànrǔ ⟨baby⟩.

weapon *n.* 武器 wǔqì.

wear *v.* ①穿 chuān ⟨clothing⟩, 佩戴 pèidài ⟨jewelry, hat, etc.⟩. ②磨损 mósǔn (damage). — *n.* ①穿着 chuānzhuó, 佩戴 pèidài ⟨clothing⟩. ②磨损 mósǔn (damage).

weary *adj.* ①疲倦的 píjuàn de (tired). ②令人厌烦的 lìng rén yànfán de (tiresome). — *v.* ①使疲倦 shǐ píjuàn (tire out). ②使厌烦 shǐ yànfán (annoy).

weasel *n.* 鼬 yòu.

weather *n.* 天气 tiānqì.

weather-beaten *adj.* 风吹雨

打的 fēngchuī-yǔdǎ de.

weathercock *n.* 风标 fēngbiāo, 风信鸡 fēngxìnjī.

weave *v.* 编织 biānzhī.

weaver *n.* 织者 zhīzhě.

web *n.* 网 wǎng, 网状物 wǎngzhuàngwù (net). *~ browser* 全球信息网络浏览器 quánqiú xìnxī wǎngluò liúlǎnqì / 全球资讯网路浏览器 quánqiú zīxùn wǎngluò liúlǎnqì. *~ page* 网页 wǎngyè.

website *n.* 网站 wǎngzhàn.

wed *v.* 跟……结婚 gēn... jiéhūn (get married to), 嫁 jià ⟨said of a woman⟩, 娶 qǔ ⟨said of a man⟩.

wedding *n.* 婚礼 hūnlǐ.

wedge *n.* 楔 xiē (V-shaped piece of wood). — *v.* 以楔固定 yǐ xiē gùdìng.

wedlock *n.* 婚姻生活 hūnyīn shēnghuó (married life).

Wednesday *n.* 星期三 Xīngqīsān / Xīngqísān.

weed *n.* 杂草 zácǎo (unwanted wild plant). — *v.* 除杂草 chú zácǎo.

week *n.* 星期 xīngqī / xīngqí, 周 zhōu.

weekday *n.* 平日 píngrì, 工作日 gōngzuòrì.

weekend *n.* 周末 zhōumò.

weekly *adj. & adv.* 每周的 měi zhōu de. — *n.* 周刊 zhōukān.

weep *v.* 哭泣 kūqì, 流泪 liúlèi.

weigh *v.* ①称重 chēngzhòng ⟨measure⟩. ②考虑 kǎolǜ, 斟酌 zhēnzhuó (consider). ③具有重要性 jùyǒu zhòngyàoxìng, 有分量 yǒu fènliàng (be important).

weight *n.* ①重 zhòng, 重量

zhòngliàng (heaviness). ②重要
性 zhòngyàoxìng (importance).
— v. 加重 jiāzhòng.

weighty adj. 重要的
zhòngyào de.

weird adj. 怪异的 guàiyì de.

welcome n. & interj. 欢迎
huānyíng. — adj. 受欢迎的
shòu huānyíng de.

weld v. 焊接 hànjiē (solder).

welfare n. 幸福 xìngfú (well-
being), 福利 fúlì (benefits).
social ~ 社会福利 shèhuì fúlì.

well adv. 很好 hěn hǎo (in a
good way). — adj. 健康的
jiànkāng de (healthy).
— n. ①井 jǐng 〈water〉. ②油井
yóujǐng 〈oil〉.

well-being n. 幸福 xìngfú.

well-bred adj. 有教养的 yǒu
jiàoyǎng de (of good upbring-
ing), 客气的 kèqi de (polite).

well-done adj. 完全煮熟的
wánquán zhǔshú de /
wánquán zhǔshóu de (cook).

well-known adj. 著名的
zhùmíng de.

were v. 是 shì.

west n. ①西 xī 〈direction〉. ②西
方 xīfāng (western region). ③西
边 xībiān, 西部 xībù (western
part). — adv. 西 xī, 向西 xiàng
xī, 往西 wǎng xī. — adj. ①西 xī
(of the west). ②西方的 xīfāng
de (of the western region). ③西
部的 xībù de (of the western
part).

western adj. 西方的 xīfāng
de.

westward adj. 西方的 xīfāng
de. — adv. 向西方 xiàng
xīfāng.

wet adj. 湿的 shī de (not dry).
— n. 湿气 shīqì (humid weather),

雨天 yǔtiān (rainy day).

whale n. 鲸 jīng.

whaling n. 捕鲸 bǔ jīng.

wharf n. 码头 mǎtou.

what adj. & pron. 什么
shénme.

whatever adj. & pron. 不论什
么 búlùn shénme (no matter
what).

wheat n. 小麦 xiǎomài.

wheel n. 轮 lún, 车轮 chēlún.

wheelchair n. 轮椅 lúnyǐ.

wheeze v. 喘息 chuǎnxī /
chuǎnxí.

when adv. 何时 héshí, 什么时
候 shénme shíhou. — conj. 当
……时 dāng...shí (at some
time).

whenever conj. 无论何时
wúlùn héshí (at whatever time).
— adv. 随时都可以 suíshí
dōu kěyǐ (anytime is good).

where adv. 哪里 nǎli, 何处
héchù (at what place).

whereabouts adv. 靠近何处
kàojìn héchù, 在哪里附近 zài
nǎli fùjìn (near what place).
— n. 所在 suǒzài, 下落
xiàluò.

whereas conj. ①然而 rán'ér
(although). ②鉴于 jiànyú, 兹因
zīyīn (because of the fact that).

wherever adv. 无论何处
wúlùn héchù.

whether conj. 是否 shìfǒu, 抑
或 yìhuò (if).

which adj. & pron. 哪一个
nǎ yí ge.

whichever adj. & pron. 任何
一个 rènhé yí ge.

whiff n. 一阵 yí zhèn.

while n. 短暂时间 duǎnzàn
shíjiān / duǎnzhàn shíjiān,
一会儿 yíhuìr / yìhuǐr (short

time). — *conj.* 当……的时候
dāng...de shíhòu (during the
time that).

whim *n.* 突然的念头 tūrán de
niàntou / túrán de niàntou.

whimper *v.* 啜泣 chuòqì, 呜
咽 wūyè.

whimsical *adj.* 异想天开的
yìxiǎng-tiānkāi de.

whine *v.* 哀泣 āiqì. — *n.* 哀泣
声 āiqìshēng.

whinny *n.* 马嘶声
mǎsīshēng. — *v.* 发出马嘶声
fāchū mǎsīshēng.

whip *n.* 鞭 biān. — *v.* 鞭打
biāndǎ.

whirl *n.* & *v.* 旋转 xuánzhuǎn.

whirlpool *n.* 漩涡 xuánwō.

whirlwind *n.* 旋风 xuànfēng.

whisker *n.* 颊髭 jiázī, 须 xū.

whisky *n.* 威士忌酒
wēishìjìjiǔ.

whisper *n.* & *v.* 低语 dīyǔ, 耳
语 ěryǔ.

whistle *v.* ①吹口哨 chuī
kǒushào (mouth). ②鸣笛 míng
dí (blow). ③吹笛子 chuī dízi
(flute). — *n.* ①口哨声
kǒushàoshēng (sound of
whistling). ②哨子 shàozi, 笛 dí
(instrument). ③鸣笛声
míngdíshēng (sound of whistle
blowing).

white *n.* & *adj.* 白色 báisè.

whitewash *v.* ①粉刷 fěnshuā
(paint). ②粉饰 fěnshì (cover
up). — *n.* 石灰水 shíhuīshuǐ
⟨liquid⟩.

who *pron.* 谁 shéi.

whoever *pron.* 不论谁 búlùn
shéi (no matter who).

whole *adj.* 全部的 quánbù de,
整个的 zhěngge de. — *n.* 全体
quántǐ.

wholesale *n.* 批销 pīxiāo, 批
发 pīfā. — *adj.* 批销的 pīxiāo
de, 批发的 pīfā de.

wholesome *adj.* ①卫生的
wèishēng de (sanitary). ②有益
健康的 yǒuyì jiànkāng de
(healthy).

whom *pron.* 谁 shéi.

whoop *n.* 呼喊声
hūhǎnshēng. — *v.* 呼喊 hūhǎn.

whore *n.* 娼妓 chāngjì, 妓女
jìnǚ ⟨female⟩. ②男妓 nánjì
⟨male⟩.

whose *pron.* 谁的 shéi de.

why *adv.* 为什么 wèishénme.

wick *n.* 芯 xīn.

wicked *adj.* 邪恶的 xié'è de,
坏心眼的 huàixīnyǎn de.

wicker *n.* 柳条 liǔtiáo.

wide *adj.* 宽的 kuān de, 广阔
的 guǎngkuò de.

widely *adv.* ①广大地 guǎngdà
de, 广泛地 guǎngfàn de
(generally). ②相当地
xiāngdāng de (to a great
extent).

widen *v.* 使……变宽 shǐ...
biànkuān.

widespread *adj.* 流传广的
liúchuán guǎng de.

widow *n.* 寡妇 guǎfù.

widower *n.* 鳏夫 guānfū.

width *n.* 宽度 kuāndù.

wife *n.* 妻子 qīzi, 太太 tàitai.

wig *n.* 假发 jiǎfà / jiǎfǎ.

wiggle *v.* 扭动 niǔdòng, 摆动
bǎidòng.

wild *adj.* ①野生的 yěshēng
de (undomesticated). ②野蛮的
yěmán de (barbaric). ③未开化
的 wèi kāihuà de (uncivilized).
④粗暴的 cūbào de (riotous).
⑤无人烟的 wú rényān de
(uninhabited). ⑥狂暴的

kuángbào de (turbulent).
⑦疯狂的 fēngkuáng de
(crazy). — adv. 粗暴地 cūbào
de. — n. 荒野 huāngyě.

wilderness n. 荒野 huāngyě.

wiles n. (pl.) 诡计 guǐjì.

will aux. v. ①将 jiāng (be going
to). ②想要 xiǎngyào (wish).
— n. ①意志 yìzhì (determination). ②遗嘱 yízhǔ (testament).

willful adj. ①任性的 rènxìng
de, 刚愎的 gāngbì de (strong-
willed). ②故意的 gùyì de
(done on purpose).

willing adj. 愿意的 yuànyì de,
情愿的 qíngyuàn de (of one's
own accord), 乐意的 lèyì de
(happily).

willingly adv. 愿意地 yuànyì
de.

willow n. 柳树 liǔshù.

wilt v. 枯萎 kūwěi / kūwēi,
凋谢 diāoxiè.

wily adj. 狡猾的 jiǎohuá de.

win v. 赢 yíng, 获胜 huòshèng.
— n. 胜利 shènglì.

wince v. 畏缩 wèisuō.

winch n. 绞盘 jiǎopán, 绞车
jiǎochē.

wind n. ①风 fēng (air-current).
②气味 qìwèi (scent). ③胀气
zhàngqì (flatulence). — v. ①蜿
蜒 wānyán (road). ②缠绕
chánrào (thread).

windmill n. 风车 fēngchē.

window n. 窗 chuāng, 窗户
chuānghù.

windshield n. 挡风玻璃
dǎngfēng bōli.

windy adj. ①多风的 duōfēng
de (breezy). ②迎风的 yíngfēng
de (wind-swept).

wine n. ①酒 jiǔ (alcoholic
drink). ②葡萄酒 pútáojiǔ

(grape wine).

wing n. 翼 yì, 翅 chì, 翅膀
chìbǎng.

wink v. ①眨眼 zhǎyǎn (eye).
②闪烁 shǎnshuò (flash).

winner n. 胜利者 shènglìzhě.

winning adj. ①胜利的
shènglì de (triumphant). ②迷
人的 mírén de (charming).

winnings n. 赢得的奖金
yíngdé de jiǎngjīn.

winter n. 冬季 dōngjì, 冬天
dōngtiān.

wintry adj. 冬的 dōng de.

wipe n. & v. 擦 cā, 拭 shì.

wire n. ①金属线 jīnshǔxiàn,
铁丝 tiěsī (metal). ②电缆
diànlǎn (cable). ③电报 diànbào
(telegram). — v. ①用铁丝固定
yòng tiěsī gùdìng (fasten).
②装电线 zhuāng diànxiàn
(install). ③拍电报 pāi diànbào
(telegram).

wireless adj. 无线的 wúxiàn
de. — n. 无线电 wúxiàndiàn.

wiring n. 架线 jiàxiàn, 配线
pèixiàn.

wisdom n. 智慧 zhìhuì
(understanding), 知识 zhīshi
(knowledge).

wise adj. 有智慧的 yǒu zhìhuì
de, 明智的 míngzhì de.

wish v. 意欲 yìyù (want), 希望
xīwàng (hope). — n. 愿望
yuànwàng.

wisp n. 小束 xiǎoshù ⟨hair,
hay, etc.⟩.

wistful adj. ①企盼的 qǐpàn
de / qìpàn de ⟨wish⟩. ②伤感的
shānggǎn de ⟨sad⟩.

wit n. ①机智 jīzhì, 智力 zhìlì
(understanding). ②幽默感
yōumògǎn (sense of humor).

witch n. 女巫 nǚwū, 巫婆

wūpó.

witchcraft n. 巫术 wūshù.

with prep. ①跟 gēn, 与 yǔ (accompanied by). ②具有 jùyǒu (having). ③用 yòng (by means of).

withdraw v. ①撤回 chèhuí (take back). ②撤退 chètuì (retreat). ③退出 tuìchū (leave). ④提取 tíqǔ (take out).

withdrawn adj. 孤独的 gūdú de (solitary).

wither v. 凋谢 diāoxiè, 枯萎 kūwěi / kūwēi.

withhold v. ①制止 zhìzhǐ (prevent). ②扣留 kòuliú (hold).

within prep. 在……之内 zài...zhīnèi. — adv. 在内部 zài nèibù.

without prep. 没有 méiyǒu, 无 wú (lacking). — adv. 在外部 zài wàibù.

withstand v. ①抵抗 dǐkàng, 反抗 fǎnkàng (resist). ②耐 nài, 禁得起 jīndeqǐ (weather).

witness n. ①目击者 mùjīzhě / mùjízhě, 证人 zhèngrén (person). ②证据 zhèngjù (evidence). — v. 目击 mùjī / mùjí, 目睹 mùdǔ.

witticism n. 诙谐语 huīxiéyǔ, 隽语 juànyǔ.

witty adj. 幽默的 yōumò de, 诙谐的 huīxié de.

wizard n. 男巫 nánwū.

woe n. 悲哀 bēi'āi, 悲痛 bēitòng.

wolf n. 狼 láng.

woman n. 女性 nǚxìng, 女人 nǚrén, 妇女 fùnǚ.

womb n. 子宫 zǐgōng.

wonder n. ①惊奇 jīngqí (amazement). ②奇观 qíguān (spectacle), 奇迹 qíjì / qíjī

(marvel). — v. ①想知道 xiǎng zhīdao (would like to know). ②感到好奇 gǎndào hàoqí (feel curious).

wonderful adj. 极好的 jí hǎo de (excellent).

wonderland n. 奇境 qíjìng, 仙境 xiānjìng.

wondrous adj. 令人惊奇的 lìng rén jīngqí de.

woo v. 求爱 qiú'ài (court).

wood n. ①木材 mùcái (timber). ②树林 shùlín (forest).

woodcut n. 木刻 mùkè.

woodcutter n. 樵夫 qiáofū.

wooden adj. ①木制的 mùzhì de (made of wood). ②不自然的 bú zìrán de, 死板的 sǐbǎn de (stilted).

woodland n. 森林地区 sēnlín dìqū.

woodpecker n. 啄木鸟 zhuómùniǎo.

wool n. 羊毛 yángmáo.

woolen adj. 羊毛制的 yángmáo zhì de.

woolly adj. ①羊毛的 yángmáo de (of wool), 羊毛似的 yángmáo shì de / yángmáo sì de (like wool). ②毛茸茸的 máoróngróng de (fuzzy). ③不清楚的 bù qīngchu de (unclear).

word n. ①字 zì, 词 cí (term). ②话 huà, 言辞 yáncí (utterance). ③消息 xiāoxi (news). ④诺言 nuòyán (promise), 保证 bǎozhèng (guarantee). ⑤命令 mìnglìng (command).

work n. ①工作 gōngzuò 〈job〉. ②职业 zhíyè (profession). ③作品 zuòpǐn (artistic product). — v. ①工作 gōngzuò, 做事

W

zuòshì ⟨labor⟩. ②运转
yùnzhuǎn ⟨function⟩. ③有效
yǒuxiào (be effective), 有用
yǒuyòng (be useful).

worker *n.* 工作者
gōngzuòzhě, 工人 gōngrén.

working *n.* 作用 zuòyòng
⟨function⟩. ~ *girl* ①娼妓
chāngjì (prostitute). ②职业妇
女 zhíyè fùnǚ (woman who
works). ~ *mother* 在职妈妈
zàizhí māma.

workman *n.* 劳工 láogōng.

workmanship *n.* 手艺
shǒuyì, 技艺 jìyì.

workshop *n.* ①工厂
gōngchǎng (factory). ②研讨会
yántǎohuì, 工作坊
gōngzuòfáng / gōngzuòfāng
⟨seminar⟩.

world *n.* ①世界 shìjiè ⟨uni-
verse⟩. ②界 jiè (group).

worldly *adj.* ①世俗的 shìsú
de (temporal). ②物质的 wùzhì
de / wùzhí de (material).

world-wide *adj.* 全世界的
quánshìjiè de.

worm *n.* 虫 chóng, 蠕虫
rúchóng. — *v.* 蠕行 rúxíng.

worn *adj.* 磨破的 mópò de
⟨damaged⟩.

worn-out *adj.* ①磨破的 mópò
de (damaged). ②精疲力尽的
jīngpí-lìjìn de (exhausted).

worried *adj.* 担心的 dānxīn
de.

worry *v.* ①困扰 kùnrǎo (cause
anxiety). ②担心 dānxīn (feel
anxious). — *n.* 问题 wèntí
(problem), 烦恼的事 fánnǎo
de shì (annoyance).

worse *adj.* & *adv.* 更坏的
gèng huài de.

worsen *v.* 恶化 èhuà (become

worse), 变坏 biàn huài
(become bad).

worship *n.* ①崇拜 chóngbài,
尊敬 zūnjìng (reverence). ②礼
拜 lǐbài ⟨ceremony⟩. — *v.* 崇拜
chóngbài.

worst *adj.* & *adv.* 最坏的
zuìhuài de.

worth *prep.* ①值得 zhíde
(deserving of). ②值 zhí (of the
value of). — *n.* 价值 jiàzhí.

worthless *adj.* 无价值的 wú
jiàzhí de.

worthwhile *adj.* 值得的
zhíde de.

worthy *adj.* ①值得的 zhíde
de (worthwhile). ②可敬的
kějìng de (respectable).

wound *n.* 伤口 shāngkǒu, 创
伤 chuāngshāng. — *v.* 伤害
shānghài.

wrangle *n.* & *v.* 争吵
zhēngchǎo, 口角 kǒujiǎo.

wrap *v.* 包 bāo, 裹 guǒ. — *n.* 披
肩 pījiān.

wrath *n.* 愤怒 fènnù.

wreath *n.* 花圈 huāquān, 花
冠 huāguān.

wreck *n.* ①毁坏 huǐhuài (ruin).
②船难 chuánnàn (shipwreck).

wrench *v.* ①猛扭 měngniǔ,
扭转 niǔzhuǎn (twist). ②扳手
bānshou ⟨tool⟩. — *v.* 扭 niǔ, 拧
nǐng (twist).

wrestle *n.* & *v.* 摔角 shuāijiǎo.

wrestling *n.* 摔角 shuāijiǎo.

wretch *n.* ①可怜的人 kělián
de rén, 苦命人 kǔmìngrén
(pitiable person). ②恶劣的人
èliè de rén, 坏小子 huài
xiǎozi (vile person).

wretched *adj.* ①可怜的
kělián de, 悲惨的 bēicǎn de
(pitiable). ②恶劣的 èliè de

W

(vile).

wriggle *v.* 蠕动 rúdòng.

wring *v.* ①绞 jiǎo, 拧 níng / nǐng (squeeze). ②紧握 jǐnwò (grip).

wrinkle *n.* 皱纹 zhòuwén (furrow). – *v.* 使起皱纹 shǐ qǐ zhòuwén.

wrist *n.* 腕 wàn.

writ *n.* 令状 lìngzhuàng ⟨law⟩.

write *v.* 书写 shūxiě, 写字 xiězì.

writer *n.* 作者 zuòzhě, 作家 zuòjiā.

writhe *v.* 扭动 niǔdòng.

writing *n.* ①书写 shūxiě (activity of writing). ②笔迹 bǐjī / bǐjī (handwriting). ③写作

xiězuò (composition).

written *adj.* 书写的 shūxiě de.

wrong *adj.* ①错误的 cuòwù de, 不正确的 bú zhèngquè de, 不对的 búduì de (incorrect). ②不正当的 bú zhèngdàng de (improper).

wrongdoing *n.* 犯罪 fànzuì, 罪行 zuìxíng / zuìxíng.

WTO 世界贸易组织 Shìjiè Màoyì Zǔzhī (World Trade Organization).

WWW 万维网 wànwéiwǎng, 环球网 huánqiúwǎng / 全球资讯网 quánqiú zīxùnwǎng (World Wide Web).

X

Xmas *n.* 圣诞节 Shèngdànjié.

X-rated *adj.* X级的 X jí de, 色情的 sèqíng de (obscene).

X ray *n.* X 光线 X guāngxiàn.

xylophone *n.* 木琴 mùqín.

Y

yacht *n.* 游艇 yóutǐng, 快艇 kuàitǐng.

yak *n.* 犛牛 líniú.

yam *n.* 甘薯 gānshǔ.

Yangtze River 长江 Chángjiāng.

yap *n.* 犬吠 quǎnfèi (bark).

yard *n.* ①庭院 tíngyuàn (garden). ②码 mǎ ⟨measurement⟩.

yarn *n.* 纱 shā, 线 xiàn (thread).

yawn v. 打呵欠 dǎhēqiàn.
— n. 呵欠 hēqiàn.

yeah adv. 是 shì.

year n. ①年 nián ⟨time⟩. ②岁 suì ⟨age⟩.

yearly adj. 每年一次的 měi nián yícì de. — adv. 一年一度 yìnián-yídù, 每年 měi nián.

yearn v. 渴望 kěwàng, 向往 xiàngwǎng ⟨long⟩.

yeast n. 酵母 jiàomǔ / xiàomǔ.

yell v. 嘶喊 sīhǎn, 大声叫 dàshēngjiào.

yellow n. 黄色 huángsè.
— adj. 黄色的 huángsè de.

Yellow River 黄河 Huánghé.

yes adv. 是 shì, 对 duì.

yesterday n. & adv. 昨天 zuótiān.

yet adv. 还 hái, 尚 shàng, 迄今 qìjīn ⟨still⟩. — conj. 然而 rán'ér, 但是 dànshì.

yew n. 紫杉 zǐshān.

yield v. ①出产 chūchǎn, 生产 shēngchǎn ⟨produce⟩. ②屈服 qūfú, 投降 tóuxiáng ⟨surrender to⟩. — n. ①生产 shēngchǎn, 生产量 shēngchǎnliàng ⟨product⟩. ②收益 shōuyì ⟨profit⟩.

yoga n. 瑜伽 yújiā.

yogurt n. 酸牛奶 suānniúnǎi / 优酪乳 yōuluòrǔ ⟨curds⟩.

yoke n. ①轭 è ⟨harness⟩. ②束缚 shùfù / shùfú ⟨burden⟩. — v. 驾以轭 jià yǐ è ⟨harness⟩.

yolk n. 蛋黄 dànhuáng.

yonder adv. 在那边 zài nàbiān.

you pron. ①你 nǐ ⟨singular, familiar⟩, 您 nín ⟨singular, respectful⟩. ②你们 nǐmen ⟨plural, familiar⟩, 您们 nínmen ⟨plural, respectful⟩.

young adj. 年轻的 niánqīng de ⟨youthful⟩.

youngster n. 儿童 értóng ⟨child⟩, 少年 shàonián ⟨youth⟩.

your pron. ①你的 nǐ de ⟨singular, familiar⟩, 您的 nín de ⟨singular, respectful⟩. ②你们的 nǐmen de ⟨plural, familiar⟩, 您们的 nínmen de ⟨plural, respectful⟩.

yours pron. ①你的 nǐ de ⟨singular, familiar⟩, 您的 nín de ⟨singular, respectful⟩. ②你们的 nǐmen de ⟨plural, familiar⟩, 您们的 nínmen de ⟨plural, respectful⟩.

yourself pron. ①你自己 nǐ zìjǐ ⟨singular, familiar⟩, 您自己 nín zìjǐ ⟨singular, respectful⟩. ②你们自己 nǐmen zìjǐ ⟨plural, familiar⟩, 您们自己 nínmen zìjǐ ⟨plural, respectful⟩.

youth n. ①年轻 niánqīng, 青春 qīngchūn ⟨being young⟩. ②青春时期 qīngchūn shíqí / qīngchūn shíqī ⟨adolescence⟩.

youthful adj. 年轻的 niánqīng de, 青春的 qīngchūn de.

yo-yo n. 溜溜球 liūliūqiú ⟨toy⟩.

yummy adj. 好吃的 hǎochī de ⟨delicious⟩.

yuppie n. 雅皮士 yǎpíshì / 雅痞 yǎpǐ.

Zei

zany *n.* ①丑角 chǒujué (clown). ②笨蛋 bèndàn (fool).

zapper *n.* ①遥控器 yáokòngqì (remote control). ②电蚊拍 diànwénpāi (insects).

zeal *n.* 热心 rèxīn, 热诚 rèchéng.

zealous *adj.* 热心的 rèxīn de, 热诚的 rèchéng de.

zebra *n.* 斑马 bānmǎ. BĀN MĂ

zenith *n.* ①天顶 tiāndǐng (highest point). ②顶点 dǐngdiǎn (top).

zero *n.* 零 líng.

zest *n.* ①强烈的兴趣 qiángliè de xìngqù (enthusiasm). ②风味 fēngwèi, 滋味 zīwèi (flavor).

③趣味 qùwèi (enjoyment).

zigzag *v.* 作锯齿形 zuò jùchǐxíng. — *n.* 锯齿形 jùchǐxíng.

zinc *n.* 锌 xīn.

zip *n.* 飕飕声 sōusōushēng ⟨sound⟩. ~ *up* 拉上 lāshang.

zipper *n.* 拉链 lāliàn.

zone *n.* 地带 dìdài, 地区 dìqū.

zoo *n.* 动物园 dòngwùyuán.

zoology *n.* 动物学 dòngwùxué. Dig

zoom *v.* ①放大 fàngdà (zoom in). ②缩小 suōxiǎo (zoom out). ③陡升 dǒushēng (go upward). ~ *lens* 变焦镜头 biànjiāo jìngtóu.

Z

Countries · Cities · Regions

国家　　都市　　地区

guójiā　　dūshì　　dìqū

Afghanistan	阿富汗 Āfùhàn
Africa	非洲 Fēizhōu
Albania	阿尔巴尼亚 Ā'ěrbāníyà
Algeria	阿尔及利亚 Ā'ěrjílìyà
America	美洲 Měizhōu
Amsterdam	阿姆斯特丹 Āmǔsītèdān
Angola	安哥拉 Āngēlā
Antarctic	南极洲 Nánjízhōu
Argentina	阿根廷 Āgēntíng
Armenia	亚美尼亚 Yàměiníyà
Asia	亚洲 Yàzhōu
Athens	雅典 Yǎdiǎn
Auckland	奥克兰 Àokèlán
Australia	澳大利亚 Àodàlìyà
Austria	奥地利 Àodìlì
Azerbaijan	阿塞拜疆 Āsàibàijiāng / 亚塞拜然 Yàsàibàirán
Baghdad	巴格达 Bāgédá
Bahamas	巴哈马 Bāhāmǎ
Bahrain	巴林 Bālín
Bangkok	曼谷 Màngǔ
Bangladesh	孟加拉国 Mèngjiālāguó / 孟加拉 Mèngjiālā
Barcelona	巴塞罗那 Bāsàiluónà / 巴塞隆纳 Bāsàilóngnà
Beijing	北京 Běijīng
Beirut	贝鲁特 Bèilǔtè
Belarus	白俄罗斯 Bái'éluósī
Belgium	比利时 Bǐlìshí
Belize	伯利兹 Bólìzī / 贝里斯 Bèilǐsī

Berlin	柏林 Bólín
Bermuda	百慕大 Bǎimùdà / 百慕达 Bǎimùdà
Bern	伯尔尼 Bó'ěrní / 伯恩 Bó'ēn
Bhutan	不丹 Bùdān
Bolivia	玻利维亚 Bōlìwéiyà
Bonn	波恩 Bō'ēn / 波昂 Bō'áng
Bosnia and Herzegovina	波斯尼亚和黑塞哥维那 Bōsīníyà hé Hēisàigēwéinà / 波士尼亚赫塞哥维纳 Bōshìníyà Hèsègēwéinà
Brazil	巴西 Bāxī
Brunei	文莱 Wénlái / 汶莱 Wènlái
Budapest	布达佩斯 Bùdápèisī
Buenos Aires	布宜诺斯艾利斯 Bùyínuòsī'àilìsī
Bulgaria	保加利亚 Bǎojiālìyà
Burundi	布隆迪 Bùlóngdí / 蒲隆地 Púlóngdì
Cairo	开罗 Kāiluó
Cambodia	柬埔寨 Jiǎnpǔzhài
Cameroon	喀麦隆 Kāmàilóng
Canada	加拿大 Jiānádà
Central African Republic	中非 Zhōngfēi
Chad	乍得 Zhàdé / 查德 Chádé
Chicago	芝加哥 Zhījiāgē
Chile	智利 Zhìlì
China	中国 Zhōngguó
Colombia	哥伦比亚 Gēlúnbǐyà
Congo, Democratic Republic of the	刚果民主共和国 Gāngguǒ Mínzhǔ Gònghéguó
Congo, Republic of the	刚果共和国 Gāngguǒ Gònghéguó
Copenhagen	哥本哈根 Gēběnhāgēn
Costa Rica	哥斯达黎加 Gēsīdálíjiā / 哥斯大黎加 Gēsīdàlíjiā
Cote d'Ivoire	科特迪瓦 Kētèdíwǎ / 象牙海岸 Xiàngyá Hǎi'àn
Croatia	克罗地亚 Kèluódìyà / 克罗埃西亚 Kèluó'āixīyà

Cuba	古巴 Gǔbā
Cyprus	塞浦路斯 Sàipǔlùsī / 赛普勒斯 Sàipǔlèsī
Czech Republic	捷克 Jiékè
Denmark	丹麦 Dānmài
Dominican Republic	多米尼加 Duōmǐníjiā / 多明尼加 Duōmíngníjiā
Dublin	都柏林 Dūbólín
East Timor	东帝汶 Dōng Dìwèn
Ecuador	厄瓜多尔 Èguāduō'ěr / 厄瓜多 Èguāduō
Egypt	埃及 Āijí
El Salvador	萨尔瓦多 Sà'ěrwǎduō
Estonia	爱沙尼亚 Àishāníyà
Ethiopia	埃塞俄比亚 Āisài'ébǐyà / 衣索比亚 Yīsuǒbǐyà
Europe	欧洲 Ōuzhōu
Fiji	斐济 Fěijì
Finland	芬兰 Fēnlán
France	法国 Fǎguó / 法兰西 Fǎlánxī
Gabon	加蓬 Jiāpéng / 加彭 Jiāpéng
Gambia	冈比亚 Gāngbǐyà / 甘比亚 Gānbǐyà
Georgia	格鲁吉亚 Gélǔjíyà / 乔治亚 Qiáozhìyà
Germany	德国 Déguó / 德意志 Déyìzhì
Ghana	加纳 Jiānà / 迦纳 Jiānà
Greece	希腊 Xīlà
Greenland	格陵兰 Gélínglán
Grenada	格林纳达 Gélínnàdá / 格瑞那达 Géruìnàdá
Guam	关岛 Guāndǎo
Guangzhou	广州 Guǎngzhōu
Guatemala	危地马拉 Wēidìmǎlā / 瓜地马拉 Guādìmǎlā
Guinea	几内亚 Jǐnèiyà
Guyana	圭亚那 Guīyànà / 盖亚那 Gàiyànà
Hague	海牙 Hǎiyá
Haiti	海地 Hǎidì
Hanoi	河内 Hénèi
Helsinki	赫尔辛基 Hè'ěrxīnjī

Ho Chi Minh City	胡志明市 Húzhìmíngshì
Holy See (Vatican City)	梵蒂冈 Fàndìgāng / 教廷 Jiàotíng
Honduras	洪都拉斯 Hóngdūlāsī / 宏都拉斯 Hóngdūlāsī
Hong Kong	香港 Xiānggǎng
Hungary	匈牙利 Xiōngyálì
Iceland	冰岛 Bīngdǎo
India	印度 Yìndù
Indonesia	印度尼西亚 Yìndùníxīyà
Iran	伊朗 Yīlǎng
Iraq	伊拉克 Yīlākè
Ireland	爱尔兰 Àiěrlán
Israel	以色列 Yǐsèliè
Italy	意大利 Yìdàlì / 义大利 Yìdàlì
Jakarta	雅加达 Yǎjiādá
Jamaica	牙买加 Yámǎijiā
Japan	日本 Rìběn
Java	爪哇 Zhǎowā
Jordan	约旦 Yuēdàn
Kaohsiung	高雄 Gāoxióng
Kashmir	克什米尔 Kèshímǐěr / 喀什米尔 Kāshímǐěr
Kazakhstan	哈萨克斯坦 Hāsàkèsītǎn / 哈萨克 Hāsàkè
Kenya	肯尼亚 Kěnníyà / 肯亚 Kěnyà
Korea, North	朝鲜 Cháoxiǎn / 朝鲜（北韩）Cháoxiǎn (Běihán)
Korea, South	大韩民国（韩国）Dàhánmínguó (Hánguó) / 大韩民国（南韩）Dàhánmínguó (Nánhán)
Kuala Lumpur	吉隆坡 Jílóngpō
Kuwait	科威特 Kēwēitè
Kyoto	京都 Jīngdū
Kyrgyzstan	吉尔吉斯斯坦 Jíěrjísīsītǎn / 吉尔吉斯 Jíěrjísī
Laos	老挝 Lǎowō / 寮国 Liáoguó
Latvia	拉脱维亚 Lātuōwéiyà
Lebanon	黎巴嫩 Líbānèn
Lesotho	莱索托 Láisuǒtuō / 赖索托 Làisuǒtuō

Liberia	利比里亚 Lìbǐlǐyà / 赖比瑞亚 Làibǐruìyà
Libya	利比亚 Lìbǐyà
Liechtenstein	列支敦士登 Lièzhīdūnshìdēng / 列支敦斯登 Lièzhīdūnsīdēng
Lithuania	立陶宛 Lìtáowǎn
London	伦敦 Lúndūn
Los Angeles	洛杉矶 Luòshānjī
Luxembourg	卢森堡 Lúsēnbǎo
Macao	澳门 Àomén
Macedonia	马其顿 Mǎqídùn
Madagascar	马达加斯加 Mǎdájiāsījiā
Madrid	马德里 Mǎdélǐ
Malawi	马拉维 Mǎlāwéi / 马拉威 Mǎlāwēi
Malaysia	马来西亚 Mǎláixīyà
Maldives	马尔代夫 Mǎ'ěrdàifū / 马尔地夫 Mǎ'ěrdìfū
Malta	马耳他 Mǎ'ěrtā / 马尔他 Mǎ'ěrtā
Manila	大马尼拉市 Dàmǎnílāshì / 马尼拉市 Mǎnílāshì
Marshall Islands	马绍尔群岛 Mǎshào'ěr Qúndǎo
Mauritania	毛里塔尼亚 Máolǐtǎníyà / 茅利塔尼亚 Máolìtǎníyà
Mauritius	毛里求斯 Máolǐqiúsī / 模里西斯 Mólǐxīsī
Melbourne	墨尔本 Mò'ěrběn
Mexico	墨西哥 Mòxīgē
Moldova	摩尔多瓦 Mó'ěrduōwǎ
Monaco	摩纳哥 Mónàgē
Mongolia	蒙古 Měnggǔ / Ménggǔ
Morocco	摩洛哥 Móluògē
Moscow	莫斯科 Mòsīkē
Mozambique	莫桑比克 Mòsāngbǐkè / 莫三比克 Mòsānbǐkè
Namibia	纳米比亚 Nàmǐbǐyà
Nanjing	南京 Nánjīng
Nauru	瑙鲁 Nǎolǔ / 诺鲁 Nuòlǔ
Nepal	尼泊尔 Níbó'ěr
Netherlands	荷兰 Hélán

New Delhi	新德里 Xīndélǐ
New York	纽约 Niǔyuē
New Zealand	新西兰 Xīnxīlán / 纽西兰 Niǔxīlán
Nicaragua	尼加拉瓜 Níjiālāguā
Niger	尼日尔 Nírì'ěr / 尼日 Nírì
Nigeria	尼日利亚 Nírìlìyà / 奈及利亚 Nàijílìyà
North America	北美洲 Běiměizhōu
Norway	挪威 Nuówēi
Oceania	大洋洲 Dàyángzhōu
Oman	阿曼 Āmàn
Osaka	大阪 Dàbǎn
Oslo	奥斯陆 Àosīlù
Pakistan	巴基斯坦 Bājīsītǎn
Palau	帕劳 Pàláo / 帛琉 Bóliú
Palestine	巴勒斯坦 Bālèsītǎn
Panama	巴拿马 Bānámǎ
Papua New Guinea	巴布亚新几内亚 Bābùyà Xīnjǐnèiyà /
	巴布亚纽几内亚 Bābùyà Niǔjǐnèiyà
Paraguay	巴拉圭 Bālāguī
Paris	巴黎 Bālí
Peru	秘鲁 Bìlǔ
Philippines	菲律宾 Fēilǜbīn
Poland	波兰 Bōlán
Polynesia	波利尼西亚 Bōlìníxīyà / 玻里尼西亚
	Bōlǐníxīyà
Portugal	葡萄牙 Pútáoyá
Prague	布拉格 Bùlāgé
Puerto Rico	波多黎各 Bōduōlígè
Pyongyang	平壤 Píngrǎng
Qatar	卡塔尔 Kǎtǎ'ěr / 卡达 Kǎdá
Rio de Janeiro	里约热内卢 Lǐyuē Rènèilú
Romania	罗马尼亚 Luómǎníyà
Rome	罗马 Luómǎ
Russia	俄罗斯 Éluósī
Rwanda	卢旺达 Lúwàngdá / 卢安达 Lú'āndá

San Francisco	旧金山 Jiùjīnshān
San Marino	圣马力诺 Shèngmǎlìnuò / 圣马利诺 Shèngmǎlìnuò
Saudi Arabia	沙特阿拉伯 Shātè Ālābó / 沙乌地阿拉伯 Shāwūdì Ālābó
Senegal	塞内加尔 Sàinèijiā'ěr / Sènèijiā'ěr
Seoul	首尔 Shǒu'ěr
Shanghai	上海 Shànghǎi
Sierra Leone	塞拉利昂 Sàilālì'áng / 狮子山 Shīzishān
Sikkim	锡金 Xíjīn / Xíjīn
Singapore	新加坡 Xīnjiāpō
Slovakia	斯洛伐克 Sīluòfákè / Sīluòfākè
Slovenia	斯洛文尼亚 Sīluòwénníyà / 斯洛维尼亚 Sīluòwéiníyà
Solomon Islands	所罗门群岛 Suǒluómén Qúndǎo / 索罗门群岛 Suǒluómén Qúndǎo
Somalia	索马里 Suǒmǎlǐ / 索马利亚 Suǒmǎlìyà
South Africa	南非 Nánfēi
South America	南美洲 Nánměizhōu
Spain	西班牙 Xībānyá
Sri Lanka	斯里兰卡 Sīlǐlánkǎ
Stockholm	斯德哥尔摩 Sīdégē'ěrmó
St. Petersburg	圣彼得堡 Shèngbǐdébǎo
Sudan	苏丹 Sūdān
Suriname	苏里南 Sūlǐnán / 苏利南 Sūlìnán
Swaziland	斯威士兰 Sīwēishìlán / 史瓦济兰 Shǐwǎjìlán
Sweden	瑞典 Ruìdiǎn
Switzerland	瑞士 Ruìshì
Sydney	悉尼 Xīní / 雪梨 Xuělí
Syria	叙利亚 Xùlìyà
Taichung	台中 Táizhōng
Taipei	台北 Táiběi
Taiwan	台湾 Táiwān
Tajikistan	塔吉克斯坦 Tǎjíkèsītǎn / 塔吉克 Tǎjíkè
Tanzania	坦桑尼亚 Tǎnsāngníyà / 坦尚尼亚 Tǎnshàngníyà

	Tǎnshàngníyà
Thailand	泰国 Tàiguó
Tibet	西藏 Xīzàng
Tokyo	东京 Dōngjīng
Tonga	汤加 Tāngjiā / 东加 Dōngjiā
Tunisia	突尼斯 Tūnísī / 突尼西亚 Túníxīyà
Turkey	土耳其 Tǔ'ěrqí
Turkmenistan	土库曼斯坦 Tǔkùmànsītǎn / 土库曼 Tǔkùmàn
Uganda	乌干达 Wūgāndá
Ukraine	乌克兰 Wūkèlán
Union of Myanmar (Burma)	缅甸 Miǎndiàn
United Arab Emirates	阿拉伯联合酋长国 Ālābó Liánhé Qiúzhǎngguó / 阿拉伯联合大公国 Ālābó Liánhé Dàgōngguó
United Kingdom	英国 Yīngguó
United States	美国 Měiguó
Uruguay	乌拉圭 Wūlāguī
Uzbekistan	乌兹别克斯坦 Wūzībiékèsītǎn / 乌兹别克 Wūzībiékè
Vancouver	温哥华 Wēngēhuá
Vanuatu	瓦努阿图 Wǎnǔ'ātú / 万那杜 Wànnàdù
Venezuela	委内瑞拉 Wěinèiruìlā
Vienna	维也纳 Wéiyěnà
Vietnam	越南 Yuènán
Warsaw	华沙 Huáshā
Washington, DC	华盛顿哥伦比亚特区 Huáshèngdùn Gēlúnbǐyà Tèqū / 华盛顿特区 Huáshèngdùn Tèqū
Western Samoa	西萨摩亚 Xīsàmóyà
Yemen	也门 Yěmén / 叶门 Yèmén
Zambia	赞比亚 Zànbǐyà / 尚比亚 Shàngbǐyà
Zimbabwe	津巴布韦 Jīnbābùwéi / 辛巴威 Xīnbāwēi

Important Chinese Festivals

Chinese New Year (Chūnjié 春节)

It falls on the 1st day of the 1st month in the Lunar Calendar. Chinese New Year ranks on the top of the national festivals in terms of importance. On the New Year's Eve the families reunite and have good meals together. The celebration may last for up to 15 days. According to tradition, the New Year holidays end on the first full moon.

Lantern Festival (Yuánxiāojié 元宵节)

It is a Chinese festival celebrated on the 15th day of the 1st month in the Lunar Calendar. During the Lantern Festival, children go out at night to temples carrying lanterns and guess the answer to riddles. In addition to eating tāngyuán (汤圆, stuffed dumplings made of glutinous rice flour and served in soup), another popular activity at this festival is watching informal lantern parades. The Lantern Festival is also known as the Xiǎoguònián (小过年, Little New Year) since it marks the end of the series of celebrations starting from the Chinese New Year.

Tomb-Sweeping Day (Qīngmíngjié 清明节)

On the 5th day of April, you will see many families troop off to the graveyards on the hillside on the edge of towns. This is the day when people visit their ancestors, cutback weeds, maintain the graves, and say their prayers.

Dragon Boat Festival (Duānwǔjié 端午节)

Falling on the 5th day of the 5th month in the Lunar Calendar, Dragon Boat Festival marks the beginning of summer. Legend has it that Qū Yuán (屈原), a poet and patriot from the Warring States Period (475-222 B.C.), drown himself in the river on this day. To protect his body from being consumed by the fish, people threw rice dumplings into the river and went out on the river to look for his body — hence the boat race we have today.

Ghost Festival (Zhōngyuánjié 中元节)

Chinese people believe that the 7th month in the Lunar Calendar is the time when ghosts rise from the Underworld and walk the earth, so it's not a good time for weddings, funerals, moving house, swimming, you name it. The 15th day of the 7th month in the Lunar Calendar is known as Ghost Festival. On this day, people present their offerings to the dead, out of fear and out of compassion at the same time.

Moon Festival / Mid-Autumn Festival (Zhōngqiūjié 中秋节)

As indicated by its name, this festival falls in the middle of the fall season, i.e. the 15th day of the 8th month in the Lunar Calendar. It is the time to gaze at the moon, eat moon cakes, and tell the romantic story of Cháng'é (嫦娥), a lonesome beauty now looking down from the moon.

Double Ninth Festival
(Chóngyángjié 重阳节)

According to the Chinese tradition, nine is the yáng (阳, active, masculine cosmic principle) number; the 9th day of the 9th month in the Lunar Calender has too much yáng (阳, active, masculine cosmic principle). Hence, the day is also called "Double Yang Festival." On this day, people climb a high mountain, drink chrysanthemum wine, and wear the zhūyú (茱萸, a kind of plant with fragrance, can ward off evil spirits) plant. Also on this holiday, some Chinese visit the graves of their ancestors to pay their respects.

Introduction to Chinese Culture

Tradition

Chinese Medicine

The philosophy behind Chinese medicine is that man lives between heaven and earth, comprising a miniature universe in himself. The imbalance of "yīn (阴)" and "yáng (阳)" causes illness. The doctor analyzes the patient's loss of balance and prescribes a method to correct the imbalance.

Within a Chinese pharmacy, row after row of little drawers contain herbs, minerals, and animal products. The pharmacist selects particular ingredients based on the doctor's prescription. The patient then takes the Chinese medicine home, boils it into a "soup," and drinks it. Once the imbalances are adjusted, physical and mental health and balance can be restored.

Acupuncture

Acupuncture is a method of treatment in Chinese medicine that has been used for centuries. Acupuncture is often used to relieve pain, usually done by inserting thin needles into certain points of the body. It is based on the theory that there is energy, called "qì (气)," flowing through the body. "Qì" is thought to flow along energy pathways called meridians. If the flow of "qì" is blocked or unbalanced at any point on the pathway, it may result in illness. Chinese people believe that acupuncture

unblocks and balances the flow of "qì" to restore health.

Martial Arts

Wǔshù (武术) is a traditional sport of the Chinese people, and is often called kungfu or martial arts. In ancient China, Wǔshù was used for fighting. It has now developed into a sport. Along with its exercise benefit, it has rich artistic content and entertainment value. Wǔshù has different classical systems of fighting, each with its own style and traditions. However, they all have certain features in common. They are not intended to be used to provoke aggression, but merely to promote health, well-being and a sense of moral responsibility, as well as a means of self-defense. Students of Wǔshù become disciplined in martial art techniques, principles of self-defense, meditation, breathing, and internal cultivation. These disciplines become priceless assets throughout one's life.

Tai Chi

Tàijíquán (太极拳), also known to western people as Tai Chi, is a system of gentle exercises derived from Tai Chi Kungfu. Doing Tai Chi requires the movements of one's head, eyes, arms, hands, body, legs, and feet in coordination with one's mind and respiration. There are five secrets for Tai Chi practice: 1) the tranquility of the mind; 2) the relaxation and agility of the body; 3) the gathering of the qì (气), to penetrate the entire body; 4) the unification of strength throughout the whole body; and 5) the development of the qì into spirit. The

whole routine of Tai Chi is usually difficult to remember, requiring years of supervised instruction to become proficient. If one is just learning Tai Chi for health purposes, but not for its value as a martial art, practicing some simple Tai Chi forms repeatedly will be enough for one's physical well-being.

Silk Road

The "Silk Road" is one of the world's oldest and most historically important trade routes. During the Han Dynasty (founded in 202 B.C.), traders from ancient Persia (now Iran) bought richly colored silk from Chinese merchants and transported it by camel caravans to Damascus, from where silk was taken to the Roman Empire. For 12,000 kilometers, this ancient trade route starts in the old capitals of Luo-yang and Xi'an (then called Chang'an), reaches the Yellow River at Lanzhou, then goes westward along deserts and mountains before dividing into three routes at the oasis of Dunhuang. The great part of the Silk Road threads its way through Xin-jiang. The "Silk Road" linked the Chinese culture with the Indian, Roman and Persian cultures, spreading Chinese inventions such as silk, papermaking, and printing far into the West while intruding Buddhism, and Islamic cultures and arts to China.

Culture Concept

Chinese Dragon

Lóng (龙) are imaginary animals created in ancient China, and are composites of many real

animals: snake-like bodies, fish's scales and tail, tiger's claws, horse or donkey's head, rabbit's eyes, ox's ears, and deer's horns. Dragons can fly, walk, and swim, and live in the sky behind the clouds, inside caves deep in the mountains, and at the bottom of rivers and oceans. Dragons are auspicious animals in Chinese culture. They are considered good and friendly creatures, symbolizing China and its people. They are also the emblems of the emperors and royalty. In addition, the Dragon Dance is an important tradition during Chinese New Year celebrations. It expresses the hopes that lóng will bring rain for good harvests and other good fortunes in the coming year.

Chinese Jades

Chinese people value jade above any other stone because of its durability, rarity, and beauty. For millennia, jade has been an intimate part of the lives of Chinese. The majority of carved jade items are ornamental. A round jade with a hole in the center is a popular ornament, representing the round heaven and designed to honor the gods of heaven. Today, it is still common for Chinese people to purchase, wear, and give jade items as gifts. The Chinese believe that jade has the power to ward off evil and bring good fortune. Jade is an everlasting symbol of Chinese civilization.

God of Longevity

"老寿星 (Lǎo Shòuxīng)" or "寿星" is the Chinese name for the God of Longevity.

Shòuxīng is depicted as a smiling old man who

carries a staff and a peach as a symbol of immortality. Shòuxīng is often displayed with characters such as 寿比南山, 福如东海 (shòu bǐ Nánshān, fú rú Dōnghǎi) as birthday wishes for family elders to live long and have health and good fortunes. Shòuxīng is one of the three-star gods of 福禄寿 (Fú Lù Shòu). These three gods often appear together as popular symbols in Chinese paintings and cards, representing people's wishes for good fortune, prosperity, and longevity.

Chinese Symbolism

Peony (牡丹 mǔdān), Lotus (荷花 héhuā), Chrysanthemum (菊花 júhuā), and Plum (梅花 méihuā) symbolize the four seasons individually. Peony, the king of flowers, is used as a symbol of love, beauty and wealth; lotus as purity and perfection; chrysanthemum as cheerfulness; and plum, which blossoms at the end of winter, as courage and hope for the spring.

Horse (马 mǎ): indicates speed and strength. Eight horses racing together means a booming business or career.

Crane (仙鹤 xiānhè): emblem of longevity and wisdom.

Peach (桃子 táozi): a fairy fruit symbolizing immortality.

Peacock (孔雀 kǒngquè): emblem of beauty and dignity.

Pomegranate (石榴 shíliú): symbolizes fertility and many children.

Bat (蝠 fú): indicates good luck and fortune because in Chinese, 蝠 (bat) sounds like 福 (good luck). The Wu Fu, or five bats or happiness, stand

for the five blessings of old age, wealth, health, virtue, and natural death.

Arts

Calligraphy Scrolls

Chinese calligraphy is an abstract art that co-ordinates the mind and the body to choose the best expression of the passage's content. To appreciate the astonishing beauty of Chinese calligraphy, Chinese people like to decorate their homes with scrolls containing single words from works of master calligraphers. The techniques for mounting Chinese brushwork are believed to have begun two thousand years ago. The basic idea for mounting is to glue calligraphy paper onto several layers of backing and cover it with four silk borders. With a roller on each end, such scrolls can be kept level for several hundreds of years.

Practice Makes Perfect

Since ancient China, practice has been considered the key to the success of learning Chinese calligraphy. Wang Xizhi (王羲之), a great calligrapher of the Eastern Jin (317-420 A.D.), told his son Wang Xianzhi (王献之) that to master the skill of calligraphy, he must use up to eighteen large jars of water for practice. Following his father's advice, Wang Xianzhi practiced calligraphy diligently, eventually becoming one of the greatest calligraphers. This tradition continues even today, with Chinese children still required to practice calligraphy by coping Zìtiě (字帖), which contains calligraphy

rubbings of ancient tombstones.

Chinese Zither

Guzheng, or Chinese zither, is a long-bridged instrument with varying sizes and differing numbers of strings. It is one of the most ancient Chinese musical instruments, originated during the Warring Period over 2,500 years ago. In the early times "zhēng (筝)" had 5 strings; today, most instruments have anywhere from 21 to 25 strings. These strings pass over individual bridges, which can be moved to adjust the pitch. Guzheng has been a popular instrument since ancient times and is considered one of the main chamber, as well as solo, instruments of traditional Chinese music.

Society

Marriage in China

Traditionally, marriages in China were arranged by the parents. The arranged marriage was actually marriage by purchase. Women were treated as possessions to be bought and sold. The parents would begin marriage arrangements even before their children were born. Once the boy's parents found a suitable bride, they sent the matchmaker to bring gifts to the girl's parents as means of negotiation. With the arranged marriage based on the girl's family's social status, wealth, and background, the girl's desires or opinions were never considered.

In present day Chinese society, marriages are based on mutual love and a sense of equality between

husband and wife. Women have finally gained the right of self-determination in marriage. Other rights that are now guaranteed include a woman's right to divorce and remarriage.

Chinese Wedding

At a traditional Chinese wedding, the bride's head is covered with a red silk veil with tassels that hang from the phoenix crown. The bridegroom is dressed in a long gown, red shoes, and a red silk sash with a silk ball on his chest. During the ceremony, the couple kowtows to Heaven and Earth, the family ancestors, and their parents. They then bow to each other. After the ceremony, a grand feast is held.

Today's Chinese wedding combines aspects of Western tradition with those of Chinese tradition. The bride wears a Western-style, white wedding gown during the wedding ceremony, as well as at the start of the wedding banquet. The bride then changes into the traditional Chinese red wedding outfit. She will change one more time into a beautiful going-way outfit, which is a fancy, vibrantly colored ball gown.

Internet

According to the information provided by CNNIC (China Internet Network Information Center), on September 20, 1987, Professor Qian Tianbai sent China's first e-mail titled "Crossing the Great Wall to Join the World," marking the beginning of the use of Internet in China. In 1990, CN was registered as China's top domain name and since then, the international e-mail communication service

with CN has been available. In CNNIC's Statistic Report on Internet Development in China issued in January 2003, by the end of 2002, China had more than 20,830,000 PCs connected to the Internet and 179,000 registered domain names of CN, 371,000 WWW web. Also, the total number of Internet users in China ranked second in the world after the United States of America. However, the number of Internet users includes only 0.6% of China's population, showing the great potential for Internet development in China.

Scenic Spots

Emperor's Glory

The Forbidden City, situated at the center of Beijing, was completed in 1420 during the Ming Dynasty. It was the home of 24 emperors of the Ming and Qing dynasties. In Chinese, the Forbidden City is called "紫禁城 (Zǐjìnchéng)." It is said that purple is the symbolic color of the Emperor of Heaven. In ancient days, the Forbidden City was inaccessible to the common people. It has now been renamed as the Palace Museum and is open to the general public.

The National Palace Museum is located in Taipei, Taiwan. Accumulated over a thousand years by Chinese emperors and royal families, its collections include ceramics, porcelain, calligraphy, painting and ritual bronzes. The Museum also possesses many fine examples of jade, lacquer wares, curio cabinets, enamel wares, writing accessories, carving, embroidery, and rare books.

Nine Dragon Wall

The Nine Dragon Wall (九龙壁Jiǔlóngbì) is in Beihai Park (北海公园 Běihǎi Gōngyuán), an extremely popular park in the center of Beijing. Previously, this park was the royal garden of the Kin, Yuan, Ming, and Qing emperors. The Nine Dragon Wall was built in 1756 during the reign of Emperor Qianlong. It is 87-feet long and over 15-feet high. The surface of the screen is comprised of 424 seven-color ceramic tiles. At the center of the wall, there is a giant dragon, flanked by four dragons on each side. The ancient Chinese regarded nine to be the largest numeral, and the dragon as an auspicious beast to ward off evil spirits. In addition to these nine large dragons, the wall is covered from edge to edge with 635 smaller dragons. The Nine Dragon Wall is a very popular tourist site in Beijing.

Guilin

Guìlín (桂林), located in the northeast section of Guangxi, is one of the most celebrated scenic cities in China. It is famous for its karst landscape created by the erosion of limestone. The Li Jiang, Guilin's main waterway, winds among clusters of steep hills, which seem to rise abruptly out of the ground. Along the Li Jiang, between Gulin and Yangshuo, the green hills in all kinds of shapes merge with their reflections in the placid blue waters.

Other scenic sites include the Solitary Beauty Peak, Elephant Trunk Peak, Folded Brocade Hill, Underground Water Hill, Crescent Moon Hill, South Steam Hill, Seven-Star Cave, and Reed Flute Cave. Thus, it is no wonder that the old Chinese saying

goes "East or west, Guilin scenery is best. (桂林山水甲天下 Guìlín shānshuǐ jiǎ tiānxià.)"

Alishan

Ālīshān (阿里山) is a famous scenic spot of Taiwan and is formed by a cluster of 18 great mountains. It takes four hours by the mountaineering train from Jiayi County to reach Alishan scenic spots. The 72 kilometers railway starts 30 meters above sea level and rises up to 2,450 meters above sea level, the gradient of which is so large that is rare in the world. The mountain is renowned for its four beautiful scenes of mystical tree, oriental cherry, clouds, and sunrise. In the summer, the temperature of Mt. Ali area is very comfortable, making it the most wonderful place in Taiwan to avoid sunstroke.

Principles of Simplified Characters

When learning Chinese characters, one immediately confronts a hard-to-tackle issue: Shall I learn the traditional characters? Or should I learn the simplified characters? In the so-called Kanji world, traditional characters are used in Taiwan, Hong Kong, Japan, and Korea, while China, Singapore, and many overseas Chinese communities in Southeast Asia use simplified characters. The choice is more than just national affiliation. Most Chinese classics and most of pre-modern documents are still available only in traditional characters. Thus, it seems that knowledge of both types of characters is a must to students of the Chinese language today.

The Simplification Movement

Simplifying the strokes of characters for either faster writing or for aesthetic purposes has had a long history in China, but such simplified forms were in most cases not used in print, especially not in official documents. The simplification of Chinese characters as promoted by the government of Mainland China was motivated primarily by two factors:

*Reduce the number of strokes

*Renew the phonetic element in a character

In 1956 the government published "Plan on the Simplification of Chinese Characters" and in 1964 issued a "List of Simplified Characters," which included reference to 2,261 traditional characters with a total number of strokes at 36,236, averaging 16 strokes per character. In that list, 2,235 simplified characters were announced with an average of 10.3 strokes per character. The reduction of number of strokes averaged six.

In 1977, the Chinese government issued "The Second List of Simplified Characters" with an aim to further reduce the number of strokes and to incorporate common practices of simplification. The list met with severe criticism and was later rescinded. In 1986, it republished its "List of Simplified Characters" and this is where simplified characters currently stands.

Note that a major difference between the traditional practice of simplification and the 1964 list lies in the important fact that after 1964, the simplified forms are the only state-sanctioned forms with no variants permitted and that simplified forms are to appear in print for public consumption.

Principles of Simplification

The simplification of traditional characters in the 50's and 60's underwent complex processes and aroused in the 70's and 80's much heated discussion among different walks of life in China and even more markedly between China and Taiwan. What is given below are some general and obvious principles underlying the simplification movement, though such principles were never officially spelled out as such. There are many instances of idiosyncrasies, which can not be dealt with herein.

1. Omission of Components

Non-prominent or non-distinctive components of characters are deleted in simplification, with no special attention given to the Six Categories or "radicals," nor to the pronunciation of the character. The concern here is the reduction of strokes.

Traditional	Simplified	Traditional	Simplified
聲	声	習	习
shēng "sound"		xí "to practice"	

Traditional	Simplified	Traditional	Simplified
業	业	廠	厂
yè "career"		chǎng "factory"	

2. Rephoneticization

This is by far the most important principle in simplification, and has the greatest number of categories for simplified characters. Usually a commoner and simpler character substitutes the old phonetic element, or is built into the new character to indicate the sound.

Traditional	Simplified	Traditional	Simplified
達	达	鐘	钟
dá "reach"		zhōng "clock"	

Sometimes, in the process of rephoneticization, the radical element is adjusted as well.

Traditional	Simplified
驚	惊

jīng "fright;" with a new radical "heart" to replace the old "horse" radical.

Traditional	Simplified
護	护

hù "protect;" with "speech" replaced by "hand."

Occasionally, rephoneticization is accompanied by an adjustment to the entire character for no apparent motivation except for the general shape of the original character.

Traditional Simplified

華　　　华

huá "flower; China"

3. New Semantic Compounds

There is a small number of simplified characters that result from a new implementation of the old principle of "semantic compound."

Traditional Simplified

泪　　　泪

lèi "tears," where the components 氵 "water" and 目 "eye" refer hopefully to something obvious. The original traditional character is a phonetic compound with an uncommon and now less obvious phonetic element 戾 lì.

Traditional Simplified

孫　　　孙

sūn "grandchild," with the components 子 "child" and 小 "small," though the simplified form can be argued as a result of omitting components.

4. New Phonetic Borrowing

This makes use of the traditional category of "phonetic borrowing 假借" to achieve the same effect as the principle of rephoneticization.

Traditional   Simplified

穀   谷

gǔ "grains;" the entire character is substituted by
a commoner and phonetically obvious character
originally meaning "ravine." As a result, the
simplified form is at least two-way ambiguous.

Traditional   Simplified

後   后

hòu "after;" the entire character replaced by
another meaning "queen," making the latter two-
way ambiguous.

5. Adoption of the Cursive

The cursive form of writing has had a long
history in China, and some cursive forms have
been adopted in simplification, with the now
controversial assumption that cursive writing is
faster. The cursive form suggests the original shape
of the character quite faithfully, at least to native
Chinese readers/writers.

Traditional	Simplified	Traditional	Simplified
書	书	東	东

shū "book"   dōng "east"

Traditional	Simplified	Traditional	Simplified
發	发	為	为

fā "prosper"   wèi "for the sake of "

6. Adoption of Ancient Forms

Some characters in the present stock of simplified characters are results from substituting the pre-1964 forms with their ancient counterparts, but only when the ancient forms are simpler in structure than the pre-1964 forms.

Traditional Simplified

從   从

cóng "follow; from," where does not result from the omission of components, though it can be so interpreted, but from adopting the ancient, original form for "following."

Traditional Simplified

雲   云

yún "cloud"

7. Non-unique Substitution

In this category, a simple symbol, for example, is used to replace various components of characters, resulting in non-one-to-one recovery, unlike in the other categories of simplified characters.

Symbol "又"

Traditional Simplified

雞   鸡

jī "chicken," where 又 replaces 奚, and 隹 "short-tailed bird" (the right side of the traditional) is replaced by a regular bird 鸟. Otherwise, "chicken" would merge with "difficult" 难.

Traditional	Simplified
對	对

duì "correct," where 又 replaces 䇂.

Traditional	Simplified
歡	欢

huān "like," where 又 replaces 雚.

Traditional	Simplified
難	难

nán "difficult," where 又 replaces 𦰩.

Traditional	Simplified
樹	树

shù "tree," where 又 replaces 壴.

Traditional	Simplified
戲	戏

xì "drama," where 又 replaces 虍.

Traditional	Simplified
鳳	凤

fèng "male phoenix," where 又 replaces 鳥.

Simplified vs. Traditional Character Comparison Chart

简体	繁体	简体	繁体	简体	繁体	简体	繁体
a		**ai**		**bi**		**变**	**變**
鳌	鰲	祎	禕	辩	辯	宾	賓
钢	鋼					摈	擯
ba						殡	殯
皑	皚			笔	筆	膑	臏
蔼	藹			哔	嗶	髌	髕
霭	靄			币	幣	鬓	鬢
嗳	噯			毕	畢	**bing**	
嫒	嬡			筚	篳	饼	餅
爱	愛			荜	蓽	**bo**	
暧	曖			跸	蹕	拨	撥
瑷	璦			铋	鉍	钵	缽
碍	礙			闭	閉	饽	餑
叇	靉			毙	斃	卜	蔔
an		**ban**		鳖	鱉	铂	鉑
谙	諳	板	闆	瘪	癟	驳	駁
鹌	鵪	绊	絆	**bian**		鹁	鵓
ang		办	辦	笾	籩	**bu**	
肮	骯	**bang**		编	編	补	補
ao		帮	幫	鳊	鯿	**cai**	
				边	邊		
				贬	貶		

简体	繁体	简体	繁体	简体	繁体
绑	綁			标	標
谤	謗			飙	飆
镑	鎊			镖	鏢
bao		**biao**		镳	鑣
饱	飽			表	錶
鸨	鴇			鳔	鰾
宝	寶			**bie**	
报	報			别	彆
鲍	鮑			**bin**	
bei		傧	儐		
备	備	槟	檳		
惫	憊	滨	濱		
贝	貝	濒	瀕		
辈	輩	缤	繽		
钡	鋇				
bian					
狈	狽				
ben					
笾	籩				
贲	賁				
锛	錛				
边	邊				
beng					
贬	貶				

		cen			chen		迟	遲	雏	雛
才	纔	简体	繁体	葳	葳	简体	繁体	齿	齒	储	儲
财	財			诶	諳			炽	熾	础	礎
can		参	參	铲	鏟	尘	塵	饬	飭	处	處
简体	繁体	ceng		阐	闡	谌	諶	chong		绌	絀
骖	驂	简体	繁体	忏	懺	陈	陳	简体	繁体	触	觸
参	參	层	層	chang		榇	櫬	冲	衝	chuan	
惭	慚	cha		简体	繁体	衬	襯	虫	蟲	简体	繁体
残	殘	简体	繁体	伥	倀	谶	讖	宠	寵	传	傳
蚕	蠶	诧	詫	阊	閶	龀	齔	铳	銃	钏	釧
惨	慘	chai		偿	償	cheng		chou		chuang	
灿	燦	简体	繁体	尝	嘗	简体	繁体	简体	繁体	简体	繁体
cang		钗	釵	肠	腸	柽	檉	绸	紬	疮	瘡
简体	繁体	侪	儕	长	長	蛏	蟶	俦	儔	闯	闖
仓	倉	虿	蠆	场	場	枪	槍	畴	疇	怆	愴
伧	傖	chan		厂	廠	赪	赬	筹	籌	创	創
沧	滄	简体	繁体	怅	悵	称	稱	绸	綢	chui	
舱	艙	搀	攙	畅	暢	铛	鐺	雠	讎	简体	繁体
苍	蒼	单	單	chao		柽	棖	踌	躊	锤	錘
鸧	鶬	婵	嬋	简体	繁体	诚	誠	丑	醜	chun	
ce		缠	纏	钞	鈔	惩	懲	chu		简体	繁体
简体	繁体	蝉	蟬	che		骋	騁	简体	繁体	纯	純
侧	側	谗	讒	简体	繁体	chi		出	齣	莼	蒓
恻	惻	馋	饞	车	車	简体	繁体	刍	芻	鹑	鶉
测	測	禅	禪	彻	徹	鸱	鴟	锄	鋤	chuo	
厕	廁	产	產	辙	轍	驰	馳				

chuo

简体	繁体
绰	綽
辍	輟
龊	齪

ci

简体	繁体
词	詞
辞	辭
鹚	鶿

cong

简体	繁体
聪	聰
骢	驄
枞	樅
丛	叢
从	從

cou

简体	繁体
辏	輳

cu

简体	繁体
数	數

cuan

简体	繁体
撺	攛
镩	鑹
蹿	躥
攒	攢
窜	竄

cui

简体	繁体
缞	縗

cuo

简体	繁体
鹾	鹺
锉	銼
错	錯

da

简体	繁体
鞑	韃
达	達

dai

简体	繁体
带	帶
贷	貸
骀	駘

dan

简体	繁体
殚	殫
郸	鄲
单	單
担	擔
胆	膽
掸	撣
诞	誕
瘅	癉
弹	彈

dang

简体	繁体
当	當
当	噹
裆	襠
铛	鐺
档	檔
党	黨
挡	擋
荡	蕩

dao

简体	繁体
导	導
岛	島
捣	搗
祷	禱

deng

简体	繁体
灯	燈
邓	鄧
镫	鐙

di

简体	繁体
涤	滌
籴	糴
觌	覿
镝	鏑
敌	敵
诋	詆
谛	諦
递	遞
缔	締

dian

简体	繁体
巅	巔
颠	顛
癫	癲
点	點
垫	墊
淀	澱
钿	鈿
电	電

diao

简体	繁体
鲷	鯛
鸟	鳥
钓	釣
调	調
铫	銚

die

简体	繁体
叠	疊
绖	絰
谍	諜
鲽	鰈

ding

简体	繁体
钉	釘
顶	頂
订	訂
锭	錠

diu

简体	繁体
铥	銩

dong

简体	繁体
东	東
冬	鼕
动	動
栋	棟
冻	凍

dou

简体	繁体
窦	竇
斗	鬥
读	讀

du

简体	繁体
椟	櫝
犊	犢
牍	牘
黩	黷
渎	瀆
读	讀
笃	篤
赌	賭

简体	繁体								
镀	鍍	简体	繁体	发	髮	奋	奮	凫	鳬

duan			fan			愤	憤	庑	無
简体	繁体	讹	訛	简体	繁体	抚	撫	简体	繁体

gan

断	斷	额	額	烦	煩	辅	輔	尴	尷
缎	緞	鹅	鵝	矾	礬	妇	婦	干	乾
锻	鍛	谔	諤	钒	釩	复	復	赶	趕

		轭	軛	范	範	复	複	绀	紺

dui | | | | | | **feng** | | |

简体	繁体	锷	鍔	贩	販	复	覆	赣	贛
对	對	饿	餓	饭	飯	讣	訃	干	幹
怼	懟	鹗	鶚			负	負		

队	隊	恶	惡	**fang**		赋	賦	**gang**	

dun | | 阏 | 閼 | 简体 | 繁体 | 赗 | 賵 | 简体 | 繁体 |

简体	繁体			鲂	魴	驸	駙	刚	剛

er | | | | 纺 | 紡 | 鲋 | 鮒 | 冈 | 岡 |

趸	躉	简体	繁体	访	訪	冯	馮	岗	崗
吨	噸	儿	兒			讽	諷	纲	綱
钝	鈍	尔	爾	**fei**		凤	鳳	钢	鋼
饨	飩	铒	鉺	简体	繁体				
顿	頓	饵	餌	绯	緋	**fu**		**gao**	

		迩	邇	飞	飛	简体	繁体	简体	繁体

duo | | | | 诽 | 誹 | 钆 | 釓 | 缟 | 縞 |

简体	繁体	贰	貳	废	廢	轧	軋	镐	鎬
夺	奪			费	費			搅	攪

铎	鐸	**fa**		**fen**		**gai**		诰	誥

驮	馱	简体	繁体	简体	繁体	简体	繁体	锆	鋯
堕	墮	发	發	纷	紛	该	該		

		罚	罰	坟	墳	赅	賅	**ge**	

e | | 阀 | 閥 | | | 钙 | 鈣 | 简体 | 繁体 |

						盖	蓋	搁	擱

简体	繁体	简体	繁体	简体	繁体	简体	繁体	简体	繁体	简体	繁体
鸽	鴿	沟	溝	诖	詿	诡	詭	颏	頦	阂	閡
锎	鐦	缑	緱	guan		轨	軌	骇	駭	阃	閫
阁	閣	钩	鈎	简体	繁体	柜	櫃	han		鹃	鵑
合	閤	构	構	关	關	贵	貴	简体	繁体	贺	賀
盖	蓋	觏	覯	鳏	鰥	鳜	鱖	顸	頇	鹤	鶴
铬	鉻	诟	詬	观	觀	会	會	干	幹	吓	嚇
个	個	购	購	纶	綸	绘	繪	韩	韓	hong	
gei		gu		馆	館	gun		汉	漢	简体	繁体
简体	繁体	简体	繁体	惯	慣	绲	緄	焊	釺	轰	轟
给	給	鸪	鴣	掼	摜	鲧	鯀	颔	頷	荭	葒
geng		钴	鈷	贯	貫	guo		hang		讧	訌
简体	繁体	鹘	鶻	鹳	鸛	简体	繁体	简体	繁体	鸿	鴻
赓	賡	谷	穀	guang		蝈	蟈	颃	頏	黉	黌
鹒	鶊	蛊	蠱	简体	繁体	锅	鍋	hao		红	紅
绠	緪	诂	詁	犷	獷	涡	渦	简体	繁体	hou	
鲠	鯁	毂	轂	广	廣	帼	幗	灏	灝	后	後
颈	頸	鹄	鵠	gui		国	國	颢	顥	鲎	鱟
gong		贾	賈	简体	繁体	掴	摑	镐	鎬	hu	
龚	龔	锢	錮	归	歸	馃	餜	号	號	简体	繁体
红	紅	顾	顧	沩	溈	过	過	he		戏	戲
巩	鞏	gua		规	規	ha		简体	繁体	壶	壺
贡	貢	简体	繁体	闺	閨	简体	繁体	诃	訶	胡	鬍
gou		蜗	蝸	鲑	鮭	虾	蝦	纥	紇	鹕	鶘
简体	繁体	刮	颳	龟	龜	hai		铪	鉿	鹘	鶻
		鸹	鴰			还	還	合	閤	鹕	鶘

简体	繁体	简体	繁体	简体	繁体	简体	繁体	简体	繁体	简体	繁体
鹘	鶻	缓	緩	珲	琿	鸡	雞	济	濟	缄	緘
浒	滸	鲩	鯇	馄	餛	饥	饑	齐	齊	缣	縑
沪	滬	**huang**		浑	渾	赍	齎	系	繫	艰	艱
护	護	简体	繁体	诨	諢	齑	齏	**jia**		鞯	韉
hua		谎	謊	**huo**		藉	藉	简体	繁体	鲣	鰹
简体	繁体	**hui**		简体	繁体	击	擊	家	傢	鹣	鶼
哗	嘩	简体	繁体	伙	夥	极	極	镓	鎵	鲣	鰹
华	華	挥	揮	钬	鈥	辑	輯	夹	夾	间	間
骅	驊	诙	詼	获	獲	鹡	鶺	荚	莢	浅	淺
桦	樺	辉	輝	祸	禍	给	給	郏	郟	拣	揀
画	畫	回	迴	鹱	鸌	挤	擠	铗	鋏	捡	撿
话	話	诲	誨	获	穫	虮	蟣	颊	頰	检	檢
划	劃	烩	燴	货	貨	剂	劑	槚	檟	睑	瞼
huai		绘	繪	镬	鑊	纪	紀	钾	鉀	笕	筧
简体	繁体	荟	薈	**ji**		继	繼	贾	賈	茧	繭
怀	懷	讳	諱	简体	繁体	蓟	薊	价	價	裥	襇
坏	壞	贿	賄	几	幾	荠	薺	驾	駕	谏	諫
huan		汇	彙	叽	嘰	觊	覬	**jian**		碱	鹼
简体	繁体	会	會	机	機	计	計	简体	繁体	俭	儉
欢	歡	**hun**		玑	璣	际	際	坚	堅	钱	錢
还	還	简体	繁体	矶	磯	霁	霽	戋	戔	剑	劍
环	環	阍	閽	积	積	骥	驥	歼	殲	渐	漸
缳	繯	荤	葷	绩	績	鲫	鯽	监	監	涧	澗
镮	鐶	讦	訐	羁	羈	跻	躋	笺	箋	溅	濺

简体 / 繁体 对照表（简化字—繁体字）

jian（续）

简体	繁体
舰	艦
荐	薦
见	見
谏	諫
贱	賤
践	踐
键	鍵
锏	鐧
鉴	鑑
饯	餞
槛	檻

jiang

简体	繁体
将	將
姜	薑
缰	韁
浆	漿
桨	槳
奖	獎
蒋	蔣
讲	講
绛	絳
酱	醬

jiao

简体	繁体
娇	嬌
浇	澆
胶	膠
骄	驕
鲛	鮫
鹪	鷦
挢	撟
矫	矯
绞	絞
铰	鉸
饺	餃
缴	繳
搅	攪
侥	僥
峤	嶠
较	較
轿	轎

jie

简体	繁体
阶	階
讦	訐
诘	詰
洁	潔
节	節
疖	癤
结	結
颉	頡
诫	誡
借	藉

jin

简体	繁体
仅	僅
尽	盡
紧	緊
谨	謹
锦	錦
馑	饉
进	進
烬	燼
尽	儘
缙	縉

jing

简体	繁体
泾	涇
茎	莖
惊	驚
鲸	鯨
颈	頸
劲	勁
径	徑
竞	競
胫	脛
镜	鏡
靓	靚
痉	痙
请	請

jiu

简体	繁体
纠	糾
阄	鬮
鸠	鳩
旧	舊
鹫	鷲

ju

简体	繁体
驹	駒
榉	櫸
举	舉
龃	齟
剧	劇
屦	屨
惧	懼
据	據
讵	詎
飓	颶
锯	鋸
窭	窶

juan

简体	繁体
鹃	鵑
卷	捲
绢	絹

jue

简体	繁体
绝	絕
诀	訣
觉	覺
谲	譎

jun

简体	繁体
龟	龜
军	軍
皲	皸
钧	鈞
骏	駿

kai

简体	繁体
开	開
凯	凱
剀	剴
恺	愷
铠	鎧
闿	闓
忾	愾

kan

简体	繁体
龛	龕
槛	檻
阚	闞

kang

简体	繁体
闶	閌
钪	鈧

kao

简体	繁体
铐	銬

ke

简体	繁体
颏	頦
轲	軻
钶	鈳
颗	顆
壳	殼
克	剋
缂	緙
课	課

ken

简体	繁体
垦	墾
恳	懇

keng

简体	繁体
铿	鏗

kou

简体	繁体
抠	摳

ku

简体	繁体
裤	褲
库	庫

kua

简体	繁体
夸	誇

kuai

简体	繁体
会	會
刽	劊
侩	儈
块	塊
桧	檜
浍	澮
狯	獪
脍	膾
郐	鄶

kuan

简体	繁体
宽	寬

kuang

简体	繁体
诓	誆
圹	壙
旷	曠
矿	礦
纩	纊
邝	鄺

kui

简体	繁体
岿	巋
窥	窺
亏	虧
匮	匱
愦	憒
溃	潰
篑	簣
聩	聵
蒉	蕢
馈	饋

kun

简体	繁体
锟	錕
鲲	鯤
壶	壺
阃	閫

kuo

简体	繁体
扩	擴
阔	闊

la

简体	繁体
腊	臘
蜡	蠟
镴	鑞

lai

简体	繁体
来	來
崃	崍
徕	徠
莱	萊
铼	錸
涞	淶
濑	瀨
睐	睞
籁	籟
赉	賚
赖	賴
癞	癩

lan

简体	繁体
岚	嵐
拦	攔
斓	斕
栏	欄
篮	籃
褴	襤
蓝	藍
兰	蘭
谰	讕
阑	闌
澜	瀾
懒	懶
揽	攬
榄	欖
缆	纜
览	覽
滥	濫
烂	爛

lang

简体	繁体
锒	鋃
阆	閬

lao

简体	繁体
捞	撈
唠	嘮
崂	嶗
劳	勞
铑	鐒
涝	澇
络	絡

le

简体	繁体
乐	樂

lei

简体	繁体
缧	縲
累	纍
镭	鐳
诔	誄
垒	壘
类	類

li

简体	繁体
篱	籬
缡	縭
离	離
骊	驪
鹂	鸝
礼	禮
里	裡
锂	鋰

li

简体	繁体	简体	繁体
鲤	鲤	砾	礫
逦	邐	粝	糲
俪	儷	蛎	蠣
励	勵	轹	轢
厉	厲	郦	酈
历	曆	雳	靂
历	歷	丽	麗
栎	櫟	疠	癘
枥	櫪	隶	隸
沥	瀝		
砺	礪		

lia

简体	繁体
俩	俩

lian

简体	繁体
奁	奩
怜	憐
涟	漣
琏	璉
帘	簾
联	聯
裢	褳
莲	蓮
镰	鐮
鲢	鰱
连	連
脸	臉
敛	斂
恋	戀
㳠	㵽
炼	煉
练	練
蔹	薟
链	鏈

liang

简体	繁体
粮	糧
两	兩
唡	啢
魉	魎

liao

简体	繁体
缭	繚
鹩	鷯
辽	遼
疗	療
镣	鐐
钌	釕
了	瞭

lie

简体	繁体
猎	獵
䴕	鴷

lin

简体	繁体
辚	轔
邻	鄰
鳞	鱗
蔺	藺
赁	賃
躏	躪
临	臨

ling

简体	繁体
铃	鈴
灵	靈
鲮	鯪
鸰	鴒
龄	齡
绫	綾
岭	嶺
领	領

liu

简体	繁体
刘	劉
浏	瀏
骝	駵
绺	綹
馏	餾

long

简体	繁体
龙	龍
泷	瀧
垄	壟
拢	攏
陇	隴
砻	礱
笼	籠
聋	聾
咙	嚨
昽	曨
胧	朧
眬	矓
珑	瓏
栊	櫳
茏	蘢

lou

简体	繁体
娄	婁
偻	僂
喽	嘍
楼	樓
蝼	螻
蒌	蔞
髅	髏
篓	簍
搂	摟
瘘	瘺
镂	鏤

lu

简体	繁体
噜	嚕
橹	櫓
泸	瀘
炉	爐
卢	盧
垆	壚
舻	艫
芦	蘆
轳	轤
颅	顱
鲈	鱸
鸬	鸕
庐	廬
栌	櫨
鲁	魯
卤	鹵
虏	虜
掳	擄
赂	賂
辂	輅
辘	轆
录	錄
鹭	鷺

陆 陸	乱 亂	简体 繁体	缦 縵	简体 繁体	简体 繁体
lü	lun	妈 媽	镘 鏝	蒙 濛	灭 滅
简体 繁体	简体 繁体	么 麼	mang	蒙 矇	蔑 衊
榈 櫚	伦 倫	玛 瑪	简体 繁体	锰 錳	min
闾 閭	囵 圇	码 碼	铓 鋩	梦 夢	简体 繁体
驴 驢	抡 掄	蚂 螞	mao	mi	缗 緡
屡 屢	沦 淪	马 馬	简体 繁体	简体 繁体	悯 憫
缕 縷	轮 輪	骂 罵	锚 錨	弥 彌	闵 閔
褛 褸	纶 綸	吗 嗎	贸 貿	弥 瀰	闽 閩
铝 鋁	论 論	mai	me	猕 獼	黾 黽
虑 慮	luo	简体 繁体	简体 繁体	谜 謎	渑 澠
滤 濾	简体 繁体	买 買	么 麼	祢 禰	ming
绿 綠	啰 囉	卖 賣	mei	觅 覓	简体 繁体
垒 壘	猡 玀	麦 麥	简体 繁体	谧 謐	铭 銘
luan	箩 籮	迈 邁	霉 黴	mian	鸣 鳴
简体 繁体	罗 羅	man	镁 鎂	简体 繁体	miu
娈 孌	萝 蘿	简体 繁体	men	绵 綿	简体 繁体
孪 孿	锣 鑼	瞒 瞞	简体 繁体	缅 緬	缪 繆
峦 巒	骡 騾	蛮 蠻	闷 悶	面 麵	谬 謬
挛 攣	逻 邏	谩 謾	扪 捫	miao	mo
栾 欒	荦 犖	蹒 蹣	门 門	简体 繁体	简体 繁体
滦 灤	骆 駱	颟 顢	懑 懣	缈 緲	谟 謨
脔 臠	泺 濼	馒 饅	焖 燜	缪 繆	馍 饃
銮 鑾	络 絡	鳗 鰻	们 們	庙 廟	么 麼
鸾 鸞	ma	满 滿	meng	mie	蓦 驀

mou		聂 聶	nu		pa		辟 闢
简体	繁体	摄 攝	简体	繁体	简体	繁体	pian
谋	謀	蹑 躡	弩 駑		钯 鈀		简体 繁体
缪	繆	镍 鎳	nü		pan		谝 諞
mu		镍 鎳	简体	繁体	简体	繁体	骈 駢
简体	繁体	颞 顳	钕 釹		盘 盤		骗 騙
亩	畝	拟 擬	啮 齧	nüe		pang	piao
钼	鉬	祢 禰	ning		简体 繁体		简体 繁体
na		腻 膩	简体	繁体	谑 謔	庞 龐	飘 飄
简体	繁体	nian	咛 嚀	疟 瘧		pei	缥 縹
纳	納	简体	繁体	柠 檸	nuo		骠 驃
钠	鈉	鲶 鯰	狞 獰	简体	繁体	赔 賠	pin
nan		撵 攆	宁 寧	难 難	銮 鑾		简体 繁体
简体	繁体	辇 輦	拧 擰	诺 諾		pen	嫔 嬪
难	難	niang	泞 濘	ou		简体 繁体	贫 貧
nao		简体 繁体	niu	简体	繁体	喷 噴	频 頻
简体	繁体	酿 釀	简体	繁体	欧 歐	peng	颦 顰
挠	撓	niao	钮 鈕	殴 毆		简体 繁体	苹 蘋
桡	橈	简体 繁体	纽 紐	瓯 甌		鹏 鵬	ping
铙	鐃	袅 裊	nong	讴 謳		pi	简体 繁体
恼	惱	茑 蔦	简体 繁体	鸥 鷗		简体 繁体	冯 馮
脑	腦	鸟 鳥	侬 儂	沤 漚		纰 紕	凭 憑
闹	鬧	nie	浓 濃	区 區		罢 罷	评 評
ne		简体 繁体	脓 膿	呕 嘔		罴 羆	苹 蘋
简体	繁体	嗫 囁	农 農	怄 慪		铍 鈹	po

po

简体	繁体
泼	潑
颇	頗
钋	釙

pu

简体	繁体
扑	撲
铺	鋪
朴	樸
仆	僕
谱	譜
镨	鐯

qi

简体	繁体
脐	臍
蛴	蠐
蕲	蘄
颀	頎
骐	騏
骑	騎
鳍	鰭
荠	薺
齐	齊
绮	綺
岂	豈
启	啟
气	氣
碛	磧
缉	緝
讫	訖

qian

简体	繁体
佥	僉
悭	慳
牵	牽
签	簽
签	籤
谦	謙
铅	鉛
千	韆
骞	騫
迁	遷
钤	鈐
钳	鉗
钱	錢
缱	繾
遣	譴
浅	淺
堑	塹
椠	槧
纤	縴

qiang

简体	繁体
枪	槍
玱	瑲
锵	鏘
将	將
嫱	嬙
樯	檣
墙	牆
蔷	薔
锖	錆
抢	搶
呛	嗆
跄	蹌

qiao

简体	繁体
硗	磽
跷	蹺
锹	鍬
侨	僑
乔	喬
桥	橋
荞	蕎
谯	譙
窍	竅
诮	誚
翘	翹

qie

简体	繁体
惬	愜
窃	竊
箧	篋
锲	鍥

qin

简体	繁体
嵚	嶔
钦	欽
骎	駸
亲	親
寝	寢
揿	撳

qing

简体	繁体
倾	傾
氢	氫
轻	輕
鲭	鯖
顷	頃
请	請
庆	慶
亲	親

qiong

简体	繁体
茕	煢
琼	瓊
穷	窮
䓖	藭

qiu

简体	繁体
龟	龜
秋	鞦
鳅	鰍
鹙	鶖

qu

简体	繁体
曲	麯
觑	覷
岖	嶇
诎	詘
趋	趨
躯	軀
驱	驅
区	區
鸲	鴝

quan

简体	繁体
权	權
诠	詮
铨	銓
颧	顴
绻	綣
劝	勸

que

简体	繁体
悫	慤
确	確
阕	闋
鹊	鵲
阙	闕

rang

简体	繁体
让	讓

rao

简体	繁体
荛	蕘

简体	繁体
饶	饒
扰	擾
绕	繞

re

简体	繁体
热	熱

ren

简体	繁体
纫	紉
纴	紝
认	認
轫	軔
韧	韌
饪	飪

rong

简体	繁体
嵘	嶸
荣	榮
绒	絨
蝾	蠑
鳙	鱅

ru

简体	繁体
铷	銣
缛	縟

ruan

简体	繁体
软	軟

rui

简体	繁体
锐	銳

run

简体	繁体
润	潤
闰	閏

sa

简体	繁体
洒	灑
萨	薩
飒	颯

sai

简体	繁体
鳃	鰓
赛	賽

san

简体	繁体
伞	傘
糁	糝

sang

简体	繁体
丧	喪
颡	顙

sao

简体	繁体
缫	繅
骚	騷
缲	繰
扫	掃

se

简体	繁体
铯	銫
啬	嗇
涩	澀
穑	穡

sha

简体	繁体
纱	紗
铩	鎩
鲨	鯊
杀	殺

shai

简体	繁体
筛	篩
杀	殺

shan

简体	繁体
钐	釤
闪	閃
陕	陝
禅	禪
单	單
掸	撣
缮	繕
讪	訕
赡	贍
鳝	鱔
鳣	鱣

shang

简体	繁体
伤	傷
殇	殤
觞	觴
汤	湯
赏	賞

shao

简体	繁体
烧	燒
绍	紹

she

简体	繁体
赊	賒
舍	捨
设	設
摄	攝

shei

简体	繁体
谁	誰

shen

简体	繁体
参	參
绅	紳
审	審
婶	嬸
沈	瀋
谂	諗
谞	諝
渗	滲
肾	腎

sheng

简体	繁体
声	聲
绳	繩
渑	澠
圣	聖
胜	勝

shi

简体	繁体
师	師
狮	獅
诗	詩
湿	濕
时	時
蚀	蝕
莳	蒔
鲥	鰣
实	實
驶	駛
势	勢
视	視
试	試
谥	謚
贳	貰
轼	軾
释	釋
饰	飾
识	識
适	適

shou

简体	繁体

shou
寿/壽, 兽/獸, 绶/綬

shu
摅/攄, 书/書, 枢/樞, 纾/紓, 输/輸, 赎/贖, 属/屬, 树/樹, 术/術, 数/數

shuai
帅/帥

shuan
闩/閂

shuang
泷/瀧, 双/雙

shui
说/說

shun
顺/順

shuo
说/說, 数/數, 烁/爍, 硕/碩, 铄/鑠

si
丝/絲, 缌/緦, 蛳/螄, 锶/鍶, 鸶/鷥, 赐/賜, 饲/飼, 驷/駟

song
松/鬆, 讼/訟, 诵/誦, 颂/頌

sou
飕/颼, 馊/餿, 擞/擻, 薮/藪

su
苏/蘇, 肃/肅, 诉/訴, 谡/謖, 数/數

sui
绥/綏, 虽/雖, 随/隨, 岁/歲, 谇/誶

sun
孙/孫, 狲/猻, 荪/蓀, 损/損

suo
缩/縮, 唢/嗩, 琐/瑣, 锁/鎖

ta
铊/鉈, 挞/撻, 獭/獺

tai
台/檯, 台/臺, 台/颱, 骀/駘, 态/態, 钛/鈦

tan
摊/攤, 滩/灘, 贪/貪, 瘫/癱, 弹/彈, 昙/曇, 坛/壇, 坛/壜, 谈/談, 谭/譚, 叹/嘆

tang
铴/鐋, 镗/鏜, 烫/燙

tao
绦/縧, 韬/韜, 涛/濤, 焘/燾, 讨/討

te
铽/鋱

teng
誊/謄, 腾/騰

ti
绨/綈, 缇/緹, 题/題, 鹈/鵜, 体/體, 锑/銻

tian
阗/闐

tiao
条/條, 龆/齠

调	調	tuan		湾	灣	匙	韃	诬	誣	系	係
铫	銚	简体	繁体	纨	紈	鲔	鮪	无	蕪	细	餼
粜	糶	团	團	顽	頑	伪	偽	妩	嫵	饩	閱
tie		团	糰	绾	綰	卫	衛	忤	憮	阅	繫
简体	繁体	抟	摶	万	萬	谓	謂	鹉	鵡	系	戲
贴	貼	tui		wang		遗	遺	鹉	鵡	戏	xia
铁	鐵	简体	繁体	简体	繁体	wen		庑	廡	简体	繁体
ting		颓	頹	网	網	简体	繁体	恶	惡	虾	蝦
简体	繁体	tuo		辋	輞	鳁	鰮	务	務	侠	俠
厅	廳	简体	繁体	wei		纹	紋	坞	塢	峡	峽
听	聽	驼	駝	简体	繁体	闻	聞	误	誤	挟	挾
铤	鋌	驮	馱	帏	幃	稳	穩	雾	霧	狭	狹
tong		鸵	鴕	围	圍	问	問	骛	鶩	辖	轄
简体	繁体	鼍	鼉	潍	濰	wo		鹜	鶩	吓	嚇
铜	銅	椭	橢	维	維	简体	繁体	xi		xian	
统	統	箨	籜	闱	闈	窝	窩	简体	繁体	简体	繁体
恸	慟	择	擇	韦	韋	莴	萵	牺	犧	纤	纖
tou		wa		违	違	涡	渦	诶	誒	跹	躚
简体	繁体	简体	繁体	为	為	醒	齷	觇	覘	鲜	鮮
头	頭	娲	媧	伟	偉	wu		湿	濕	娴	嫻
tu		洼	窪	炜	煒	简体	繁体	习	習	贤	賢
简体	繁体	袜	襪	玮	瑋	乌	烏	锡	錫	衔	銜
涂	塗	wan		纬	緯	呜	嗚	鳃	鰓	闲	閑
图	圖	简体	繁体	苇	葦	邬	鄔	玺	璽	咸	鹹
钍	釷	弯	彎	逶	諉	钨	鎢				

简体	繁体
痫	癇
狝	獮
薛	薛
铣	銑
险	險
显	顯
癣	癬
岘	峴
宪	憲
献	獻
现	現
线	線
县	縣
苋	莧
馅	餡
xiang	
缃	緗
芗	薌
乡	鄉
镶	鑲
骧	驤
详	詳
响	響
饷	餉
飨	饗
象	像
向	嚮
项	項
xiao	
嚣	囂
枭	梟
潇	瀟
箫	簫
绡	綃
蟏	蠨
萧	蕭
销	銷
骁	驍
鸮	鴞
晓	曉
啸	嘯
xie	
协	協
缬	纈
鲑	鮭
胁	脅
谐	諧
颉	頡
写	寫
泻	瀉
绁	紲
亵	褻
谢	謝
xin	
䜣	訢
锌	鋅
衅	釁
xing	
兴	興
陉	陘
饧	餳
铏	鉶
荥	滎
xiong	
讻	訩
xiu	
馐	饈
鸺	鵂
绣	繡
锈	鏽
xu	
须	須
须	鬚
许	許
诩	詡
谞	諝
绪	緒
续	續
xuan	
谖	諼
轩	軒
悬	懸
选	選
绚	絢
铉	鉉
旋	鏇
xue	
学	學
鳕	鱈
xun	
荤	葷
寻	尋
挦	撏
浔	潯
荨	蕁
询	詢
驯	馴
鲟	鱘
训	訓
讯	訊
逊	遜
ya	
压	壓
鸦	鴉
鸭	鴨
哑	啞
亚	亞
娅	婭
讶	訝
轧	軋
yan	
阎	閻
恹	懨
阉	閹
铅	鉛
严	嚴
颜	顏
盐	鹽
俨	儼
魇	魘
餍	饜
厌	厭
滟	灩
砚	硯
谚	諺
谳	讞
艳	艷
赝	贋
酽	釅
验	驗
yang	

简体	繁体
yang	
鸯	鴦
扬	揚
杨	楊
炀	煬
阳	陽
疡	瘍
痒	癢
养	養
样	樣
yao	
尧	堯
峣	嶢
谣	謠
轺	軺
铫	銚
侥	僥
药	藥
鹞	鷂
钥	鑰
乐	樂
ye	
爷	爺
晔	曄
业	業
叶	葉
谒	謁
邺	鄴
页	頁
yi	
怿	懌
译	譯
诣	詣
谊	誼
议	議
轶	軼
镒	鎰
驿	驛
亿	億
呓	囈
忆	憶
医	醫
鹥	鷖
仪	儀
诒	詒
贻	貽
颐	頤
饴	飴
遗	遺
蚁	蟻
钇	釔
铱	銥
yin	
铟	銦
阴	陰
银	銀
龈	齦
隐	隱
瘾	癮
饮	飲
ying	
婴	嬰
撄	攖
樱	櫻
璎	瓔
缨	纓
莺	鶯
鹰	鷹
鹦	鸚
应	應
茔	塋
荧	熒
莹	瑩
营	營
萦	縈
萤	螢
蝇	蠅
赢	贏
荥	滎
颍	潁
颖	穎
瘿	癭
yong	
佣	傭
痈	癰
颙	顒
拥	擁
you	
优	優
忧	憂
犹	猶
莸	蕕
邮	郵
鱿	魷
铕	銪
诱	誘
铀	鈾
yu	
纡	紆
欤	歟
渔	漁
觎	覦
谀	諛
与	與
余	餘
鱼	魚
伛	傴
屿	嶼
语	語
龉	齬
龋	齲
妪	嫗
狱	獄
御	禦
吁	籲
蓣	蕷
谕	諭
誉	譽
钰	鈺
阈	閾
预	預
饫	飫
驭	馭
郁	鬱
yuan	
渊	淵
鸢	鳶
鸳	鴛

园	園	恽	惲	脏	臟	赠	贈	zhang	侦	偵
圆	圓	缊	縕	zao		zha		简体 繁体	桢	楨
缘	緣	蕴	蘊	简体 繁体	简体 繁体	张	張	祯	禎
辕	轅	郓	鄆	凿	鑿	铡	鍘	长	長	贞	貞
鼋	黿	酝	醞	枣	棗	闸	閘	涨	漲	针	針
员	員	韫	韞	缲	繰	诈	詐	帐	帳	缜	縝
远	遠	运	運	ze		zhai		胀	脹	诊	診
愿	願	za		简体 繁体	简体 繁体	账	賬	轸	軫
yue		简体 繁体	则	則	斋	齋	zhao		赈	賑
简体 繁体	杂	雜	帻	幘	债	債	简体 繁体	镇	鎮
约	約	zai		帧	幀	zhan		刽	劊	阵	陣
栎	櫟	简体 繁体	择	擇	简体 繁体	诏	詔	鸠	鴆
乐	樂	载	載	泽	澤	毡	氈	赵	趙	zheng	
钺	鉞	zan		箦	簀	觇	覘	zhe		简体 繁体
阅	閱	简体 繁体	责	責	鹯	鸇	简体 繁体	征	徵
跃	躍	趱	趲	赜	賾	鳣	鱣	慑	懾	诤	諍
yun		攒	攢	zei		崭	嶄	折	摺	钲	鉦
简体 繁体	赞	贊	简体 繁体	斩	斬	谪	讁	铮	錚
晕	暈	鉴	鑒	贼	賊	盏	盞	辄	輒	症	癥
纭	紜	zang		zen		辗	輾	辙	轍	帧	幀
芸	蕓	简体 繁体	简体 繁体	战	戰	锗	鍺	证	證
云	雲	赃	贓	谮	譖	zeng		鹧	鷓	郑	鄭
员	員	脏	臟	zeng		栈	棧	这	這	zhi	
殒	殞	脏	髒	简体 繁体	绽	綻	zhen		简体 繁体
陨	隕	驵	駔	缯	繒	颤	顫	简体 繁体	织	織

简体	繁体
只	隻
执	執
掷	擲
絷	縶
职	職
蛰	蟄
蹰	躕
质	質
只	祇
纸	紙
识	識
帜	幟
挚	摯
滞	滯
致	緻
制	製
赘	贅
踬	躓
轾	輊
锧	鑕
骘	騭
鸷	鷙
迟	遲

zhong

简体	繁体
终	終
钟	鍾
钟	鐘
肿	腫
种	種
众	眾

zhou

简体	繁体
赒	賙
鸼	鵃
轴	軸
昼	晝
皱	皺
纣	紂
绉	縐

zhu

简体	繁体
朱	硃
诛	誅
诸	諸
铢	銖
烛	燭
筑	築
属	屬
嘱	囑
瞩	矚
贮	貯
铸	鑄
驻	駐

zhua

简体	繁体
挝	撾

zhuan

简体	繁体
专	專
砖	磚
颛	顓
啭	囀
转	轉
传	傳
赚	賺
馔	饌

zhuang

简体	繁体
妆	妝
桩	樁
装	裝
庄	莊
壮	壯
戆	戇
状	狀

zhui

简体	繁体
锥	錐
骓	騅
坠	墜
缀	綴
缒	縋

zhun

简体	繁体
谆	諄
准	準

zhuo

简体	繁体
诼	諑
缴	繳
浊	濁
涿	涿
镯	鐲

zi

简体	繁体
齐	齊
缁	緇
谘	諮
资	資
辎	輜
锱	錙
镃	鎡
龇	齜
渍	漬

zong

简体	繁体
枞	樅
总	總
综	綜
纵	縱

zou

简体	繁体
诹	諏
邹	鄒
驺	騶
鲰	鯫
骤	驟

zu

简体	繁体
镞	鏃
组	組
诅	詛
驵	駔

zuan

简体	繁体
缵	纘
钻	鑽

Comparison Chart for Hanyu Pinyin (HP) and Mandarin Phonetic Symbols (MPS)

Initials			
MPS	HP	MPS	HP
ㄅ	b	ㄐ	j
ㄆ	p	ㄑ	q
ㄇ	m	ㄒ	x
ㄈ	f	ㄓ	zh
ㄉ	d	ㄔ	ch
ㄊ	t	ㄕ	sh
ㄋ	n	ㄖ	r
ㄌ	l	ㄗ	z
ㄍ	g	ㄘ	c
ㄎ	k	ㄙ	s
ㄏ	h		

Finals			
MPS	HP	MPS	HP
ㄚ	a	ㄧㄢ	ian
ㄛ	o	ㄧㄣ	in
ㄜ	e	ㄧㄤ	iang
ㄝ	ê	ㄧㄥ	ing
ㄞ	ai	ㄨ	u
ㄟ	ei	ㄨㄚ	ua
ㄠ	ao	ㄨㄛ	uo
ㄡ	ou	ㄨㄞ	uai
ㄢ	an	ㄨㄟ	ui
ㄣ	en	ㄨㄢ	uan
ㄤ	ang	ㄨㄣ	un
ㄥ	eng	ㄨㄤ	uang
ㄦ	er	ㄨㄥ	ong
ㄧ	i	ㄩ	ü
ㄧㄚ	ia	ㄩㄝ	üe
ㄧㄝ	ie	ㄩㄢ	üan
ㄧㄞ	iai	ㄩㄣ	ün
ㄧㄠ	iao	ㄩㄥ	iong
ㄧㄡ	iu		

Tones		
	MPS	HP
1st tone		ˉ
2nd tone	ˊ	ˊ
3rd tone	ˇ	ˇ
4th tone	ˋ	ˋ
neutral tone	·	

erling

9270566